RPG II, RPG III, AND RPG/400

GARY B. SHELLY

THOMAS J. CASHMAN

HAL GOODWIN

Boyd & Fraser

The Shelly/Cashman Series
Boyd & Fraser Publishing Company

THE SHELLY/CASHMAN SERIES

Essential Computer Concepts
Computer Concepts
Computer Concepts with BASIC
   ClassNotes and Study Guide to Accompany Computer Concepts and Computer Concepts with BASIC
Computer Concepts with Microcomputer Applications (Lotus® version)
Computer Concepts with Microcomputer Applications (VP-Planner Plus® version)
   ClassNotes and Study Guide to Accompany Computer Concepts with Microcomputer Applications
   (VP-Planner Plus® and Lotus® versions)
Learning to Use WordPerfect® (version 4.2), Lotus 1-2-3®, and dBASE III PLUS®
   ClassNotes and Study Guide to Accompany Learning to Use WordPerfect® (version 4.2), Lotus 1-2-3®, and dBASE III PLUS®
Learning to Use WordPerfect® 5.0/5.1, Lotus 1-2-3®, and dBASE III PLUS®
   ClassNotes and Study Guide to Accompany Learning to Use WordPerfect® 5.0/5.1, Lotus 1-2-3®, and dBASE III PLUS®
Learning to Use WordPerfect® 5.0/5.1, Lotus 1-2-3® Release 2.2, and dBASE III PLUS®
   ClassNotes and Study Guide to Accompany Learning to Use WordPerfect® 5.0/5.1, Lotus 1-2-3® Release 2.2, and dBASE III PLUS®
Learning to Use WordPerfect® (version 4.2), VP-Planner Plus®, and dBASE III PLUS®
   ClassNotes and Study Guide to Accompany Learning to Use WordPerfect® (version 4.2), VP-Planner Plus®, and dBASE III PLUS®
Learning to Use WordPerfect® (version 4.2)
   ClassNotes and Study Guide to Accompany Learning to Use WordPerfect® (version 4.2)
Learning to Use WordPerfect® 5.0/5.1
   ClassNotes and Study Guide to Accompany Learning to Use WordPerfect® 5.0/5.1
Learning to Use VP-Planner Plus®
   ClassNotes and Study Guide to Accompany Learning to Use VP-Planner Plus®
Learning to Use Lotus 1-2-3®
   ClassNotes and Study Guide to Accompany Learning to Use Lotus 1-2-3®
Learning to Use Lotus 1-2-3® Release 2.2
   ClassNotes and Study Guide to Accompany Learning to Use Lotus 1-2-3® Release 2.2
Learning to Use dBASE III PLUS®
   ClassNotes and Study Guide to Accompany Learning to Use dBASE III PLUS®
Learning to Use dBASE IV®
Computer Fundamentals with Application Software
   Workbook and Study Guide to Accompany Computer Fundamentals with Application Software
Learning to Use SuperCalc®3, dBASE III®, and WordStar® 3.3: An Introduction
Learning to Use SuperCalc®3: An Introduction
Learning to Use dBASE III®: An Introduction
Learning to Use WordStar® 3.3: An Introduction
BASIC Programming for the IBM Personal Computer
RPG II, RPG III, and RPG/400

The forms used in this book are reprinted from the publications of International Business Machines Corporation with permission of International Business Machines Corporation.

© 1990 by boyd & fraser publishing company
A Division of South-Western Publishing Company
Boston, MA 02116

Developed by Susan Solomon Communications
Produced by Mary Douglas

Manufactured in the United States of America

Library of Congress Cataloging-in-Publication Data

Shelly, Gary B.
    RPG II, RPG III, and RPG/400 / by Gary B. Shelly, Thomas J.
Cashman, Hal Goodwin.
        p.   cm. -- (The Shelly/Cashman series)
    ISBN 0-87835-246-5
    1. RPG (Computer program language)   I. Cashman, Thomas J.
II. Goodwin, Hal.   III. Title.   IV. Title: RPG 2, RPG 3, and
RPG/400.   V. Series: Shelly, Gary B.   Shelly/Cashman series.
QA76.73.R25S56   1990
650'.0285'5242--dc20   89-71214
                                                          CIP

4 5 6 H 3 2

CONTENTS IN BRIEF

CONTENTS

▶ **Chapter 3**   **RPG Calculation Specifications, Arithmetic Operations,**
& Edit Codes   **3.1**

▶ **Chapter 6   Array Processing & Compiler Directive Statements**   6.1

▶ **Chapter 9   Looping Techniques, Exception Output, & Move Operations   9.1**

▶ **Chapter 12   Interactive Processing, Screen Format Design, Programming,
                    & System/36 Screen Design Aid**   **12.1**

▶ Chapter 13 Sequential File Updating Using Matching Records 13.1

▶ Chapter 14 RPG III & RPG/400 Enhancements 14.1

▸ Appendix A   RPG Coding Checklist & Programming Standards

A.1

▸ Appendix B   RPG Debugging Techniques

B.1

▸ Appendix C   RPG Operation Code Summary

C.1

In the early 1960s the IBM Corporation introduced the Report Program Generator language, also known as RPG. Since then RPG has evolved. RPG II and then RPG III were announced to meet users' needs; and, with the recent introduction of RPG /400, IBM has demonstrated its continued support of the language.

RPG is the language of choice in many small- to medium-size business computer installations. Moreover, because IBM has added RPG to its System Application Architecture base, RPG is likely to become more widely used in microcomputer and mainframe environments. This book is the only book currently available that addresses the needs of RPG installations in computer environments of all sizes.

THE SHELLY CASHMAN METHOD

This book is designed to be used in one- or two-term RPG programming courses. It is a derivative of an earlier work by Shelly and Cashman. Great care has been taken to maintain the relevant content and philosophy of the original work, as well as the Shelly Cashman pedagogy and teaching style—a style which has proven effective in educating millions of students.

A "problem oriented" approach is used throughout this book. That is, students are introduced to programming concepts and techniques by a series of programs illustrating typical business applications. Only those statements and segments of the language necessary for the solution of the problem are explained. The students, therefore, learn RPG programming in relation to the total problem and are not burdened with the task of remembering a series of isolated facts concerning individual segments of the language. Each chapter in the book introduces additional programming concepts. Upon completion of the book students will have been exposed to the most frequently used characteristics of the language and should have the ability to write a wide variety of programs using RPG.

COVERAGE OF RPG CONTENT

This book presents RPG in a clear and pedagogically sound manner and helps prepare students to be capable and knowledgeable RPG programmers.

The Fixed Logic Cycle

Students must completely understand the fixed logic cycle to become effective RPG programmers. Thus, each chapter in this book presents a programming problem to be solved. The chapter then presents portions of the logic cycle as they are needed until the entire logic cycle has been presented and the problem is solved.

Indicators

Indicators are unique concepts to RPG. This book introduces each type of indicator as needed and emphasizes the timing of particular types of indicators. Students learn not only how and when to use indicators but also when the logic cycle turns indicators on and off.

Multiple Specification Forms

Unlike other programming languages, RPG uses several different specification forms, each of which serves a specific function within the program. This book provides a brief introduction to all RPG specification forms in Chapter 1—allowing students to learn about each form and its use in context.

Non-Machine-Specific RPG Environment

This book can be used to teach RPG in any machine environment. The text identifies concepts that are specific to a particular vendor or machine. In addition, four different compilers are used throughout the book to demonstrate programs. This variety shows students that although the listing format of a particular compiler may be slightly different from the one they are using, the information provided by the compiler is the same.

Standard and Enhanced Formats

This book shows both the standard calculation formats used in all RPG compilers and the enhanced formats used on current RPG II, RPG III, and RPG/400 compilers.

Operation Code Summaries

Every calculation operation is summarized. The summary includes a description of the operation's function, the coding format used, and coded examples of the operation. All of the operation descriptions appear together in Appendix C—an alphabetized, quick-reference appendix.

Programming Hints and Suggestions

Wherever applicable, hints and suggestions are included to help students avoid some of the errors most commonly made by beginning and even experienced programmers.

ORGANIZATION OF RPG CONTENT

Content Flow

The chapters in this book are arranged to provide a logical flow of material.

▸ Chapter 1 provides a complete overview of the RPG language and three pre-coded RPG programming exercises which familiarize students with the program entry utility and the compiler they will use.
▸ Chapter 6 on array processing is followed by coverage of table and array lookup in Chapter 7. The random reading of table and array data in this chapter leads to the random retrieval of data records using the CHAIN operation in Chapter 8. Chapter 9 covers the random writing of data using the EXCPT operation.
▸ RPG structured operation codes are presented where they make the most sense. Those that are available with most versions of RPG are in Chapter 11; those limited to RPG III and RPG/400 are in Chapter 14.

Flexibility

Care has been taken to present the material in as flexible a manner as possible.

▸ The discussion of keyed (indexed) files in Chapter 8 can be taught as early as Chapter 4.
▸ The discussion of interactive programming and screen design in Chapter 12 can be taught at anytime.
▸ Chapter 14 covers features of RPG that are available only in RPG III and RPG/400. Thus, this chapter can be skipped altogether or taught at any time the instructor desires.
▸ Several appendices include material that can be taught or referenced at any time.

STUDY AIDS AND EXERCISES

Each chapter in this book concludes with the following:

Chapter Summary

This summary helps students study by listing the key points presented in the chapter.

Review Questions

These questions help students review the key concepts of the chapter.

Student Exercises: RPG Program Code

These exercises test students' grasp of the programming presented in the chapter by requiring students to develop short blocks of code based on the chapter's content.

Student Exercises: RPG Debugging Programs

These exercises require students to correct coding errors commonly made in RPG syntax and logic.

Student Exercises: RPG Program Maintenance

In these exercises students make and explain modifications to the sample program shown in the chapter.

Student Exercises: Programming in RPG

These exercises allow students to apply the chapter's concepts to the solution of typical data processing problems. Exercises range from simple, which closely parallel the program presented in the chapter, to difficult, in which students work with more demanding applications. These exercises require students to apply not only the concepts they have learned in this chapter but also the concepts mastered in previous chapters. Thus, they reinforce cumulative learning. Several of these exercises are built upon earlier, simpler Programming Exercises and instructors can assign them as new programs or allow students to build upon previously completed programming exercises.

SUPPLEMENTS

Instructor's Materials

Two teaching materials supplement this book. They are the Instructor's Materials and Instructor's Diskette.

Instructor's Materials

This manual includes three items to help improve instruction and learning.

▸ **Lesson Plans** These plans begin with chapter behavioral objectives. Next an overview of each chapter is included to help the instructor quickly identify the purpose and key concepts. Detailed outlines of each chapter follow. They are annotated with the page number of the textbook on which the outlined material is covered; notes, teaching tips, and additional activities that the instructor can use to embellish the lesson; and a key for using the transparency masters.

▶ **Answers/Solutions** Complete answers and solutions for all of the Review Questions and Student Exercises are included to ease course administration.

▶ **Transparency Masters** This section of the Instructor's Materials includes 150 key illustrations from the text.

Instructor's Diskette

This free supplement contains data sets for all of the programs in the book in both 5 1/4'' and 3 1/2'' formats.

═ ACKNOWLEDGMENTS ═

This book is the result of the contributions of many people. We would like to thank those who worked diligently to assure a quality publication: Yvonne Howell, copyeditor; Victoria Vandeventer, text design; Janet Bollow, cover design; Jeanne Huntington, typesetter; Charles Garbarino, computer operator; Ken Russo, Michael Broussard, layout; and John Foster, artist; Martha Simmons, editorial assistant; Becky Herrington, production coordinator; Mary Douglas, director of art and production; and Susan Solomon, director of development.

RPG II, RPG III, & RPG/400:
History &
Language Concepts

The data processing industry has undergone dramatic changes since it began in the late 1940s. Much of the drama has centered around changes and improvements in computer hardware and software. Devices such as card readers, card punches, and paper tape readers and punches have all but disappeared from computer installations. Peripheral devices such as magnetic tape units, disk storage devices, and other input/output units used with the computer have undergone enormous improvements in speed and capacity. As computer hardware has evolved, so too has the art and science of programming. This includes the job done by programmers and the tools available to the programmer for solving problems.

Programming can be broken down into two broad categories: systems programming and applications programming. **Systems programming** is concerned with programs that control the computer and make it easier to operate and program, whereas **applications programming** is concerned with programs that use the computer to perform a task or solve a problem.

Systems programmers develop operating system software. The **operating system** monitors and controls the microsecond-by-microsecond operation of the computer by means of programs that control input/output equipment, detect errors and malfunctions within the computer, and control the simultaneous operation of as many as several hundred jobs. Systems programmers also design and develop utility programs, which provide for easy manipulation of data, and programming language translators, which are then available for the applications programmer to use to solve problems. In addition, systems programmers are responsible for making changes to the operating system and utility programs.

Applications programmers usually work in the areas of scientific programming and business programming. **Scientific applications programmers** normally write programs requiring a large number of complex mathematical calculations. In many cases, they are mathematicians or engineers who are using the computer to solve problems with which they are directly concerned. **Business applications programmers**, on the other hand, write programs to solve problems relating to the business transactions of a company. Payroll, sales, billing, accounts payable, accounts receivable, production control, and inventory control are examples of such business problems. Business programming is normally performed by a professional programmer working in the data processing department, rather than by computer users, such as accountants. Thus, business programmers are required to write programs for a variety of applications within a company and should be not only skilled in computer programming but also knowledgable about business in general and about the company for which they work.

An applications programmer can use numerous programming languages. Some of these languages are designed to solve a specific type of problem and are, therefore, of limited use. Others, such as COBOL, BASIC, Assembler, and RPG, are capable of solving a variety of business problems and are in widespread use. One of the most productive and easiest to use languages for business applications programming is RPG.

HISTORY OF RPG PROGRAMMING LANGUAGES

The RPG II, RPG III, and RPG/400 languages are based on the **RPG** language developed in the early 1960s by International Business Machines (IBM) for use on their small-scale computer systems. At that time, many companies were converting from electromechanical punched card equipment controlled by hand-wired plug boards to electronic computers controlled by stored programs. The IBM employees created RPG to permit data processing departments to generate the same reports on their new computers that the older equipment had been providing. With RPG this could be accomplished with almost no interruption of a company's required data processing activities. The name RPG, **Report Program Generator,** is based on this original purpose: to easily generate programs for the production of printed reports. Much of the terminology of the language is based on terms used with the older, electromechanical equipment, which was made obsolete by the development of the small, transistorized computers.

RPG has gained wide acceptance as a programming language not only in small-scale computer installations but also in medium- and large-scale installations. Several versions of RPG are now available for use on such desktop computers as the IBM PC and PS/2; in addition, it has been implemented on computer systems by a variety of other manufacturers. RPG is widely used for business applications.

The original RPG language has undergone many changes. With the introduction of the System/3 computer in the mid-1960s, IBM released the RPG II language. **RPG II,** an enhanced version of the original RPG, contains features that enable it to be used for more than just generating printed reports. RPG II itself has been enhanced many times since its introduction (though it has kept nearly all its original features) and is the primary programming language for IBM's mid-range series of computers. The IBM System/38 uses a more advanced version of the language, **RPG III,** which was designed to take advantage of System/38 internal hardware. RPG III, also supported by the IBM Application System/400 (AS/400), contains features not available in RPG II. Some of these features make it possible for a single RPG III program instruction to perform operations that require several instructions in RPG II; RPG III also permits the use of types of databases that cannot be used by RPG II programs. However, every enhancement to RPG II has reduced the differences between RPG II and RPG III, and some operations that were originally available only with RPG III have been added to RPG II, which is available on various computers. Today, differences between the two languages are few.

In June 1989, IBM introduced the AS/400 series of computers and a new version of RPG, RPG/400. **RPG/400** contains all the features of RPG III and, for the first time, deletes some features of RPG that were available in all previous versions. The most notable of these deletions is support of the punched card as a data input or output medium. Other than this deletion, few differences exist between RPG III and RPG/400. Figure 1-1 briefly summarizes the development of RPG.

To avoid confusion in this text, the name RPG will be used to refer to RPG II, RPG III, and RPG/400. If a statement refers to RPG II, RPG III, or RPG/400 only, we will use the full name of the language.

HOW IS DATA ORGANIZED?

Data must be organized before it can be processed. This is true whether the data will be processed by hand or by computer. If someone threw all the forms and documents about the students at your school into unlabeled boxes, it would be impossible to find information needed for grades, scheduling, and so on. So documents about students are organized and kept in file cabinets. Perhaps there is one file folder for each student, and the folders are kept in order by name or student identification number. Each folder probably contains all the documents about a single student. The documents contain specific information, such as home address, health information, last semester's grades, and scholarship information.

Data to be processed by computer is also organized. The units of computer data organization are the field, record, and file. A **record,** the basic unit of data organization, is made up of a group of **fields,** each of which contains a specific unit of information such as part number, description, price, unit of measure, or quantity. Data is read into the computer and processed one record at a time. A **file** is a series of records containing the same type of information. Figure 1-2 shows the relationship of fields, records, and files.

	Introduced	Features
RPG	Early 1960s	Card oriented, limited arithmetic ability, program logic totally controlled by RPG, designed as a conversion aid from punched card equipment to computers
RPG II	Mid-1960s	Based on IBM System/3 computer, expanded disk and tape processing abilities, logic only partially controlled by RPG with some logic controllable by programmer, interactive programming ability
RPG III	1980	Based on IBM System/38 computer, structured operation codes, source program entry utility, screen design aid
RPG/400	June 1989	Based on IBM Application System/400, expanded file handling operations, elimination of obsolete data processing functions such as punched card processing

Figure 1-1   RPG language development

Field: Area in a record reserved and used for a particular item of data

Record: Group of related fields

File: Group of related records

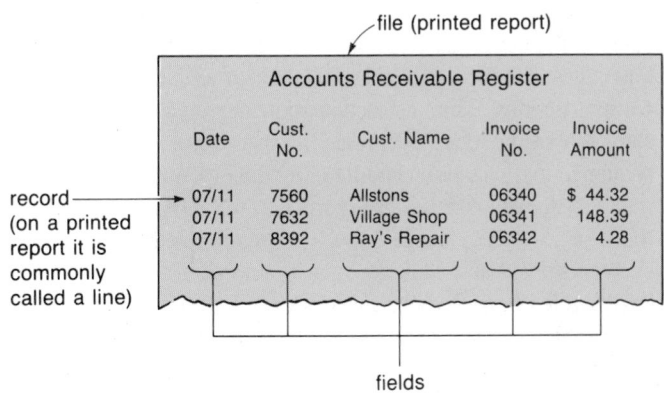

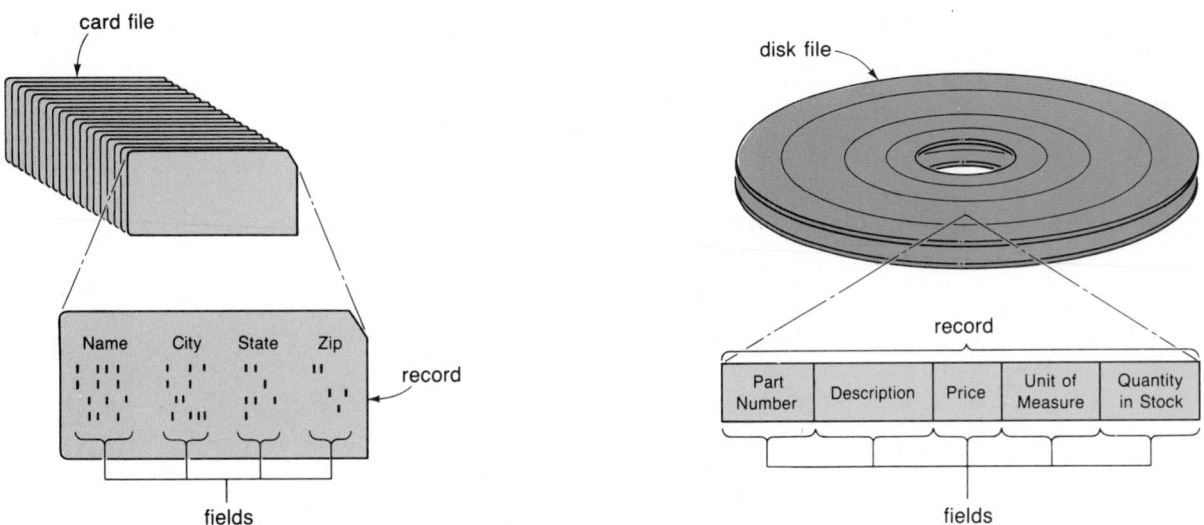

Figure 1-2   Field, record, and file relationship

Unlike the file cabinet system, a computer may or may not keep all information about a student in a single file. Computer information is often organized in the form of a database, which is one very large file containing all the information about every student. Another method is to organize data into a series of smaller files, each of which contains a single type of data. For example, a student master file contains one record for each student. Each record contains several fields of information, such as name, date of birth, and street address, that apply to the same student. The student grade file has for each student, a record containing all information about his or her previous grades. If your school keeps its information in separate files, you are probably listed in five or six different computer data files.

RPG IS DIFFERENT

RPG differs from other widely used programming languages in three important ways:

- ▸ RPG programs are controlled by a fixed logic cycle.
- ▸ RPG uses different specification sheets to describe different parts of the program.
- ▸ RPG uses indicators.

The RPG Fixed Logic Cycle

A **computer program** is a series of instructions. These instructions are executed in a specific sequence, causing the computer to process data in an orderly manner and develop the needed result. In most programming languages, the most difficult and error-prone part of the programming process is to determine the proper sequence for instructions. This instruction sequence is called the **logic** of the program. RPG uses an automatic sequence of steps to execute every program. In other words, all RPG programs have identical logic. This logic is a predefined sequence that was built into RPG by the systems programmers who developed the language.

As you can see in Figure 1-3, the **RPG logic cycle** is a continuous loop containing twelve steps. Some of these steps, such as steps 2 and 11, are completely automatic and cannot be controlled by the programmer. Others, such as steps 7 and 12, may or may not occur depending on the instructions written by the programmer. The RPG logic cycle contains those functions that are found in almost every computer program. Among these are reading input data (step 3), stopping the program when there is no more data to be processed (steps 4 and 9), and performing calculations (steps 7 and 12). Because the logic of all RPG programs is based on this cycle, an understanding of the cycle's sequence of events is fundamental to developing RPG programming skills.

It may appear that the fixed logic cycle would limit the ability of a programmer to work with RPG. This was true when RPG was first developed. Some programming techniques could not be used due to the limitations caused by this fixed logic. Other techniques could be used only if the programmer wrote some of the instructions in another programming language and merged them into the RPG program. However, the development of RPG II, RPG III, and RPG/400 eliminated these restrictions. RPG II, RPG III, and RPG/400 contain operations that permit the programmer to "break" the cycle and perform operations whenever needed.

RPG Specification Sheets

Most programming languages use a single coding sheet. A **coding sheet** is a form on which a programmer writes the instructions that make up a program. Because one form is used for all the different types of program instructions, a programmer must memorize or look up the way in which each part of the program must be coded. RPG programmers use a different **specification sheet** for each part of the program. Figure 1-4 shows one of the seven common specification sheets. Each of the seven has a different format because each sheet serves a unique function within the program. For example, RPG uses one specification sheet to describe the data being read into the computer by the program, a different one for the operations being performed on the input data, and a still different one for the output that the program will generate.

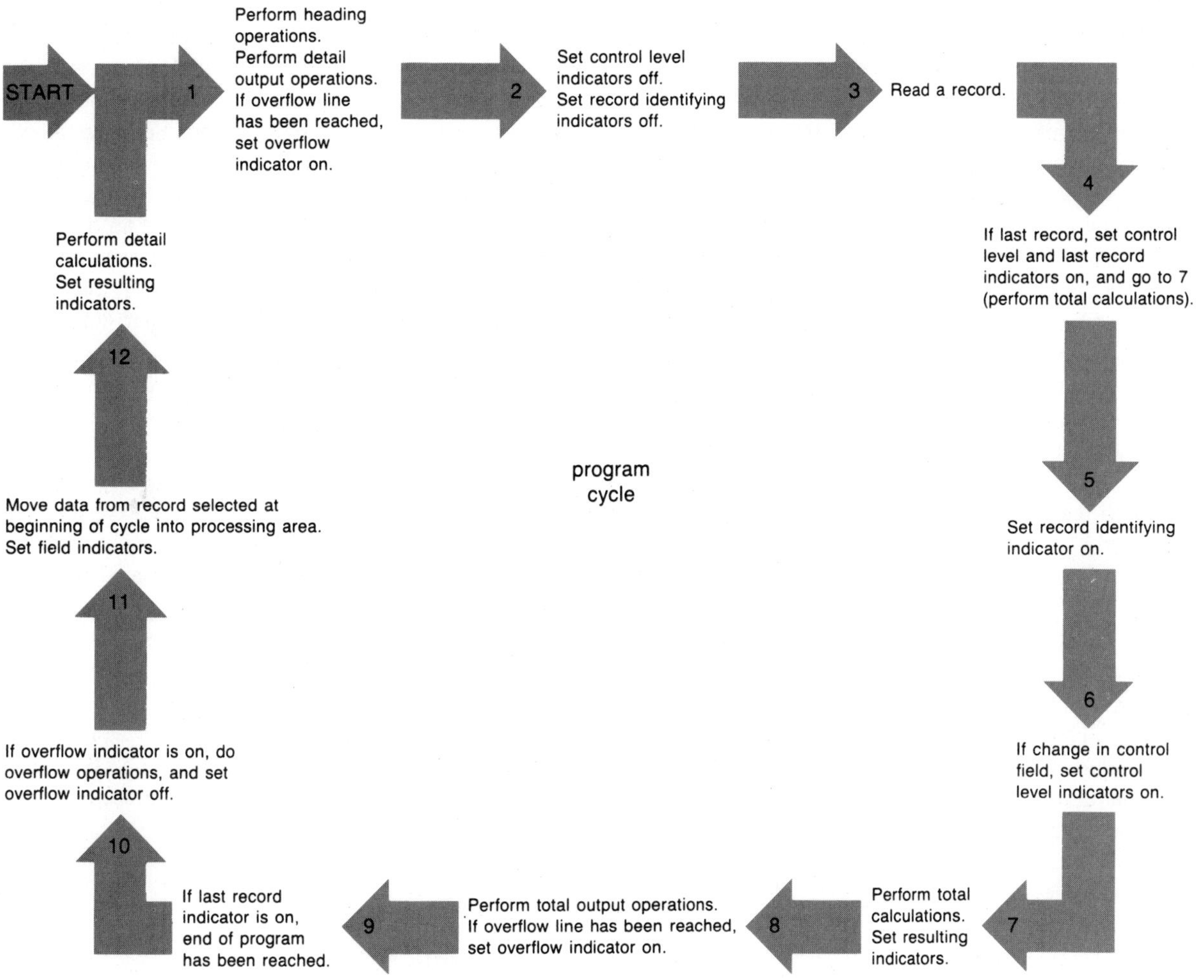

START
1
Perform heading operations.
Perform detail output operations.
If overflow line has been reached, set overflow indicator on.
2
Set control level indicators off.
Set record identifying indicators off.
3
Read a record.
4
If last record, set control level and last record indicators on, and go to 7 (perform total calculations).
5
Set record identifying indicator on.
6
If change in control field, set control level indicators on.
7
Perform total calculations.
Set resulting indicators.
8
Perform total output operations.
If overflow line has been reached, set overflow indicator on.
9
If last record indicator is on, end of program has been reached.
10
If overflow indicator is on, do overflow operations, and set overflow indicator off.
11
Move data from record selected at beginning of cycle into processing area.
Set field indicators.
12
Perform detail calculations.
Set resulting indicators.
program cycle

Figure 1-3 RPG logic cycle

program name
keying instructions
page area
program identification
RPG INPUT SPECIFICATIONS
Program ANALYSIS REPORT
Programmer GOODWIN
Date 5-17-91
Page 02 of
ANLRPT
programmer name
date written
position numbers
form type area
line area
Filename or Record Name
Field Location
From
To
RPG Field Name
Field Indicators
Plus
Minus
Zero or Blank

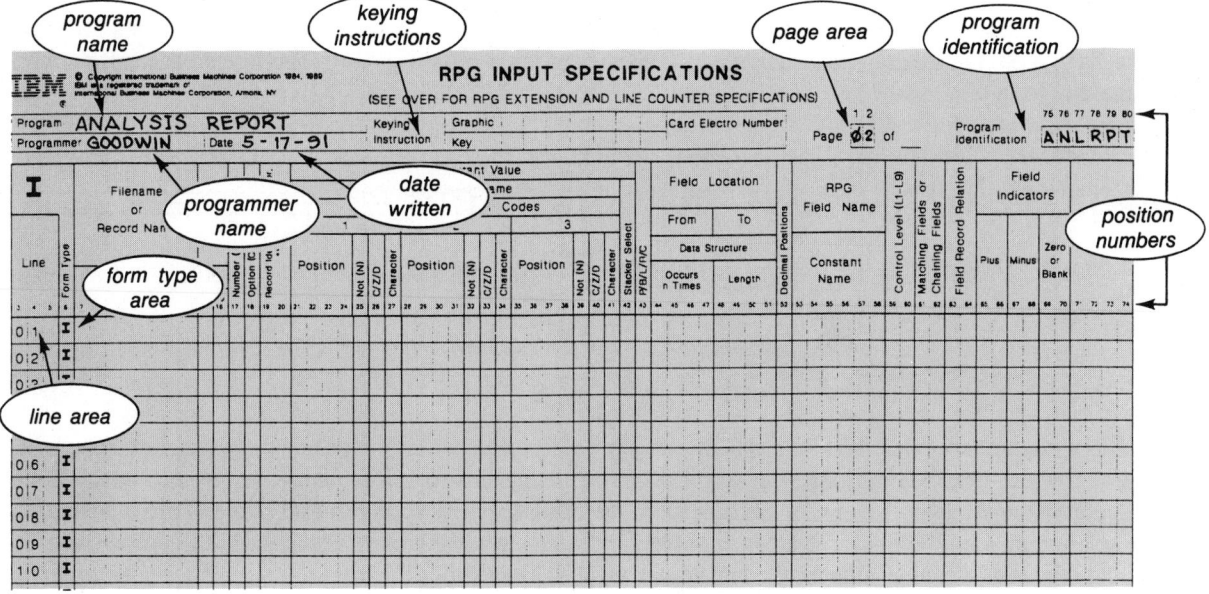

Figure 1-4 RPG coding sheet

An **area** is a part of a specification sheet into which a programmer writes specific information. All areas of every RPG specification sheet are identified by headings that specify the name of the area. The area name iden-tifies the information the programmer will enter. All the RPG specification sheets contain several **common areas**. Some of these areas—such as Program, Programmer, Date, and Keying Instructions—are for reference only and are not part of the program. Areas that are a part of the program are also identified by small numbers that show the position of the area within the line of the specification sheet.

The **Page area** identifies each page of the program and its sequence within the program; it is used in con-junction with the **Line area** at the left of the specification sheet to assign a sequence to every line of an RPG pro-gram. These areas were of vital importance when programs were punched into decks of cards, with each card representing a single line of code. If a program deck was dropped or the cards somehow became out of order, the page and line areas were used to restore the proper sequence. In a modern programming environment, where pro-grams are entered directly onto a computer disk, these areas have lost their importance; (they remain on the speci-fication sheets because a small number of card-based computer systems are still in use). Although programmers still number pages to ensure their proper order, they usually do not enter the page and line numbers since the com-puter automatically keeps specifications in the order in which they are keyed.

The **Program Identification area** is normally used to assign a name that will uniquely identify the pro-gram. If the programmer makes no entry in this area, most versions of RPG will assign the name **RPGOBJ** to the program.

The one remaining area common to all specification sheets is located in position 6 of the main body of the sheet. This is the **Form Type area**, which provides a unique identifier for each of the different RPG specification types. Because this entry is preprinted on every line of every RPG specification sheet, it is sometimes overlooked when one enters the program into the computer. This entry is required, and it must be keyed as part of every line of program code.

The area labeled **Keying Instructions** is used to eliminate any confusion caused by differences in print-ing. Figure 1-5 shows how this area can be used to prevent confusion between the letter O and the digit 0, the let-ter I and the digit 1. The Keying Instructions area is generally used only if the program will be entered, or keyed, into the computer by a person other than the programmer who wrote it.

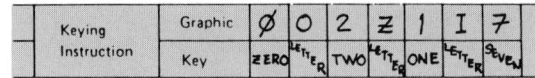

Figure 1-5 Keying instructions

To understand how the information a programmer writes on these specification sheets forms a complete program, you must understand what kind of information each specification provides. Remember that not every pro-gram needs to use all of these specification sheets. Whether or not a certain specification is used depends on the requirements of the program.

TYPES OF RPG SPECIFICATION SHEETS

Most versions of RPG use seven types of RPG specification sheets: Control, File Description, Extension, Line Counter, Input, Calculation, and Output.

Control Specification

The **control specification** (form type H), Figure 1-6, provides information about the program and the computer on which it will be run. Every program must contain one control specification, and it must be the first specification in the program. No entries are needed on the control specification form other than form type and, generally, program identification. The areas left blank in this figure are used for special machine control com-mands and often differ from computer to computer. If any of these additional entries are needed for your computer, they will be specified by your instructor or computer center manager.

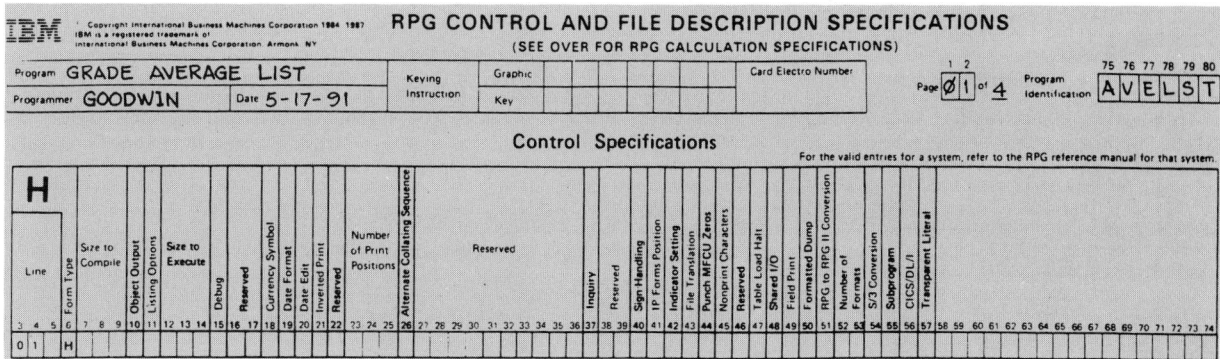

Figure 1-6   RPG Control Specifications

File Description Specifications

File description specifications (form type F), Figure 1-7, provide the description of each data file used within a program, the input/output device that will access the file, and the way in which the file will be used. RPG requires a separate file description for every file in the program. If a file is not described by a file description specification, it cannot be processed by the program.

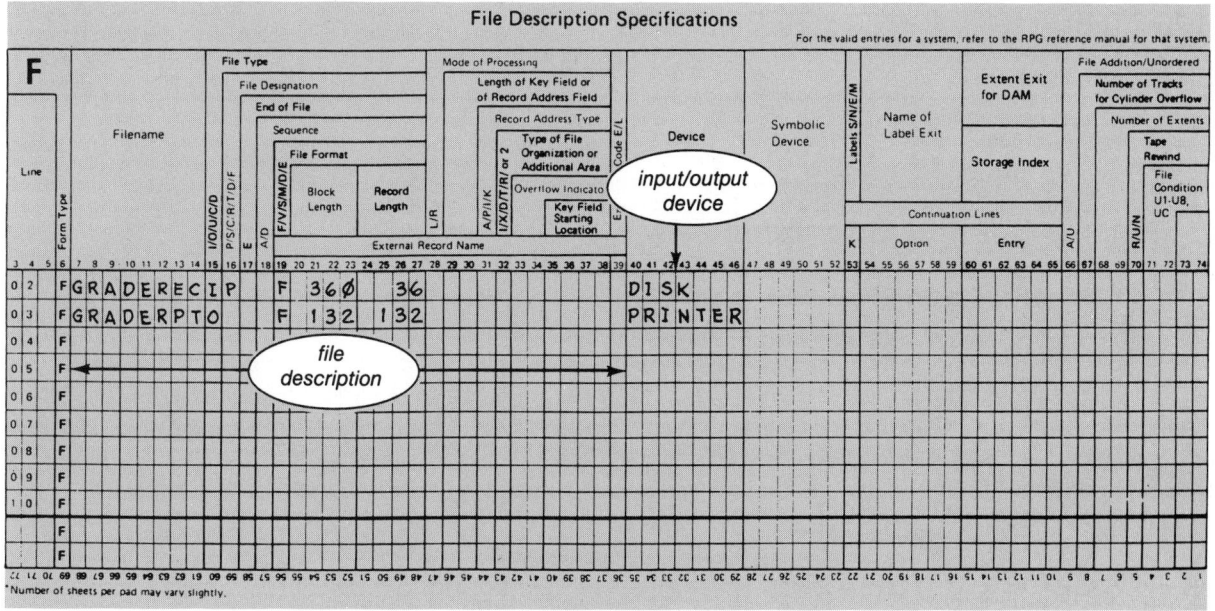

Figure 1-7   RPG File Description Specifications

Extension Specifications

Extension specifications (form type E), Figure 1-8, are used to describe three special data types: record address files, tables, and arrays. Extension specifications are used only if these types of data appear in your program. This specification, in conjunction with other specifications, is used to fully describe these data types.

IBM RPG EXTENSION AND LINE COUNTER SPECIFICATIONS
(SEE OVER FOR RPG INPUT SPECIFICATIONS)
Printed in U.S.A.
Program | Keying Instruction | Graphic | Key | Card Electro Number | Page of | Program Identification
Programmer | Date
Extension Specifications
E | Line | Form Type | Record Sequence of the Chaining File | Number of the Chaining Field | From Filename | To Filename | Table or Array Name | Number of Entries Per Record | Number of Entries Per Table or Array | Length of Entry | P/B/L/R | Decimal Positions | Sequence (A/D) | Table or Array Name (Alternating Format) | Length of Entry | P/B/L/R | Decimal Positions | Sequence (A/D) | Comments

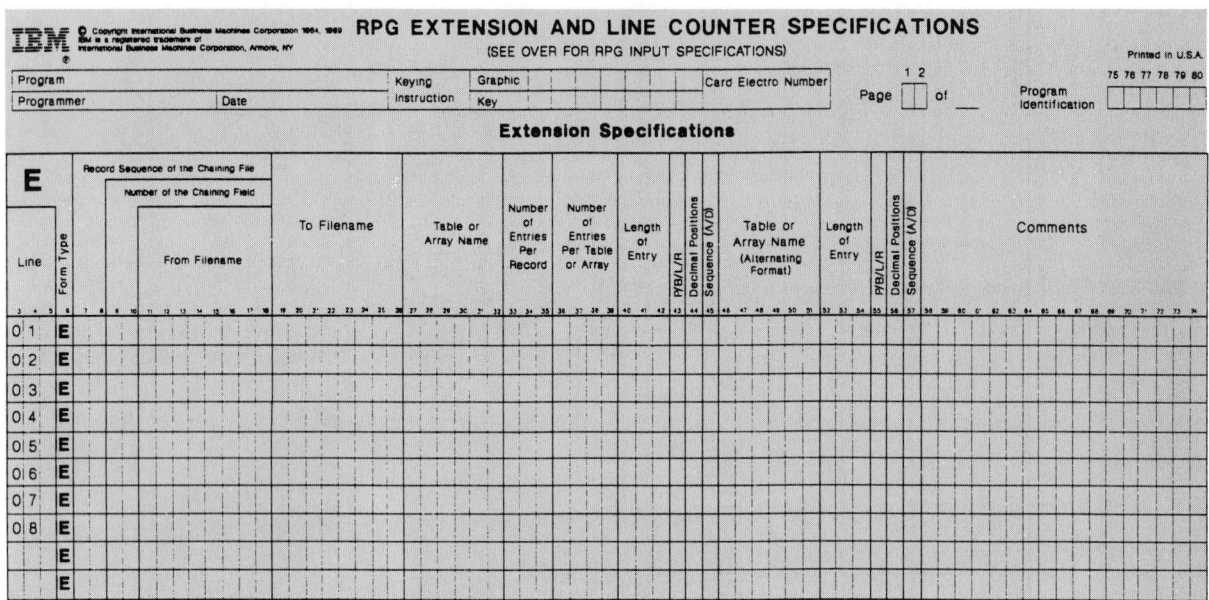

Figure 1-8 RPG Extension Specifications

Line Counter Specifications

Line counter specifications (form type L), Figure 1-9, are used only with printed output files. These specifications indicate the length of the printed page and the point at which the program should advance to a new page. The IBM System/36, System/38, and AS/400 can use other methods for determining this information; they do not use this specification for standard sized paper (11 inches long), but do use it for nonstandard sizes. In addition, some versions of RPG use the line counter to control the movement of paper to a specific line on a page before data is printed. For example, information must be printed on specific lines of a check in order for the check to be accepted by a bank. The line counter specification can control the proper positioning of the checks for printing.

Line Counter Specifications
L | Line | Form Type | Filename | 1 Line Number, FL or Channel Number | 2 Line Number, OL or Channel Number | 3–12 Line Number, Channel Number

* Number of sheets per pad may vary slightly.

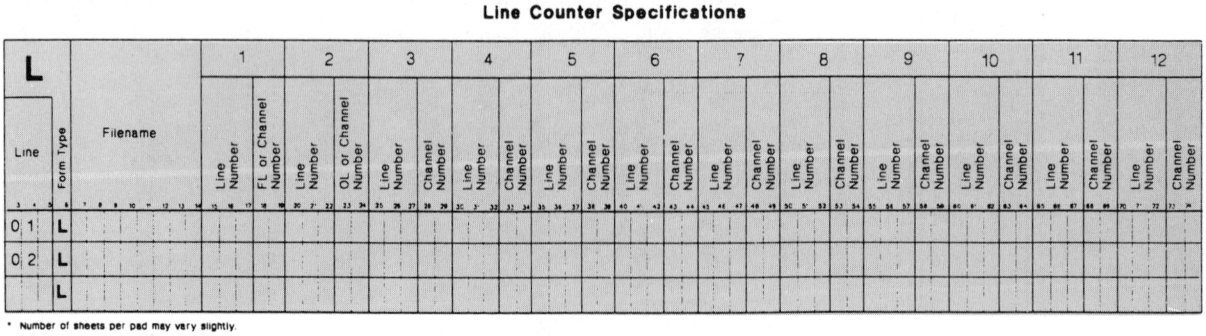

Figure 1-9 RPG Line Counter Specifications

Input Specifications

Input specifications (form type I), Figure 1-10, are used to describe the records and fields contained in the data files being read into a program. RPG requires that only the fields used by a program need to be described on the input specifications. Unused fields need not be shown. This feature makes the description of input data with RPG much easier than, for example, with COBOL, which requires that every field in a record be described, even if it is not used by the program. The input specifications also make it easy to describe the different record types that are identified by a data code in a specific position. An input specification can describe a record by coding entries in positions 7–42 or describe a field by coding entries in positions 43–70; an input specification line may contain either of these entries but not both. This sheet is best thought of as serving two functions: The left side describes input records, and the right side describes data fields within the records.

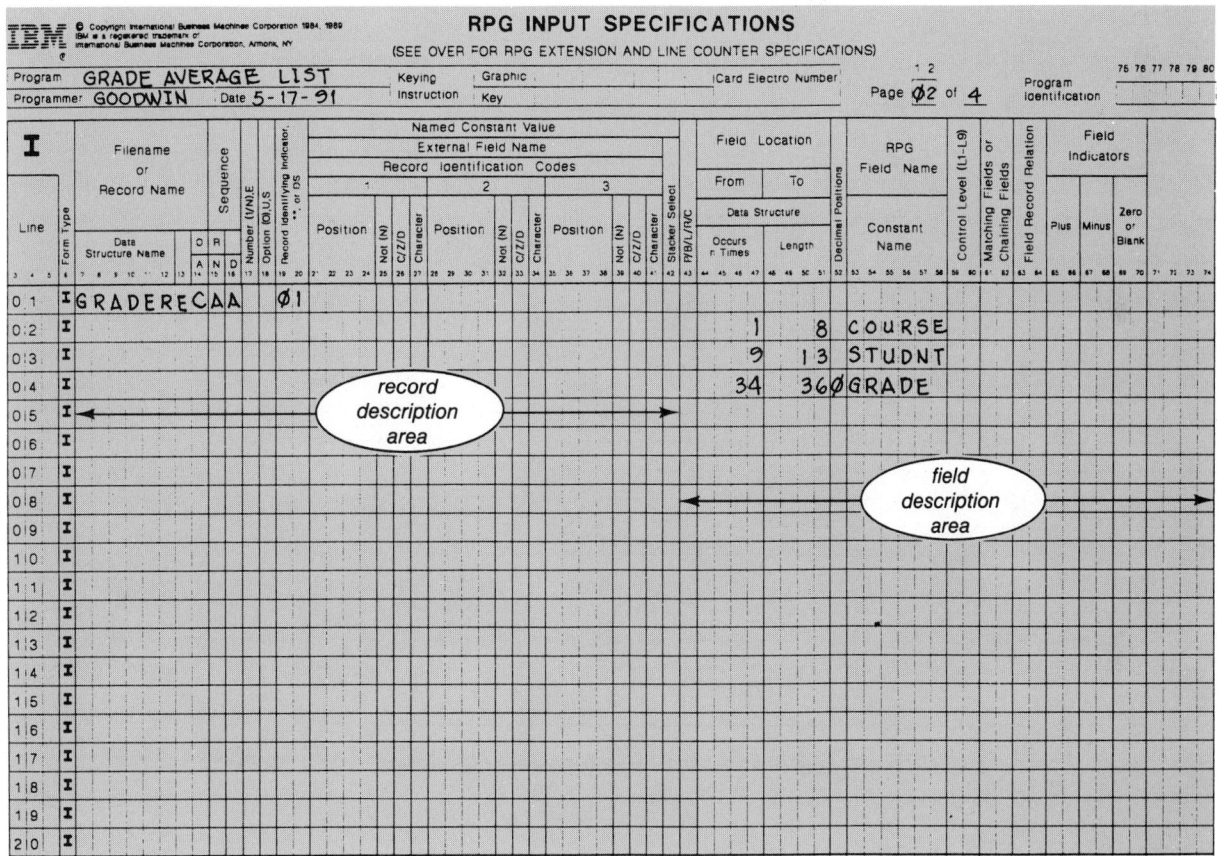

Figure 1-10   RPG Input Specifications

Calculation Specifications

The word *calculation* usually means an arithmetic operation, but this is not necessarily the case in RPG. The **calculation specifications** (form type C), Figure 1-11, are used to describe any operation that is not under automatic control of RPG fixed logic. In addition to arithmetic operations, the calculation specifications are also used to describe data movement, comparison, and some input and output operations. The programmer can control when (or if) an operation is to be performed, the type of operation to be performed, and tests to provide information about the results of an operation.

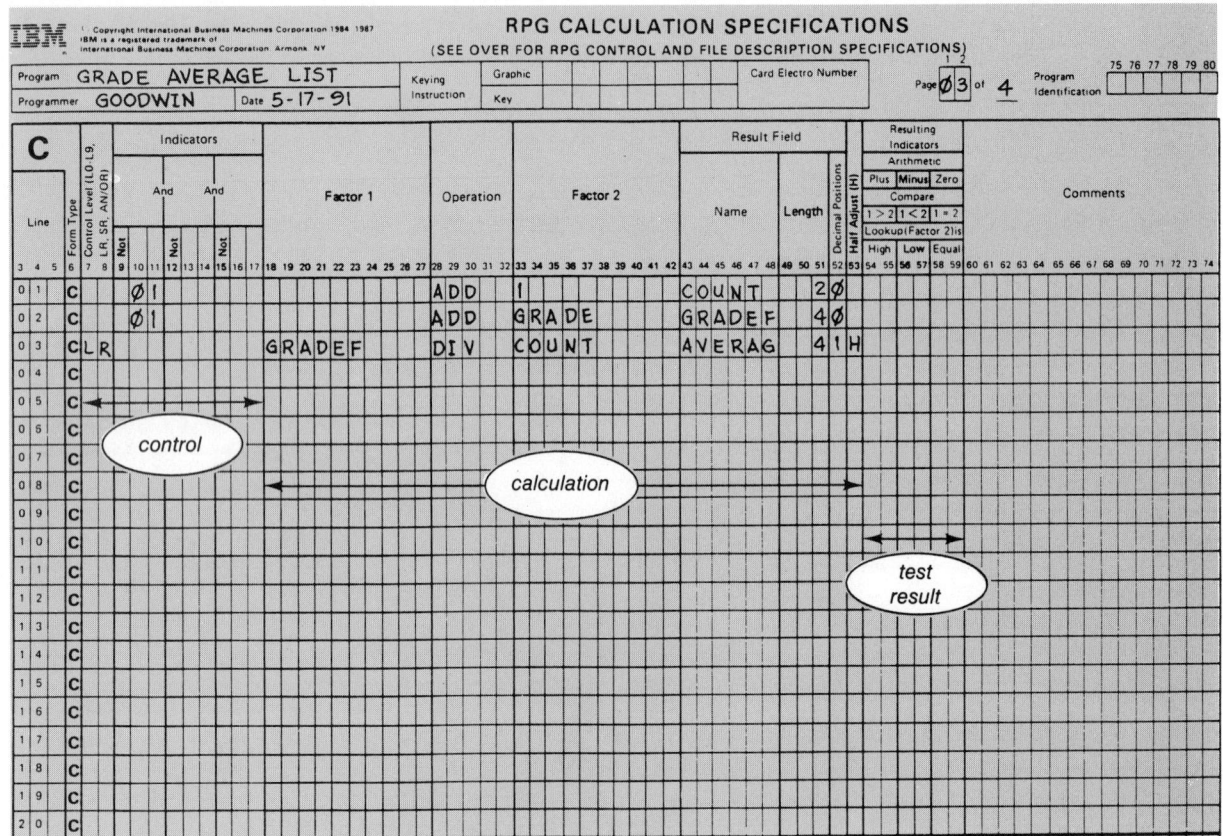

Figure 1-11 RPG Calculation Specifications

Output Specifications

Output specifications (form type O), Figure 1-12, describe the records and fields contained in output files. They appear in almost every RPG program. Coding of the output specification is similar to that of the input specification. Use the left side of the specification (positions 7–37) to describe output records and the right side (positions 23–70) to describe fields. Also like the input specification, an output specification line may contain either a record description or a field description but not both. Note that the division between record and field description areas is not clear cut in this case. Positions 23–37 comprise an overlap area and may be used with positions 7–22 as part of a record description *or* with positions 38–70 as part of a field description.

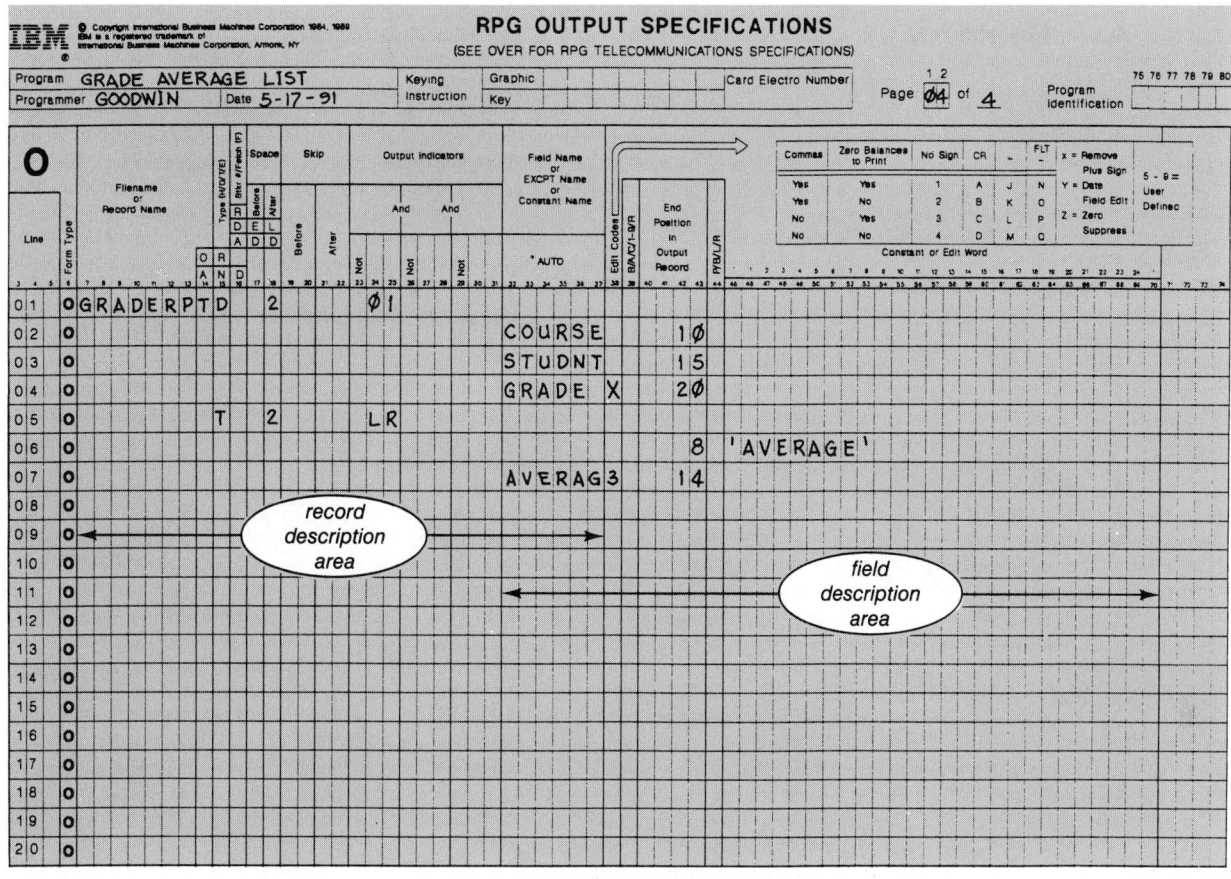

Figure 1-12   RPG Output Specifications

SPECIFICATION SEQUENCE

You must always use the specifications in a program in the correct sequence. Otherwise, RPG will not be able to process them properly. The correct sequence for RPG specifications is the following:

    Control Specification
    File Description Specifications
    Extension Specifications
    Line Counter Specifications
    Input Specifications
    Calculation Specifications
    Output Specifications

If a specification type is not used, the remaining specifications must still be in the proper sequence. For example, if a program contains no extension and no line counter specifications, then the input specifications immediately follow the file descriptions.

ADDITIONAL SPECIFICATION TYPES

A few additional types of specifications are listed separately from the commonly used specification types, for the reasons stated.

Indicator Summary

The **indicator summary** (Figure 1-13) is not a specification sheet but helps the programmer keep track of internal switches used by the program. Although the indicator summary is shown as form type F in this figure, the programmer may use it anywhere in the program, with the appropriate form type code.

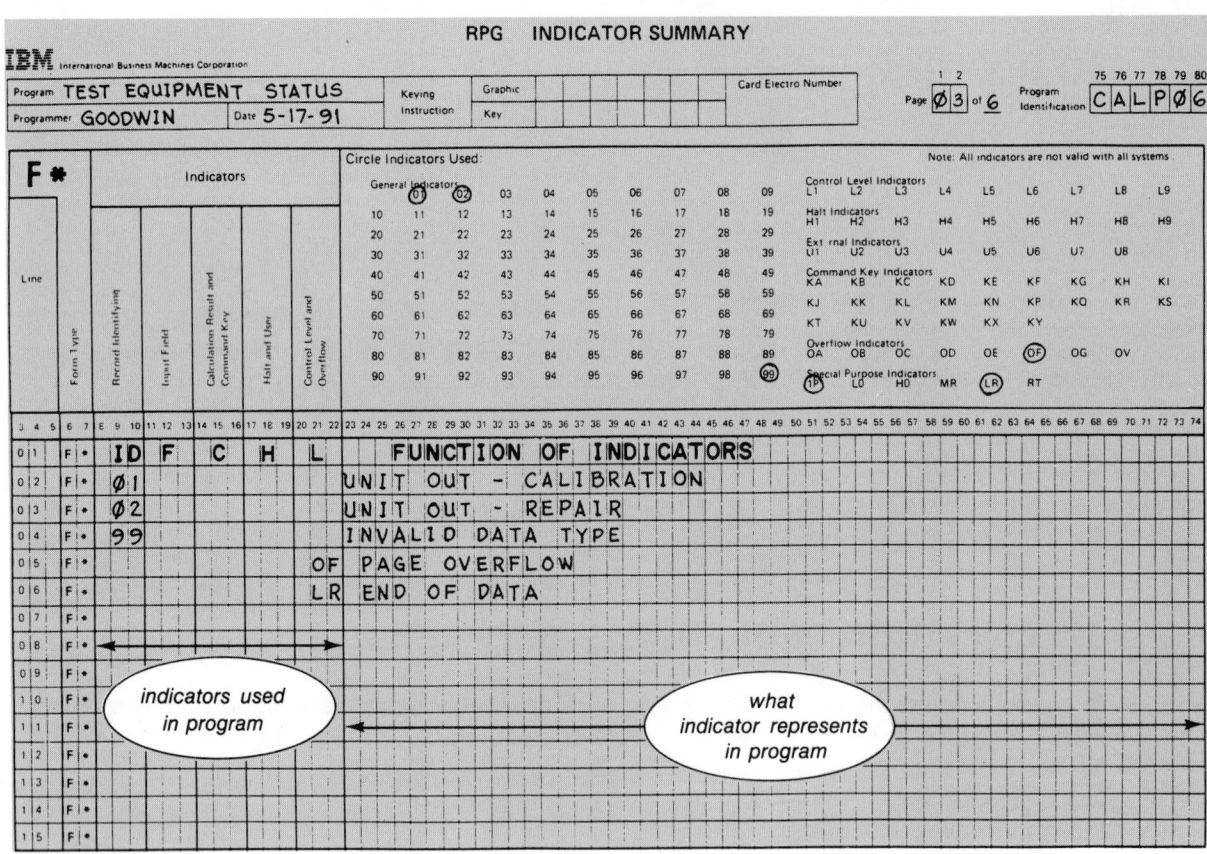

Figure 1-13   RPG Indicator Summary

Display Format Specifications

The **display format specifications** (Figure 1-14) are not a part of RPG. They are part of a separate system program, the System/36 Screen Design Aid, and are used to design and code screen displays in programs that interact with an operator at a terminal. The IBM Screen Design Aid software can translate display format specifications into System/36 RPG II input and output specifications for inclusion in a program. Display format specifications are also used with several micro-computer versions of RPG.

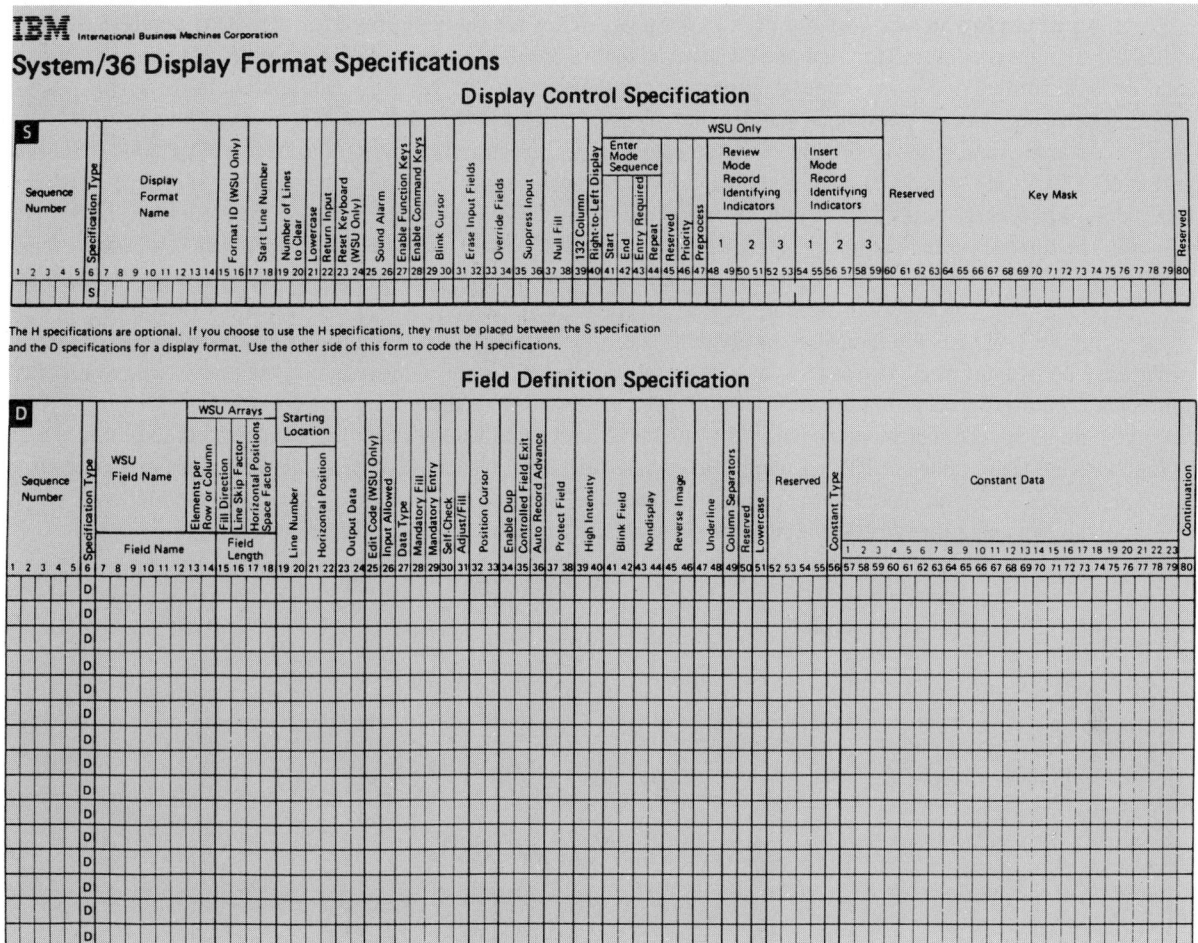

Figure 1-14   System/36 Display Format Specifications

INDICATORS: THEIR USES AND IMPORTANCE

An **RPG indicator** is a switch that can be turned on or off to provide information about the result of an instruction performed in by the program. Indicators are not switches in the physical sense. They are not like the push buttons on a television set or stereo system, and they are not like the toggle switches that turn room lights on or off. Indicators are positions of computer memory that contain either of two data values, which can be thought of as representing yes or no, on or off, or any two values needed by the programmer. Every programming language has some means by which the programmer can define and set switches. These program switches are used for many purposes: to show the result of a comparison, to indicate that there is no more input data to be processed, or to indicate any other condition needed by the programmer.

Switches also have the ability to communicate information from one portion of a program to another. Once a switch is turned on or off, its setting remains unchanged until the program resets it. Because of this ability, it is possible to compare two data fields in one part of a program, set a switch to indicate the result of the comparison, and base an operation or group of operations, much later in the program, on the result of the comparison. For example, early in the processing of an employee's payroll record an indicator could be turned on to show that the employee had authorized a payroll deduction for a charitable donation. Later in the processing, after the employee's gross pay had been calculated, this same indicator could control instructions to calculate the deduction and subtract it from the gross pay.

An RPG programmer does not need to define switches for use in a program since RPG contains over 150 indicators that are predefined for such use. These indicators are used to control, for example, whether or not a calculation is performed and when output data records are to be produced. Not only can operations be performed if an indicator is on, but it is possible to specify that an operation be performed only if a given indicator is off.

As is the case with fixed logic, an understanding of indicators is important to becoming a good RPG programmer. As you saw when you studied the RPG logic cycle in Figure 1-3, indicators play a major role in RPG fixed logic. Every step, except for step 3, either sets indicators or bases an operation on the setting of an indicator.

The number of indicators and complexity of steps in the logic cycle may at first appear somewhat overwhelming. Their use, however, is introduced in stages in this book. As you learn about each function of RPG, the logic steps and indicator functions needed for that function are presented.

Figure 1-15 lists the indicators available to the programmer. Each is identified by a two-character code, which may be two numbers, two letters, or a letter and a number. Some of these indicators may not be available on your system, however, because they are used for specific functions. If these functions are not available on the computer you are using, the indicators also are not available. Some manufacturers have added indicators to permit the use of functions they have added to RPG. Figure 1-15 is based on IBM System/36 RPG II. If you are using a different computer, check with your instructor or computer center manager to determine which indicators are available.

The two categories of RPG indicators are special purpose and general purpose.

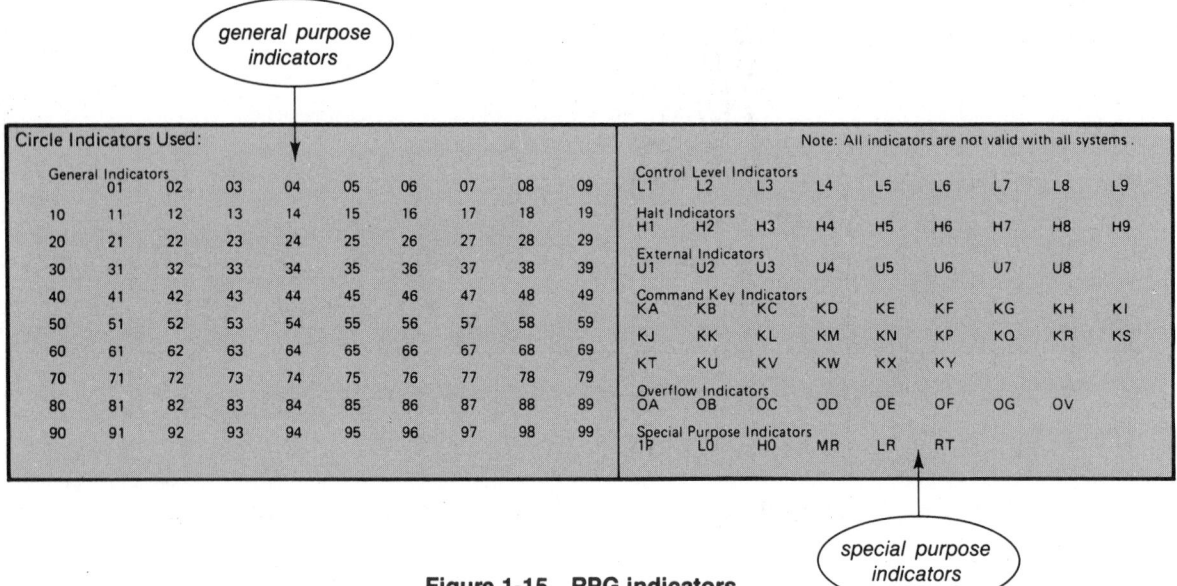

Figure 1-15   RPG indicators

Special-Purpose Indicators

Special-purpose indicators are those that have a predefined meaning to RPG. They are meant to be used for specific functions and must be used as defined by the RPG language. All these codes contain at least one letter. Note that several groups of special purpose indicators, such as the U and K indicators, share the same first letter. Each indicator in these groups works in the same way and performs essentially the same function. Having more than one indicator with the same function enables several similar conditions to be determined and communicated within a program. Examples are the H, or Halt, indicators. Setting any of these indicators on causes the program to stop executing, generally because of an error condition. By having ten halt indicators, a programmer is able to check as many as ten different error conditions, stopping the program if any of them occurs. When a program halts due to an H indicator, the program shows the indicator causing the halt. From this the computer operator is able to identify the error condition that stopped, or terminated, the program.

General-Purpose Indicators

General-purpose indicators are used whenever the programmer needs an indicator within a program and no special purpose indicator exists for the function. The codes for these indicators consist of two numbers from 01 through 99. You do not need to use these indicators in any specific sequence. Any one of them can be used wherever a general purpose indicator is required in the program.

PROGRAMS ARE DEVELOPED NOT JUST WRITTEN

Whenever a problem is to be solved by use of a computer, the programmer must write a program that will process data on the computer. Contrary to popular belief, however, not all of a programmer's time is spent in **coding** the program, that is, writing instructions in a programming language. Most of the time, a programmer is analyzing the problem, determining the best solution to the problem, testing the program to ensure that it works properly under all conditions, and documenting the program. The **program development process** begins with a request that one or more programs be written to solve a problem or meet a need. The process ends when the program is in regular use and the need has been met. The steps needed to convert this programming request into a business application are the following:

Problem definition
Problem analysis
Coding
Desk checking
Program entry
Program compilation
Program testing
Documentation

Problem Definition

Traditionally, systems analysts have designed the overall system, which is composed of one or more programs, and then this design has been turned over to a programmer who develops the application program. Recently, however, in companies with small or medium-sized computer installations, these tasks are often performed by a programmer analyst, who both designs and develops the programs for the system.

Problem Analysis

The **problem analysis** process determines the needs of the individual programs based on information gathered from several sources. These sources include the eventual end users of the system, management, and past experience in the development of similar systems and application programs. This information is then organized into a form that can be used as a guide to program development. Typically, the information takes the form of the following three formats: a definition or layout of the input data files and records used in the program; a definition or layout of the output, which the program must generate; and some type of written narrative that describes in detail the processing that is to take place within the program. Figure 1-16 shows an example of information gathered for a typical program.

PROBLEM

Write an RPG program to produce an Author's Royalty Report. Authors receive a 10% royalty if the net quantity of books sold (quantity sold – quantity returned) is less than 10,000. If the net quantity of books sold is 10,000 or more, the authors receive a 12% royalty. The royalty is calculated by multiplying the total sales (net quantity × unit price) by the royalty rate.

INPUT

Input consists of the Book Sales File containing author identification, book title, quantity sold, quantity returned, and unit price. The format of the input file is:

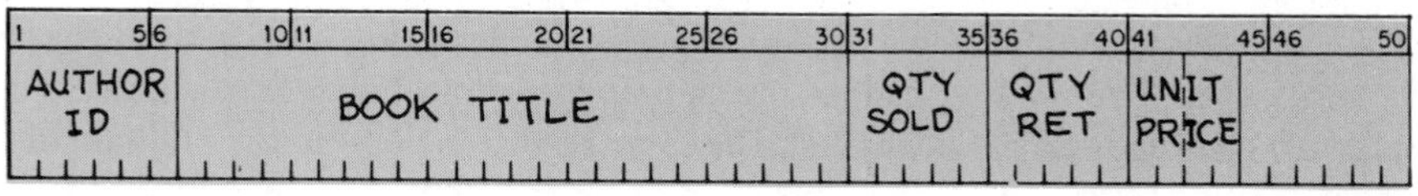

OUTPUT

The output report that is to be produced is

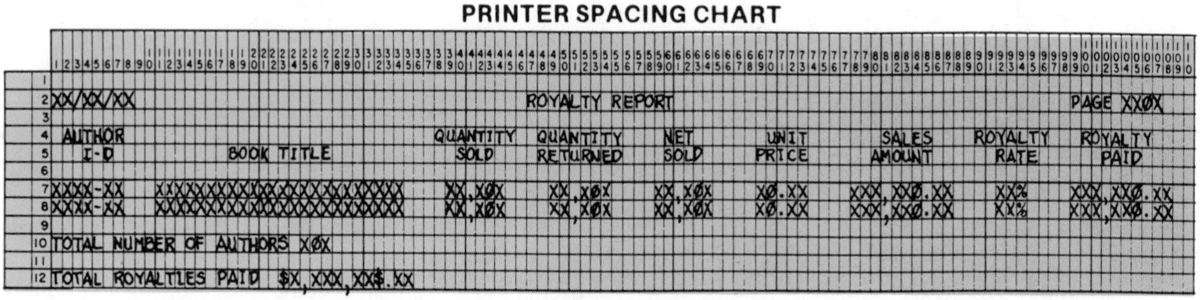

PRINTER SPACING CHART

Figure 1-16 Programming specifications

Too much emphasis cannot be placed on the requirement that a programmer fully understand the processing that is to occur within the program. If the requirements of a program are not fully understood, it is impossible to write a program that will properly process data under all conditions. The purpose of the input layout, output layout, and written narrative developed during the systems analysis process is to communicate specific information to the programmer. This information pertains to one of the three fundamental areas of the basic data processing cycle: input, processing, and output.

▶ **Program Output** Analysis of a program begins with a complete understanding of the output that the program must generate. This output can be a printed report, a screen panel to display on a terminal, or a data file to be stored on disk or magnetic tape. It may, at first, seem strange to begin the analysis process with the final result. But it is impossible to properly determine the input that is needed and the processing steps required to develop the output data unless, first, the analyst clearly understands the objective of the program.

One common form of program output is the printed report. Figure 1-17 shows a printer spacing chart annotated with the types of information it provides about the report to be generated by the program. The **printer spacing chart** is a guide to the coding of the RPG output specifications and shows the location and format of the output fields, any punctuation to be used in numeric data, field names to be used within the program, and the spacing to be used between lines of the report. In addition, the printer spacing chart may provide information to be used in coding the file description specification for the printed file.

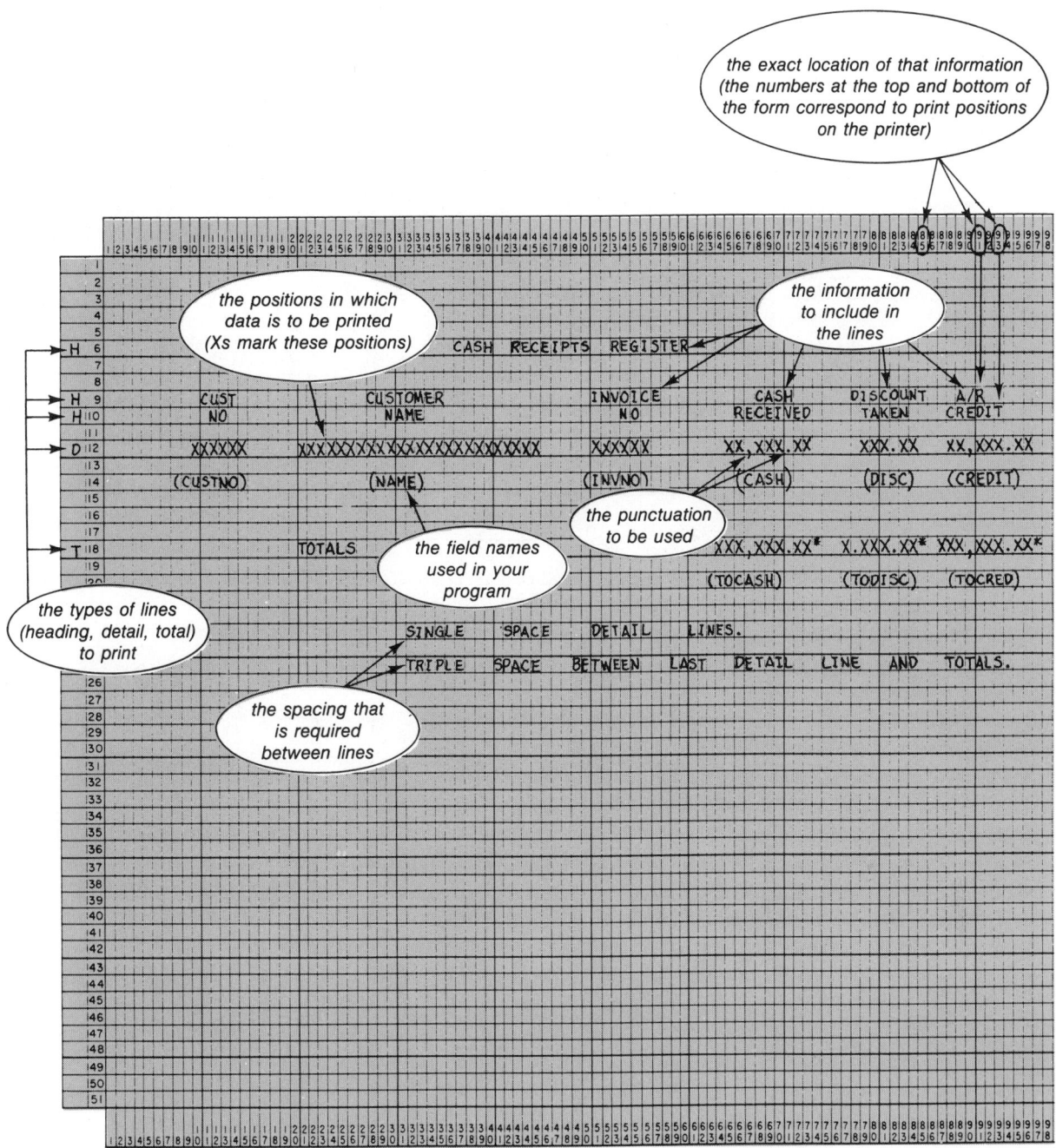

Figure 1-17   Printer spacing chart

▸ **Program Input**   The **proportional record layout form** (Figure 1-18 on the next page) is a guide to coding the file description specifications for the input data file and to coding the input specifications. This form provides information about the input file, record formats within the file, and the location, format, and size of data fields within the input record. As is the case with the printer spacing chart, you can use the record layout form to provide field names for use within the program. It is important to remember that the program does not necessarily use all data fields shown on a record layout form even though the record layout shows the complete structure of a record within a data file. As you have seen, RPG is not like other programming languages such as COBOL; RPG does not require that all data fields be defined. You need to define only those fields used within a program. Defining a field that is not used will result in a warning message when the program is translated into machine language prior to being executed.

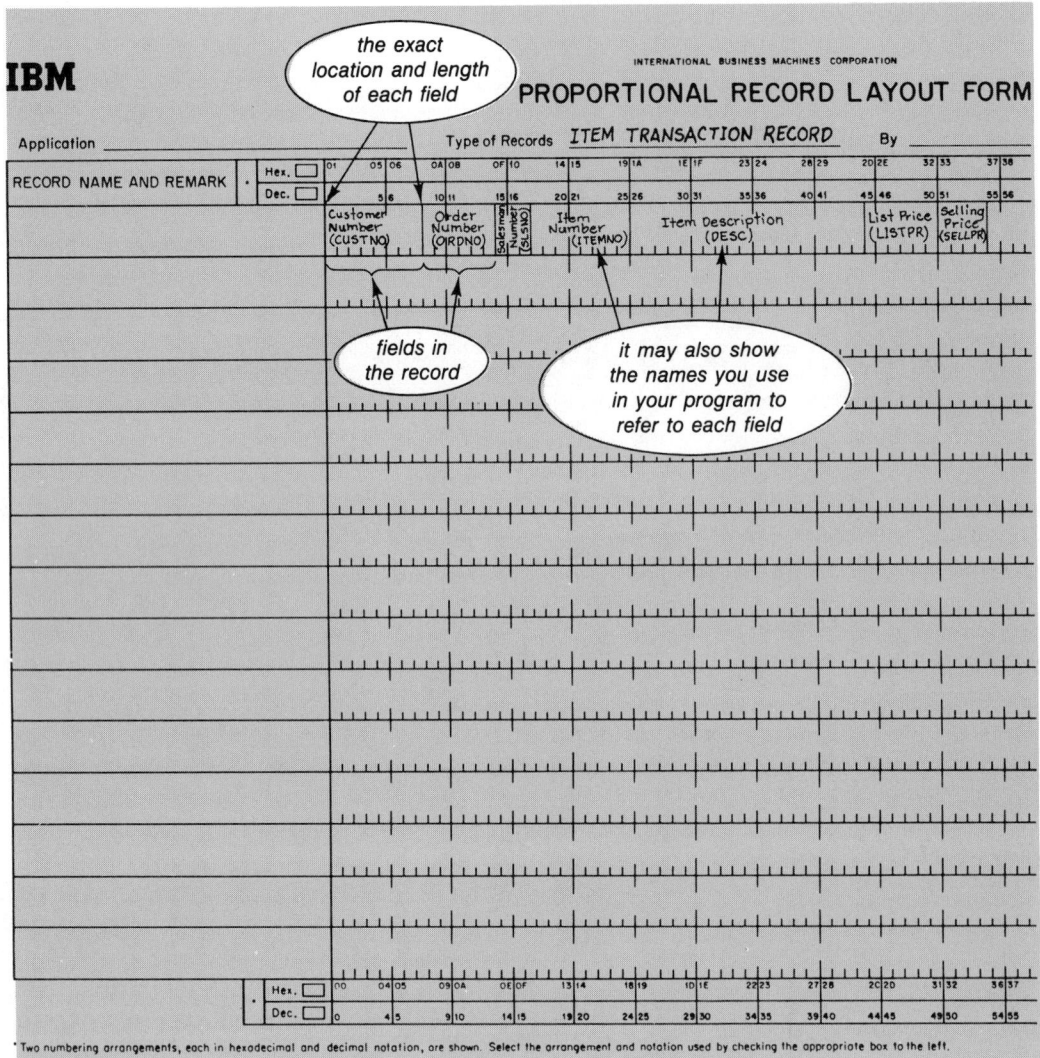

Figure 1-18   Input record layout

▸ **Program Processing**   The **processing** phase of problem analysis involves determining the program logic needed to get the correct results. This is, in most cases, the most difficult step in problem analysis. Flowcharts are the most commonly used tool for logic definition. Due to the internal logic of RPG, however, flowcharts are not widely used with this language. An exception to this occurs in RPG III and RPG/400 environments, as some RPG functions available in these versions are best planned by using flowcharts. Program processing is based on the narrative instructions (Figure 1-19) developed during the systems analysis phase. The narrative provides specific processing instructions to be followed when coding the calculation specifications. In addition, comparing the record layout and printer spacing forms shows the programmer those fields that must be generated within the program as a result of processing.

It is essential that the programmer take whatever time is necessary to fully understand the desired objective of a program and the steps needed to reach that objective, before proceeding to the next step in the program development process.

PROGRAM OBJECTIVE

Develop a program to calculate and print an amortization schedule for all loans granted. This schedule shows the amount of the monthly payment, the portion of the monthly payment applied against interest, and the portion of the monthly payment applied against principal. This information will be developed for each month that the loan is in force. The account number, client name, interest rate, and loan amount information are in the Loan Application File. The month field will begin with 1 and be incremented by 1 for each payment shown on the report. The beginning principal, payment amount, interest due, principal payment, and new principal data will be calculated in accordance with the following processing instructions.

PROCESSING

To calculate the information for the amortization schedule, the following calculations must be performed:

1. Since each payment is to be made monthly, and since the interest is compounded monthly, the yearly interest rate on the input record must be divided by 12 to determine the interest charged each month. This is necessary so that the compound interest can be determined accurately.

2. To determine the payment that is due each month, the following formula is used:

$$\text{Payment} = \frac{A}{\left(\frac{\left[\frac{(1 + i)^n - 1}{(1 + i)^n}\right]}{i}\right)}$$

where A = amount of loan
    n = number of monthly payments
    i = interest rate for one month (interest rate / 12) as calculated in step 1

It is important that the calculations in the formula above are performed in the proper sequence as indicated by the parentheses and brackets. Therefore, the calculations should take place in the following sequence:

   a. Determine $(1 + i)^n$
   b. Determine $(1 + i)^n - 1$
   c. Determine $\dfrac{(1 + i)^n - 1}{(1 + i)^n}$
   d. Divide the answer determined in step c.
   e. Divide A by the answer determined in step d.

The result of the calculation in step e is the monthly payment that is due.

3. Multiply the beginning principal value by the interest rate for one month (calculated in step 1) to obtain the interest that will be paid by the payment. The result is the interest due.

4. The interest due (calculated in step 3) is subtracted from the payment amount (calculated in step 2). The difference is the principal payment, that is, the amount of the payment that is applied to the principal.

5. Subtract the principal payment (calculated in step 3) from the beginning principal. The result is the new principal.

6. The new principal becomes the beginning principal for the next month's payments.

Note that steps 1 and 2 are performed only once, but steps 3–6 are performed for every month a payment is to be made. In addition, the maximum number of decimal places allowed when using RPG should be utilized in all the calculations to ensure maximum accuracy. Rounding should be performed on all calculations. If, after all payments have been made a balance remains, this balance should be added to the last payment.

Figure 1-19   Program narrative

≡ Coding

After thoroughly understanding and planning the logic of the program, the programmer writes code to reflect the required processing. The programmer should take great care when coding the program to include all the steps that are required for the solution of the problem. Attention to detail and accuracy in coding the program will result in far fewer errors when the program is tested. Program code must be written following the rules, or **syntax**, of the RPG language. The entries made in each area of the coding sheets must conform to the rules of the language. An example of an RPG program is shown in Figure 1-20.

A program should also conform to accepted programming practices and standards. A good, well-written program and a quick-and-dirty program that simply does a job are vastly different. Programs are rarely written to be used only once and then discarded; almost all are written to be used on a daily, weekly, or monthly basis over a period of years. A program will often be changed or modified several times during its lifetime. For example, every time changes are made to federal income tax laws, employers must change programs that perform payroll. The task of making program changes is given to a maintenance programmer. A **maintenance programmer** spends most of his or her time changing programs rather than developing new programs. A well-written program makes the job of understanding and changing the program easier; it is easily maintained because it can be changed with a minimum of time and effort. If a program was poorly written, the maintenance programmer has to spend a large amount of time understanding the program before being able to make the required changes. In many cases, errors are made during this modification process due to misunderstanding the way a program functions; and such misunderstandings can be the result of poor programming technique.

Appendix A contains a set of **programming standards** for use with

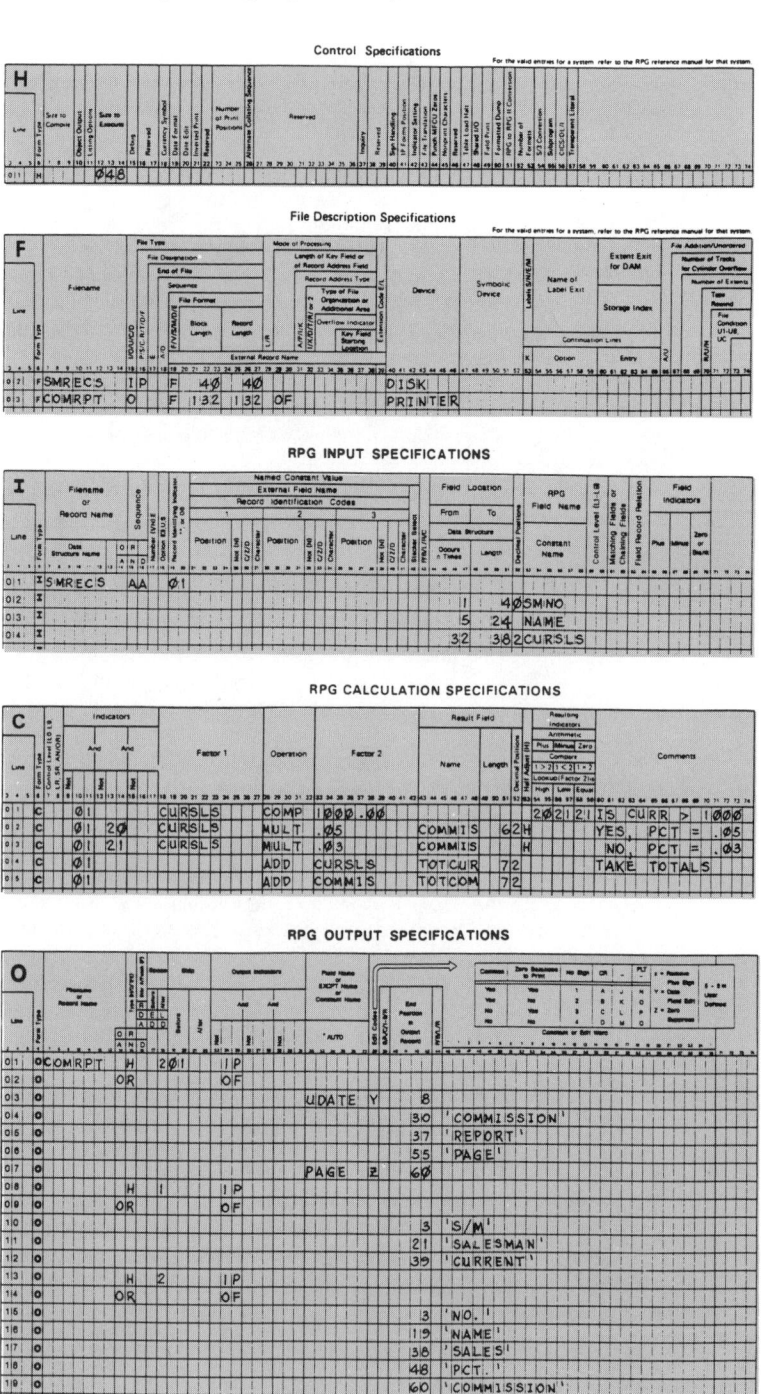

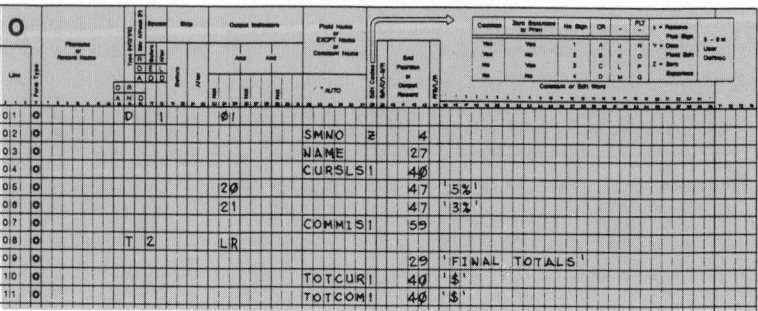

Figure 1-20   RPG program code

RPG. These standards are not language rules. They are guides for good programming practice. These standards are typical of those that are used in most computer installations. The purpose of standards is to cause all programmers to develop programs using a common set of guidelines to minimize confusion.

Desk Checking

Desk checking is the portion of a programmer's job spent, away from the computer, verifying the accuracy of what has been done. Desk checking is the most commonly overlooked part of the program development process. Programmers, especially student programmers, have a tendency to go from the coding phase directly to the computer to enter the program. Before doing that, take time to read the code that you have written and to verify its accuracy. Time taken at this point will eliminate many coding errors and result in less computer time being needed during program development. Desk checking is not only a matter of looking at code to determine that no language syntax errors were made; it is also an excellent time to rethink the development process and detect errors in planning or logic. Although syntax errors can be detected by the computer, logic errors cannot. Errors in program logic become apparent only when the program is run, and they can take many hours, sometimes days, to locate and correct. It is not unheard of for extremely complex programs to contain errors that become apparent only after a program has been in use for several years.

Desk checking is an excellent time in the program development process to check a program against the installation programming standards. Also, at this time, you can check the program against Appendix A, the **RPG coding checklist**, a list of the most common areas in which coding errors are made. This is not a complete list of every possible RPG error but is an aid in the avoidance of the most frequently made coding mistakes.

Program Entry

After the RPG specifications have been coded and thoroughly desk checked, they must be entered in some form that can be processed by the computer. Generally, the program is placed on disk using a program entry utility or text editor. These are programs, developed by systems programmers, that permit programs, data files, and other information to be keyed into the computer and stored on disk.

▶ **Text Editors** A **text editor**, such as DEC's EDT editor, is a general purpose entry program. It is designed to allow the entry of any type of information and is used mainly for word processing applications. The page you are reading now was first written using a microcomputer text editor rather than pencil and paper. Although text editors can be used for the entry of program code, they lack most of the features found in source program entry utilities. Because of this lack of features, program entry with a text editor is slower and more difficult than with a program entry utility.

▶ **Program Entry Utilities** **Program entry utilities**, such as IBM's Source Entry Utility (SEU), IBM's Program Development Manager (PDM), and DEC's RPGESP editor are designed to be used for the entry of programs. Because these utility programs are designed for this specific task, they contain features that make program entry easier and more error free. Most program entry utilities provide automatic formatting of RPG specifications as they are keyed in. All you need to do is enter the form-type letter (H, F, E, L, I, C, or O) of the specification you are keying. The entry utility then displays information showing all the separate areas of the specification and indicates which of these areas are required by RPG.

In addition, program entry utilities provide limited error checking of the specifications as they are entered. For example, you may have coded alphabetic characters into an area that, based on the rules of the RPG language, requires numeric information. When you key this incorrect code into the computer, the program entry utility detects the violation of RPG rules and identifies the error. The way in which you are alerted to the error varies, based on the entry utility you are using. A utility may cause the incorrect entry to flash on the screen of your terminal, cause the incorrect entry to appear more brightly than other information of the screen, or cause your terminal to beep or buzz. Some utilities use a combination of these features to alert you to the error. Program entry utilities cannot detect all possible errors, only those that are commonly made when keying the program into the computer. Appendix D provides a brief introduction to the program entry utilities available on the IBM mid-range computer systems.

⊟ Program Compilation

Regardless of the type of utility used, each line of RPG specification is keyed in as a separate entry. All the specifications a programmer writes and keys into the computer are called the **source program**. This program cannot be executed by the computer. It must first be translated into machine language that can be "understood" by the computer when data is to be processed. This translation of the RPG specifications into machine language is accomplished through use of an RPG compiler.

The **compiler** is a computer program, generally supplied by the computer manufacturer, for the purpose of translating RPG source programs into a set of machine language instructions. Figure 1-21 illustrates the steps in compiling a program.

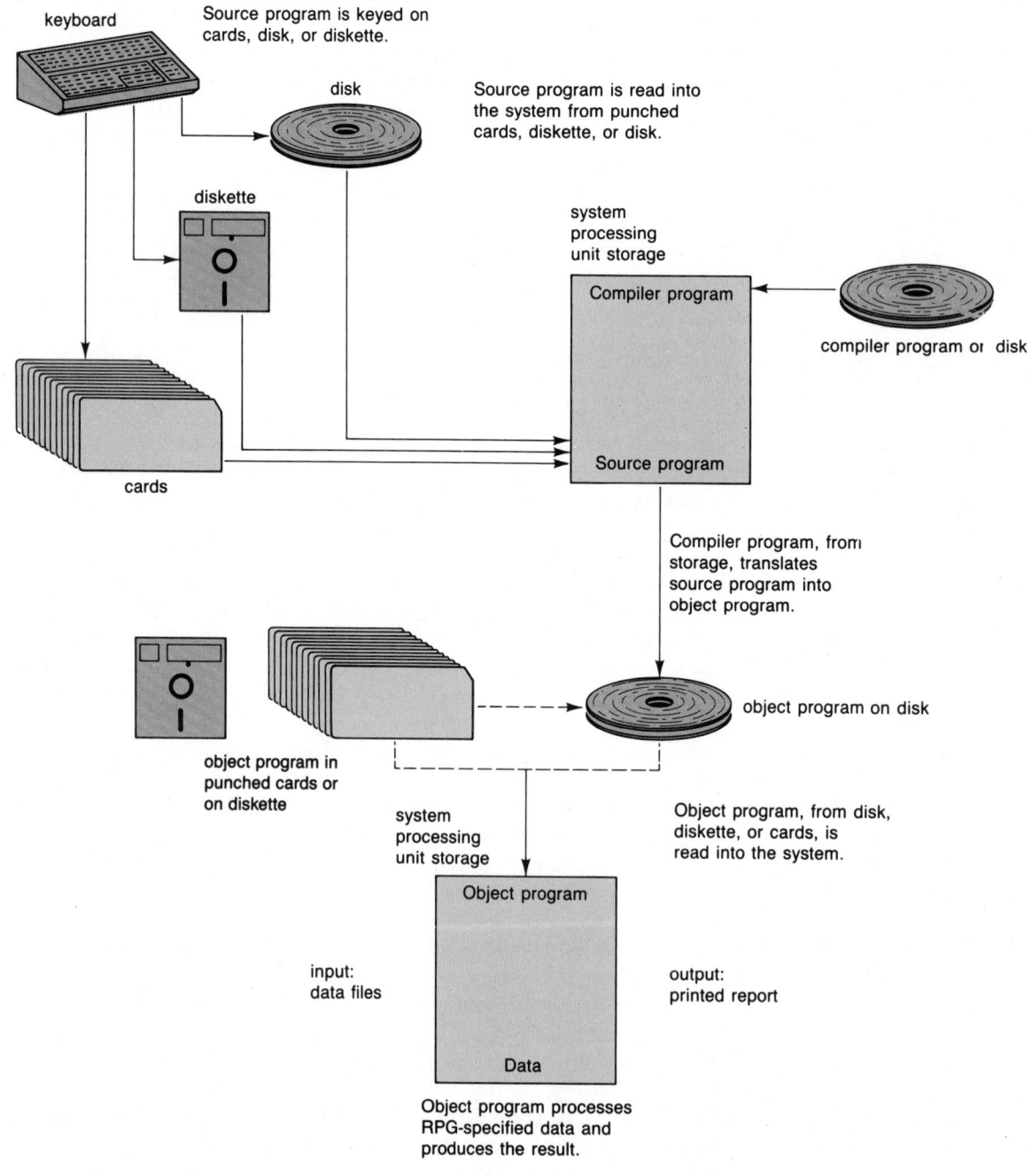

Figure 1-21 Compiling an RPG source program

To convert an RPG source program into machine language form, the computer reads the compiler into the storage unit of the computer from its permanent location on magnetic disk. The compiler is, in fact, copied into main storage and remains available to other users. It is not uncommon for several programs to be compiling at the same time. After the compiler is in storage, the computer reads the RPG source program. The compiler then translates the specifications into machine language form and creates an **object program**, also called a **load member**. When the program is to be executed, this object program, or load member, is read into memory. It is this object program that is executed to process input data and produce the required output.

The compiler also provides auxiliary functions that assist the programmer in checking and documenting programs. Some of these functions are: Source program listings, Cross reference listings, and Error indications.

▸ **Source Program Listing**   The **source program listing** (Figure 1-22) is a computer printout of all the specifications in your source program. This listing may also show any errors that you made when coding or entering the source program.

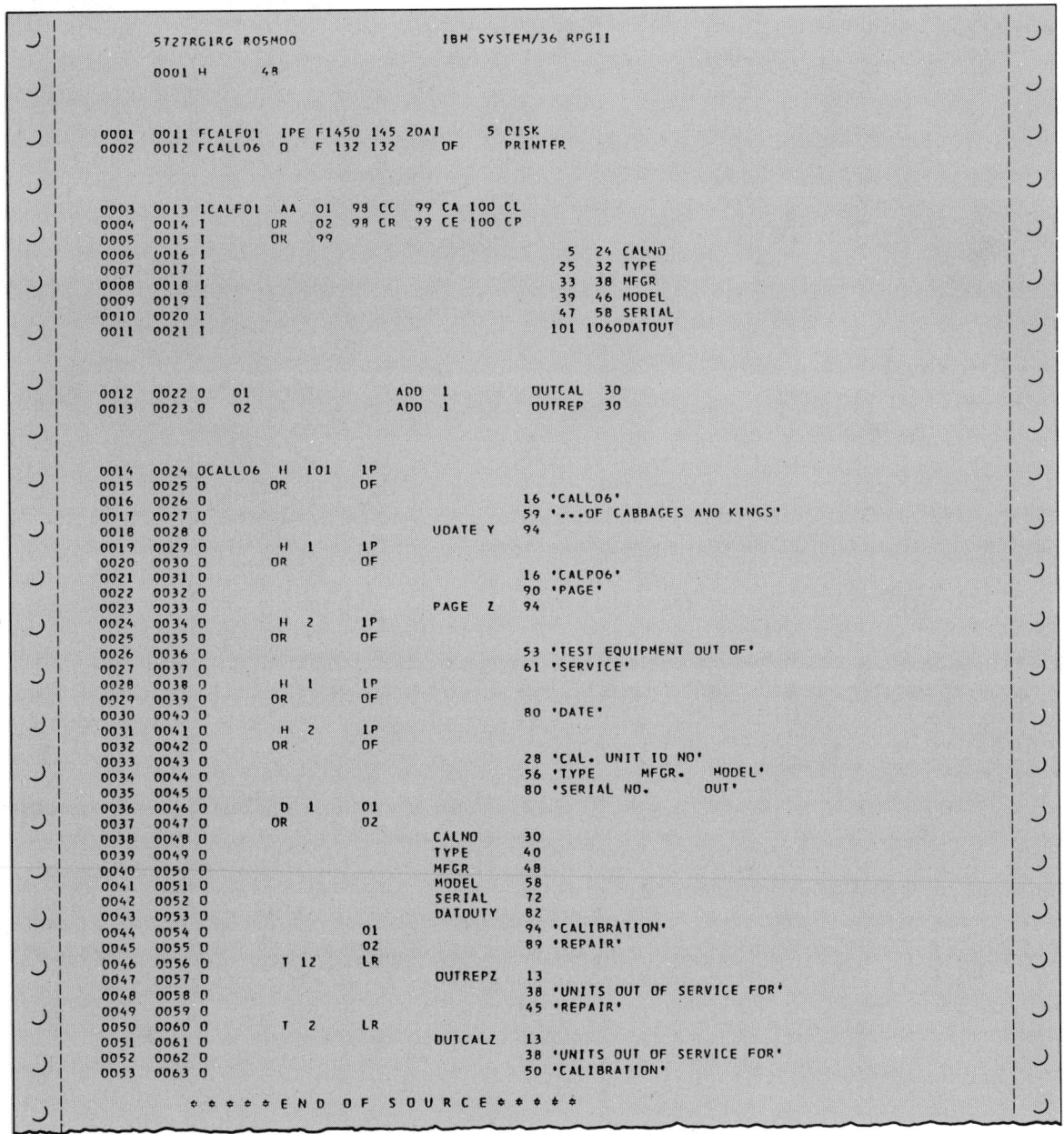

Figure 1-22   RPG source program listing

▸ **Cross Reference Listing** The compiler has the ability to generate a listing of every file and field name used in the program. This **cross reference listing** (Figure 1-23) shows the line number of the specification in which a file or field name is first used, as well as the number of every specification that uses the name throughout the program.

```
                              CALP01    CROSS REFERENCE LISTING


        ** FIELD AND DATA STRUCTURE LEGEND **

    SYMBOL    LNG   DEC   DEFN     REFERENCES


    ACQCST    0008         0017    0025*  0062   0097
    ACQDAT    0006    0    0016    0096   0110   0159
    BLANK     0024         0052*   0053
    CALDAT    0006    0    0018    0055   0056   0098   0112   0161
    CALINT    0002    0    0020    0057   0100   0115   0163
    CALMO     0002    0    0055*   0057*  0058   0059*  0061
    CALNO     0020         0009    0049   0089   0104   0147
    COUNT     0004    0    0084*   0166
    CSTOUT    0006    2    0080*   0111   0160
    DATA      0145         0023
    DONEBY    0006         0019    0099   0114   0162
    FAIDNO    0020         0010    0090   0116   0148
    LOCATN    0004         0015    0095   0109   0158
    MESSAG    0024         0040*   0050*  0053*  0101
    MFGR      0006         0012    0092   0106   0155
    MODEL     0008         0013    0093   0107   0156
    NXTDAT    0006    0    0056*   0060*  0061*  0113   0164
    PAGE      0004    0    0128
    SERIAL    0012         0014    0094   0108   0157
    TYPE      0008         0011    0091   0105   0154
    UDATE     0006    0    0121
    X         0001    0    0063*   0069*  0071   0073   0075   0077
    Y         0001    0    0064*   0066*  0077
```

Figure 1-23   RPG cross reference listing

▸ **Error Indications** As a source program is compiled, it is analyzed for actual or potential errors in the use of the RPG language. Detected errors are indicated as part of the program listing. The RPG compiler can detect two types of errors: terminal errors and warning errors.

▸ **Terminal Errors** A **terminal (or type T) error** (also called a **fatal error**) is a major error that requires correction before a program can be successfully compiled. This type of error represents a serious violation of the rules of RPG. If one or more terminal errors exists in a program, no object program is generated by the compiler. A terminal error usually causes the specification to be ignored by the compiler, which can lead to the generation of other terminal errors. Terminal errors should be corrected from the top down, and all terminal errors should be corrected before attempting to compile the program again.

▸ **Warning Errors** A **warning (or type W) error** indicates an abnormal condition in the source program. A warning may be a syntax error or may represent some condition that the compiler considers unusual. Even if warning errors are present, the compiler will create an object program. Although warning errors do not prevent the creation and execution of an object program, they should be checked carefully since, in most cases, the program will not execute properly. In some cases, warnings will list actions taken by the compiler to permit the program compilation to be completed. Warning messages are also called **informational (or type I)** messages by some versions of RPG. Figure 1-24 shows a typical RPG II error listing. The type of error is indicated by the letter T or W under the heading Severity to the left of the error description text. The error number at the left of each line helps the programmer look up the message in a reference manual if a more complete explanation is needed.

```
ERROR NUMBER   STATEMENT NUMBER
   RPG-0558        0029
   RPG-0901        0079

   ERROR SEVERITY                                    TEXT
   RPG-0305    W    INDICATOR IS ASSIGNED BUT IS NOT USED TO CONDITION OPERATIONS.
   RPG-0314    W    FIELD, TABLE, OR ARRAY NAME IS DEFINED BUT NEVER USED.
   RPG-0315    T    FIELD NAME IS USED BUT NEVER DEFINED, OR TABLE NAME OR ARRAY ELEMENT IS USED AS AN ARRAY INDEX.
   RPG-0558    W    INVALID USE OF, OR MISSING, RESULTING INDICATORS WITH THIS OPERATION CODE. INVALID RESULTING
                    INDICATORS ARE ASSUMED TO BE BLANK.
   RPG-0901    W    MOVING ALPHAMERIC DATA TO A NUMERIC RESULT FIELD MAY PRODUCE UNPREDICTABLE RESULTS.

              * * * * * E N D   O F   C O M P I L E * * * * *
```

Figure 1-24   RPG error message listing

Program testing

After a program has been successfully compiled and all syntax errors have been eliminated, it must be tested to determine that the program is correct and that the data is being processed properly. Program testing involves several important steps that must be followed to ensure that a program contains no logic errors and will operate correctly. These steps are:

Desk checking
Preparing test data
Program debugging

▸ **Desk Checking**   During the compilation process, if any terminal or warning errors are detected, changes are made to the source program to correct these errors. After changes are made, the program should again be desk checked before continuing with the testing process. The program should be checked to be certain it still conforms to the programming standards, and the logic should be reviewed. If any problems are discovered and changes made, the program must again be compiled and desk checked. If no problems are found, the programmer should **"play computer"** by examining each source statement within the program as if the computer were processing the statements. It is important, at this point, that the programmer disassociate from the program and look at each statement as the computer would, with no preconceptions of what the statement should do. If the logic cycle calls for the reading of an input record, the programmer should simulate the read operation by writing down the contents of the fields on a sheet of paper. If a statement adds two numbers together, the programmer should perform the addition and record the result on the work sheet. By performing this process carefully, the programmer can trace the logic that the computer will use when the program executes and find errors that would otherwise not be found until the program is actually processed on the computer.

▸ **Preparing Test Data**   When a program is to be tested, one should use data prepared specifically to test the various routines within the program. One should not test the program using data that will eventually be processed by the program. The reason for this is that a small sampling of "live" data, no matter how it is chosen, is not likely to contain all the situations that may occur in the program. Thus, some occurrences that are programmed for will never be adequately tested if well-prepared test data is not used; it is these untested routines that are likely to fail when the program is in production. Thus, the programmer should design data that can be used to test all aspects of the program so that all routines and processing decisions are tested. Properly prepared test data should include some erroneous data in order to test error detection routines within the program. The preparation of test data is a difficult and time-consuming task, but a necessary one.

▸ **Program Debugging**   After the program has been desk checked and test data has been prepared, the program can be tested on the computer. This process, commonly referred to as **debugging**, is the detection, location, and correction of all program errors. The number of test runs that are required to completely debug a program usually depends on the size and complexity of the program, the thoroughness of the programmer, and the care with which test data was prepared. After each test run of the program, the output must be analyzed. It is possible to predict, based on the test data used, precisely what the output should be. The actual output should be compared against the predicted output, and three questions should be answered:

Was any output generated that should not have been?
Was any predicted output not generated?
Was all generated output correct?

When the answers to the first two questions are no and the answer to the third is yes, the program has been debugged. This process can be both tedious and time-consuming; however, it is important that any program released by the programmer for production use be completely free of errors.

Documentation

Documentation is the process of recording in an organized form all the facts concerning a computer program. The two categories of documentation are internal documentation, which is coded as part of the program onto the RPG specification forms, and external documentation, which is not part of the source specifications.

Internal documentation generally consists of brief explanations of individual parts of the code. It is used to answer questions that a programmer might have about a specific line or group of lines of code. RPG internal documentation is normally not extensive. Figure 1-25 shows a portion of the calculation specifications for a program that uses internal documentation not only to explain coding but also to separate coding segments. The details of internal documentation are discussed in Chapter 4, after you have learned the fundamentals of RPG program code.

External documentation normally contains data record layouts, printer spacing charts, a program narrative describing the routines and programming techniques used in the program, the function of all indicators used in the program, source listings, listings of the input data used in the sample run, and all output produced by the program. If the computer requires special command statements, called **control language**, to run the program, a sample of the control language statements is also included.

Program documentation is an often neglected part of an application programmer's job. This neglect may be caused either by data processing managers, who want the programmer to begin writing new programs, or by the programmer, who does not enjoy the rather mundane task of preparing program narratives, drawing file and record layouts, and so on. It has been found, however, that proper documentation of a program is absolutely vital to the smooth functioning of the data processing department. As has been stated earlier, all programs must be changed at some time during their useful life, and often the maintenance programmer is not the original application programmer. Thus, it is the application programmer's responsibility to supply adequate documentation to permit the maintenance programmer to make needed changes easily and quickly.

IN CONCLUSION

The purpose of this chapter is to introduce you to all parts of the RPG language, including features that are not part of any other programming language. In the chapters that follow, you will use these features as you plan, design, code, test, and debug application programs to solve typical business problems. Chapter 2 will teach you to program for applications that require the reading of a data file and the production of a printed report listing information from the input file.

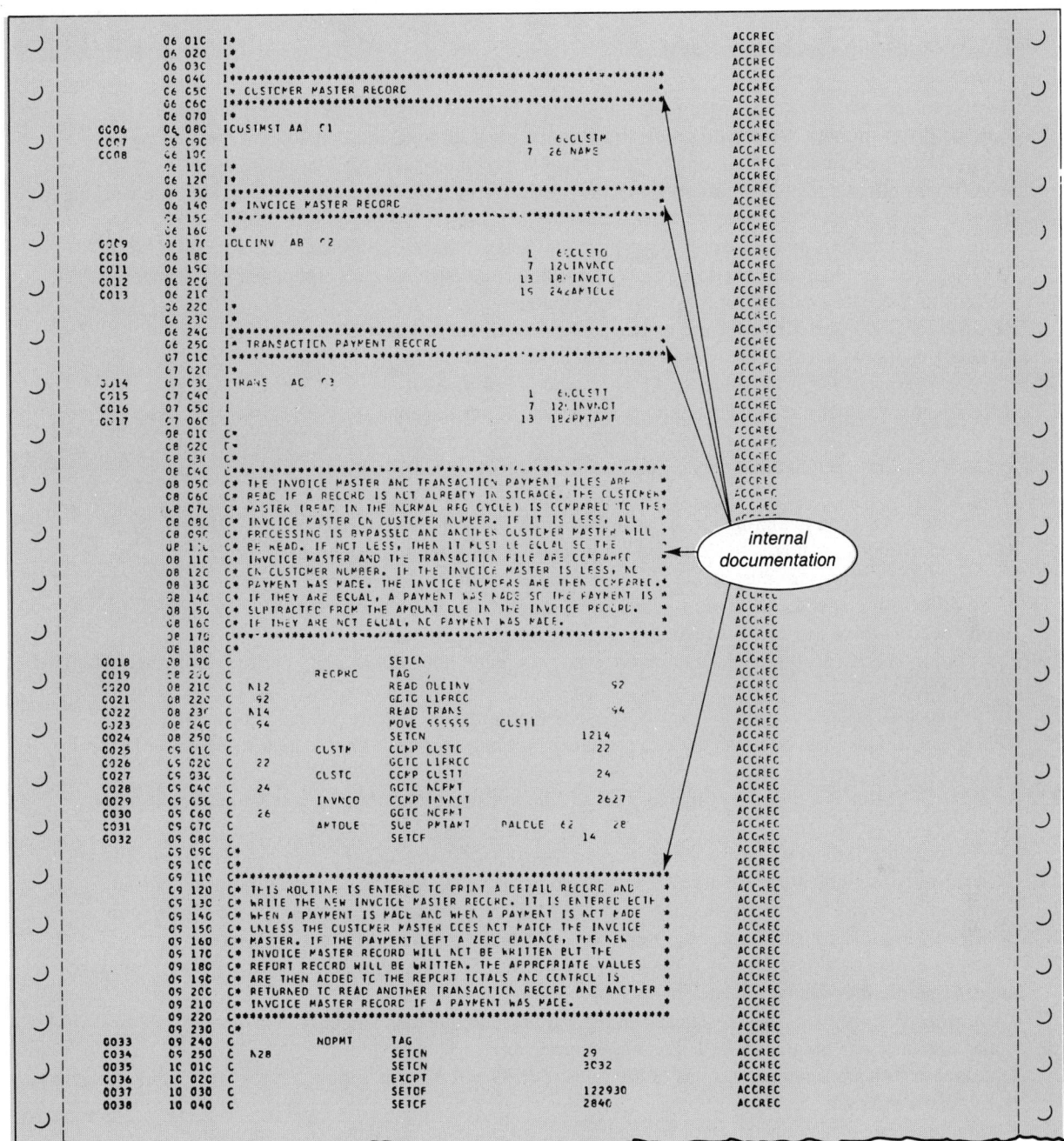

Figure 1-25   RPG internal documentation

CHAPTER SUMMARY

1. The two major categories of programming are systems programming and applications programming.
2. **Systems programmers** develop programs to aid in the programming and operation of computers.
3. **Applications programmers** develop programs to solve problems using the computer.
4. **Scientific applications programmers** are usually directly concerned with the problems they are working to solve.
5. **Business applications programmers** write programs related to the overall business of their company.
6. **RPG** was developed initially to allow an easy transition from punched card equipment to computer use.
7. Versions of RPG are available for a variety of computers.
8. **RPG II**, **RPG III**, and **RPG/400** are enhanced versions of the original RPG.
9. A **record** is the basic unit of data organization in RPG.
10. A **file** is a series of records containing the same type of information.
11. A **field** is a portion of a record containing a single unit of information.
12. RPG logic is based on a **fixed, predefined logic cycle** that is the basis for all RPG programs.
13. RPG uses various **specification sheets**, each of which provides a description of a separate part of the program being written.
14. If no name is assigned to a program, most versions of RPG will assign the name **RPGOBJ**.
15. RPG specifications are uniquely identified by the **form type entry** in position 6.
16. The **control specification** must be the first specification in an RPG program.
17. A **file description specification** must be prepared for each file used by a program.
18. **Input specifications** describe the records and fields read by a program.
19. **Calculation specifications** are used to describe any operation not automatically performed by the RPG fixed-logic cycle.
20. **Output specifications** are used to describe the output records and fields generated by the program.
21. RPG specifications must be in the **correct sequence** within a program. This sequence, based on form type, is **H, F, E, L, I, C, and O.**
22. An **RPG indicator** is a position of memory set to either of two values to represent a condition that has occurred within a program.
23. **Special-purpose indicators** have a predefined meaning to RPG and must be used exactly as defined by RPG.
24. **General-purpose indicators** are used for any function for which there is no special purpose indicator.
25. A programmer must fully understand the purpose of a program before beginning to code the program.
26. **Desk checking** is a critical, frequently overlooked part of the program development process.
27. The code written by a programmer is the **source program**. Source programs must be translated into machine language before they can be executed by the computer.
28. A **compiler** is a program that translates source programs into machine language.
29. A machine language program is called an **object program**.
30. **Terminal errors** are serious violations of the rules of RPG and make it impossible for the compiler to generate an object program.
31. A **warning error** may not be an error but an unusual coding condition detected by the compiler.
32. The compiler cannot detect errors in program logic.
33. **Test data** must be carefully prepared to test every part of a program. Live data should not be used for testing because it may not test every condition.
34. **Debugging** is the detection, location, and correction of all program errors.
35. **Documentation** is the process of recording all the facts concerning a program.

REVIEW QUESTIONS

1. What do the initials RPG stand for?
2. Briefly explain the RPG fixed logic cycle.
3. Name, in proper order, the seven commonly used RPG specification forms and briefly explain the purpose of each.
4. What type of information should be included in the Keying Instructions area of the RPG specification sheet? Under what circumstances should this area be used?
5. If no name is assigned to an RPG program, what name is assigned by RPG?
6. What is the purpose of the Form Type entry?
7. What is an indicator?
8. Name the two categories of RPG indicators and briefly explain their difference.
9. Why is problem analysis the crucial first step in program development?
10. What is the purpose of the Printer Spacing Chart?
11. List five types of information that may be found on a printer spacing chart.
12. What is the purpose of the proportional record layout form?
13. Why are flowcharts not commonly used when planning an RPG program?
14. Why are programming standards important in a data processing department?
15. What is the difference between a source program and an object program?
16. What is a compiler?
17. List and explain the two types of errors that can be detected by the compiler.
18. Why should live data not be used to test a program?
19. What is debugging?
20. What three questions should a programmer ask when reviewing the output of a program test?
21. What are the two types of program documentation?
22. Why is program documentation important?

STUDENT EXERCISES: PROGRAM ENTRY

The purpose of these exercises is to train you in the use of the program entry utility and compiler available on your computer. You are not expected to understand the RPG programs that you will be entering but to enter the code correctly into your computer and to use the compiler to successfully generate and run an object program.

1. Enter the RPG program in Figure 1-26 on the next page into your computer system and then compile and execute it. The File Description specifications were written for an IBM System/36. If you are using a different computer, verify these specifications with your instructor or computer center manager. Use test data set PE-1.

Figure 1-26 Name and Address List Program, specification sheets

IBM

RPG CONTROL AND FILE DESCRIPTION SPECIFICATIONS
(SEE OVER FOR RPG CALCULATION SPECIFICATIONS)

Program NAME & ADDRESS LIST
Programmer GOODWIN   Date 4-25-91

Keying Instruction — Graphic Ø O 2 Z 1 I — Key ZERO LETTER TWO LETTER ONE LETTER

Card Electro Number

Page Ø1 of 3   Program Identification NALIST

Control Specifications

Line	Form Type	...	Size to Execute	...
0 1	H		Ø48	

File Description Specifications

Line	Form Type	Filename	File Type	File Designation	F/V/S/M/D/E	Block Length	Record Length	Device
0 2	F	NAFILE	I P E		F	8Ø	8Ø	DISK
0 3	F	NALIST	O		F	132	132	PRINTER
0 4	F							
0 5	F							
0 6	F							
0 7	F							
0 8	F							
0 9	F							
1 0	F							

Figure 1-26 (1)

IBM

RPG INPUT SPECIFICATIONS
(SEE OVER FOR RPG EXTENSION AND LINE COUNTER SPECIFICATIONS)

Program NAME & ADDRESS LIST
Programmer — Date

Keying Instruction — Graphic — Key

Card Electro Number

Page Ø2 of 3   Program Identification NALIST

Line	Form Type	Filename or Record Name	Sequence	Number (1/N)	Record Identifying Indicator	Position	From	To	Decimal Positions	Field Name	Field Indicators
0 1	I	NAFILE	AA		Ø1						
0 2	I						1	25		NAME	
0 3	I						26	5Ø		ADDRES	
0 4	I						51	75		CITYST	
0 5	I						76	8Ø		ZIP	
0 6	I										
0 7	I										
0 8	I										
0 9	I										
1 0	I										
1 1	I										
1 2	I										
1 3	I										
1 4	I										

Figure 1-26 (2)

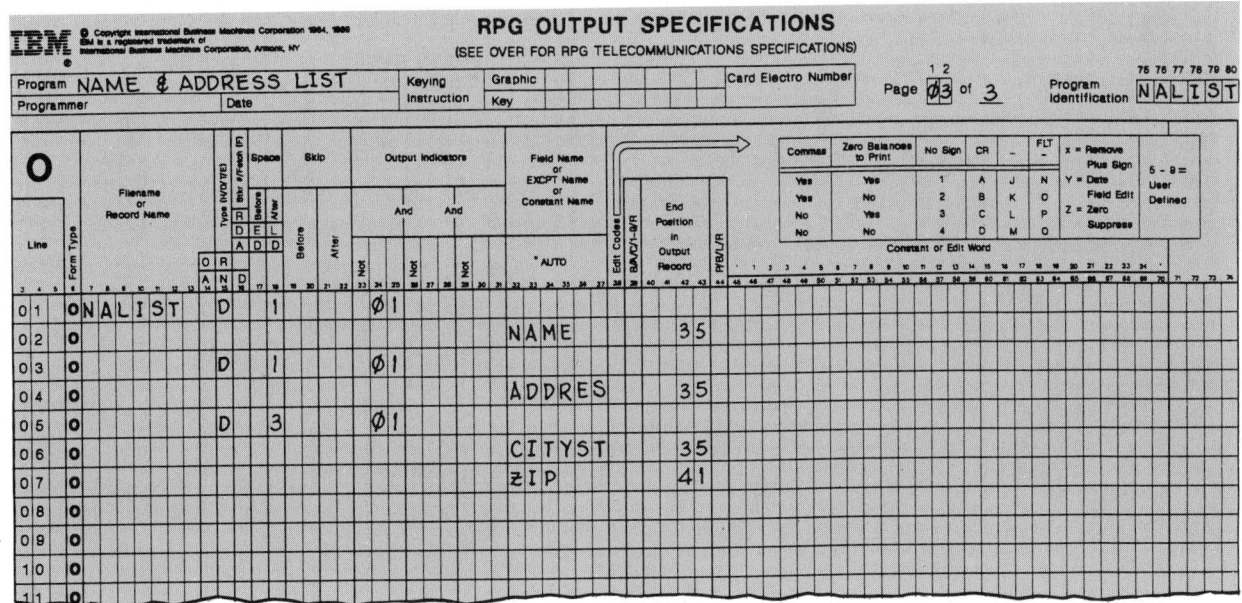

Figure 1-26 (3)

2. Enter the RPG program in Figure 1-27 into your computer system and then compile and execute it. The File Description specifications were written for an IBM System/36. If you are using a different computer, verify these specifications with your instructor or computer center manager. Use test data set PE-2.

Figure 1-27   Sales Report Program, specification sheets

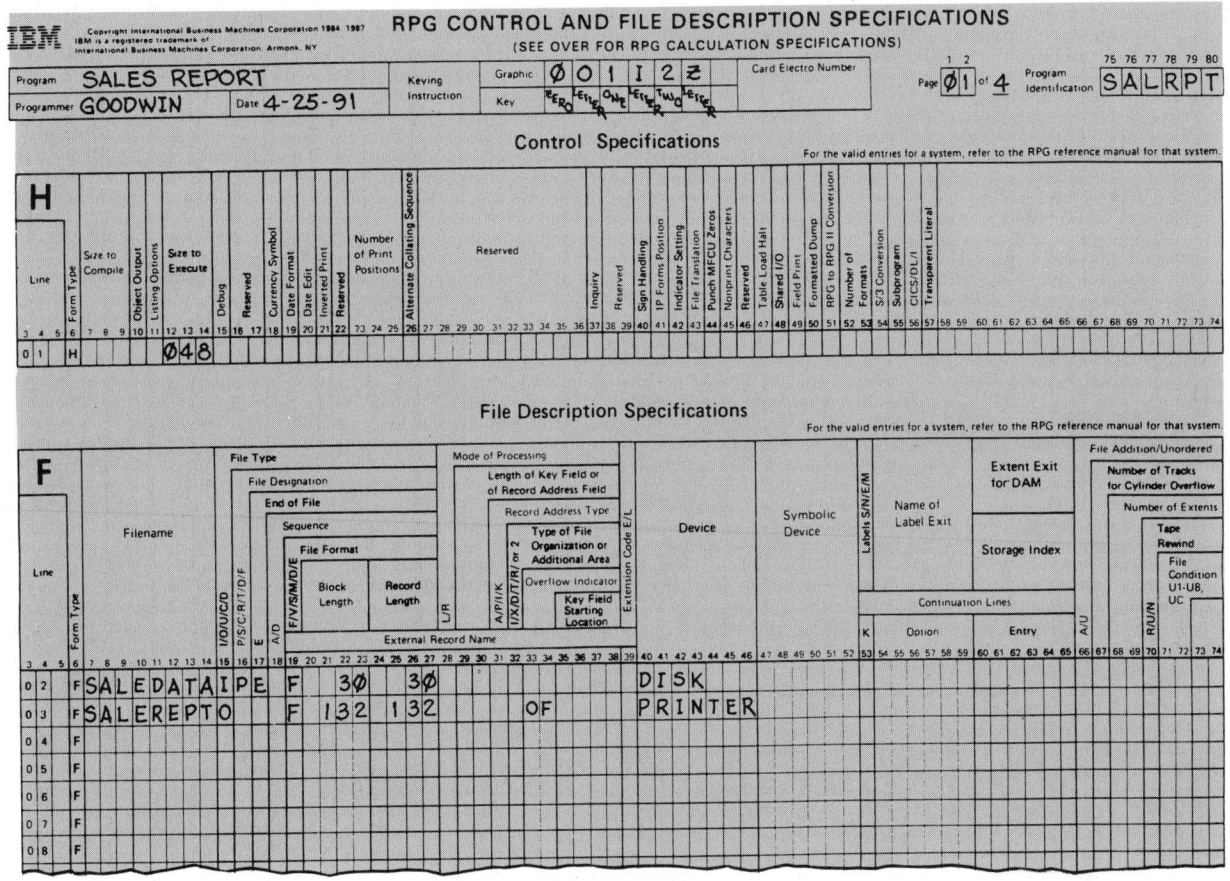

Figure 1-27 (1)

continued

IBM — © Copyright International Business Machines Corporation 1984, 1989

RPG INPUT SPECIFICATIONS

(SEE OVER FOR RPG EXTENSION AND LINE COUNTER SPECIFICATIONS)

Program: SALES REPORT — Page Ø2 of 4 — Program Identification: SALRPT

Line	Form Type	Filename or Record Name	Record Identifying Indicator	Field Location From	Field Location To	Decimal Positions	RPG Field Name
01	I	SALEDATAAA	Ø1				
02	I			1	5		ITEM
03	I			6	2Ø		DESCR
04	I			21	25	2	SALAMT
05	I			26	3Ø	2	COSAMT

Figure 1-27 (2)

IBM — © Copyright International Business Machines Corporation 1984, 1987

RPG CALCULATION SPECIFICATIONS

(SEE OVER FOR RPG CONTROL AND FILE DESCRIPTION SPECIFICATIONS)

Program: SALES REPORT — Page Ø3 of 4 — Program Identification: SALRPT

Line	Form Type	Indicators	Factor 1	Operation	Factor 2	Result Field Name	Length	Decimal Positions	Comments
01	C	Ø1	SALAMT	SUB	COSAMT	PROFIT	5	2	USE THESE LINES
02	C	Ø1		ADD	SALAMT	TOTSAL	7	2	FOR SYSTEM/36,
03	C	Ø1		ADD	COSAMT	TOTCOS	7	2	SYSTEM/38,
04	C	Ø1		ADD	PROFIT	TOTPRO	7	2	AS/4ØØ, ETC.
09	C	Ø1	SALAMT	SUB	COSAMT	PROFIT	5	2	USE THESE LINES
10	C	Ø1	TOTSAL	ADD	SALAMT	TOTSAL	7	2	FOR ALL OTHER
11	C	Ø1	TOTCOS	ADD	COSAMT	TOTCOS	7	2	COMPUTER
12	C	Ø1	TOTPRO	ADD	PROFIT	TOTPRO	7	2	SYSTEMS

*Number of sheets per pad may vary slightly.

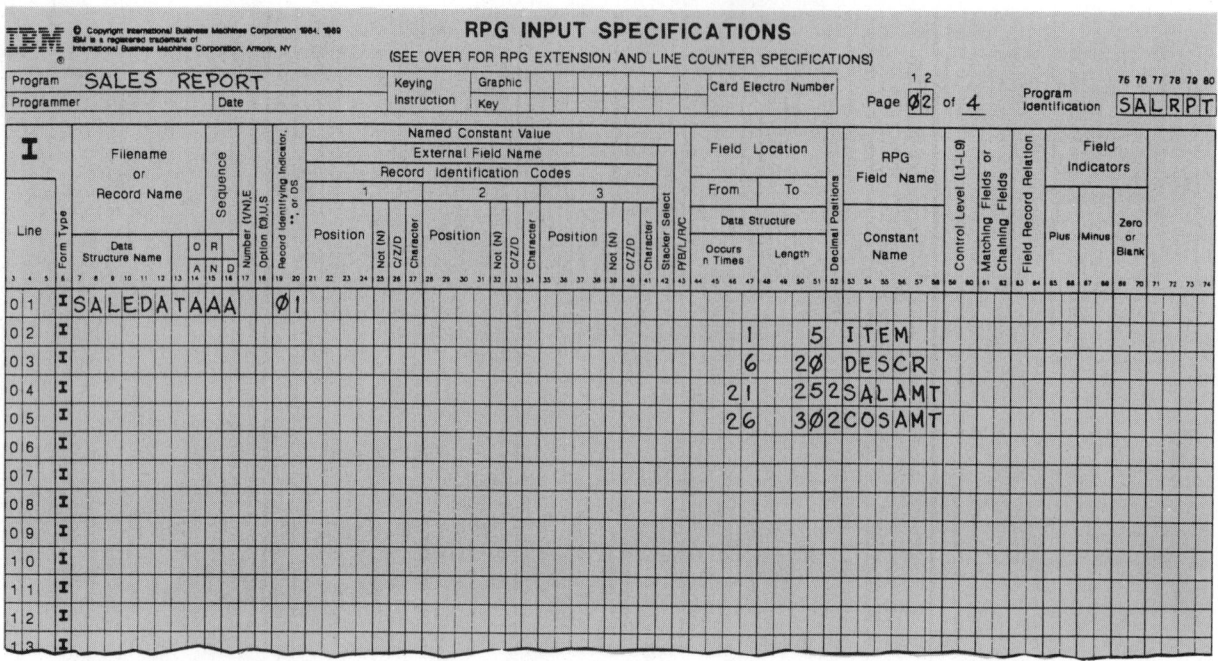

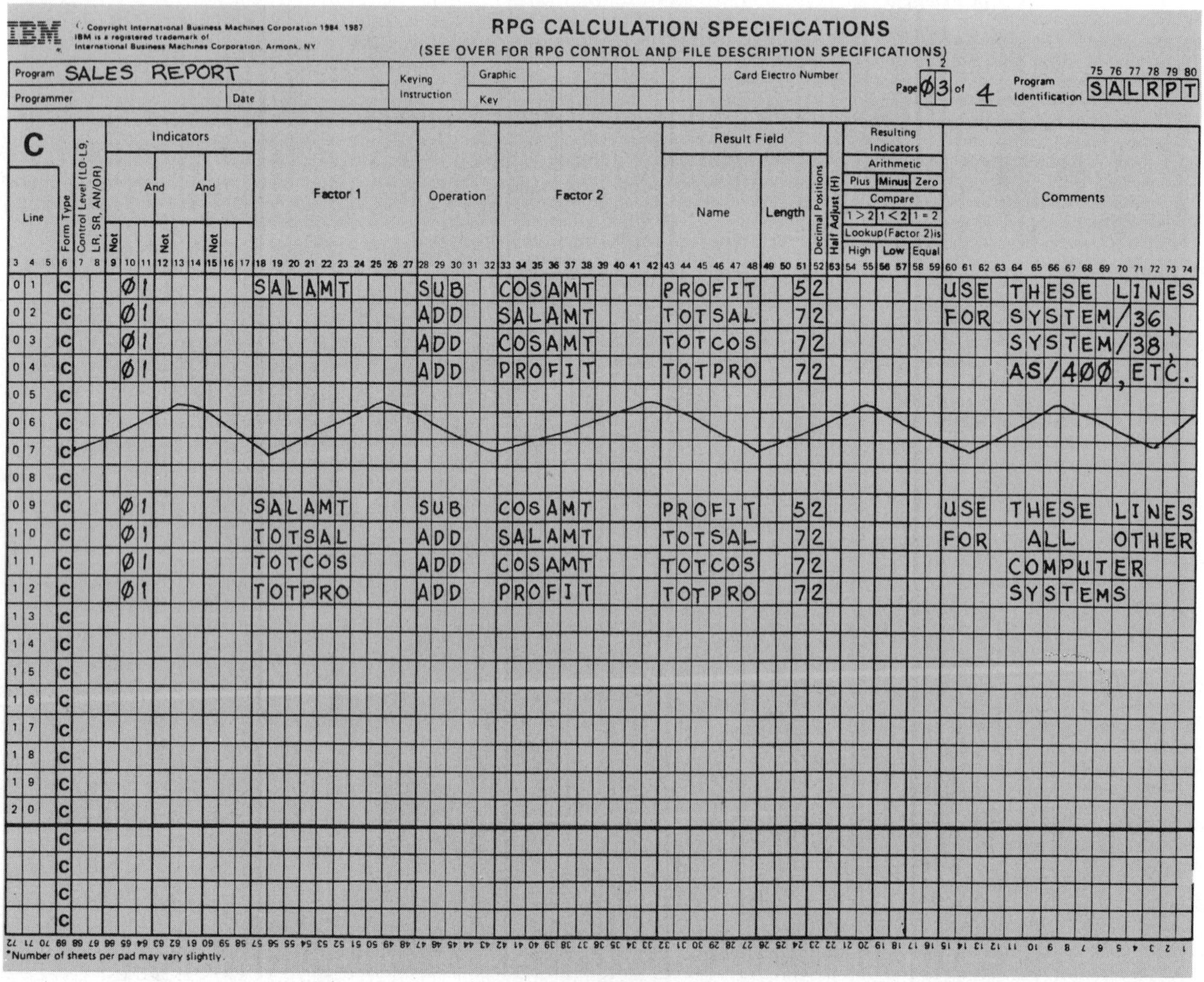

Figure 1-27 (3)

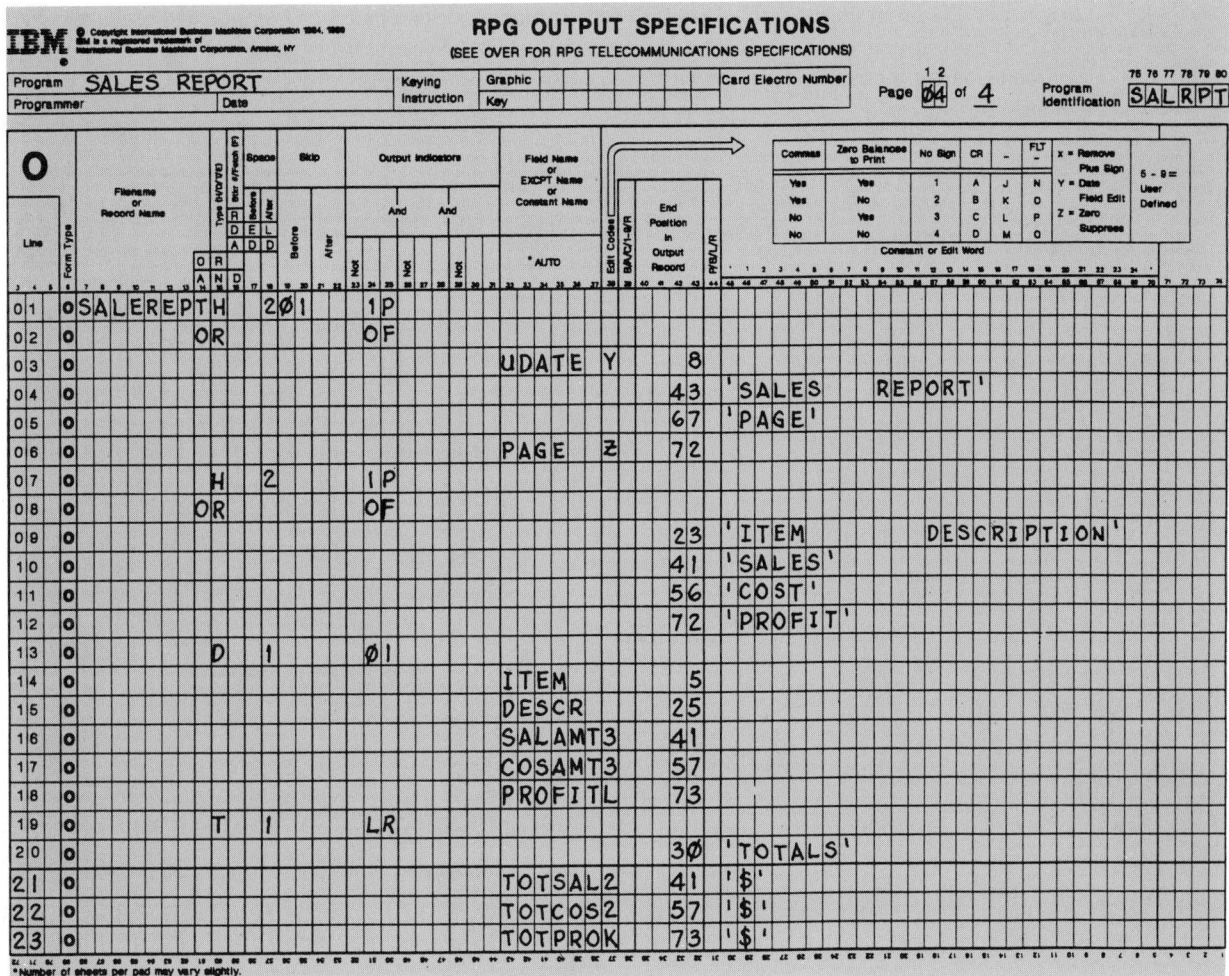

Figure 1-27 (4)

3. Enter the RPG program in Figure 1-28 into your computer system and then compile and execute it. The File Description specifications were written for an IBM System/36. If you are using a different computer, verify these specifications with your instructor or computer center manager. Use test data set PE-3.

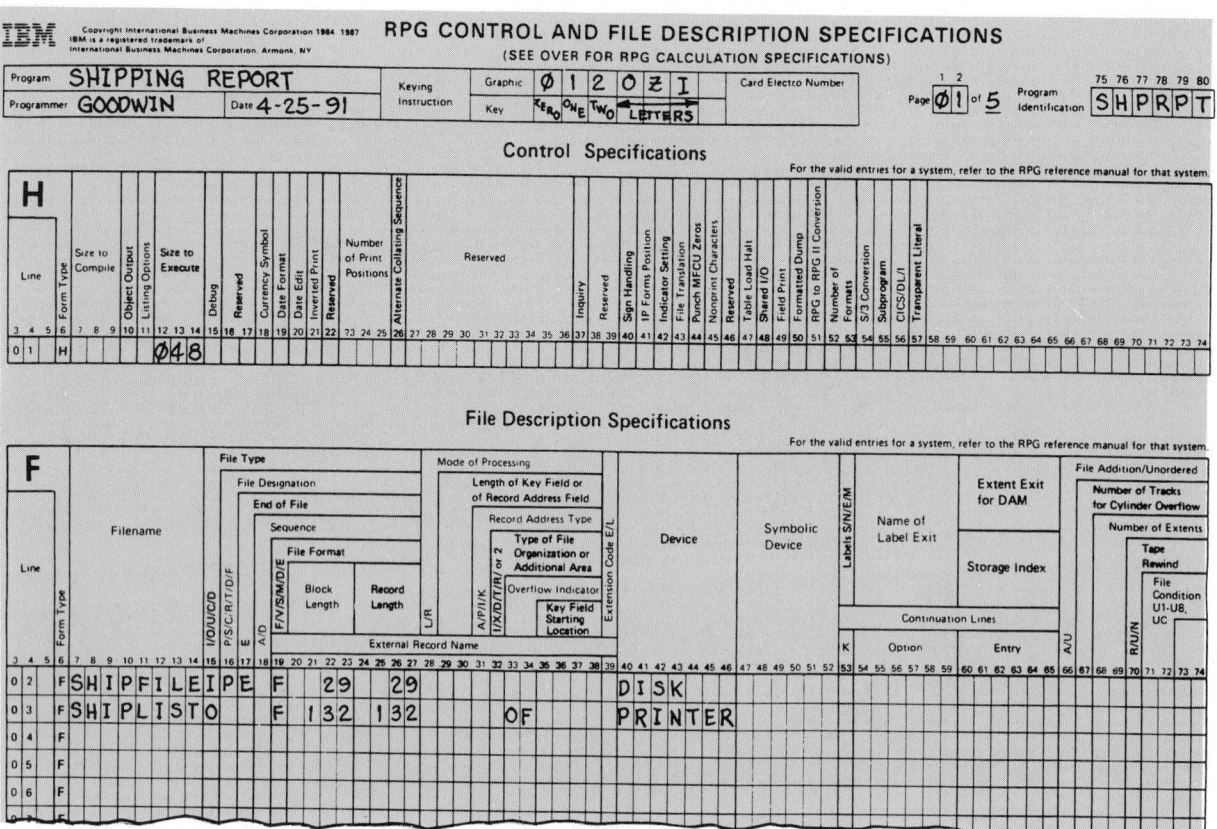

Figure 1-28 (1)

Figure 1-28 (2)

IBM — RPG CALCULATION SPECIFICATIONS
(SEE OVER FOR RPG CONTROL AND FILE DESCRIPTION SPECIFICATIONS)

Program: SHIPPING REPORT — Page 03 of 5 — Program Identification: SHPRPT

Line	Form Type	Indicators	Factor 1	Operation	Factor 2	Result Field Name	Length	Resulting Indicators	Comments
01	C	01	WEIGHT	COMP	500			99	FOR SYSTEM/36
02	C	01 99		ADD	1	AIR	30		SYSTEM/38,
03	C	01N99		ADD	1	TRUCK	30		AS/400, ETC.
04	C								
05	C								
06	C								
07	C	01	WEIGHT	COMP	500			99	FOR ALL OTHER
08	C	01 99	AIR	ADD	1	AIR	30		COMPUTER
09	C	01N99	TRUCK	ADD	1	TRUCK	30		SYSTEMS
10	C								
11	C								
12	C								

Figure 1-28 (3)

IBM — RPG OUTPUT SPECIFICATIONS
(SEE OVER FOR RPG TELECOMMUNICATIONS SPECIFICATIONS)

Program: SHIPPING REPORT — Page 04 of 5 — Program Identification: SHPRPT

Line	Form Type	Filename or Record Name	Type	Space/Skip	Output Indicators	Field Name	Edit Code	End Position	Constant or Edit Word
01	O	SHIPLIST	H	201	1P				
02	O		OR		OF				
03	O					UDATE	Y	8	
04	O							35	'SHIPPING REPORT'
05	O							50	'PAGE'
06	O					PAGE	Z	55	
07	O		H	1	1P				
08	O		OR		OF				
09	O							4	'ITEM'
10	O		H	2	1P				
11	O		OR		OF				
12	O							23	'NO. DESCRIPTION'
13	O							53	'WEIGHT SHIP VIA'
14	O		D	1	01				
15	O					ITEM		5	
16	O					DESCR		28	
17	O					WEIGHT	2	36	
18	O							41	'LBS.'
19	O				99			55	'AIR FREIGHT'
20	O				N99			49	'TRUCK'

*Number of sheets per pad may vary slightly.

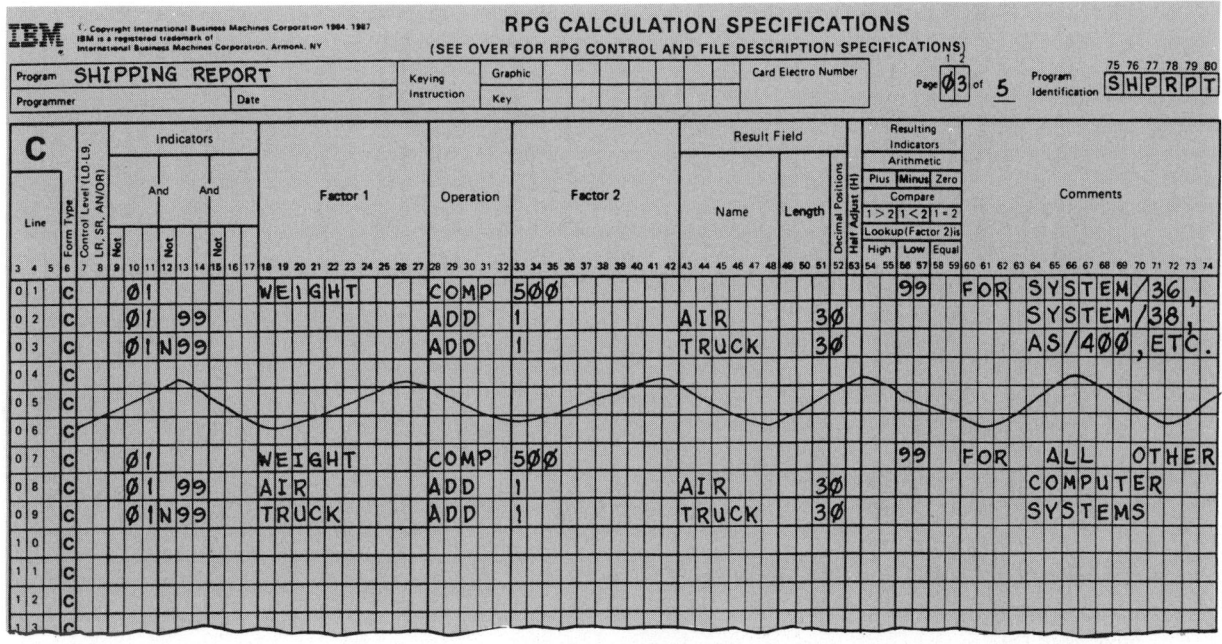

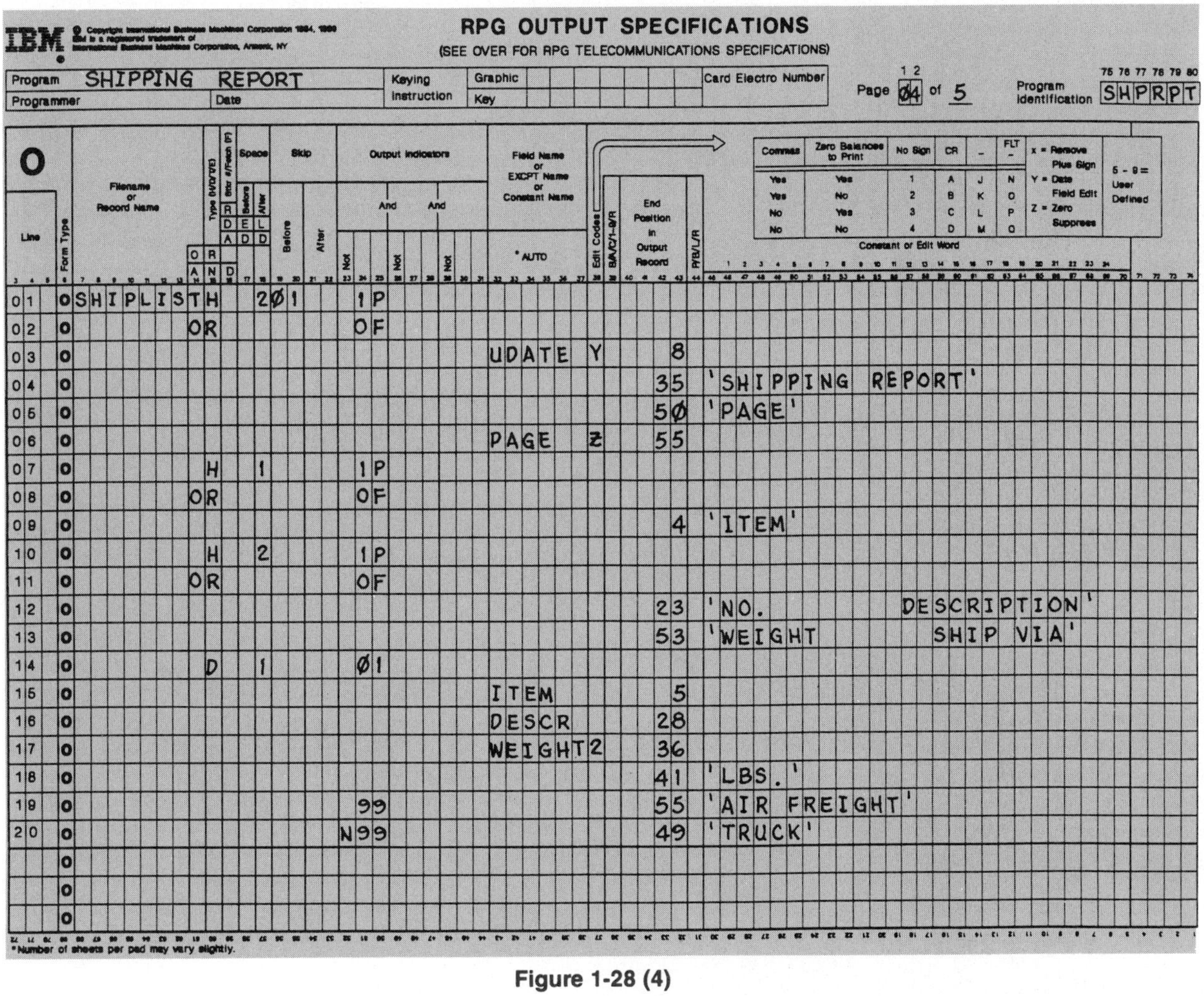

Figure 1-28 (4)

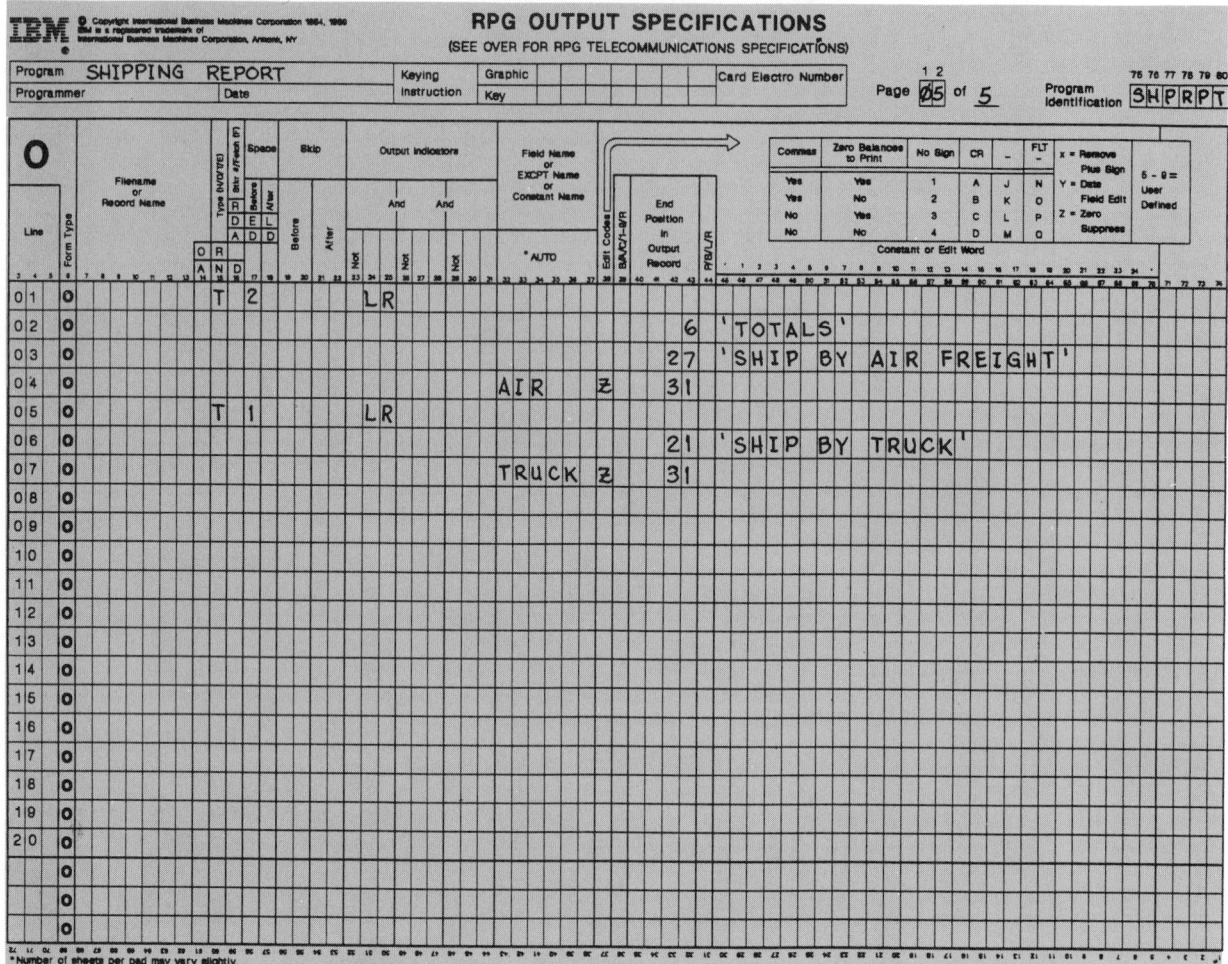

Figure 1-28 (5)   Shipping Report Program, specification sheets

Input/Output Programming & Report Generation

The simplest type of program reads input data, performs no calculations or other processing steps, and produces a printed output report. Chapter 2 introduces the RPG coding specifications needed to develop this type of program and, like all the chapters to come, is formed around a sample program. The sample program for this chapter demonstrates the RPG specifications needed to:

Describe a disk input file
Describe a printed output file
Describe the input record and fields
Describe the output records and fields

ANALYSIS OF THE SAMPLE PROGRAM

Input

Input to the sample program is the Employee Seniority File (SENFILE) shown in Figure 2-1. As you can see, this file contains five data fields that are used by the program. These fields are employee number, employee name, department code, store number, and date hired. Note that a portion of the input record is not identified as a field; this area, located in positions 31–34 of the input record, is not needed by the sample program. However, you cannot assume that this area contains no data just because it is unidentified in the program specifications. The lack of a name for this area only shows that the program to be developed does not use positions 31–34 of the input record. Because the area is not used, we do not define positions 31–34 as part of the input specifications.

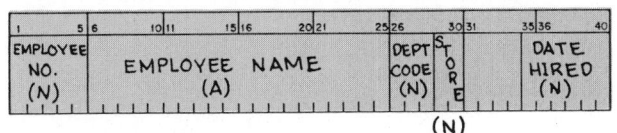

(A) = alphameric data
(N) = numeric data

Figure 2-1   SENFILE record layout

Notice also that one of the fields, Employee Name, is identified as an alphameric field, whereas the other fields are identified as numeric. An **alphameric** data field may contain any type of data: letters, numbers, and special characters such as punctuation marks. A **numeric** data field may contain only numeric data: the digits 0–9 and a sign, either positive or negative. A numeric data field cannot contain any punctuation marks such as commas or decimal points, which we normally use to make numbers easier to read. Although these punctuation marks are not a part of the input data, they can be created on printed output reports by a process called output editing.

Output

The program output report is the Employee Seniority List (SENLIST), which lists all the input fields, (Figure 2-2). In addition, this report contains **headings**, which identify the report and the individual fields listed on the report.

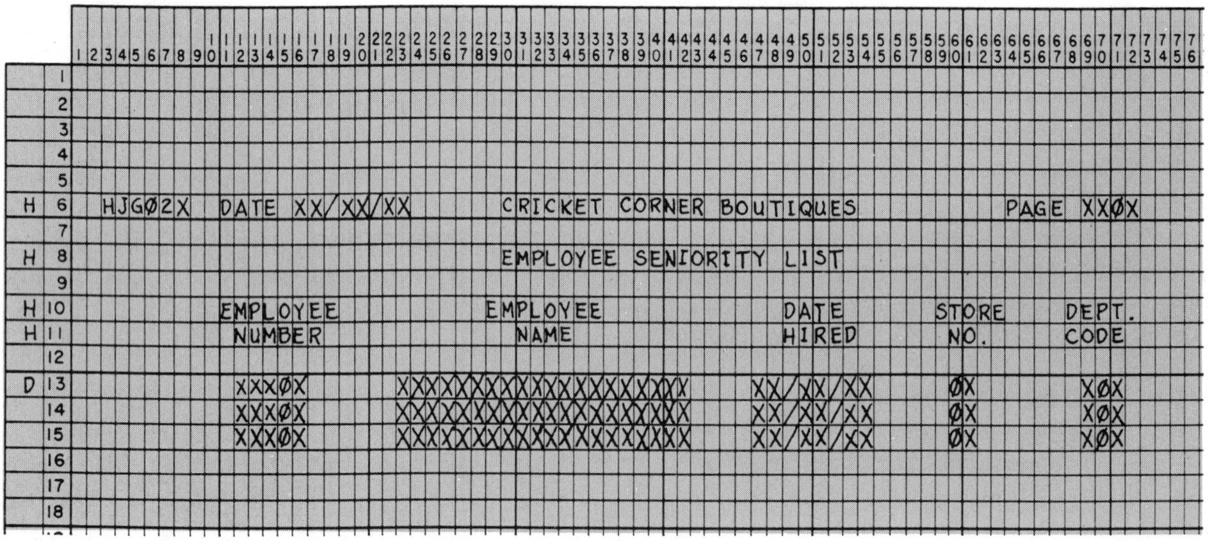

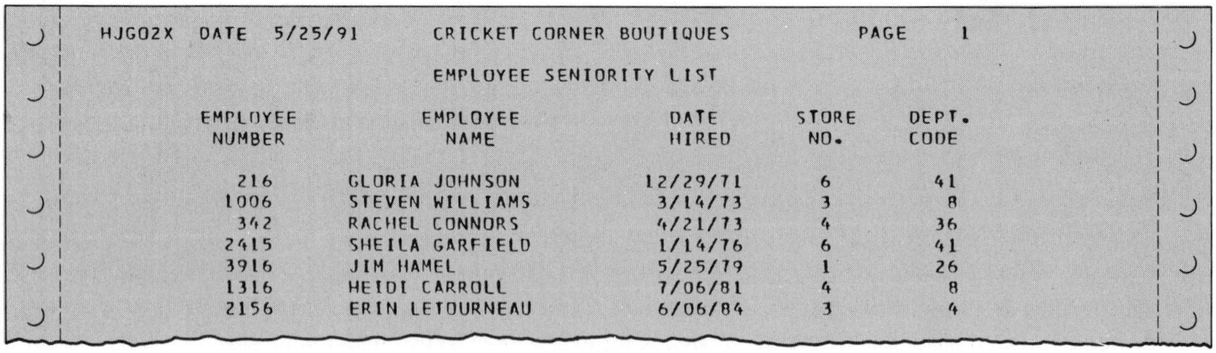
HJG02X DATE 5/25/91 CRICKET CORNER BOUTIQUES PAGE 1

EMPLOYEE SENIORITY LIST

EMPLOYEE NUMBER	EMPLOYEE NAME	DATE HIRED	STORE NO.	DEPT. CODE
216	GLORIA JOHNSON	12/29/71	6	41
1006	STEVEN WILLIAMS	3/14/73	3	8
342	RACHEL CONNORS	4/21/73	4	36
2415	SHEILA GARFIELD	1/14/76	6	41
3916	JIM HAMEL	5/25/79	1	26
1316	HEIDI CARROLL	7/06/81	4	8
2156	ERIN LETOURNEAU	6/06/84	3	4

Figure 2-2 SENLIST output report

The Printer Spacing Chart

Figure 2-3 shows the printer spacing chart for the output report that the sample program produces. A well-drawn printer spacing chart provides all necessary information about the report that a program produces and the data lines within the report. The letters H and D at the left edge of each line identify the type of line.

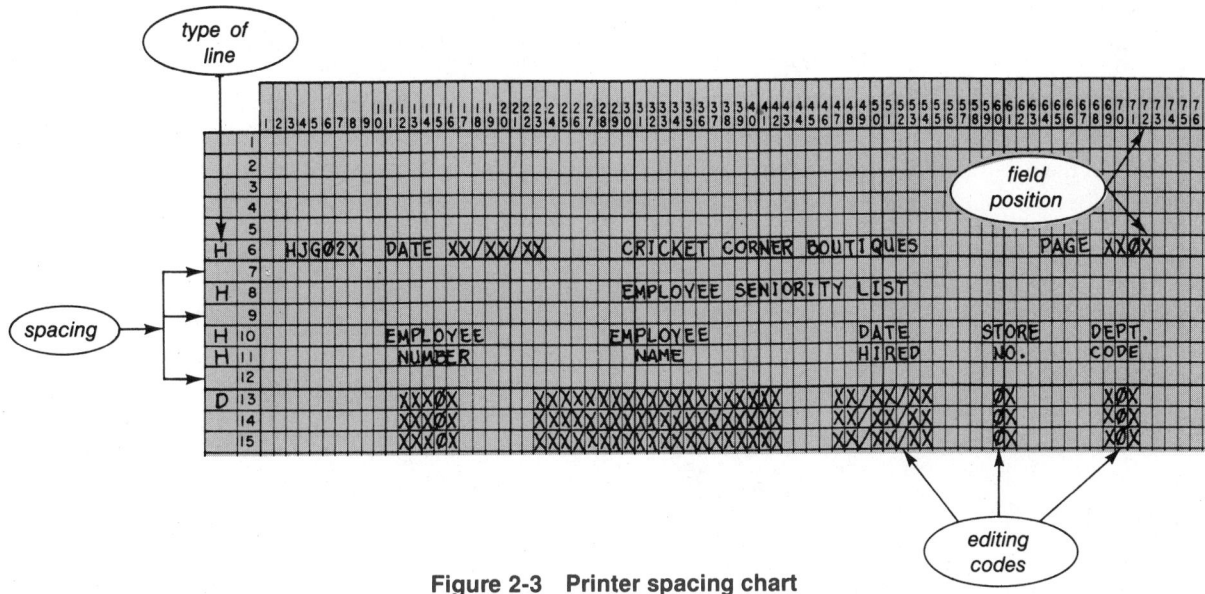

Figure 2-3   Printer spacing chart

▶ **Headings**   Let's start by looking at the type H, or heading, lines. Two categories of heading lines are commonly found on printed reports: report headings and column headings. **Report headings** contain information that identifies the entire report. In Figure 2-3, the first two H lines are report headings; the first shows:

> Name of the program creating the report
> Date the report was printed
> Name of the company
> Page number

The second heading line contains the name of the report. **Column headings**, which identify each column of printed data, are shown in the third and fourth heading lines.

▶ **Detail Output Data**   The line identified by D in Figure 2-3 is a detail line. **Detail lines** are output lines containing data that is based directly on the input data read by the program. Detail output data can be the input data itself or data produced by calculations performed on the input data. Generally, one detail output line is printed for each input record read by the program. The location of output data within the printed line is denoted by the small numbers at the top of the printer spacing chart; each of these numbers represents one of the 132 print positions used by most printers. To specify the position of each field of a detail or heading line, we place strings of Xs and other characters in certain locations within the 132-position print line. For example, the Employee Name field is shown as a string of 20 Xs, one for each of the 20 positions of the input field. By looking at the position numbers above the first and last Xs, you can see that the employee name data prints in positions 23–42.

▶ **Data Editing Codes**   In addition to the Xs to show data positions, we use codes to show the format of printed numeric data. The zero in the Employee Number, Store Number, and Department Code fields indicates that these fields are to be zero suppressed. **Zero suppression** is a process by which unnecessary zeros are removed from the beginning of a printed field; it is a form of output editing. **Output editing** makes numeric data more readable by removing meaningless zeros and inserting punctuation such as commas, decimal points, and dollar signs. Another form of output editing is shown in the Date Hired field, where slashes (/) are inserted to separate the month, day, and year, making the date easier to read. Note that these codes are also used in the first heading line as part of the report date and page number.

▶ **Line Spacing**   The printer spacing chart also shows the spacing between lines of the printed report. The report generated by the sample program has one blank line, or **double spacing**, between the first, second, and third heading lines as well as double spacing between the last heading line and the first detail line. Three identical detail line formats are shown on the printer spacing chart to demonstrate the spacing between consecutive detail lines: These lines are to be **single spaced**, that is, they are to be printed on consecutive lines of the report.

▸ **Field Sequence** Figure 2-4 shows the sequence of data fields within the input record and the detail line. As you can see, the order of data fields in the input record does not have to be the same as the order of data fields within the detail line. *There is no relationship between the positions occupied by an input field and the positions in which that same field is printed as part of the detail line.*

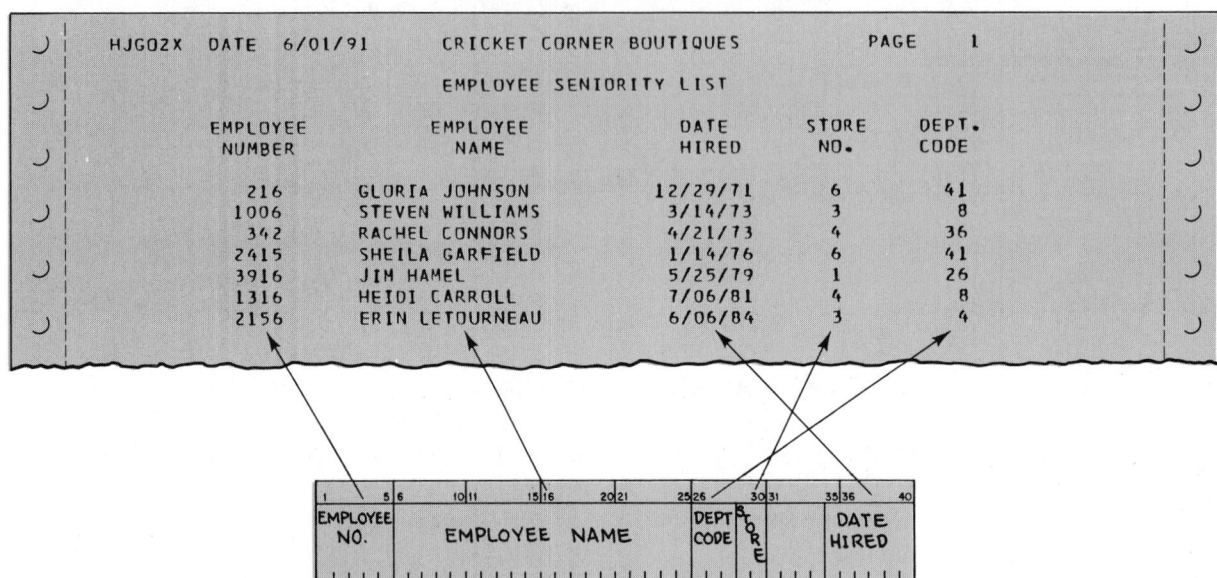

Figure 2-4   Comparison of input record and output line

RPG Fixed Logic: Input/Output Programming

Figure 2-5 shows the parts of the RPG fixed logic cycle that are used in a simple input/output program. All the logic steps and operations that are not required for this type of program have been eliminated.

▸ **Step 1: Detail Output** The first step of the logic cycle performs output operations, even though no input data has yet been read. At this point, if the program specifications call for them, headings are printed at the top of the first page of the output report.

▸ **Step 2: Turn Off Record Identifying Indicators** Every time an input data record is read, the program specifications cause a general-purpose indicator to be turned on. This indicator is called a **record identifying indicator** because it shows that a record has been read. Record identifying indicators can also identify the type of record read if the program uses several different types of records. Because all the records in the sample program have the same format and are the same type, the record identifying indicator only shows that a new record has been read. For this indicator to have meaning, it must be reset every time a new record is read by the program. Therefore, step 2 of the logic cycle turns off the indicator just before a read operation is performed in step 3.

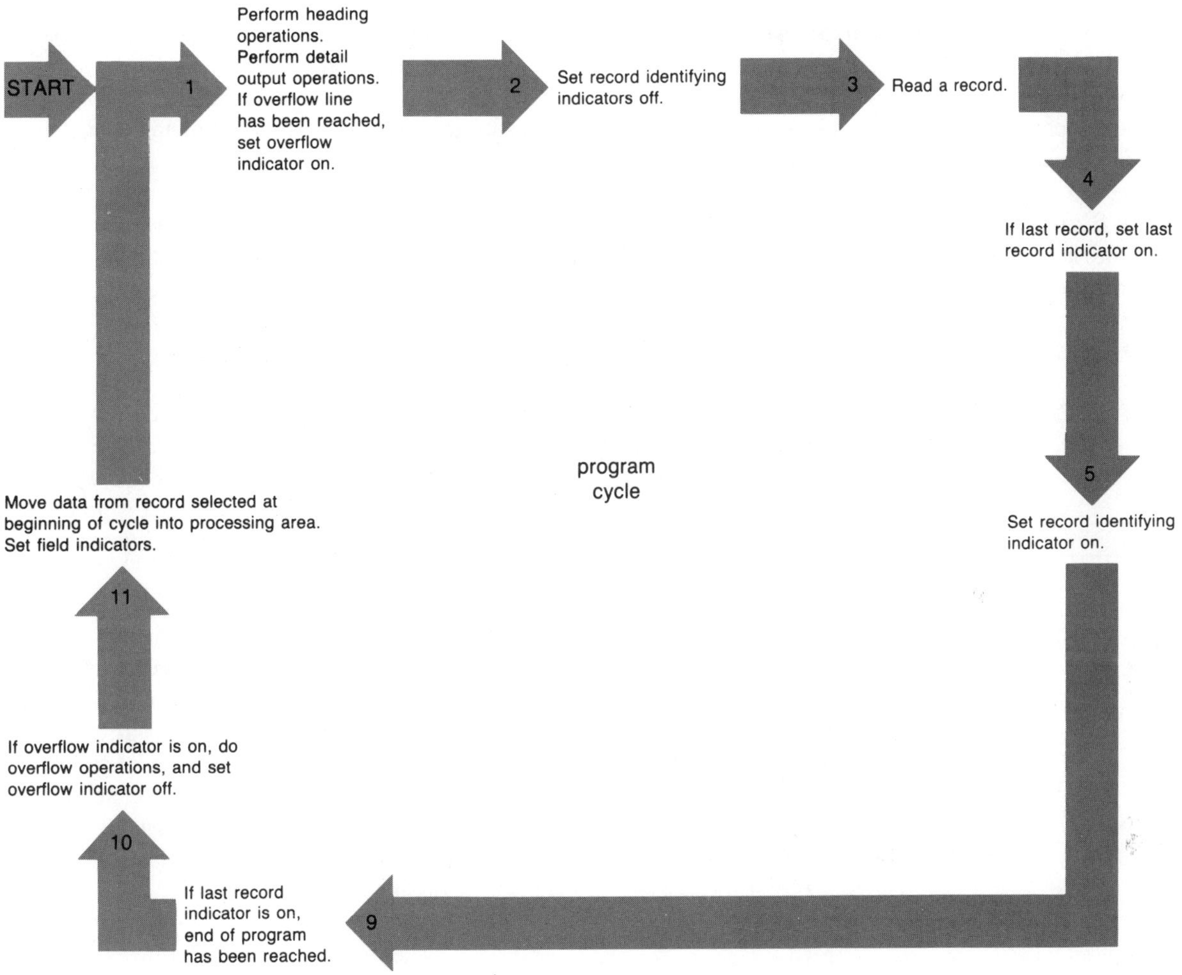

START → 1

Perform heading operations. Perform detail output operations. If overflow line has been reached, set overflow indicator on.

2 Set record identifying indicators off.

3 Read a record.

4

If last record, set last record indicator on.

5

Set record identifying indicator on.

program cycle

Move data from record selected at beginning of cycle into processing area. Set field indicators.

11

If overflow indicator is on, do overflow operations, and set overflow indicator off.

10

If last record indicator is on, end of program has been reached.

9

Figure 2-5 Logic cycle for input/output programs

▸ **Step 3: Read a Record**   At this point in the logic cycle, RPG attempts to read the next record from the input file. If there is a record to be read, RPG places the entire record into an area of computer memory called the **record input area**, as in Figure 2-6. This area is automatically reserved by RPG based on the source program specifications. After the read operation has been performed, RPG proceeds to step 5 of the logic cycle. If all the input data has already been processed and there is no record to be read, RPG executes step 4 of the logic cycle. If a data record is read in step 3, the logic cycle proceeds to step 5.

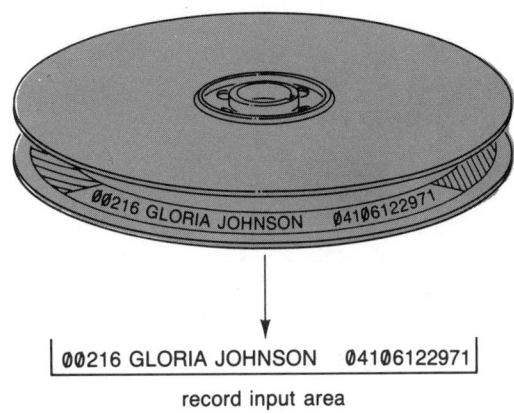

| 00216 GLORIA JOHNSON   04106122971 |

record input area

Figure 2-6 Data record is read

▸ **Step 4: Last-Record Processing**   When RPG reaches the end of an input file and there is no more data to be processed, indicator LR, the **last record indicator**, is turned on. **Indicator LR** is a special-purpose indicator reserved for end-of-program processing. This indicator controls operations that are performed only at the end of the program and tells RPG when the program is to stop executing. If indicator LR was turned on, RPG does not execute step 5 of the logic cycle.

▸ **Step 5: Set Record Identifying Indicator**   Based on the source program specifications, one record identifying indicator is turned on to show that a record has been read. If the input file contains more than one type of record, the indicator shows which type of record was read.

▸ **Step 9: End of Program**   If indicator LR was turned on in step 4, the program ends.

▸ **Step 11: Data Movement**   As shown in Figure 2-7, the input data is moved from the record input area to the separate **input field areas** in main memory. Like the record input area, these field areas are reserved by RPG based on the specifications written by the programmer. The data is processed from these field areas during the remainder of the program.

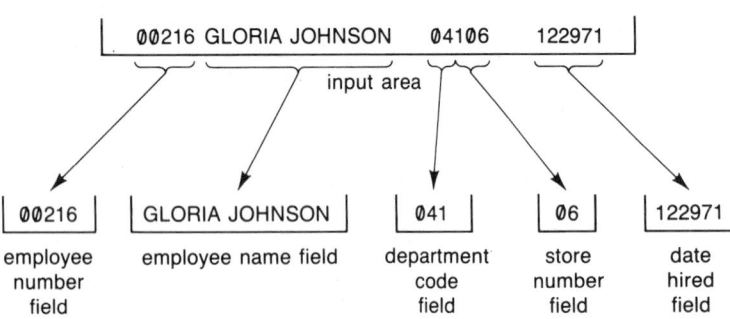

Figure 2-7   **Data is moved to input fields**

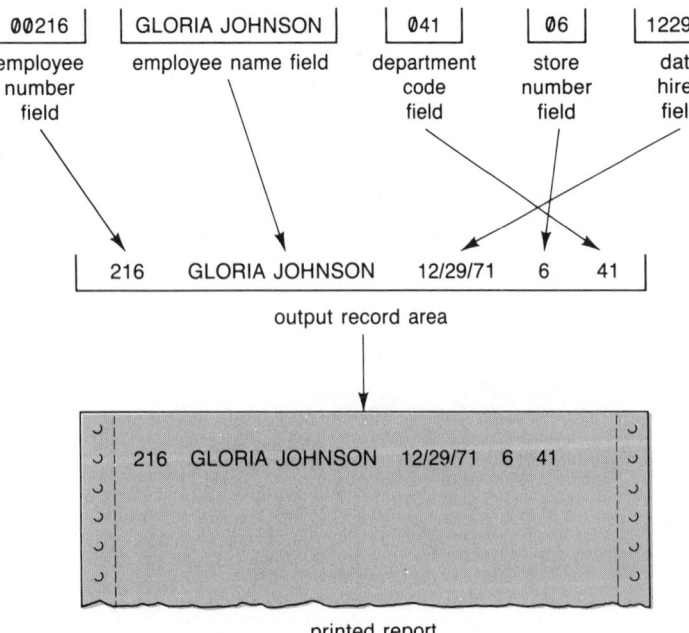

Figure 2-8   **Data is moved to the output area**

▸ **Step 1: Detail Output**   The logic cycle now returns to step 1. At this point, the necessary data is moved from the input fields areas into an **output record area**, as shown in Figure 2-8. After all the needed data has been moved to the output record area and output editing has been performed, the record is printed on the output report as a single line.

This series of operations is a cycle that is performed for every data record in the input file. After enough lines are printed to fill the usable lines on a page, the computer recognizes that a page overflow condition exists. **Page overflow** means that all available lines have been printed and the paper must be advanced to the next page. RPG then turns on a special-purpose **overflow indicator** to identify the need for page overflow. This overflow indicator remains on until the next time step 10 is reached.

▸ **Step 10: Page Overflow Operations**   When step 10 of the logic cycle is reached, RPG determines if an overflow indicator is on. If it is, RPG performs any operations controlled by the indicator. Generally, these operations cause the program to advance to the next page and print the headings. The overflow indicator then turns off automatically, and the logic cycle continues.

RPG PROGRAM CODE: EMPLOYEE SENIORITY LISTING

Figure 2-9 shows the entire coded source program for the Employee Seniority List. Notice that this program does not use all the RPG specification forms. The only forms needed to code this type of program are the Control Specification, the File Description Specifications, the Input Specifications, and the Output Specifications. Because none of the RPG functions coded on the remaining specifications are needed for this program, the other specification forms are not used.

Figure 2-9 RPG source program

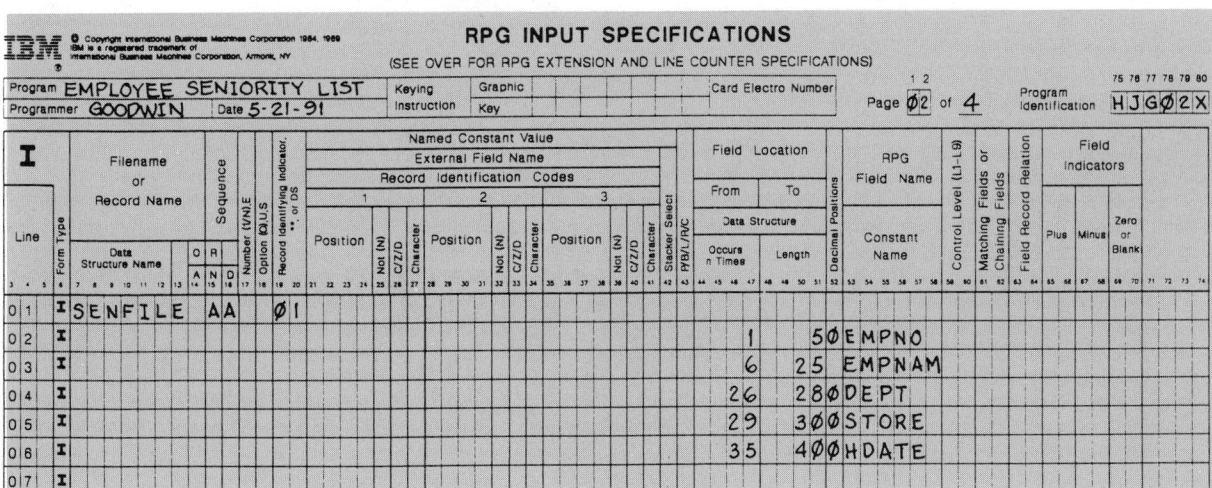

Figure 2-9 (1)

continued

RPG OUTPUT SPECIFICATIONS

(SEE OVER FOR RPG TELECOMMUNICATIONS SPECIFICATIONS)

Program EMPLOYEE SENIORITY LIST
Programmer GOODWIN Date 5-21-91
Page 03 of 4
Program Identification HJG02X

Line	Form Type	Filename or Record Name	Type	Space Before	Space After	Skip Before	Skip After	Output Indicators			Field Name or EXCPT Name or Constant Name	Edit Codes	End Position in Output Record	P/B/L/R	Constant or Edit Word
01	O	SENLIST	H	2 06				1P							
02	O	OR						OF							
03	O												8		'HJG02X'
04	O												14		'DATE'
05	O										UDATE	Y	23		
06	O												53		'CRICKET CORNER BOUTIQUES'
07	O												67		'PAGE'
08	O										PAGE		72		
09	O		H	2				1P							
10	O	OR						OF							
11	O												52		'EMPLOYEE SENIORITY LIST'
12	O		H	1				1P							
13	O	OR						OF							
14	O												18		'EMPLOYEE'
15	O												36		'EMPLOYEE'
16	O												52		'DATE'
17	O												72		'STORE DEPT'
18	O														
19	O														
20	O														

* Number of sheets per pad may vary slightly.

RPG OUTPUT SPECIFICATIONS

(SEE OVER FOR RPG TELECOMMUNICATIONS SPECIFICATIONS)

Program EMPLOYEE SENIORITY LIST
Programmer GOODWIN Date 5-21-91
Page 04 of 4
Program Identification HJG02X

Line	Form Type	Filename or Record Name	Type	Space Before	Space After	Skip Before	Skip After	Output Indicators			Field Name or EXCPT Name or Constant Name	Edit Codes	End Position in Output Record	P/B/L/R	Constant or Edit Word
01	O		H	2				1P							
02	O	OR						OF							
03	O												17		'NUMBER'
04	O												34		'NAME'
05	O												62		'HIRED NO.'
06	O												71		'CODE'
07	O		D	1				01							
08	O										EMPNO	Z	16		
09	O										EMPNAM		42		
10	O										HDATE	Y	54		
11	O										STORE	Z	61		
12	O										DEPT	Z	71		

Figure 2-9 (2)

Note: A careful study of this source program and a comparison of the code with the programming standards in Appendix A will show that some of the standards have not been followed. A standard is followed only if its RPG entries have been discussed in a preceding chapter or if the standard is introduced in the current chapter.

RPG CONTROL SPECIFICATION

The RPG Control Specification (Figure 2-10) must be the first specification of every RPG program. The only entries required by most versions of RPG are the Form Type entry H in position 6 and the Program Identification entry in positions 75–80.

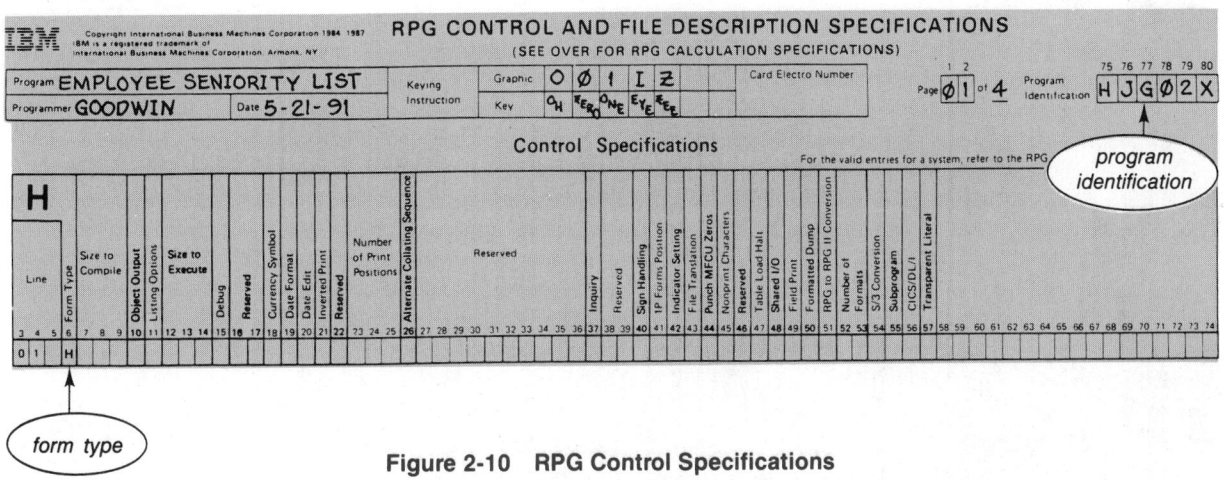

Figure 2-10   RPG Control Specifications

A program identification must be from 1 to 6 characters long and must begin with an alphabetic character. The remaining characters may be either alphabetic or numeric. No special characters may be used in a program identification, and no blank spaces may appear between characters. Some IBM computers treat the characters #, $, and @ as alphabetic. If you are using one of these systems, you cannot use any of these three characters as the first character of a program identification.

Unused Control Specification Entries

Use of the remaining areas of the Control Specification vary based on the computer being used. Some of these areas, positions 7–9 and 12–14, for example, provide information about the computer on which the program is to be compiled. Other areas, such as positions 18–20, control the way that data is read and stored in memory. Still others give the computer operator control over the program when it is executed. If any of these areas must be used for your computer, the entries will be provided to you by your instructor or computer center manager.

Defaults

All the unused entries, as well as many areas of other RPG specification forms, work under the default concept. A **default** is an entry that has been built in to the RPG compiler by the systems programming team that developed the compiler. If the application programmer makes no entry in an area for which there is a built-in default, the RPG compiler automatically uses the default. If the application programmer provides an entry, the built-in default is ignored. In some cases, the RPG compiler generates a warning message to notify the application programmer of the default that was taken when the program was compiled. In most cases, however, these entries are simple yes/no choices, with the default being no. In these cases, no warning message is generated.

RPG FILE DESCRIPTION SPECIFICATIONS

The File Description Specifications (Figure 2-11) must immediately follow the Control Specification. File Description Specifications are identified by the Form Type entry F in position 6. There must be a separate File Description Specification line for each file used by a program. Although there is no required sequence for the file descriptions, programmers normally describe input files before output files since this was a requirement of the original RPG language. This accepted practice is followed throughout this book, and accordingly, the first file description line describes the input file.

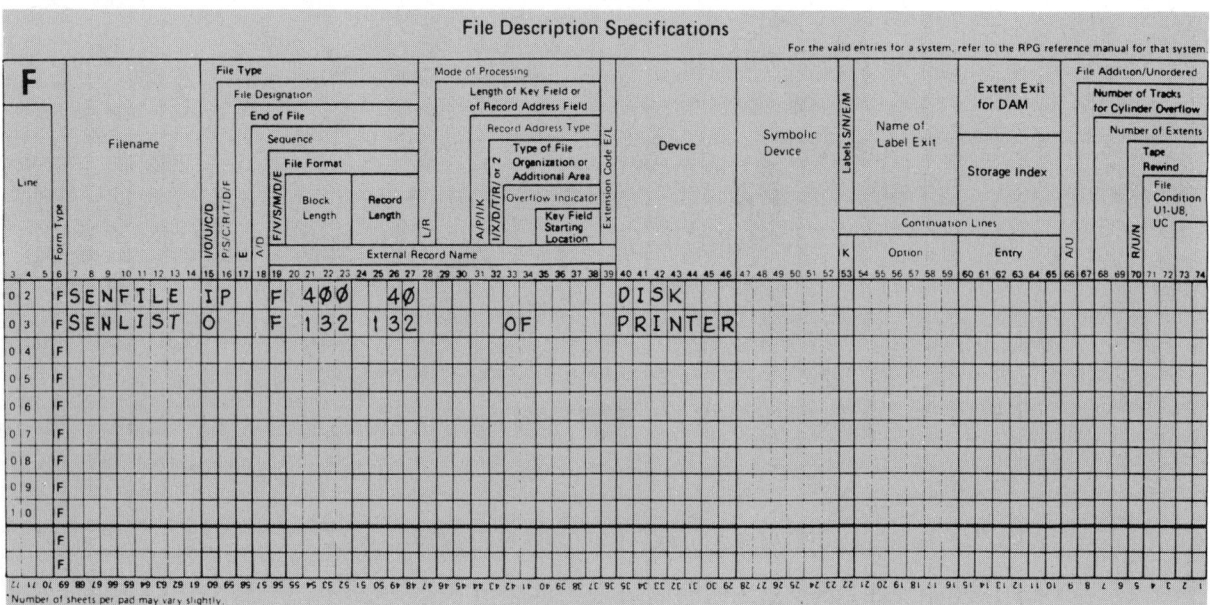

Figure 2-11 RPG File Description Specifications

Filename Entries

Figure 2-12 shows the Filename area and the disk file that it describes. As with most names given to data in an RPG program, the choice of file names is up to the programmer. However, certain syntax rules must be followed when creating file names:

Each file name must be **unique**. No name may be used for more than one file.

A file name may be from 1 to 8 characters long. (Note: Some RPG compilers use only the first 6 or 7 characters to uniquely identify the file.)

The file name must begin with an alphabetic character. In addition to the letters A–Z, some versions of RPG consider the dollar sign ($), the at sign (@), and the pound sign (#) to be alphabetic when used in file names; these characters may be used as the first character of a file name.

The remainder of the file name may consist of either alphabetic or numeric characters. No special characters (other than the three just listed, if your computer treats them as alphabetic) or embedded blanks may appear in the name. An **embedded blank** is a space that appears between two characters.

The Filename entry must begin in position 7.

One other factor should be considered when choosing file names. Data files stored on magnetic disk or tape are assigned permanent names when they are created. Although it is not necessary to use these assigned names in an RPG program, it is good programming practice to use the assigned name if that name conforms to the rules for RPG file names. If the assigned name is not used, the name chosen should be meaningful and should relate to the file being described.

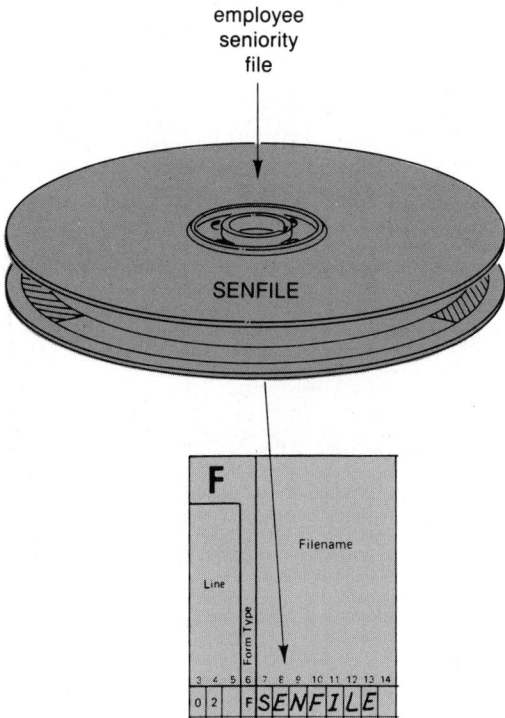

Figure 2-12   Use of the Filename entry

File Type and File Designation Entries

Positions 15 and 16 are used to specify file type and file designation, respectively (Figure 2-13). Look first at the File Type area. Note that a series of letters (I/O/U/C/D) appears above the position number (15); these letters are the possible valid entries in this area. This system of listing the valid entries is used, when space permits, in many areas of the RPG specification forms. A blank is also valid in some areas that list possible entries.

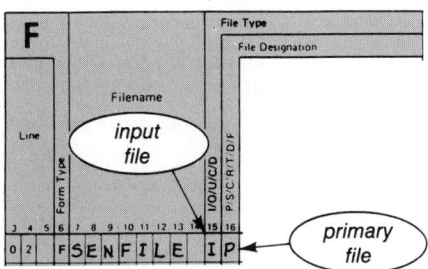

Figure 2-13   Example of the File Type and File Designation entries

The **File Type** entry specifies how a file is used in a program; it tells RPG if a file is used for input only, output only, or both. In Figure 2-13 the entry is I, which indicates that SENFILE is an input file from which data is read by the program.

The **File Designation** entry P indicates that SENFILE is the primary file in the program. Some programs use more than one input file. When this is the case, one of the files must be designated as the primary file, and all remaining input files are designated as secondary. The **primary** or **secondary** designation determines the order in which multiple input files are read by a program. Since there is only one input file in the program, it must be designated as the primary file. Every file that provides input data to the program must have a File Designation entry.

File Format, Block Length, and Record Length Entries

The entries discussed thus far have given a name, SENFILE, to the file and have indicated to RPG that SENFILE is the primary input file. The next entries specify the attributes, or characteristics, of the file. The attributes that must be described for the input file are the format and size of the records in the file and the device from which the records will be read. Figure 2-14 shows the entries that describe the format and size attributes. In the figure, an F has been entered in the File Format area, position 19. The entry F specifies that the file contains **fixed length records**, that is, each record in the file contains the same number of characters.

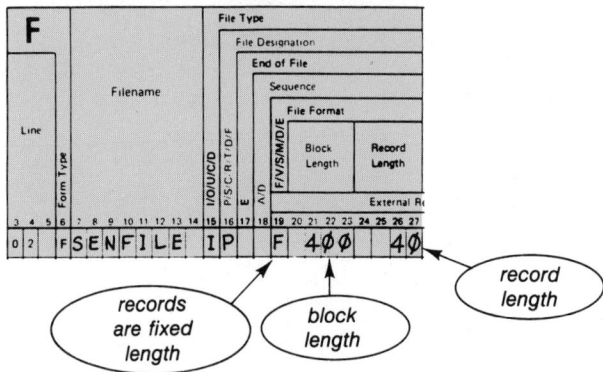

Figure 2-14   Example of the File Format, Block Length, and Record Length entries

The entry in the **Record Length** area, positions 24–27, specifies the number of characters in each record. When you are describing disk or tape files, this entry must be the same as the record length that was defined when the file was created. The entry in this area is right-justified, that is, the rightmost character of the entry must be in the rightmost position of the area. The entry 40 must be in positions 26–27 of the Record Length area. The Record Length area is four positions long because the maximum length of a record may be up to 9999 characters for input from some devices. For entries not requiring all four positions, leading zeros need not be used to fill the beginning positions.

The entry that is placed in the Block Length area, positions 20–23, depends on the computer and input/output device being used. A **block** is a group of individual data records read into or written out of computer memory as a group. By **blocking** a group of separate records, the number of input/output operations can be reduced. Since input and output operations are the most time-consuming instructions executed by a program, reducing the number of these operations speeds up the program. Blocking speeds up execution of the program, but at the cost of memory usage. If blocking is specified, the entire block of records is read into memory at once, increasing the amount of memory needed for input data. This is generally a problem only on smaller computer systems with lesser amounts of memory.

Block length must be an exact multiple of the record length. In Figure 2-14, SENFILE has been given a block length of 400. This results in ten records being read into memory at a time, reducing the number of disk-read operations by 90%. It is not necessary to perform any specific programming to cause the program to process each record individually. Even though records are read in groups of ten, RPG processes them one at a time.

Device and Symbolic Device Entries

After the file attributes have been described, an entry must be made to specify the input device from which the data file will be read. The Device and Symbolic Device entries describe specific hardware attached to the computer system. Because of this, these entries are machine dependent. A **machine dependent** entry is one that changes according to the computer hardware being used. The Device and Symbolic Device entries in this book are valid for IBM System/36, System/38, AS/400, and many microcomputer RPG compilers. If you are using other computer hardware, your instructor or computer center manager will provide the correct entries for your system.

Figure 2-15 shows the Device entry in positions 40–46 for SENFILE. The Device entry DISK indicates that the file is to be read from the system's disk unit. Because the IBM System/3X family and many other RPG compilers do not use the Symbolic Device entry (positions 47–52), this area has been left blank. Again, verify the entries for these areas with your instructor or computer center manager.

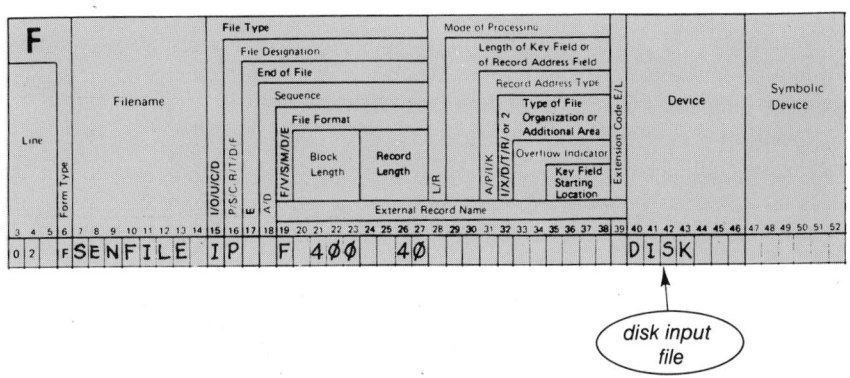

Figure 2-15   Example of the Device entry

Output File Definition

Although Figure 2-15 shows all the entries needed to describe SENFILE, the output printer file must also be defined. The File Description Specifications needed to define the output file are shown in Figure 2-16.

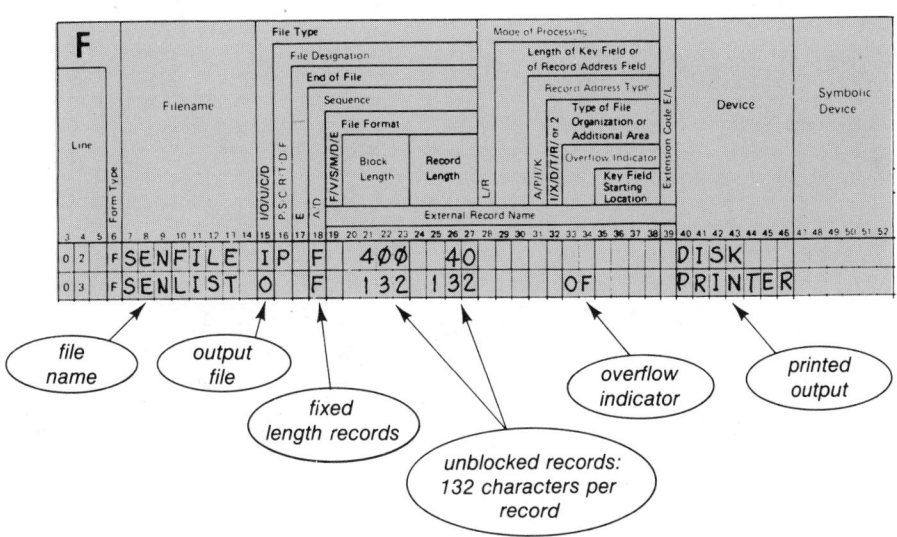

Figure 2-16   Example of entries for the printed output file

In Figure 2-16, the printer output file has been given the name SENLIST. The name SENLIST follows the rules for formation of file names, which were explained earlier. The entry in the File Type area is the letter O, which indicates that SENLIST is an output file; the File Type entry O is required for all files that are used only for data output. A printer is always an output device, unlike a disk, which can be used as an input and an output device.

The records for the SENLIST output file are fixed in length, and each record is 132 characters long (132 is the full length of a standard print line). The Block Length entry 132 indicates that the lengths of the record and block are the same, making this an unblocked file. When an **unblocked file** is processed, each record is independent of all other records. No grouping of records is performed. Output files that create printed reports are always unblocked files.

The entry in the Device area for a printed report is PRINTER. This device name must be used for all printed files. Like the specifications for the input file, the output file Symbolic Device entry is machine dependent.

‣ **Overflow Indicator** As you can see, the output file description entries are very similar to the entries made for the input file. One new entry is required, however, to describe an output printer file. The **overflow indicator** is a special-purpose indicator used on the Output Specifications form to control the printing of headings. Eight special-purpose indicators can be used as overflow indicators: OA, OB, OC, OD, OE, OF, OG, and OV. Any one of these indicators could be selected, but the most commonly used is indicator OF. Indicator **OF** is usually used because it is thought of as an abbreviation for the word OverFlow. Figure 2-16 shows that indicator OF has been entered in positions 33 and 34 to be used as the Overflow indicator for SENLIST.

RPG INPUT SPECIFICATIONS

The File Description Specifications are used to define each file that is to be processed by the program. Each input file contains individual records to be processed. The fields within these records must be defined so that the RPG compiler can generate the instructions needed to process each field. For example, in the sample program, the Employee Number, Employee Name, Department Code, Store Number, and Date Hired fields must be defined. Records within an input file and the fields within these records are defined on the Input Specifications form. Figure 2-17 shows the entries required to describe SENFILE.

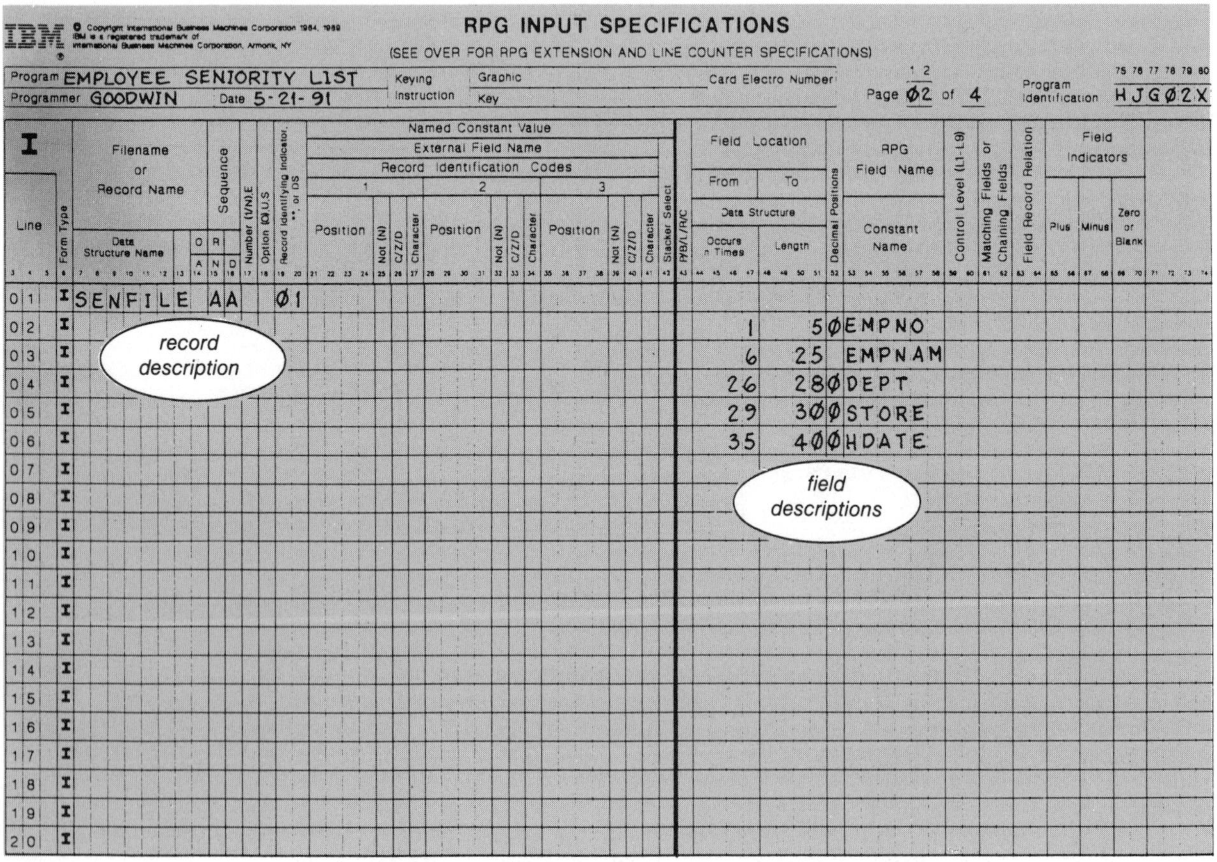

Figure 2-17 Example of Input Specifications

≡ Form Type and Filename Entries

In Chapter 1 you were shown that the Input Specifications form is used to describe records in positions 7–42 and fields in positions 43–70. It was also noted that either type of description can appear on a single input specification line, but not both. Note that in Figure 2-17 the first line of specifications is the record description, whereas the five specifications that follow are field descriptions. When you code RPG Input Specifications, remember to use a separate line for the first input field description.

On the Input Specifications form, as on all other RPG specification forms, the form type has been preentered in position 6. The first entry to be coded by the programmer is the Filename entry (positions 7–14), the name of the input file in which the records appear. In this example, the file name is SENFILE because this is the name that was given to the file when the File Description Specifications were coded. The relationship between the File Description Specification, which defines the file, and the Input Specifications form is illustrated in Figure 2-18.

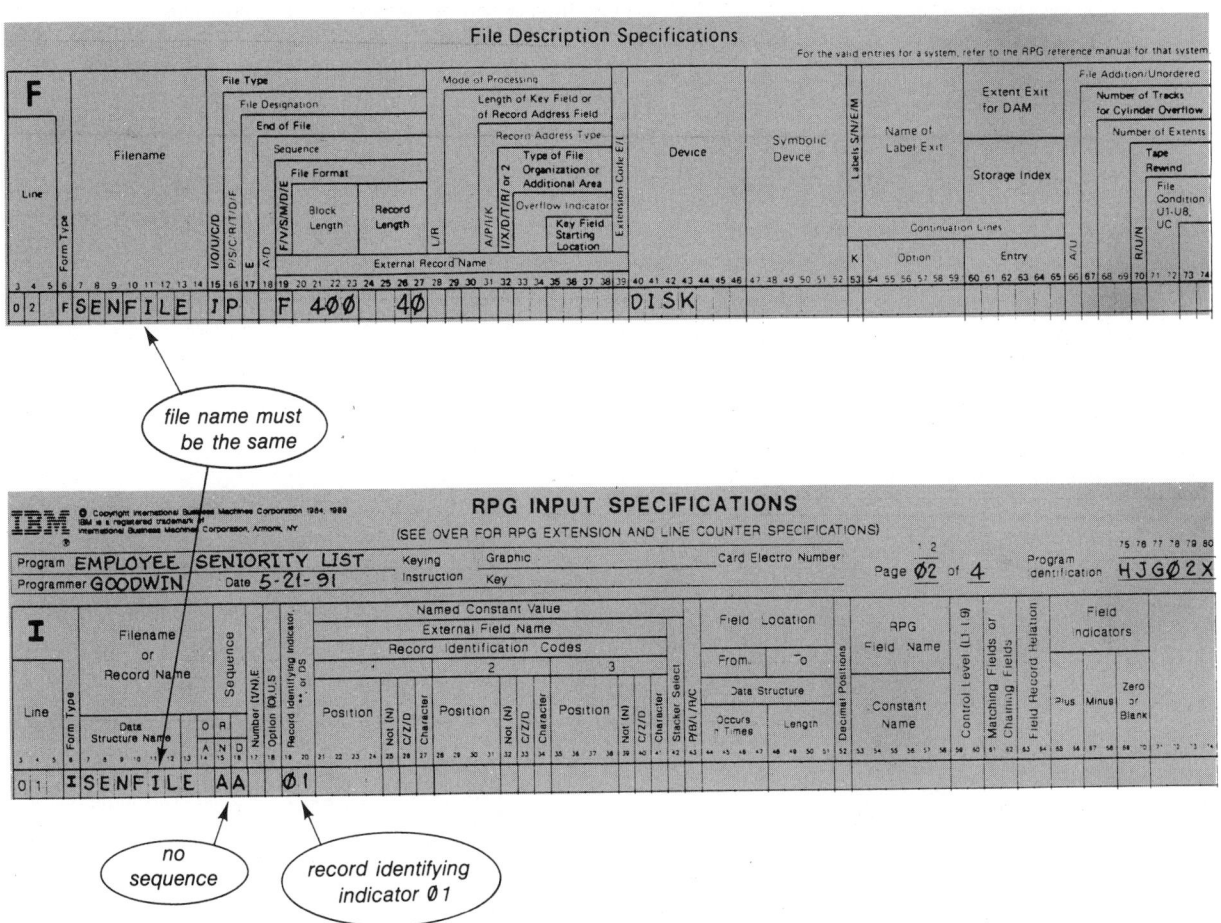

Figure 2-18   Relationship between the Filename entry on the File Description and the Input Specifications

Figure 2-18 shows that the Filename entries are identical on the Input and File Description Specification forms. As was stated earlier, the programmer can select almost any desired name for a file when coding the File Description Specifications. However, once the name is chosen, that identical name must be used for every reference to that file within the program.

≡ Sequence Entry

The **Sequence** entry can be used to specify a required sequence, or order, of records within a file. The sample program does not require that this technique be used. However, RPG requires that an entry be made in the Sequence area of the Input Specifications. The entry in positions 15–16 may be any two letters of the alphabet, except that the letters **ND** should not be used as a Sequence entry because some older versions of the RPG compiler confuses a sequence entry of ND in positions 15–16 with the entry AND in positions 14–16. This confusion by the compiler may result in a Terminal error message when the program is compiled.

≡ Record Identifying Indicator Entry

Step 5 of the fixed logic cycle (Figure 2-19) shows that a record identifying indicator is turned on to show that a new record has been read by the program. The **record identifying indicator** entry in positions 19–20 (see Figure 2-18) specifies which of the 99 general-purpose indicators is to be used for this purpose. Any of these general-purpose indicators may be used for record identification. Use of indicator 01 is based on the RPG Programming Standards in Appendix A: Standard 1 on Indicator Usage specifies that indicators 01–19 are to be used for record identification. Remember that this is not a rule of the RPG language but is a technique for uniform programming practice. In theory, any of the 99 general-purpose indicators could be used.

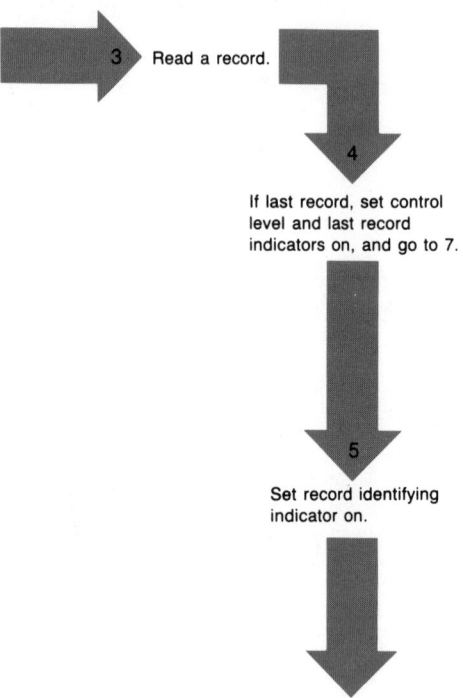

Figure 2-19   Logic cycle: steps 3, 4, and 5

Since RPG turns off all record identifying indicators before the program attempts to read an input record, each time a record is read, the record identifying indicator is turned on to show that there is new data to be processed.

▤ Data Field Definition

The input data fields to be processed by an RPG program must be defined before they can be processed. If a field is not fully and accurately defined, it cannot be processed correctly, if at all, by the program. A **field definition** provides three facts about the field being defined:

Length, the Field Location entry, indicates how much computer memory must be reserved for the data.
Data class, the Decimal Positions entry, indicates what type of data is to be stored in the field and what types of operations may be performed on the field.
Name, the Field Name entry, indicates how the programmer will identify and refer to the data.

Every field used in an RPG program must be defined in terms of its length, data class, and name. Figure 2-20 shows the relationship between the input record layout and the Input Specifications that define the fields. Note again that the unused area of the input layout is not defined on the Input Specifications.

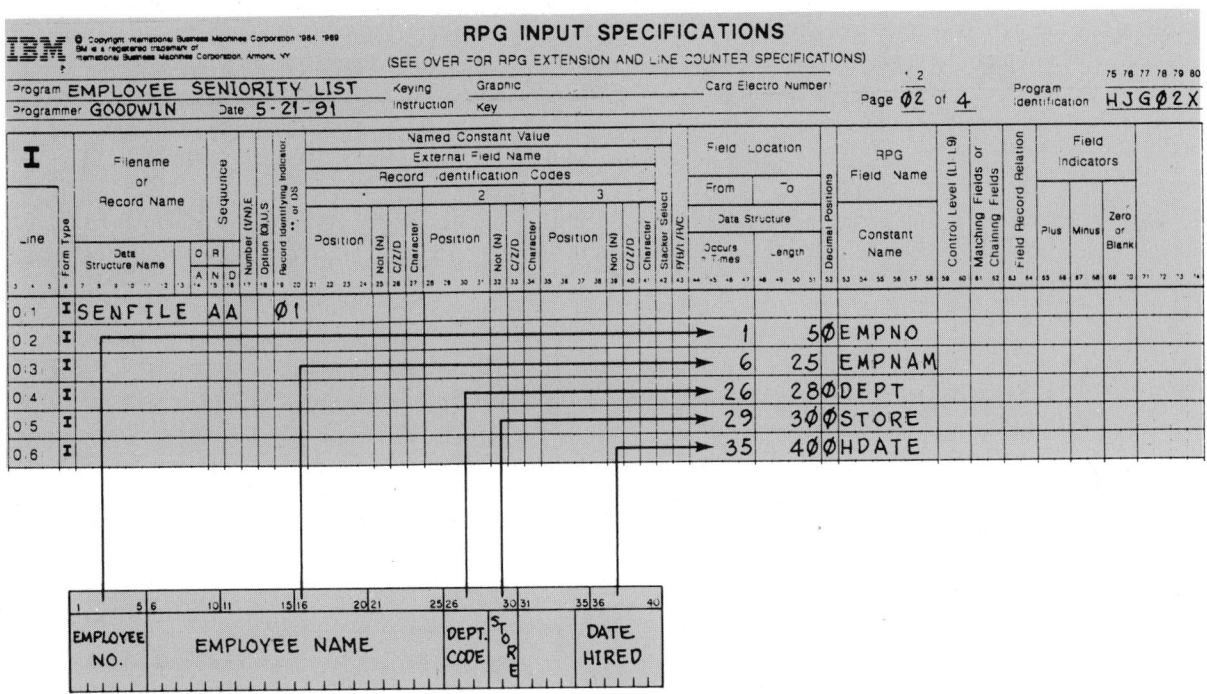

Figure 2-20   Input field definition

▶ **Field Location, From and To Entries**   These entries specify the location of a field within the input record. The From entry in positions 44–47 is used to specify where a field begins. The To entry in positions 48–51 specifies where a field ends. For example, (see Figure 2-20), a From entry of 6 and a To entry of 25 have been entered for the Employee Name field because the record layout shows that this field occupies positions 6–25 of the input record. These entries are always right-justified in their areas. The From entry must end in position 47 of the specification line; the To entry must end in position 51.

These entries also provide the first of the three needed data definition facts, field length, in addition to specifying the starting and ending positions of a data field. Field length is determined by RPG by comparing the starting and ending positions of the field. In other words, if RPG knows where a field starts and where that field ends, the compiler can determine its length.

▸ **Decimal Positions Entry** The Decimal Positions entry in position 52 establishes the second of the three facts needed to define a field: the data class. The data class of a field can be either numeric or alphameric. A numeric data field must contain only the digits 0–9 and either a plus or minus sign. Two RPG program functions require numeric data fields:

A field must be defined as numeric if it will be used in arithmetic operations.
A field must be defined as numeric if it will be edited when it is used as part of an output record.

An alphameric data field may contain any character that the computer understands: letters, numbers, and special characters. *You cannot use an alphameric data field for arithmetic operations or output editing.*

Data class must be correctly described. If a field described as numeric contains nonnumeric characters, such as letters or punctuation, the program will fail during execution. Depending on the version of RPG being used, the program may stop completely or may convert the letters and punctuation to numbers. If this conversion takes place, the program will appear to execute correctly. This type of error cannot be detected until the program output is verified during program testing.

Data class is defined by the entry in the Decimal Positions area. If the programmer makes no entry in position 52, the field is defined as alphameric. If a number is placed in the Decimal Positions area, the field is defined with a numeric data class. The number used to define a numeric field represents the number of decimal places in the data field. If the field is an integer (or whole number) field, the Decimal Positions entry is the digit zero. If the field contains decimal positions (a money amount, for example), the number placed in the Decimal Positions area is the number of positions after the decimal point location. In the case of a money amount, the normal Decimal Positions entry would be the digit 2.

In Figure 2-21, four of the input fields have a Decimal Positions entry of zero, defining them as numeric integer fields. They have been defined as numeric because the printer spacing chart shows that zero suppression (a form of editing) is to be performed on these fields.

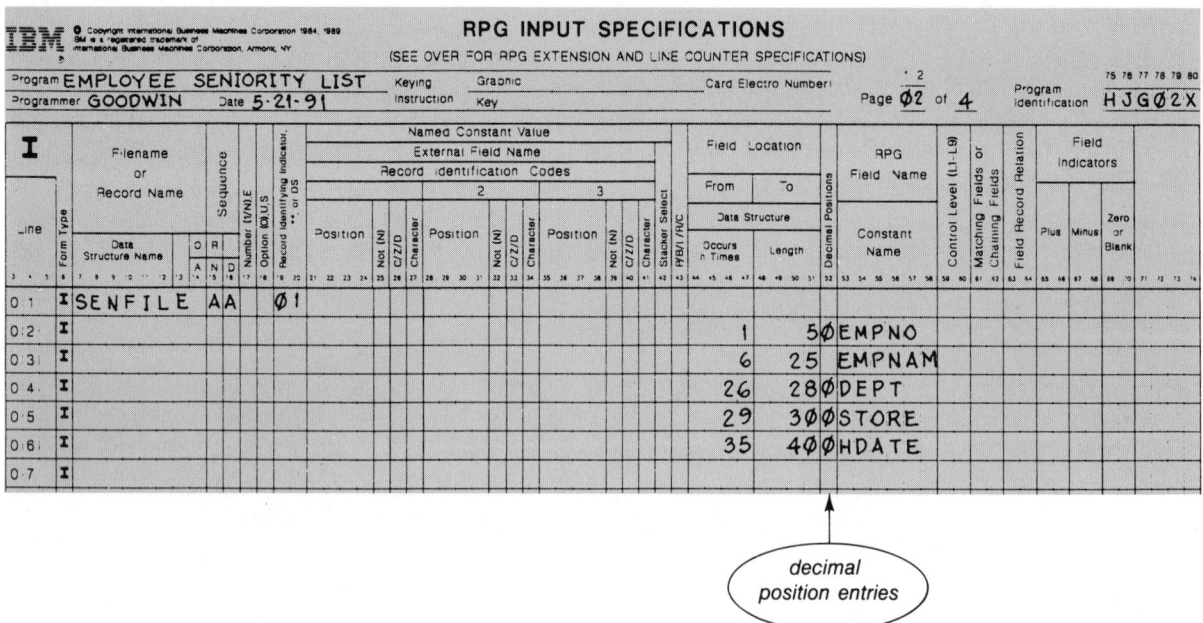

Figure 2-21   Examples of Decimal Positions entries

▸ **Field Name Entries** The third fact needed to define a field is the name of the field. The Field Name entry in positions 53–58 is used by RPG to identify the memory area in which the field data is stored. The rules for field name formation are similar to the rules for file name formation. The single exception is the length of the field name, which is a maximum of 6 characters. Briefly, a field name

Must be unique
Can be from 1 to 6 six characters long
Must begin with an alphabetic character
Can have either alphabetic characters or digits after the first character
Must begin in position 53 of the Input Specifications form

In addition, field names should, whenever possible, be a description or abbreviation of the field being named rather than a random selection of characters. A common problem in RPG stems from the fact that RPG allows only six positions for a field name. One common method used to overcome this problem is the elimination of letters from the full name of the field being described. An Employee Name field could be named EMPNAM within the program, a Billing Date field could be named BILDAT, and so on. Figure 2-21 also shows the field names assigned to the input data fields in the sample program.

RPG OUTPUT CONCEPTS

The output file contains records and fields that must be defined to RPG in a manner similar to the definition of the input data. Figure 2-22 shows the printer spacing chart and printed output for the sample program.

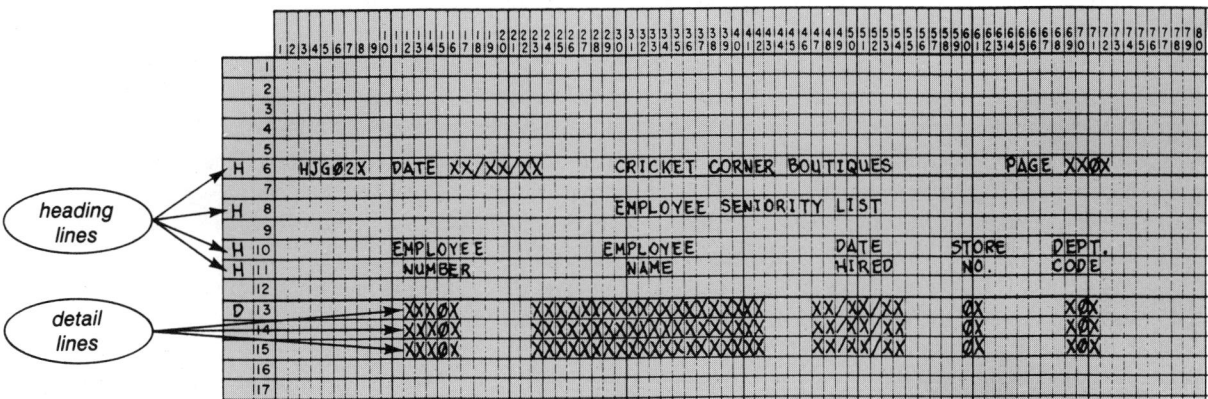

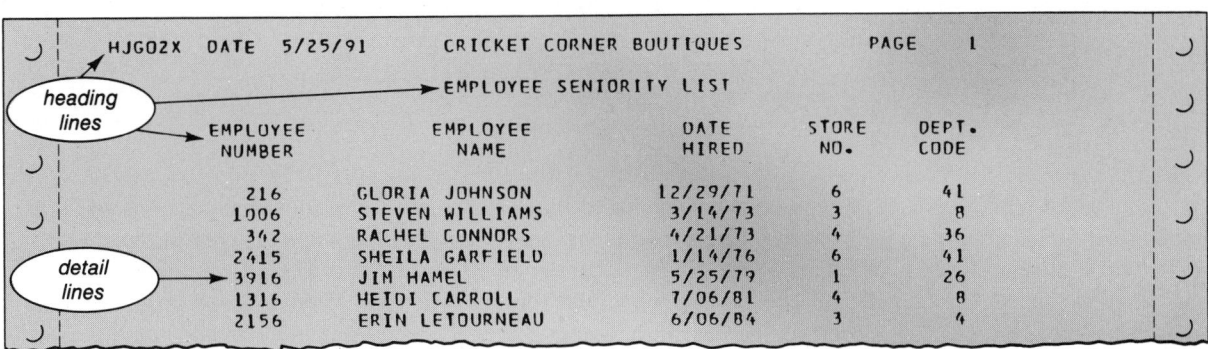

Figure 2-22   Examples of heading and detail lines

In Figure 2-22, four heading lines are described as part of the output report. Also note that there is one detail line. The detail line is described only once in the Output Specifications, even though it is shown several times. The repetition of the detail line on the printer spacing chart is done to show the correct spacing between consecutive detail lines.

Types of Output Data

The information that is to appear on the printed report is divided into two types, or categories: data fields and constants. You are already familiar with data fields. A **data field** is an area of an input record or computer memory that contains data taken from an input field or created as the result of a calculation. These data fields are often referred to as **variables** because their contents change, or vary, depending on the data that has been read or calculated. Two variables appear in the first heading line (Figure 2-22): the Date field and the Page Number field. All the fields in the detail line are variables. The term *variable* is not used as commonly in RPG as in other languages such as BASIC and FORTRAN. In this book, the terms *field* and *data field*, are used to refer to a variable.

A **constant** is a unit of data that never changes in a program. The words that are part of the heading lines are constants; they remain unchanged within the program no matter how often the program is executed, and no matter how many pages of output data are printed. Another word for unchanging data is **literal**. In RPG, unchanging data that appears in the Output Specifications is called a constant, whereas unchanging data used in calculations is referred to as a literal. The use of literals is discussed in the chapters dealing with calculations.

Output Records and Fields

Figure 2-23 shows the RPG Output specifications for the sample program. Note that the left side of the form is used to describe each of the five output records (lines) required by this program. The right side of the form is used to describe the constants and data fields in each of these records. Each record, data field, or constant description appears on a separate line. The record and field description areas cannot both be used on the same output specification line. The figure also shows the basic format of output specification coding. Each of the five record descriptions on the left side of the Output Specifications form is followed by the field descriptions for that record. A rule in coding RPG Output Specifications is that *after a record is described, all the fields within the record are described before beginning the next record description.*

Headings are an excellent example of one additional fact that a programmer must remember when writing RPG Output Specifications. The sample program contains four heading lines to be printed at the top of every page. Heading lines print at the top of the first page of the report and at the top of every succeeding page. In other words, these four output records are printed under the same conditions. *When several lines are to be printed under the same conditions, they must appear on the Output Specifications form in their correct order.* The first heading line must be coded first, followed by the second, then the third, and so on. RPG treats all output that occurs under identical conditions on a top-to-bottom basis. You will see this demonstrated as the four heading lines of the program are coded.

Page Overflow

Printed reports, except for those in programming textbook examples, are rarely single-page reports. It is not unusual for an application program to generate reports that are several hundred pages long. Most reports are printed on **continuous forms**, which are a series of pages connected by perforations. These perforations can be easily torn to separate a group of connected pages into individual pages. The most common length for these pages is 11 inches. As most computers print six lines per inch, a normal report page could have a maximum of 66 lines printed on it.

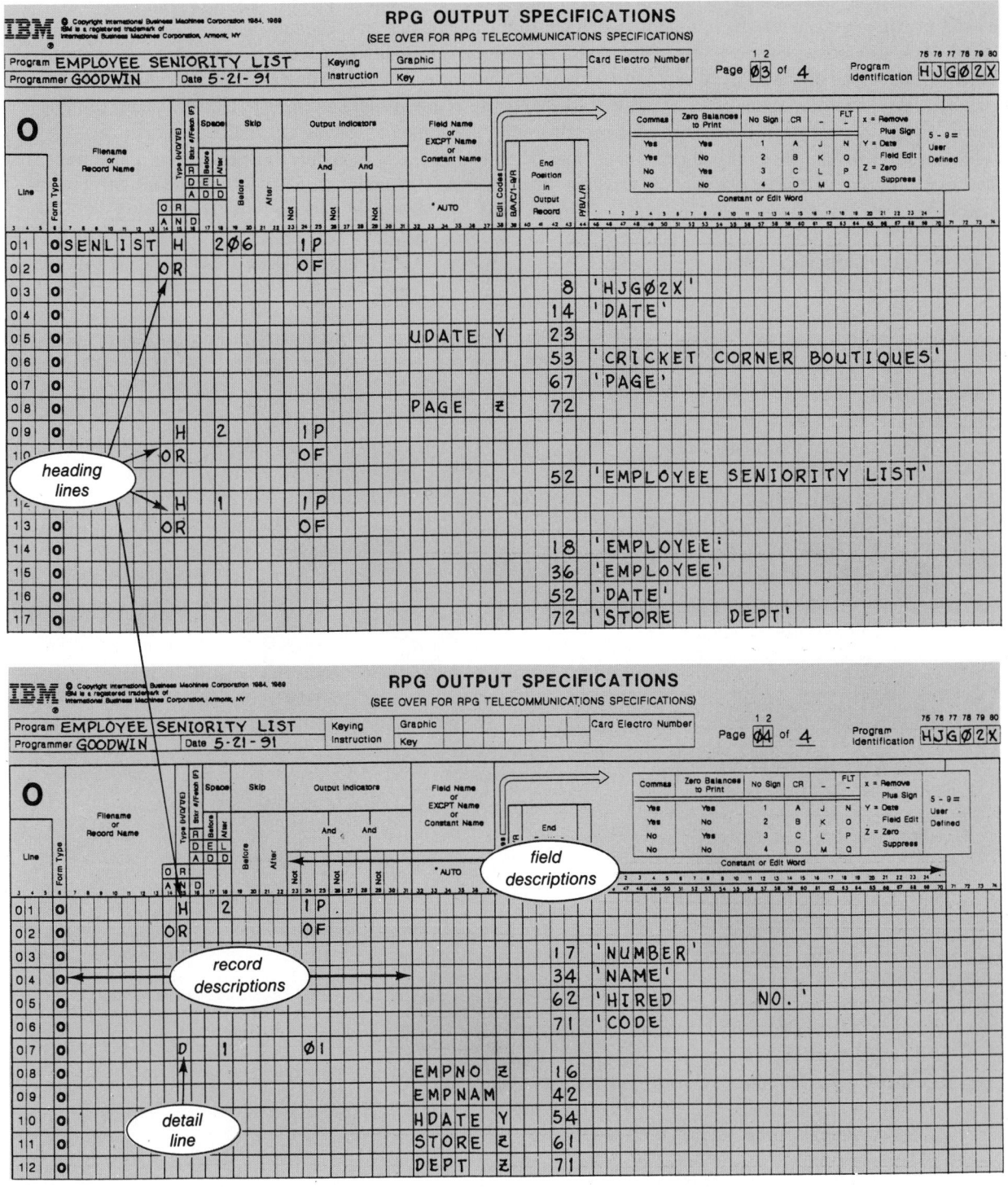

Figure 2-23   RPG Output Specifications

A report does not usually print on all 66 of these lines. The standard practice when writing a report, memo, or letter by hand is to leave a blank margin at the top and bottom of each page. This practice is also followed when a report is generated using a computer. Printed reports usually have a margin of 1 inch, or six print lines, at the top and bottom of each page. Program instructions determine when the last print line of the page has been reached, and advance the paper to line 6 of the next page before resuming printing. The last usable printing line of a page, normally line 60, is called the **overflow line**. In addition to leaving top and bottom margins, this process also avoids the possibility of printing an unreadable line on the page-connecting perforation. **Page overflow** is the process of leaving margins and avoiding the connecting perforation. Figure 2-24 illustrates the continuous forms used on a computer.

▸ **Form Skipping** When the overflow line is reached, the paper is moved to the first usable line of the next page by skipping the form. **Skipping** is the process of moving a continuous form to a predetermined line on the page regardless of the distance to the line. For example, a skip instruction might cause the paper to move to print line 55 before a total is printed. If the program has just finished printing line 10 of the page, the form will advance more than 7 inches. If, however, the program has just finished printing line 51, the paper will advance only half an inch. In both cases, regardless of distance, the paper is set at the same line for the printing of the total.

▸ **Page Overflow, Skipping, and Headings** The most common use of page overflow is to cause headings to be printed at the top of every report page except the first. A different programming technique is used to control first page headings because overflow can, by definition, only occur after at least one page has been printed.

overflow line, the last line to be printed on a page

when overflow line is printed, overflow then occurs

Figure 2-24 Continuous forms

When the overflow line is reached on a page, the overflow indicator that was specified as part of the file description is turned on. The next time step 10 of the logic cycle (Figure 2-25) is reached, the overflow indicator causes overflow processing to take place. During overflow processing:

> The continuous forms are advanced to the next page
> Headings print
> The overflow indicator is turned off
> The next detail line prints
> The logic cycle continues to the next step

If no overflow indicator was specified in the File Description Specifications, no overflow processing takes place. However, some versions of RPG perform an automatic advance to the top of the next page after reaching the overflow line, even if no overflow processing has been included in the program.

Move data from record selected at beginning of cycle into processing area. Set field indicators.

11

If overflow indicator is on, do overflow operations, and set overflow indicator off.

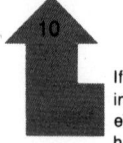

10

If last record indicator is on, end of program has been reached.

Figure 2-25 Logic cycle: step 10

Filename Entry

The first entry on the Output Specifications form is the Filename entry in positions 7–14. The file name must be the same as the output file name specified on the File Description Specifications. Figure 2-26 shows this relationship. The file name SENLIST is entered in the Filename area of the form. It is through this entry that RPG is able to relate the Output Specifications to the file description. The Filename entry must be left-justified, that is, it must begin in position 7 of the Filename area.

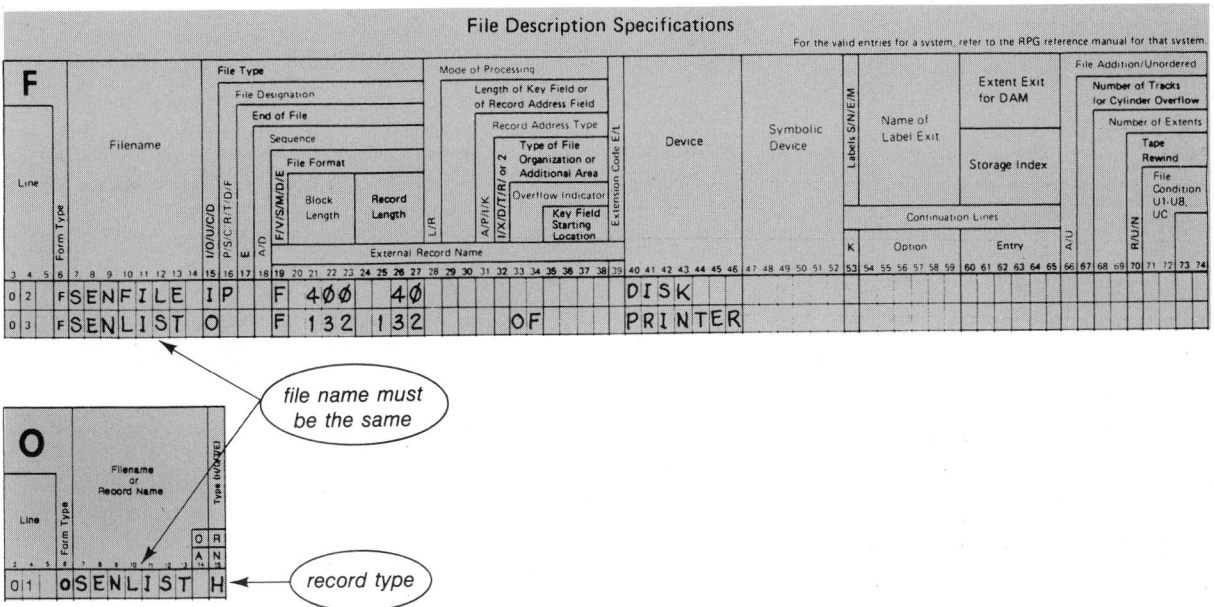

Figure 2-26   Example of Filename and Type entries

The Filename entry is used only once for each file, as part of the first record description. RPG assumes that all records described after a Filename entry are part of that file. If a program contains more than one output file, each Filename entry marks the beginning of the description of a different output file.

Type Entry

The **Type** entry, position 15, performs two functions in the RPG Output Specifications. The first function is to mark the beginning of a record description. Just as the Filename entry tells RPG that a different file description is beginning, an entry in the Type area specifies the beginning of a record description.

The second Type area function is to specify to RPG the type of record being described. The type of output record determines the point in the RPG logic cycle during which the record output can take place. The sample program uses two types of records: **type H**, or heading, records and **type D**, or detail, records. Although heading and detail lines use different Type entries, the H and D entries have identical meanings to the RPG compiler; these two different entries exist for the convenience of application and maintenance programmers. Separate H and D entries provide an easy distinction between these two types of output records. This book follows the accepted programming practice of identifying all heading lines as type H and all detail lines as type D.

Heading Control

Figure 2-27 shows the Output Specifications that control the conditions under which the first heading line will print, as well as the specifications for the movement of the output form before and after the first heading line is printed. The Output Indicators area controls when an output record is produced. The Space and the Skip areas control the movement of the form through the printer.

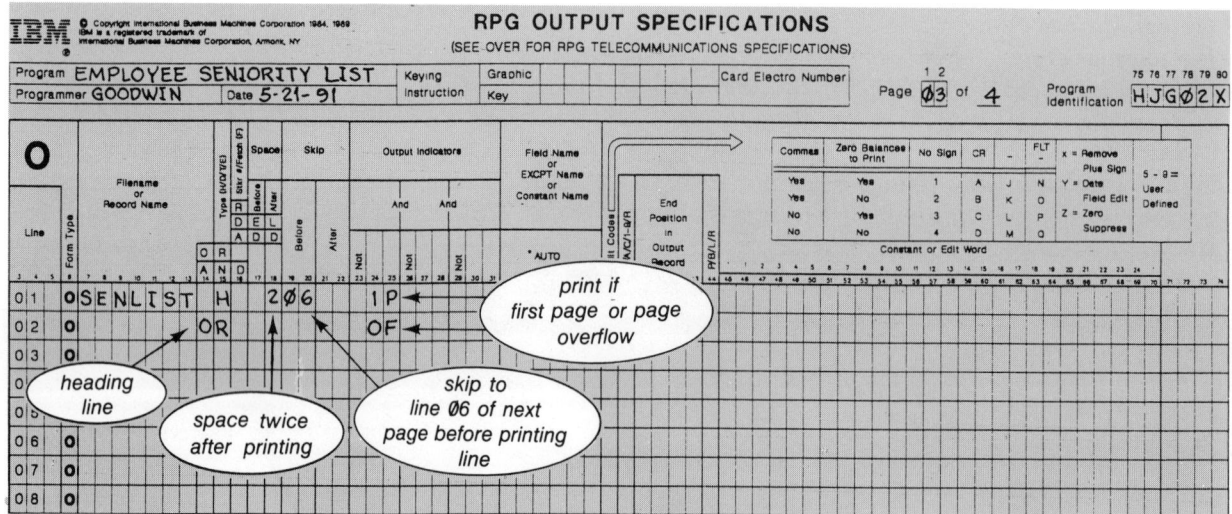

Figure 2-27   Example of heading control entries

▸ **Space Area**   Spacing is the movement of the output form a fixed number of lines. You have already learned that a skipping operation causes the form to be moved to a predetermined point on a page regardless of how far the form must move. Spacing moves the form a fixed number of lines regardless of position on the form. The Space entries cause the output form to move a specific number of lines **before** (position 17) or **after** (position 18) a line is printed. The maximum number of lines that can be spaced is three in most versions of RPG. Figure 2-27 shows that there will be double spacing after the first heading line is printed.

▸ **Skip Area**   The entry of 06 in the **Skip Before** area, positions 19-20, specifies that the form will be advanced to line 6 before printing. As line 6 is the first line to be used for printing, the form is advanced to the top of the next page before the first heading line prints. This Skip Before entry is normally used only with the first heading line. Some versions of RPG use an entry of 01 to specify the first printing line of a page. Verify the proper entry with your instructor or computer center manager. If no entry is made in either the Space or the Skip areas of a record description for a printed report, most versions of RPG default to a single space after printing occurs. If no entry is made in either Skip area, and if one of the Space areas contains an entry of zero, no form movement takes place. This technique, called **space suppression**, is used if it is necessary to print two or more records on the same line of a form.

The Space and Skip areas of the Output Specifications are used only with printed output files. If these entries are used with a file that is described as using any device other than a printer, an error message is generated during program compilation.

▸ **Output Indicators**   The Output Indicator area controls when the line is printed; this area is divided into three separate areas in which indicators may be specified to control the printing of an output line. An output indicator can be specified in positions 24–25, 27–28, or 30–31. You may use two or more of these areas if an output line is to be printed only when more than one indicator is on at the same time.

Headings must be printed under two different conditions during a program:

At the beginning of a program at the top of the first page
At the top of every succeeding page when a page overflow condition occurs

▶ **Indicator 1P** RPG uses a special-purpose indicator to control first-page headings. **Indicator 1P**, the first-page indicator, is turned on at the beginning of program execution. This indicator remains on until step 1 of the logic cycle is executed, and then it is turned off. Indicator 1P turns on and then off before the first input record is read by the object program. Because step 1 of the logic cycle permits detail and heading output to occur, any H and D output records that are controlled by indicator 1P are written. Note that indicator 1P is not available at any other point in the program. This is a fully automatic special-purpose indicator.

▶ **Indicator OF** All page headings after the first page are treated as overflow headings. These headings are controlled by the overflow indicator that was selected when the File Description Specifications were written. As was explained earlier, the overflow indicator is turned on when the overflow line is reached on a page. The overflow indicator causes overflow operations to occur during the next detail output operation at step 1 of the logic cycle.

▶ **OR Relation** The first-page and overflow indicators are joined by the use of the word **OR** (Figure 2-28) in positions 14–15 of the second record description line. When the OR is used in positions 14–15 it indicates that the output record is to be printed if either indicator 1P or indicator OF is on. This **OR relation** causes the output to print when either of these two conditions occurs during program execution.

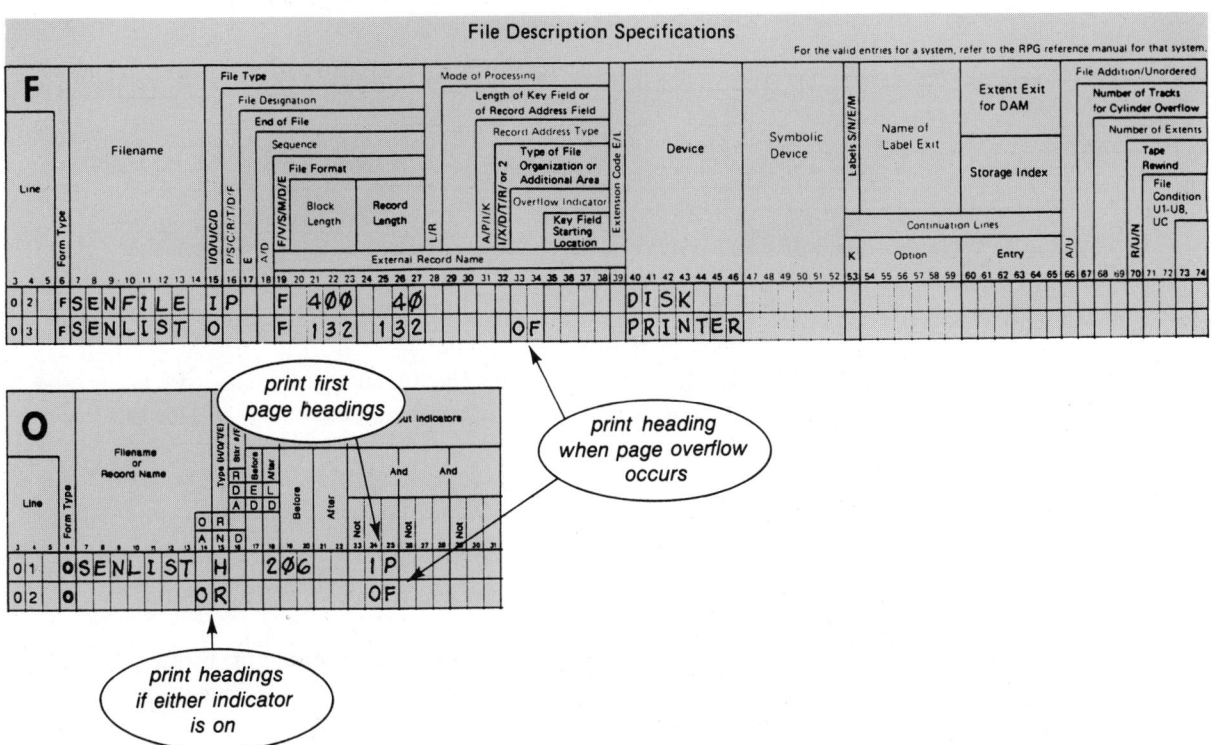

Figure 2-28 File Description and Output Specifications

Output Data Description

After the skipping and spacing of the heading line have been defined and the controlling indicators have been specified, the information to be printed on the heading line must be described. The entries needed to complete the description of the first heading line are shown in Figure 2-29.

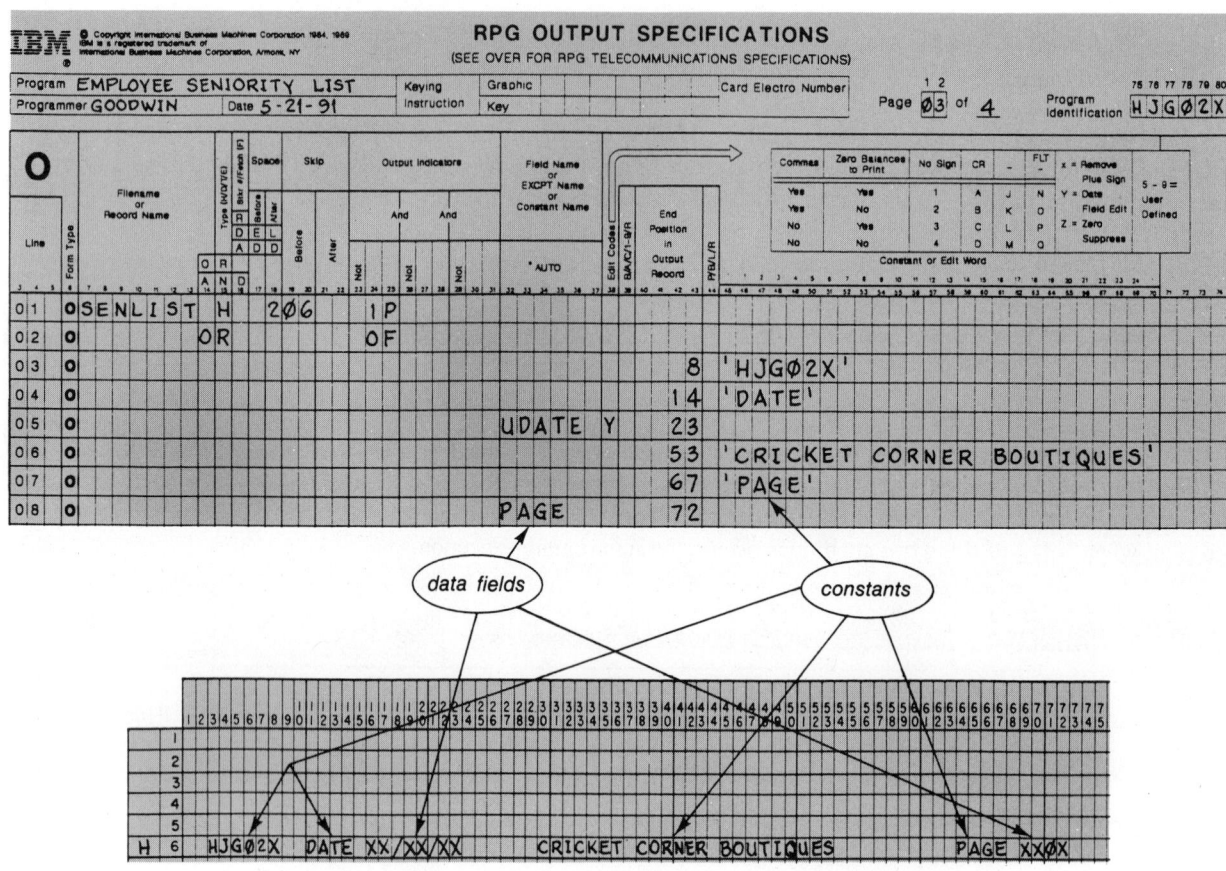

Figure 2-29 Output Specifications for first heading line

The first heading line contains both data fields and constants. The date and page number are taken from data fields when the program executes. All other information in the first heading line consists of constants that are written as part of the Output Specifications.

Output Constant Description

▶ **Constant Area** The first entry in the heading line is the constant HJG02X, which identifies the program creating the report. Values of constants are entered in the Constant or Edit Word area, positions 45–70. Line 03 of the Output Specifications form shows the entry for the constant HJG02X. You must write constant entries exactly as they are to appear on the printed report. All constants coded on the Output Specifications must be enclosed within apostrophes. These **apostrophes** do not appear on the printed report but act as **delimiters**, marking the start and end of the constant. Between the apostrophes, any letter, number, or special character desired by the programmer may be specified. As is illustrated on line 06 of Figure 2-29, blanks or spaces may be used within a constant.

Note that all constant entries begin in position 45 of the specification. Line 03 shows the entry 'HJG02X' beginning in position 45. A constant may be a single word, as shown on lines 03, 04, and 07, or a group of words, as shown on line 06. The constant is taken from the report layout developed on the printer spacing chart.

All the letters used in the constant are capital, or uppercase, letters. This is traditional for output constants because most minicomputer and mainframe computer printers can print only in capital letters. If you are using a printer that supports both uppercase and lowercase letters, either type may be used in a constant.

▸ **End Position in Output Record** The End Position area in positions 40–43 indicates the last, or rightmost, printing position to be used by a constant or data field. Figure 2-30 illustrates the relation between the printer spacing chart and the End Position entry in the Output Specifications. Note that the first constant, HJG02X is 6 characters long. Since this constant has been given an End Position entry of 8, the constant will print in positions 3–8 of the output line. Likewise, the DATE constant will print in positions 11–14.

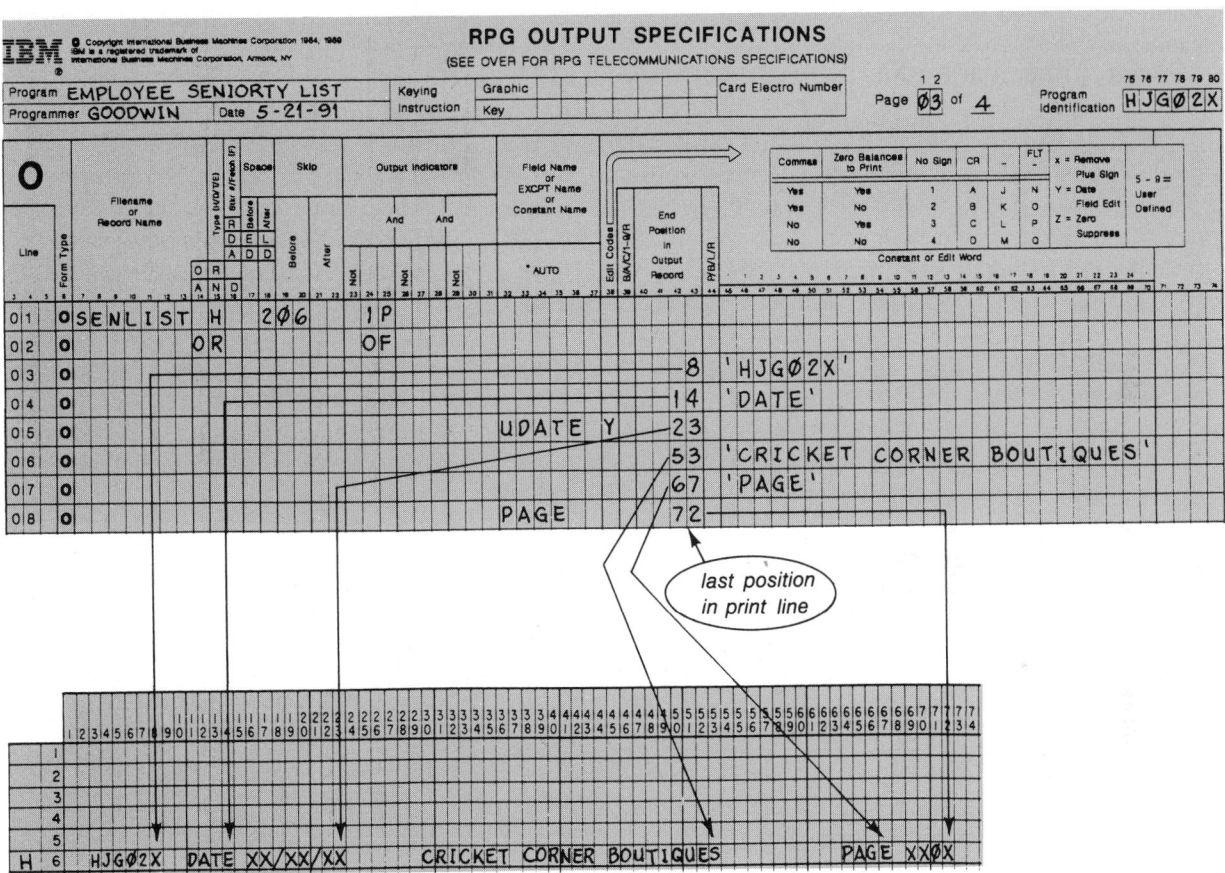

Figure 2-30 Relation between End Position entry and printer spacing chart

Earlier you learned that data fields must be defined with name, length, and data class. Constants are unnamed, but they are assigned a length (the number of positions between apostrophes) and data class (always alphameric). RPG is able to calculate the proper starting position in the print line because the Output Specification for a constant specifies both the length and end position.

▬ Data Field Output

All data fields that are to be part of an output record must have been defined earlier in the program. However, neither of the two data fields appearing in the first heading line has been previously defined. These two data fields, UDATE and PAGE, are special fields that are predefined within the RPG language. These predefined, or

reserved, fields do not have to be defined anywhere within the program. They are part of the RPG compiler and can be used on the Output Specifications just as any programmer-defined field would be.

▶ **System Date Field** The printer spacing chart shows that a date is to appear in the first heading line. This is the report date, the date on which the report is printed. The reserved field, **UDATE**, is a 6-position numeric field containing the current, or report, date. UDATE is normally stored within the computer in MMD-DYY format: The first two positions contain the month, the middle two positions contain the day, and the last two positions contain the last two digits of the year. For example, the UDATE for July 23, 1944 is 072344 and the UDATE for November 18, 1963 is 111863. Usually, the current date is set into the UDATE area when the computer is started at the beginning of the day. At midnight, if the computer is still running, the current date is automatically advanced by the operating system software so that UDATE always contains the current date. RPG also permits access to the individual month, day, and year of the current date by means of the reserved fields **UMONTH, UDAY,** and **UYEAR.** Each of these is a two-position numeric data field.

▶ **Page Number Field** The other reserved field to appear in the first heading line is **PAGE**, which is a 4-position, numeric field containing the page number of each page of the report. Each time that page overflow occurs, RPG adds 1 to the numeric value of the page field. This page count is kept automatically by the object program. When the first page headings are printed, the value in PAGE is 1. The value in PAGE when headings are printed the second time is 2; the third time the value is 3, and so on. Unless special programming techniques are used to vary the contents, the PAGE field always starts at a value of 1.

▶ **Field Name Entry** The names of output data fields are placed in positions 32–37, the Field Name area, as shown in Figure 2-31. Remember, as was noted earlier, that all field names used in the Output specifications must have been defined in the program or must be RPG reserved field names. The field name is left-justified into the Field Name area, starting in position 32. Line 05 shows the entry of the UDATE field with an end position of 23, as specified on the printer spacing chart. Line 08 shows the PAGE entry.

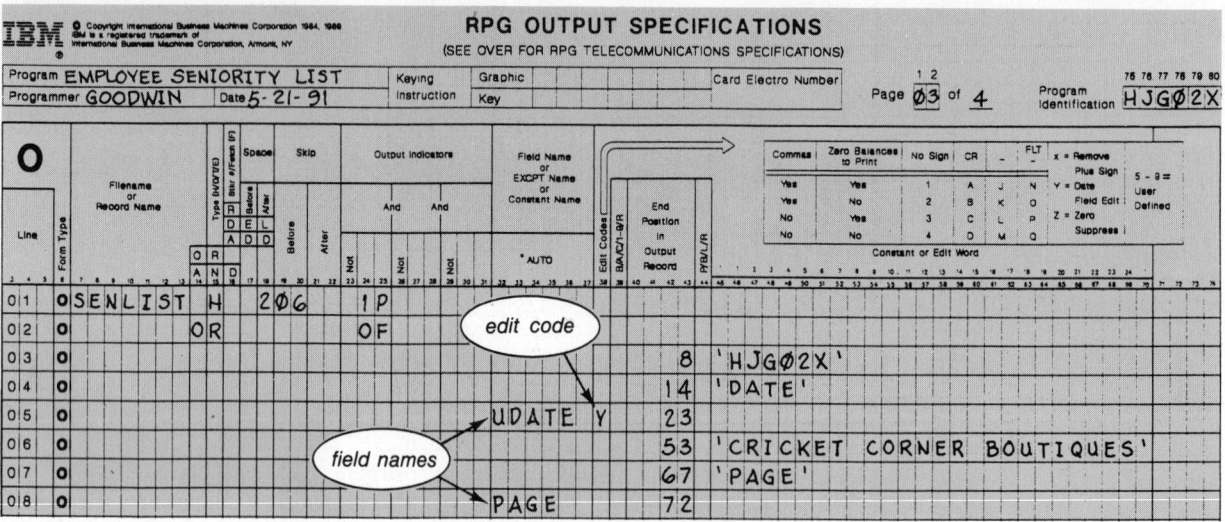

Figure 2-31 Examples of use of output field name and edit code

▶ **Edit Code Entry and Date Editing** When a numeric data field is printed, it is normally edited. **Editing** is the insertion of punctuation between digits to make the number more readable. The unedited date 052988 is less easily read than the edited date 05/29/88. One method of editing output data is to place an **edit code** in position 38 of the Output specification for the field. Edit codes can be used only with data that has been defined as numeric. As many as 20 edit codes may be available for use with your version of RPG. At this time, only one of these codes is needed. The other codes are discussed as their need arises.

The edit code **Y** is reserved for editing data fields containing dates. Use of the Y edit code is shown in Figure 2-31. The Y entry causes the 6-position UDATE field to print in edited format with slashes separating the month, day, and year portions of the date.

The PAGE field, shown on line 08, also requires editing; however, this editing is automatic. PAGE, as was stated earlier, is a 4-position numeric field. The page number for the first page is stored as 0001 within the computer. Usually, however, leading zeros are not included in printed output. These unnecessary zeros are replaced by blanks before the data is printed. The process of replacing leading zeros with blanks is called **zero suppression**. The PAGE field uses the only fully automatic edit process in the RPG language: PAGE is always zero suppressed, with no need for an edit code in position 38. The result of the automatic zero suppression of PAGE is illustrated in Figure 2-32. Note that the nonsignificant (meaningless) leading zeros have been changed to blanks so that they do not print on the report.

The second, third, and fourth heading lines are specified in the same manner as the first heading line and with the same output indicators. The only differences are the spacing of the lines and the lack of a skip specification for lines other than the first. Figure 2-33 shows the completed heading specifications.

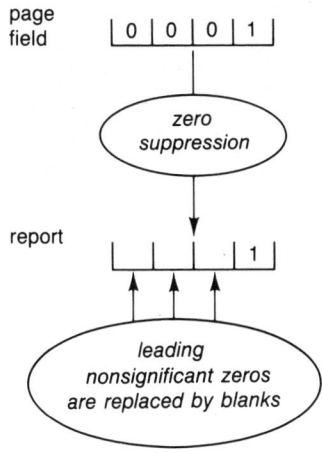

Figure 2-32 Zero suppression of the PAGE field

Figure 2-33 Heading line specifications and printed headings

Line	Form Type	Filename/Record Name	Type	Space Before	Space After	Skip Before	Skip After	Output Indicators			Field Name/EXCPT Name/Constant Name	Edit Codes	End Position in Output Record	Constant or Edit Word
01	O	SENLIST	H	2	06			1P						
02	O		OR					OF						
03	O												8	'HJG02X'
04	O												14	'DATE'
05	O											UDATE Y	23	
06	O												53	'CRICKET CORNER BOUTIQUES'
07	O												67	'PAGE'
08	O											PAGE	72	
09	O		H	2				1P						
10	O		OR					OF						
11	O												52	'EMPLOYEE SENIORITY LIST'
12	O		H	1				1P						
13	O		OR					OF						
14	O												18	'EMPLOYEE'
15	O												36	'EMPLOYEE'
16	O												52	'DATE'
17	O												72	'STORE DEPT'
18	O		H	2				1P						
19	O		OR					OF						
20	O												17	'NUMBER'
	O												34	'NAME'
	O												62	'HIRED NO.'
	O												71	'CODE'

RPG OUTPUT SPECIFICATIONS
(SEE OVER FOR RPG TELECOMMUNICATIONS SPECIFICATIONS)

Program EMPLOYEE SENIORITY LIST Programmer GOODWIN Date 5-21-91 Page 03 of 4 Program Identification HJG02X

*Number of sheets per pad may vary slightly.

Figure 2-33 (1)

continued

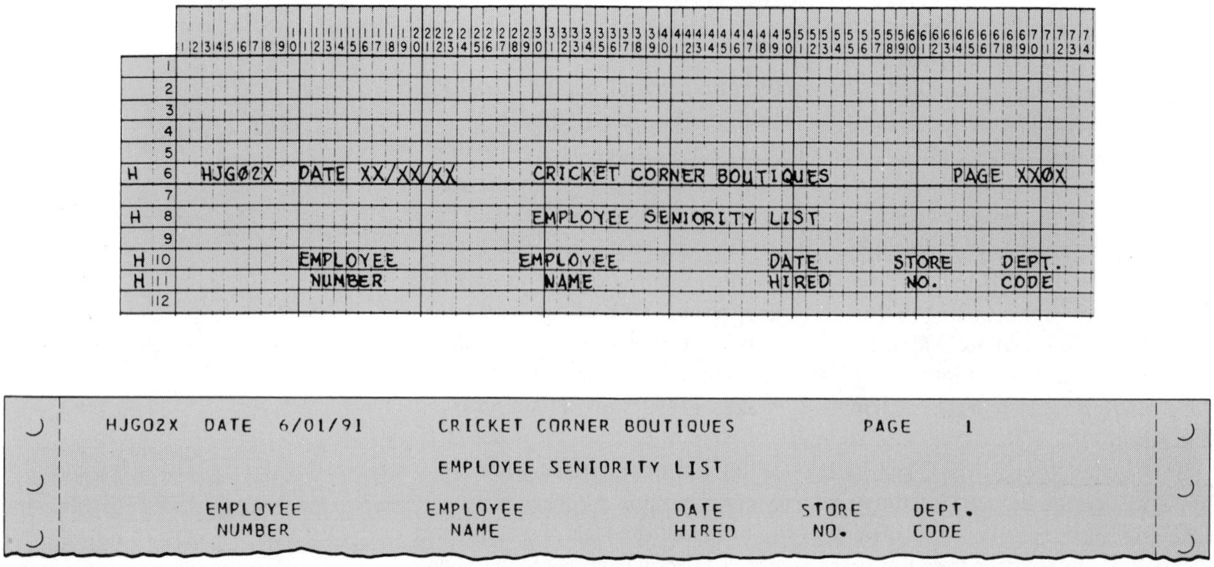

Figure 2-33 (2)

In the example in Figure 2-33, you can see that all four heading records are identified by an H entry in position 15 and that each of them will be printed when either the 1P or the OF indicator is on. The printer will space twice after the first, second, and fourth heading lines and once after the third line is printed.

Detail Output Data

As was stated earlier, a detail output record contains data that is based on each input record and, generally, is produced each time an input record is read. Figure 2-34 shows the relationship between the Input Specifications, detail Output Specifications, and the detail line of the printer spacing chart.

As shown in this figure, the indicator chosen as the record identifying indicator is specified on the Output Specifications to control the printing of the detail output line. Each time indicator 01 is turned on by the reading of an input record, an output line is printed. The program prints exactly as many detail output lines as there are records in the input file. All the detail line data is in the form of data fields since the printer spacing chart shows no constants in the detail line. Constants can appear within a detail line, but none are required for this program.

Also note that although the position of the output fields is based on the printer spacing chart, these positions are not the same as the input field locations. As was stated earlier, there is no relationship between the location of a data field within the input record and its position within a printed line. The three detail lines shown on the printer spacing chart are drawn on consecutive lines, indicating that the detail output is to be single spaced. This is accomplished by the entry of 1 in position 18 of the detail record description.

As shown in Figure 2-34, the Date Hired field, HDATE, is edited into MM/DD/YY format by the edit code Y in position 38 of line 04. The edit code will perform the same function that it performed in the first heading line. Three fields – EMPNO, STORE, and DEPT – have been edited with edit code Z. The Z edit code causes leading zeros to be removed from each of these fields. This zero suppression operation is the same function that RPG performs automatically on the PAGE field within the heading.

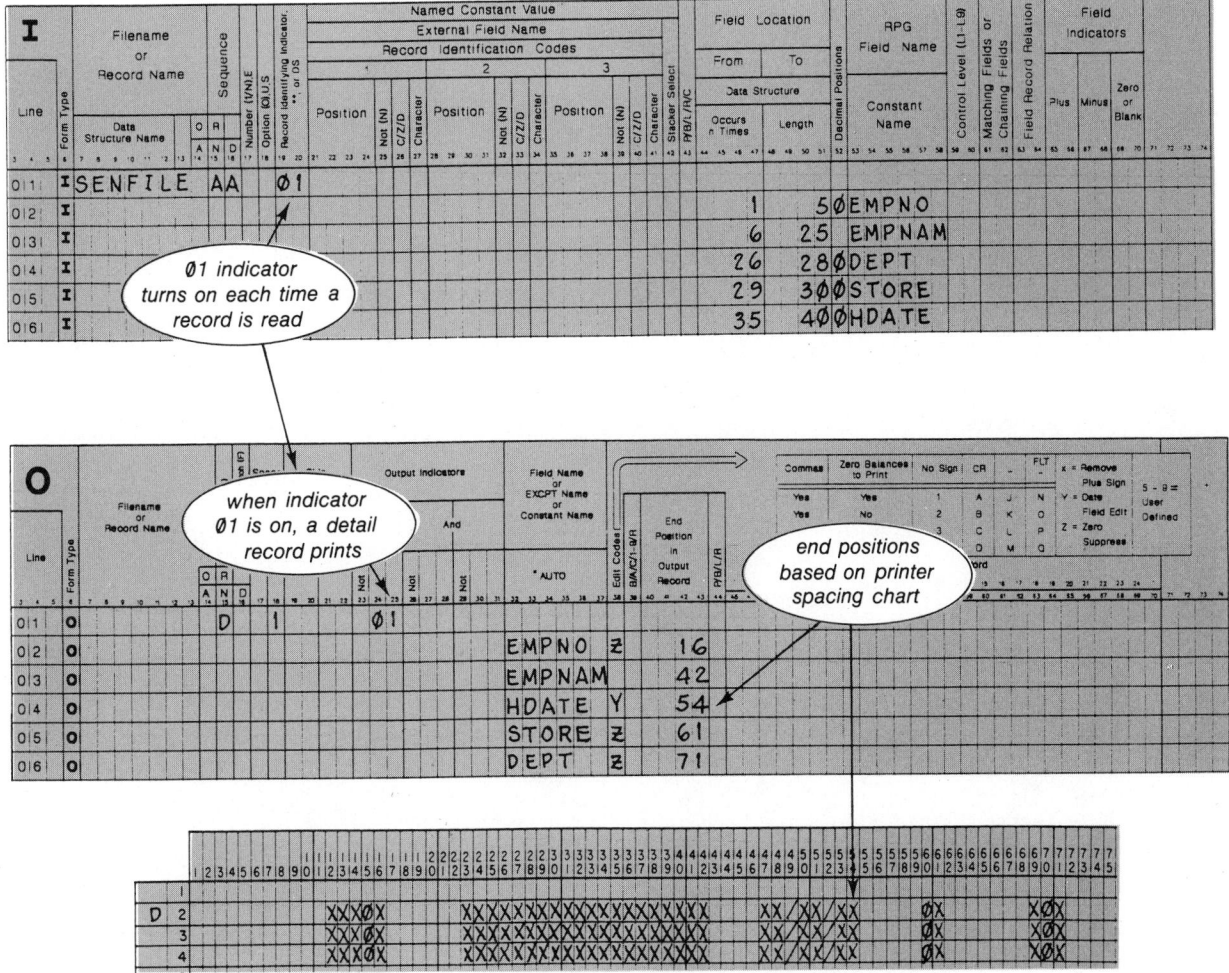

Figure 2-34   Record identification indicator and output fields

If you need to review the entire source program, refer to Figure 2-9. Figure 2-35 on the next page shows the compilation listing produced for the sample program.

≡ IN CONCLUSION ≡

This chapter has shown the coding techniques needed to develop a simple program that requires only that data be read and printed. Most RPG programs, however, require more than just the reading and writing of data records. Chapter 3 develops programs using the Calculation Specifications Form to perform arithmetic operations and accumulate totals to be printed at the end of the report. In addition, it shows how output specifications are written to print these totals.

```
        5727RG1RG R05M00                IBM SYSTEM/36 RPGII                05/25/91  10.33

        0001 H                                                                    HJG02X


0001   0002 FSENFILE IP  F 400  40              DISK
0002   0003 FSENLIST O   F 132 132      OF      PRINTER


0003   0004 ISENFILE AA  01
0004   0005 I                                          1   50EMPNO
0005   0006 I                                          6   25 EMPNAM
0006   0007 I                                         26  280DEPT
0007   0008 I                                         29  300STORE
0008   0009 I                                         35  400HDATE


0009   0010 OSENLIST H  206    1P
0010   0011 O       OR         OF
0011   0012 O                                   8 "HJG02X"
0012   0013 O                                  14 "DATE"
0013   0014 O                          UDATE Y  23
0014   0015 O                                  53 "CRICKET CORNER BOUTIQUES"
0015   0016 O                                  67 "PAGE"
0016   0017 O                          PAGE    72
0017   0018 O       H  2    1P
0018   0019 O       OR      OF
0019   0020 O                                  52 "EMPLOYEE SENIORITY LIST"
0020   0021 O       H  1    1P
0021   0022 O       OR      OF
0022   0023 O                                  18 "EMPLOYEE"
0023   0024 O                                  36 "EMPLOYEE"
0024   0025 O                                  52 "DATE"
0025   0026 O                                  72 "STORE     DEPT."
0026   0027 O       H  2    1P
0027   0028 O       OR      OF
0028   0029 O                                  17 "NUMBER"
0029   0030 O                                  34 "NAME"
0030   0031 O                                  62 "HIRED       NO."
0031   0032 O                                  71 "CODE"
0032   0033 O       D  1    01
0033   0034 O                          EMPNO Z  16
0034   0035 O                          EMPNAM   42
0035   0036 O                          HDATE Y  54
0036   0037 O                          STORE Z  61
0037   0038 O                          DEPT  Z  71

        ✿ ✿ ✿ ✿ ✿ E N D  O F  S O U R C E ✿ ✿ ✿ ✿ ✿


        5727RG1RG R05M00                IBM SYSTEM/36 RPGII                05/25/91  10.33

INDICATORS USED
      OF 1P 01

   FIELD NAMES USED
   STMT#  NAME   DEC  LNG   DISP
   0016 PAGE    0  0004  0127
   0013 UDATE   0  0006  00A7
   0004 EMPNO   0  0005  0118
   0005 EMPNAM     0020  0113
   0006 DEPT    0  0003  011B
   0007 STORE   0  0002  011D
   0008 HDATE   0  0006  0123


        ✿ ✿ ✿ ✿ ✿ E N D  O F  C O M P I L E ✿ ✿ ✿ ✿ ✿
```

Figure 2-35   Compile listing for program HJG02X

CHAPTER SUMMARY

1. An **alphameric** data field may contain letters, numbers, and special characters.
2. A **numeric** data field may contain the digits 0–9 and a sign, either positive or negative.
3. **Report headings** contain information that identifies the entire output report.
4. **Column headings** contain information that identifies columns of output information.
5. There is generally a one-to-one relationship between the number of input records read and the number of **detail lines** printed.
6. Detail lines contain information based on the data in a single input record.
7. **Zero suppression** is the elimination of meaningless zeros from the beginning of a number.
8. **Output editing** makes printed numeric data more readable by zero suppression and the insertion of punctuation such as dollar signs, decimal points, and commas. In addition, output editing can be used to insert characters into a date in order to separate the month, day, and year.
9. **Double spacing** inserts a blank line between consecutive lines of an output report.
10. There is no relationship between the positions occupied by an input field and the output positions in which that field will be printed.
11. The **record identifying indicator** shows that a record has been read by the object program.
12. **Indicator LR** is a special-purpose indicator used to signal end-of-job to the object program.
13. Indicator LR turns on when no data remains in the input file.
14. RPG moves the contents of a record from the **record input area** to the **input fields area** before the fields are processed.
15. A **default** is a built-in entry used by RPG if the programmer leaves an entry blank.
16. A **filename** must be unique, can be from 1 to 8 characters long, must start with an alphabetic character, and cannot contain embedded blanks.
17. The **file designation** entry is not used with files that are output only.
18. A file is **fixed length** if all records within the file contain the same number of characters.
19. A **block** is a group of records read into memory as a unit. **Blocking** data saves time when the program executes, but uses additional computer memory.
20. **Block length** must be an exact multiple of the **record length**.
21. A **machine-dependent** entry is based on the specific computer hardware being used.
22. The input **sequence** entry may be any two letters except **ND**.
23. **Name**, **length**, and **data class** entries are required to define a data field.
24. A data field is called a **variable** because the contents of the field may change during program execution.
25. A **constant** is data that does not change during program execution.
26. All fields within a record are described before beginning the next record description.
27. Output records that are controlled by the same **output indicators** must be described in the order in which the records are to be printed.
28. The **overflow line** is the last printed line on an output page.
29. **Page overflow** is used to leave top and bottom margins on a printed page as well as to avoid printing on the connecting page perforation.
30. **Skipping** is the process of moving a continuous form to a fixed point on a page.
31. The RPG compiler does not differentiate between **type H** and **type D** output lines. The two different **type** entries are used for program clarity.
32. **Space suppression** can be used to cause two or more print operations to occur on the same line of a report.

33. **Indicator 1P** is automatically turned on at the beginning of the program. First-page headings print while indicator 1P is on. Indicator 1P is turned off after step 1 of the logic cycle has been performed for the first time. Indicator 1P cannot be used for any purpose other than the printing first-page headings.
34. An **OR relation** causes an output record to print if either of two indicators is on.
35. Output constants must be enclosed in apostrophes.
36. **UDATE** is a reserved field containing the current date stored within the system.
37. **PAGE** is a reserved field containing the page number of the current page of a printed report. PAGE is automatically zero suppressed by the RPG object program.
38. Editing can be specified only for data fields that have been defined as numeric.
39. The edit code **Y** is used to insert slashes in a date field. The date 122588 prints as 12/25/88 when edited with code Y.
40. The edit code **Z** is used for zero suppression.

REVIEW QUESTIONS

1. Explain the difference between report headings and column headings.
2. How are field and constant locations identified on the printer spacing chart?
3. Define *default*.
4. List the five rules for the formation of file names.
5. Explain why the technique of blocking is used with disk files.
6. What is the overflow indicator used for? How many indicators are available for this use?
7. What entries are required in the Sequence area, positions 15–16, of the Input Specifications, if the input records are in no prescribed sequence? What entry may not be used in this area?
8. What are the two functions of the record identifying indicator?
9. Name and explain each of the three facts required to define a data field.
10. What characters may an alphameric data field contain?
11. What characters may a numeric data field contain?
12. What is a constant?
13. Why are data fields referred to as variables?
14. Explain the difference between the Spacing and Skipping forms-movement operations.
15. When does indicator 1P turn on? When does it turn off?
16. Describe the format and contents of the reserved field UDATE.
17. Describe the format and contents of the reserved field PAGE.
18. What is the function of the edit code Y?
19. Explain zero suppression. What edit code is used to cause an output field to be zero suppressed?
20. Why does RPG require that the beginning and the ending positions of a field be specified as part of the Input Specifications but only requires that the end position be specified on the Output Specifications?

STUDENT EXERCISES: RPG PROGRAM CODE

1. On the File Description Specifications form (Figure 2-36), code the entries to define a disk file named OVRDUE. All records in OVRDUE are 46 characters long. Block OVRDUE in groups of 15 records. This is the only input file. Also code the entries to define a printed output file named OVRRPT. This printed file will print a minimum of eight pages. The printer has a standard 132 character line.

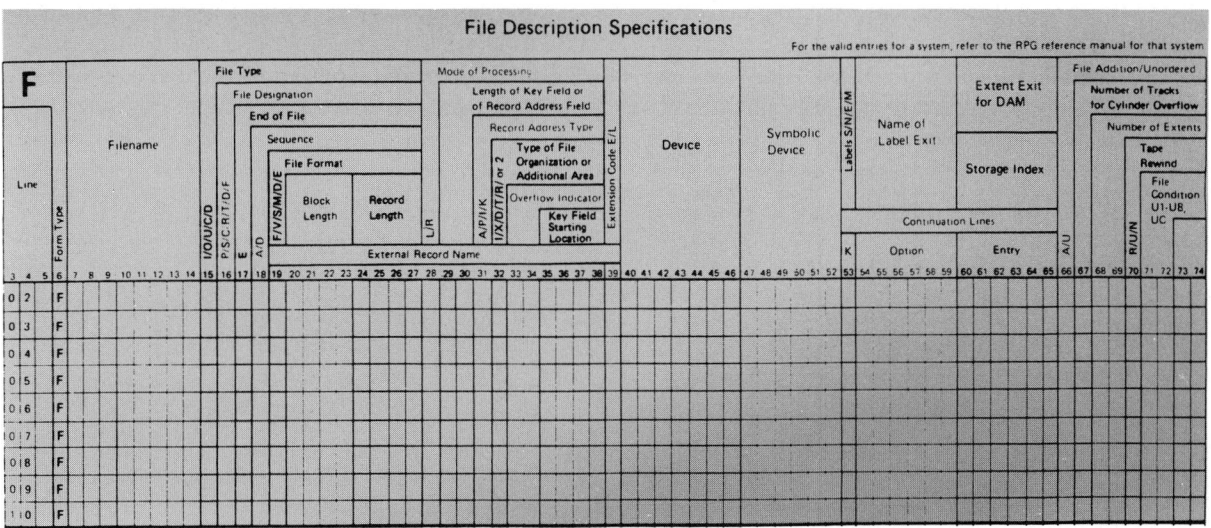

Figure 2-36   File Description Specifications form

2. On the Input Specifications form (Figure 2-37), code the entries needed to define the record and fields contained within OVRDUE in Exercise 1. The fields are:

Positions 1–8   Account identification
Positions 21–40   Account name
Positions 41–46   Date due (MMDDYY format)

You may choose any field name you determine to be appropriate as well as the record identifying indicator to be used.

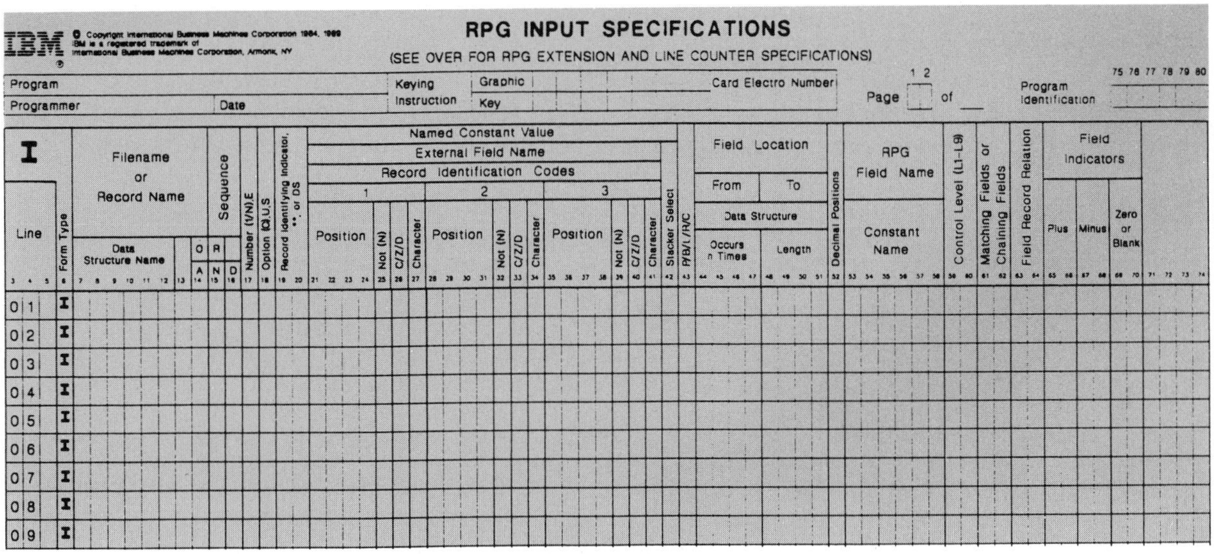

Figure 2-37   Input Specifications form

3. On the Output Specifications form (Figure 2-38), code the Output Specifications needed to produce a detail printed report of the file described in Exercises 1 and 2. No headings are required for this report. The detail lines are to be double spaced. The Date Due field is to be edited in date format. The fields are to be printed in the same order in which they appear in the input record, however, they are to be separated by four spaces.

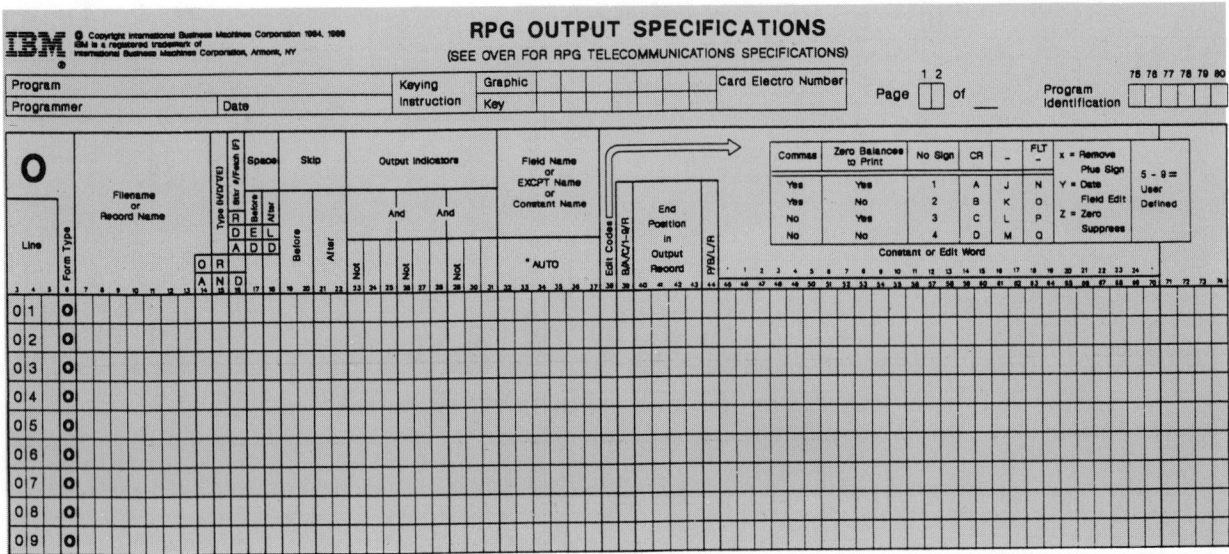

Figure 2-38   Output Specifications form

STUDENT EXERCISES: DEBUGGING RPG PROGRAMS

≣ Problem 1

The following RPG program (Figure 2-39) contains one or more errors detected by the compiler. Circle each error and record the corrected entry directly on the listing. Explain the error and method of correction.

Figure 2-39   Debugging Problem 1

```
          5727RG1RG R05M00              IBM SYSTEM/36 RPGII           05/25/91   10.36

          0001 H                                                            HJG02X


     0001  0002 FSENFILE IP  F 400  40            DISK
     0002  0003 FSENLIST O   F 132 132     OF     PRINTER


     0003  0004 ISENFILE AA  01
     0004  0005 I                                      1    50EMPLY
     0005  0006 I                                      6    25 EMPNAM
     0006  0007 I                                     26    280DEPT
     0007  0008 I                                     29    300STORE
     0008  0009 I                                     35    400HDATE


     0009  0010 OSENLIST H  206      1P
     0010  0011 O            OR      OF
     0011  0012 O                                       8  'HJG02X'
     0012  0013 O                                      14  'DATE'
     0013  0014 O                       UDATE Y        23
     0014  0015 O                                      53  'CRICKET CORNER BOUTIQUES'
     0015  0016 O                                      67  'PAGE'
     0016  0017 O                       PAGE           72
     0017  0018 O            H  2      1P
     0018  0019 O            OR      OF
     0019  0020 O                                      52  'EMPLOYEE SENIORITY LIST'
     0020  0021 O            H  1      1P
     0021  0022 O            OR      OF
     0022  0023 O                                      18  'EMPLOYEE'
     0023  0024 O                                      36  'EMPLOYEE'
     0024  0025 O                                      52  'DATE'
     0025  0026 O                                      72  'STORE    DEPT.'
     0026  0027 O            H  2      1P
     0027  0028 O            OR      OF
     0028  0029 O                                      17  'NUMBER'
     0029  0030 O                                      34  'NAME'
     0030  0031 O                                      62  'HIRED      NO.'
     0031  0032 O                                      71  'CODE'
     0032  0033 O            D  1      01
     0033  0034 O                       EMPNO Z        16
     0034  0035 O                       EMPNAM         42
     0035  0036 O                       HDATE Y        54
     0036  0037 O                       STORE Z        61
     0037  0038 O                       DEPT  Z        71

          * * * * * E N D   O F   S O U R C E * * * * *
```

Figure 2-39 (1)

```
          5727RG1RG R05M00              IBM SYSTEM/36 RPGII           05/25/91   10.36

     INDICATORS USED
          OF 1P 01

     RPG-0315 UNDEFINED FIELD NAMES
       STMT# NAME
        0033 EMPNO

     RPG-0314 UNREFERENCED FIELD NAMES
       STMT# NAME
        0004 EMPLY

       FIELD NAMES USED
       STMT# NAME  DEC  LNG   DISP
        0016 PAGE   0   0004  0122
        0013 UDATE  0   0006  00A7
        0005 EMPNAM     0020  0113
        0006 DEPT   0   0003  0116
        0007 STORE  0   0002  0118
        0008 HDATE  0   0006  011E

       ERROR SEVERITY                              TEXT

     RPG-0314   W    FIELD, TABLE, OR ARRAY NAME IS DEFINED BUT NEVER USED.
     RPG-0315   T    FIELD NAME IS USED BUT NEVER DEFINED, OR TABLE NAME OR ARRAY ELEMENT IS USED AS AN ARRAY INDEX.

          * * * * * E N D   O F   C O M P I L E * * * * *
```

Figure 2-39 (2)

≡ Problem 2

The following RPG program (Figure 2-40) contains one or more errors detected by the compiler. Circle each error and record the corrected entry directly on the listing. Explain the error and method of correction.

Figure 2-40   Debugging Problem 2

```
        5727RG1RG R05M00              IBM SYSTEM/36 RPGII              05/25/91   10.40

        0001 H                                                                 HJGO2X


0001   0002 FSENFILE IP  F 400  40          DISK
0002   0003 FSENLIST O   F 132 132     OF   PRINTER


0003   0004 ISENFILE AA  01
0004   0005 I                                    1    50EMPNO
0005   0006 I                                    6    25 EMPNAM
0006   0007 I                                   26   280DEPT
0007   0008 I                                   29   300STORE
0008   0009 I                                   35   400HDATE


0009   0010 OSENLIST H  206    1P
0010   0011 O           OR     OF
0011   0012 O                             8  'HJGO2X'
0012   0013 O                            14  'DATE'
0013   0014 O              UDATE Y        23
0014   0015 O                            53  'CRICKET CORNER BOUTIQUES'
0015   0016 O                            67  'PAGE'
0016   0017 O              PAGE           72
0017   0018 O       H   2    1P
0018   0019 O           OR     OF
0019   0020 O                            52  'EMPLOYEE SENIORITY LIST'
0020   0021 O       H   1    1P
0021   0022 O           OR     OF
0022   0023 O                            18  'EMPLOYEE'
0023   0024 O                            36  'EMPLOYEE'
0024   0025 O                            52  'DATE'
0025   0026 O                            72  'STORE      DEPT.'
0026   0027 O       H   2    1P
0027   0028 O           OR     OF
0028   0029 O                            17  'NUMBER'
0029   0030 O                            34  'NAME'
0030   0031 O                            62  'HIRED       NO.'
0031   0032 O                            71  'CODE'
0032   0033 O       D   1    28
0033   0034 O              EMPNO Z        16
0034   0035 O              EMPNAM         42
0035   0036 O              HDATE Y        54
0036   0037 O              STORE Z        61
0037   0038 O              DEPT  Z        71

        * * * * END OF SOURCE * * * * *
```

Figure 2-40 (1)

```
        5727RG1RG R05M00              IBM SYSTEM/36 RPGII              05/25/91   10.40


INDICATORS USED
      OF 1P 01 28

RPG-0305 INDICATORS UNREFERENCED
      01

RPG-0306 INDICATORS UNDEFINED
      28

   FIELD NAMES USED
  STMT#  NAME  DEC  LNG   DISP
   0016 PAGE    0   0004  0127
   0013 UDATE   0   0006  00A7
   0004 EMPNO   0   0005  0118
   0005 EMPNAM      0020  0113
   0006 DEPT    0   0003  011B
   0007 STORE   0   0002  011D
   0008 HDATE   0   0006  0123

   ERROR SEVERITY                                 TEXT

RPG-0305   W    INDICATOR IS ASSIGNED BUT IS NOT USED TO CONDITION OPERATIONS.
RPG-0306   T    INDICATOR IS USED TO CONDITION OPERATIONS BUT IS NOT ASSIGNED.

      * * * * * END OF COMPILE * * * * *
```

Figure 2-40 (2)

Problem 3

The following RPG program (Figure 2-41) contains one or more errors detected while checking output from the program. Circle each error and record the corrected entry directly on the listing. Explain the error and method of correction.

Figure 2-41   Debugging Problem 3

```
        5727RG1RG R05M00              IBM SYSTEM/36 RPGII              05/25/91  10.44

            0001 H                                                          HJG02X


   0001  0002 FSENFILE IP  F 400  40           DISK
   0002  0003 FSENLIST O   F 132 132       OF  PRINTER


   0003  0004 ISENFILE AA  01
   0004  0005 I                                        1    50EMPNO
   0005  0006 I                                        6    25 EMPNAM
   0006  0007 I                                       26    28DDEPT
   0007  0008 I                                       29    30STORE
   0008  0009 I                                       35    40HDATE


   0009  0010 OSENLIST H  206     1P
   0010  0011 O          OR       OF
   0011  0012 O                                    8 *HJG02X*
   0012  0013 O                                   14 *DATE*
   0013  0014 O                   UDATE Y         23
   0014  0015 O                                   53 *CRICKET CORNER BOUTIQUES*
   0015  0016 O                                   67 *PAGE*
   0016  0017 O                   PAGE            72
   0017  0018 O       H  2        1P
   0018  0019 O          OR       OF
   0019  0020 O                                   52 *EMPLOYEE SENIORITY LIST*
   0020  0021 O       H  1        1P
   0021  0022 O          OR       OF
   0022  0023 O                                   18 *EMPLOYEE*
   0023  0024 O                                   36 *EMPLOYEE*
   0024  0025 O                                   52 *DATE*
   0025  0026 O                                   72 *STORE     DEPT.*
   0026  0027 O       H  2        1P
   0027  0028 O          OR       OF
   0028  0029 O                                   17 *NUMBER*
   0029  0030 O                                   34 *NAME*
   0030  0031 O                                   62 *HIRED      NO.*
   0031  0032 O                                   71 *CODE*
   0032  0033 O       D  1        01
   0033  0034 O                   EMPNO Z         16
   0034  0035 O                   EMPNAM         42
   0035  0036 O                   HDATE Y        54
   0036  0037 O                   STORE Z        68
   0037  0038 O                   DEPT  Z        71

        * * * * * E N D   O F   S O U R C E * * * * *


        5727RG1RG R05M00              IBM SYSTEM/36 RPGII              05/25/91  10.44


   INDICATORS USED
        OF 1P 01

   FIELD NAMES USED
   STMT# NAME  DEC  LNG   DISP
   0016 PAGE    0   0004  0127
   0013 UDATE   0   0006  00A7
   0004 EMPNO   0   0005  0118
   0005 EMPNAM      0020  0113
   0006 DEPT    D   0003  011B
   0007 STORE   0   0002  011D
   0008 HDATE   D   0006  0123


        * * * * * E N D   O F   C O M P I L E * * * * *
```

Figure 2-41 (1)   *continued*

```
 HJGO2X  DATE  5/25/91       CRICKET CORNER BOUTIQUES        PAGE    1

                        EMPLOYEE SENIORITY LIST

        EMPLOYEE            EMPLOYEE           DATE      STORE    DEPT.
         NUMBER               NAME            HIRED       NO.     CODE

           216        GLORIA  JOHNSON        12/29/71      6       41
          1006        STEVEN  WILLIAMS        3/14/73      3        8
           342        RACHEL  CONNORS         4/21/73      4       36
          2415        SHEILA  GARFIELD        1/14/76      6       41
          3916        JIM  HAMEL              5/25/79      1       26
          1316        HEIDI  CARROLL          7/06/81      4        8
          2156        ERIN  LETOURNEAU        6/06/84      3        4
```

Figure 2-41 (2)

Problem 4

The following RPG program (Figure 2-42) contains one or more errors detected while checking output from the program. Circle each error and record the corrected entry directly on the listing. Explain the error and method of correction.

Figure 2-42   Debugging Problem 4

```
     5727RG1RG R05M00            IBM SYSTEM/36 RPGII           05/25/91  11.22

     0001 H                                                            HJGO2X


0001  0002 FSENFILE IP  F 400  40         DISK
0002  0003 FSENLIST O   F 132 132    OF   PRINTER


0003  0004 ISENFILE AA  01
0004  0005 I                                 1   50EMPNO
0005  0006 I                                 6   25 EMPNAM
0006  0007 I                                26   280DEPT
0007  0008 I                                29   300STORE
0008  0009 I                                35   400HDATE


0009  0010 OSENLIST H  206    1P
0010  0011 O        OR        OF
0011  0012 O                            8 *HJGO2X*
0012  0013 O                           14 *DATE*
0013  0014 O                UDATE Y     23
0014  0015 O                           53 *CRICKET CORNER BOUTIQUES*
0015  0016 O                           67 *PAGE*
0016  0017 O                PAGE        72
0017  0018 O        H   1    1P
0018  0019 O        OR        OF
0019  0020 O                           52 *EMPLOYEE SENIORITY LIST*
0020  0021 O        H   1    1P
0021  0022 O        OR        OF
0022  0023 O                           18 *EMPLOYEE*
0023  0024 O                           36 *EMPLOYEE*
0024  0025 O                           52 *DATE*
0025  0026 O                           72 *STORE    DEPT.*
0026  0027 O        H   2    1P
0027  0028 O        OR        OF
0028  0029 O                           17 *NUMBER*
0029  0030 O                           34 *NAME*
0030  0031 O                           62 *HIRED      NO.*
0031  0032 O                           71 *CODE*
0032  0033 O        D   1    01
0033  0034 O                    EMPNO Z  16
0034  0035 O                    EMPNAM   42
0035  0036 O                    HDATE Y  54
0036  0037 O                    STORE Z  61
0037  0038 O                    DEPT  Z  71


     * * * * * E N D  O F  S O U R C E * * * * *


     5727RG1RG R05M00            IBM SYSTEM/36 RPGII           05/25/91  11.22


INDICATORS USED
       OF 1P 01
```

Figure 2-42 (1)

```
      5727RG1RG R05M00              IBM SYSTEM/36 RPGII              05/25/91  11.22

          0001 H                                                          HJG02X
      FIELD NAMES USED
    STMT#  NAME  DEC  LNG   DISP
    0016  PAGE    0   0004  0127
    0013  UDATE   0   0006  00A7
    0004  EMPNO   0   0005  0118
    0005  EMPNAM      0020  0113
    0006  DEPT    0   0003  011B
    0007  STORE   0   0002  011D
    0008  HDATE   0   0006  0123


           * * * * * E N D   O F   C O M P I L E * * * * *
```

```
HJG02X  DATE  5/25/91        CRICKET CORNER BOUTIQUES            PAGE   1

                          EMPLOYEE SENIORITY LIST
        EMPLOYEE              EMPLOYEE           DATE      STORE    DEPT.
        NUMBER                 NAME             HIRED       NO.     CODE

          216           GLORIA JOHNSON         12/29/71      6       41
         1006           STEVEN WILLIAMS         3/14/73      3        8
          342           RACHEL CONNORS          4/21/73      4       36
         2415           SHEILA GARFIELD         1/14/76      6       41
         3916           JIM HAMEL               5/25/79      1       26
         1316           HEIDI CARROLL           7/06/81      4        8
         2156           ERIN LETOURNEAU         6/06/84      3        4
```

heading lines are not correctly spaced

Figure 2-42 (2)

STUDENT EXERCISES: PROGRAMMING IN RPG

PROGRAMMING ASSIGNMENT 1
TEST EQUIPMENT INVENTORY REPORT

INSTRUCTIONS

Plan, code, enter, and test an RPG program to produce the Test Equipment Inventory Report.

INPUT

Input is the Test Equipment File. Each record contains the unit I.D. number, description, location, date purchased, and date last calibrated. The format of the test equipment records is shown in Figure 2-43. Use test data set 1 for this problem.

01	05	06	0A	0B	0F	10	14	15	19	1A	1E	1F	23	24	28	29	2D	2E	32	33	37	38	3C	3D	41
1		5	6		10	11		15	16		20	21		25	26		30	31		35	36		40	41		45	46		50	51		55	56		60	61		65

| UNIT ID (A) | DESCRIPTION (A) | LOCATION (A) | PURCHASE DATE (N) | DATE LAST CALIBRAT. (N) | |

Figure 2-43 Format of test equipment records

OUTPUT

Output is the Test Equipment Inventory Report. The report format is shown in Figure 2-44 on the next page.

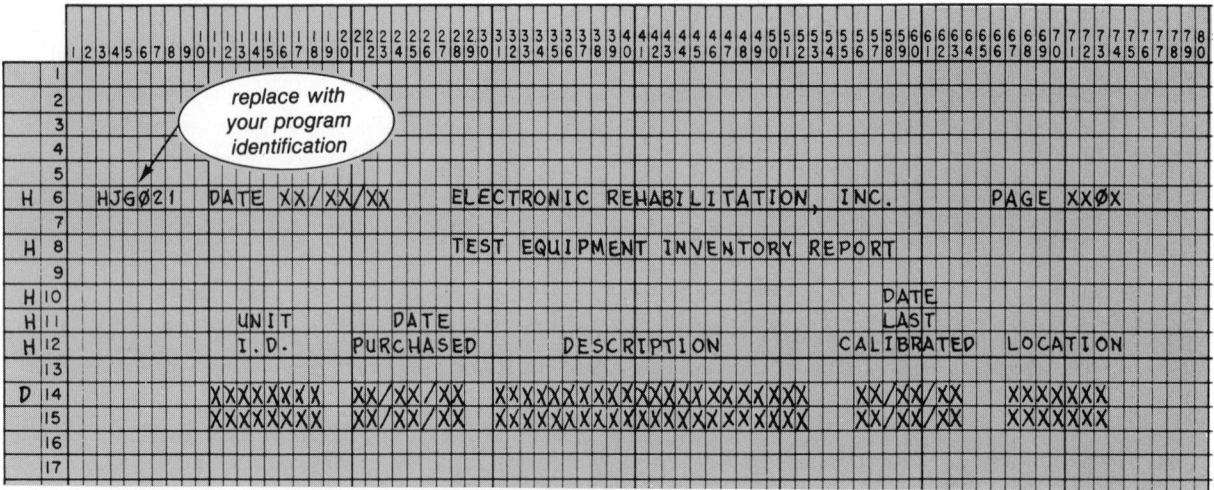

Figure 2-44   Format of test Equipment Inventory Report

═══ PROGRAMMING ASSIGNMENT 2 ═══
MAILING LABELS

INSTRUCTIONS

Plan, code, enter, and test an RPG program to produce mailing labels.

INPUT

Input is the Employee Master File containing employee name, street address, city/state, and ZIP code. The format of the Employee Master File is shown in Figure 2-45. Use test data set 2 for this problem.

Figure 2-45   Format of records for Mailing Label File

OUTPUT

Output is a group of mailing labels. The label format is shown in Figure 2-46. Note that three output lines are to be printed for each record read. There is a double space between the first and second of these lines. Also note that the third line will be followed by three blank lines. No headings are to be printed.

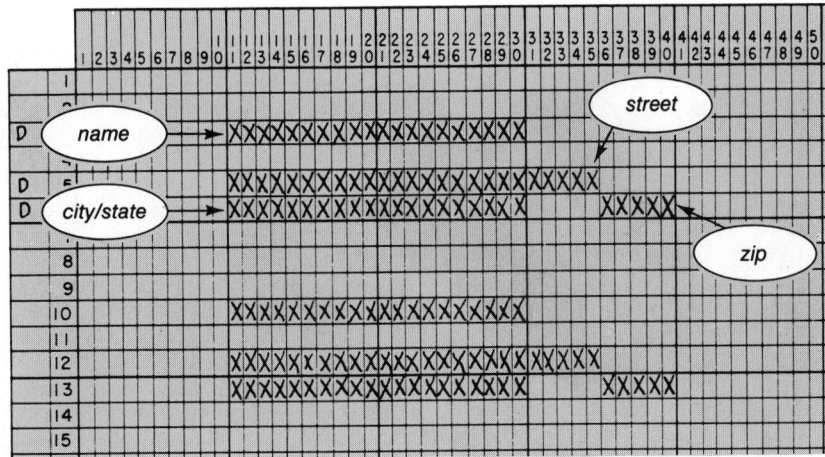

Figure 2-46 Format of mailing label

═══ PROGRAMMING ASSIGNMENT 3 ═══
COMPUTER USER IDENTIFIER REPORT

INSTRUCTIONS

Plan, code, enter, and test an RPG program to produce the Computer User Identifier Report.

Input

Input is the Computer User Master File. This file contains the user name, year of graduation, and student I.D. number. The format of the records for this file is shown in Figure 2-47. Use test data set 3 for this problem.

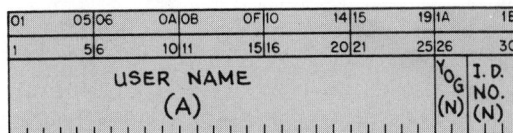

Figure 2-47 Format of Records for Computer User Master File

OUTPUT

Output is the Computer User Identifier Report. The report format is shown in (Figure 2-48 on the next page). The User Code field is an 8-position field made up of information from other fields. The first two positions are the student's year of graduation. The next three positions are the student's I.D. number, and the last three positions are the first three positions of the student's name.

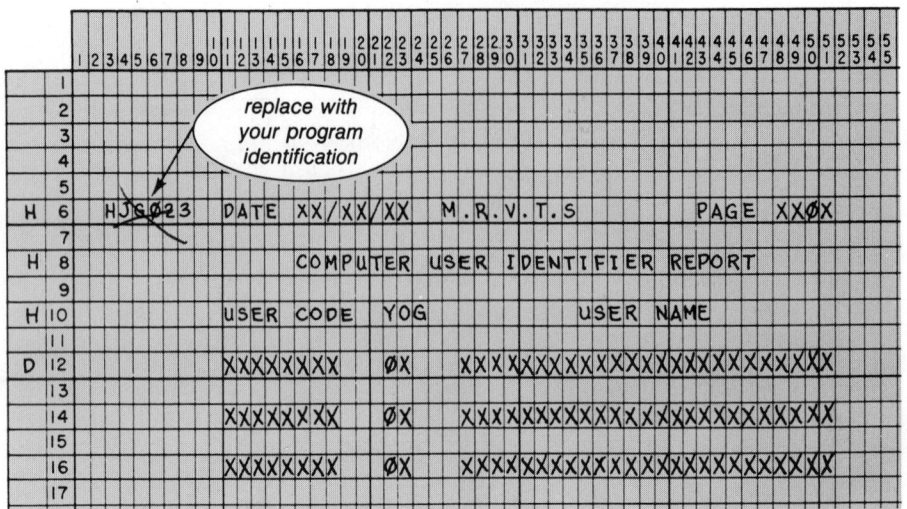

Figure 2-48 Format of Computer User Identifier Report

Hint 1 A single input field can appear twice in an output line.

Hint 2 It is possible, in RPG, to define only a portion of the field as a separate field. RPG permits positions of an input record to be defined twice; once as a separate field and again as part of a larger field.

═══ PROGRAMMING ASSIGNMENT 4 ═══
SUBSCRIBER LABELS, TWO-ACROSS FORMAT

INSTRUCTIONS

Plan, code, enter, and test an RPG program to produce subscriber mailing labels in two-across format.

INPUT

Input is the Subscriber File containing name, street address, city/state, and ZIP code. The format of the Subscriber File is shown in Figure 2-49. Use test data set 2 for this problem.

01	05	06	0A	0B	0F	10	14	15	19	1A	1E	1F	23	24	28	29	2D	2E	32	33	37	38	3C	3D	41	42	46
1	5	6	10	11	15	16	20	21	25	26	30	31	35	36	40	41	45	46	50	51	55	56	60	61	65	66	70

EMPLOYEE NAME	STREET ADDRESS	CITY / STATE	ZIP CODE (A)

Figure 2-49 Format of record for Subscriber File

OUTPUT

Output is a set of mailing labels printed in two-across (two-up) format. Each input record will produce a set of two identical labels side by side. The first line of each label will contain the subscriber I.D. number. This is a 14-position field made up of the ZIP code, the first three positions of the Name field, the first three positions of the Street Address field, and the first three positions of the City/State field. Note that two blank lines follow each label. No headings are required. The format of the subscriber labels is shown in Figure 2-50.

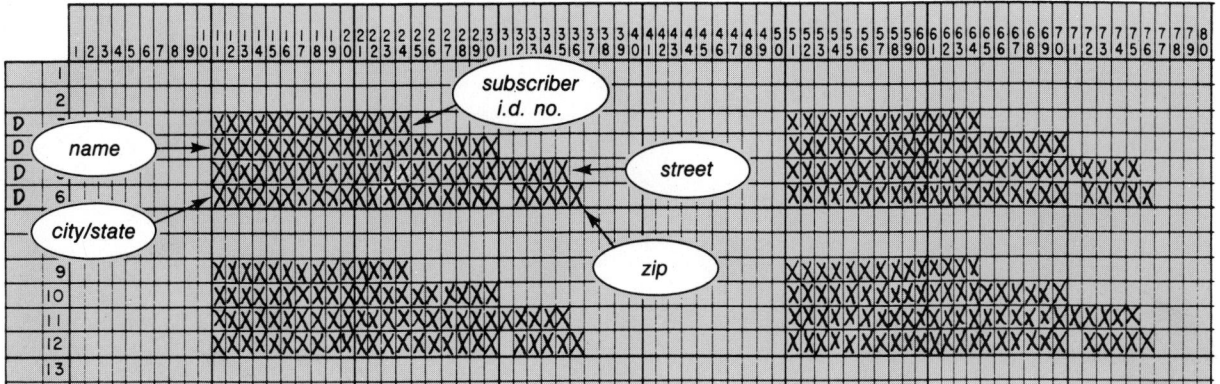

Figure 2-50   Format for subscriber labels

T H R E E

RPG Calculation Specifications, Arithmetic Operations, & Edit Codes

Computers are generally thought of as machines capable of performing thousands of mathematical calculations in a very short time. The word *compute* is defined in most dictionaries in a mathematical sense: To compute is to calculate.

The earliest computers were designed primarily to perform complex mathematical operations, and little thought was given to the printing of large amounts of information. In the nineteenth century, Charles Babbage designed (but did not build) a "difference engine," which was to have been a calculating machine capable of dealing with numbers only. The first working digital computer, the Harvard Mark I, was designed to calculate ballistic trajectories for the U.S. Army during World War II.

In Chapter 2, you learned to write programs that could read information from a disk file and print that information in a predetermined format. Most business application programs written today require far more than a simple listing; almost all require that some arithmetic be performed. Chapter 3 introduces the RPG entries needed to code the four basic arithmetic operations: addition, subtraction, multiplication, and division. In addition, the sample problem in this chapter demonstrates the full use of the RPG edit codes and shows the techniques needed to accumulate and print end-of-job totals.

ANALYSIS OF SAMPLE PROBLEM

Input

Input for the sample problem is the Employee Payroll File. The format of the employee payroll records is shown in Figure 3-1. The employee payroll record is 60 characters long and contains the employee number, employee name, regular earnings, and overtime earnings.

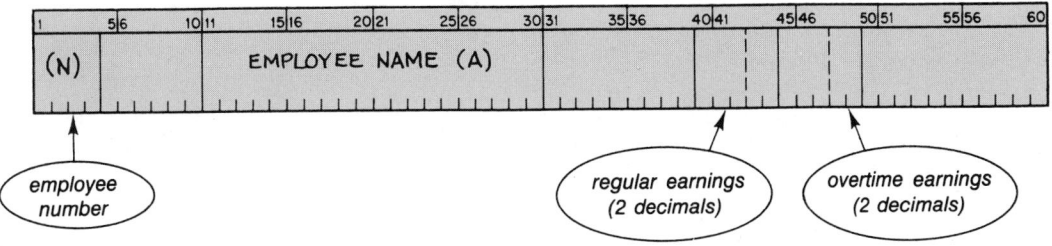

Figure 3-1   Format of Employee Payroll records

This input layout differs somewhat from those you have seen previously in this book. Because of the relatively small field sizes, some of the field names and descriptions have been listed separately below the record. This method is used to ensure readability of the layout. The Regular Earnings and Overtime Earnings fields are money amounts, expressed in dollars and cents. The vertical dotted line between positions 42–43, and 47–48 shows the position of an implied decimal point. As was shown in Chapter 2, numeric data fields cannot contain special characters such as a decimal point. The input record layout shows that the decimal point is only implied because no position is occupied by the dotted line.

≡ Output

The output of the sample problem is the Earnings Report shown in Figure 3-2. The Earnings Report contains three heading lines, a detail line for each input record read by the program, and, at the bottom of the report, a total line. This line is identified at the left of the printer spacing chart by the letters T-LR. The T specifies that this line is a type T, or total, line. The entry LR shows that this total line is to be printed at the end of the job as a **final total**.

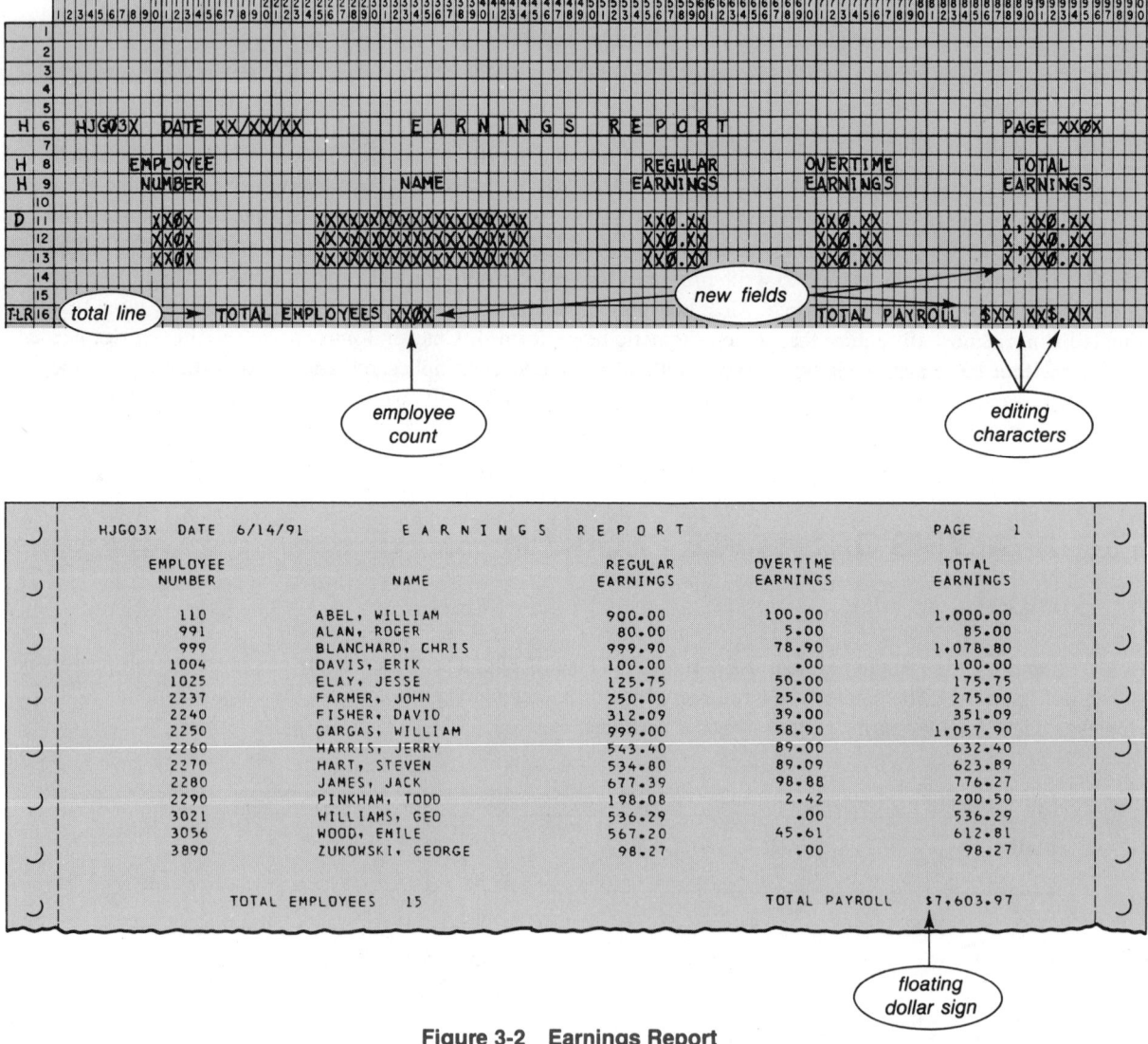

Figure 3-2   Earnings Report

Three output fields that appear in the report are not part of the input layout; these are the two fields within the total line and the field listed under the TOTAL EARNINGS column heading. These fields are created on the Calculation Specifications form. All numeric fields are shown as edited fields. In addition to zero suppression and date editing, all money amount fields are shown with decimal points. The Total Earnings and Total Payroll fields are shown with an edited comma.

The editing format of the Total Payroll field is shown in Figure 3-3. The editing format of this field does not show a zero suppression code. Instead, a dollar sign is shown at the beginning of the field and also to the left of the decimal point. This editing format indicates that a **floating dollar sign** is to be used. This editing function requires that the field be zero suppressed and that a dollar sign be placed to the left of the first field digit to be printed. The placement of the floating dollar sign on the printed report is shown in Figure 3-2.

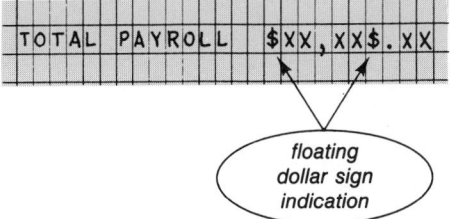

Figure 3-3   Total Payroll field

Processing Steps

The three new fields shown in Figure 3-2 are based on input data. The information to be printed from these fields is developed as follows:

Total earnings = regular earnings + overtime earnings.
The end-of-job total below the total earnings column is the sum of all the amounts in the total earnings column.
The Total Employees field is a count of all input records.

Program Logic

Figure 3-4 on the next page shows the parts of the RPG logic cycle needed for this type of problem. As in Chapter 2, only the logic cycle steps needed for the problem are shown. All these steps perform the same functions they performed for a simple input/output program. Two additional functions are needed for the Chapter 3 sample problem. Steps 8 and 12 of the logic cycle perform these needed functions.

▸ **Step 12: Detail Calculations**   After data is moved from the input record area to the input fields areas in step 11, the RPG logic cycle provides the opportunity to perform calculations. These detail calculations are controlled by the record identification indicator that was turned on when the input record was read. **Detail calculations** generally are performed using data read as part of an input record. Unless special instructions are used to vary their sequence, RPG calculations are performed in a top-down order. In other words, all RPG calculations are executed in the order in which they appear on the Calculation Specifications form. You must plan your calculations carefully so that they are written in the order needed to solve the programming problem.

▸ **Step 8: Total Output Operations**   Step 8 is the point in the RPG logic cycle when totals may be printed or total records written to disk or tape. The sample program requires only that end-of-job or final totals be produced; so this step is executed only once by the program, immediately before the program is ended by step 9 of the RPG logic cycle.

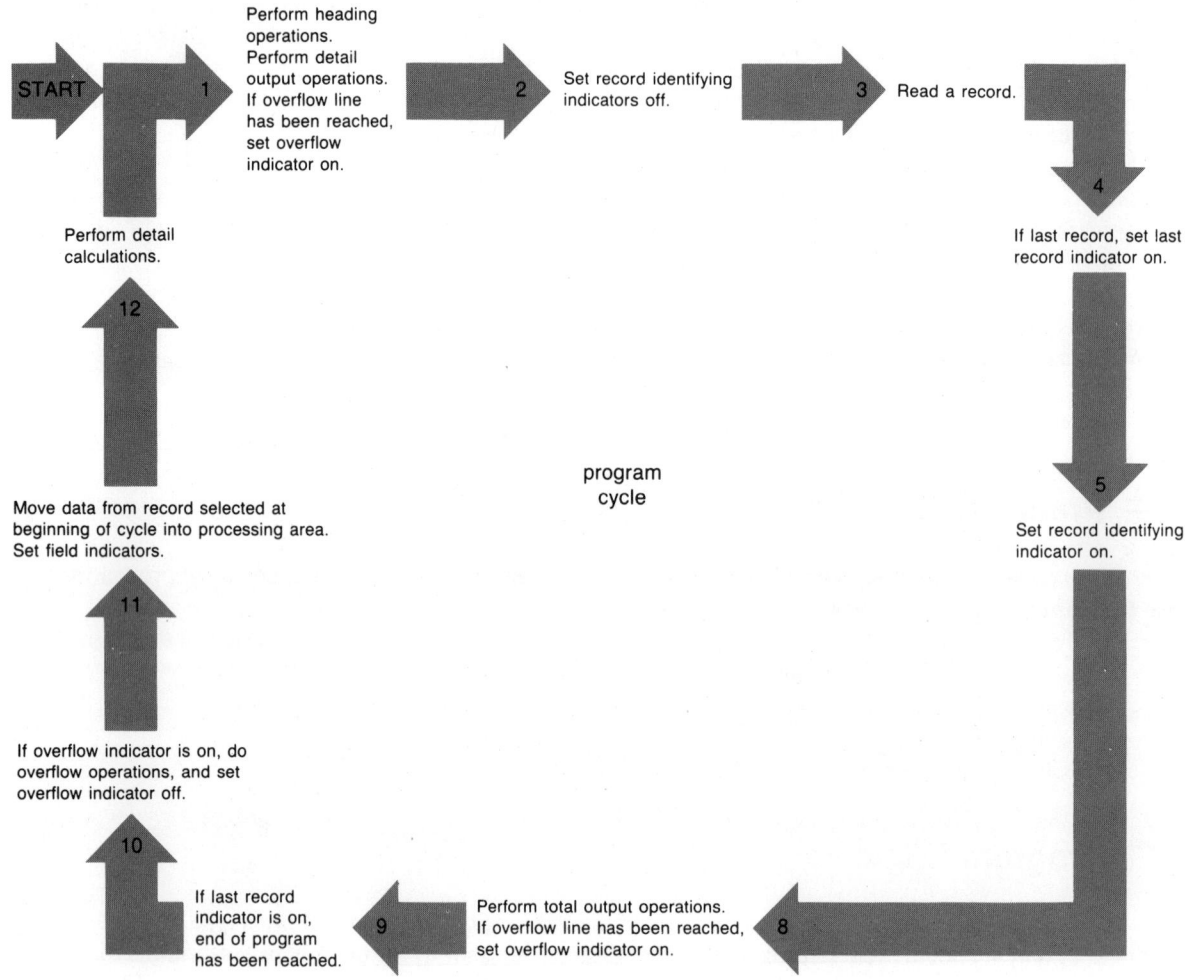

Figure 3-4   Logic cycle for detail calculations and final totals

PROGRAM CODE: EARNINGS REPORT

The coded program to prepare the Earnings Report is shown in Figure 3-5. The general format is similar to program HJG02X, which was developed in Chapter 2. Note, however, the insertion of the Calculation Specifications in their proper sequence between the Input and Output Specifications.

Figure 3-5   RPG source program

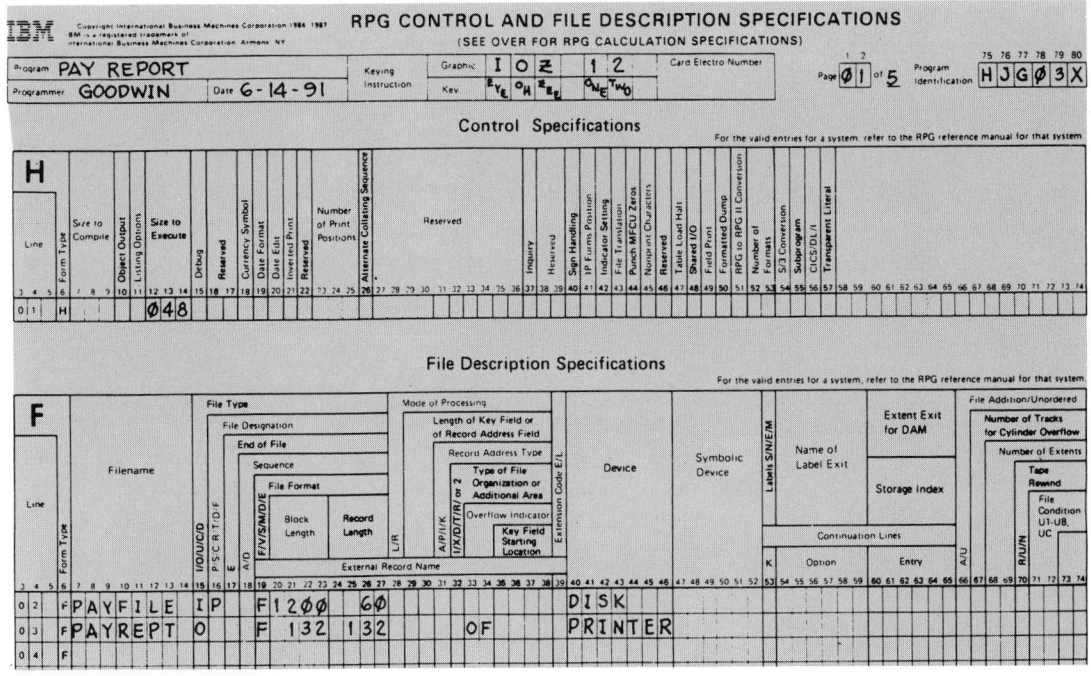

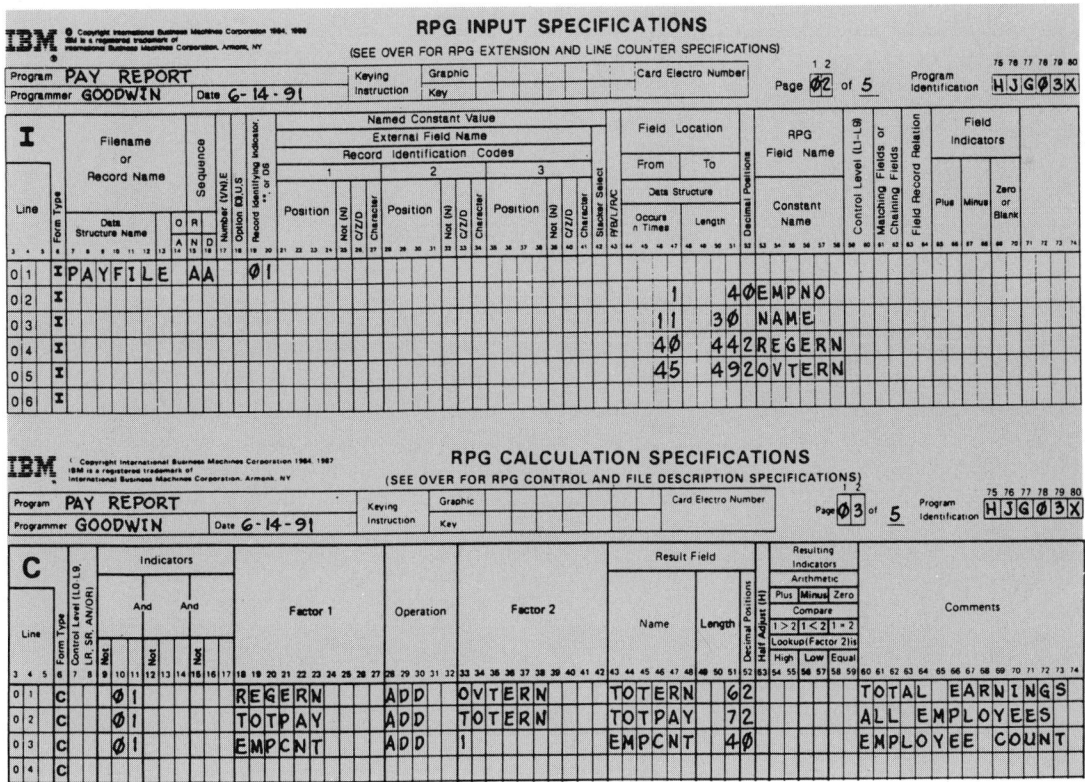

Figure 3-5 (1)

continued

RPG OUTPUT SPECIFICATIONS
(SEE OVER FOR RPG TELECOMMUNICATIONS SPECIFICATIONS)

Program: PAY REPORT
Programmer: GOODWIN   Date 6-14-91
Keying Instruction
Graphic / Key
Card Electro Number
Page 04 of 5
Program Identification: HJG03X

Line	Form Type	Filename or Record Name	Type H/D/T/E	Space Before	Space After	Skip Before	Skip After	Output indicators And And Not	Field Name or EXCPT Name or Constant Name	Edit Codes	End Position in Output Record	P/B/L/R	Constant or Edit Word
01	O	PAYREPT	H	2	0	6		1P					
02	O	OR						OF					
03	O										14		'HJG03X DATE'
04	O								UDATE	Y	23		
05	O										48		'EARNINGS'
06	O										62		'REPORT'
07	O										91		'PAGE'
08	O								PAGE		96		
09	O		H	1				1P					
10	O	OR						OF					
11	O										15		'EMPLOYEE'
12	O										77		'REGULAR OVERTIME'
13	O										93		'TOTAL'
14	O		H	2				1P					
15	O	OR						OF					
16	O										14		'NUMBER'
17	O										36		'NAME'
18	O										61		'EARNINGS'
19	O										77		'EARNINGS'
20	O										95		'EARNINGS'

RPG OUTPUT SPECIFICATIONS
(SEE OVER FOR RPG TELECOMMUNICATIONS SPECIFICATIONS)

Program: PAY REPORT
Programmer: GOODWIN   Date 6-14-91
Keying Instruction
Graphic / Key
Card Electro Number
Page 05 of 5
Program Identification: HJG03X

Line	Form Type	Filename or Record Name	Type D/T	Space Before	Output indicators And And Not	Field Name or EXCPT Name or Constant Name	Edit Codes	End Position in Output Record	P/B/L/R	Constant or Edit Word
01	O		D	1	01					
02	O					EMPNO	Z	13		
03	O					NAME		44		
04	O					REGERN	1	60		
05	O					OVTERN	1	76		
06	O					TOTERN	1	95		
07	O		T	2	LR					
08	O							30		'TOTAL EMPLOYEES'
09	O					EMPCNT	Z	35		
10	O							83		'TOTAL PAYROLL'
11	O					TOTPAY	1	95		'$'
12	O									

Figure 3-5 (2)

FILE DESCRIPTION SPECIFICATIONS

As with program HJG02X (Chapter 2), the input disk file and printed output file used in the sample program must be defined on the File Description Specifications form. The entries to describe these files are shown in Figure 3-6.

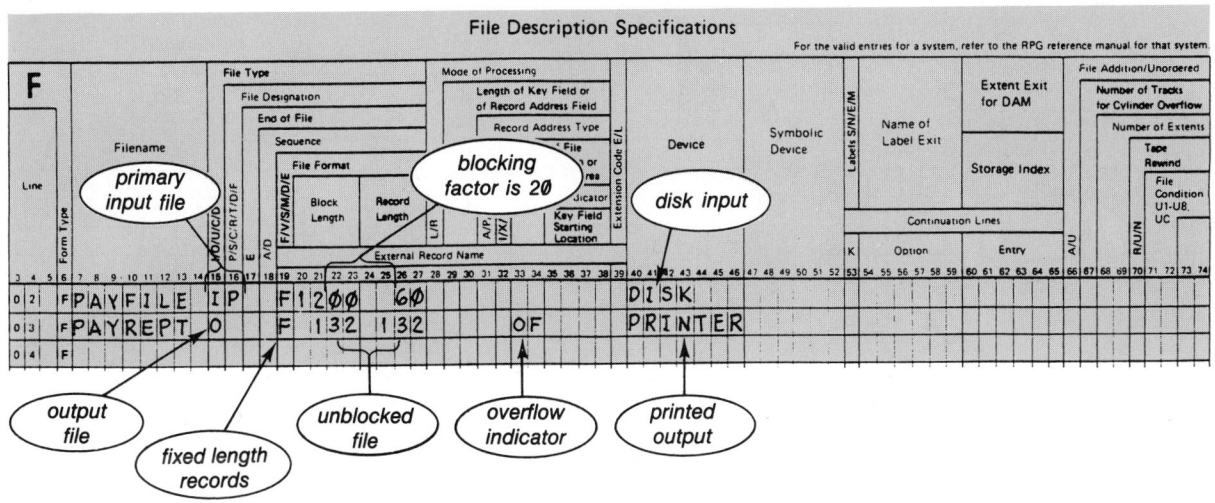

Figure 3-6   RPG File Description Specifications

The File Description Specifications show that the entries for the disk input file PAYFILE and the printed output file PAYREPT are similar to those used in Chapter 2. PAYFILE is designated as the primary input file by the entries in positions 15 and 16. PAYFILE records are fixed length and contain 60 characters each. These records have been blocked in groups of 20, creating a block length of 1200. The file is to be read from disk.

The PAYREPT output file contains fixed-length, 132-character records and will be printed. Indicator OF has been chosen as the overflow indicator.

INPUT SPECIFICATIONS

The data contained within PAYFILE is described on the Input Specifications form, shown in Figure 3-7 on the next page. Because PAYFILE has no required record sequence, an alphabetic entry (AA) has been made in positions 15–16 of the record description. Indicator 01 has been selected for use as the record identifying indicator. Remember that any of the 99 general-purpose indicators could be used, but our programming standards, not RPG rules, determine the indicator used. Every time a new record is read from PAYFILE, indicator 01 is turned on. You should also note that when the end of the data file is reached and indicator LR is turned on by RPG logic, indicator 01 is not turned on.

The four data fields contained in the input record have been defined by assigning a name, length, and data class to each. All the selected field names relate to the content of the field being described, in accordance with good RPG programming practice. The EMPNO, REGERN, and OVTERN fields have been defined as numeric by means of the entry in position 52, the Decimal Positions entry. EMPNO has been defined as numeric because it is to be zero suppressed.

The Decimal Positions entry is 2 for the regular earnings (REGERN) and overtime earnings (OVTERN) fields; it specifies that two of the digits in the field are to the right of the decimal point location. This is the normal description of dollars-and-cents money fields. You must remember that this description specifies the number of digits to the right of the decimal point location, not the actual decimal point. You learned in Chapter 2 that RPG numeric data fields may contain only the digits 0–9 and a plus or minus sign. Numeric data fields cannot, by definition, contain a decimal point. Instead, the location of the implied decimal point is shown by the Decimal Positions entry.

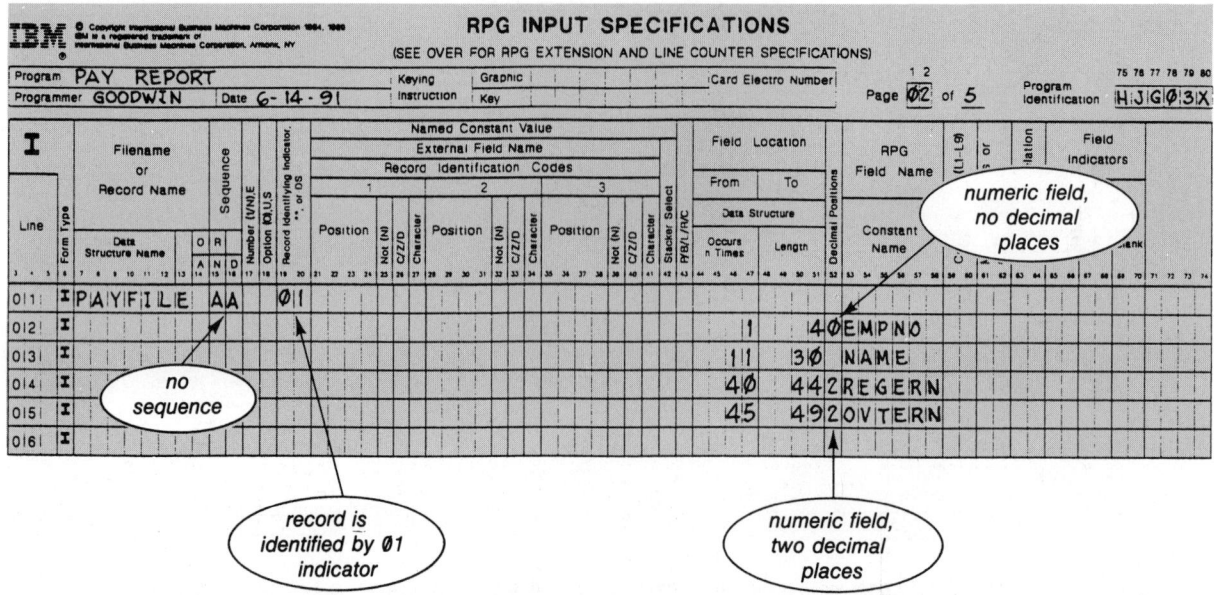

Figure 3-7 RPG Input Specifications

The **implied decimal point** location is used to indicate to the RPG compiler where it should assume the decimal point to be, so that proper decimal alignment can take place during arithmetic operations and output editing. If an incorrect number is specified as the Decimal Positions entry, the RPG compiler cannot detect the error. The error will be detected only during program testing when output data is found to be incorrect. This is an example of a logic error made in a program.

A **logic error** is an entry that is correct according to the rules of RPG but is incorrect based upon the program specifications. Other examples of logic errors include incorrect From or To locations for a field definition and an incorrect End Position on the Output Specification form.

CALCULATION SPECIFICATIONS FORM

Introducing RPG Calculations

Although the word *calculation* usually refers to an arithmetic operation, the RPG Calculation Specifications form (Figure 3-8) has a much broader usage. Contrary to its name, this specification sheet is not limited to arithmetic. You learned in Chapter 2 that the RPG logic cycle automatically performs normal input/output operations. All **operations** to be performed within an RPG program that are not controlled by the fixed logic cycle must be described on the RPG Calculations Specification form.

The Calculation Specifications form should be thought of as divided into seven areas. Six of these areas answer a specific question about the operation being written, and the seventh area can be used to provide a brief description of the operation.

▶ **Indicators: When Is the Operation Performed?** Positions 7–17 (Figure 3-9) of the coding sheet are used to specify when the operation is to be performed. This is accomplished by entering an indicator or indicators to control the operation. If no indicators are shown for an operation, it will be performed every time step 12 of the logic cycle is reached during the execution of the program.

▶ **Operation: What Operation Is Being Performed?** Positions 28–32 (Figure 3-10) specify the type of operation to be performed. This entry must be a valid RPG **operation code**, and must start in position 28. A list of valid RPG operation codes is contained in Appendix C, the RPG Operation Code Summary.

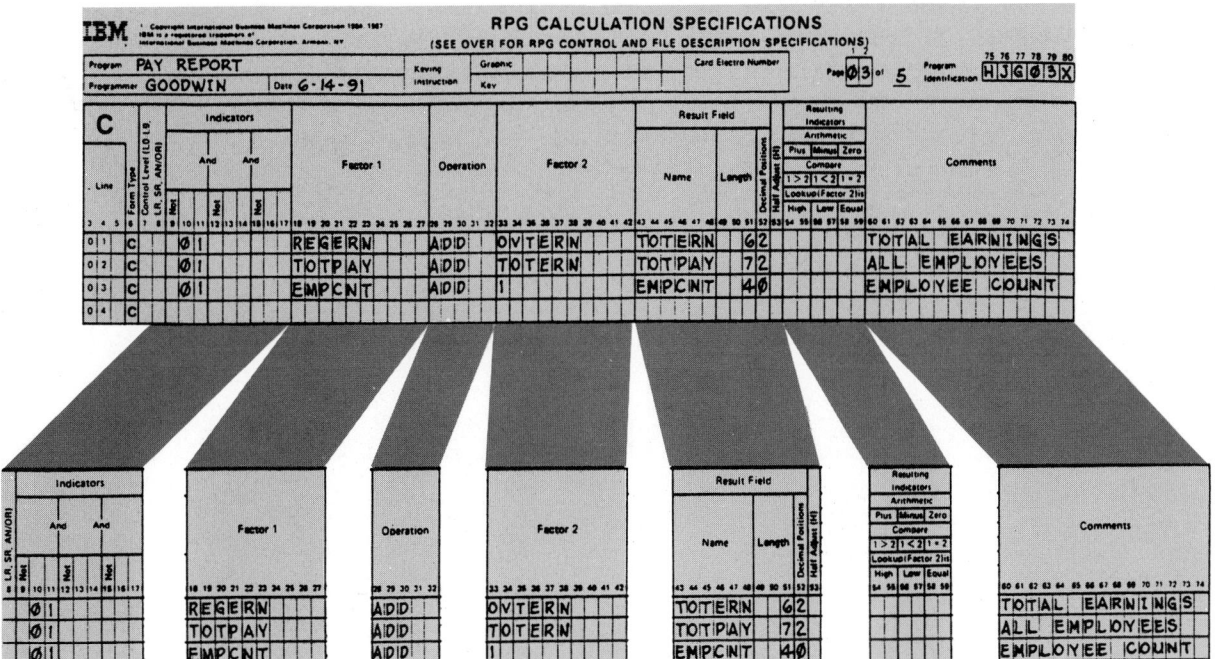

Figure 3-8   RPG Calculation Specifications for program HJG03X

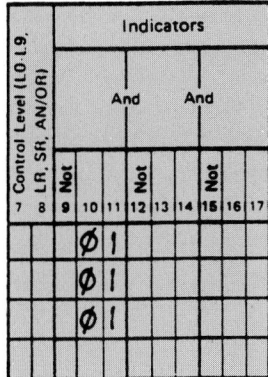

Figure 3-9   Indicators: When is the operation performed?

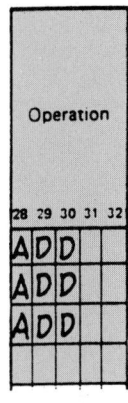

Figure 3-10   Operation: What operation is being performed?

▸ **Factor 1, Factor 2: What Does the Operation Work Upon?**   Positions 18–27 and 33–42 (Figure 3-11) are used to describe the object or subject of the operation or the limits of the operation. The entries in these two areas depend on the operation being described. Some operations require entries in both of these areas, some use neither; and in others the use of one or both of these areas is optional and depends on the way the operation is to be performed. As each RPG operation is introduced in this book, you will be shown the rules relating to its Factor 1 and Factor 2 entries.

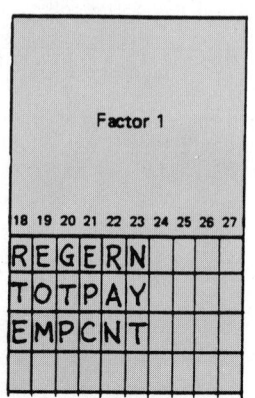 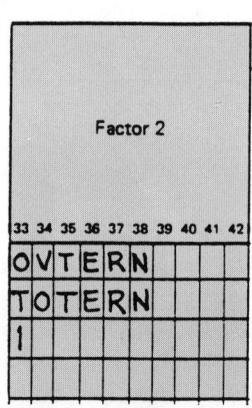

Figure 3-11   Factor 1, Factor 2: What does the operation work upon?

▸ **Result Field: Where Does the Result Go?**   In operations that place data in a result field, such as data movement and arithmetic, positions 43–53 (Figure 3-12) specify where that result is to go. This area can specify that the result is to be placed in a data field that already exists, or it can be used to create and describe a new data field to hold the result. In addition, this portion of the specification form can be used to control the rounding of the result of an arithmetic operation.

▸ **Resulting Indicators: Is Information Available About the Result?**   Positions 54–59 (Figure 3-13) are used to provide information about the result of certain operations by specifying indicators that are to be turned on or off based on the result of the operation. For example, indicators can be designated to show whether one field is greater than, less than, or equal to another field during a compare operation.

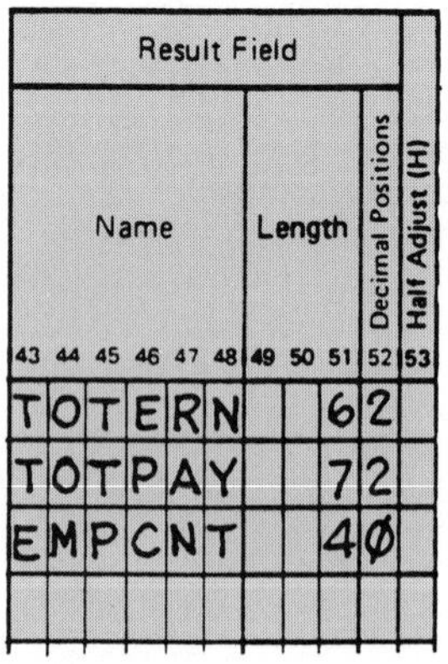

Figure 3-12   Result Field: Where does the result go?

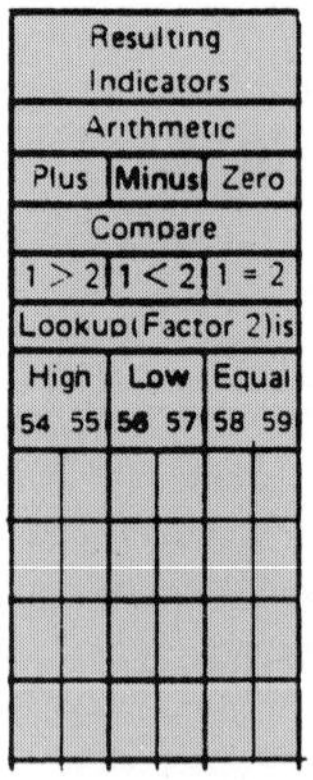

Figure 3-13   Resulting Indicators: Is information available about the result?

▸ **Comment Area**   The Calculation Specification form has an area for comments. Positions 60–74 (Figure 3-14) can be used to provide a brief description of an operation or group of operations. These **comments** are not part of the program code and have no effect on the object program that is generated during the compilation. Although the use of comments is optional, it is good programming practice to briefly describe the functions being performed.

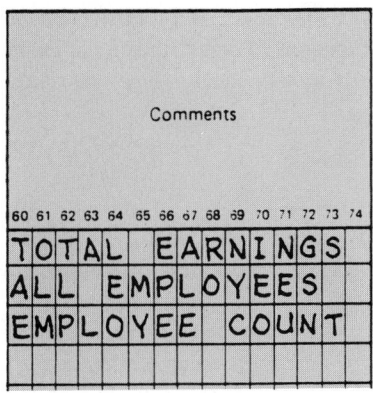

Figure 3-14   Comments

Types Of RPG Operations

RPG operations are grouped according to the type of function they perform. The following descriptions of these categories include the most common operations of each type.

▸ **Arithmetic Operations**   These operations (ADD, SUB, MULT, DIV, Z-ADD, Z-SUB) can be performed only on numeric data. RPG arithmetic is performed algebraically, and the result of the operation is a signed number (plus or minus). Sign control is automatic in RPG. Unlike languages such as COBOL, RPG always maintains the proper sign, either positive or negative, of a number. RPG issues a warning message if, based on the rules of arithmetic, the result of an arithmetic operation may require more positions than are available in the field designated to hold the result.

▸ **Data Movement Operations**   Move operations (MOVE, MOVEA, MOVEL) are, in fact, copy operations. When one of these operations is performed, the original data is not moved to another location in computer memory but is copied into that location with the original data remaining unchanged.

▸ **Compare and Testing Operations**   The COMP operation tests fields for certain conditions and sets indicators on or off depending on the result of the test. These indicators can be used to condition the performance of other operations within the program.

▸ **Structured Compare and Testing Operations**   These operations (DO, DOWxx, DOUxx, IFxx, ELSE) allow one or more other operations to occur based on the result of comparison of data. Several of these operations (DO, DOWxx, and DOUxx) are normally used for the control of loops within the program and are similar to COBOL's PERFORM and BASIC's FOR statements. A **loop** is a series of operations executed repeatedly until a program condition causes the series to stop. The RPG fixed logic cycle is a loop that executes until indicator LR is turned on.

The IFxx and ELSE operations are used to control the execution of one group of operations if a specified indicator is on and a different group of operations if the same indicator is off. The IFxx and ELSE are similar to the IF statement in COBOL and BASIC.

▸ **Indicator Control Operations**   The SETON and SETOF operations are used to turn indicators on or off. These operations can be used with all general-purpose indicators and most special-purpose indicators.

▶ **Sequence Control Operations**   RPG normally performs operations in the order in which they appear on the Calculation Specifications form. Sequence control operations (GOTO, EXSR, CASxx) permit the programmer to vary this sequence in order to skip operations, repeat operations, or perform operations only under certain conditions.

▶ **Input/Output Control Operations**   Although RPG uses a fixed, predefined logic cycle to control input and output, this group of operations (EXCPT, READ, CHAIN) enables the programmer to vary this logic. These operations cause input and output functions to occur during the calculation portion of the logic cycle rather than at normal input and output times.

≡ Operation Formats

Throughout this book, as each operation is introduced, you will be shown the format of the operation and a summary of the way the operation works. Figure 3-15 shows a summary and format for the COMP operation.

COMP Operation Summary

The COMP operation compares the value in Factor 1 against the value in Factor 2. Both factors must have the same data class. Fields are automatically aligned prior to the comparison. At least one resulting indicator must be specified. Comparison results are as follows:

High Factor 1 > Factor 2
Low   Factor 1 < Factor 2
Equal Factor 1 = Factor 2

Control Level Indicators	Indicators	Factor 1	Operation Name	Factor 2	Result Field	Resulting Indicators		
7–8	9–17	18–27	28–32	33–42	43–53	54–55	56–57	58–59
optional	optional	required	COMP	required	blank	optional	optional	optional

one required

Figure 3-15   Operation summary: COMP operation

The **format** shows each of the areas of the Calculation Specification form as they are used for the operation. Note that the Factor 1 and Factor 2 areas contain the word *required*. This means that when the COMP operation is used, these areas must contain an entry. The word *optional* in an area means that an entry may or may not be made in that area based on the requirements of the program. The Result Field area contains the word *blank*. This indicates that you may not make and entry in the Result Field area when coding a COMP operation. The presence of an entry where no entry is permitted will result in an error during program compilation.

The **operation summary** is a brief explanation of the way the instruction works. This summary is not a complete explanation of the operation. The operation summary explains what the operation does, not how it is written.

Enhanced Format and Standard Format

Some instructions have two sets of instruction formats and operation summaries. Figures 3-16 and 3-17 show the format and summary for the addition operation (ADD). Figure 3-16 is the **standard format**, and Figure 3-17 is the **enhanced format**. Computers in the current IBM midrange series – such as the System/36, System/38, and AS/400 – as well as some microcomputer versions of RPG permit several instructions to be written in an abbreviated format, eliminating the duplication of some code. This abbreviated format is an addition or **enhancement** to RPG; therefore, it is called the enhanced format. When these instructions are explained, both formats will be shown. Note that in Figure 3-16, the standard format shows Factor 1 as required, whereas in Figure 3-17 the enhanced format shows Factor 1 to be optional.

ADD Operation Summary, Standard Format
The value of the field or literal specified in Factor 2 is added to the value of the field or literal specified in Factor 1. The sum is placed in the Result Field. Neither Factor 1 nor Factor 2 is changed by the ADD operation.

Control Level Indicators	Indicators	Factor 1	Operation Name	Factor 2	Result Field	Resulting Indicators		
7–8	9–17	18–27	28–32	33–42	43–53	54–55	56–57	58–59
optional	optional	required	ADD	required	required	optional	optional	optional

Figure 3-16   Operation Summary: ADD operation, standard format

ADD Operation Summary, Enhanced Format
The value of the field or literal specified in Factor 2 is added to the value of the field or literal specified in Factor 1. The sum is placed in the Result Field. Neither Factor 1 nor Factor 2 is changed by the ADD operation. If Factor 1 is not specified, Factor 2 is added to the Result Field and the sum placed in the Result Field.

Control Level Indicators	Indicators	Factor 1	Operation Name	Factor 2	Result Field	Resulting Indicators		
7–8	9–17	18–27	28–32	33–42	43–53	54–55	56–57	58–59
optional	optional	optional	ADD	required	required	optional	optional	optional

Figure 3-17   Operation summary: ADD operation, enhanced format

The standard format should be considered universal and will work on those computers that also support the enhanced format. The reverse is not true. Computers that support only the standard format cannot accept operations written in enhanced format.

ARITHMETIC OPERATIONS FOR PROGRAM HJG03X

As noted at the beginning of this chapter, the program must add the values in the Regular Earnings field to the values in the Overtime Earnings field to determine the total earnings of an employee. In addition, the program must accumulate a separate total of the total earnings for all of the employees. This total prints after all the detail records have been processed. Whenever calculations are to be performed within an RPG program, the Calculation Specifications form is used; the form used in this program is illustrated in Figure 3-18.

IBM — RPG CALCULATION SPECIFICATIONS (SEE OVER FOR RPG CONTROL AND FILE DESCRIPTION SPECIFICATIONS)

Program: PAY REPORT — Programmer: GOODWIN — Date: 6-14-91 — Page Ø3 of 5 — Program Identification: HJGØ3X

Line	Form Type	Indicators	Factor 1	Operation	Factor 2	Result Field Name	Length	Decimal Positions	Comments
01	C	Ø1	REGERN	ADD	OVTERN	TOTERN	6	2	TOTAL EARNINGS
02	C	Ø1	TOTPAY	ADD	TOTERN	TOTPAY	7	2	ALL EMPLOYEES
03	C	Ø1	EMPCNT	ADD	1	EMPCNT	4	Ø	EMPLOYEE COUNT
04	C								

Figure 3-18 Calculation Specifications for program HJG03X

Figure 3-18 shows that the Calculation Specifications form (as do all RPG forms) contains space for the date, the program name, the programmer's name, the keying instructions, the page number, and the program identification. Note that the letter C is preprinted in form type, position 6.

When calculations are to be performed on data that is read as input, the RPG compiler must be informed when the calculations are to be done. This is accomplished through the use of indicators, which may be on at the time the calculation is to take place. The use of the indicators in the sample program is shown in Figure 3-19. As was noted previously, when the input record in the sample program is read, the 01 indicator is turned on by the object program. The entry 01 in the Indicators area, positions 10–11, indicates that the calculation on that line is to take place only when the 01 indicator is on. Thus, when a record is read, record-identifying indicator 01 is turned on; and when indicator 01 is on, calculations are performed.

Addition Operation

The regular earnings in the input record is to be added to the overtime earnings in the input record to give the total earnings of the employee. The **ADD operation** is used to add two numbers together. When the ADD operation takes place, the value stored in the field specified in Factor 2 is added to the value stored in the field specified in Factor 1, and the answer is stored in the field specified in the Result Field area of the form.

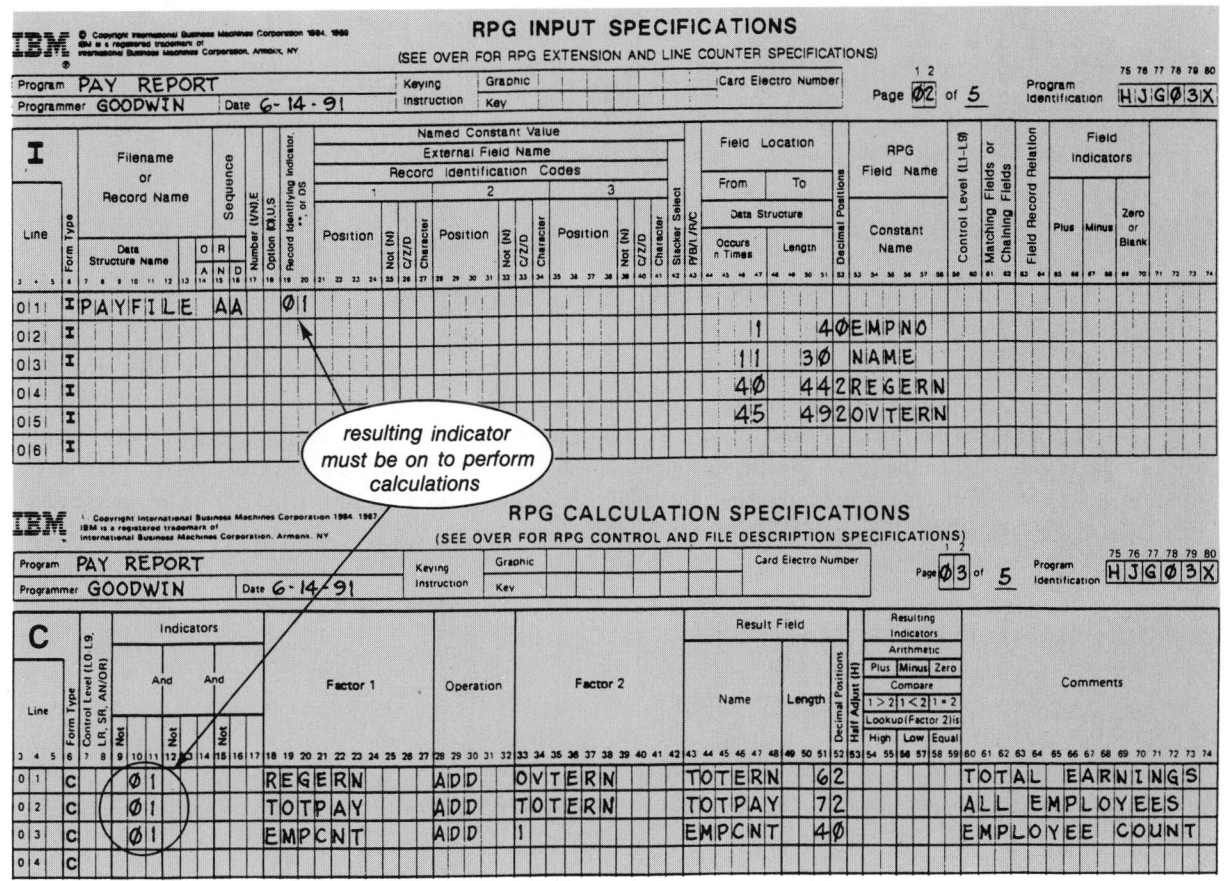

Figure 3-19   Indicator control of calculations

As can be seen in Figure 3-20 on the next page, the addition operation takes place only when the 01 indicator is on because the value 01 is specified in positions 10–11. To cause an addition operation to take place, the word ADD must be placed in the Operation area, positions 28–32. Note that the word ADD must be left-justified, that is, it must begin in position 28. The field name entered in the Factor 1 portion of the form, positions 18–27, is REGERN, which is the name of the Regular Earnings field in the input record (see Figure 3-7). The field name entered in the Factor 2 portion of the form is OVTERN, which is the name of the Overtime Earnings field in the input record. Note that these names are left-justified in their respective fields on the form.

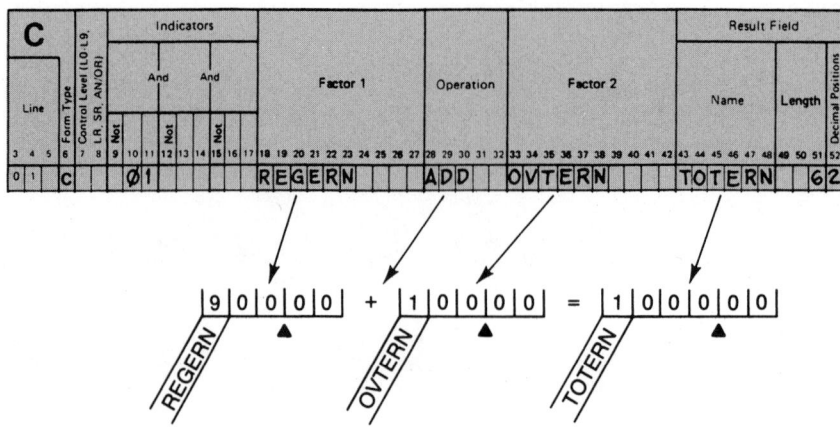

▲ is position of the implied decimal point

Figure 3-20   Example of ADD operation

After the addition operation takes place, the answer is stored in the area referenced by the name specified in the Result Field, positions 43–48. From the example in Figure 3-20, you can see that the name in the Result Field is TOTERN. This field is to be used to store the total earnings of each employee. The field TOTERN has not been previously defined on the Input Specifications because it is not part of the input record. Thus, in addition to specifying the name of the result field, the Calculation Specifications form must be used to define the length and data class of the result field. Figure 3-21 illustrates this definition.

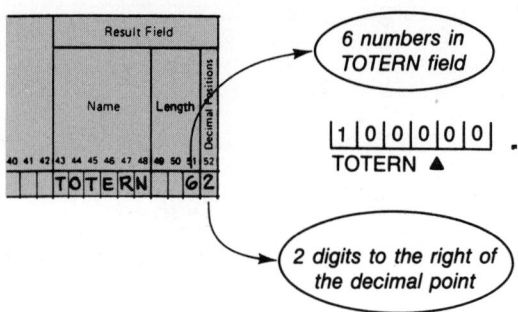

Figure 3-21   Definition of result field

Figure 3-21 shows that the name TOTERN is used to define the field that is to contain the result of the addition of the values in the REGERN and OVTERN fields. A result field defined on the Calculation Specifications form must have a name that follows the same rules as those used when defining field names on the Input Specifications form.

The Field Length entry, positions 49–51, is used to specify the total length of the Result Field. In the example, you can see that the value 6 is specified in position 51, indicating that the field TOTERN is to contain 6 numeric digits. The entry for the length of the field must be right-justified in the Field Length area, and leading zeros need not be included. *The maximum length that can be specified for a result field of an arithmetic operation, or any numeric data field, is 15 digits in RPG, RPG II, and RPG III. The maximum length is 30 digits in RPG/ 400.* You must make sure that the entry in the Field Length area specifies an area large enough to contain the maximum size answer that can develop. In this example, based on information contained in the printer spacing chart, no result will exceed 6 digits in length. Determining the length of the result of addition is difficult; it depends on the length of the longest field being added and on how many numbers are being summed. As a general rule, the result field should be one or two digits larger than the fields being added.

The Decimal Positions specification, position 52, is used to state the number of positions that are to be assumed to the right of the implied decimal point. This field performs the same function as the Decimal Positions area of the Input Specifications form. It must be noted, however, that the decimal positions specified are not in addition to the length specified in the Field Length entry. Thus, as shown in Figure 3-21, the Field Length entry 6 specifies the total number of digits in the field. The 2 in the Decimal Positions area states that within the 6 digits in TOTERN, two digits are to the right of the assumed decimal point. The definition in Figure 3-21 shows that there will be 4 digits to the left of the decimal place and two digits to the right of the decimal place in the TOTERN field.

A result field should be defined only once on the Calculation Specifications form. Therefore, if the field TOTERN is used as a result in subsequent calculations, its length and the number of digits to the right of the decimal place need not be indicated. Once a field is defined in RPG, its length and data class cannot be changed.

Figure 3-20 shows that the value in the REGERN field (900.00) will be added to the value in the OVTERN field (100.00), and the answer (1000.00) will be stored in the TOTERN field.

A second addition operation is also required in the sample program. The total earnings for each employee are to be added so that a final total of all of the employees' earnings can be printed after all input records have been processed (see Figure 3-2). For this total to be accumulated, the value in TOTERN must be added to a field that will accumulate these values. This is illustrated in Figure 3-22.

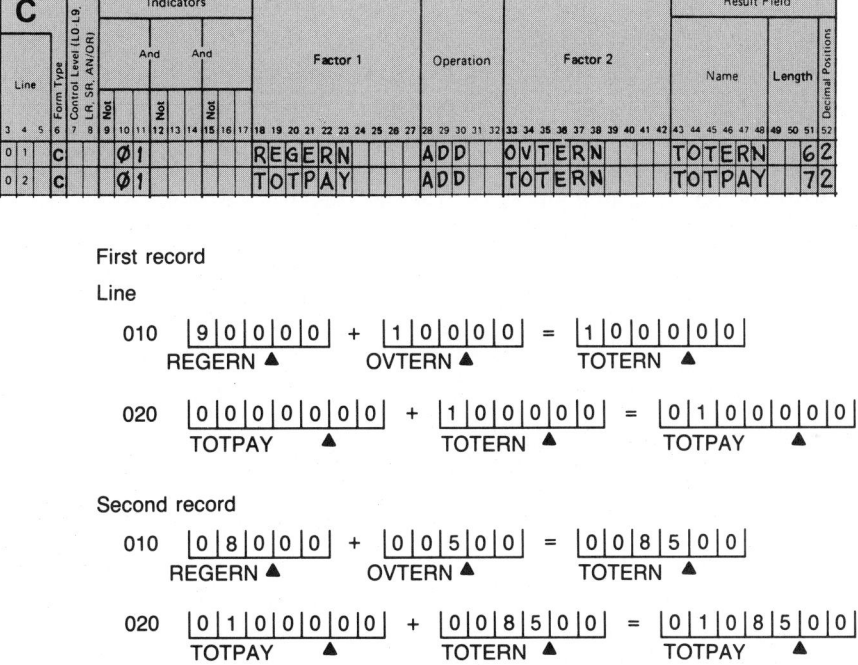

Figure 3-22 Accumulating a final total

Figure 3-22 shows that the field used to accumulate the final total, TOTPAY, is defined on the Calculation Specifications form as containing seven numeric digits, positions 49–51, with two positions to the right of the decimal point, position 52. A field such as TOTPAY that is used to accumulate a total from a series of records is called an **accumulator**.

You have already seen that when the ADD operation is executed, the field referenced in Factor 2 is added to the field referenced in Factor 1, and the answer that develops is stored in the area referenced by the Result Field. Thus, in Figure 3-22, line 02 shows that TOTERN will be added to the TOTPAY accumulator and the answer will be stored in TOTPAY.

When the first input record is processed (see Figure 3-22), the value in the Regular Earnings field (REGERN) is added to the value in the Overtime Earnings field (OVTERN), and the result is stored in the Total Earnings field (TOTERN). The value just calculated in the TOTERN field is then added to the value in the Total Pay field (TOTPAY). When processing of the first record begins, the value in TOTPAY is equal to zero. This is because the RPG compiler sets all numeric fields defined on the Calculation Specifications form to zero prior to beginning the processing of the program. After the addition takes place, the field TOTPAY contains the value 1000.00, which is the total earnings of the first employee processed.

When the second record is read, the value in the Regular Earnings field is again added to the value in the Overtime Earnings field to determine the total earnings of the second employee. Note that the result is again stored in the TOTERN field and that the value from the first record is no longer available. Thus, after the addition on line 01 takes place, the TOTERN field always contains the total earnings of the employee being processed.

The total earnings of the second employee, which is stored in the TOTERN field, is then added to the value stored in TOTPAY. When the second record is processed, however, the value in TOTPAY is not equal to zero as it was when the first record was processed. Instead, it contains the total earnings from the first employee. Thus, when the value in TOTERN is added to the value in TOTPAY for the second employee, the field TOTPAY contains the total of the first employee's pay plus the second employee's pay. This is the desired result because the contents of the field TOTPAY are to be printed at the conclusion of the processing of the input data and should contain the total pay for all of the employee records processed.

Literals

In the previous examples of the addition operations, both Factor 1 and Factor 2 have been fields that contained values to be added. However, it is also possible to specify actual numeric values, which are called **numeric literals**, to be used in arithmetic operations instead of data fields. A numeric literal used on the Calculation Specifications form may be 1–10 characters in length and may contain a decimal point and a plus or minus sign.

In the sample program, the number of employees processed is to be accumulated and the total printed after all of the employee records have been processed. The statement that will cause this accumulation is shown in Figure 3-23.

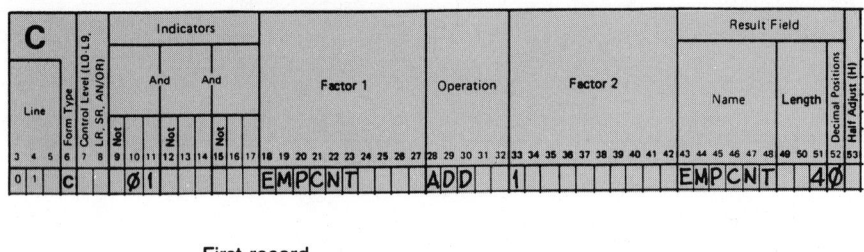

Figure 3-23 Using a literal value

Note in Figure 3-23 that the addition operation takes place only when the 01 indicator is on. The field specified in the Factor 1 area is EMPCNT and is to be used to accumulate the number of employee records processed. The number of employees processed is the same as the number of input records read. Thus, by adding one to this field each time a record is processed, the total number of employees will be accumulated. The operation code is ADD. The value 1, which is a numeric literal, is specified in position 33 of the Factor 2 area. Note that this value is not the name of a field; rather, it is the actual value to be used in the addition operation. In the example, the value 1 is added to EMPCNT, and the answer is stored in EMPCNT.

The result field is the field with the name EMPCNT. Since EMPCNT has not been defined on the Input specifications, its length and number of decimal positions must be specified on the Calculation Specifications form. Note that the field EMPCNT is defined as 4 digits in length. Thus, the maximum size answer that can be developed cannot exceed 4 digits (9999). The zero in Decimal Positions, position 52, specifies that EMPCNT is a whole number, or integer, field with no values to the right of the decimal point. As with input specifications, if a field contains a value that is to be used in an arithmetic operation or is to be zero-suppressed or edited, it must be defined as a numeric field by specifying a value in the Decimal Positions area. If there are no decimal values in the field, the number 0 must be placed in the Decimal Positions area.

The ADD operation is summarized in Figures 3-24 and 3-25. Note that Figure 3-24 shows the standard format of the ADD, whereas Figure 3-25 on the next page shows the ADD format for use with enhanced RPG compilers. The coding examples in these figures point out the difference in writing these two formats. Note that lines 02 and 03 of the enhanced format calculations do not use a Factor 1 entry. In the enhanced format, Factor 2 may be added directly to the Result Field. Although the format of the instructions differs, there is no difference in the totals developed by these two sets of calculations.

Line	Form Type	Control Level (L0–L9, LR, SR, AN/OR)	Indicators							Factor 1	Operation	Factor 2	Result Field				Resulting Indicators			Comments
01	C	Ø1								REGERN	ADD	OVTERN	TOTERN	62						
02	C	Ø1								TOTPAY	ADD	TOTERN	TOTPAY	72						
03	C	Ø1								EMPCNT	ADD	1	EMPCNT	4Ø						

ADD Operation Summary, Standard Format

The value of the field or literal specified in Factor 2 is added to the value of the field or literal specified in Factor 1. The sum is placed in the Result Field. Neither Factor 1 nor Factor 2 is changed by the ADD operation.

Control Level Indicators	Indicators	Factor 1	Operation Name	Factor 2	Result Field	Resulting Indicators		
7–8	9–17	18–27	28–32	33–42	43–53	54–55	56–57	58–59
optional	optional	required	ADD	required	required	optional	optional	optional

Figure 3-24 ADD summary, standard format

3.20 · Chapter 3 RPG Calculation Specifications, Arithmetic Operations, & Edit Codes

C						Factor 1	Operation	Factor 2	Name	Length		
0 1	C		0 1			REGERN	ADD	OVTERN	TOTERN	6 2		
0 2	C		0 1				ADD	TOTERN	TOTPAY	7 2		
0 3	C		0 1				ADD	1	EMPCNT	4 0		

ADD Operation Summary, Enhanced Format

The value of the field or literal specified in Factor 2 is added to the value of the field or literal specified in Factor 1. The sum is placed in the Result Field. Neither Factor 1 nor Factor 2 is changed by the ADD operation. If Factor 1 is not specified, Factor 2 is added to the Result Field and the sum placed in the Result Field.

Control Level Indicators	Indicators	Factor 1	Operation Name	Factor 2	Result Field	Resulting Indicators		
7–8	9–17	18–27	28–32	33–42	43–53	54–55	56–57	58–59
optional	optional	optional	ADD	required	required	optional	optional	optional

Figure 3-25   ADD Summary, enhanced format

OUTPUT SPECIFICATIONS

Report Editing: Detail Lines

Business reports normally require some form of editing, that is, the insertion of special characters such as a dollar sign or period or the suppression of leading zeros to make the information on the report more meaningful. Editing and zero suppression are easily accomplished in RPG through the use of special edit codes placed on the Output Specifications form; the example in Figure 3-26 illustrates the form used to edit the detail lines of the Payroll Report.

The Output Specifications in Figure 3-26 shows that the line described is a detail line that is to be printed when the 01 indicator is on. The printer is to be spaced once after each line is printed on the report. Note the entries in Edit Codes, position 38. These entries are used to edit the fields on the report.

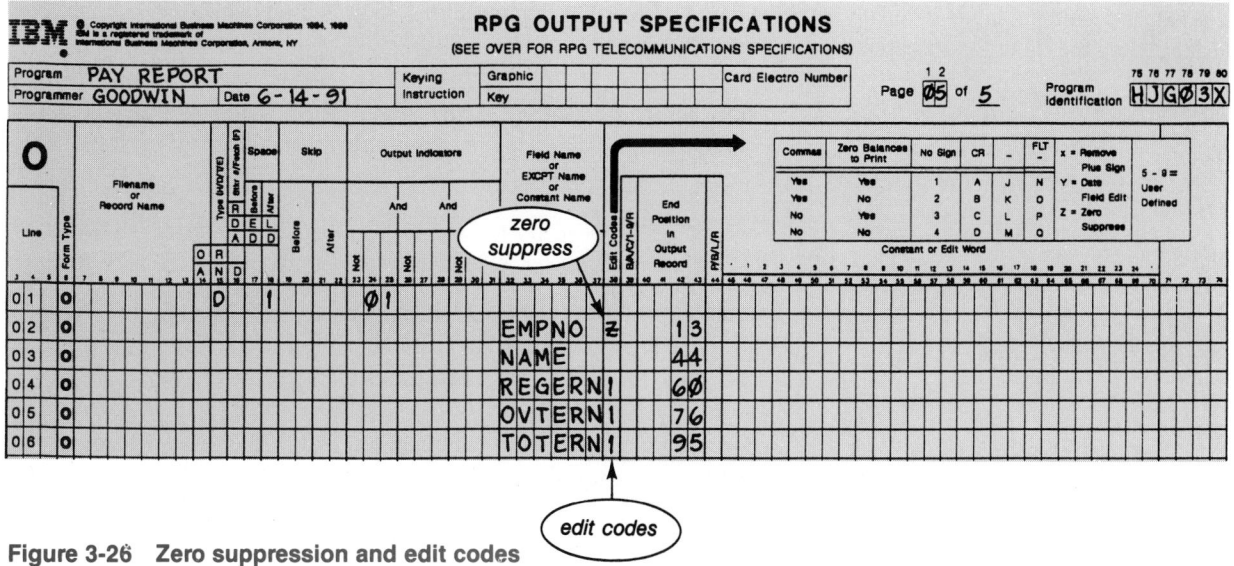

Figure 3-26   Zero suppression and edit codes

As in Chapter 2, when a field is zero suppressed on a report, the leading, nonsignificant zeros in the field are changed to blanks so that the zeros do not appear on the report. To zero suppress a field, the letter Z is entered in position 38 of the Output Specifications form, as in Figure 3-26 for the EMPNO field. This entry causes a field to be zero suppressed. The example in Figure 3-27 shows the results of zero suppressing a field.

Data in Storage	Printed Output
00001	1
02132	2132
10032	10032
07045	7045
00000	(blank)

Figure 3-27   Examples of zero suppression

Editing

When special characters such as commas, periods, and dollar signs are to be placed in a field that is to be printed, special edit codes are used. A summary of the edit codes and their functions is in Figure 3-28.

The Format of Edited Data column on the left indicates how the numeric field is to appear after it has been edited. The Negative Balance Indication columns on the right are used to specify the appearance of the field if it contains a negative number. The edit codes are 1–4, A–D, and J–M. To illustrate the use of the edit codes,

Format of Edited Data	Negative Balance Indication		
	None	CR	—
Prints with commas, prints zero balance	1	A	J
Prints with commas, zero balance suppressed	2	B	K
Prints without commas, prints zero balance	3	C	L
Prints without commas, zero balance suppressed	4	D	M

Figure 3-28   Summary of edit codes and their functions

a numeric field six digits in length with two digits to the right of the decimal point is used. This field can be defined on the Input Specifications form (Figure 3-29).

RPG INPUT SPECIFICATIONS

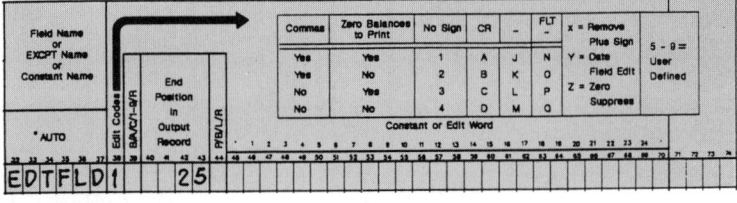

Figure 3-29   Definition of field to be edited

▸ **Edit Code 1**   Edit Code 1 is used to print a numeric field with commas and, if the value is zero, to print the zero value. In addition, all the edit codes perform several functions automatically:

If the field has no positions to the right of the decimal place, no decimal point is printed for the field.
If the field has one or more positions to the right of the decimal place, a decimal point is automatically printed in its proper position.
All fields are zero suppressed.

The example in Figure 3-30 displays the results of editing the field EDTFLD with the Edit Code 1. This figure shows that when the six-digit field EDTFLD contains six significant digits (123456), it is edited with a decimal point and a comma. The decimal point is automatically placed in the proper place, which is dependent on the number of decimal places specified for the field when it was defined (see Figure 3-29). When Edit Code 1 is used, commas are inserted at the proper places.

When five significant digits (023456) are contained in the field, blanks are substituted for the leading, nonsignificant zeros and also for any punctuation that is not required. Thus, there are two leading blanks when there are five significant digits, one for the leading zero in the field and one for the comma, which is not required.

When there are two significant digits, both are to the right of the decimal place. In this case, the decimal point and the two digits are printed, but the remainder of the field, including the positions for the comma, contains blanks.

When there is one significant digit (000007), it is to the right of the decimal point. As with two digits, the decimal point and all values to the right of the decimal point are printed.

RPG OUTPUT SPECIFICATIONS

Value in EDTFLD	Edited results
123456	1,234.56
023456	234.56
000023	.23
000007	.07
000000	.00

▲ indicates location of assumed decimal point

Figure 3-30   Example Of Edit Code 1

With Edit Code 1, the value zero (000000) is printed because that is one of the attributes of Edit Code 1. Therefore, the value .00 is printed when the value in the field being edited is zero.

Note that Edit Code 1 can be used with fields of any size. For example, a five-digit numeric field can be specified with Edit Code 1 and a comma will not be included because the field is not large enough.

▸ **Edit Code 2**   Edit Code 2 works in the same manner as Edit Code 1 except that when the value in the field is zero, no printing occurs for the field because all zeros are replaced by blanks.

As Figures 3-30 and 3-31 show, the only difference between the results from Edit Code 1 and the results from Edit Code 2 is that when the value in the field to be edited is zero, nothing is printed with Edit Code 2 whereas the value .00 is printed with Edit Code 1.

RPG OUTPUT SPECIFICATIONS

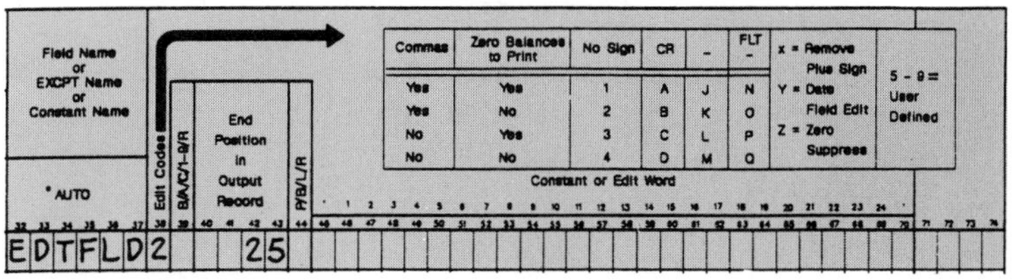

Value in EDTFLD	Edited results
123456	1,234.56
023456	234.56
000023	.23
000007	.07
000000	(blank)

Figure 3-31   Example Of Edit Code 2

▸ **Edit Code 3**   When you use Edit Code 3, no commas are contained in the edited results, and the zero balance prints. The results obtained from Edit Code 3 are in Figure 3-32. Note in the figure that the editing with Edit Code 3 takes place as with Edit Code 1 except that commas are not printed in the edited result. The decimal point is still printed in the proper place and, as with Edit Code 1, if the value in the field is zero, the zero value to the right of the decimal place is printed, together with the decimal point.

RPG OUTPUT SPECIFICATIONS

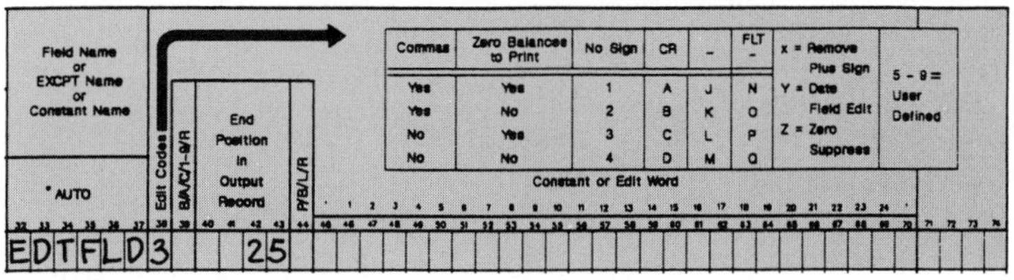

Value in EDTFLD	Edited results
123456	1234.56
023456	234.56
000023	.23
000007	.07
000000	.00

Figure 3-32   Example Of Edit Code 3

▸ **Edit Code 4** When you use Edit Code 4, no commas are printed, and the zero balances in the field to be edited are not printed. The example in Figure 3-33 illustrates the use of Edit Code 4. Note from this figure that no commas are printed in the result field and that when the value is zero in the field to be edited, blanks are printed on the report.

RPG OUTPUT SPECIFICATIONS

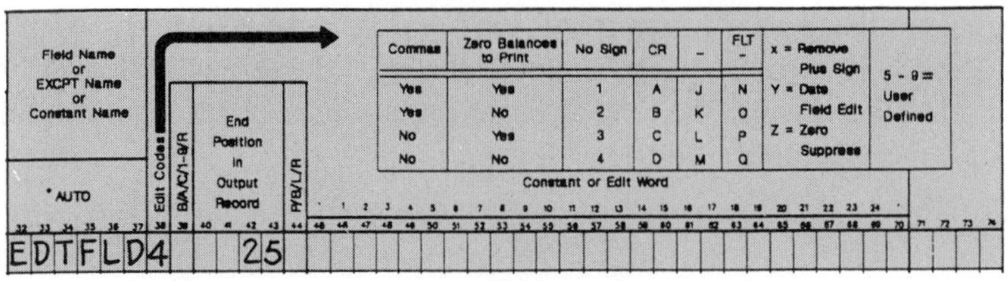

Value in EDTFLD	Edited results
123456	1234.56
023456	234.56
000023	.23
000007	.07
000000	(blank)

Figure 3-33   Example Of Edit Code 4

You can see from the previous examples that the four edit codes allow for many of the ways in which numeric data is edited on a printed report. The table at the top-right of the Output Specifications form summarizes the functions of each of the codes and should be referenced as a reminder of the results using the edit codes.

▸ **Editing Negative Values** All the previous examples contained positive values in the field to be edited, but on many business reports one must differentiate between positive and negative values. When you use only Edit Codes 1–4, the negative values on the report will look exactly the same as positive values. Therefore, other edit codes must be used so that negative values can be distinguished from positive values.

In most data processing applications, there are two ways to indicate a negative value: Either a **minus sign** (–) is printed following the numeric value or the **letters CR** are printed to indicate a credit value. The CRedit indication is often used in accounting applications.

Edit codes can be used to cause the minus sign (–) or the credit sign (CR) to print when the field being edited contains a negative value. Edit Codes A–D edit exactly like Edit Codes 1–4, except that the CR indication is included with the edited field if the field to be edited is negative. The codes J–M edit exactly like Edit Codes 1–4, except that the minus sign is included with the edited field if the field being edited is negative (Figure 3-34).

FIELD VALUE	CODE 1	A	J	2	B	K	3	C	L	4	D	M
102025	1,020.25	1,020.25	1,020.25	1,020.25	1,020.25	1,020.25	1020.25	1020.25	1020.25	1020.25	1020.25	1020.25
102025	1,020.25	1,020.25CR	1,020.25–	1,020.25	1,020.25CR	1,020.25–	1020.25	1020.25CR	1020.25–	1020.25	1020.25CR	1020.25–
102025	102,025	102,025	102,025	102,025	102,025	102,025	102025	102025	102025	102025	102025	102025
102025	102,025	102,025CR	102,025–	102,025	102,025CR	102,025–	102025	102025CR	102025–	102025	102025CR	102025–
000251	2.51	2.51	2.51	2.51	2.51	2.51	2.51	2.51	2.51	2.51	2.51	2.51
000251	2.51	2.51CR	2.51–	2.51	2.51CR	2.51–	2.51	2.51CR	2.51–	2.51	2.51CR	2.51–
000000	.00	.00	.00				.00	.00	.00			
000000	0	0	0				0	0	0			

▲ - is implied decimal place   – - above the low order position indicates negative amount

Figure 3-34   Example of all edit codes

Note that in Figure 3-34 the Edit Codes 1, A, and J edit the numeric data in exactly the same fashion except that Edit Code A places the letters CR following the field if the field contains a negative value, and Edit Code J places a minus sign (–) following the field if the field contains a negative value. In this figure, a negative value is shown by a horizontal line over the rightmost digit of the field value.

When these negative indications are used, you must allow space for the minus sign or CR indication to print. The output end position for the field must be the position occupied by the minus sign or R. If this space is not planned, the field will print in the wrong positions.

The Edit Codes 2, B, and K edit data in the same manner, except for the negative fields, as do the Edit Codes 3, C, L and 4, D, M. When a whole value (without digits to the right of the decimal place) is edited, no decimal point is printed. In addition, when a zero value (without values to the right of the decimal place) is edited, the value 0 is printed by those edit codes that print zeros.

▸ **Dollar Signs** In business applications, the fields printed are often dollar values. In many instances, a programmer wants to print a dollar sign on the report with the dollar value. To print a **floating dollar sign**, that is, one which is printed to the left of and adjacent to the first significant character in the edited output field, the value '$' must be placed in positions 45–47 of the Output Specifications form. An example of this is Figure 3-35. Generally, in RPG, you cannot place a constant and an edit code on the same output field line. The floating dollar sign is one of the few exceptions to this rule.

RPG OUTPUT SPECIFICATIONS

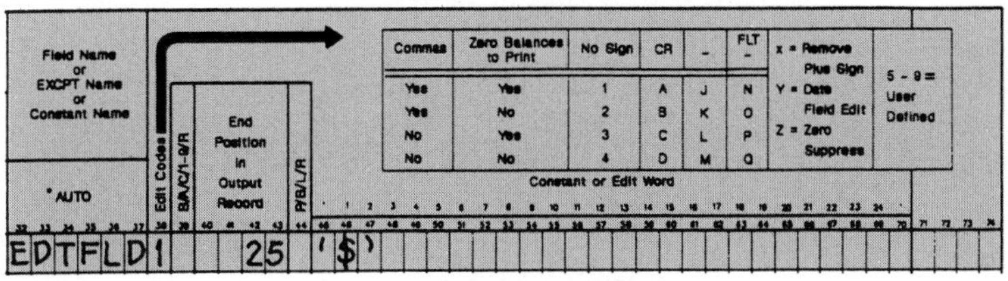

Value in EDTFLD	Edited results
123456	$1,234.56
023456	$234.56
000023	$.23
000007	$.07
000000	$.00

Figure 3-35 Example of floating dollar sign

In Figure 3-35, the dollar sign is enclosed between apostrophes in positions 45–47 of the Output Specifications form, and as a result, it will be printed adjacent to the leftmost digit of the number being edited. Note that if a floating dollar sign is specified for Edit Codes 2, 4, B, D, K, or M, and the value in the field is zero, the dollar sign does not print.

In some applications, a **fixed dollar sign** is used; this is a dollar sign that prints in the same position regardless of the size of the value in the field. To print a fixed dollar sign, the dollar sign is not placed in positions 45–47 with the field to be edited; instead, the dollar sign is specified as a constant that appears on a coding line by itself.

Printing Total Lines

As noted previously, two totals are accumulated during the processing of the input data: a total of the number of employees processed and the total pay for all of the employees. These totals are to be printed after all the input records have been processed. To print them, a specification must be made on the Output Specifications form to indicate that a Total line is to be printed.

Figure 3-36 is the Output Specifications form used in the sample program. When a line is to be printed on the report after each input record is read, the line is considered to be a Detail Line and the letter D is entered in position 15 of the Output Specifications form to indicate this. When a **Total line** is to be printed – such a line is printed only at a specified time and not for each input record that is read – the letter T must be entered in the Type field, position 15. As can be seen in the figure, the letter T is entered in position 15 after the specifications for the detail line.

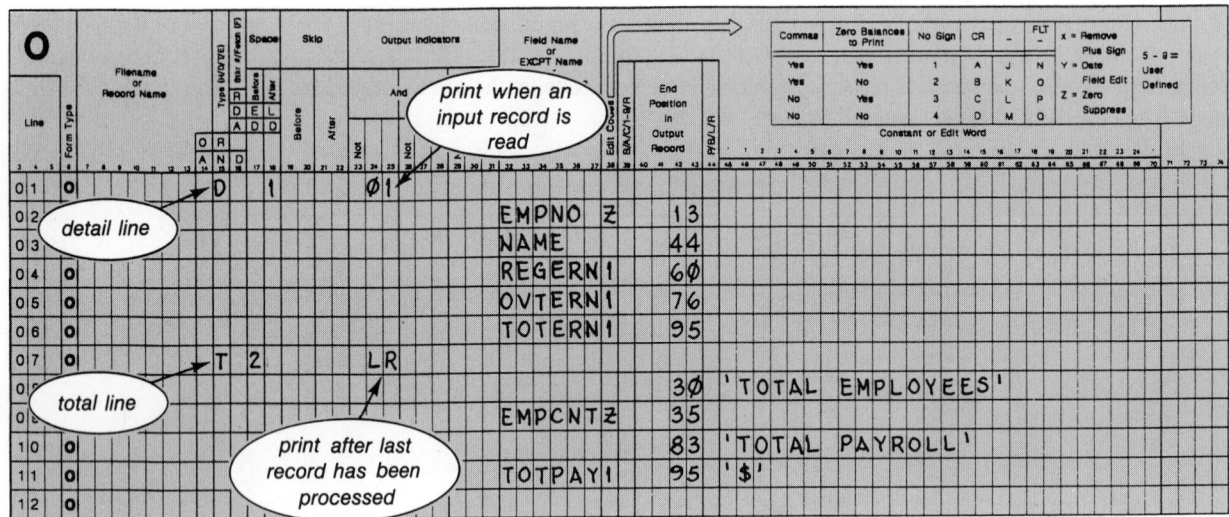

Figure 3-36   Example of total line

Figure 3-36 also shows that the Total line is to be printed on the report after two line spaces because the value 2 is entered in position 17. Thus, as in Figure 3-2, the Total line is separated from the detail lines by two spaces. The total line is to be printed only after all the input detail records have been read and processed. The fact that it is to be printed after the last record has been processed is indicated by the entry LR in the Output Indicators area of the form, in positions 24–25. The **LR** entry specifies that the Total line is to be printed only after the last record has been processed. Thus, by making the LR entry, a Total line is processed only after all the input records have been read and processed. Indicator LR is fully automatic and need not be defined by the programmer.

Note that the field specifications for the Total line, as with the detail line, are placed on the next coding line after the entries that define the type of record to be printed. The specifications for the fields to be printed begin on line 08 of the coding form, and the specifications for the type of record to be printed are on line 07.

As a result of the entries shown in Figure 3-36, the total line, as illustrated in Figure 3-2, is printed after all the input records have been read. Figure 3-37 shows the compilation listing and output report for program HJG03X.

Figure 3-37 Compilation listing and sample output report

```
      5727RG1RG R05M00              IBM SYSTEM/36 RPGII           06/14/91  11.34

            H                                                          HJG03X


      0001      FPAYFILE IP  F1200  60            DISK
      0002      FPAYREPT O   F 132 132     OF     PRINTER


      0003      IPAYFILE AA  01
      0004      I                                    1     40EMPNO
      0005      I                                   11     30 NAME
      0006      I                                   40     442REGERN
      0007      I                                   45     4920VTERN


      0008      C    01       REGERN    ADD  OVTERN    TOTERN 62      TOTAL EARNINGS
      0009      C    01       TOTPAY    ADD  TOTERN    TOTPAY 72      ALL EMPLOYEES
      0010      C    01       EMPCNT    ADD  1         EMPCNT 40      EMPLOYEE COUNT


      0011      OPAYREPT H  206   1P
      0012      O        OR       OF
      0013      O                                   14 'HJG03X  DATE'
      0014      O                      UDATE Y       23
      0015      O                                   48 'E A R N I N G S'
      0016      O                                   62 'R E P O R T'
      0017      O                                   91 'PAGE'
      0018      O                      PAGE         96
      0019      O        H  1   1P
      0020      O        OR       OF
      0021      O                                   15 'EMPLOYEE'
      0022      O                                   77 'REGULAR        OVERTIME'
      0023      O                                   93 'TOTAL'
      0024      O        H  2   1P
      0025      O        OR       OF
      0026      O                                   14 'NUMBER'
      0027      O                                   36 'NAME'
      0028      O                                   61 'EARNINGS'
      0029      O                                   77 'EARNINGS'
      0030      O                                   95 'EARNINGS'
      0031      O        D  1   01
      0032      O                      EMPNO Z      13
      0033      O                      NAME         44
      0034      O                      REGERN1      60
      0035      O                      OVTERN1      76
      0036      O                      TOTERN1      95
      0037      O        T  2   LR
      0038      O                                   30 'TOTAL EMPLOYEES'
      0039      O                      EMPCNTZ      35
      0040      O                                   83 'TOTAL PAYROLL'
      0041      O                      TOTPAY1      95 '$'

              * * * * * E N D   O F   S O U R C E * * * * *


      5727RG1RG R05M00              IBM SYSTEM/36 RPGII           06/14/91  11.34


INDICATORS USED
      LR OF 1P 01

  FIELD NAMES USED
  STMT#  NAME  DEC  LNG   DISP
  0018  PAGE    0  0004  0136
  0014  UDATE   0  0006  00A7
  0004  EMPNO   0  0004  0117
  0005  NAME       0020  0113
  0006  REGERN  2  0005  0110
  0007  OVTERN  2  0005  0121
  0008  TOTERN  2  0006  0127
  0009  TOTPAY  2  0007  012E
  0010  EMPNOS  0  0004  0132

         * * * * * E N D   O F   C O M P I L E * * * * *
```

Figure 3-37 (1)   *continued*

```
HJG03X   DATE  6/14/91            E A R N I N G S   R E P O R T                         PAGE     1

       EMPLOYEE                                          REGULAR        OVERTIME          TOTAL
        NUMBER                      NAME                 EARNINGS        EARNINGS         EARNINGS

          110           ABEL, WILLIAM                    900.00          100.00         1,000.00
          991           ALAN, ROGER                       80.00            5.00            85.00
          999           BLANCHARD, CHRIS                 999.90           78.90         1,078.80
         1004           DAVIS, ERIK                      100.00             .00           100.00
         1025           ELAY, JESSE                      125.75           50.00           175.75
         2237           FARMER, JOHN                     250.00           25.00           275.00
         2240           FISHER, DAVID                    312.09           39.00           351.09
         2250           GARGAS, WILLIAM                  999.00           58.90         1,057.90
         2260           HARRIS, JERRY                    543.40           89.00           632.40
         2270           HART, STEVEN                     534.80           89.09           623.89
         2280           JAMES, JACK                      677.39           98.88           776.27
         2290           PINKHAM, TODD                    198.08            2.42           200.50
         3021           WILLIAMS, GEO                    536.29             .00           536.29
         3056           WOOD, EMILE                      567.20           45.61           612.81
         3890           ZUKOWSKI, GEORGE                  98.27             .00            98.27


              TOTAL EMPLOYEES    15                                TOTAL PAYROLL    $7,603.97
```

Figure 3-37 (2)

ADDITIONAL ARITHMETIC OPERATIONS

Subtraction

Although not illustrated in the sample problem, the entries for a subtraction operation are very similar to those for addition. As noted, the ADD operation code is used to add the values that appear in two fields. To subtract one field from another, the SUB operation is used. The **SUB operation** subtracts the contents of the field or literal specified in Factor 2 from the contents of the field or literal specified in Factor 1. The result of the subtraction, the difference, is placed in the Result Field, as in Figure 3-38. Based on the rules of arithmetic, the length of the Result Field should be the same as the length of either Factor 1 or Factor 2, whichever is longer.

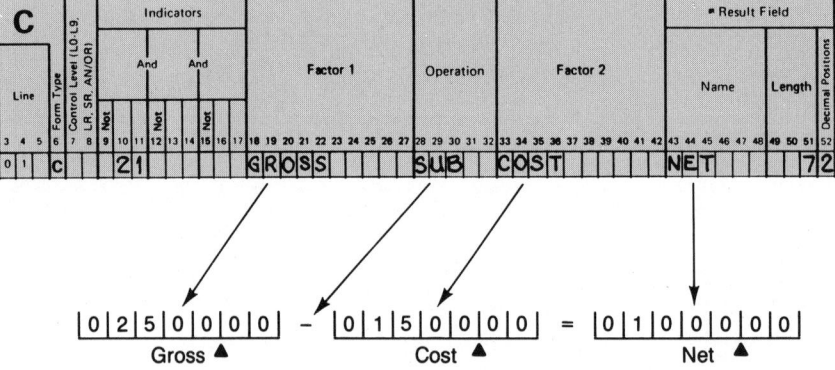

Figure 3-38   Example of SUB operation

Figure 3-38 shows that the subtraction operation is to take place if indicator 21 is on. The field that is specified in Factor 1, positions 18–27, is the **minuend** of the subtraction operation, and the field that is specified in Factor 2, positions 33–42, is the **subtrahend**. Thus, the value in the field in Factor 2 is subtracted from the value in the field in Factor 1; in this example, the value in the field COST is subtracted from the value in the field GROSS. The **difference**, or result of the subtraction operation, is stored in the Result Field specified in positions 43–48; thus, the difference between GROSS and COST is stored in the field NET. As can be seen, the length of the NET field is seven digits, with two digits to the right of the decimal place. In the figure, note that the value 1500.00 in the COST field is subtracted from the value 2500.00 in the GROSS field, and the answer 1000.00 stored in the NET field.

Figures 3-39 and 3-40 on the next page summarize the SUB operation.

C		Indicators		Factor 1	Operation	Factor 2	Result Field			Resulting Indicators	Comments
01	C	14		ONHAND	SUB	SOLD	ONHAND				
02	C	14		COUNT	SUB	1	COUNT				
03	C	14		AMOUNT	SUB	AMOUNT	AMOUNT				SETS AMOUNT TO
04	C										ZERO

SUB Operation Summary, Standard Format

The value of the field or literal specified in Factor 2 is subtracted from the value of the field or literal specified in Factor 1. The difference is placed in the Result Field. Neither Factor 1 nor Factor 2 is changed by the SUB operation. Subtracting a field from itself can be used to set a field to a value of zero.

Control Level Indicators	Indicators	Factor 1	Operation Name	Factor 2	Result Field	Resulting Indicators		
7–8	9–17	18–27	28–32	33–42	43–53	54–55	56–57	58–59
optional	optional	required	SUB	required	required	optional	optional	optional

Figure 3-39   SUB summary, standard format

Line	Form Type	Control Level	Indicators	Factor 1	Operation	Factor 2	Result Field Name	Length	Decimal Positions	Half Adjust (H)	Resulting Indicators	Comments
01	C		14		SUB	SOLD	ONHAND					
02	C		14		SUB	1	COUNT					
03	C		14		SUB	AMOUNT	AMOUNT					SETS AMOUNT TO
04	C											ZERO

SUB Operation Summary, Enhanced Format

The value of the field or literal specified in Factor 2 is subtracted from the value of the field or literal specified in Factor 1. The difference is placed in the Result Field. Neither Factor 1 nor Factor 2 is changed by the SUB operation. Subtracting a field from itself can be used to set a field to a value of zero. If Factor 1 is not specified, Factor 2 is subtracted from the Result Field and the difference placed in the Result Field.

Control Level Indicators	Indicators	Factor 1	Operation Name	Factor 2	Result Field	Resulting Indicators		
7–8	9–17	18–27	28–32	33–42	43–53	54–55	56–57	58–59
optional	optional	optional	SUB	required	required	optional	optional	optional

Figure 3-40 SUB summary, enhanced format

Multiplication

When you program in RPG, multiplication is accomplished through the use of the **MULT operation**. In any multiplication operation, manual or with a computer, the maximum size of the answer that can develop may be determined by adding the number of digits in the multiplier to the number of digits in the multiplicand. For example, as shown in Figure 3-41, if a three-digit Rate field is multiplied by a two-digit Hours field in order to obtain the pay of an employee, the maximum size of the result that can develop is five digits. Similarly, the maximum number of decimal places in the product is calculated by adding the number of decimal positions in the multiplier to the number of decimal positions in the multiplicand.

$3.20	Rate	(multiplicand)
40	Hours	(multiplier)
$128.00	Pay	(maximum size answer, 5 digits in length)

Figure 3-41 Length of multiplication product

It is important that the programmer understand this basic concept of arithmetic to properly perform multiplication operations using the computer.

Figure 3-42 shows the entries that are required to multiply a three-digit (X.XX) Rate field by a three-digit (XX.X) Hours field. The MULT operation multiplies the contents of the field or literal specified in Factor 1, **the multiplicand**, by the contents of the field or literal specified in Factor 2, **the multiplier**. The result (**product**) of this operation is placed in the Result Field.

In the example in Figure 3-42, you can see that the value in the field RATE is to be multiplied by the value in the field HOURS and the result is to be stored in the field PAY. The RATE field contains three digits with two digits to the right of the decimal point, as defined on the Input Specifications. The HOURS field also contains three digits with one digit to the right of the decimal point; therefore, the answer (PAY) is six digits in length with three digits to the right of the decimal point.

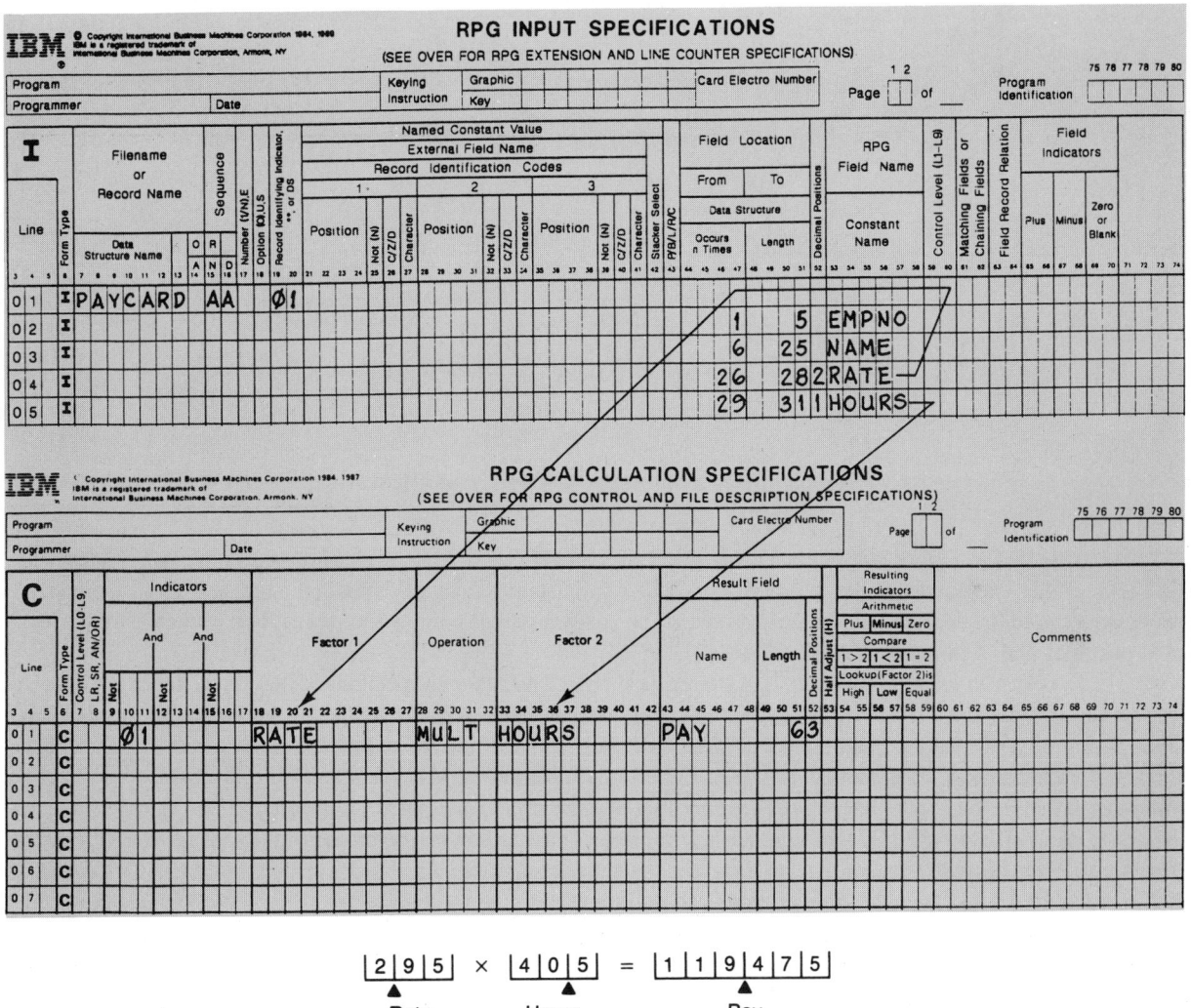

Figure 3-42   Example of MULT operation

▸ **Rounding**   In programming for business applications involving decimal positions in the answer, it is frequently desirable to **round** the answer. For example, if the answer is developed as $1.254, you may want to round the answer to $1.25 so that the amount can be expressed in terms of dollars and cents. If the answer is developed as $1.255, the amount would normally be rounded upward to $1.26. (Note that if the low-order position is less than 5, the amount is not rounded upward. If the low-order position is 5 or greater, the amount is rounded upward.)

In the example in Figure 3-42, the value in the field PAY contains three digits to the right of the decimal point. Normally, when dealing with dollar amounts, the result of this multiplication would be rounded so that there are only two digits to the right of the decimal point. Figure 3-43 shows the entries to accomplish this.

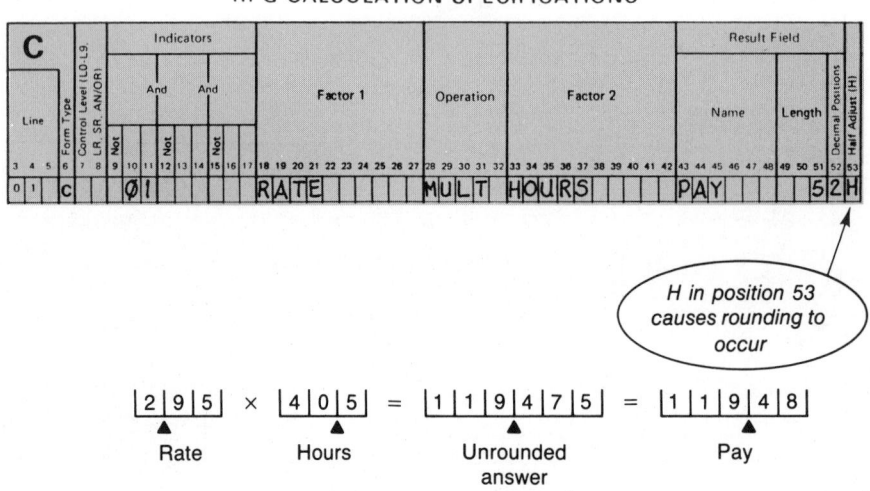

RPG CALCULATION SPECIFICATIONS

Figure 3-43   Rounding the product of multiplication

Note that in Figure 3-43 the values in the RATE and HOURS fields are multiplied in the same manner as in Figure 3-42. The answer to the multiplication operation is stored in a work area that is created by RPG. This work area cannot be accessed by the programmer. The answer stored in the work area is then rounded to two decimal positions and is stored in the PAY field.

To round an answer, the letter H is placed in the Half Adjust area, position 53, on the Calculation Specifications form. This entry indicates that rounding or **half-adjusting** is to occur on the answer stored in Result Field. Note in Figure 3-43 that the length of the PAY field is specified as 5 and the number of decimal positions is specified as 2, rather than 6 for the length and 3 for the decimal positions as was specified in Figure 3-42. Whenever rounding is to take place, the length specified and the number of decimal positions specified must refer to the length of the field after the half-adjusting has taken place. Thus, as you can see from Figure 3-43, the PAY field is five digits in length with two positions to the right of the decimal place.

Figures 3-44 and 3-45 summarize the MULT operation.

C			Indicators						Factor 1	Operation	Factor 2		Result Field				Resulting Indicators						Comments
			And		And								Name	Length			Arithmetic						
																	Plus	Minus	Zero				
																	Compare						
																	1>2	1<2	1=2				
																	Lookup(Factor 2)is						
Line				Not		Not		Not									High	Low	Equal				
3 4 5	6	7	8	9 10	11	12 13	14	15 16	17	18 19 20 21 22 23 24 25 26 27	28 29 30 31 32	33 34 35 36 37 38 39 40 41 42	43 44 45 46 47 48	49 50 51	52	53	54 55	56 57	58 59	60 61 62 63 64 65 66 67 68 69 70 71 72 73 74
0 1	C		Ø3						AMOUNT	MULT	DISCNT	AMOUNT								
0 2	C		Ø4						AMTDUE	MULT	.Ø15	AMTDUE			H					
0 3	C																			
0 4	C																			

Figure 3-44   MULT summary, standard format

continued

	MULT Operation Summary, Standard Format
	The value of the field or literal specified in Factor 1 is multiplied by the contents of the field or literal specified in Factor 2. The product is placed in the Result Field. Neither Factor 1 nor Factor 2 is changed by the MULT operation.

Control Level Indicators	Indicators	Factor 1	Operation Name	Factor 2	Result Field	Resulting Indicators		
7–8	9–17	18–27	28–32	33–42	43–53	54–55	56–57	58–59
optional	optional	required	MULT	required	required	optional	optional	optional

Figure 3-44   (continued)

	MULT Operation Summary, Enhanced Format
	The value in the field or literal specified in Factor 1 is multiplied by the value in the field or literal specified in Factor 2. The product is placed in the Result Field. Neither Factor 1 nor Factor 2 is changed by the MULT operation. If Factor 1 is not specified, the Result Field is multiplied by Factor 2 and the product placed in the Result Field.

Control Level Indicators	Indicators	Factor 1	Operation Name	Factor 2	Result Field	Resulting Indicators		
7–8	9–17	18–27	28–32	33–42	43–53	54–55	56–57	58–59
optional	optional	optional	MULT	required	required	optional	optional	optional

Figure 3-45   MULT summary, enhanced format

▆ Division

When division is to be performed in an RPG program, the **DIV operation** is specified on the Calculation Specifications form. In Figure 3-46, a Year-to-Date Sales field is to be divided by the Months field to determine an Average Monthly Sales for the employee. The Year-to-Date Sales field is the **dividend**, the Months field is the **divisor**, and the answer or **quotient** is the Average Monthly Sales. The **remainder** after dividing is zero. In this figure, the value 1200.00 is divided by the value 04, and the answer is 300.00 with a remainder of zero.

In any division problem, the maximum number of digits that the quotient (result) can have equal to the number of digits in the dividend. This is illustrated in Figure 3-47.

The maximum number of digits that the remainder can have after a division operation is equal to the number of digits in the divisor. This is illustrated in Figure 3-48: The remainder, 1111, contains the same number of digits as the divisor, 2222. It is important that the programmer understand these functions of the division operation in order to properly use the Divide statement in RPG.

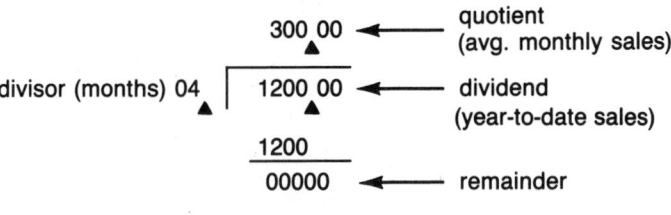

Figure 3-46 Division

Figure 3-47 Determining maximum quotient size

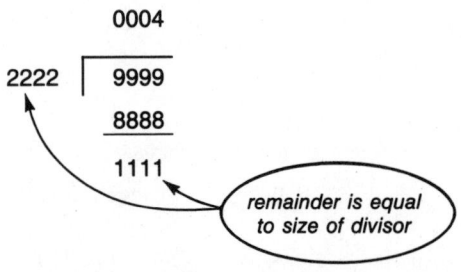

Figure 3-48 Determining remainder size

▶ **The DIV Operation** To divide two numbers using the RPG language, the DIV operation is specified on the Calculation Specifications form as in Figure 3-49.

When the divide operation (DIV) is executed, the contents of the field or literal specified in Factor 1 (the dividend) is divided by the contents of the field or literal specified in Factor 2 (the divisor). The result of this

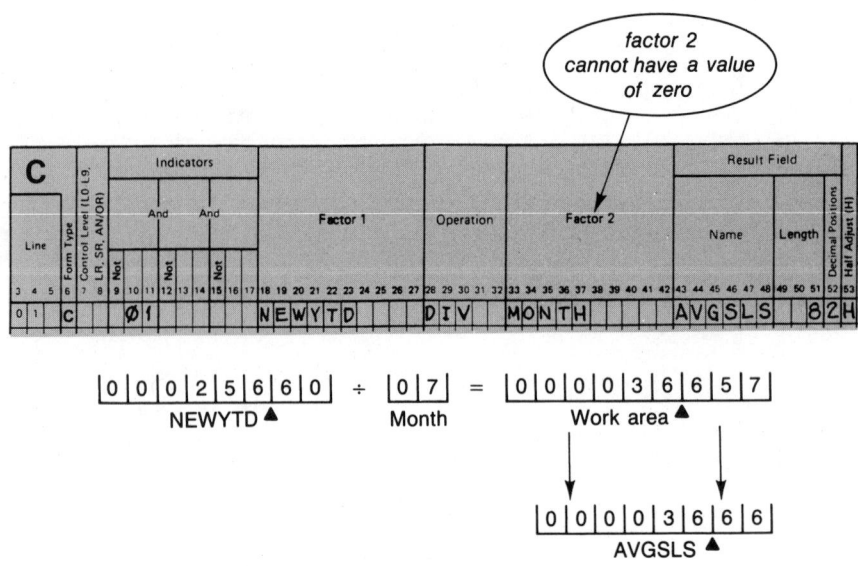

Figure 3-49 Example Of DIV operation

operation (the quotient) is placed in the area specified in the Result Field. The contents of the field or literal in Factor 2 cannot be zero because the rules of arithmetic forbid division by zero. If this is attempted, program execution will terminate.

Note in the example in Figure 3-49 that the value in the field NEWYTD is divided by the value in the field MONTH and the result is stored in the field AVGSLS. The dividend is placed in the Factor 1 area of the form (positions 18–27), the divisor is placed in the Factor 2 area of the form (positions 33–42), and the field to be used for the quotient is placed in the Result Field area (positions 43–48). The length of the field to be used for the quotient is specified in positions 49–51. As noted previously, it should be equal to the size of the dividend, which, in the example, is eight digits with two digits to the right of the decimal point. Note also that half-adjusting is specified by the character H in position 53. Thus, the division is carried out to three places to the right of the decimal location, and then the quotient is rounded to two decimal places as specified by the 2 in position 52. The field length and decimal positions specified for the result field in a Division operation must be the values that are to be used after the half-adjusting has taken place.

Figures 3-50 and 3-51 summarize the DIV operation.

DIV Operation Summary, Standard Format

The value in the field or literal specified in Factor 1 is divided by the value in the field or literal specified in Factor 2. The quotient is placed in the Result Field. Neither Factor 1 nor Factor 2 is changed as a result of the DIV operation. If Factor 1 is zero, the quotient will be zero. Factor 2 cannot be zero. If it is, the program stops immediately.

Control Level Indicators	Indicators	Factor 1	Operation Name	Factor 2	Result Field	Resulting Indicators		
7–8	9–17	18–27	28–32	33–42	43–53	54–55	56–57	58–59
optional	optional	required	DIV	required	required	optional	optional	optional

Figure 3-50   DIV summary, standard format

Line	Form Type	Control Level	Indicators	Factor 1	Operation	Factor 2	Result Field Name	Length	Decimal Positions	Half Adjust (H)	Resulting Indicators	Comments
01	C		Ø1		DIV	EMPCNT	TOTAL			H		
02	C		Ø1		DIV	9	YARDS					
03	C											
04	C											

DIV Operation Summary, Enhanced Format

The value in the field or literal specified in Factor 1 is divided by the value in the field or literal specified in Factor 2. The quotient is placed in the Result Field. Neither Factor 1 nor Factor 2 is changed as a result of the DIV operation. If Factor 1 is zero, the quotient will be zero. Factor 2 cannot be zero. If it is, the program stops immediately. If Factor 1 is not specified, the Result Field is divided by Factor 2 and the quotient placed in the Result Field.

Control Level Indicators	Indicators	Factor 1	Operation Name	Factor 2	Result Field	Resulting Indicators		
7–8	9–17	18–27	28–32	33–42	43–53	54–55	56–57	58–59
optional	optional	optional	DIV	required	required	optional	optional	optional

Figure 3-51 DIV summary, enhanced format

Remainders and the MVR Operation If it is necessary to save the remainder of the division operation, the **MVR (move remainder) operation** must be used. An example of the division and MVR operations is shown in Figure 3-52. In this example, the value in the MINUTE field is to be divided by the literal 60, and the quotient is to be stored in the HOURS field. Immediately following the DIV operation is the MVR (move remainder) operation code. This instruction causes the **remainder** that resulted from the division operation to be moved to the field specified in the Result Field of the Calculation Specifications form, positions 43–48. In the example in Figure 3-52, this is the MINS field.

There are two restrictions that you must remember when using the MVR operation. First, the MVR must immediately follow the DIV operation from which the remainder is to be retrieved. No operations may appear between the DIV and MVR operations. Second, the MVR cannot be used if the result of the DIV was half-adjusted. Half-adjust and MVR are mutually exclusive operations, that is, if one is used the other cannot be used.

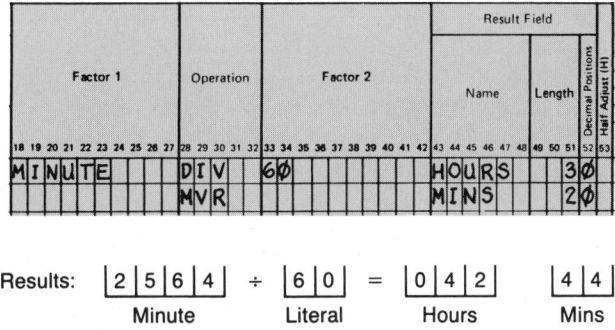

Results: $2\ 5\ 6\ 4$ ÷ $6\ 0$ = $0\ 4\ 2$ $4\ 4$
Minute ÷ Literal = Hours Mins

Figure 3-52   Example of DIV and MVR operations

The size of the field to be used for the remainder value is quite important in order for the MVR operation to take place properly. The value specified in the Length area of the form, positions 49–51, must be equal to the length of the field specified in Factor 2 of the Division operation. In the example, this is the literal 60, which is two digits in length. Therefore, the length specified for the Result Field (MINS) of the MVR operation is 2. The reason that the remainder field must be the same size as the field specified in Factor 2 is that the maximum size of the remainder in a division operation is always the length of the divisor, and the divisor must be specified in Factor 2 of the DIV operation.

Figure 3-53 summarizes the MVR operation

Line	Form Type	Control Level (L0 L9) LR, SR, AN/OR)	Not	Not	Not	Factor 1	Operation	Factor 2	Name	Length	Decimal Positions	Half Adjust (H)	Plus	Minus	Zero	High	Low	Equal	Comments
0 1	C	Ø2				AREA	DIV	144	SQRFT	4Ø									
0 2	C	Ø2					MVR		SQRIN	3Ø									
0 3	C																		
0 4	C																		

MVR Operation Summary

The MVR operation causes the remainder created by the preceding DIV operation to be moved into the field specified as the result field. Factors 1 and 2 must be blank. MVR may not be used if the quotient of the preceding DIV operation was half-adjusted.

Control Level Indicators	Indicators	Factor 1	Operation Name	Factor 2	Result Field	Resulting Indicators		
7–8	9–17	18–27	28–32	33–42	43–53	54–55	56–57	58–59
optional	optional	blank	MVR	blank	required	optional	optional	optional

Figure 3-53   MVR summary

═══ IN CONCLUSION ═══

In this chapter you have learned to use the addition, subtraction, multiplication, and division operations and how to accumulate final totals. In addition, you have seen how the Half Adjust entry is used to round numbers and how to use the MVR operation to capture the remainder of a division operation.

The sample problem in this chapter performed the same operations on every data record read. In Chapter 4 you will learn to use the COMP (compare) operation to determine the relative values of two data fields and to perform different processing operations based on the result of the comparison.

CHAPTER SUMMARY

1. Most business application programs require the use of arithmetic operations.
2. A vertical dotted line in an input layout represents the decimal point location.
3. A **final total** is a Total line printed at the end of a report.
4. **Detail calculations** use data read from an input record.
5. Detail calculations that are controlled by the same indicator are performed in the order in which they are written. Special operations may be used to change the sequence of execution.
6. Data to be used in arithmetic operations must be defined as numeric.
7. An **implied** or **assumed decimal point** is used for correct decimal alignment during arithmetic and output editing. An implied decimal point does not appear in the data.
8. A **logic error** is an entry that is correct according to the rules of RPG but is incorrect based on the program specifications.
9. Logic errors can not be detected by the compiler; they become apparent only during program testing.
10. If no indicator is used to control an operation, the operation will be performed every time step 12 of the logic cycle is performed.
11. The **operation** entry must be a valid RPG operation code.
12. A **comment** is not part of the program code and has no effect on the object program. Comments are used to briefly explain calculation specification operations.
13. Sign control is automatic in RPG. You do not need to make a special entry to keep the sign of a number.
14. RPG **move operations** copy data into a new location, leaving the original data unchanged.
15. **Instruction formats** show which portions of the calculation specification line are used for a given operation.
16. The **operation summary** is a brief explanation of the way an instruction works.
17. The **enhanced** format permits some operations to be written in a manner that eliminates the duplication of some portions of the operation code.
18. The **ADD operation** adds the value in Factor 2 to the value in Factor 1 and places the sum in the Result Field.
19. The maximum length of a numeric data field is 15 digits in RPG, RPG II, and RPG III. It is 30 digits in RPG/400.
20. A numeric result field is automatically set to zero at the beginning of program execution.
21. The length and data class of a result field should be specified only the first time the result field appears.
22. An **accumulator** is a data field used to store the total of data from a series of records.
23. A **numeric literal** is data that is specified as a factor in an arithmetic operation. The maximum length of a numeric literal is ten digits. If a decimal point or sign is part of the literal, each occupies one digit position.
24. An **edit code** can perform several editing functions on the same field.
25. A chart of edit codes appears on every Output Specifications form.

26. Negative data fields can be identified by a **minus sign** or **CR indication**. If either of these is used, the end position of the output field must be adjusted to allow space for these characters.
27. A **floating dollar sign** prints to the left of the first significant digit of a field.
28. A **fixed dollar sign** prints in the same position regardless of the size of the value in a field.
29. The **SUB operation** subtracts the value in Factor 2 from the value in Factor 1 and places the difference in the Result Field.
30. The **MULT operation** multiplies the value in Factor 1 by the value in Factor 2 and places the product in the Result Field.
31. **Half-adjust** should be used whenever the maximum number of decimal places that can develop is greater than the number of decimal places allowed in the result field.
32. The **DIV operation** divides the value in Factor 1 by the value in Factor 2 and places the quotient in the Result Field.
33. The **MVR operation** places the remainder of the preceding DIV operation into the Result Field. The MVR operation must immediately follow a DIV operation and cannot be used if half-adjust was specified for the DIV operation.

REVIEW QUESTIONS

1. In what sequence are detail calculations normally executed?
2. How does a logic error differ from a syntax error?
3. What are comments used for on the Calculation Specifications form?
4. Name, and briefly explain, the eight types of RPG operations.
5. Explain the operation of the ADD statement.
6. What is the maximum length of a numeric data field?
7. What is a numeric literal?
8. What is the maximum length of a numeric literal?
9. What functions are automatically performed by all edit codes?
10. What two symbols may be used to identify a negative value on a printed report?
11. Explain the difference between a floating dollar sign and a fixed dollar sign.
12. Explain the operation of the SUB statement.
13. Explain the operation of the MULT statement.
14. When is a half-adjust entry needed?
15. Explain the operation of the DIV statement.
16. Explain the operation of the MVR statement.
17. Where must the MVR statement appear? If an MVR statement is used, what RPG function cannot be used?

STUDENT EXERCISES: RPG PROGRAM CODE

1. Code the calculation specification to subtract the contents of RETURN from the contents of SALES, placing the result in NETSAL. NETSAL is a 7-position field with two decimal positions. This calculation is to be done when indicator 46 is on.

2. Code the calculation specifications to multiply the value in HOURS by the value in RATE and place the result in GROSS. HOURS is a 3-position field with one decimal position. RATE is a 3-position field with two decimal positions. GROSS is to have two decimal positions. After the multiplication has been done, subtract the value in DEDUCT from GROSS and place the answer in NET. These calculations are to be done when indicator 22 is on.

3. Code the calculation specifications to divide the value in DISTNC by 3 and place the result in YARDS. Any remainder is to be placed in FEET. DISTNC is a 4-position field with no decimal positions. These operations are to be performed when indicator 01 is on.

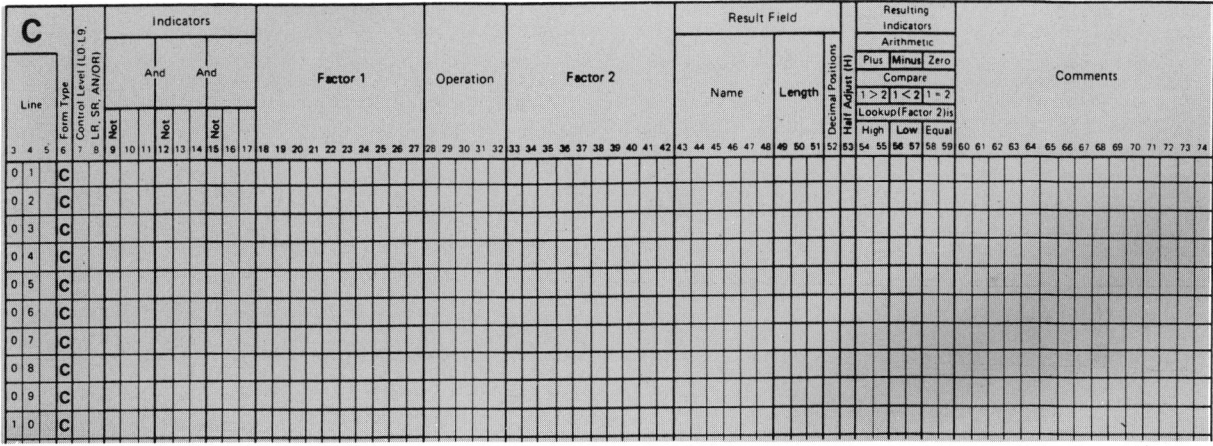

4. Code the calculation specifications to perform the following arithmetic operations. Use field names that relate to the data being defined.

a. Subtract CURRENT VALUE (7 positions, two decimal positions) from PURCHASE PRICE (8 positions, two decimal positions) giving DEPRECIATION.

b. Divide DEPRECIATION by YEARS OWNED (3 positions, no decimals) giving ANNUAL COST.

STUDENT EXERCISES: DEBUGGING RPG PROGRAMS

Problem 1

The following RPG program (Figure 3-54 on the next page) contains one or more errors detected by the compiler. Circle each error and record the corrected entry directly on the listing. Explain the error and the method of correction.

Figure 3-54   Debugging Problem 1

```
        5721RG1RG R05M00                  IBM SYSTEM/36 RPGII              06/14/91  11.34

              H                                                            HJG03X
   0001      FPAYFILE IP  F1200  60               DISK
   0002      FPAYREPT O   F 132 132        OF     PRINTER


   0003      IPAYFILE AA  01
   0004      I                                       1    4CEMPNO
   0005      I                                      11   30 NAME
   0006      I                                      40   44 REGERN
   0007      I                                      45   492OVTERN


   0008      C   01      REGERN    ADD  OVTERN    TOTERN  62       TOTAL EARNINGS
   0009      C   01      TOTPA     ADD  TOTERN    TOTPAY  72       ALL EMPLOYEES
   0010      C   01      EMPCNT    ADD  1         EMPCNT  40       EMPLOYEE COUNT


   0011      OPAYREPT H  206    1P
   0012      O           OR        OF
   0013      O                                    14 'HJG03X  DATE'
   0014      O                             UDATE Y 23
   0015      O                                    48 'E A R N I N G S'
   0016      O                                    62 'R E P O R T'
   0017      O                                    91 'PAGE'
   0018      O                             PAGE   96
   0019      O           H   1    1P
   0020      O           OR        OF
   0021      O                                    15 'EMPLOYEE'
   0022      O                                    77 'REGULAR         OVERTIME'
   0023      O                                    93 'TOTAL'
   0024      O           H   2    1P
   0025      O           OR        OF
   0026      O                                    14 'NUMBER'
   0027      O                                    36 'NAME'
   0028      O                                    61 'EARNINGS'
   0029      O                                    77 'EARNINGS'
   0030      O                                    95 'EARNINGS'
   0031      O           D   1    01
   0032      O                          EMPNO Z   13
   0033      O                          NAME      44
   0034      O                          REGERN1   60
   0035      O                          OVTERN1   76
   0036      O                          TOTERN1   95
   0037      O           T   2    LR
   0038      O                                    30 'TOTAL EMPLOYEES'
   0039      O                          EMPCNTZ   35
   0040      O                                    83 'TOTAL PAYROLL'
   0041      O                          TOTPAY1   95 '$'

              * * * * * E N D  O F  S O U R C E * * * * *
```

Figure 3-54 (1)

```
        5727RG1RG R05M00                  IBM SYSTEM/36 RPGII              06/14/91  11.41

   INDICATORS USED
       LR OF 1P 01

   RPG-0315 UNDEFINED FIELD NAMES
     STMT#  NAME
     0009  TOTPA

     FIELD NAMES USED
     STMT#  NAME   DEC  LNG   DISP
     0018  PAGE    0   0004   0136
     0014  UDATE   0   0006   00A7
     0004  EMPNO   0   0004   011C
     0005  NAME        0020   0113
     0006  REGERN      0005   0118
     0007  OVTERN  2   0005   0121
     0008  TOTERN  2   0006   0127
     0009  TOTPAY  2   0007   012E
     0010  EMPCNT  0   0004   0132

     ERROR NUMBER   STATEMENT NUMBER
       RPG-0207         0008
       RPG-0278         0034

     ERROR SEVERITY                           TEXT
   RPG-0207    T    FIELD TYPE, ALPHAMERIC OR NUMERIC, IS INVALID FOR OPERATION SPECIFIED.
   RPG-0278    T    EDIT CODES ARE INVALID WITH FIELDS OTHER THAN UNPACKED NUMERIC FIELDS OR WITH CONSTANTS OTHER
                    THAN CURRENCY SYMBOL.
   RPG-0315    T    FIELD NAME IS USED BUT NEVER DEFINED, OR TABLE NAME OR ARRAY ELEMENT IS USED AS AN ARRAY INDEX.

              * * * * * E N D  O F  C O M P I L E * * * * *
```

Figure 3-54 (2)

Problem 2

The following RPG program (Figure 3-55) contains one or more errors detected by the compiler. Circle each error and record the corrected entry directly on the listing. Explain the error and the method of correction.

Figure 3-55   Debugging Problem 2

```
       5727RG1RG R05M00                    IBM SYSTEM/36 RPGII                    06/14/91   11.56

               H                                                                        HJG03X


       0001      FPAYFILE IP  F1200  60              DISK
       0002      FPAYREPT O   F 132 132      OF      PRINTER


       0003      IPAYFILE AA
       0004      I                                        1   40EMPNO
       0005      I                                       11   30 NAME
       0006      I                                       40   442REGERN
       0007      I                                       45   4920VTERN


       0008      C   01      REGERN     ADD  OVTERN    TOTERN  62      TOTAL EARNINGS
       0009      C   01      TOTPAY     ADD  TOTERN    TOTPAY  72      ALL EMPLOYEES
       0010      C   01      EMPCNT     ADD  1         EMPCNT          EMPLOYEE COUNT


       0011      OPAYREPT H  206    1P
       0012      O         OR       OF
       0013      O                                14  'HJG03X   DATE'
       0014      O                        UDATE Y  23
       0015      O                                48  'E A R N I N G S'
       0016      O                                62  'R E P O R T'
       0017      O                                91  'PAGE'
       0018      O                        PAGE    96
       0019      O         H  1    1P
       0020      O         OR       OF
       0021      O                                15  'EMPLOYEE'
       0022      O                                77  'REGULAR        OVERTIME'
       0023      O                                93  'TOTAL'
       0024      O         H  2    1P
       0025      O         OR       OF
       0026      O                                14  'NUMBER'
       0027      O                                36  'NAME'
       0028      O                                61  'EARNINGS'
       0029      O                                77  'EARNINGS'
       0030      O                                95  'EARNINGS'
       0031      O         D  1    01
       0032      O                        EMPNO Z  13
       0033      O                        NAME     44
       0034      O                        REGERN1  60
       0035      O                        OVTERN1  76
       0036      O                        TOTERN1  95
       0037      O         T  2    LR
       0038      O                                30  'TOTAL EMPLOYEES'
       0039      O                        EMPCNTZ  35
       0040      O                                83  'TOTAL PAYROLL'
       0041      O                        TOTPAY1  95  '$'

        * * * * * E N D   O F   S O U R C E * * * * *
```

Figure 3-55 (1)

continued

```
            5727RG1RG R05M00              IBM SYSTEM/36 RPGII              06/14/91  11.56

     INDICATORS USED
            LR OF 1P 01

     RPG-0306 INDICATORS UNDEFINED
            01

     RPG-0315 UNDEFINED FIELD NAMES
       STMT#  NAME
        0010  EMPCNT
        0010  EMPCNT
        0039  EMPCNT

       FIELD NAMES USED
       STMT#  NAME   DEC  LNG   DISP
        0018  PAGE    0   0004  0132
        0014  UDATE   0   0006  00A7
        0004  EMPNO   0   0004  0117
        0005  NAME        0020  0113
        0006  REGERN  2   0005  011C
        0007  OVTERN  2   0005  0121
        0008  TOTERN  2   0006  0127
        0009  TOTPAY  2   0007  012E

       ERROR NUMBER   STATEMENT NUMBER
         RPG-0159          0003

       ERROR SEVERITY                              TEXT
       RPG-0159   W     MISSING RECORD-IDENTIFYING INDICATOR IN COLUMNS 19-20.
       RPG-0306   T     INDICATOR IS USED TO CONDITION OPERATIONS BUT IS NOT ASSIGNED.
       RPG-0315   T     FIELD NAME IS USED BUT NEVER DEFINED, OR TABLE NAME OR ARRAY ELEMENT IS USED AS AN ARRAY INDEX.

         * * * * * E N D   O F   C O M P I L E * * * * *
```

Figure 3-55 (2)

≡ Problem 3

The following RPG program (Figure 3-56) contains one or more errors detected while checking output from the program. Circle each error and record the corrected entry directly on the listing. Explain the error and method of correction.

Figure 3-56 Debugging Problem 3

```
            5727RG1RG R05M00              IBM SYSTEM/36 RPGII            ·06/14/91   12.09

            0001 H                                                               HJG03X


     0001  0002 FPAYFILE IP   F1200  60            DISK
     0002  0003 FPAYREPT O    F 132 132      OF    PRINTER


     0003  0004 IPAYFILE AA  01
     0004  0005 I                                     1   40EMPNO
     0005  0006 I                                    11   30 NAME
     0006  0007 I                                    40   442REGERN
     0007  0008 I                                    45   492OVTERN


     0008  0009 C    01     REGERN   ADD  OVTERN   TOTERN  62    TOTAL EARNINGS
     0009  0010 C    01     TOTPAY   ADD  TOTERN   TOTPAY  72    ALL EMPLOYEES
     0010  0011 C    01     EMPCNT   ADD  1        EMPCNT  40    EMPLOYEE COUNT
```

Figure 3-56 (1a)

```
0011   0012 OPAYREPT H    206      1P
0012   0013 O         OR           OF
0013   0014 O                              14 'HJG03X  DATE'
0014   0015 O             UDATE Y           23
0015   0016 O                              48 'E A R N I N G S'
0016   0017 O                              62 'R E P O R T'
0017   0018 O                              91 'PAGE'
0018   0017 O             PAGE             96
0019   0020 O         H  1      1P
0020   0021 O         OR           OF
0021   0022 O                              15 'EMPLOYEE'
0022   0023 O                              77 'REGULAR          OVERTIME'
0023   0024 O                              93 'TOTAL'
0024   0025 O         H  2      1P
0025   0026 O         OR           OF
0026   0027 O                              14 'NUMBER'
0027   0028 O                              36 'NAME'
0028   0029 O                              61 'EARNINGS'
0029   0030 O                              61 'EARNINGS'
0030   0031 O                              61 'EARNINGS'
0031   0032 O         D  1      01
0032   0033 O             EMPNO Z           13
0033   0034 O             NAME              44
0034   0035 O             REGERN1           60
0035   0036 O             OVTERN            76
0036   0037 O             TOTERN1           95
0037   0038 O         T  2      LR
0038   0039 O                              30 'TOTAL EMPLOYEES'
0039   0040 O             EMPCNTZ           35
0040   0041 O                              83 'TOTAL PAYROLL'
0041   0042 O             TOTPAY1           95


        * * * * * E N D   O F   S O U R C E * * * * *


        5727RG1RG R05M00              IBM SYSTEM/36 RPGII              06/14/91  12.09


INDICATORS USED
        LR OF 1P 01

  FIELD NAMES USED
  STMT#  NAME  DEC   LNG   DISP
  0018   PAGE   0    0004  0136
  0014   UDATE  0    0006  00A7
  0004   EMPNO  0    0004  0117
  0005   NAME        0020  0113
  0006   REGERN 2    0005  0110
  0007   OVTERN 2    0005  0121
  0008   TOTERN 2    0006  0127
  0009   TOTPAY 2    0007  012E
  0010   EMPCNT 0    0004  0132


        * * * * * E N D   O F   C O M P I L E * * * * *
```

Figure 3-56 (1b)

```
HJG03X  DATE  6/14/91            E A R N I N G S   R E P O R T                    PAGE    1

    EMPLOYEE                                 REGULAR        OVERTIME        TOTAL
     NUMBER                NAME              EARNINGS

        110        ABEL, WILLIAM             900.00          10000        1,000.00
        991        ALAN, ROGER                80.00          00500           85.00
        999        BLANCHARD, CHRIS          999.90          07890        1,078.80
       1004        DAVIS, ERIK               100.00          00000          100.00
       1025        ELAY, JESSE               125.75          05000          175.75
       2237        FARMER, JOHN              250.00          02500          275.00
       2240        FISHER, DAVID             312.09          03900          351.09
       2250        GARGAS, WILLIAM           999.00          05890        1,057.90
       2260        HARRIS, JERRY             543.40          08900          632.40
       2270        HART, STEVEN              534.80          08909          623.89
       2280        JAMES, JACK               677.39          09888          776.27
       2290        PINKHAM, TODD             198.08          00242          200.50
       3021        WILLIAMS, GEO             536.29          00000          536.29
       3056        WOOD, EMILE               567.20          04561          612.81
       3890        ZUKOWSKI, GEORGE           98.27          00000           98.27


        TOTAL EMPLOYEES   15                        TOTAL PAYROLL        7,603.97
```

Figure 3-56 (2)

Problem 4

The following RPG program (Figure 3-57) contains one or more errors detected while checking output from the program. Circle each error and record the corrected entry directly on the listing. Explain the error and method of correction.

Figure 3-57   Debugging Problem 4

```
     5727RG1RG R05M00                 IBM SYSTEM/36 RPGII              06/14/91  12.51

       0001 H                                                             HJG03X


  0001  0002 FPAYFILE IP  F1200  60          DISK
  0002  0003 FPAYREPT O   F 132 132     OF    PRINTER


  0003  0004 IPAYFILE AA  01
  0004  0005 I                                     1   40EMPNO
  0005  0006 I                                    11   30 NAME
  0006  0007 I                                    40  442REGERN
  0007  0008 I                                    45  492OVTERN


  0008  0009 C    01      REGERN    ADD  OVTERN    TOTERN  62       TOTAL EARNINGS
  0009  0010 C    01      TOTPAY    ADD  TOTERN    TOTPAY  72       ALL EMPLOYEES
  0010  0011 C    01      EMPCNT    ADD  1         EMPCNT  40       EMPLOYEE COUNT


  0011  0012 OPAYREPT H   206   1P
  0012  0013 O        OR        OF
  0013  0014 O                           14 'HJG03X   DATE'
  0014  0015 O                  UDATE Y   23
  0015  0016 O                           48 'E A R N I N G S'
  0016  0017 O                           62 'R E P O R T'
  0017  0018 O                           91 'PAGE'
  0018  0019 O                  PAGE      96
  0019  0020 O        H   1      01
  0020  0021 O        OR        OF
  0021  0022 O                           15 'EMPLOYEE'
  0022  0023 O                           77 'REGULAR       OVERTIME'
  0023  0024 O                           93 'TOTAL'
  0024  0025 O        H   2     1P
  0025  0026 O        OR        OF
  0026  0027 O                           14 'NUMBER'
  0027  0028 O                           36 'NAME'
  0028  0029 O                           61 'EARNINGS'
  0029  0030 O                           77 'EARNINGS'
  0030  0031 O                           95 'EARNINGS'
  0031  0032 O        D   1      01
  0032  0033 O                  EMPNO Z   13
  0033  0034 O                  NAME      44
  0034  0035 O                  REGERN1   60
  0035  0036 O                  OVTERN1   95
  0036  0037 O                  TOTERN1   76
  0037  0038 O        T   2      LR
  0038  0039 O                           30 'TOTAL EMPLOYEES'
  0039  0040 O                  EMPCNTZ   35
  0040  0041 O                           83 'TOTAL PAYROLL'
  0041  0042 O                  TOTPAY1   95 '$'

       * * * * * E N D  O F  S O U R C E * * * * *


     5727RG1RG R05M00                 IBM SYSTEM/36 RPGII              06/14/91  12.51

  INDICATORS USED
       LR OF 1P 01

   FIELD NAMES USED
  STMT#  NAME  DEC  LNG   DISP
   0018  PAGE   0   0004  0136
   0014  UDATE  0   0006  00A7
   0004  EMPNO  0   0004  0117
   0005  NAME       0020  0113
   0006  REGERN 2   0005  0110
   0007  OVTERN 2   0005  0121
   0008  TOTERN 2   0006  0127
   0009  TOTPAY 2   0007  012E
   0010  EMPCNT 0   0004  0132

       * * * * E N D  O F  C O M P I L E * * * *
```

Figure 3-57 (1)

```
HJG03X  DATE  6/14/91           E A R N I N G S   R E P O R T                    PAGE    1

      NUMBER                   NAME              EARNINGS          EARNINGS          EARNINGS

    EMPLOYEE                                      REGULAR          OVERTIME           TOTAL
      110             ABEL, WILLIAM               900.00          1,000.00           100.00
    EMPLOYEE                                      REGULAR          OVERTIME           TOTAL
      991             ALAN, ROGER                  80.00            85.00             5.00
    EMPLOYEE                                      REGULAR          OVERTIME           TOTAL
      999             BLANCHARD, CHRIS            999.90          1,078.80           78.90
    EMPLOYEE                                      REGULAR          OVERTIME           TOTAL
      1004            DAVIS, ERIK                 100.00           100.00             .00
    EMPLOYEE                                      REGULAR          OVERTIME           TOTAL
      1025            ELAY, JESSE                 125.75           175.75            50.00
    EMPLOYEE                                      REGULAR          OVERTIME           TOTAL
      2237            FARMER, JOHN                250.00           275.00            25.00
    EMPLOYEE                                      REGULAR          OVERTIME           TOTAL
      2240            FISHER, DAVID               312.09           351.09            39.00
    EMPLOYEE                                      REGULAR          OVERTIME           TOTAL
      2250            GARGAS, WILLIAM             999.00          1,057.90           58.90
    EMPLOYEE                                      REGULAR          OVERTIME           TOTAL
      2260            HARRIS, JERRY               543.40           632.40            89.00
    EMPLOYEE                                      REGULAR          OVERTIME           TOTAL
      2270            HART, STEVEN                534.80           623.89            89.09
    EMPLOYEE                                      REGULAR          OVERTIME           TOTAL
      2280            JAMES, JACK                 677.39           776.27            98.88
    EMPLOYEE                                      REGULAR          OVERTIME           TOTAL
      2290            PINKHAM, TODD               198.08           200.50             2.42
    EMPLOYEE                                      REGULAR          OVERTIME           TOTAL
      3021            WILLIAMS, GEO               536.29           536.29             .00
    EMPLOYEE                                      REGULAR          OVERTIME           TOTAL
      3056            WOOD, EMILE                 567.20           612.81            45.61
    EMPLOYEE                                      REGULAR          OVERTIME           TOTAL
      3890            ZUKOWSKI, GEORGE             98.27            98.27             .00

            TOTAL EMPLOYEES    15                           TOTAL PAYROLL    $7,603.97
```

Figure 3-57 (2)

STUDENT EXERCISES: PROGRAMMING IN RPG

PROGRAMMING ASSIGNMENT 1
REPAIR COST SUMMARY

INSTRUCTIONS

Plan, code, enter, and test an RPG program to produce the Repair Cost Summary Report.

INPUT

Input is the Repair Work Order file containing the job number, customer name, labor cost, and parts cost. The format of the Repair Work Order file is shown in Figure 3-58. Use test data set 4 for this problem.

1	5	6	10	11	15	16	20	21	25	26	30	31	35	36	40	41	45	46	50	51	55	56	60	61
		JOB NO. (N)		CUSTOMER NAME (A)																LABOR COST (N)		PARTS COST (N)		

Figure 3-58 Repair Work Order file

OUTPUT

Output is the Repair Cost Summary, the format of which is shown in Figure 3-59.

H 6	HJG031 XX/XX/XX			PAGE XX0X
H 7	REPAIR COST SUMMARY			
H 9	JOB	LABOR	PARTS	JOB
H 10	NO. CUSTOMER NAME	COST	COST	TOTAL
D 12	XXX XXXXXXXXXXXXXXXXXXXXXX	XX0.XX	XX0.XX	X,XX.XX
13	XXX XXXXXXXXXXXXXXXXXXXXXX	XX0.XX	XX0.XX	X,XX.XX
T-LR 16		XX,XX0.XX	XX,XX0.XX	XXX,XX.XX

Figure 3-59 Repair Cost Summary

◼ Processing Requirements

The Job Total field is the sum of the Labor Cost and Parts Cost fields. The program must accumulate and print final totals for the three cost fields.

◼ PROGRAMMING ASSIGNMENT 2
SALES REPORT

INSTRUCTIONS

Plan, code, enter, and test an RPG program to produce the Sales Report.

INPUT

Input is the Customer Sales file containing the customer number, item description, number of units purchased, unit cost, and rate of discount. Figure 3-60 shows the format of the Customer Sales file. Use test data set 5 for this problem.

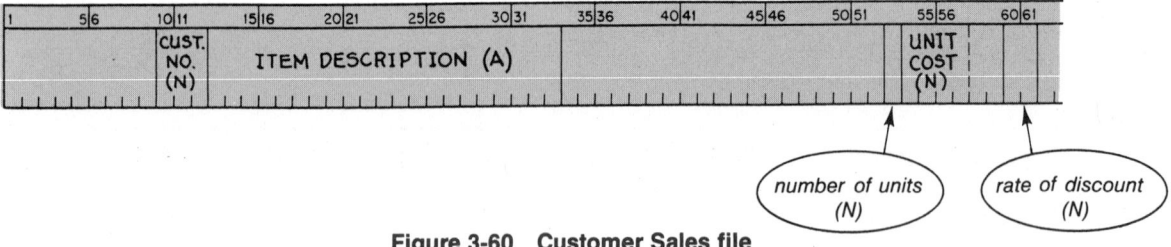

Figure 3-60 Customer Sales file

Output is the Sales Report, the format of which is shown in Figure 3-61.

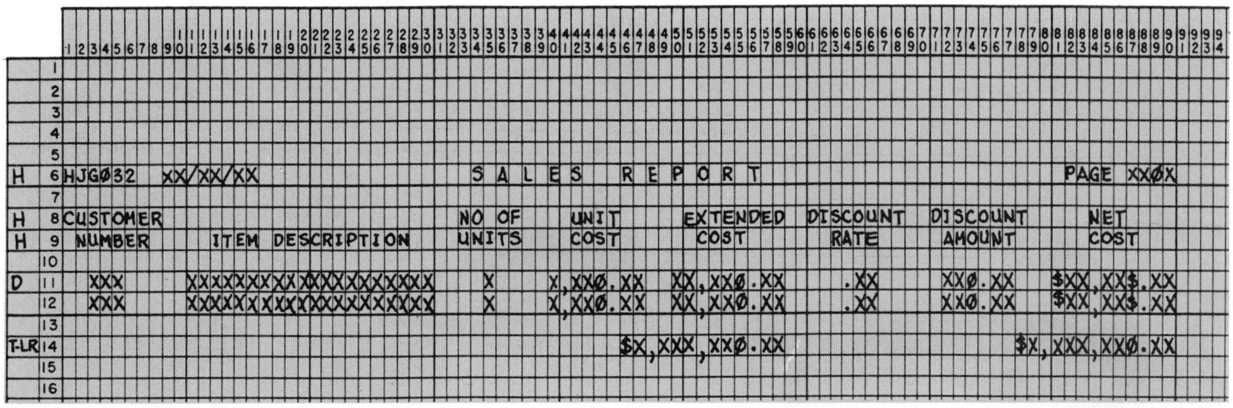

Figure 3-61   Sales Report

Processing Requirements

Extended cost is calculated by multiplying number of units by unit cost. Discount amount is the product of multiplying extended cost by rate of discount. Note that the rate of discount is a 2-position field with two decimal places. Net cost is obtained by subtracting discount amount from extended cost. The program must accumulate final totals for the Extended Cost and Net Cost fields.

PROGRAMMING ASSIGNMENT 3
ACCOUNT BALANCE REGISTER

INSTRUCTIONS

Plan, code, enter, and test an RPG program to produce the Account Balance Register.

INPUT

Input is the Account Status file containing account number, customer name, old balance, payment, and purchases. The format of the Account Status file is shown in Figure 3-62. Use test data set 6 for this problem.

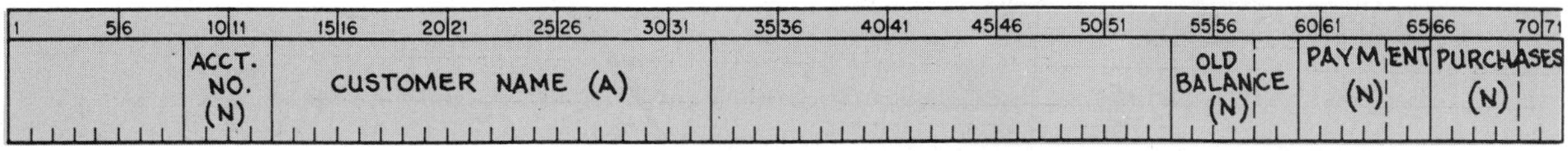

Figure 3-62   Account Status file

OUTPUT

Output is the Account Balance Register, the format of which is shown in Figure 3-63. Note the format of the final totals.

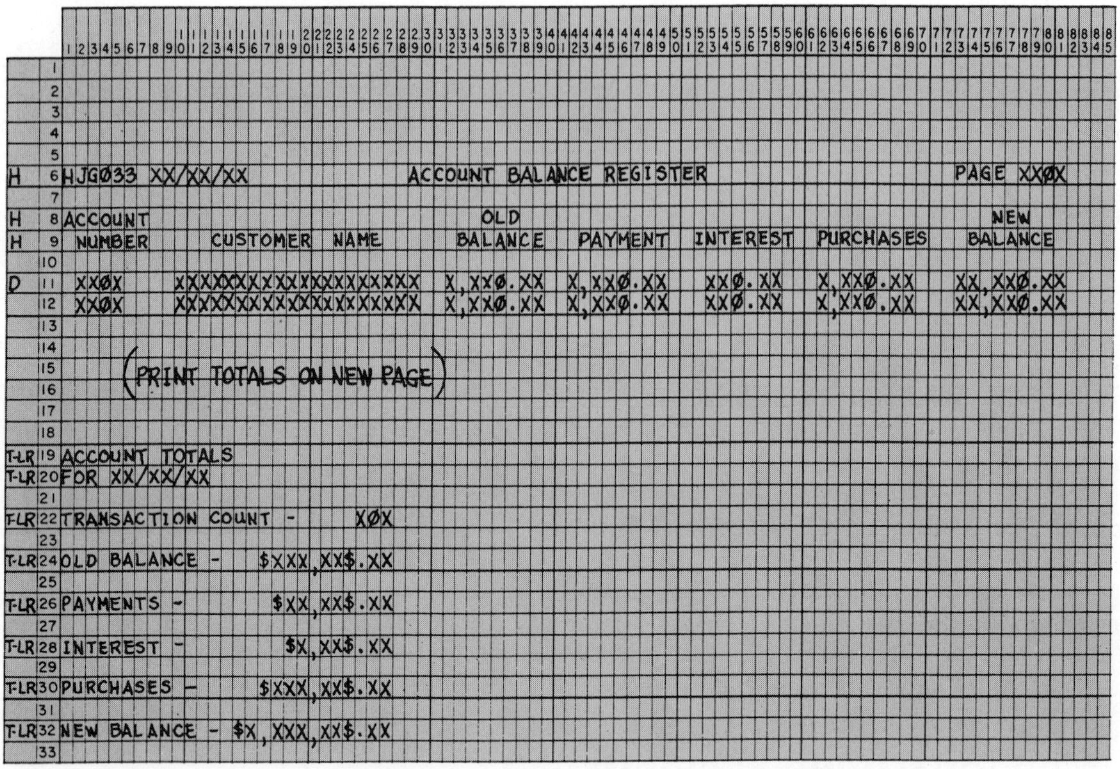

Figure 3-63 Account Balance Register

Processing Requirements

interest = (old balance – payment * 0.015)
new balance = old balance – payment + interest + purchases

PROGRAMMING ASSIGNMENT 4 CUSTOMER FINANCING REPORT

INSTRUCTIONS

Plan, code, enter, and test an RPG program to produce the Customer Financing Report.

INPUT

Input is the Finance Contract File containing customer number, customer name, invoice number, purchase amount, down payment, interest rate, and number of payments. The format of the Finance Contract file is shown in Figure 3-64. Use test data set 7 for this problem.

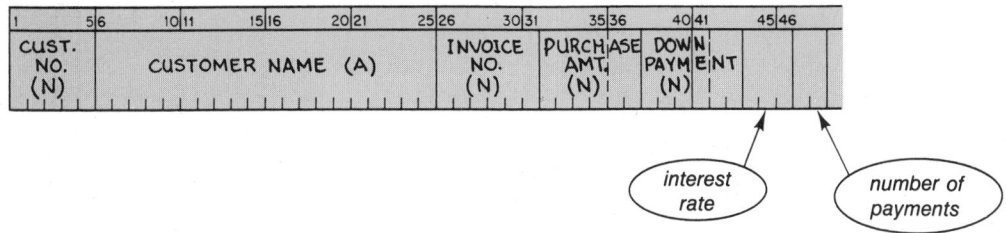

Figure 3-64   Finance Contract file

OUTPUT

Output is the Customer Financing Report, the format of which is shown in Figure 3-65. This report contains no final totals.

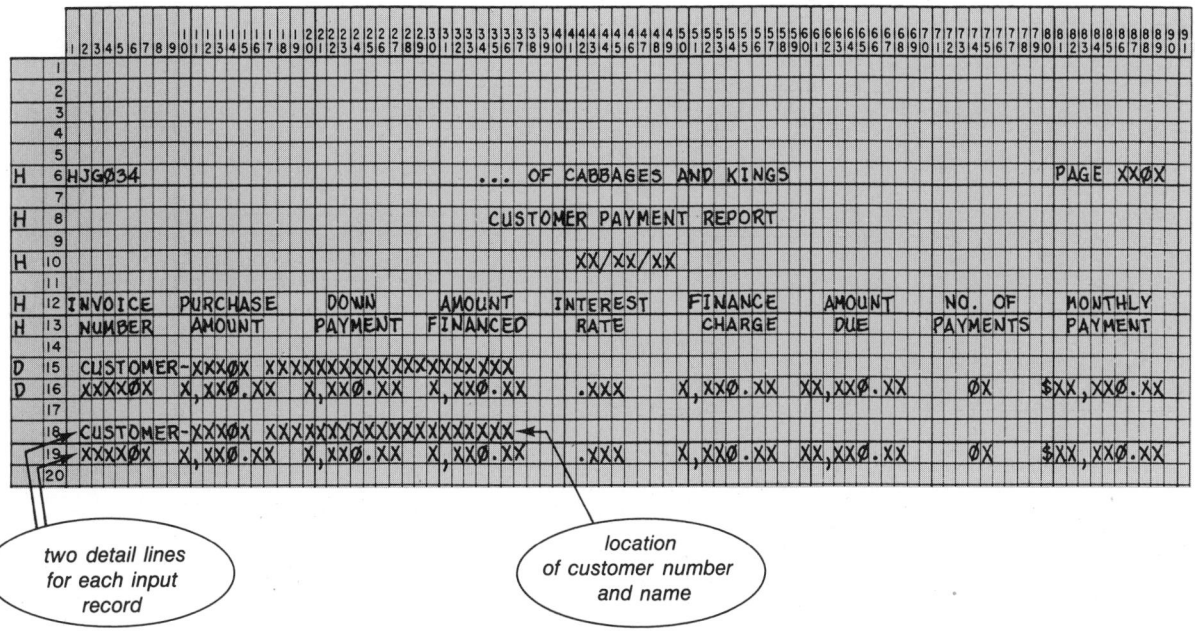

Figure 3-65   Customer Financing Report

▤ Processing Requirements

amount financed = purchase amount – down payment
finance charge = amount financed * interest rate
amount due = amount financed + finance charge
monthly payment = amount due / number of payments

F O U R

Comparing Operations & Internal Documentation

In Chapter 3 you learned to write programs that read a data record, performed arithmetic operations on the data in the record, accumulated final totals, and printed the results of the processing. In those programs, every record was treated identically; the same operations were performed on every record because the processing requirements were the same for every record. The program specifications did not require the use of one of the most powerful tools available to a programmer – conditional operations.

CONDITIONAL PROCESSING

Conditional operations enable you to control, based on the result of a previous operation, whether or not another operation is performed. Because of this ability, you can use the data in an input record to determine what processing is performed on that record. An example is found in payroll applications that compute the earnings of employees who are paid on an hourly basis.

An employee is paid at one-and-a-half times the usual pay rate for hours worked in excess of 40 per week (overtime hours). When an input record is read, the program determines if the employee has worked more than 40 hours. If this is the case, operations must be performed to determine how many overtime hours were worked. The pay for these hours must then be calculated at the overtime rate. If an employee worked 40 or less hours, the overtime calculations are not performed. Figure 4-1 is a flowchart of the logic of these conditional operations.

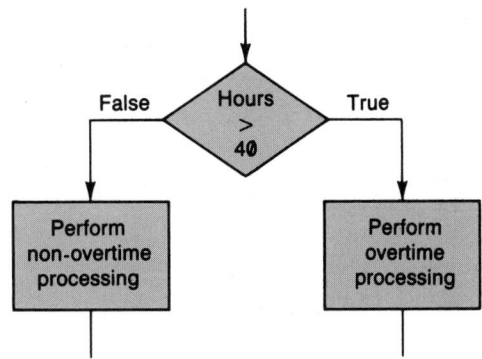

Figure 4-1   Conditional processing logic

In Chapter 1, you learned that flowcharts are not often used with RPG. Although this is true in the case of the overall RPG program, flowcharts are sometimes used to diagram or explain portions of the RPG calculations. Figure 4-1 shows a **condition**, or test, that is to be performed on the data. The test is expressed in the form of a statement: Hours > 40. The symbol > stands for the words **is greater than**. When an input record is read, if the Hours field contains a value greater than 40, the processing path labeled True is followed. If the Hours field does not contain a value greater than 40, the processing path labeled False is followed.

This example illustrates the concept of **conditional processing**. A test is made, and based on the result of this test, one of the possible paths, or groups of operations, is performed. You can see in Figure 4-1 that it is impossible for both sets of steps to be executed. A number can be either greater than 40 or not greater than 40. It cannot be both.

In this chapter, you will learn to write programs that use the compare operation to test data and set indicators based on the result of the comparison. You will learn to use these resulting indicators to control calculation operations and program output.

RPG COMPARING CONCEPTS

The RPG **compare operation** determines the relative values of two fields, or one field and one literal, and turns on one or more indicators to communicate the result of the comparison to the object program. RPG is able to determine if the values of the two fields are:

Equal   The value in field 1 is exactly the same as the value in field 2
Greater than   The value in field 1 is higher than the value in field 2
Less than   The value in field 1 is lower than the value in field 2

In RPG, the relationship between the two data fields is always expressed in terms of how field 1 relates to field 2. You would never say "field 2 is less than field 1." You would always say "field 1 is greater than field 2" because the RPG compare operation (COMP) always expresses the comparison result as Factor 1 is equal or greater than or less than Factor 2.

Notice that RPG always expresses the result of a comparison in a **positive** sense. RPG cannot turn on an indicator to show that two fields are not equal, but it can turn on an indicator to show that two fields are equal. If, after a compare operation is performed, the equal indicator is off, the two fields were not equal.

Comparison Restrictions

RPG syntax places a restriction on fields to be compared with one another: Both fields must be of the same data class, either numeric or alphameric. RPG does not permit the comparison of numeric data with alphameric data. If a compare operation contains fields of different data classes, the compiler generates an error message. This is a terminal error in most versions of RPG.

The way that RPG executes the comparison depends on the data class of the fields being compared and whether or not the data fields are of the same length.

Numeric Comparison

If both data fields are numeric, a **numeric comparison** is performed. Numeric comparisons are performed **algebraically**, that is, both the digit value and the sign of the number are compared by RPG. Because the comparison is algebraic, any negative value is lower than any positive value, regardless of the digit values. For example, a field containing a negative value of 99999 is lower than a field containing a positive value of 1.

In addition, RPG performs automatic **decimal alignment** of the two data fields based on the field definitions. RPG can properly position the implied decimal point in compare operations just as it does when performing arithmetic.

▸ **Equal-Length Numeric Data Fields** In the examples that follow, the contents of the YTDEXP (year-to-date expenditures) field are compared with the contents of the BUDGET (budgeted amount) field to illustrate the basic concepts of comparison.

In Figure 4-2, the contents of the YTDEXP and BUDGET fields are identical. Both fields contain the value 0326587.16, and both have a plus sign (+) over the rightmost digit to indicate that the values are positive numbers. When RPG compares these two values, the result of the compare indicates that the two fields are equal, so the program then processes data based on equal values.

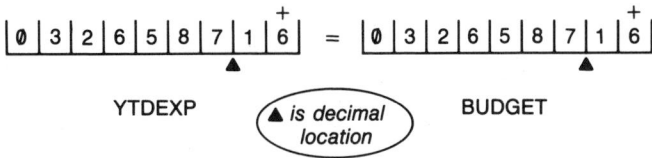

Figure 4-2   Numeric comparison: YTDEXP = BUDGET

In Figure 4-3, both fields contain positive numbers of different values. YTDEXP contains a value of 0009963.00, which is less than the value of 1000000.00 contained in BUDGET. The result of the compare would show that YTDEXP is less than BUDGET. Further processing could be based on this result. Just as the symbol = represents the words **is equal to**, the symbol < represents the words **is less than**.

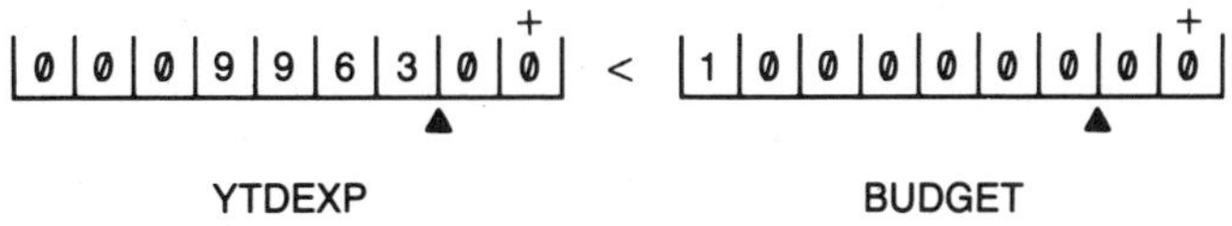

$$\boxed{0}\boxed{0}\boxed{0}\boxed{9}\boxed{9}\boxed{6}\boxed{3}\boxed{0}\boxed{\overset{+}{0}} \quad < \quad \boxed{1}\boxed{0}\boxed{0}\boxed{0}\boxed{0}\boxed{0}\boxed{0}\boxed{0}\boxed{\overset{+}{0}}$$

YTDEXP   BUDGET

Figure 4-3   Numeric comparison: YTDEXP < BUDGET

In Figure 4-4, YTDEXP contains a positive value of 2675316.84, which is greater than (>) the value of 2500000.00 stored in the BUDGET field.

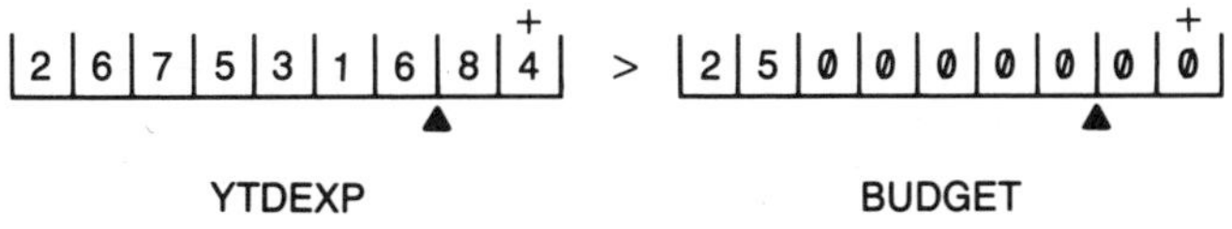

$$\boxed{2}\boxed{6}\boxed{7}\boxed{5}\boxed{3}\boxed{1}\boxed{6}\boxed{8}\boxed{\overset{+}{4}} \quad > \quad \boxed{2}\boxed{5}\boxed{0}\boxed{0}\boxed{0}\boxed{0}\boxed{0}\boxed{0}\boxed{\overset{+}{0}}$$

YTDEXP   BUDGET

Figure 4-4   Numeric comparison: YTDEXP > BUDGET

Figure 4-5 shows the result of the comparison of fields with different signs. Although the digit value in the AMT1 field (21346.88) is higher than the digit value in the AMT2 field (4136.53), AMT1 is less than AMT2 because AMT1 is a negative number. Again, in an algebraic comparison, any negative value is less than any positive value.

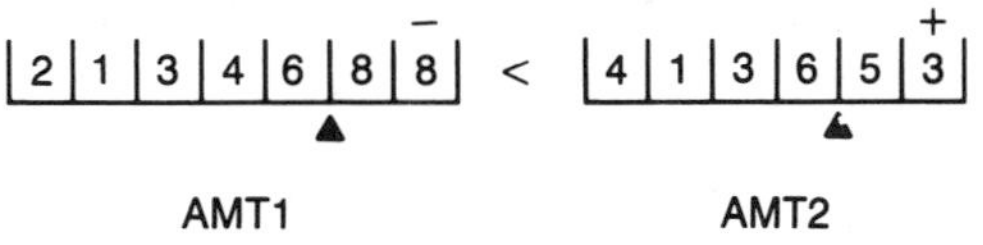

$$\boxed{2}\boxed{1}\boxed{3}\boxed{4}\boxed{6}\boxed{8}\boxed{\overset{-}{8}} \quad < \quad \boxed{4}\boxed{1}\boxed{3}\boxed{6}\boxed{5}\boxed{\overset{+}{3}}$$

AMT1   AMT2

Figure 4-5   Numeric comparison: AMT1 < AMT2

▸ **Unequal-Length Numeric Data Fields** Figures 4-6 and 4-7 illustrate RPG comparison of unequal-length numeric fields. Before the comparison takes place, RPG fills out the shorter of the two fields with zeros, thus making both fields the same length. The process by which the length of the shorter field is adjusted is called **filling**. The zeros that are attached to the field are referred to as **filled zeros**. Note that filling takes place before the compare is performed so that RPG always compares equal-length data fields. The filled version of the field is not, however, available to the programmer for use in any calculation operation or output record. After filling has been done, the comparison proceeds exactly as it would with fields of equal length. After the comparison is completed, the fill characters are automatically removed and the field restored to its original size. As Figure 4-6 shows, RPG fills two zeros to the left of AMT1 before the comparison is performed. In Figure 4-7, FIELDY is an integer field with no decimal positions. Before RPG performs the comparison against FIELDX, the object program fills two zeros to the right of the assumed decimal position.

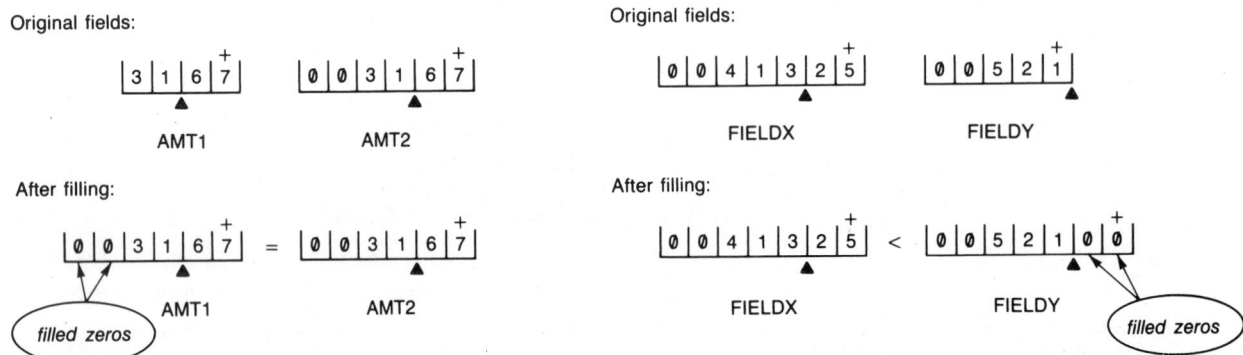

Figure 4-6 Filling of numeric data, left side

Figure 4-7 Filling of numeric data, right side

Figure 4-8 shows that RPG can fill both the left and the right sides of a field prior to the comparison, and Figure 4-9 illustrates that, in some cases, it is necessary for RPG to fill both fields before comparing them.

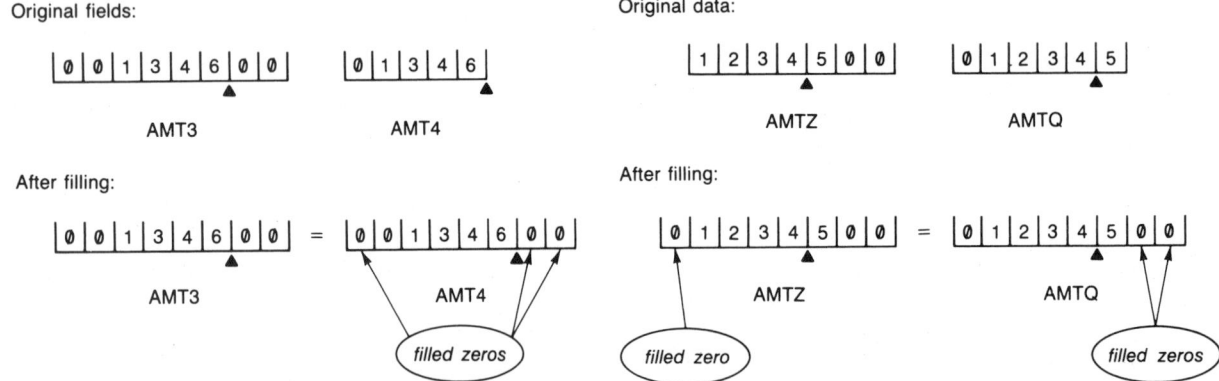

Figure 4-8 Filling of numeric data, both sides

Figure 4-9 Filling of numeric data, both sides

Alphameric Comparison

If both fields being compared are described with an alphameric data class, an **alphameric comparison** is performed. Alphameric comparisons are **left-justified**, which means that the leftmost positions of both fields are aligned, and the comparison proceeds from left to right, comparing one character at a time from each field until the comparison is complete. An alphameric comparison is complete when either of two conditions is detected by RPG:

1. The two characters being compared are not equal. RPG makes a greater than or less than determination and ends the comparison.
2. All characters have compared equally, and the end of both fields is reached. If this happens, the result of the comparison is equal.

▸ **Equal-Length Alphameric Data Fields** Figure 4-10 illustrates the comparison of two alphameric data fields. FLDA and FLDB are of equal length, and both contain the characters JOHNSTON. The comparison starts with the first character of each field, proceeds to the second character, then the third, and so on. When all positions have been compared and no unequal condition detected, the comparison is complete and the fields are determined to be equal.

▸ **Collating Sequence** In Figure 4-11, the fields are equal in length but contain different data. The first two characters (letters S and J) are not equal, but the result of comparing two letters is not as obvious as the comparison of two numbers. Is the letter S greater than or less than the letter J? The answer is found by referring to the collating sequence for your computer. The **collating sequence** for a computer is the order of characters from lowest value to highest value, which was determined when the computer was installed.

Every character stored in computer memory is stored in the form of a numeric code. The character that has the lowest numeric code value has the lowest order in the collating sequence. The character with the highest numeric code value has the highest collating sequence position. Figure 4-12 shows one widely used collating sequence. This figure is not a complete collating sequence but shows the most common characters: letters, numbers, and some punctuation characters. Although there is no need to memorize the collating sequence, a few general concepts are useful to remember:

A blank space has the lowest value of the characters shown.

All lowercase letters (a, b, ..., x, y, z) have lower values than all uppercase (A, B, ..., X, Y, Z) letters.

The beginning of the alphabet is lowest in value; the end of the alphabet is highest. For example, B is higher than A, C is higher than B, and so on. Likewise, m is higher than k, z is higher than x and so on.

Numbers are higher than letters, and, of course, zero is low and nine is high.

As the collating sequence shows, S is higher in value than J; therefore, the comparison in Figure 4-11 would result in NAME1 > NAME2. Remember that an alphameric comparison stops as soon as an unequal condition is found and that this result becomes the result of the comparison.

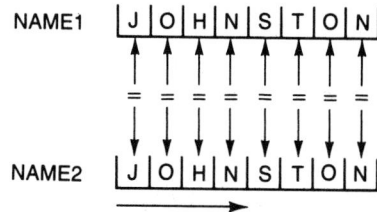

Figure 4-10 Alphameric comparison:
NAME1 = NAME2

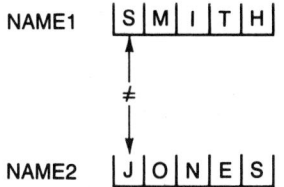

Figure 4-11 Alphameric comparison:
NAME1 > NAME2

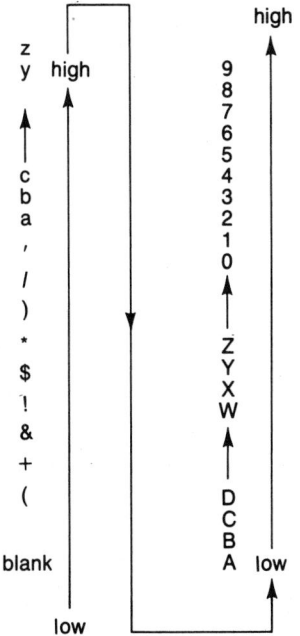

Figure 4-12 Collating sequence

▸ **Unequal-Length Alphameric Data Fields**   When unequal-length alphameric data fields are compared, the shorter of the two fields is filled automatically, as was the case with numeric data fields. However, because alphameric comparisons are left-adjusted, all filling is done to the right end of the shorter field. The fill character used with alphameric data is the blank, or space, character. Figure 4-13 illustrates the filling of a short field for alphameric comparison. As with numeric comparisons, the fill characters are automatically removed after the comparison, and the filled version of the field is not available to the programmer.

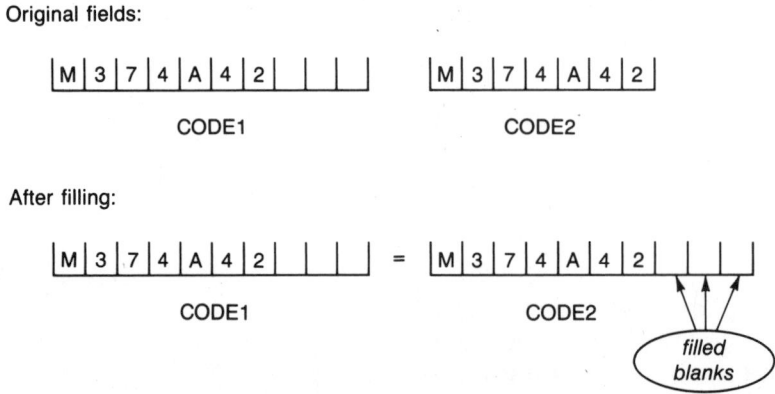

Figure 4-13   Filling of alphameric data

THE COMP OPERATION

To compare two values when programming in RPG, the **COMP** operation is specified on the Calculation Specifications form. Figure 4-14 is an example of the use of the COMP operation.

C	Form Type	Control Level (L0-L9, LR, SR, AN/OR)	Indicators						Factor 1	Operation	Factor 2	Result Field		Decimal Positions	Half Adjust (H)	Resulting Indicators			Comments
				And		And						Name	Length			Arithmetic			
			Not		Not		Not									Plus	Minus	Zero	
																Compare			
																1>2	1<2	1=2	
																Lookup(Factor 2)is			
																High	Low	Equal	
0 1	C		0 1						SALAMT	COMP	QUOTA					40	41	42	
0 2	C																		

Figure 4-14   Example of the COMP operation

When the compare operation (COMP) is performed, the contents of the field or the literal specified in Factor 1 are compared with the contents of the field or literal specified in Factor 2. The outcome of this operation can be used to set on indicators that have been specified in the **Resulting Indicators** area, positions 54–59.

In Figure 4-14, the value in the field SALAMT is compared with the value in the field QUOTA. Note that the field name SALAMT is placed in the Factor 1 area of the Calculation Specification form, positions 18–27, and the field name QUOTA is placed in the Factor 2 area, positions 33–42. Note that no entry is made in the Result Field area, positions 43–52, because the COMP operation does not use the Result Field area. The operation code to compare two values is COMP, which must be placed in positions 28–31 of the Calculation Specifications form.

When comparisons between the values in two fields are performed, there must be some indication of the results of the comparisons so that alternative processing can be based on the results. When you are programming in RPG, these results are indicated by use of the resulting indicators that are specified in positions 54–59 on the Calculation Specifications form. Note in the example that resulting indicator 40 has been entered in positions 54–55, resulting indicator 41 in positions 56–57, and resulting indicator 42 in positions 58–59.

In Figure 4-15, which shows again the resulting indicators used in Figure 4-14, you can see that three resulting conditions are possible after the comparison has taken place:

The value in Factor 1 is greater than the value in Factor 2: 1 > 2.
The value in Factor 1 is less than the value in Factor 2: 1 < 2.
The values in the two fields are equal: 1 = 2.

Resulting indicators are used so that the program can test for these conditions. As you have seen, a record identifying indicator was specified on the Input Specifications forms of previous sample programs to indicate the type of record that was read. This indicator can then be tested on the Calculation Specifications form and on the Output Specifications form to determine if calculations are to be performed or if data output records are to be written. The use of the record identifying indicator to control whether or not a calculation or output operation is to be performed is itself a form of conditional processing.

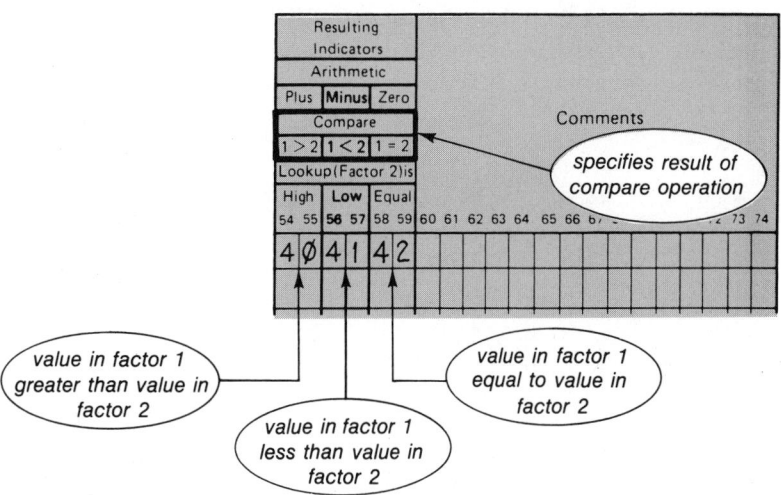

Figure 4-15   Resulting indicators

The resulting indicators from a COMP operation are used in a similar manner. Testing the status of a resulting indicator enables different processing to take place in the program.

In Figure 4-15, note that if the value in Factor 1 is greater than the value in Factor 2, indicator 40 is turned on. If the value in Factor 1 is less than the value in Factor 2, then indicator 41 is turned on, and if the fields contain equal values, indicator 42 is turned on.

The examples in Figure 4-16 give the status of these resulting indicators, which is based on the comparison that has taken place. Note that when one of the resulting indicators is on, the other resulting indicators are off. For example, as Example 1 in the figure shows, when the value in the area referenced by Factor 1 is greater than the value in the area referenced in Factor 2, resulting indicator 40 is turned on, and resulting indicators 41 and 42 are off. As you can see in Figure 4-16, only one resulting indicator may be turned on to show the result of a COMP operation.

Example 1:   Sales amount high (Factor 1 > Factor 2)

| 6 | 4 | 0 | 9 | 1 | > | 4 | 1 | 2 | 7 | 3 | Indicator 40 on
     SALAMT   QUOTA   Indicator 41 off
                                                   Indicator 42 off

Example 2:   Sales amount low (Factor 1 < Factor 2)

| 2 | 8 | 7 | 5 | 4 | < | 4 | 8 | 6 | 3 | 2 | Indicator 40 off
     SALAMT   QUOTA   Indicator 41 on
                                                   Indicator 42 off

Example 3:   Equal (Factor 1 = Factor 2)

| 1 | 7 | 3 | 5 | 4 | = | 1 | 7 | 3 | 5 | 4 | Indicator 40 off
     SALAMT   QUOTA   Indicator 41 off
                                                   Indicator 42 on

Figure 4-16   Resulting indicators from a COMP operation

Resulting Indicator Control of Calculations

Figure 4-17 illustrates the use of resulting indicators to control operations that are to be performed based on the result of a comparison. Recall that the entries made in the Indicators area, positions 9–17, are used to specify when an operation on the Calculation Specifications form is to be performed. Thus, in the example in Figure 4-17, the comparison takes place only when the 01 indicator is on. After the comparison, either indicator 40, 41, or 42 is on, depending on the results of the comparison. These indicators can then be specified in positions 9-17 to control other operations. The figure also shows that if the value in SALAMT is greater than the value in QUOTA, indicator 40 is turned on. When indicator 40 is on, the value in QUOTA is subtracted from the value in SALAMT. If the value in SALAMT is less than the value in QUOTA, indicator 41 is on and the value in SALAMT is subtracted from the value in QUOTA. Note that no operations are performed if the values are equal (indicator 42 is on). Thus, through the use of the indicators, different operations can be performed based upon the results of a comparison. Note that in this and the following examples any of the 99 general-purpose indicators could have been used.

Figure 4-17   Testing resulting indicators

Testing for Not-Equal Conditions

In some applications, it is necessary to perform alternative operations depending on whether the data in two fields are equal or not equal. As you have seen, the Calculation Specifications form does not have a Resulting Indicator area for not-equal. Instead, there are entries for Factor 1 greater than Factor 2, Factor 1 less than Factor 2, and Factor 1 equal to Factor 2. Two methods that can be used to test for an unequal condition are shown in Figures 4-18 and 4-19.

Figure 4-18   Testing for not-equal condition, method 1

Figure 4-19   Testing for not-equal condition, method 2

Note that in Figure 4-18 the value in the field CODEIN is compared with the value in the field LASTCD. If the value in CODEIN is either greater than or less than the value in LASTCD, then indicator 25 is turned on. The only other possibility is that the fields are equal. Therefore, by specifying the same indicator in both the Less Than area (positions 56–57) and the Greater Than area (positions 54–55) of the Calculation Specifications form, the **not-equal condition** can be tested. In the example in Figure 4-18, if the fields are not equal, the value in FLD1 is added to the value in FLD2, and the sum is stored in FLD3.

In Figure 4-19, the value in CODEIN is compared with the value in LASTCD. If the fields are equal, indicator 25 is turned on; if the fields are not equal, indicator 25 is not turned on. Therefore, to perform calculations when the fields are not equal, the entry N25 is specified in the Indicators area of line 02. This entry says that if indicator 25 is **NOT** on, perform the calculation; that is, if the fields are not equal, perform the calculation. The N in position 9 is used to indicate that a calculation is to be performed when the indicator is not on.

Literal Comparisons

It is also possible to specify alphameric or numeric literals in Factor 1 or Factor 2 when comparing. Figure 4-20 illustrates comparing the contents of the field referenced by MONTHS with the literal JANUARY and comparing the field SALES with the literal 1000.00.

Line	Form Type	Indicators	Factor 1	Operation	Factor 2	Result Field Name	Length	High	Low	Equal	Comments
01	C	Ø1	MONTHS	COMP	'JANUARY'					55	ALPHAMERIC
02	C										
03	C	Ø1	SALES	COMP	1ØØØ.ØØ				21		NUMERIC
04	C										

Figure 4-20 Comparing alphameric literals

▸ **Comparing Alphameric Literals** In line 01 of Figure 4-20, the field MONTHS is compared with the alphameric literal JANUARY, and if the fields are equal, indicator 55 is turned on. As the figure shows, an alphameric literal must be contained within apostrophes and a numeric literal cannot be contained within apostrophes. The apostrophes are not included in the comparison, that is, the value to be compared in Factor 2 is JANUARY, not 'JANUARY'. The apostrophes merely indicate that the literal is an alphameric literal. Although the Factor area is ten positions long, two of these positions are required for the apostrophes, making the maximum length of an alphameric literal eight positions.

Comparing Numeric Literals

In line 03 of Figure 4-20, the field SALES is compared with the numeric literal 1000.00. If SALES is less than 1000.00, indicator 21 is turned on. The decimal point included in the 1000.00 is used to indicate where the decimal point is assumed to be. The value in SALES does not have to include a decimal point to be equal to the literal. The value actually compared with SALES is 100000, with two zeros to the right of the assumed decimal place. RPG automatically removes the decimal point from the numeric literal after decimal alignment is performed, and the comparison proceeds as an ordinary numeric comparison.

Figure 4-21 summarizes the COMP operation.

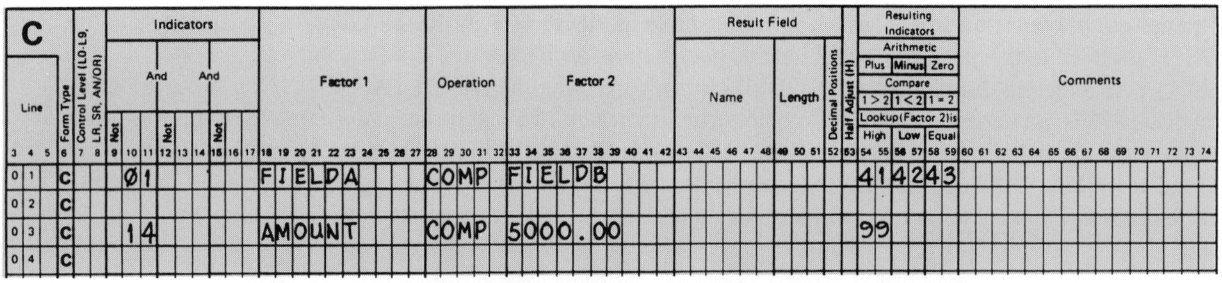

C		Indicators		Factor 1	Operation	Factor 2	Result Field			Resulting Indicators			Comments
Line	Form Type / Control Level (L0-L9, LR, SR, AN/OR)	And (Not)	And (Not) (Not)	Factor 1	Operation	Factor 2	Name	Length	Decimal Positions / Half Adjust (H)	Arithmetic: Plus / Minus / Zero; Compare 1>2 1<2 1=2; Lookup(Factor 2)is High Low Equal			Comments
0 1	C	Ø1		FIELDA	COMP	FIELDB				41 42 43			
0 2	C												
0 3	C	14		AMOUNT	COMP	5000.00				99			
0 4	C												

COMP Operation Summary

The COMP operation compares the value in Factor 1 against the value in Factor 2. Both factors must have the same data class. Fields are automatically aligned prior to the comparison. At least one resulting indicator must be specified. Comparison results are as follows:

High Factor 1 > Factor 2
Low   Factor 1 < Factor 2
Equal Factor 1 = Factor 2

Control Level Indicators	Indicators	Factor 1	Operation Name	Factor 2	Result Field	Resulting Indicators		
7–8	9–17	18–27	28–32	33–42	43–53	54–55	56–57	58–59
optional	optional	required	COMP	required	blank	optional	optional	optional

one required

Figure 4-21   COMP operation summary

ANALYSIS OF SAMPLE PROBLEM HJG04X: Inventory Status Report

Input

Input for the sample problem is the Inventory file; its format is shown in Figure 4-22. Each inventory record is 38 characters long and contains the stock number, unit cost, previous quantity on hand, quantity shipped, quantity received, and re-order point. The field in positions 1-8, even though it is named Stock Number, is an alphameric data field.

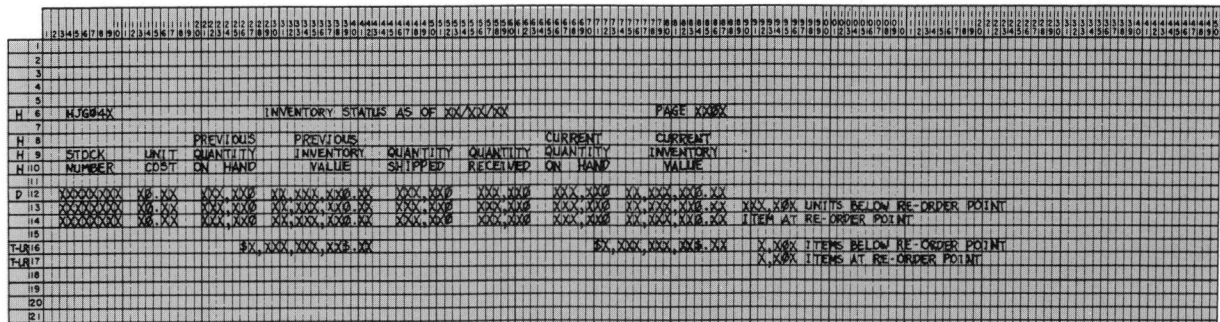

Figure 4-22 Inventory file layout

Output

The output of the sample problem is the Inventory Status Report (Figure 4-23). The four quantity fields show the zero-suppression zero in the rightmost position of the output area. This indicates that if the field consists of all zeros, the field is to be completely zero suppressed. That is, nothing is to print for a zero balance.

Figure 4-23 Inventory status report layout

Processing Steps

The data for the new fields created by the program is to be developed as follows:

previous inventory value = previous quantity on hand * unit cost
current quantity on hand = previous quantity on hand – quantity shipped + quantity received
current inventory value = current quantity on hand * unit cost

The program accumulates final totals of the previous and current inventory values.

If the current quantity on hand is equal to or less than the reorder point quantity, the program generates a message beginning in position 90 of the print line, as shown on lines 13 and 14 of the printer spacing chart. If an item develops a current quantity that is less than the reorder point, the generated message indicates the difference between the current quantity and the reorder point. The difference prints in positions 90–96 as shown on line 13.

The word **if** in the preceding paragraph is your clue that the solution to the problem requires the use of conditional statements or conditional processing techniques. When you read a set of problem specifications, make special note of instructions that begin with the words *if* or *when*. Instructions beginning with these words usually require conditional techniques.

The program accumulates counts of the number of items (input records) that develop a current quantity equal to the reorder point and the number of items that generate a current quantity below the reorder point.

≡ Program Logic

This problem requires no additional RPG logic cycle steps. However, the RPG logic cycle, shown in Figure 4-24, now includes one additional statement: Step 12 now includes the statement "Set resulting indicators" to permit the setting of resulting indicators by the COMP operation. All the conditional operations required to program this problem are performed during step 12 (detail calculations) and step 1 (detail output).

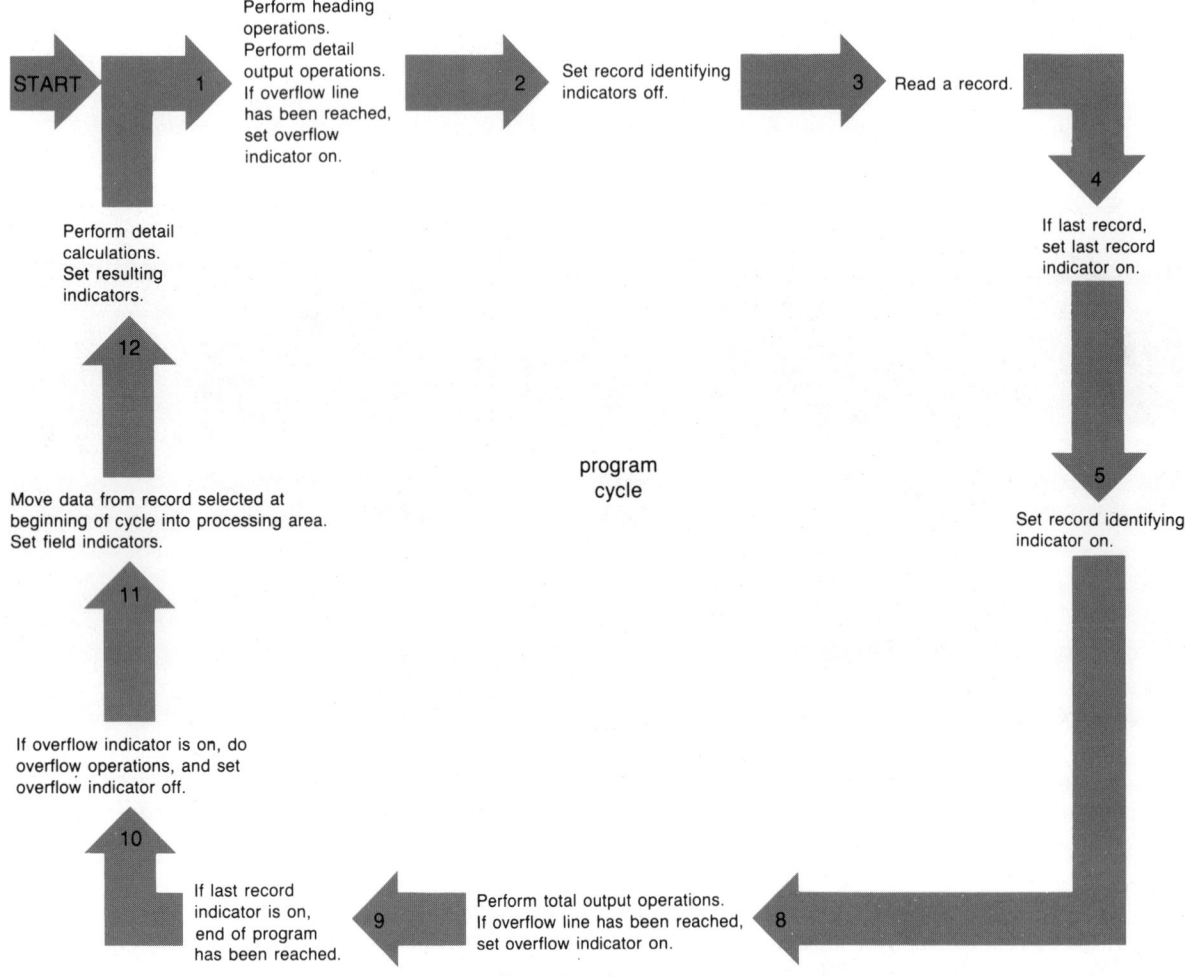

Figure 4-24 RPG fixed logic cycle

≡ CONTROL AND FILE DESCRIPTION SPECIFICATIONS ≡ FOR PROGRAM HJG04X

The Control and File Description specifications for program HJG04X, Inventory Status Report, contain no new programming specifications. However, this sample program does include internal program documentation. Recall from Chapter 1, that internal documentation is used to provide information about the program to anyone working with the actual program code. Internal documentation is important to maintenance programmers as well as to the original program authors.

▤ Comment Lines

Internal documentation is placed in a program by using comment lines. A **comment line** is identified to the RPG compiler by an asterisk (*) in position 7. Comment lines are printed on the compiler listing but are not translated into object program code. Comment lines, therefore, have no effect on the object program that is generated by the compilation process.

Figure 4-25 shows the Control and File Description Specification form. You can see that lines 02–10 of the file description specifications comprise a comment box that contains the name of the program, the name of the programmer, the date the program was written, and a brief description of the function of the program. The placement of comments is arbitrary. RPG accepts comments at any point in the program, with one exception: Some versions of RPG require that the first record read as part of the source program be the control specification. Because of this, the example shows the comment box placed after the control specification which works in all versions of RPG.

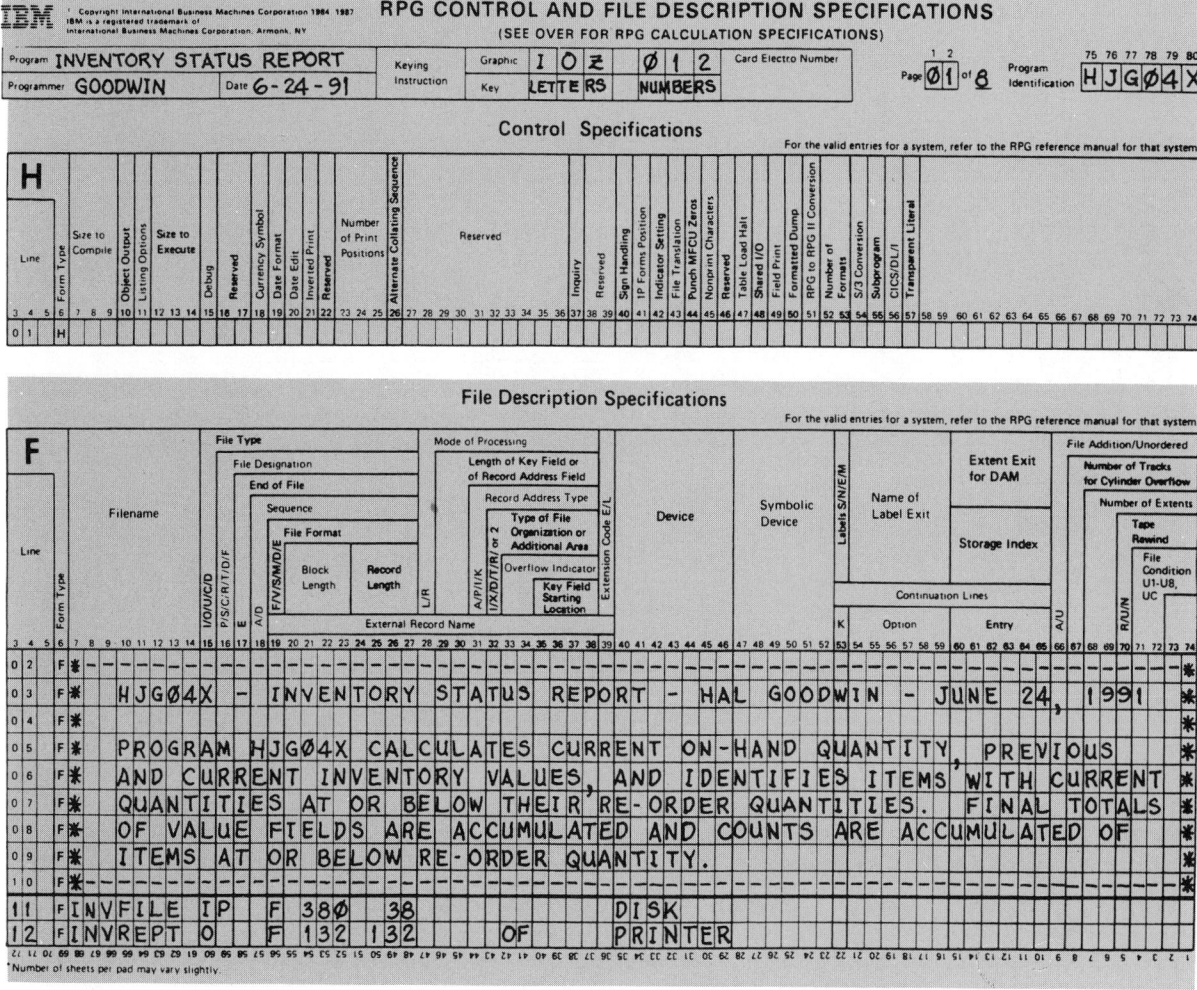

Figure 4-25 RPG Control and File Description specifications

▸ **RPG Indicator Summary**   Page 02 of program HJG04X (Figure 4-26) shows an RPG form that you have not used before. This form is the RPG **Indicator Summary** form, which is a comment form, not a program coding form. The Indicator Summary form is used to record, for internal documentation, the indicators used in the program and their assigned functions; it also provides a work sheet for the programmer while the program is being written.

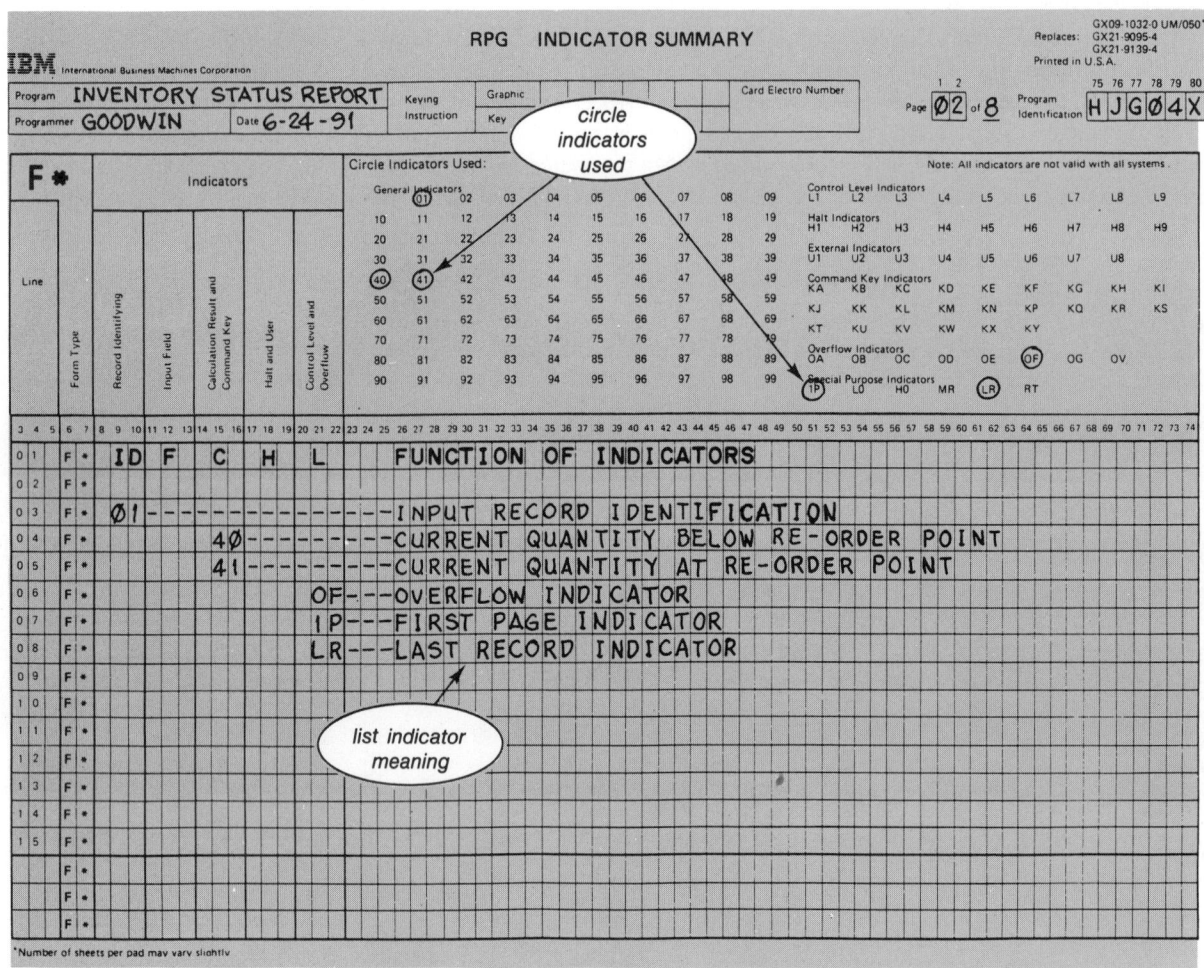

Figure 4-26   RPG Indicator Summary form

Every time an indicator is assigned during the coding of the program, the name of the indicator is circled at the top of the form, and the indicator function is written below. This record of indicator function prevents the accidental use of an indicator for two different functions. Each indicator used in an RPG program should have one, and only one, meaning or function.

Because the indicator summary consists of comments only (note that the asterisk is preprinted in position 7), it could be placed anywhere in the source program by changing the Form Type entry in position 6. Usually, however, the indicator summary is placed at or near the beginning of the source code. This is why form type F is preprinted on the form. If a programmer chooses to place these comments elsewhere in the program, perhaps at the beginning of the calculations, the Form Type entry must be changed.

The indicator summary is written at the same time as the program code. You should not attempt to write the summary first and then proceed to code the RPG program. Instead, keep the Indicator Summary form to one side, code your program in the usual way, and make an Indicator Summary entry whenever you first assign a meaning to an indicator. When the program code is complete, place the Indicator Summary form at the desired point in the coding sheet sequence.

INPUT SPECIFICATIONS FOR PROGRAM HJG04X

No new Input Specifications (Figure 4-27) entries are required for this program. Note, however, the use of comments on lines 01, 02, and 03 to provide an identifier for the input record description. Also note that although the data field in positions 1–8 of the input record is called 'Stock Number' (see Figure 4-22), it is described as an alphameric data field. Remember that fields should be described as numeric only if they are to be used in arithmetic operations or if they are to be edited as part of the output. Because the program specifications require neither arithmetic nor editing for Stock Number, it is described as an alphameric data field.

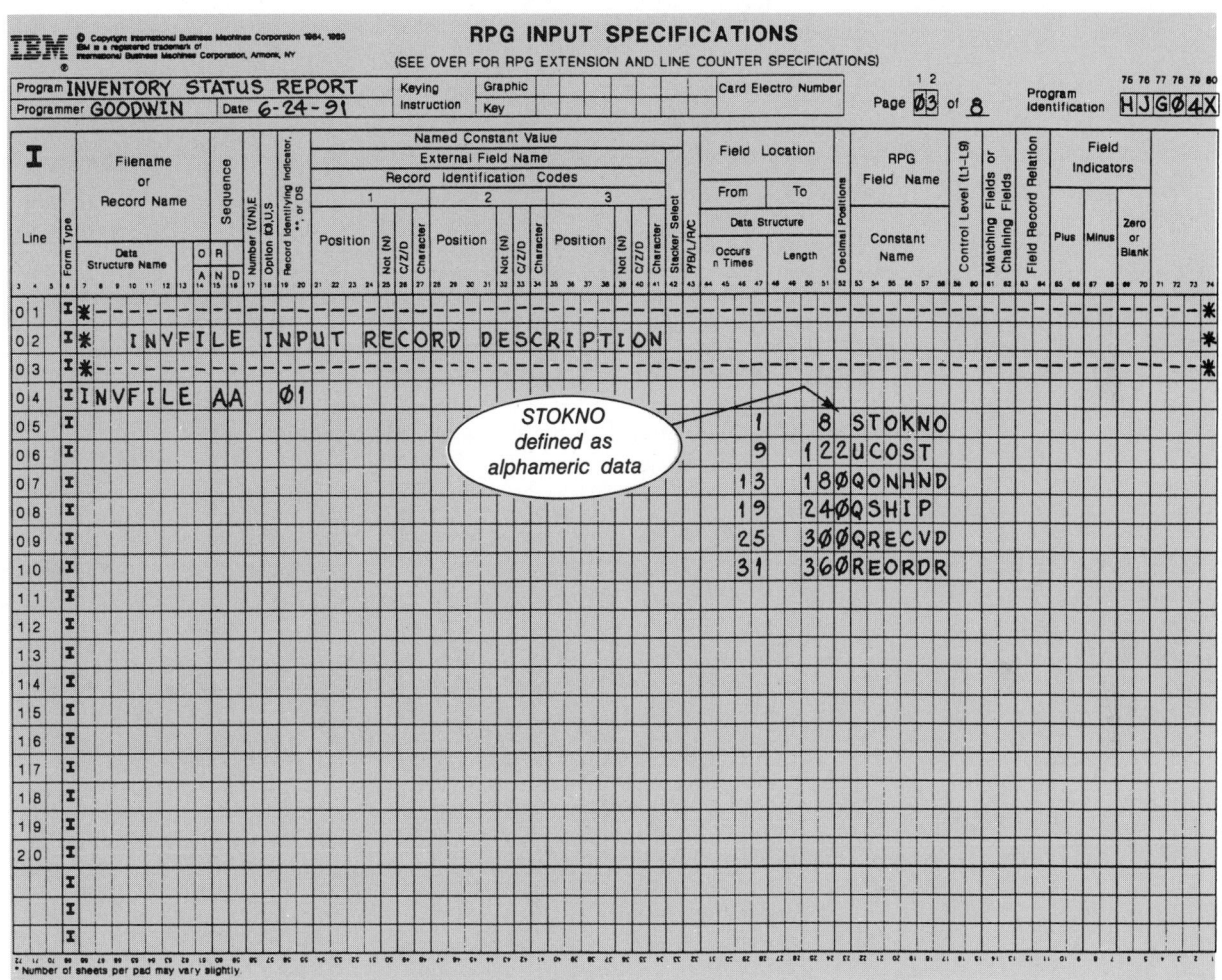

Figure 4-27   RPG Input specifications

CALCULATION SPECIFICATIONS FOR PROGRAM HJG04X

Figures 4-28 and 4-29 show Calculation Specifications forms for the sample program. These sets of calculations are identical in function. Figure 4-28 on the next page shows the calculations written in the RPG standard format, and Figure 4-29 shows the same calculations written in the enhanced format.

The only difference between these formats appears on lines 06, 12, 13, 14, and 15. Recall that Factor 1 can be eliminated in the enhanced format when an arithmetic operation requires that Factor 2 be added to the result field. Other than this, there is no difference between the two sets of calculation specifications. (The enhanced format is shown for illustration only; the remainder of this chapter uses the standard format calculation specifications.)

RPG CALCULATION SPECIFICATIONS
(SEE OVER FOR RPG CONTROL AND FILE DESCRIPTION SPECIFICATIONS)

Program: INVENTORY STATUS REPORT
Programmer: GOODWIN   Date 6-24-91
Page 04 of 8   Program Identification HJG04X

Line	Form Type	Control Level	Indicators And Not / And Not	Factor 1	Operation	Factor 2	Result Field Name	Length	Dec	Resulting Indicators	Comments
01	C*			———————						*	
02	C*			STANDARD FORMAT CALCULATIONS						*	
03	C*			———————						*	
04	C		01	QONHND	MULT	UCOST	PVAL	102			PREVIOUS VALUE
05	C		01	QONHND	SUB	QSHIP	QCURNT	60			
06	C		01	QCURNT	ADD	QRECVD	QCURNT				CURRENT QTY.
07	C		01	QCURNT	MULT	UCOST	CVAL	102			CURRENT VALUE
08	C*										
09	C		01	QCURNT	COMP	REORDR				4041	CHECK RE-ORDER
10	C		01 40	REORDR	SUB	QCURNT	UBELOW	60			UNITS UNDER
11	C*										
12	C		01	PVALLR	ADD	PVAL	PVALLR	122			ADD TO FINAL
13	C		01	CVALLR	ADD	CVAL	CVALLR	122			TOTAL
14	C		01 40	LOWLR	ADD	1	LOWLR	40			ACCUMULATORS
15	C		01 41	RORDLR	ADD	1	RORDLR	40			

Figure 4-28   RPG Calculation specifications, standard format

RPG CALCULATION SPECIFICATIONS
(SEE OVER FOR RPG CONTROL AND FILE DESCRIPTION SPECIFICATIONS)

Program: INVENTORY STATUS REPORT
Programmer: GOODWIN   Date 6-24-91
Page 04 of 8   Program Identification HJG04X

Line	Form Type	Control Level	Indicators And Not / And Not	Factor 1	Operation	Factor 2	Result Field Name	Length	Dec	Resulting Indicators	Comments
01	C*			———————						*	
02	C*			ENHANCED FORMAT CALCULATIONS						*	
03	C*			———————						*	
04	C		01	QONHND	MULT	UCOST	PVAL	102			PREVIOUS VALUE
05	C		01	QONHND	SUB	QSHIP	QCURNT	60			
06	C		01		ADD	QRECVD	QCURNT				CURRENT QTY.
07	C		01	QCURNT	MULT	UCOST	CVAL	102			CURRENT VALUE
08	C*										
09	C		01	QCURNT	COMP	REORDR				4041	CHECK RE-ORDER
10	C		01 40	REORDR	SUB	QCURNT	UBELOW	60			UNITS UNDER
11	C*										
12	C		01		ADD	PVAL	PVALLR	122			ADD TO FINAL
13	C		01		ADD	CVAL	CVALLR	122			TOTAL
14	C		01 40		ADD	1	LOWLR	40			ACCUMULATORS
15	C		01 41		ADD	1	RORDLR	40			
16	C										
17	C										
18	C										
19	C										
20	C										

factor 1 unused on lines 06, 12, 13, 14, 15

Figure 4-29   RPG Calculation specifications, enhanced format

▤ Calculation Comments

The calculation specifications for program HJG04X contain several different forms of internal documentation. Lines 01, 02, and 03 provide three comment lines for identifying the calculations. These comments have been used in the sample problem to differentiate between the standard and the enhanced format calculations.

In addition, the Comments area (positions 60–74) provides information about several of the calculations. The Comments area entries on lines 04, 06, 07, and 10 identify the contents of the result field developed in each of these calculations, and the Comments entries on lines 12, 13, and 14 identify the function of the group of calculations on lines 12–15. The Comments entry CHECK REORDER on line 09 shows that this line compares the reorder point.

The use of **blank comments** on lines 08 and 11 merely provides visual separation to make the calculations easier to read.

▤ Calculation Operations

The specifications for program HJG04X require that the calculations develop eight new fields. The first six calculations develop the fields that are printed as part of the detail line, and the last four calculations develop the Final Total fields.

In these two groups of calculations, the new fields have been developed in a **left-to-right** order. Although, because of program specifications, this is not always possible, it is good programming practice to work top-to-bottom and left-to-right when possible. All calculations are controlled by the record identifying indicator 01 (Figure 4-29) and therefore can be performed every time an input record is read.

▸ **Lines 04, 05, 06, and 07** These four lines develop the Previous Inventory Value, Current Quantity on Hand, and Current Inventory Value fields. Two calculations are required to develop the Current Quantity on Hand field. RPG does not have the ability to perform two different arithmetic functions, such as addition and subtraction, in a single operation. There is no RPG equivalent of COBOL's Compute statement or BASIC's Let statement. Also unlike those statements, RPG arithmetic statements cannot do arithmetic with more than two factors.

Statement 05 subtracts the quantity shipped from the previous quantity on hand and places the difference in the Current Quantity on Hand field. Statement 06 then adds the quantity received to the value stored in the Current Quantity on Hand field. Notice that QCURNT is defined on line 05 and used again as the result field on line 06. The length and data class of QCURNT are specified only the first time QCURNT is used as a Result Field entry.

▸ **Line 09** Line 09 compares the value in QCURNT with the value in REORDR (the reorder point for the item). If the value in QCURNT is less than the value in REORDR, indicator 40 turns on. If the value in QCURNT is equal to the value in REORDR, indicator 41 turns on. These indicators will be used to control further calculations and output operations. Note that if the value in QCURNT is greater than the value in REORDR, neither indicator turns on.

Resulting indicators used in COMP operations are automatically turned off by RPG immediately before the comparison is made. Then, depending on the result of the comparison, one resulting indicator may turn on. In this program, if the value in QCURNT is greater than the value in REORDR, no resulting indicator is on after the comparison.

A resulting indicator turned on by a COMP operation stays on until the same operation is performed again, or until the programmer turns the indicator off by using one of the indicator control operations, SETOF. The use of the SETOF operation is described later in this chapter.

▸ **AND Relationship of Indicators** Line 10 is controlled by two indicators: indicator 01 in positions 10–11 and indicator 40 in positions 13–14. Because these two indicators appear on the same line as the calculation, they must BOTH be on for the calculation to be performed. This relationship, in which two or more indicators must all be on for an operation to be performed is called an **AND relationship**. The AND relationship links two or more indicators that must all be on for the desired result to occur.

Figure 4-30 shows several examples of the use of the AND relationship to control operations on the Calculation Specifications form. Example One shows the use of three indicators to control an operation. For the MULT operation, indicators 43, 02, and 51 must be on. If one or more of these indicators are not on, the MULT operation is not performed. Note that multiple indicators in an AND relationship do not have to be coded in any particular order.

Line	Form Type	Control Level	And Not	And Not	Not	Factor 1	Operation	Factor 2	Result Field Name	Length	Dec	H	Comments
01	C*		EXAMPLE ONE										
02	C		43	02	51	RATE	MULT	1.5	OTRATE	52		H	
03	C*												
04	C*		EXAMPLE TWO										
05	C		48										
06	C AN		49	61	53	GROSS	SUB	DEDUCT	NET	82			
07	C*												
08	C*		EXAMPLE THREE										
09	C		04	31	16								
10	C AN		44	53	54								
11	C AN		62	12	38	AMT1	DIV	AMT2	AMT3	52		H	
12	C*												
13	C*		EXAMPLE FOUR										
14	C		35	N18	27	TOTAL	COMP	10000					99
15	C*												
16	C*		EXAMPLE FIVE										
17	C		N03	N05		TOTAL1	ADD	1	TOTAL1	40			
18	C												
19	C												
20	C												

Figure 4-30   AND relationship examples

Example Two shows four indicators being used to control a calculation. Because there is only room for three indicators on a calculation line, two lines must be linked. Placing **AN** in positions 7–8 of line 06 links lines 05 and 06 and extends indicator capability. All four indicators (48, 49, 53, and 61) must be on for the subtraction to be performed. Most versions of RPG permit the linking of up to seven lines in an AND relationship, thus making it possible to use up to 21 indicators to control an operation.

Example Three links three lines containing nine indicators to control a DIV operation. Note that the AN entry is not used on the first of the three lines. If the program requires that the DIV operation be followed by an MVR operation, the same indicators are used to control the MVR.

Example Four shows that you can control calculations by requiring that indicators be off as well as on. For the COMP to be executed, indicators 35 and 27 must be on and indicator 18 must be off. The entry N in position 9, 12, or 15 represents the word NOT. The NOT entry specifies that the indicator must NOT be on for the operation to be performed. Although it is valid to control operations by both on and off indicators, there is one circumstance (see Example Five) that you should avoid.

Example Five shows the control of a calculation by two indicators, both of which must be off for the operation to be performed. Because RPG turns all general-purpose indicators off at the beginning of program execution, controlling an operation by the use of all N indicators is the same as using no indicators at all to control the operation. This results in the operation being performed every time the RPG logic cycle reaches a calculation point and can cause undesired results. *Every RPG operation should be controlled by at least one on indicator.*

▸ **OR Relationship of Indicators** You are already familiar with the OR relationship. You have been using the OR relationship to control output heading lines in all programming examples so far. The programs have printed heading lines if either indicator 1P **OR** indicator OF was on. The **OR relationship** links two or more indicators so that if one or more of them are on, the desired result (a calculation or output record) takes place.

The OR relationship can also be used to control operations on the Calculation Specification form (Figure 4-31). In Example One, the literal 1 is added to the COUNT field if either indicator 38 or indicator 41 is on. Unlike the AND relationship, the OR relationship requires only that one or more of the listed indicator conditions be met. If either or both of the listed indicators is on, the addition is performed.

Line	Form Type	Control Level (L0-L9, LR, SR, AN/OR)	Indicators	And	And	Factor 1	Operation	Factor 2	Result Field Name	Length	Decimal Positions	Half Adjust (H)	Resulting Indicators Plus/High	Minus/Low	Zero/Equal	Comments
01	C	*	EXAMPLE ONE													
02	C		38													
03	C	OR	41			COUNT	ADD	1	COUNT	4	0					
04	C	*														
05	C	*	EXAMPLE TWO													
06	C		58	59												
07	C	OR	43	47		TOTAL	SUB	DISCNT	NET	7	2					
08	C															
09	C															
10	C															
11	C															
12	C															
13	C															
14	C															
15	C															
16	C															
17	C															
18	C															
19	C															
20	C															

Figure 4-31 OR relationship examples

Example Two is a combined AND/OR relationship. The SUB operation is executed if both indicators 58 and 59, or both indicators 43 and 47, are on. Each pair of indicators on the same line represents an AND relationship. The two AND relationships are linked in an OR relationship. As is the case with linking AND lines, most versions of RPG permit the linking of up to seven OR lines.

▸ **Line 10** Line 10 (see Figure 4-28) is controlled by the AND relationship of indicators 01 and 40. If both these indicators are on, meaning that the record being processed contains a current quantity on hand that is less than the reorder point, the current quantity is subtracted from the reorder point quantity, giving the number of units below reorder point (UBELOW). The program specifications require that UBELOW be printed as part of the detail record when the Current Quantity field is less than the reorder point.

▸ **Lines 12, 13, 14, and 15** As you can see from the comments associated with these calculations (see Figure 4-28), lines 12–15 add detail amounts to the final total accumulators. Lines 12–13 add the previous and current inventory values to the final totals for these fields. Lines 14–15 are counting operations. Line 14, controlled by indicators 01 (record identification) and 40 (QCURNT < REORDR), counts the number of records that contain a current quantity that is less than the reorder point quantity. Line 15, controlled by indicators 01 (record identification) and 41 (QCURNT = REORDR), counts the number of records that contain a current quantity equal to the reorder point quantity.

OUTPUT SPECIFICATIONS FOR PROGRAM HJG04X

Figure 4-32 shows pages 05 and 06 of the program specifications. Note the use of comment lines to identify the four heading lines. Note also that the Page Number field in Heading Line One has been zero suppressed with an edit code Z. This is because this sample program was written to be compiled by a microcomputer RPG compiler that does not support the automatic zero suppression of the Page Number field. If edit code Z is used with an RPG compiler that provides automatic zero suppression, it does not cause an error message to be generated.

Figure 4-33 shows the output specifications for the detail print line. Lines 13–16 show the use of indicators to control a particular field or constant in an output record.

Figure 4-32 RPG Output specifications: heading lines

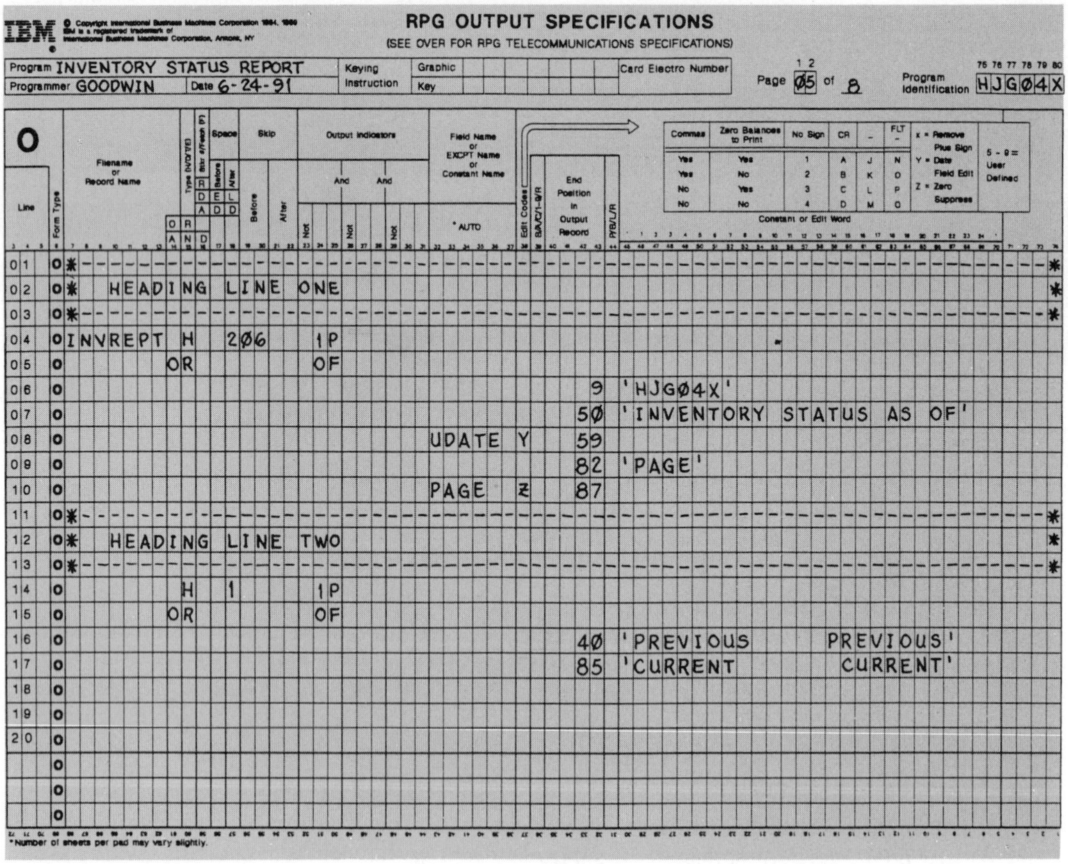
RPG OUTPUT SPECIFICATIONS

Program INVENTORY STATUS REPORT — Programmer GOODWIN — Date 6-24-91 — Page 05 of 8 — Program Identification HJGØ4X

```
01 O*----------------------------------------------------------------*
02 O*     HEADING LINE ONE                                           *
03 O*----------------------------------------------------------------*
04 OINVREPT  H  2Ø6   1P
05 O       OR         OF
06 O                              9 'HJGØ4X'
07 O                             5Ø 'INVENTORY STATUS AS OF'
08 O                  UDATE Y    59
09 O                             82 'PAGE'
10 O                  PAGE  Z    87
11 O*----------------------------------------------------------------*
12 O*    HEADING LINE TWO                                            *
13 O*----------------------------------------------------------------*
14 O         H  1     1P
15 O       OR         OF
16 O                             4Ø 'PREVIOUS              PREVIOUS'
17 O                             85 'CURRENT                CURRENT'
```

Figure 4-32 (1)

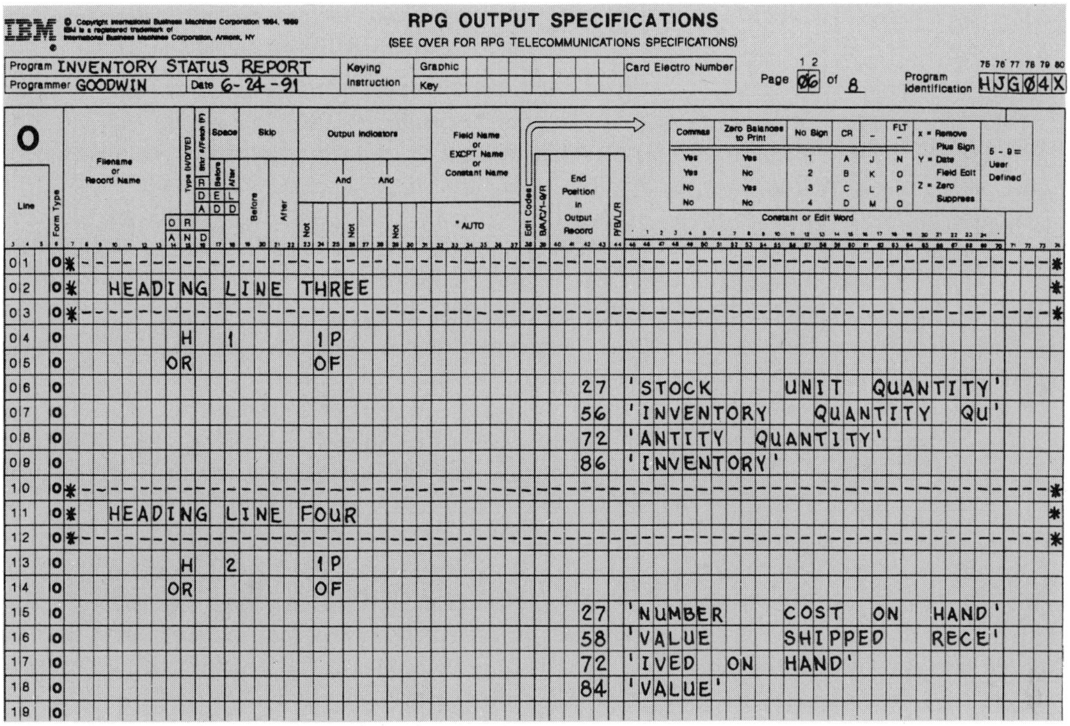

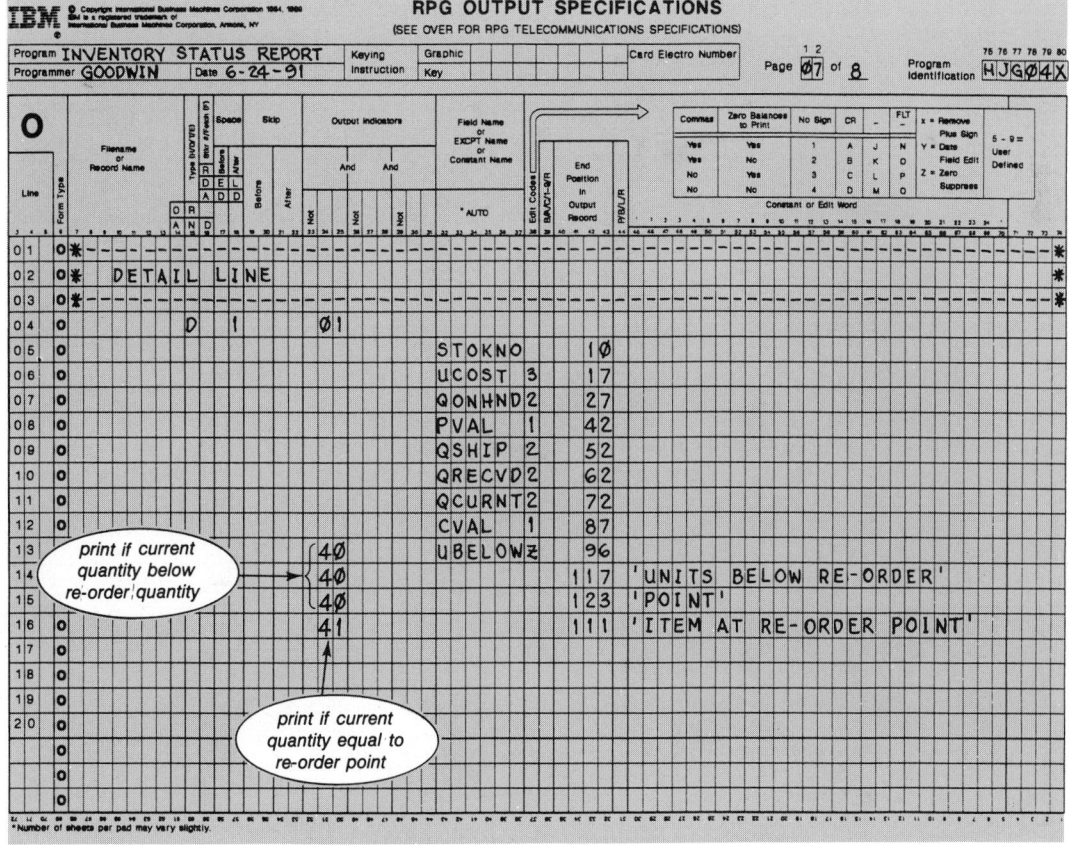

RPG OUTPUT SPECIFICATIONS

Program INVENTORY STATUS REPORT — Programmer GOODWIN — Date 6-24-91 — Page 06 of 8 — Program Identification HJG04X

```
01 O*------------------------------------------------------------------*
02 O*     HEADING LINE THREE                                           *
03 O*------------------------------------------------------------------*
04 O          H  1      1P
05 O        OR          OF
06 O                                      27 'STOCK      UNIT   QUANTITY'
07 O                                      56 'INVENTORY      QUANTITY   QU'
08 O                                      72 'ANTITY   QUANTITY'
09 O                                      86 'INVENTORY'
10 O*------------------------------------------------------------------*
11 O*     HEADING LINE FOUR                                            *
12 O*------------------------------------------------------------------*
13 O          H  2      1P
14 O        OR          OF
15 O                                      27 'NUMBER      COST    ON     HAND'
16 O                                      58 'VALUE       SHIPPED        RECE'
17 O                                      72 'IVED    ON     HAND'
18 O                                      84 'VALUE'
19 O
```

Figure 4-32 (2)

RPG OUTPUT SPECIFICATIONS

Program INVENTORY STATUS REPORT — Programmer GOODWIN — Date 6-24-91 — Page 07 of 8 — Program Identification HJGØ4X

```
01 O*------------------------------------------------------------------*
02 O*   DETAIL LINE                                                    *
03 O*------------------------------------------------------------------*
04 O          D  1      Ø1
05 O                          STOKNO      1Ø
06 O                          UCOST  3    17
07 O                          QONHND2     27
08 O                          PVAL   1    42
09 O                          QSHIP  2    52
10 O                          QRECVD2     62
11 O                          QCURNT2     72
12 O                          CVAL   1    87
13 O                    4Ø    UBELOWZ     96
14 O                    4Ø               117 'UNITS BELOW RE-ORDER'
15 O                    4Ø               123 'POINT'
16 O                    41               111 'ITEM AT RE-ORDER POINT'
17 O
18 O
19 O
20 O
```


Figure 4-33 RPG Output specifications: detail line

▤ Field Control of Output Specifications

The use of indicator 01 in line 04 specifies that the detail record is to be printed whenever a new record has been read. The indicators in lines 13–16 specify that, in the detail line, these individual fields and constants are subject to further indicator control. If indicator 40 is on when a detail record is printed, the data field (UBELOW) and constants controlled by indicator 40 also are printed. If indicator 40 is not on, lines 13, 14, and 15 are ignored by the RPG object program. This is another form of AND relationship. Indicator 01 controls the printing of the record, whereas indicator 40 controls the printing of one field and two constants within the record. For lines 13–15 to be active, indicators 01 AND 40 must both be on.

Indicator 41 is also in an AND relationship with indicator 01. Indicator 41 controls printing of the constant that is specified on line 16. If neither indicator 40 nor indicator 41 is on when the detail record is printed, only the fields specified in lines 05–12 appear on the output report.

The final total output specifications are shown in Figure 4-34. Note that indicators 40 and 41 are not used to control the final totals, but they were used to control whether or not the value 1 was added to the LOWLR and RORDLR accumulators. These indicators controlled operations that were performed on the basis of conditions found in the detail input data. Because indicators 40 and 41 control detail calculation operations, they are not used to control end-of-job totals, which are printed at the end of the program regardless of the state of indicators 40 and 41.

Note the use of the **Skip After** entry on line 13. This entry causes the printer to advance the continuous form to the top of a new page after the last Final Total line has printed. Advancing the form makes it easier for the computer operator to remove the report after printing is completed. The use of the Skip After entry with the last final total line also eliminates the possibility that the next report will print on the same page if it does not contain a Skip Before entry (which advances the form before printing the first heading line).

Figure 4-35 is the completed RPG source program for the Inventory Status Report problem. Note that only the standard format calculations are shown.

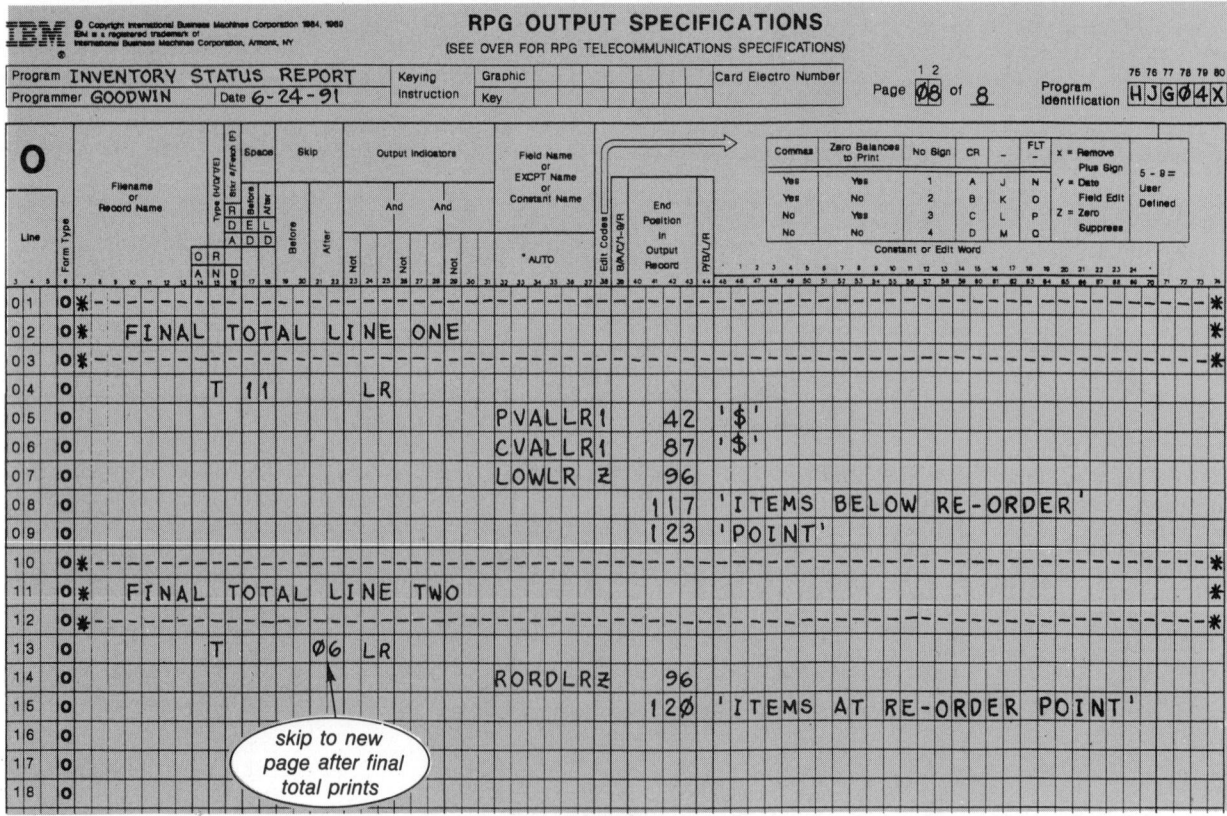

Figure 4-34 RPG Output specifications: total lines

Figure 4-35   RPG source program for program HJG04X

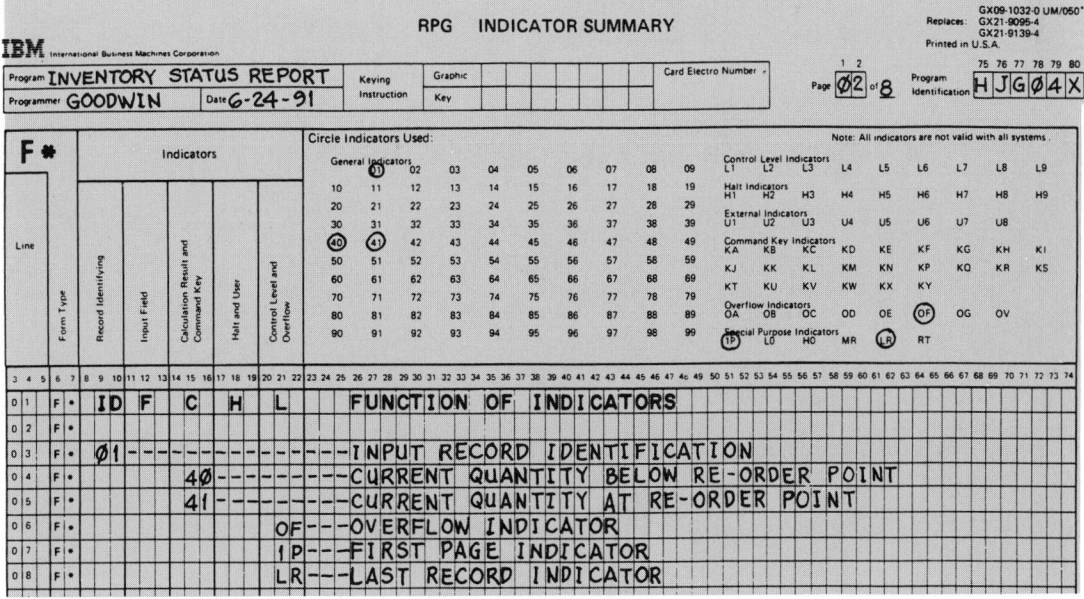

Figure 4-35 (1)

Figure 4-35 (2)

continued

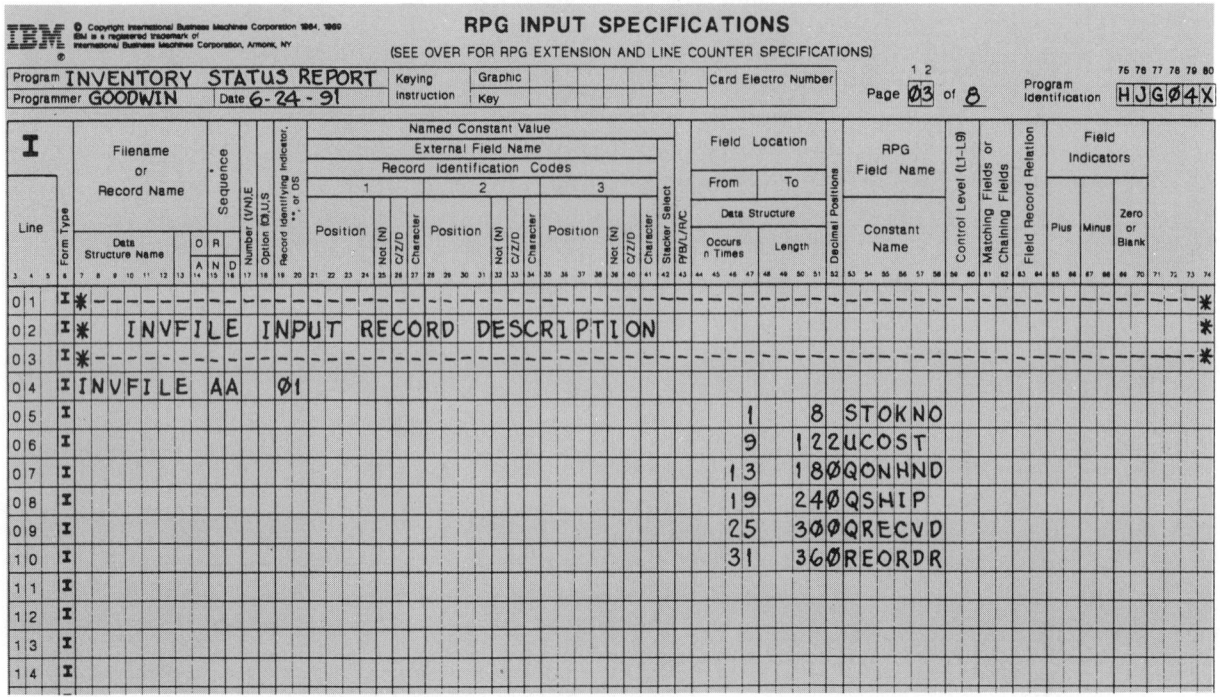

Figure 4-35 (3)

Figure 4-35 (4)

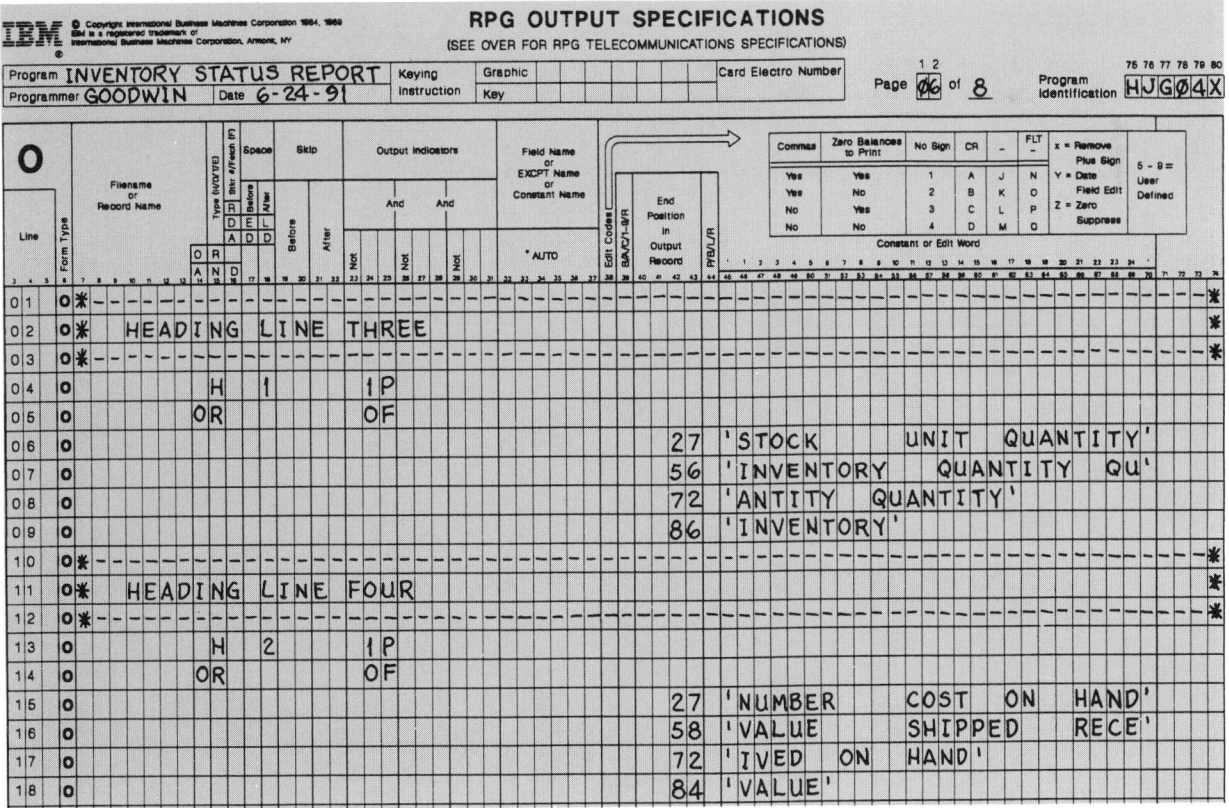

Figure 4-35 (5)

Figure 4-35 (6)

continued

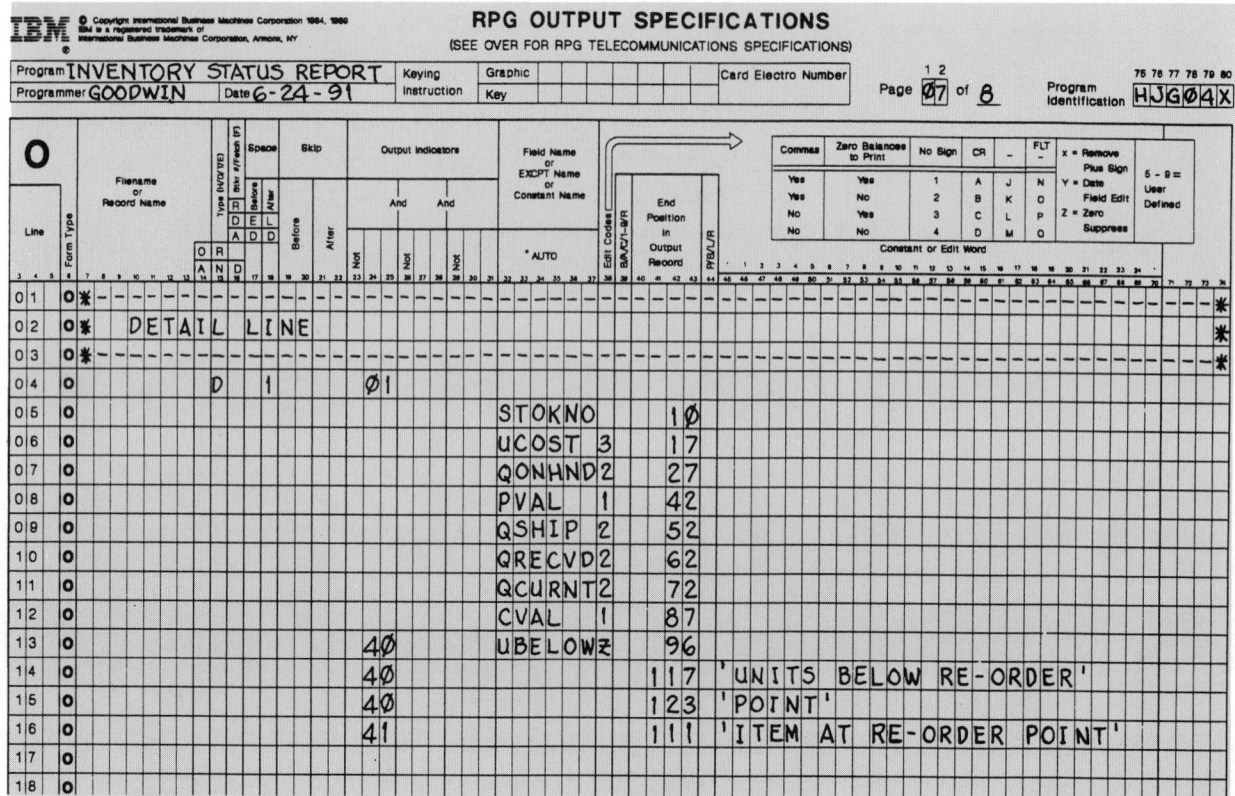

Figure 4-35 (7)

Figure 4-35 (8)

RPG Program Compilation Listing

Figure 4-36 shows the compilation listing of the sample program. This listing differs slightly from the listings in the previous chapters because program HJG04X was compiled on an IBM PC/AT microcomputer rather than the minicomputer used in previous examples. Although the format of the listing is slightly different, the compiler has generated the same information and performed the same functions. You will see several different compiler listings in this book, to familiarize you with the types of compiler listings produced by different versions of RPG. Figure 4-37 on the next page is the output report produced by the sample program.

Figure 4-36   Compilation listing for program HJG04X

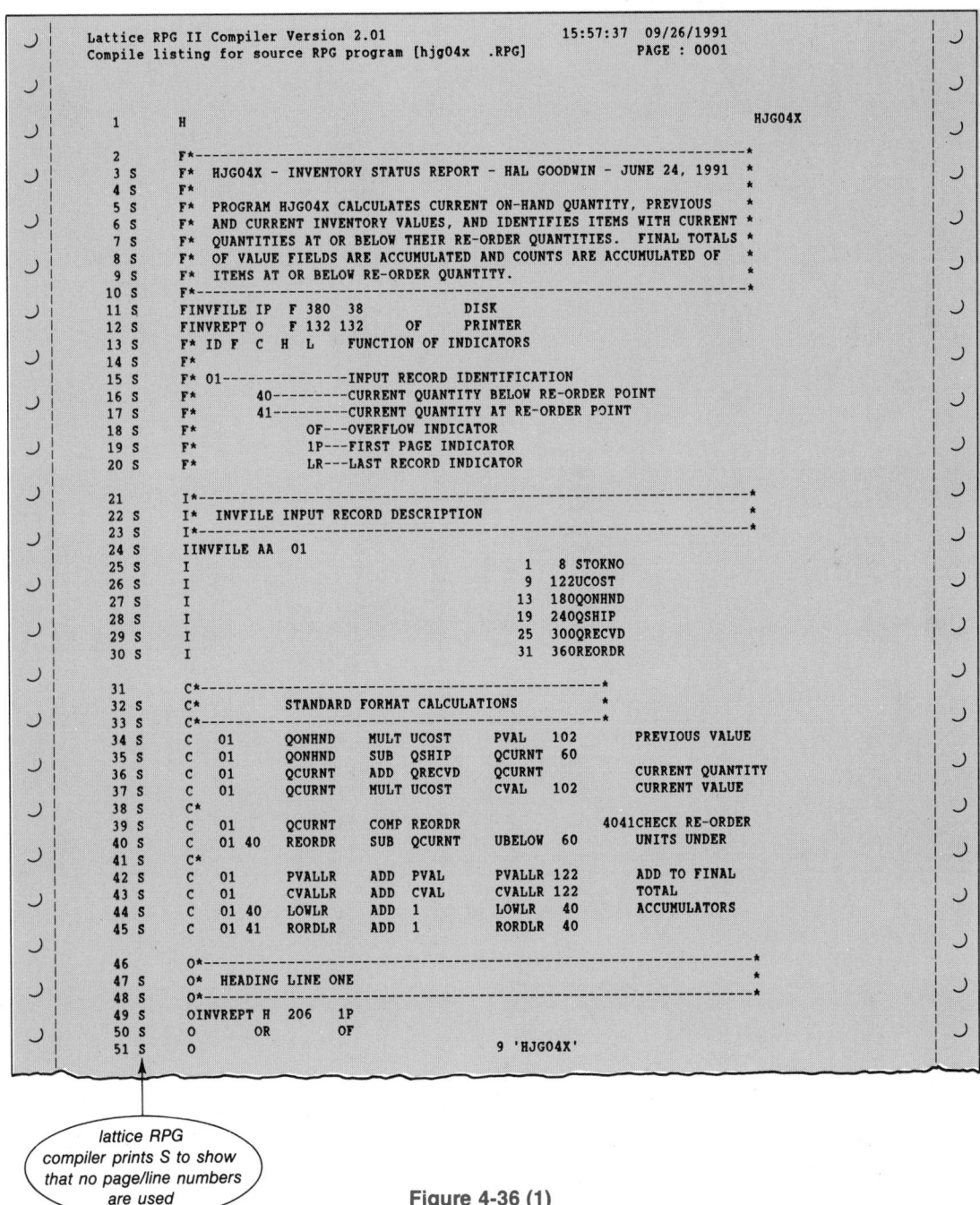

```
Lattice RPG II Compiler Version 2.01                 15:57:37 09/26/1991
Compile listing for source RPG program [hjg04x  .RPG]          PAGE : 0001


  1      H                                                            HJG04X

  2      F*------------------------------------------------------------*
  3 S    F*  HJG04X - INVENTORY STATUS REPORT - HAL GOODWIN - JUNE 24, 1991 *
  4 S    F*                                                           *
  5 S    F*  PROGRAM HJG04X CALCULATES CURRENT ON-HAND QUANTITY, PREVIOUS  *
  6 S    F*  AND CURRENT INVENTORY VALUES, AND IDENTIFIES ITEMS WITH CURRENT *
  7 S    F*  QUANTITIES AT OR BELOW THEIR RE-ORDER QUANTITIES.  FINAL TOTALS *
  8 S    F*  OF VALUE FIELDS ARE ACCUMULATED AND COUNTS ARE ACCUMULATED OF   *
  9 S    F*  ITEMS AT OR BELOW RE-ORDER QUANTITY.                      *
 10 S    F*------------------------------------------------------------*
 11 S    FINVFILE IP  F 380  38          DISK
 12 S    FINVREPT  O  F 132 132     OF    PRINTER
 13 S    F* ID F  C  H  L    FUNCTION OF INDICATORS
 14 S    F*
 15 S    F* 01--------------INPUT RECORD IDENTIFICATION
 16 S    F*        40---------CURRENT QUANTITY BELOW RE-ORDER POINT
 17 S    F*        41---------CURRENT QUANTITY AT RE-ORDER POINT
 18 S    F*           OF---OVERFLOW INDICATOR
 19 S    F*           1P---FIRST PAGE INDICATOR
 20 S    F*           LR---LAST RECORD INDICATOR

 21      I*------------------------------------------------------------*
 22 S    I*  INVFILE INPUT RECORD DESCRIPTION                         *
 23 S    I*------------------------------------------------------------*
 24 S    IINVFILE AA  01
 25 S    I                                     1   8 STOKNO
 26 S    I                                     9  122UCOST
 27 S    I                                    13  180QONHND
 28 S    I                                    19  240QSHIP
 29 S    I                                    25  300QRECVD
 30 S    I                                    31  360REORDR

 31      C*------------------------------------------*
 32 S    C*          STANDARD FORMAT CALCULATIONS    *
 33 S    C*------------------------------------------*
 34 S    C    01       QONHND   MULT UCOST     PVAL   102    PREVIOUS VALUE
 35 S    C    01       QONHND   SUB  QSHIP     QCURNT  60
 36 S    C    01       QCURNT   ADD  QRECVD    QCURNT         CURRENT QUANTITY
 37 S    C    01       QCURNT   MULT UCOST     CVAL   102    CURRENT VALUE
 38 S    C*
 39 S    C    01       QCURNT   COMP REORDR          4041CHECK RE-ORDER
 40 S    C    01 40    REORDR   SUB  QCURNT    UBELOW  60    UNITS UNDER
 41 S    C*
 42 S    C    01       PVALLR   ADD  PVAL      PVALLR 122    ADD TO FINAL
 43 S    C    01       CVALLR   ADD  CVAL      CVALLR 122    TOTAL
 44 S    C    01 40    LOWLR    ADD  1         LOWLR   40    ACCUMULATORS
 45 S    C    01 41    RORDLR   ADD  1         RORDLR  40

 46      O*------------------------------------------------------------*
 47 S    O*  HEADING LINE ONE                                         *
 48 S    O*------------------------------------------------------------*
 49 S    OINVREPT H  206     1P
 50 S    O    OR           OF
 51 S    O                              9 'HJG04X'
```

lattice RPG compiler prints S to show that no page/line numbers are used

Figure 4-36 (1)

```
Lattice RPG II Compiler Version 2.01                15:57:38  09/26/1991
Compile listing for source RPG program [hjg04x  .RPG]        PAGE : 0002


   52 S    O                                    50 'INVENTORY STATUS AS OF'
   53 S    O                         UDATE Y    59
   54 S    O                                    82 'PAGE'
   55 S    O                         PAGE  Z    87
   56 S    O*-----------------------------------------------------------------*
   57 S    O*  HEADING LINE TWO                                               *
   58 S    O*-----------------------------------------------------------------*
   59 S    O        H  1    1P
   60 S    O        OR      OF
   61 S    O                                    40 'PREVIOUS      PREVIOUS'
   62 S    O                                    85 'CURRENT       CURRENT'
   63 S    O*-----------------------------------------------------------------*
   64 S    O*  HEADING LINE THREE                                             *
   65 S    O*-----------------------------------------------------------------*
   66 S    O        H  1    1P
   67 S    O        OR      OF
   68 S    O                                    27 'STOCK     UNIT  QUANTITY'
   69 S    O                                    56 'INVENTORY    QUANTITY  QU'
   70 S    O                                    72 'ANTITY  QUANTITY'
   71 S    O                                    86 'INVENTORY'
   72 S    O*-----------------------------------------------------------------*
   73 S    O*  HEADING LINE FOUR                                              *
   74 S    O*-----------------------------------------------------------------*
   75 S    O        H  2    1P
   76 S    O        OR      OF
   77 S    O                                    27 'NUMBER     COST  ON  HAND'
   78 S    O                                    58 'VALUE      SHIPPED    RECE'
   79 S    O                                    72 'IVED  ON  HAND'
   80 S    O                                    84 'VALUE'
   81 S    O*-----------------------------------------------------------------*
   82 S    O*  DETAIL LINE                                                    *
   83 S    O*-----------------------------------------------------------------*
   84 S    O        D  1    01
   85 S    O                         STOKNO     10
   86 S    O                         UCOST 3    17
   87 S    O                         QONHND2    27
   88 S    O                         PVAL  1    42
   89 S    O                         QSHIP 2    52
   90 S    O                         QRECVD2    62
   91 S    O                         QCURNT2    72
   92 S    O                         CVAL  1    87
   93 S    O                  40     UBELOWZ    96
   94 S    O                  40                117 'UNITS BELOW RE-ORDER'
   95 S    O                  40                123 'POINT'
   96 S    O                  41                111 'ITEM AT RE-ORDER POINT'
   97 S    O*-----------------------------------------------------------------*
   98 S    O*  FINAL TOTAL LINE ONE                                           *
   99 S    O*-----------------------------------------------------------------*
  100 S    O        T  11   LR
  101 S    O                         PVALLR1    42 '$'
  102 S    O                         CVALLR1    87 '$'
  103 S    O                         LOWLR Z    96
  104 S    O                                    117 'ITEMS BELOW RE-ORDER'
  105 S    O                                    123 'POINT'
  106 S    O*-----------------------------------------------------------------*
```

Figure 4-36 (2)

```
Lattice RPG II Compiler Version 2.01                    15:57:39  09/26/1991
Compile listing for source RPG program [hjg04x  .RPG]            PAGE : 0003


107 S    O*  FINAL TOTAL LINE TWO                                          *
108 S    O*-------------------------------------------------------------*
109 S    O       T    06 LR
110 S    O                              RORDLRZ    96
111 S    O                                         120 'ITEMS AT RE-ORDER POINT'
112 /*



Warning Severe
Errors  Errors
   0      0
```

Figure 4-36 (3)

```
HJG04X                    INVENTORY STATUS AS OF  7/06/91              PAGE    1

                PREVIOUS     PREVIOUS                       CURRENT    CURRENT
STOCK    UNIT   QUANTITY     INVENTORY  QUANTITY  QUANTITY  QUANTITY   INVENTORY
NUMBER   COST   ON  HAND     VALUE      SHIPPED   RECEIVED  ON  HAND   VALUE
A35-2621 1.30       251          326.30                         251        326.30
A35-2738  .04   137,850       5,514.00   47,365              90,485     3,619.40
A76-3184  .10    87,416       8,741.60   80,000               7,416       741.60    2584 UNITS BELOW RE-ORDER POINT
B31-1004  .07   638,412      44,688.84            100,000   738,412    51,688.84
C42-1411 1.00   427,631     427,631.00  146,218   200,000   481,413   481,413.00   18587 UNITS BELOW RE-ORDER POINT
F31-2600  .01   800,000       8,000.00  700,000   200,000   300,000     3,000.00  ITEM AT RE-ORDER POINT
G46-384X 21.16      835      17,668.60      400                 435     9,204.60      65 UNITS BELOW RE-ORDER POINT
H39-874J 46.12        6         276.72              100         106     4,888.72      94 UNITS BELOW RE-ORDER POINT
L86-4166 12.37      742       9,178.54      142                 600     7,422.00  ITEM AT RE-ORDER POINT
L93-2147 1.48     8,575      12,691.00    8,575                               .00    5000 UNITS BELOW RE-ORDER POINT
P40-0250 2.71     3,162       8,569.02      485             2,677       7,254.67      17 UNITS BELOW RE-ORDER POINT
P86-M1.1  .99     7,583       7,507.17    2,000             5,583       5,527.17

                            $550,792.79                              $575,086.30       6 ITEMS BELOW RE-ORDER POINT
                                                                                       2 ITEMS AT RE-ORDER POINT
```

Figure 4-37   Output report for program HJG04X

SPECIAL CASES IN COMPARING

Although they are not used by sample program HJG04X, two common comparing situations require discussion because they are potential problems for the student or beginning programmer.

Date Comparisons

Comparing dates is a special problem because of the format in which dates are stored. Recall that dates are often stored in MMDDYY format, the first two positions being the month, the middle two the day, and the last two the year. The method that RPG usually uses to compare numeric fields does not work with date fields because the major component, the year, is at the end of the field rather than the beginning. The beginning of a date field contains the month.

If dates in MMDDYY format are compared, the results are usually incorrect. Take, for example, a comparison between September 18, 1947 (091847) and December 3, 1907 (120307). RPG does not know that these are dates and are stored in a special format; it simply looks at each as a six-position numeric field and compares them. The rules of algebraic comparison determine that 120,307 is greater than 091,847. Therefore, RPG sets a resulting indicator showing that December 3, 1907 is greater than September 18, 1947. If the month fields were interchanged, RPG would indicate that December 18, 1947 is greater than September 3, 1907. As you can see, RPG determines the result of comparison between two MMDDYY fields by comparing month first, then day, then year.

For a date comparison to work correctly, RPG must compare year first, then month, then day. To do this, the dates are converted from MMDDYY format to YYMMDD format and then compared. This conversion can be performed in a single step by the use of the MULT operation.

To convert an MMDDYY date to YYMMDD format, multiply the MMDDYY date by the literal 10000.01. Limit the product of the multiplication to six positions with no decimal places. This limited product is then in YYMMDD format (Figure 4-38). When 070476 is multiplied by 10000.01, a product value of 0704760704.76 is developed. When excess positions are eliminated and the product is limited to six positions with no decimal places, the result is 760704. The date is thus converted from MMDDYY format (070476) to YYMMDD format (760704), which can now be successfully used for comparison. Figure 4-39 illustrates the coding of this conversion. Note that the Result Field Length entry is 6 and the Decimal Positions entry is 0.

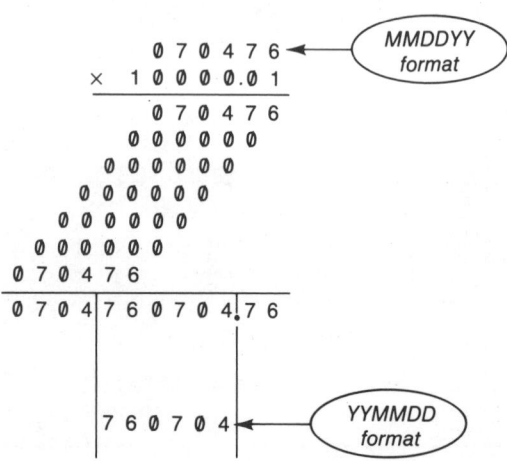

Figure 4-38   Date conversion example

C			Indicators				Factor 1	Operation	Factor 2	Result Field				Resulting Indicators				Comments
			Name	Length														
0 1	C						DATE	MULT	10000.01	DATEWK	60							
0 2	C																	
0 3	C																	

Figure 4-39   Date conversion calculation specifications

There is one peculiarity of this method of conversion. The rules of arithmetic show that the product of this multiplication is a 12-position field with two decimal positions (see Figure 4-38). When this conversion is performed by the RPG MULT operation, a warning message commonly results, indicating that the result field may not be long enough. This warning message should be ignored. The MULT operation will execute properly and the product will be correct.

Dates can also be converted from YYMMDD format to MMDDYY format by a multiplication step. To restore a date to MMDDYY format, multiply the YYMMDD date by the literal 100.0001 and limit the product to six positions with zero decimal positions (Figure 4-40). Be aware that the conversion multiplication from YYMMDD format to MMDDYY format may also generate a warning message.

C		Indicators				Factor 1	Operation	Factor 2	Result Field				Resulting Indicators			Comments
	Form Type	Control Level (L0, L9, LR, SR, AN/OR)	And		And				Name	Length	Decimal Positions	Half Adjust (H)	Arithmetic			
Line				Not		Not								Plus / Compare 1>2 High	Minus / 1<2 Low	Zero / 1=2 Lookup(Factor 2)is Equal	
3 4 5	6	7	8	9 10 11	12 13 14	15 16 17	18 19 20 21 22 23 24 25 26 27	28 29 30 31 32	33 34 35 36 37 38 39 40 41 42	43 44 45 46 47 48	49 50 51	52	53	54 55	56 57	58 59	60 61 62 63 64 65 66 67 68 69 70 71 72 73 74
0 1	C*						TO CONVERT A DATE IN YYMMDD FORMAT TO MMDDYY										
0 2	C*						FORMAT, MULTIPLY BY 100.0001										
0 3	C*																
0 4	C			1 9			YYMMDD	MULT	100.0001	MMDDYY	60						
0 5	C*																
0 6	C			1 2			WORKDT	MULT	100.0001	OUTDT	60						
0 7	C																

Figure 4-40   Date conversion to original format

═══ Comparisons Controlled by Previous Comparisons

COMP operations that are controlled by resulting indicators from previous COMP operations present a potentially serious trap for the unwary programmer. Note that the previous sentence did not say "the unwary student programmer"; the pitfall generated by the problem of compares that are controlled by other compares has caught many experienced programmers. An understanding and awareness of this problem will help you avoid it when a program requires this type of logic. Consider the following programming problem:

Holders of the Spenditol bank credit card have credit limits that govern the maximum amount they may charge to their credit card accounts. If the account balance reaches or exceeds the credit limit, no further purchases may be charged to the account. However, account holders who have an excellent payment history for over five years may exceed their credit limit. Part of the data record for each account contains the following three fields:

BALANC   the current account balance
LIMIT   the credit limit for the account
YEARS   length of excellent payment history

If BALANC exceeds LIMIT the YEARS field is to be tested.
If YEARS is greater than 5, processing is to continue.
If, however, BALANC exceeds LIMIT and YEARS is not greater than 5, the program must turn on indicator 99. Indicator 99 is used later in the program to cut off further credit to the holder of the account.

Figure 4-41 on the next page demonstrates the problem that can be caused by an incorrect understanding of COMP operations that are controlled by earlier COMP operations. The calculation specifications show that BALANC is COMPared with LIMIT and that indicator 45 is turned on if BALANC exceeds LIMIT. If 45 is on, the second COMPare is performed. If, after the second comparison, indicator 99 is on, the message on the Output Specifications form is printed, and the credit card holder will no longer be able to use the account.

In the first record in Figure 4-41, BALANC is greater than LIMIT and indicator 45 is turned on by the COMP operation on line 01. The program then performs the COMP on line 02; and because YEARS contains a value less than 5, indicator 99 turns on. Based on indicator 99, the output message is printed and use of the credit card is stopped.

Later, when the second record is processed, because the value in BALANC is less than the value in LIMIT, indicator 45 is not turned on and the second COMP operation is not performed. However, indicator 99 is still on, and, as you know *resulting indicators used in a COMP operation are not reset until the same COMP operation is performed again*. Because the COMP operation on line 02 is not performed during processing of the second record, indicator 99 is not reset. This logic error results in an invalid error message. If the error is not detected during the testing and debugging of the program, the result could be the improper cancellation of credit privileges.

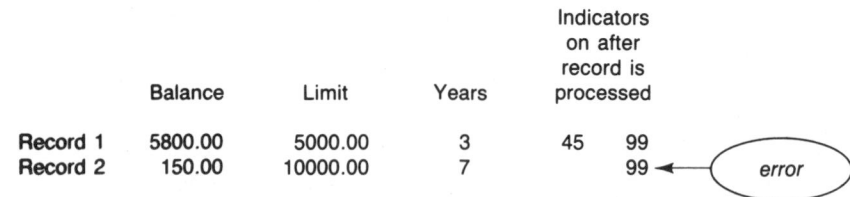

	Balance	Limit	Years	Indicators on after record is processed	
Record 1	5800.00	5000.00	3	45	99
Record 2	150.00	10000.00	7		99 ◄ ─ error

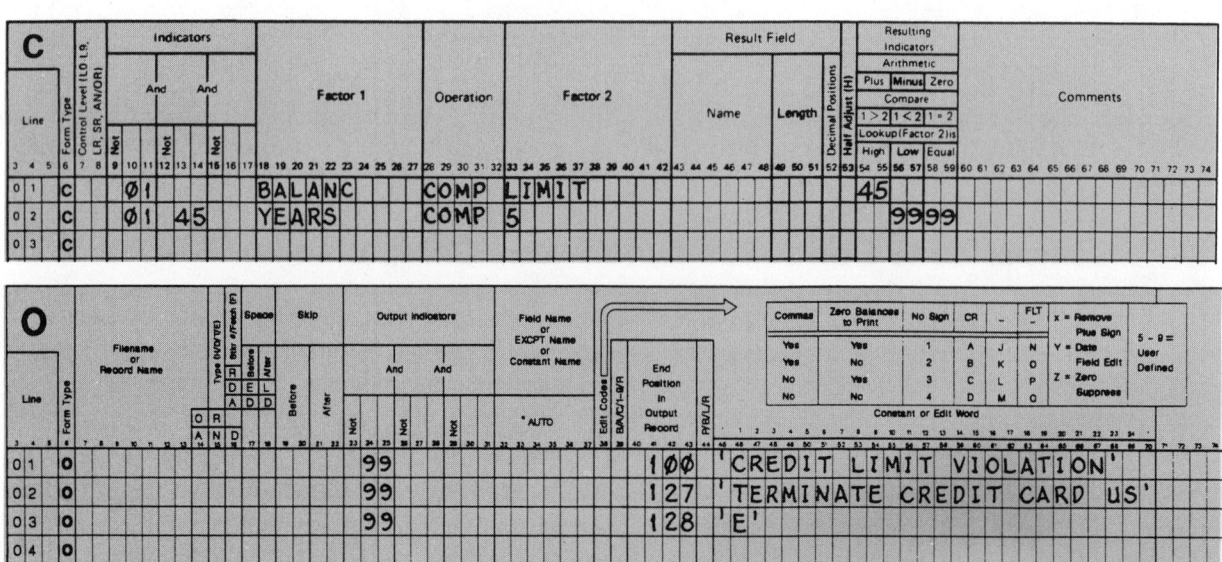

Figure 4-41   Improper coding of dependent COMP operation

▸ **The SETOF Operation**   A simple way to prevent the preceding logic error is by the use of the SETOF operation. The **SETOF** operation can turn off up to three indicators specified in the Resulting Indicators area. Figure 4-42 illustrates the use of the SETOF operation to eliminate the problem with indicator 99 by turning it off at the beginning of the comparison sequence. In this case, even though the second record does not cause the second COMP operation to be performed, indicator 99 cannot be left on incorrectly. Whenever a COMP operation is controlled by the resulting indicators of a preceding COMP operation, use of the SETOF operation should be considered. Figure 4-43 summarizes the SETOF operation.

═ IN CONCLUSION ═

In this chapter you have learned to use the most basic of the RPG conditional operations, the COMP operation. Even though it is a relatively simple operation, knowledge of the COMP operation extends your programming capabilities tremendously. With the ability to perform conditional operations, you can write programs that do far more than electronic calculator operations. Conditional operations are the first of the operations that enable you to control RPG program logic.

In Chapter 5 you will use control break techniques to accumulate and print totals that print automatically when the content of a controlling data field changes.

	Balance	Limit	Years	Indicators on after record is processed	
Record 1	5800.00	5000.00	3	45	99
Record 2	150.00	10000.00	7		

99 off for second record

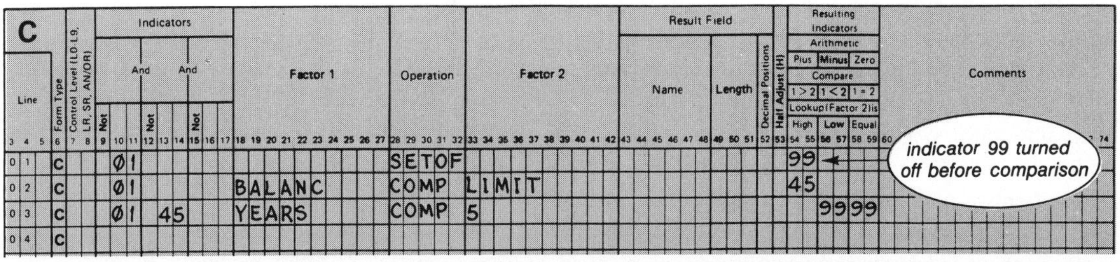

indicator 99 turned off before comparison

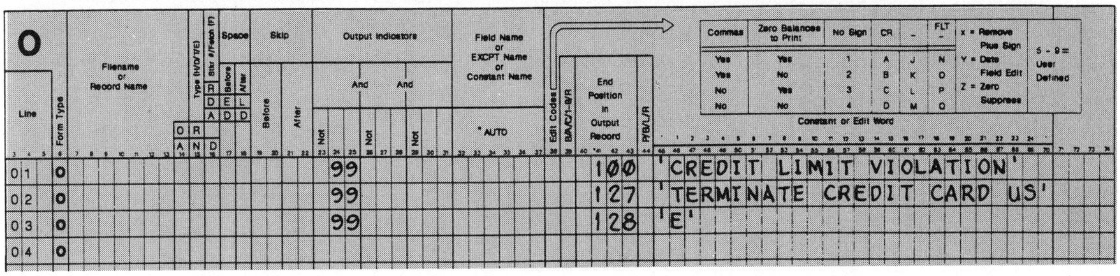

Calculation specification:

Line	Form Type	Control Level	Indicators And / And Not	Factor 1	Operation	Factor 2	Result Field Name	Length	Resulting Indicators
01	C	01			SETOF				99
02	C	01		BALANC	COMP	LIMIT			45
03	C	01	45	YEARS	COMP	5			99 99
04	C								

Output specification:

Line	Form Type	Output Indicators	Field Name	End Position	Constant
01	O	99		100	'CREDIT LIMIT VIOLATION'
02	O	99		127	'TERMINATE CREDIT CARD US'
03	O	99		128	'E'
04	O				

Figure 4-42 Proper coding of dependent COMP operation

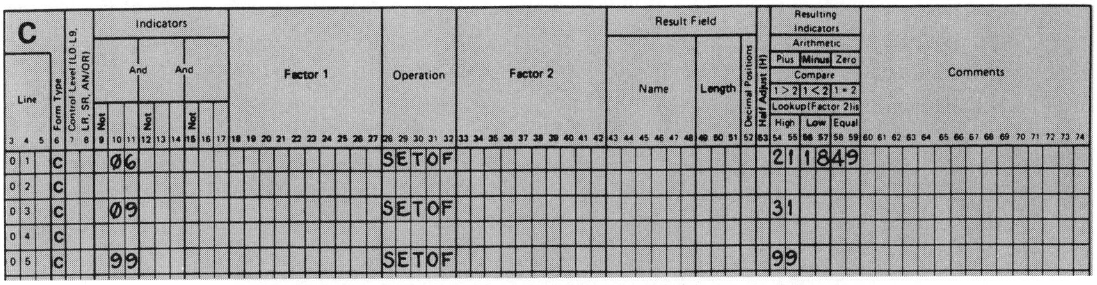

Calculation specification:

Line	Form Type	Control Level	Indicators	Factor 1	Operation	Factor 2	Result Field	Resulting Indicators
01	C	06			SETOF			21 18 49
02	C							
03	C	09			SETOF			31
04	C							
05	C	99			SETOF			99

SETOF Operation Summary

The SETOF operation turns off all indicators specified in positions 54–55, 56–57, and 58–59. At least one resulting indicator must be specified in a SETOF operation.

Control Level Indicators	Indicators	Factor 1	Operation Name	Factor 2	Result Field	Resulting Indicators		
7–8	9–17	18–27	28–32	33–42	43–53	54–55	56–57	58–59
optional	optional	blank	SETOF	blank	blank	optional	optional	optional

one required (56–57, 58–59)

Figure 4-43 SETOF operation summary

CHAPTER SUMMARY

1. **Conditional operations** permit the program to control whether or not an operation is performed, based on the result of a previous operation.
2. A **compare operation** can determine the relative values of two data fields.
3. RPG cannot compare two data fields of different data classes: Both fields must be numeric, or both fields must be alphameric.
4. If both fields are numeric, a **numeric comparison** is performed taking both the sign and digit values of the fields into consideration.
5. When a numeric comparison is performed, a short field is **filled** with zeros to make its length equal that of the longer field. The filled version of the field is not available for use by the programmer.
6. If both fields are alphameric, an **alphameric comparison** is performed.
7. Alphameric comparisons are left-justified, comparing one position of each field at a time. An alphameric comparison ends when an unequal condition is found or both fields have been completely compared.
8. Alphameric comparison results are based on the **collating sequence** used by the computer.
9. The RPG COMP operation can use up to three **resulting indicators** to indicate the result of a comparison.
10. The possible results of a COMP operation are Factor 1 > Factor 2, Factor 1 < Factor 2, and Factor 1 = Factor 2.
11. Only one resulting indicator can be turned on by a COMP operation.
12. RPG cannot turn on an indicator to show a not-equal comparison result. Not-equal results are shown by the equal indicator being off.
13. The use of the letter **N** before an indicator specifies a test for that indicator being off.
14. **Alphameric literals** must be preceded and followed by apostrophes. The apostrophes are not part of the literal.
15. The maximum length of an alphameric literal is eight characters.
16. A **comment line** is identified by an asterisk in position 7 of the line. Comment lines are used for internal documentation only and are not compiled into the object program.
17. The **indicator summary** is a form used for the documentation of indicator use in a program.
18. An **AND relationship** specifies that two or more indicators must meet the conditions being tested for a calculation or output operation to take place.
19. An **OR relationship** specifies that one or more of the indicator conditions being tested must occur for a calculation or output operation to take place.
20. If date fields in the MMDDYY format are compared, the result of the comparison is probably not accurate.
21. Date fields can be converted to the YYMMDD format for accurate comparison by multiplying the date by the literal 10000.01 and limiting the answer to six positions with no decimal places.
22. Resulting indicators turned on by a COMP operation stay on until the same COMP operation is performed again. If a COMP is controlled by the resulting indicators from a previous COMP operation, special steps should be taken to assure that resulting indicators are not left on incorrectly.
23. The **SETOF** operation can turn off up to three indicators and can be used to solve the problem of resulting indicators left on incorrectly.

REVIEW QUESTIONS

1. Under what circumstances does RPG perform a numeric comparison? How is a numeric comparison performed?
2. How is an alphameric comparison performed?
3. How does RPG compare two fields of different lengths?
4. RPG cannot turn on an indicator to show that two fields are not equal. What two methods can be used to show a not-equal comparison result?

5. How are comment lines specified within an RPG program? What does the RPG compiler do with comment lines?

6. What is the function of the RPG indicator summary?

7. How does an AND relationship affect indicator use?

8. How does an OR relationship affect indicator use?

9. What is the difference between an output indicator specified on the same line as a file name and an output indicator that is specified on the same line as a field name?

10. Why cannot dates in the MMDDYY format be compared accurately?

11. When a resulting indicator is turned on by a COMP operation, how long does it stay on?

STUDENT EXERCISES: RPG PROGRAM CODE

1. For each of the following examples (Figure 4-44), indicate the type of comparison (numeric or alphameric) that will be performed and the result of the comparison. Some of the fields contain a series of digits and an actual decimal point; these fields should be considered numeric fields. In addition, unsigned numeric data fields should be considered to be positive numbers.

	FIELDA	FIELDB	Type of Comparison	Result A > B, A < B, A = B
1a.	JAMES, FRANK	JAMES, JESSE		
1b.	12.789	127.89		
1c.	+.000005	000.005		
1d.	1568.99	1568.99		
1e.	98357	14		
1f.	003.76	3.7600000		
1g.	HALIBUT	HAL		
1h.	83750.226	83750.236		
1i.	1.1	000001.100000		

Figure 4-44 Comparison exercises

2. Write the RPG statement to compare the contents of the MONSAL field against the contents of the LIMIT field. If MONSAL is less than LIMIT, turn on indicator 51. If MONSAL is greater than LIMIT, turn on indicator 53. If the two fields are equal, turn on indicator 55. Use the following Calculation Specifications form.

RPG CALCULATION SPECIFICATIONS

(SEE OVER FOR RPG CONTROL AND FILE DESCRIPTION SPECIFICATIONS)

Line	Form Type	Control Level (L0-L9, LR, SR, AN/OR)	Indicators (And / And)	Factor 1	Operation	Factor 2	Result Field — Name	Length	Decimal Positions	Half Adjust (H)	Resulting Indicators — Arithmetic Plus/Minus/Zero, Compare 1>2 1<2 1=2, Lookup (Factor 2) is High/Low/Equal	Comments
0 1	C											
0 2	C											
0 3	C											
0 4	C											
0 5	C											
0 6	C											
0 7	C											
0 8	C											
0 9	C											
1 0	C											
1 1	C											
1 2	C											

3. Write the RPG operations necessary to determine that the starting date (STDATE) is earlier than the ending date (ENDATE). Both date fields are in MMDDYY format. Use the following Calculation Specifications form.

RPG CALCULATION SPECIFICATIONS

(SEE OVER FOR RPG CONTROL AND FILE DESCRIPTION SPECIFICATIONS)

Line	Form Type	Control Level (L0-L9, LR, SR, AN/OR)	Indicators (And / And)	Factor 1	Operation	Factor 2	Result Field — Name	Length	Decimal Positions	Half Adjust (H)	Resulting Indicators — Arithmetic Plus/Minus/Zero, Compare 1>2 1<2 1=2, Lookup (Factor 2) is High/Low/Equal	Comments
0 1	C											
0 2	C											
0 3	C											
0 4	C											
0 5	C											
0 6	C											
0 7	C											
0 8	C											
0 9	C											
1 0	C											
1 1	C											
1 2	C											

4. Each time an input record is read, one of three fields (FIELDA, FIELDB, or FIELDC) is printed depending on the values stored in the three fields. Write the calculation specifications needed to set the indicators that specify which field is to print and the output specifications to print the proper field. The conditions controlling which field will print are the following:

   If the value in FIELDA is less than the value in FIELDB and the value in FIELDC is greater than the value in FIELDA, then FIELDA will print.
   If the value in FIELDA is greater than the value in FIELDB and is less than the value in FIELDC, then FIELDB will print.

If the value in FIELDA is greater than the value in FIELDB and is greater than the value in FIELDC, then FIELDC will print.

FIELDA will print ending in position 15, FIELDB will end in position 56, and FIELDC will end in position 90. Use the following specification sheets.

STUDENT EXERCISES: DEBUGGING RPG PROGRAMS

Problem 1

The following RPG program (Figure 4-45) contains one or more errors detected by the compiler. Circle each error and record the corrected entry directly on the listing. Explain the error and the method of correction.

Figure 4-45 Debugging Problem 1

```
Lattice RPG II Compiler Version 2.01                    08:52:31  07/11/1991
Compile listing for source RPG program [HJG04X   .RPG]           PAGE : 0001


     1       H                                                            HJG04X

     2       F*-------------------------------------------------------------------*
     3 S     F*  HJG04X - INVENTORY STATUS REPORT - HAL GOODWIN - JUNE 24, 1991   *
     4 S     F*                                                                   *
     5 S     F*  PROGRAM HJG04X CALCULATES CURRENT ON-HAND QUANTITY, PREVIOUS     *
     6 S     F*  AND CURRENT INVENTORY VALUES, AND IDENTIFIES ITEMS WITH CURRENT  *
     7 S     F*  QUANTITIES AT OR BELOW THEIR RE-ORDER QUANTITIES.  FINAL TOTALS  *
     8 S     F*  OF VALUE FIELDS ARE ACCUMULATED AND COUNTS ARE ACCUMULATED OF    *
     9 S     F*  ITEMS AT OR BELOW RE-ORDER QUANTITY.                             *
    10 S     F*-------------------------------------------------------------------*
    11 S     FINVFILE IP  F 380  38            DISK
    12 S     FINVREPT O   F 132 132      OF    PRINTER
    13       F* ID F  C   H   L    FUNCTION OF INDICATORS
    14 S     F*
    15 S     F* 01--------------INPUT RECORD IDENTIFICATION
    16 S     F*          40---------CURRENT QUANTITY BELOW RE-ORDER POINT
    17 S     F*          41---------CURRENT QUANTITY AT RE-ORDER POINT
    18 S     F*          OF---OVERFLOW INDICATOR
    19 S     F*          1P---FIRST PAGE INDICATOR
    20 S     F*          LR---LAST RECORD INDICATOR

    21       I*-------------------------------------------------------------------*
    22 S     I*  INVFILE INPUT RECORD DESCRIPTION                                 *
    23 S     I*-------------------------------------------------------------------*
    24 S     IINVFILE AA  01
    25 S     I                                          1   8 STOKNO
    26 S     I                                          9 122UCOST
    27 S     I                                         13 180QONHND
    28 S     I                                         19 240QSHIP
    29 S     I                                         25 300QRECVD
    30 S     I                                         31 360REORDR

    31       C*-----------------------------------------------------*
    32 S     C*          STANDARD FORMAT CALCULATIONS               *
    33 S     C*-----------------------------------------------------*
    34 S     C   01       QONHND    MULT UCOST     PVAL    102       PREVIOUS VALUE
    35 S     C   01       QONHND    SUB  QSHIP     QCURNT   60
    36 S     C   01       QCURNT    ADD  QRECVD    QCURNT            CURRENT QUANTITY
    37 S     C   01       QCURNT    MULT UCOST     CVAL    102       CURRENT VALUE
    38 S     C*
    39 S     C   01       QCURNT    COMP           REORDR           4041CHECK RE-ORDER
  T215 Factor 1, factor 2, or result field entry missing.
  T220 Result field entry in columns 43-48 invalid for this operation.
    40 S     C   01 40    REORDR    SUB  QCURNT    UBELOW   60       UNITS UNDER
    41 S     C*
    42 S     C   01       PVALLR    ADD  PVAL      PVALLR  122       ADD TO FINAL
    43 S     C   01       CVALLR    ADD  CVAL      CVALLR  122       TOTAL
    44 S     C   01 40    LOWLR     ADD  1         LOWLR    40       ACCUMULATORS
    45 S     C   01 41    RORDLR    ADD  1         RORDLR   40

    46       O*-----------------------------------------------------------------*
    47 S     O*  HEADING LINE ONE                                                *
    48 S     O*-----------------------------------------------------------------*
    49 S     OINVREPT H  206    1P
```

error messages refer to line 39

Figure 4-45 (1)

```
Lattice RPG II Compiler Version 2.01                08:52:32  07/11/1991
Compile listing for source RPG program [HJG04X  .RPG]         PAGE : 0002


   50 S    O        OR        OF
   51 S    O                                      9 'HJG04X'
   52 S    O                                     50 'INVENTORY STATUS AS OF'
   53 S    O                           UDATE Y    59
   54 S    O                                     82 'PAGE'
   55 S    O                           PAGE  Z    87
   56 S    O*---------------------------------------------------------------*
   57 S    O* HEADING LINE TWO                                              *
   58 S    O*---------------------------------------------------------------*
   59 S    O        H  1     1P
   60 S    O        OR        OF
   61 S    O                                     40 'PREVIOUS     PREVIOUS'
   62 S    O                                     85 'CURRENT       CURRENT'
   63 S    O*---------------------------------------------------------------*
   64 S    O* HEADING LINE THREE                                            *
   65 S    O*---------------------------------------------------------------*
   66 S    O        H  1     1P
   67 S    O        OR        OF
   68 S    O                                     27 'STOCK     UNIT  QUANTITY'
   69 S    O                                     56 'INVENTORY   QUANTITY  QU'
   70 S    O                                     72 'ANTITY  QUANTITY'
   71 S    O                                     86 'INVENTORY'
   72 S    O*---------------------------------------------------------------*
   73 S    O* HEADING LINE FOUR                                             *
   74 S    O*---------------------------------------------------------------*
   75 S    O        H  2     1P
   76 S    O        OR        OF
   77 S    O                                     27 'NUMBER     COST  ON   HAND'
   78 S    O                                     58 'VALUE       SHIPPED    RECE'
   79 S    O                                     72 'IVED  ON  HAND'
   80 S    O                                     84 'VALUE'
   81 S    O*---------------------------------------------------------------*
   82 S    O* DETAIL LINE                                                   *
   83 S    O*---------------------------------------------------------------*
   84 S    O        D  1     01
   85 S    O                           STOKNO    10
   86 S    O                           UCOST 3   17
   87 S    O                           QONHND2   27
   88 S    O                           PVAL  1   42
   89 S    O                           QSHIP 2   52
   90 S    O                           QRECVD2   62
   91 S    O                           QCURNT2   72
   92 S    O                           CVAL  1   87
   93 S    O                   40      UBELOWZ   96
   94 S    O                   40                117 'UNITS BELOW RE-ORDER'
   95 S    O                   40                123 'POINT'
   96 S    O                   41                111 'ITEM AT RE-ORDER POINT'
   97 S    O*---------------------------------------------------------------*
   98 S    O* FINAL TOTAL LINE ONE                                          *
   99 S    O*---------------------------------------------------------------*
  100 S    O        T 11     LR
  101 S    O                           PVALLR1   42 '$'
  102 S    O                           CVALLR1   87 '$'
  103 S    O                           LOWLR Z   96
  104 S    O                                    117 'ITEMS BELOW RE-ORDER'
```

Figure 4-45 (2)

```
Lattice RPG II Compiler Version 2.01                08:52:33  07/11/1991
Compile listing for source RPG program [HJG04X  .RPG]         PAGE : 0003


  105 S    O                                    123 'POINT'
  106 S    O*---------------------------------------------------------------*
  107 S    O* FINAL TOTAL LINE TWO                                          *
  108 S    O*---------------------------------------------------------------*
  109 S    O        T    06  LR
  110 S    O                           RORDLRZ   96
  111 S    O                                    120 'ITEMS AT RE-ORDER POINT'
  112  /*


Warning Severe
Errors  Errors
   0       2
```

Figure 4-45 (3)

Problem 2

The following RPG program (Figure 4-46) contains one or more errors detected by the compiler. Circle each error and record the corrected entry directly on the listing. Explain the error and the method of correction.

Figure 4-46 Debugging Problem 2

```
Lattice RPG II Compiler Version 2.01                    09:00:24  07/11/1991
Compile listing for source RPG program [HJG04X   .RPG]           PAGE : 0001


    1        H                                                              HJG04X

    2        F*--------------------------------------------------------------*
    3  S     F* HJG04X - INVENTORY STATUS REPORT - HAL GOODWIN - JUNE 24, 1991 *
    4  S     F*                                                              *
    5  S     F*  PROGRAM HJG04X CALCULATES CURRENT ON-HAND QUANTITY, PREVIOUS  *
    6  S     F*  AND CURRENT INVENTORY VALUES, AND IDENTIFIES ITEMS WITH CURRENT *
    7  S     F*  QUANTITIES AT OR BELOW THEIR RE-ORDER QUANTITIES.  FINAL TOTALS *
    8  S     F*  OF VALUE FIELDS ARE ACCUMULATED AND COUNTS ARE ACCUMULATED OF  *
    9  S     F*  ITEMS AT OR BELOW RE-ORDER QUANTITY.                          *
   10  S     F*--------------------------------------------------------------*
   11  S     FINVFILE IP  F 380  38        DISK
   12  S     FINVREPT  O  F 132 132    OF    PRINTER
   13  S     F* ID F   C   H   L    FUNCTION OF INDICATORS
   14  S     F*
   15  S     F* 01---------------INPUT RECORD IDENTIFICATION
   16  S     F*        40---------CURRENT QUANTITY BELOW RE-ORDER POINT
   17  S     F*        41---------CURRENT QUANTITY AT RE-ORDER POINT
   18  S     F*            OF---OVERFLOW INDICATOR
   19  S     F*            1P---FIRST PAGE INDICATOR
   20  S     F*            LR---LAST RECORD INDICATOR

   21        I*--------------------------------------------------------------*
   22  S     I*  INVFILE INPUT RECORD DESCRIPTION                            *
   23  S     I*--------------------------------------------------------------*
   24  S     IINVFILE AA  01
   25  S     I                                          1   8 STOKNO
   26  S     I                                          9 122UCOST
   27  S     I                                         13 180QONHND
   28  S     I                                         19 240QSHIP
   29  S     I                                         25 300QRECVD
   30  S     I                                         31 360REORDR

   31        C*--------------------------------------------------------------*
   32  S     C*          STANDARD FORMAT CALCULATIONS              *
   33  S     C*--------------------------------------------------------------*
   34  S     C   01     QONHND    MULT UCOST     PVAL   102     PREVIOUS VALUE
   35  S     C   01     QONHND    SUB  QSHIP     QCURNT  60
   36  S     C   01     QCURNT    ADD  QRECVD    QCURNT          CURRENT QUANTITY
   37  S     C   01     QCURNT    MULT UCOST     CVAL   102     CURRENT VALUE
   38  S     C*
   39  S     C   01     QCURNT    COMP REORDR                   CHECK RE-ORDER
W200 Resulting indicators in columns 54-59 required or not allowed for operation specified.
   40  S     C   01 40  REORDR    SUB  QCURNT    UBELOW  60     UNITS UNDER
   41  S     C*
   42  S     C   01     PVALLR    ADD  PVAL      PVALLR 122     ADD TO FINAL
   43  S     C   01     CVALLR    ADD  CVAL      CVALLR 122     TOTAL
   44  S     C   01 40  LOWLR     ADD  1         LOWLR   40     ACCUMULATORS
   45  S     C   01 41  RORDLR    ADD  1         RORDLR  40

   46        O*--------------------------------------------------------------*
   47  S     O*  HEADING LINE ONE                                            *
   48  S     O*--------------------------------------------------------------*
   49  S     OINVREPT H  206    1P
   50  S     O      OR          OF
```

Figure 4-46 (1)

```
Lattice RPG II Compiler Version 2.01                09:00:25  07/11/1991
Compile listing for source RPG program [HJG04X  .RPG]        PAGE : 0002

    51 S     O                                     9 'HJG04X'
    52 S     O                                    50 'INVENTORY STATUS AS OF'
    53 S     O                       UDATE Y      59
    54 S     O                                    82 'PAGE'
    55 S     O                       PAGE  Z      87
    56 S     O*--------------------------------------------------------------*
    57 S     O* HEADING LINE TWO                                             *
    58 S     O*--------------------------------------------------------------*
    59 S     O          H  1    1P
    60 S     O      OR          OF
    61 S     O                                    40 'PREVIOUS    PREVIOUS'
    62 S     O                                    85 'CURRENT      CURRENT'
    63 S     O*--------------------------------------------------------------*
    64 S     O* HEADING LINE THREE                                           *
    65 S     O*--------------------------------------------------------------*
    66 S     O          H  1    1P
    67 S     O      OR          OF
    68 S     O                                    27 'STOCK     UNIT  QUANTITY'
    69 S     O                                    56 'INVENTORY   QUANTITY  QU'
    70 S     O                                    72 'ANTITY  QUANTITY'
    71 S     O                                    86 'INVENTORY'
    72 S     O*--------------------------------------------------------------*
    73 S     O* HEADING LINE FOUR                                            *
    74 S     O*--------------------------------------------------------------*
    75 S     O          H  2    1P
    76 S     O      OR          OF
    77 S     O                                    27 'NUMBER    COST  ON   HAND'
    78 S     O .                                  58 'VALUE     SHIPPED    RECE'
    79 S     O                                    72 'IVED  ON  HAND'
    80 S     O                                    84 'VALUE'
    81 S     O*--------------------------------------------------------------*
    82 S     O* DETAIL LINE                                                  *
    83 S     O*--------------------------------------------------------------*
    84 S     O          D  1    01
    85 S     O                       STOKNO       10
    86 S     O                       UCOST 3      17
    87 S     O                       QONHND2      27
    88 S     O                       PVAL  1      42
    89 S     O                       QSHIP 2      52
    90 S     O                       QRECVD2      62
    91 S     O                       QCURNT2      72
    92 S     O                       CVAL  1      87
    93 S     O                  40   UBELOWZ      96
    94 S     O                  40              117 'UNITS BELOW RE-ORDER'
    95 S     O                  40              123 'POINT'
    96 S     O                  41              111 'ITEM AT RE-ORDER POINT'
    97 S     O*--------------------------------------------------------------*
    98 S     O* FINAL TOTAL LINE ONE                                         *
    99 S     O*--------------------------------------------------------------*
   100 S     O          T 11    LR
   101 S     O                       PVALLR1      42 '$'
   102 S     O                       CVALLR1      87 '$'
   103 S     O                       LOWLR Z      96
   104 S     O                                   117 'ITEMS BELOW RE-ORDER'
   105 S     O                                   123 'POINT'
```

Figure 4-46 (2)

```
Lattice RPG II Compiler Version 2.01                09:00:26  07/11/1991
Compile listing for source RPG program [HJG04X  .RPG]        PAGE : 0003

   106 S     O*--------------------------------------------------------------*
   107 S     O* FINAL TOTAL LINE TWO                                         *
   108 S     O*--------------------------------------------------------------*
   109 S     O          T    06 LR
   110 S     O                       RORDLRZ      96
   111 S     O                                   120 'ITEMS AT RE-ORDER POINT'
   112 /*

Warning Severe
Errors Errors
   1      0
```

Figure 4-46 (3)

continued

```
HJG04X                    INVENTORY STATUS AS OF  7/06/91                    PAGE   1

              PREVIOUS     PREVIOUS                          CURRENT      CURRENT
   STOCK    UNIT  QUANTITY   INVENTORY   QUANTITY   QUANTITY  QUANTITY    INVENTORY
  NUMBER    COST  ON  HAND     VALUE     SHIPPED    RECEIVED  ON  HAND      VALUE
  A35-2621  1.30      251       326.30                            251        326.30
  A35-2738   .04   137,850    5,514.00    47,365                90,485     3,619.40
  A76-3184   .10    87,416    8,741.60    80,000                 7,416       741.60
  B31-1004   .07   638,412   44,688.84              100,000    738,412    51,688.84
  C42-1411  1.00   427,631  427,631.00   146,218    200,000    481,413   481,413.00
  F31-2600   .01   800,000    8,000.00   700,000    200,000    300,000     3,000.00
  G46-384X  21.16      835   17,668.60       400                   435     9,204.60
  H39-874J  46.12        6      276.72                 100         106     4,888.72
  L86-4166  12.37      742    9,178.54       142                   600     7,422.00
  L93-2147  1.48     8,575   12,691.00     8,575                                .00
  P40-0250  2.71     3,162    8,569.02       485                 2,677     7,254.67
  P86-M1.1   .99     7,583    7,507.17     2,000                 5,583     5,527.17

                             $550,792.79                               $575,086.30    ITEMS BELOW RE-ORDER POINT
                                                                                      ITEMS AT RE-ORDER POINT
```

Figure 4-46 (4)

▤ Problem 3

The following RPG program (Figure 4-47) contains one or more errors detected while checking output from the program. Circle each error and record the corrected entry directly on the listing. Explain the error and method of correction.

Figure 4-47   Debugging Problem 3

```
Lattice RPG II Compiler Version 2.01                09:04:41 07/11/1991
Compile listing for source RPG program [HJG04X  .RPG]        PAGE : 0001


   1       H                                                              HJG04X

   2       F*------------------------------------------------------------------*
   3  S    F*  HJG04X - INVENTORY STATUS REPORT - HAL GOODWIN - JUNE 24, 1991  *
   4  S    F*                                                                  *
   5  S    F*  PROGRAM HJG04X CALCULATES CURRENT ON-HAND QUANTITY, PREVIOUS    *
   6  S    F*  AND CURRENT INVENTORY VALUES, AND IDENTIFIES ITEMS WITH CURRENT *
   7  S    F*  QUANTITIES AT OR BELOW THEIR RE-ORDER QUANTITIES.  FINAL TOTALS *
   8  S    F*  OF VALUE FIELDS ARE ACCUMULATED AND COUNTS ARE ACCUMULATED OF   *
   9  S    F*  ITEMS AT OR BELOW RE-ORDER QUANTITY.                            *
  10  S    F*------------------------------------------------------------------*
  11  S    FINVFILE IP  F 380  38          DISK
  12  S    FINVREPT  O  F 132 132     OF    PRINTER
  13  S    F* ID F  C  H  L    FUNCTION OF INDICATORS
  14  S    F*
  15  S    F* 01----------------INPUT RECORD IDENTIFICATION
  16  S    F*       40---------CURRENT QUANTITY BELOW RE-ORDER POINT
  17  S    F*       41---------CURRENT QUANTITY AT RE-ORDER POINT
  18  S    F*         OF---OVERFLOW INDICATOR
  19  S    F*         1P---FIRST PAGE INDICATOR
  20  S    F*         LR---LAST RECORD INDICATOR

  21       I*------------------------------------------------------------------*
  22  S    I*  INVFILE INPUT RECORD DESCRIPTION                                *
  23  S    I*------------------------------------------------------------------*
  24  S    IINVFILE AA  01
  25  S    I                                       1   8 STOKNO
  26  S    I                                       9  122UCOST
  27  S    I                                      13  180QONHND
  28  S    I                                      19  240QSHIP
  29  S    I                                      25  300QRECVD
  30  S    I                                      31  360REORDR

  31       C*------------------------------------------------------------------*
  32  S    C*         STANDARD FORMAT CALCULATIONS                             *
  33  S    C*------------------------------------------------------------------*
  34  S    C    01      QONHND    MULT UCOST    PVAL    102      PREVIOUS VALUE
  35  S    C    01      QONHND    SUB  QSHIP    QCURNT   60
  36  S    C    01      QCURNT    ADD  QRECVD   QCURNT            CURRENT QUANTITY
  37  S    C    01      QCURNT    MULT UCOST    CVAL    102      CURRENT VALUE
  38  S    C*
  39  S    C    01      QCURNT    COMP REORDR           4041CHECK RE-ORDER
  40  S    C    01 40   REORDR    SUB  QCURNT   UBELOW   60      UNITS UNDER
  41  S    C*
  42  S    C    01      PVALLR    ADD  PVAL     PVALLR  122      ADD TO FINAL
  43  S    C    01      CVALLR    ADD  CVAL     CVALLR  122      TOTAL
  44  S    C    01 41   LOWLR     ADD  1        LOWLR    40      ACCUMULATORS
  45  S    C    01 40   RORDLR    ADD  1        RORDLR   40

  46       O*------------------------------------------------------------------*
  47  S    O*  HEADING LINE ONE                                                *
  48  S    O*------------------------------------------------------------------*
  49  S    OINVREPT H  206    1P
  50  S    O          OR      OF
  51  S    O                            9 'HJG04X'
```

Figure 4-47 (1)

```
Lattice RPG II Compiler Version 2.01                    09:04:41  07/11/1991
Compile listing for source RPG program [HJG04X  .RPG]            PAGE : 0002


    52 S   O                                         50 'INVENTORY STATUS AS OF'
    53 S   O                              UDATE Y    59
    54 S   O                                         82 'PAGE'
    55 S   O                              PAGE  Z    87
    56 S   O*----------------------------------------------------------------*
    57 S   O*  HEADING LINE TWO                                              *
    58 S   O*----------------------------------------------------------------*
    59 S   O        H  1      1P
    60 S   O        OR        OF
    61 S   O                                         40 'PREVIOUS     PREVIOUS'
    62 S   O                                         85 'CURRENT      CURRENT'
    63 S   O*----------------------------------------------------------------*
    64 S   O*  HEADING LINE THREE                                            *
    65 S   O*----------------------------------------------------------------*
    66 S   O        H  1      1P
    67 S   O        OR        OF
    68 S   O                                         27 'STOCK     UNIT  QUANTITY'
    69 S   O                                         56 'INVENTORY  QUANTITY  QU'
    70 S   O                                         72 'ANTITY  QUANTITY'
    71 S   O                                         86 'INVENTORY'
    72 S   O*----------------------------------------------------------------*
    73 S   O*  HEADING LINE FOUR                                             *
    74 S   O*----------------------------------------------------------------*
    75 S   O        H  2      1P
    76 S   O        OR        OF
    77 S   O                                         27 'NUMBER    COST  ON   HAND'
    78 S   O                                         58 'VALUE     SHIPPED   RECE'
    79 S   O                                         72 'IVED  ON   HAND'
    80 S   O                                         84 'VALUE'
    81 S   O*----------------------------------------------------------------*
    82 S   O*  DETAIL LINE                                                   *
    83 S   O*----------------------------------------------------------------*
    84 S   O        D  1      01
    85 S   O                              STOKNO    10
    86 S   O                              UCOST 3   17
    87 S   O                              QONHND2   27
    88 S   O                              PVAL  1   42
    89 S   O                              QSHIP 2   52
    90 S   O                              QRECVD2   62
    91 S   O                              QCURNT2   72
    92 S   O                              CVAL  1   87
    93 S   O                40            UBELOWZ   96
    94 S   O                40                      117 'UNITS BELOW RE-ORDER'
    95 S   O                40                      123 'POINT'
    96 S   O                41                      111 'ITEM AT RE-ORDER POINT'
    97 S   O*----------------------------------------------------------------*
    98 S   O*  FINAL TOTAL LINE ONE                                          *
    99 S   O*----------------------------------------------------------------*
   100 S   O        T 11      LR
   101 S   O                              PVALLR1   42 '$'
   102 S   O                              CVALLR1   87 '$'
   103 S   O                              LOWLR Z   96
   104 S   O                                        117 'ITEMS BELOW RE-ORDER'
   105 S   O                                        123 'POINT'
   106 S   O*----------------------------------------------------------------*
```

Figure 4-47 (2)

```
Lattice RPG II Compiler Version 2.01                    09:04:43  07/11/1991
Compile listing for source RPG program [HJG04X  .RPG]            PAGE : 0003


   107 S   O*  FINAL TOTAL LINE TWO                                         *
   108 S   O*----------------------------------------------------------------*
   109 S   O        T     06  LR
   110 S   O                              RORDLRZ   96
   111 S   O                                        120 'ITEMS AT RE-ORDER POINT'
   112  /*

Warning Severe
Errors  Errors
   0       0
```

Figure 4-47 (3)

continued

```
HJG04X                    INVENTORY STATUS AS OF  7/06/91                      PAGE    1

                     PREVIOUS    PREVIOUS                       CURRENT     CURRENT
          STOCK   UNIT QUANTITY   INVENTORY  QUANTITY  QUANTITY  QUANTITY   INVENTORY
          NUMBER  COST ON  HAND     VALUE     SHIPPED  RECEIVED  ON  HAND     VALUE

          A35-2621  1.30      251      326.30                         251      326.30
          A35-2738   .04  137,850    5,514.00   47,365            90,485    3,619.40
          A76-3184   .10   87,416    8,741.60   80,000             7,416      741.60   2584 UNITS BELOW RE-ORDER POINT
          B31-1004   .07  638,412   44,688.84           100,000  738,412   51,688.84
          C42-1411  1.00  427,631  427,631.00  146,218  200,000  481,413  481,413.00  18587 UNITS BELOW RE-ORDER POINT
          F31-2600   .01  800,000    8,000.00  700,000  200,000  300,000    3,000.00  ITEM AT RE-ORDER POINT
          G46-384X  21.16      835   17,668.60      400                435    9,204.60     65 UNITS BELOW RE-ORDER POINT
          H39-874J  46.12        6      276.72                100       106    4,888.72     94 UNITS BELOW RE-ORDER POINT
          L86-4166  12.37      742    9,178.54      142                600    7,422.00  ITEM AT RE-ORDER POINT
          L93-2147   1.48    8,575   12,691.00    8,575                 .00   5000 UNITS BELOW RE-ORDER POINT
          P40-0250   2.71    3,162    8,569.02      485              2,677    7,254.67
          P86-M1.1    .99    7,583    7,507.17    2,000              5,583    5,527.17     17 UNITS BELOW RE-ORDER POINT

                              $550,792.79                                  $575,086.30    2 ITEMS BELOW RE-ORDER POINT
                                                                                          6 ITEMS AT RE-ORDER POINT
```

final total counts do not agree with number of messages

Figure 4-47 (4)

▬ Problem 4

The following RPG program (Figure 4-48) contains one or more errors detected while checking output from the program. Circle each error and record the corrected entry directly on the listing. Explain the error and method of correction.

Figure 4-48   Debugging Problem 4

```
Lattice RPG II Compiler Version 2.01                    09:41:03  07/11/1991
Compile listing for source RPG program [HJG04X  .RPG]            PAGE : 0001


    1       H                                                          HJG04X

    2 S     F*-------------------------------------------------------------------*
    3 S     F*  HJG04X - INVENTORY STATUS REPORT - HAL GOODWIN - JUNE 24, 1991  *
    4 S     F*                                                                  *
    5 S     F*  PROGRAM HJG04X CALCULATES CURRENT ON-HAND QUANTITY, PREVIOUS    *
    6 S     F*  AND CURRENT INVENTORY VALUES, AND IDENTIFIES ITEMS WITH CURRENT *
    7 S     F*  QUANTITIES AT OR BELOW THEIR RE-ORDER QUANTITIES.  FINAL TOTALS *
    8 S     F*  OF VALUE FIELDS ARE ACCUMULATED AND COUNTS ARE ACCUMULATED OF   *
    9 S     F*  ITEMS AT OR BELOW RE-ORDER QUANTITY.                            *
   10 S     F*-------------------------------------------------------------------*
   11 S     FINVFILE IP  F 380 38           DISK
   12 S     FINVREPT O   F 132 132     OF    PRINTER
   13 S     F* ID F  C   H   L    FUNCTION OF INDICATORS
   14 S     F*
   15 S     F* 01--------------INPUT RECORD IDENTIFICATION
   16 S     F*        40---------CURRENT QUANTITY BELOW RE-ORDER POINT
   17 S     F*        41---------CURRENT QUANTITY AT RE-ORDER POINT
   18 S     F*           OF---OVERFLOW INDICATOR
   19 S     F*           1P---FIRST PAGE INDICATOR
   20 S     F*           LR---LAST RECORD INDICATOR

   21       I*-------------------------------------------------------------------*
   22 S     I*  INVFILE INPUT RECORD DESCRIPTION                                 *
   23 S     I*-------------------------------------------------------------------*
   24 S     IINVFILE AA  01
   25 S     I                                         1   8 STOKNO
   26 S     I                                         9 122UCOST
   27 S     I                                        13 180QONHND
   28 S     I                                        19 240QSHIP
   29 S     I                                        25 300QRECVD
   30 S     I                                        31 360REORDR

   31       C*-------------------------------------------------------------------*
   32 S     C*          STANDARD FORMAT CALCULATIONS              *
   33 S     C*-------------------------------------------------------------------*
   34 S     C    01   QONHND   MULT UCOST    PVAL   102    PREVIOUS VALUE
   35 S     C    01   QONHND   SUB  QSHIP    QCURNT  60
   36 S     C    01   QCURNT   ADD  QRECVD   QCURNT         CURRENT QUANTITY
   37 S     C    01   QCURNT   MULT UCOST    CVAL   102     CURRENT VALUE
   38 S     C*
   39 S     C    01   QCURNT   COMP REORDR          4140CHECK RE-ORDER
   40 S     C    01 40 REORDR   SUB  QCURNT   UBELOW  60    UNITS UNDER
   41 S     C*
   42 S     C    01   PVALLR   ADD  PVAL     PVALLR 122     ADD TO FINAL
   43 S     C    01   CVALLR   ADD  CVAL     CVALLR 122     TOTAL
   44 S     C    01 40 LOWLR    ADD  1        LOWLR   40     ACCUMULATORS
   45 S     C    01 41 RORDLR   ADD  1        RORDLR  40

   46       O*-------------------------------------------------------------------*
   47 S     O*  HEADING LINE ONE                                                 *
   48 S     O*-------------------------------------------------------------------*
   49 S     OINVREPT H  206     1P
   50 S     O      OR       OF
   51 S     O                        9 'HJG04X'
```

Figure 4-48 (1)

```
Lattice RPG II Compiler Version 2.01                    09:41:04 07/11/1991
Compile listing for source RPG program [HJG04X  .RPG]          PAGE : 0002

 52 S    O                                          50 'INVENTORY STATUS AS OF'
 53 S    O                              UDATE Y     59
 54 S    O                                          82 'PAGE'
 55 S    O                              PAGE  Z     87
 56 S    O*-----------------------------------------------------------------*
 57 S    O*  HEADING LINE TWO                                               *
 58 S    O*-----------------------------------------------------------------*
 59 S    O        H  1     1P
 60 S    O   OR         OF
 61 S    O                                          40 'PREVIOUS     PREVIOUS'
 62 S    O                                          85 'CURRENT      CURRENT'
 63 S    O*-----------------------------------------------------------------*
 64 S    O*  HEADING LINE THREE                                             *
 65 S    O*-----------------------------------------------------------------*
 66 S    O        H  1     1P
 67 S    O   OR         OF
 68 S    O                                          27 'STOCK     UNIT QUANTITY'
 69 S    O                                          56 'INVENTORY    QUANTITY QU'
 70 S    O                                          72 'ANTITY   QUANTITY'
 71 S    O                                          86 'INVENTORY'
 72 S    O*-----------------------------------------------------------------*
 73 S    O*  HEADING LINE FOUR                                              *
 74 S    O*-----------------------------------------------------------------*
 75 S    O        H  2     1P
 76 S    O   OR         OF
 77 S    O                                          27 'NUMBER    COST ON  HAND'
 78 S    O                                          58 'VALUE     SHIPPED   RECE'
 79 S    O                                          72 'IVED  ON  HAND'
 80 S    O                                          84 'VALUE'
 81 S    O*-----------------------------------------------------------------*
 82 S    O*  DETAIL LINE                                                    *
 83 S    O*-----------------------------------------------------------------*
 84 S    O        D  1     01
 85 S    O                              STOKNO     10
 86 S    O                              UCOST 3    17
 87 S    O                              QONHND2    27
 88 S    O                              PVAL  1    42
 89 S    O                              QSHIP 2    52
 90 S    O                              QRECVD2    62
 91 S    O                              QCURNT2    72
 92 S    O                              CVAL  1    87
 93 S    O                        40    UBELOWZ    96
 94 S    O                        40               117 'UNITS BELOW RE-ORDER'
 95 S    O                        40               123 'POINT'
 96 S    O                        41               111 'ITEM AT RE-ORDER POINT'
 97 S    O*-----------------------------------------------------------------*
 98 S    O*  FINAL TOTAL LINE ONE                                           *
 99 S    O*-----------------------------------------------------------------*
100 S    O        T 11     LR
101 S    O                              PVALLR1    42 'S'
102 S    O                              CVALLR1    87 'S'
103 S    O                              LOWLR Z    96
104 S    O                                         117 'ITEMS BELOW RE-ORDER'
105 S    O                                         123 'POINT'
106 S    O*-----------------------------------------------------------------*
```

Figure 4-48 (2)

```
Lattice RPG II Compiler Version 2.01                    09:41:05 07/11/1991
Compile listing for source RPG program [HJG04X  .RPG]          PAGE : 0003


107 S    O*  FINAL TOTAL LINE TWO                                           *
108 S    O*-----------------------------------------------------------------*
109 S    O        T    06 LR
110 S    O                              RORDLRZ    96
111 S    O                                         120 'ITEMS AT RE-ORDER POINT'
112 /*


Warning Severe
Errors  Errors
   0      0
```

Figure 4-48 (3)

continued

```
HJG04X                    INVENTORY STATUS AS OF  7/06/91                       PAGE   1

            PREVIOUS      PREVIOUS                           CURRENT      CURRENT
 STOCK      UNIT  QUANTITY  INVENTORY  QUANTITY  QUANTITY   QUANTITY    INVENTORY
 NUMBER     COST  ON  HAND    VALUE    SHIPPED   RECEIVED   ON  HAND      VALUE

 A35-2621   1.30      251      326.30                           251       326.30
 A35-2738    .04   137,850    5,514.00   47,365              90,485     3,619.40
 A76-3184    .10    87,416    8,741.60   80,000               7,416       741.60   ITEM AT RE-ORDER POINT
 B31-1004    .07   638,412   44,688.84            100,000   738,412    51,688.84
 C42-1411   1.00   427,631  427,631.00  146,218  200,000   481,413   481,413.00   ITEM AT RE-ORDER POINT
 F31-2600    .01   800,000    8,000.00  700,000  200,000   300,000     3,000.00   UNITS BELOW RE-ORDER POINT
 G46-384X  21.16       835   17,668.60      400                 435     9,204.60   ITEM AT RE-ORDER POINT
 H39-874J  46.12         6      276.72               100        106     4,888.72   ITEM AT RE-ORDER POINT
 L86-4166  12.37       742    9,178.54      142                 600     7,422.00   UNITS BELOW RE-ORDER POINT
 L93-2147   1.48     8,575   12,691.00    8,575                 .00   ITEM AT RE-ORDER POINT
 P40-0250   2.71     3,162    8,569.02      485               2,677     7,254.67
 P86-M1.1    .99     7,583    7,507.17    2,000               5,583     5,527.17   ITEM AT RE-ORDER POINT

                             $550,792.79                              $575,086.30   2 ITEMS BELOW RE-ORDER POINT
                                                                                    6 ITEMS AT RE-ORDER POINT
```

Figure 4-48 (4)

STUDENT EXERCISES: PROGRAMMING IN RPG

All four programming exercises for this chapter are based on programming requests from the personnel department, and all the programs are based on data found in the Employee Payroll File. The format of the employee payroll records is shown in Figure 4-49. As you can see, this format differs from those you have seen in earlier examples.

As record descriptions become more detailed, the graphic illustration format we have used so far becomes inconvenient. As the number of fields increases and some fields occupy only a single position, it becomes difficult to write the needed descriptive information within the record layout.

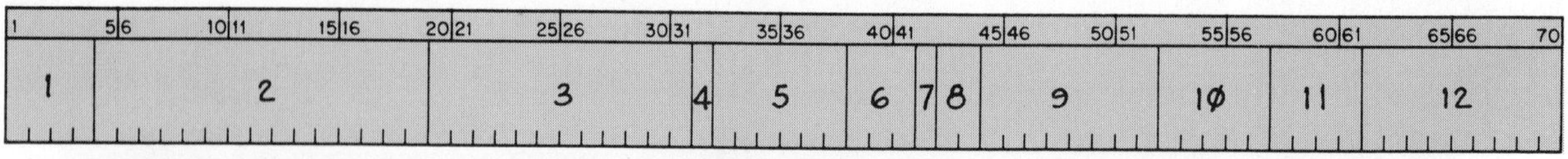

	5 6	10 11	15 16	20 21	25 26	30 31	35 36	40 41	45 46	50 51	55 56	60 61	65 66	70
1		2			3		4	5	6	7	8	9	10	11	12

EMPLOYEE PAYROLL RECORD						
Record Length 70						
Field No.	Field Name	Field Description	Field Position	Field Length	Dec. Pos.	Data Class
1	EMPLID	Employee Number	1–4	4	0	N
2	LNAME	Last Name	5–19	15		A
3	FNAME	First Name	20–31	12		A
4	SCODE	Sex Code (M/F)	32	1		A
5	DTHIRE	Date Hired	33–38	6	0	N
6	DEPTNO	Department Number	39–41	3	0	N
7	PAYCAT	Pay Category (H/S)	42	1		A
8	RATCOD	Pay Rate Code	43–44	2	0	N
9	ANNSAL	Annual Salary	45–52	8	2	N
10	HRATE	Hourly Pay Rate	53–57	5	3	N
11	HOURS	Hours Worked Last Pay Period	58–61	4	1	N
12		UNUSED AREA	62–70			

Figure 4-49   Format of employee payroll records

Figure 4-49 shows the standard layout; but instead of field descriptions, each field area is identified by a number. Below the layout is a chart that contains the needed information about each of the fields in the record. The field number column at the left of the chart relates each line to the field area in the layout. In addition to field number, each line shows the following information for each field:

Field name Can appear in a record description if standardized field names have been assigned for use in all programming applications

Field description Brief description of the data contained within the field

Field position Location of the field within the record; shows the starting (FROM) and ending (TO) positions occupied by the field

Field length Number of positions occupied by the field

Dec. Pos. Number of decimal positions in a numeric data field

Data Class Data class of the field

Note that this description contains all the fields found in the record. A specific program may not use all these fields. As you analyze each program, you must determine which fields are needed for that program. Remember that unused data fields are normally not described in the RPG Input specifications. Data for the employee payroll file is contained in test data set 8.

PROGRAMMING ASSIGNMENT 1
WEEKLY EARNINGS REPORT

INSTRUCTIONS

Plan, code, enter, and test an RPG program to produce the Weekly Earnings Report based on input data found in the employee payroll file.

INPUT

Input is the Employee Payroll Record shown in Figure 4-49.

OUTPUT

Output is the Weekly Earnings Report, the format of which is shown in Figure 4-50.

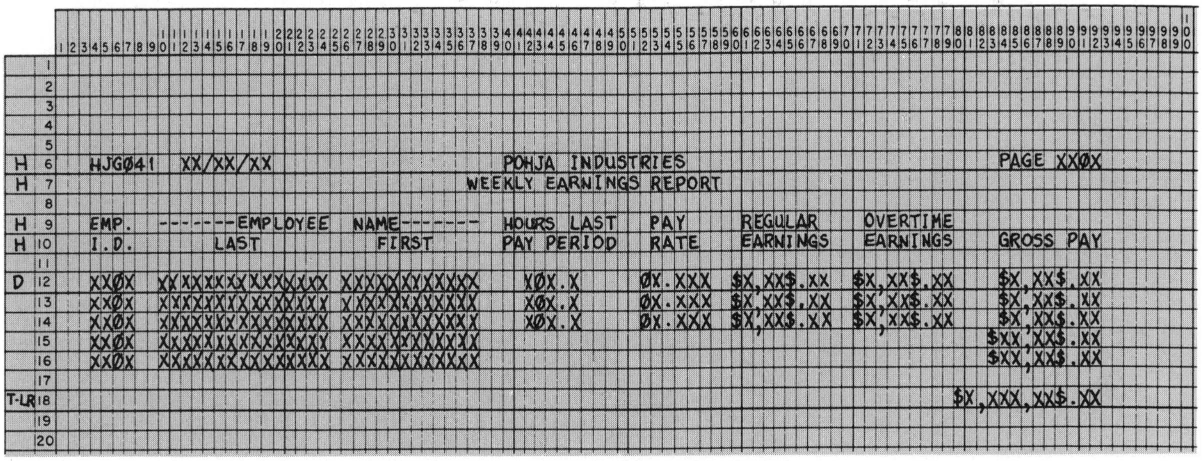

Figure 4-50 Weekly Earnings Report

Processing Requirements

The Weekly Earnings Report is a detail report showing the weekly earnings for each employee of Pohja Industries. The company employs both salaried and hourly employees. The category of employee is determined by the contents of the Pay Category field. The Pay Category field has been verified and contains no invalid entries. Salaried employees are identified by an S in this field. When a salaried employee's record is processed, the detail output shown on lines 15 and 16 of the printer spacing chart is produced. The weekly gross pay for a salaried employee is calculated by dividing the Annual Salary field by 52.

Hourly employees are identified by a Pay Category entry of H. The earnings for hourly employees are calculated as follows:

If hours worked last pay period is not greater than 40.000, then regular earnings = hours worked last pay period * hourly pay rate; overtime earnings = 0.

If hours worked last pay period is greater than 40, then regular earnings = hourly pay rate * 40; overtime earnings = (hours worked last pay period – 40) * hourly pay rate * 1.5. For example, if an employee worked 47 hours at an hourly pay rate of $5.60, she would be paid as follows:

Regular earnings $224.00 (or 40 * 5.60)

Overtime earnings $58.80 (or 7 * (5.60 * 1.5))

Gross pay for hourly employees is the sum of regular earnings + overtime earnings. The detail line format for hourly employees is shown on lines 12, 13, and 14 of the printer spacing chart.

Gross pay for all employees is to be accumulated and the sum printed as a final total.

PROGRAMMING ASSIGNMENT 2
VACATION STATUS REPORT

INSTRUCTIONS

Plan, code, enter, and test an RPG program to produce the Vacation Status Report.

INPUT

Input is the employee payroll record shown in Figure 4-49.

OUTPUT

Output is the Vacation Status Report, the format of which is shown in Figure 4-51.

Processing Requirements

The Vacation Status Report lists each employee and the number of weeks of vacation to which the employee is entitled. Note that only the initial of the first name is printed.

Vacation entitlement is based upon the Date Hired field according to the following rules:

If the employee was hired after January 1, 1990, the employee receives no vacation. Note that the word NONE is printed in the weeks of vacation column.

If date hired is between June 1, 1989 and December 30, 1989, the employee receives one vacation week.

If date hired is between June 1, 1984 and May 31, 1989, the employee receives two vacation weeks.

If date hired is between June 1, 1979 and May 31, 1984, the employee receives three vacation weeks.

If date hired is earlier than June 1, 1979, the employee receives four vacation weeks.

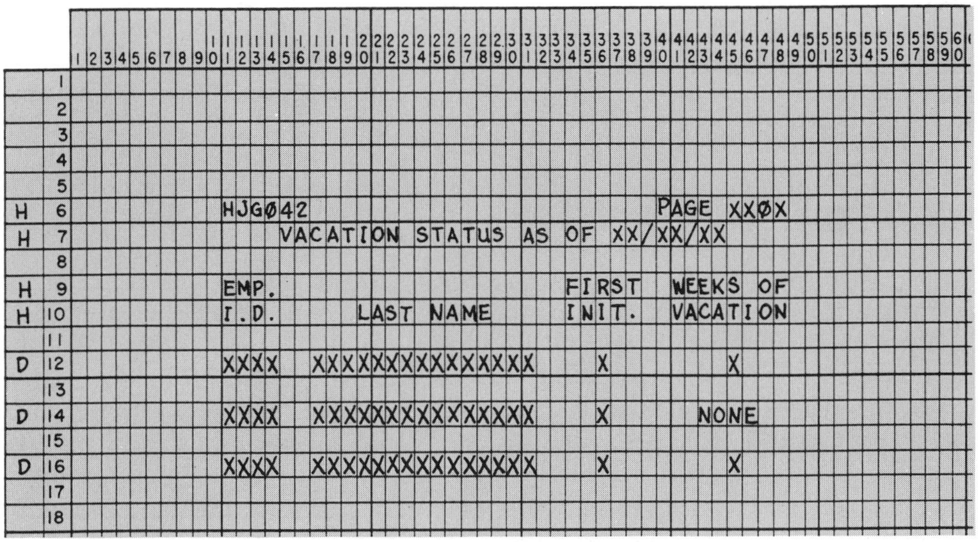

Figure 4-51   Vacation Status Report

PROGRAMMING ASSIGNMENT 3
EMPLOYEE LIST

INSTRUCTIONS

Plan, code, enter, and test an RPG program to produce the Employee List.

INPUT

Input is the employee payroll record shown in Figure 4-49.

OUTPUT

Output is the Employee List, the format of which is shown in Figure 4-52.

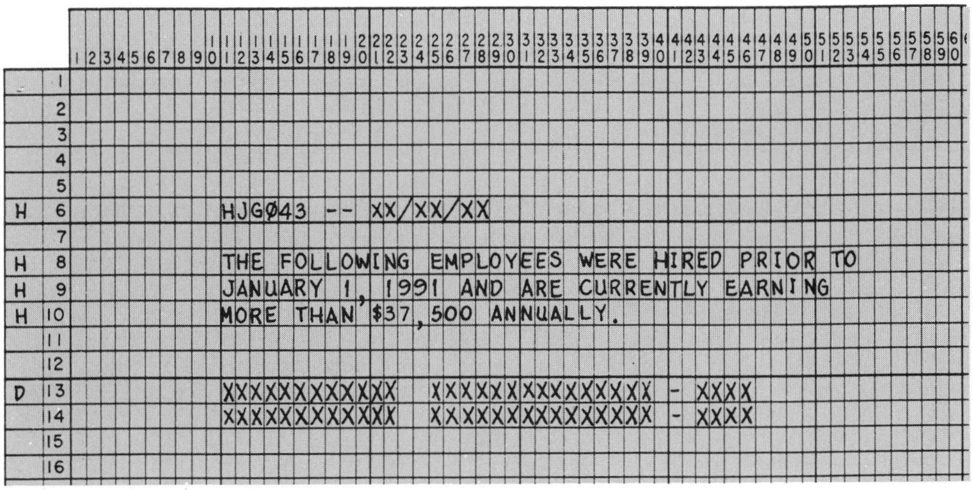

Figure 4-52   Employee List

The report contains headings only on the first page. Your program must not contain any coding that would cause overflow headings to print. Note: The lack of an overflow indicator in the output file description specification can cause a warning message in some versions of RPG. This warning message should be ignored. Each detail line printed will contain the first name in positions 11–22, the last name in positions 25–39, and the employee number in positions 43–46.

▤ Processing Requirements

The program must test each input record for two conditions. If both conditions exist, a detail line is printed. If either or both of these conditions do not exist, no detail output is produced for the input record. An output record is printed if the following conditions hold:

The employee was hired prior to January 1, 1985, and the employee is a salaried employee with an annual salary greater than $37,500.00.

▤ PROGRAMMING ASSIGNMENT 4 ▤ EMPLOYEE SUMMARY REPORT

INSTRUCTIONS

Plan, code, enter, and test an RPG program to produce the Employee Summary Report.

INPUT

Input is the employee payroll record shown in Figure 4-49.

OUTPUT

Output is the Employee Summary Report, the format of which is shown in Figure 4-53.

Because this report occupies only one page, it contains no detail output and no overflow headings. The report consists of four heading lines and ten total lines, which are printed at the end of the program.

▤ Processing Requirements

The program will count, based on the contents of the Sex Code field and the Pay Rate Code field, the number of male and female employees within pay rate categories 01, 02, 03, 04, 05, 06, 07, 08, 09, and 10. The Sex Code field has been verified and contains the letters M for male employees and F for female employees. There are no incorrect Sex Code entries.

If the program determines that a Pay Rate Code entry is greater than ten, no further processing is to be performed for the record.

Twenty counts will be accumulated, one each for the number of male and female employees in each of the pay rate categories 01–10. The program will print the 20 counts at the end of the program.

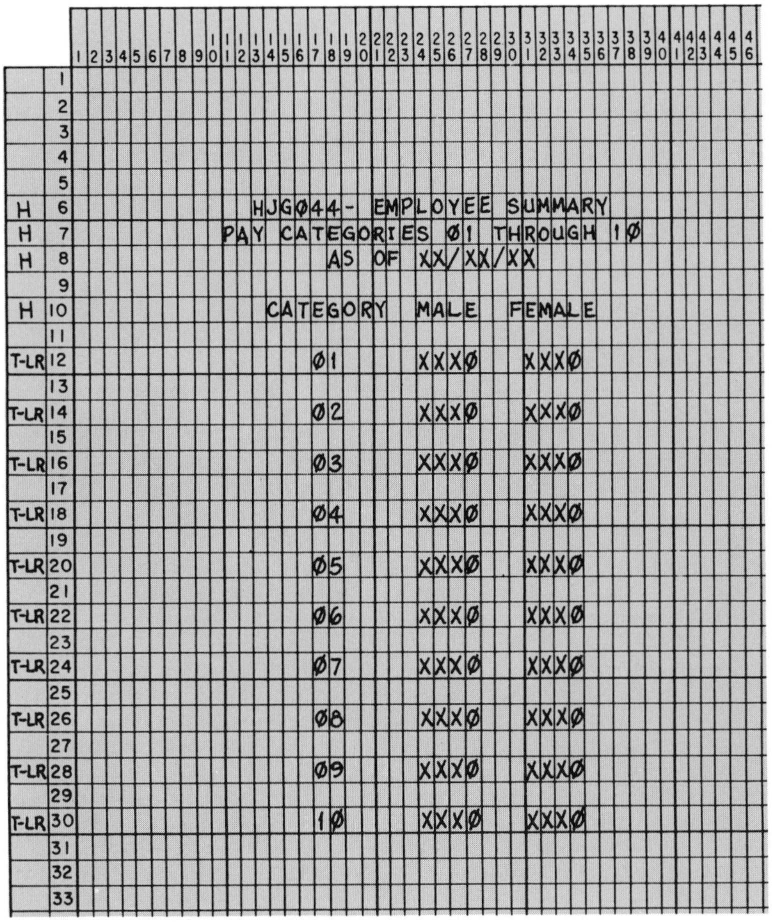
H 6 HJGØ44- EMPLOYEE SUMMARY
H 7 PAY CATEGORIES Ø1 THROUGH 1Ø
H 8 AS OF XX/XX/XX
H 10 CATEGORY MALE FEMALE
T-LR 12 Ø1 XXXØ XXXØ
T-LR 14 Ø2 XXXØ XXXØ
T-LR 16 Ø3 XXXØ XXXØ
T-LR 18 Ø4 XXXØ XXXØ
T-LR 20 Ø5 XXXØ XXXØ
T-LR 22 Ø6 XXXØ XXXØ
T-LR 24 Ø7 XXXØ XXXØ
T-LR 26 Ø8 XXXØ XXXØ
T-LR 28 Ø9 XXXØ XXXØ
T-LR 30 1Ø XXXØ XXXØ

Figure 4-53 Employee Summary Report

Control Breaks, Group Indication, Group Printing, & Fetch Overflow

CONTROL BREAK PROCESSING

In all the programming examples that you have seen and developed thus far, the records in the input data file have been treated as a single unit. After program execution began, the detail processing cycle continued until the program ended. Each input record was read, calculated, and printed in an uninterrupted series of operations. This continuous detail processing cycle is not always suited to business programs. Many business programming applications require the temporary interruption of detail processing, usually for printing totals that have accumulated from the preceding group of input records. Printing these totals is usually effected by a programming technique called control break processing.

The Control Break, A Temporary Pause

A **control break** is a pause in detail processing and is usually used for printing group totals. A control break occurs when the value in a specific input field differs from the value in that field in the previous record.

▸ **Control Fields** The field on which control break processing is based is called the **control field**. Figure 5-1 on the next page shows a series of nine records in a data file. Only the Store Number field is shown in detail because Store Number is being used as the control field in this example.

In programs that use control break logic, the fixed logic cycle performs automatic functions to determine if the value in the control field has changed from the value in the previous record. RPG sets up a special area in memory to store the control field value of each record after the record is read by the program. When the next record is read, the control field is compared with the special area. If the two values are the same, no control break occurs. If the two values are not equal, the program turns on a special-purpose indicator that enables you to perform control break processing.

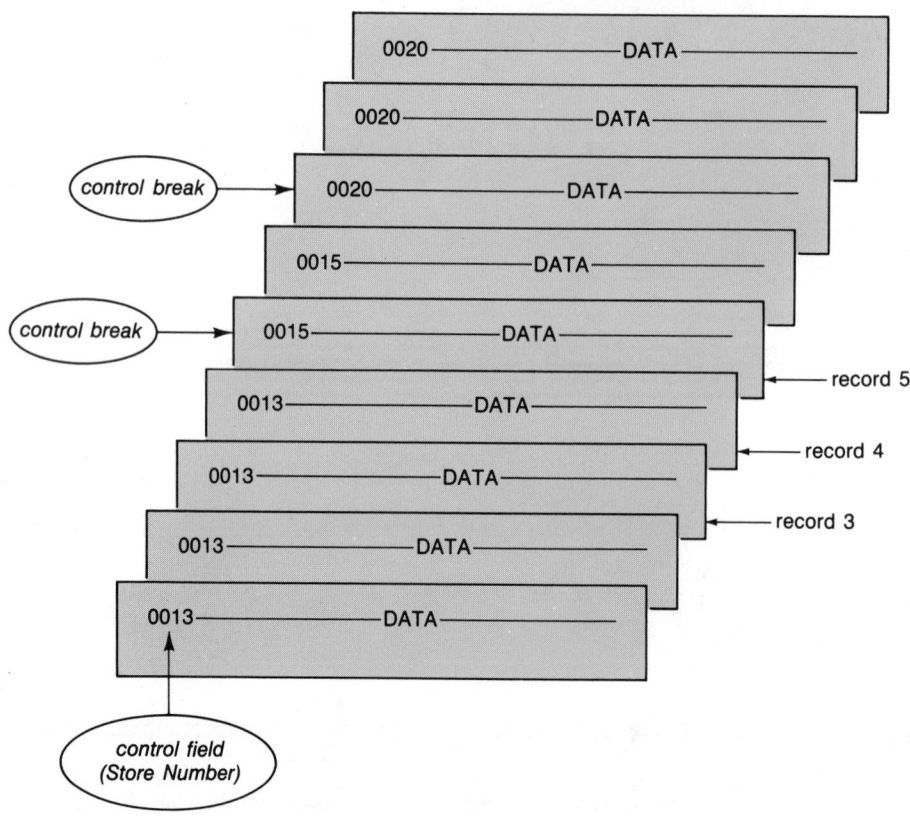

Figure 5-1   Data file records in ascending sequence

Figure 5-2 shows this comparison for records three, four, and five of the sample data file, which illustrates the comparing logic used for control break testing. When the control field value in record three is compared with the value in the compare area, no control break occurs because the two values are equal. The control field from record three is saved in the compare area and is compared with the control field value from record four. Again, the two values are equal; thus, no control break occurs, and the control field value is saved.

When record five is read, its control field value (0015) is compared with the saved value from record four (0013). Because the two fields are not equal, RPG turns on a special-purpose indicator that specifies that a control break has occurred. The control field value from record five is saved, and after control break processing has been performed, the program continues and performs the detail processing of record five.

Although control break testing is performed by comparing techniques, there is one major difference between control break comparisons and comparisons performed by the RPG COMP operation. The COMP operation compares both the sign and the digits of numeric data fields. However, when control break testing is performed on a numeric control field, only the digit portion of the field is compared. If the control fields in two consecutive records contain the same digits but different signs (+ and –), no control break occurs.

The designation of a field as a control field is specific to an individual program. The fact that Store Number is the control field in this file example does not mean that Store Number is a control field every time the file is used. The designation of a field as a control field is made by an entry in the source program and does not carry over from one program to another.

▸ **Control Groups**   The sample data file in Figure 5-1 is shown in a sequence based on the contents of the Store Number field. The group of four records with lowest control field value (0013) is first; the next group contains two records with a higher control field value (0015); the last group contains three records with the highest control field value in the example (0020). Each of these groups of records is a control group. A **control group** is a series of consecutive records in a file, all of which have the same control field value. Control breaks occur between control groups.

▸ Control Group Sequence

Note that control groups need not have consecutive values. There are no records for store number 0014: control group 0013 is followed by control group 0015. Likewise, control group 0015 is followed by control group 0020, with no records for store numbers 0016, 0017, 0018, or 0019. Although control groups need not be consecutive, they must be sequential. A report that listed information for store 0027 first, then store 0010, then store 0036, and so on would be almost meaningless.

Control groups can be in ascending or descending sequence. A file is in **ascending sequence** if the file begins with the record containing the lowest control field value and every record that follows has a control field value equal to or higher than the one before it. The file in Figure 5-1 is in ascending sequence. A file is in **descending sequence** if every record has a control field value equal to or lower than the value in the preceding record. The sample data file in Figure 5-3 is in descending sequence. Although data is usually processed in ascending sequence, control break processing can just as easily be performed on data files that are in descending sequence.

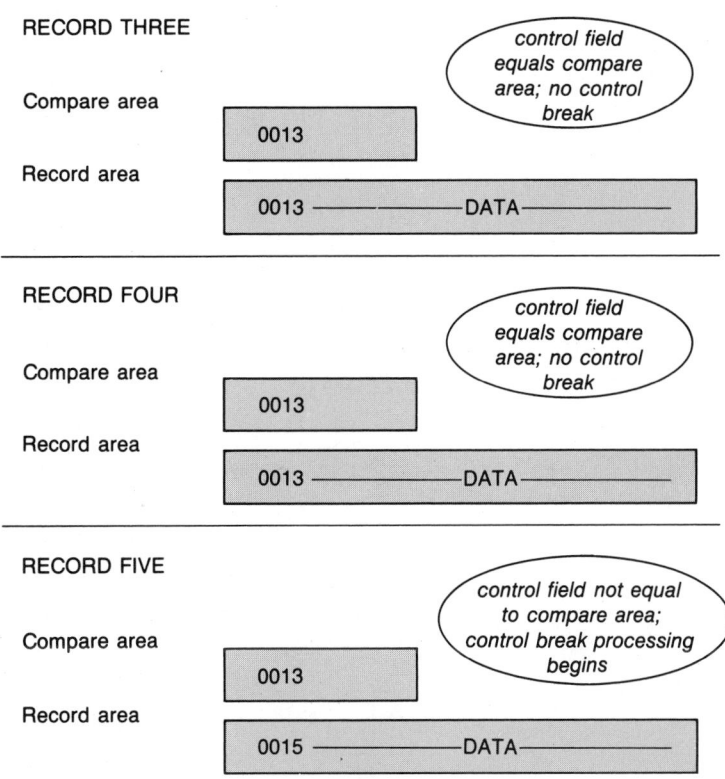

Figure 5-2   Comparing input data with compare area

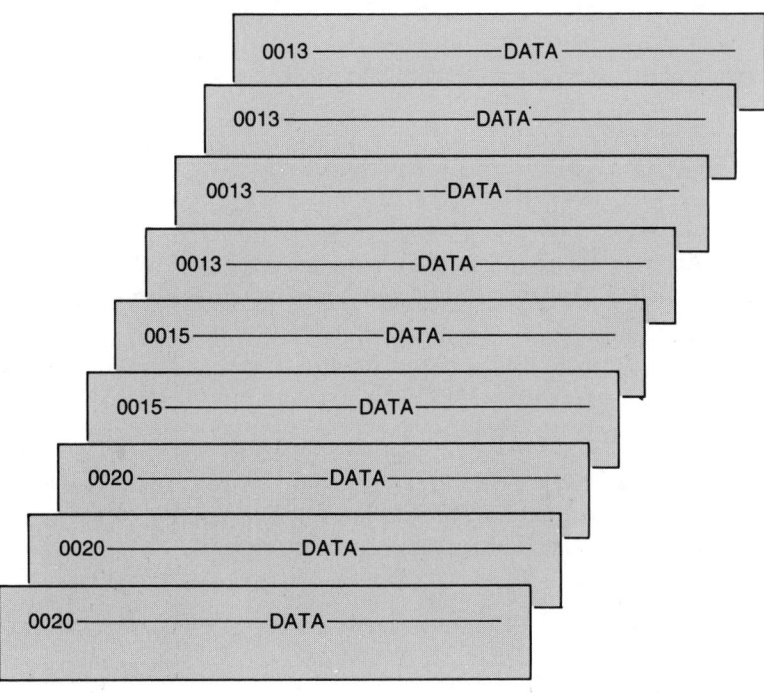

Figure 5-3   Data file records in descending sequence

Control group records must be together in a file. Records for the same control field value do not appear as a group in the data file in Figure 5-4. This file is called an unsequenced file, that is, the data records appear in no particular order. When this file is processed, control breaks occur after almost every record (see figure). The result of this processing is useless because the records are not arranged into meaningful groups.

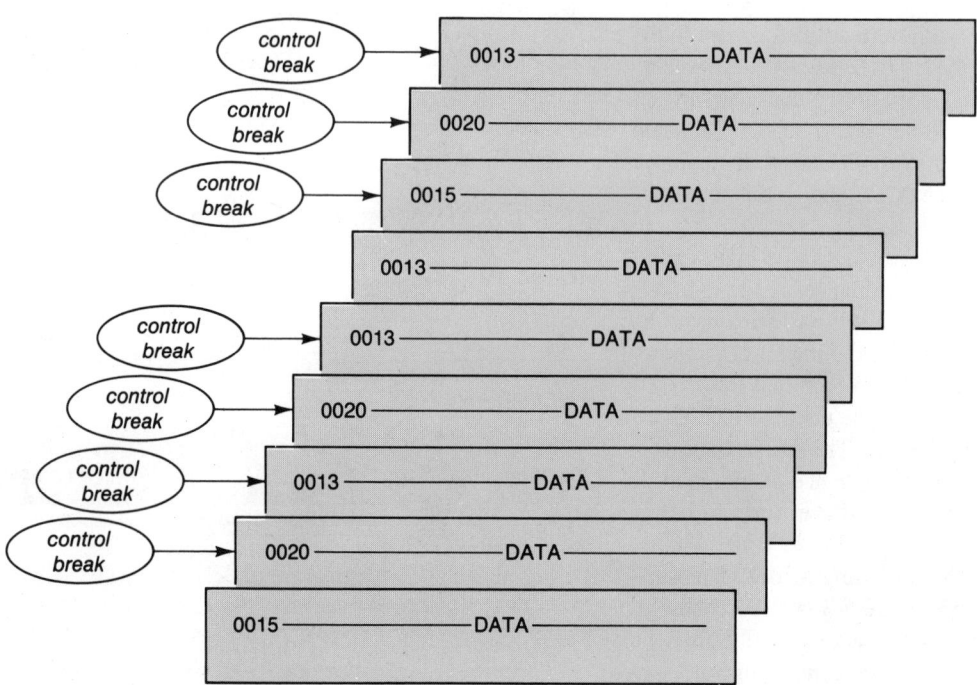

Figure 5-4   Unsequenced data file records

═══ SAMPLE PROBLEM: SALES SUMMARY REPORT ═══

This first sample problem uses program HJG05X to produce a Sales Summary Report for the first six months of 1991.

═ Input

Input is the Sales Analysis Record (Figure 5-5). Note that positions 31–54 of the input record contain a series of six identical fields, each of which contains the number of units sold during one of the first six months of the year.

═ Output

Program output is the Sales Summary Report (Figure 5-6). As you can see, every time the store number changes, detail processing is interrupted and a total line is printed. This printing occurs as part of control break processing. Also note that a final total line prints at the end of the program.

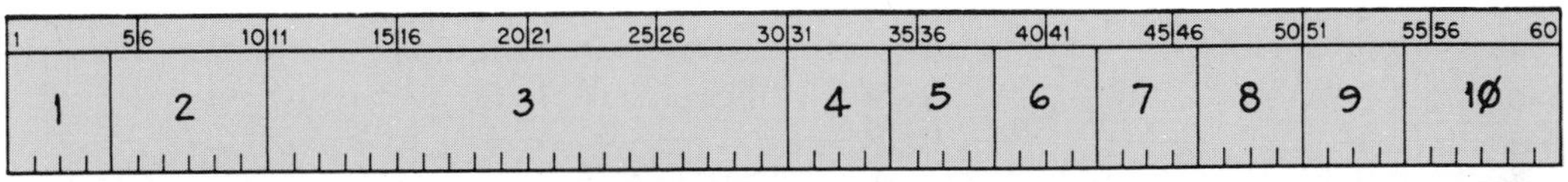

| 1 | 5 | 6 | 10 | 11 | 15 | 16 | 20 | 21 | 25 | 26 | 30 | 31 | 35 | 36 | 40 | 41 | 45 | 46 | 50 | 51 | 55 | 56 | 60 |

| 1 | 2 | 3 | 4 | 5 | 6 | 7 | 8 | 9 | 10 |

	SALES ANALYSIS RECORD					
	Record Length 60					
Field No.	Field Name	Field Description	Field Position	Field Length	Dec. Pos.	Data Class
1	STORE	Store Number	1–4	4	0	N
2		UNUSED AREA	5–10			
3	DESC	Item Description	11–30	20		A
4	JANSAL	Units Sold, Jan.	31–34	4	0	N
5	FEBSAL	Units Sold, Feb.	35–38	4	0	N
6	MARSAL	Units Sold, March	39–42	4	0	N
7	APRSAL	Units Sold, April	43–46	4	0	N
8	MAYSAL	Units Sold, May	47–50	4	0	N
9	JÛNSAL	Units Sold, June	51–54	4	0	N
10		UNUSED AREA	55–60			

Figure 5-5   Sales Analysis Record

Figure 5-6   Sales Summary Report

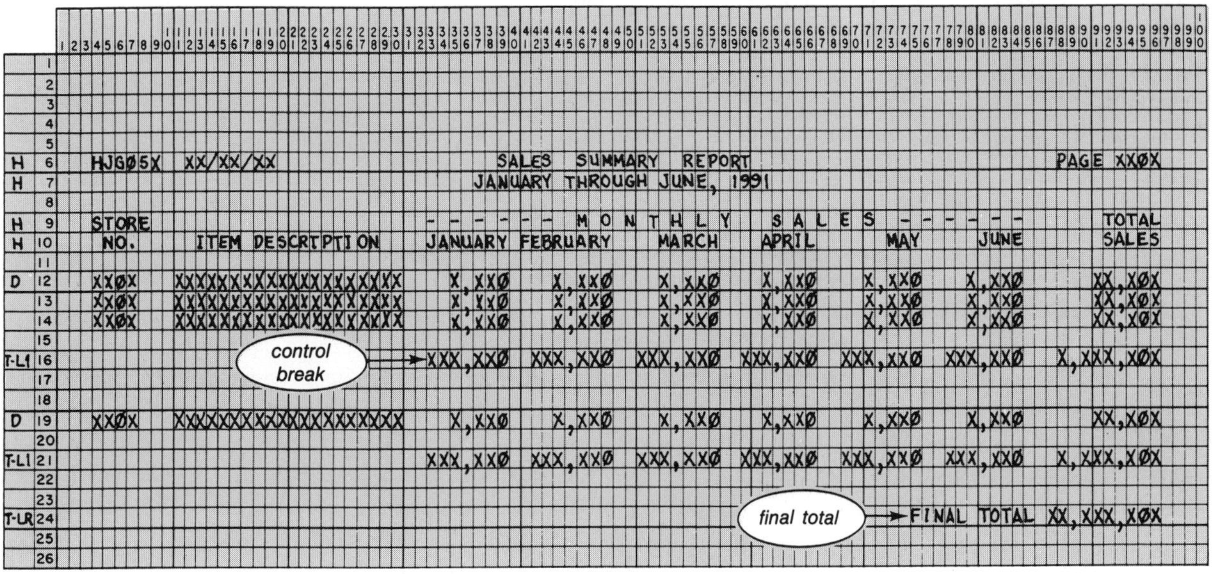

Figure 5-6 (1)

continued

```
HJG05X    7/20/91                 SALES  SUMMARY  REPORT                  PAGE    1
                               JANUARY THROUGH JUNE, 1991

   STORE                     - - - - - - M O N T H L Y   S A L E S - - - - - -        TOTAL
    NO.      ITEM DESCRIPTION   JANUARY FEBRUARY    MARCH     APRIL      MAY     JUNE   SALES

     13    CRT STAND AND PAD        203        5       18        10       28       43      307
     13    5 1/4" DISKETTES       3,056    8,500      750     2,780    4,540      100   19,726
     13    3 1/2" DISKETTES         151    7,000      800     1,750    3,060    6,000   18,761
     13    0911 COMPUTER FORMS        3    1,805       18        10       88       43    1,967
     13    1411 COMPUTER FORMS    3,010    8,136      750     2,760    4,870      909   20,435
     13    CRT WORKSTATION            3       10    3,422     3,020       68       21    6,544
     13    COBOL CODING PADS        150    2,001    3,800     1,753    3,030    6,003   16,737

 (control                         6,576   27,457    9,558    12,083   15,684   13,119   84,477
  break)

     15    RPG INPUT FORMS           3        5    1,018        10      358       43    1,437
     15    RPG OUTPUT FORMS      3,000    8,500      150     2,780    4,530      103   19,063
     15    3 1/2" DISKETTES        150    2,003      310     1,750    3,042    6,030   13,285
     15    0911 COMPUTER FORMS       3        5    2,011        10    1,228    3,343    6,600
     15    1411 COMPUTER FORMS   3,000    8,500      750     1,783    4,543    3,400   21,976
     15    TERMINAL COVERS           3               25       118        5       65      216
     15    SURGE PROTECTORS        150    2,000      800     1,760    3,037    6,000   13,747

 (control                         6,309   21,013    5,064     8,211   16,743   18,984   76,324
  break)

     20    CRT STAND AND PAD         3    3,005       16     5,011    4,308       43   12,386
     20    5 1/4" DISKETTES      3,000    8,760      750     2,782    3,508    9,100   27,900
     20    FLOWCHARTING TMPLTS     150    2,008      800     1,744    3,100    9,000   16,802
     20    0911 COMPUTER FORMS       3        5    9,018        90       18    9,042   18,176
     20    CRT WORKSTATION           3               75        60        8       21      167
     20    COBOL CODING PADS         3        5       18        20        8    3,243    3,297

 (control                         3,162   13,783   10,677     9,707   10,950   30,449   78,728
  break)

     21    5 1/4" DISKETTES      3,000    8,500      750     3,750    4,500      210   20,710
     21    3 1/2" DISKETTES        150    2,000      800     1,230    3,000    6,601   13,781
     21    0911 COMPUTER FORMS       3        5       18        20        8      323      377
     21    1411 COMPUTER FORMS   3,000    8,500      750     2,785    4,500      100   19,635
     21    CRT WORKSTATION           3               25        10    7,808       21    7,867
     21    COBOL CODING PADS       150    2,000      800     1,750    3,090      580    8,370

 (control                         6,306   21,005    3,143     9,545   22,906    7,835   70,740
  break)

                                  (final total)  ──►  FINAL TOTAL             310,269
```

Figure 5-6 (2)

Processing Requirements

The Sales Summary Report is a detail printed report, with a control break on a change in store number. The six monthly sales fields are to be summed and a total of the six fields printed as part of each detail line under the TOTAL SALES heading. The six monthly sales fields, as well as the Total Sales field, are to be added into separate totals that print as control break totals. In addition, the program must accumulate a final total of the Total Sales field.

Program Logic

In the RPG logic cycle for a control break program (Figure 5-7), steps 2 and 4 contain entries that you have not seen before, and steps 6 and 7 have been added. These entries complete the RPG logic cycle chart. Although some areas of the chart are explained in greater detail in later parts of this book, all the fundamental steps of the fixed logic cycle are now present. Let's review these additions to the logic cycle, beginning with the step in which RPG determines that a control break must occur.

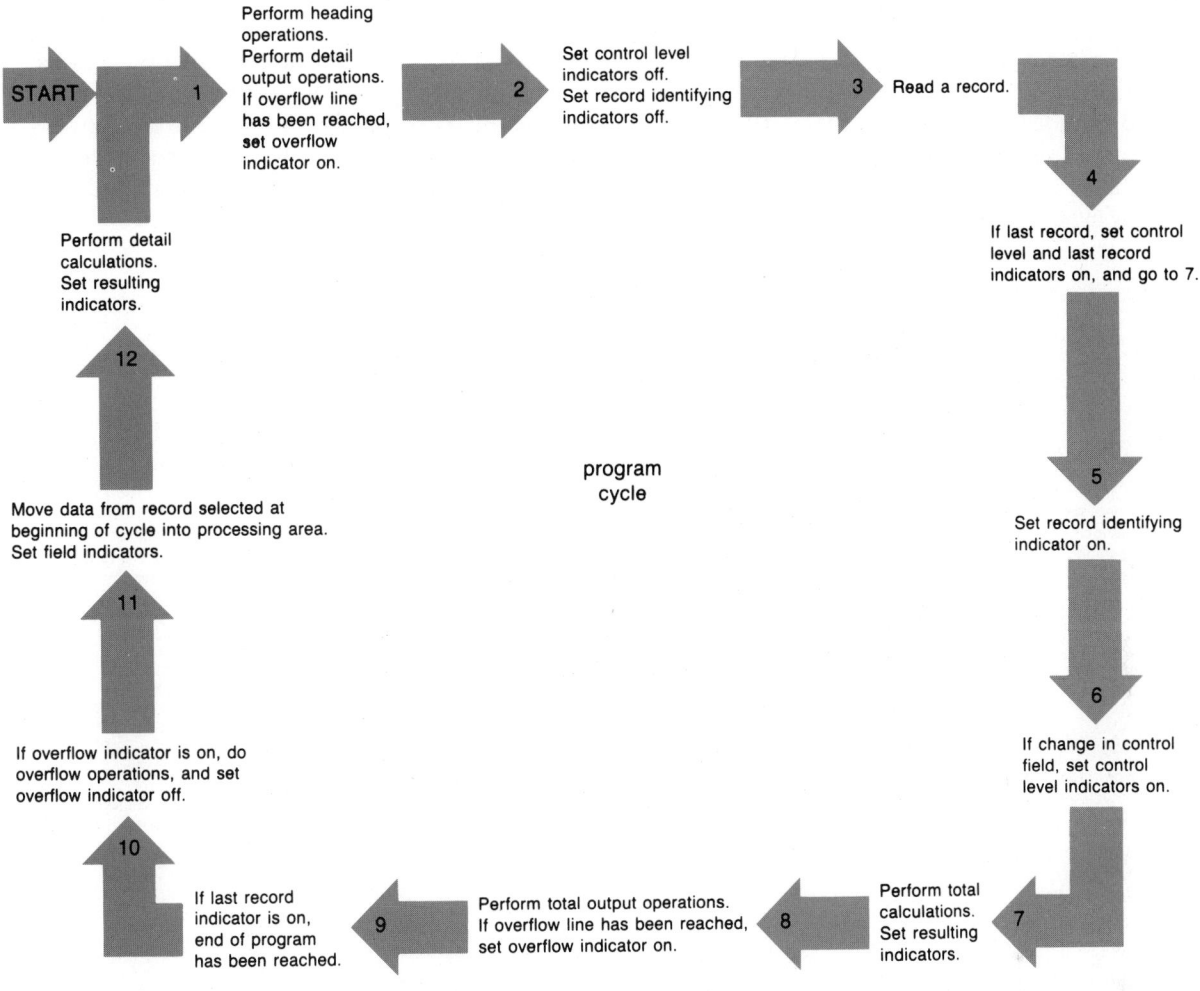

Figure 5-7 RPG fixed logic cycle

▶ **Step 6: Test for Control Break** Step 6 is the point in the fixed logic cycle during which RPG performs the comparison of the input record, read during step 3, with the value stored in the compare area during processing of the prior record. If these value are not equal, a special-purpose control level indicator is turned on. The **control level indicator** is used to control calculations and output operations needed during the control break.

▶ **Step 7: Total Calculations** Just as step 12 provides a time in the logic cycle when calculation operations can be performed on input data, step 7 provides a time when calculations can be performed between records during the control break. Note the use of the word *time* in the preceding sentence. Steps in the RPG fixed logic cycle are often referred to as times. Step 12 is usually referred to as the **detail calculation time**, step 1 the **detail output time**, and so on. Generally, the term *time* is applied only to those steps of the logic cycle during which calculations are performed or output is produced. However, the term can be applied to almost every step of the logic cycle.

Step 7 (**total calculation time**) enables the programmer to specify calculations that are to be performed with data accumulated from an entire control group. In this chapter's sample program, we use total calculation time to add a control group total to the final total.

▶ **Step 2: Set Off Indicators** Control-level indicators are turned off in step 2 at the same time and for the same reason that record identifying indicators are turned off. The record identifying indicators are turned off prior to reading a new record so that they can be tested and reset to represent the record just read. The same is true of control-level indicators. They are turned off in step 2 so that after a record is read in step 3, a new control break comparison can be made and the control-level indicator set.

It is important to understand and remember at what times these control-level indicators turn off. They are turned on in step 6, are used primarily to control operations in steps 7 and 8, but stay on until the next time step 2 is reached. This means that a control-level indicator is on during the entire detail processing of the first record of the new control group. In the logic cycle (Figure 5-8), an arrow has been added to show the duration of control level indicators in a cycle. Later in this chapter you will see one of the programming techniques that takes advantage of this indicator duration.

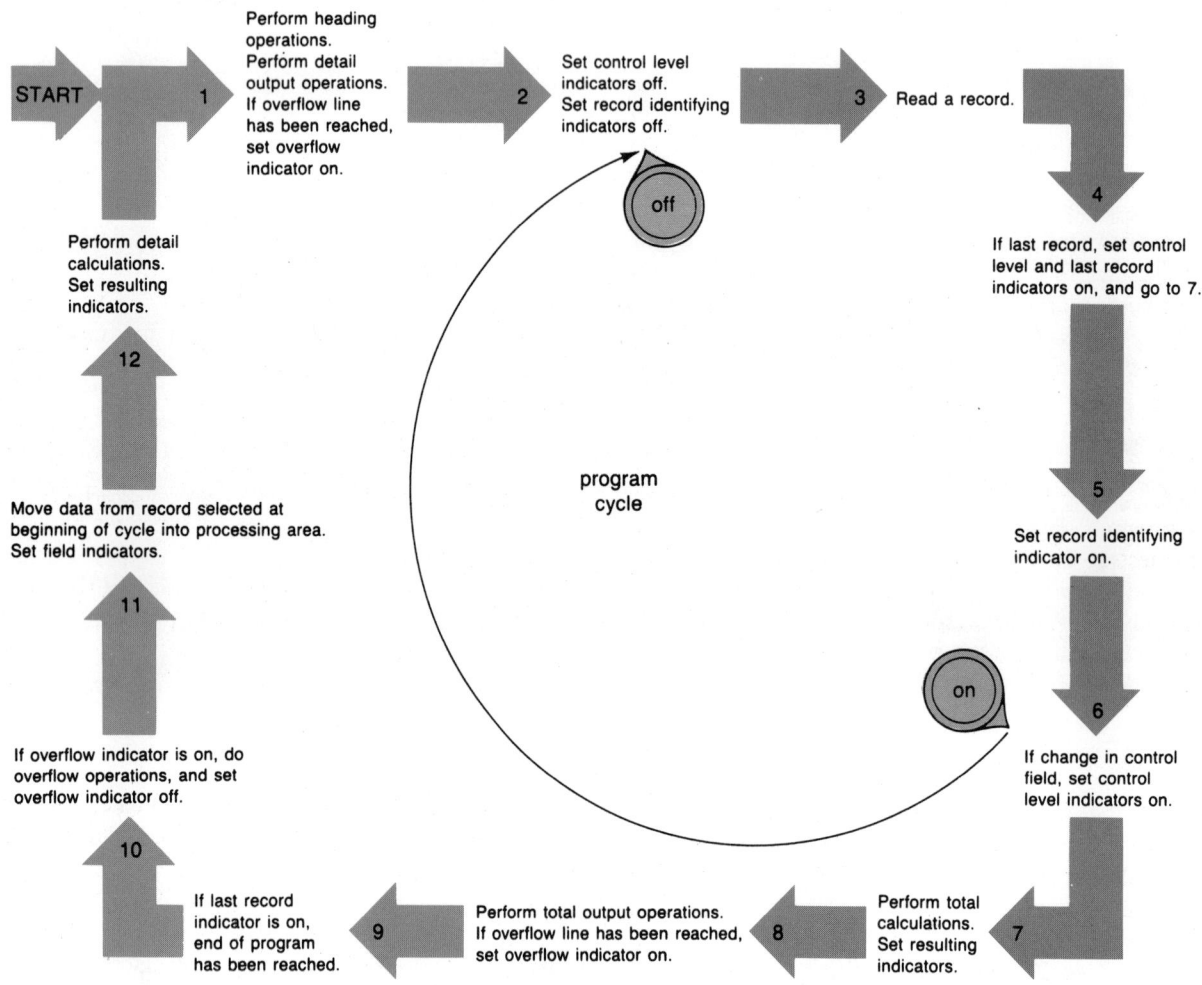

Figure 5-8   Control level indicator cycle

▶ **Step 4: Last Record Time**   So far, step 4 has looked as in Figure 5-9. If all records had been processed, step 4 turned on indicator LR, which was used for the printing of final totals. Now, with the completed logic cycle, step 4 not only turns on indicator LR but it also turns on any control level indicators used in the program. This is required for printing totals for the last control group.

Because control breaks and the printing of control break totals are based on the comparison of a record with the previous record, a logic problem occurs at the end of the program. Because there is no record to compare with the control field value saved from the last input record of the data file, no control break occurs. RPG resolves this problem by causing an automatic control break at the end of the program.

When indicator LR turns on, RPG assumes that the end of the last control group has been reached and automatically turns on the control level indicator needed to cause the last control break. Turning on a control-level indicator in reaction to the LR indicator is called **forcing** a control break. The control break at the end of the program is called a **forced control break** and is shown in step 4 of Figure 5-8.

If, at last record time, indicator LR and needed control-level indicators are turned on, the logic cycle then proceeds to step 7, total calculation time. After any needed total-time calculations are performed, the program continues to step 8, total output time. After output for the last control group and any necessary final totals are printed, the program continues to step 9, which ends the program.

▸ **First Record Processing** Before continuing, you must understand another part of the fixed logic cycle, which does not appear in the logic cycle chart because it is transparent to a programmer. **Transparent** means that a function is fully automatic and is not displayed. You can do nothing that is based on the function and the function does nothing that you can see, either during compilation or when the object program is executed.

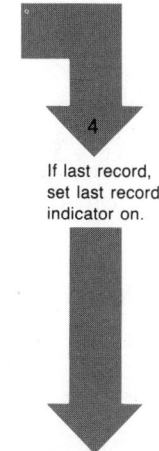

Figure 5-9 Old version of logic cycle step 4

An example of a transparent function is the way that RPG handles the first input record in a program that uses control breaks. Recall that every input record is compared with the control field value from the previous record, but there is nothing to compare the first record with. Because RPG automatically sets all numeric compare fields to zeros and all alphameric compare fields to spaces at the beginning of the program, an erroneous control break occurs when the first record is read and compared unless the control field also contains similar values.

To avoid this error, RPG automatically bypasses control break operations for the first input record read by the program. Figure 5-10 shows the logic that RPG uses to bypass the first record. After step 6 of the logic cycle, RPG tests to determine if it is executing the logic cycle for the first time. If it is the first cycle, RPG bypasses total calculation time and total output time and goes directly to step 9. This **first cycle test** eliminates unwanted control breaks before the first record has been processed. On all cycles after the first, the test result is negative, and processing continues from step 6 to step 7.

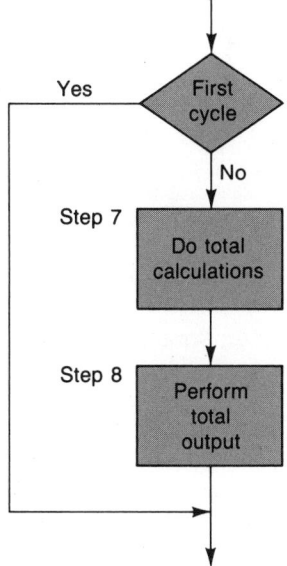

Figure 5-10 Logic to avoid incorrect first record control break

Input Specifications for Control Breaks

To process control breaks, the control field must be identified on the Input Specifications form. The input specifications for the sample program Sales Summary Report are in Figure 5-11. The entries that identify the record and define the data fields are similar to those you have seen in previous examples. The only new entry appears in the Control Level (L1–L9) area, positions 59–60. The entry L1 in this area identifies STORE (the Store Number field) as a control field and specifies that special–purpose indicator L1 is to be turned on to identify a control break. Although STORE is the first field in the record, RPG does not require that the control field be identified first in the record description. A control field can appear in any location in the input record. The remainder of the field descriptions are coded as they have been in previous examples.

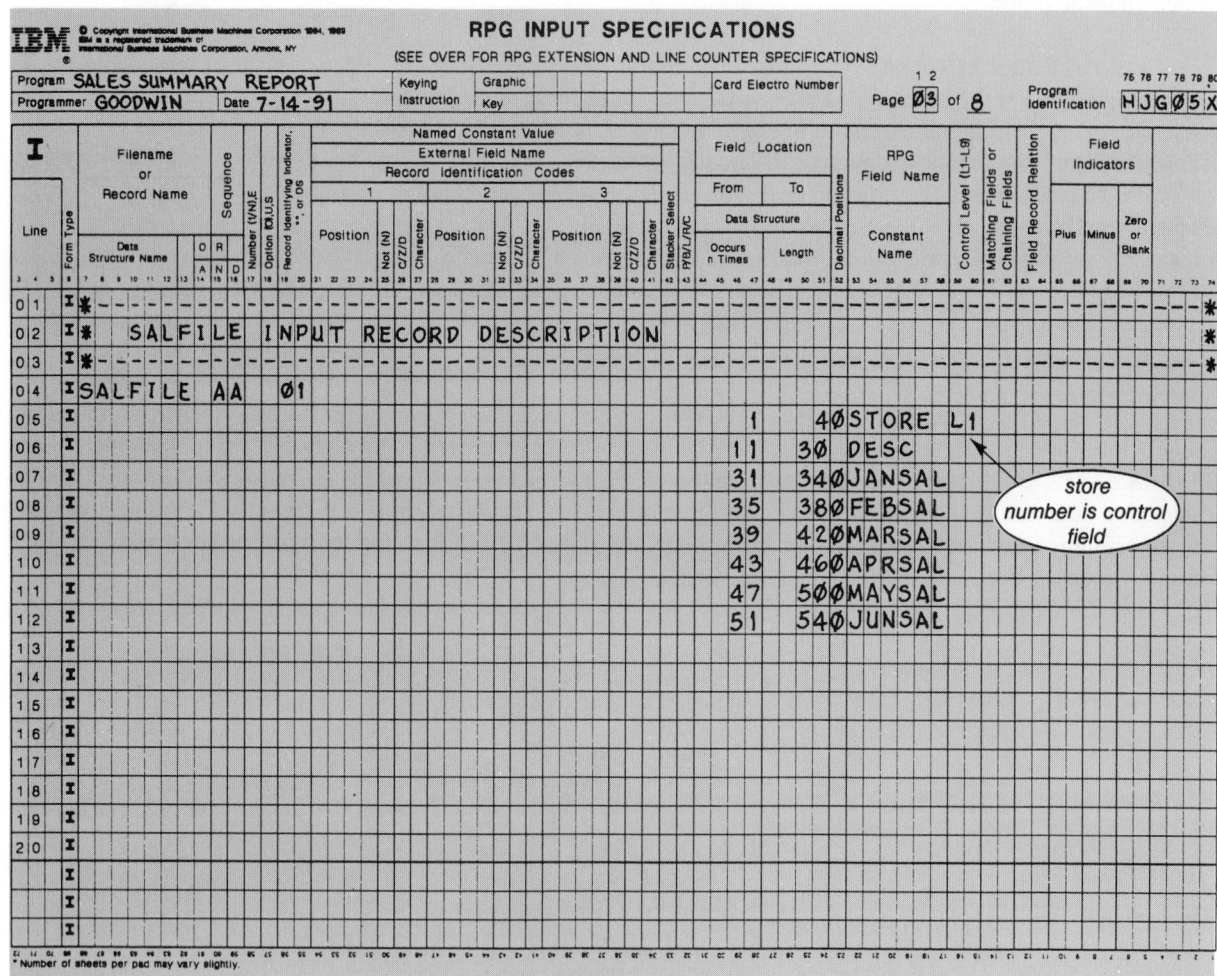

Figure 5-11   Control field designation

Calculation Specifications for Control Breaks

▸ **Detail Calculations**   The Calculation Specifications form for the sample program (Figure 5-12) shows that lines 02–07 execute every time a detail record is read and add the monthly sales fields (JANSAL, FEBSAL, etc.) to the total sales field (TOTSAL). Notice that TOTSAL is defined on line 02 by the entries in the Length and Decimal Positions areas. On lines 03–07, TOTSAL is specified as the Result Field but is not redefined. Remember that a field is defined only the first time that it is used as a result. As each input record is processed, the sum of all six of the monthly sales fields are accumulated in the TOTSAL field, which is printed as part of each detail output line.

RPG CALCULATION SPECIFICATIONS
(SEE OVER FOR RPG CONTROL AND FILE DESCRIPTION SPECIFICATIONS)

Program: SALES SUMMARY REPORT
Programmer: GOODWIN Date 7-14-91
Page 04 of 8 Program Identification HJG05X

Line	Form Type	Control Level	And (Not)	And (Not)	(Not)	Factor 1	Operation	Factor 2	Result Field Name	Length	Dec	HA	Comments
01	C	*				ACCUMULATE TOTAL SALES FOR EACH RECORD							
02	C		01			TOTSAL	ADD	JANSAL	TOTSAL	50			
03	C		01			TOTSAL	ADD	FEBSAL	TOTSAL				
04	C		01			TOTSAL	ADD	MARSAL	TOTSAL				
05	C		01			TOTSAL	ADD	APRSAL	TOTSAL				
06	C		01			TOTSAL	ADD	MAYSAL	TOTSAL				
07	C		01			TOTSAL	ADD	JUNSAL	TOTSAL				
08	C	*											
09	C	*				ACCUMULATE CONTROL BREAK TOTALS							
10	C		01			JANTOT	ADD	JANSAL	JANTOT	60			
11	C		01			FEBTOT	ADD	FEBSAL	FEBTOT	60			
12	C		01			MARTOT	ADD	MARSAL	MARTOT	60			
13	C		01			APRTOT	ADD	APRSAL	APRTOT	60			
14	C		01			MAYTOT	ADD	MAYSAL	MAYTOT	60			
15	C		01			JUNTOT	ADD	JUNSAL	JUNTOT	60			
16	C		01			SALTOT	ADD	TOTSAL	SALTOT	70			
17	C	*											
18	C	*				ACCUMULATE FINAL TOTAL SALES							
19	C	L1				SALFIN	ADD	SALTOT	SALFIN	80			
20	C												

calculation done during control break

Figure 5-12 Control break calculations

Lines 10–16 add the seven detail fields – the six monthly sales fields and the TOTSAL field – into total fields. These seven calculations are also performed for every input record when indicator 01 is on. Each of the seven new total fields (JANTOT, FEBTOT, MARTOT, APRTOT, MAYTOT, JUNTOT, and SALTOT) is defined, and thereby created, by the calculation that adds to it. The contents of these seven fields is printed during every control break and at the end of the program.

▸ **Total Time Calculations** Line 19 is a total time calculation controlled by control level indicator L1. Note that indicator L1 has been specified in the Control Level (L0–L9, LR, SR, AN/OR) area, positions 7–8. The entry of a control level indicator in this area specifies that the calculation is to be performed at total time (step 7) rather than at detail time (step 12) of the logic cycle (Figure 5-13). Thus, RPG performs all total time calculations before producing total time output. The same is true of the relationship between detail calculations and detail output. It is important to remember that, during a specific time, either detail or total, all calculations are performed before any output is produced under control of the fixed logic cycle. In addition, remember that *all total time calculations and output are performed before detail processing of the record that caused the control break.*

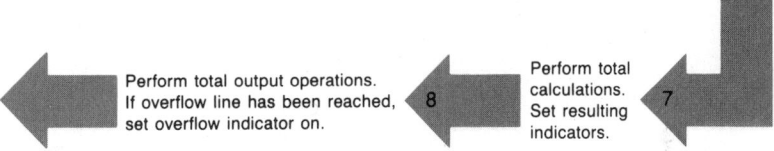

Perform total output operations. If overflow line has been reached, set overflow indicator on. **8**

Perform total calculations. Set resulting indicators. **7**

Figure 5-13 Total time

Line 19 (see Figure 5-12) adds the sales total (SALTOT) for a control group to the final sales total (SALFIN), which is to be printed at the end of the program. This process of adding a control break total to a final total is called **rolling** a total.

The same result could be achieved by adding the contents of the TOTSAL field directly to SALFIN at every detail cycle (Figure 5-14). Adding TOTSAL to both the SALTOT and SALFIN fields every time an input record was processed would develop the same totals. However, this would cause the addition to SALFIN to be performed for every input record and would slightly increase processing time. Although the extremely fast internal processing speed of modern computers would render the additional time unnoticeable, the customary method of adding totals to larger totals is by rolling rather than multiple ADD statements.

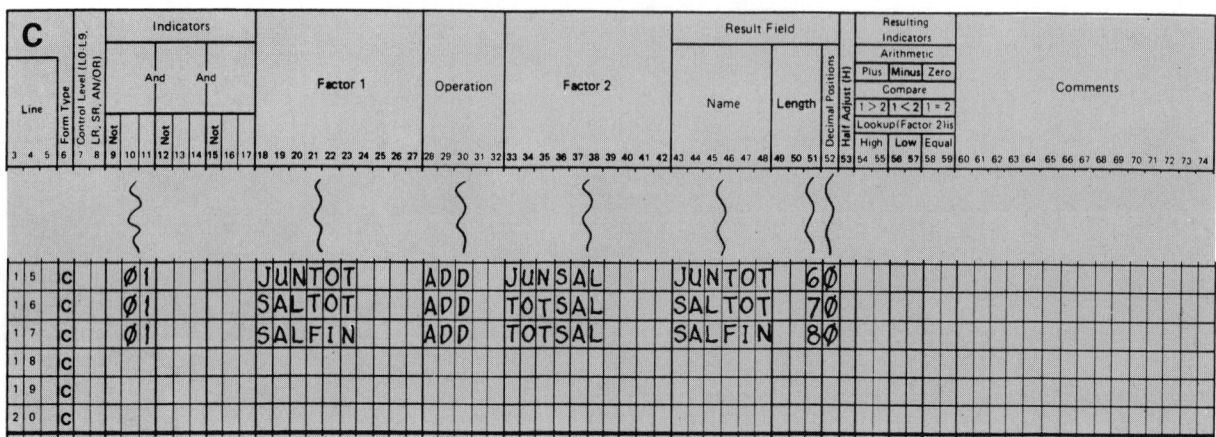

Figure 5-14 Detail time addition to final total

▆▆ Output Specifications for Control Breaks

▸ **Control Break Total Lines** The detail and total output specifications (pages 07 and 08) of the program are shown in Figure 5-15. Note that the first total line, (T in position 15), which begins on line 17 of page 07, prints whenever indicator L1 is on and is, therefore, a control break total line. This line prints the seven total accumulators every time the store number changes.

After these accumulated totals have been printed, the accumulators must be reset to zero so that when the monthly sales amounts for the next store are added, the accumulators do not contain the total of both stores. Instead, they contain only the totals for the current control group. If the accumulators are not reset after the control break totals are printed, the totals will be incorrect for all control groups after the first.

In the incorrect sample of the output report in Figure 5-16 on page 5.14, the total accumulators have not been properly reset after printing. Note that with each successive control break the totals increase. Also note that, after the first control break, none of the totals is the sum of the amounts listed above it. When you are debugging a program that uses control break processing and find that each control break total is larger than the preceding total, you should check to see if the accumulators are reset to zero.

▸ **Blank After** To reset an accumulator to zero after the printing of control break totals, the Blank After entry is used. The **Blank After** entry causes a numeric field to be reset to zero after the field is printed. If a Blank After entry is used for an alphameric data field, the field is reset to spaces, not zeros. Blank after is specified by the entry B in position 39 (B/A/C/1–9/R) of the line on which the output field appears.

Figure 5-15 Sequence of total time output specifications

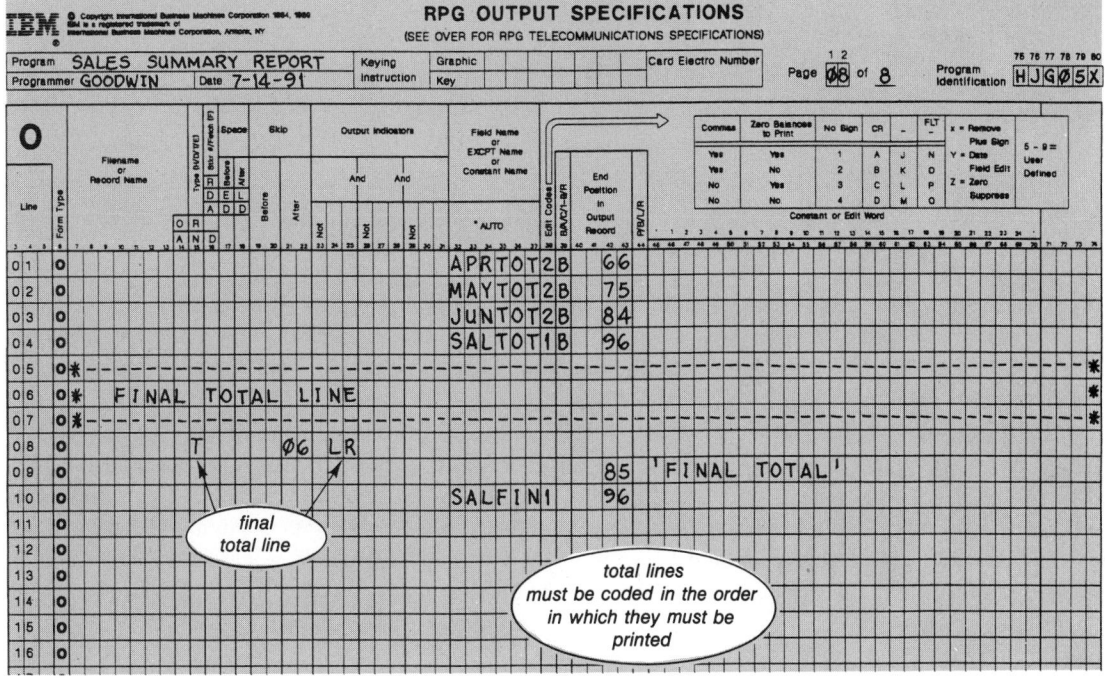

Figure 5-15 (1)

Figure 5-15 (2)

```
HJG05X    7/20/91              SALES  SUMMARY  REPORT                      PAGE    1
                             JANUARY THROUGH JUNE, 1991

   STORE                  - - - - - - M O N T H L Y    S A L E S - - - - - -         TOTAL
    NO.    ITEM DESCRIPTION  JANUARY FEBRUARY   MARCH    APRIL     MAY     JUNE       SALES

     13    CRT STAND AND PAD     203        5       18       10       28       43       307
     13    5 1/4" DISKETTES    3,056    8,500      750    2,780    4,540      100    19,726
     13    3 1/2" DISKETTES      151    7,000      800    1,750    3,060    6,000    18,761
     13    0911 COMPUTER FORMS     3    1,805       18       10       88       43     1,967
     13    1411 COMPUTER FORMS 3,010    8,136      750    2,760    4,870      909    20,435
     13    CRT WORKSTATION         3       10    3,422    3,020       68       21     6,544
     13    COBOL CODING PADS     150    2,001    3,800    1,753    3,030    6,003    16,737

                              6,576   27,457    9,558   12,083   15,684   13,119    84,477


     15    RPG INPUT FORMS         3        5    1,018       10      358       43     1,437
     15    RPG OUTPUT FORMS    3,000    8,500      150    2,780    4,530      103    19,063
     15    3 1/2" DISKETTES      150    2,003      310    1,750    3,042    6,030    13,285
     15    0911 COMPUTER FORMS     3        5    2,011       10    1,228    3,343     6,600
     15    1411 COMPUTER FORMS 3,000    8,500      750    1,783    4,543    3,400    21,976
     15    TERMINAL COVERS         3                25      118        5       65       216
     15    SURGE PROTECTORS      150    2,000      800    1,760    3,037    6,000    13,747
           ( incorrect
             totals )        12,885   48,470   14,622   20,294   32,427   32,103   160,801

     20    CRT STAND AND PAD       3    3,005       16    5,011    4,308       43    12,386
     20    5 1/4" DISKETTES    3,000    8,760      750    2,782    3,508    9,100    27,900
     20    FLOWCHARTING TMPLTS   150    2,008      800    1,744    3,100    9,000    16,802
     20    0911 COMPUTER FORMS     3        5    9,018       90       18    9,042    18,176
     20    CRT WORKSTATION         3                75       60        8       21       167
     20    COBOL CODING PADS       3        5       18       20        8    3,243     3,297
           ( incorrect
             totals )        16,047   62,253   25,299   30,001   43,377   62,552   239,529

     21    5 1/4" DISKETTES    3,000    8,500      750    3,750    4,500      210    20,710
     21    3 1/2" DISKETTES      150    2,000      800    1,230    3,000    6,601    13,781
     21    0911 COMPUTER FORMS     3        5       18       20        8      323       377
     21    1411 COMPUTER FORMS 3,000    8,500      750    2,785    4,500      100    19,635
     21    CRT WORKSTATION         3                25       10    7,808       21     7,867
     21    COBOL CODING PADS     150    2,000      800    1,750    3,090      580     8,370
           ( incorrect
             totals )        22,353   83,258   28,442   39,546   66,283   70,387   310,269

                           ( incorrect
                             total )                           FINAL TOTAL   795,076
```

Figure 5-16   Incorrect output: blank after not used

Figure 5-17 again shows pages 07 and 08 of the source program. You can see that the Blank After entry B has been placed in position 39 for each of the seven control break total fields. No Blank After entry has been made for SALFIN in the final total line because the final total prints only once, at the end of the program, and no other amounts are accumulated into it.

Blank after should always be used when control break totals are printed so as to reset the accumulators to zero before processing the first record of the next control group. The resetting of a field occurs immediately after the output is produced. The contents of the field are no longer available for further processing. In some programs, it is necessary to use the same field two or more times as output. For example, the program might print the contents of the field and then, in a separate output file, write the data to a disk file. If a field is used as output more than once and if blank after is necessary, the B entry should appear only on the last output specification for that field. The last entry is the one that produces output last; it may or may not be the last one written in the source program.

Figure 5-17   Blank after entries

RPG OUTPUT SPECIFICATIONS
(SEE OVER FOR RPG TELECOMMUNICATIONS SPECIFICATIONS)

Program SALES SUMMARY REPORT Programmer GOODWIN Date 7-14-91 Page 07 of 8 Program Identification HJG05X

Line	Form Type	Filename or Record Name		Field Name or EXCPT or Constant Name	End Position in Output Record	Constant or Edit Word
01	O*	---------				
02	O*	DETAIL LINE				
03	O*	---------				
04	O		D 1 01			
05	O			STORE Z	7	
06	O			DESC	30	
07	O			JANSAL2	39	
08	O			FEBSAL2	48	
09	O			MARSAL2	57	
10	O			APRSAL2	66	
11	O			MAYSAL2	75	
12	O			JUNSAL2	84	
13	O			TOTSAL1B	96	
14	O*	---------				
15	O*	CONTROL BREAK (L1) TOTAL LINE				
16	O*	---------				
17	O		T 13 L1			
18	O			JANTOT2B	39	
19	O			FEBTOT2B	48	
20	O			MARTOT2B	57	

blank after (annotations pointing to TOTSAL1B and to line 17 T 13 L1)

Figure 5-17 (1)

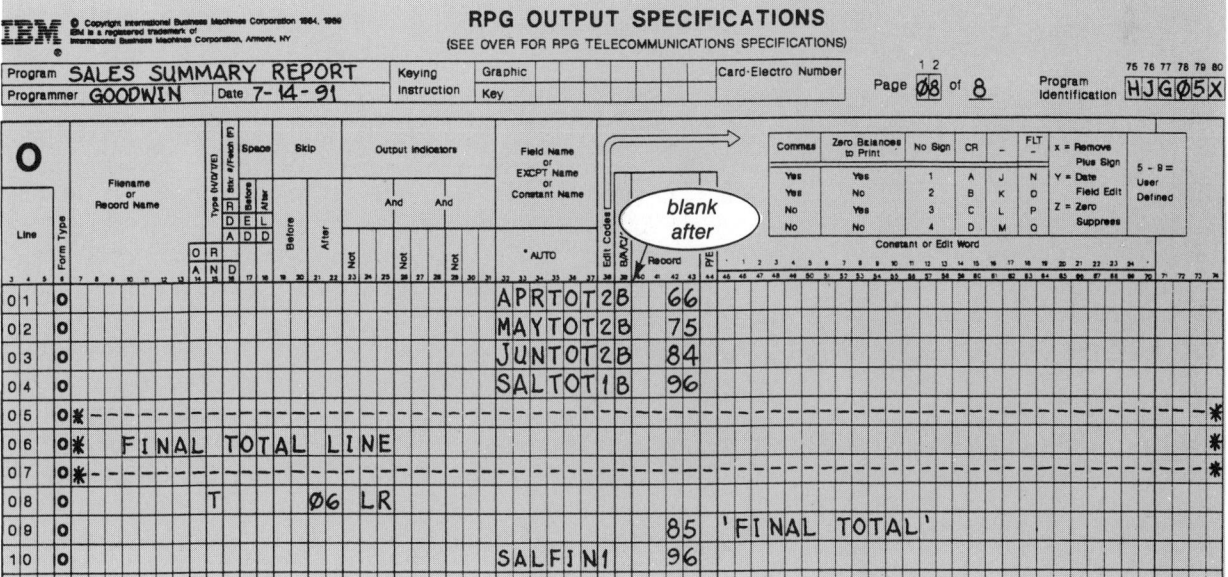

RPG OUTPUT SPECIFICATIONS
(SEE OVER FOR RPG TELECOMMUNICATIONS SPECIFICATIONS)

Program SALES SUMMARY REPORT Programmer GOODWIN Date 7-14-91 Page 08 of 8 Program Identification HJG05X

Line	Form Type	Filename or Record Name		Field Name or EXCPT or Constant Name	End Position in Output Record	Constant or Edit Word
01	O			APRTOT2B	66	
02	O			MAYTOT2B	75	
03	O			JUNTOT2B	84	
04	O			SALTOT1B	96	
05	O*	---------				
06	O*	FINAL TOTAL LINE				
07	O*	---------				
08	O		T 06 LR			
09	O				85	'FINAL TOTAL'
10	O			SALFIN1	96	

blank after

Figure 5-17 (2)

▸ **Final Total Lines** Line 08 on page 08 of the Sales Summary Report program (see Figure 5-17) is the final total line and is controlled by indicator LR. Note that the final total line follows the control break total line specifications. Just as heading lines must be specified in the order in which they are to be printed, total lines that are to be printed at the same point in the RPG logic cycle must also be specified in the order in which they are to print.

Step 8 of the logic cycle says "perform total output operations." At the end of the program, when both indicator L1 and indicator LR are on, both of these total lines must print. Because they both print during step 8 of the logic cycle, at total output time, they must be coded in the required order. If the final total line is coded before the control break total line, the last two totals will be in the wrong order at the end of the program output listing. Total lines (type T) must be coded in the source program in the order in which they are to be printed.

▤ Compile Listing for Sample Program HJG05X

Figures 5-18 and 5-19 (on page 5.18) show the compile listing and program output for the sample program.

Figure 5-18   Compilation listing for program HJG05X

```
Lattice RPG II Compiler Version 2.01                09:41:33  07/15/1991
Compile listing for source RPG program [HJG05X  .RPG]        PAGE : 0001


    1      H                                                       HJG05X

    2      F*----------------------------------------------------------*
    3 S    F* HJG05X - SALES SUMMARY REPORT - HAL GOODWIN - JULY 14, 1991   *
    4 S    F*                                                          *
    5 S    F* PROGRAM HJG05X LISTS MONTHLY SALES FOR EACH ITEM.  THE SIX    *
    6 S    F* MONTHLY SALES FIELDS ARE ADDED TO ACCUMULATE TOTAL SALES.     *
    7 S    F* WHEN STORE NUMBER CHANGES, TOTALS OF THE SEVEN SALES FIELDS WILL*
    8 S    F* PRINT.  IN ADDITION, A FINAL TOTAL OF THE TOTAL SALES FIELD    *
    9 S    F* WILL BE PRINTED.                                          *
   10 S    F*----------------------------------------------------------*
   11 S    FSALFILE IP  F 360  60            DISK
   12 S    FSALREPT O   F 132 132     OF     PRINTER
   13 S    F* ID F  C  H  L   FUNCTION OF INDICATORS
   14 S    F* 01--------------SALFILE RECORD IDENTIFICATION
   15 S    F*            1P---FIRST PAGE INDICATOR
   16 S    F*            OF---OVERFLOW INDICATOR
   17 S    F*            L1---CONTROL BREAK - STORE NUMBER CHANGE
   18 S    F*            LR---END OF JOB

   19      I*----------------------------------------------------------*
   20 S    I* SALFILE INPUT RECORD DESCRIPTION                          *
   21 S    I*----------------------------------------------------------*
   22 S    ISALFILE AA  01
   23 S    I                                1   40STORE L1
   24 S    I                               11   30 DESC
   25 S    I                               31  340JANSAL
   26 S    I                               35  380FEBSAL
   27 S    I                               39  420MARSAL
   28 S    I                               43  460APRSAL
   29 S    I                               47  500MAYSAL
   30 S    I                               51  540JUNSAL

   31      C* ACCUMULATE TOTAL SALES FOR EACH RECORD
   32 S    C   01      TOTSAL   ADD JANSAL   TOTSAL 50
   33 S    C   01      TOTSAL   ADD FEBSAL   TOTSAL
   34 S    C   01      TOTSAL   ADD MARSAL   TOTSAL
   35 S    C   01      TOTSAL   ADD APRSAL   TOTSAL
   36 S    C   01      TOTSAL   ADD MAYSAL   TOTSAL
   37 S    C   01      TOTSAL   ADD JUNSAL   TOTSAL
   38 S    C*
   39 S    C* ACCUMULATE CONTROL BREAK TOTALS
   40 S    C   01      JANTOT   ADD JANSAL   JANTOT 60
   41 S    C   01      FEBTOT   ADD FEBSAL   FEBTOT 60
   42 S    C   01      MARTOT   ADD MARSAL   MARTOT 60
   43 S    C   01      APRTOT   ADD APRSAL   APRTOT 60
   44 S    C   01      MAYTOT   ADD MAYSAL   MAYTOT 60
   45 S    C   01      JUNTOT   ADD JUNSAL   JUNTOT 60
   46 S    C   01      SALTOT   ADD TOTSAL   SALTOT 70
   47 S    C*
   48 S    C* ACCUMULATE FINAL TOTAL SALES
   49 S    CL1         SALFIN   ADD SALTOT   SALFIN 80

   50      O*----------------------------------------------------------*
   51 S    O* HEADING LINE ONE                                         *
```

Figure 5-18 (1)

```
Lattice RPG II Compiler Version 2.01                    09:41:34  07/15/1991
Compile listing for source RPG program [HJG05X  .RPG]            PAGE : 0002


  52 S    O*------------------------------------------------------------*
  53 S    OSALREPT H  106     1P
  54 S    O      OR          OF
  55 S    O                                        9 'HJG05X'
  56 S    O                          UDATE Y      19
  57 S    O                                       60 'SALES  SUMMARY  REPORT'
  58 S    O                                       91 'PAGE'
  59 S    O                          PAGE  Z      96
  60 S    O*------------------------------------------------------------*
  61 S    O*  HEADING LINE TWO                                          *
  62 S    O*------------------------------------------------------------*
  63 S    O       H  2     1P
  64 S    O      OR          OF
  65 S    O                                       56 'JANUARY THROUGH JUNE'
  66 S    O                                       62 ', 1991'
  67 S    O*------------------------------------------------------------*
  68 S    O*  HEADING LINE THREE                                        *
  69 S    O*------------------------------------------------------------*
  70 S    O       H  1     1P
  71 S    O      OR          OF
  72 S    O                                        8 'STORE'
  73 S    O                                       56 '- - - - -  M O N T H L'
  74 S    O                                       80 'Y   S A L E S - - - -'
  75 S    O                                       96 '- -      TOTAL'
  76 S    O*------------------------------------------------------------*
  77 S    O*  HEADING LINE FOUR                                         *
  78 S    O*------------------------------------------------------------*
  79 S    O       H  2     1P
  80 S    O      OR          OF
  81 S    O                                       28 'NO.     ITEM DESCRIPTION'
  82 S    O                                       56 'JANUARY FEBRUARY    MARC'
  83 S    O                                       75 'H   APRIL      MAY'
  84 S    O                                       96 'JUNE      SALES'
  85 S    O*------------------------------------------------------------*
  86 S    O*  DETAIL LINE                                               *
  87 S    O*------------------------------------------------------------*
  88 S    O       D  1     01
  89 S    O                          STORE Z       7
  90 S    O                          DESC         30
  91 S    O                          JANSAL2      39
  92 S    O                          FEBSAL2      48
  93 S    O                          MARSAL2      57
  94 S    O                          APRSAL2      66
  95 S    O                          MAYSAL2      75
  96 S    O                          JUNSAL2      84
  97 S    O                          TOTSAL1B     96
  98 S    O*------------------------------------------------------------*
  99 S    O*  CONTROL BREAK (L1) TOTAL LINE                             *
 100 S    O*------------------------------------------------------------*
 101 S    O       T 13     L1
 102 S    O                          JANTOT2B     39
 103 S    O                          FEBTOT2B     48
 104 S    O                          MARTOT2B     57
 105 S    O                          APRTOT2B     66
 106 S    O                          MAYTOT2B     75
```

Figure 5-18 (2)

```
Lattice RPG II Compiler Version 2.01                    09:41:35  07/15/1991
Compile listing for source RPG program [HJG05X  .RPG]            PAGE : 0003


 107 S    O                          JUNTOT2B     84
 108 S    O                          SALTOT1B     96
 109 S    O*------------------------------------------------------------*
 110 S    O*  FINAL TOTAL LINE                                          *
 111 S    O*------------------------------------------------------------*
 112 S    O       T    06 LR
 113 S    O                                       85 'FINAL TOTAL'
 114 S    O                          SALFIN1      96
 115 /*

Warning Severe
Errors  Errors
   0       0
```

Figure 5-18 (3)

```
HJG05X   7/20/91              SALES  SUMMARY  REPORT                PAGE    1
                           JANUARY THROUGH JUNE, 1991

STORE                - - - - - M O N T H L Y   S A L E S - - - - - -     TOTAL
 NO.    ITEM DESCRIPTION  JANUARY FEBRUARY   MARCH   APRIL     MAY    JUNE    SALES

  13    CRT STAND AND PAD     203       5      18      10      28      43      307
  13    5 1/4" DISKETTES    3,056   8,500     750   2,780   4,540     100   19,726
  13    3 1/2" DISKETTES      151   7,000     800   1,750   3,060   6,000   18,761
  13    0911 COMPUTER FORMS     3   1,805      18      10      88      43    1,967
  13    1411 COMPUTER FORMS 3,010   8,136     750   2,760   4,870     909   20,435
  13    CRT WORKSTATION         3      10   3,422   3,020      68      21    6,544
  13    COBOL CODING PADS     150   2,001   3,800   1,753   3,030   6,003   16,737

                          6,576  27,457   9,558  12,083  15,684  13,119   84,477


  15    RPG INPUT FORMS         3       5   1,018      10     358      43    1,437
  15    RPG OUTPUT FORMS    3,000   8,500     150   2,780   4,530     103   19,063
  15    3 1/2" DISKETTES      150   2,003     310   1,750   3,042   6,030   13,285
  15    0911 COMPUTER FORMS     3       5   2,011      10   1,228   3,343    6,600
  15    1411 COMPUTER FORMS 3,000   8,500     750   1,783   4,543   3,400   21,976
  15    TERMINAL COVERS         3              25     118       5      65      216
  15    SURGE PROTECTORS      150   2,000     800   1,760   3,037   6,000   13,747

                          6,309  21,013   5,064   8,211  16,743  18,984   76,324


  20    CRT STAND AND PAD       3   3,005      16   5,011   4,308      43   12,386
  20    5 1/4" DISKETTES    3,000   8,760     750   2,782   3,508   9,100   27,900
  20    FLOWCHARTING TMPLTS   150   2,008     800   1,744   3,100   9,000   16,802
  20    0911 COMPUTER FORMS     3       5   9,018      90      18   9,042   18,176
  20    CRT WORKSTATION         3              75      60       8      21      167
  20    COBOL CODING PADS       3       5      18      20       8   3,243    3,297

                          3,162  13,783  10,677   9,707  10,950  30,449   78,728


  21    5 1/4" DISKETTES    3,000   8,500     750   3,750   4,500     210   20,710
  21    3 1/2" DISKETTES      150   2,000     800   1,230   3,000   6,601   13,781
  21    0911 COMPUTER FORMS     3       5      18      20       8     323      377
  21    1411 COMPUTER FORMS 3,000   8,500     750   2,785   4,500     100   19,635
  21    CRT WORKSTATION         3              25      10   7,808      21    7,867
  21    COBOL CODING PADS     150   2,000     800   1,750   3,090     580    8,370

                          6,306  21,005   3,143   9,545  22,906   7,835   70,740


                                                   FINAL TOTAL          310,269
```

Figure 5-19   Program output for program HJG05X

GROUP INDICATION

As you have seen, program HJG05X detail prints all the output fields on every line of the report. In programs that perform control breaks, the control field is duplicated on the print line created by every record in the control group. If a control group contains 200 records, the same control field information prints on all 200 output lines generated by the group. The repetition of control-field information can be confusing because the control-field identification may not be immediately obvious to the person reading the printed report. In many applications, it is preferable to have the control-field data print only once, as part of the first output record for the control group.

Group indication is a programming technique by which the control field is printed only on the first detail line of the group. Figure 5-20 shows a group indicated version of the sample report developed earlier in this chapter.

```
HJG05X   7/20/91                 SALES  SUMMARY  REPORT                    PAGE    1
                               JANUARY THROUGH JUNE, 1991

 STORE                     - - - - - -  M O N T H L Y   S A L E S  - - - - - -     TOTAL
  NO.    ITEM DESCRIPTION   JANUARY FEBRUARY    MARCH   APRIL     MAY    JUNE       SALES

   13    CRT STAND AND PAD      203        5       18      10      28      43        307
         5 1/4" DISKETTES     3,056    8,500      750   2,780   4,540     100     19,726
         3 1/2" DISKETTES       151    7,000      800   1,750   3,060   6,000     18,761
         0911 COMPUTER FORMS      3    1,805       18      10      88      43      1,967
         1411 COMPUTER FORMS  3,010    8,136      750   2,760   4,870     909     20,435
         CRT WORKSTATION         3       10    3,422   3,020      68      21      6,544
         COBOL CODING PADS      150    2,001    3,800   1,753   3,030   6,003     16,737

                            6,576   27,457    9,558  12,083  15,684  13,119     84,477


   15    RPG INPUT FORMS         3        5    1,018      10     358      43      1,437
         RPG OUTPUT FORMS    3,000    8,500      150   2,780   4,530     103     19,063
         3 1/2" DISKETTES       150    2,003      310   1,750   3,042   6,030     13,285
         0911 COMPUTER FORMS      3        5    2,011      10   1,228   3,343      6,600
         1411 COMPUTER FORMS  3,000    8,500      750   1,783   4,543   3,400     21,976
         TERMINAL COVERS         3              25     118       5      65        216
         SURGE PROTECTORS       150    2,000      800   1,760   3,037   6,000     13,747

                            6,309   21,013    5,064   8,211  16,743  18,984     76,324


   20    CRT STAND AND PAD       3    3,005       16   5,011   4,308      43     12,386
         5 1/4" DISKETTES     3,000    8,760      750   2,782   3,508   9,100     27,900
         FLOWCHARTING TMPLTS    150    2,008      800   1,744   3,100   9,000     16,802
         0911 COMPUTER FORMS      3        5    9,018      90      18   9,042     18,176
         CRT WORKSTATION         3              75      60       8      21        167
         COBOL CODING PADS       3        5       18      20       8   3,243      3,297

                            3,162   13,783   10,677   9,707  10,950  30,449     78,728


   21    5 1/4" DISKETTES     3,000    8,500      750   3,750   4,500     210     20,710
         3 1/2" DISKETTES       150    2,000      800   1,230   3,000   6,601     13,781
         0911 COMPUTER FORMS      3        5       18      20       8     323        377
         1411 COMPUTER FORMS  3,000    8,500      750   2,785   4,500     100     19,635
         CRT WORKSTATION         3              25      10   7,808      21      7,867
         COBOL CODING PADS      150    2,000      800   1,750   3,090     580      8,370

                            6,306   21,005    3,143   9,545  22,906   7,835     70,740


                                                               FINAL TOTAL   310,269
```

group
indication

Figure 5-20 Group indication

In the figure, the Store Number field prints only once for each control group, as part of the first detail line. All subsequent lines in the same control group are blank in the store number column. Many people consider group indicated reports easier to read and work with because meaningless, repetitive information is eliminated.

▶ **Group Indication Logic**   A report can be group indicated only if control breaks occur in the program; otherwise there are no groups to indicate. The logic of group indication is based on the control break indicator and takes advantage of the time in the RPG logic cycle during which the control break indicator is on.

In the logic cycle in Figure 5-21, the duration of the control break indicator is shown as a dark arrow. If a control break occurs, the control break indicator is on not only during total time but also stays on through the next detail calculation and output times. During this next detail output step, the output for the first record of the next control group is printed. Step 2 of the logic cycle then turns the control break indicator off, and it stays off until the next control break.

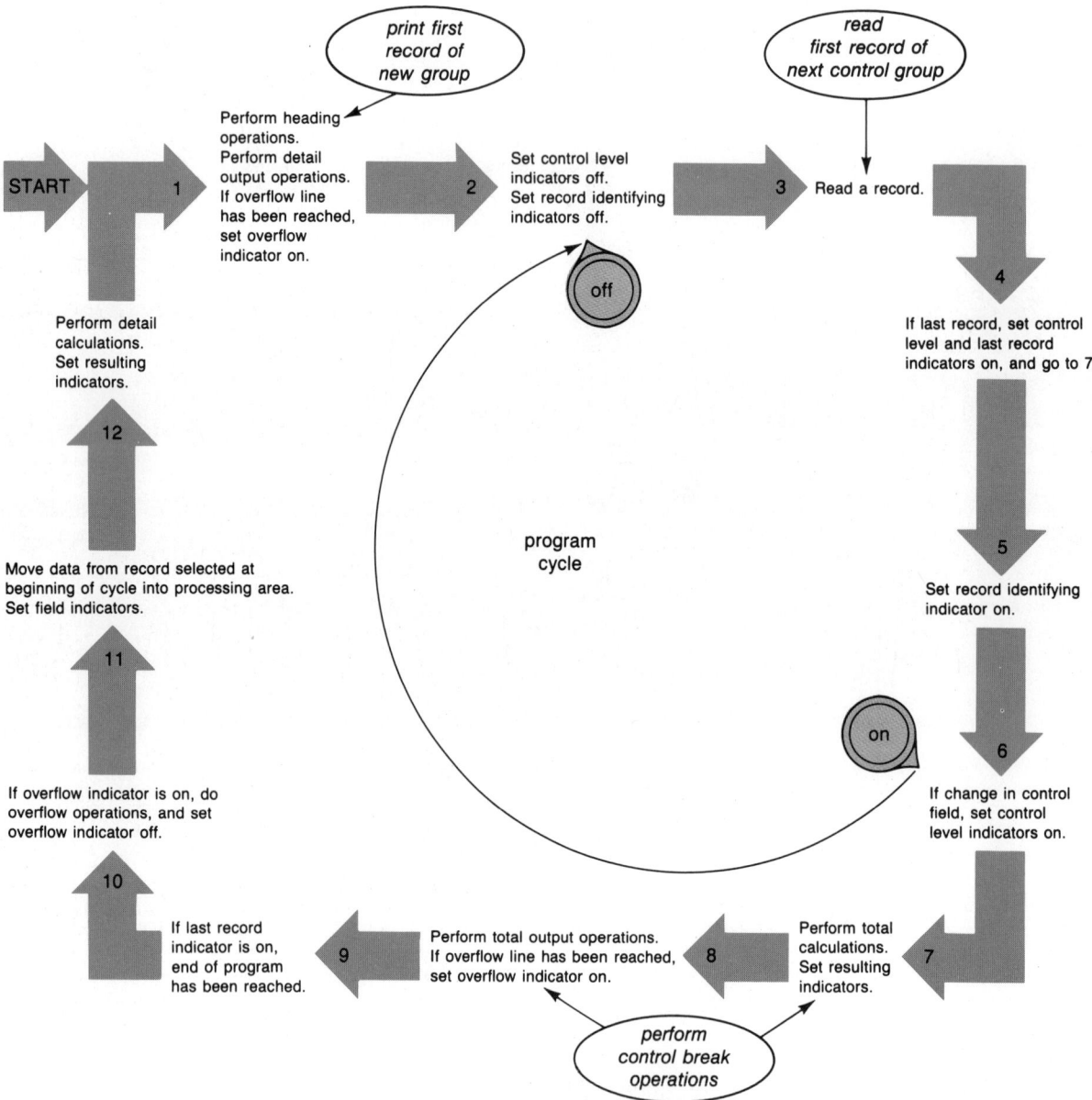

Figure 5-21   Group indication logic

Using the control level indicator to control an output field (Figure 5-22) causes the control field to print only for the first record of the control group. The STORE field is controlled by two indicators in an AND relationship. The detail line prints whenever indicator 01 is on. If indicator L1 is also on, as it is for the first record of each control group, the STORE field prints. If indicator L1 is not on, STORE does not print as part of the detail line.

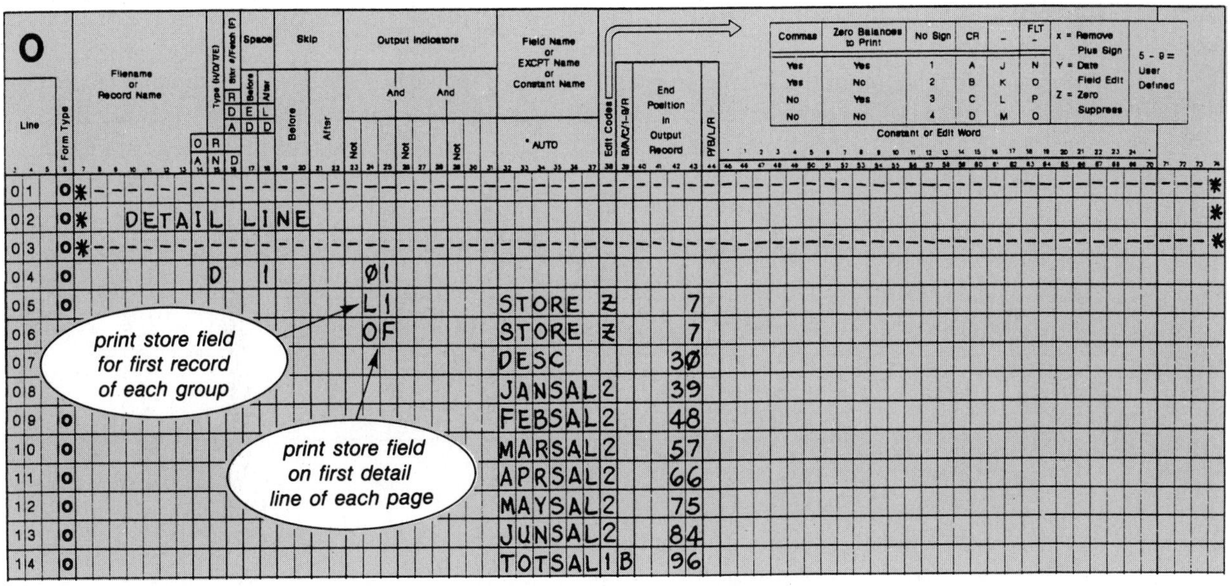

Figure 5-22   Group indication coding

Note that there are two output entries for the STORE field, the second one controlled by indicator OF. This second output entry for a group indicated field causes the field to print at the top of a new page when page overflow occurs. If this second entry is not used, a group indicated report could contain a page in which the control group is not identified.

▸ **Group Indication of the First Record**   By now you may be wondering about group indication of the first control group, since the first detail record is not preceded by a control break. Refer to Figure 5-10. RPG tests all input records, including the first, for a control break. As the figure shows, the bypass of logic steps 7 and 8 (total calculations and output) occurs after the control level indicator has been turned on. Although the control level indicator is not used for steps 7 and 8, it is available at detail output time for the first input record and thus group indication takes place.

At this point your instructor may assign one or more of the single level control break exercises at the end of this chapter or may instruct you to continue and learn about multiple level control breaks.

MULTIPLE LEVEL CONTROL BREAKS

RPG does not limit control breaking to a single control field; its programs can use up to nine different fields as control fields. This permits the development of programs that produce reports containing totals within other, larger totals. This technique of using several control fields to produce totals within totals is called **multiple level control breaks**.

ANALYSIS OF SAMPLE PROBLEM: SALES REPORT

The second sample problem uses program HJG05Y to create a Sales Report in which three fields are used as control fields. This section begins the problem description and logic used.

Input

The input record layout for the sample program HJG05Y is shown in Figure 5-23. Each input record contains fields for branch number, salesperson number, customer number, sales amount, and sales type. The Branch Number, Salesperson Number, and Customer Number fields are the control fields in the record. Each of these control fields causes a separate level of control break.

Field No.	Field Name	Field Description	Field Position	Field Length	Dec. Pos.	Data Class
1	BRANCH	Branch Number	1–2	2	0	N
2	SPRSON	Salesperson Number	3–4	2	0	N
3	CUSTMR	Customer Number	5–9	5	0	N
4	AMOUNT	Sales Amount	10–14	5	2	N
5	TYPE	Sale Type	15–15	1	0	N
6		UNUSED AREA	16–50			

SALES RECORD — Record Length 50

Figure 5-23   Input record layout

Output

The output of the sample program is the Sales Report; its format is shown in Figure 5-24.

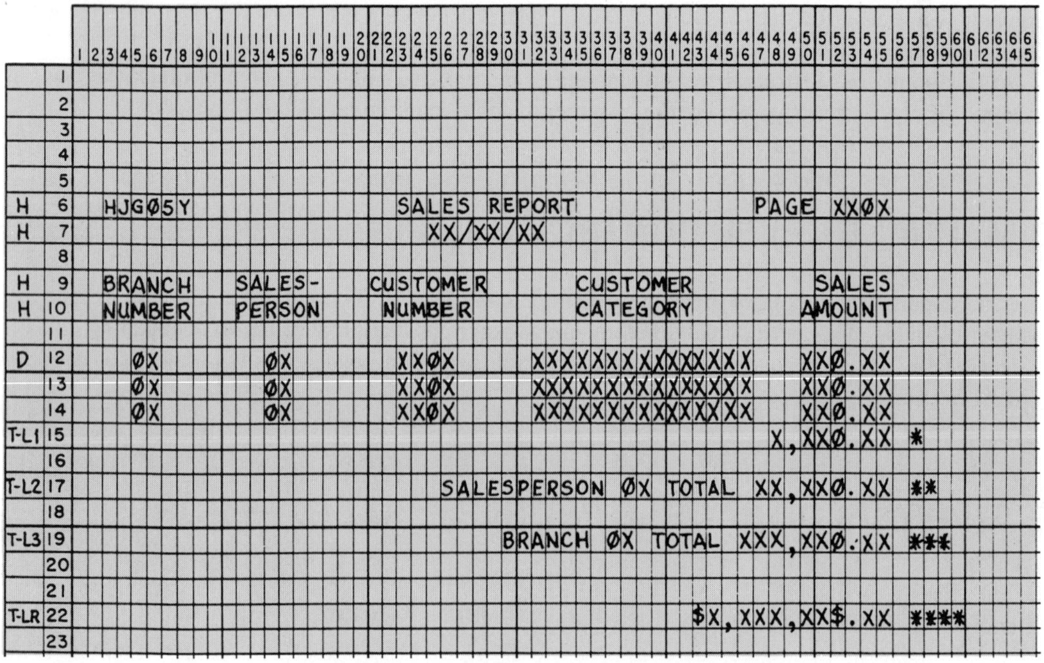

Figure 5-24   Format of Sales Report

▤ Processing Requirements

The Sales Report is to be detail printed with control breaks occurring whenever there is a change in the Customer Number, Salesperson Number, or Branch Number fields. The sum of the Sales Amount fields in the group is printed during each control break. Each total amount is identified by asterisks, as shown on the printer spacing chart.

Each detail line contains a customer category constant, beginning in position 32. The constant is based on the contents of the Customer Category (TYPE) input field. The following table lists each of the valid TYPE values and the constant that is printed:

Type	Constant
1	Cash sale
2	Credit card
3	School
4	Municipality
5	State
6	Corporate

If the TYPE field does not contain one of the six valid entries, the constant INVALID TYPE*** is printed in the Customer Category field.

▤ MULTIPLE LEVEL CONTROL BREAK CONCEPTS ▤

▤ Input Data Records

In Figure 5-25 on the next page, every control field change in the data file is indicated to show the relationship of the three control fields. The Customer Number field is the lowest of the three control levels. Every time the customer number changes, a total of the amounts contained in all the customer's records is printed. Because customer number is the lowest level control field, it has been assigned control level L1.

The second-level control field (L2) is the salesperson number. Every time the salesperson number changes, a total of all the amounts contained in the records for that salesperson are printed. This total can be thought of in two ways: The total is the sum of all detail records within the salesperson group, but it is also the total of the customer number (L1) totals within the salesperson group.

Branch number is the highest level control field (L3) used in the sample program. Every time the branch number changes, a total of all the amounts within the branch group is printed. Again, this total can be thought of either as the sum of a series of detail amounts or as the sum of a series of lower level (L2) totals.

▸ **Control Groups within Control Groups** Note in Figure 5-25 that the term **multiple control levels** refers to control groups that are within larger control groups. When you plan a program that uses multiple control levels, it is important that you understand the **hierarchy** of these groups, that is, which group is a subdivision of a larger group.

The program specifications often clearly indicate the hierarchy of control fields and the indicator to be used with each field by statements such as "When there is a change in part number, an L1 total is to be printed." If statements of this type are not part of the program specifications, you often see a statement such as "Control breaks are to be taken on a change in customer number, within salesperson number, within branch number." The key word in that sentence is *within*. The use of *within* indicates that a control group is contained in, or is a subdivision of, another control group. The quoted statement tells you that each customer group is part of a salesperson group, and that each salesperson group is part of a branch group. From this, you can determine that branch number is the highest level of control, customer number is the lowest, and salesperson number is in the middle.

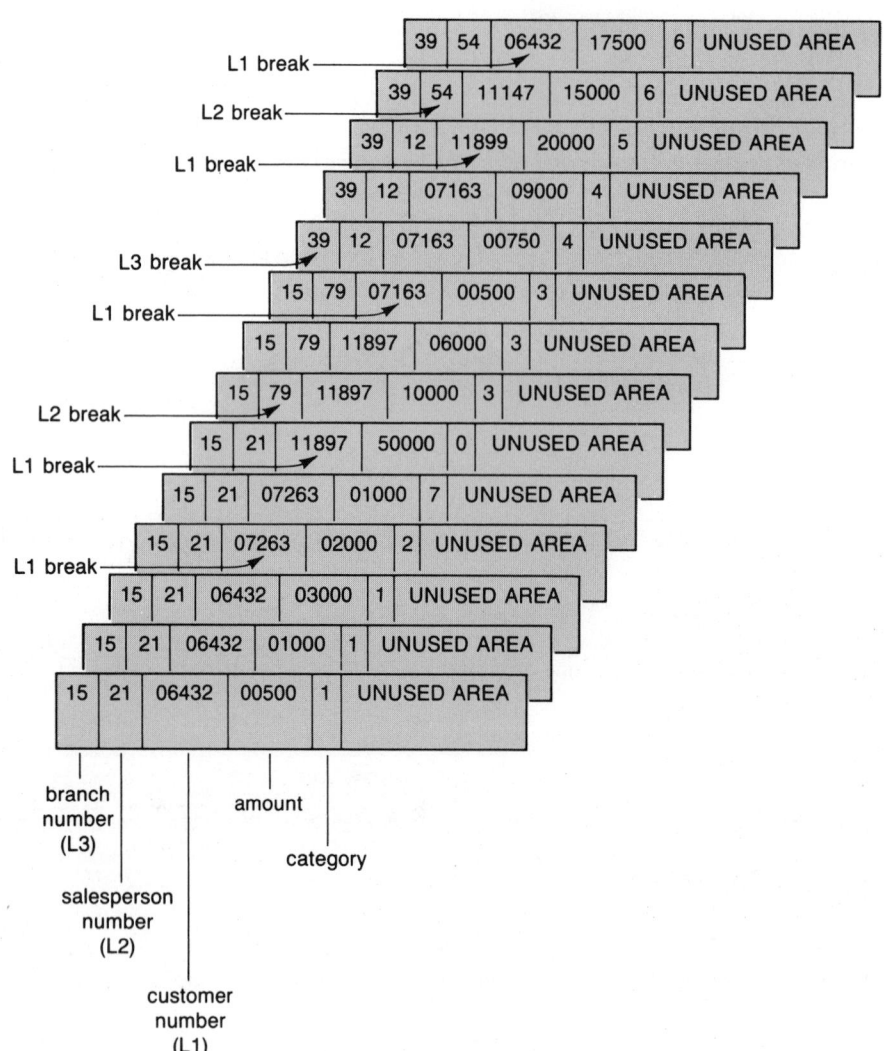

Figure 5-25 Input data file

Some program specifications just state that "the control fields are branch number, salesperson number, and customer number". In this case your knowledge of the company or programming application might provide you with the information necessary to determine the hierarchy. Another clue can often be found by reviewing the input record layout. Usually, but not always, control fields appear in the record in a left-to-right, high-to-low order. The first control field in the record is usually the highest level control field, and the last control field in the record is usually the lowest.

It is imperative that you understand the hierarchy of the control fields when you plan a multiple level control break program. If you do not understand the hierarchy, you cannot plan the program correctly. If the programming specifications do not clearly identify the hierarchy of the control fields, consult the systems analyst who developed the program specifications.

▸ **Multiple Control Level Indicators**   Recall that an RPG program can contain up to nine control levels, each identified by a special-purpose indicator, L1–L9. The lowest level of control field hierarchy is assigned control level L1, the next level L2, and so on. Note that these control level assignments should start with level L1 and proceed consecutively. If three control levels are used in a program, they should be assigned control level indicators L1, L2, and L3. If five levels are used, you should assign indicators L1, L2, L3, L4, and L5.

Some versions of RPG do not require that control level indicators be assigned consecutively; if three levels are needed, indicators L2, L5, and L8 could be used. However, consecutive assignment starting with level L1 not only works in all versions of RPG but also is good, accepted programming practice.

Output Reports and Multiple Control Break Totals

The processing needed to accumulate multiple control break totals can be easily shown by the relationship of the totals fields as they appear on the printed output report. The following examples relate to the sample report in Figure 5-26 (generated from the data file of Figure 5-25).

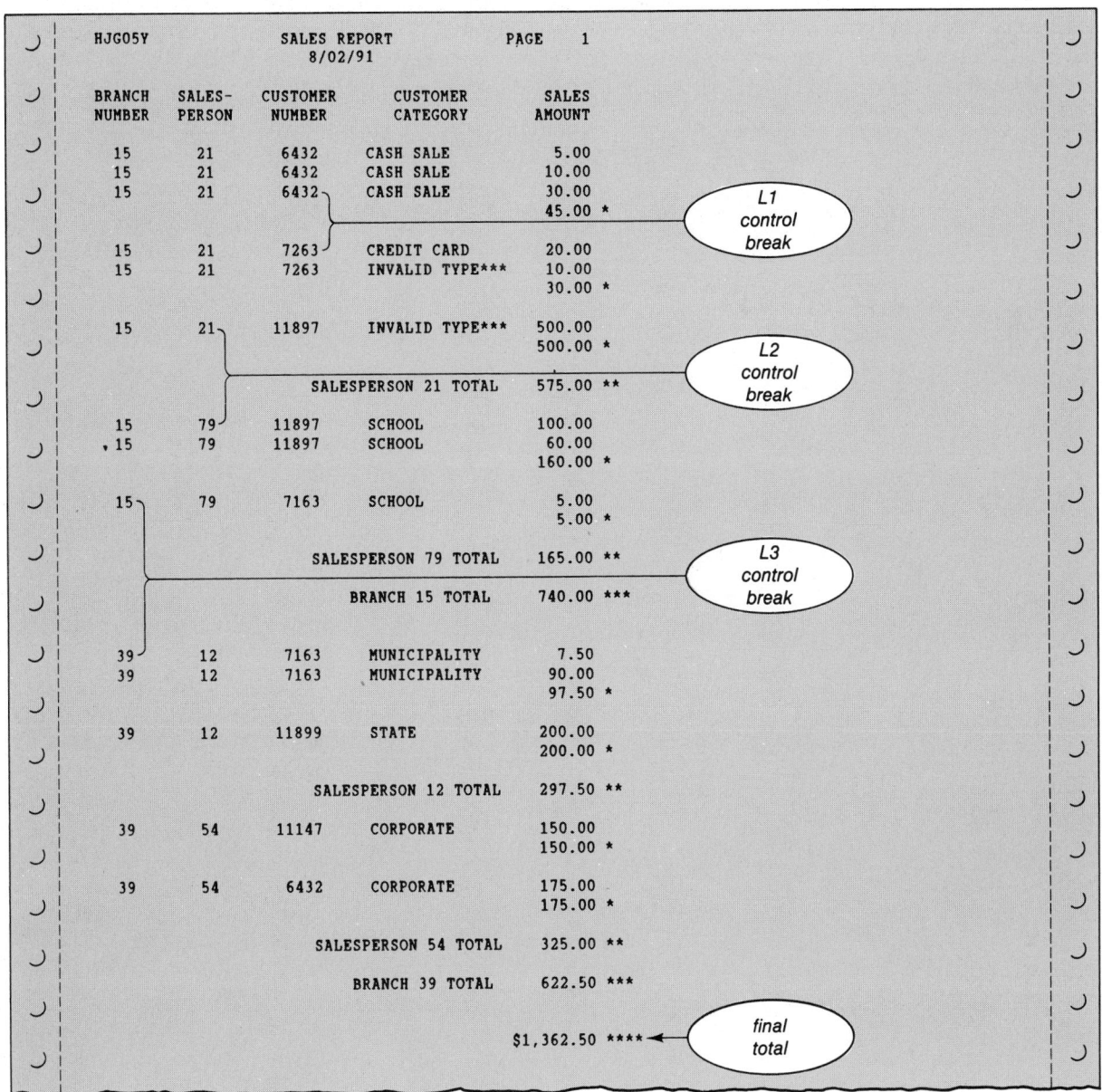

Figure 5-26   Output report with L1, L2, and L3 control breaks

▶ **Output: L1, L2, and L3 Control Breaks** The report shows that when there is a change in the Customer Number field, an L1 control break occurs, and the total of the Sales Amount fields for all customers in the control group is printed. When an L2 control break occurs because of a change in the Salesperson Number field, the total for the last customer number within the salesperson group prints, followed by a total of all the sales amounts for the salesperson. When there is an L3 control break, that is, when there is a change in the branch number, the total for the last customer is printed, followed by a salesperson total, and then by the total of all the sales amounts for the branch. At the end of the program, after all data records have been processed, the customer, salesperson, branch, and final totals are printed. Because it is extremely important that you understand the processing that must take place at total time during an L1, L2, or L3 control break, the following paragraphs and illustrations demonstrate the processing that occurs during each of the three control breaks.

▶ **L1 Total Time Processing** At every L1 control break, the sales amount total for each customer is added to the salesperson total accumulator and then printed, (Figure 5-27). In this example, the total for salesperson 21 is 575.00, which is the sum of the totals for each of the customers within salesperson 21. As this illustration shows, the salesperson total (L2) is the sum of the totals for each customer (L1).

Figure 5-27 L1 total time calculation

▶ **L2 Total Time Processing** During each L2 control break, the total for the last customer group is added to the salesperson total and then printed (Figure 5-28). The salesperson total is then added to the branch total accumulator and then printed. Just as the L2 total is the sum of L1 totals, the L3 total is the sum of the L2 totals. The branch total is, therefore, the sum of all salesperson totals within the branch.

```
HJG05Y                SALES REPORT              PAGE    1
                        8/02/91

     BRANCH    SALES-    CUSTOMER    CUSTOMER       SALES
     NUMBER    PERSON    NUMBER      CATEGORY       AMOUNT

       15        21       6432      CASH SALE         5.00
       15        21       6432      CASH SALE        10.00
       15        21       6432      CASH SALE        30.00
                                                     45.00 *

       15        21       7263      CREDIT CARD      20.00
       15        21       7263      INVALID TYPE***  10.00
                                                     30.00 *

       15        21      11897      INVALID TYPE***  500.00
                                                    500.00 *

                        SALESPERSON 21 TOTAL        575.00 **

       15        79      11897      SCHOOL          100.00
       15        79      11897      SCHOOL           60.00
                                                    160.00 *

       15        79       7163      SCHOOL            5.00
                                                      5.00 *

                        SALESPERSON 79 TOTAL        165.00 **

                        BRANCH 15 TOTAL             740.00 ***

       39        12       7163      MUNICIPALITY      7.50
       39        12       7163      MUNICIPALITY     90.00
                                                     97.50 *

       39        12      11899      STATE           200.00
                                                    200.00 *

                        SALESPERSON 12 TOTAL        297.50 **

       39        54      11147      CORPORATE       150.00
                                                    150.00 *

       39        54       6432      CORPORATE       175.00
                                                    175.00 *

                        SALESPERSON 54 TOTAL        325.00 **

                        BRANCH 39 TOTAL             622.50 ***


                                                 $1,362.50 ****
```

each time there is an L2 control break (a change in the salesperson number), the total for the salesperson is added to the branch total accumulator

Figure 5-28 L2 Total time calculation

Earlier in this chapter you saw that at the end of the program the indicator LR forces indicator L1 to be turned on in order to print the last control break total. In Figure 5-28, whenever there is an L2 control break, an L1 control break is forced. At the end of the salesperson 21 group, even though customer number does not change, an L1 control break occurs. *Any control break greater than L1 causes all lower level control break indicators to be turned on.* Thus, whenever an L2 control break occurs, an L1 control break also occurs.

▸ **L3 Total Time Processing**   From the sample report in Figure 5-29, you can see that when an L3 control break is caused by a change in the Branch Number field, the L1 and L2 processing just described occurs because the L3 control break forces L2 and L1 breaks. The branch total is then added to the final total accumulator, and the branch total is printed.

```
 HJG05Y                SALES REPORT          PAGE    1
                         8/02/91

 BRANCH     SALES-    CUSTOMER     CUSTOMER        SALES
 NUMBER     PERSON    NUMBER       CATEGORY        AMOUNT

   15         21       6432        CASH SALE          5.00
   15         21       6432        CASH SALE         10.00
   15         21       6432        CASH SALE         30.00
                                                     45.00 *

   15         21       7263        CREDIT CARD       20.00
   15         21       7263        INVALID TYPE***   10.00
                                                     30.00 *

   15         21      11897        INVALID TYPE***  500.00
                                                    500.00 *

                      SALESPERSON 21 TOTAL          575.00 **

   15         79      11897        SCHOOL           100.00
   15         79      11897        SCHOOL            60.00
                                                    160.00 *

   15         79       7163        SCHOOL             5.00
                                                      5.00 *

                      SALESPERSON 79 TOTAL          165.00 **

                      BRANCH 15 TOTAL               740.00 ***

   39         12       7163        MUNICIPALITY       7.50
   39         12       7163        MUNICIPALITY      90.00
                                                     97.50 *

   39         12      11899        STATE            200.00
                                                    200.00 *

                      SALESPERSON 12 TOTAL          297.50 **

   39         54      11147        CORPORATE        150.00
                                                    150.00 *

   39         54       6432        CORPORATE        175.00
                                                    175.00 *

                      SALESPERSON 54 TOTAL          325.00 **

                      BRANCH 39 TOTAL               622.50 ***

                                              $1,362.50 ****
```

each time there is an L3 control break (a change in the branch number), the branch total is added to the final total accumulator

Figure 5-29   L3 Total time calculation

▸ **LR Total Time Processing**   At the end of the program, RPG turns on indicator LR and all other control level indicators, L1–L9. This is the method by which RPG forces control break totals at the end of the program. Because all control level indicators are on, the program performs L1, L2, L3, and LR processing before ending program execution.

RPG Fixed Logic Cycle for Multiple Control Breaks

When multiple control break processing is used in a program, several of the steps of the logic cycle perform more complex functions than are shown on the cycle chart. The flowchart in Figure 5-30 expands on steps 4–10 of the logic cycle and shows several of the logic steps in more detail. Steps 5 and 10 are not discussed here because they are not part of control break processing, and there is no change in their operation. Although this flowchart is based on a program that uses three levels of control, the same logic applies to a program using any number of control levels. The only differences are the number of tests performed and the number of indicators turned on in step 6.

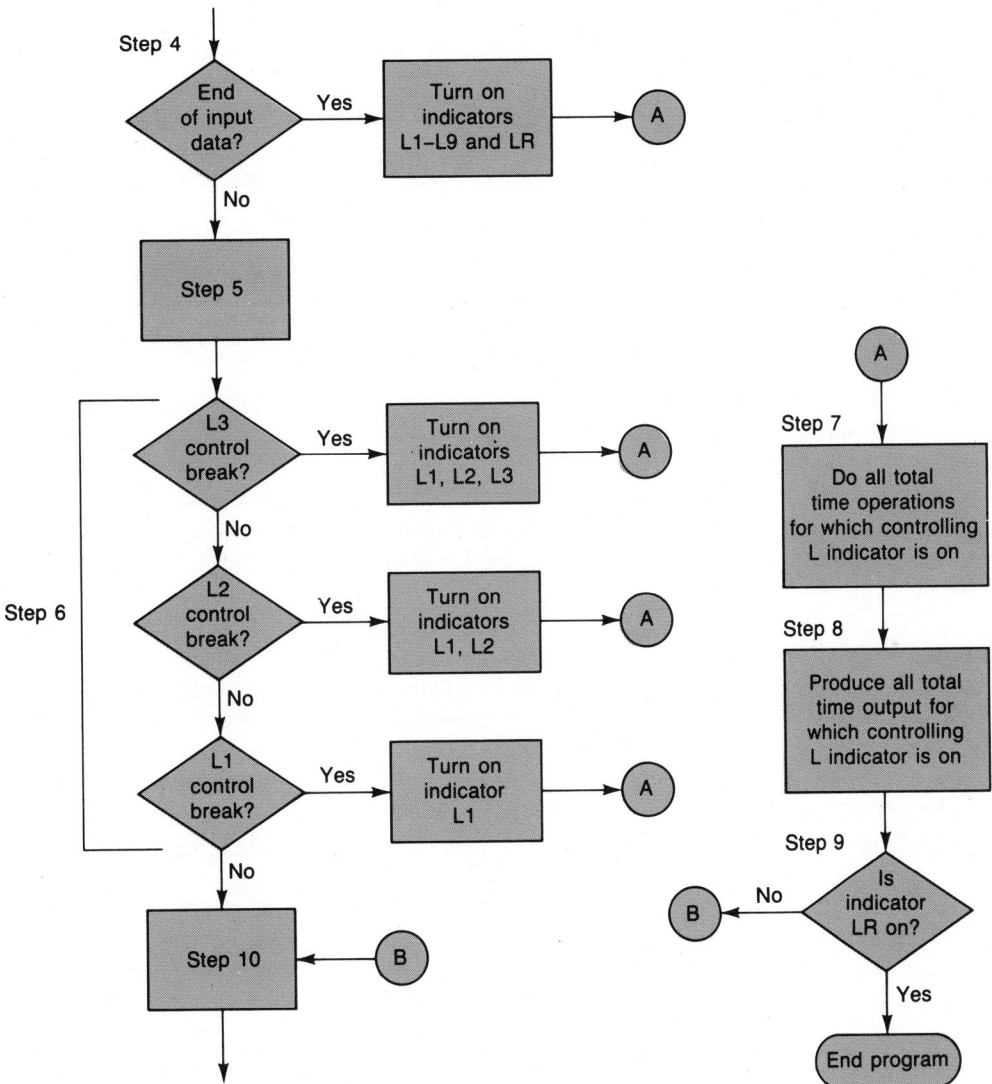

Figure 5-30 Control break processing flowchart

▸ **Step 4: Test for End of Job** When the end of the input data file is detected by RPG, indicator LR and all control level indicators, L1–L9, are turned on. The nine control level indicators are turned on when the end of the data is reached in every RPG program, regardless of whether or not these indicators are used in the program. After turning on these indicators, the program logic proceeds directly to step 7, total calculation time.

▸ **Step 6: Control Break Test** The flowchart shows that when multiple control levels are used in a program, step 6 consists of a series of tests, one for each level of control. Control break testing always starts with the highest level control field (branch number, L3, in this example).

If there is a control break on the highest level control field, RPG turns on the control level indicator for that field and all lower control level indicators. If there is an L3 control break, indicators L3, L2, and L1 are turned on. After turning on the control level indicators, program logic proceeds to step 7.

If there is no change in the highest level control field, RPG then tests the next control field (salesperson number, L2). If this control field has changed, RPG turns on the L2 and L1 control level indicators and then proceeds to step 7.

If there is no change in the L2 control field, RPG tests the L1 field. If there is a change in the L1 control field, RPG turns on indicator L1 and proceeds to step 7. If there is no change in the L1 field, the program continues with normal detail processing in step 10.

Remember that RPG starts control break testing with the highest level of control and continues to test each lower level field until either a control break is detected or RPG determines that there is no control break. This series of tests takes place regardless of the number of control fields in the program. If there is only one control field, only one test occurs; if there are nine control fields, nine tests are performed. At each level, if a control break is detected by the test, the indicator for that control level and all lower control level indicators are turned on. With the exception of L1, any control break forces all lower level control breaks.

▸ **Step 7: Total Calculation Time** During step 7, all total time calculations are performed in a top-down sequence, with each operation being performed if its controlling indicator is on. **Top-down** means that the calculations are performed in the sequence in which they appear on the coding sheet or program listing, starting at the top of the calculation specifications and continuing to the bottom.

RPG looks at every calculation specification line that has a control level indicator in positions 7 and 8. If the indicator is on, the operation is performed; if the indicator is not on, the operation is not performed. Because RPG tests the indicator status of the calculations in a top-down sequence, the calculations must be written in the order in which they are to be performed. When working with multiple level control breaks, this usually means that all L1 total time calculations are coded first, all L2 total time calculations are coded second, and so on; the LR total time calculations should be coded last. Within each level of total time calculations, each operation should be coded in the sequence in which it must be performed.

▸ **Step 8: Total Output Time** Total time output records are also produced in a top-down sequence. The indicators that control each total time output record (type T) are tested. If the controlling indicator is on, the line is printed; if the controlling indicator is not on, the line is not printed. Because these output records are tested in a top-down sequence, the output records must be coded in the order in which they are to be printed. The L1 total line(s) should be coded first, the L2 line(s) second, and so on. The LR total lines are usually coded last. If multiple lines are to be printed during a single control break, these lines must also be coded in the correct order. The general rule for the coding of output lines is that they are coded in the order in which they are to appear on the printed report.

▸ **Step 9: Indicator LR Testing** Step 9 determines if indicator LR is on. If LR is on, the program ends. If LR is not on, the program continues with normal detail processing at step 10 of the logic cycle.

SPECIFICATIONS FOR SAMPLE PROGRAM HJG05Y

This section presents the program specifications for solving this problem.

Input Specifications

The program Input Specification form (Figure 5-31) contains entries in positions 59–60 to identify the three control fields. CUSTMR (customer number) has been assigned as the L1 control field, SPRSON (salesperson number) is the L2 control field, and BRANCH is the L3 control field.

I	Filename or Record Name		Sequence	Number (1/N),E	Option (O),U,S	Record Identifying Indicator, or DS		Named Constant Value																	Field Location			RPG Field Name		Control Level (L1-L9)	Matching Fields or Chaining Fields	Field Record Relation	Field Indicators		
								External Field Name																		From	To							Plus	Minus	Zero or Blank
								Record Identification Codes																												
								1				2				3										Data Structure			Constant Name							
Line								Position	Not (N)	C/Z/D	Character	Position	Not (N)	C/Z/D	Character	Position	Not (N)	C/Z/D	Character	Stacker Select	P/B/L/R/C					Occurs n Times	Length	Decimal Positions								
0 1	I	SALEFILE	AA				01																			1	20		BRANCH		L3					
0 2	I																									3	40		SPRSON		L2					
0 3	I																									5	90		CUSTMR		L1					
0 4	I																									10	142		AMOUNT							
0 5	I																									15	150		TYPE					40	40	
0 6	I																																			
0 7	I																																			
0 8	I																																			

Figure 5-31 Input specifications for Program HJG05Y

Note that the control fields are assigned in descending control sequence: The L3 field is first, the L2 field second, and the L1 field third. This is a matter of coincidence and input record format, rather than a function of RPG syntax. Control fields do not have to be assigned in any specific order. The accepted programming practice is to describe the input data fields in the usual sequence, assigning control fields wherever they are needed.

▸ **Field Indicators (Positions 65–66, 67–68, and 69–70)** RPG has the ability to provide some information about the contents of an input data field by means of entries in the Field Indicators area, positions 65–70 of the Input Specifications form. The Field Indicators area is divided into three smaller areas headed Plus, Minus, and Zero or Blank. Although all three areas can be used to test the contents of a numeric data field, only the Zero or Blank area can be used with alphameric data.

These areas are used to determine if an alphameric field is completely blank or if a numeric field contains a positive number, negative number, or zero. If the program is testing a numeric field, an indicator placed in positions 65–66 (Plus) turns on if the field named in positions 53–58 contains a value greater than zero. If the field contains a value less than zero, the indicator placed in positions 67–68 (Minus) turns on. An indicator placed in positions 69–70 (Zero or Blank) turns on if the input field contains a value of zero.

When field indicators are used with alphameric data fields, only positions 69–70 can be used. This area is used to indicate that an alphameric data field is blank, that is, the field contains a space in every position. The Plus and Minus entries cannot be used with alphameric data fields.

Several examples of the use of input field indicators are shown in Figure 5-32. On line 01, indicator 10 turns on if the QTY field contains a value of zero when an input record is read. Indicator 10 could then be used to control the execution or nonexecution of calculations or program output. For example, if QTY is the divisor in a DIV operation, the DIV could be performed only when indicator 10 is off (N10) because division by zero is not permitted in RPG.

I	Filename or Record Name		Sequence	Number (1/N),E	Option (O),U,S	Record Identifying Indicator, or DS		Named Constant Value																	Field Location			RPG Field Name		Control Level (L1-L9)	Matching Fields or Chaining Fields	Field Record Relation	Field Indicators		
								External Field Name																		From	To							Plus	Minus	Zero or Blank
								Record Identification Codes																												
								1				2				3										Data Structure			Constant Name							
Line								Position	Not (N)	C/Z/D	Character	Position	Not (N)	C/Z/D	Character	Position	Not (N)	C/Z/D	Character	Stacker Select	P/B/L/R/C					Occurs n Times	Length	Decimal Positions								
0 1	I																									1	40		QTY							10
0 2	I																																			
0 3	I																									13	202		AMOUNT					99	20	
0 4	I																																			
0 5	I																									21	40		NAME							98
0 6	I																																			
0 7	I																									21	40		NAME							H1
0 8	I																																			

Figure 5-32 Input field indicator usage

Line 03 shows that two indicators can be set for the same field. In this example, indicator 20 is turned on if AMOUNT contains a value of zero, and indicator 99 is turned on if AMOUNT contains a negative value. If AMOUNT contains a positive amount, neither 99 nor 20 turns on.

Lines 05 and 07 both show testing of the alphameric data field NAME. In the example on line 05, indicator 98 turns on if the NAME field is blank in all 20 positions. Because NAME is an alphameric data field, it cannot be tested for Plus or Minus values. Line 07 shows the use of the Field Indicator area to turn on a halt indicator on an error condition. In this example, indicator H1 turns on if the NAME field is blank. This causes the program to stop at the end of the detail processing cycle for the input record. All current versions of RPG permit the use of general-purpose and halt indicators in the Field Indicators area. Some newer versions of the language also permit the use of other types of indicators.

In the sample program (Figure 5-31), an entry has been made in the Zero or Blank and the Minus areas for the TYPE field. Because the valid TYPE entries are 1–6, the Field Indicators entry has been used to check for an entry that is less than the lowest valid TYPE field entry. These entries are used in conjunction with COMP operations on the Calculation Specifications form to test for incorrect TYPE entries.

Calculation Specifications

On the Calculation Specifications form for the sample program (Figure 5-33), lines 01 and 02 are used to SETOF the indicators that are used to show the result of testing the TYPE field to determine which valid code it contains. Testing the TYPE field involves comparisons controlled by other comparisons, a subject discussed in Chapter 4.

Line	Form Type	Control Level	Indicators And/And	Factor 1	Operation	Factor 2	Result Field Name	Length	Dec Pos	Resulting Indicators Plus High	Minus Low	Zero Equal	Comments
01	C		01		SETOF					41	42	43	
02	C		01		SETOF					44	45	46	
03	C		01N40	TYPE	COMP	6				40		46	
04	C		01N40	TYPE	COMP	5						45	
05	C		01N40	TYPE	COMP	4						44	
06	C		01N40	TYPE	COMP	3						43	
07	C		01N40	TYPE	COMP	2						42	
08	C		01N40	TYPE	COMP	1						41	
09	C		01	CUSTOT	ADD	AMOUNT	CUSTOT	62					
10	C	L1		SPTOT	ADD	CUSTOT	SPTOT	72					
11	C	L2		BRTOT	ADD	SPTOT	BRTOT	82					
12	C	L3		FINTOT	ADD	BRTOT	FINTOT	92					
13	C												
14	C												

Figure 5-33 Calculation specifications for program HJG05Y

Lines 03–08 are controlled by indicators 01 and N40. Indicator 40 is turned on as an input field indicator to show that TYPE contains an invalid entry. If the TYPE entry is determined to be invalid by the input specifications, there is no need to test the TYPE field further. If indicator 40 is not on, line 03 compares the TYPE field with the numeric literal 6. If TYPE is greater than 6, indicator 40 is turned on. Thus, indicator 40 represents an invalid TYPE field entry because it is turned on if the TYPE is less than 1 or greater than 6. Both conditions represent an invalid TYPE entry. If TYPE is equal to 6, indicator 46 is turned on. Lines 04–08 compare the TYPE field with the other five valid codes and set a separate indicator to show which code the field contains.

Line 09 adds the contents of the Sales Amount field to the CUSTOT accumulator, which is printed during an L1 control break. Line 10 adds the CUSTOT accumulator to the L2 accumulator SPTOT. Recall that the logic cycle performs calculations before output, and therefore CUSTOT is added before it is printed. When CUSTOT is printed, a Blank After entry resets the accumulator. Line 11 rolls the L2 accumulator SPTOT into the L3 accumulator BRTOT. On line 12, the L3 accumulator is rolled into FINTOT, which is the final total accumulator for the Sales Amount field.

Output Specifications

In the detail and total output specifications for the sample program (Figure 5-34), the detail line prints when indicator 01 is on. Lines 05–11 of the detail line control the printing of the customer category message, depending on the indicators that were turned on as the result of comparison of the TYPE field (see Figure 5-33, lines 03–08). Because only one of these indicators can be on during any one detail cycle, a single message is printed.

Figure 5-34   Output specifications for program HJG05Y

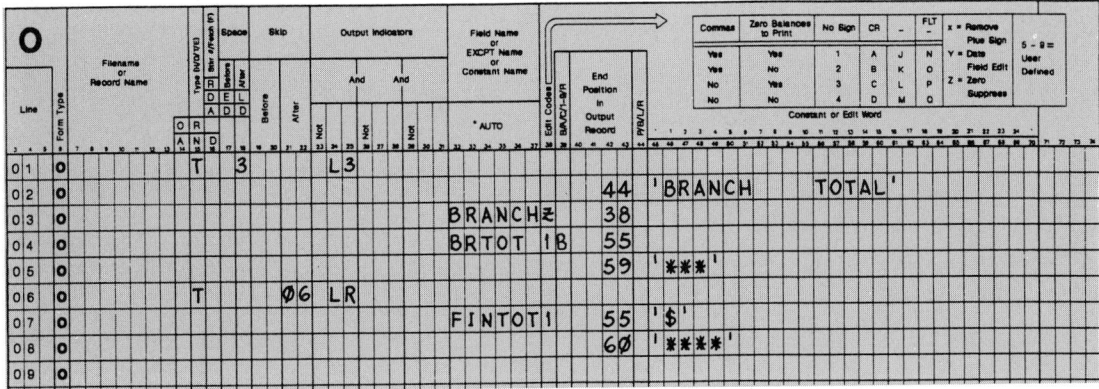

Figure 5-34 (1)

Figure 5-34 (2)

Note that the four total lines are coded in the sequence in which they must be printed. The L1 total line appears first, followed by the L2 line, the L3 line, and the LR line. When multiple control level indicators are on, as happens at L2, L3, and LR total times, RPG tests the indicator status of each total line in a top-down manner, and if the controlling indicator is on, prints the record.

As in earlier examples, the salesperson total line contains the salesperson number and the branch total line contains the branch number. The L2 and L3 total line coding (Figure 5-34) shows two methods of coding the insertion of a data field into an output constant.

In the L2 total line, the constant 'SALESPERSON' is printed first, followed by the contents of the SPRSON field and then the constant 'TOTAL'. These three entries result in the needed total identification, such as SALESPERSON 21 TOTAL.

The L3 total line coding takes advantage of the top-down functioning of RPG. RPG not only processes output records in a top-down order, but also processes fields and constants within an output record in a top-down manner. The first L3 total line entry causes the constant 'BRANCH   TOTAL' to be placed in the output area, ending in position 44. The second entry causes the branch number to be moved to the output area, ending in position 38. This causes the branch number to overlay two of the blank positions in the 'BRANCH   TOTAL' constant. The result of this overlay is to position the branch number in the output, for example, BRANCH 15 TOTAL. As you can see, there is no difference between the results of these two methods of field insertion. The only difference is that the second method eliminates one line of RPG output coding.

SOURCE LISTING FOR SAMPLE PROGRAM HJG05Y

The source listing for the sample program (Figure 5-35) which is not a compiled listing, is the type of listing that might be generated from the source entry utility used to enter the source program code into the computer.

Figure 5-35 Source code listing for program HJG05Y

```
     LIBRARY -  HALSLIB                              Date: 8/12/91  Page:   1
     Member  Suf    Bytes    Date    Time            Time:12:28:54
     --------  ---    ------   --------  -----

     HJG05Y  .S      3440   08/12/91  12:28

     0001 H                                                          HJG05Y
     0002 FSALEFILEIP  F 500  50          DISK
     0003 FSALELISTO   F 132 132    OF    PRINTER
     0004 ISALEFILEAA  01
     0005 I                             1    20BRANCHL3
     0006 I                             3    40SPRSONL2
     0007 I                             5    90CUSTMRL1
     0008 I                            10   142AMOUNT
     0009 I                            15   150TYPE          4040
     0010 C    01              SETOF             414243
     0011 C    01              SETOF             444546
     0012 C    01N40   TYPE    COMP 6            40  46
     0013 C    01N40   TYPE    COMP 5                45
     0014 C    01N40   TYPE    COMP 4                44
     0015 C    01N40   TYPE    COMP 3                43
     0016 C    01N40   TYPE    COMP 2                42
     0017 C    01N40   TYPE    COMP 1                41
     0018 C    01      CUSTOT  ADD AMOUNT   CUSTOT 62
     0019 CL1          SPTOT   ADD CUSTOT   SPTOT  72
     0020 CL2          BRTOT   ADD SPTOT    BRTOT  82
     0021 CL3          FINTOT  ADD BRTOT    FINTOT 92
     0022 OSALELISTH   106    1P
     0023 O       OR          OF
     0024 O                             8 'HJG05Y'
     0025 O                            34 'SALES REPORT'
     0026 O                            50 'PAGE'
     0027 O                    PAGE    55
```

Figure 5-35 (1a)

```
0028 O        H  2   1P
0029 O        OR     OF
0030 O                      UDATE   Y   32
0031 O        H  1   1P
0032 O        OR     OF
0033 O                              26  'BRANCH    SALES-   CUSTOM'
0034 O                              42  'ER        CUSTOMER'
0035 O                              55  'SALES'
0036 O        H  2   1P
0037 O        OR     OF
0038 O                              26  'NUMBER    PERSON     NUMBE'
0039 O                              42  'R         CATEGORY'
0040 O                              55  'AMOUNT'
0041 O        D  1   01
0042 O                      BRANCHZ  6
0043 O                      SPRSONZ 15
0044 O                      CUSTMRZ 26
0045 O                40            46  'INVALID TYPE***'
0046 O                41            40  'CASH SALE'
0047 O                42            42  'CREDIT CARD'
0048 O                43            37  'SCHOOL'
0049 O                44            43  'MUNICIPALITY'
0050 O                45            36  'STATE'
0051 O                46            40  'CORPORATE'
0052 O                      AMOUNT3 55
```

Figure 5-35 (1b)

```
LIBRARY -  HALSLIB                         Date: 8/12/91  Page:    2
Member  Suf    Bytes   Date    Time        Time:12:28:54
-------- ---   ------  ------  ------
HJG05Y  .S      3440  08/12/91 12:28

0053 O        T  2   L1
0054 O                      CUSTOT1B 55
0055 O                               57  '*'
0056 O        T  2   L2
0057 O                               36  'SALESPERSON'
0058 O                      SPRSONZ  39
0059 O                               45  'TOTAL'
0060 O                      SPTOT 1B 55
0061 O                               58  '**'
0062 O        T  3   L3
0063 O                               44  'BRANCH    TOTAL'
0064 O                      BRANCHZ  38
0065 O                      BRTOT 1B 55
0066 O                               59  '***'
0067 O        T     06  LR
0068 O                      FINTOT1  55  '$'
0069 O                               60  '****'
```

Figure 5-35 (2)

GROUP PRINTING OF REPORTS
Introduction to Group Printing

Recall that data is group indicated by printing the control field data only for the first record of each control group. Another common technique for business reports is group printing. In **group printing**, no detail lines are printed on a report, and output lines are printed on the report only when a control break occurs. A group printed report consists only of headings and total lines.

The differences between the detail printed and group printed output reports are shown in Figure 5-36 on the next page. In the detail printed report, one detail line is printed for every input record read. In addition, totals are printed every time a change occurs in any of the three control fields. Note that the group printed report does not contain any detail lines. Instead, printed output lines appear only when a control field value changes. Note also that the customer, salesperson, branch, and final totals on the group printed report are the same as the totals on the detail printed report.

Figure 5-36   Detail printed and group printed reports

```
DETAIL PRINTED

HJG05Y                      SALES REPORT              PAGE    1
                              7/28/91

BRANCH    SALES-    CUSTOMER    CUSTOMER        SALES
NUMBER    PERSON    NUMBER      CATEGORY        AMOUNT
   15       21       6432      CASH SALE          5.00
   15       21       6432      CASH SALE         10.00
   15       21       6432      CASH SALE         30.00
                                                 45.00 *

   15       21       7263      CREDIT CARD        20.00
   15       21       7263      INVALID TYPE***    10.00
                                                  30.00 *

   15       21      11897      INVALID TYPE***   500.00
                                                 500.00 *

                   SALESPERSON 21 TOTAL          575.00 **

   15       79      11897      SCHOOL            100.00
   15       79      11897      SCHOOL             60.00
                                                 160.00 *

   15       79       7163      SCHOOL              5.00
                                                   5.00 *

                   SALESPERSON 79 TOTAL          165.00 **

                   BRANCH 15 TOTAL               740.00 ***

   39       12       7163      MUNICIPALITY        7.50
   39       12       7163      MUNICIPALITY       90.00
                                                  97.50 *

   39       12      11899      STATE             200.00
                                                 200.00 *

                   SALESPERSON 12 TOTAL          297.50 **

   39       54      11147      CORPORATE         150.00
                                                 150.00 *

   39       54       6432      CORPORATE         175.00
                                                 175.00 *

                   SALESPERSON 54 TOTAL          325.00 **

                   BRANCH 39 TOTAL               622.50 ***

                                              $1,362.50 ****
```

Figure 5-36 (1)

```
GROUP PRINTED

HJG05Y      SALES REPORT      PAGE    1
               8/02/91

BRANCH   SALES-    CUSTOMER  CUSTOMER
NUMBER   PERSON     NUMBER    TOTAL

  15       21        6432     45.00
  15       21        7263     30.00
  15       21       11897    500.00
     SALESPERSON 21 TOTAL    575.00

  15       79       11897    160.00
  15       79        7163      5.00
     SALESPERSON 79 TOTAL    165.00

        BRANCH 15 TOTAL      740.00


  39       12        7163     97.50
  39       12       11899    200.00
     SALESPERSON 12 TOTAL    297.50

  39       54       11147    150.00
  39       54        6432    175.00
     SALESPERSON 54 TOTAL    325.00

        BRANCH 39 TOTAL      622.50


                           $1,362.50
```

Figure 5-36 (2)

▶ **Calculations for Group Printed Reports**   The group printed program generates no detail output, so the comparisons needed to determine the customer category have been removed from the calculation specifications (Figure 5-37). The only remaining calculations are the addition steps needed to accumulate the totals of the sales amount. As you can see, total accumulation in a group printed report is no different from total accumulation in a detail printed report.

Line	Form Type	Control Level (L0-L9, LR, SR, AN/OR)	Indicators And Not	And Not		Factor 1	Operation	Factor 2	Result Field Name	Length	Decimal Positions	Half Adjust (H)	Resulting Indicators Arithmetic Plus/Minus/Zero Compare 1>2 1<2 1=2 High/Low/Equal Lookup(Factor 2)is	Comments
0 1	C		01			CUSTOT	ADD	AMOUNT	CUSTOT	62				
0 2	C	L1				SPTOT	ADD	CUSTOT	SPTOT	72				
0 3	C	L2				BRTOT	ADD	SPTOT	BRTOT	82				
0 4	C	L3				FINTOT	ADD	BRTOT	FINTOT	92				
0 5	C													
0 6	C													

Figure 5-37   Calculation specifications for program HJG05Y

▸ **Output Specifications for Group Printed Reports** The heading lines for the group printed version of the report (Figure 5-38) are specified in the same manner as for the detail printed report. Note that the heading lines have been changed because a detail field (customer category) has been eliminated. The program contains no detail output lines because the only output lines required in a group printed report are total lines. The three fields that identify the totals (branch number, salesperson number, and customer number) have been made a part of the L1 total line.

Figure 5-38 Output specifications for program HJG05Y

Line	Form Type	Filename or Record Name	Type	Space Before	Space After	Skip Before	Skip After	Output Indicators And/And	Field Name or EXCPT Name or Constant Name	End Position in Output Record	Constant or Edit Word
01	O	SALELIST	H			106		1P			
02	O		OR					OF			
03	O									8	'HJG05Y'
04	O									25	'SALES REPORT'
05	O									33	'PAGE'
06	O								PAGE	38	
07	O		H	2				1P			
08	O		OR					OF			
09	O								UDATE Y	23	
10	O		H	1				1P			
11	O		OR					OF			
12	O									26	'BRANCH SALES- CUSTOM'
13	O									37	'ER CUSTOMER'
14	O		H	2				1P			
15	O		OR					OF			
16	O									26	'NUMBER PERSON NUMBE'
17	O									36	'R TOTAL'

Figure 5-38 (1)

Line	Form Type	Type	Space Before	Space After	Skip Before	Skip After	Output Indicators	Field Name or EXCPT Name or Constant Name	End Position in Output Record	Edit Codes	Constant or Edit Word
01	O	T	1				L1				
02	O							BRANCHZ	6		
03	O							SPRSONZ	15		
04	O							CUSTMRZ	26		
05	O							CUSTOT	35	1B	
06	O	T	2				L2				
07	O								16		'SALESPERSON'
08	O							SPRSONZ	19		
09	O										'TOTAL'
10	O							SPTOT	35	1B	
11	O	T	3				L3				
12	O								24		'BRANCH TOTAL'
13	O							BRANCHZ	18		
14	O							BRTOT	35	1B	
15	O	T			06		LR				
16	O							FINTOT	35	1	'$'

Figure 5-38 (2)

Combining Group Indication with Group Printing

The reasons for group indication of a detail printed report are also valid for group indicated reports. Group indication can be used to make the control fields more obvious in a group printed report as well as in a detail printed report. This combination of group indication and group printing is demonstrated in program HJG05Z, the fourth programming example in this chapter.

▸ **Output Report for Sample Program HJG05Z**   The output report generated by program HJG05Z (Figure 5-39) is a group printed report with one output line for each customer number group. In addition, however, the branch number and a salesperson number have been group indicated and appear only for the first record of each control group.

```
HJG05Z      SALES REPORT     PAGE   1
              8/02/91

BRANCH      SALES-      CUSTOMER  CUSTOMER
NUMBER      PERSON       NUMBER    TOTAL

  15          21          6432     45.00
                          7263     30.00
                         11897    500.00
          SALESPERSON 21 TOTAL    575.00

              79         11897    160.00
                          7163      5.00
          SALESPERSON 79 TOTAL    165.00

            BRANCH 15 TOTAL       740.00


  39          12          7163     97.50
                         11899    200.00
          SALESPERSON 12 TOTAL    297.50

              54         11147    150.00
                          6432    175.00
          SALESPERSON 54 TOTAL    325.00

            BRANCH 39 TOTAL       622.50


                      $1,362.50
```

Figure 5-39   Group indication and group printing for program HJG05Z

▸ **Output Specifications for Sample Program HJG05Z**   The calculations for combining group indication and group printing remain the same as for a group indicated output report. All the coding changes needed to combine group printing and group indication are made on the Output Specifications form. Because no changes need to be made to the heading lines, Figure 5-40 on the next page shows only the detail and total lines necessary for combining these two techniques.

When group indication and group printing are used together, a detail line must be coded as part of the output specifications. The detail line is needed to perform the group indication of all control fields other than the L1 control field. In this example, the detail line causes group printing of the branch number (L3) and salesperson number (L2) control fields. Because the detail line is controlled by indicator 01, it prints every time a detail input record is processed.

The detail line in this example, however, has additional indicators that control the individual fields in the line. Note that each of the four field entries is controlled by an indicator. The BRANCH field prints only if indicator L3 or indicator OF is on, and the SPRSON field prints only if indicator L2 or indicator OF is on. The L2 and L3 indicators cause the printing of the control fields only when the detail record being processed is the first record of a control group. This, as you have seen in earlier examples, is the standard method of group indication.

Line	Form Type	Type (H/D/T/E)	Space After	Skip Before	Output Indicators	Field Name or Constant Name	Edit Codes	Blank After	End Position in Output Record	Constant or Edit Word
01	O	D	Ø		Ø1					
02	O				L3	BRANCH	Z		6	
03	O				L2	SPRSON	Z		15	
04	O				OF	BRANCH	Z		6	
05	O				OF	SPRSON	Z		15	
06	O	T	1		L1					
07	O					CUSTMR	Z		26	
08	O					CUSTOT	1	B	35	
09	O	T	2		L2					
10	O								16	'SALESPERSON'
11	O					SPRSON	Z		19	
12	O								25	'TOTAL'
13	O					SPTOT	1	B	35	
14	O	T	3		L3					
15	O								24	'BRANCH TOTAL'
16	O					BRANCH	Z		18	
17	O					BRTOT	1	B	35	
18	O	T		Ø6	LR					
19	O					FINTOT			35	

Figure 5-40 Output specifications for program HJG05Z

The OF (overflow) indicator causes the control fields to print on the first line of every new page of the report, regardless of whether there has been a change in the BRANCH or SPRSON control fields. This assures that group identifying information appears at the top of every page, in case the pages of a report are separated. Note that even though a detail line is specified, if indicators L2, L3, and OF are all off, nothing is printed during detail output time.

Another important fact about the detail line (Figure 5-40) is that the report is not spaced after the detail line is printed. The entry 0 (zero) in position 18 of the detail line causes **space suppression**, the deliberate elimination of forms movement either before or after the printing of a line. Because of space suppression of the detail line, the form is positioned in the printer to print the first customer total line on the same print line as the group indicated fields. All other customer total lines print normally.

The entry 0 in position 18 is important and cannot be left blank. In most versions of RPG, if no entry is made in any Space/Skip area, RPG generates an automatic single space after printing. If spacing occurs after the detail line is printed, two problems will be evident on the output report. First, because most detail output records are not the first output record of a control group, there will be one blank line for each input record read. RPG performs the detail output operation, including spacing, even though none of the individual fields can print. The second problem is that the customer total output will not print on the same line as the group indicated information.

In summary, whenever group indication and group printing are used in the same report, the data to be group indicated must be specified as a detail line, with the proper control level and overflow indicator specified for each field to be group indicated. The detail line must be space suppressed by an entry 0 in either position 17 or 18. The remainder of the report output is coded in the same way as any group printed report.

FETCH OVERFLOW

In every program example so far, page overflow occurs when the last usable print line of a page is reached. At that time, the overflow indicator is turned on, and before the next detail line is printed, page overflow operations take place and headings are printed.

Some applications require that page overflow take place at other than the normal time in the RPG fixed logic cycle. To illustrate this, let's make two additions to the processing requirements of program HJG05Y, the detail version of our sample program. These two modifications are as follows:

1. Each branch must begin printing on a new page, regardless of whether or not the end of the previous page has been reached.
2. The final total must print on a separate page and be preceded by page headings.

Thus, every time a new branch number is read, the report advances to a new page (Figure 5-41). All data related to branch 15 is printed on the first page, all data for branch 39 is on the second page, and so on. In addition, the final total is printed on a page by itself regardless of where the last line was printed on the previous page. To accomplish these two functions, you must include two operations in the program:

1. The overflow indicator (OF) must be turned on as part of the total time processing.
2. For the final total to print on a separate page, fetch overflow must be used. **Fetch overflow** is a technique by which overflow processing can be forced to occur outside of its normal place in the RPG logic cycle.

Figure 5-41 Example of forced page overflow

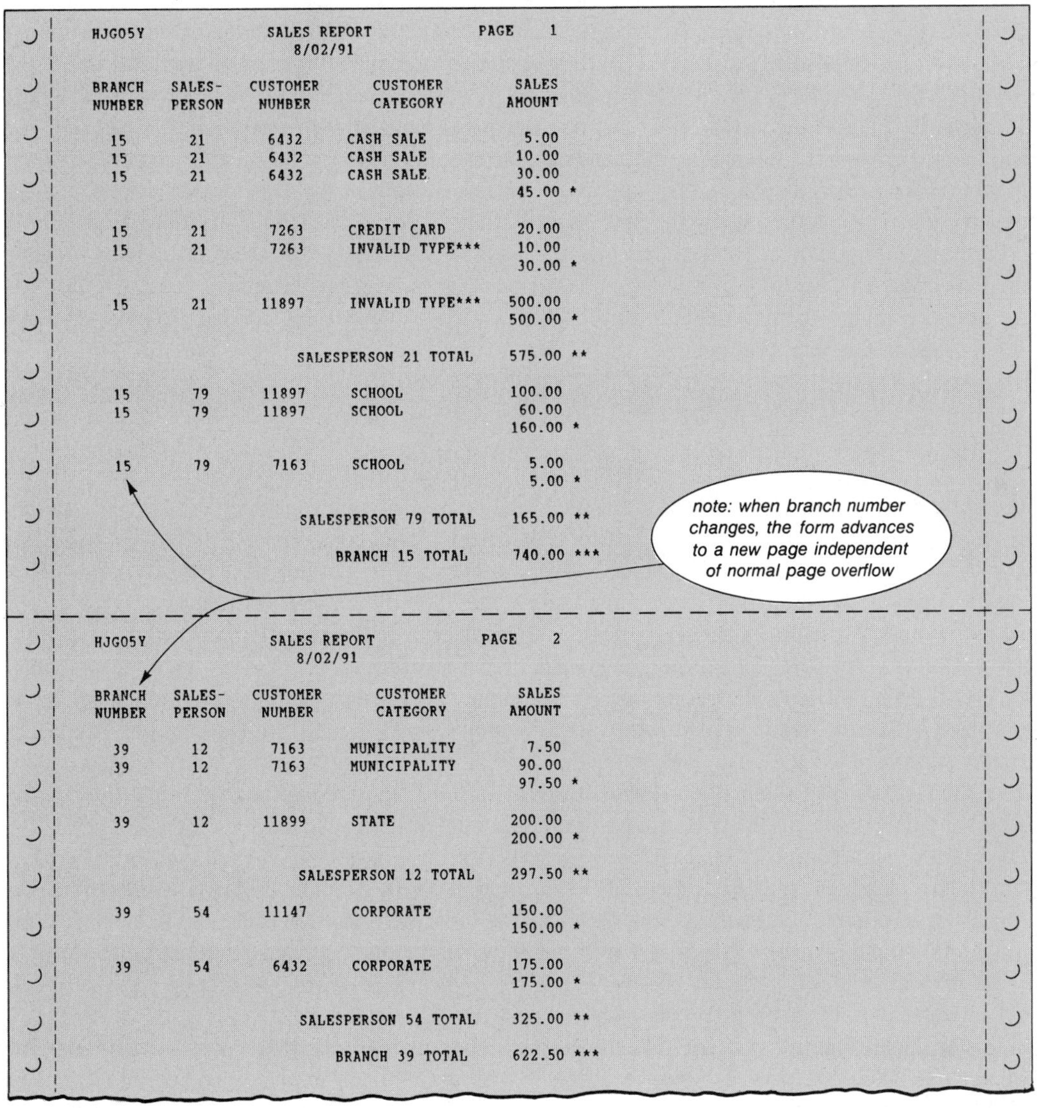

```
HJG05Y              SALES REPORT              PAGE    1
                      8/02/91

BRANCH  SALES-   CUSTOMER      CUSTOMER          SALES
NUMBER  PERSON   NUMBER        CATEGORY          AMOUNT

  15      21      6432      CASH SALE              5.00
  15      21      6432      CASH SALE             10.00
  15      21      6432      CASH SALE             30.00
                                                  45.00 *

  15      21      7263      CREDIT CARD           20.00
  15      21      7263      INVALID TYPE***       10.00
                                                  30.00 *

  15      21     11897      INVALID TYPE***      500.00
                                                 500.00 *

                      SALESPERSON 21 TOTAL       575.00 **

  15      79     11897      SCHOOL               100.00
  15      79     11897      SCHOOL                60.00
                                                 160.00 *

  15      79      7163      SCHOOL                 5.00
                                                   5.00 *

                      SALESPERSON 79 TOTAL       165.00 **

                          BRANCH 15 TOTAL        740.00 ***
```



```
HJG05Y              SALES REPORT              PAGE    2
                      8/02/91

BRANCH  SALES-   CUSTOMER      CUSTOMER          SALES
NUMBER  PERSON   NUMBER        CATEGORY          AMOUNT

  39      12      7163      MUNICIPALITY           7.50
  39      12      7163      MUNICIPALITY          90.00
                                                  97.50 *

  39      12     11899      STATE                200.00
                                                 200.00 *

                      SALESPERSON 12 TOTAL       297.50 **

  39      54     11147      CORPORATE            150.00
                                                 150.00 *

  39      54      6432      CORPORATE            175.00
                                                 175.00 *

                      SALESPERSON 54 TOTAL       325.00 **

                          BRANCH 39 TOTAL        622.50 ***
```

Figure 5-41 (1)

continued

```
HJG05Y              SALES REPORT           PAGE    3
                       8/02/91

BRANCH   SALES-    CUSTOMER    CUSTOMER       SALES
NUMBER   PERSON    NUMBER      CATEGORY       AMOUNT
                                          $1,362.50 ****
```

Figure 5-41 (2)

Total Time Overflow Logic

The first of the two modification to the processing requirements for program HJG05Y can be accomplished easily by the SETON operation.

▸ **The SETON Operation** Besides the SETOF operation to turn indicators off, RPG contains a comparable operation, SETON, to turn indicators on during calculations. The SETON operation can turn on up to three indicators. After an indicator is turned on by a SETON operation, the indicator stays on until the end of the program unless it is reset by the RPG logic cycle or turned off by a SETOF operation. With the exception of indicator 1P, all the indicators you have dealt with so far can be turned on by the SETON operation. Indicator 1P is automatically turned on and off prior to calculation time and cannot be controlled by a calculation operation.

Figure 5-42 summarizes the SETON operation. As line 01 shows, the overflow indicator OF can be turned on during total calculation time by the SETON operation. If this is done, the indicator stays on until step 10 of the logic cycle (see Figure 5-7). Step 10 performs the overflow operations that are controlled by indicator OF. These operations cause an advance to a new page and the printing of headings. The next detail line, the first of the new control group, prints on the new page. With this method, you can cause any control group at any level to begin on a new page of the output report.

Final Totals

The second modification requires that the final total be printed on a separate page. The separation of final totals from the main report is a common requirement in business applications. However, the logic cycle chart shows that with the technique previously illustrated, the page overflow processing does not take place properly for the final total it is printed at total output time of the logic cycle, before the overflow indicator is tested. Therefore, another technique must be used to cause page overflow to occur prior to the point in the fixed logic cycle at which the overflow indicator is checked. This technique is called fetch overflow.

By use of fetch overflow, any output line on the output specifications can be conditioned so that headings are always printed before the line is printed if the overflow indicator (OF) is on. In this example, it is necessary to print the headings before the final total. Therefore, the OF indicator must be turned on during last record (LR) processing on the Calculation Specifications form. In addition, the final total line on the Output Specifications form must be conditioned to print the headings before the final total line is printed.

The entries that accomplish fetch overflow are illustrated in Figure 5-43. When the LR Indicator is on, that is, after the last detail record is read, the SETON instruction on the Calculation Specifications form turns on indicator OF. Prior to printing the final total line, the heading lines are printed because of the entry F in position 16 of the final total output record description. The F (fetch overflow) entry indicates that before the final total line is printed, the program is to test indicator OF. If the overflow indicator is on, the program is to print headings immediately rather than waiting for the proper step in the logic cycle.

In this example (Figure 5-43), the OF indicator is on because it was set during total calculation time. Thus, when you use Fetch Overflow, it is not necessary to wait until the OF indicator is checked in the RPG fixed logic; it can be turned on and headings can be printed at any time that other lines are printed, during either total or detail output time.

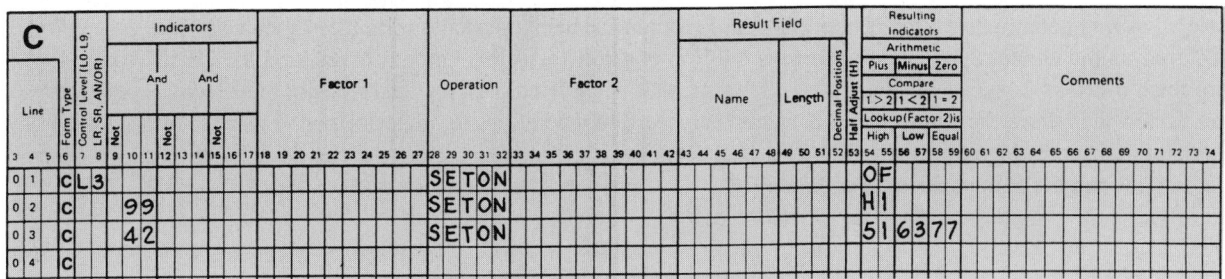

SETON Operation Summary

The SETON operation turns on all indicators specified in positions 54–55, 56–57, and 58–59. At least one indicator must be specified as part of a SETON operation.

Control Level Indicators	Indicators	Factor 1	Operation Name	Factor 2	Result Field	Resulting Indicators		
7–8	9–17	18–27	28–32	33–42	43–53	54–55	56–57	58–59
optional	optional	blank	SETON	blank	blank	optional	optional	optional

at least one entry required

Figure 5-42   SETON operation summary

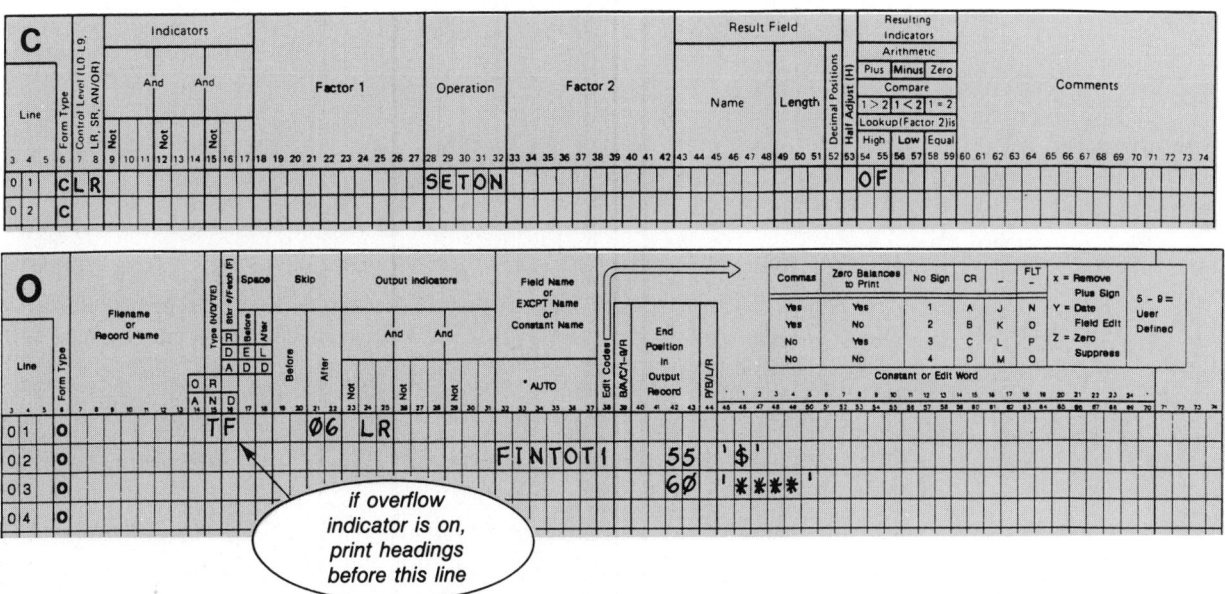

if overflow indicator is on, print headings before this line

Figure 5-43   Example of fetch overflow

The use of fetch overflow is not limited to total time, but can also be used to cause heading lines to be printed during detail output time if multiple detail records are being printed during the same cycle. The only entry required on the Output Specifications form is the F in position 16. If this entry is made, and the OF indicator is on, fetch overflow is activated. Remember, however, that when fetch overflow takes place, the heading operations are performed before the output line that caused the overflow operations to be performed. Figure 5-44 shows the complete source listing of program HJG05Y after fetch overflow is added. Note the two SETON instructions (lines 22 and 23) and the F in position 16 of line 69.

Figure 5-44   Program HJG05Y with fetch overflow

```
HJG05Y     08-02-91  15:16:52       IBM PC       RPG II        Version 3.5  Page   1

            ....+....1....+....2....+....3....+....4....+....5....+....6....+....7....

     1 0001 H                                                                HJG05Y


     2 0002 FSALEFILEIP  F 500  50            DISK
     3 0003 FSALELISTO   F 132 132      OF    PRINTER


     4 0004 ISALEFILEAA  01
     5 0005 I                                      1   20BRANCHL3
     6 0006 I                                      3   40SPRSONL2
     7 0007 I                                      5   90CUSTMRL1
     8 0008 I                                     10  142AMOUNT
     9 0009 I                                     15  150TYPE            4040


    10 0010 C    01            SETOF                    414243
    11 0011 C    01            SETOF                    444546
    12 0012 C    01N40  TYPE   COMP 6                 40 46
    13 0013 C    01N40  TYPE   COMP 5                    45
    14 0014 C    01N40  TYPE   COMP 4                    44
    15 0015 C    01N40  TYPE   COMP 3                    43
    16 0016 C    01N40  TYPE   COMP 2                    42
    17 0017 C    01N40  TYPE   COMP 1                    41
    18 0018 C    01     CUSTOT ADD  AMOUNT    CUSTOT 62
    19 0019 CL1         SPTOT  ADD  CUSTOT    SPTOT  72
    20 0020 CL2         BRTOT  ADD  SPTOT     BRTOT  82
    21 0021 CL3         FINTOT ADD  BRTOT     FINTOT 92
    22 0022 CL3         SETON                    OF
    23 0023 CLR         SETON                    OF


    24 0024 OSALELISTH  106    1P
    25 0025 O       OR         OF
    26 0026 O                                    8 'HJG05Y'
    27 0027 O                                   34 'SALES REPORT'
    28 0028 O                                   50 'PAGE'
    29 0029 O                           PAGE    55
    30 0030 O       H   2      1P
    31 0031 O       OR         OF
    32 0032 O                           UDATE Y 32
    33 0033 O       H   1      1P
    34 0034 O       OR         OF
    35 0035 O                                   26 'BRANCH   SALES-   CUSTOM'
    36 0036 O                                   42 'ER        CUSTOMER'
    37 0037 O                                   55 'SALES'
    38 0038 O       H   2      1P
    39 0039 O       OR         OF
    40 0040 O                                   26 'NUMBER   PERSON   NUMBE'
    41 0041 O                                   42 'R         CATEGORY'
```

seton indicator OF

Figure 5-44 (1)

```
HJG05Y      08-02-91  15:16:52        IBM PC        RPG II        Version 3.5  Page  2

            ....+....1....+....2....+....3....+....4....+....5....+....6....+....7....

   42 0042 O                                        55 'AMOUNT'
   43 0043 O       D  1    01
   44 0044 O                        BRANCHZ     6
   45 0045 O                        SPRSONZ    15
   46 0046 O                        CUSTMRZ    26
   47 0047 O              40                    46 'INVALID TYPE***'
   48 0048 O              41                    40 'CASH SALE'
   49 0049 O              42                    42 'CREDIT CARD'
   50 0050 O              43                    37 'SCHOOL'
   51 0051 O              44                    43 'MUNICIPALITY'
   52 0052 O              45                    36 'STATE'
   53 0053 O              46                    40 'CORPORATE'
   54 0054 O                        AMOUNT3    55
   55 0055 O       T  2    L1
   56 0056 O                        CUSTOT1B   55
   57 0057 O                                   57 '*'
   58 0058 O       T  2    L2
   59 0059 O                                   36 'SALESPERSON'
   60 0060 O           .              SPRSONZ    39
   61 0061 O                                   45 'TOTAL'
   62 0062 O                        SPTOT 1B   55
   63 0063 O                                   58 '**'
   64 0064 O       T  3    L3
   65 0065 O                                   44 'BRANCH    TOTAL'
   66 0066 O                        BRANCHZ    38
   67 0067 O                        BRTOT 1B   55
   68 0068 O                                   59 '***'
   69 0069 O       TF      06 LR
   70 0070 O                        FINTOT1    55 '$'
   71 0071 O                                   60 '****'
   72 /*
   73 /*         fetch
                 overflow

        THE FOLLOWING INDICATORS APPEARED IN THIS PROGRAM

        01  40  41  42  43  44  45  46  LR  L1  L2  L3  1P  OF
   No Warning Errors
   No Fatal Errors
```

Figure 5-44 (2)

IN CONCLUSION

In this chapter you have learned to use control break processing to cause a program to pause between groups of records and to print totals. In Chapter 6 you will study two of the same sample programs used in this chapter and learn to use array processing techniques to reduce the amount of RPG code needed to obtain the same output. In addition, the Chapter 6 programming assignments will give you further opportunity to develop your control break programming skills.

CHAPTER SUMMARY

1. A **control break** is a temporary pause in detail processing, usually used for printing group totals.
2. A control break is caused by a change in the contents of a **control field**.
3. A **control group** is a series of consecutive records, all of which have the same control field value.
4. In a program that uses control breaks, control field values must be sequential.
5. A file is in **ascending sequence** if the control field value of a record is equal to or greater than the control field value of the previous record.

6. A file is in **descending sequence** if the control field value of a record is equal to or less than the control field value of the previous record.

7. The RPG fixed logic cycle turns on a **control level indicator** when a control break is detected.

8. The term **time** refers to a point in the RPG fixed logic cycle.

9. A **forced control break** occurs at the end of a program when indicator LR is turned on.

10. A **transparent** function is fully automatic and cannot be used by the programmer. Transparent functions cannot be detected when the object program is executed.

11. **First cycle** testing by the RPG fixed logic cycle eliminates the possibility of an unwanted control break before the first input record has been processed.

12. The entry of **L1** on the Input Specifications form specifies a control field.

13. **Rolling totals** is a process by which totals are added to higher level group totals.

14. The **Blank After** entry causes numeric fields to be reset to zero after printing. It also causes alphameric fields to be reset to spaces.

15. If a field is used as output more than once, blank after should be specified for the field in the record that is to be written last.

16. **Group indication** is a technique by which control field data is printed only with the first output record of a control group.

17. As many as nine different fields can be used as control fields in an RPG program.

18. When more than one control field is used in a program, these fields are processed as **multiple level control fields**.

19. The **hierarchy** of control groups refers to their relationship in terms of which group is a subdivision of another group.

20. The hierarchy·of control fields must be understood to correctly assign control level indicators.

21. Control level indicator L1 should be assigned to the lowest level control group, and control level indicators should be assigned consecutively to each higher level group.

22. Any control break that has a level greater than L1 causes all lower level control break indicators to be turned on.

23. At the end of the program, indicator LR and all control level indicators are automatically turned on.

24. The RPG fixed logic tests control fields starting with the highest level field, and then tests them in order from high to low.

25. All total time calculations are performed in a **top-down** order and should, therefore, be coded in the sequence in which they are to be performed.

26. All total time output lines are printed in a top-down order and should, therefore, be coded in the sequence in which they are to appear on the printed report.

27. Control fields can be assigned to fields in any order on the Input Specifications form.

28. Field indicators can be used to determine if data in a numeric input field is a positive number, a negative number, or zero.

29. Field indicators can be used to determine if an alphameric input field is completely blank. Alphameric data fields cannot be tested for plus or minus conditions.

30. A **group printed** report contains no detail output but consists of headings and totals only.

31. When a report is both group printed and group indicated, the control fields must print as part of a **space suppressed** detail line.

32. If no entries are made in the spacing and skipping areas of an output report line, most versions of RPG cause an automatic single space after printing.

33. **Fetch overflow** is a process by which the overflow routine is performed before the printing of an output line even though the last print line of a page has not been reached.

34. The SETON operation can turn on up to three indicators. Indicators turned on by the SETON operation stay on until the end of the program unless turned off by normal RPG fixed logic or by a SETOF operation.

REVIEW QUESTIONS

1. What input specification entry designates a field as a control field?
2. What is a control group?
3. Because there is no record for the first input record to be compared with, how is an erroneous control break avoided at the beginning of the program?
4. Because no control break occurs at the end of the program, what causes the printing of the last set of control break totals?
5. Why cannot a report be group indicated if there are no control breaks specified?
6. What is the relationship between the portion of the logic cycle during which the control break indicator is on and the printing of group indicated information during detail time?
7. What is meant by the hierarchy of control groups?
8. When an L6 control break is detected, how many control level indicators are turned on?
9. Why must total time calculations be written in a top-down sequence when multiple level control breaks are used in a program?
10. What information can be determined about a numeric input field by the use of field indicators?
11. What is a group printed report?
12. What is fetch overflow? When is it used?
13. If no entries are made in the spacing and skipping areas of an output record description, what default action does RPG take?

STUDENT EXERCISES: RPG PROGRAM CODE

1. An input record contains the following data fields:

   Positions 1–6 Vendor number
   Positions 7–11 ZIP code
   Positions 12–13 State code
   Positions 14–19 Invoice amount (2 decimal places)

   These records are in sequence by vendor number, within ZIP code, within state code, and these three fields are control fields. Code the proper entries on the Input Specification form (Figure 5-45) to define this file and assign the proper control level indicators to the control fields.

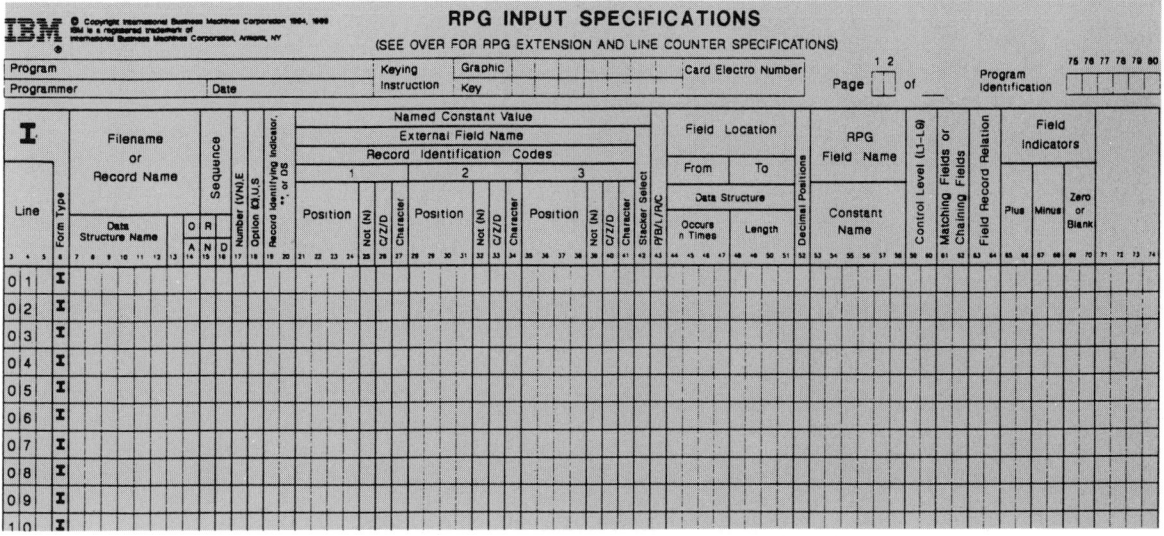

Figure 5-45 Input specifications form

2. Use the Calculations Specifications form (Figure 5-46) to code the entries to accumulate L1, L2, L3, and LR totals of the Invoice Amount field defined in Exercise 1. Allow sufficient room in the accumulators for the expansion of the totals beyond the original size of the Invoice Amount field.

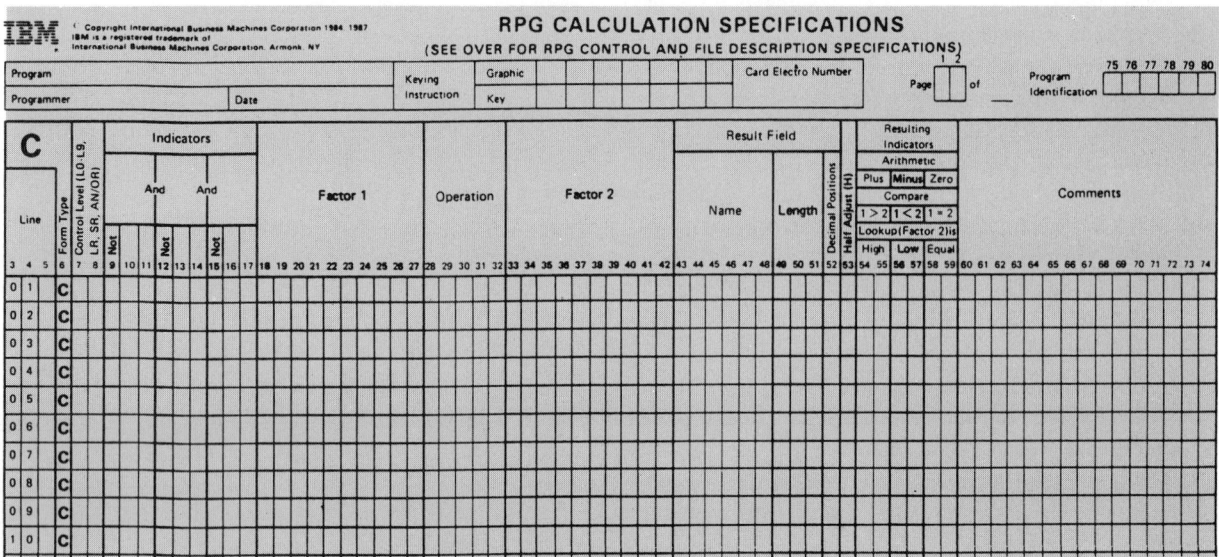

Figure 5-46 Calculation specifications form

3. Use the Output Specifications form (Figure 5-47) to code the necessary entries to produce a group printed report based on the specifications coded in Exercises 1 and 2. The L2 and L3 control fields are to be group indicated. This report does not require headings.

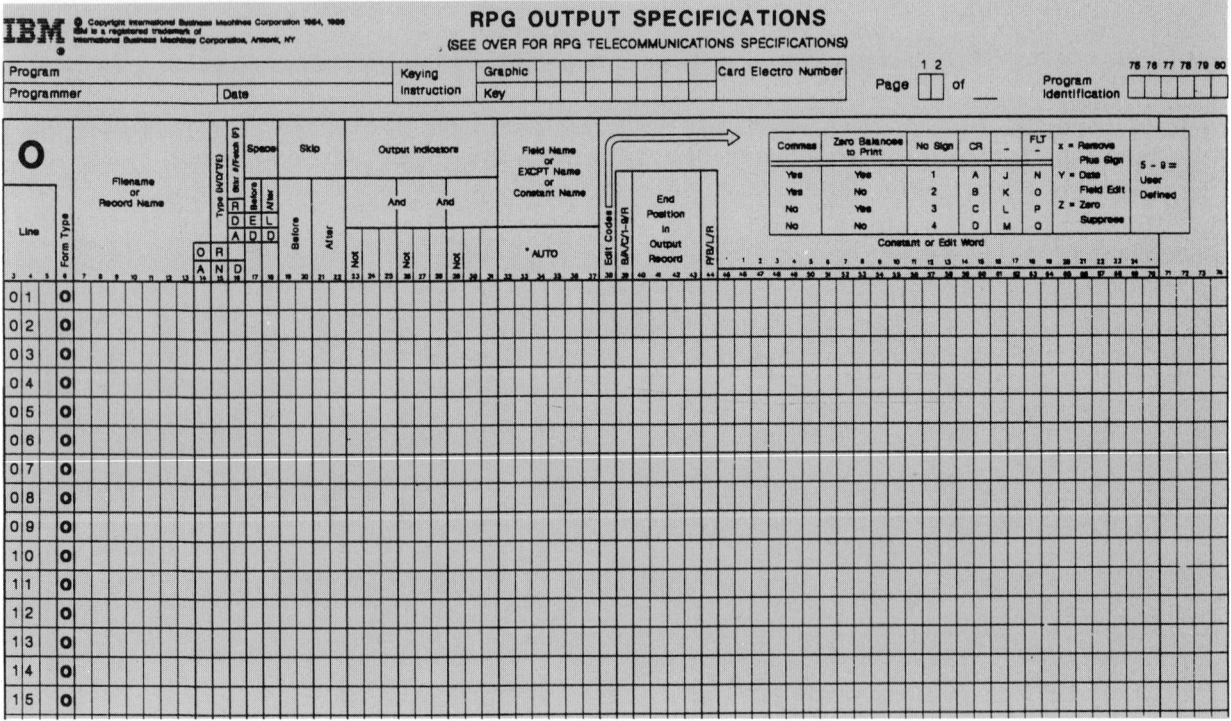

Figure 5-47 Output specifications form

STUDENT EXERCISES: DEBUGGING RPG PROGRAMS

Problem 1

The following RPG program (Figure 5-48) contains one or more errors detected while checking output from the program. Circle each error and record the corrected entry directly on the listing. Explain the error and the method of correction.

Figure 5-48   Debugging Problem 1

```
Lattice RPG II Compiler Version 2.01                14:01:42  07/20/1991
Compile listing for source RPG program [HJG05X  .RPG]          PAGE : 0001


     1      H                                                          HJG05X

     2        F*----------------------------------------------------------------*
     3 S      F* HJG05X - SALES SUMMARY REPORT - HAL GOODWIN - JULY 14, 1991  *
     4 S      F*                                                             *
     5 S      F* PROGRAM HJG05X LISTS MONTHLY SALES FOR EACH ITEM.  THE SIX  *
     6 S      F* MONTHLY SALES FIELDS ARE ADDED TO ACCUMULATE TOTAL SALES.   *
     7 S      F* WHEN STORE NUMBER CHANGES, TOTALS OF THE SEVEN SALES FIELDS WILL*
     8 S      F* PRINT.  IN ADDITION, A FINAL TOTAL OF THE TOTAL SALES FIELD  *
     9 S      F* WILL BE PRINTED.                                            *
    10 S      F*----------------------------------------------------------------*
    11 S      FSALFILE IP  F 360  60              DISK
    12 S      FSALREPT O   F 132 132     OF       PRINTER
    13 S      F* ID F  C  H  L   FUNCTION OF INDICATORS
    14 S      F* 01---------------SALFILE RECORD IDENTIFICATION
    15 S      F*          1P---FIRST PAGE INDICATOR
    16 S      F*          OF---OVERFLOW INDICATOR
    17 S      F*          L1---CONTROL BREAK - STORE NUMBER CHANGE
    18 S      F*          LR---END OF JOB

    19        I*----------------------------------------------------------------*
    20 S      I* SALFILE INPUT RECORD DESCRIPTION                            *
    21 S      I*----------------------------------------------------------------*
    22 S      ISALFILE AA  01
    23 S      I                              1    40STORE L1
    24 S      I                             11    30 DESC
    25 S      I                             31   340JANSAL
    26 S      I                             35   380FEBSAL
    27 S      I                             39   420MARSAL
    28 S      I                             43   460APRSAL
    29 S      I                             47   500MAYSAL
    30 S      I                             51   540JUNSAL

    31        C* ACCUMULATE TOTAL SALES FOR EACH RECORD
    32 S      C   01    TOTSAL    ADD JANSAL    TOTSAL 50
    33 S      C   01    TOTSAL    ADD FEBSAL    TOTSAL
    34 S      C   01    TOTSAL    ADD MARSAL    TOTSAL
    35 S      C   01    TOTSAL    ADD APRSAL    TOTSAL
    36 S      C   01    TOTSAL    ADD MAYSAL    TOTSAL
    37 S      C   01    TOTSAL    ADD JUNSAL    TOTSAL
    38 S      C*
    39 S      C* ACCUMULATE CONTROL BREAK TOTALS
    40 S      C   01    JANTOT    ADD JANSAL    JANTOT 60
    41 S      C   01    FEBTOT    ADD FEBSAL    FEBTOT 60
    42 S      C   01    MARTOT    ADD MARSAL    MARTOT 60
    43 S      C   01    APRTOT    ADD APRSAL    APRTOT 60
    44 S      C   01    MAYTOT    ADD MAYSAL    MAYTOT 60
    45 S      C   01    JUNTOT    ADD JUNSAL    JUNTOT 60
    46 S      C   01    SALTOT    ADD TOTSAL    SALTOT 70
    47 S      C*
    48 S      C* ACCUMULATE FINAL TOTAL SALES
    49 S      C   L1    SALFIN    ADD SALTOT    SALFIN 80

    50        O*----------------------------------------------------------------*
    51 S      O* HEADING LINE ONE                                           *
```

Figure 5-48 (1)

continued

```
Lattice RPG II Compiler Version 2.01          14:01:43 07/20/1991
Compile listing for source RPG program [HJG05X  .RPG]      PAGE : 0002


  52 S    O*-------------------------------------------------------------*
  53 S    OSALREPT H 106    1P
  54 S    O     OR         OF
  55 S    O                             9 'HJG05X'
  56 S    O                       UDATE Y  19
  57 S    O                            60 'SALES  SUMMARY  REPORT'
  58 S    O                            91 'PAGE'
  59 S    O                       PAGE Z  96
  60 S    O*-------------------------------------------------------------*
  61 S    O*  HEADING LINE TWO                                           *
  62 S    O*-------------------------------------------------------------*
  63 S    O        H  2    1P
  64 S    O     OR         OF
  65 S    O                            56 'JANUARY THROUGH JUNE'
  66 S    O                            62 ', 1991'
  67 S    O*-------------------------------------------------------------*
  68 S    O*  HEADING LINE THREE                                         *
  69 S    O*-------------------------------------------------------------*
  70 S    O        H  1    1P
  71 S    O     OR         OF
  72 S    O                             8 'STORE'
  73 S    O                            56 '- - - - -  M O N T H L'
  74 S    O                            80 'Y   S A L E S - - - -'
  75 S    O                            96 '- -     TOTAL'
  76 S    O*-------------------------------------------------------------*
  77 S    O*  HEADING LINE FOUR                                          *
  78 S    O*-------------------------------------------------------------*
  79 S    O        H  2    1P
  80 S    O     OR         OF
  81 S    O                            28 'NO.    ITEM DESCRIPTION'
  82 S    O                            56 'JANUARY FEBRUARY     MARC'
  83 S    O                            75 'H    APRIL       MAY'
  84 S    O                            96 'JUNE       SALES'
  85 S    O*-------------------------------------------------------------*
  86 S    O*  DETAIL LINE                                                *
  87 S    O*-------------------------------------------------------------*
  88 S    O        D  1    01
  89 S    O                       STORE Z   7
  90 S    O                       DESC     30
  91 S    O                       JANSAL2  39
  92 S    O                       FEBSAL2  48
  93 S    O                       MARSAL2  57
  94 S    O                       APRSAL2  66
  95 S    O                       MAYSAL2  75
  96 S    O                       JUNSAL2  84
  97 S    O                       TOTSAL1B 96
  98 S    O*-------------------------------------------------------------*
  99 S    O*  CONTROL BREAK (L1) TOTAL LINE                              *
 100 S    O*-------------------------------------------------------------*
 101 S    O        T 13    L1
 102 S    O                       JANTOT2B 39
 103 S    O                       FEBTOT2B 48
 104 S    O                       MARTOT2B 57
 105 S    O                       APRTOT2B 66
 106 S    O                       MAYTOT2B 75
 107 S    O                       JUNTOT2B 84
 108 S    O                       SALTOT1B 96
 109 S    O*-------------------------------------------------------------*
 110 S    O*  FINAL TOTAL LINE                                           *
 111 S    O*-------------------------------------------------------------*
 112 S    O        T   06 LR
 113 S    O                            85 'FINAL TOTAL'
 114 S    O                       SALFIN1  96
 115 /*


  Warning Severe
  Errors  Errors
     0      0
```

Figure 5-48 (2)

```
HJG05X    7/20/91              SALES  SUMMARY  REPORT                    PAGE  · 1
                            JANUARY THROUGH JUNE, 1991

  STORE                 - - - - - - M O N T H L Y    S A L E S - - - - - -      TOTAL
   NO.    ITEM DESCRIPTION   JANUARY FEBRUARY   MARCH    APRIL    MAY    JUNE   SALES

    13   CRT STAND AND PAD      203       5      18      10      28      43      307
    13   5 1/4" DISKETTES     3,056   8,500     750   2,780   4,540     100   19,726
    13   3 1/2" DISKETTES       151   7,000     800   1,750   3,060   6,000   18,761
    13   0911 COMPUTER FORMS      3   1,805      18      10      88      43    1,967
    13   1411 COMPUTER FORMS  3,010   8,136     750   2,760   4,870     909   20,435
    13   CRT WORKSTATION          3      10   3,422   3,020      68      21    6,544
    13   COBOL CODING PADS      150   2,001   3,800   1,753   3,030   6,003   16,737

                           6,576  27,457   9,558  12,083  15,684  13,119   84,477


    15   RPG INPUT FORMS          3       5   1,018      10     358      43    1,437
    15   RPG OUTPUT FORMS     3,000   8,500     150   2,780   4,530     103   19,063
    15   3 1/2" DISKETTES       150   2,003     310   1,750   3,042   6,030   13,285
    15   0911 COMPUTER FORMS      3       5   2,011      10   1,228   3,343    6,600
    15   1411 COMPUTER FORMS  3,000   8,500     750   1,783   4,543   3,400   21,976
    15   TERMINAL COVERS          3              25     118       5      65      216
    15   SURGE PROTECTORS       150   2,000     800   1,760   3,037   6,000   13,747

                           6,309  21,013   5,064   8,211  16,743  18,984   76,324


    20   CRT STAND AND PAD        3   3,005      16   5,011   4,308      43   12,386
    20   5 1/4" DISKETTES     3,000   8,760     750   2,782   3,508   9,100   27,900
    20   FLOWCHARTING TMPLTS    150   2,008     800   1,744   3,100   9,000   16,802
    20   0911 COMPUTER FORMS      3       5   9,018      90      18   9,042   18,176
    20   CRT WORKSTATION          3              75      60       8      21      167
    20   COBOL CODING PADS        3       5      18      20       8   3,243    3,297

                           3,162  13,783  10,677   9,707  10,950  30,449   78,728


    21   5 1/4" DISKETTES     3,000   8,500     750   3,750   4,500     210   20,710
    21   3 1/2" DISKETTES       150   2,000     800   1,230   3,000   6,601   13,781
    21   0911 COMPUTER FORMS      3       5      18      20       8     323      377
    21   1411 COMPUTER FORMS  3,000   8,500     750   2,785   4,500     100   19,635
    21   CRT WORKSTATION          3              25      10   7,808      21    7,867
    21   COBOL CODING PADS      150   2,000     800   1,750   3,090     580    8,370

                           6,306  21,005   3,143   9,545  22,906   7,835   70,740


                                                        FINAL TOTAL   34,840
```

final total is wrong

Figure 5-48 (3)

Problem 2

The following RPG program (Figure 5-49 on the next page) contains one or more errors detected while checking output from the program. Circle each error and record the corrected entry directly on the listing. Explain the error and the method of correction.

Figure 5-49 Debugging Problem 2

```
Lattice RPG II Compiler Version 2.01                    13:29:51  07/20/1991
Compile listing for source RPG program [HJG05X  .RPG]       PAGE : 0001


   1       H                                                              HJG05X

   2       F*------------------------------------------------------------------*
   3 S     F* HJG05X - SALES SUMMARY REPORT - HAL GOODWIN - JULY 14, 1991     *
   4 S     F*                                                                 *
   5 S     F* PROGRAM HJG05X LISTS MONTHLY SALES FOR EACH ITEM.  THE SIX      *
   6 S     F* MONTHLY SALES FIELDS ARE ADDED TO ACCUMULATE TOTAL SALES.       *
   7 S     F* WHEN STORE NUMBER CHANGES, TOTALS OF THE SEVEN SALES FIELDS WILL*
   8 S     F* PRINT.  IN ADDITION, A FINAL TOTAL OF THE TOTAL SALES FIELD     *
   9 S     F* WILL BE PRINTED.                                                *
  10 S     F*------------------------------------------------------------------*
  11 S     FSALFILE IP  F 360 60          DISK
  12 S     FSALREPT O   F 132 132    OF   PRINTER
  13 S     F* ID F  C  H  L    FUNCTION OF INDICATORS
  14 S     F* 01----------------SALFILE RECORD IDENTIFICATION
  15 S     F*              1P---FIRST PAGE INDICATOR
  16 S     F*              OF---OVERFLOW INDICATOR
  17 S     F*              L1---CONTROL BREAK - STORE NUMBER CHANGE
  18 S     F*              LR---END OF JOB

  19       I*------------------------------------------------------------------*
  20 S     I* SALFILE INPUT RECORD DESCRIPTION                               *
  21 S     I*------------------------------------------------------------------*
  22 S     ISALFILE AA  01
  23 S     I                                      1   40STORE L1
  24 S     I                                     11   30 DESC
  25 S     I                                     31  340JANSAL
  26 S     I                                     35  380FEBSAL
  27 S     I                                     39  420MARSAL
  28 S     I                                     43  460APRSAL
  29 S     I                                     47  500MAYSAL
  30 S     I                                     51  540JUNSAL

  31       C* ACCUMULATE TOTAL SALES FOR EACH RECORD
  32 S     C   01     TOTSAL    ADD  JANSAL    TOTSAL 50
  33 S     C   01     TOTSAL    ADD  FEBSAL    TOTSAL
  34 S     C   01     TOTSAL    ADD  MARSAL    TOTSAL
  35 S     C   01     TOTSAL    ADD  APRSAL    TOTSAL
  36 S     C   01     TOTSAL    ADD  MAYSAL    TOTSAL
  37 S     C   01     TOTSAL    ADD  JUNSAL    TOTSAL
  38 S     C*
  39 S     C* ACCUMULATE CONTROL BREAK TOTALS
  40 S     C   01     JANTOT    ADD  JANSAL    JANTOT 60
  41 S     C   01     FEBTOT    ADD  FEBSAL    FEBTOT 60
  42 S     C   01     MARTOT    ADD  MARSAL    MARTOT 60
  43 S     C   01     APRTOT    ADD  APRSAL    APRTOT 60
  44 S     C   01     MAYTOT    ADD  MAYSAL    MAYTOT 60
  45 S     C   01     JUNTOT    ADD  JUNSAL    JUNTOT 60
  46 S     C   01     SALTOT    ADD  TOTSAL    SALTOT 70
  47 S     C*
  48 S     C* ACCUMULATE FINAL TOTAL SALES
  49 S     CL1        SALFIN    ADD  SALTOT    SALFIN 80

  50       O*------------------------------------------------------------------*
  51 S     O* HEADING LINE ONE                                              *
  52 S     O*------------------------------------------------------------------*
  53 S     OSALREPT H 106    1P
  54 S     O        OR        OF
  55 S     O                                   9 'HJG05X'
  56 S     O                           UDATE Y 19
  57 S     O                                  60 'SALES  SUMMARY  REPORT'
  58 S     O                                  91 'PAGE'
  59 S     O                           PAGE Z 96
  60 S     O*------------------------------------------------------------------*
  61 S     O* HEADING LINE TWO                                              *
  62 S     O*------------------------------------------------------------------*
  63 S     O        H 2      1P
  64 S     O        OR        OF
```

Figure 5-49 (1)

```
Lattice RPG II Compiler Version 2.01              13:29:52  07/20/1991
Compile listing for source RPG program [HJG05X  .RPG]         PAGE : 0002

  65 S    O                                    56 'JANUARY THROUGH JUNE'
  66 S    O                                    62 ', 1991'
  67 S    O*----------------------------------------------------------*
  68 S    O*  HEADING LINE THREE                                      *
  69 S    O*----------------------------------------------------------*
  70 S    O       H  1     1P
  71 S    O       OR       OF
  72 S    O                                     8 'STORE'
  73 S    O                                    56 '- - - - - M O N T H L'
  74 S    O                                    80 'Y   S A L E S - - - -'
  75 S    O                                    96 '- -      TOTAL'
  76 S    O*----------------------------------------------------------*
  77 S    O*  HEADING LINE FOUR                                       *
  78 S    O*----------------------------------------------------------*
  79 S    O       H  2     1P
  80 S    O       OR       OF
  81 S    O                                    28 'NO.    ITEM DESCRIPTION'
  82 S    O                                    56 'JANUARY FEBRUARY    MARC'
  83 S    O                                    75 'H   APRIL      MAY'
  84 S    O                                    96 'JUNE       SALES'
  85 S    O*----------------------------------------------------------*
  86 S    O*  DETAIL LINE                                             *
  87 S    O*----------------------------------------------------------*
  88 S    O       D  1     01
  89 S    O                       STORE Z    7
  90 S    O                       DESC      30
  91 S    O                       JANSAL2B  39
  92 S    O                       FEBSAL2B  48
  93 S    O                       MARSAL2B  57
  94 S    O                       APRSAL2B  66
  95 S    O                       MAYSAL2B  75
  96 S    O                       JUNSAL2B  84
  97 S    O                       TOTSAL1B  96
  98 S    O*----------------------------------------------------------*
  99 S    O*  CONTROL BREAK (L1) TOTAL LINE                           *
 100 S    O*----------------------------------------------------------*
 101 S    O       T 13     01
 102 S    O                       JANTOT2   39
 103 S    O                       FEBTOT2   48
 104 S    O                       MARTOT2   57
 105 S    O                       APRTOT2   66
 106 S    O                       MAYTOT2   75
 107 S    O                       JUNTOT2   84
 108 S    O                       SALTOT1   96
 109 S    O*----------------------------------------------------------*
 110 S    O*  FINAL TOTAL LINE                                        *
 111 S    O*----------------------------------------------------------*
 112 S    O       T    06 LR
 113 S    O                                    85 'FINAL TOTAL'
 114 S    O                       SALFIN1   96
 115 /*

Warning Severe
Errors Errors
   0    0
```

Figure 5-49 (2)

continued

```
HJG05X    7/20/91                 SALES  SUMMARY  REPORT                    PAGE    1
                               JANUARY THROUGH JUNE, 1991
```

STORE NO.	ITEM DESCRIPTION	JANUARY	FEBRUARY	MARCH	APRIL	MAY	JUNE	TOTAL SALES
			— — — — — M O N T H L Y		S A L E S — — — — —			
13	CRT STAND AND PAD	203	5	18	10	28	43	307
		203	5	18	10	28	43	307
13	5 1/4" DISKETTES	3,056	8,500	750	2,780	4,540	100	19,726
		3,259	8,505	768	2,790	4,568	143	20,033
13	3 1/2" DISKETTES	151	7,000	800	1,750	3,060	6,000	18,761
		3,410	15,505	1,568	4,540	7,628	6,143	38,794
13	0911 COMPUTER FORMS	3	1,805	18	10	88	43	1,967
		3,413	17,310	1,586	4,550	7,716	6,186	40,761
13	1411 COMPUTER FORMS	3,010	8,136	750	2,760	4,870	909	20,435
		6,423	25,446	2,336	7,310	12,586	7,095	61,196
13	CRT WORKSTATION	3	10	3,422	3,020	68	21	6,544
		6,426	25,456	5,758	10,330	12,654	7,116	67,740
13	COBOL CODING PADS	150	2,001	3,800	1,753	3,030	6,003	16,737
		6,576	27,457	9,558	12,083	15,684	13,119	84,477
15	RPG INPUT FORMS	3	5	1,018	10	358	43	1,437
		6,579	27,462	10,576	12,093	16,042	13,162	85,914
15	RPG OUTPUT FORMS	3,000	8,500	150	2,780	4,530	103	19,063
		9,579	35,962	10,726	14,873	20,572	13,265	104,977
15	3 1/2" DISKETTES	150	2,003	310	1,750	3,042	6,030	13,285
		9,729	37,965	11,036	16,623	23,614	19,295	118,262
15	0911 COMPUTER FORMS	3	5	2,011	10	1,228	3,343	6,600
		9,732	37,970	13,047	16,633	24,842	22,638	124,862
15	1411 COMPUTER FORMS	3,000	8,500	750	1,783	4,543	3,400	21,976
		12,732	46,470	13,797	18,416	29,385	26,038	146,838
15	TERMINAL COVERS	3		25	118	5	65	216
		12,735	46,470	13,822	18,534	29,390	26,103	147,054

Figure 5-49 (3)

```
HJG05X   7/20/91              SALES SUMMARY REPORT                    PAGE   2
                           JANUARY THROUGH JUNE, 1991
```

STORE NO.	ITEM DESCRIPTION	JANUARY	FEBRUARY	MARCH	APRIL	MAY	JUNE	TOTAL SALES
		------ M O N T H L Y	S A L E S ------					
15	SURGE PROTECTORS	150	2,000	800	1,760	3,037	6,000	13,747
		12,885	48,470	14,622	20,294	32,427	32,103	160,801
20	CRT STAND AND PAD	3	3,005	16	5,011	4,308	43	12,386
		12,888	51,475	14,638	25,305	36,735	32,146	173,187
20	5 1/4" DISKETTES	3,000	8,760	750	2,782	3,508	9,100	27,900
		15,888	60,235	15,388	28,087	40,243	41,246	201,087
20	FLOWCHARTING TMPLTS	150	2,008	800	1,744	3,100	9,000	16,802
		16,038	62,243	16,188	29,831	43,343	50,246	217,889
20	0911 COMPUTER FORMS	3	5	9,018	90	18	9,042	18,176
		16,041	62,248	25,206	29,921	43,361	59,288	236,065
20	CRT WORKSTATION	3		75	60	8	21	167
		16,044	62,248	25,281	29,981	43,369	59,309	236,232
20	COBOL CODING PADS	3	5	18	20	8	3,243	3,297
		16,047	62,253	25,299	30,001	43,377	62,552	239,529
21	5 1/4" DISKETTES	3,000	8,500	750	3,750	4,500	210	20,710
		19,047	70,753	26,049	33,751	47,877	62,762	260,239
21	3 1/2" DISKETTES	150	2,000	800	1,230	3,000	6,601	13,781
		19,197	72,753	26,849	34,981	50,877	69,363	274,020
21	0911 COMPUTER FORMS	3	5	18	20	8	323	377
		19,200	72,758	26,867	35,001	50,885	69,686	274,397
21	1411 COMPUTER FORMS	3,000	8,500	750	2,785	4,500	100	19,635
		22,200	81,258	27,617	37,786	55,385	69,786	294,032
21	CRT WORKSTATION	3		25	10	7,808	21	7,867
		22,203	81,258	27,642	37,796	63,193	69,807	301,899
21	COBOL CODING PADS	150	2,000	800	1,750	3,090	580	8,370
							FINAL TOTAL	795,076

Figure 5-49 (4)

Problem 3

The following RPG program (Figure 5-50) contains one or more errors detected while checking output from the program. Circle each error and record the corrected entry directly on the listing. Explain the error and method of correction.

Figure 5-50 Debugging Problem 3

```
HJG05Y   08-12-91  14:38:52      IBM PC        RPG II        Version 3.5  Page  1

         ....+....1....+....2....+....3....+....4....+....5....+....6....+....7....

    1 0001 H                                                                 HJG05Y


    2 0002 FSALEFILEIP  F 500  50        DISK
    3 0003 FSALELISTO   F 132 132    OF  PRINTER


    4 0004 ISALEFILEAA  01
    5 0005 I                                 1   20BRANCHL3
    6 0006 I                                 3   40SPRSONL2
    7 0007 I                                 5   90CUSTMRL1
    8 0008 I                                10  142AMOUNT


    9 0009 C    01       CUSTOT   ADD  AMOUNT   CUSTOT  62
   10 0010 CL1          SPTOT    ADD  CUSTOT   SPTOT   72
   11 0011 CL2          BRTOT    ADD  SPTOT    BRTOT   82
   12 0012 CL3          FINTOT   ADD  BRTOT    FINTOT  92


   13 0013 OSALELISTH  106    1P
   14 0014 O       OR         OF
   15 0015 O                                   8 'HJG05Y'
   16 0016 O                                  25 'SALES REPORT'
   17 0017 O                                  33 'PAGE'
   18 0018 O                          PAGE    38
   19 0019 O       H   2    1P
   20 0020 O       OR         OF
   21 0021 O                          UDATE Y 23
   22 0022 O       H   1    1P
   23 0023 O       OR         OF
   24 0024 O                                  26 'BRANCH    SALES-   CUSTOM'
   25 0025 O                                  37 'ER CUSTOMER'
   26 0026 O       H   2    1P
   27 0027 O       OR         OF
   28 0028 O                                  26 'NUMBER    PERSON    NUMBE'
   29 0029 O                                  36 'R    TOTAL'
   30 0030 O       D   1    01
   31 0031 O                L3       BRANCHZ   6
   32 0032 O                L2       SPRSONZ  15
   33 0033 O                OF       BRANCHZ   6
   34 0034 O                OF       SPRSONZ  15
   35 0035 O       T   1    L1
   36 0036 O                         CUSTMRZ  26
   37 0037 O                         CUSTOT1B 35
   38 0038 O       T   2    L2
   39 0039 O                                  16 'SALESPERSON'
   40 0040 O                         SPRSONZ  19
   41 0041 O                                  25 'TOTAL'
```

Figure 5-50 (1)

```
HJG05Y    08-12-91  14:38:52      IBM PC        RPG II         Version 3.5  Page  2

        ....+....1....+....2....+....3....+....4....+....5....+....6....+....7....
     42 0042 O                          SPTOT 1B  35
     43 0043 O        T  3    L3
     44 0044 O                                     24 'BRANCH    TOTAL'
     45 0045 O                          BRANCHZ    18
     46 0046 O                          BRTOT 1B   35
     47 0047 O        T      06 LR
     48 0048 O                          FINTOT1    35 '$'
     49 /*
     50 /*


        THE FOLLOWING INDICATORS APPEARED IN THIS PROGRAM

           01  LR  L1  L2  L3  1P  OF
 No Warning Errors
 No Fatal Errors
```

Figure 5-50 (2)

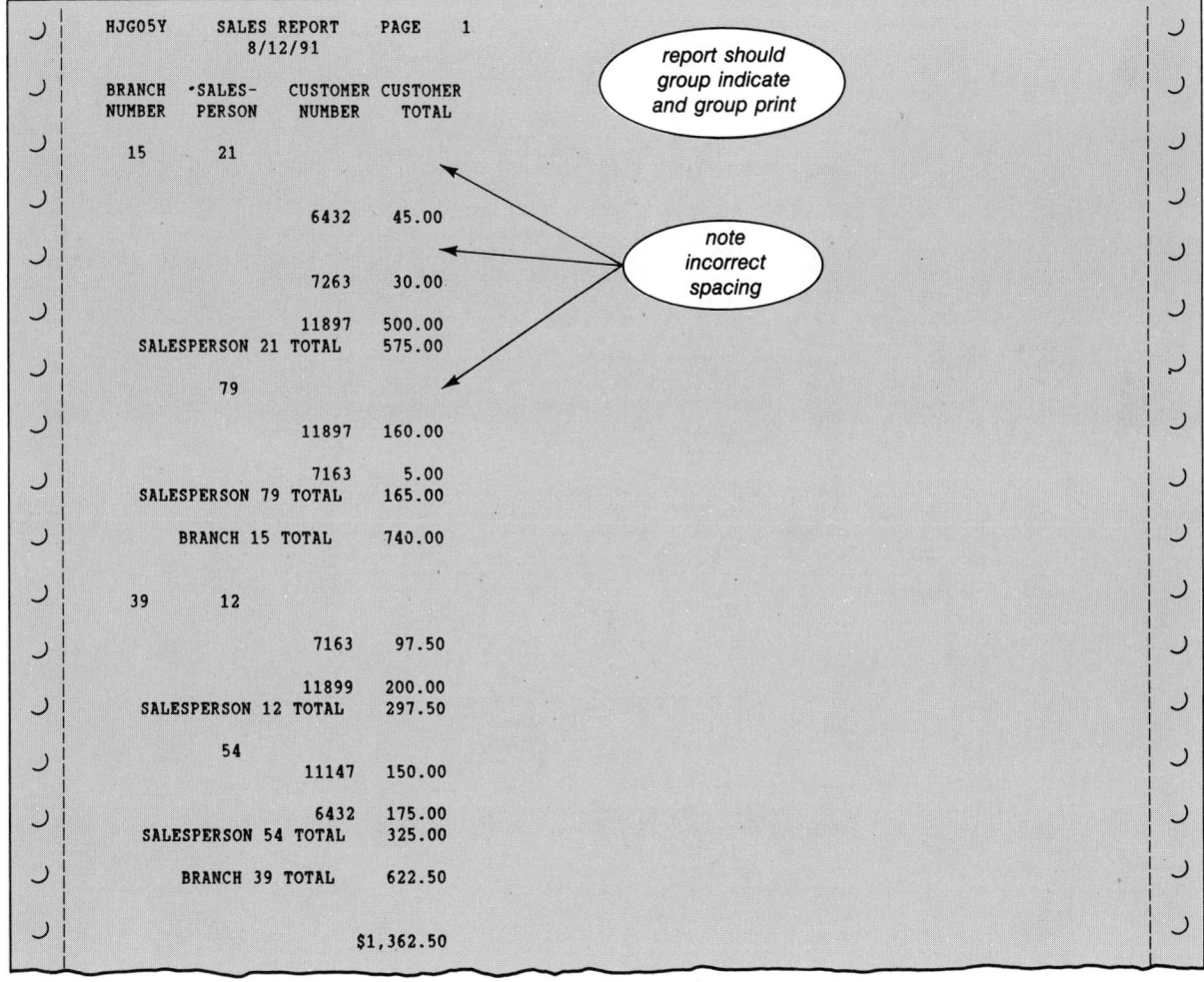

Figure 5-50 (3)

▤ Problem 4

Problem 4 is different from any of the exercises or problems you have done so far. This problem requires that you determine how to make a needed change to a working program. It is a problem in program maintenance, which can be thought of as a form of debugging because the program no longer performs the needed function. In this case, however, the program must be corrected because the problem description has been changed not because the program contains errors. (As you sharpen your debugging skills by writing and testing the sample programs at the end of each chapter, the debugging problems will be replaced by program maintenance problems, enabling you to develop and sharpen your skills in program maintenance.)

In sample program HJG05X, the year has been placed in the heading by means of a literal. For heading line 02 to read other than 1990, the source program must be changed and the program recompiled. Indicate on Figure 5-51 how you would modify the program so that the current year would print in heading line 02 whenever the program is run.

Hint: Review the part of Chapter 2 dealing with the UDATE field.

Figure 5-51   Debugging Problem 4

```
Lattice RPG II Compiler Version 2.01                  14:21:05  07/20/1991
Compile listing for source RPG program [HJG05X   .RPG]          PAGE : 0001


     1       H                                                                    HJG05X

     2       F*-------------------------------------------------------------------*
     3 S     F* HJG05X - SALES SUMMARY REPORT - HAL GOODWIN - JULY 14, 1991      *
     4 S     F*                                                                  *
     5 S     F* PROGRAM HJG05X LISTS MONTHLY SALES FOR EACH ITEM.  THE SIX       *
     6 S     F* MONTHLY SALES FIELDS ARE ADDED TO ACCUMULATE TOTAL SALES.        *
     7 S     F* WHEN STORE NUMBER CHANGES, TOTALS OF THE SEVEN SALES FIELDS WILL*
     8 S     F* PRINT.  IN ADDITION, A FINAL TOTAL OF THE TOTAL SALES FIELD      *
     9 S     F* WILL BE PRINTED.                                                 *
    10 S     F*-------------------------------------------------------------------*
    11 S     FSALFILE IP  F 360  60          DISK
    12 S     FSALREPT O   F 132 132     OF    PRINTER
    13 S     F* ID F  C   H  L    FUNCTION OF INDICATORS
    14 S     F* 01----------------SALFILE RECORD IDENTIFICATION
    15 S     F*              1P---FIRST PAGE INDICATOR
    16 S     F*              OF---OVERFLOW INDICATOR
    17 S     F*              L1---CONTROL BREAK - STORE NUMBER CHANGE
    18 S     F*              LR---END OF JOB

    19       I*-------------------------------------------------------------------*
    20 S     I* SALFILE INPUT RECORD DESCRIPTION                                  *
    21 S     I*-------------------------------------------------------------------*
    22 S     ISALFILE AA  01
    23 S     I                                      1   40STORE L1
    24 S     I                                     11   30 DESC
    25 S     I                                     31  340JANSAL
    26 S     I                                     35  380FEBSAL
    27 S     I                                     39  420MARSAL
    28 S     I                                     43  460APRSAL
    29 S     I                                     47  500MAYSAL
    30 S     I                                     51  540JUNSAL

    31       C* ACCUMULATE TOTAL SALES FOR EACH RECORD
    32 S     C   01     TOTSAL    ADD  JANSAL    TOTSAL 50
    33 S     C   01     TOTSAL    ADD  FEBSAL    TOTSAL
    34 S     C   01     TOTSAL    ADD  MARSAL    TOTSAL
    35 S     C   01     TOTSAL    ADD  APRSAL    TOTSAL
    36 S     C   01     TOTSAL    ADD  MAYSAL    TOTSAL
    37 S     C   01     TOTSAL    ADD  JUNSAL    TOTSAL
    38 S     C*
    39 S     C* ACCUMULATE CONTROL BREAK TOTALS
    40 S     C   01     JANTOT    ADD  JANSAL    JANTOT 60
    41 S     C   01     FEBTOT    ADD  FEBSAL    FEBTOT 60
```

Figure 5-51 (1)

```
Lattice RPG II Compiler Version 2.01                14:21:06  07/20/1991
Compile listing for source RPG program [HJG05X   .RPG]        PAGE : 0002

   42 S   C   01     MARTOT    ADD  MARSAL    MARTOT 60
   43 S   C   01     APRTOT    ADD  APRSAL    APRTOT 60
   44 S   C   01     MAYTOT    ADD  MAYSAL    MAYTOT 60
   45 S   C   01     JUNTOT    ADD  JUNSAL    JUNTOT 60
   46 S   C   01     SALTOT    ADD  TOTSAL    SALTOT 70
   47 S   C*
   48 S   C* ACCUMULATE FINAL TOTAL SALES
   49 S   CL1        SALFIN    ADD  SALTOT    SALFIN 80

   50     O*-------------------------------------------------------*
   51 S   O* HEADING LINE ONE                                      *
   52 S   O*-------------------------------------------------------*
   53 S   OSALREPT H  106      1P
   54 S   O       OR        OF
   55 S   O                                 9 'HJG05X'
   56 S   O                    UDATE Y      19
   57 S   O                                60 'SALES  SUMMARY  REPORT'
   58 S   O                                91 'PAGE'
   59 S   O                    PAGE  Z      96
   60 S   O*-------------------------------------------------------*
   61 S   O* HEADING LINE TWO                                      *
   62 S   O*-------------------------------------------------------*
   63 S   O        H  2       1P
   64 S   O       OR        OF
   65 S   O                                56 'JANUARY THROUGH JUNE'
   66 S   O                                62 ', 1991'
   67 S   O*-------------------------------------------------------*
   68 S   O* HEADING LINE THREE                                    *
   69 S   O*-------------------------------------------------------*
   70 S   O        H  1       1P
   71 S   O       OR        OF
   72 S   O                                 8 'STORE'
   73 S   O                                56 '- - - - - M O N T H L'
   74 S   O                                80 'Y   S A L E S - - - -'
   75 S   O                                96 '- -     TOTAL'
   76 S   O*-------------------------------------------------------*
   77 S   O* HEADING LINE FOUR                                     *
   78 S   O*-------------------------------------------------------*
   79 S   O        H  2       1P
   80 S   O       OR        OF
   81 S   O                                28 'NO.     ITEM DESCRIPTION'
   82 S   O                                56 'JANUARY FEBRUARY    MARC'
   83 S   O                                75 'H     APRIL     MAY'
   84 S   O                                96 'JUNE        SALES'
   85 S   O*-------------------------------------------------------*
   86 S   O* DETAIL LINE                                           *
   87 S   O*-------------------------------------------------------*
   88 S   O        D  1       01
   89 S   O                    STORE Z       7
   90 S   O                    DESC         30
   91 S   O                    JANSAL2      39
   92 S   O                    FEBSAL2      48
   93 S   O                    MARSAL2      57
   94 S   O                    APRSAL2      66
   95 S   O                    MAYSAL2      75
   96 S   O                    JUNSAL2      84
   97 S   O                    TOTSAL1B     96
   98 S   O*-------------------------------------------------------*
   99 S   O* CONTROL BREAK (L1) TOTAL LINE                         *
  100 S   O*-------------------------------------------------------*
  101 S   O        T 13       L1
  102 S   O                    JANTOT2B     39
  103 S   O                    FEBTOT2B     48
  104 S   O                    MARTOT2B     57
  105 S   O                    APRTOT2B     66
  106 S   O                    MAYTOT2B     75
```

Figure 5-51 (2)

continued

```
Lattice RPG II Compiler Version 2.01              14:21:08  07/20/1991
Compile listing for source RPG program [HJG05X  .RPG]        PAGE : 0003


  107 S    O                        JUNTOT2B  84
  108 S    O                        SALTOT1B  96
  109 S    O*------------------------------------------------------*
  110 S    O*  FINAL TOTAL LINE                                    *
  111 S    O*------------------------------------------------------*
  112 S    O        T      06 LR
  113 S    O                                  85 'FINAL TOTAL'
  114 S    O                        SALFIN1   96
  115 /*


Warning Severe
Errors  Errors
   0      0
```

Figure 5-51 (3)

STUDENT EXERCISES: PROGRAMMING IN RPG

PROGRAMMING ASSIGNMENT 1
FLEET USAGE REPORT

INSTRUCTIONS

Plan, code, enter, and test an RPG program to produce the Fleet Usage Report.

INPUT

The format of the Vehicle Mileage File is shown in Figure 5-52. Use test data set 9 for this problem.

VEHICLE MILEAGE FILE						
Record Length 60						
Field No.	Field Name	Field Description	Field Position	Field Length	Dec. Pos.	Data Class
1	VEHID	Vehicle I.D. No.	1–4	4		A
2	DATE	Date Vehicle Used	5–10	6	0	N
3	DRIVER	Driver Name	11–35	25		A
4	MILES	Miles Driven	36–39	4	0	N
5		UNUSED AREA	40–60	21		

Figure 5-52   Vehicle Mileage File

OUTPUT

Output is the Fleet Usage Report, the format of which is shown in Figure 5-53.

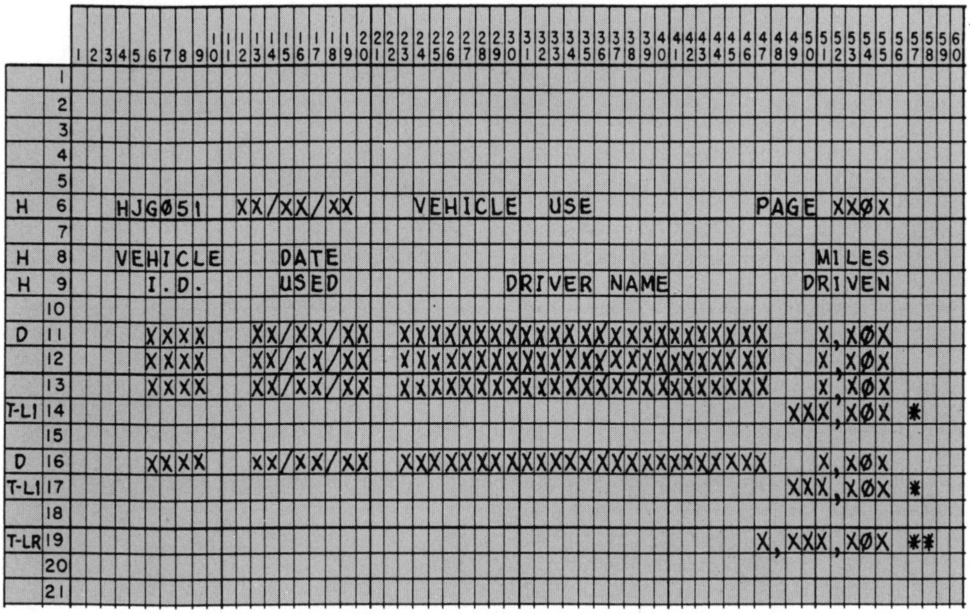

```
        1 2 3 4 5 6 7 8 9 0 1 2 3 4 5 6 7 8 9 0 1 2 3 4 5 6 7 8 9 0 1 2 3 4 5 6 7 8 9 0 1 2 3 4 5 6 7 8 9 0 1 2 3 4 5 6 7 8 9 0
H   6   HJG051    XX/XX/XX      VEHICLE  USE                    PAGE XX0X
H   8   VEHICLE      DATE                                       MILES
H   9     I.D.      USED                 DRIVER NAME            DRIVEN
D   11      XXXX    XX/XX/XX   XXXXXXXXXXXXXXXXXXXXXXXXXX        X,X0X
    12      XXXX    XX/XX/XX   XXXXXXXXXXXXXXXXXXXXXXXXXX        X,X0X
    13      XXXX    XX/XX/XX   XXXXXXXXXXXXXXXXXXXXXXXXXX        X,X0X
T-L1 14                                                      XXX,X0X *
    16      XXXX    XX/XX/XX   XXXXXXXXXXXXXXXXXXXXXXXXXX        X,X0X
T-L1 17                                                      XXX,X0X *
T-LR 19                                                    X,XXX,X0X **
```

Figure 5-53   Fleet Usage Report

Processing Requirements

The program takes a control break whenever the vehicle I.D. number changes. During the control break, the total of miles driven for that vehicle is printed. At the end of the program, a final total is printed that shows the total miles driven for all vehicles.

PROGRAMMING ASSIGNMENT 2
GATE USAGE REPORT

INSTRUCTIONS

Plan code, enter, and test an RPG program to produce the Gate Usage Report.

INPUT

The format of the Flight Departure File is shown in Figure 5-54 on the next page. Use test data set 10 for this problem.

FLIGHT DEPARTURE FILE						
Record Length 23						
Field No.	Field Name	Field Description	Field Position	Field Length	Dec. Pos.	Data Class
1	GATE	Departure Gate	1–3	3		A
2	FLIGHT	Flight Number	4–7	4		A
3		UNUSED AREA	8–16	9		
4	DEPTIM	Flight Departure Time	17–20	4	0	N
5	NOPASS	Number of Passengers	21–23	3	0	N

Figure 5-54   Flight Departure File

OUTPUT

Output is the Gate Usage Report, the format of which is shown in Figure 5-55.

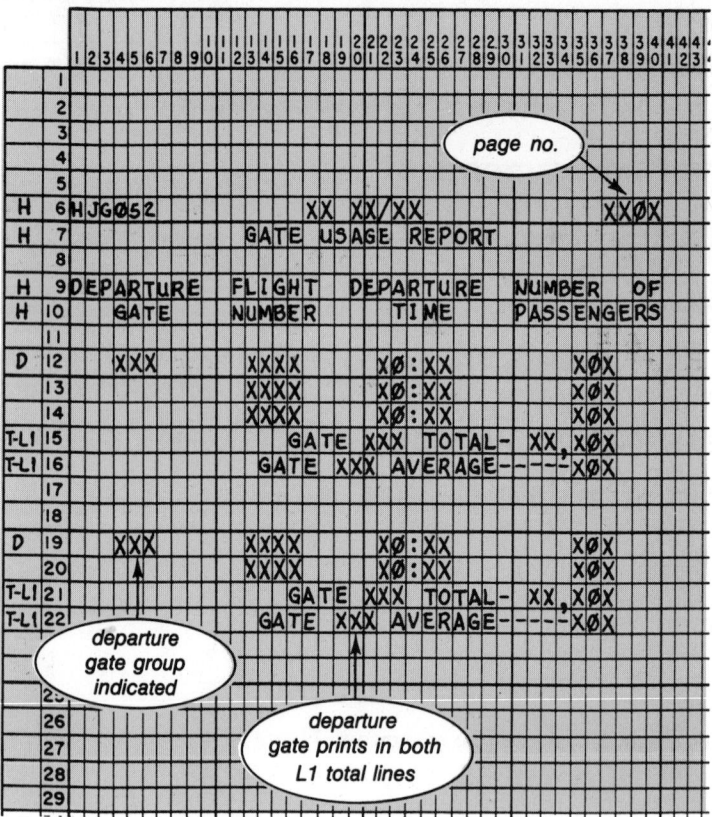

Figure 5-55   Gate Usage Report

Processing Requirements

The program takes a control break whenever the departure gate changes. During the control break, a total line is printed containing the total number of passengers using the gate. This total is the sum of the Number of Passengers fields from all records in the control group. In addition, the control break total shows the average number of passengers for all flights in the control group. This average is calculated by dividing the total number of passengers by the number of flights in the control group. Note that the number of flights does not print as part of the total and cannot be reset by use of a Blank After, entry.

PROGRAMMING ASSIGNMENT 3
LOAD FACTOR REPORT

INSTRUCTIONS

Plan, code, enter, and test an RPG program to produce the Load Factor Report.

INPUT

The format of the Flight Load File is shown in Figure 5-56. Use test data set 14 for this problem.

FLIGHT LOAD FILE						
Record Length 33						
Field No.	Field Name	Field Description	Field Position	Field Length	Dec. Pos.	Data Class
1	DATE	Flight Date	1–6	6	0	N
2	CITY	Departure City	7–25	19		A
3	FLITNO	Flight Number	26–29	4		A
4	NOPASS	Passenger Load	30–32	3	0	N
5	C	Flight Capacity Code	33–33	1	0	N

Figure 5-56   Flight Load File

OUTPUT

Output is the Load Factor Report, the format of which is shown in Figure 5-57.

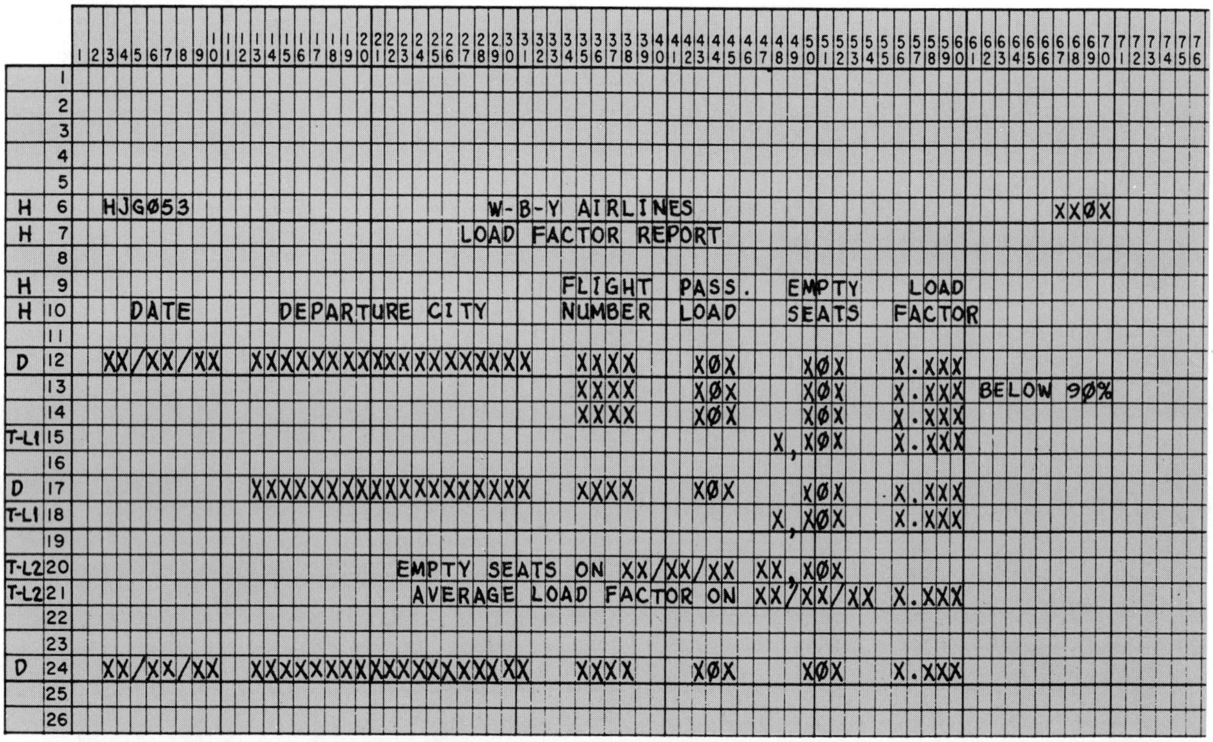

Figure 5-57 Load Factor Report

The print chart contains the following layout:

```
H  6  HJGØ53                          W-B-Y AIRLINES                    XXØX
H  7                                 LOAD FACTOR REPORT
H  9                            FLIGHT  PASS.   EMPTY    LOAD
H 10     DATE      DEPARTURE CITY    NUMBER  LOAD    SEATS   FACTOR
D 12  XX/XX/XX  XXXXXXXXXXXXXXXXXX    XXXX    XØX     XØX   X.XXX
  13                                  XXXX    XØX     XØX   X.XXX BELOW 9Ø%
  14                                  XXXX    XØX     XØX   X.XXX
T-L1 15                                              X,XØX  X.XXX
D 17            XXXXXXXXXXXXXXXXXX    XXXX    XØX     XØX   X.XXX
T-L1 18                                               X,XØX  X.XXX
T-L2 20                    EMPTY SEATS ON XX/XX/XX  XX,XØX
T-L2 21                    AVERAGE LOAD FACTOR ON XX/XX/XX X.XXX
D 24  XX/XX/XX  XXXXXXXXXXXXXXXXXX    XXXX    XØX     XØX   X.XXX
```

Processing Requirements

The load factor on an airline flight is the fraction (or percentage) of available seats on the airliner that were actually sold. If, for example, ten percent of the seats on a flight were not sold, the flight has a load factor of .90 (or 90%). This program determines the load factor by dividing the Passenger Load, which is the number of seats actually sold, by the number of available seats on each flight. The number of seats on the airplane is based on the Flight Capacity Code. This code has been verified for accuracy, so you do not have to test for a valid code in your program. The codes and seating capacities are as follows:

Code	Seats
1	150
2	180
3	225
4	280
5	300
6	325

Each line of the detail printed report contains the flight date, departure city, flight number, passenger load, number of empty seats, and load factor. The number of empty seats is calculated by subtracting passenger load from flight capacity. In addition, if the load factor is less than .90, the message BELOW 90% prints beginning in position 62 of the detail line.

This report control breaks on Departure City within Date. At each control break, the total number of empty seats and the average load factor for the control group are printed. There are no final totals in this report.

PROGRAMMING ASSIGNMENT 4
INVENTORY VALUE REPORT

INSTRUCTIONS

Plan, code, enter, and test an RPG program to produce the Inventory Value Report.

INPUT

The format of the Inventory File is shown in Figure 5-58. Use test data set 15 for this problem.

INVENTORY FILE						
Record Length 25						
Field No.	Field Name	Field Description	Field Position	Field Length	Dec. Pos.	Data Class
1	PLANT	Plant Number	1–3	3		A
2	DIV	Division Number	4–5	2		A
3	AREA	Area	6–8	3		A
4	STKRM	Stockroom	9–11	3		A
5	PART	Part Number	12–16	5		A
6	QTY	Quantity on Hand	17–20	4	0	N
7	UPRICE	Unit Price	21–25	5	3	N

Figure 5-58   Inventory File

OUTPUT

Output is the Inventory Value Report, the format of which is shown in Figure 5-59.

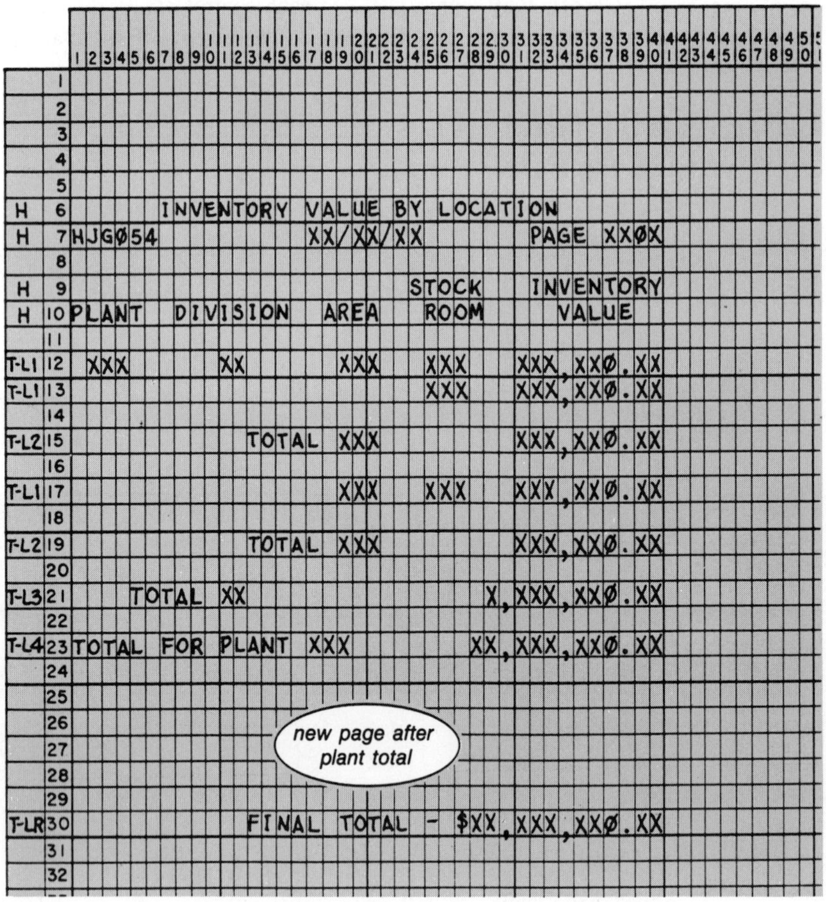

Figure 5-59 Inventory Value Report

Processing Requirements

This program produces a group printed, group indicated report. Control breaks are based on plant number (L4), division number (L3), area (L2), and stockroom (L1). Each control break prints the total inventory value for the group. Total inventory value is calculated by multiplying the unit price by the quantity on hand each time an input record is read. The product of this multiplication is added to the L1 total accumulator. The L1 total is rolled into each higher level accumulator. Note that the report advances to a new page after plant totals have been printed. Use fetch overflow to print headings on the final total page.

Array Processing & Compiler Directive Statements

ARRAY PROCESSING

In all RPG programming examples you have studied so far, every field has been assigned a unique name when it was defined on either the Input or Calculation Specifications form. A separate definition was needed for each field being used in the program. In some programming applications, it is possible to define a group of fields with a single RPG specification by using **array processing** techniques.

An **array** is a series of identical data fields defined as a single unit. Arrays can be used to simplify programming and program maintenance by eliminating some program code. In addition, because arrays define a group of fields with a single statement, program modifications affecting several fields can be made by changing a single line of source code when arrays are used. To illustrate how arrays can be used to simplify program code, we use two sample programs (which also were studied in Chapter 5).

Types of Arrays

RPG uses three types of arrays: compile time, preexecution time, and execution time. The type of array is determined by when data is loaded into the array. Thus, the type of array used in a specific program is based on the requirements of the program.

▶ **Compile Time Arrays** Because **compile time arrays** are part of the RPG source program, the array data is coded as part of the source program. These arrays are usually used only when changes in the array data are expected to be infrequent because a change in the array data requires that the program be recompiled.

▶ **Preexecution (Prerun) Time Arrays** The data is loaded into **preexecution time arrays**, usually from a disk file, at the beginning of program execution before any input, calculation, or output operations have been performed. The file containing the array data is a separate file from the input file processed by the program.

▸ **Execution (Run) Time Arrays** Execution time arrays are loaded with data during program execution. The data usually is read in as part of an input record or is created by the program. The first sample program that we examine uses execution time arrays to process input data and accumulate control break totals.

Array Concepts

Array techniques can only be used if the fields have identical characteristics that is, the fields must have the same length, data class, and number of decimal positions. If the fields are not identical in these three respects, array techniques cannot be used. Let's review the input record for program HJG06X.

The six monthly sales fields meet the requirements for array definition (Figure 6-1); each has the same length (four positions), the same data class (numeric), and the same number of decimal positions (none). Because these fields meet the requirements, the sample program can be modified to use array techniques. As you will see in program HJG06X, which is a modification of program HJG05X, array techniques permit the elimination of several lines of program code and still perform the same functions as non-array programming techniques.

SALES ANALYSIS RECORD						
Record Length 60						
Field No.	Field Name	Field Description	Field Position	Field Length	Dec. Pos.	Data Class
1	STORE	Store Number	1–4	4	0	N
2		UNUSED AREA	5–10			
3	DESC	Item Description	11–30	20		A
4	JANSAL	Units Sold, Jan.	31–34	4	0	N
5	FEBSAL	Units Sold, Feb.	35–38	4	0	N
6	MARSAL	Units Sold, March	39–42	4	0	N
7	APRSAL	Units Sold, April	43-46	4	0	N
8	MAYSAL	Units Sold, May	47–50	4	0	N
9	JUNSAL	Units Sold, June	51–54	4	0	N
10		UNUSED AREA	55–60			

monthly sales fields

Figure 6-1   Sales Analysis Record

Array Elements

Figure 6-2 shows the six monthly sales fields in the form of an array that consists of six consecutive fields. Each field in an array is called an **element**, and every element has the same characteristics. In this file, all elements of the array are four positions long, contain numeric data, and have no decimal positions. The six monthly sales fields, located in positions 31–54 of the input file records, are read into memory and stored in the form of an array. The elements of the array are used to perform all the same functions as the six separate monthly sales input fields in program HJG05X.

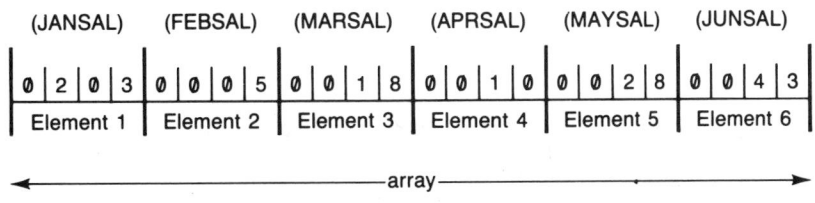

Figure 6-2　Monthly sales array

Execution Time Array Definition

RPG requires that entries be made on both the Input and Extension Specifications forms in order to describe and define an array that is to be read as part of an input record. Figure 6-3 shows the relationship between the input record and the input and extension specifications needed to define an array.

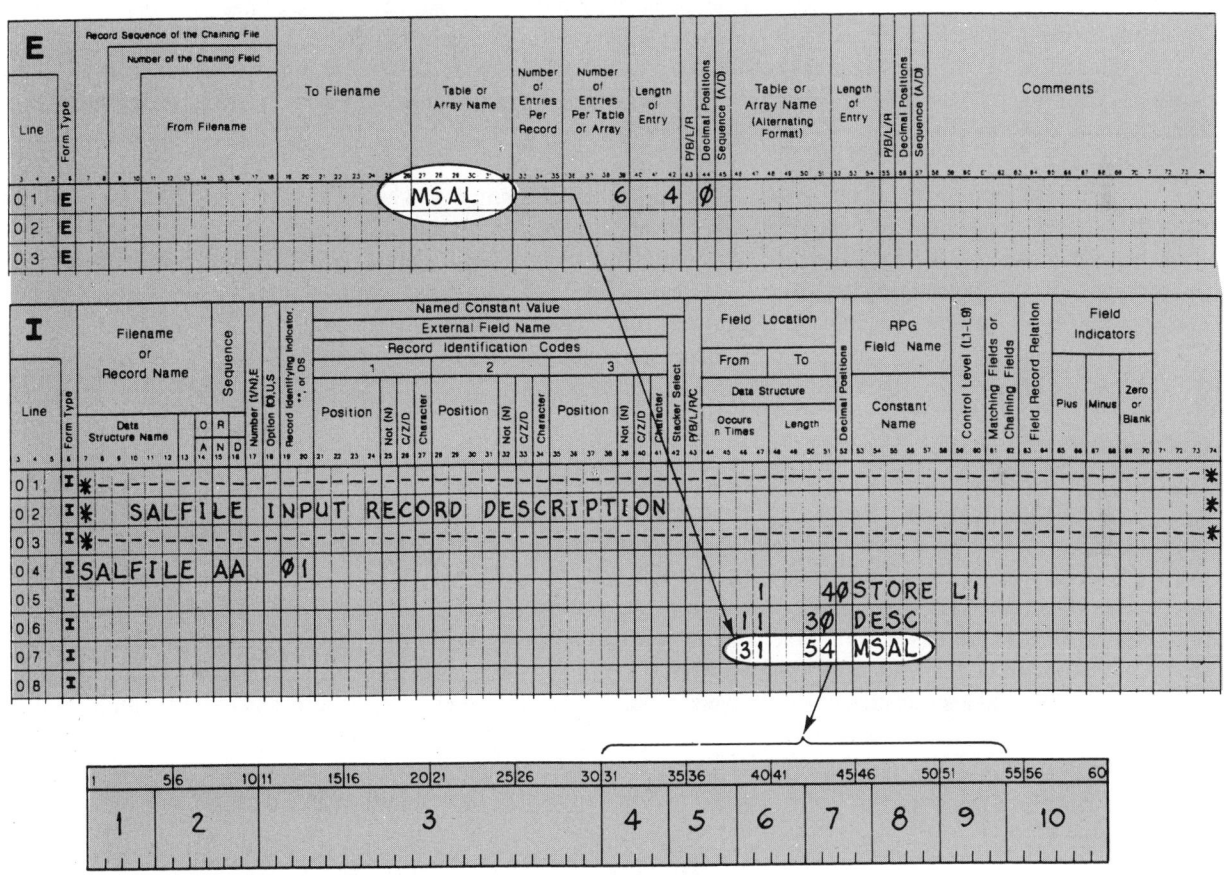

Figure 6-3　Execution time array definition

▸ **Input Specifications**　The input specification entry for an array defines the entire array, as is shown on line 07 of the Input Specifications form (middle of Figure 6-3). The array is defined as a single area, starting in position 31 of the input record and ending in position 54. The name assigned to the array is MSAL. These positions encompass the entire area occupied by the six monthly sales fields in the input record. Although the individual fields are numeric, there is no entry in the Decimal Positions area. Most current versions of RPG obtain the Decimal Positions entry for the array elements from the array description coded on the Extension Specifications form. However, some older versions of RPG require that the Decimal Positions entry also be made on the Input Specifications form. Your instructor or data center manager can tell you if a Decimal Positions entry is required on the Input Specifications form when defining an array.

▸ **Extension Specifications**   Although the array area is described on the Input Specifications form, it is still necessary to define the array and describe the attributes of each of the elements within the array and the number of elements in the array. The entries to provide this information are made on the **Extension Specifications** form (top of Figure 6-3). The array description on the Extension Specifications form causes the computer to reserve the memory needed to store the array data.

The array name is entered in the **Table or Array Name** area, positions 27–32. This entry must be the same name used on the Input Specifications form and is, in this example, MSAL. Positions 36–39 of the Extension Specifications form tell RPG the **number of entries per table or array**. This entry specifies the number of elements in the array. Since the MSAL array contains six elements, or fields, the number 6 has been entered in position 39. Positions 40–42 specify the **length of entry** (the length of each array element). A 4 has been entered in position 42 because each of the monthly sales fields is four positions long. Position 44 of the Extension Specifications form is the Decimal Positions area. This area serves the same purpose as on the Input and Calculations forms, that is, it specifies the data class of the elements within the array. An entry 0 (zero) has been made in this area because each of the array elements is a numeric field with no decimal positions.

In addition to the array that has been defined as part of the input data record, one additional array is needed if the program is to take full advantage of array processing techniques. This array is used to accumulate the control break total amounts for the six monthly sales fields and must also be defined on the Extension Specifications form.

The definition of this second array, TSAL, is shown in Figure 6-4. The six elements of TSAL are used to store the totals of the six monthly sales elements contained in the MSAL array. Because the program specifications show that the control break total areas could contain up to six digits, each element of TSAL has been defined as six positions long by the entry 6 in position 42. The data for TSAL is not read from an input record, so there is no entry for TSAL on the Input Specifications form. As is the case with all numeric data fields, each element of the TSAL array is automatically set to a value of zero at the beginning of program execution.

▤ Array Calculations

The Calculation Specifications form for program HJG06X (Figure 6-5) shows that by using array techniques, you can reduce the amount of coding needed to perform the calculations. With non-array techniques, program HJG05X required 14 calculation operations to solve the problem (see Figure 5-12). With array techniques, the number of operations has been reduced to 4, yet both of these programs perform identical functions and produce exactly the same results. Overall, the number of actual RPG statements (not including comments) is reduced from 70 in program HJG05X to 52 in program HJG06X, a reduction of over 25 percent. This amount of coding reduction can result in a substantial saving in the amount of time needed to develop, test, and maintain an RPG program.

As you saw in program HJG05X, the first calculations to be performed must add the six monthly sales fields to determine total sales (TOTSAL). Line 02 performs all six of these additions in a single step by use of the XFOOT instruction.

IBM RPG EXTENSION AND LINE COUNTER SPECIFICATIONS GX09-1033-02 UM/050

(SEE OVER FOR RPG INPUT SPECIFICATIONS) Printed in U.S.A.

Program SALES SUMMARY REPORT Programmer GOODWIN Date 7-14-91 Page 03 of 9 Program Identification HJG06X

Extension Specifications

Line	Form Type	To Filename	Table or Array Name	Number of Entries Per Record	Number of Entries Per Table or Array	Length of Entry	Decimal Positions
01	E		MSAL		6	4	0
02	E		TSAL		6	6	0
03	E						
04	E						
05	E						
06	E						
07	E						
08	E						

Line Counter Specifications

Line	Form Type	Filename
01	L	
02	L	

* Number of sheets per pad may vary slightly.

Figure 6-4 Extension specifications for program HJG06X

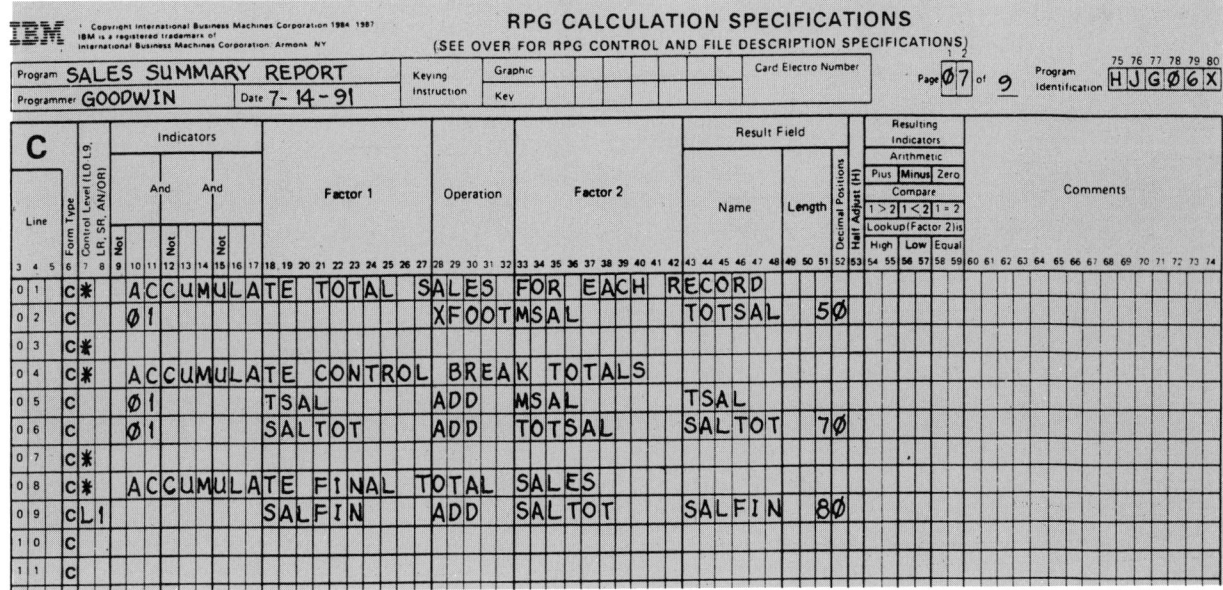

Figure 6-5 Calculation specifications for program HJG06X

▸ **The XFOOT Operation** The **XFOOT** operation (Figure 6-6), which can be used only with arrays containing numeric data, adds the contents of all the elements and places the sum of the elements in the data field named in the Result Field area. The name of the array being added is specified in the Factor 2 area. Factor 1 must be blank. In this example, the XFOOT operation is used to add each element of the array to the TOTSAL total area. XFOOT can be used with any numeric array, regardless of the number of elements in the array. When using the XFOOT operation, you should be aware of the size of each element and the number of elements so that you define the result field with a length adequate to hold the maximum size sum that may develop. Figure 6-7 summarizes the XFOOT operation.

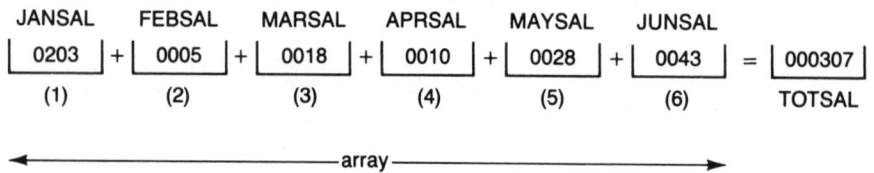

Figure 6-6   Example of XFOOT operation

C										

The coding sheet shows:

Line 01: C, Control Level 01, Operation XFOOT, Factor 2 ARR1, Result Field Name ARRTOT, Length 7, Decimal Position 2

XFOOT Operation Summary

XFOOT adds the contents of all of the elements of the numeric array named in Factor 2 and places the sum in the Result Field. Factor 2 must be a numeric array. Factor 1 may not be used.

Control Level Indicators	Indicators	Factor 1	Operation Name	Factor 2	Result Field	Resulting Indicators		
7–8	9–17	18–27	28–32	33–42	43–53	54–55	56–57	58–59
optional	optional	blank	XFOOT	required	required	optional	optional	optional

Figure 6-7   XFOOT operation summary

▸ **Adding Arrays**   You have seen how the XFOOT operation is used to simplify adding all the elements in the MSAL array to a total field. The next step in the sample problem requires that the individual array elements be added to totals that will print when a control break occurs. The TSAL array has been defined to hold the control break totals. Each element of the MSAL array can be added to the corresponding element of the TSAL array by using the ADD operation.

As discussed earlier, the ADD operation adds the contents of two data fields and places the sum in a result area. When the ADD operation is used to add two arrays, it works as a series of separate ADD operations, adding individual elements of both arrays, as in Figure 6-8.

C	Form Type	Control Level (L0-L9, LR, SR, AN/OR)	Indicators						Factor 1	Operation	Factor 2	Result Field		Decimal Positions	Half Adjust (H)	Resulting Indicators		
			And		And							Name	Length			Arithmetic		
			Not		Not		Not									Plus	Minus	Zero
Line																Compare		
																1>2	1<2	1=2
																Lookup(Factor 2)is		
																High	Low	Equal
0 1	C		Ø1						TSAL	ADD	MSAL	TSAL						
0 2	C																	
0 3	C																	
0 4	C																	

First record

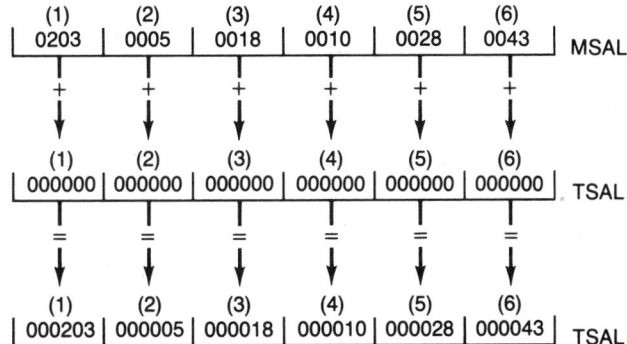

Second record

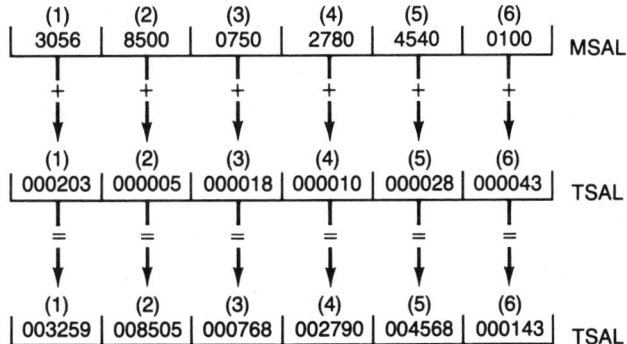

Figure 6-8   Example of addition of arrays

The calculation specification shows that MSAL (Factor 2) is to be added to TSAL (Factor 1) and the sum stored in TSAL (Result Field). Because MSAL and TSAL are arrays, the addition works somewhat differently from an ADD operation performed on normal data fields. When the ADD operation is executed, the first element of MSAL is added to the first element of TSAL and the sum stored in the first element of TSAL. Then the second element of MSAL is added to the second element of TSAL and the sum stored in the second element of TSAL. This continues on an element-by-element basis until all elements of the arrays have been added. This series of additions is repeated every time the ADD operation is performed.

This method of arithmetic between arrays is not limited to the ADD operation. **Array arithmetic** can also be performed using the SUB, MULT, and DIV operations. Remember that if arrays are used as factors in these arithmetic operations, the result field must also be an array.

Array Output

As you have seen, it is possible to reference all the elements of an array as a single unit by using the array name. This was done as part of the input specifications as well as in the XFOOT and ADD operations in the calculation specifications. It is also possible to reference individual array elements for calculation and output operations.

The array name not only identifies the entire array but also is the name of each of the elements within the array. For example, the name MSAL identifies seven separate data items. MSAL is not only the name of the entire 24 position array, it is the name of each of the six elements within the array as well.

▶ **Array Element Identification**   When an array name is used in a program, RPG assumes that it refers to the entire array. To reference an element within an array, a value known as an index must be used. An **index**, also called a **subscript**, is a number that identifies the position of the element within the array. Figure 6-9 shows the MSAL array with each element identified by its name and index value, that is, by the array name, a comma, and then a numeric literal that indicates the element being referenced. The first element is MSAL,1 (the array name, comma, and the literal 1). The second element is MSAL,2, and so on. To print each element of the array, the elements are referenced on the Output Specification form (Figure 6-10).

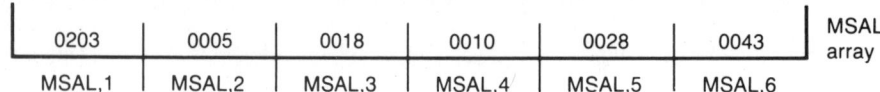

| 0203 | 0005 | 0018 | 0010 | 0028 | 0043 | MSAL array |
| MSAL,1 | MSAL,2 | MSAL,3 | MSAL,4 | MSAL,5 | MSAL,6 | |

Figure 6-9   Examples of literal index

▶ **Output of Individual Array Elements**   As in Figure 6-10, each element of the array MSAL is referenced by the array name followed by a **literal index** number. The first element of MSAL will print ending in position 39, the second element in position 48, the third element in position 57, and so on. Thus, by specifying the array name followed by a comma and a literal index, you can reference each element of an array individually.

However, you must consider field length when naming arrays if elements are to be referenced by this method. Because the Field Name area of the specification form is only six positions long, the combined length of the array name, the comma, and the literal index cannot exceed six characters. If the combined length is greater than six characters, the indexed array name cannot fit in the Field Name area. If a one-digit index is all that is needed (the array contains up to nine elements), the array name can be up to four characters in length. If a two-digit index is needed (the array contains between 10 and 99 elements), the array name cannot exceed three characters.

▶ **Output of an Array As a Single Unit**   There is another way in which you can take advantage of the ease of working with arrays. Under some conditions, it is possible to output an entire array with a single output specification. If an array name is used as an output field name, with no index, the entire array is printed, and each array element is separated by two spaces. Figure 6-11 shows the printer spacing chart for the sample program.

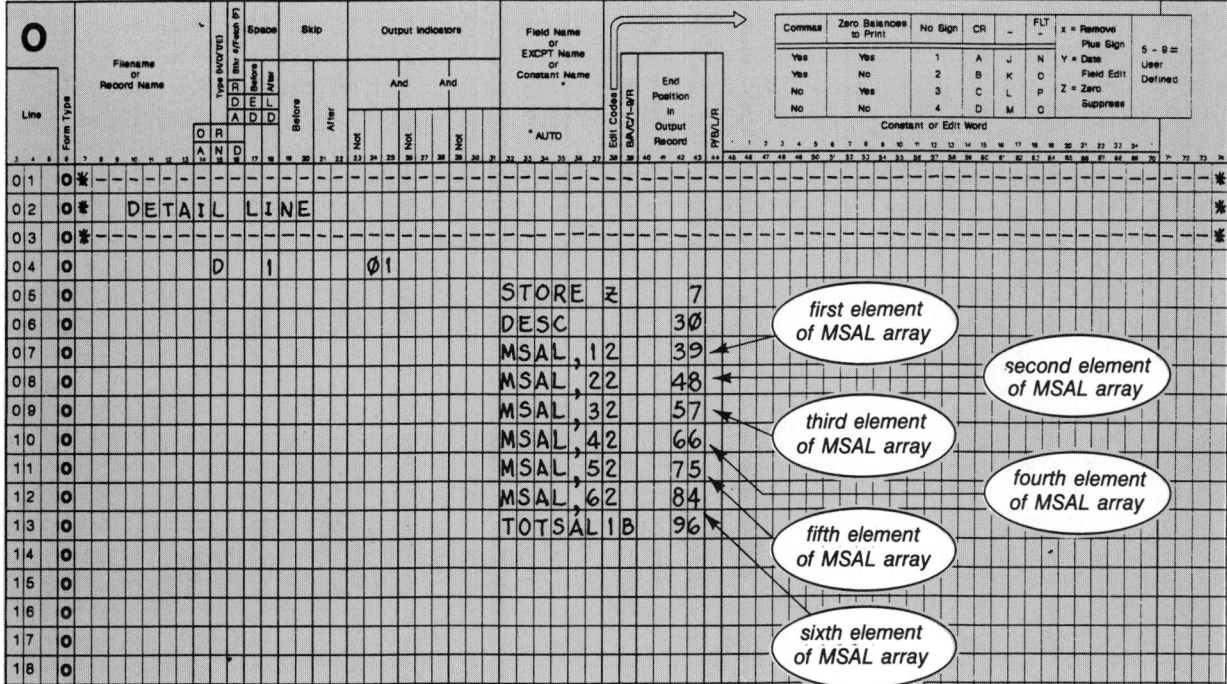

Figure 6-10   Output of individual array elements

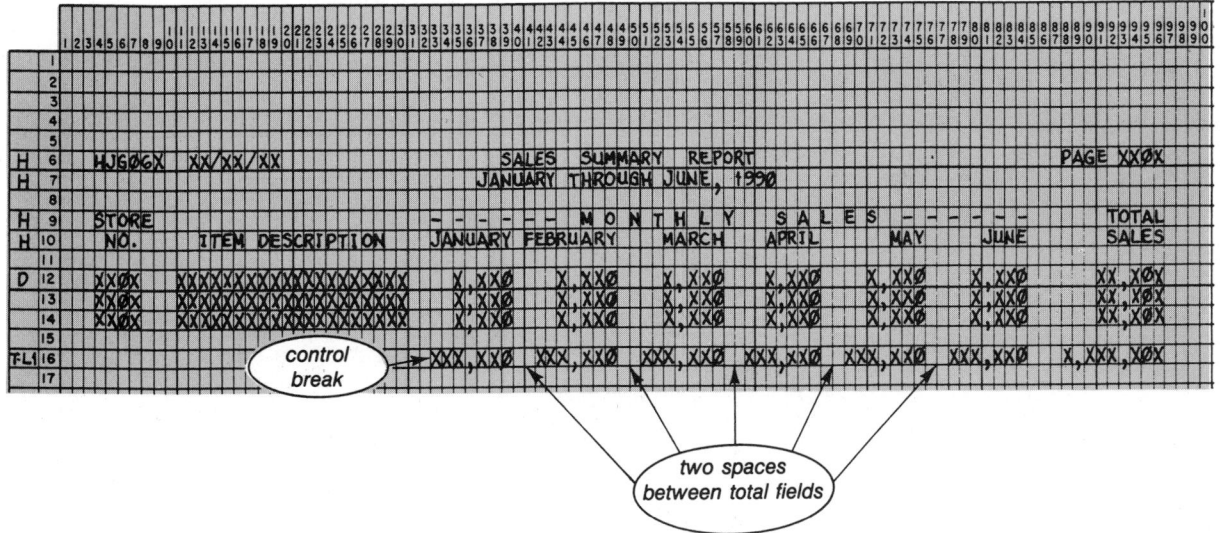

Figure 6-11   Automatic spacing of array elements

Notice that the six monthly sales control break totals are to be printed with two spaces separating each total field. Because a two-space separation is needed, we can take advantage of the automatic element-spacing feature of array output. Figure 6-12 shows the output specifications for the L1 total line. Note that the name of the L1 total array is used with no literal index. Because of this, the entire array is printed, and each element is separated by two spaces. The end position used (84) is the end position of the last element of the array. This entry causes TSAL,6 to print in positions 78–84, TSAL,5 in positions 69–75, TSAL,4 in positions 60–66, and so on. Note the two-space separation between each of the L1 total fields. Edit Code 2, used for the array, is also used for each array element as it prints.

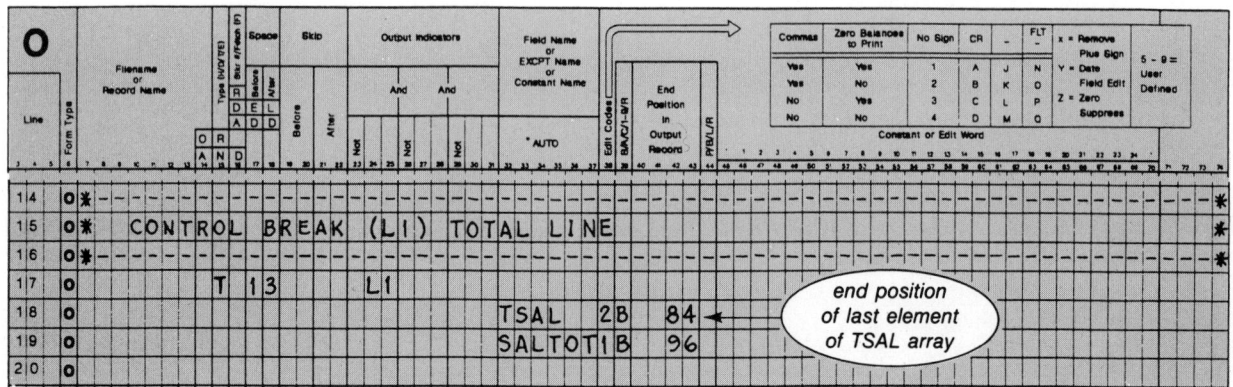

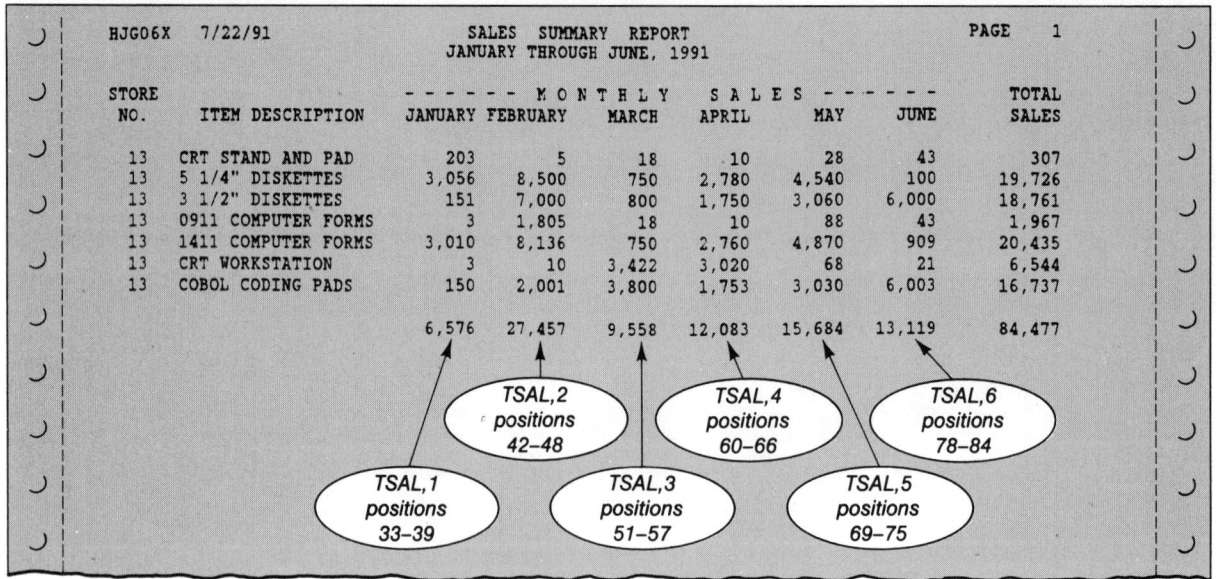

Figure 6-12   Output of an entire array

Sample Program HJG06X

The compile listing and sample output for program HJG06X are shown in Figure 6-13. Although the program is considerably shorter due to the use of array techniques, the output report is identical to that of program HJG05X.

Figure 6-13   Sample program HJG06X

```
Lattice RPG II Compiler Version 2.01                19:25:37  07/19/1991
Compile listing for source RPG program [HJG06X  .RPG]        PAGE : 0001


     1      H                                                        HJG06Z

     2      F*-------------------------------------------------------------
     3 S    F* HJG06X - SALES SUMMARY REPORT - HAL GOODWIN - JULY 14, 1991  *
     4 S    F*                                                               *
     5 S    F* PROGRAM HJG06X LISTS MONTHLY SALES FOR EACH ITEM.  THE SIX    *
     6 S    F* MONTHLY SALES FIELDS ARE ADDED TO ACCUMULATE TOTAL SALES.     *
     7 S    F* WHEN STORE NUMBER CHANGES, TOTALS OF THE SEVEN SALES FIELDS WILL*
     8 S    F* PRINT.  IN ADDITION, A FINAL TOTAL OF THE TOTAL SALES FIELD   *
     9 S    F* WILL BE PRINTED.                                              *
    10 S    F*-------------------------------------------------------------
    11 S    FSALFILE IP  F 360 60          DISK
    12 S    FSALREPT O   F 132 132    OF   PRINTER
    13 S    F* ID F  C  H  L   FUNCTION OF INDICATORS
    14 S    F* 01---------------SALFILE RECORD IDENTIFICATION
    15 S    F*               1P---FIRST PAGE INDICATOR
    16 S    F*               OF---OVERFLOW INDICATOR
    17 S    F*               L1---CONTROL BREAK - STORE NUMBER CHANGE
    18 S    F*               LR---END OF JOB

    19      E               MSAL      6  4 0
    20 S    E               TSAL      6  6 0

    21      I*-------------------------------------------------------------*
    22 S    I* SALFILE INPUT RECORD DESCRIPTION                            *
    23 S    I*-------------------------------------------------------------*
    24 S    ISALFILE AA  01
    25 S    I                                       1    40STORE L1
    26 S    I                                      11    30 DESC
    27 S    I                                      31    54 MSAL

    28      C* ACCUMULATE TOTAL SALES FOR EACH RECORD
    29 S    C   01             XFOOTMSAL      TOTSAL 50
    30 S    C*
    31 S    C* ACCUMULATE CONTROL BREAK TOTALS
    32 S    C   01   TSAL      ADD  MSAL      TSAL
    33 S    C   01   SALTOT    ADD  TOTSAL    SALTOT 70
    34 S    C*
    35 S    C* ACCUMULATE FINAL TOTAL SALES
    36 S    CL1      SALFIN    ADD  SALTOT    SALFIN 80

    37      O*-------------------------------------------------------------*
    38 S    O* HEADING LINE ONE                                            *
    39 S    O*-------------------------------------------------------------*
    40 S    OSALREPT H 106  1P
    41 S    O        OR      OF
    42 S    O                               9 'HJG06X'
    43 S    O                UDATE Y       19
    44 S    O                              60 'SALES  SUMMARY  REPORT'
    45 S    O                              91 'PAGE'
    46 S    O                PAGE Z        96
    47 S    O*-------------------------------------------------------------*
    48 S    O* HEADING LINE TWO                                            *
    49 S    O*-------------------------------------------------------------*
    50 S    O        H  2    1P
    51 S    O        OR      OF
    52 S    O                              56 'JANUARY THROUGH JUNE'
    53 S    O                              62 ', 1991'
    54 S    O*-------------------------------------------------------------*
    55 S    O* HEADING LINE THREE                                          *
    56 S    O*-------------------------------------------------------------*
    57 S    O        H  1    1P
    58 S    O        OR      OF
    59 S    O                               8 'STORE'
    60 S    O                              56 '- - - - - M O N T H L'
    61 S    O                              80 'Y  S A L E S - - -'
    62 S    O                              96 '- -    TOTAL'
    63 S    O*-------------------------------------------------------------*
    64 S    O* HEADING LINE FOUR                                           *
    65 S    O*-------------------------------------------------------------*
    66 S    O        H  2    1P
    67 S    O        OR      OF
    68 S    O                              28 'NO.    ITEM DESCRIPTION'
    69 S    O                              56 'JANUARY FEBRUARY   MARC'
    70 S    O                              75 'H     APRIL     MAY'
    71 S    O                              96 'JUNE     SALES'
    72 S    O*-------------------------------------------------------------*
    73 S    O* DETAIL LINE                                                 *
    74 S    O*-------------------------------------------------------------*
```

Figure 6-13 (1)   *continued*

```
Lattice RPG II Compiler Version 2.01                    19:25:38 07/19/1991
Compile listing for source RPG program [HJG06X  .RPG]        PAGE : 0002

   75 S    O       D 1     01
   76 S    O                        STORE Z   7
   77 S    O                        DESC      30
   78 S    O                        MSAL,12   39
   79 S    O                        MSAL,22   48
   80 S    O                        MSAL,32   57
   81 S    O                        MSAL,42   66
   82 S    O                        MSAL,52   75
   83 S    O                        MSAL,62   84
   84 S    O                        TOTSAL1B  96
   85 S    O*-----------------------------------------------------------*
   86 S    O*  CONTROL BREAK (L1) TOTAL LINE                            *
   87 S    O*-----------------------------------------------------------*
   88 S    O       T 13    L1
   89 S    O                        TSAL   2B 84
   90 S    O                        SALTOT1B  96
   91 S    O*-----------------------------------------------------------*
   92 S    O*  FINAL TOTAL LINE                                         *
   93 S    O*-----------------------------------------------------------*
   94 S    O       T       06 LR
   95 S    O                        85 'FINAL TOTAL'
   96 S    O                        SALFIN1   96
   97 /*

Warning Severe
Errors  Errors
   0      0
```

Figure 6-13 (2)

```
HJG06X  7/20/91                 SALES  SUMMARY  REPORT                PAGE    1
                              JANUARY THROUGH JUNE, 1991

STORE                  - - - - - - M O N T H L Y   S A L E S - - - - - -      TOTAL
 NO.   ITEM DESCRIPTION   JANUARY FEBRUARY   MARCH    APRIL     MAY     JUNE   SALES

  13   CRT STAND AND PAD      203       5      18       10      28       43      307
  13   5 1/4" DISKETTES     3,056   8,500     750    2,780   4,540      100   19,726
  13   3 1/2" DISKETTES       151   7,000     800    1,750   3,060    6,000   18,761
  13   0911 COMPUTER FORMS      3   1,805      18       10      88       43    1,967
  13   1411 COMPUTER FORMS  3,010   8,136     750    2,760   4,870      909   20,435
  13   CRT WORKSTATION         3      10    3,422    3,020      68       21    6,544
  13   COBOL CODING PADS      150   2,001   3,800    1,753   3,030    6,003   16,737

                          6,576  27,457   9,558   12,083  15,684   13,119   84,477


  15   RPG INPUT FORMS         3       5    1,018      10     358       43    1,437
  15   RPG OUTPUT FORMS     3,000   8,500     150    2,780   4,530      103   19,063
  15   3 1/2" DISKETTES       150   2,003     310    1,750   3,042    6,030   13,285
  15   0911 COMPUTER FORMS      3       5    2,011      10   1,228    3,343    6,600
  15   1411 COMPUTER FORMS  3,000   8,500     750    1,783   4,543    3,400   21,976
  15   TERMINAL COVERS         3              25      118       5       65      216
  15   SURGE PROTECTORS       150   2,000     800    1,760   3,037    6,000   13,747

                          6,309  21,013   5,064    8,211  16,743   18,984   76,324


  20   CRT STAND AND PAD       3   3,005      16    5,011   4,308       43   12,386
  20   5 1/4" DISKETTES     3,000   8,760     750    2,782   3,508    9,100   27,900
  20   FLOWCHARTING TMPLTS    150   2,008     800    1,744   3,100    9,000   16,802
  20   0911 COMPUTER FORMS      3       5    9,018      90      18    9,042   18,176
  20   CRT WORKSTATION         3              75      60       8       21      167
  20   COBOL CODING PADS       3       5      18       20       8    3,243    3,297

                          3,162  13,783  10,677    9,707  10,950   30,449   78,728


  21   5 1/4" DISKETTES     3,000   8,500     750    3,750   4,500      210   20,710
  21   3 1/2" DISKETTES       150   2,000     800    1,230   3,000    6,601   13,781
  21   0911 COMPUTER FORMS      3       5      18       20       8      323      377
  21   1411 COMPUTER FORMS  3,000   8,500     750    2,785   4,500      100   19,635
  21   CRT WORKSTATION         3              25      10    7,808       21    7,867
  21   COBOL CODING PADS      150   2,000     800    1,750   3,090      580    8,370

                          6,306  21,005   3,143    9,545  22,906    7,835   70,740


                                                    FINAL TOTAL           310,269
```

Figure 6-13 (3)

COMPILE TIME ARRAYS

The previous example demonstrated how execution time array techniques can be used to simplify coding when the input data contains a series of identical data fields. In the next sample program, a revision of program HJG05Y, another type of array is used to eliminate some of the code needed to determine which of the six customer category codes is contained in a record. We can also use the same array to produce the output messages more easily. The type of array that can be used to solve this type of coding problem is the compile time array.

A **compile time array** is a part of the RPG source program. Because of this, compile time arrays are normally used only for applications in which the array data does not change very often. Data that does not change frequently is called **static data**. Data that changes often is **dynamic data**. Generally, compile time arrays are used when the array data is static and execution and preexecution time arrays are used with dynamic data.

A compile time array is coded as part of the RPG source program and appears at the end of the source code (Figure 6-14). During program compilation, the data from the array records is loaded into the array area. Because the data is loaded during compilation, it is available at the start of program execution. When compile time arrays are used, the source program is entered first, followed by the array data. A record containing asterisks in positions 1 and 2 is entered between the last statement of the source program and the first array data record. This ** record marks the beginning of the array data. Some versions of RPG require that the last array record be followed by a record containing the characters /* in positions 1 and 2. In addition, some versions of RPG that do not require the use of a /* record generate one or more of these records as part of the compilation listing. You will see examples of this in the debugging exercises in this and other chapters. Your instructor or data center manager can tell you if you are using an RPG compiler that either requires or generates a /* record.

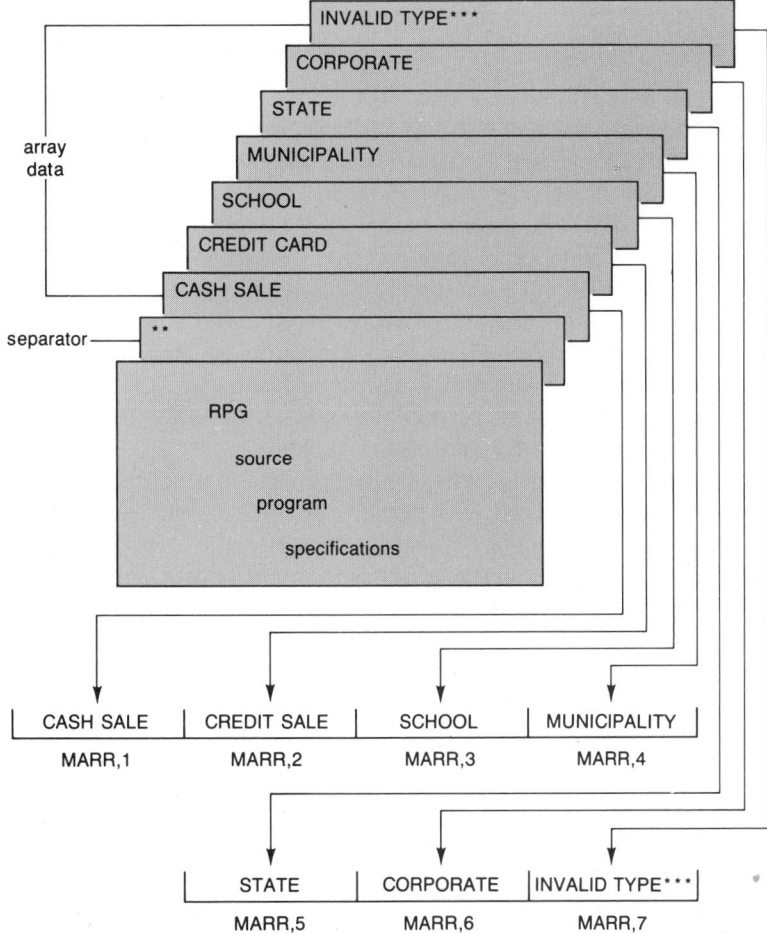

Figure 6-14   Compile time array placement

Compile Time Array Description

The extension specification needed to define the compile time array used in the sample program is shown in Figure 6-15. Most of these entries are similar to those used to describe the execution time arrays in the first sample program. The array name (MARR) has been entered starting in position 27, the number of entries in the array (7) has been entered in position 39, and the length of each element (15) is in positions 41 and 42.

Extension Specifications

E	Record Sequence of the Chaining File		To Filename	Table or Array Name	Number of Entries Per Record	Number of Entries Per Table or Array	Length of Entry	P/B/L/R	Decimal Positions	Sequence (A/D)	Table or Array Name (Alternating Format)	Length of Entry	P/B/L/R	Decimal Positions	Sequence (A/D)	Comments
	Number of the Chaining Field															
Line / Form Type	From Filename															
0 1 E				MARR	1	7	15									
0 2 E																
0 3 E																
0 4 E																
0 5 E																
0 6 E																
0 7 E																
0 8 E																
E																
E																

Figure 6-15   Compile time array definition

The number entered in the Length of Entry area is based on the length of the longest element in the array, element 7 (INVALID TYPE***). Because all elements in an array must be the same length, each element occupies a 15-position area. Those elements that appear to contain shorter entries are still considered to be 15 positions long. For example, element 5 (STATE) will contain the word STATE followed by ten blanks. When you plan compile time arrays, remember to base the length of entry on the longest array element.

The Number of Entries per Record entry specifies how many array elements are contained in each array data record at the end of the program. In addition, this entry tells RPG that a compile time array is being described. The number of elements contained in each array data record is determined by the programmer. In this example, each message (array element) is contained in a separate data record. The first array data record contains the message 'CASH SALE   ', the second contains the message 'CREDIT CARD   ', and so on. Note that each array data record contains 15 characters of data including blanks.

The format used in this example is not a requirement of RPG. It is not necessary to enter each array element in a separate array data record. For example, it would be possible to describe this array as containing two entries per data record by an entry 2 in position 35. If this were done, each array data record would contain two elements, each of which would be 15 characters long. If this format were used, the array data records would contain the following entries:

```
CASH SALE       CREDIT CARD
SCHOOL          MUNICIPALITY
STATE           CORPORATE
INVALID TYPE***
```

As you can see, entering two elements per array data record reduces the number of data records. The number of elements that can be entered in an array data record is limited by the length of each entry and by the maximum length of an RPG entry as permitted on your computer; this maximum length is generally either 80 or 96 characters, depending on the version of RPG being used. This array could be entered in two array data records by specifying that four entries are contained in each array data record.

If multiple elements are contained in each array data record, the first element in each record must start in position 1. In addition, all array data records except the last must contain the same number of elements. RPG permits the last array data record to be short because the number of elements in the array may not be evenly divisible by the number of elements in each record. In the format just shown, the fourth array data record is a **short record** containing only one element.

Describing Multiple Arrays

If two or more compile time arrays are used in a program, each must be described with a separate extension specification. The sequence of the arrays at the end of the source code must be the same as the sequence of the extension specifications. Each of the arrays must be preceded by a ** separator record.

Processing Compile Time Arrays

The source program listing for the array version of the sample program HJG06Y (Figure 6-16) shows that the use of an array has reduced the number of calculation and output specifications needed in the program. The number of specification lines has been reduced from 69 in the original version of program HJG05Y to 58 in program HJG06Y. Although eight lines have been added by the array data records at the end of the program, this could have been reduced to as few as three additional lines by specifying that each data record contain four array elements.

Figure 6-16   Source code list for program HJG06Y

```
    LIBRARY  -  HALSLIB                              Date: 8/02/91  Page:    1
    Member   Suf    Bytes    Date     Time           Time:18:07:02
    --------  ---   ------  --------  -----
    HJG06Y  .S      2825   08/02/91  18:06

    0001 H                                                            HJG06Y
    0002 FSALEFILEIP F 500  50                  DISK
    0003 FSALELISTO  F 132 132       OF         PRINTER
    0004 E                     MARR   1   7 15
    0005 ISALEFILEAA  01
    0006 I                                 1    20BRANCHL3
    0007 I                                 3    40SPRSONL2
    0008 I                                 5    90CUSTMRL1
    0009 I                                10   142AMOUNT
    0010 I                                15   150T          4040
    0011 C    01N40    T       COMP 6                 40
    0012 C    01       CUSTOT  ADD  AMOUNT    CUSTOT 62
    0013 CL1           SPTOT   ADD  CUSTOT    SPTOT  72
    0014 CL2           BRTOT   ADD  SPTOT     BRTOT  82
    0015 CL3           FINTOT  ADD  BRTOT     FINTOT 92
    0016 OSALELISTH  106    1P
    0017 O       OR          OF
    0018 O                                8 'HJG06Y'
    0019 O                               34 'SALES REPORT'
    0020 O                               50 'PAGE'
    0021 O                     PAGE     55
    0022 O       H   2     1P
    0023 O       OR          OF
    0024 O                     UDATE Y  32
    0025 O       H   1     1P
    0026 O       OR          OF
    0027 O                               26 'BRANCH    SALES-   CUSTOM'
    0028 O                               42 'ER       CUSTOMER'
    0029 O                               55 'SALES'
    0030 O       H   2     1P
    0031 O       OR          OF
    0032 O                               26 'NUMBER    PERSON    NUMBE'
    0033 O                               42 'R        CATEGORY'
    0034 O                               55 'AMOUNT'
    0035 O       D   1     01
```

Figure 6-16 (1)

continued

```
LIBRARY -  HALSLIB                                                    Date: 8/02/91   Page:    2
 Member   Suf      Bytes     Date        Time                         Time:18:07:02
--------  ---     ------   --------     -----
HJG06Y   .S         2825  08/02/91   18:06

0036 O                              BRANCHZ      6
0037 O                              SPRSONZ     15
0038 O                              CUSTMRZ     26
0039 O                     40       MARR,7      46
0040 O                    N40       MARR,T      46
0041 O                              AMOUNT3     55
0042 O          T  2       L1
0043 O                              CUSTOT1B    55
0044 O                                          57 '*'
0045 O          T  2       L2
0046 O                                          36 'SALESPERSON'
0047 O                              SPRSONZ     39
0048 O                                          45 'TOTAL'
0049 O                              SPTOT 1B    55
0050 O                                          58 '**'
0051 O          T  3       L3
0052 O                                          44 'BRANCH     TOTAL'
0053 O                              BRANCHZ     38
0054 O                              BRTOT 1B    55
0055 O                                          59 '***'
0056 O          T      06 LR
0057 O                              FINTOT1     55 '$'
0058 O                                          60 '****'
**
CASH SALE
CREDIT CARD
SCHOOL
MUNICIPALITY
STATE
CORPORATE
INVALID TYPE***
```

Figure 6-16 (2)

▸ **Input Specifications** Figure 6-17 shows the Input Specifications form for program HJG06Y. The only change made to the input specifications for the data file is a change to the name assigned to the Customer Category field. The field name has been changed to T, a single character, because this field is used on the output specifications as an index to control array element printing. Note that indicator 40 still is turned on to show that the customer category is either zero or a negative number.

Line	Form Type	Filename or Record Name	Sequence	Record Identifying Indicator	Field Location From	Field Location To	Decimal Positions	RPG Field Name	Control Level (L1–L9)	Field Indicators Plus	Field Indicators Minus	Field Indicators Zero or Blank
01	I	SALEFILE	AA	Ø1								
02	I				1	2	Ø	BRANCH	L3			
03	I				3	4	Ø	SPRSON	L2			
04	I				5	9	Ø	CUSTMR	L1			
05	I				1Ø	14	2	AMOUNT				
06	I				15	15	Ø	T			4Ø	4Ø
07	I											
08	I											

Figure 6-17 Input specifications for program HJG06Y

▸ **Calculation Specifications** On the Calculation Specifications form (Figure 6-18), you can see immediately that the number of calculations has been reduced from 12, in program HJG05Y to 5. The use of an array has permitted us to eliminate the SETOF operations and all but one of the COMP operations. Line 01 compares the Customer Category field (T) against the numeric literal 6. If the customer category is greater than 6, indicator 40 is turned on. Note that this comparison is performed only if indicator 40 was not turned on as a field indicator.

Line	Form Type	Control Level	Indicators	Factor 1	Operation	Factor 2	Result Field Name	Length	Decimal Positions	Resulting Indicators High (1>2)	Low (1<2)	Equal (1=2)	Comments
01	C		01 N40	T	COMP	6				40			
02	C		01	CUSTOT	ADD	AMOUNT	CUSTOT	6	2				
03	C	L1		SPTOT	ADD	CUSTOT	SPTOT	7	2				
04	C	L2		BRTOT	ADD	SPTOT	BRTOT	8	2				
05	C	L3		FINTOT	ADD	BRTOT	FINTOT	9	2				
06	C												
07	C												

Figure 6-18 Calculation specifications for program HJG06Y

As a result of the use of indicator 40 as both a field indicator and as the resulting indicator of the COMP operation, indicator 40 is on if the customer category is either greater than six or less than one. Indicator 40 is off if the customer category contains a valid entry in the range of one through six.

▸ **Output Specifications** Figure 6-19 shows the output specifications for the detail print line. Line 05 uses the literal 7 as an index to print the seventh element of the MARR array if indicator 40 is on. Remember that indicator 40 was turned on to specify that the customer category code is invalid. If the code is invalid, the message INVALID TYPE***, contained in element 7 of the array is printed.

Line	Form Type	Filename or Record Name	Type	Space After	Output Indicators	Field Name or Constant	Edit Codes	End Position in Output Record
01	O		D	1	01			
02	O					BRANCH	Z	6
03	O					SPRSON	Z	15
04	O					CUSTMR	Z	26
05	O				40	MARR,7		46
06	O				N40	MARR,T		46
07	O					AMOUNT	3	55
08	O							
09	O							

Figure 6-19 Detail output specifications for program HJG06Y

Line 06 also prints an element of the MARR array. This element prints if indicator 40 is not on, meaning that the code is valid. The Field Name entry, MARR,T, uses the Customer Category field name (T) as an index. If indicator 40 is not on, the element of MARR identified by the number in field T is printed. If T contains the value 3, the third element, SCHOOL, is printed. If T contains the value 6, the sixth element is printed. The selection of which element to print is controlled by the value in the data field used as an index. A data field used as an index is called a variable index.

▸ **Variable Indexes** A **variable index** is a numeric integer data field used to index an array. Because an index must be a whole number, the field used as a variable index must be described as an integer field, that is, a numeric field with no decimal places. The value in a variable index cannot be either zero or a value higher than the number of elements in the array being indexed. If, when the program executes, the index value is either zero or greater than the highest element number in the array, the program usually terminates because the index is invalid. The possibility of an invalid index must be handled by program code. In program HJG06Y, the index has been tested on the input and calculations specifications to assure that it contains a valid number (1–6).

COMPILER DIRECTIVE STATEMENTS

Throughout this chapter, the program examples have been shown without any comment entries. This has been done to permit you to concentrate on the RPG code. In the examples that follow, comments have been added to program HJG06Y. In addition, several compiler directive statements have been added to control the format of the listing generated during the program compilation. **Compiler directive statements**, like comment lines, are not part of the RPG source program in that they are not translated into object program code. Unlike comment lines, compiler directive statements do have an effect on the compilation process. These statements cause the compiler to perform specific operations that alter the format of the listing generated during the compilation.

The three compiler directive statements used in this example are the /TITLE, /SPACE, and /EJECT statements. All three share several common characteristics:

1. They can be used at any point in the RPG source program.
2. They cause an action to be taken by the compiler at the point in the source code where the compiler directive statement is placed.
3. The compiler directive statement is not printed on the compiler listing.
4. Compiler directive statements begin in position 7 of the specification form.

The source listing of program HJG06Y in Figure 6-20 contains added comments and compiler directive statements. This is not a compiler listing but was generated by the source program entry utility used for this program. The paragraphs that follow refer to lines on this listing.

Figure 6-20   Compiler directive statements

```
        LIBRARY -  HALSLIB                          Date: 8/03/91  Page:   1
        Member  Suf   Bytes    Date    Time         Time:11:08:39
        --------  ---  ------  --------  -----

        HJG06Y  .S    4649  08/03/91  11:08

        0001 H/TITLE HJG06Y -- SALES REPORT -- HAL GOODWIN -        /title
        0002 H                                                      directive      HJG06Y
        0003 F*----------------------------------------------------------------*
        0004 F*  HJG06Y - SALES REPORT - HAL GOODWIN - JULY 25, 1991            *
        0005 F*                                                                 *
        0006 F*  PROGRAM HJG06Y LISTS AND ACCUMULATES THE SALES AMOUNT OF EACH  *
        0007 F*  RECORD READ.  CONTROL BREAK TOTALS ARE PRINTED ON A CHANGE IN  *
        0008 F*  BRANCH NUMBER, SALESPERSON NUMBER, OR CUSTOMER NUMBER.  THE    *
        0009 F*  PROGRAM PRINTS THE CUSTOMER CATEGORY BASED ON A RETRIEVAL FROM *
        0010 F*  THE MARR ARRAY, USING THE CUSTOMER CATEGORY FIELD AS A VARIABLE*
        0011 F*  INDEX.  IF THE INDEX IS INVALID, THE MESSAGE 'INVALID TYPE***' *
        0012 F*  WILL PRINT IN THE CUSTOMER CATEGORY AREA OF THE DETAIL LINE.   *
        0013 F*----------------------------------------------------------------*
        0014 F/SPACE 2
        0015 FSALEFILEIP  F 500  50            DISK
        0016 FSALELISTO   F 132 132     OF     PRINTER
        0017 F/SPACE 2
        0018 F* ID F  C  H  L    FUNCTION OF INDICATORS
        0019 F* 01----------------SALEFILE RECORD IDENTIFICATION
        0020 F*    40 40----------INVALID CUSTOMER CATEGORY CODE
        0021 F*       N40---------VALID CUSTOMER CATEGORY CODE
        0022 F*             L1---CUSTOMER NUMBER CHANGE
        0023 F*             L2---SALESPERSON NUMBER CHANGE
        0024 F*             L3---BRANCH NUMBER CHANGE
```

Figure 6-20 (1)

```
LIBRARY - HALSLIB                              Date: 8/03/91  Page:   2
Member  Suf   Bytes   Date    Time             Time:11:08:39
-------- ---  -----  --------  -----
HJG06Y  .S    4649   08/03/91  11:08

0025 F*           LR---LAST RECORD INDICATOR
0026 F*           OF---OVERFLOW INDICATOR
0027 E            MARR    1   7 15
0028 ISALEFILEAA 01
0029 I                                   1   20BRANCHL3
0030 I                                   3   40SPRSONL2
0031 I                                   5   90CUSTMRL1
0032 I                                  10  142AMOUNT
0033 I                                  15  150T               4040
0034 C   01N40   T      COMP 6                      40
0035 C   01      CUSTOT   ADD AMOUNT   CUSTOT  62
0036 CL1         SPTOT    ADD CUSTOT   SPTOT   72
0037 CL2         BRTOT    ADD SPTOT    BRTOT   82
0038 CL3         FINTOT   ADD BRTOT    FINTOT  92
0039 O/EJECT
0040 O* HEADING LINE ONE
0041 OSALELISTH 106  1P
0042 O      OR         OF
0043 O                             8 'HJG06Y'
0044 O                            34 'SALES REPORT'
0045 O                            50 'PAGE'
0046 O                    PAGE    55
0047 O/SPACE 1
0048 O*  HEADING LINE TWO
0049 O         H   2   1P
0050 O      OR         OF
0051 O                    UDATE Y 32
0052 O/SPACE 1
0053 O*  HEADING LINE THREE
0054 O         H   1   1P
0055 O      OR         OF
0056 O                            26 'BRANCH    SALES-   CUSTOM'
0057 O                            42 'ER      CUSTOMER'
0058 O                            55 'SALES'
0059 O/SPACE 1
0060 O*  HEADING LINE FOUR
0061 O         H   2   1P
0062 O      OR         OF
0063 O                            26 'NUMBER    PERSON    NUMBE'
0064 O                            42 'R      CATEGORY'
0065 O                            55 'AMOUNT'
0066 O/SPACE 3
0067 O*  DETAIL LINE
0068 O         D   1   01
0069 O                    BRANCHZ   6
0070 O                    SPRSONZ  15
0071 O                    CUSTMRZ  26
0072 O              40    MARR,7   46
0073 O             N40    MARR,T   46
0074 O                    AMOUNT3  55
0075 O/SPACE 3
0076 O*  L1 TOTAL LINE
0077 O         T   2   L1
0078 O                    CUSTOT1B 55
0079 O                            57 '*'
0080 O/SPACE 1
0081 O*  L2 TOTAL LINE
0082 O         T   2   L2
0083 O                            36 'SALESPERSON'
0084 O                    SPRSONZ  39
0085 O                            45 'TOTAL'
0086 O                    SPTOT 1B 55
0087 O                            58 '**'
0088 O/SPACE 1
0089 O*  L3 TOTAL LINE
0090 O         T   3   L3
0091 O                            44 'BRANCH    TOTAL'
0092 O                    BRANCHZ  38
0093 O                    BRTOT 1B 55
0094 O                            59 '***'
0095 O/SPACE 1
0096 O*  FINAL TOTAL LINE
0097 O         T      06 LR
0098 O                    FINTOT1  55 '$'
0099 O                            60 '****'
0100 O/SPACE 3
0101 O*  MARR ARRAY DATA RECORDS FOLLOW
**
CASH SALE
CREDIT CARD
```

/EJECT directive

/SPACE directive

Figure 6-20 (2)

continued

```
LIBRARY  -  HALSLIB                                             Date: 8/03/91   Page:    3
Member   Suf     Bytes     Date       Time                      Time:11:08:39
-------- ---    ------   --------   -----
HJGO6Y   .S       4649   08/03/91   11:08

SCHOOL
MUNICIPALITY
STATE
CORPORATE
INVALID TYPE***
```

Figure 6-20 (3)

/TITLE Compiler Directive

The **/TITLE** compiler directive statement causes a title to be printed at the top of each page of the compiler listing. This heading appears at the top of every page of the listing unless another /TITLE statement is used. By using the /TITLE statement, you can provide an easier identification of a compiler listing by showing information such as program name and programmer on every page of the compile listing.

The /TITLE statement causes the listing to advance to a new page and the title to print at the top of that page and every following page. If you need a title on the first page of the compile listing, the /TITLE statement must be placed before the Control (H) specification. Line 0001 of the source listing in Figure 6-20 shows the placement of the /TITLE statement. Line 01 of Figure 6-21 shows an example of the /TITLE statement. Note that the entry /TITLE begins in position 7 and that the title to appear on the compile list begins in position 14. This is standard in all versions of RPG that use this statement. The maximum length of a title depends on the version of RPG you are using. Your instructor or computer center manager can provide this information.

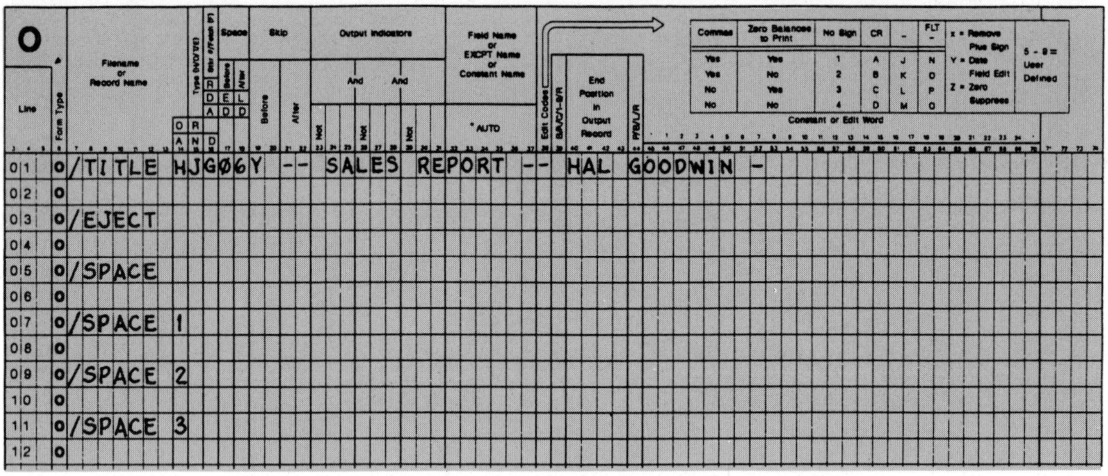

```
01 O/TITLE HJGØ6Y -- SALES REPORT -- HAL GOODWIN -
02 O
03 O/EJECT
04 O
05 O/SPACE
06 O
07 O/SPACE 1
08 O
09 O/SPACE 2
10 O
11 O/SPACE 3
12 O
```

Figure 6-21 Examples of compiler directive statements

/EJECT Compiler Directive

The **/EJECT** compiler directive causes the compiler listing to advance to a new page and print any headings and title normally printed by the compiler. Line 03 of Figure 6-21 shows an example of the /EJECT statement. Note that there is no information following the entry /EJECT. Line 0039 of Figure 6-20 shows an /EJECT statement that is used to cause the output specifications to begin printing on a new page.

/SPACE Compiler Directive

The **/SPACE** compiler directive causes blank lines to be inserted into the compiler listing. You can insert 1, 2, or 3 blank lines by using the /SPACE statement. The entry /SPACE begins in position 7 of the specification form, and the number of blank lines to be inserted is coded in position 14. Lines 05, 07, 09, and 11 of Figure 6-21 show examples of the /SPACE statement. The line 07 entry inserts one blank line, the line 09 entry inserts two, and the line 11 entry inserts three blank lines. Note that the entry on line 05 has no number in position 14. If no number is entered with a /SPACE statement, a single blank line is inserted. Therefore, lines 05 and 07 of Figure 6-21 do the same thing. The source listing in Figure 6-20 shows several examples of the /SPACE statement, the first of which are on lines 0014, 0017, and 0047.

Figure 6-22 shows the compiler listing for program HJG06Y, including comments and compiler directive statements. As you can see, none of the compiler directive statements appear on the listing. Instead, the action directed by the statement has been taken. Note that each page of the compiler listing has a title that shows program identification, program name, and author's name. Also note that the output specifications begin on a new page as the result of the /EJECT statement. /SPACE statements have been used to separate the heading detail and total lines. This could have been done with blank comment lines, but many programmers feel that these compiler directives provide a neater looking compiler listing.

Figure 6-22 Compile listing with compiler directives

```
HJG06Y    08-03-91  11:10:41  HJG06Y -- SALES REPORT -- HAL GOODWIN -Version 3.5  Page  1

          ....+....1....+....2....+....3....+....4....+....5....+....6....+....7....

        3 0002 H                                                                  HJG06Y

       4 0003 F*---------------------------------------------------------------------*
        5 0004 F*  HJG06Y - SALES REPORT - HAL GOODWIN - JULY 25, 1991                 *
        6 0005 F*                                                                     *
        7 0006 F*  PROGRAM HJG06Y LISTS AND ACCUMULATES THE SALES AMOUNT OF EACH       *
        8 0007 F*  RECORD READ.  CONTROL BREAK TOTALS ARE PRINTED ON A CHANGE IN       *
        9 0008 F*  BRANCH NUMBER, SALESPERSON NUMBER, OR CUSTOMER NUMBER.  THE         *
       10 0009 F*  PROGRAM PRINTS THE CUSTOMER CATEGORY BASED ON A RETRIEVAL FROM      *
       11 0010 F*  THE MARR ARRAY, USING THE CUSTOMER CATEGORY FIELD AS A VARIABLE     *
       12 0011 F*  INDEX.  IF THE INDEX IS INVALID, THE MESSAGE 'INVALID TYPE***'      *
       13 0012 F*  WILL PRINT IN THE CUSTOMER CATEGORY AREA OF THE DETAIL LINE.        *
       14 0013 F*---------------------------------------------------------------------*


       17 0015 FSALEFILEIP  F 500  50            DISK
       18 0016 FSALELISTO   F 132 132     OF     PRINTER


       21 0018 F* ID F  C  H  L     FUNCTION OF INDICATORS
       22 0019 F* 01---------------SALEFILE RECORD IDENTIFICATION
       23 0020 F*     40 40---------INVALID CUSTOMER CATEGORY CODE
       24 0021 F*       N40---------VALID CUSTOMER CATEGORY CODE
       25 0022 F*              L1---CUSTOMER NUMBER CHANGE
       26 0023 F*              L2---SALESPERSON NUMBER CHANGE
       27 0024 F*              L3---BRANCH NUMBER CHANGE
       28 0025 F*              LR---LAST RECORD INDICATOR
       29 0026 F*              OF---OVERFLOW INDICATOR



       30 0027 E                   MARR    1   7 15



       31 0028 ISALEFILEAA  01
       32 0029 I                                            1   20BRANCHL3
       33 0030 I                                            3   40SPRSONL2
       34 0031 I                                            5   90CUSTMRL1
       35 0032 I                                           10  142AMOUNT
       36 0033 I                                           15  150T             4040


       37 0034 C    01N40    T         COMP 6                  40
       38 0035 C    01       CUSTOT    ADD  AMOUNT    CUSTOT  62
       39 0036 CL1           SPTOT     ADD  CUSTOT    SPTOT   72
       40 0037 CL2           BRTOT     ADD  SPTOT     BRTOT   82
       41 0038 CL3           FINTOT    ADD  BRTOT     FINTOT  92
```

compile list title

page eject

Figure 6-22 (1) *continued*

```
HJG06Y     08-03-91  11:10:41  HJG06Y -- SALES REPORT -- HAL GOODWIN -Version 3.5  Page  2
           ....+....1....+....2....+....3....+....4....+....5....+....6....+....7....


    44 0040 O*  HEADING LINE ONE
    45 0041 OSALELISTH  106   1P
    46 0042 O     OR          OF
    47 0043 O                                        8 'HJG06Y'
    48 0044 O                                       34 'SALES REPORT'
    49 0045 O                                       50 'PAGE'
    50 0046 O                              PAGE      55

    53 0048 O*  HEADING LINE TWO
    54 0049 O          H  2   1P
    55 0050 O     OR          OF
    56 0051 O                              UDATE Y   32

    59 0053 O*  HEADING LINE THREE
    60 0054 O          H  1   1P
    61 0055 O     OR          OF
    62 0056 O                                       26 'BRANCH   SALES-   CUSTOM'
    63 0057 O                                       42 'ER      CUSTOMER'
    64 0058 O                                       55 'SALES'

    67 0060 O*  HEADING LINE FOUR
    68 0061 O          H  2   1P
    69 0062 O     OR          OF
    70 0063 O                                       26 'NUMBER   PERSON    NUMBE'
    71 0064 O                                       42 'R       CATEGORY'
    72 0065 O                                       55 'AMOUNT'

    75 0067 O*  DETAIL LINE
    76 0068 O          D  1   01
    77 0069 O                              BRANCHZ    6
    78 0070 O                              SPRSONZ   15
    79 0071 O                              CUSTMRZ   26
    80 0072 O                   40         MARR,7    46
    81 0073 O                   N40        MARR,T    46
    82 0074 O                              AMOUNT3   55

    85 0076 O*  L1 TOTAL LINE
    86 0077 O          T  2   L1
    87 0078 O                              CUSTOT1B  55
    88 0079 O                                        57 '*'

    91 0081 O*  L2 TOTAL LINE
    92 0082 O          T  2   L2
    93 0083 O                                        36 'SALESPERSON'
    94 0084 O                              SPRSONZ   39
    95 0085 O                                        45 'TOTAL'
    96 0086 O                              SPTOT 1B  55
    97 0087 O                                        58 '**'

   100 0089 O*  L3 TOTAL LINE
   101 0090 O          T  3   L3
   102 0091 O                                        44 'BRANCH    TOTAL'
   103 0092 O                              BRANCHZ   38
   104 0093 O                              BRTOT 1B  55
   105 0094 O                                        59 '***'

   108 0096 O*  FINAL TOTAL LINE
   109 0097 O          T     06 LR
   110 0098 O                              FINTOT1   55 '$'
   111 0099 O                                        60 '****'
```

space (annotation pointing to line 50 0046)

Figure 6-22 (2)

```
HJG06Y    08-03-91  11:10:41  HJG06Y -- SALES REPORT -- HAL GOODWIN -Version 3.5  Page  3

          ....+....1....+....2....+....3....+....4....+....5....+....6....+....7....

    114 0101 O*  HARR ARRAY DATA RECORDS FOLLOW
    115 **
    116 CASH SALE
    117 CREDIT CARD
    118 SCHOOL
    119 MUNICIPALITY
    120 STATE
    121 CORPORATE
    122 INVALID TYPE***
    123 /*
    124 /*


        THE FOLLOWING INDICATORS APPEARED IN THIS PROGRAM

          01  40  LR  L1  L2  L3  1P  OF
No Warning Errors
No Fatal Errors
```

Figure 6-22 (3)

IN CONCLUSION

This chapter has provided you with several powerful tools for your RPG programmer's tool kit. These tools, however, have limitations. Compile time arrays, for example, can be used efficiently only if the index values begin with 1 and continue consecutively. In Chapter 7, you will learn to use techniques that permit random retrieval of data without the restriction of consecutive indexes.

CHAPTER SUMMARY

1. An **array** is a series of identical data fields defined as a single unit.
2. Each data field within an array is called an **element**.
3. , A **compile time array** is part of the RPG source program.
4. A **preexecution time** or **prerun time** array is loaded with data at the beginning of the program before any input, calculation, or output operations have occurred.
5. An **execution time** or **run time** array is loaded with data during program execution. These arrays usually are loaded with data from input files.
6. The **XFOOT** operation sums up all the elements of a numeric array in a single operation.
7. **Array arithmetic** is performed on an element-by-element basis between arrays.
8. An **index**, or **subscript**, is a number used to identify a specific element within an array.
9. A **compile time array** is coded as part of the RPG source program.
10. **Static data** does not change frequently.
11. **Dynamic data** does change frequently.
12. The data for a compile time array follows the last RPG source specification and is preceded by a record that contains asterisks in positions 1 and 2.
13. All data records for a compile time array must contain the same number of array elements except for the last record, which can be a **short record**.

14. A **variable index** is a numeric integer field containing a number to be used as an array index.
15. A variable index cannot contain the value zero or a value higher than the number of elements in the array being indexed.
16. **Compiler directive statements** cause the RPG compiler to perform an action during program compilation.
17. The **/TITLE** statement causes a title to be printed at the top of each page of an RPG compile listing.
18. The **/EJECT** statement causes the RPG compile listing to advance to a new page.
19. The **/SPACE** statement may be used to insert up to three blank lines in an RPG compile listing.

REVIEW QUESTIONS

1. What is an array?
2. When is data loaded into a compile time array? When is data loaded into an execution time array?
3. Why are compile time arrays generally used only for static data?
4. What entries are needed to define the number of elements in an array and the attributes of the elements.
5. Explain the operation of the XFOOT operation.
6. Explain the operation of the ADD operation when two arrays are added together.
7. What is the function of an array index?
8. What occurs if an array name is specified on the Output Specification form but no index is used?
9. What must be contained in the separator record that appears between the last source program statement and the beginning of a compile time array?
10. What is a variable index?
11. What is a compiler directive statement?

STUDENT EXERCISES: RPG PROGRAM CODE

1. An input record contains the following data fields:

   Positions 1–6   Employee number
   Positions 7–41   Series of seven daily earnings fields. Each field contains 2 decimal places.
   Positions 42–46 Branch number

   Use Figures 6-23 and 6-24 to Code the needed extension and input specifications to describe these records. The Branch Number field is to be used to start a control break. The daily earnings fields are used for arithmetic operations and must be defined and calculated using array techniques. Use appropriate names for all data descriptions.

IBM © Copyright International Business Machines Corporation 1964, 1969
IBM is a registered trademark of International Business Machines Corporation, Armonk, NY

RPG EXTENSION AND LINE COUNTER SPECIFICATIONS
(SEE OVER FOR RPG INPUT SPECIFICATIONS)

GX09-1033-02 UM/050 *
Printed in U.S.A.

Program | Keying Instruction | Graphic | Key | Card Electro Number
Programmer | Date
Page 1 2 of ___ Program Identification 75 76 77 78 79 80

Extension Specifications

E | Line | Form Type | Record Sequence of the Chaining File | Number of the Chaining Field | From Filename | To Filename | Table or Array Name | Number of Entries Per Record | Number of Entries Per Table or Array | Length of Entry | P/B/L/R | Decimal Positions | Sequence (A/D) | Table or Array Name (Alternating Format) | Length of Entry | P/B/L/R | Decimal Positions | Sequence (A/D) | Comments

01 E
02 E
03 E
04 E
05 E
06 E
07 E
08 E
E
E

Line Counter Specifications

L | Line | Form Type | Filename | 1 Line Number | FL or Channel Number | 2 Line Number | OL or Channel Number | 3 Line Number | Channel Number | 4 Line Number | Channel Number | 5 Line Number | Channel Number | 6 Line Number | Channel Number | 7 Line Number | Channel Number | 8 Line Number | Channel Number | 9 Line Number | Channel Number | 10 Line Number | Channel Number | 11 Line Number | Channel Number | 12 Line Number | Channel Number

01 L
02 L
L

* Number of sheets per pad may vary slightly.

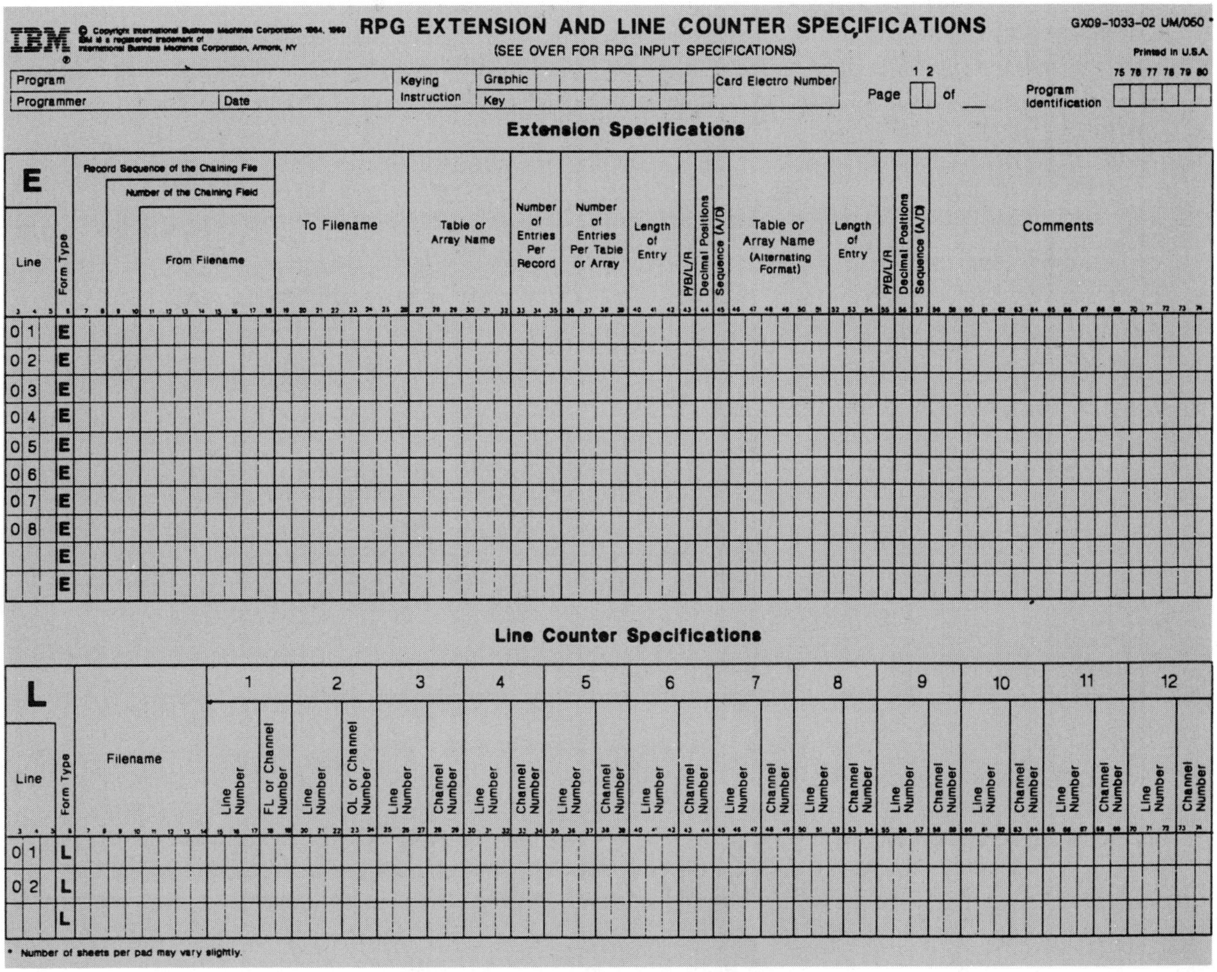

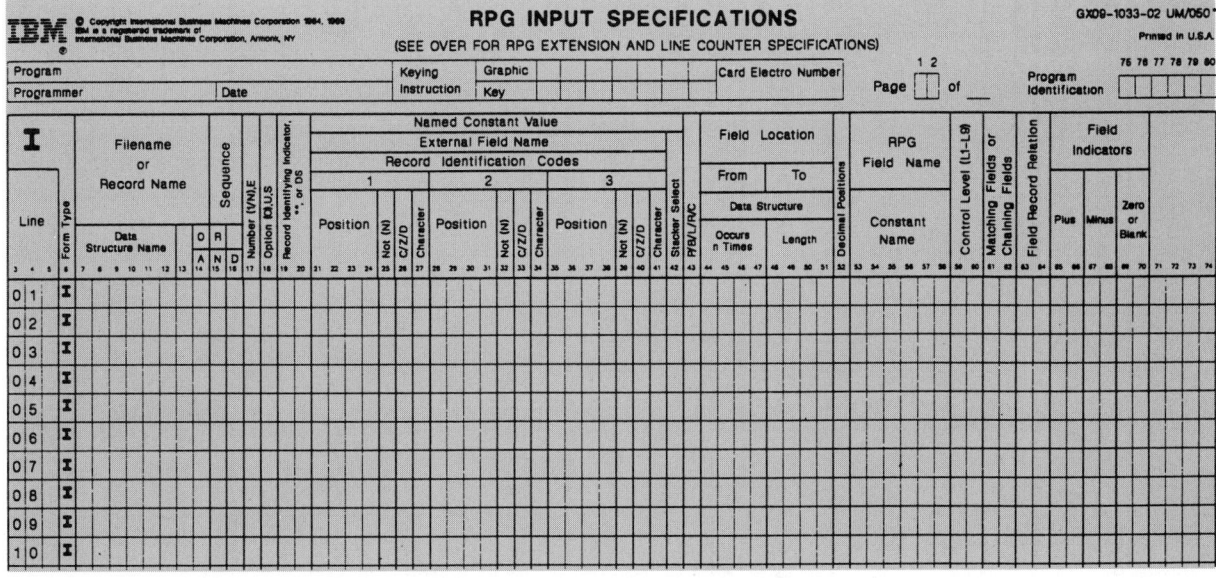

Figure 6-23 Extension Specifications form

IBM © Copyright International Business Machines Corporation 1964, 1969
IBM is a registered trademark of International Business Machines Corporation, Armonk, NY

RPG INPUT SPECIFICATIONS
(SEE OVER FOR RPG EXTENSION AND LINE COUNTER SPECIFICATIONS)

GX09-1033-02 UM/050 *
Printed in U.S.A.

Program | Keying Instruction | Graphic | Key | Card Electro Number
Programmer | Date
Page 1 2 of ___ Program Identification 75 76 77 78 79 80

I | Line | Form Type | Filename or Record Name | Data Structure Name | Sequence | O R | A N D | Number (1/N),E | Option (O),U,S | Record Identifying Indicator, **, or DS | Named Constant Value | External Field Name | Record Identification Codes 1: Position, Not (N), C/Z/D, Character | 2: Position, Not (N), C/Z/D, Character | 3: Position, Not (N), C/Z/D, Character | Stacker Select | P/B/L/R/C | Field Location: From, To | Data Structure: Occurs n Times, Length | Decimal Positions | RPG Field Name | Constant Name | Control Level (L1-L9) | Matching Fields or Chaining Fields | Field Record Relation | Field Indicators: Plus, Minus, Zero or Blank

01 I
02 I
03 I
04 I
05 I
06 I
07 I
08 I
09 I
10 I

Figure 6-24 Input Specifications form

2. Using Figure 6-25 and the specifications coded in Exercise 1, write the calculations necessary to compute a weekly earnings amount for each employee. In addition, calculate daily earnings totals for each branch. The total number of employees in all branches is to be accumulated.

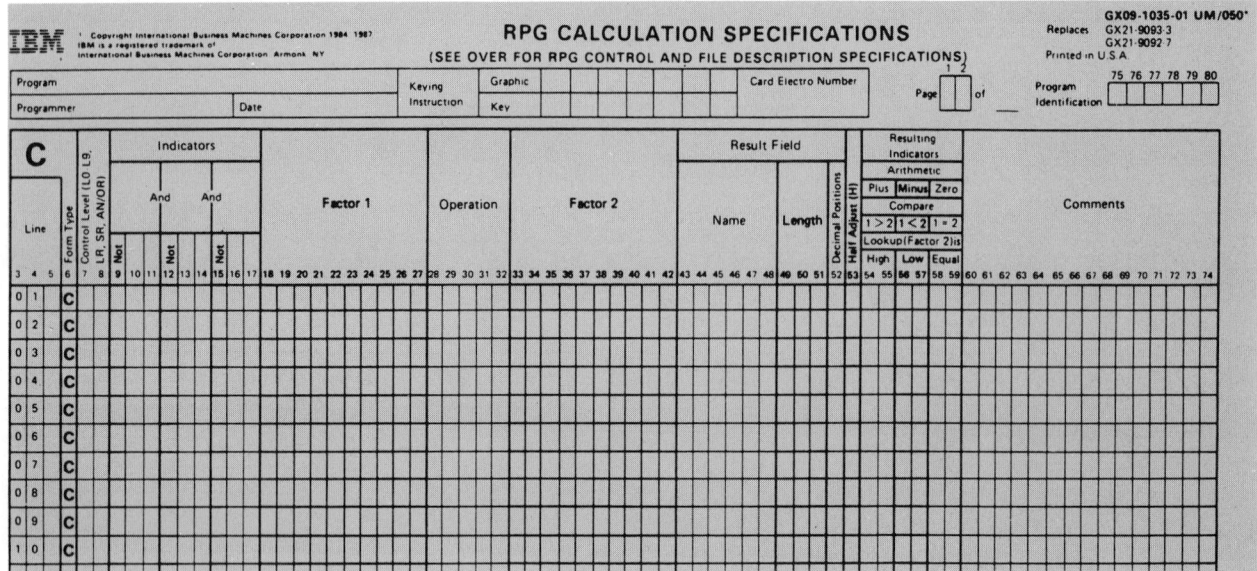

Figure 6-25 Calculation Specifications form

3. Using Figure 6-26 and the specifications coded in Exercises 1 and 2, code the output specifications needed to print the detail, control break, and final total lines for a printed file named EARNREPT. The detail line is to contain all input data plus the weekly earnings for the employee. The control break line is to contain totals of the seven daily earnings fields and the weekly earnings amounts. The final total line is to contain the employee count.

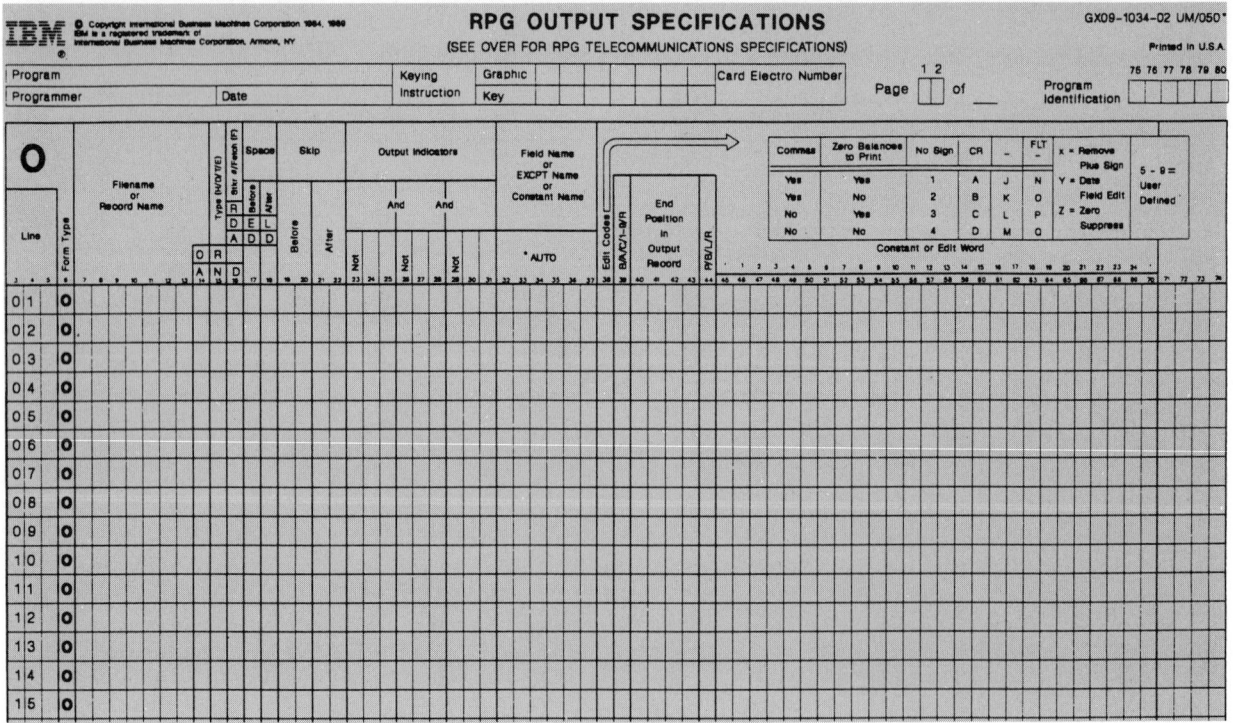

Figure 6-26 Output Specifications form

STUDENT EXERCISES: DEBUGGING RPG PROGRAMS

Problem 1

The following RPG program (Figure 6-27) contains one or more errors detected by the compiler. Circle each error and record the corrected entry directly on the listing. Explain the error and the method of correction.

Figure 6-27   Debugging Problem 1

```
Lattice RPG II Compiler Version 2.01              13:21:39  07/20/1991
Compile listing for source RPG program [HJG06X  .RPG]       PAGE : 0001


    1    H                                              HJG06X

    2    F*------------------------------------------------*
    3 S  F*  HJG06X - SALES SUMMARY REPORT - HAL GOODWIN - JULY 14, 1991  *
    4 S  F*                                                               *
    5 S  F*  PROGRAM HJG06X LISTS MONTHLY SALES FOR EACH ITEM.  THE SIX   *
    6 S  F*  MONTHLY SALES FIELDS ARE ADDED TO ACCUMULATE TOTAL SALES.    *
    7 S  F*  WHEN STORE NUMBER CHANGES, TOTALS OF THE SEVEN SALES FIELDS WILL*
    8 S  F*  PRINT.  IN ADDITION, A FINAL TOTAL OF THE TOTAL SALES FIELD  *
    9 S  F*  WILL BE PRINTED.                                             *
   10 S  F*------------------------------------------------*
   11 S  FSALFILE IP  F 360  60         DISK
   12 S  FSALREPT O   F 132 132    OF   PRINTER
   13 S  F* ID F  C  H  L    FUNCTION OF INDICATORS
   14 S  F* 01-----------SALFILE RECORD IDENTIFICATION
   15 S  F*          1P---FIRST PAGE INDICATOR
   16 S  F*          OF---OVERFLOW INDICATOR
   17 S  F*          L1---CONTROL BREAK - STORE NUMBER CHANGE
   18 S  F*          LR---END OF JOB

   19    E             MSAL    6 4
   20 S  E             TSAL    6 6

   21    I*------------------------------------------------*
   22 S  I*  SALFILE INPUT RECORD DESCRIPTION                *
   23 S  I*------------------------------------------------*
   24 S  ISALFILE AA  01
   25 S  I                            1   40STORE L1
   26 S  I                           11  30 DESC
   27 S  I                           31  54 MSAL

   28    C*  ACCUMULATE TOTAL SALES FOR EACH RECORD
   29 S  C   01        XFOOTMSAL     TOTSAL  50
T207 Field type, alphameric or numeric, invalid for operation specified.
   30 S  C*
   31 S  C*  ACCUMULATE CONTROL BREAK TOTALS
   32 S  C   01   TSAL     ADD MSAL     TSAL
T207 Field type, alphameric or numeric, invalid for operation specified.
T207 Field type, alphameric or numeric, invalid for operation specified.
T207 Field type, alphameric or numeric, invalid for operation specified.
   33 S  C   01   SALTOT   ADD TOTSAL   SALTOT  70
   34 S  C*
   35 S  C*  ACCUMULATE FINAL TOTAL SALES
   36 S  CL1        SALFIN   ADD SALTOT   SALFIN  80

   37    O*------------------------------------------------*
   38 S  O*  HEADING LINE ONE                              *
   39 S  O*------------------------------------------------*
   40 S  OSALREPT H 106   1P
   41 S  O      OR      OF
   42 S  O                         9 'HJG06X'
   43 S  O               UDATE Y  19
   44 S  O                        60 'SALES SUMMARY REPORT'
   45 S  O                        91 'PAGE'
   46 S  O               PAGE Z  96
```

Figure 6-27 (1)

continued

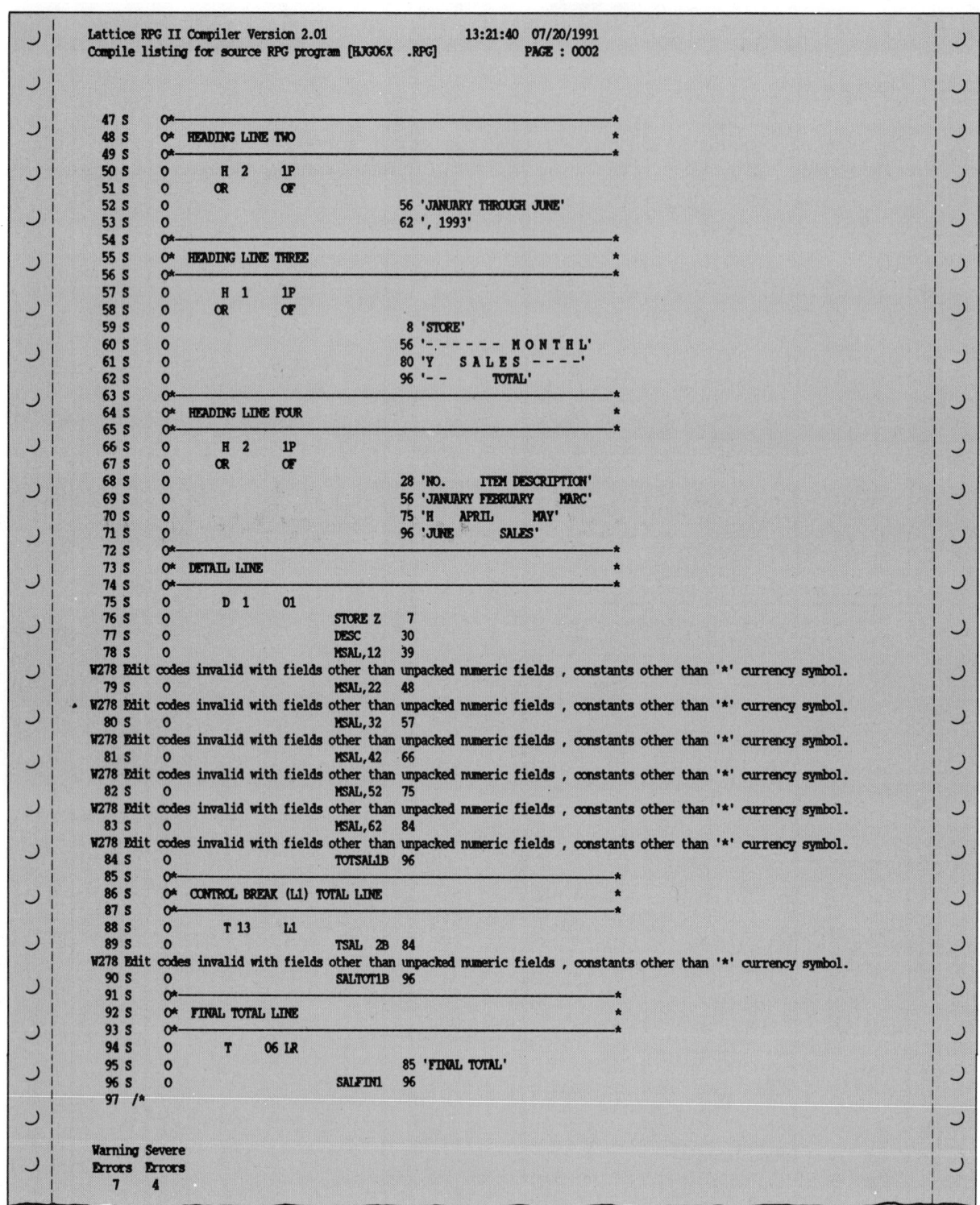

```
Lattice RPG II Compiler Version 2.01                    13:21:40  07/20/1991
Compile listing for source RPG program [HJGO6X  .RPG]          PAGE : 0002


   47 S   O*----------------------------------------------------------------*
   48 S   O* HEADING LINE TWO                                                *
   49 S   O*----------------------------------------------------------------*
   50 S   O      H  2    1P
   51 S   O      OR      OF
   52 S   O                                 56 'JANUARY THROUGH JUNE'
   53 S   O                                 62 ', 1993'
   54 S   O*----------------------------------------------------------------*
   55 S   O* HEADING LINE THREE                                              *
   56 S   O*----------------------------------------------------------------*
   57 S   O      H  1    1P
   58 S   O      OR      OF
   59 S   O                                  8 'STORE'
   60 S   O                                 56 '-.- - - - -  M O N T H L'
   61 S   O                                 80 'Y  S A L E S - - - -'
   62 S   O                                 96 '- -       TOTAL'
   63 S   O*----------------------------------------------------------------*
   64 S   O* HEADING LINE FOUR                                               *
   65 S   O*----------------------------------------------------------------*
   66 S   O      H  2    1P
   67 S   O      OR      OF
   68 S   O                                 28 'NO.    ITEM DESCRIPTION'
   69 S   O                                 56 'JANUARY FEBRUARY    MARC'
   70 S   O                                 75 'H    APRIL       MAY'
   71 S   O                                 96 'JUNE       SALES'
   72 S   O*----------------------------------------------------------------*
   73 S   O* DETAIL LINE                                                     *
   74 S   O*----------------------------------------------------------------*
   75 S   O      D  1    01
   76 S   O                    STORE Z    7
   77 S   O                    DESC       30
   78 S   O                    MSAL,12    39
W278 Edit codes invalid with fields other than unpacked numeric fields , constants other than '*' currency symbol.
   79 S   O                    MSAL,22    48
W278 Edit codes invalid with fields other than unpacked numeric fields , constants other than '*' currency symbol.
   80 S   O                    MSAL,32    57
W278 Edit codes invalid with fields other than unpacked numeric fields , constants other than '*' currency symbol.
   81 S   O                    MSAL,42    66
W278 Edit codes invalid with fields other than unpacked numeric fields , constants other than '*' currency symbol.
   82 S   O                    MSAL,52    75
W278 Edit codes invalid with fields other than unpacked numeric fields , constants other than '*' currency symbol.
   83 S   O                    MSAL,62    84
W278 Edit codes invalid with fields other than unpacked numeric fields , constants other than '*' currency symbol.
   84 S   O                    TOTSAL1B   96
   85 S   O*----------------------------------------------------------------*
   86 S   O* CONTROL BREAK (L1) TOTAL LINE                                   *
   87 S   O*----------------------------------------------------------------*
   88 S   O      T 13    L1
   89 S   O                    TSAL 2B    84
W278 Edit codes invalid with fields other than unpacked numeric fields , constants other than '*' currency symbol.
   90 S   O                    SALTOT1B   96
   91 S   O*----------------------------------------------------------------*
   92 S   O* FINAL TOTAL LINE                                                *
   93 S   O*----------------------------------------------------------------*
   94 S   O      T  06   LR
   95 S   O                                 85 'FINAL TOTAL'
   96 S   O                    SALFIN1     96
   97 /*


Warning Severe
Errors  Errors
   7       4
```

Figure 6-27 (2)

≡ Problem 2

The following RPG program (Figure 6-28) contains one or more errors detected by the compiler. Circle each error and record the corrected entry directly on the listing. Explain the error and the method of correction.

Figure 6-28   Debugging Problem 2

```
HJG06Y    08-12-91  14:44:09  HJG06Y -- SALES REPORT -- HAL GOODWIN -Version 3.5  Page  1

          ....+....1....+....2....+....3....+....4....+....5....+....6....+....7....

     3 0002 H                                                                  HJG06Y


     4 0003 F*------------------------------------------------------------------*
     5 0004 F*  HJG06Y - SALES REPORT - HAL GOODWIN - JULY 25, 1991             *
     6 0005 F*                                                                  *
     7 0006 F*  PROGRAM HJG06Y LISTS AND ACCUMULATES THE SALES AMOUNT OF EACH   *
     8 0007 F*  RECORD READ.  CONTROL BREAK TOTALS ARE PRINTED ON A CHANGE IN   *
     9 0008 F*  BRANCH NUMBER, SALESPERSON NUMBER, OR CUSTOMER NUMBER.  THE     *
    10 0009 F*  PROGRAM PRINTS THE CUSTOMER CATEGORY BASED ON A RETRIEVAL FROM  *
    11 0010 F*  THE MARR ARRAY, USING THE CUSTOMER CATEGORY FIELD AS A VARIABLE *
    12 0011 F*  INDEX.  IF THE INDEX IS INVALID, THE MESSAGE 'INVALID TYPE***'  *
    13 0012 F*  WILL PRINT IN THE CUSTOMER CATEGORY AREA OF THE DETAIL LINE.    *
    14 0013 F*------------------------------------------------------------------*


    17 0015 FSALEFILEIP  F 500  50          DISK
    18 0016 FSALELISTO   F 132 132      OF  PRINTER


    21 0018 F* ID F  C  H  L    FUNCTION OF INDICATORS
    22 0019 F*  01---------------SALEFILE RECORD IDENTIFICATION
    23 0020 F*     40 40---------INVALID CUSTOMER CATEGORY CODE
    24 0021 F*        N40--------VALID CUSTOMER CATEGORY CODE
    25 0022 F*              L1---CUSTOMER NUMBER CHANGE
    26 0023 F*              L2---SALESPERSON NUMBER CHANGE
    27 0024 F*              L3---BRANCH NUMBER CHANGE
    28 0025 F*              LR---LAST RECORD INDICATOR
    29 0026 F*              OF---OVERFLOW INDICATOR


    30 0027 ISALEFILEAA  01
    31 0028 I                               1   20BRANCHL3
    32 0029 I                               3   40SPRSONL2
    33 0030 I                               5   90CUSTMRL1
    34 0031 I                              10  142AMOUNT
    35 0032 I                              15  150T          4040


    36 0033 C    01N40   T        COMP 6                    40
    37 0034 C    01      CUSTOT   ADD  AMOUNT  CUSTOT  62
    38 0035 CL1          SPTOT    ADD  CUSTOT  SPTOT   72
    39 0036 CL2          BRTOT    ADD  SPTOT   BRTOT   82
    40 0037 CL3          FINTOT   ADD  BRTOT   FINTOT  92
    43 0039 O* HEADING LINE ONE
    44 0040 OSALELISTH  106   1P
    45 0041 O      OR        OF
    46 0042 O                               8 'HJG06Y'
    47 0043 O                              34 'SALES REPORT'
    48 0044 O                              50 'PAGE'
    49 0045 O                     PAGE     55

    52 0047 O* HEADING LINE TWO
    53 0048 O      H  2      1P
    54 0049 O      OR        OF
    55 0050 O                     UDATE Y  32

    58 0052 O* HEADING LINE THREE
    59 0053 O      H  1      1P
    60 0054 O      OR        OF
```

Figure 6-28 (1)   *continued*

```
HJG06Y    08-12-91  14:44:09  HJG06Y -- SALES REPORT -- HAL GOODWIN -Version 3.5  Page  2
          ....+....1....+....2....+....3....+....4....+....5....+....6....+....7....

        61 0055 O                                    26 'BRANCH    SALES-  CUSTOM'
        62 0056 O                                    42 'ER      CUSTOMER'
        63 0057 O                                    55 'SALES'

        66 0059 O*  HEADING LINE FOUR
        67 0060 O           H  2    1P
        68 0061 O           OR       OF
        69 0062 O                                    26 'NUMBER    PERSON    NUMBE'
        70 0063 O                                    42 'R      CATEGORY'
        71 0064 O                                    55 'AMOUNT'


        74 0066 O*  DETAIL LINE
        75 0067 O           D  1    01
        76 0068 O                           BRANCHZ    6
        77 0069 O                           SPRSONZ   15
        78 0070 O                           CUSTMRZ   26
        79 0071 O                 40        MARR,7    46
****-0106- Field Name has not been defined.
****-0137- Field Name is indexed but is not defined as an array.
        80 0072 O                N40        MARR,T    46
****-0106- Field Name has not been defined.
****-0137- Field Name is indexed but is not defined as an array.
        81 0073 O                           AMOUNT3   55


        84 0075 O*  L1 TOTAL LINE
        85 0076 O           T  2    L1
        86 0077 O                           CUSTOT1B  55
        87 0078 O                                     57 '*'

        90 0080 O*  L2 TOTAL LINE
        91 0081 O           T  2    L2
        92 0082 O                                     36 'SALESPERSON'
        93 0083 O                           SPRSONZ   39
        94 0084 O                                     45 'TOTAL'
        95 0085 O                           SPTOT 1B  55
        96 0086 O                                     58 '**'

        99 0088 O*  L3 TOTAL LINE
       100 0089 O           T  3    L3
       101 0090 O                                     44 'BRANCH     TOTAL'
       102 0091 O                           BRANCHZ   38
       103 0092 O                           BRTOT 1B  55
       104 0093 O                                     59 '***'


       107 0095 O*  FINAL TOTAL LINE
       108 0096 O           T    06 LR
       109 0097 O                           FINTOT1   55 '$'
       110 0098 O                                     60 '****'



       113 0100 O*  MARR ARRAY DATA RECORDS FOLLOW
       114 **
****-A002W-End of source file expected at this point.
       115 CASH SALE
       116 CREDIT CARD
       117 SCHOOL
       118 MUNICIPALITY
       119 STATE
       120 CORPORATE
       121 INVALID TYPE***
       122 /*



           THE FOLLOWING INDICATORS APPEARED IN THIS PROGRAM

            01  40  LR  L1  L2  L3  1P  OF
       1 Warning Errors
       4 Fatal Errors
```

Figure 6-28 (2)

Problem 3

The following RPG program (Figure 6-29) contains one or more errors detected while checking output from the program. Circle each error and record the corrected entry directly on the listing. Explain the error and the method of correction.

Figure 6-29   Debugging Problem 3

```
HJG06Y    08-12-91  16:01:22  HJG06Y -- SALES REPORT -- HAL GOODWIN -Version 3.5  Page  1

          ....+....1....+....2....+....3....+....4....+....5....+....6....+....7....

    3 0002 H                                                                    HJG06Y


    4 0003 F*------------------------------------------------------------------*
    5 0004 F*  HJG06Y - SALES REPORT - HAL GOODWIN - JULY 25, 1991             *
    6 0005 F*                                                                  *
    7 0006 F*  PROGRAM HJG06Y LISTS AND ACCUMULATES THE SALES AMOUNT OF EACH   *
    8 0007 F*  RECORD READ.  CONTROL BREAK TOTALS ARE PRINTED ON A CHANGE IN   *
    9 0008 F*  BRANCH NUMBER, SALESPERSON NUMBER, OR CUSTOMER NUMBER.  THE     *
   10 0009 F*  PROGRAM PRINTS THE CUSTOMER CATEGORY BASED ON A RETRIEVAL FROM  *
   11 0010 F*  THE MARR ARRAY, USING THE CUSTOMER CATEGORY FIELD AS A VARIABLE *
   12 0011 F*  INDEX.  IF THE INDEX IS INVALID, THE MESSAGE 'INVALID TYPE***'  *
   13 0012 F*  WILL PRINT IN THE CUSTOMER CATEGORY AREA OF THE DETAIL LINE.    *
   14 0013 F*------------------------------------------------------------------*


   17 0015 FSALEFILEIP  F 500  50           DISK
   18 0016 FSALELISTO   F 132 132     OF    PRINTER


   21 0018 F* ID F  C  H  L    FUNCTION OF INDICATORS
   22 0019 F* 01--------------SALEFILE RECORD IDENTIFICATION
   23 0020 F*     40 40--------INVALID CUSTOMER CATEGORY CODE
   24 0021 F*     N40---------VALID CUSTOMER CATEGORY CODE
   25 0022 F*              L1---CUSTOMER NUMBER CHANGE
   26 0023 F*              L2---SALESPERSON NUMBER CHANGE
   27 0024 F*              L3---BRANCH NUMBER CHANGE
   28 0025 F*              LR---LAST RECORD INDICATOR
   29 0026 F*              OF---OVERFLOW INDICATOR


   30 0027 E              MARR   1   7 15


   31 0028 ISALEFILEAA  01
   32 0029 I                                1   20BRANCHL1
   33 0030 I                                3   40SPRSONL2
   34 0031 I                                5   90CUSTMRL3
   35 0032 I                               10  142AMOUNT
   36 0033 I                               15  150T          4040


   37 0034 C  01N40    T        COMP 6                  40
   38 0035 C  01       CUSTOT   ADD  AMOUNT   CUSTOT 62
   39 0036 CL1         SPTOT    ADD  CUSTOT   SPTOT  72
   40 0037 CL2         BRTOT    ADD  SPTOT    BRTOT  82
   41 0038 CL3         FINTOT   ADD  BRTOT    FINTOT 92
   44 0040 O*  HEADING LINE ONE
   45 0041 OSALELISTH  106   1P
   46 0042 O       OR        OF
   47 0043 O                              8 'HJG06Y'
   48 0044 O                             34 'SALES REPORT'
   49 0045 O                             50 'PAGE'
   50 0046 O                 PAGE        55

   53 0048 O*  HEADING LINE TWO
   54 0049 O       H   2   1P
   55 0050 O       OR        OF
   56 0051 O                 UDATE Y    32

   59 0053 O*  HEADING LINE THREE
   60 0054 O       H   1   1P
   61 0055 O       OR        OF
```

Figure 6-29 (1)

continued

```
HJG06Y   08-12-91  16:01:22  HJG06Y -- SALES REPORT -- HAL GOODWIN -Version 3.5  Page  2
         ....+....1....+....2....+....3....+....4....+....5....+....6....+....7....

        62 0056 O                                    26 'BRANCH   SALES-   CUSTOM'
        63 0057 O                                    42 'ER       CUSTOMER'
        64 0058 O                                    55 'SALES'

        67 0060 O*  HEADING LINE FOUR
        68 0061 O            H  2     1P
        69 0062 O            OR       OF
        70 0063 O                                    26 'NUMBER   PERSON   NUMBE'
        71 0064 O                                    42 'R        CATEGORY'
        72 0065 O                                    55 'AMOUNT'

        75 0067 O*  DETAIL LINE
        76 0068 O            D  1     01
        77 0069 O                         BRANCHZ    6
        78 0070 O                         SPRSONZ   15
        79 0071 O                         CUSTMRZ   26
        80 0072 O                40       MARR,7    46
        81 0073 O               N40       MARR,T    46
        82 0074 O                         AMOUNT3   55

        85 0076 O*  L1 TOTAL LINE
        86 0077 O            T  2     L1
        87 0078 O                         CUSTOT1B  55
        88 0079 O                                   57 '*'

        91 0081 O*  L2 TOTAL LINE
        92 0082 O            T  2     L2
        93 0083 O                                   36 'SALESPERSON'
        94 0084 O                         SPRSONZ   39
        95 0085 O                                   45 'TOTAL'
        96 0086 O                         SPTOT 1B  55
        97 0087 O                                   58 '**'

       100 0089 O*  L3 TOTAL LINE
       101 0090 O            T  3     L3
       102 0091 O                                   44 'BRANCH      TOTAL'
       103 0092 O                         BRANCHZ   38
       104 0093 O                         BRTOT 1B  55
       105 0094 O                                   59 '***'

       108 0096 O*  FINAL TOTAL LINE
       109 0097 O            T     06 LR
       110 0098 O                         FINTOT1   55 '$'
       111 0099 O                                   60 '****'

       114 0101 O*  MARR ARRAY DATA RECORDS FOLLOW
       115 **
       116 CASH SALE
       117 CREDIT CARD
       118 SCHOOL
       119 MUNICIPALITY
       120 STATE
       121 CORPORATE
       122 INVALID TYPE***
       123 /*
       124 /*


              THE FOLLOWING INDICATORS APPEARED IN THIS PROGRAM

              01  40  LR  L1  L2  L3  1P  OF
      No Warning Errors
      No Fatal Errors
```

Figure 6-29 (2)

```
· HJG06Y              SALES REPORT          PAGE   1
                        8/12/91

  BRANCH    SALES-    CUSTOMER     CUSTOMER        SALES
  NUMBER    PERSON    NUMBER       CATEGORY        AMOUNT
   15        21       6432       CASH SALE          5.00
   15        21       6432       CASH SALE         10.00
   15        21       6432       CASH SALE         30.00
                                                   45.00 *

                          SALESPERSON 21 TOTAL     45.00 **

                             BRANCH 15 TOTAL       45.00 ***


   15        21       7263       CREDIT CARD        20.00
   15        21       7263       INVALID TYPE***    10.00
                                                    30.00 *

                          SALESPERSON 21 TOTAL      30.00 **

                             BRANCH 15 TOTAL        30.00 ***


   15        21      11897       INVALID TYPE***   500.00
                                                   500.00 *

                          SALESPERSON 21 TOTAL     500.00 **

   15        79      11897       SCHOOL            100.00
   15        79      11897       SCHOOL             60.00
                                                   160.00 *

                          SALESPERSON 79 TOTAL     160.00 **

                             BRANCH 15 TOTAL       660.00 ***


   15        79       7163       SCHOOL              5.00
                                                     5.00 *

                          SALESPERSON 79 TOTAL       5.00 **

   39        12       7163       MUNICIPALITY        7.50
   39        12       7163       MUNICIPALITY       90.00
                                                    97.50 *

                          SALESPERSON 12 TOTAL      97.50 **

                             BRANCH 39 TOTAL       102.50 ***


   39        12      11899       STATE             200.00
                                                   200.00 *

                          SALESPERSON 12 TOTAL     200.00 **

                             BRANCH 39 TOTAL       200.00 ***

   39        54      11147       CORPORATE         150.00
                                                   150.00 *

                          SALESPERSON 54 TOTAL     150.00 **

                             BRANCH 39 TOTAL       150.00 ***


   39        54       6432       CORPORATE         175.00
                                                   175.00 *

                          SALESPERSON 54 TOTAL     175.00 **

                             BRANCH 39 TOTAL       175.00 ***


                                              $1,362.50 ****
```

incorrect total lines are printing on L2 and L3 control breaks

Figure 6-29 (3)

Problem 4

Problem 4 (Figure 6-30) is an exercise in program maintenance. Modify program HJG06Y to permit the use of three additional customer category codes:

Code 7   Nonbillable
Code 8   Credit memo
Code 9   Company use

Indicate on Figure 6-30 how you would modify the program to add these three categories.

Figure 6-30   Debugging Problem 4

```
HJG06Y    08-02-91  17:32:19         IBM PC        RPG II          Version 3.5  Page  1
          ....+....1....+....2....+....3....+....4....+....5....+....6....+....7...

 1 0001 H                                                                          HJG06Y


 2 0002 FSALEFILEIP  F 500  50          DISK
 3 0003 FSALELISTO   F 132 132     OF   PRINTER


 4 0004 E                     MARR    1   7 15


 5 0005 ISALEFILEAA  01
 6 0006 I                                         1   20BRANCHL3
 7 0007 I                                         3   40SPRSONL2
 8 0008 I                                         5   90CUSTMRL1
 9 0009 I                                        10  142AMOUNT
10 0010 I                                        15  150T                4040


11 0011 C     01N40   T          COMP 6                      40
12 0012 C     01      CUSTOT     ADD  AMOUNT    CUSTOT  62
13 0013 CL1           SPTOT      ADD  CUSTOT    SPTOT   72
14 0014 CL2           BRTOT      ADD  SPTOT     BRTOT   82
15 0015 CL3           FINTOT     ADD  BRTOT     FINTOT  92


16 0016 OSALELISTH  106   1P
17 0017 O        OR       OF
18 0018 O                                      8 'HJG06Y'
19 0019 O                                     34 'SALES REPORT'
20 0020 O                                     50 'PAGE'
21 0021 O                            PAGE     55
22 0022 O        H  2   1P
23 0023 O        OR       OF
24 0024 O                            UDATE Y  32
25 0025 O        H  1   1P
26 0026 O        OR       OF
27 0027 O                                     26 'BRANCH    SALES-   CUSTOM'
28 0028 O                                     42 'ER       CUSTOMER'
29 0029 O                                     55 'SALES'
30 0030 O        H  2   1P
31 0031 O        OR       OF
32 0032 O                                     26 'NUMBER    PERSON    NUMBE'
33 0033 O                                     42 'R        CATEGORY'
34 0034 O                                     55 'AMOUNT'
35 0035 O        D  1   01
36 0036 O                            BRANCHZ   6
37 0037 O                            SPRSONZ  15
38 0038 O                            CUSTMRZ  26
```

Figure 6-30 (1)

```
HJG06Y    08-02-91  17:32:19       IBM PC        RPG II        Version 3.5  Page  2

          ....+....1....+....2....+....3....+....4....+....5....+....6....+....7....
    39 0039 O                     40          MARR,7      46
    40 0040 O                     N40         MARR,T      46
    41 0041 O                                 AMOUNT3     55
    42 0042 O        T    2    L1
    43 0043 O                                 CUSTOT1B    55
    44 0044 O                                             57 '*'
    45 0045 O        T    2    L2
    46 0046 O                                             36 'SALESPERSON'
    47 0047 O                                 SPRSONZ     39
    48 0048 O                                             45 'TOTAL'
    49 0049 O                                 SPTOT 1B    55
    50 0050 O                                             58 '**'
    51 0051 O        T    3    L3
    52 0052 O                                             44 'BRANCH    TOTAL'
    53 0053 O                                 BRANCHZ     38
    54 0054 O                                 BRTOT 1B    55
    55 0055 O                                             59 '***'
    56 0056 O        T       06 LR
    57 0057 O                                 FINTOT1     55 '$'
    58 0058 O                                             60 '****'
    59 **
    60 CASH SALE
    61 CREDIT CARD
    62 SCHOOL
    63 MUNICIPALITY
    64 STATE
    65 CORPORATE
    66 INVALID TYPE***
    67 /*
    68 /*


          THE FOLLOWING INDICATORS APPEARED IN THIS PROGRAM

          01  40  LR  L1  L2  L3  1P  OF
 No Warning Errors
 No Fatal Errors
```

Figure 6-30 (2)

STUDENT EXERCISES: PROGRAMMING IN RPG

PROGRAMMING ASSIGNMENT 1
STATION SALES SUMMARY

INSTRUCTIONS

Plan, code, enter, and test an RPG program to produce the Station Sales Summary Report.

INPUT

The format of the Work Order File is shown in Figure 6-31 on the next page. Use test data set 11 for this problem. The six amount fields in the input record must be described and processed using array techniques.

WORK ORDER FILE						
Record Length 41						
Field No.	Field Name	Field Description	Field Position	Field Length	Dec. Pos.	Data Class
1	STATN	Station ID No.	1–4	4	0	N
2	WRKORD	Work Order	5–11	7		A
3	GAS	Gasoline Amount	12–16	5	2	N
4	OIL	Oil Amount	17–21	5	2	N
5	PARTS	Parts Amount	22–26	5	2	N
6	LABOR	Labor Amount	27–31	5	2	N
7	TOW	Towing Amount	32–36	5	2	N
8	ACCESS	Accessory Amount	37–41	5	2	N

Figure 6-31   Work Order File

OUTPUT

Output is the Station Sales Summary report, the format of which is shown in Figure 6-32.

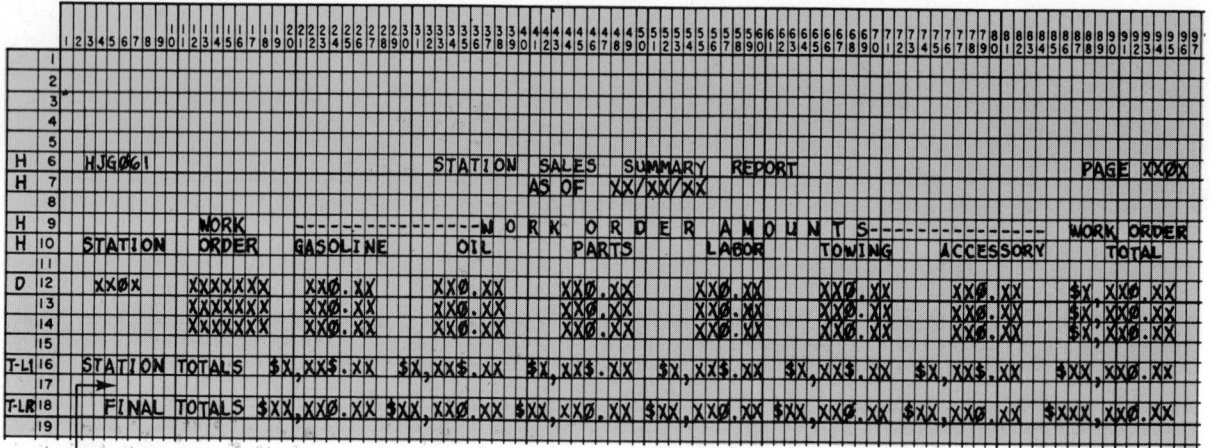

Figure 6-32   Station Sales Summary Report

Processing Requirements

The program takes a control break whenever the station I.D. number changes. The six input amount fields are added to calculate the work order total. Totals of the six amount fields and the Work Order Total field are printed during each control break. The program also accumulates final totals of these fields. Each control break total is followed by two blank lines.

PROGRAMMING ASSIGNMENT 2
STUDENT GRADE REPORT

INSTRUCTIONS

Plan, code, enter, and test an RPG program to produce the Student Grade Report.

INPUT

The format of the Student Grade File is shown in Figure 6-33. Use test data set 12 for this problem. The six grade fields in the input record must be described and processed using array techniques.

STUDENT GRADE FILE						
Record Length 40						
Field No.	Field Name	Field Description	Field Position	Field Length	Dec. Pos.	Data Class
1		UNUSED AREA	1–10			
2	COURSE	Course Number	11–16	6		A
3	STUDID	Student Number	17–22	6	0	N
4	GR1	Grade, Test 1	23–25	3	0	N
5	GR2	Grade, Test 2	26–28	3	0	N
6	GR3	Grade, Test 3	29–31	3	0	N
7	GR4	Grade, Test 4	32–34	3	0	N
8	GR5	Grade, Test 5	35–37	3	0	N
9	GR6	Grade, Test 6	38–40	3	0	N

Figure 6-33 Student Grade File

OUTPUT

Output is the Student Grades report, the format of which is shown in Figure 6-34 on the next page.

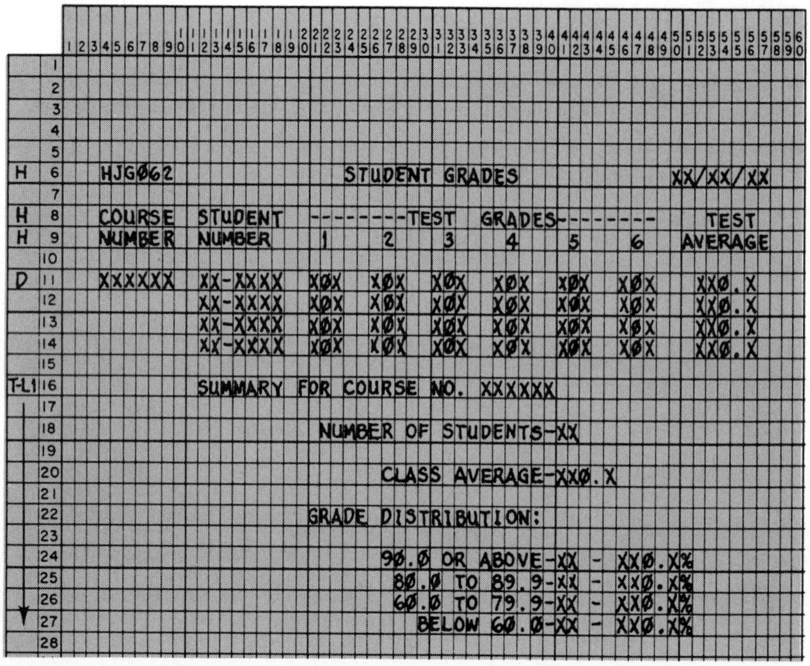

Figure 6-34   Student Grades report format

Processing Requirements

The program takes a control break whenever the course number changes. A detail line is printed for each input record read, showing all input fields and the average of the six test grades. The average is rounded to one decimal place.

The program determines which of four categories the grade average falls into:

Category 1   90.0 or above
Category 2   80.0 to 89.9
Category 3   60.0 to 79.9
Category 4   Below 60.0

The program then counts the number of students falling into each of these grade categories.

During the control break, the program prints the following information:

1. The number of students in the course.
2. The course average, calculated by dividing the total of all grades by the number of student grades in the course.
3. The number of students whose grade average falls into each of the four grade categories. In addition, the program calculates and prints the percentage that each of these counts represents. The percentage for each category can be calculated by dividing the number of students in the category by the number of students in the course and multiplying by 100.
4. Each course begins printing on a new page.

PROGRAMMING ASSIGNMENT 3
RETURNS REPORT

INSTRUCTIONS

Plan, code, enter, and test an RPG program to produce the Returns Report.

INPUT

The format of the Return File is shown in Figure 6-35. Use test data set 13 for this problem.

RETURN FILE						
Record Length 22						
Field No.	Field Name	Field Description	Field Position	Field Length	Dec. Pos.	Data Class
1	STATE	State	1–2	2		A
2	STORE	Store Identifier	3–8	6		A
3	STOCK	Stock Number	9–15	7		A
4	RETQTY	Number of Units Returned	16–18	3	0	N
5	UCOST	Unit Cost	19–22	4	2	N

Figure 6-35   Return File format

OUTPUT

Output is the Returns Report, the format of which is shown in Figure 6-36.

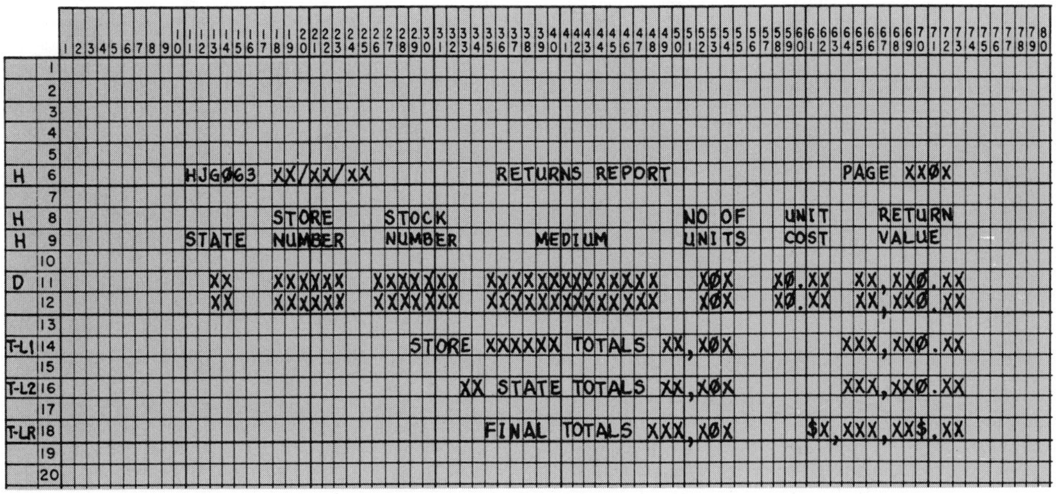

Figure 6-36   Returns Report

⊫ Processing Requirements

This program produces a detail printed report that control breaks on a change in store number (L1) within state (L2). The program accumulates totals of the number of units and the return value calculated from each input record. Return value is obtained by multiplying unit cost by the number of units.

The entry printed in the Medium output field is determined by retrieval from a compile time array. All Medium entries print beginning in position 35 of the print line. The index used for the retrieval is the rightmost position of the Stock Number field. The medium associated with each of the four valid codes is as follows:

Code	Medium
1	Record
2	Compact disk
3	Audio cassette
4	Video tape

If any other entry is in the code position, the medium output message is *INVALID CODE*.

☰ PROGRAMMING ASSIGNMENT 4 ☰
EMPLOYEE PRODUCTION REPORT

INSTRUCTIONS

Plan, Code, enter, and test an RPG program to produce the Employee Production Report.

INPUT

The format of the Employee Production File is shown in Figure 6-37. Use test data set 16 for this problem.

EMPLOYEE PRODUCTION FILE						
Record Length 19						
Field No.	Field Name	Field Description	Field Position	Field Length	Dec. Pos.	Data Class
1	DATE	Date	1–6	6	0	N
2	DIV	Division Number	7–8	2	0	N
3	DEPT	Department Number	9–10	2	0	N
4	EMPNO	Employee Number	11–14	4		A
5	PROD	Units Produced	15–18	4	0	N
6	CAT	Category	19–19	1	0	N

Figure 6-37   Employee Production File format

OUTPUT

Output is the Employee Production Report, the format of which is shown in Figure 6-38.

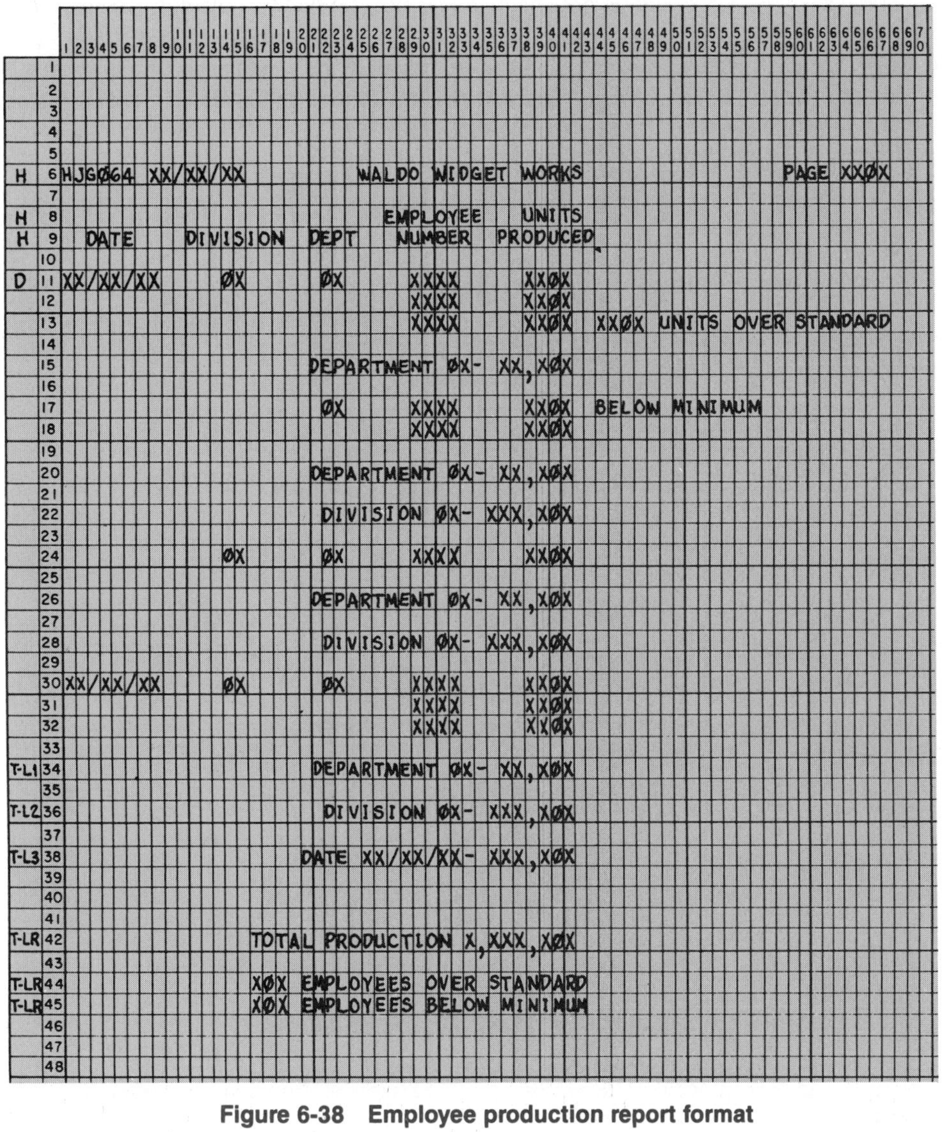

Figure 6-38 Employee production report format

Processing Requirements

The Employee Production Report is a group indicated, detail printed report with control breaks on department number, within division number, within date.

The units produced by each employee are compared against the standard quantity and minimum quantity figures retrieved from the compile time arrays shown in Figure 6-39. The Category field is used as the index for these retrievals. Note: The data in the Category field has been verified and contains no invalid entries. The nine standard quantity and the nine minimum quantity values should be defined and loaded as separate arrays.

	Standard Quantity	Minimum Quantity
1	50	45
2	75	67
3	90	81
4	100	90
5	125	112
6	150	135
7	200	180
8	300	270
9	500	450

Figure 6-39   Production standard array data

If an employee's unit production is below the minimum for the employee's category, the message BELOW MINIMUM is printed, beginning in position 44 of the detail line. In addition, a total of the number of employees below minimum is accumulated.

If an employee's unit production is above the standard quantity for the employee's category, a message is printed beginning in position 44 of the detail line. This message shows the number of units produced over the standard value. The program also accumulates a total of the number of employees whose production exceeds the standard quantity.

Table Lookup & Array Lookup

In the previous chapter you learned to use array processing techniques to retrieve messages for use in a program. Although arrays are an important RPG programming tool, they are limited because successful retrieval of an element from an array depends on knowledge of its position within the array. If the position is not known or cannot be determined, retrieval is difficult.

The method of array retrieval used in Chapter 6 depends on a numeric integer index. If the field used to access data within an array is not numeric, the techniques you have learned cannot be used. Also, the index values must begin with a value of 1 and continue consecutively for array retrieval to be efficient. If, for instance, the variable index field contains values in the range of 1000 to 1200, the array would have to begin with 999 blank entries or else the index value would have to be recalculated to begin with a value of 1. Two techniques that can be used to access information randomly without these limitations are table lookup and array lookup.

DEFINITIONS AND USE OF TABLE LOOKUP

Table Lookup Technically Defined

Table lookup is a process by which a known value, called a **search argument**, is compared with a series of values of the same type, called an **argument table**, until an exact match is found or until it is determined that the argument table contains no match. If a match is found, a related value, called the **function**, is retrieved.

Table Lookup in Friendly Terms

You have probably performed the table lookup process manually many times. Think about the last time you used a telephone directory to look up a telephone number. You started with a known value, the name of the person or company whose number you needed. You compared the known value against a series of similar values, the list of names in the telephone directory, until you found the name you were looking for or until you determined that the name was not listed in the directory. If you found the name, you retrieved a related value, the telephone number.

In this example, the name you start out with is the search argument, the list of names in the telephone directory is the argument table, and the telephone number is the function. The function (telephone number) is also part of a list or series called the **function table**.

≡ Table Lookup in Application Programs

Many business application programs use table lookup to minimize the amount of information that must be keyed into an input data record. The first sample program in this chapter produces a video tape rental list showing the membership numbers and names of persons renting tapes and the titles of the video tapes rented. This application could be coded as a simple detail list by keying in all the required information for every tape rented. Instead, by using table lookup techniques, this program requires the input only of the membership number of the renter and the identification number of the tape in order to determine the name of the person renting the tape and the title of the tape.

▸ **Positional Relationship of Table Elements** In Figure 7-1, the member number column is the argument table, and the member name column is the function table. Note that although the argument table is in numeric sequence, the function table is not; table lookup does not require table entries to be in any sequence. The only requirement is that the first argument correspond to the first function, the second argument to the second function, and so on. In the figure, member number 723144 corresponds to member name RICK THALER, number 816125 corresponds to the name CAROLYN MOES, and so on. This positional relationship between the argument and the function tables is necessary. Think again about using a telephone directory. If the first name did not relate to the first number, the 200th name to the 200th number, and so on, the directory would be useless. Whatever order, if any, the two tables are in, this **positional relationship** between elements in the argument and function tables is essential.

Table lookup techniques are based on this positional relationship. When the two tables are stored in computer memory, the program searches through the argument table until the needed item (search argument) is found; the program then retrieves the function that occupies the same position in the function table. If the search argument is found in the eighth position of the argument table, RPG retrieves the data that is stored in the eighth position of the function table (Figure 7-2).

The member number table in the figure consists of a series of membership numbers that occupy consecutive positions in main computer memory when the program is run. The member name table contains a series of name entries that also occupy a series of consecutive memory locations. The first entry in the member number table (723144) corresponds to the first element of the member name table (RICK·THALER); the entries in the two tables have the same positional relationship.

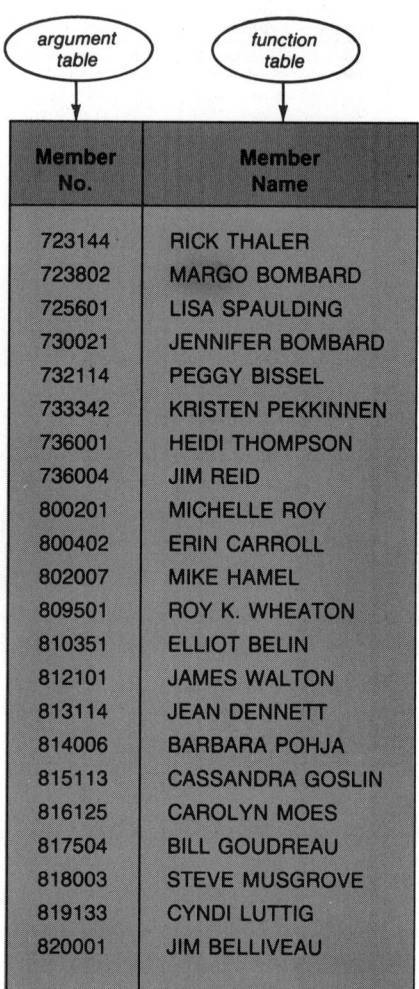

Figure 7-1 **Member numbers and names**

member no. table (arguments)

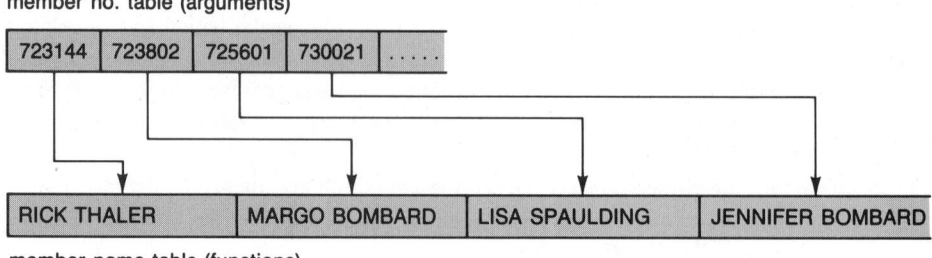

member name table (functions)

Figure 7-2 **Positional relationship of argument and function table elements**

There is no other relationship between the two tables. Each table is a completely separate series of data elements. The only connection between the tables is the way in which the member number table is used to retrieve a name from the member name table.

TABLE LOOKUP: COMPILE TIME TABLES

Figure 7-3 is the format of the input file and output report of our first sample program, HJG07X, which produces a Tape Rental Report that is based on information read from the video tape rental file.

INPUT

VIDEO TAPE RENTAL RECORD						
Record Length 20						
Field No.	Field Name	Field Description	Field Position	Field Length	Dec. Pos.	Data Class
1	MEMBER	Membership Number	1–6	6		A
2		UNUSED AREA	7–9			
3	TAPENO	Video Tape Number	10–14	5	0	N
4		UNUSED AREA	15–20			

OUTPUT

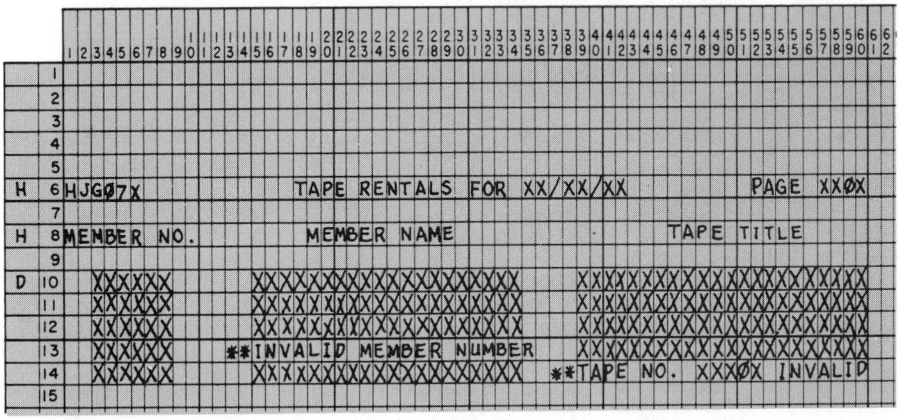

```
H  6 HJG07X              TAPE RENTALS FOR XX/XX/XX           PAGE XX0X
H  8 MEMBER NO.           MEMBER NAME                TAPE TITLE
D 10 XXXXXX       XXXXXXXXXXXXXXXXXXXX        XXXXXXXXXXXXXXXXXXXXXXXXXX
  11 XXXXXX       XXXXXXXXXXXXXXXXXXXX        XXXXXXXXXXXXXXXXXXXXXXXXXX
  12 XXXXXX       XXXXXXXXXXXXXXXXXXXX        XXXXXXXXXXXXXXXXXXXXXXXXXX
  13 XXXXXX     **INVALID MEMBER NUMBER       XXXXXXXXXXXXXXXXXXXXXXXXXX
  14 XXXXXX       XXXXXXXXXXXXXXXXXXXX    **TAPE NO.  XXX0X INVALID
```

```
HJG07X            TAPE RENTALS FOR  8/23/91          PAGE    1

MEMBER NO.           MEMBER NAME               TAPE TITLE

   723144      RICK THALER            FLASHDANCE
   723802      MARGO BOMBARD          MUTINY ON THE BOUNTY
   723802      MARGO BOMBARD          THE STING
   732114      PEGGY BISSEL           A CHRISTMAS CAROL
   733342      KRISTEN PEKKINNEN      ALICE IN WONDERLAND
   812007      **INVALID MEMBER NUMBER  STAR TREK
   820001      JIM BELLIVEAU          CONAN THE BARBARIAN
   813114      JEAN DENNETT           TRON
   810351      ELLIOT BELIN           GREMLINS
   815113      CASSANDRA GOSLIN       WOODSTOCK
   817504      BILL GOUDREAU          **TAPE NO.  8802 INVALID
```

Figure 7-3 Video tape rental record

As the figure shows, the input data records contain only the membership number and the video tape number of the tape that was rented. The report contains not only the membership number but also the member name and the tape title, which must be retrieved by table lookup techniques. The membership number is be used to search the member name table shown in Figure 7-1. The Video Tape Number field of the input record is the argument used to search the tape number table to retrieve the tape title.

If the input membership number is not found in the table, the message **INVALID MEMBER NUMBER prints in the Member Name field of the report; and if the input video tape number is not found, the message **TAPE NO. xxxxx INVALID prints in the Tape Title field of the detail line (the characters xxxxx represent the invalid video tape number that was found in the input record). Figure 7-4 shows the tape number and title tables that you will use.

Tape No.	Title	Tape No.	Title
00100	2001: A SPACE ODYSSEY	04238	A CHRISTMAS CAROL
00203	REAR WINDOW	04611	HIGH ROAD TO CHINA
00500	STAR WARS	04801	KING KONG
00900	THE PHILADELPHIA STORY	04922	SPIRIT OF ST. LOUIS
01001	CLOSE ENCOUNTERS-3RD	05110	GREMLINS
01101	E.T.	05340	MUTINY ON THE BOUNTY
01301	TRON	05462	THE 39 STEPS
01332	GUYS AND DOLLS	05602	VERTIGO
01472	POLTERGEIST	06001	CONAN THE BARBARIAN
01501	GHOSTBUSTERS	06401	STAR TREK
01502	EMPIRE STRIKES BACK	06433	STAR TREK II
01816	ALICE IN WONDERLAND	06481	STAR TREK III
02117	FLASHDANCE	06495	STAR TREK IV
02283	MY FAIR LADY	06501	THE STING
02400	WAR GAMES	06601	RETURN OF THE JEDI
02533	RIO BRAVO	07203	SANDS OF IWO JIMA
02788	BLUE THUNDER	07401	BLADE RUNNER
02791	THE FINAL COUNTDOWN	08202	WOODSTOCK
03101	RISKY BUSINESS	08801	THE QUIET MAN
03105	TOP GUN	09003	BELL, BOOK, AND CANDLE
03301	THE GODFATHER	09501	TOPPER
03401	GODFATHER II	10101	METROPOLIS
03601	THE GALLANT HOURS	10301	ALIEN
03901	CLOUD DANCER	10305	ALIENS
04060	THE RIGHT STUFF	10386	THE ALAMO

Figure 7-4   Tape numbers and titles

Location of Compile Time Tables

The sample program HJG07X uses **compile time tables**, which (like compile time arrays) are a part of the RPG source program and are placed at the end of the source program (Figure 7-5). Each compile time table is preceded by a separator record that contains ** in positions 1 and 2. Note that Figure 7-5 shows the location of the two sets of compile time tables, and remember that two tables, the argument table and the function table, are used in every lookup operation. In this sample program the membership number and name tables are the first set of tables, and the tape number and title tables are the second set. This relationship is arbitrary; the program could have been written as easily and as well with the table sets in reverse order.

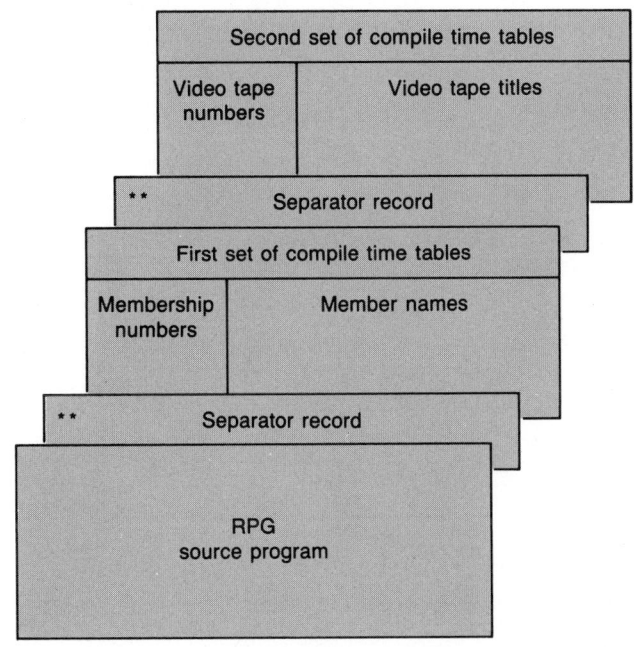

Figure 7-5 Source program sequence: Multiple compile time tables

▤ Format of Compile Time Table Record

Figure 7-6 shows the format of the first set of compile time table data records. Note that every record contains an argument entry (Member No.) followed by a function entry (Member Name). As in this example, the first entry in an argument table record must begin in position 1 of the record, and the first position of the function table entry must be in the next position after the argument. No unused positions can separate the argument and function entries.

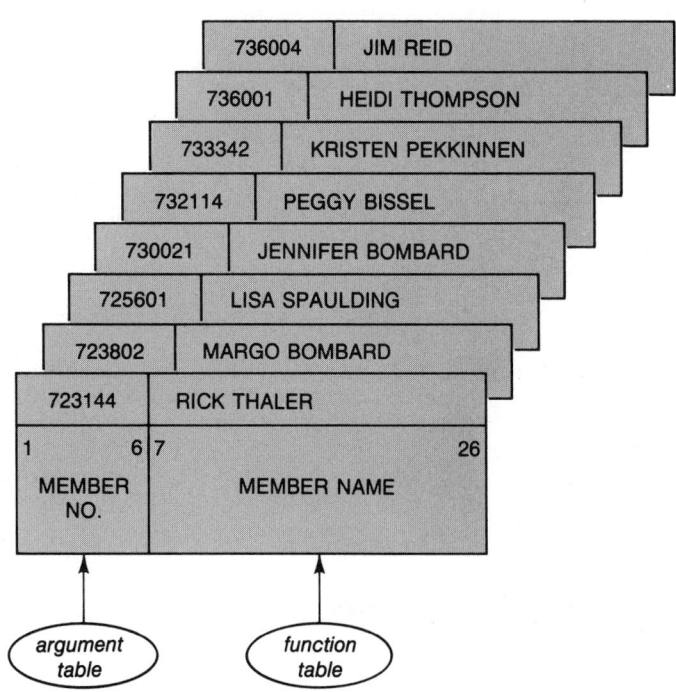

Figure 7-6 Data format of membership tables

Figure 7-7 shows the layout of the second set of tables. Note that the argument entry in every record begins in position 1 and that the function entry immediately follows the argument.

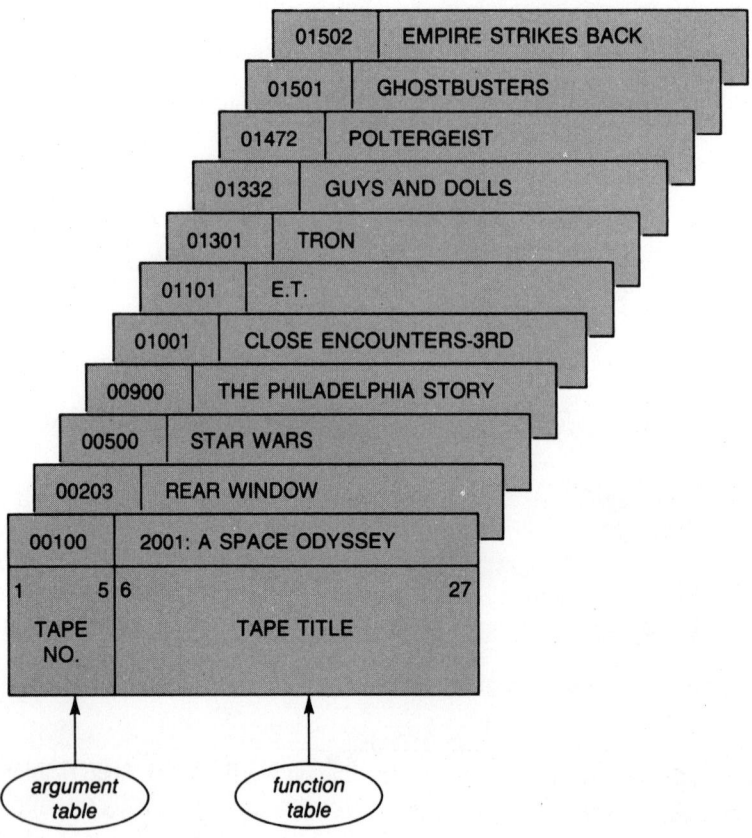

Figure 7-7   Data format of video tape tables

When tables are arranged in this manner, the program reads and stores the first argument, then the first function, the second argument, the second function, and so on. This alternating arrangement of table data (argument, function, argument, function) is called the **alternating format**. When tables are read in the alternating format, they are stored in computer memory as in Figure 7-8. As this figure shows, the table data is stored in the sequence in which it was read.

ARG,1	FUNCT,1	ARG,2	FUNCT,2	ARG,3	FUNCT,3	ARG,4	FUNCT,4	ARG,5	FUNCT,5	

Figure 7-8   Alternating tables in computer memory

≡ SAMPLE PROGRAM HJG07X ≡

≡ Control And File Description Specifications

Figure 7-9 shows the Control and File Description Specifications form for this program. Note that the use of compile time tables does not result in any new entries to these specifications.

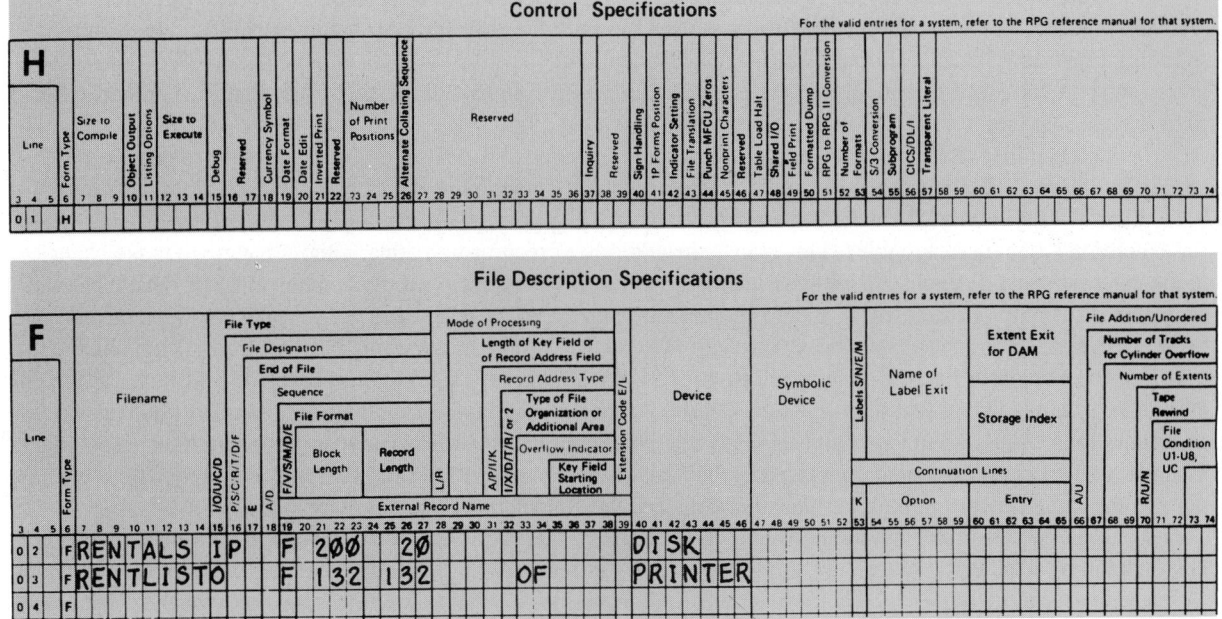

Figure 7-9 Control and file description specifications for program HJG07X

Extension Specifications

▶ **Argument Table Definition** When the table data is in the alternating format, the argument table and the function table must both be defined on the same coding line on the Extension Specifications form (Figure 7-10). The table name that is entered in the Table or Array Name area (positions 27–32) must be the name of the argument table. Thus, the name of the table that contains the member numbers is TABMEM. *Table names used in RPG programs must be four to six characters long and must begin with the letters TAB.* This argument table name is used on the Calculation Specifications form to reference data in the table.

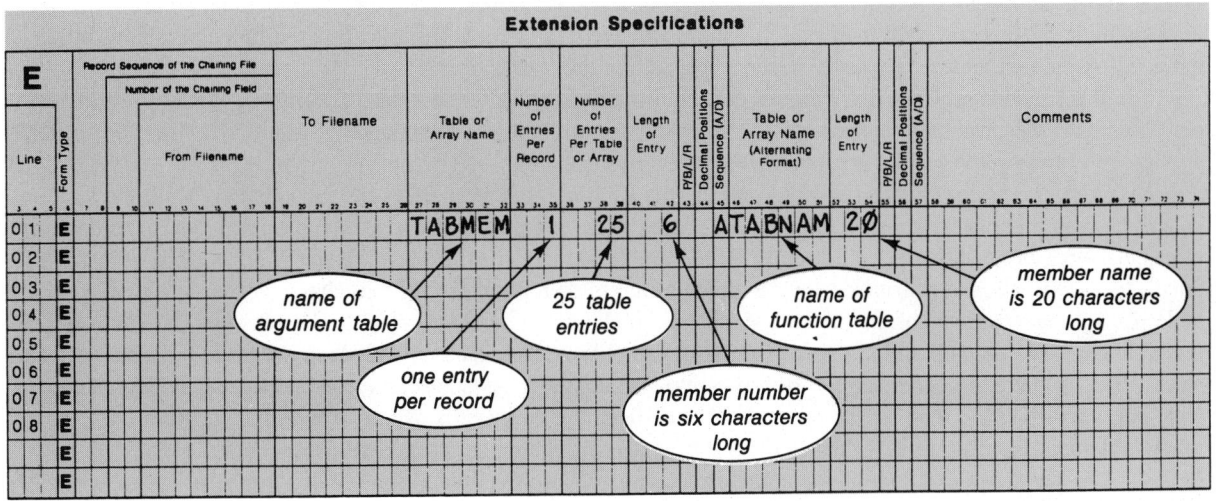

Figure 7-10 Table definition specifications

The Number of Entries per Record area (positions 33–35) is used to specify the number of entries in each table data record. When the alternating format is used, an **entry** is defined as an argument value and its corresponding function value. Recall that there is one argument and one function in each table data record. Thus, there is one entry in each record, and the value 1 is entered in position 35 to indicate this. Note that the number in this field is right-justified with no required leading zeros.

The Number of Entries per Table or Array area (positions 36–39) specifies the number of entries in the tables. In Figure 7-10, the value in this field is 25, which is the maximum number of entries that the table can hold. Figure 7-1 had only 22 entries in the member tables. It is good programming technique to leave some room for expansion when defining tables. This allows the addition of records to a table without having to make changes to the extension specifications. However, if there is little or no possibility that the number of entries in a table will change (e.g., a table of state names), there is no need to leave room for expansion. As you will see when the compile listing is shown later in this chapter, leaving room for expansion results in a warning message during compilation.

The Length of Entry area in positions 40–42 is used to specify the length of each element in the argument table. The example shows that the value 6 is specified in position 42, indicating that each member number is 6 characters long. Thus, when the computer reads the table input data, the first six positions of each table record are assumed to be the argument and are placed in the TABMEM table. The Decimal Positions area (position 44) functions in the same way as on the Input Specifications and the Calculation Specifications forms.

The Sequence field (position 45) is used to specify whether the argument table is in an ascending (A) or descending (D) sequence. Figure 7-10 shows the value A in position 45, indicating that the values in the argument table are in ascending sequence. The letter D would indicate that the values are in descending sequence. RPG does not require that the argument table be in any sequence, but table lookup is more efficient if it is, because RPG is then able to determine if the lookup has passed the point in the table where the entry should be and can terminate the lookup operation if the entry was not found. Think again of the telephone directory. You do not look through the entire directory for a name that begins with the letter A, you stop as soon as you find that the name is not listed in the A's because you know that the directory names are listed in ascending sequence. When an argument table is sequential, RPG has the same capability. If there is no sequence, the Sequence field in position 45 is left blank, and RPG searches the entire table before determining that the entry cannot be located.

▶ **Function Table Definition** Positions 46–57 pertain to the function table: the table that contains the second portion of every entry in the input table data, the member name table in this example. The table name is to be TABNAM. Note again that the first three characters of a table name must be TAB. The Length of Entry area (positions 52–54) is used to indicate the length of each element in the TABNAM table. The example specifies the value 20 because each Member Name field is 20 characters long. Because the member name is alphameric, there is no entry in the Decimal Positions area. The member name is not necessarily in any sequence, so the Sequence area (position 57) is blank. You will find that in almost every table lookup application the function table is unsequenced. Argument tables are usually in sequence but not the function table.

The function table TABNAM does not require a Number of Entries per Record or a Number of Entries per Table entry because these entries must be the same for both the argument and the function tables, and so RPG applies the entries given for the argument table to the function table.

From the extension specifications entries, the RPG compiler generates instructions that cause the table data to be read and placed in the defined tables. When a table data record is read, the program places the data in the first six positions of the record in the TABMEM table because the elements are specified as six characters in length (position 42). The instructions in the object program then place the next 20 characters in the TABNAM table because each element of the TABNAM table is 20 characters in length. The object program continues to read the table data records until all have been read. If the number of table data records does not exactly fill the specified tables, (i.e., if there are either too few or too many), the compiler generates an error message. If the number of table data records is too few, so that the table is not filled, the message is usually a warning. If there are too many table data records, so that they cannot all be placed in the table, a fatal error may occur.

The second line of code in the completed extension specifications (Figure 7-11) describes the tape number and title tables. These entries are similar to those in the first set of tables. TABTAP, the name assigned to the tape number table, contains one entry in each table data record. The program allocates space for a total of 50 entries in the table. Each TABTAP entry is five positions long, is numeric, and has no decimal places. Note that TABTAP

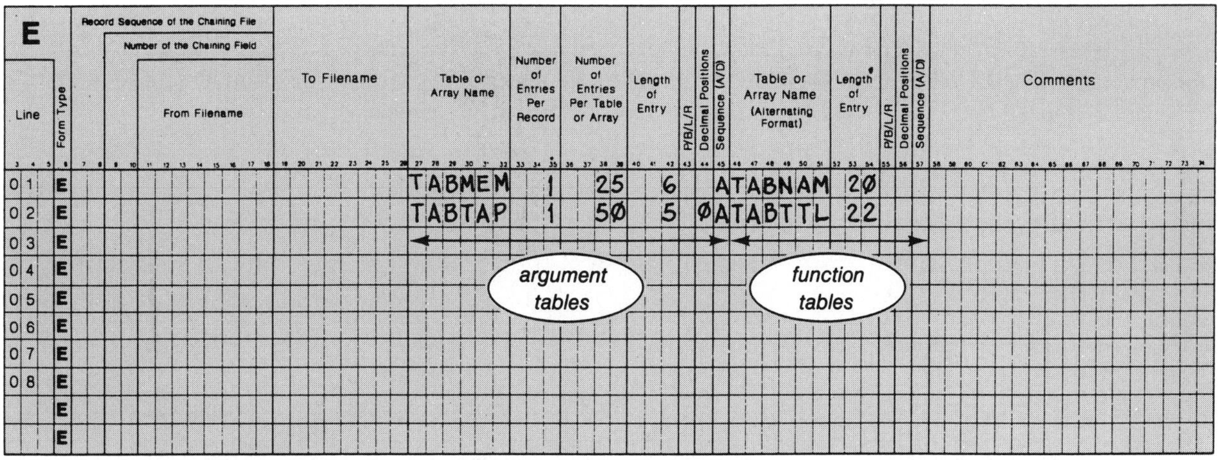

Extension Specifications

Line	Form Type	From Filename	To Filename	Table or Array Name	Number of Entries Per Record	Number of Entries Per Table or Array	Length of Entry	P/B/L/R	Decimal Positions	Sequence (A/D)	Table or Array Name (Alternating Format)	Length of Entry	P/B/L/R	Decimal Positions	Sequence (A/D)	Comments
01	E			TABMEM	1	25	6			A	TABNAM	20				
02	E			TABTAP	1	50	5		0	A	TABTTL	22				
03	E															
04	E															
05	E															
06	E															
07	E															
08	E															
	E															
	E															

Figure 7-11 Extension specifications for program HJG07X

is in ascending sequence. The name TABTTL has been assigned to the title table; each entry is 22 positions long, and, like the member name table, is alphameric and unsequenced.

The sequence of table descriptions in the extension specifications determines the order in which compile time tables must be placed at the end of the source program. Because the TABMEM/TABNAM set has been described on the first line and the TABTAP/TABTTL set on the second line, RPG expects these tables to be in this same order when the compiler reads the source program.

Input Specifications

Note that there is no reference to the tables on the Input Specifications form for the sample program (Figure 7-12). In table lookup operations, the tables are not described on the Input Specifications form because the tables are fully described on the Extension Specifications form. The only data described on the Input Specifications form is the input data file, which contains the arguments used to search the tables.

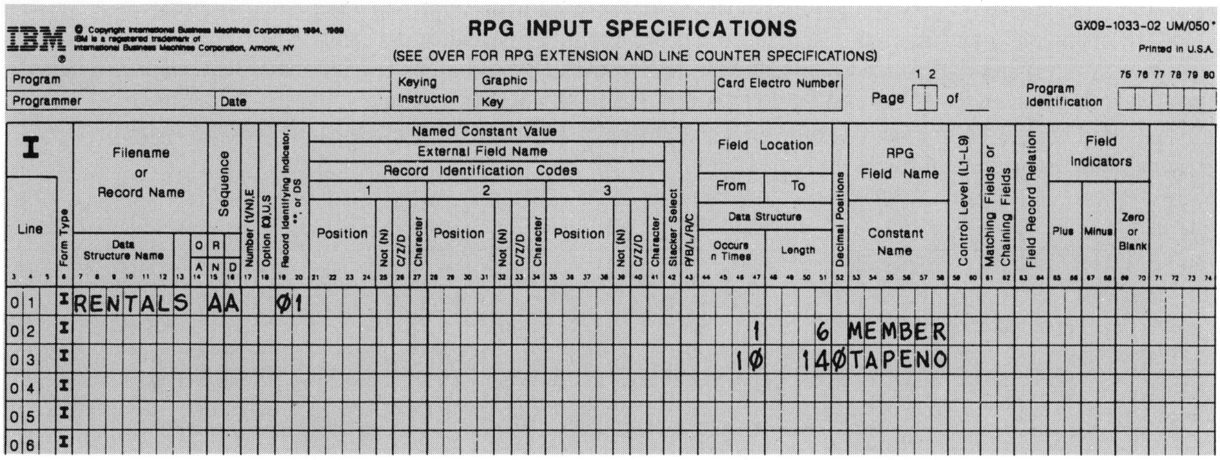

RPG INPUT SPECIFICATIONS

(SEE OVER FOR RPG EXTENSION AND LINE COUNTER SPECIFICATIONS)

Line	Form Type	Filename or Record Name	Sequence	Record Identifying Indicator	Field Location From	Field Location To	Decimal Positions	RPG Field Name
01	I	RENTALS	AA	01				
02	I				1	6		MEMBER
03	I				10	14	0	TAPENO
04	I							
05	I							
06	I							

Figure 7-12 Input specifications for program HJG07X

▬ Calculation Specifications

When tables are defined on the Extension Specifications form, the table data is stored in main memory for processing. The **LOKUP** operation searches the tables and retrieves the needed entry from the function table. A separate LOKUP operation is used for each of the sets of tables to be searched (Figure 7-13).

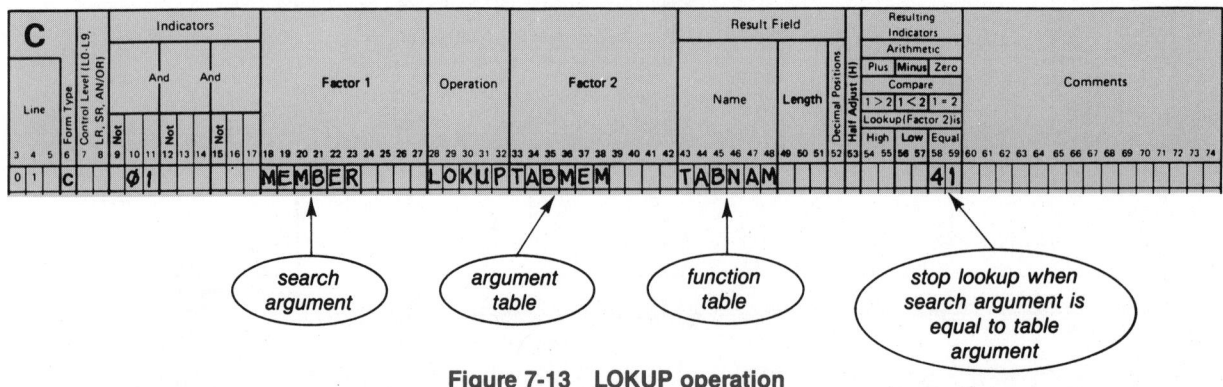

Figure 7-13 LOKUP operation

The table lookup operation (LOKUP) is performed when the 01 indicator is on. RPG requires that the length and data class of the search argument be the same as the length and data class of the elements in the argument table. The LOKUP operation code causes the value in the search argument field, which is specified in the Factor 1 area (MEMBER), to be compared with each element in the argument table, which is specified in the Factor 2 area (TABMEM). If the condition specified by the resulting indicators is found, the lookup ends, and the corresponding function from the function table specified in the Result Field area (TABNAM) is made available for processing. Note in Figure 7-13 that indicator 41 is specified in positions 58–59, which means that the table lookup operation proceeds until an element in the TABMEM table is found to be equal to the value in the MEMBER field. At that time, the corresponding element in the TABNAM table is made available, and indicator 41 is turned on.

Indicators can be placed in positions 54–55 to stop the search when the value in the Factor 2 table is the next higher value to that contained in the Factor 1 search argument. An indicator can also be placed in positions 56–57 to stop the search when the value in the Factor 2 table is the next lower value to that contained in the Factor 1 search argument. RPG does not permit indicators to be placed in all three Resulting Indicator areas. In a LOKUP operation, a maximum of two indicators is permitted. These indicators can be placed in both the HIGH (positions 54–55) and EQUAL (positions 58–59) areas or the LOW (positions 56–57) and EQUAL areas; if indicators are coded in both the HIGH and the LOW areas, the LOW entry is ignored.

In Figure 7-14, the search argument value in Factor 1 (MEMBER) is compared with the values in the argument table specified in Factor 2 (TABMEM).

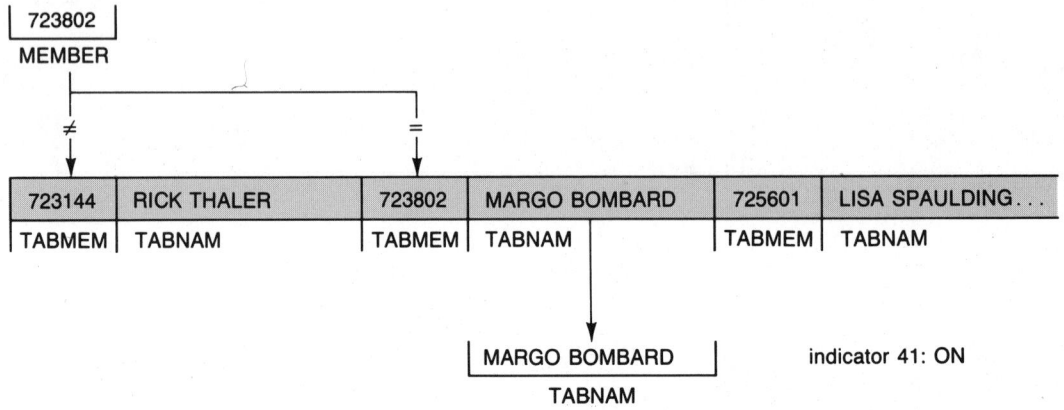

Figure 7-14 Example of LOKUP Operation

When an equal condition is found, that is, when the member number in the MEMBER field equals a member number in the TABMEM table, the corresponding member name in the TABNAM table is retrieved and placed in a field named TABNAM. Because the value 732802 in the MEMBER field equals the second member number in the TABMEM table, the second member name (MARGO BOMBARD) is retrieved from the TABNAM table and placed in the TABNAM field. Note also that because an equal condition is found, indicator 41 is turned on. If an equal condition is not found, that is, if the value in the MEMBER field is compared with all the member numbers in the TABMEM table and none are equal, indicator 41 is not turned on; and no new member name is moved to the TABNAM field.

Remember that LOKUP resulting indicators, like those in the COMP operation, stay on until the same LOKUP is performed again. If a LOKUP operation is conditional, based on the result of a previous LOKUP or COMP operation, consider the use of the SETOF operation to turn the resulting indicators off.

Figure 7-15 is the completed Calculation Specifications form. The second LOKUP operation uses the TAPENO field as a search argument to search the TABTAP table. If an equal condition is detected (indicator 42 in positions 58–59), the corresponding function is retrieved from the TABTTL table and placed in a field named TABTTL. Figure 7-16 summarizes the LOKUP operation code.

Line (3–5)	Form Type (6)	Control Level (7–8)	Indicators (9–17)	Factor 1 (18–27)	Operation (28–32)	Factor 2 (33–42)	Result Field Name (43–48)	Length (49–51)	Decimal Positions (52)	Half Adjust (53)	Plus / > / High (54–55)	Minus / < / Low (56–57)	Zero / = / Equal (58–59)	Comments (60–74)
01	C		Ø1	MEMBER	LOKUP	TABMEM	TABNAM						41	
02	C		Ø1	TAPENO	LOKUP	TABTAP	TABTTL						42	
03	C													

Figure 7-15 Calculation specifications for program HJG07X

Line (3–5)	Form Type (6)	Control Level (7–8)	Indicators (9–17)	Factor 1 (18–27)	Operation (28–32)	Factor 2 (33–42)	Result Field Name (43–48)	Length (49–51)	Decimal Positions (52)	Half Adjust (53)	Plus / > / High (54–55)	Minus / < / Low (56–57)	Zero / = / Equal (58–59)	Comments (60–74)
01	C		Ø1	UNIT	LOKUP	TABCAR	TABPRI						5Ø	

LOKUP Operation Summary

The LOKUP operation performs a search for a specific element in a table or array. The table or array to be searched is named in Factor 2. Factor 1 is the search argument. If table lookup is being performed, the function table may be named in the Result Field area. If array lookup is being performed, the Result Field area cannot be used. At least one resulting indicator must be used with the LOKUP operation.

Control Level Indicators	Indicators	Factor 1	Operation Name	Factor 2	Result Field	Resulting Indicators		
7–8	9–17	18–27	28–32	33–42	43–53	54–55	56–57	58–59
optional	optional	required	LOKUP	required	optional	optional	optional	optional

Figure 7-16 LOKUP operation summary

Output Specifications

After the table lookup operations have been performed during detail calculation time, the program must print the information retrieved from the function tables as well as the Member Number from the detail input record as part of the detail output line. Figure 7-17 shows the output specifications for the sample program.

IBM RPG OUTPUT SPECIFICATIONS (SEE OVER FOR RPG TELECOMMUNICATIONS SPECIFICATIONS) GX09-1034-02 UM/050*

Line	Form Type	Filename or Record Name	Type (H/D/T/E)	Space Before	Skip Before	Output Indicators	Field Name or EXCPT Name or Constant Name	Edit Codes	End Position in Output Record	Constant or Edit Word
01	O	RENTLIST	H	2	Ø6	1P				
02	O	OR				OF				
03	O								6	'HJGØ7X'
04	O								33	'TAPE RENTALS FOR'
05	O						UDATE	Y	42	
06	O								55	'PAGE'
07	O						PAGE		6Ø	
08	O		H	2		1P				
09	O	OR				OF				
10	O								1Ø	'MEMBER NO.'
11	O								29	'MEMBER NAME'
12	O								55	'TAPE TITLE'
13	O		D	1		Ø1				
14	O						MEMBER		8	
15	O					41	TABNAM		34	
16	O					42	TABTTL		6Ø	
17	O					N41			35	'**INVALID MEMBER NUMBER'
18	O					N42			46	'**TAPE NO.'
19	O					N42	TAPENO	Z	52	
20	O					N42			6Ø	'INVALID'

Figure 7-17 Output specifications for program HJG07X

Line 14 of the Output Specifications form causes the contents of the MEMBER field to be printed every time a detail record is processed. If indicator 41 is on, the member name retrieved from the TABNAM table prints, ending in position 34 as is shown on line 15. If the member number is not valid, and no match is found during the LOKUP operation that searches the TABMEM table, indicator 41 does not turn on and the message **INVALID MEMBER NUMBER prints, as shown on line 17.

If the lookup of the TABTAP table is successful, and a match is found, indicator 42 turns on and the corresponding function from the TABTTL table prints as shown on line 16. If the lookup does not find a matching entry in the argument table, indicator 42 does not turn on and the **TAPE NO. xxxxx INVALID message is printed as shown on lines 18, 19, and 20.

Compile Listing

Figure 7-18 is the compile listing for program HJG07X. Comments have been deleted from the source code to enable you to read the RPG specifications of the program more easily.

Figure 7-18   Compile listing for program HJG07X

```
HJG07X    08-28-91  14:47:24     IBM PC     RPG II        Version 3.5  Page 1

           ....+....1....+....2....+....3....+....4....+....5....+....6....+....7....

  1 0001 H                                                                  HJG07X


  2 0002 FRENTALS IP  F 200  20          DISK
  3 0003 FRENTLISTO   F 132 132     OF   PRINTER


  4 0004 E              TABMEM  1 25  6 ATABNAM 20
  5 0005 E              TABTAP  1 50  5 OATABTTL 22


  6 0006 IRENTALS AA  01
  7 0007 I                                       1   6 MEMBER
  8 0008 I                                      10  140TAPENO


  9 0009 C    01     MEMBER     LOKUPTABMEM    TABNAM      41
 10 0010 C    01     TAPENO     LOKUPTABTAP    TABTTL      42


 11 0011 ORENTLISTH  206    1P
 12 0012 O      OR          OF
 13 0013 O                                 6 'HJG07X'
 14 0014 O                                33 'TAPE RENTALS FOR'
 15 0015 O                    UDATE Y     42
 16 0016 O                                55 'PAGE'
 17 0017 O                    PAGE        60
 18 0018 O       H  2         1P
 19 0019 O      OR          OF
 20 0020 O                                10 'MEMBER NO.'
 21 0021 O                                29 'MEMBER NAME'
 22 0022 O                                55 'TAPE TITLE'
 23 0023 O       D  1         01
 24 0024 O                    MEMBER       8
 25 0025 O                41  TABNAM      34
 26 0026 O                42  TABTTL      60
 27 0027 O               N41              35 '**INVALID MEMBER NUMBER'
 28 0028 O               N42              46 '**TAPE NO.'
 29 0029 O               N42  TAPENOZ     52
 30 0030 O               N42              60 'INVALID'
 31 **
 32 723144RICK THALER
 33 723802MARGO BOMBARD
 34 725601LISA SPAULDING
 35 730021JENNIFER BOMBARD
 36 732114PEGGY BISSEL
 37 733342KRISTEN PEKKINNEN
 38 736001HEIDI THOMPSON
 39 736004JIM REID
 40 800201MICHELLE ROY
 41 800402ERIN CARROLL
 42 802007MIKE HAMEL
 43 809501ROY K. WHEATON
 44 810351ELLIOT BELIN
 45 812101JAMES WALTON
 46 813114JEAN DENNETT
 47 814006BARBARA POHJA
 48 815113CASSANDRA GOSLIN
 49 816125CAROLYN MOES
 50 817504BILL GOUDREAU
 51 818003STEVE MUSGROVE
 52 819133CYNDI LUTTIG
 53 820001JIM BELLIVEAU
 54 **
```

Figure 7-18 (1)   *continued*

```
HJG07X     08-28-91  14:47:24        IBM PC        RPG II        Version 3.5  Page  2
           ....+....1....+....2....+....3....+....4....+....5....+....6....+....7....

****-A001W-Less than the total number of table or array data elements were provided.
           55 001002001: A SPACE ODYSSEY
           56 00203REAR WINDOW
           57 00500STAR WARS
           58 00900THE PHILADELPHIA STORY
           59 01001CLOSE ENCOUNTERS-3RD
           60 01101E. T.
           61 01301TRON
           62 01332GUYS AND DOLLS
           63 01472POLTERGEIST
           64 01501GHOSTBUSTERS
           65 01502EMPIRE STRIKES BACK
           66 01816ALICE IN WONDERLAND
           67 02117FLASHDANCE
           68 02283MY FAIR LADY
           69 02400WAR GAMES
           70 02533RIO BRAVO
           71 02788BLUE THUNDER
           72 02791THE FINAL COUNTDOWN
           73 03101RISKY BUSINESS
           74 03105TOP GUN
           75 03301THE GODFATHER
           76 03401GODFATHER II
           77 03601THE GALLANT HOURS
           78 03901CLOUD DANCER
           79 04060THE RIGHT STUFF
           80 04238A CHRISTMAS CAROL
           81 04611HIGH ROAD TO CHINA
           82 04801KING KONG
           83 04922SPIRIT OF ST. LOUIS
           84 05110GREMLINS
           85 05340MUTINY ON THE BOUNTY
           86 05462THE 39 STEPS
           87 05602VERTIGO
           88 06001CONAN THE BARBARIAN
           89 06401STAR TREK
           90 06433STAR TREK 11
           91 06481STAR TREK III
           92 06495STAR TREK IV
           93 06501THE STING
           94 06601RETURN OF THE JEDI
           95 07203SANDS OF IWO JIMA
           96 07401BLADE RUNNER
           97 08202WOODSTOCK
           98 08801THE QUIET MAN
           99 09003BELL, BOOK, AND CANDLE
          100 09501TOPPER
          101 10101METROPOLIS
          102 10301ALIEN
          103 10305ALIENS
          104 10386THE ALAMO
          105 /*
          106 /*


              THE FOLLOWING INDICATORS APPEARED IN THIS PROGRAM

              01  41  42  1P  OF
         1 Warning Errors
         No Fatal Errors
```

Figure 7-18 (2)

The warning message at the end of the first set of compile time tables, between lines 54 and 55 of the compile listing, indicates that there are too few compile time table data records in the program to fill the table. The program contains only 22 table data records for the TABMEM/TABNAM set of tables though the extension specifications on line 4 indicates 25 entries in the tables. This warning message is only a reminder that there are too few records; the program will compile successfully with a short table and will execute correctly. As was stated earlier, it is not uncommon to have extra table entry spaces to allow for expansion of a table without having to change the extension specifications. Note that no such message appears at the end of the second set of tables because the number of entries in the table data records is equal to the Number of Entries per Table entry on the Extension Specifications form.

Figure 7-19 is the output report developed by the sample program.

```
HJG07X          TAPE RENTALS FOR  8/23/91          PAGE    1

MEMBER NO.         MEMBER NAME                 TAPE TITLE

   723144      RICK THALER            FLASHDANCE
   723802      MARGO BOMBARD          MUTINY ON THE BOUNTY
   723802      MARGO BOMBARD          THE STING
   732114      PEGGY BISSEL           A CHRISTMAS CAROL
   733342      KRISTEN PEKKINNEN      ALICE IN WONDERLAND
   812007      **INVALID MEMBER NUMBER  STAR TREK
   820001      JIM BELLIVEAU          CONAN THE BARBARIAN
   813114      JEAN DENNETT           TRON
   810351      ELLIOT BELIN           GREMLINS
   815113      CASSANDRA GOSLIN       WOODSTOCK
   817504      BILL GOUDREAU          **TAPE NO.   8802 INVALID
```

Figure 7-19   Tape Rental Report

Separate Table Format

Although table lookup is normally performed using the alternating table format, the program can be coded by describing each table as a completely separate entity (Figure 7-20). Each table is described with a separate extension specification line, and each table requires entries in Number of Entries per Record and Number of Entries per Table areas.

Line	Form Type	Record Sequence of the Chaining File / Number of the Chaining Field / From Filename	To Filename	Table or Array Name	Number of Entries Per Record	Number of Entries Per Table or Array	Length of Entry	P/B/L/R	Decimal Positions / Sequence (A/D)	Table or Array Name (Alternating Format)	Length of Entry	P/B/L/R	Decimal Positions / Sequence (A/D)	Comments
0 1	E			TABMEM	1	25	6		A					
0 2	E			TABNAM	1	25	20							
0 3	E			TABTAP	1	50	5		0A					
0 4	E			TABTTL	1	50	22							
0 5	E													
0 6	E													
0 7	E													
0 8	E													
	E													
	E													

Figure 7-20   Separate table definition

If the compile time tables for program HJG07X are described in this way, the source program is arranged as in Figure 7-21.

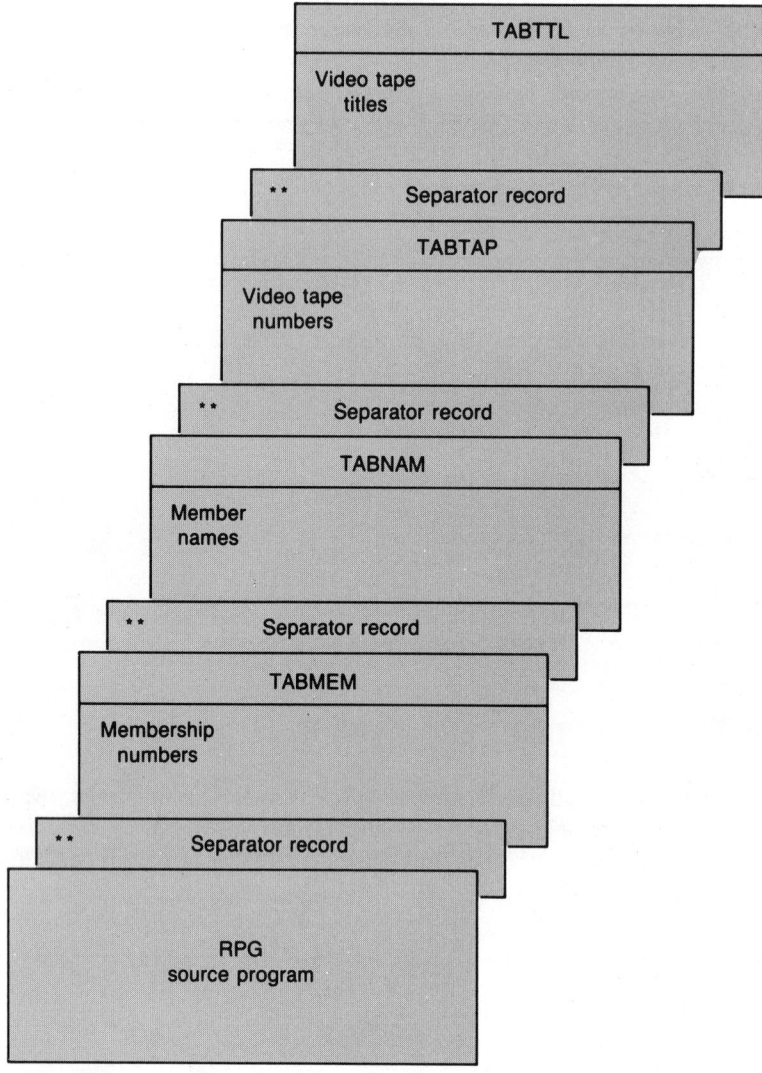

Figure 7-21 Source program sequence using multiple compile time tables and separate table format

There are no differences in the rest of the source program code when the separate table format is used. The LOKUP operations are performed in the calculations, and any output operations pertaining to the tables are coded exactly as they were in the previous sample program.

TABLE LOOKUP: PREEXECUTION (PRERUN) TIME TABLES

Because the compile time tables are part of the RPG source program, any change made to a compile time table makes it necessary to recompile the RPG source program. To avoid the need to recompile, data for each table is often stored in a separate data file. The data from these separate files is loaded into the tables prior to the execution of the RPG object program. Because the data is loaded before the program begins to execute, or run, such tables are called **preexecution** or **prerun** time tables. The two terms are interchangeable; some newer versions of RPG use the term prerun.

Loading Preexecution Time Tables

Because loading of data into preexecution time tables is a fully transparent function of the RPG logic cycle, it is not normally shown as part of the RPG logic cycle. Figure 7-22 is an RPG fixed logic cycle that has been modified to show that table loading takes place before step 1 of the cycle.

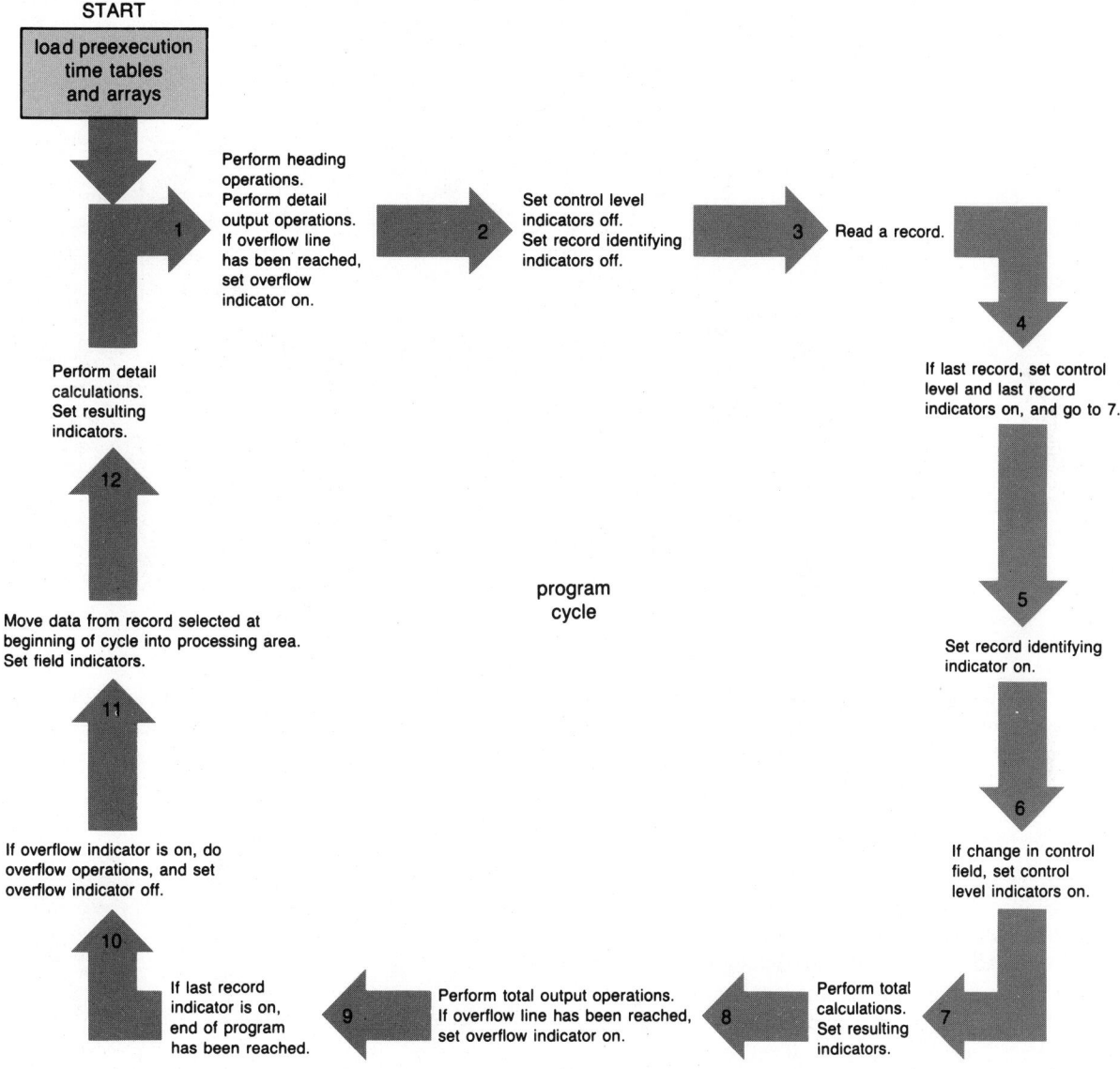

Figure 7-22 RPG logic cycle modified to show preexecution table loading

SAMPLE PROGRAM HJG07Y

Our second sample Program, HJG07Y, performs the same functions as program HJG07X, the only difference between them being HJG07Y uses preexecution time tables instead of compile time tables.

File Description Specifications for Table Files

Each data file that contains preexecution time table data must be described as a separate file on the File Description Specifications form. (Figure 7-23). Note that four files have been described instead of the two that were described in sample program HJG07X. The first two files, MEMBERS and TAPES, are **table files** that contain data to be loaded into preexecution time tables. The description of the table files at the beginning of the file description specifications is not a requirement of RPG. These files can be described either before or after the normal input data file. The table files are described like any other input files but must have two additional entries for each file description.

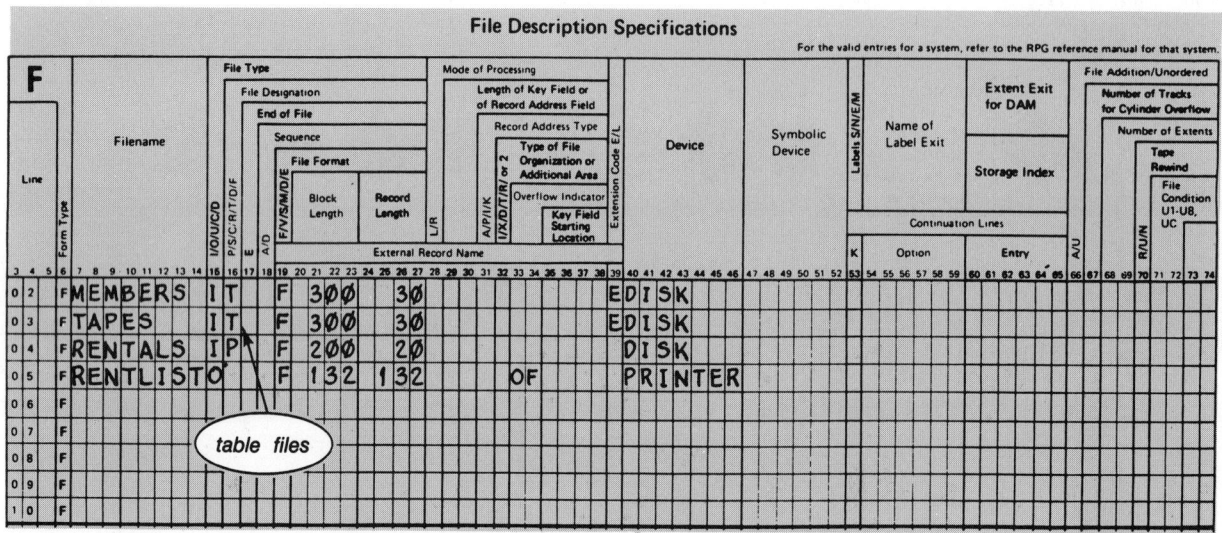

Figure 7-23   File description specifications for table files

▸ **File Designation of Table Files**   Each of the two files used to load table data must contain a File Designation entry T in position 16 which indicates that these files contain data to be loaded into tables at preexecution time. Although most versions of RPG can read table files from any input device, the IBM System/36 requires a Device entry DISK (positions 40–46) for table files.

▸ **Extension Code E/L**   Entry E in position 39 specifies that all the table files are further described on the Extension Specifications form. Without this entry, RPG would look for further description of an input file on the Input Specifications form and, not finding it, would generate an error message during program compilation. However, when a file has an E in the Extension Code area (position 39), the compiler does not expect input specifications for the file but, instead, expects a further description of the file as part of the Extension Specifications form. Figure 7-24 shows the four files used in program HJG07Y.

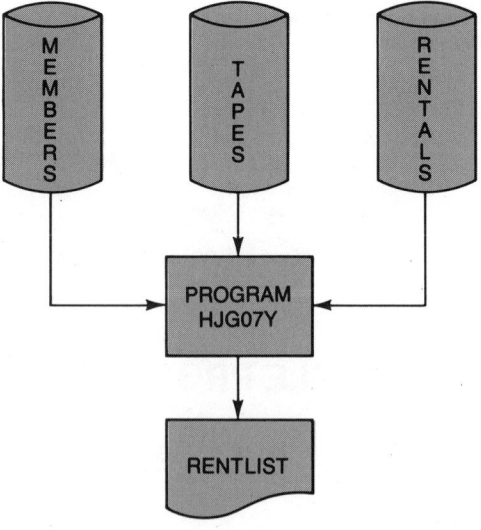

Figure 7-24   Data flow for program HJG07Y

Extension Specifications Form for Preexecution Time Tables

The entries on the Extension Specifications form that are used to describe preexecution time tables (Figure 7-25) are the same for this program as those used in the first sample program. Note that the only modification is the addition of an entry in the From Filename area, positions 11–18, which tells RPG the name of the data file from which the table data is to be loaded and also connects the file description of the table file to the extension specification description of the file. Without this entry, RPG could not associate the table file description with the correct table description on the Extension Specifications form.

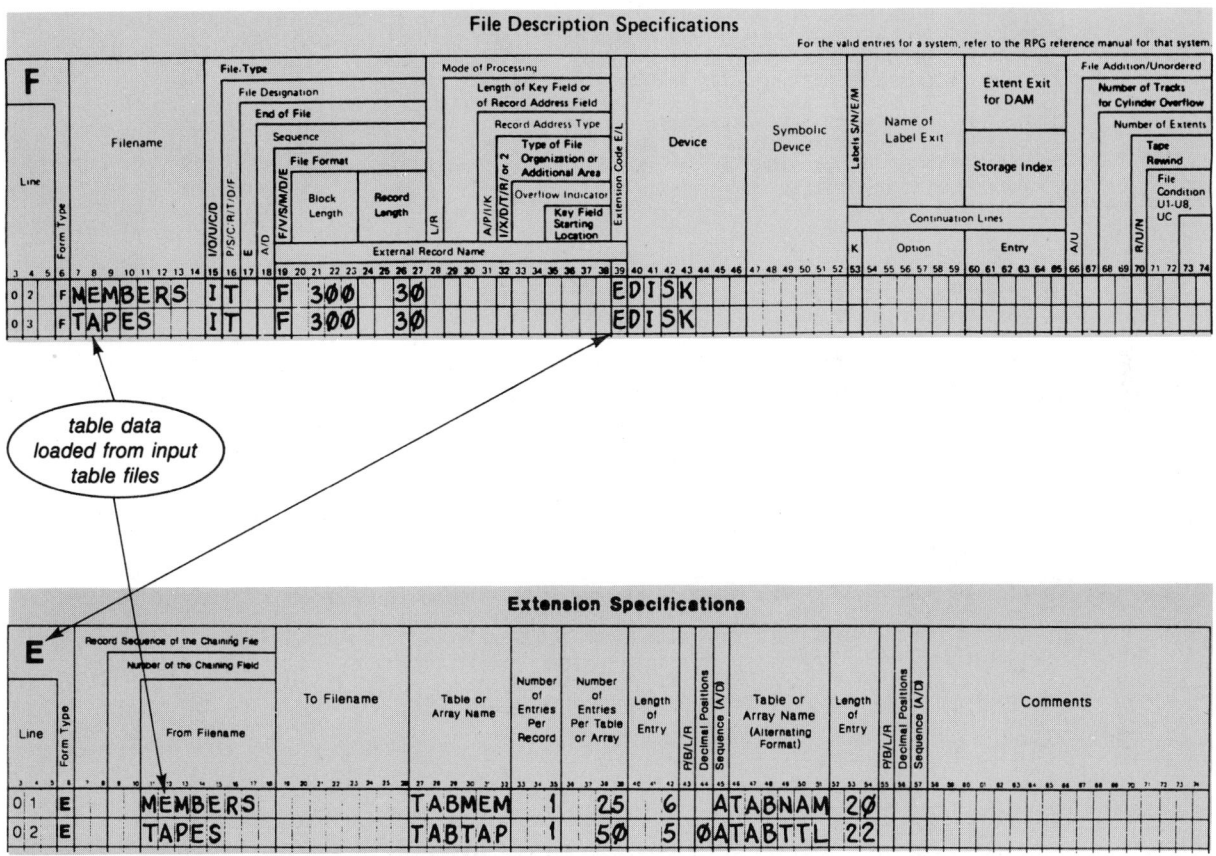

Figure 7-25 Extension specifications for preexecution time tables

Calculation and Output Specifications for Preexecution Time Tables

The remainder of the specifications for program HJG07Y are the same as those for HJG07X. There is no difference between the processing of compile time tables and preexecution time tables often the tables have been loaded into computer memory. Figure 7-26 shows the compile listing for program HJG07Y.

Figure 7-26   Compile listing for program HJG07Y

```
HJG07Y     08-23-91  14:55:23  HJG07Y -- TAPE RENTAL REPORT          .Version 3.5  Page  1

           ....+....1....+....2....+....3....+....4....+....5....+....6....+....7....

     3 0002 H                                                                          HJG07Y


     4 0003 F*-------------------------------------------------------------------*
     5 0004 F*  HJG07Y - TAPE RENTAL REPORT - HAL GOODWIN - AUGUST 19, 1991      *
     6 0005 F*                                                                   *
     7 0006 F*  PROGRAM HJG07Y READS AN INPUT DATA FILE CONTAINING THE MEMBER-   *
     8 0007 F*  SHIP NUMBER AND VIDEO TAPE NUMBER OF A TAPE RENTED BY THE CLUB    *
     9 0008 F*  MEMBER.  THESE TWO NUMBERS ARE USED TO SEARCH PRE-EXECUTION TIME*
    10 0009 F*  TABLES TO DETERMINE THE NAME OF THE RENTER AND TITLE OF THE      *
    11 0010 F*  TAPE.  THE TABLE DATA IS LOADED FROM THE 'MEMBERS' AND 'TAPES'    *
    12 0011 F*  INPUT FILES.  IF EITHER ENTRY IN THE INPUT RECORD IS INVALID      *
    13 0012 F*  AND NO CORRESPONDING TABLE ENTRY IS FOUND, AN ERROR MESSAGE WILL*
    14 0013 F*  PRINT ON THE OUTPUT REPORT IN PLACE OF THE MEMBER NAME AND/OR     *
    15 0014 F*  THE TAPE TITLE.                                                   *
    16 0015 F*-------------------------------------------------------------------*


    19 0017 F*  TABLE FILE DESCRIPTIONS
    20 0018 FMEMBERS IT  F 300  30          EDISK
    21 0019 FTAPES   IT  F 300  30          EDISK


    24 0021 FRENTALS IP  F 200  20          DISK


    27 0023 FRENTLISTO   F 132 132     OF   PRINTER


    28 0024 E*-------------------------------------------------------------------*
    29 0025 E*  THE 'MEMBERS' FILE CONTAINS A MAXIMUM OF 25 RECORDS.  EACH        *
    30 0026 E*  RECORD CONTAINS A MEMBER NUMBER IN POSITIONS 1-6 AND A MEMBER     *
    31 0027 E*  NAME IN POSITIONS 7-26.  THE FILE IS SEQUENCED BY MEMBER NUMBER.*
    32 0028 E*                                                                   *
    33 0029 E*  THE 'TAPES' FILE CONTAINS A MAXIMUM OF 50 RECORDS.  EACH RECORD  *
    34 0030 E*  CONTAINS A VIDEO TAPE NUMBER IN POSITIONS 1-5, AND A TAPE TITLE  *
    35 0031 E*  IN POSITIONS 6-27.  THE FILE IS SEQUENCED BY VIDEO TAPE NUMBER.  *
    36 0032 E*-------------------------------------------------------------------*
    37 0033 E    MEMBERS        TABMEM 1  25  6 ATABNAM 20
    38 0034 E    TAPES          TABTAP 1  50  5 OATABTTL 22


    39 0035 I*  TAPE RENTAL RECORDS
    40 0036 I*---------------------
    41 0037 IRENTALS AA  01
    42 0038 I                                    1   6 MEMBER
    43 0039 I                                   10  140TAPENO


    44 0040 C*  TABLE LOOKUP OPERATIONS
    45 0041 C*-------------------------
    46 0042 C   01      MEMBER    LOKUPTABMEM   TABNAM        41
    47 0043 C   01      TAPENO    LOKUPTABTAP   TABTTL        42


    48 0044 O*  HEADING LINE ONE
    49 0045 O*------------------
    50 0046 ORENTLISTH  206    1P
    51 0047 O     OR         OF
    52 0048 O                             6 'HJG07Y'
    53 0049 O                            33 'TAPE RENTALS FOR'
    54 0050 O                   UDATE Y  42
    55 0051 O                            55 'PAGE'
    56 0052 O                   PAGE     60
```

Figure 7-26 (1)

```
HJG07Y    08-23-91  14:55:23  HJG07Y -- TAPE RENTAL REPORT         Version 3.5  Page  2
          ....+....1....+....2....+....3....+....4....+....5....+....6....+....7....

     59 0054 O*   HEADING LINE TWO
     60 0055 O*------------------
     61 0056 O         H   2      1P
     62 0057 O        OR          OF
     63 0058 O                                 10 'MEMBER NO.'
     64 0059 O                                 29 'MEMBER NAME'
     65 0060 O                                 55 'TAPE TITLE'

     68 0062 O*   DETAIL LINE
     69 0063 O*-----------
     70 0064 O         D   1      01
     71 0065 O                          MEMBER      8
     72 0066 O                     41   TABNAM     34
     73 0067 O                     42   TABTTL     60

     76 0069 O*               ----------------------
     77 0070 O*               *   ERROR MESSAGES    *
     78 0071 O*               ----------------------
     79 0072 O                     N41             35 '**INVALID MEMBER NUMBER'
     80 0073 O                     N42             46 '**TAPE NO.'
     81 0074 O                     N42   TAPENOZ   52
     82 0075 O                     N42             60 'INVALID'
     83 /*
     84 /*


          THE FOLLOWING INDICATORS APPEARED IN THIS PROGRAM

              01  41  42  1P  OF
     No Warning Errors
     No Fatal Errors
```

Figure 7-26 (2)

ARRAY LOOKUP

Chapter 6 presented the use of arrays for storing input values and values calculated by arithmetic statements and for retrieving messages based on the value of an index field. Arrays can also be used for lookup purposes in a manner similar to that used for tables. You have seen that an array and a table appear similar in computer storage; that is, they are composed of a series of elements in adjacent storage positions, have identical characteristics, and contain the same type of information. Unlike tables, however, the elements of the array are referenced by the array name and an index value.

To illustrate the use of arrays in a lookup operation, program HJG07Y is rewritten for arrays. To reference each element in the array, the array name, followed by a comma and an index, must be used in (Figure 7-27).

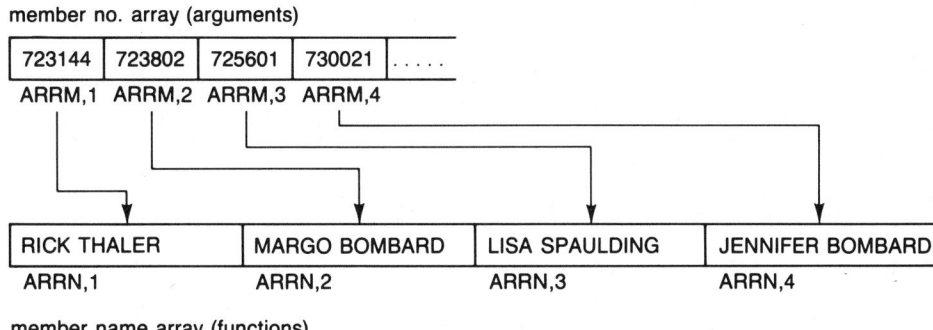

Figure 7-27 Example of arrays

Definition of Arrays

Note in the figure that the first element of the ARRM array (member number array) is referenced by the name ARRM,1. ARRM is the name of the array and 1 is its index. Similarly, the elements in the ARRN array (member name array) are referenced by the array name and an index. When the lookup operation takes place, the index is defined as a numeric field with no decimal positions so that it can be incremented to search the member number array for the correct element. Prior to specifying the lookup operation on the Calculation Specifications form, however, you must define the table file on the File Description Specifications form and the Extension Specifications form (Figure 7-28).

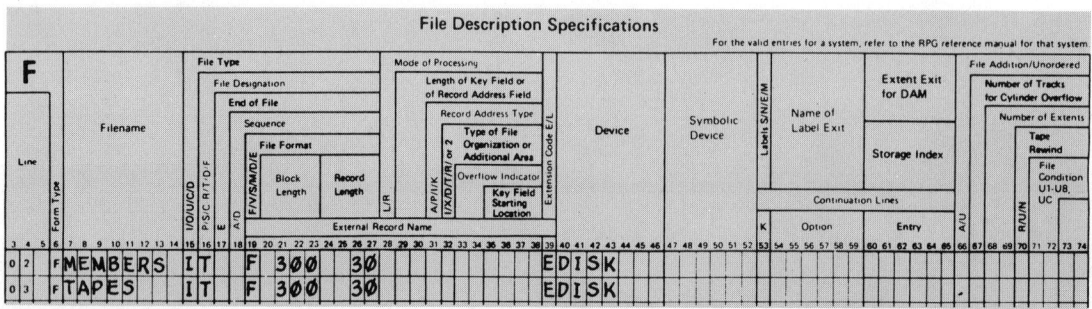

Figure 7-28   Preexecution Time Array Definition

Note from the example in Figure 7-28 that the definition of the table file MEMBERS on the File Description Specifications form for the array is the same as that for the preexecution time tables in program HJG07Y. It is important to note that the File Designation, position 16, must be T and that the E entry must be made in position 39. Unlike the examples of arrays in Chapter 6, these arrays are read into the program from the MEMBERS and TAPES files prior to reading the first data record because they are preexecution time arrays.

The entries on the Extension Specifications form specify the alternating array format; that is, each array data record in the MEMBERS file contains a member number element (ARRM) followed by a member name element (ARRN). This is the same way that the table file was defined in our earlier use of this program (see Figure 7-25). Each record contains one entry consisting of the member number and member name (specified by the entry in position 35). The total number of entries in the array is 25. The member number array consists of alphameric elements, each six characters long (position 42); this array is in ascending sequence, as indicated by the entry A in position 45. The member name array consists of alphameric elements, each with 20 characters (positions 53–54).

Array Lookup Calculations

After the arrays are defined, the array look-up can take place. The processing that occurs is illustrated in the following examples.

▸ **Setting the Index**   The **Z-ADD** (zero and add) operation is used to initialize the index to the value 1; this is step 1 (Figure 7-29). The **zero and add** operation is equivalent to adding the data contained in Factor 2 to a field of zeros and placing the result in the Result Field area. In effect, the value in Factor 2 is placed in the Result Field. Thus, as shown in the figure, after the Z-ADD instruction is executed, the index field I contains a numeric value of 1 and can then be used as the index to begin the array search.

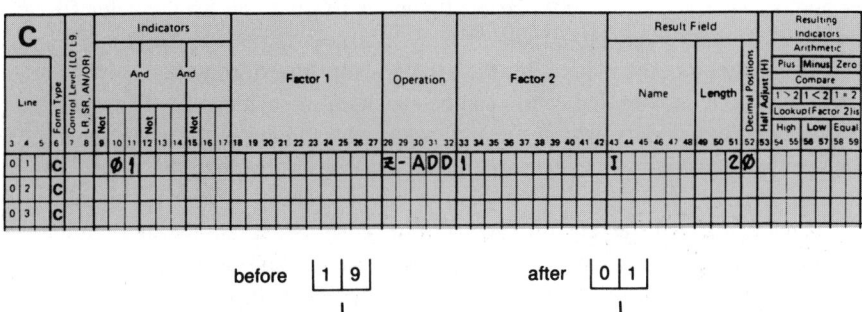

Figure 7-29   Step 1: Index is initialized by the Z-ADD operation to point
to the first element in the argument array.

▸ **Searching the Array**   The LOKUP operation code is used to search the ARRM array for a member number that equals the member number found in the MEMBER input field; this is step 2 (Figure 7-30). When arrays are used in a lookup operation, the entry in Factor 2 must be the name of the array to be searched, followed immediately by a comma and then the name of the index to be used in the search. The figure shows that the array name specified is ARRM, which is the array that contains the member numbers. A comma and then the index I immediately follow the ARRM name. In step 1, I was initialized with the value 1; therefore, the lookup operation begins with the first element in the array ARRM. If the index I had been initialized with another value, the search would begin with that element. For example, if the value 5 had been placed in the index prior to the LOKUP operation, the lookup would have begun with the fifth element in the array and then would have continued to the end. The LOKUP operation automatically causes the value in the index to be incremented by 1 during the lookup process so that each element in the argument array is compared with the search argument.

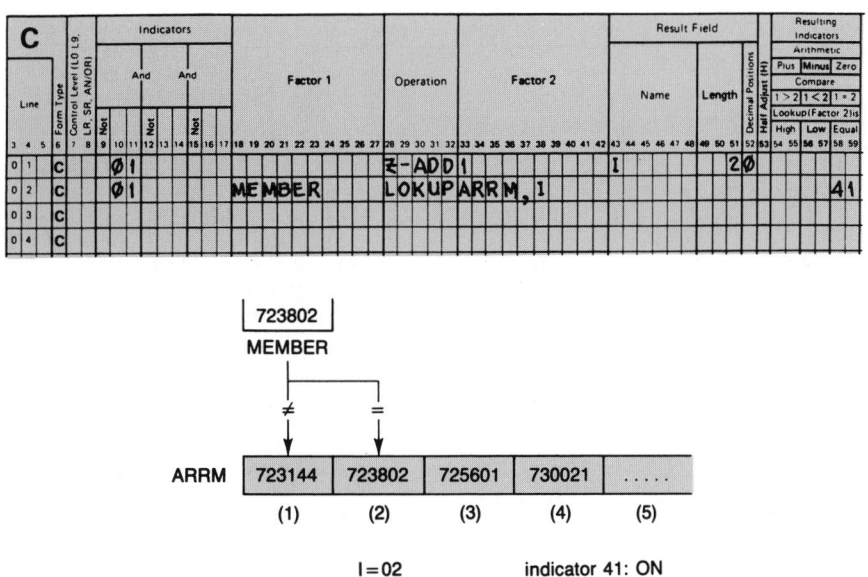

Figure 7-30   Step 2: Array lookup is performed to examine the argument array
and set the index at the correct value.

The LOKUP operation is terminated in one of two ways. First, if an item in the array is found to be equal to the item in the Factor 1 field, the resulting indicator is turned on, and the index is set to reference the number of the array element. Thus, in Figure 7-30, the second element in the ARRM array is found equal to the member number in the MEMBER field. Therefore, indicator 41 is turned on, and the index is set to the value 02. The second way in which the search is terminated is if no element in the array is found to be equal to the value in the Factor 1 field, in which case, the index is reset to the value 1 and the indicator is not turned on. Thus, in Figure 7-30, if an equal member number were not found in the array, the index I would contain the value 01, and indicator 41 would not be turned on. Note that (unlike table lookup) array lookup does not use the Result Field. The function is determined by the value contained in the index after the array lookup is performed.

As is the case with table lookup, indicators can be specified in positions 54–55 to indicate that the search is to terminate when the next higher value than the search argument is found in the array specified in Factor 2, or in positions 56–57 when the search is to terminate when the next lower value than the search argument is found in the Factor 2 array.

Figure 7-31 is the completed Calculation Specifications form. Note that the lookup procedure for the second set of arrays – ARRV (video tape number) and ARRT (video tape title) – is similar to the operations used to retrieve the member name from the ARRN array. Notice also that a separate field has been defined as the index for the ARRV array. The same index cannot be used for both array lookup operations because the second LOKUP would destroy the index setting of the first. This logic error would not be detected by the compiler but would result in incorrect output data. Figure 7-32 summarizes the Z-ADD operation.

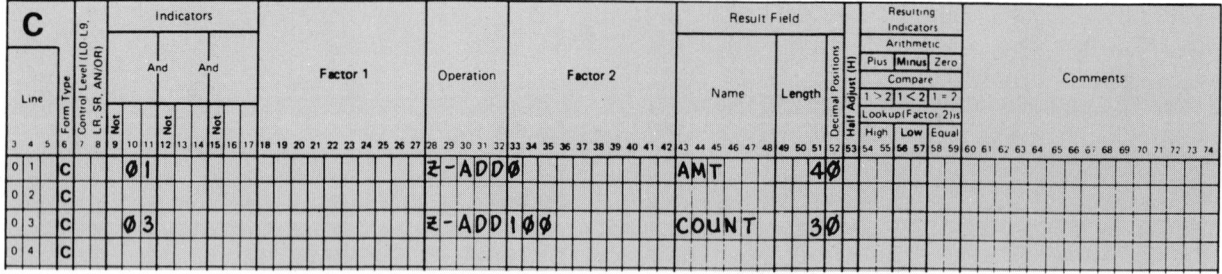

Figure 7-31   Array lookup calculations

Z-ADD Operation Summary
Factor 2 is added to a field of zeros. The sum is then placed into the Result Field. Factor 1 is not used.

Figure 7-32 (1)   Z-ADD operation summary

continued

Control Level Indicators	Indicators	Factor 1	Operation Name	Factor 2	Result Field	Resulting Indicators		
7–8	9–17	18–27	28–32	33–42	43–53	54–55	56–57	58–59
optional	optional	blank	Z-ADD	required	required	optional	optional	optional

Figure 7-32 (2)   (continued)

Output Specifications

After the array lookup is completed and the location of the array argument is stored in the index, the program uses the index to retrieve the related item from the function array. The sample program retrieves from the ARRN array the member name that corresponds to the member number in the ARRM array. To do this, the ARRN array is specified with the index used in the lookup operation (Figure 7-33).

On line 05 in Figure 7-33, the entry ARRN,I is placed in the Field Name area, positions 32–37, which instructs the program to print the element in the ARRN array that is specified by the value in the index I. Note that the element is printed only if indicator 41 is on, that is, if a member number is found in the ARRM array (see Figure 7-31). If indicator 41 is not on, the message **INVALID MEMBER NUMBER is printed on the report.

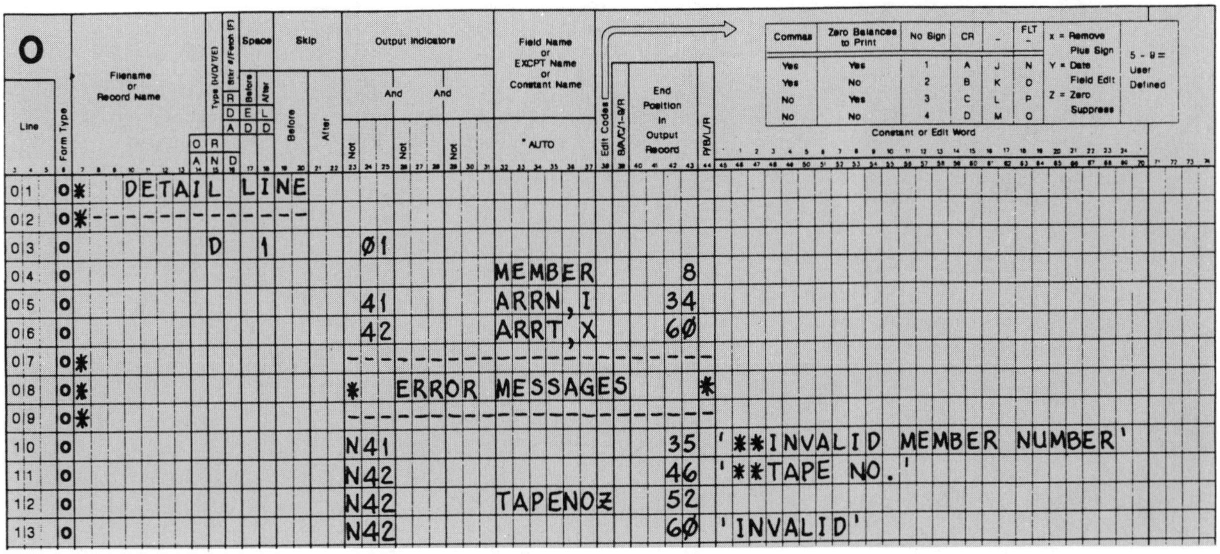

Figure 7-33   Output specifications for program HJG07Z

The same technique is used to print the video tape title (ARRT,X) if indicator 42 is on (line 06 of Figure 7-33). Lines 11–13 print the error message **TAPE NO. xxxxx INVALID if indicator 42 is not on. Figure 7-34 is the compiled array lookup program and program output. Note that the output of the array lookup program is identical to the output from the two previous table lookup examples.

Figure 7-34 Compilation listing and output for program HJG07Z

```
HJG07Z    08-23-91  14:16:54  HJG07Z -- TAPE RENTAL REPORT           Version 3.5  Page  1

          ....+....1....+....2....+....3....+....4....+....5....+....6....+....7....

   3 0002 H                                                                    HJG07Z


   4 0003 F*-----------------------------------------------------------------*
   5 0004 F*  HJG07Y - TAPE RENTAL REPORT - HAL GOODWIN - AUGUST 19, 1991     *
   6 0005 F*                                                                  *
   7 0006 F*  PROGRAM HJG07Y READS AN INPUT DATA FILE CONTAINING THE MEMBER-  *
   8 0007 F*  SHIP NUMBER AND VIDEO TAPE NUMBER OF A TAPE RENTED BY THE CLUB  *
   9 0008 F*  MEMBER.  THESE TWO NUMBERS ARE USED TO SEARCH PRE-EXECUTION TIME*
  10 0009 F*  ARRAYS TO DETERMINE THE NAME OF THE RENTER AND TITLE OF THE     *
  11 0010 F*  TAPE.  THE ARRAY DATA IS LOADED FROM THE 'MEMBERS' AND 'TAPES'  *
  12 0011 F*  INPUT FILES.  IF EITHER ENTRY IN THE INPUT RECORD IS INVALID    *
  13 0012 F*  AND NO CORRESPONDING ARRAY ENTRY IS FOUND, AN ERROR MESSAGE WILL*
  14 0013 F*  PRINT ON THE OUTPUT REPORT IN PLACE OF THE MEMBER NAME AND/OR   *
  15 0014 F*  THE TAPE TITLE.                                                 *
  16 0015 F*-----------------------------------------------------------------*


  19 0017 F*  ARRAY FILE DESCRIPTIONS
  20 0018 FMEMBERS IT  F 300  30         EDISK
  21 0019 FTAPES   IT  F 300  30         EDISK

  24 0021 FRENTALS IP  F 200  20         DISK

  27 0023 FRENTLISTO   F 132 132    OF   PRINTER


  28 0024 E*-----------------------------------------------------------------*
  29 0025 E*  THE 'MEMBERS' FILE CONTAINS A MAXIMUM OF 25 RECORDS.  EACH      *
  30 0026 E*  RECORD CONTAINS A MEMBER NUMBER IN POSITIONS 1-6 AND A MEMBER   *
  31 0027 E*  NAME IN POSITIONS 7-26.  THE FILE IS SEQUENCED BY MEMBER NUMBER.*
  32 0028 E*                                                                  *
  33 0029 E*  THE 'TAPES' FILE CONTAINS A MAXIMUM OF 50 RECORDS.  EACH RECORD *
  34 0030 E*  CONTAINS A VIDEO TAPE NUMBER IN POSITIONS 1-5, AND A TAPE TITLE *
  35 0031 E*  IN POSITIONS 6-27.  THE FILE IS SEQUENCED BY VIDEO TAPE NUMBER. *
  36 0032 E*-----------------------------------------------------------------*
  37 0033 E    MEMBERS          ARRM  1 25 6 AARRN    20
  38 0034 E    TAPES            ARRV  1 50 5 0AARRT   22


  39 0035 I*  TAPE RENTAL RECORDS
  40 0036 I*---------------------
  41 0037 IRENTALS AA  01
  42 0038 I                                    1   6 MEMBER
  43 0039 I                                   10  140TAPENO


  44 0040 C*  ARRAY LOOKUP OPERATIONS
  45 0041 C*----------------------
  46 0042 C    01            Z-ADD1      I      20
  47 0043 C    01   MEMBER   LOKUPARRM,I                41
  48 0044 C    01            Z-ADD1      X      20
  49 0045 C    01   TAPENO   LOKUPARRV,X                42


  50 0046 O*  HEADING LINE ONE
  51 0047 O*-------------------
  52 0048 ORENTLISTH  206   1P
  53 0049 O      OR        OF
  54 0050 O                            6 'HJG07Z'
  55 0051 O                           33 'TAPE RENTALS FOR'
  56 0052 O              UDATE Y      42
  57 0053 O                           55 'PAGE'
  58 0054 O              PAGE         60
```

Figure 7-34 (1)

```
HJG07Z    08-23-91  14:16:54  HJG07Z -- TAPE RENTAL REPORT        Version 3.5  Page  2

          ....+....1....+....2....+....3....+....4....+....5....+....6....+....7....

   61 0056 O*  HEADING LINE TWO
   62 0057 O*------------------
   63 0058 O        H  2    1P
   64 0059 O       OR        OF
   65 0060 O                                  10 'MEMBER NO.'
   66 0061 O                                  29 'MEMBER NAME'
   67 0062 O                                  55 'TAPE TITLE'


   70 0064 O*  DETAIL LINE
   71 0065 O*------------
   72 0066 O        D  1    01
   73 0067 O                      MEMBER      8
   74 0068 O                41    ARRN,I     34
   75 0069 O                42    ARRT,X     60


   78 0071 O*                  --------------------
   79 0072 O*                  *  ERROR MESSAGES    *
   80 0073 O*                  --------------------
   81 0074 O                N41            35 '**INVALID MEMBER NUMBER'
   82 0075 O                N42            46 '**TAPE NO.'
   83 0076 O                N42  TAPENOZ  52
   84 0077 O                N42            60 'INVALID'
   85 /*
   86 /*



          THE FOLLOWING INDICATORS APPEARED IN THIS PROGRAM


               01  41  42  1P  OF
       No Warning Errors
       No Fatal Errors
```

Figure 7-34 (2)

```
HJG07Z              TAPE RENTALS FOR  8/23/91          PAGE     1

       MEMBER NO.         MEMBER NAME              TAPE TITLE

         723144      RICK THALER          FLASHDANCE
         723802      MARGO BOMBARD         MUTINY ON THE BOUNTY
         723802      MARGO BOMBARD         THE STING
         732114      PEGGY BISSEL          A CHRISTMAS CAROL
         733342      KRISTEN PEKKINNEN     ALICE IN WONDERLAND
         812007      **INVALID MEMBER NUMBER  STAR TREK
         820001      JIM BELLIVEAU         CONAN THE BARBARIAN
         813114      JEAN DENNETT          TRON
         810351      ELLIOT BELIN          GREMLINS
         815113      CASSANDRA GOSLIN      WOODSTOCK
         817504      BILL GOUDREAU         **TAPE NO.  8802 INVALID
```

Figure 7-34 (3)

IN CONCLUSION

This chapter has shown you how to use tables and arrays to retrieve data based on the contents of an input field. Table and array lookup have two major limitations, however. First, when table and array lookup are being performed, each LOKUP operation can access only a single function field. If the program needs to access five fields, even though they are all based on the same search argument, five separate LOKUPs would be required.

Second, table and array lookup require the entire table or array to be stored in memory while the program is executing, which greatly limits the amount of data that can be stored in a table or array. In Chapter 8, we will learn to use the CHAIN command to retrieve an entire record from a separate disk file. The techniques of randomly accessing a data file will enable you to retrieve many fields with a single operation. Because the data is stored in a disk file rather than in computer memory, the limitations of table and array lookup are eliminated.

CHAPTER SUMMARY

1. **Table lookup** is a process by which a known value, called a **search argument**, is compared with a series of similar values, called an **argument table**, until either a match is found or it is determined that no match exists. If a match is found, a related value, called the **function**, is retrieved.
2. The function is one of a series of values called the **function table**.
3. Although tables used in table lookup can be in any sequence, there must be a **positional relationship** between elements in the argument and the function table. The first argument must correspond to the first function, the second argument to the second function, and so on.
4. A **compile time table** is part of the RPG source program. Each compile time table must be preceded by a separator record containing ** in positions 1 and 2.
5. If a single table data input record contains both an argument and a function, the table is in the **alternating format**.
6. When the alternating format is used, an **entry** consists of two fields, an argument and a function.
7. The number of table data records can be less than the number specified in the Number of Entries per Table area of the Extension Specifications form. The number of records cannot be greater than the Extension form entry.
8. Table names can be from four to six characters long and must begin with the letters **TAB**.
9. If multiple compile time tables are used in a program, they must appear at the end of the RPG source code in the sequence in which they were described on the Extension Specifications form.
10. The **LOKUP** operation searches tables and retrieves the needed entries from the function table.
11. If a table lookup operation is successful, the retrieved function is placed in the field that has the same name as the function table.
12. When the argument table and function tables are in separate table data records, the data is in the **separate table** format.
13. A **preexecution** or **prerun** time table contains data that is loaded into the table area from a disk data file. These tables are loaded at the beginning of program execution, prior to step 1 of the RPG logic cycle.
14. Data files used to load preexecution time tables must be described on the File Description Specifications form with the entry T in position 16 and the entry E in position 39.
15. When array lookup is performed, the array index must be loaded with the number of the first array element to be tested. This value is normally 1 but can be any valid array element number.
16. The **Z-ADD** operation adds the numeric value in Factor 2 to zero and places the sum in the field specified in the Result Field area.

REVIEW QUESTIONS

1. List two limitations of array retrieval.
2. Define search argument.
3. Define table argument.
4. Define function.
5. Why is a positional relationship necessary between elements of the argument and function tables?
6. What is the main difference between compile time tables and preexecution time tables?
7. Why does the LOKUP operation work more efficiently when a sequential argument table is used?
8. What does each of the three resulting indicators that can be used in a LOKUP operation specify?
9. What is the difference in the use of the Result Field area when doing table lookup as opposed to array lookup?
10. What three letters must be used to start every table name?
11. When performing array lookup, how is the index set to the starting position of the argument array?
12. What value does RPG place in the index field if no match is found during an array lookup operation and the resulting indicator has been placed in the = position?

STUDENT EXERCISES: RPG PROGRAM CODE

1. Use Figure 7-35 to code the File Description Specifications and Extension Specifications form entries needed to define the table that is to be loaded from the following disk data file:

   Each data file record contains five table entries. Each argument entry is an Item Number, which is seven positions long and contains alphameric data. Each function entry is a Unit Cost field, which is a four-position, numeric data field with three decimal places. The data records in this file are 70 characters long.

   You may select any appropriate names for the data file, the argument table, and the function table. The maximum number of table entries is 100.

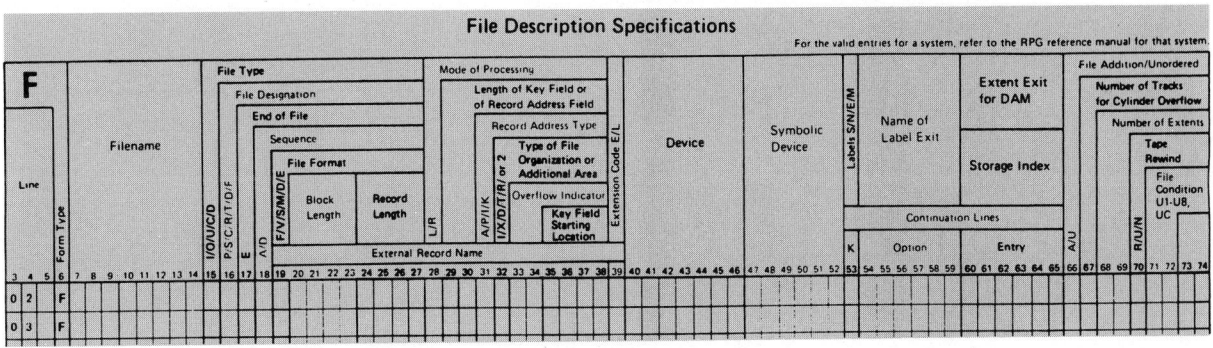

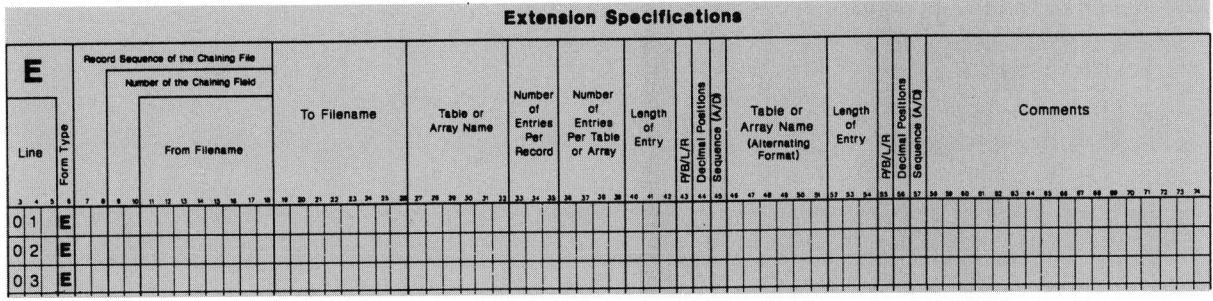

Figure 7-35   File description and extension specifications forms

2. Use Figure 7-36 on the next page to code the calculation operations needed to retrieve the unit cost of an item identified in the ITEM data field. Use table lookup for this retrieval. If the corresponding item number is found and unit cost retrieved, multiply the unit cost by the QTY field. The product of the multiplication is a money (dollars and cents) amount. If no corresponding item number is found, the multiplication is not performed.

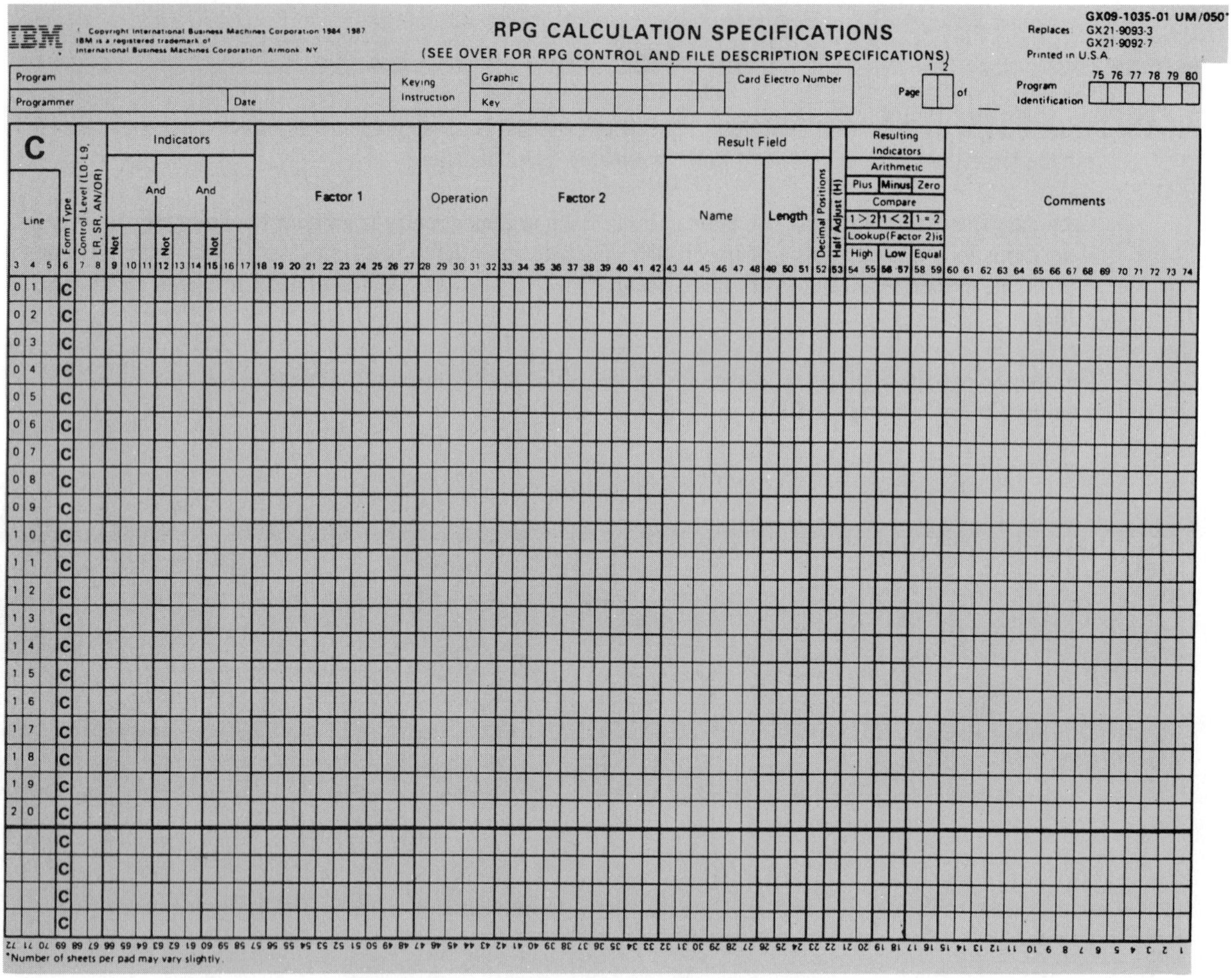

IBM © Copyright International Business Machines Corporation 1984 1987 IBM is a registered trademark of International Business Machines Corporation Armonk NY

RPG CALCULATION SPECIFICATIONS

(SEE OVER FOR RPG CONTROL AND FILE DESCRIPTION SPECIFICATIONS)

GX09-1035-01 UM/050*
Replaces GX21-9093-3 GX21-9092-7
Printed in U.S.A.

Program | Programmer | Date | Keying Instruction | Graphic | Key | Card Electro Number | Page of | Program Identification

C | Line | Form Type | Control Level (L0-L9, LR, SR, AN/OR) | Indicators (And, And, Not) | Factor 1 | Operation | Factor 2 | Result Field (Name, Length) | Decimal Positions | Half Adjust (H) | Resulting Indicators (Arithmetic: Plus, Minus, Zero; Compare: 1>2, 1<2, 1=2; Lookup(Factor 2)is: High, Low, Equal) | Comments

*Number of sheets per pad may vary slightly.

Figure 7-36 Calculation Specifications form

STUDENT EXERCISES: DEBUGGING RPG PROGRAMS

Problem 1

The following RPG program (Figure 7-37) contains a fatal error detected by the compiler. The error is message number A106 following line 105 of the compiler listing. Explain the cause of this error and two possible methods of eliminating the error.

Figure 7-37   Debugging Problem 1

```
HJG07X · 08-24-91 17:01:02        IBM PC        RPG II        Version 3.5  Page  1

    ....+....1....+....2....+....3....+....4....+....5....+....6....+....7....

    1 0001 H                                                              HJG07X


    2 0002 FRENTALS IP  F 200  20           DISK
    3 0003 FRENTLISTO   F 132 132     OF    PRINTER


    4 0004 E                    TABMEM  1  25  6 ATABNAM 20
    5 0005 E                    TABTAP  1  50  5 OATABTTL 22


    6 0006 IRENTALS AA  01
    7 0007 I                                     1   6 MEMBER
    8 0008 I                                    10  140TAPENO


    9 0009 C   01      MEMBER    LOKUPTABMEM    TABNAM        41
   10 0010 C   01      TAPENO    LOKUPTABTAP    TABTTL        42


   11 0011 ORENTLISTH    206   1P
   12*0012 O        OR         OF
   13 0013 O                                    6 'HJG07X'
   14 0014 O                                   33 'TAPE RENTALS FOR'
   15 0015 O                         UDATE Y    42
   16 0016 O                                   55 'PAGE'
   17 0017 O                         PAGE       60
   18 0018 O        H  2   1P
   19 0019 O        OR         OF
   20 0020 O                                   10 'MEMBER NO.'
   21 0021 O                                   29 'MEMBER NAME'
   22 0022 O                                   55 'TAPE TITLE'
   23 0023 O        D  1   01
   24 0024 O                         MEMBER      8
   25 0025 O                   41    TABNAM     34
   26 0026 O                   42    TABTTL     60
   27 0027 O                  N41               35 '**INVALID MEMBER NUMBER'
   28 0028 O                  N42               46 '**TAPE NO.'
   29 0029 O                  N42    TAPENOZ    52
   30 0030 O                  N42               60 'INVALID'
   31 **
   32 723144RICK THALER
   33 723802MARGO BOMBARD
   34 725601LISA SPALDING
   35 730021JENNIFER BOMBARD
   36 732114PEGGY BISSEL
   37 733342KRISTEN PEKKINNEN
   38 736001HEIDI THOMPSON
   39 736004JIM REID
   40 800201MICHELLE ROY
   41 800402ERIN CARROLL
   42 802007MIKE HAMEL
   43 809501ROY K. WHEATON
   44 810351ELLIOT BELIN
   45 812101JAMES WALTON
   46 813114JEAN DENNETT
   47 814006BARBARA POHJA
   48 815113CASSANDRA GOSLIN
   49 816125CAROLYN MOES
   50 817504BILL GOUDREAU
   51 818003STEVE MUSGROVE
   52 819133CYNDI LUTTIG
   53 820001JIM BELLIVEAU
```

Figure 7-37 (1)   *continued*

```
HJG07X     08-24-91  17:01:02         IBM PC       RPG II        Version 3.5  Page  2
           ....+....1....+....2....+....3....+....4....+....5....+....6....+....7....

      54 **
****-A001W-Less than the total number of table or array data elements were provided.
      55 001002001: A SPACE ODYSSEY
      56 00203REAR WINDOW
      57 00500STAR WARS
      58 00900THE PHILADELPHIA STORY
      59 01001CLOSE ENCOUNTERS-3RD
      60 01101E. T.
      61 01301TRON
      62 01332GUYS AND DOLLS
      63 01472POLTERGEIST
      64 01501GHOSTBUSTERS
      65 01502EMPIRE STRIKES BACK
      66 01816ALICE IN WONDERLAND
      67 02117FLASHDANCE
      68 02283MY FAIR LADY
      69 02400WAR GAMES
      70 02533RIO BRAVO
      71 02788BLUE THUNDER
      72 02791THE FINAL COUNTDOWN
      73 03101RISKY BUSINESS
      74 03105TOP GUN
      75 03301THE GODFATHER
      76 03401GODFATHER II
      77 03601THE GALLANT HOURS
      78 03901CLOUD DANCER
      79 04060THE RIGHT STUFF
      80 04238A CHRISTMAS CAROL
      81 04611HIGH ROAD TO CHINA
      82 04801KING KONG
      83 04922SPIRIT OF ST. LOUIS
      84 05110GREMLINS
      85 05340MUTINY ON THE BOUNTY
      86 05462THE 39 STEPS
      87 05602VERTIGO
      88 06001CONAN THE BARBARIAN
      89 06401STAR TREK
      90 06433STAR TREK 11
      91 06481STAR TREK III
      92 06495STAR TREK IV
      93 06501THE STING
      94 06601RETURN OF THE JEDI
      95 07203SANDS OF IWO JIMA
      96 07401BLADE RUNNER
      97 08202WOODSTOCK
      98 08801THE QUIET MAN
      99 09003BELL, BOOK, AND CANDLE
     100 09501TOPPER
     101 10101METROPOLIS
     102 10301ALIEN
     103 10305ALIENS
     104 10386THE ALAMO
     105 14589PLAN 9 FROM OUTER SPCE
****-A106- Too many table or array data elements were provided.
     106 /*
     107 /*


          THE FOLLOWING INDICATORS APPEARED IN THIS PROGRAM

          01  41  42  1P  OF
    1 Warning Errors
    1 Fatal Errors
```

Figure 7-37 (2)

Problem 2

The following RPG program (Figure 7-38) contains one or more errors detected while checking output from the program. Circle the errors and record the corrected entries directly on the listing. Explain the error and method of correction.

Figure 7-38   Debugging Problem 2

```
HJG07Z    08-24-91  17:05:23  HJG07Z -- TAPE RENTAL REPORT          Version 3.5  Page  1

          ....+....1....+....2....+....3....+....4....+....5....+....6....+....7....

     3 0002 H                                                                  HJG07Z


     4 0003 F*-----------------------------------------------------------------*
     5 0004 F*  HJG07Z - TAPE RENTAL REPORT - HAL GOODWIN - AUGUST 19, 1991    *
     6 0005 F*                                                                 *
     7 0006 F*  PROGRAM HJG07Z READS AN INPUT DATA FILE CONTAINING THE MEMBER- *
     8 0007 F*  SHIP NUMBER AND VIDEO TAPE NUMBER OF A TAPE RENTED BY THE CLUB  *
     9 0008 F*  MEMBER.  THESE TWO NUMBERS ARE USED TO SEARCH PRE-EXECUTION TIME*
    10 0009 F*  ARRAYS TO DETERMINE THE NAME OF THE RENTER AND TITLE OF THE     *
    11 0010 F*  TAPE.  THE ARRAY DATA IS LOADED FROM THE 'MEMBERS' AND 'TAPES'  *
    12 0011 F*  INPUT FILES.  IF EITHER ENTRY IN THE INPUT RECORD IS INVALID    *
    13 0012 F*  AND NO CORRESPONDING ARRAY ENTRY IS FOUND, AN ERROR MESSAGE WILL*
    14 0013 F*  PRINT ON THE OUTPUT REPORT IN PLACE OF THE MEMBER NAME AND/OR   *
    15 0014 F*  THE TAPE TITLE.                                                 *
    16 0015 F*-----------------------------------------------------------------*


    19 0017 F* ARRAY FILE DESCRIPTIONS
    20 0018 FMEMBERS IT  F 300  30              EDISK
    21 0019 FTAPES   IT  F 300  30              EDISK


    24 0021 FRENTALS IP  F 200  20              DISK


    27 0023 FRENTLISTO   F 132 132       OF     PRINTER



    28 0024 E*-----------------------------------------------------------------*
    29 0025 E*  THE 'MEMBERS' FILE CONTAINS A MAXIMUM OF 25 RECORDS.  EACH      *
    30 0026 E*  RECORD CONTAINS A MEMBER NUMBER IN POSITIONS 1-6 AND A MEMBER   *
    31 0027 E*  NAME IN POSITIONS 7-26.  THE FILE IS SEQUENCED BY MEMBER NUMBER.*
    32 0028 E*                                                                  *
    33 0029 E*  THE 'TAPES' FILE CONTAINS A MAXIMUM OF 50 RECORDS.  EACH RECORD *
    34 0030 E*  CONTAINS A VIDEO TAPE NUMBER IN POSITIONS 1-5, AND A TAPE TITLE *
    35 0031 E*  IN POSITIONS 6-27.  THE FILE IS SEQUENCED BY VIDEO TAPE NUMBER. *
    36 0032 E*-----------------------------------------------------------------*
    37 0033 E    MEMBERS        ARRM   1  25  6 AARRN   20
    38 0034 E    TAPES          ARRV   1  50  5 0AARRT   22


    39 0035 I* TAPE RENTAL RECORDS
    40 0036 I*-------------------
    41 0037 IRENTALS AA  01
    42 0038 I                                  1   6 MEMBER
    43 0039 I                                 10  140TAPENO


    44 0040 C* ARRAY LOOKUP OPERATIONS
    45 0041 C*--------------------
    46 0042 C   01             Z-ADD1     I      20
    47 0043 C   01     MEMBER  LOKUPARRM                41
    48 0044 C   01             Z-ADD1     X      20
    49 0045 C   01     TAPENO  LOKUPARRV                42
```

Figure 7-38 (1)

```
HJG07Z    08-24-91  17:05:23  HJG07Z -- TAPE RENTAL REPORT        Version 3.5  Page  2

          :...+....1....+....2....+....3....+....4....+....5....+....6....+....7....

      50 0046 O*  HEADING LINE ONE
      51 0047 O*------------------
      52 0048 ORENTLISTH    206     1P
      53 0049 O         OR          OF
      54 0050 O                                    6 'HJG07Z'
      55 0051 O                                   33 'TAPE RENTALS FOR'
      56 0052 O                      UDATE Y       42
      57 0053 O                                   55 'PAGE'
      58 0054 O                      PAGE          60

      61 0056 O*  HEADING LINE TWO
      62 0057 O*------------------
      63 0058 O             H  2     1P
      64 0059 O         OR          OF
      65 0060 O                                   10 'MEMBER NO.'
      66 0061 O                                   29 'MEMBER NAME'
      67 0062 O                                   55 'TAPE TITLE'

      70 0064 O*  DETAIL LINE
      71 0065 O*------------
      72 0066 O             D  1     01
      73 0067 O                      MEMBER     8
      74 0068 O                41    ARRN,I    34
      75 0069 O                42    ARRT,X    60

      78 0071 O*                  --------------------
      79 0072 O*                  *  ERROR MESSAGES   *
      80 0073 O*                  --------------------
      81 0074 O                N41              35 '**INVALID MEMBER NUMBER'
      82 0075 O                N42              46 '**TAPE NO.'
      83 0076 O                N42   TAPENOZ    52
      84 0077 O                N42              60 'INVALID'
      85 /*
      86 /*


          THE FOLLOWING INDICATORS APPEARED IN THIS PROGRAM

              01  41  42  1P  OF
      No Warning Errors
      No Fatal Errors
```

Figure 7-38 (2)

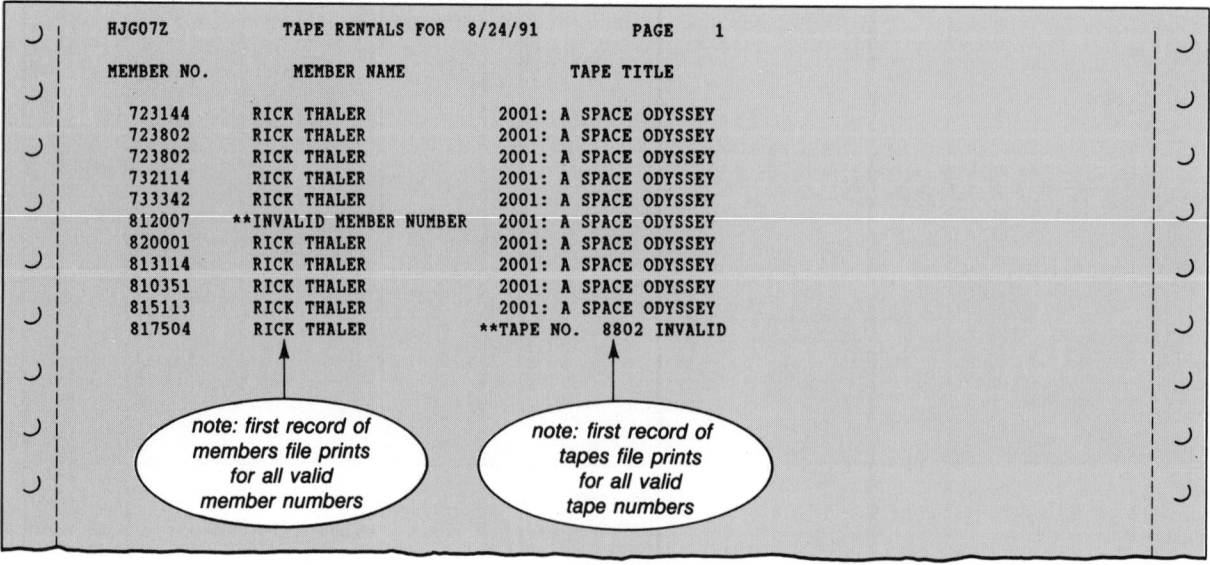

Figure 7-38 (3)

STUDENT EXERCISES: RPG PROGRAM MAINTENANCE

Problem 1

The user of the Tape Rental Report has indicated that extra space is needed in both of the compile time tables used in program HJG07X. Print the changes needed to double the number of allowable entries in each of the two sets of tables directly on the program listing (Figure 7-39). Explain your modifications and their effect on the program.

Figure 7-39   Program Maintenance Problem 1

```
HJG07X     08-24-91  17:16:38       IBM PC       RPG II        Version 3.5  Page  1
           ....+....1....+....2....+....3....+....4....+....5....+....6....+....7....

    1 0001 H                                                             HJG07X


    2 0002 FRENTALS IP  F 200  20           DISK
    3 0003 FRENTLISTO   F 132 132      OF   PRINTER


    4 0004 E                  TABMEM  1  25   6  ATABNAM 20
    5 0005 E                  TABTAP  1. 50   5 0ATABTTL 22


    6 0006 IRENTALS AA   01
    7 0007 I                                      1   6 MEMBER
    8 0008 I                                     10  14OTAPENO


    9 0009 C    01     MEMBER     LOKUPTABMEM    TABNAM       41
   10 0010 C    01     TAPENO     LOKUPTABTAP    TABTTL       42


   11 0011 ORENTLISTH    206    1P
   12 0012 O       OR           OF
   13 0013 O                                  6 'HJG07X'
   14 0014 O                                 33 'TAPE RENTALS FOR'
   15 0015 O                        UDATE Y  42
   16 0016 O                                 55 'PAGE'
   17 0017 O                        PAGE     60
   18 0018 O       H  2   1P
   19 0019 O       OR           OF
   20 0020 O                                 10 'MEMBER NO.'
   21 0021 O                                 29 'MEMBER NAME'
   22 0022 O                                 55 'TAPE TITLE'
   23 0023 O       D  1   01
   24 0024 O                        MEMBER    8
   25 0025 O                    41  TABNAM   34
   26 0026 O                    42  TABTTL   60
   27 0027 O                   N41           35 '**INVALID MEMBER NUMBER'
   28 0028 O                   N42           46 '**TAPE NO.'
   29 0029 O                   N42  TAPENOZ  52
   30 0030 O                   N42           60 'INVALID'
   31 **
   32 723144RICK THALER
   33 723802MARGO BOMBARD
   34 725601LISA SPALDING
   35 730021JENNIFER BOMBARD
   36 732114PEGGY BISSEL
   37 733342KRISTEN PEKKINNEN
   38 736001HEIDI THOMPSON
   39 736004JIM REID
   40 800201MICHELLE ROY
   41 800402ERIN CARROLL
   42 802007MIKE HAMEL
   43 809501ROY K. WHEATON
```

Figure 7-39 (1)   *continued*

```
HJG07X      08-24-91  17:16:38       IBM PC       RPG II        Version 3.5  Page  2

            ....+....1....+....2....+....3....+....4....+....5....+....6....+....7....

        44 810351ELLIOT BELIN
        45 812101JAMES WALTON
        46 813114JEAN DENNETT
        47 814006BARBARA POHJA
        48 815113CASSANDRA GOSLIN
        49 816125CAROLYN MOES
        50 817504BILL GOUDREAU
        51 818003STEVE MUSGROVE
        52 819133CYNDI LUTTIG
        53 820001JIM BELLIVEAU
        54 **
****-A001W-Less than the total number of table or array data elements were provided.
        55 001002001: A SPACE ODYSSEY
        56 00203REAR WINDOW
        57 00500STAR WARS
        58 00900THE PHILADELPHIA STORY
        59 01001CLOSE ENCOUNTERS-3RD
        60 01101E. T.
        61 01301TRON
        62 01332GUYS AND DOLLS
        63 01472POLTERGEIST
        64 01501GHOSTBUSTERS
        65 01502EMPIRE STRIKES BACK
        66 01816ALICE IN WONDERLAND
        67 02117FLASHDANCE
        68 02283MY FAIR LADY
        69 02400WAR GAMES
        70 02533RIO BRAVO
        71 02788BLUE THUNDER
        72 02791THE FINAL COUNTDOWN
        73 03101RISKY BUSINESS
        74 03105TOP GUN
        75 03301THE GODFATHER
        76 03401GODFATHER II
        77 03601THE GALLANT HOURS
        78 03901CLOUD DANCER
        79 04060THE RIGHT STUFF
        80 04238A CHRISTMAS CAROL
        81 04611HIGH ROAD TO CHINA
        82 04801KING KONG
        83 04922SPIRIT OF ST. LOUIS
        84 05110GREMLINS
        85 05340MUTINY ON THE BOUNTY
        86 05462THE 39 STEPS
        87 05602VERTIGO
        88 06001CONAN THE BARBARIAN
        89 06401STAR TREK
        90 06433STAR TREK 11
        91 06481STAR TREK III
        92 06495STAR TREK IV
        93 06501THE STING
        94 06601RETURN OF THE JEDI
        95 07203SANDS OF IWO JIMA
        96 07401BLADE RUNNER
        97 08202WOODSTOCK
        98 08801THE QUIET MAN
        99 09003BELL, BOOK, AND CANDLE
       100 09501TOPPER
       101 10101METROPOLIS
       102 10301ALIEN
       103 10305ALIENS
       104 10386THE ALAMO
       105 /*
       106 /*


          THE FOLLOWING INDICATORS APPEARED IN THIS PROGRAM

             01  41  42  1P  OF
      1 Warning Errors
      No Fatal Errors
```

Figure 7-38 (3)

▦ Problem 2

Modify program HJG07Y (Figure 7-40) so that the detail line prints only if both the member number (MEMBER) and the video tape number (TAPENO) are valid and are found in the program tables. If only one, or neither, of the input fields can be found by the table lookup operations, indicator H1 is to be turned on and the program halted. Print the necessary modifications to the program on the compile listing. Explain your modifications and their effect on the program.

```
   HJG07Y    08-17-91  16:05:37      IBM PC      RPG II       Version 3.5  Page  1

            ....+....1....+....2....+....3....+....4....+....5....+....6....+....7....

     1 0001 H                                                                HJG07Y


     2 0002 FMEMBERS  IT  F 300   30            EDISK
     3 0003 FTAPES    IT  F 300   30            EDISK
     4 0004 FRENTALS  IP  F 200   20            DISK
     5 0005 FRENTLISTO    F 132  132        OF  PRINTER


     6 0006 E    MEMBERS       TABMEM  1  25  6 ATABNAM 20
     7 0007 E    TAPES         TABTAP  1  50  5 0ATABTTL 22


     8 0008 IRENTALS AA   01
     9 0009 I                                    1    6 MEMBER
    10 0010 I                                   10  140TAPENO


    11 0011 C   01      MEMBER    LOKUPTABMEM   TABNAM        41
    12 0012 C   01      TAPENO    LOKUPTABTAP   TABTTL        42


    13 0013 ORENTLISTH   206    1P
    14 0014 O       OR          OF
    15 0015 O                               6 'HJG07Y'
    16 0016 O                              33 'TAPE RENTALS FOR'
    17 0017 O                    UDATE Y   42
    18 0018 O                              55 'PAGE'
    19 0019 O                    PAGE      60
    20 0020 O         H  2       1P
    21 0021 O       OR          OF
    22 0022 O                              10 'MEMBER NO.'
    23 0023 O                              29 'MEMBER NAME'
    24 0024 O                              55 'TAPE TITLE'
    25 0025 O         D  1       01
    26 0026 O                    MEMBER     8
    27 0027 O                41  TABNAM    34
    28 0028 O                42  TABTTL    60
    29 0029 O               N41            35 '**INVALID MEMBER NUMBER'
    30 0030 O               N42            46 '**TAPE NO.'
    31 0031 O               N42  TAPENOZ   52
    32 0032 O               N42            60 'INVALID'
    33 /*
    34 /*


            THE FOLLOWING INDICATORS APPEARED IN THIS PROGRAM

               01  41  42  1P  OF
    No Warning Errors
    No Fatal Errors
```

Figure 7-40   Program Maintenance Problem 2

STUDENT EXERCISES: PROGRAMMING IN RPG

PROGRAMMING ASSIGNMENT 1
EQUIPMENT LOCATION STATUS REPORT

INSTRUCTIONS

Plan, code, enter, and test an RPG program to produce the Equipment Location Status Report.

INPUT

The format of the Equipment Inventory File is shown in Figure 7-41. Use test data set 1 for this problem. Note that positions 5–6 of the Unit I.D. field contain the description code of the unit, and positions 7–8 contain the location code.

EQUIPMENT INVENTORY RECORD						
Record Length 65						
Field No.	Field Name	Field Description	Field Position	Field Length	Dec. Pos.	Data Class
1	UNITID	Unit ID	1–8	8		A
		Description Code	5–6			
		Location Code	7–8			
2		UNUSED AREA	9–65			

Figure 7-41 Equipment inventory record layout

OUTPUT

Output is the Equipment Location Status Report, the format of which is shown in Figure 7-42.

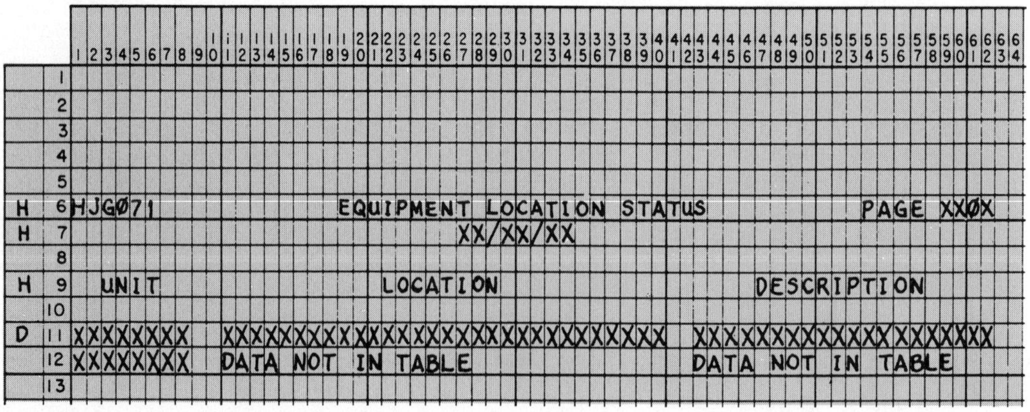

Figure 7-42 Equipment Location Status Report

⊨ Processing Requirements

This program produces a detail printed report. Each detail line contains unit I.D. read from the input record and the Description and Location of the unit. The description and location are obtained from the compile time tables shown in Figure 7-43.

LOCATION TABLE DATA	
Code	Location
AA	Warehouse One, First Floor
AB	Warehouse One, Second Floor
AC	Warehouse Two, First Floor
AD	Warehouse Two, Second Floor
AE	Warehouse Two, Third Floor
BA	Showroom One
BB	Showroom Two
BC	Showroom Three

DESCRIPTION TABLE DATA	
Code	Description
CD	CD player
SP	Speaker unit
CS	Cassette deck
CT	Twin cassette deck
AM	Amplifier
GE	Graphic equalizer
FM	FM receiver

Figure 7-43   Table data

The description and location are retrieved by table lookup techniques. If either of these items is not found by the table lookup operation, the message DATA NOT IN TABLE prints in the output area.

⊨ PROGRAMMING ASSIGNMENT 2 ⊨
EQUIPMENT LOCATION STATUS REPORT

INSTRUCTIONS

Write the program described in Programming Assignment 1 using ARRAY lookup techniques instead of table lookup. Use the same test data and table data for this program.

⊨ PROGRAMMING ASSIGNMENT 3 ⊨
ACCOUNT NUMBER AVAILABILITY REPORT

INSTRUCTIONS

Plan, code, enter, and test an RPG program to produce the Account Number Availability Report.

INPUT

The format of the Account File is shown in Figure 7-44 on the next page. Use test data set 6 for this problem. Use the list of valid account numbers as compile time table data for this problem.

ACCOUNT RECORD LAYOUT

ACCOUNT RECORD						
Record Length 71						
Field No.	Field Name	Field Description	Field Position	Field Length	Dec. Pos.	Data Class
1	ACCTNO	Account Number	9–12	4	0	N
2		UNUSED AREA	13–71			

VALID ACCOUNT NUMBERS

0013	0015	0016	0017	0020	0035	0047	0091	0111	0112	0113	0114	0115
0116	0117	0118	0119	0120	0200	0231	0248	0249	0256	0273	0275	0278
0281	0349	0350	0351	0468	0500	0502	0503	0671	0679	0700	0838	0943
1367												

Figure 7-44   Input layout and table data

OUTPUT

Output is the Account Number Availability Report, the format of which is shown in Figure 7-45.

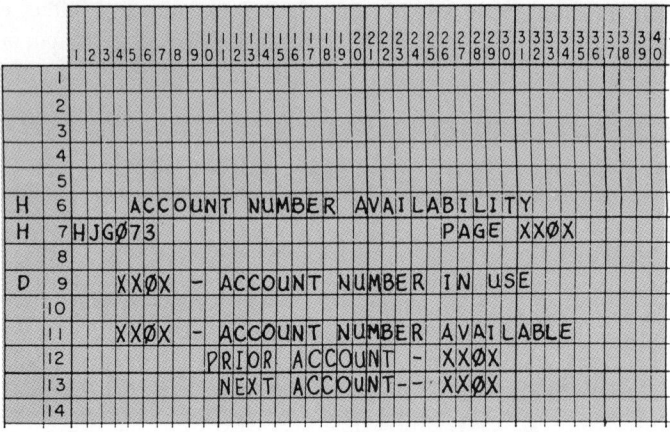

Figure 7-45   Account Number Availability Report

◢◢ Processing Requirements

Load the list of valid account numbers into a compile time table. As each input record is read, use table lookup to determine whether or not the account number read from the input record appears in the table of valid account numbers. If the account number is in the list, print the ACCOUNT NUMBER IN USE message shown on the report layout.

If the account number does not appear in the list, perform the necessary lookup operations to determine the next highest and next lowest account numbers that do appear on the list. If the account number is not in the list, the three detail lines starting with the ACCOUNT NUMBER AVAILABLE line will print.

PROGRAMMING ASSIGNMENT 4
SHIPMENT REPORT

INSTRUCTIONS

Plan, code, enter, and test an RPG program to produce the Shipment Report.

INPUT

The format of the Shipment File is shown in Figure 7-46. Use test data set 17 for this problem.

SHIPMENT DATA RECORD						
Record Length 16						
Field No.	Field Name	Field Description	Field Position	Field Length	Dec. Pos.	Data Class
1	SHIPNO	Shipment Number	1–8	8		A
2		UNUSED AREA	9–14	6		
3	WEIGHT	Shipment Weight	15–16	2	0	N

Figure 7-46   Shipment record layout

OUTPUT

Output is the Shipping Report, the format of which is shown in Figure 7-47.

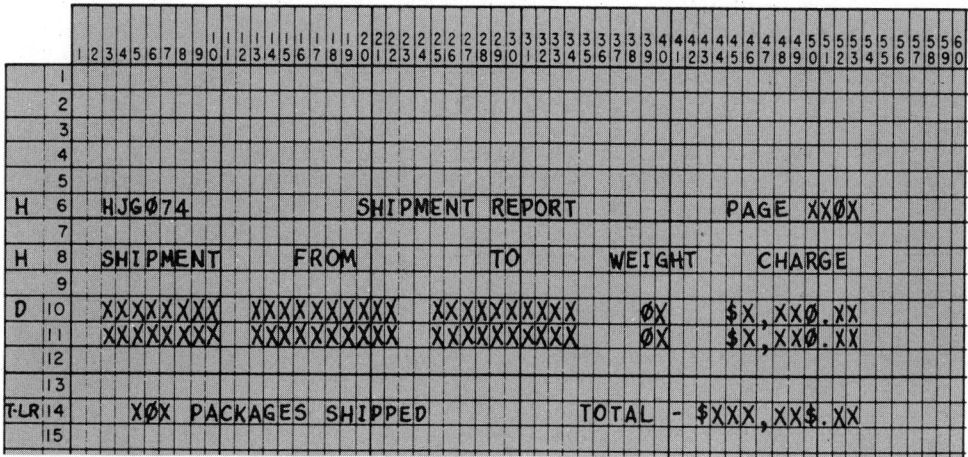

Figure 7-47   Shipment Report

▤ Processing Requirements

Each input record contains the shipment number and shipment weight of a package shipped by Katie's Kourier Service. This service provides pick up and same-day delivery of packages between the capitol cities of the six New England states. The charge for the service is based on the weight of the package and the distance between the city the package was shipped from and the city to which the package was shipped. Katie's Kourier Service also provides local transportation of packages within the six cities. The objective of this program is to determine the amount charged for the shipment of each package. The program also accumulates a final total of all charges and a count of the number of packages shipped.

The first two positions of the Shipment Number field contain a code specifying the city shipped FROM. Positions 3 and 4 of the Shipment Number field contain the code for the city shipped TO. The names of the FROM and TO cities are determined by either table or array lookup, using the data in Table One, which is shown in Figure 7-48.

Table One: State Capital Codes	
CN	Hartford
MA	Boston
ME	Augusta
NH	Concord
RI	Providence
VT	Montpelier

Table Two: Distances						
	CN	MA	ME	NH	RI	VT
CN	local	107	272	185	74	196
MA	107	local	165	78	51	187
ME	272	165	local	153	216	181
NH	185	78	153	local	129	128
RI	74	51	216	129	local	247
VT	196	187	181	128	247	local

Figure 7-48   Programming Assignment 4 table data

The distance between the FROM and TO cities is contained in Table Two, which must be accessed by using table lookup techniques. The charge amount for each package shipped is based on the following rules:

1. If the FROM and TO cities are the same, the package is a local shipment. The charge for a local shipment is $3.00 per pound for the first 10 pounds of shipment weight, and $1.50 for every pound over 10 pounds. For example, if a package weighs 12 pounds, the charge would be $33.00. (10 pounds @ $3.00 = $30.00 plus 2 pounds @ $1.50 = $3.00; total, $33.00.) The minimum charge is for 5 pounds: If a package weighs less than 5 pounds, it is charged at the 5-pound rate, or $15.00.

2. If the package is not a local shipment, the charges are based on the distance between cities as shown in Table Two. The rate for these intercity shipments is 15 cents per pound per mile for the first 10 pounds of package weight, and 12.5 cents ($.125) per pound per mile for every pound over 10 pounds. For example, if a 12-pound package is shipped between Boston, Massachusetts and Providence, Rhode Island (51 miles), the charge is $89.25, determined as follows:

$$
\begin{array}{rcl}
10 \text{ lb} \times 51 \text{ miles} \times \$.15 & = & \$76.50 \\
2 \text{ lb} \times 51 \text{ miles} \times \$.125 & = & \underline{\$12.75} \\
& & \$89.25
\end{array}
$$

As is the case for local shipments, there is a 5-pound minimum weight charge for intercity shipments.

Random Record Retrieval Using Keyed (Indexed) Sequence Access Path Processing

In all the RPG programs you have worked with so far, the input data file is processed as a unit. These programs process the first record in the file, then the second record, then the third, and so on, until the entire file has been read and processed. Many business programming applications require the processing of individual records from a data file. However, to process an individual record without having to process all records in a file, you must use a different method of describing and accessing input data.

ACCESS PATHS

All RPG programs that process a file as a single unit use the RPG fixed logic cycle to control the input and output processing of data. When coding the program specifications, you describe the data files to be used on the File Description Specifications form and provide information about the records in the file on either the Input or Output Specifications form. With these descriptions, the RPG compiler generates the machine language instructions for reading or writing the data file. The specific machine language instructions developed from RPG program specifications are based on the type of access path defined for the data file.

The **access path** of a data file is the method used by the computer to retrieve input file data and write output file data. Although the term *access path* can be applied to a file that uses any type of input or output device, it is important only with disk files. *Disk is the only device that permits you to use more than one type of access path.* Data files stored on disk can be accessed by either an arrival sequence access path or a keyed sequence access path. Other devices, such as tape drives and printers, use only the arrival sequence access path.

Arrival Sequence Access Path

In Lewis Carroll's *Alice In Wonderland*, the King of Hearts told the White Rabbit to "Begin at the beginning, go on until you come to the end: then stop," which is how **arrival sequence processing** takes place. The **arrival sequence access path** is based on the order in which the data records are stored in the disk file (Figure 8-1). Processing files by an arrival sequence access path begins with the first record of the file and then proceeds, record-by-record, to the end of the file.

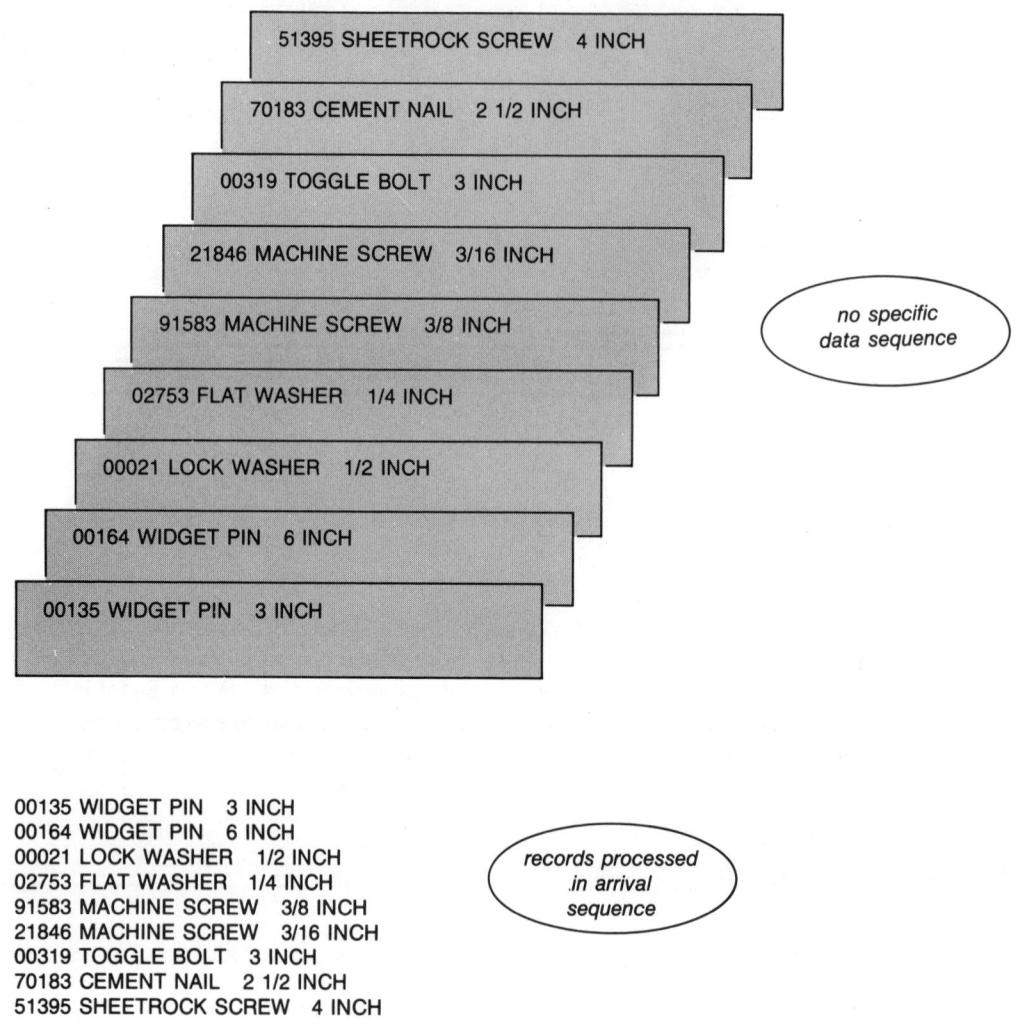

00135 WIDGET PIN   3 INCH
00164 WIDGET PIN   6 INCH
00021 LOCK WASHER   1/2 INCH
02753 FLAT WASHER   1/4 INCH
91583 MACHINE SCREW   3/8 INCH
21846 MACHINE SCREW   3/16 INCH
00319 TOGGLE BOLT   3 INCH
70183 CEMENT NAIL   2 1/2 INCH
51395 SHEETROCK SCREW   4 INCH

*records processed
.in arrival
sequence*

Figure 8-1   Arrival sequence processing

In earlier versions of RPG, arrival sequence processing was called sequential processing because most files processed by this path are arranged into either ascending or descending sequence based on the order of one or more fields in the data records. However, the term *sequential* is not necessarily accurate because a so-called sequential file is usually processed without regard for the order of the data records. Unless special programming techniques are used, the object program pays no attention to the sequence of the records because the processing is actually based on the order in which the records arrive in computer memory. Therefore, the term *arrival sequence* has been adopted to accurately describe the access path used to process these files.

▤ Keyed Sequence Access Path

Keyed sequence access path processing is based on the contents of a particular data field in each record. This field, called the **key field** or **key** of the record, contains a value that identifies the record. For example, in a student record file, the student number might be the key field that identifies each individual record. Because access to the data records is based on this key field, the file can be processed in either of two ways. The first is keyed sequential processing. **Keyed sequential** processing is true **sequential processing** of the file, based on key field values. When keyed sequential processing is used in a program, the data file is not read in a beginning-to-end order but in key field order (Figure 8-2). Although the records are not in sequence in the data file, they are processed sequentially based on the Member Number field.

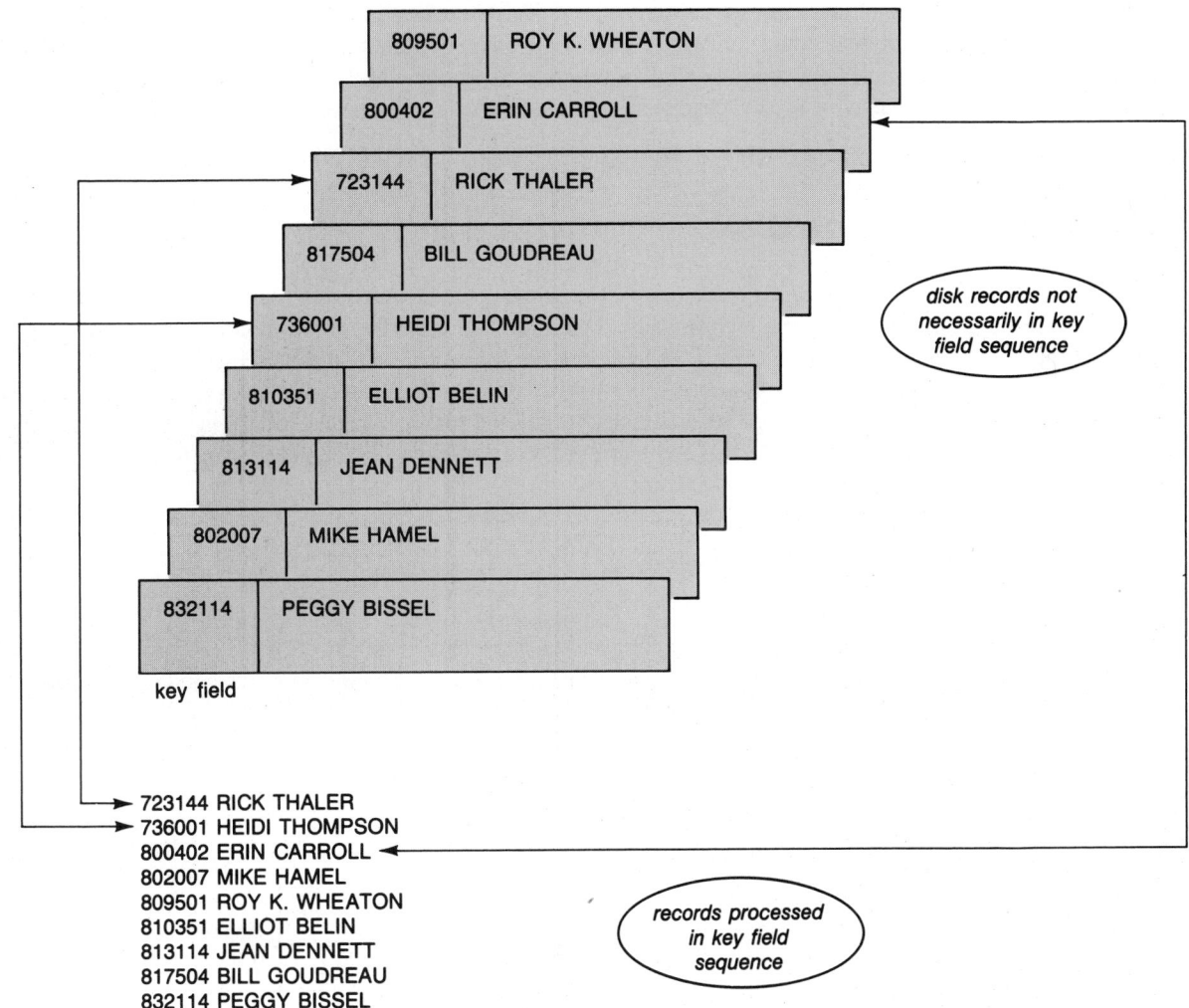

Figure 8-2   Keyed sequence processing

Programmers could eliminate arrival sequence processing completely by describing all arrival sequence files using a keyed sequence access path, but files described with a keyed sequence access path require more disk storage space and are slightly slower to process. Because of these two drawbacks, it is often more efficient, when processing data files that contain a large number of records, to sort the data into the required sequence before the RPG program is run and then to process the data in arrival sequence.

The second method of retrieving data records using the keyed sequence access path is based on the use of the key field to identify a particular record in the data file. Because the key field value can identify any record, it is possible to access records in a file by using random access techniques. **Random access** techniques use RPG operations that instruct the program to read a record that contains a specified key field value. When these operations are used, RPG uses the keyed sequence access path to go directly to the required disk record and read its contents into main computer memory. When a program uses random access techniques, the reading of a file is controlled by the programmer rather than by the RPG fixed logic cycle; and so it can be performed during detail or total calculation time instead of at input time.

Figure 8-2 illustrates the random accessing of a data file using a keyed sequence access path. To understand how random access is performed, you must understand how areas of a disk storage unit are identified.

DISK PROCESSING CONCEPTS

The most commonly used medium for the storage of large amounts of data is the magnetic disk because it offers the best combination of large storage capacity, speed of data retrieval, and relatively low cost. Although the capacity, speed, and cost of disk storage units vary greatly depending on the type of computer they are used with, we will discuss basic principles that apply to all disk storage devices, whether you work with a personal computer using a diskette with a capacity of 80,000 characters or a mainframe computer with several billion characters of disk storage.

Data Storage on Disk

The **disk pack** in Figure 8-3 is made up of 11 separate disks mounted on a central support shaft. It somewhat resembles a group of phonograph records stacked on a turntable spindle. However, although records on a turntable spindle rest upon one another, the disks in a pack are separated, so that the **access arms** can move between them. At the end of each access arm is a **read–write head**, which reads data from and writes data onto the magnetic surface of a disk. There is a separate read–write head for each usable surface in the disk pack. Note that all the access arms and read–write heads are connected to a common control mechanism, which moves all the access arms between all the surfaces at the same time.

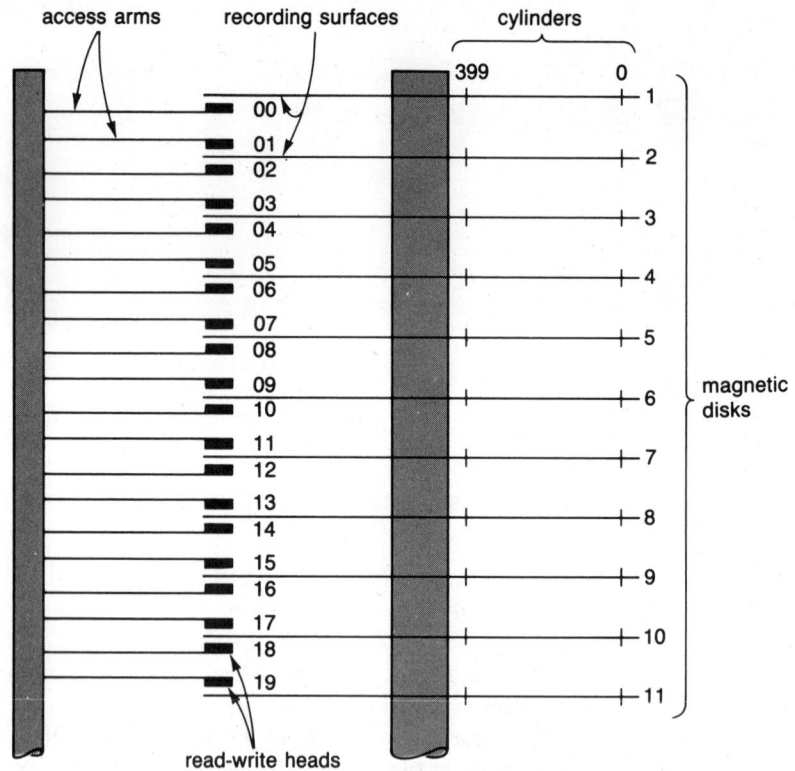

Figure 8-3   Magnetic disk

▶ **Surface Number**   Although the disk pack has 11 disks, each with two sides, there are only 20 usable **surfaces**. Disk drives that use removable, interchangeable disk packs generally do not use the top and bottom surfaces for recording data, because these surfaces are exposed to dirt and damage and may not, be reliable. Computers with fixed, internal disk drives that cannot be removed usually use all available surfaces for data storage.

The usable surfaces of a disk pack are numbered. The top usable surface (the underside of the first disk) is surface number 00, and the bottom usable surface is number 19. This number is called the surface number, or head number. Remember that the actual number of disks depends on the computer you are using.

▶ **Track Number** Figure 8-4 is a diagram of a disk surface. Data is recorded on the surface of a disk along circular paths called **tracks**. The disk surface in the figure contains 400 tracks numbered from track zero on the outer edge to track 399 on the inner edge of the disk surface. Do not confuse these tracks with the grooves in a phonograph record. A phonograph record's information has been recorded in a single, spiral-shaped groove, whereas the tracks on a disk surface are separate circular areas. Also unlike a phonograph record, in which the groove is physically cut into the surface of the record, a track on a disk is an area where data can be recorded. The surface of a disk looks (and is) perfectly smooth. The data is recorded onto the surface in the form of magnetic lines of force. (You also cannot see the data recorded on an audio or video cassette, but it is there and can be read by a VCR or cassette player.)

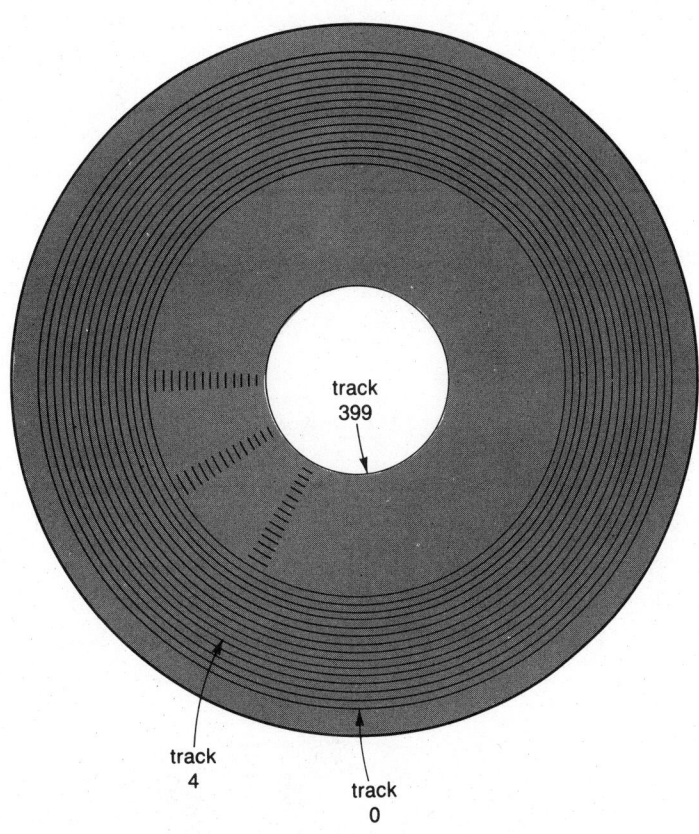

track
399

track
4

track
0

Figure 8-4 Tracks on a disk surface

▶ **The Cylinder Concept of Data Addressing** Because all the read–write heads move in or out of the disk pack at the same time as a unit, all the read–write heads are positioned at the same track of every surface. The like-numbered tracks on the surfaces of a disk pack are called a **cylinder**. (Figure 8-5 on the next page). If, for example, all the tracks numbered 200 in the illustrated disk pack were to be connected vertically, the resulting shape would be a cylinder. Storing data on such a cylinder rather than across a disk surface minimizes the number of movements of the access arms. Every time the access arms are positioned, the read–write heads can access, in this example, 20 separate tracks of data.

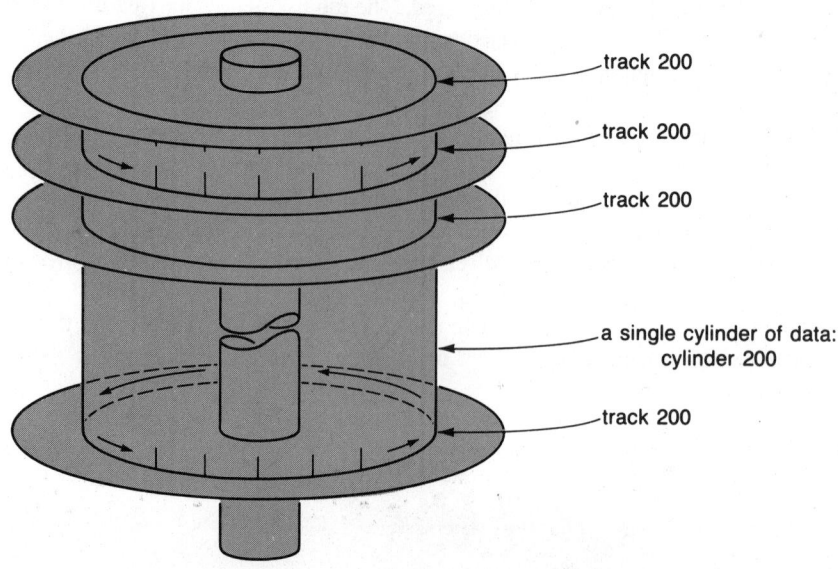

Figure 8-5   The cylinder concept

▸ **Sectors**   Each track on a disk surface is divided into areas called **sectors** (Figure 8-6). The sector is the smallest area of a disk that has a unique identifying address. The number of data characters stored in a sector varies, like the number of surfaces and cylinders, depending on the type of disk unit used. However, most computers use a sector size of either 256 or 512 characters of data.

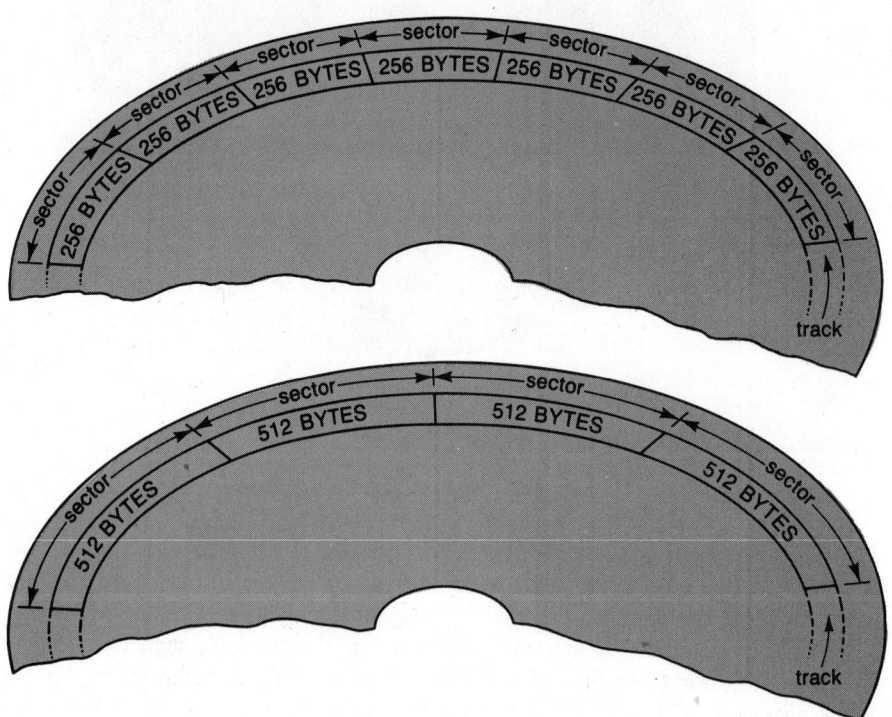

Figure 8-6   Disk sectors

Even though sectors vary in size (Figure 8-6), all sectors on a disk contain exactly the same amount of data because the length of a sector within a track is based on a percentage of the track circumference, not a linear distance. Each sector is capable of storing the same number of characters as every other sector on the same disk.

Similarly, every track of a disk has the same storage capacity as every other track, whether the data is stored on the outermost track, which has the largest circumference, or the innermost track, which has the smallest circumference.

Disk Addressing

Each area of a disk can be **addressed** by its cylinder, surface, and sector numbers (Figure 8-7). Although a disk pack can contain as many as several hundred million characters of data, it is possible to identify an area as small as 256 characters by referencing the cylinder, surface, and sector numbers. To read the data stored in a specific sector, the program need only generate commands to move the access mechanism to the required cylinder, activate the read–write head for the required track, and perform the read operation when the required sector has rotated under the read–write head.

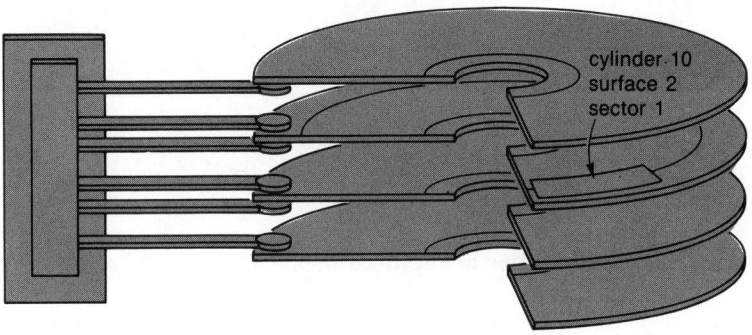

Figure 8-7 Disk addressing

KEYED SEQUENCE ACCESS PATH PROCESSING

When data is written onto a disk using a keyed sequence access path, the computer not only writes the data to disk but also develops a **file index**. The file index is stored on disk, usually at the beginning of the file area. The development and use of the index is another transparent function of RPG. You have only to make the correct entries on the File Description Specifications form, and RPG will use those entries to perform all needed index functions.

The index contains two units of information (Figure 8-8 on the next page): the key field value for each record in the file, which is the value that identifies a record, and the disk address of the data record identified by the key field value. By referencing the key field value and using the associated disk address, the RPG program can access any data record in the file regardless of its location. Because of the use of an index to access data records, this type of processing was referred to as **indexed sequential access method (ISAM)** processing. This terminology was used in RPG and RPG II but has been replaced in RPG III and RPG/400, by the term **keyed access path** processing. Files accessed by the **keyed access path** are commonly called **keyed** files.

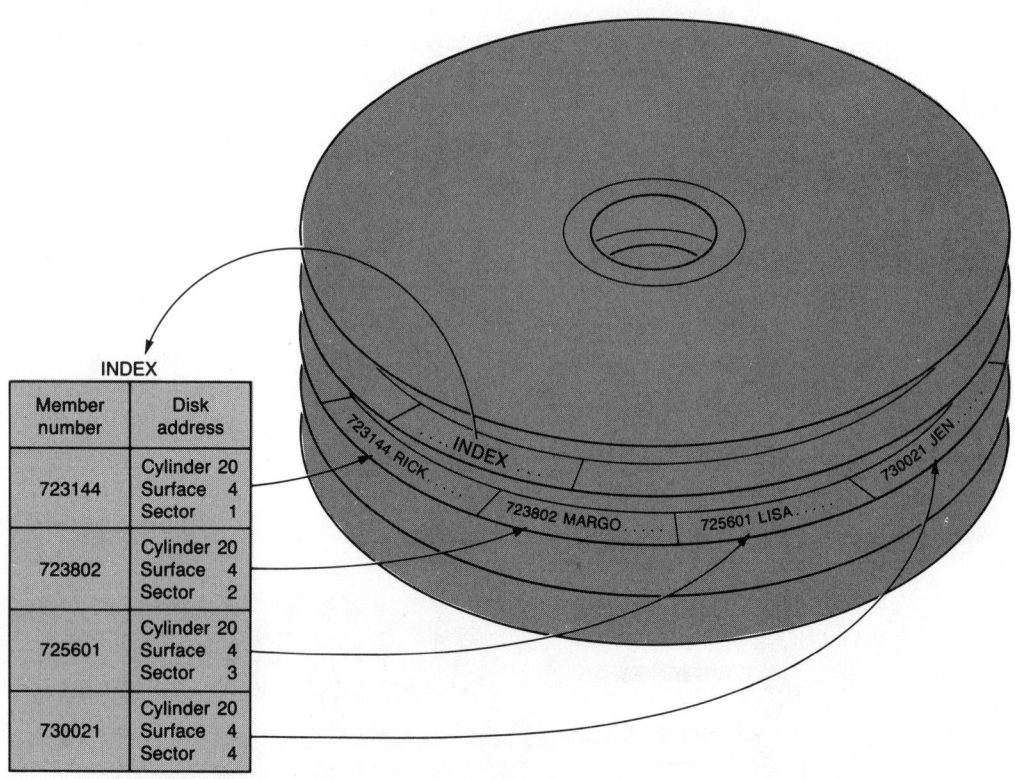

Figure 8-8   Use of keyed sequence access path index

The following examples explain how a file's index can be used to access data records. Remember, however, that every computer uses an indexing system that is designed for its particular architecture, so these explanations should be understood to be generalized examples and not specific examples of the way your computer functions internally. For example, many computer systems use several separate indexes to access data in a single file. Such computers can have a different index for each cylinder and track used by the file.

Sequential Processing

When a keyed file is processed sequentially, data records are accessed in order according to the sequence of the keys in the index. Generally, because the index of a file is maintained in sequence, the object program need only access the data records through the index, starting with the record identified by the first key, then the record identified by the second key, and so on. Because the index is in a sequence based on the key field values and the file is accessed through the index, the data file is processed in the keyed sequence rather than in arrival sequence. The data records are not necessarily in key field sequence when stored on disk. If records were to be processed in arrival sequence, they would not be in key field sequence.

Random or Direct Access Processing

The index of a keyed file also makes it possible to process data records on a random basis. Recall that RPG contains operations that permit the random reading of any individual data record (see Figure 8-8). The RPG program uses the member number of the needed record to access the file index, which provides the disk address of the record, and the object program then retrieves the record from the addressed area of the disk.

If this logic appears similar to the logic that RPG uses to perform table lookup, it is. From the viewpoint of the programmer, there is little difference between the way that a table lookup operation is coded and the way that direct access of a record is performed using the keyed sequence access path. The main difference is that table lookup accesses only a single function field, whereas use of the keyed sequence access path for random access of a data file retrieves an entire data record.

DESCRIPTION OF SAMPLE PROGRAM HJG08X

Program HJG08X is another application dealing with video tape rentals. This sample program prints the Overdue Tape Report using input data from three disk files; the data file flow is illustrated in Figure 8-9. The returns file is an arrival sequence file on which processing is based; the members and tapes files are keyed files, which are accessed on a random basis to provide data about specified members and video tapes.

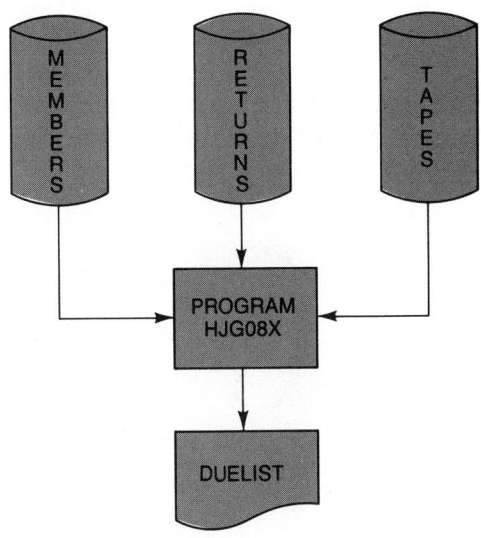

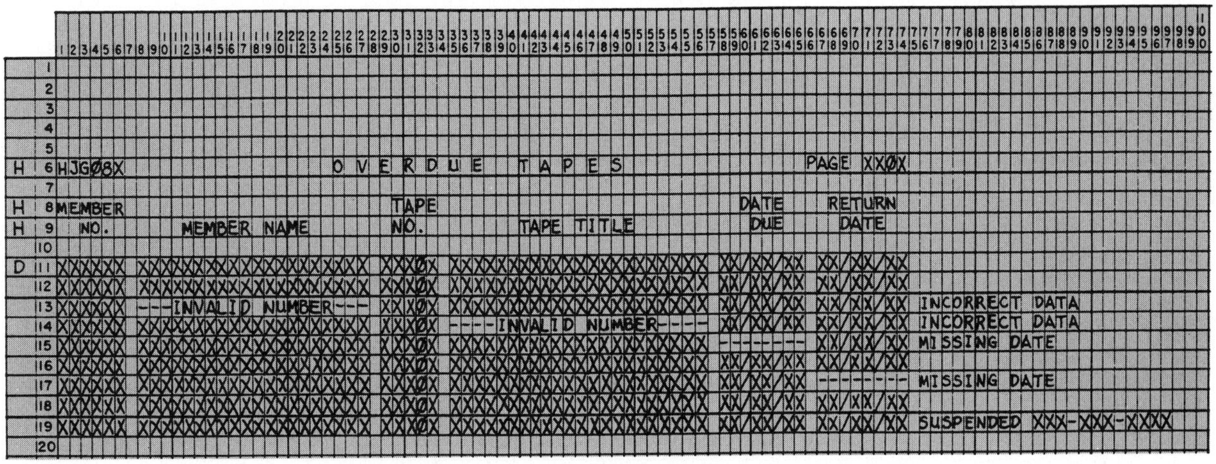

Figure 8-9 Data flow for program HJG08X

Output Description

Output from the sample program is the Overdue Tapes Report (Figure 8-10). Although this is a detail printed report, it does not require that an output line be printed for every input record read. The printing of a detail line is based on the result of a comparison of the Date Due field and the Return Date field. If the return date is later than the date due, or if either of the date fields is blank, the program prints a detail line. If

```
HJG08X                    O V E R D U E   T A P E S            PAGE    1

MEMBER                         TAPE                           DATE   RETURN
  NO.      MEMBER NAME         NO.        TAPE TITLE          DUE     DATE

730021 JENNIFER BOMBARD        1101 E.T.                    6/07/91  6/08/91
736004 JIM REID                2400 WAR GAMES               -------- -------- MISSING DATE
809501 ROY K. WHEATON          1002 ----INVALID NUMBER----  -------- -------- INCORRECT DATA
813114 JEAN DENNETT            1301 TRON                    6/08/91  6/09/91  SUSPENDED 413-555-7435
814006 BARBARA POHJA           2283 MY FAIR LADY            6/09/91  6/10/91
```

Figure 8-10 Overdue Tapes Report

the return date is earlier than or equal to the date due, the program produces no output. Note that several error messages could be printed. The processing to test for these errors is explained later in the Processing Requirements section.

Input Descriptions

The primary file for this program is the returns file; the record layout is shown in Figure 8-11. As you can see, this file contains member number, video tape number, due date, and date returned. Returns is an arrival sequence file and has been sorted in ascending member number sequence.

The members file, is a keyed file, keyed on member number in positions 1–6 (Figure 8-12). Records in this file are accessed to obtain the member name, telephone number, and number of late returns if needed.

Figure 8-13 shows the record layout for the tapes file, which is also a keyed file, keyed on tape number in positions 1–5. Records from this file are accessed to obtain the video tape title if needed.

RETURNS RECORD						
Record Length 40						
Field No.	Field Name	Field Description	Field Position	Field Length	Dec. Pos.	Data Class
1	MEMBER	Member Number	1–6	6		A
2	VIDEO	Video Tape Number	7–11	5	0	N
3	DUEDAT	Due Date	12–17	6	0	N
4	RETDAT	Date Returned	18–23	6	0	N

Figure 8-11   Returns Record

MEMBERS FILE RECORD						
Record Length 90		Key Location 1–6 (MEMBNO)				
Field No.	Field Name	Field Description	Field Position	Field Length	Dec. Pos.	Data Class
1	MEMBNO	Member Number	1–6	6		A
2	NAME	Member Name	7–26	20		A
3		Telephone Number	27–36	10		A
4	NUMBER	Late Return Count	37–38	2	0	N

Figure 8-12   Members File Record

TAPES FILE RECORD						
Record Length 50		Key Location 1–5 (TAPENO)				
Field No.	Field Name	Field Description	Field Position	Field Length	Dec. Pos.	Data Class
1	TAPENO	Video Tape Number	1–5	5	0	N
2	TITLE	Video Tape Title	6–27	22		A

Figure 8-13   Tapes File Record

Processing Requirements

1. The program prints a detail line only if the return date is later than the date due or if either of the date fields is blank. When a line is printed, a blank date field area is filled with a line of hyphens, as shown on the printer spacing chart.
2. If either or both of the date fields is blank, the program does not compare the return date and date due but prints a MISSING DATE message beginning in position 76 of the detail line.
3. If a detail line is to be printed, the program directly accesses the members file to obtain the member name and the tapes file to obtain the video tape title. If the member number and/or tape number cannot be found on the member or tapes files, the INVALID NUMBER message prints in place of the member name and/or video tape title, as shown on lines 13 and 14 of the printer spacing chart. In addition, the detail line contains the message INCORRECT DATA beginning in position 76.
4. If both a blank date field and an invalid member or tape number are found in the same input record, the INCORRECT DATA message prints as part of the detail line.
5. If the tape was returned after the due date and if the number of late returns is greater than 10, the message SUSPENDED followed by the telephone number of the member, prints beginning in position 76 of the detail line.

SPECIFICATIONS FOR PROGRAM HJG08X

File Description Specifications

Figure 8-14 shows the first two lines of the file description specifications. Note that no new entries have been made for the returns file because this is an arrival sequence file. The members file, however, requires several new entries to enable the program to access it on a random basis using a keyed sequence access path.

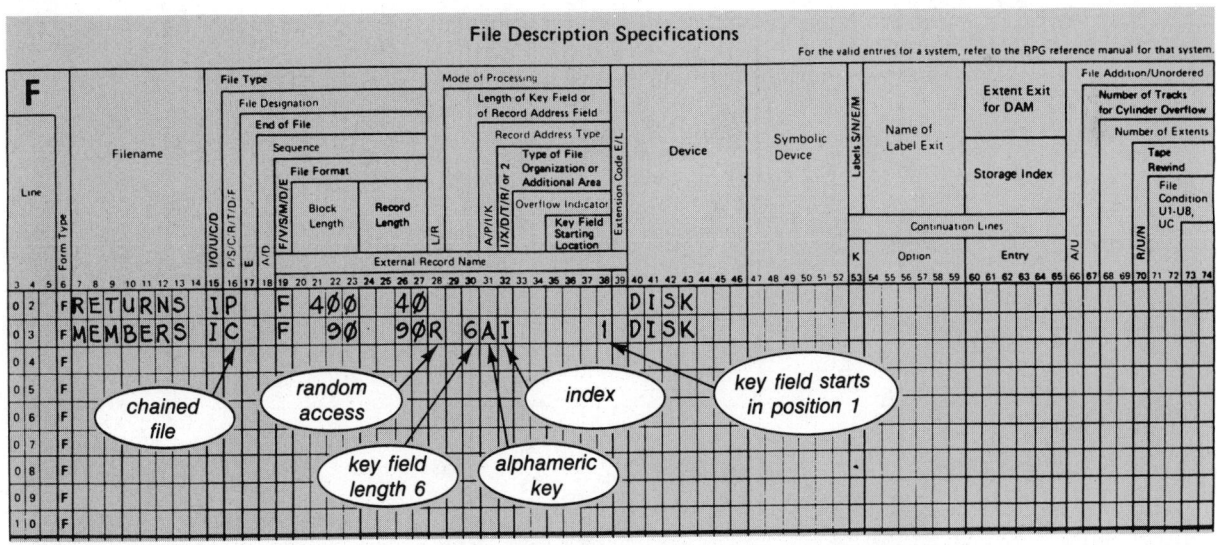

Figure 8-14   File description for keyed sequence access path

▸ **File Designation C**   The file designation C (position 16) has been entered for members because this file is to be accessed using the **CHAIN** operation code to read individual records on a random access basis. The file designation C can be used only with keyed disk files accessed by the CHAIN operation.

▸ **Block Length and Record Length** Note that the members file has been described as an unblocked file by entering the record length in both areas. Because this file is accessed one record at a time on a random basis, there is no advantage to specifying a blocking factor for the file.

▸ **Mode of Processing** The entry R in the Mode of Processing area, position 28, specifies that records in the file are to be accessed randomly by means of the contents of the key field.

▸ **Length of Key Field** The Length of Key Field area (positions 29–30) specifies the length of the field used as the key for random access of the file. The length of the file key is determined when the file is created. The entry in this area must be exactly the same as the key length defined for the file during file creation.

▸ **Record Address Type** The entry A in the Record Address Type area (position 31) specifies that the key field is either an alphameric field or a numeric field that is stored in the zoned format. Unless special coding is used, numeric data is stored in the **zoned format**, with each digit occupying one position of disk storage or computer memory.

Numeric data can also be stored in the packed format. When the **packed format** is used, each storage position on disk or in computer memory can store up to two numeric digits. The packed format is usually used to reduce the amount of storage needed for large amounts of numeric data in a record. If the file or record layout does not specify that the packed format has been used for a field, you can assume that the field is in the zoned format. Because the Member field is described as alphameric, the A entry is used in the Record Address Type area.

▸ **Type of File Organization** The entry I in position 32 specifies that the file is a keyed file. The letter I is used because the former term for this type of file was *indexed*. If a keyed file is being described, the entry I must be used in position 32.

▸ **Key Field Starting Location** This entry in positions 35–38 and the entry in positions 29–30 specify the location of the key field in the record. As was the case with the Length of Key Field entry, the starting position of the key field is defined when the file is created. The entry made in positions 35–38 must be the same as the original definition of the file.

Figure 8-15 shows the completed File Description Specifications form, in which the entries for the Tapes file are similar to the entries made for the members file. Note that tapes is also a CHAINed file, is unblocked, and is randomly accessed by a zoned format numeric key located in positions 1–5 of the record.

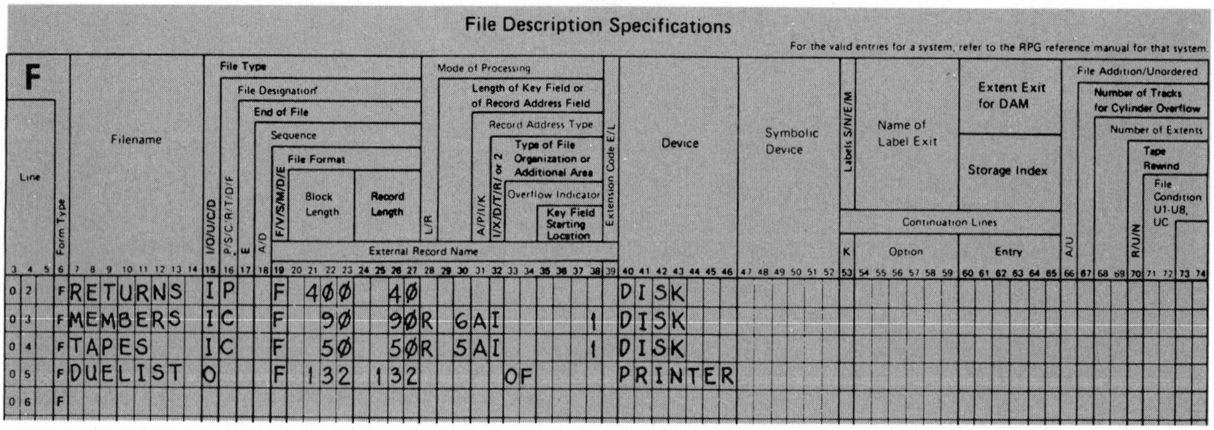

Figure 8-15 Completed file description specifications for program HJG08X

Recall that RPG does not have a required sequence for file descriptions, but accepted industry practice is to describe the primary input file first and the output last.

Indicator Summary

As described in the specifications, this program performs many different tests on the input data. Each test uses a separate indicator to show the result. Figure 8-16, the indicator summary sheet for program HJG08X, is provided for reference as you study the remaining program specifications.

Line	Form Type	Record Identifying	Input Field	Calculation Result and Command Key	Halt and User	Control Level and Overflow	FUNCTION OF INDICATORS
01	F*	ID	F	C	H	L	FUNCTION OF INDICATORS
02	F*	Ø1					RETURNS RECORD IDENTIFICATION
03	F*	Ø2					MEMBERS RECORD IDENTIFICATION (UNUSED)
04	F*	Ø3					TAPES RECORD IDENTIFICATION (UNUSED)
05	F*		41				BLANK MEMBER FIELD
06	F*		42				ZERO VIDEO FIELD
07	F*		43				ZERO DUEDAT FIELD
08	F*		44				ZERO RETDAT FIELD
09	F*			45			RETDAT LATER THAN DUEDAT (LATE RETURN)
10	F*			46			MORE THAN TEN LATE RETURNS
11	F*					1P	FIRST PAGE INDICATOR
12	F*					OF	OVERFLOW INDICATOR
13	F*						

Circle Indicators Used — General Indicators circled: 01, 02, 03, 41, 42, 43, 44, 45, 46; Overflow Indicators: OF; Special Purpose Indicators: 1P.

Figure 8-16   Indicator summary sheet

Input Specifications

Figure 8-17 on the next page shows the Input Specifications form for this sample program. Although it requires no new entries, this program uses a technique that you have not encountered before. Note that three separate files are described on the Input Specifications form. Each file description begins with a Filename entry in positions 7–14 and uses a different record identifying indicator. Note also that each file uses a different alphabetic sequence entry. Again, this is not a requirement of RPG but follows standard programming practice.

The input specifications for the three files are in the same order as were the file description specifications. Returns is described first, then members, then tapes. This ordering is not required by current versions of the RPG language but was required by some older versions. For this reason, the accepted practice is to use the same file sequence on both the File Description and the Input Specifications forms. Note that indicators 41, 42, 43, and 44 test for blank or zero input fields in the returns file.

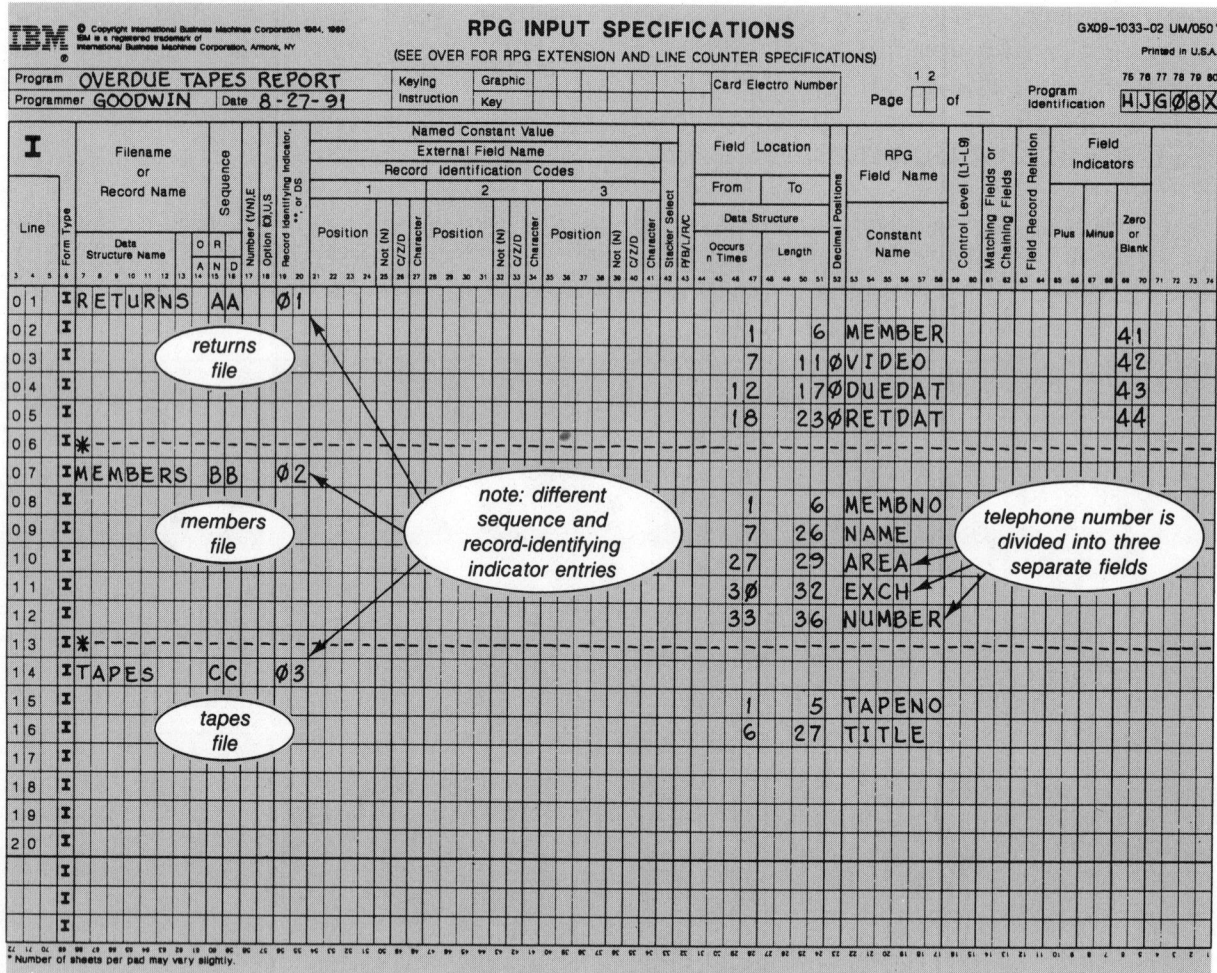

Figure 8-17   Input specifications for program HJG08X

The telephone number in the members file has been described as three separate fields – AREA, EXCH, and PHONE – to enable the program to print the Telephone Number field with hyphens separating the area code, the exchange, and the four-digit number. A telephone number is not usually printed as 11 consecutive digits, such as 5085552185, but is separated into three parts by hyphens: 508-555-2185. This program edits the Telephone Number field by dividing the number into its three components and prints each component as a separate field, with hyphen constants as dividers.

▸ **Unreferenced Record Identifying Indicators**   The input descriptions of the members and tapes files cause a problem in RPG code to which there is no single correct solution. The problem is caused by the requirement of most versions of RPG that a record identifying indicator be specified in positions 19–20 of the record description for a file. In Figure 8-17, indicator 02 has been specified for the members file and indicator 03 for the tapes file. Neither of these indicators is used in the sample program to condition either a calculation operation or output specification.

When the compile listing is shown later in this chapter, you will see that this results in a warning that these indicators have not been used to condition operations. If, however, the resulting indicator entries were omitted for these files, most versions of RPG would generate a message warning you that no record identifying indicator had been specified. Some language versions also default to an entry of indicator 01 as the record identifying indicator if none is specified. This is a classic "wrong if you do, wrong if you don't" situation in that whichever choice you make when coding the program, the compiler generates a warning message. There is nothing you as a programmer can do to eliminate these messages. Remember that they are only warnings and do not interfere with the correct compilation of the program.

Program Calculations

The calculations for program HJG08X are somewhat more complex than those you have seen so far because of the number of tests that must be performed on the input data. The program not only requires that the four fields in each returns record be tested to assure that they are not blank but also requires that the two input dates be compared and that the member number and video tape number be used to access the members and tapes files. Figure 8-18 illustrates the logic in the calculations. Note that at several points in the flowchart the decision whether or not to perform a calculation is made. At two of these points, the decision is whether or not a group of calculations should be performed. Two new operations, GOTO and TAG, are used to bypass groups of operations when they are not required by the program.

▶ **GOTO and TAG** The GOTO and TAG operations are **sequence control** operations, which enable you to alter the sequence in which operations are performed in RPG calculations. Sequence control operations are more commonly called **branching** operations, and the execution of a branching operation is generally referred to as a **branch**.

Branching operations bypass the top–down sequence of RPG calculations. They can be used to go directly to an operation later in the calculations or to repeat an earlier calculation. After a branch has been made by using GOTO and TAG, the operations again proceed in top-down order unless another pair of GOTO and TAG operations occurs.

If you are familiar with another programming language such as BASIC, COBOL, or FORTRAN, you have probably used branching operations. GOTO and TAG are similar to branching operations in other programming languages. However, there is one restriction on RPG branching that does not exist in other languages. Because the RPG logic cycle automatically separates detail and total time calculations and performs them at separate points in the logic cycle, RPG syntax does not permit branching between detail time calculations and total time calculations.

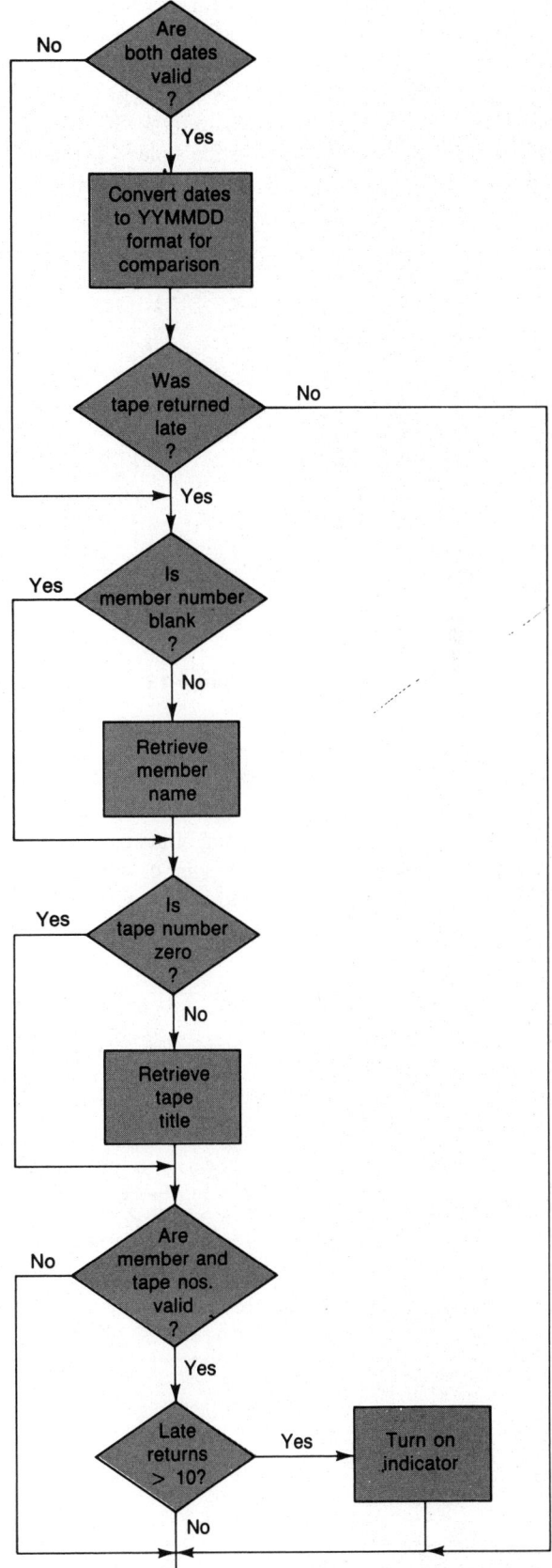

Figure 8-18 Calculation flowchart for program HJG08X

The GOTO and TAG operations are always used in combination. The **GOTO operation** directs the program to go to (or branch to) another operation, skipping all operations between the GOTO and the operation branched to. The **TAG operation** provides a name, or label, for the operation to which the GOTO is branching.

When the GOTO is executed, the program proceeds directly to the operation following the TAG operation (Figure 8-19). All operations between the GOTO and the TAG are skipped. The TAG operation does not do anything. Its only function is to provide a place for the GOTO to branch to. The TAG operation performs the same function as a paragraph name in COBOL or a statement number in BASIC.

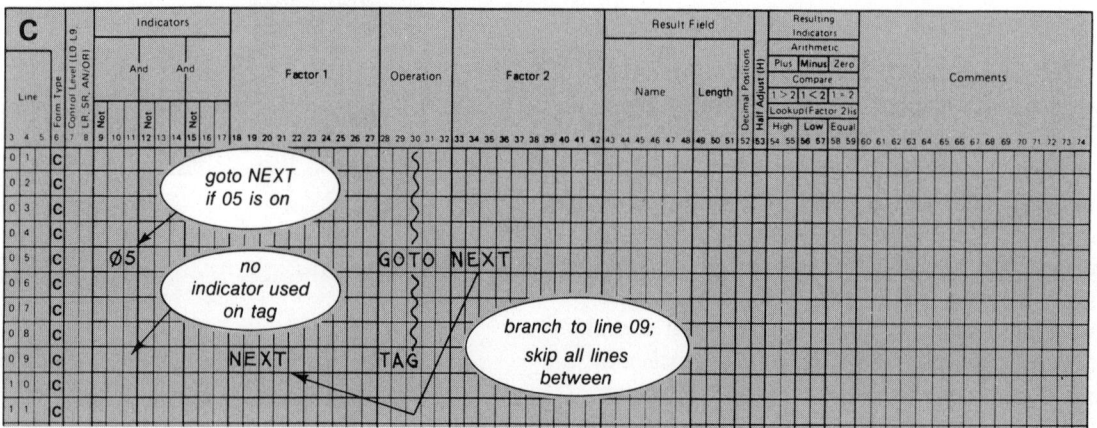

Figure 8-19 GOTO and TAG for bypassing operations

Figure 8-20 shows that GOTO can be used to branch to a preceding point in the calculations. As you can see, the GOTO on line 12 causes a branch to the TAG on line 04 whenever indicators 01 and 06 are on. Because the TAG operation performs no function other than to provide a branch-to point, line 04 is ignored if it is reached during normal top-down processing of the calculations. Note that no indicators are used with the TAG operation; because the TAG is the branch-to point of GOTO, the TAG is, in effect, controlled by the GOTO. The only indicators permitted with a TAG operation are total time indicators (L1–L9 and LR) in positions 7–8. If the GOTO is conditioned by a total time indicator, the TAG operation must have the same total time indicator in positions 7–8.

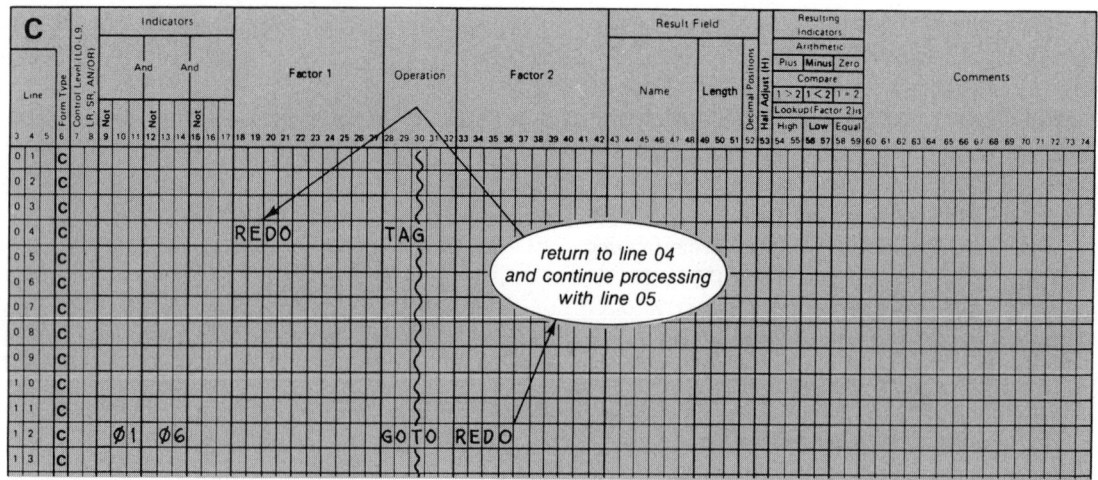

Figure 8-20 GOTO and TAG for repeating operations

Because the GOTO is conditioned by indicators 01 and 06, you can assume that some condition in the calculations will cause either or both of these indicators to be off at some point when line 12 is reached. If indicators 01 and 06 are always on, the calculations will never be able to proceed past line 12, resulting in a never–ending

loop, or repetitive series of operations. A GOTO operation that is controlled, or conditioned, by one or more indicators is called a **conditional** GOTO operation because it may or may not be executed, depending on the setting of the indicator that controls the operation. A GOTO that is not controlled by any indicators and is therefore always executed is called an **unconditional** GOTO operation. Figures 8-21 and 8-22 summarize the GOTO and TAG operations.

GOTO Operation Summary

The GOTO operation causes a branch to another instruction. The instruction being branched to must be immediately preceded by a TAG operation. The GOTO can cause a branch to a previous or succeeding operation. A GOTO cannot be used to branch from a detail time operation to a total time operation or from a total time operation to a detail time operation. Factor 2 must contain the name of the operation to which the branch is being made. This same name must be used in Factor 1 of the TAG operation to which the branch is being made. Factor 1 and the Result Field are not used by the GOTO operation.

Control Level Indicators	Indicators	Factor 1	Operation Name	Factor 2	Result Field	Resulting Indicators		
7–8	9–17	18–27	28–32	33–42	43–53	54–55	56–57	58–59
optional	optional	blank	GOTO	required	blank	blank	blank	blank

Figure 8-21   GOTO operation summary

TAG Operation Summary

The TAG operation names an operation being branched to by a GOTO operation. Factor 1 contains the name assigned to the operation and must be the same as the name used in Factor 2 of the associated GOTO operation. The same name cannot be used for two or more TAG operations. Factor 2 and the Result Field are not used by the TAG operation. The Indicators area (positions 9–17) must be blank.

Control Level Indicators	Indicators	Factor 1	Operation Name	Factor 2	Result Field	Resulting Indicators		
7–8	9–17	18–27	28–32	33–42	43–53	54–55	56–57	58–59
optional	blank	required	TAG	blank	blank	blank	blank	blank

Figure 8-22   TAG operation summary

Calculation Specifications

Figure 8-23 shows the calculation specifications for the sample program. As you study the explanations that follow, refer to Figure 8-16 as necessary for review of the functions of the indicators.

Line	Form Type	Control Level (L0-L9, LR, SR, AN/OR)	And Not	And Not	And Not	Factor 1	Operation	Factor 2	Result Field Name	Length	Decimal Positions	Half Adjust (H)	Arithmetic Plus	Arithmetic Minus	Arithmetic Zero	Compare 1>2 High	Compare 1<2 Low	Compare 1=2 Equal	Comments
01	C		Ø1				SETOF									45	46		RESET TESTS
02	C		Ø1	43															MISSING DATE
03	COR		Ø1	44			GOTO	BYPASS											
04	C*																		
05	C		Ø1			DUEDAT	MULT	10000.01	DUE	60									CONVERT DATES
06	C		Ø1			RETDAT	MULT	10000.01	RETURN	60									
07	C		Ø1			RETURN	COMP	DUE								45			COMPARE DATES
08	C		Ø1	N45			GOTO	END											
09	C*																		
10	C					BYPASS	TAG												
11	C		Ø1	N41		MEMBER	CHAIN	MEMBERS								41			GET MEMBER DATA
12	C		Ø1	N42		VIDEO	CHAIN	TAPES								42			GET TAPE DATA
13	C		Ø1	N41	N42	NUMBER	COMP	10								46			EXCESS OVERDUE
14	C					END	TAG												

Figure 8-23   Calculation specifications for program HJG08X

▶ **Clearing the Results of Previous Tests**   Line 01 uses a SETOF operation to turn off indicators 45 and 46. These indicators can be turned on later in the calculations as the result of comparisons. Recall from Chapter 4 that when compare operations are based on the result of other operations, a SETOF should be used to reset the resulting indicators. Indicators 45 and 46 are resulting indicators for the COMP operations on lines 07 and 13. Because these two comparisons may not be performed for every input record, the indicators must be reset by a SETOF.

▶ **Bypassing Date Comparison**   Indicators 43 and 44 are used to show a blank date field in a returns record. If either the Date Due or Return Date field is blank, the program must skip the date comparison that determines if a video tape was returned late. Lines 02 and 03 are linked in an OR relationship and use GOTO to bypass lines 05, 06, and 07 if either date field is blank. If this condition occurs, the program proceeds directly from the GOTO on line 03 to the TAG on line 10. Note that Factor 2 of the GOTO and Factor 1 of the TAG contain the same name. Remember that Factor 2 of a GOTO and Factor 1 of its related TAG must have the same name. Figure 8-24 illustrates the sequence of calculations if either of the date fields is blank and line 03 is executed.

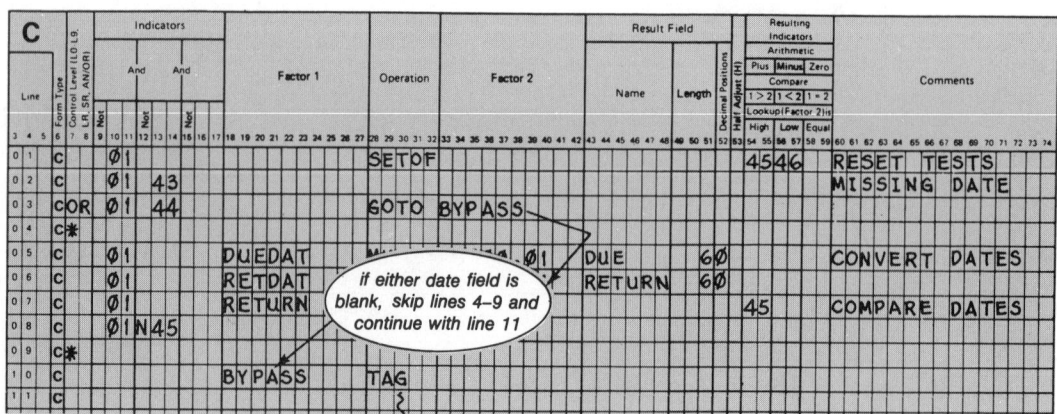

Figure 8-24   Use of GOTO and TAG

▸ **Date Comparison** Lines 05, 06, and 07 (see Figure 8-23) compare the return date and the date due to determine if the tape was returned late. Lines 05 and 06 convert the date from MMDDYY format to YYMMDD format prior to the comparison. The COMP operation on line 07 turns on indicator 45 if the converted return date (RETURN) is later than the converted date due (DUE). If the tape was not returned late and indicator 45 is not turned on, line 08 branches to the end of the calculations because the program specifications require further processing only for overdue tapes. Although it is not a requirement of RPG, the TAG name END is commonly used when branching to the end of the calculations.

▸ **The CHAIN Operation** Lines 11 and 12 use the **CHAIN operation** to perform a random read of the members and tapes files. CHAIN is one of several operations that enable the programmer, rather than the RPG fixed logic cycle, to control input and output operations. The two CHAIN operations are conditioned by input field indicators and are not performed if the field named in Factor 1 is blank or contains only zeros.

Factor 1 is the key value of the record needed from the file named in Factor 2 (Figure 8-25). Factor 1 can contain a literal that specifies the key value, or (as in the figure) it can be a variable field name. The length and data class of the field or literal used in Factor 1 must be the same as the length and data class of the key field of the file named in Factor 2. When a field name is used in Factor 1, the value of the field is the key that is used to access the Factor 2 file. In this example, the member field contains the value 809501. RPG searches the index of the members file until the value is found or until RPG determines that the value 809501 is not in the index. If the key value is found, the keyed sequence access path retrieves the record for that member number from the members file. The retrieved data is placed in the field areas described for members file on the Input Specifications form.

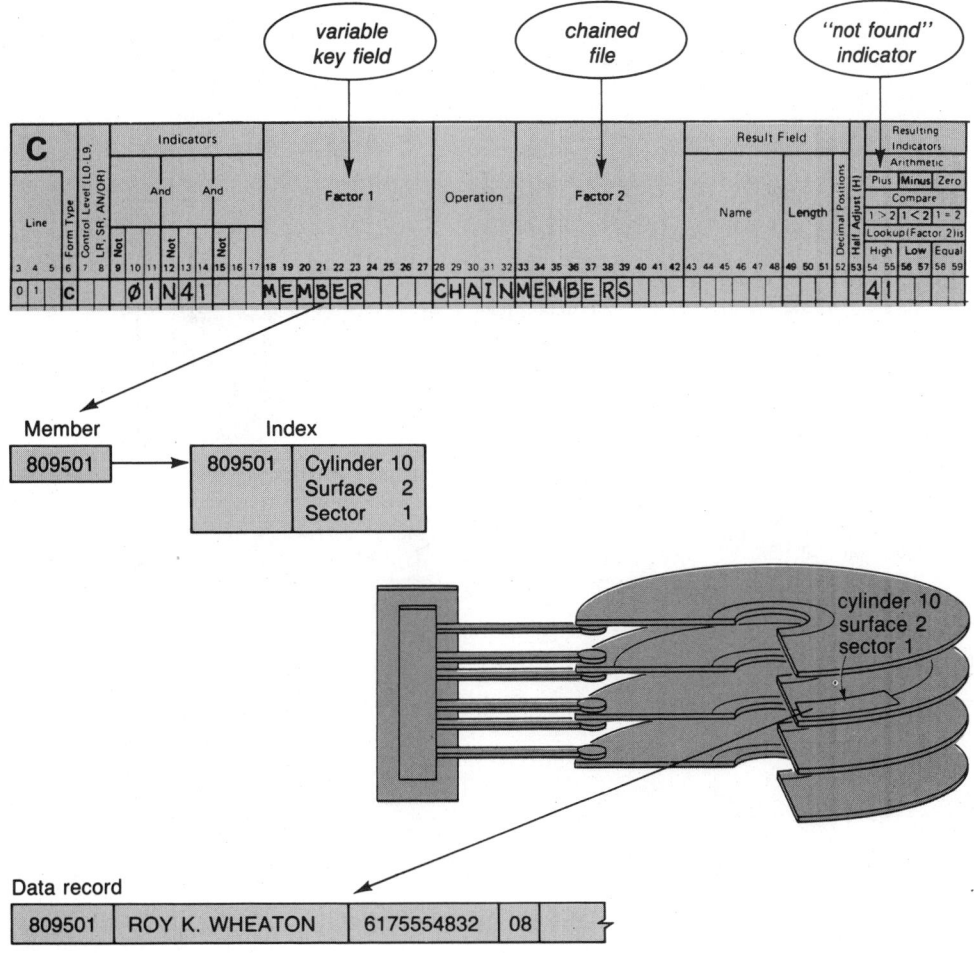

Figure 8-25 Random access using the CHAIN operation

If RPG does not find the Factor 1 value in the index for members, the indicator specified in positions 54 and 55 is turned on. The resulting indicator, 41 in this example, used with a CHAIN operation is turned on if the CHAIN operation is not successful and no record is found in the index for the Factor 2 file. RPG II does not require that a resulting indicator be used with a CHAIN operation, but if you do not use an indicator and the CHAIN operation does not find the needed entry in the index, the program halts. In this case, the person running the program can restart the job. RPG III and RPG/400 require a resulting indicator in positions 54 and 55.

Note in the figure that one indicator is apparently used to represent two different conditions. Indicator 41 is used as an input field indicator to represent a blank member number and is also used to show that the record could not be found in the index for the members file. One indicator is rarely used for two different conditions, but this program displays the error message INVALID NUMBER and shows the member number on the output report when either condition is detected. Because the member number is printed, it will be apparent to the report user whether the field was blank or was not found by the CHAIN operation. Figure 8-26 summarizes the CHAIN operation.

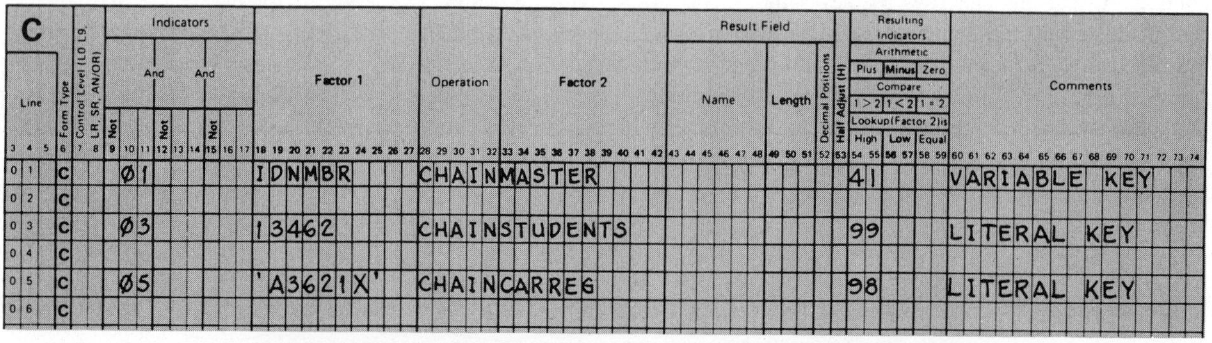

CHAIN Operation Summary

The CHAIN operation reads one record from a keyed sequence access path file. Factor 1 can be either a literal or field name containing the key field value of the record to be read. Factor 2 is the name of the file containing the record. The Result Field is not used. Positions 54 and 55 should contain an indicator that is turned on if the record identified in Factor 1 is not in the file. If no indicator is specified in positions 54 and 55 and the requested record is not found, the program stops but can be restarted.

Control Level Indicators	Indicators	Factor 1	Operation Name	Factor 2	Result Field	Resulting Indicators		
7–8	9–17	18–27	28–32	33–42	43–53	54–55	56–57	58–59
optional	optional	required	CHAIN	required	blank	optional	optional	blank

compiler dependent

Figure 8-26   CHAIN operation summary

Figure 8-27 shows lines 11–14 of the calculation specifications. Line 12 performs the CHAIN to the tapes file using the VIDEO field to provide the key for the random access retrieval. The resulting indicator, 42, is used in a similar manner to indicator 41 on line 11.

Line 13 performs the comparison needed to determine if a member has had more than ten previous late tape returns. This COMP operation is performed only if both the Member Number and Video Tape Number fields contain valid values. If both field values are valid (indicators N41 and N42) and the contents of the NUMBER field is greater than ten, indicator 46 is turned on.

Line 14 is the TAG used with the GOTO on line 08 to bypass the CHAIN and COMP operations if the video tape was returned on time.

Line	Form Type	Indicators	Factor 1	Operation	Factor 2	Resulting Indicators (High)	Comments
11	C	Ø1 N41	MEMBER	CHAIN	MEMBERS	41	GET MEMBER DATA
12	C	Ø1 N42	VIDEO	CHAIN	TAPES	42	GET TAPE DATA
13	C	Ø1 N41 N42	NUMBER	COMP	1Ø	46	EXCESS OVERDUE
14	C		END	TAG			

Figure 8-27 CHAIN operations for program HJG08X

Output Specifications

The detail output specifications for the sample program (Figure 8-28) show that three separate sets of indicators linked in an OR relationship are used to control printing of the detail line. The line prints if DUEDAT contains a value of zero (01 and 43), if RETDAT contains a value of zero (01 and 44), or if the return date is later than the date due (01 and 45).

Line	Form Type	Type / AND-OR	Space After	Output Indicators	Field Name	Edit Codes	End Position in Output Record	Constant or Edit Word
01	O	D	1	Ø1 43				
02	O	OR		Ø1 44				
03	O	OR		Ø1 45				
04	O				MEMBER		6	
05	O			N41	NAME		27	
06	O			41			27	'---INVALID NUMBER---'
07	O				VIDEO	Z	33	
08	O			N42	TITLE		56	
09	O			42			56	'----INVALID NUMBER----'
10	O			N43	DUEDATY		65	
11	O			43			65	'--------'
12	O			N44	RETDATY		74	
13	O			44			74	'--------'
14	O			41			89	'INCORRECT DATA'
15	O			42			89	'INCORRECT DATA'
16	O			43N41N42			87	'MISSING DATE'
17	O			44N41N42			87	'MISSING DATE'
18	O			46			93	'SUSPENDED - -'
19	O			46	AREA		88	
20	O			46	EXCH		92	
21	O			46	PHONE		97	

Figure 8-28 Detail output specifications

Lines 05 and 06 are an example of the use of both the on and the off settings of an indicator to control field printing. If indicator 41 is not on (N41), as shown on line 05, the contents of the NAME field retrieved from the members file will print. If the CHAIN operation to the members file was not successful or if the MEMBER field was blank or zero, the message ---INVALID NUMBER-- prints. In a similar manner, indicator 42 controls the printing of the TITLE field or an error message on lines 08 and 09. Indicators 41 and 42 are also used to control the error messages on lines 14, 15, 16, and 17.

The same logic is used with indicators 43 and 44 on lines 10, 11, 12, and 13 to control printing of the date fields or error messages if the fields are blank or zero.

Lines 18, 19, 20, and 21 are controlled by indicator 46 and print only if the content of the NUMBER field is greater than ten. Note that the telephone number is divided into the fields AREA, EXCH, and PHONE, which are used with the constant in line 18 for proper hyphenation of the printed telephone number.

Compilation Listing

The completed compilation listing and output report from the sample program are shown in Figure 8-29.

Figure 8-29 Compile listing and output for program HJG08X

```
HJG08X    09-12-91  18:59:49  HJG08X - OVERDUE TAPES              Version 3.5  Page  1

       ....+....1....+....2....+....3....+....4....+....5....+....6....+....7....

      3 0002 H                                                              HJG08X


      4 0003 F*-----------------------------------------------------------------*
      5 0004 F*  HJG08X - OVERDUE TAPES REPORT - HAL GOODWIN - AUGUST 19, 1991   *
      6 0005 F*                                                                  *
      7 0006 F*  PROGRAM HJG08X READS AN INPUT DATA FILE CONTAINING THE MEMBER-  *
      8 0007 F*  SHIP NUMBER, VIDEO TAPE NUMBER, DATE DUE BACK, AND DATE         *
      9 0008 F*  RETURNED OF A TAPE RENTED BY THE CLUB MEMBER.  IF NEITHER DATE  *
     10 0009 F*  IS A ZERO VALUED FIELD, THE PROGRAM CONVERTS THE DATES TO       *
     11 0010 F*  YYMMDD FORMAT AND THEN COMPARES THEM TO DETERMINE IF THE TAPE   *
     12 0011 F*  WAS RETURNED AFTER THE DUE DATE.  IF THE TAPE WAS RETURNED ON   *
     13 0012 F*  OR BEFORE THE DUE DATE, NO FURTHER PROCESSING TAKES PLACE ON    *
     14 0013 F*  THAT RECORD.  IF THE TAPE WAS RETURNED LATE, THE PROGRAM PRINTS *
     15 0014 F*  A DETAIL LINE.  IF THE RENTER HAS HAD MORE THAN TEN PREVIOUS    *
     16 0015 F*  LATE RETURNS, THE PROGRAM WILL PRINT A MESSAGE INDICATING THAT  *
     17 0016 F*  MEMBERSHIP PRIVILEGES ARE SUSPENDED, AND WILL ALSO PRINT THE    *
     18 0017 F*  MEMBER'S TELEPHONE NUMBER SO THAT HE/SHE MAY BE NOTIFIED.       *
     19 0018 F*-----------------------------------------------------------------*


     22 0020 FRETURNS IP  F 400  40        DISK
     23 0021 FMEMBERS IC  F  90  90R 6AI    1 DISK
     24 0022 FTAPES   IC  F  50  50R 5AI    1 DISK
     25 0023 FODUELISTO   F 132 132     OF     PRINTER


     28 0025 F* ID F  C  H  L   FUNCTION OF INDICATORS
     29 0026 F* 01---------------RETURNS RECORD IDENTIFICATION
     30 0027 F* 02---------------MEMBERS RECORD IDENTIFICATION (UNUSED)
     31 0028 F* 03---------------TAPES RECORD IDENTIFICATION (UNUSED)
     32 0029 F*    41------------BLANK MEMBER FIELD
     33 0030 F*    42------------ZERO VIDEO FIELD
     34 0031 F*    43------------ZERO DUEDAT FIELD
     35 0032 F*    44------------ZERO RETDAT FIELD
     36 0033 F*      45--------RETDAT LATER THAN DUEDAT (LATE RETURN)
     37 0034 F*      46--------MORE THAN TEN LATE RETURNS
     38 0035 F*          1P---FIRST PAGE INDICATOR
     39 0036 F*---OVERFLOW INDICATOR
```

Figure 8-29 (1)

```
HJG08X     09-12-91  18:59:49  HJG08X - OVERDUE TAPES          Version 3.5  Page  2

           ....+....1....+....2....+....3....+....4....+....5....+....6....+....7....


   40 0037 IRETURNS AA  01
   41 0038 I                                       1   6 MEMBER      41
   42 0039 I                                       7 110VIDEO        42
   43 0040 I                                      12 170DUEDAT       43
   44 0041 I                                      18 230RETDAT       44
   45 0042 I*--------------------------------------------------------------

   48 0044 IMEMBERS BB  02
   49 0045 I                                       1   6 MEMBNO
   50 0046 I                                       7  26 NAME
   51 0047 I                                      27  29 AREA
   52 0048 I                                      30  32 EXCH
   53 0049 I                                      33  36 PHONE
   54 0050 I                                      37  380NUMBER
   55 0051 I*--------------------------------------------------------------

   58 0053 ITAPES   CC  03
   59 0054 I                                       1   50TAPENO
   60 0055 I                                       6  27 TITLE


   61 0056 C     01              SETOF                 4546  RESET TESTS
   62 0057 C     01 43                                       MISSING DATE
   63 0058 COR   01 44           GOTO BYPASS


   66 0060 C     01     DUEDAT   MULT 10000.01 DUE     60    CONVERT DATES
   67 0061 C     01     RETDAT   MULT 10000.01 RETURN  60
   68 0062 C     01     RETURN   COMP DUE              45    COMPARE DATES
   69 0063 C     01N45           GOTO END


   72 0065 C            BYPASS   TAG
   73 0066 C     01N41  MEMBER   CHAINMEMBERS          41    GET MEMBER DATA
   74 0067 C     01N42  VIDEO    CHAINTAPES            42    GET TAPE DATA
   75 0068 C     01N41N42NUMBER  COMP 10               46    EXCESS OVERDUE
   76 0069 C            END      TAG
   77 0070 C            'DEBUG-1' DEBUGODUELIST  MEMBER


   78 0071 O*  HEADING LINE ONE
   79 0072 O*-----------------
   80 0073 OODUELISTH  206    1P
   81 0074 O       OR         OF
   82 0075 O                                    6 'HJG08X'
   83 0076 O                                   37 'O V E R D U E'
   84 0077 O                                   49 'T A P E S'
   85 0078 O                                   69 'PAGE'
   86 0079 O                         PAGE      74

   89 0081 O*  HEADING LINE TWO
   90 0082 O*-----------------
   91 0083 O          H  1    1P
   92 0084 O       OR         OF
   93 0085 O                                    6 'MEMBER'
   94 0086 O                                   33 'TAPE'
   95 0087 O                                   73 'DATE    RETURN'

   98 0089 O*  HEADING LINE THREE
   99 0090 O*-----------------
  100 0091 O          H  2    1P
  101 0092 O       OR         OF
  102 0093 O                                   22 'NO.     MEMBER NAME'
  103 0094 O                                   50 'NO.      TAPE TITLE'
  104 0095 O                                   72 'DUE     DATE'
```

Figure 8-29 (2)

continued

```
  HJG08X    09-12-91  18:59:49  HJG08X - OVERDUE TAPES              Version 3.5  Page  3

        ....+....1....+....2....+....3....+....4....+....5....+....6....+....7....
      107 0097 O*  DETAIL LINE
      108 0098 O*-------------
      109 0099 O        D  1      01 43
      110 0100 O          OR      01 44
      111 0101 O          OR      01 45
      112 0102 O                      MEMBER     6
      113 0103 O                  N41 NAME      27
      114 0104 O                  41            27 '---INVALID NUMBER---'
      115 0105 O                      VIDEO Z   33
      116 0106 O                  N42 TITLE     56
      117 0107 O                  42            56 '----INVALID NUMBER----'
      118 0108 O                  N43 DUEDATY   65
      119 0109 O                  43            65 '--------'
      120 0110 O                  N44 RETDATY   74
      121 0111 O                  44            74 '--------'
      122 0112 O                  41            89 'INCORRECT DATA'
      123 0113 O                  42            89 'INCORRECT DATA'
      124 0114 O                  43N41N42      87 'MISSING DATE'
      125 0115 O                  44N41N42      87 'MISSING DATE'
      126 0116 O                  46            93 'SUSPENDED   -   -'
      127 0117 O                  46  AREA      88
      128 0118 O                  46  EXCH      92
      129 0119 O                  46  PHONE     97
      130 /*
      131 /*



      THE FOLLOWING INDICATORS WERE SPECIFIED BUT WERE NEVER
      USED TO CONDITION OPERATIONS

        02  03



      THE FOLLOWING INDICATORS APPEARED IN THIS PROGRAM

          01  02  03  41  42  43  44  45  46  1P  OF
  No Warning Errors
  No Fatal Errors
```

Figure 8-29 (3)

```
  HJG08X                     O V E R D U E   T A P E S                PAGE    1

  MEMBER                      TAPE                      DATE    RETURN
    NO.      MEMBER NAME      NO.      TAPE TITLE       DUE     DATE

  730021 JENNIFER BOMBARD     1101 E.T.                 6/07/91 6/08/91
  736004 JIM REID             2400 WAR GAMES            ------- ------- MISSING DATE
  809501 ROY K. WHEATON       1002 ----INVALID NUMBER---- ------- ------- INCORRECT DATA
  813114 JEAN DENNETT         1301 TRON                 6/08/91 6/09/91 SUSPENDED 413-555-7435
  814006 BARBARA POHJA        2283 MY FAIR LADY         6/09/91 6/10/91
```

Figure 8-29 (4)

IN CONCLUSION

This Chapter has introduced you to the keyed sequence access path and shown you how to perform random access retrieval of data from data files using this type of access path. Later chapters demonstrate how to process this type of file sequentially, load data into these files, and perform operations that enable you to alter the data stored in the files.

Chapter 9 introduces the use of exception output, which enables you to control output operations during either detail or total calculation time. In addition, Chapter 9 shows you how to use looping techniques to perform repetitive operations that are based on a single input record.

CHAPTER SUMMARY

1. The **access path** of a file is the method used by the computer to retrieve input data and write output file data.
2. The **arrival sequence access path** processes records in the order in which they are stored in a file, without regard for the sequence of the records.
3. The **keyed sequence access path** accesses data records according to the value contained in a **key field** that identifies each record in a file. Another term for the keyed sequence access path is the **indexed sequential access method (ISAM)**.
4. Because keyed sequence access path processing is slower than arrival sequence access path processing, it is sometimes more efficient to sort a data file into the necessary sequence and then to process the file by arrival sequence techniques.
5. **Random access** techniques enable you to access a specific record in a file by means of the value of the record's key field.
6. Random access processing techniques are under programmer control and are not dependent on the RPG fixed logic cycle.
7. A **sector** of a disk track is the smallest unit of disk storage that can be identified and specifically accessed.
8. A **disk address** is usually based on a combination of surface, track, and sector numbers.
9. The **file index** of a keyed sequence access path file contains each record's identifying key and the disk address where the data record is stored.
10. The method of disk addressing and file indexing used by a computer depends on its design.
11. **Sequence control** operations enable the programmer to bypass the normal top-down processing of RPG calculation. Sequence control operations are commonly called **branching** operations.
12. RPG branching operations can be used to go directly to other operations whether they precede or follow the branching operations.
13. RPG does not permit branching between detail time and total time operations.
14. When a **GOTO** operation is executed, the program immediately branches to the operation following the associated **TAG** operation. All operations between the GOTO and the TAG are skipped.
15. No indicators can be specified in positions 9–17 of a TAG operation. However, if a GOTO is conditioned by a total time indicator in positions 7–8, the TAG must have the same conditioning indicator.
16. The **CHAIN operation** causes a random access read of a record from a keyed sequence access path data file.
17. The length and data class of the Factor 1 entry in a CHAIN operation must match the description of the key field of the file being read.
18. The resulting indicator specified in positions 54 and 55 of a CHAIN operation is turned on if the required record is not found in the file being read.

REVIEW QUESTIONS

1. What is an access path?
2. Why is the access path concept important only with disk data files?
3. How does arrival sequence access path processing differ from sequential processing of a keyed file?
4. Name two types of processing that can be performed when a keyed sequence access path file is used.
5. Name the three areas of a disk that are identified by a disk address.
6. What is a disk cylinder?
7. What is the smallest area of disk storage that can be uniquely addressed?
8. What two items are usually stored in a file index?
9. What is the key field of a file? What entries are needed to define the key field?
10. Explain the relationship between the GOTO and TAG operations used in branching.
11. Explain the coding of the CHAIN operation.
12. Why is a resulting indicator used with a CHAIN operation?

STUDENT EXERCISES: RPG PROGRAM CODE

1. Using the following file information:

   File name   STUFILE
   Access path   Keyed sequence
   Record length   75
   Key location   Positions 8–12 (alphameric)

   Code the description of STUFILE and the operation needed to access the record with the key 91X12. Turn on indicator 99 if the record does not exist in the file. Use the File Description and Calculation Specifications form below.

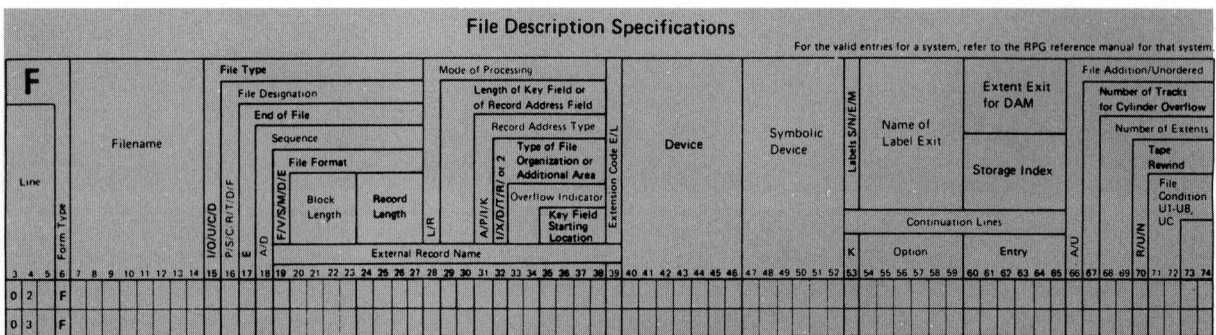

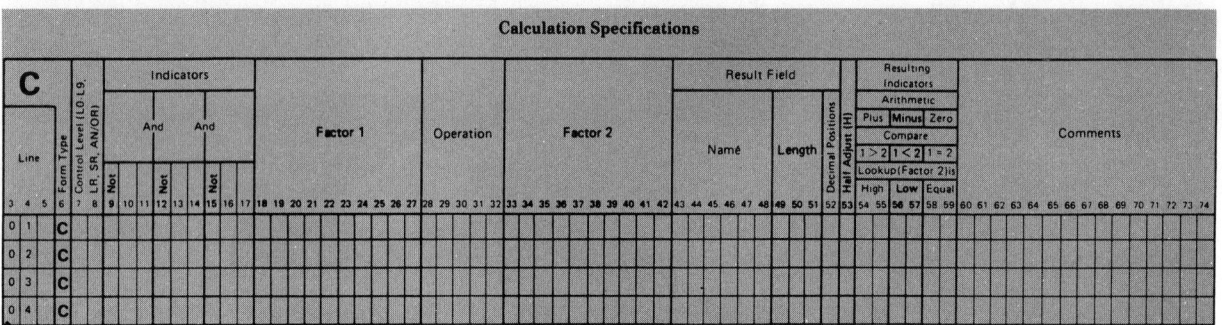

2. Using the following file information:

   File name   PAYROLL
   Access path   Keyed sequence
   Record length   51
   Key location   Positions 1–6 (zoned numeric)

   Code the description of PAYROLL on the File Description form in Figure 8-31. On the Calculation Specifications form below, code the operations necessary to access a PAYROLL record based on the value contained in the EMPNO field. If the record does not exist in the file, turn on indicator 25 and branch to ERROR.

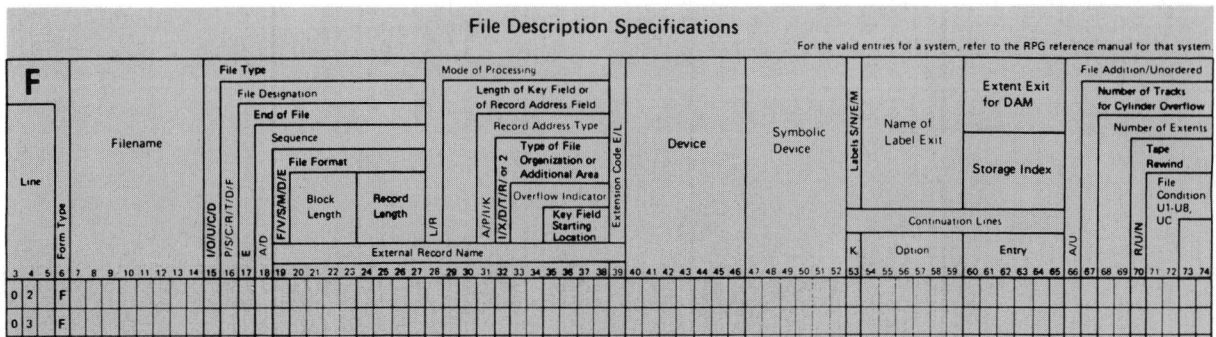

File Description Specifications

For the valid entries for a system, refer to the RPG reference manual for that system.

Calculation Specifications

STUDENT EXERCISES: DEBUGGING RPG PROGRAMS

▤ Problem 1

The following program (Figure 8-30) contains one or more errors detected by the compiler. Circle each error and record the corrected entry directly on the listing. Explain the error and the method of correction.

Figure 8-30 Debugging Problem 1

```
    HJG08X    09-11-91  17:44:57  HJG08X - OVERDUE TAPES         Version 3.5  Page  1

              ....+....1....+....2....+....3....+....4....+....5....+....6....+....7....

       3 0002 H                                                            HJG08X



       4 0003 FRETURNS IP  F 400  40           DISK
       5 0004 FMEMBERS IC  F  90  90R AI        DISK
****-F128- Indexed file requires Key Field Starting Location.
****-F129- Indexed file requires Key Length.
****-F187- Key length must be specified for an indexed or an address output file.
****-F188- Key field starting location must be specified for an indexed file.
       6 0005 FTAPES   IC  F  50  50  5AI      1 DISK
****-F140- Improper characteristics for use with a chain file.
       7 0006 FODUELISTO    F 132 132      OF    PRINTER



       8 0007 IRETURNS AA   01
       9 0008 I                                 1    6 MEMBER          41
      10 0009 I                                 7  110VIDEO            42
```

Figure 8-30 (1)

continued

```
HJG08X     09-11-91  17:44:57  HJG08X - OVERDUE TAPES              Version 3.5  Page  2

       ....+....1....+....2....+....3....+....4....+....5....+....6....+....7....

  11 0010 I                                        12  170DUEDAT         43
  12 0011 I                                        18  230RETDAT         44
  13 0012 IMEMBERS BB 02
  14 0013 I                                         1    6 MEMBNO
  15 0014 I                                         7   26 NAME
  16 0015 I                                        27   29 AREA
  17 0016 I                                        30   32 EXCH
  18 0017 I                                        33   36 PHONE
  19 0018 I                                        37  380NUMBER
  20 0019 ITAPES    CC 03
  21 0020 I                                         1   50TAPENO
  22 0021 I                                         6   27 TITLE



  23 0022 C    01              SETOF                    4546  RESET TESTS
  24 0023 C    01 43                                          MISSING DATE
  25 0024 COR  01 44           GOTO BYPASS


  28 0026 C    01      DUEDAT  MULT 10000.01  DUE      60    CONVERT DATES
  29 0027 C    01      RETDAT  MULT 10000.01  RETURN   60
  30 0028 C    01      RETURN  COMP DUE                45    COMPARE DATES
  31 0029 C    01N45           GOTO END


  34 0031 C            BYPASS  TAG
  35 0032 C    01N41   MEMBER  CHAINMEMBERS            41    GET MEMBER DATA
****-C208- Factor 1 length must match the indexed file length.
  36 0033 C    01N42   VIDEO   CHAINTAPES             42    GET TAPE DATA
  37 0034 C    01N41N42NUMBER  COMP 10                46    EXCESS OVERDUE
  38 0035 C            END     TAG
  39 0036 OODUELISTH    206   1P
  40 0037 O      OR          OF
  41 0038 O                                6 'HJG08X'
  42 0039 O                               37 'O V E R D U E'
  43 0040 O                               49 'T A P E S'
  44 0041 O                               69 'PAGE'
  45 0042 O                       PAGE    74


  48 0044 O      H  1         1P
  49 0045 O      OR          OF
  50 0046 O                                6 'MEMBER'
  51 0047 O                               33 'TAPE'
  52 0048 O                               73 'DATE    RETURN'


  55 0050 O      H  2         1P
  56 0051 O      OR          OF
  57 0052 O                               22 'NO.     MEMBER NAME'
  58 0053 O                               50 'NO.       TAPE TITLE'
  59 0054 O                               72 'DUE     DATE'


  62 0056 O      D  1         01 43
  63 0057 O      OR           01 44
  64 0058 O      OR           01 45
  65 0059 O                      MEMBER    6
  66 0060 O              N41     NAME     27
  67 0061 O              41              27 '---INVALID NUMBER---'
  68 0062 O                      VIDEO Z  33
  69 0063 O              N42     TITLE    56
  70 0064 O              42              56 '----INVALID NUMBER----'
  71 0065 O              N43     DUEDATY  65
  72 0066 O              43              65 '--------'
  73 0067 O              N44     RETDATY  74
  74 0068 O              44              74 '--------'
  75 0069 O              41              89 'INCORRECT DATA'
  76 0070 O              42              89 'INCORRECT DATA'
  77 0071 O              43N41N42        87 'MISSING DATE'
  78 0072 O              44N41N42        87 'MISSING DATE'
```

Figure 8-30 (2)

```
HJG08X    09-11-91  17:44:57  HJG08X - OVERDUE TAPES              Version 3.5  Page  3

     `....+....1....+....2....+....3....+....4....+....5....+....6....+....7....

   79 0073 O            46              .    93 'SUSPENDED   -  -'
   80 0074 O            46      AREA         88
   81 0075 O            46      EXCH         92                         -  -
   82 0076 O            46      PHONE        97
   83 /*
   84 /*



       THE FOLLOWING INDICATORS WERE SPECIFIED BUT WERE NEVER
       USED TO CONDITION OPERATIONS

       02   03

       THE FOLLOWING INDICATORS APPEARED IN THIS PROGRAM

       01  02  03  41  42  43  44  45  46  1P  OF
 No Warning Errors
 6 Fatal Errors
```

Figure 8-30 (3)

Problem 2

The following program (Figure 8-31) contains one or more errors detected by the compiler. Circle each error and record the corrected entry directly on the listing. Explain the error and the method of correction.

Figure 8-31   Debugging Problem 2

```
HJG08X    09-11-91  17:48:12  HJG08X - OVERDUE TAPES              Version 3.5  Page  1

     ....+....1....+....2....+....3....+....4....+....5....+....6....+....7....

    3 0002 H                                                         HJG08X


    4 0003 FRETURNS IP  F 400  40             DISK
    5 0004 FMEMBERS IS  F  90  90R 6AI   1 DISK
****-F139- Improper characteristics for use with a secondary file.
    6 0005 FTAPES   IC  F  50  50R 5AI   1 DISK
    7 0006 FODUELISTO   F 132 132      OF    PRINTER


    8 0007 IRETURNS AA  01
    9 0008 I                                1   6 MEMBER       41
   10 0009 I                                7  110VIDEO        42
   11 0010 I                               12  170DUEDAT       43
   12 0011 I                               18  230RETDAT       44
   13 0012 IMEMBERS BB  02
   14 0013 I                                1   6 MEMBNO
   15 0014 I                                7  26 NAME
   16 0015 I                               27  29 AREA
   17 0016 I                               30  32 EXCH
   18 0017 I                               33  36 PHONE
   19 0018 I                               37  380NUMBER
   20 0019 ITAPES   CC  03
   21 0020 I                                1   50TAPENO
   22 0021 I                                6  27 TITLE
```

Figure 8-31 (1)

continued

```
HJG08X    09-11-91  17:48:12  HJG08X - OVERDUE TAPES            Version 3.5  Page  2

          ....+....1....+....2....+....3....+....4....+....5....+....6....+....7....
     23 0022 C   01                  SETOF                      4546  RESET TESTS
     24 0023 C   01 43                                                MISSING DATE
     25 0024 COR 01 44               GOTO BYPASS


     28 0026 C   01       DUEDAT     MULT 10000.01 DUE     60    CONVERT DATES
     29 0027 C   01       RETDAT     MULT 10000.01 RETURN  60    CONVERT DATES
     30 0028 C   01       RETURN     COMP DUE              45    COMPARE DATES
     31 0029 C   01N45               GOTO END


     34 0031 C            BYPASS     TAG
     35 0032 C   01N41    MEMBER     CHAINMEMBERS         41    GET MEMBER DATA
     36 0033 C   01N42    VIDEO      CHAINTAPES           42    GET TAPE DATA
     37 0034 C   01N41N42NUMBER      COMP 10              46    EXCESS OVERDUE
     38 0035 C            END        TAG


     39 0036 OODUELISTH  206   1P
     40 0037 O     OR          OF
     41 0038 O                              6 'HJG08X'
     42 0039 O                             37 'O V E R D U E'
     43 0040 O                             49 'T A P E S'
     44 0041 O                             69 'PAGE'
     45 0042 O                    PAGE     74


     48 0044 O     H 1         1P
     49 0045 O     OR          OF
     50 0046 O                              6 'MEMBER'
     51 0047 O                             33 'TAPE'
     52 0048 O                             73 'DATE      RETURN'


     55 0050 O     H 2         1P
     56 0051 O     OR          OF
     57 0052 O                             22 'NO.    MEMBER NAME'
     58 0053 O                             50 'NO.      TAPE TITLE'
     59 0054 O                             72 'DUE    DATE'


     62 0056 O     D 1      01 43
     63 0057 O     OR       01 44
     64 0058 O     OR       01 45
     65 0059 O                   MEMBER     6
     66 0060 O              N41  NAME      27
     67 0061 O              41             27 '---INVALID NUMBER---'
     68 0062 O                   VIDEO Z   33
     69 0063 O              N42  TITLE     56
     70 0064 O              42             56 '----INVALID NUMBER----'
     71 0065 O              N43  DUEDATY   65
     72 0066 O              43             65 '--------'
     73 0067 O              N44  RETDATY   74
     74 0068 O              44             74 '--------'
     75 0069 O              41             89 'INCORRECT DATA'
     76 0070 O              42             89 'INCORRECT DATA'
     77 0071 O              43N41N42       87 'MISSING DATE'
     78 0072 O              44N41N42       87 'MISSING DATE'
     79 0073 O              46             93 'SUSPENDED  -  -'
     80 0074 O              46   AREA      88
     81 0075 O              46   EXCH      92
     82 0076 O              46   PHONE     97
     83 /*
     84 /*


          THE FOLLOWING INDICATORS WERE SPECIFIED BUT WERE NEVER
          USED TO CONDITION OPERATIONS

          02  03


          THE FOLLOWING INDICATORS APPEARED IN THIS PROGRAM

          01  02  03  41  42  43  44  45  46  1P  OF
   No Warning Errors
    1 Fatal Errors
```

Figure 8-31 (2)

STUDENT EXERCISES: RPG PROGRAM MAINTENANCE

Problem 1

Modify program HJG08X to print a detail line only if the tape was returned after the due date. If either of the date fields contains a value of zero, the program skips all detail calculations and does not print a detail line. Print the needed modifications to the program on the compile listing (Figure 8-32), and explain your modifications and their effect on the program.

```
HJG08X    09-11-91  17:49:08  HJG08X - OVERDUE TAPES              Version 3.5  Page  1
          ....+....1....+....2....+....3....+....4....+....5....+....6....+....7....

 3  0002 H                                                                 HJG08X


 4  0003 FRETURNS IP  F 400  40             DISK
 5  0004 FMEMBERS IC  F  90  90R 6AI      1 DISK
 6  0005 FTAPES   IC  F  50  50R 5AI      1 DISK
 7  0006 FODUELISTO   F 132 132       OF    PRINTER


 8  0007 IRETURNS AA  01
 9  0008 I                                        1   6 MEMBER       41
10  0009 I                                        7  110VIDEO        42
11  0010 I                                       12  170DUEDAT       43
12  0011 I                                       18  230RETDAT       44
13  0012 IMEMBERS BB  02
14  0013 I                                        1   6 MEMBNO
15  0014 I                                        7  26 NAME
16  0015 I                                       27  29 AREA
17  0016 I                                       30  32 EXCH
18  0017 I                                       33  36 PHONE
19  0018 I                                       37  380NUMBER
20  0019 ITAPES    CC  03
21  0020 I                                        1   50TAPENO
22  0021 I                                        6  27 TITLE


23  0022 C     01              SETOF                  4546  RESET TESTS
24  0023 C     01 43                                        MISSING DATE
25  0024 COR   01 44           GOTO BYPASS


28  0026 C     01        DUEDAT MULT 10000.01 DUE   60      CONVERT DATES
29  0027 C     01        RETDAT MULT 10000.01 RETURN 60
30  0028 C     01        RETURN COMP DUE             45     COMPARE DATES
31  0029 C     01N45           GOTO END


34  0031 C               BYPASS TAG
35  0032 C     01N41     MEMBER CHAINMEMBERS         41     GET MEMBER DATA
36  0033 C     01N42     VIDEO  CHAINTAPES           42     GET TAPE DATA
37  0034 C     01N41N42NUMBER   COMP 10              46     EXCESS OVERDUE
38  0035 C               END    TAG


39  0036 OODUELISTH   206    1P
40  0037 O        OR         OF
41  0038 O                                       6 'HJG08X'
42  0039 O                                      37 'O V E R D U E'
```

Figure 8-32 Compile listing for Problem 1

Problem 2

Modify program HJG08X to print a detail line for every input record. In addition to all current processing, if the video tape was returned on or before the due date, the program prints a detail line containing the message ON TIME beginning in position 76 of the detail line. Print the needed changes directly on the compile listing (Figure 8-33), and explain your modifications and their effect on the program.

```
HJG08X    09-11-91  17:49:08  HJG08X - OVERDUE TAPES              Version 3.5  Page  2

          ....+....1....+....2....+....3....+....4....+....5....+....6....+....7....

      43 0040 O                                       49 'T A P E S'
      44 0041 O                                       69 'PAGE'
      45 0042 O                          PAGE         74

      48 0044 O        H  1    1P
      49 0045 O        OR      OF
      50 0046 O                                        6 'MEMBER'
      51 0047 O                                       33 'TAPE'
      52 0048 O                                       73 'DATE     RETURN'

      55 0050 O        H  2    1P
      56 0051 O        OR      OF
      57 0052 O                                       22 'NO.      MEMBER NAME'
      58 0053 O                                       50 'NO.       TAPE TITLE'
      59 0054 O                                       72 'DUE      DATE'

      62 0056 O        D  1    01 43
      63 0057 O        OR      01 44
      64 0058 O        OR      01 45
      65 0059 O                         MEMBER         6
      66 0060 O                N41      NAME          27
      67 0061 O                41                     27 '---INVALID NUMBER---'
      68 0062 O                         VIDEO Ż       33
      69 0063 O                N42      TITLE         56
      70 0064 O                42                     56 '----INVALID NUMBER----'
      71 0065 O                N43      DUEDATY       65
      72 0066 O                43                     65 '--------'
      73 0067 O                N44      RETDATY       74
      74 0068 O                44                     74 '--------'
      75 0069 O                41                     89 'INCORRECT DATA'
      76 0070 O                42                     89 'INCORRECT DATA'
      77 0071 O                43N41N42               87 'MISSING DATE'
      78 0072 O                44N41N42               87 'MISSING DATE'
      79 0073 O                46                     93 'SUSPENDED    -  -'
      80 0074 O                46       AREA          88
      81 0075 O                46       EXCH          92
      82 0076 O                46       PHONE         97
      83 /*
      84 /*


          THE FOLLOWING INDICATORS WERE SPECIFIED BUT WERE NEVER
          USED TO CONDITION OPERATIONS

          02   03


          THE FOLLOWING INDICATORS APPEARED IN THIS PROGRAM

          01   02   03   41   42   43   44   45   46   1P   OF
No Warning Errors
No Fatal Errors
```

Figure 8-33 Compile listing for Problem 2

STUDENT EXERCISES: PROGRAMMING IN RPG

PROGRAMMING ASSIGNMENT 1
ACCOUNT NUMBER VERIFICATION REPORT

INSTRUCTIONS

Plan, code, enter, and test an RPG program that produces the Account Number Verification Report.

INPUT

The formats of the sales transaction file and the account master file (ACCOUNTS) are shown in Figure 8-34. Use test data set 18 for the sales transaction file and test data set 19 for the account master file.

SALES TRANSACTION RECORD						
Record Length 25						
Field No.	Field Name	Field Description	Field Position	Field Length	Dec. Pos.	Data Class
1		UNUSED AREA	1–7			
2	ACCTNO	Account Number	8–14	7		A
3		UNUSED AREA	15–25			

ACCOUNTS FILE RECORD						
Record Length 15		Key Location 2–8 (ACCNT)				
Field No.	Field Name	Field Description	Field Position	Field Length	Dec. Pos.	Data Class
1		UNUSED AREA	1			
2	ACCNT	Account Number	2–8	7		A
3	VCODE	Verification Code	9–12	4	0	N
4		UNUSED AREA	13–15			

Figure 8-34 Data files for programming assignment 1

OUTPUT

Output is the Account Number Verification Report, the format of which is shown in Figure 8-35.

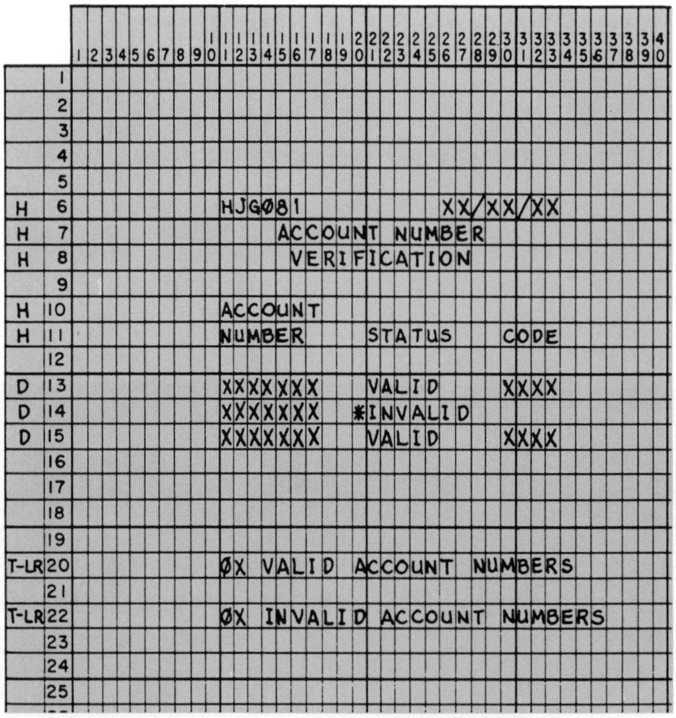

```
        |1|2|3|4|5|6|7|8|9|0|1|2|3|4|5|6|7|8|9|0|1|2|3|4|5|6|7|8|9|0|1|2|3|4|5|6|7|8|9|0|
  1
  2
  3
  4
  5
H 6           HJG081                    XX/XX/XX
H 7                ACCOUNT NUMBER
H 8                VERIFICATION
  9
H 10         ACCOUNT
H 11         NUMBER      STATUS      CODE
  12
D 13         XXXXXXX     VALID       XXXX
D 14         XXXXXXX    *INVALID
D 15         XXXXXXX     VALID       XXXX
  16
  17
  18
  19
T-LR 20          ØX VALID ACCOUNT NUMBERS
  21
T-LR 22          ØX INVALID ACCOUNT NUMBERS
  23
  24
  25
```

Figure 8-35 Account Number Verification Report format

⊨ Processing Requirements

The Account Number Verification Report is a detail printed report based on information from the sales transaction file, which is the primary file. Every time a sales transaction record is read, perform a random access read of the ACCOUNTS file. If the account number used to perform the direct access read is not found in ACCOUNTS, print the invalid account number line shown on line 14 of the printer spacing chart and add 1 to a count of invalid account numbers.

If the read of ACCOUNTS is successful, print the valid account number line shown on lines 13 and 15 of the printer spacing chart and add 1 to a count of valid account numbers. This line will contain the account number, the VALID constant, and the verification code taken from the ACCOUNTS record.

At the end of the program, print the counts of valid and invalid account numbers as shown on lines 20 and 22.

PROGRAMMING ASSIGNMENT 2
SALES REPORT

INSTRUCTIONS

Plan, code, enter, and test an RPG program to produce the Sales Report.

INPUT

The formats of the sales transaction file and the part master file (PARTMSTR) are shown in Figure 8-36. Use test data set 18 for the Sales Transaction file and test data set 19 for the Part Master file.

	SALES TRANSACTION RECORD					
	Record Length 25					
Field No.	Field Name	Field Description	Field Position	Field Length	Dec. Pos.	Data Class
1	INVNO	Invoice Number	1–7	7	0	N
2	PARTNO	Part Number	8–14	7		A
3	QTY	Quantity Purchased	15–17	3	0	N

	PARTMSTR FILE RECORD					
	Record Length 15		Key Location 2–8 (PART)			
Field No.	Field Name	Field Description	Field Position	Field Length	Dec. Pos.	Data Class
1	PART	Part Number	2–8	7		A
2	UCOST	Unit Cost	9–12	4	3	N
3	MARKUP	Markup Percentage	13–15	3	3	N

Figure 8-36   Data files for programming assignment 2

OUTPUT

Output is the Sales Report, the format of which is shown in Figure 8-37.

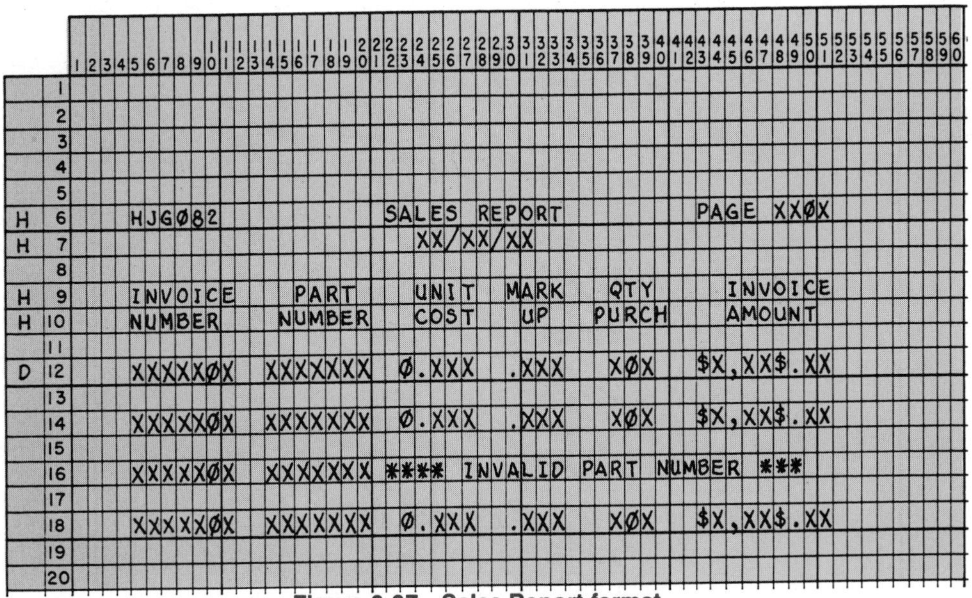

Figure 8-37   Sales Report format

Processing Requirements

The Sales Report is a detail printed report based on information from the sales transaction file, which is the primary file. Every time a sales transaction record is read, perform a random access read of the PARTMSTR file. If the part number used to perform the direct access read is not found in PARTMSTR, perform no further calculations, and print the invalid part number message as shown on the printer spacing chart.

If the read of PARTMSTR is successful, calculate the invoice amount based on the following instructions:

unit price = (unit cost × markup percentage) + unit cost
invoice amount = unit price × quantity purchased

This program does not calculate any final totals.

PROGRAMMING ASSIGNMENT 3
STUDENT CREDIT LOAD REPORT

INSTRUCTIONS

Plan, code, enter, and test an RPG program to produce the Student Credit Load Report.

INPUT

The formats of the student record file, student schedule file (STUSCHED), and the course master file (COURSMAS) are shown in Figure 8-38. Use test data set 3 for the student record file, test data set 20 for the student schedule file, and test data set 21 for the course master file.

STUDENT RECORD						
Record Length 30						
Field No.	Field Name	Field Description	Field Position	Field Length	Dec. Pos.	Data Class
1		UNUSED AREA	1–24			
2	STUDNT	Student Number	25–30	6		A

STUSCHED FILE RECORD						
Record Length 45		Key Location 1–6 (STUDNO)				
Field No.	Field Name	Field Description	Field Position	Field Length	Dec. Pos.	Data Class
1	STUDNO	Student Number	1–6	6		A
2	CRSNO1	Course Number 1	7–12	6		A
3	CRSNO2	Course Number 2	15–20	6		A
4	CRSNO3	Course Number 3	23–28	6		A
5	CRSNO4	Course Number 4	31–36	6		A
6	CRSNO5	Course Number 5	39–44	6		A

Figure 8-38   Data files for programming assignment 3   *continued*

COURSMAS FILE RECORD						
Record Length 61			Key Location 1–6 (COURSE)			
Field No.	Field Name	Field Description	Field Position	Field Length	Dec. Pos.	Data Class
1	COURSE	Course Number	1–6	6		A
2	CREDIT	Course Credits	10–10	1	0	N
3	TITLE	Course Name	11–35	25		A
4	INSTR	Instructor's Name	41–60	20		A

Figure 8-38 (continued)

OUTPUT

Output is the Student Credit Load Report, the format of which is shown in Figure 8-39.

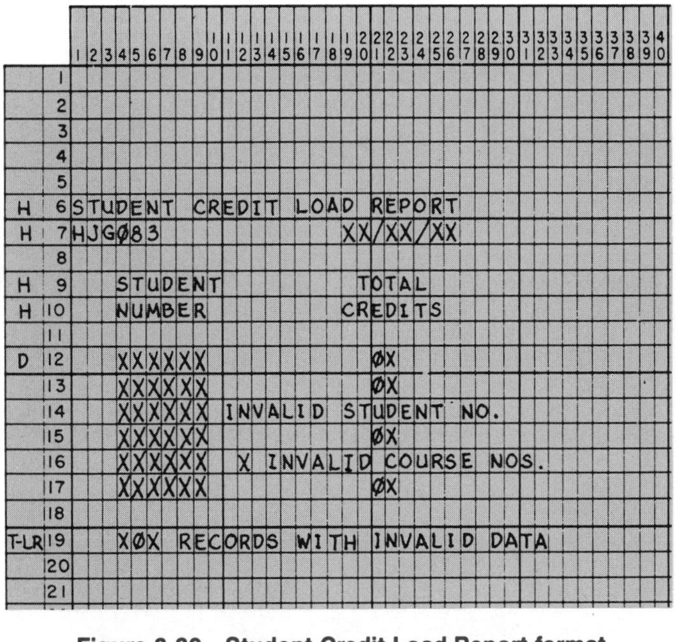

Figure 8-39   Student Credit Load Report format

Processing Requirements

The student record file is the primary input file for this program. Every time a record is read, perform a direct access read of the student schedule file to obtain the schedule record for the file. If the student number cannot be found in the student schedule file, print the error message shown on the printer spacing chart, add 1 to the final total count of records containing invalid data, and bypass all further processing for the record.

If the read of the student schedule file was performed successfully, use each of the course numbers to perform a direct access read of the course master file. Every time a record is retrieved from the course master file, add the number of course credits to an accumulator for the student. If one or more of the course numbers are invalid, clear the counter to zero, print the error message shown on the printer spacing chart, add 1 to the final total count of records containing invalid data, and bypass all further processing for the record. A student may take less than five courses. Blank course numbers are not invalid.

If all of the course numbers are valid, print the detail line shown on the printer spacing chart containing the total number of credits for the courses taken by the student.

PROGRAMMING ASSIGNMENT 4
STUDENT RECORD ERROR LIST

INSTRUCTIONS

Plan, code, enter, and test an RPG program to produce the Student Record Error List.

INPUT

The formats of the student record file, student schedule file (STUSCHED), and the course master file (COURSMAS) are shown in Figure 8-40. Use test data set 3 for the student record file, test data set 20 for the student schedule file, and test data set 21 for the course master file.

STUDENT RECORD						
Record Length 30						
Field No.	Field Name	Field Description	Field Position	Field Length	Dec. Pos.	Data Class
1		Student Name	1–24			
2	STUDNT	Student Number	25–30	6		A

STUSCHED FILE RECORD						
Record Length 45		Key Location 1–6 (STUDNO)				
Field No.	Field Name	Field Description	Field Position	Field Length	Dec. Pos.	Data Class
1	STUDNO	Student Number	1–6	6		A
2	CRSNO1	Course Number 1	7–12	6		A
3	CRSNO2	Course Number 2	15–20	6		A
4	CRSNO3	Course Number 3	23–28	6		A
5	CRSNO4	Course Number 4	31–36	6		A
6	CRSNO5	Course Number 5	39–44	6		A

Figure 8-40   Data files for programming assignment 4   *continued*

COURSMAS FILE RECORD						
Record Length 61			Key Location 1–6 (COURSE)			
Field No.	Field Name	Field Description	Field Position	Field Length	Dec. Pos.	Data Class
1	COURSE	Course Number	1–6	6		A
2	CREDIT	Course Credits	10–10	1	0	N
3	TITLE	Course Name	11–35	25		A
4	INSTR	Instructor's Name	41–60	20		A

Figure 8-40   (continued)

OUTPUT

Output is the Student Record Error List, the format of which is shown in Figure 8-41.

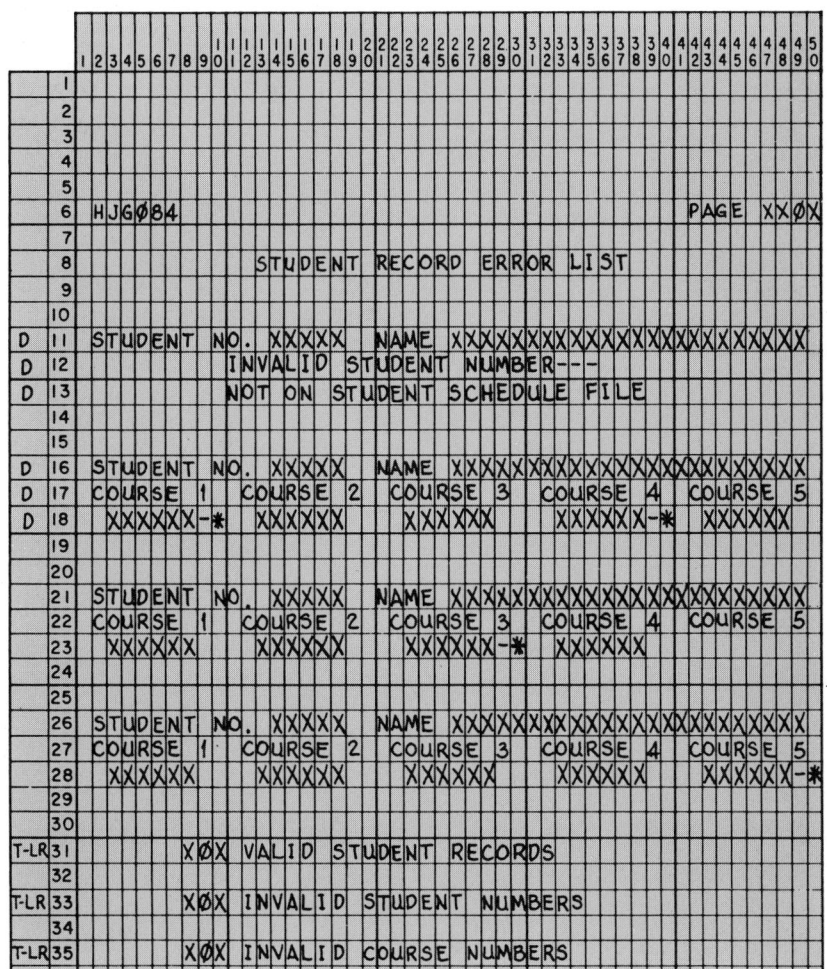

Figure 8-41   Student Record Error List format

▆ Processing Requirements

The student record file is the primary input file for this program. Every time a record is read, perform a direct access read of the student schedule file to obtain the schedule record for the student. If the student number cannot be found in the student schedule file, add 1 to the count of invalid student numbers, perform no further calculations on the record, and print the three detail lines as shown on lines 11–13 of the printer spacing chart.

If the read of the student schedule file was performed successfully, use each of the course numbers to perform a direct access read of the course master file. If one or more of the course numbers cannot be found on the course master file, add 1 to the count of invalid course numbers for each invalid course number detected and print the three detail lines as shown on lines 16–18 and 21–23 of the printer spacing chart. On the third of these lines, an invalid course number is identified by an asterisk following the course number as shown on lines 18 and 23 of the printer spacing chart. A student may take less than five courses. Blank course numbers are not invalid.

If the student number and all course numbers are valid, add 1 to the count of valid student records.

Looping Techniques, Exception Output, & Move Operations

The previous chapter introduced you to the first of the commands you will use to bypass the normal RPG fixed logic cycle for input and output operations. You learned to use the CHAIN operation to perform random reading of data from a keyed file. This chapter introduces a similar operation, EXCPT. The **EXCPT operation** performs output operations under programmer control rather than under control of the RPG fixed logic cycle. In that respect, EXCPT is similar to CHAIN. However, rather than being restricted to keyed sequence access path files, the EXCPT operation can be used with any output capable file, regardless of access path.

You also will learn to plan, design, and code program loops. A **loop** is a series of calculation operations that are executed repeatedly. Rather than executing in a top-down order, the instructions in a loop are executed over and over (from beginning to end and back to the beginning) until some condition in the program stops the repetition. Looping does not use any new instructions. Looping is a technique rather than an operation.

PROBLEM DESCRIPTION FOR PROGRAM HJG09X

This sample program introduces the EXCPT operation and the techniques used in looping. Program HJG09X reads an arrival sequence access path file and, based on data in each data record, prints a variable number of shipping labels for each record read.

Program Input: Shipping File

The format of the shipping file is shown in Figure 9-1. Each record in the shipping file contains the customer number, name, address, ZIP code, the purchase order number of the order being shipped, and the number of packages being shipped as part of the order. Note that the ZIP code is a nine-digit data field rather than a five-digit field. This data file uses the ZIP + 4 system adopted by the U.S. Postal Service and currently used by many businesses. Coding for ZIP + 4 is explained later when the input and output specifications are shown.

SHIPPING RECORD						
Record Length 185						
Field No.	Field Name	Field Description	Field Position	Field Length	Dec. Pos.	Data Class
1	CUSTNO	Customer Number	1–5	5		A
2	CUSTNA	Customer Name	6–30	25		A
3	ADDR1	Address Line 1	31–55	25		A
4	ADDR2	Address Line 2	56–80	25		A
5	ADDR3	Address Line 3	81–105	25		A
6	ZIP	ZIP Code	106–114	9		A
7	PURORD	Purchase Order No.	115–120	6		A
8	NOPACK	Number of Packages	121–122	2	0	N

Figure 9-1   Shipping File Record

The Number of Packages field controls the number of shipping labels printed for each input record. The program uses looping techniques to repeatedly print shipping labels until the number of labels printed equals the value in the Number of Packages field. As a result, the program prints one label for each package in the order.

▤ Program Output: Shipping Labels

The format of the shipping labels produced by the sample program is shown in Figure 9-2. These labels are 3 1/2 inches (35 print positions) wide and 3 inches (18 print lines) long. They are separated by the equivalent of one print line, 1/6 of an inch. The line numbers in the label description that follows are based on the top label shown on the printer spacing chart in Figure 9-2.

Note that lines 7–9 show the return (shipped-from) name and address. Lines 12–17 give the name and address to which the shipment is going (the ship-to address). Line 19 shows the customer's purchase order number, which is usually provided on a shipping to enable the person responsible for receiving incoming shipments (the receiver) to determine which purchase order is being received and which person or department is to receive the shipment.

Line 20, the last line of each label, prints a package number as well as the total number of packages being shipped to the ship-to address for the individual purchase order. This tells the receiver how many packages were part of the shipment and, if less than that number are received, which of the packages are missing. Figure 9-3 shows the labels produced for a shipment containing three packages. Note that the last line of the first label reads "Box   1 of   3." The second label reads, "Box   2 of   3," and the third label reads "Box   3 of   3."

Because this program prints a variable number of shipping labels, the usual detail printing techniques cannot be used. Instead, the program must contain a loop to control printing. Each time the instructions within the loop are executed, the EXCPT operation is used to print one shipping label. Before beginning our review of the necessary RPG specifications, let's look at the basic concepts of looping.

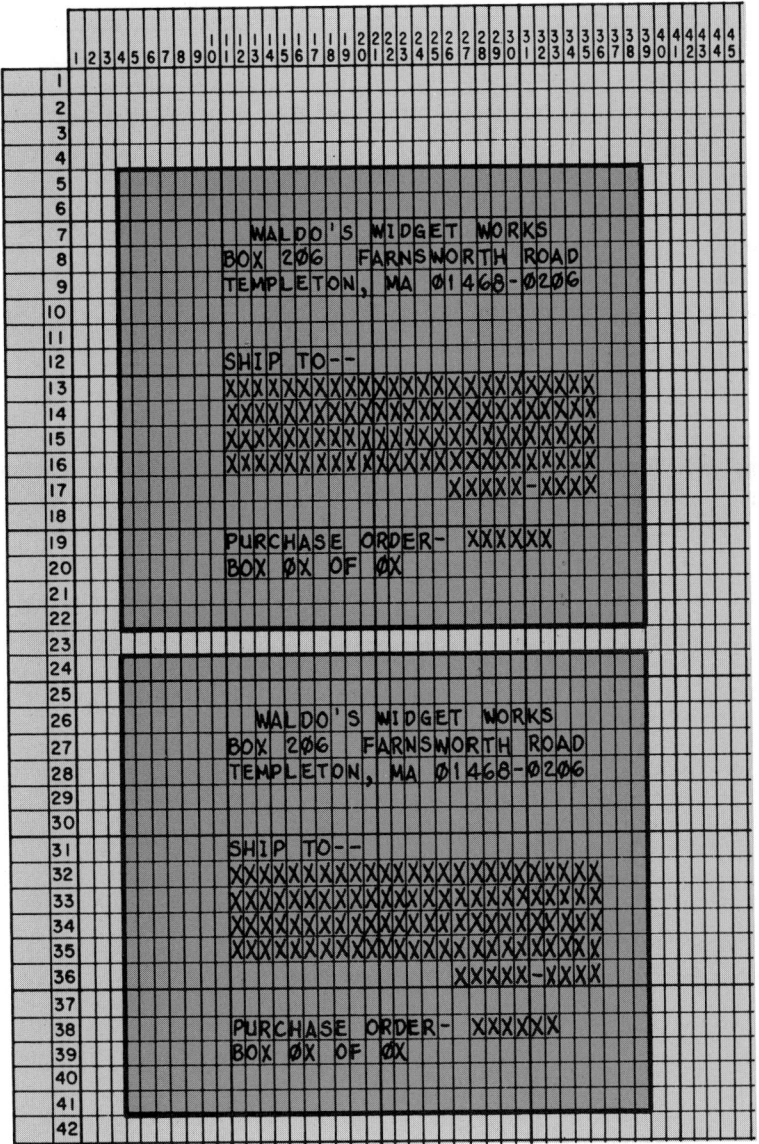

Figure 9-2   Shipping label format

```
   WALDO'S WIDGET WORKS
   BOX 206   FARNSWORTH ROAD
   TEMPLETON, MA 01468-0206


   SHIP TO--
   CRICKET'S BOUTIQUES

   6046 SUNSET BOULEVARD
   RANDOLPH, TX
                  31999-2144

   PURCHASE ORDER- 593CTZ
   BOX  1 OF  3
```

```
   WALDO'S WIDGET WORKS
   BOX 206   FARNSWORTH ROAD
   TEMPLETON, MA 01468-0206


   SHIP TO--
   CRICKET'S BOUTIQUES

   6046 SUNSET BOULEVARD
   RANDOLPH, TX
                  31999-2144

   PURCHASE ORDER- 593CTZ
   BOX  2 OF  3
```

```
   WALDO'S WIDGET WORKS
   BOX 206   FARNSWORTH ROAD
   TEMPLETON, MA 01468-0206


   SHIP TO--
   CRICKET'S BOUTIQUES

   6046 SUNSET BOULEVARD
   RANDOLPH, TX
                  31999-2144

   PURCHASE ORDER- 593CTZ
   BOX  3 OF  3
```

Figure 9-3   Shipping labels

≡ LOOPING ≡

A loop is a series of instructions or operations, that are executed repeatedly until some condition within the series of instructions causes the repetition to stop. The technique of using a loop in a program is called **looping** or **iteration**. The flowchart in Figure 9-4 shows the logic of a simple loop. As you can see, the loop is made up of six logical components:

1. Initialization
2. Incrementation
3. Processing
4. Testing
5. Branching
6. Termination

Every loop that is performed a variable number of times contains all of these components. If one or more of the logical components of a loop are omitted, the loop does not perform the work in the program that it was designed to do.

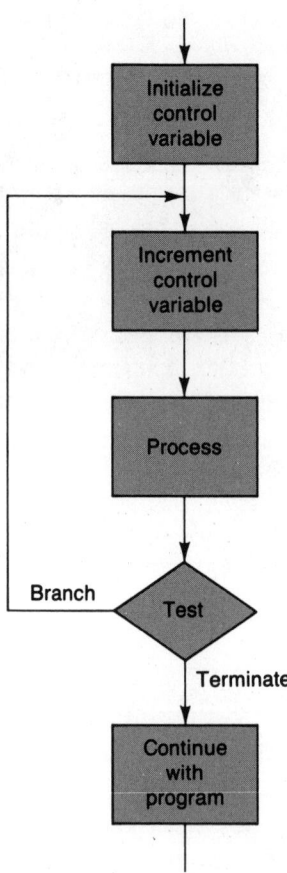

Figure 9-4 Loop component flowchart

≡ Initialization

In addition to the six logical components, the loop uses one data field to control the number of times the loop is to be performed. This data field, regardless of its name in the program, is called the control variable. The **control variable** is a data field used to count the number of times the loop has been performed. When the count in the control variable reaches a predetermined amount, performance of the loop stops, and the program continues with the next operation following the loop. Because the control variable contains a count, this field, like all counters in a program, must initially be set to zero for the count to be accurate. The process of setting the control variable to zero is called the **initialization** step. In RPG, initialization is often performed by a Z-ADD operation.

Incrementation

The **incrementation** component of a loop changes the value stored in the control variable. Usually, this is accomplished by adding 1 to the value stored in the control variable. Remember that the control variable determines the number of times that the loop is performed. If the value in the control variable is not changed, the loop can never end because the control variable always contains the value placed in it during the initialization step.

Processing

The **processing** component is the part of the loop that performs the information processing steps for which the loop was designed. In the first sample problem, the processing portion of the loop is used to cause the printing of the mailing labels. Although each of the other components of a loop usually consists of only one or two operations, the processing component can consist of any number of operations, depending on the program being written.

Testing

The **testing** component of a loop determines if the loop has been performed the required number of times. Testing is usually performed by comparing the value in the control variable with a literal or data field that contains a number equal to the number of times the loop is to be performed. If the required number of loops (iterations) has not yet been performed, the branching component is executed to cause another iteration to take place. If the loop has been performed the required number of times, the termination component is executed.

Branching

The **branching** component is usually a conditional GOTO operation that causes a branch back to the beginning of the loop so that the loop is performed again. If the branching component of the loop is omitted, the steps in the planned loop execute only once, and the program then continues with the next operation or logic cycle step.

Termination

The **termination** component of the loop is the step that causes the loop to not be executed again. In RPG, as in most programming languages, the termination component takes place if the branching step is not executed. Because the branching step is a conditional operation that is executed only if the loop has not been performed the required number of times, termination is usually the lack of a branching operation rather than a specific operation itself. Termination occurs when the program proceeds to the operation or logic step that follows the loop, that is, the program does not return to the beginning of the loop for another iteration.

CALCULATION LOOP FOR PROGRAM HJG09X

Initialization

A flowchart for the looping logic of the calculation operations needed for the sample program is shown in Figure 9-5. In the initialization step, the COUNT field is set to a value of zero. Count is the control variable that determines if the number of shipping labels printed is equal to the number of packages that are part of the customer's shipment.

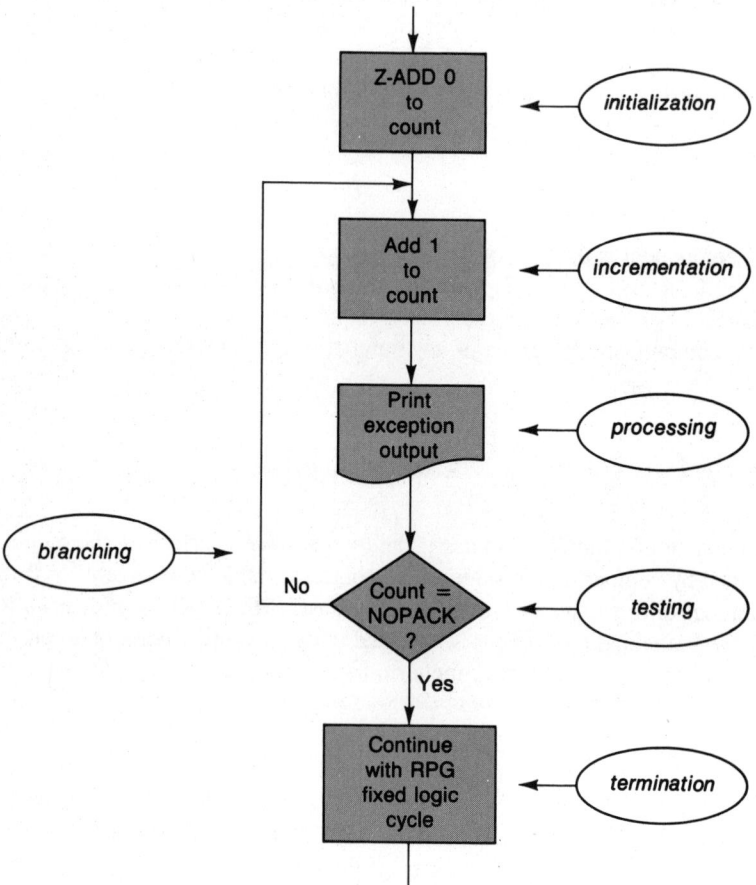

Figure 9-5   Loop flowchart for program HJG09X

Incrementation

The incrementation component of the loop adds the value 1 to the control variable. Although incrementation is performed at the beginning of the loop in this example, incrementation can be performed at almost any point in the loop. The actual placement of this component depends to a great extent on the requirements of the specific program being coded. In this sample program, incrementation takes place before the processing step because the control variable prints on each shipping label to indicate the box number of each package.

Processing

The processing component of the loop performs the printing of the shipping labels. The EXCPT operation causes printing to occur during the detail calculation portion of the logic cycle.

Testing, Branching, and Termination

In the testing component of the loop, the value in the control variable COUNT is compared with the value in the input field that contains the number of packages being shipped. If the value in the control variable is less than the value in the number of packages field, the loop performs a GOTO operation (branching component) that causes the loop to be executed again. If the value in the control variable is equal to the value in the number of packages field, the branch is not executed and the program continues according to normal RPG fixed logic (termination component).

Common Errors in Loop Design

Several errors are often made when programmers design loops.

▶ **Incorrect Placement of Initialization Component** The error in loop design that is probably made most frequently by beginning programmers is incorrect placement of the step that initializes the control variable. Figure 9-6 illustrates this error. Note that the initialization step has been placed inside the repeated portion of the loop. As a result, the control variable will be reinitialized to a value of zero every time the loop is performed. Because of reinitialization, the value in the control variable can never reach the value that terminates the loop, which results in a **never-ending loop**. The correct placement of the initialization component of a loop is *outside* the repetitive portion of the loop.

▶ **Nonincrementation of Control Variable** Figure 9-7 shows another common loop error. In this example, the incrementation step has been omitted. As a result, the value in the control variable will always be zero, which also results in a never-ending loop.

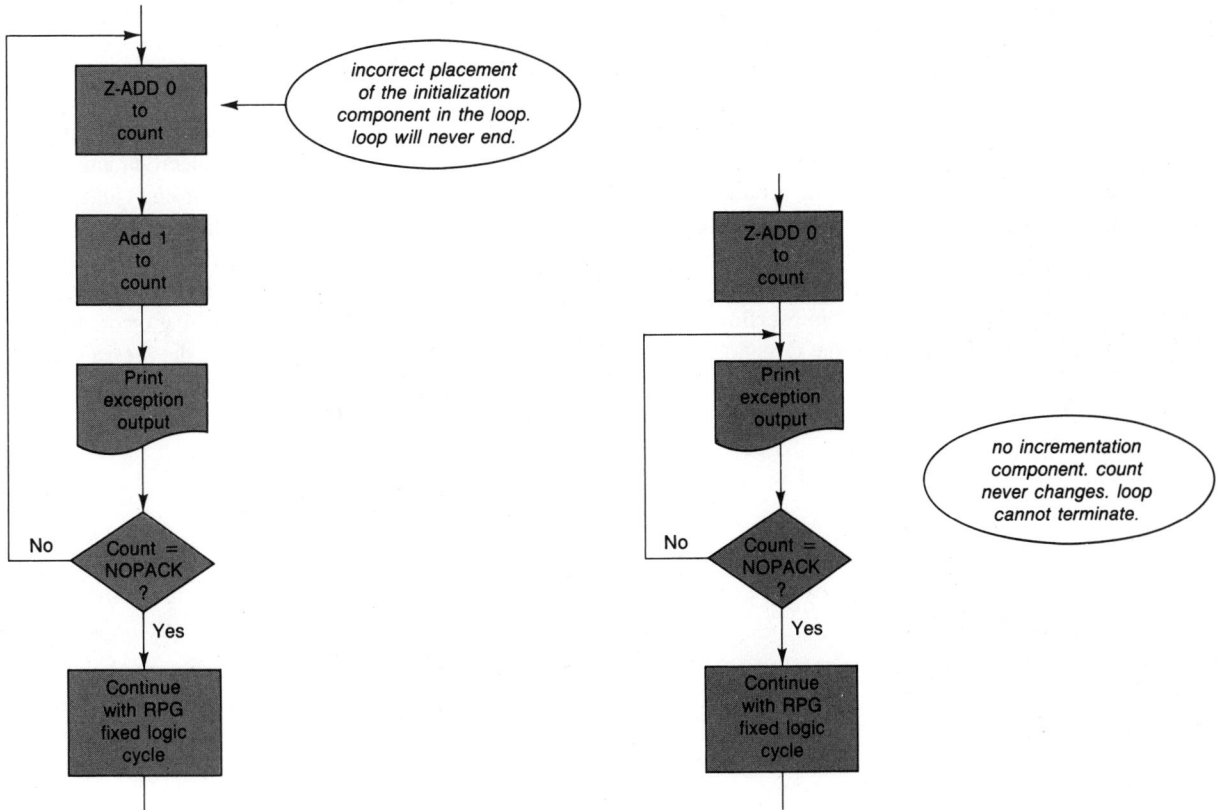

Figure 9-6   Loop logic error 1   Figure 9-7   Loop logic error 2

▸ **Incorrect Placement of Incrementation**

Step In Figure 9-8, the incrementation component has been placed after the test component. As a result, the first time the test is made, the control variable will still be zero; the second time the test is made, the value will be one; the third time the test is made, the value will be two; and so on. In every case, the value in the control variable is one less than the number of times the loop has been performed. This results in the loops being performed one extra time. If, when debugging program output, it appears that a loop has been executed one time too many in every case, check for incorrect placement of the incrementation step.

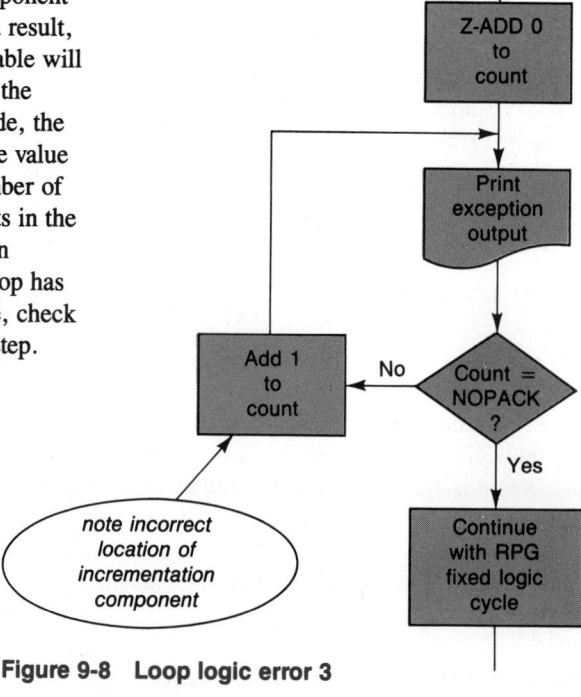

Figure 9-8   Loop logic error 3

PROGRAM CODE FOR PROGRAM HJG09X

Control and File Description Specifications

As you can see, no new entries have been introduced into the Control and File Description Specifications form for the sample program (Figure 9-9). However, one familiar entry does not appear on the specifications form.

Note that the description of the printed output file does not include an Overflow Indicator entry in positions 33–34. This is because the shipping labels printed by the sample program do not include headings and do not use page overflow. All forms movement is controlled by spacing entries on the output specifications form. Some versions of RPG generate a compiler message if no overflow indicator is specified; this is done as a reminder to the programmer because the lack of an overflow indicator is unusual and generally is a programming error. If, as is the case in this sample program, the Overflow Indicator entry has deliberately been left blank, the message can be ignored.

Input Specifications

The Input Specifications form for this program (Figure 9-10) shows that no new entries are needed. Note that the ZIP Code field has been divided into two separate fields, ZIP and ZPLUS4, because the input data in this program uses the U.S. Postal Service ZIP + 4, system.

▸ **ZIP + 4 Program Considerations** The Postal Service initiated the ZIP (zone improvement plan) Code system to move mail more quickly; the plan divides the United States (and some other countries) into areas identified by a five-digit number. When the five-digit ZIP code is used as part of the address, the Postal Service can use automated equipment to sort and direct each piece of mail. An additional four digits were added to permit the

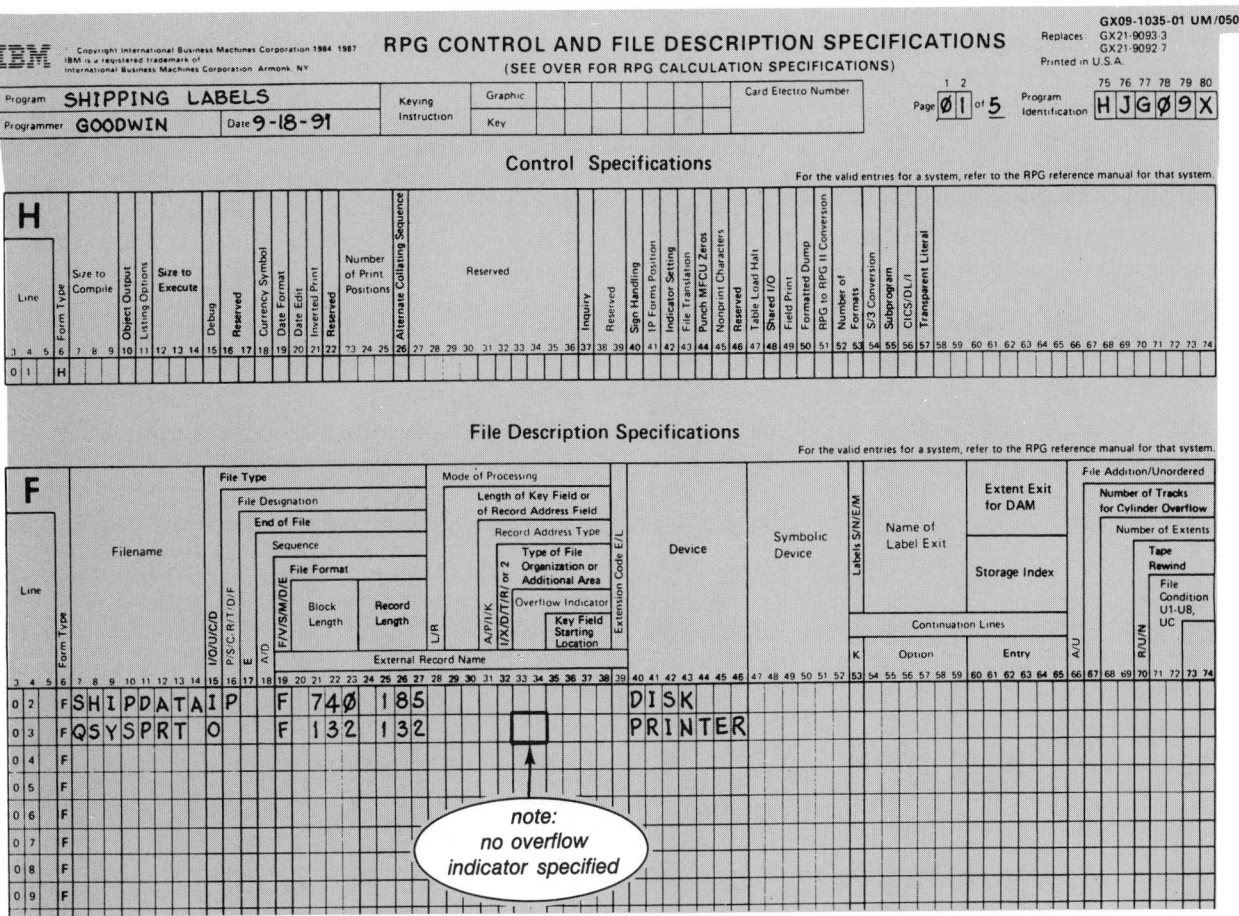

Figure 9-9 Control and file designation specifications for program HJG09X

Figure 9-10 Input specifications for program HJG09X

Postal Service to identify the destination of a piece of mail in even greater detail. Generally, the first five digits of the code identify the post office to which the mail is being sent, and the last four digits identify the specific area or street in the area served by that post office.

The problem facing the programmer when coding a program that must handle ZIP + 4 coding is that the last four digits are not always present. A ZIP + 4 code is printed in the format XXXXX- XXXX, and a five-digit ZIP code is printed in the format XXXXX. You must make provisions in your program to print or suppress the hyphen depending on whether or not the last four digits contain data. Indicator 41 is used on the Output Specifications form to control printing of the hyphen and the last four digits of the ZIP + 4 Code.

Loop Code Calculation Specifications

Figure 9-11 shows the Calculation Specifications form for program HJG09X. Except for the TAG operation on line 03, each operation contains a comment in positions 60–74 that identifies the loop component that it represents.

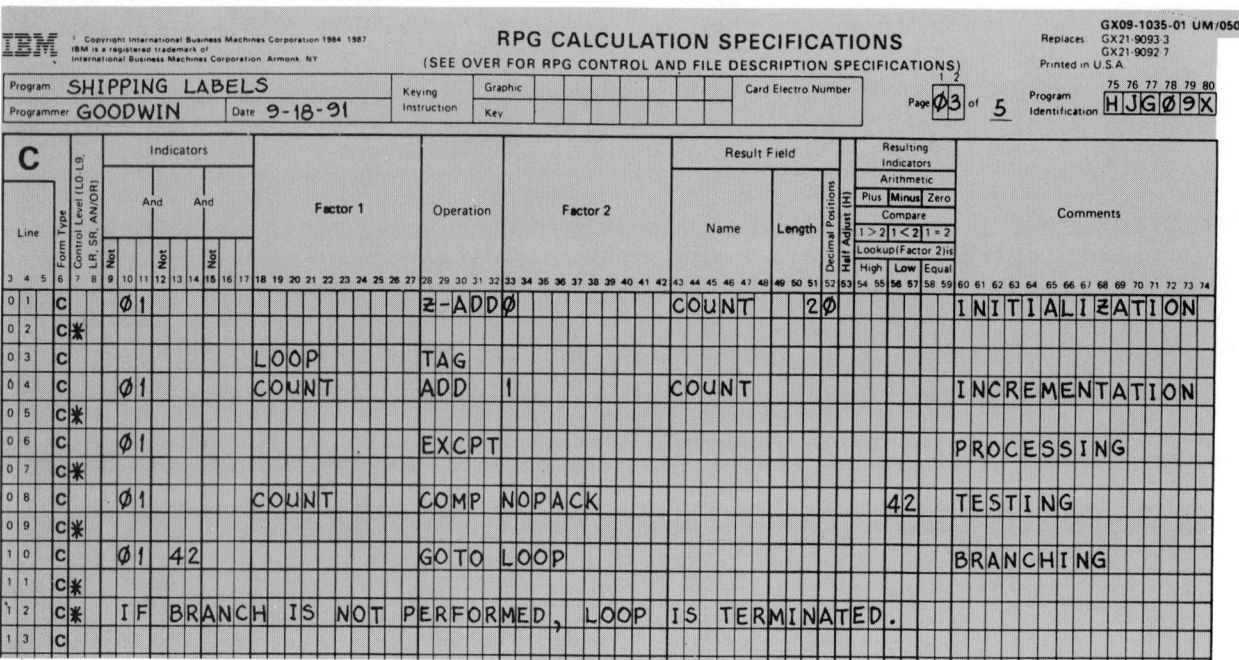

Figure 9-11 Loop code calculation specifications HJG09X

▶ **Initialization (Line 01)** Line 01 uses a Z-ADD operation to initialize the control variable that controls the number of times the loop executes. Remember that the Z-ADD operation adds the contents of Factor 2 to zero and places the sum in the Result Field area. In this example, because Factor 2 contains the literal 0, the result field is initialized to zero before the loop begins. Note that the initialization operation appears outside of the repeated portion of the loop because it precedes the TAG operation that appears on line 03.

▶ **Incrementation (Line 04)** Line 04 of the calculations increments the control variable by a value of 1. Because this is performed at the beginning of the loop portion of the calculations, before the processing and testing components, the control variable always contains a number that specifies which repetition of the loop is being executed.

▶ **Processing (Line 06)** The EXCPT operation in line 06 is the only part of the processing component of the loop that appears on the Calculation Specifications form. Every time the EXCPT operation is performed, all output records identified by an E in position 15 of the output record description are produced. After all possible type-E output has been produced, RPG continues on to the next operation on the Calculation Specifications form.

▸ **Testing (Line 08)**   The testing component of this loop is the comparison of COUNT, which contains the number of times the loop has been performed, with NOPACK, which contains the number of times the loop is to be performed. If COUNT is less than NOPACK, meaning that the loop has not been performed the required number of times, the COMP operation turns on indicator 42. When the value in COUNT equals the value in NOPACK, indicator 42 is not turned on.

▸ **Branching (Line 10)**   If indicator 42 is turned on by the testing component of the loop to indicate that the loop has not been performed the required number of times, the GOTO operation on line 10 causes the calculations to branch to the TAG on line 03 so that the loop is performed again. This repetition of the loop continues until the value in COUNT reaches the value in the NOPACK field.

▸ **Termination**   In this example, as in many RPG programs, there is no specific loop-termination operation. The loop terminates when it does not execute the branching component. When this occurs, the normal RPG logic cycle resumes, and RPG proceeds to the next calculation. In this example, because there is no calculation to proceed to, the RPG fixed logic cycle resumes, and the program continues with the next logic step – detail output – even though this program does not contain any detail output specifications.

▤ Output Specifications

The output for the sample program consists of 11 output lines, all of which contain an E in position 15 of the record description. Figure 9-12 shows the relationship between the EXCPT operation code and the type E output record descriptions. Every time the EXCPT operation is performed, RPG produces all possible type E output. Exception output records can, like any other output records, be controlled by output indicators. When type E output is produced, the output is subject to the control of the output indicators. Because no output indicators are used in this program, all 11 output lines print every time the EXCPT operation is performed. As is the case with most RPG functions, the type E lines are printed in a top-down sequence. RPG starts with the first output record description, then the second, then the third, and so on. Figure 9-13 on the next page summarizes the EXCPT operation.

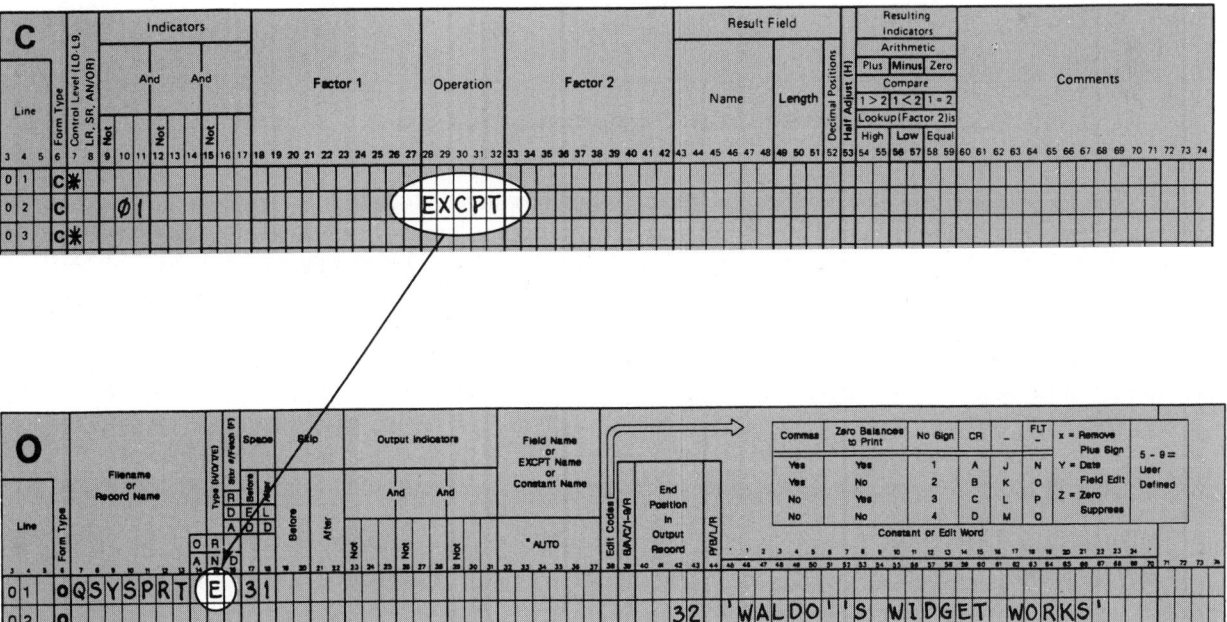

Figure 9-12   Example of EXCPT operation

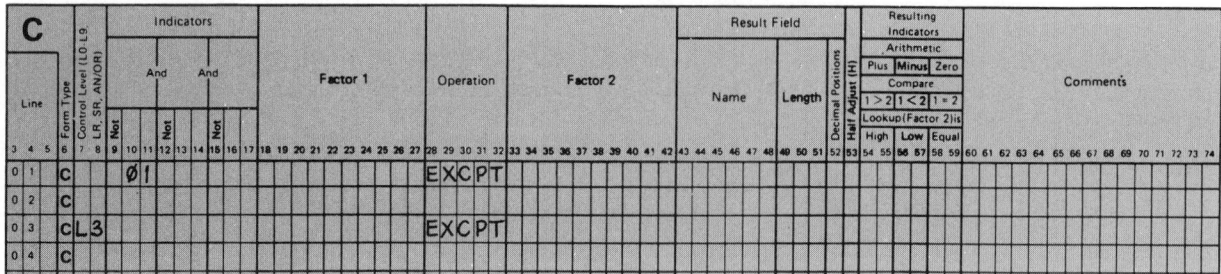

EXCPT Operation Summary, Non-3X Format

The EXCPT operation causes output records to be written during
either detail or total calculation time under control of the object program rather than the RPG fixed logic cycle. The EXCPT operation
can be conditioned by indicators in positions 7–17, but all other
entries must be blank. The output records written must be identified
by the entry E in the Type area, position 15.

Control Level Indicators	Indicators	Factor 1	Operation Name	Factor 2	Result Field	Resulting Indicators		
7–8	9–17	18–27	28–32	33–42	43–53	54–55	56–57	58–59
optional	optional	blank	EXCPT	blank	blank	blank	blank	blank

Figure 9-13   EXCPT operation, non-3X format

The Output Specifications forms for the sample program (Figure 9-14) show that all 11 of the exception
lines are printed under control of the EXCPT operation. They also show two new techniques. The first involves
insertion of an apostrophe into an output constant, and the second deals with printing the last four digits of the
nine-digit ZIP Code field.

▶ **Apostrophe Insertion in Output Constants**   The first line of each shipping label contains the company name 'WALDO'S WIDGET WORKS'. The apostrophe in the first word of the company name requires special handling in RPG because the apostrophe is the delimiter used to mark the beginning and end of every output
constant. If the entry in positions 45–70 of line 02 of the output specifications were 'WALDO'S WIDGET
WORKS', the RPG compiler would generate an error message. The compiler would assume the first apostrophe to
be the beginning delimiter of the constant and the second (between the letters O and S) to be the ending delimiter;
the compiler would then generate an error message because of the characters following the second apostrophe. To
insert an apostrophe into an output constant, two consecutive apostrophes must be used. Line 02 of Figure 9-14
shows the correct method of apostrophe insertion. Note that two consecutive apostrophes are used, making the
constant 'WALDO''S WIDGET WORKS'. RPG replaces the two consecutive apostrophes with a single apostrophe
when the constant is printed. Do not attempt to use a quotation mark (") as two apostrophes. RPG will print the
quotation mark as part of the constant.

Figure 9-14 Output specifications for program HJG09X

RPG OUTPUT SPECIFICATIONS

GX09-1034-02 UM/050*

(SEE OVER FOR RPG TELECOMMUNICATIONS SPECIFICATIONS)

Program: SHIPPING LABELS
Programmer: GOODWIN Date 9-18-91
Page 04 of 5 Program Identification HJG09X

Line	Form Type	Filename or Record Name	Type	Space Before/After	Output Indicators	Field Name or EXCPT Name or Constant Name	End Position in Output Record	Constant or Edit Word
01	O	QSYSPRT	E	31				
02	O						32	'WALDO''S WIDGET WORKS'
03	O		E	1				
04	O						34	'BOX 206 FARNSWORTH ROAD'
05	O		E	3				
06	O						34	'TEMPLETON, MA 01468-0206'
07	O		E	1				
08	O						19	'SHIP TO--'
09	O		E	1				
10	O					CUSTNA	35	
11	O		E	1				
12	O					ADDR1	35	
13	O		E	1				
14	O					ADDR2	35	
15	O		E	1				
16	O					ADDR3	35	
17	O		E	2				
18	O					ZIP	30	
19	O				N41		31	'-'
20	O				N41	ZPLUS4	35	
	O							
	O							
	O							

*Number of sheets per pad may vary slightly.

Figure 9-14 (1)

RPG OUTPUT SPECIFICATIONS

GX09-1034-02 UM/050*

(SEE OVER FOR RPG TELECOMMUNICATIONS SPECIFICATIONS)

Program: SHIPPING LABELS
Programmer: GOODWIN Date 9-18-91
Page 05 of 5 Program Identification HJG09X

Line	Form Type	Filename or Record Name	Type	Space Before/After	Output Indicators	Field Name or EXCPT Name or Constant Name	End Position in Output Record	Constant or Edit Word
01	O		E	1				
02	O						25	'PURCHASE ORDER-'
03	O					PURORD	32	
04	O		E	3				
05	O						19	'BOX OF'
06	O					COUNT Z	16	
07	O					NOPACK Z	22	
08	O							
09	O							

Figure 9-14 (2)

▸ **Control of ZIP + 4 Printing** Note the use of indicator 41 to control printing of the ZPLUS4 field and the hyphen that precedes it. The hyphen and field print only if indicator 41 is not on, that is, if the ZPLUS4 field is not blank. If the field is blank, neither the hyphen nor the field is printed. However, the five-digit portion of the ZIP code prints under all conditions.

The last type E output record uses the COUNT field and the NOPACK field to indicate the box number on each shipping label. If the COUNT field overlies the constant 'BOX   OF', the last line of the shipping label will read 'BOX   1 OF   3', 'BOX   2 OF   3', and so on.

Figure 9-15 shows the compilation listing for sample program HJG09X.

Figure 9-15   Compile listing for program HJG09X

```
HJG09X    09-12-91  19:51:10  HJG09X - SHIPPING LABELS -          Version 3.5  Page  1

        ....+....1....+....2....+....3....+....4....+....5....+....6...:+....7....

  3 0002 H                                                              HJG09X


  4 0003 F*-----------------------------------------------------------------*
  5 0004 F* HJG09X - SHIPPING LABELS - HAL GOODWIN - SEPTEMBER 20, 1991   *
  6 0005 F*                                                               *
  7 0006 F*  PROGRAM HJG09X WILL PRINT A VARIABLE NUMBER OF SHIPPING LABELS *
  8 0007 F*  FOR EACH INPUT RECORD READ.  THE NUMBER OF LABELS PRINTED WILL *
  9 0008 F*  BE BASED ON THE CONTENTS OF THE 'NOPACK' FIELD LOCATED IN     *
 10 0009 F*  POSITIONS 121-122 OF THE INPUT RECORD.                        *
 11 0010 F*-----------------------------------------------------------------*

 14 0012 FSHIPDATAIP  F 740 185          DISK
 15 0013 FLABELS  O   F 132 132          PRINTER


 16 0014 I*  SHIPPING LABEL DATA RECORDS
 17 0015 I*---------------------------
 18 0016 ISHIPDATAAA  01
 19 0017 I                                6   30 CUSTNA
 20 0018 I                               31   55 ADDR1
 21 0019 I                               56   80 ADDR2
 22 0020 I                               81  105 ADDR3
 23 0021 I                              106  110 ZIP
 24 0022 I                              111  114 ZPLUS4       41
 25 0023 I                              115  120 PURORD
 26 0024 I                              121  1220NOPACK


 27 0025 C    01                Z-ADD0      COUNT    20     INITIALIZATION
 28 0026 C*
 29 0027 C         LOOP         TAG
 30 0028 C    01   COUNT        ADD  1      COUNT           INCREMENTATION
 31 0029 C*
 32 0030 C    01                EXCPT                       PROCESSING
 33 0031 C*
 34 0032 C    01   COUNT        COMP NOPACK          42     TESTING
 35 0033 C*
 36 0034 C    01 42             GOTO LOOP                   BRANCHING
 37 0035 C*
 38 0036 C*  IF BRANCH IS NOT PERFORMED, THE LOOP IS TERMINATED.


 39 0037 O*  RETURN ADDRESS LINES
 40 0038 O*--------------------
 41 0039 OLABELS  E 31
 42 0040 O                              32 'WALDO''S WIDGET WORKS'
 43 0041 O          E  1
```

Figure 9-15 (1)

```
HJG09X    09-12-91  19:51:10  HJG09X - SHIPPING LABELS -        Version 3.5  Page  2

          ....+....1....+....2....+....3....+....4....+....5....+....6....+....7....

    44 0042 O                                           34 'BOX 206   FARNSWORTH ROAD'
    45 0043 O      E  3
    46 0044 O                                           34 'TEMPLETON, MA 01468-0206' ,


    49 0046 O*  SHIP TO LINES
    50 0047 O*---------------
    51 0048 O      E  1
    52 0049 O                                           19 'SHIP TO--'
    53 0050 O      E  1
    54 0051 O                           CUSTNA          35
    55 0052 O      E  1
    56 0053 O                           ADDR1           35
    57 0054 O      E  1
    58 0055 O                           ADDR2           35
    59 0056 O      E  1
    60 0057 O                           ADDR3           35
    61 0058 O      E  2
    62 0059 O                           ZIP             30
    63 0060 O                  N41                       31 '-'
    64 0061 O                  N41      ZPLUS4           35
    65 0062 O      E  1
    66 0063 O                                           25 'PURCHASE ORDER-'
    67 0064 O                           PURORD          32
    68 0065 O      E  3
    69 0066 O                                           19 'BOX       OF'
    70 0067 O                           COUNT Z         16
    71 0068 O                           NOPACKZ         22
    72 /*
    73 /*


          THE FOLLOWING INDICATORS APPEARED IN THIS PROGRAM

              01   41   42
  No Warning Errors
  No Fatal Errors
```

Figure 9-15 (2)

≡ SAMPLE PROBLEM HJG09Y: PAYMENT SCHEDULE ≡

Program HJG09Y introduces another version of the RPG compiler, the IBM System/38 RPG III compiler. As you will see, everything you have learned about RPG so far applies also to RPG III.

▱ Problem Description

Sample program HJG09Y is designed to demonstrate a more complex loop using the EXCPT operation. It also adds two more operations to your RPG tool kit: MOVE AND MOVEL, which transfer data from one field to another.

▸ **Output**   The output from program HJG09Y is the Payment Schedule Report (Figure 9-16 on the next page). This report contains the customer number, customer name, amount due for each payment, and date each payment is due. Note that the Customer Number and Customer Name fields are group indicated.

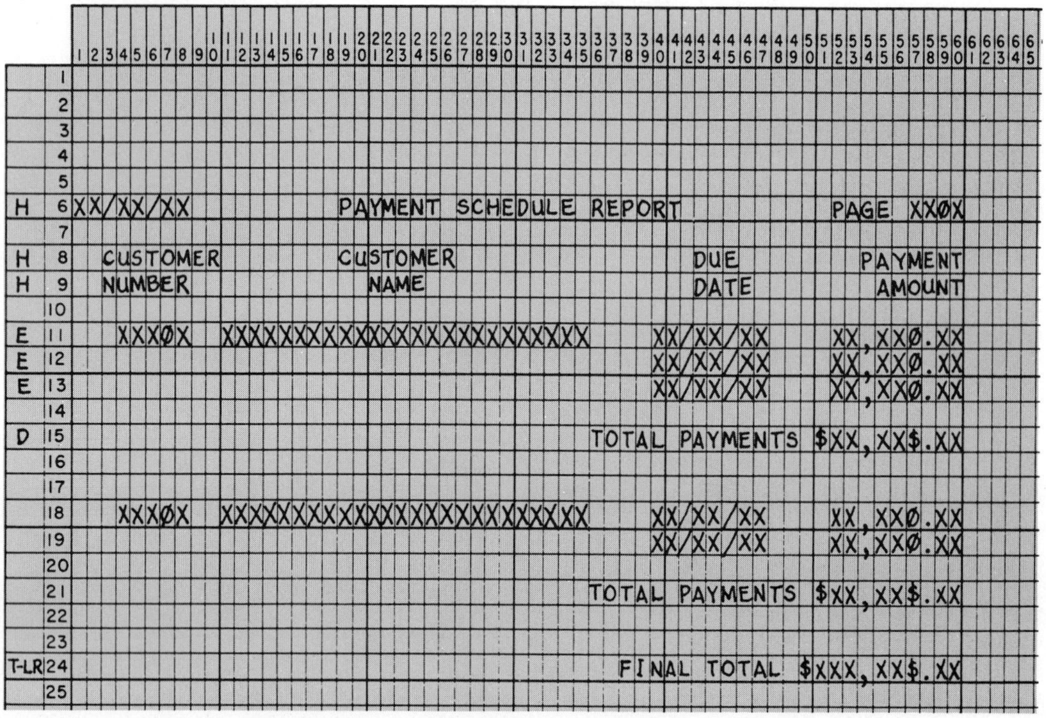

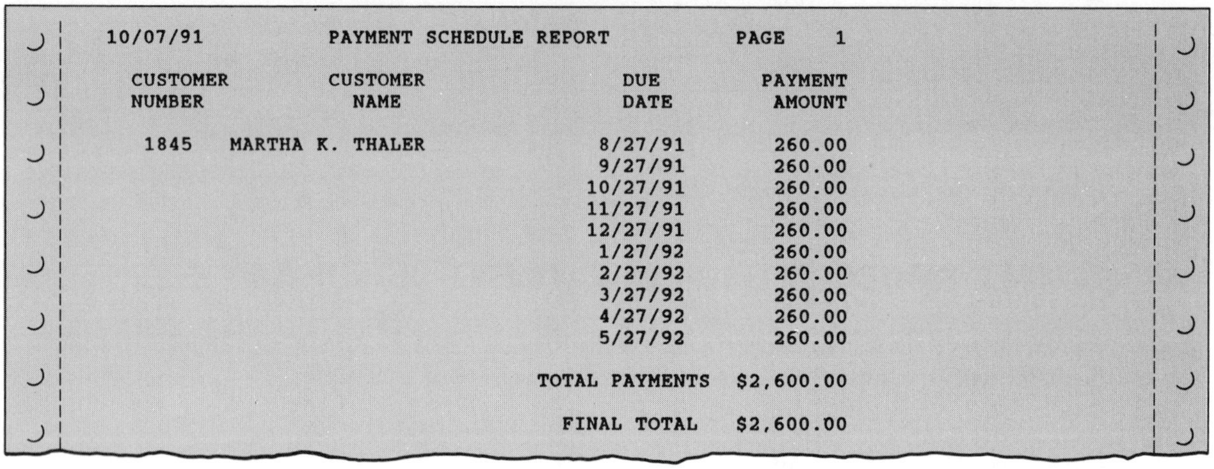

```
10/07/91            PAYMENT SCHEDULE REPORT            PAGE    1

  CUSTOMER          CUSTOMER                 DUE         PAYMENT
  NUMBER              NAME                   DATE         AMOUNT

   1845    MARTHA K. THALER               8/27/91         260.00
                                          9/27/91         260.00
                                         10/27/91         260.00
                                         11/27/91         260.00
                                         12/27/91         260.00
                                          1/27/92         260.00
                                          2/27/92         260.00
                                          3/27/92         260.00
                                          4/27/92         260.00
                                          5/27/92         260.00

                                   TOTAL PAYMENTS      $2,600.00

                                      FINAL TOTAL      $2,600.00
```

Figure 9-16 Payment Schedule Report

▸ **Input** The input record (Figure 9-17) contains the customer number, the customer name, date on which payments are to begin, number of payments to be made, and loan amount.

▸ **Processing Requirements** The amount due for each payment is determined by dividing the loan amount by the number of payments. Any remainder from the division is added to the final month's payment.

The due dates are calculated by using the beginning date as the first due date and then incrementing the month by 1 for each new payment. If the month is greater than 12, the program must increment the year by 1 and reset the month field to 1. After all the monthly payments are listed, the Total Payments field taken from the input record is printed.

PAYMENT RECORD						
Record Length 60						
Field No.	**Field Name**	**Field Description**	**Field Position**	**Field Length**	**Dec. Pos.**	**Data Class**
1	CUSTNO	Customer Number	1–5	5	0	N
2	CUSTNM	Customer Name	6–30	25		A
3	DATE	Payment Due Date	31–36	6	0	N
4	PMTS	Number of Payments	37–38	2	0	N
5	AMT	Loan Amount	39–45	7	2	N

Line	Form Type	Filename or Record Name	Sequence	Record Identifying Indicator	Field Location From	Field Location To	Decimal Positions	RPG Field Name	Control Level (L1-L9)
01	I	* PAYMENT RECORDS							
02	I	*---------------							
03	I	PMNTRECD	AA	Ø1					
04	I				1	5	Ø	CUSTNO	L1
05	I				6	30		CUSTNM	
06	I				31	36	Ø	DATE	
07	I				37	38	Ø	PMTS	
08	I				39	45	2	AMT	
09	I				31	32	Ø	MONTH	
10	I				35	36	Ø	YEAR	

Figure 9-17 Payment Record

Program HJG09Y prints a final total at the end of the report. The final total is the sum of all the total amounts due from all customers.

Because the number of payments can vary from customer to customer, the number of lines to be printed for each customer varies. The printing of this variable number of output lines for each input record is controlled by a loop containing an EXCPT operation to cause printing.

PROGRAM CODE FOR PROGRAM HJG09Y

Input Specifications

The input specifications for program HJG09Y use two techniques that you have not seen before. The first is the use of the L1 control level as part of the CUSTNO field definition even though the program does not use a control break to print totals. The L1 entry is needed because the program specifications call for group indication of the Customer Number and Customer Name fields. As demonstrated in an earlier chapter, if a program is to perform group indication, the program must use one or more control level indicators.

The second new technique involves the definition of positions 31–36 of the input record: the DATE area. Recall that the number of payments is determined by the value in the PMTS field in the input record. Because payments are to be made monthly, a new due date must be calculated for each line of the payment schedule. The due date is calculated by increasing by 1 the month of the beginning date that is in the input record. To perform calculations using the month, the month must be available as a separate field.

In addition, if the MONTH field becomes greater than 12, the YEAR field must also be incremented by 1. Again, because arithmetic is performed on the year, the year must be available as a separate data field. Note however, in Figure 9-17, that the entire date is to be edited and printed on the report as one field in MMDDYY format. Therefore, it is necessary to **redefine** the DATE field so that the month and the year can be referenced as separate fields.

Note that the DATE field is defined as a six-position field located in positions 31–36 of the input record. Because the MONTH field and the YEAR field must be used in calculations, these fields must be isolated from the entire DATE field. The entry on line 09 redefines the MONTH field in positions 31–32, and the entry on line 10 redefines the YEAR field in positions 35–36 of the input record. When the DATE field is referenced on the Calculation or Output Specifications forms, positions 31–36 of the input record are used. When the MONTH field is referenced, positions 31–32 are used, and when the YEAR field is referenced, positions 35–36 are used.

When the data in the input record is moved from the input area to the processing fields, the date data is moved to a different area from that of the month data and the year data. Even though month and year are subdivisions of the DATE input field, changing the month or year has no effect on the contents of the DATE field. Therefore, when the month is updated on the Calculation Specifications form, it is necessary to move the updated month from the MONTH field, where the arithmetic takes place, to the DATE field, so that the DATE field can be properly printed on the report.

▤ Calculation Specifications

The entries on the Calculation Specifications form not only perform the required arithmetic operations but also, by use of the EXCPT operation, control output of the printed lines on the report. The calculation specifications used in the sample program and a flowchart of the logic of the calculations are shown in Figure 9-18. The flowchart provides an overview of the operations in the calculation specifications. The first step is to calculate the amount of each payment (PAYMNT). This is accomplished on line 03 by dividing the loan amount (AMT) by the number of payments (PMTS). Line 04 uses an MVR operation to place the remainder of this division into a field (LASTPM) so that it can be added to the last payment.

▶ **The Program Loop**   The rest of the detail calculations is a loop that controls the number of output lines printed for each detail record. Several components of the loop have been identified in the comments area of the Calculation Specifications form. As you can see, no calculation is identified as the initialization component of the loop. In this program, the control variable is not defined and initialized on the Calculation Specifications form. Because the number of lines to be printed corresponds to the number of payments to be made, the input field PMTS is used as the control variable. This is possible because the PMTS field is not used as output from the program. As a result, the program can change the value in PMTS as needed to control loop execution.

▶ **Exception Output and Heading Control**   The first step in this loop is to cause all output that is specified as exception output on the output specifications to be written through the use of the EXCPT operation code, as shown on line 08. The problem description specifies that the exception output line is to contain the customer number, customer name, date, and payment amount. Because the customer number and customer name are group indicated, these fields are printed only when a control break or a page change occurs. Thus, they are printed only when the L1 indicator or OF indicator is on. Because the Customer Number field is the L1 control field and each input record contains a different customer number, each input record causes an L1 control break to occur. This means that indicator L1 is on the first time that the EXCPT operation is performed for each input record.

After the EXCPT operation prints a line, the program must determine if the overflow indicator OF is on. Because a variable number of lines are printed for each input record, and because these lines are printed by the EXCPT operation, the possibility exists that the end of the page will occur while printing the payments for one customer. When this happens, the program must advance the form to a new page and print headings. However, when the last line is printed on the page and the OF indicator is turned on, the headings are not printed until the

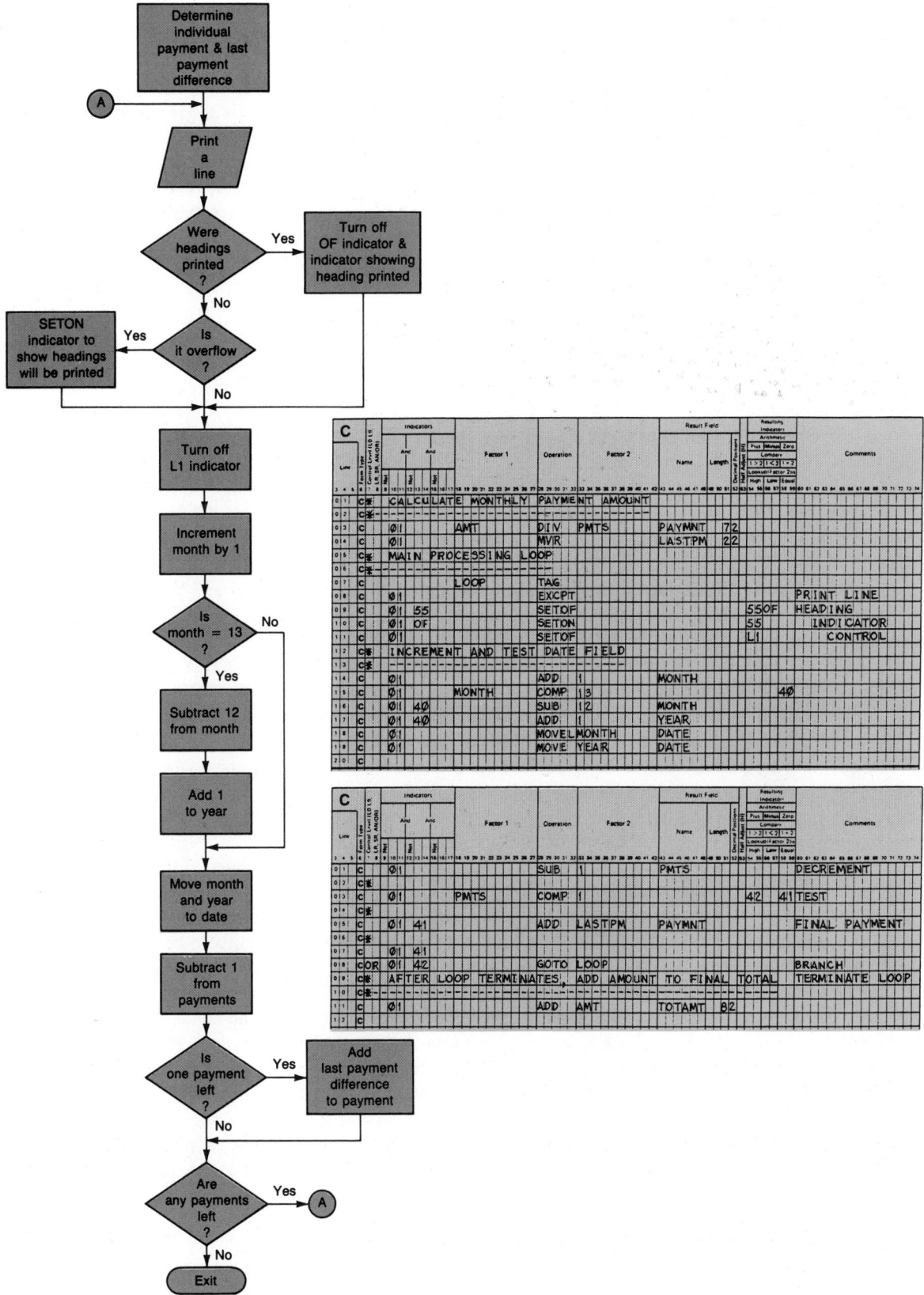

Figure 9-18   Calculations: (a) Flowchart of logic and (b) specifications

next exception output operation is performed. Therefore, the OF indicator cannot be turned off immediately after the EXCPT operation that turns it on. Instead, the program must turn on an indicator to specify that the OF Indicator is on and that, on the next pass through the loop, it should be turned off. Overflow processing ordinarily takes place under control of step 10 of the fixed logic cycle. However, because the output for this program is produced during step 12 using exception output, special methods must be used to control the printing of headings and the resetting of the overflow indicator. Indicator 55 is used for this purpose.

If the OF indicator is on, the SETON operation on line 10 turns on indicator 55. On the next iteration of the loop, the headings are printed by the EXCPT operation and fetch overflow. Line 09 then checks indicator 55; if it is on, both the OF indicator and indicator 55 are set off. Thus, the headings are properly printed within the loop without using the part of the RPG cycle that usually prints headings.

After the overflow indicator is processed, line 11 turns off the L1 indicator. It is on for the first record of each customer because of the change in the customer number; it must be turned off so that group indication takes place properly. If the control level indicator is not turned off, it remains on during the printing of all exception output lines because printing is taking place at detail calculation time and ordinary RPG processing does not turn the control level indicator off at step 2 of the logic cycle. Therefore, the L1 indicator must be turned off by a SETOF operation after the first line is printed.

▸ **Incrementation of Due Date** After the output line is printed, the MONTH field is incremented by 1 (line 14) to reflect the new payment date. The new value in the MONTH field is then compared with 13 (line 15) to determine if the YEAR field must be incremented. If the month equals 13 (indicator 40 on), line 16 subtracts 12 from the MONTH field and line 17 adds 1 to the YEAR field. As a result, the YEAR field advances, and the MONTH field is set to January (01).

▸ **MOVE and MOVEL Operations** As you saw earlier, when the MONTH and YEAR fields are defined on the Input Specifications form, the RPG compiler establishes separate areas in the processing area for these fields, even though they redefine the DATE field. However, only the DATE field is referenced on the Output Specifications form. Therefore, it is necessary to move the updated information in the MONTH and YEAR fields to the DATE field. This is accomplished by the MOVEL (MOVE left-justified) and MOVE operations.

The **MOVE** and **MOVEL** operations are called data movement operations. The word *move*, as used in a programming language, is somewhat misleading. Usually, the word refers to changing the location of something, for example, moving a chair changes the location of the chair. In the programming sense, the word has a different meaning. *When data is moved by a data movement operation, the data is, in fact, only copied into its new location and still occupies its original area of computer memory.* Data movement operations such as MOVE and MOVEL leave the original field unchanged and copy the data into a second field.

The MOVEL and MOVE operations used in the sample program are illustrated in Figure 9-19, which shows that both operation codes must be specified in the Operation area (positions 28–32) on the Calculation Specifications form. Both instructions are used to copy data from the field specified in the Factor 2 area of the form to the field specified in the Result Field area of the form (although these operations can also be used to move literals).

The MOVEL instruction causes the data in the Factor 2 field to be copied to the result field, beginning with the leftmost character and proceeding, one character at a time, to the right. The number of characters copied is determined by the length either of the field named in Factor 2 or the field named as the Result field, whichever is shorter. Figure 9-19 also shows that the data in the MONTH field is copied to the DATE field, beginning with the leftmost character in each field and that two digits are moved because this is the length of the MONTH field, which is the shorter of the two fields.

The MOVE instruction, on the other hand, begins with the rightmost character in the field specified in Factor 2 and continues to the left for as many characters as are found in the shorter of the fields specified in Factor 2 or Result Field. When the MOVE instruction in Figure 9-19 is executed, the two characters in the YEAR field are copied to the rightmost positions of the DATE field because YEAR is two digits in length. Figures 9-20 and 9-21 (on pages 9.21 and 9.22) summarize the MOVEL and MOVE operations.

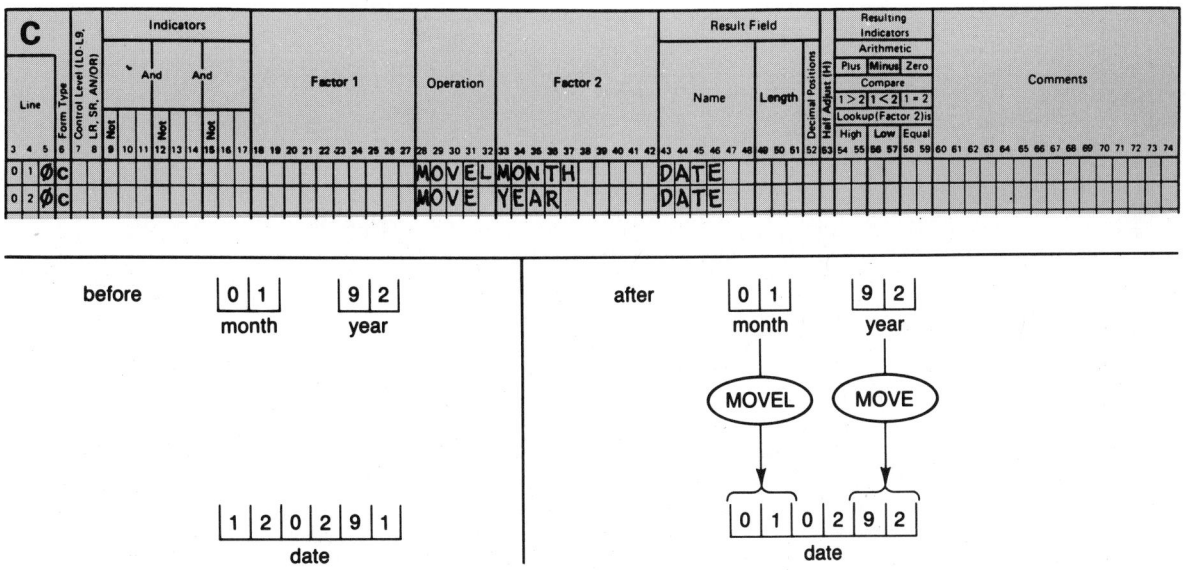

Figure 9-19 Example of MOVE and MOVEL operations

Control Level Indicators	Indicators	Factor 1	Operation	Factor 2	Result Field		Resulting Indicators		
					Name	Length			
03			MOVEL	NAMEIN	WORK	18			
99			MOVEL	'ERROR'	MESAGE				
01			MOVEL	DESC	TEMP				
01			MOVEL	19	YEAR				

MOVEL Operation Summary

The MOVEL operation transfers data from the Factor 2 field into the Result Field, one character at a time, starting with the leftmost position of the fields. The contents of Factor 2 are not changed. If Factor 2 is longer than the Result Field, the rightmost characters of Factor 2 are not transferred. If Factor 2 is shorter than the Result Field, the rightmost characters of the Result Field are not changed.

Control Level Indicators	Indicators	Factor 1	Operation Name	Factor 2	Result Field	Resulting Indicators		
7–8	9–17	18–27	28–32	33–42	43–53	54–55	56–57	58–59
optional	optional	blank	MOVEL	required	required	blank	blank	blank

optional - RPG III, RPG/400

Figure 9-20 MOVEL operation summary

C		Indicators		Factor 1	Operation	Factor 2	Result Field				Resulting Indicators			Comments
		And	And				Name	Length			Arithmetic			
Line	Form Type / Control Level (L0-L9, LR, SR, AN/OR)	Not	Not						Decimal Positions	Half Adjust (H)	Plus Minus Zero / Compare 1>2 1<2 1=2 / Lookup(Factor 2)is High Low Equal			
0 1	C	01			MOVE	INFLD	HOLD							
0 2	C													
0 3	C	99			MOVE	0	COUNT							
0 4	C													

MOVE Operation Summary

The MOVE operation transfers data from the Factor 2 field into the Result Field, one character at a time, starting with the rightmost position of the fields. The contents of Factor 2 are not changed. If Factor 2 is longer than the Result Field, the leftmost characters of Factor 2 are not transferred. If Factor 2 is shorter than the Result Field, the leftmost characters of the Result Field are not changed.

Control Level Indicators	Indicators	Factor 1	Operation Name	Factor 2	Result Field	Resulting Indicators		
7–8	9–17	18–27	28–32	33–42	43–53	54–55	56–57	58–59
optional	optional	blank	MOVE	required	required	blank	blank	blank

optional - RPG III, RPG/400

Figure 9-21 MOVE operation summary

▶ **Loop Control and Termination** Referring again to Figure 9-18, note that after the month and year are moved, the SUB operation on line 01 of the second page of calculation specifications subtracts the value 1 from the number of payments (PMTS) to determine if all payments have been made. Remember that PMTS is the control variable for the loop. In this example, the incrementation portion of the loop is performed by a SUB statement and is, in fact, **decrementation** rather than incrementation. For this reason, because some loops change the control variable by subtraction rather than addition, this component of the loop is sometimes called alteration.

After the value 1 is subtracted, the comparison on line 03 determines if the number of payments left is 1. If it is, indicator 41 is turned on, and the remainder from the DIV operation (LASTPM) is added to the last payment so that the entire amount due is accounted for. If the number of payments is greater than 1, then indicator 42 is turned on. If either indicator 41 is on (one payment left) or indicator 42 is on (more than one payment left), the GOTO operation on line 08 is executed so that the next payment is printed on the report. Note the use of the OR in positions 7–8 of line 08 to indicate that the GOTO operation should be executed if either indicator 41 or indicator 42 is on. If neither indicator is on, all the payment lines have been printed, and the loop is completed.

▶ **Addition to Final Total** Line 11 of the calculations adds the loan amount (AMT) to a final total accumulator (TOTAMT). Note that line 11 is outside of the loop and is performed only once for each record read from the input file because line 11 is executed after the loop has terminated. In this loop, as in most other RPG loops, termination is not a specific operation but is, instead, the lack of a branch back to the beginning of the loop.

▶ **Summary of Processing Loop** Recall that all this processing takes place as the result of one input record being read, that is, each input record generates the loop processing for as many cycles as there are payments. Because a variable number of output lines can be written from each input record, exception output must be used instead of the normal RPG fixed logic cycle (which performs only a single detail output cycle for each input record read).

During the detail output portion of the logic cycle, the program prints the Loan Amount field (AMT) for each record. Because this line appears after all the exception output lines created during the loop, the line has the appearance of a total. It is, however, a normal detail output line.

Output Specifications

▶ **Detail, Total, and Exception Output** When you use exception output, the heading entries on the Output Specifications form are usually the same as in previous programs. However, the Exception Output entries, differ. The entries for the detail, total, and exception output are shown in Figure 9-22.

Figure 9-22   Output specifications for detail, total, and exception output

As noted previously, the only entry required to designate the exception line is the E in position 15 of the record description line (line 15). The description of the exception line follows all other types of output description (H, D, and T). When RPG II was first developed, the placement of type E output after all other types was a requirement of the RPG II compiler. This is no longer the case. Most newer versions of RPG II as well as all versions of RPG III and RPG/400 permit exception output records to be placed in any sequence in the output specifications. Your instructor or computer center manager can tell you if the version of RPG that you are using requires that type E output record descriptions be placed after all type H, D, and T output record descriptions.

▸ **The Need for Fetch Overflow** Because the number of payments is unknown when an input record is read, there is a possibility that the end of a page on the report will occur during the loop when exception output is being printed. Therefore, it is necessary that fetch overflow be used so that if the end of a page is reached, the headings on the new page are printed properly. As can be seen from Figure 9-22, to specify fetch overflow, an F is entered in position 16 of the exception output line. This causes the headings to be printed when the end of the page is reached because before each exception line is printed, a check is made to determine if indicator OF is on. If it is, the headings are printed before the next exception line is printed.

The customer number (CUSTNO) and the customer name (CUSTNM) are printed whenever there is an L1 control break. Because each input record causes indicator L1 to be turned on, the customer number and customer name print as part of the first exception output line produced for each input record. In addition, they are printed when indicator OF is on, that is, whenever a new page is started. Thus, as in previous programs, the group indicated information is printed both when there is a control break and when there is a new page; this is to make the report as easy to read as possible.

The format of the compilation listing for program HJG09Y. (Figure 9-23) differs from the format in previous examples because this program was compiled using a System/38 RPG III compiler. However, all the information you have seen before appears, and all the familiar RPG features perform the same functions as before.

Figure 9-23   Compile listing for program HJG09Y

Figure 9-23 (1)

```
HJG09Y -- PAYMENT SCHEDULE REPORT
5714RG1 RPG R08M00  861114     HJG09Y.TEST      10/07/91  17:46:03  PAGE   3

   SEQUENCE     1       2       3       4       5       6       7     IND   DO   LAST      PAGE   PROGRAM
   NUMBER    6789012345678901234567890123456789012345678901234567890123 4  USE   NUM  UPDATE    LINE   ID

     5300  C*           INCREMENT AND TEST DATE FIELD
     5400  C*           --------------------------------
     5500  C    01               ADD  1         MONTH
     5600  C    01      MONTH    COMP 13                        40              3
     5700  C    01 40            SUB  12         MONTH
     5800  C    01 40            ADD  1          YEAR
     5900  C    01               MOVELMONTH      DATE
     6000  C    01               MOVE YEAR       DATE


     6200  C    01               SUB  1          PMTS            DECREMENT

     6400  C    01      PMTS     COMP 1                     42 41TEST          1 3

     6600  C    01 41            ADD  LASTPM     PAYMNT          FINAL PAYMENT

     6300  C    01 41            ADD  LASTPM     PAYMNT          FINAL PAYMENT
     6900  COR  01 42            GOTO LOOP                       BRANCH

     7100  C* AFTER LOOP TERMINATES, ADD AMOUNT TO FINAL TOTAL
     7200  C*------------------------------------------------
     7300  C    01               ADD  AMT        TOTAMT 82

     7400  O* HEADING LINE ONE
     7500  O*-----------------
     7600  OPMNTREPTH  206   1P
     7700  O        OR        OF
     7800  O                       UDATE Y   8
     7900  O                             41 'PAYMENT SCHEDULE REPORT'
     8000  O                             55 'PAGE'
     8100  O                       PAGE   60

     8300  O* HEADING LINE TWO
     8400  O*-----------------
     8500  O        H  1   1P
     8600  O        OR        OF
     8700  O                             26 'CUSTOMER      CUSTOMER'
     8800  O                             60 'DUE       PAYMENT'

     9000  O* HEADING LINE THREE
     9100  O*-------------------
     9200  O        H  2   1P
     9300  O        OR        OF
     9400  O                             24 'NUMBER        NAME'
     9500  O                             60 'DATE       AMOUNT'

     9700  O* DETAIL LINE PRINTED AFTER LOOP TERMINATES
     9800  O*-----------------------------------------
     9900  O        D 13   01
    10000  O                             49 'TOTAL PAYMENTS'
    10100  O                       AMT  1 60 '.'

    10300  O* FINAL TOTAL
    10400  O*-----------
    10500  O        T 00   LR
    10600  O                             48 'FINAL TOTAL'
    10700  O                       TOTAMT1 60 '.'

    10900  O* EXCEPTION OUTPUT CONTROLLED BY LOOP
    11000  O*----------------------------------
    11100  O        EF 1
    11200  O                   L1  CUSTNOZ   7
    11300  O                   L1  CUSTNM   35
    11400  O                   OF  CUSTNOZ   7
    11500  O                   OF  CUSTNM   35
    11600  O                       DATE Y  47
    11700  O                       PAYMNT1 60
  * * * * * E N D   O F   S O U R C E * * * *
```

```
MESSAGE SUMMARY

TOTAL    00    10    20    30    40    50
  1      1     0     0     0     0     0

  117 RECORDS READ FROM SOURCE FILE

  SOURCE RECORDS INCLUDE   56 SPECIFICATIONS,   0 TABLE RECORDS, AND   45 COMMENTS

  PRM HAS BEEN CALLED

  QRG0003 PROGRAM HJG09Y PLACED IN LIB TEST     00 HIGHEST SEVERITY FOUND

  * * * * * E N D   O F   C O M P I L A T I O N * * * *
```

Figure 9-23 (2)

continued

```
  10/07/91              PAYMENT SCHEDULE REPORT           PAGE   1

     CUSTOMER          CUSTOMER               DUE         PAYMENT
      NUMBER             NAME                 DATE         AMOUNT

      1845    MARTHA K. THALER              8/27/91        400.00
                                            9/27/91        400.00
                                           10/27/91        400.00
                                           11/27/91        400.00
                                           12/27/91        400.00
                                            1/27/92        400.00
                                            2/27/92        400.00
                                            3/27/92        400.00
                                            4/27/92        400.00
                                            5/27/92        400.00

                                    TOTAL PAYMENTS   $4,000.00


      2780    BARBARA E. POHJA              9/17/91        302.08
                                           10/17/91        302.08
                                           11/17/91        302.08
                                           12/17/91        302.08
                                            1/17/92        302.08
                                            2/17/92        302.08
                                            3/17/92        302.08
                                            4/17/92        302.08
                                            5/17/92        302.08
                                            6/17/92        302.08
                                            7/17/92        302.08
                                            8/17/92        302.12

                                    TOTAL PAYMENTS   $3,625.00

                                    FINAL TOTAL      $7,625.00
```

Figure 9-23 (3)

TWO COMMON LOOPING APPLICATIONS

Loops are often used in a program to perform a specific function rather than to control the execution of the primary purpose of the program. This section presents two looping routines that can be inserted into a program to solve specific programming problems. These routines can be adapted for use in any program that presents these problems.

Application 1: Removal of Editing Characters

In some applications, especially those in which the input data is keyed directly into the program from a computer terminal, numeric data fields can be read into the program with editing characters inserted into the data. As you know, according to the rules of RPG syntax, a numeric data field can contain only digits and, possibly, the sign of the number; it cannot contain editing characters such as spaces, dollar signs, commas, and decimal points. Application 1 demonstrates the use of a loop to test for these editing characters and, when they are encountered, to remove them from the Data field, leaving only the digits. Upon completion of the routine, the numeric data can be used for calculations in the program. Figure 9-24 illustrates the two fields used in this example.

The input is ACQCST, an eight-position alphameric data field. ACQCST always contains a dollar sign and decimal point and, depending on the numeric value of the field, may contain a comma and one or more spaces. Every position of ACQCST must be tested to determine if it contains a space, decimal point, comma, or dollar sign. If a position contains one of these characters, the next position is tested. If, however, the position contains a digit, the digit is saved and becomes part of the numeric result field. In this example, the numeric data taken from ACQCST is placed in a field named CSTOUT.

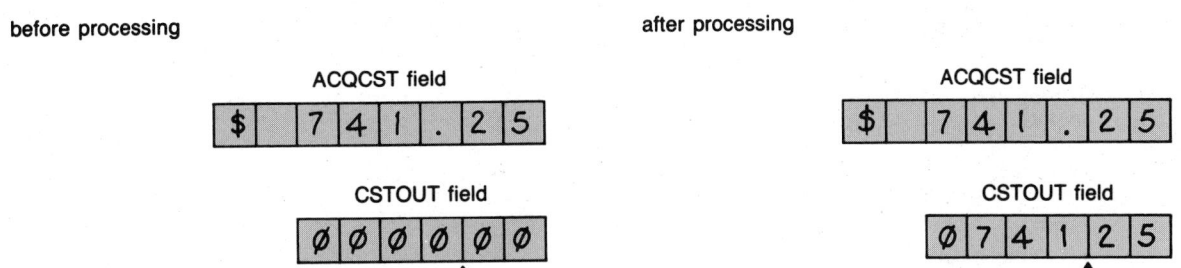

before processing   after processing

Figure 9-24   ACQCST and CSTOUT data fields

Note that CSTOUT is a six-position field. Because ACQCST is eight positions long and always contains at least two editing characters (a dollar sign and a decimal point), the maximum number of digits that can be placed in CSTOUT is six.

▸ **The Need for Arrays** Because each position in ACQCST must be examined individually, the usual techniques of field comparison cannot be used. Instead, the contents of the field must be transferred into an array and a loop performed to permit each position of the array to be compared separately. In addition, as numeric characters are found, each character must be transferred individually into an output array. The numeric characters must be transferred into an array because the field processing techniques used in RPG do not permit the program to access individual positions in the field. The two arrays used in this example are HOLD, an eight-position array that contains the contents of ACQCST, and OUT, a six-position array that contains the numeric data from ACQCST after the editing characters have been removed. Figure 9-25 shows the extension specifications used to describe the two arrays.

Extension Specifications

E	Form Type	Record Sequence of the Chaining File / Number of the Chaining Field / From Filename	To Filename	Table or Array Name	Number of Entries Per Record	Number of Entries Per Table or Array	Length of Entry	P/B/L/R	Decimal Positions	Sequence (A/D)	Table or Array Name (Alternating Format)	Length of Entry	P/B/L/R	Decimal Positions	Sequence (A/D)	Comments
0 1	E			HOLD		8	1									
0 2	E			OUT		6	1									
0 3	E															
0 4	E															
0 5	E															
0 6	E															
0 7	E															
0 8	E															
	E															
	E															

Figure 9-25   Array definitions

▸ **The MOVEA Operation** When data must be transferred between a field and an entire array, the MOVE and MOVEL operations cannot be used. MOVE and MOVEL are used to transfer data between a data field and an individual element of an array, but not between a field and an entire array. Because the contents of ACQCST must be moved into an entire array, with each character being moved into a separate element, the MOVEA command must be used.

MOVEA moves data between a field and an array or between two arrays, treating array data as one large data field and performing data movement without regard for element size or boundaries. Factor 2 of a MOVEA operation is the Sending data area and the result field specifies the Receiving area. At least one array name must be specified in a MOVEA operation.

The number of data characters moved by a MOVEA operation is determined by the length of the shorter of the two data areas involved. If the Sending data area is longer than the Receiving area and there is not enough room for all the characters, the rightmost characters of the Sending area will be lost. If the Sending area is shorter than the Receiving area, the rightmost positions of the Receiving area will not be changed by the MOVEA operation. The MOVEA operation can be used to move data in three ways:

- From a single data field to one or more consecutive array elements
- From one or more consecutive array elements to a single data field
- From consecutive elements of one array to consecutive elements of another array

Figure 9-26 illustrates the three types of move operations that can be performed by the MOVEA operation.

Figure 9-26 Examples of MOVEA operations: (a) data field to array,
(b) array to data field, and (c) array to array.

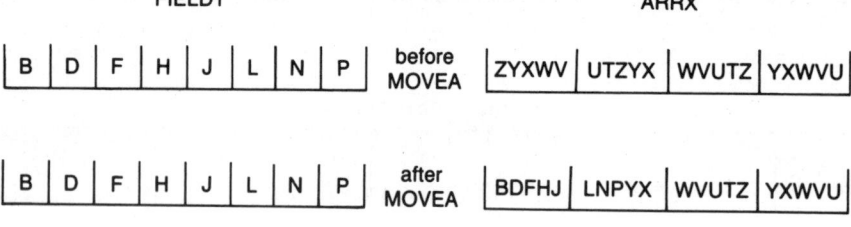

FIELD1 ARRX

| B | D | F | H | J | L | N | P | before MOVEA | ZYXWV | UTZYX | WVUTZ | YXWVU |

| B | D | F | H | J | L | N | P | after MOVEA | BDFHJ | LNPYX | WVUTZ | YXWVU |

Figure 9-26 (A)

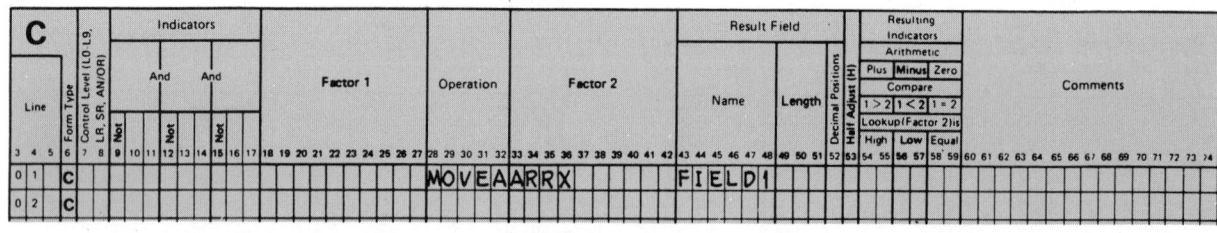

ARRX FIELD1

| 123 | 456 | 789 | 012 | before MOVEA | 9 | 8 | 7 | 6 | 5 | 4 | 3 | 2 | 1 | 9 | 8 | 7 |

| 123 | 456 | 789 | 012 | after MOVEA | 1 | 2 | 3 | 4 | 5 | 6 | 7 | 8 | 9 | 0 | 1 | 2 |

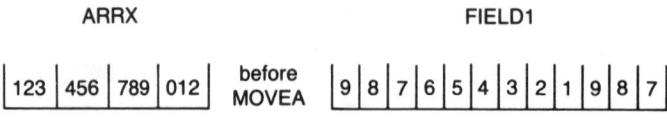

Figure 9-26 (B)

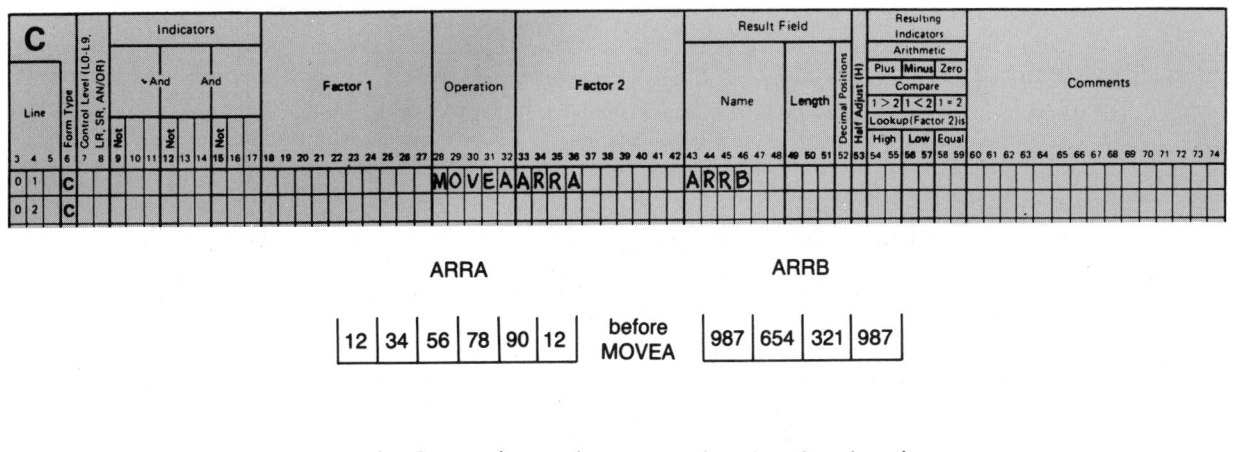

Figure 9-26 (C)

1. **Data Field to Array** Example One (Figure 9-26a) shows the use of the MOVEA operation to transfer data from a single data field into an array. Note that FIELD1 is unchanged by the MOVEA operation. As with all data movement operations, MOVEA copies data from Factor 2 into the Result Field and leaves Factor 2 unchanged. As you can see, after the MOVEA is executed, the original contents of ARRX have been replaced by the data from FIELD1. The MOVEA operation ignored the element boundaries and copied the data as a string of consecutive characters.

2. **Array to Data Field** In Example Two (Figure 9-26b), the data from ARRX has been moved into FIELD1, again without regard for the boundaries of the array elements. As you can see, each character from ARRX has been moved to a separate position of FIELD1 with no regard for the ARRX element boundaries.

3. **Array to Array** Example Three (Figure 9-26c) shows the movement of data between 2 arrays. ARRA consists of elements that are two-positions long, whereas ARRB is made up of three-position elements. The data has been moved without regard to the size of the elements. After the MOVEA is executed, the first element of ARRB contains three characters, two from the first element of ARRA and one from the second element. The second element of ARRB contains one character from the second element of ARRA and two characters from the third element.

Figure 9-27 summarizes the MOVEA operation.

Figure 9-27 MOVEA operation summary (continued)

MOVEA Operation Summary

The MOVEA operation transfers data from Factor 2 to the Result Field, starting with the leftmost position of each. At least one array must be used by the MOVEA operation. Element boundaries within the array or arrays being used are ignored, and data transfer proceeds, one character at a time, from left to right. If Factor 2 and the Result Field area are not the same length, the MOVEA operation stops when the shorter of the two areas has been completely used. The rules of data movement are similar to those of the MOVEL operation.

Control Level Indicators	Indicators	Factor 1	Operation Name	Factor 2	Result Field	Resulting Indicators		
7–8	9–17	18–27	28–32	33–42	43–53	54–55	56–57	58–59
optional	optional	blank	MOVEA	required	required	blank	blank	blank

optional - RPG III, RPG/400

Figure 9-27 (continued)

▶ **Calculation Specifications for Removal of Editing Characters** The Calculation specifications for the routine to remove editing characters from a field are shown in Figure 9-28. In the routine, the variable index X is used with the HOLD array, and the variable index Y is used with the OUT array. Both X and Y also serve as control variables to control termination of the 2 loops used in the routine. As you will see, the two variables are decremented separately, and either of them can end the routine. The line numbers in the following explanations refer to Figure 9-28 unless another illustration is specified.

▶ **Initialization of Variables and Arrays** Line 01 places a starting value of zero in each of the elements of the OUT array. The entry *ZEROS in Factor 2 is a figurative constant. A **figurative constant** is a reserved field name that represents a string of characters. The figurative constants *ZERO and *ZEROS represent a series of digits zero. The number of zeros is determined by the way that the figurative constant is used. If it is used as Factor 2 in a data movement operation, the number of zeros equals the length of the Result Field. Because OUT is a six-position array, *ZEROS moves six zeros into OUT. (The figurative constant *ZERO does exactly the same thing.) If you have studied COBOL, you have probably used figurative constants.

In addition to *ZERO and *ZEROS, RPG also provides the figurative constants ***BLANK** and ***BLANKS**. These figurative constants generate a series of spaces, that can be used in move operations to clear data from an alphameric data field. Some newer versions of RPG provide another figurative constant, *ALL. The ***ALL** figurative constant enables you to generate a series of any character you need; the format is *ALL 'x', where x represents the character needed. For example, *ALL '-' generates a series of hyphens, and *ALL '*' generates a series of asterisks.

Line 02 uses a MOVEA operation to transfer the data in ACQCST into the HOLD array for processing. Lines 03 and 04 initialize the indices that are used to reference the input and output arrays. Because the logic used in the loops subtracts 1 from the index values at the beginning of the loop, these fields are initialized to a value that is one more than the number of elements in the arrays that they are indexing. Note that these indices are set to a value that corresponds to the rightmost positions of the arrays. Because the purpose of the routine is to move numeric data, and numeric data is usually right-justified, this routine must work through the arrays from right to left. Figure 9-29 shows the contents of the two arrays and the two index fields after lines 01–04 have been executed.

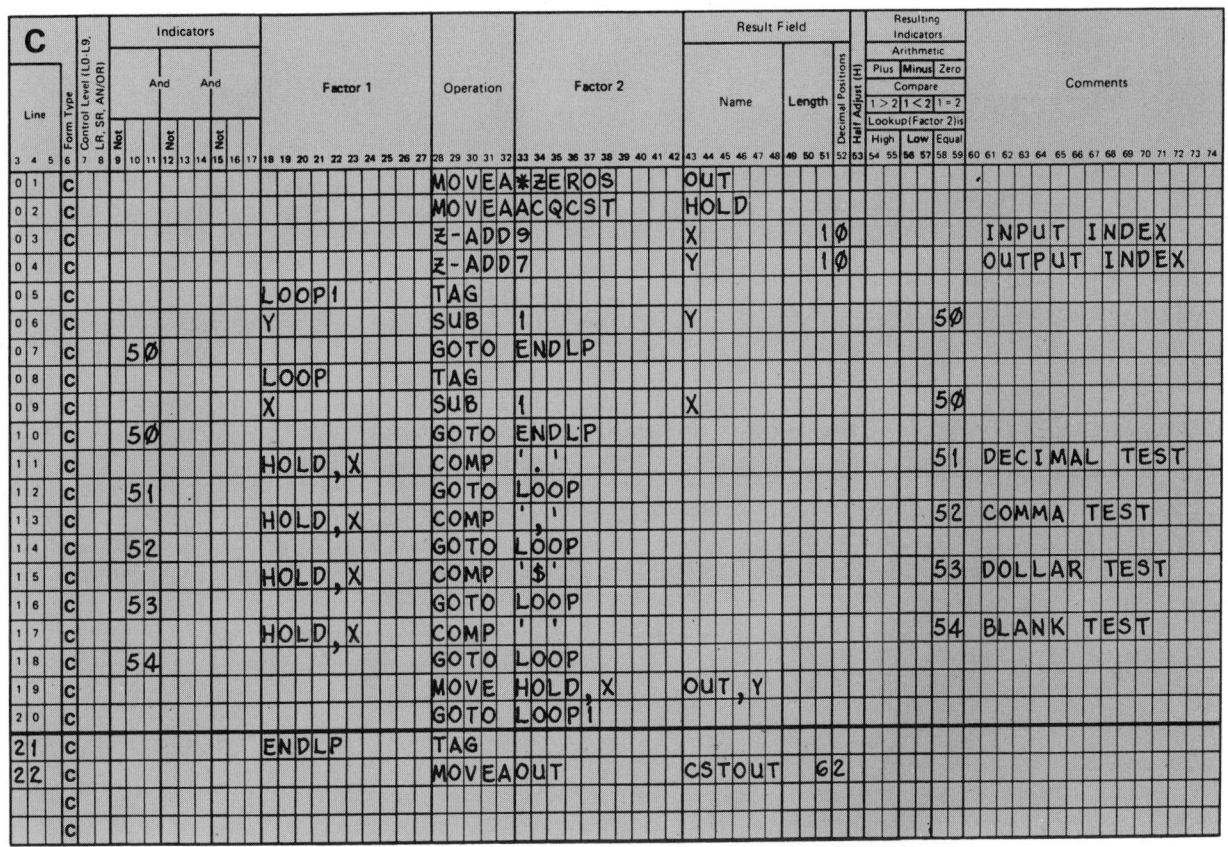

C	Line	Form Type	Control Level (L0-L9, LR, SR, AN/OR)	Indicators						Factor 1	Operation	Factor 2	Result Field				Resulting Indicators		Comments
				And		And							Name	Length	Decimal Positions	Half Adjust (H)	Arithmetic Plus/Minus/Zero Compare 1>2 1<2 1=2 Lookup(Factor 2)is High Low Equal		
0 1	C										MOVEA	*ZEROS	OUT						'
0 2	C										MOVEA	CQCST	HOLD						
0 3	C										Z-ADD	9	X		1Ø				INPUT INDEX
0 4	C										Z-ADD	7	Y		1Ø				OUTPUT INDEX
0 5	C									LOOP1	TAG								
0 6	C									Y	SUB	1	Y					5Ø	
0 7	C			5Ø							GOTO	ENDLP							
0 8	C									LOOP	TAG								
0 9	C									X	SUB	1	X					5Ø	
1 0	C			5Ø							GOTO	ENDLP							
1 1	C									HOLD,X	COMP	'.'						51	DECIMAL TEST
1 2	C			51							GOTO	LOOP							
1 3	C									HOLD,X	COMP	','						52	COMMA TEST
1 4	C			52							GOTO	LOOP							
1 5	C									HOLD,X	COMP	'$'						53	DOLLAR TEST
1 6	C			53							GOTO	LOOP							
1 7	C									HOLD,X	COMP	' '						54	BLANK TEST
1 8	C			54							GOTO	LOOP							
1 9	C										MOVE	HOLD,X	OUT,Y						
2 0	C										GOTO	LOOP1							
2 1	C									ENDLP	TAG								
2 2	C										MOVEA	OUT	CSTOUT	62					
	C																		
	C																		

Figure 9-28 Calculation specifications for data conversion

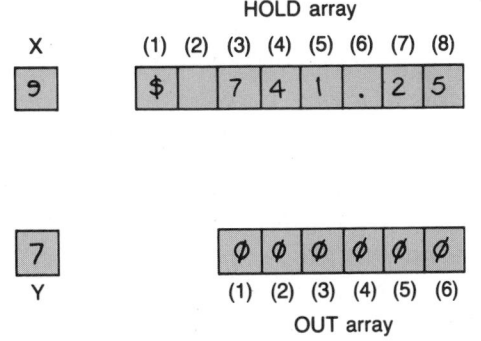

HOLD array

X   (1) (2) (3) (4) (5) (6) (7) (8)

9      $ | 7 | 4 | 1 | . | 2 | 5

7

Y   Ø Ø Ø Ø Ø Ø

      (1) (2) (3) (4) (5) (6)

OUT array

Figure 9-29 Elimination of editing characters

▸ **LOOP1 Processing** Line 05 of the calculations is the TAG operation for LOOP1. LOOP1 controls the decrementation of the Y field, which is used as the index for the OUT array. The decrementation is performed by the SUB operation on line 06, where the value 1 is subtracted from the contents of Y. Line 06 is shown in Figure 9-30 on the next page.

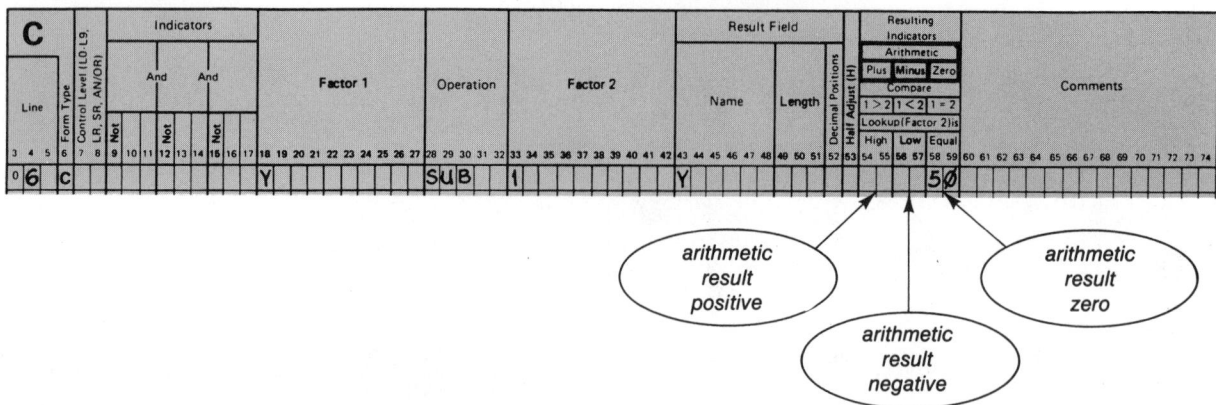

Figure 9-30   Arithmetic resulting indicators

▶ **Resulting Indicators in Arithmetic Operations**   Note in Figure 9-30 the entry of indicator 50 in positions 58–59 of the SUB operation line. The Resulting Indicators area (positions 54–59) can be used to test the contents of the result of an arithmetic operation. RPG enables you to determine whether the result of an arithmetic operation is greater than zero, less than zero, or equal to zero by specifying a resulting indicator in positions 54–55, 56–57, and/or 58–59.

If the result of an arithmetic operation is greater than zero, the indicator specified in positions 54–55 (PLUS) is turned on. If the result of an arithmetic operation is less than zero, the indicator specified in positions 56–57 (MINUS) is turned on. If the result of an arithmetic operation is equal to zero, the indicator specified in positions 58–59 (ZERO) is turned on. The PLUS, MINUS, and ZERO indicators can be used with any RPG arithmetic operation.

Line 06 specifies that indicator 50 turns on when the value in Y equals zero. This occurs when all positions of the output array (OUT) are filled and is one way to terminate the processing loop. Because line 04 initialized Y to a value of 7, this first subtraction decreases Y by 1 to a value of 6, and indicator 50 is not turned on at this time. Because indicator 50 is not on, line 07 is not executed.

Lines 08, 09, and 10 perform a similar function but act on the index field X, which is used with the HOLD array. Lines 06, 07, 09, and 10 of the calculations perform the decrementation, testing, and termination components of the loops.

▶ **Data Testing**   Figure 9-31 shows the setting of the index fields after the SUB operations are performed for the first time. Note that these indices point to the rightmost elements of both the input array (HOLD) and the output array (OUT). Lines 11–18 of the calculations perform the tests to determine if each array element contains an editing character or a digit. If any COMP operation (line 11, 13, 15, or 17) finds an editing character in the HOLD element that is being tested, a resulting indicator is turned on, and the following line (line 12, 14, 16, or 18) performs a branch to LOOP. Because HOLD,8 does not contain an editing character, none of the GOTO operations is performed, and processing continues to line 19, where the digit from the HOLD array is moved to the OUT array (Figure 9-32). Line 20 then branches to LOOP1 to begin another iteration of the loop.

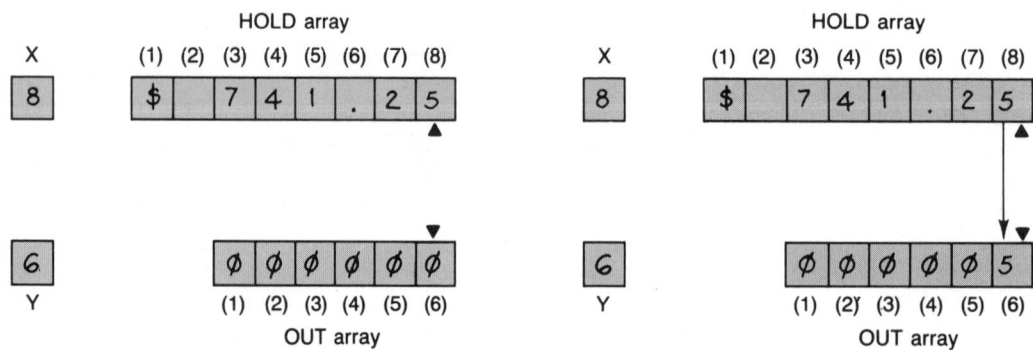

Figure 9-31   Elimination of editing characters   **Figure 9-32   Elimination of editing characters**

After the branch to LOOP1, line 06 decreases the value in Y to 5, line 09 decreases the value in X to 7, and element HOLD,7 is tested by lines 11–18. Because HOLD,7 contains a digit, processing continues to line 19, where the value in HOLD,7 is moved into OUT,5 (Figure 9-33).

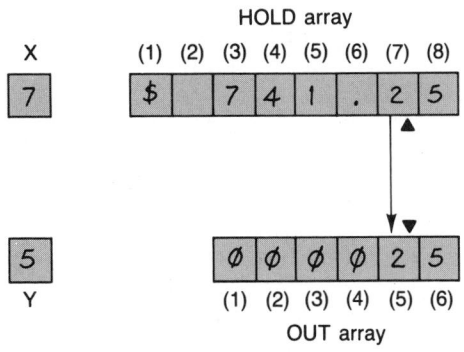

Figure 9-33   Elimination of editing characters

The program then branches to LOOP1, and the following operations decrease the value of X to 6 and the value of Y to 4 (Figure 9-34). Because HOLD,6 contains a decimal point, the COMP operation on line 11 causes indicator 51 to be turned on and causes the GOTO on line 12 to be executed, resulting in a branch to LOOP on line 08. Processing continues with line 09, decreasing the value in X by 1 and leaving a value of 5 in X. Note that in these circumstances processing does not return to line 06, and the value in Y is not changed. After line 09 is executed, the tests on lines 11–18 are again performed. Because HOLD,5 does not contain an editing character, processing continues to line 19, where the MOVE operation is again performed (Figure 9-35). Note that the decimal point located in HOLD,6 has been eliminated, and the digit 1 in HOLD,5 has been moved.

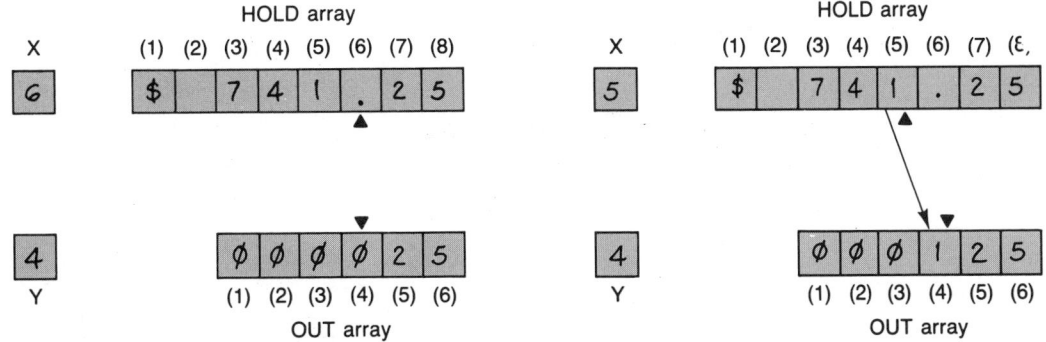

Figure 9-34   Elimination of editing characters   **Figure 9-35   Elimination of editing characters**

The looping routine continues to execute, moving digits and eliminating editing characters, until after several iterations it reaches line 08; the status of the arrays and indices is shown in Figure 9-36 on the next page. At this point, all the digits have been moved from HOLD to OUT, and both indices X and Y contain a value of 1. The SUB operation on line 09 then subtracts 1 from X, leaving a result of zero and turning on indicator 50. Because indicator 50 is on, line 10 causes a branch to ENDLP on line 21, and the routine is ended.

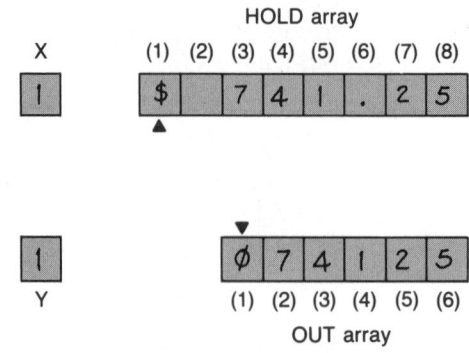

Figure 9-36 Elimination of editing characters

Because the loop has been terminated, top-down processing resumes, and line 22 is executed. The MOVEA operation on line 22 transfers the contents of the OUT array into the CSTOUT field (Figure 9-37). CSTOUT can then be used by the program for normal numeric field processing.

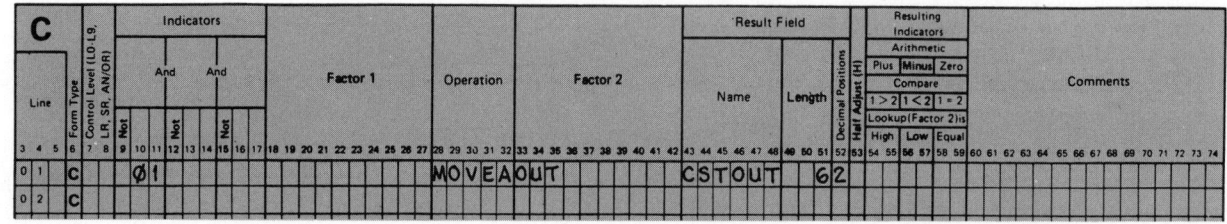

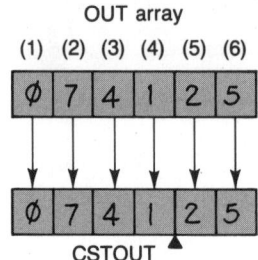

Figure 9-37 Movement of OUT array to CSTOUT

▆▆ Application 2: The Name Game

This sample looping application demonstrates the solution to a problem that often occurs when several fields must be printed consecutively and when the consecutively printed fields contain variable length data entries.

A compilation listing of SAMPLE1, a short program used to print names, is shown in Figure 9-38. As you can see, the input specifications describe three data fields: LAST, which contains the person's last name; FRST, which contains the first name; and INIT, which contains the middle initial. The output specifications print FRST ending in position 15, INIT ending in position 17, and LAST ending in position 34. However, because the First Name field may not be completely filled and because some people do not have or use middle initials, the resulting listing (Figure 9-39) can be difficult to read and simply does not look good. Note the large gaps between the first name and middle initial or, in the case of the third name on the list, between the first and last name.

```
SAMPLE1   09-29-91  16:45:44      IBM PC        RPG II        Version 3.5  Page  1
        ....+....1....+....2....+....3....+....4....+....5....+....6....+....7....

    1 0001 H                                                              SAMPLE1


    2 0002 FEMPLOYEEIP  F  51  51          DISK
    3 0003 FNAMELISTO   F 132 132          PRINTER


    4 0004 IEMPLOYEEAA  01
    5 0005 I                                    19  34 LAST
    6 0006 I                                    35  48 FRST
    7 0007 I                                    51  51 INIT


    8 0008 ONAMELISTD  2      01
    9 0009 O                        FRST     15
   10 0010 O                        INIT     17
   11 0011 O                        LAST     34
   12 /*
   13 /*


        THE FOLLOWING INDICATORS APPEARED IN THIS PROGRAM

        01
No Warning Errors
No Fatal Errors
```

Figure 9-38   Program SAMPLE1

```
GARY        B SHELLY

THOMAS      J CASHMAN

HAL           GOODWIN

KATHRYN     D WHEELER

ELIZABETH   A CASE
```

Figure 9-39   Program SAMPLE1 output

Contrast Figure 9-39 with the output listing in Figure 9-40. In the latter, the names are printed with normal spacing between parts: a single space between the first name, middle initial, and last name. In the third name, the excess spacing has been eliminated, and there is a single space between the first and last names. Although this application of looping and array techniques is shown here as a complete program, the necessary code could easily be incorporated into a larger program. This type of processing is often used in applications such as printing checks to make name alteration more difficult. The example that follows deals with names but could also be applied to other types of data, such as addresses.

```
GARY B SHELLY

THOMAS J CASHMAN

HAL GOODWIN

KATHRYN D WHEELER

ELIZABETH A CASE
```

Figure 9-40   Program SAMPLE2 output

Program SAMPLE2: Name Condensation

Figure 9-41 shows the compilation listing for program SAMPLE2, which performs the name condensation routine. The control and file description specifications contain no new or unusual entries. The program includes three extension specifications describing execution time arrays NAME, LAST, and FRST. The NAME array contains the condensed name after excess spaces have been eliminated. The LAST and FRST arrays appear in the input specifications and contain the last name and first name data. In this example, as in the example to remove editing characters, the data must be described in array form to enable the program to index through the data on a character-by-character basis. INIT does not require array description because it is a single-position data field.

In the following explanation of the calculation specifications for program SAMPLE2, the line numbers refer to those in Figure 9-41.

Figure 9-41   Program SAMPLE2

```
SAMPLE2    10-04-91   16:09:38        IBM PC         RPG II          Version 3.5  Page  1

           ....+....1....+....2....+....3....+....4....+....5....+....6....+....7....

     1 0001 H                                                                    SAMPLE2


     2 0002 FEMPLOYEEIP  F  51  51            DISK
     3 0003 FNAMELISTO   F 132 132            PRINTER


     4 0004 E                      NAME      33  1
     5 0005 E                      LAST      16  1
     6 0006 E                      FRST      14  1


     7 0007 IEMPLOYEEAA  01
     8 0008 I                                      19  34 LAST
     9 0009 I                                      35  48 FRST
    10 0010 I                                      51  51 INIT              16


    11 0011 C                      MOVEA*BLANKS  NAME
    12 0012 C*
    13 0013 C                      SETOF                    55
    14 0014 C*
    15 0015 C                      Z-ADD0    X        20
    16 0016 C                      Z-ADD0    Y        20
    17 0017 C                      Z-ADD0    Z        20
    18 0018 C*
    19 0019 C*       ----------------
    20 0020 C             FSTNAM   TAG                             MOVE FIRST NAME
    21 0021 C*       ----------------                              TO NAME ARRAY
    22 0022 C                      ADD  1    X                     X INDEXES
    23 0023 C          X           COMP 15                     51 INPUT FIRST
    24 0024 C  51                  GOTO INITL                     NAME
    25 0025 C*
    26 0026 C          FRST,X      COMP ' '                    50 Z INDEXES
    27 0027 C  50                  SETON                    55 NAME ARRAY
    28 0028 C  50                  GOTO FSTNAM                    FOR OUTPUT
    29 0029 C*
    30 0030 C  55                  ADD  1    Z
    31 0031 C  55                  SETOF                    55
    32 0032 C*
    33 0033 C                      ADD  1    Z
    34 0034 C                      MOVE FRST,X  NAME,Z
    35 0035 C                      GOTO FSTNAM
    36 0036 C*
    37 0037 C*       ----------------
    38 0038 C             INITL    TAG                             MOVE INITIAL,
    39 0039 C*       ----------------                              IF NOT BLANK
```

Figure 9-41 (1)

```
SAMPLE2   10-04-91  16:09:38        IBM PC        RPG II          Version 3.5  Page  2

         ....+....1....+....2....+....3....+....4....+....5....+....6....+....7....

40 0040 C  N16                 ADD  2         Z
41 0041 C  N16                 MOVE INIT      NAME,Z
42 0042 C*
43 0043 C*  ----------------
44 0044 C*     LAST NAME PROCESSING ROUTINE              MOVE LAST NAME
45 0045 C*  ----------------                             TO NAME ARRAY
46 0046 C                      ADD  1         Z
47 0047 C*
48 0048 C*  ----------------
49 0049 C     LAST     TAG
50 0050 C*  ----------------
51 0051 C                      ADD  1         Y          Y INDEXES
52 0052 C           Y          COMP 17                52 INPUT LAST
53 0053 C    52                GOTO OUT                   NAME
54 0054 C                      ADD  1         Z
55 0055 C                      MOVE LAST,Y    NAME,Z
56 0056 C                      GOTO LAST
57 0057 C*
58 0058 C*  ----------------
59 0059 C     OUT      TAG
60 0060 C*  ----------------
61 0061 C                      MOVEANAME      NAMOUT 33


62 0062 ONAMELISTD  2      01
63 0063 O                      NAMOUT      34
64 /*
65 /*


         THE FOLLOWING INDICATORS APPEARED IN THIS PROGRAM

              01  16  50  51  52  55
No Warning Errors
No Fatal Errors
```

Figure 9-41 (2)

▸ **Initialization**   Lines 11–17 set all the initial values needed in the routine. Line 11 uses a MOVEA operation to move the figurative constant *BLANKS into the NAME array, which holds the condensed name. Line 13 is a SETOF operation, which assures that indicator 55, used later in the routine, is off when the calculations begin. Lines 15, 16, and 17 set the three index fields X, Y, and Z to beginning values of zero. X is used to index the FRST array, Y the LAST array, and Z the NAME array. Figure 9-42 shows the contents of the arrays and indices after the initialization steps have been executed.

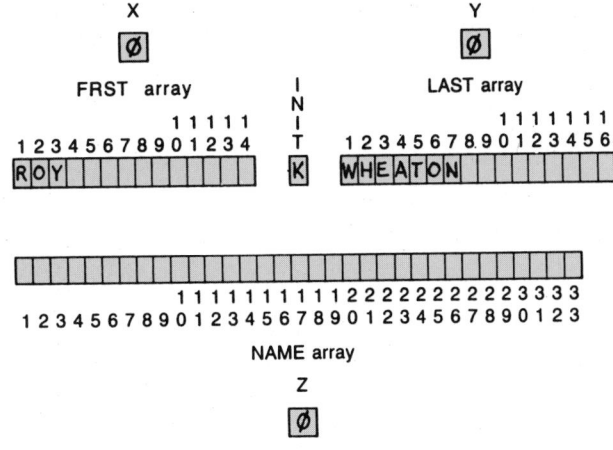

Figure 9-42   Name condensation

▶ **First Name Processing** The TAG, FSTNAM, marks the beginning of the portion of the routine that processes the first name array, FRST. Line 22 adds 1 to the index X, which is compared with 15 on line 23. Because the length of the FRST array is 14, first name processing terminates when the index reaches 15, which is 1 greater than the number of elements in the array. When the value in X reaches 15, indicator 51 is turned on by the COMP operation, and line 24 causes a branch to INITL, the portion of the routine that processes the middle initial. Figure 9-43 shows the contents of the arrays and indices after line 24 has been reached for the first time. Note that the index X now points to the first element of FRST.

Line 26 uses a COMP operation to determine if the element of FRST being tested contains a blank. Because lines 27–31 are performed only if the tested element is blank and if FRST,1 is not blank, let's proceed directly to line 33. Line 33 adds 1 to Z, the index for the NAME array. Line 34 then moves the contents of the FRST,X array element to the indexed element of the NAME array, as illustrated in Figure 9-44. After the element has been moved, the GOTO on line 35 causes a branch back to FSTNAM, and the routine is executed again. The FSTNAM routine continues to execute, moving one character at a time, until the COMP operation on line 26 determines that the FRST array contains a blank element.

When a blank is detected in an element of FRST, the COMP operation turns on indicator 50. Indicator 50 controls the turning on of indicator 55 on line 27 and, on line 28, the branch to FSTNAM. If all the remaining characters in FRST are blank, the loop consisting of lines 20–28 continues until all elements of FRST have been tested and X reaches a value of 15, at which point the program branches to INITL. Figure 9-45 shows the array contents and index settings when this point is reached in the example.

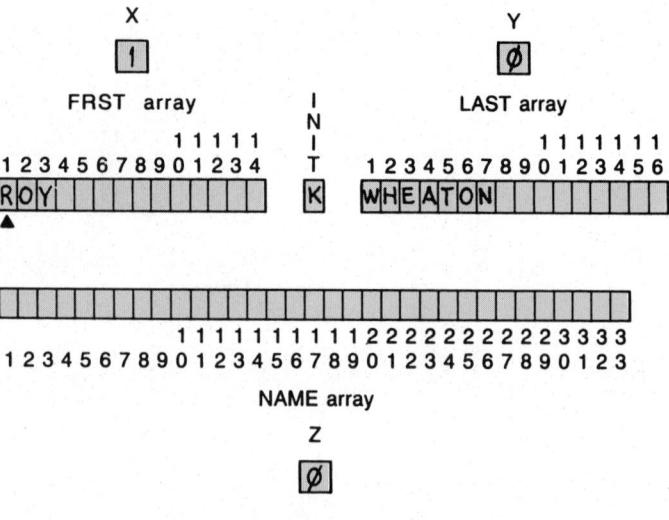

Figure 9-43 Name condensation

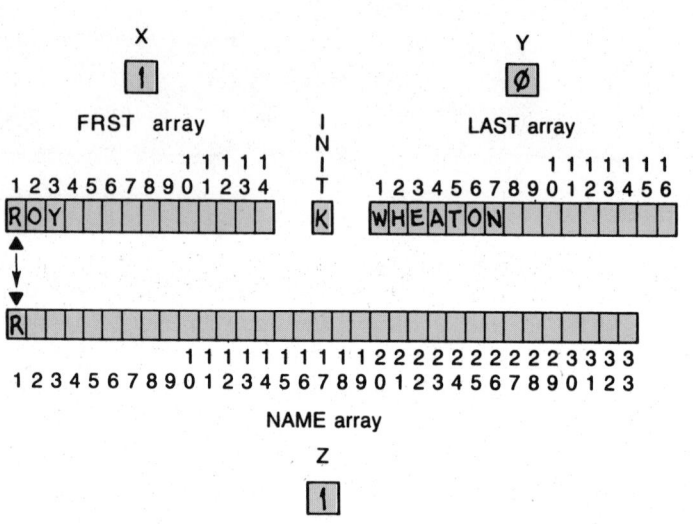

Figure 9-44 Name condensation

Lines 30 and 31 are executed only if the first name contains a blank followed by a letter or other nonblank character. This enables the routine to deal with names that contain the first initial followed by the full middle name, such as 'J Quincy Adams'. Because only one position has been allowed for the middle initial, the FRST array must contain both the first initial and the middle name in this circumstance. When this occurs, the blank after the initial J turns on indicator 50 on line 26 and indicator 55 on line 27, and then causes a branch to FSTNAM. The routine then increments X by 1 and continues processing. The COMP on line 26 detects the non-blank (the letter Q) that follows the blank, and so indicator 50 is not turned on. Because indicator 50 is not on, the GOTO on line 28 is not executed, and the program continues to line 30.

Because indicator 55 was turned on by the blank character, lines 30 and 31 are performed. Line 30 increments Z by 1, and then line 31 will SETOF indicator 55. Processing then continues to line 33, where Z is incremented and the first letter of the middle name is moved.

▸ **Middle Initial Processing**   After the FSTNAM routine is completed, processing proceeds to the INITL routine for processing the middle initial of the name. Note that the two operations in this routine are controlled by indicator N16, which indicates that the INIT field is not blank. If the field is blank, indicator 16 is on, and both the instructions in INITL are bypassed. Figure 9-46 shows the contents of the arrays and indices after the INITL routine has been completed for this example. After completion of the INITL routine, processing continues to the last name processing routine, which begins on line 46.

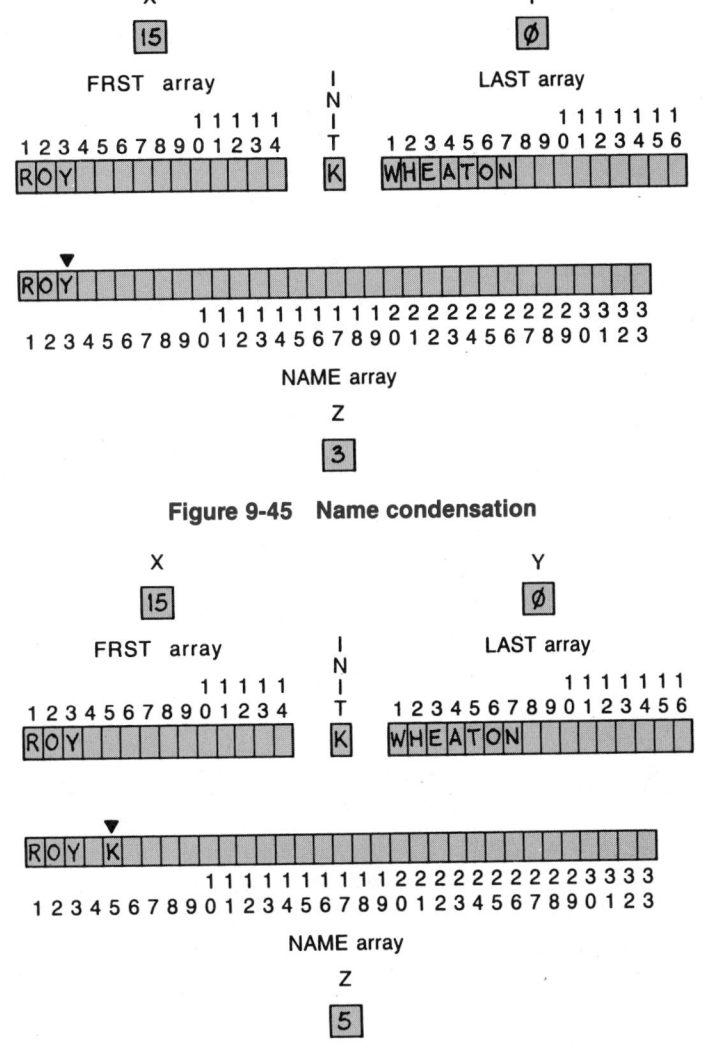

Figure 9-45   Name condensation

Figure 9-46   Name condensation

▸ **Last Name Processing**   The first operation of the last name routine occurs on line 46, where the index Z is incremented by 1. This leaves a blank between the initial and the last name. The remainder of the last name routine is similar to the processing that was done to the FRST array.

Line 51 increments the Y index by 1, initially setting it to the first position of the LAST array. On line 52, the program then compares Y with 17 to determine if the entire LAST array has been processed. If Y is equal to 17, indicator 52 is turned on, and on line 53 the program branches to OUT, ending the routine. If the GOTO on line 53 is not performed, the program adds 1 to Z and then on line 55 moves an element of LAST into an element on NAME. Figure 9-47 shows the contents of the arrays and indices after line 55 has been executed for the first time.

Line 56 then causes a branch to line 49, and the last name routine repeats. Lines 49–56 are repeated until all 16 positions of the LAST array have been moved into the NAME array, after which, as you saw earlier, the program exits the name condensation routine and branches to OUT. Figure 9-48 shows the contents of the arrays and indices after completion of the entire name condensation routine.

After the branch to OUT occurs, the program then uses a MOVEA (line 61) to move the contents of the NAME array into the NAMOUT field where it becomes available for further processing.

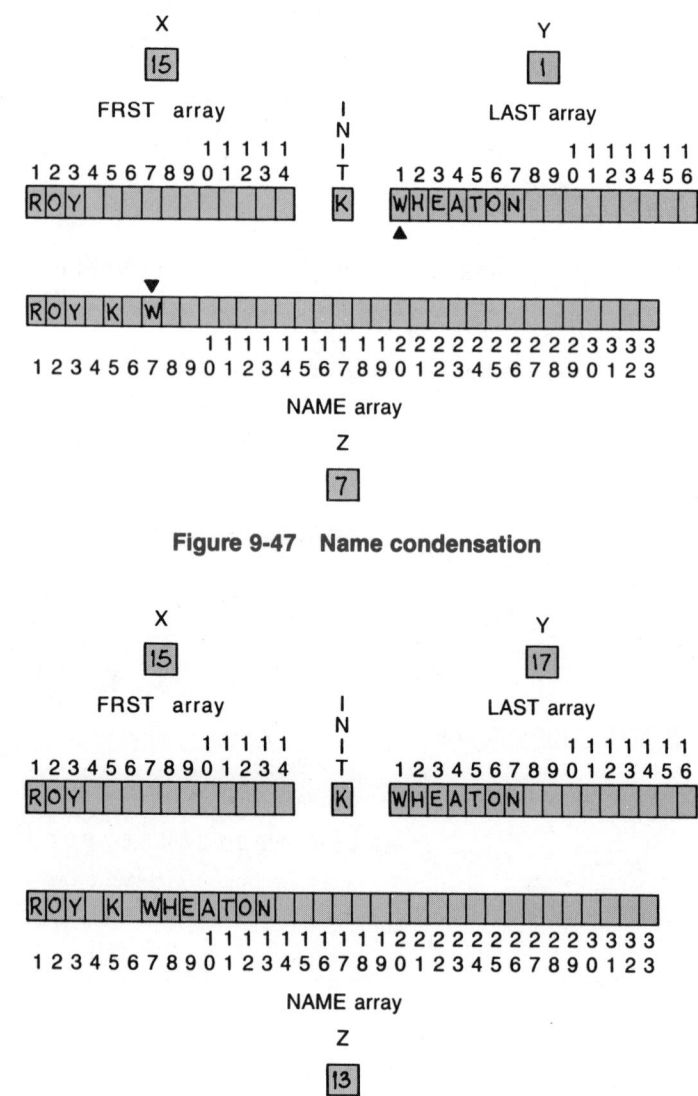

Figure 9-47 Name condensation

Figure 9-48 Name condensation

≡ IN CONCLUSION ≡

This chapter has added several powerful programming operations and techniques to your growing list of RPG tools. You can now control output based on the needs of the program rather than on the requirements of the RPG compiler by using the EXCPT operation; you can transfer data between arrays and data fields; and you can use looping operations to perform a series of instructions several times. Chapter 10 expands on these and other familiar techniques as you learn to load data into keyed sequence access path data files.

CHAPTER SUMMARY

1. The **EXCPT operation** performs output operations under programmer control rather than under control of the RPG fixed logic cycle.
2. A **loop** is a series of calculation operations that are executed repeatedly.
3. **Looping** is a technique, not an operation.
4. The six components of every loop are initialization, incrementation, processing, testing, branching, and termination.
5. The **initialization** component of a loop assigns a beginning value to the **control variable**, which is the field that controls the number of times the loop is performed.
6. The **incrementation** component of a loop alters the value in the control variable. This component can be either an addition or a subtraction operation.
7. The **processing** component of a loop performs the work for which the loop was designed.
8. The **testing** component of a loop determines if the loop has been performed the required number of times.
9. The **branching** component of a loop causes the loop to return to the beginning so that the loop will be performed again.
10. The **termination** component of a loop causes the loop to end. In RPG, as in most programming languages, the termination component takes place when the branching component is not executed, it is not a specific step.
11. Exception output records are identified by an E in position 15.
12. If an apostrophe is needed in an output constant, two consecutive apostrophes must be used in the constant.
13. The **MOVE operation** copies data from Factor 2 into the Result Field, one character at a time, starting with the rightmost position of both fields. The Factor 2 field is unchanged by the MOVE operation.
14. The **MOVEL operation** copies data from Factor 2 into the result field, one character at a time, starting with the leftmost position of both fields. The Factor 2 field is unchanged by the MOVE operation.
15. Although most newer versions of RPG permit type E output lines to appear anywhere in the output specifications, older versions of RPG require that all type E output lines appear at the end of the output specifications.
16. The **MOVEA operation** permits data to be moved between a data field and an array or between two arrays. The MOVEA operation does not recognize element boundaries within the array or arrays used.
17. A **figurative constant** is a reserved field name that represents a string of characters. The four common figurative constants are *ZERO, *ZEROS, *BLANK, and *BLANKS. Some newer versions of RPG also support the figurative constant *ALL.
18. The Resulting Indicators area (positions 54–59) of the Calculation Specifications form can be used to test the contents of the Result Field in an arithmetic operation. Resulting indicators can be set to specify whether the result is positive, negative, or zero.

REVIEW QUESTIONS

1. Name and briefly explain the function of each of the six components of a loop.
2. What is a control variable? What is its importance in the control of a loop?
3. What is the purpose of the EXCPT operation?
4. When the EXCPT operation is executed, what type of output lines are printed?
5. What special coding must be used to insert an apostrophe into an output constant?
6. Why is it necessary to use fetch overflow when all printed output, other than headings, is controlled by the EXCPT operation?
7. What is the main difference between the execution of the MOVE and the MOVEL operations?
8. Why can MOVE and MOVEL not be used to transfer data between a data field and an array?
9. What effect do the MOVE, MOVEL, and MOVEA operations have on the Factor 2 data field or array?
10. What is a figurative constant? Name the five figurative constants.

STUDENT EXERCISES: RPG PROGRAM CODE

1. Code the entries on the given Calculation and Output Specifications forms to produce 100 return address labels for Waldo's Widget Works. The format of the return address labels is shown in Figure 9-49.

Figure 9-49   Return address label coding exercise

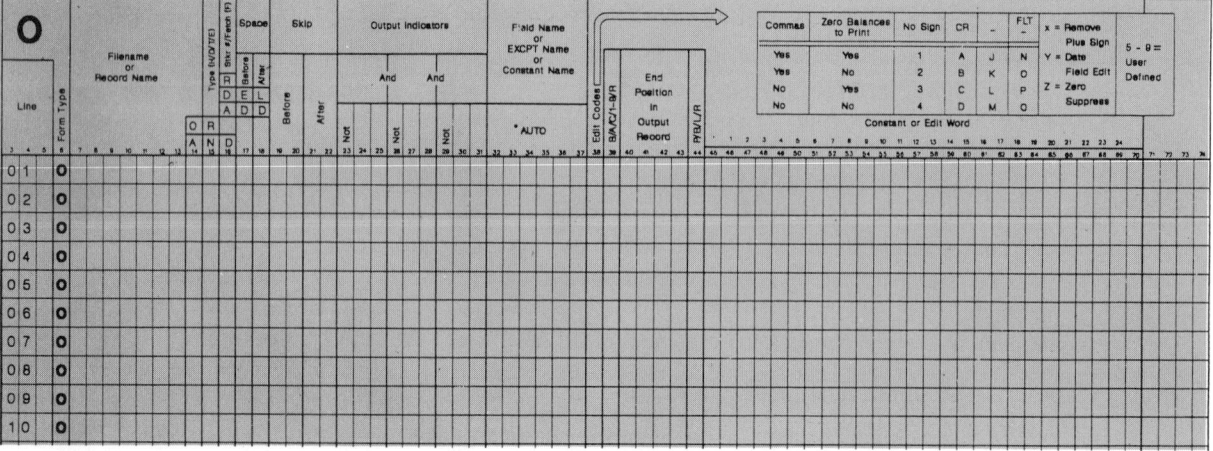

Figure 9-49 (1)

Figure 9-49 (2)

2. Using the given Calculation Specifications form, code the program segment shown in the following flowchart (Figure 9-50). Use appropriate names for all fields. How many times will the TEST subroutine be executed?

Figure 9-50 Flowchart coding exercise

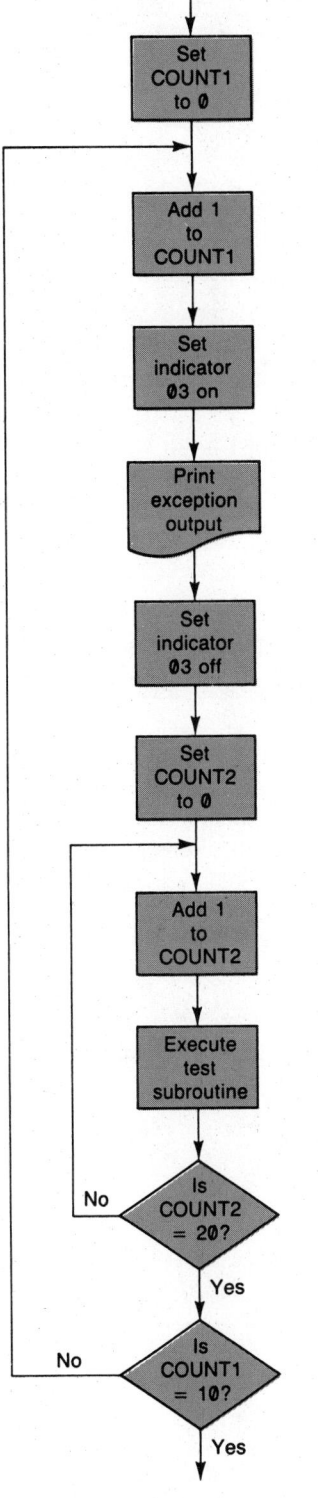

Figure 9-50 (1)

continued

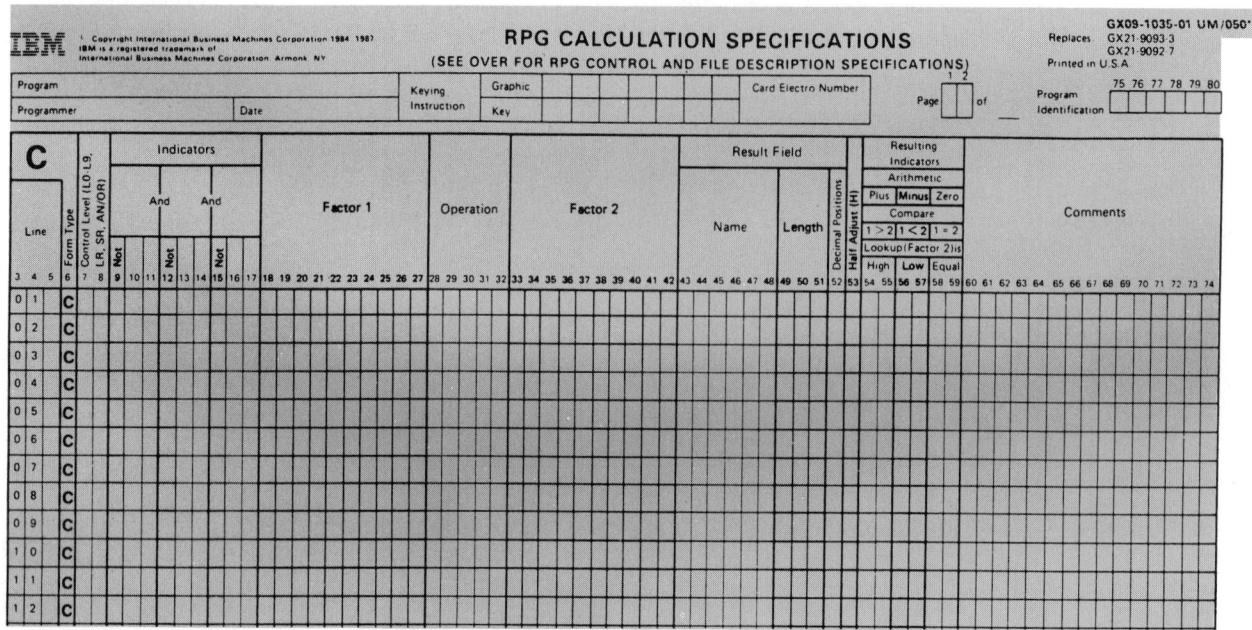

Figure 9-50 (2)

STUDENT EXERCISES: DEBUGGING RPG PROGRAMS

Problem 1

The following listing (Figure 9-51) contains one or more errors detected while testing program HJG09X. Circle each error in program code and record the corrected error on the listing. Explain the error and the method of correction.

Figure 9-51   Debugging Problem 1

```
  )   HJG09X    10-07-91  17:12:40  HJG09X - SHIPPING LABELS -           Version 3.5  Page  1      )

  )            ....+....1....+....2....+....3....+....4....+....5....+....6....+....7....                )

             3 0002 H

  )

  )           4 0003 F*------------------------------------------------------------------*            )
             5 0004 F*  HJG09X - SHIPPING LABELS - HAL GOODWIN - SEPTEMBER 20, 1991    *
             6 0005 F*                                                                  *
  )           7 0006 F*  PROGRAM HJG09X WILL PRINT A VARIABLE NUMBER OF SHIPPING LABELS  *            )
             8 0007 F*  FOR EACH INPUT RECORD READ.  THE NUMBER OF LABELS PRINTED WILL  *
             9 0008 F*  BE BASED ON THE CONTENTS OF THE 'NOPACK' FIELD LOCATED IN       *
  )          10 0009 F*  POSITIONS 121-122 OF THE INPUT RECORD.                         *            )
            11 0010 F*------------------------------------------------------------------*

  )          14 0012 FSHIPDATAIP  F 740 185            DISK                                           )
            15 0013 FLABELS   O   F 132 132            PRINTER

  )

  )          16 0014 I*  SHIPPING LABEL DATA RECORDS                                                  )
            17 0015 I*-------------------------------
  )          18 0016 ISHIPDATAAA  01                                                                  )
            19 0017 I                                    6   30 CUSTNA
            20 0018 I                                   31   55 ADDR1
```

Figure 9-51 (1)

```
HJG09X    10-07-91  17:12:40  HJG09X - SHIPPING LABELS -          Version 3.5  Page  2

          ....+....1....+....2....+....3....+....4....+....5....+....6....+....7....

       21 0019 I                                    56  80 ADDR2
       22 0020 I                                    81 105 ADDR3
       23 0021 I                                   106 110 ZIP
       24 0022 I                                   111 114 ZPLUS4          41
       25 0023 I                                   115 120 PURORD
       26 0024 I                                   121 1220NOPACK


       27 0025 C    01              Z-ADD0      COUNT   20      INITIALIZATION
       28 0026 C*
       29 0027 C         LOOP       TAG
       30 0028 C*
       31 0029 C    01              EXCPT               PROCESSING
       32 0030 C    01   COUNT      ADD  1      COUNT           INCREMENTATION
       33 0031 C*
       34 0032 C    01   COUNT      COMP NOPACK             42  TESTING
       35 0033 C*
       36 0034 C    01 42           GOTO LOOP               BRANCHING
       37 0035 C*
       38 0036 C*  IF BRANCH IS NOT PERFORMED, THE LOOP IS TERMINATED.


       39 0037 O*  RETURN ADDRESS LINES
       40 0038 O*---------------------
       41 0039 OLABELS  E 31
       42 0040 O                            32 'WALDO''S WIDGET WORKS'
       43 0041 O       E 1
       44 0042 O                            34 'BOX 206  FARNSWORTH ROAD'
       45 0043 O       E 3
       46 0044 O                            34 'TEMPLETON, MA 01468-0206'


       49 0046 O*  SHIP TO LINES
       50 0047 O*---------------
       51 0048 O       E 1
       52 0049 O                            19 'SHIP TO--'
       53 0050 O       E 1
       54 0051 O              CUSTNA        35
       55 0052 O       E 1
       56 0053 O              ADDR1         35
       57 0054 O       E 1
       58 0055 O              ADDR2         35
       59 0056 O       E 1
       60 0057 O              ADDR3         35
       61 0058 O       E 2
       62 0059 O              ZIP           30
       63 0060 O          N41               31 '-'
       64 0061 O          N41 ZPLUS4        35
       65 0062 O       E 1
       66 0063 O                            25 'PURCHASE ORDER-'
       67 0064 O              PURORD        32
       68 0065 O       E 3
       69 0066 O                            19 'BOX     OF'
       70 0067 O              COUNT Z       16
       71 0068 O              NOPACKZ       22
       72 /*
       73 /*


          THE FOLLOWING INDICATORS APPEARED IN THIS PROGRAM

              01  41  42
No Warning Errors
No Fatal Errors
```

Figure 9-51 (2)   *continued*

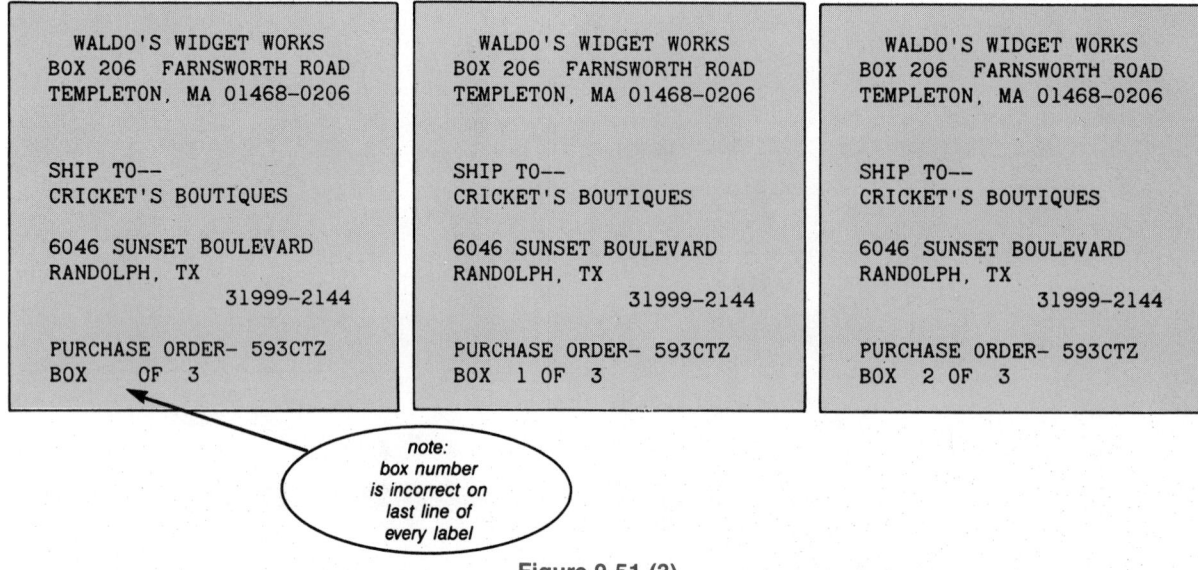

Figure 9-51 (3)

Problem 2

The following listing (Figure 9-52) contains one or more errors detected while testing program HJG09X. Circle each error in program code and record the corrected error on the listing. Explain the error and the method of correction.

Figure 9-52 Debugging Problem 2

```
HJG09X    10-07-91  17:17:30  HJG09X - SHIPPING LABELS -              Version 3.5  Page  1

          ....+....1....+....2....+....3....+....4....+....5....+....6....+....7....

       3 0002 H


       4 0003 F*---------------------------------------------------------------*
       5 0004 F*  HJG09X - SHIPPING LABELS - HAL GOODWIN - SEPTEMBER 20, 1991   *
       6 0005 F*                                                                *
       7 0006 F*  PROGRAM HJG09X WILL PRINT A VARIABLE NUMBER OF SHIPPING LABELS *
       8 0007 F*  FOR EACH INPUT RECORD READ.  THE NUMBER OF LABELS PRINTED WILL *
       9 0008 F*  BE BASED ON THE CONTENTS OF THE 'NOPACK' FIELD LOCATED IN      *
      10 0009 F*  POSITIONS 121-122 OF THE INPUT RECORD.                         *
      11 0010 F*---------------------------------------------------------------*


      14 0012 FSHIPDATAIP  F 740 185          DISK
      15 0013 FLABELS   O  F 132 132          PRINTER


      16 0014 I*  SHIPPING LABEL DATA RECORDS
      17 0015 I*-----------------------------
      18 0016 ISHIPDATAAA  01
      19 0017 I                            6   30 CUSTNA
      20 0018 I                           31   55 ADDR1
      21 0019 I                           56   80 ADDR2
      22 0020 I                           81  105 ADDR3
      23 0021 I                          106  110 ZIP
```

Figure 9-52 (1)

```
HJG09X    10-07-91  17:17:30  HJG09X - SHIPPING LABELS -          Version 3.5  Page  2

          ....+....1....+....2....+....3....+....4....+....5....+....6....+....7....

   24 0022 I                                    111 114 ZPLUS4         41
   25 0023 I                                    115 120 PURORD
   26 0024 I                                    121 1220NOPACK


   27 0025 C    01              Z-ADD1      COUNT    20       INITIALIZATION
   28 0026 C*
   29 0027 C          LOOP      TAG
   30 0028 C    01    COUNT     ADD 1       COUNT             INCREMENTATION
   31 0029 C*
   32 0030 C    01              EXCPT                         PROCESSING
   33 0031 C*
   34 0032 C    01    COUNT     COMP NOPACK           42      TESTING
   35 0033 C*
   36 0034 C    01 42           GOTO LOOP                     BRANCHING
   37 0035 C*
   38 0036 C*  IF BRANCH IS NOT PERFORMED, THE LOOP IS TERMINATED.


   39 0037 O*  RETURN ADDRESS LINES
   40 0038 O*----------------------
   41 0039 OLABELS  E 31
   42 0040 O                            32 'WALDO''S WIDGET WORKS'
   43 0041 O       E 1
   44 0042 O                            34 'BOX 206  FARNSWORTH ROAD'
   45 0043 O       E 3
   46 0044 O                            34 'TEMPLETON, MA 01468-0206'


   49 0046 O*  SHIP TO LINES
   50 0047 O*---------------
   51 0048 O       E 1
   52 0049 O                            19 'SHIP TO--'
   53 0050 O       E 1
   54 0051 O              CUSTNA        35
   55 0052 O       E 1
   56 0053 O              ADDR1         35
   57 0054 O       E 1
   58 0055 O              ADDR2         35
   59 0056 O       E 1
   60 0057 O              ADDR3         35
   61 0058 O       E 2
   62 0059 O              ZIP           30
   63 0060 O         N41                31 '-'
   64 0061 O         N41  ZPLUS4        35
   65 0062 O       E 1
   66 0063 O                            25 'PURCHASE ORDER-'
   67 0064 O              PURORD        32
   68 0065 O       E 3
   69 0066 O                            19 'BOX    OF'
   70 0067 O              COUNT Z       16
   71 0068 O              NOPACKZ       22
   72 /*
   73 /*


          THE FOLLOWING INDICATORS APPEARED IN THIS PROGRAM

          01  41  42
No Warning Errors
No Fatal Errors
```

Figure 9-52 (2)

continued

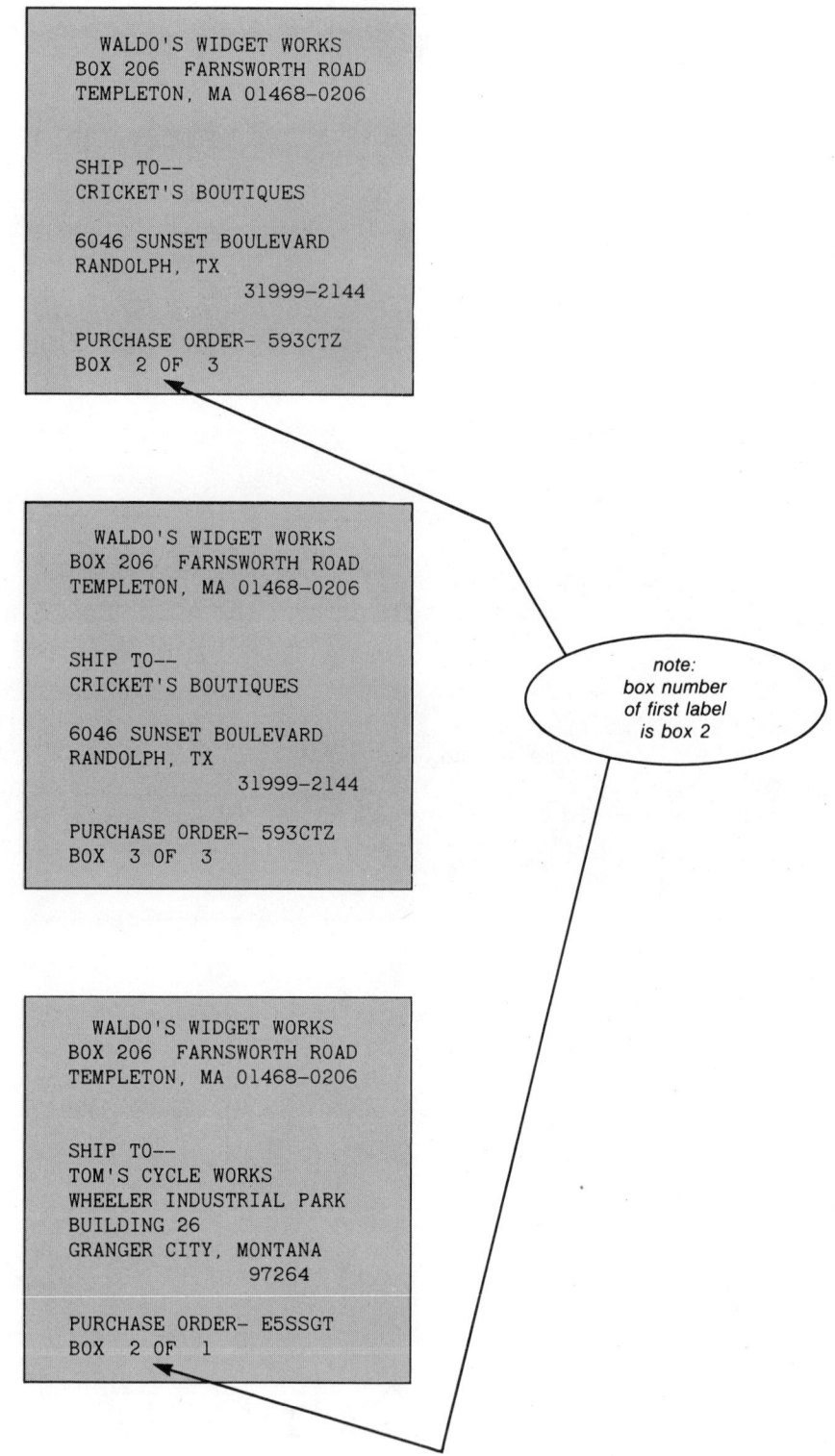

Figure 9-52 (3)

STUDENT EXERCISES: RPG PROGRAM MAINTENANCE

Problem 1

The code used in program HJG09X (Figure 9-53) is based on the assumption that the input data records have been verified and contain valid data. If the Number of Packages field (NOPACK) contains a value of zero in any input record, the program will print 100 labels, ending the loop only when the Count field contains a value of 00. Modify program HJG09X to eliminate the need to verify the contents of the NOPACK field and print only 1 label if the value in NOPACK is zero. Explain your modifications and their effect on the program.

Figure 9-53 Compile listing for program HJG09X

```
HJG09X    09-12-91  19:51:10  HJG09X - SHIPPING LABELS -          Version 3.5  Page  1

          ....+....1....+....2....+....3....+....4....+....5....+....6....+....7....

     3 0002 H                                                              HJG09X


     4 0003 F*------------------------------------------------------------------*
     5 0004 F*  HJG09X - SHIPPING LABELS - HAL GOODWIN - SEPTEMBER 20, 1991    *
     6 0005 F*                                                                 *
     7 0006 F*  PROGRAM HJG09X WILL PRINT A VARIABLE NUMBER OF SHIPPING LABELS *
     8 0007 F*  FOR EACH INPUT RECORD READ.  THE NUMBER OF LABELS PRINTED WILL *
     9 0008 F*  BE BASED ON THE CONTENTS OF THE 'NOPACK' FIELD LOCATED IN      *
    10 0009 F*  POSITIONS 121-122 OF THE INPUT RECORD.                         *
    11 0010 F*------------------------------------------------------------------*

    14 0012 FSHIPDATAIP  F 740 185          DISK
    15 0013 FLABELS   O    F 132 132          PRINTER


    16 0014 I*  SHIPPING LABEL DATA RECORDS
    17 0015 I*---------------------------------
    18 0016 ISHIPDATAAA  01
    19 0017 I                                     6   30 CUSTNA
    20 0018 I                                    31   55 ADDR1
    21 0019 I                                    56   80 ADDR2
    22 0020 I                                    81  105 ADDR3
    23 0021 I                                   106  110 ZIP
    24 0022 I                                   111  114 ZPLUS4          41
    25 0023 I                                   115  120 PURORD
    26 0024 I                                   121  1220NOPACK


    27 0025 C     01                Z-ADD0     COUNT   20    INITIALIZATION
    28 0026 C*
    29 0027 C            LOOP       TAG
    30 0028 C     01     COUNT      ADD  1     COUNT         INCREMENTATION
    31 0029 C*
    32 0030 C     01                EXCPT                    PROCESSING
    33 0031 C*
    34 0032 C     01     COUNT      COMP NOPACK         42   TESTING
    35 0033 C*
    36 0034 C     01 42             GOTO LOOP                BRANCHING
    37 0035 C*
    38 0036 C*  IF BRANCH IS NOT PERFORMED, THE LOOP IS TERMINATED.


    39 0037 O*  RETURN ADDRESS LINES
    40 0038 O*---------------------
    41 0039 OLABELS  E 31
    42 0040 O                              32 'WALDO''S WIDGET WORKS'
    43 0041 O         E  1
```

Figure 9-53 (1)

continued

```
HJG09X    09-12-91  19:51:10  HJG09X - SHIPPING LABELS -          Version 3.5  Page  2

          ....+....1....+....2....+....3....+....4....+....5....+....6....+....7....

    44 0042 O                                      34 'BOX 206  FARNSWORTH ROAD'
    45 0043 O          E 3
    46 0044 O                                      34 'TEMPLETON, MA 01468-0206'


    49 0046 O*  SHIP TO LINES
    50 0047 O*----------------
    51 0048 O          E 1
    52 0049 O                                      19 'SHIP TO--'
    53 0050 O          E 1
    54 0051 O                         CUSTNA        35
    55 0052 O          E 1
    56 0053 O                         ADDR1         35
    57 0054 O          E 1
    58 0055 O                         ADDR2         35
    59 0056 O          E 1
    60 0057 O                         ADDR3         35
    61 0058 O          E 2
    62 0059 O                         ZIP           30
    63 0060 O                  N41                  31 '-'
    64 0061 O                  N41    ZPLUS4        35
    65 0062 O          E 1
    66 0063 O                                      25 'PURCHASE ORDER-'
    67 0064 O                         PURORD        32
    68 0065 O          E 3
    69 0066 O                                      19 'BOX     OF'
    70 0067 O                         COUNT Z       16
    71 0068 O                         NOPACKZ       22
    72 /*
    73 /*



          THE FOLLOWING INDICATORS APPEARED IN THIS PROGRAM

              01  41  42
    No Warning Errors
    No Fatal Errors
```

Figure 9-53 (2)

▤ Problem 2

When program HJG09Y was written, company accounting policy determined that no loans would be granted during the last five days of any month. Because of this, the program does not take the number of days in a month into consideration when modifying the date that each payment is due. Recent changes in the accounting department have made it possible for a loan to be granted on any day of the month. This change in policy has made it possible for incorrect payment due dates to appear on an output report. For example, if a loan is granted on January 31, the first payment would be due on February 31, a nonexistent date. The third payment would be due on April 31, which is also nonexistent.

Modify program HJG09Y (Figure 9-54) so that these nonexistent due dates cannot appear. If a payment is due on a date that does not occur in a month, change the day to the last day of the month. All months in which the payment due date is valid will show the original due date. For example, if a loan is granted on August 31, the first payment due date will be September 30, the second payment October 31, the third payment November 30, and so on. Use a compile-time table to determine the last date of a month and table lookup to retrieve the last date for comparison purposes. Assume that February always contains 28 days. Do not attempt to program for leap years.

Figure 9-54   Compile listing for program HJG09Y

```
HJG09Y -- PAYMENT SCHEDULE REPORT
5714KG1 RPG  R08M00  861114      HJG09Y.TEST      10/07/91  17:46:03  PAGE   2

SEQUENCE      1         2         3         4         5         6         7     IND   DO   LAST      PAGE   PROGRAM
NUMBER    67890123456789012345678901234567890123456789012345678901234567890123  USE   NUM  UPDATE    LINE   ID


    200  F*-----------------------------------------------------------------*
    300  F*  HJG09Y - PAYMENT SCHEDULE REPORT - MAL GOODWIN - 9-18-91        *
    400  F*  PROGRAM HJG09Y CREATES A PAYMENT SCHEDULE REPORT FOR CUSTOMERS  *
    500  F*  MAKING MONTHLY PAYMENTS.  THE INPUT RECORDS CONTAIN THE CUSTOMER*
    600  F*  NUMBER AND NAME, BEGINNING PAYMENT DATE, TOTAL AMOUNT OWED, AND *
    700  F*  THE NUMBER OF PAYMENTS TO BE MADE.  THE PROGRAM DIVIDES THE     *
    800  F*  AMOUNT OWED BY THE NUMBER OF PAYMENTS TO DETERMINE THE AMOUNT OF*
    900  F*  EACH PAYMENT.  THE PROGRAM THEN LISTS THE PAYMENT AMOUNTS AND   *
   1000  F*  THE DATE EACH PAYMENT IS DUE.  THE DUE DATE IS CALCULATED BY    *
   1100  F*  ADDING 1 TO THE MONTH FIELD FOR EACH PAYMENT.  WHEN THE MONTH   *
   1200  F*  FIELD REACHES 13, THE MONTH IS RESET TO 1 AND THE YEAR IS       *
   1300  F*  INCREMENTED BY 1.                                               *
   1400  F*-----------------------------------------------------------------*




              H
   1600  FPMNTRECDIP F    60          DISK

   1800  FPMNTREPTO  F   132    OF    PRINTER


   2000  F* ID F C  M  L   FUNCTION OF INDICATORS
   2100  F* 01--------------RECORD IDENTIFICATION - PAYMENT RECORD
   2200  F*      40-----------MONTH GREATER THAN 12
   2300  F*      41-----------NUMBER OF PAYMENTS REMAINING EQUAL TO ONE
   2400  F*      42-----------NUMBER OF PAYMENTS REMAINING EXCEEDS ONE
   2500  F*      55-----------OVERFLOW CONTROL SWITCH
   2600  F*                L1---CONTROL BREAK ON CUSTOMER NUMBER CHANGE
   2700  F*                LR---END OF JOB
   2800  F*                OF---OVERFLOW INDICATOR
   2900  F*                1P---FIRST PAGE INDICATOR


   3000  I* PAYMENT RECORDS
   3100  I*-----------------
   3200  IPMNTRECDAA  01
   3300  I                                      1   50CUSTNOL1
   3400  I                                      6   30 CUSTNM
   3500  I                                     31   360DATE
   3600  I                                     37   330PMTS
   3700  I                                     39   452AMT
   3800  I                                     31   320MONTH
   3900  I                                     35   360YEAR


   4000  C* CALCULATE MONTHLY PAYMENT AMOUNT
   4100  C*-------------------------------
   4200  C   01      AMT       DIV PMTS      PAYMNT Y2
   4300  C   01                MVR           LASTPM 22

   4500  C* MAIN PROCESSING LOOP
   4600  C*-------------------
   4700  C           LOOP      TAG
   4800  C   01                EXCPT                          PRINT LINE
   4900  C   01 55             SETOF              550F HEADING   1 2
   5000  C   01 OF             SETON              55   INDICATOR  1
   5100  C   01                SETOF              L1   CONTROL    1

   5300  C*        INCREMENT AND TEST DATE FIELD
   5400  C*        -----------------------------
   5500  C   01                ADD  1        MONTH
   5600  C   01      MONTH     COMP 13                  40              3
   5700  C   01 40             SUB  12       MONTH
   5800  C   01 40             ADD  1        YEAR
   5900  C   01                MOVELMONTH    DATE
   6000  C   01                MOVE YEAR     DATE


   6200  C   01                SUB  1        PMTS          DECREMENT

   6400  C   01      PMTS      COMP 1                  42 41TEST        1 3

   6600  C   01 41             ADD  LASTPM   PAYMNT        FINAL PAYMENT

   6800  C   01 41
   6900  C0R 01 42             GOTO LOOP                   BRANCH

   7100  C* AFTER LOOP TERMINATES, ADD AMOUNT TO FINAL TOTAL
   7200  C*------------------------------------------------
   7300  C   01                ADD  AMT      TOTAMT 82


   7400  O* HEADING LINE ONE
   7500  O*-----------------
   7600  OPMNTREPTH 206   1P
   7700  O          OR    OF
   7800  O                              UDATE Y   8
   7900  O                                     41 *PAYMENT SCHEDULE REPORT*
   8000  O                                     55 *PAGE*
   8100  O                              PAGE   60

   8300  O* HEADING LINE TWO
   8400  O*-----------------
   8500  O          H  1   1P
   8600  O          OR    OF
   8700  O                                     26 *CUSTOMER      CUSTOMER*
   8800  O                                     60 *DUE      PAYMENT*

   9000  O* HEADING LINE THREE
   9100  O*-------------------
   9200  O          H  2   1P
   9300  O          OR    OF
   9400  O                                     24 *NUMBER         NAME*
   9500  O                                     60 *DATE      AMOUNT*
```

Figure 9-54 (1)

continued

```
HJG09Y -- PAYMENT SCHEDULE REPORT
5714RG1 RPG R08M00  861114      HJG09Y.TEST      10/07/91  17:46:03  PAGE    3

SEQUENCE      1         2         3         4         5         6         7    IND  DO  LAST      PAGE  PROGRAM
NUMBER     67890123456789012345678901234567890123456789012345678901234  USE  NUM  UPDATE    LINE  ID

   9700  O* DETAIL LINE PRINTED AFTER LOOP TERMINATES
   9800  O*-----------------------------------------
   9900  O       D 13      01
  10000  O                            49 'TOTAL PAYMENTS'
  10100  O                 AMT  1     60 '$'

  10300  O* FINAL TOTAL
  10400  O*------------
  10500  O       T 00      LR
  10600  O                            48 'FINAL TOTAL'
  10700  O                 TOTAMT1    60 '$'

  10900  O* EXCEPTION OUTPUT CONTROLLED BY LOOP
  11000  O*-----------------------------------------
  11100  O       EF 1
  11200  O            L1  CUSTNOZ     7
  11300  O            L1  CUSTNM     35
  11400  O            OF  CUSTNOZ     7
  11500  O            OF  CUSTNM     35
  11600  O                DATE  Y    47
  11700  O                PAYMNT1    60
* * * * * E N D  O F  S O U R C E * * * *
```

```
MESSAGE SUMMARY

TOTAL    00    10    20    30    40    50
  1       1     0     0     0     0     0

117 RECORDS READ FROM SOURCE FILE
SOURCE RECORDS INCLUDE   56 SPECIFICATIONS,   0 TABLE RECORDS, AND   45 COMMENTS
PRM HAS BEEN CALLED
QRG0003 PROGRAM HJG09Y PLACED IN LIB TEST    00 HIGHEST SEVERITY FOUND

* * * * * E N D  O F  C O M P I L A T I O N * * * * *
```

Figure 9-54 (2)

```
10/07/91           PAYMENT SCHEDULE REPORT           PAGE    1

   CUSTOMER          CUSTOMER               DUE        PAYMENT
   NUMBER            NAME                   DATE       AMOUNT

    1845   MARTHA K. THALER              8/27/91        400.00
                                         9/27/91        400.00
                                        10/27/91        400.00
                                        11/27/91        400.00
                                        12/27/91        400.00
                                         1/27/92        400.00
                                         2/27/92        400.00
                                         3/27/92        400.00
                                         4/27/92        400.00
                                         5/27/92        400.00

                                   TOTAL PAYMENTS   $4,000.00


    2780   BARBARA E. POHJA              9/17/91        302.08
                                        10/17/91        302.08
                                        11/17/91        302.08
                                        12/17/91        302.08
                                         1/17/92        302.08
                                         2/17/92        302.08
                                         3/17/92        302.08
                                         4/17/92        302.08
                                         5/17/92        302.08
                                         6/17/92        302.08
                                         7/17/92        302.08
                                         8/17/92        302.12

                                   TOTAL PAYMENTS   $3,625.00


                                      FINAL TOTAL   $7,625.00
```

Figure 9-54 (3)

STUDENT EXERCISES: PROGRAMMING IN RPG

PROGRAMMING ASSIGNMENT 1
INSPECTION LOG SHEETS

INSTRUCTIONS

Plan, code, enter, and test an RPG program to produce Inspection Log sheets.

INPUT

The format of the Extinguisher File Record is shown in Figure 9-55. Use test data set 19 for this problem.

EXTING FILE RECORD						
Record Length 15			Key Location 2–8 (EXTNO)			
Field No.	Field Name	Field Description	Field Position	Field Length	Dec. Pos.	Data Class
1	EXTNO	Extinguisher No.	2–8	7		A
2		UNUSED AREA	9–15			

Figure 9-55   Extinguisher File Record

OUTPUT

Output is a series of Inspection Log sheets, the format or which is shown in Figure 9-56.

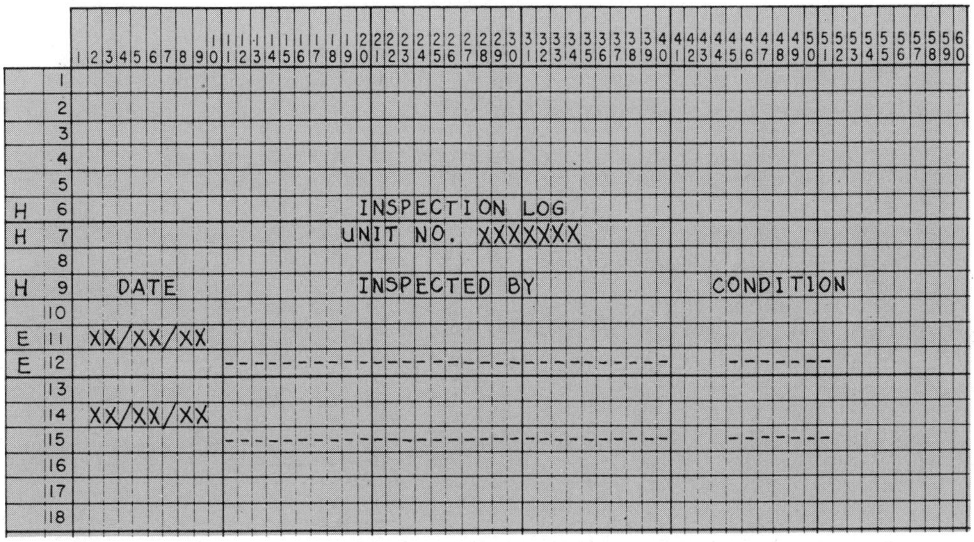

Figure 9-56   Inspection Log layout

Processing Requirements

For each input record read, the program prints a separate Inspection Log sheet. The extinguisher number prints as part of the second heading line of the sheet. The remainder of the Inspection Log sheet contains a series of exception output lines. Each set of output lines contains an inspection date and lines for the signature of the person conducting the inspection and for the condition of the extinguisher. The inspection dates are monthly dates for the 12-month period beginning on the first of next month.

PROGRAMMING ASSIGNMENT 2
DEPRECIATION SCHEDULE

INSTRUCTIONS

Plan, code, enter, and test an RPG program to produce the Depreciation Schedule.

INPUT

The format of the Depreciation Record is shown in Figure 9-57. Use test data set 22 for this problem.

DEPRECIATION RECORD						
Record Length 38						
Field No.	Field Name	Field Description	Field Position	Field Length	Dec. Pos.	Data Class
1	ITEM	Item Number	1–5	5		A
2	DESCR	Item Description	6–20	15		A
3	DATACQ	Date Acquired	21–26	6	0	N
4	COST	Original Cost	27–36	10		A
5	ESTLIF	Estimated Life	37–38	2	0	N

Figure 9-57   Depreciation Record

OUTPUT

Output is the Depreciation Schedule, the format of which is shown in Figure 9-58.

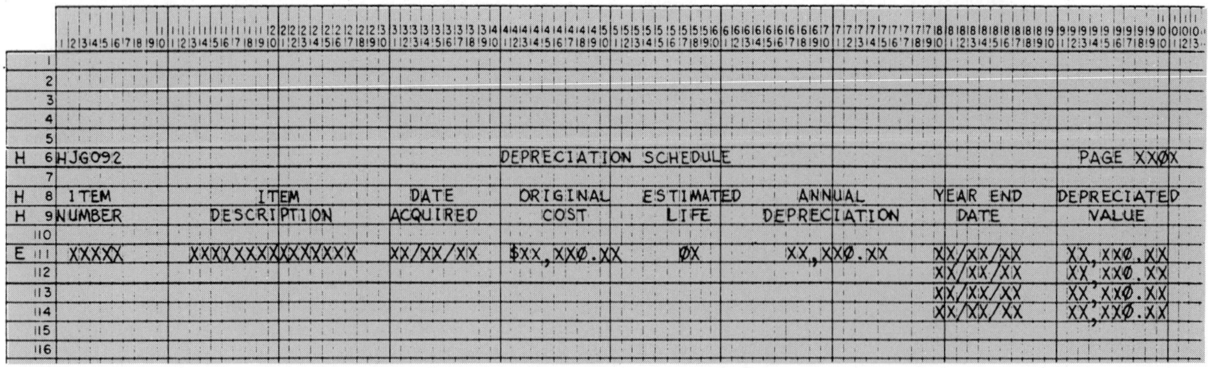

Figure 9-58   Depreciation Schedule layout

▤ Processing Requirements

In addition to the input fields, the program requires an annual depreciation amount. This amount is calculated by dividing the Original Cost field by the Estimated Life field, which contains the number of years the item is expected to last. The Original Cost field, however, is an edited numeric field. The editing characters in the field must be removed before the data can be used in an arithmetic operation.

The report also contains the depreciated value of the item at the end of each year for the life of the item. The first year-end date is one year after the date on which the item was acquired, the second year-end date is two years after acquisition, and so on. All items are to be depreciated to a value of zero. Any remainder from dividing cost by life is the final year's depreciated value.

▤ PROGRAMMING ASSIGNMENT 3 PASSENGER MANIFEST

INSTRUCTIONS

Plan, Code, Enter, and test an RPG program to produce the Passenger Manifest.

INPUT

The format of the Flight Departure File is shown in Figure 9-59. Use test data set 10 for this problem.

FLIGHT DEPARTURE FILE						
Record Length 23						
Field No.	Field Name	Field Description	Field Position	Field Length	Dec. Pos.	Data Class
1	GATE	Departure Gate	1–3	3		A
2	FLIGHT	Flight Number	4–7	4		A
3		UNUSED AREA	8–16	9		
4	DEPTIM	Flight Departure Time	17–20	4	0	N
5	NOPASS	Number of Passengers	21–23	3	0	N

Figure 9-59   Flight Departure File

OUTPUT

Output is the Passenger Manifest, the format of which is shown in Figure 9-60 on the next page. Note that the manifest for each flight must begin on a new page. The program prints headings only on the first page of a manifest.

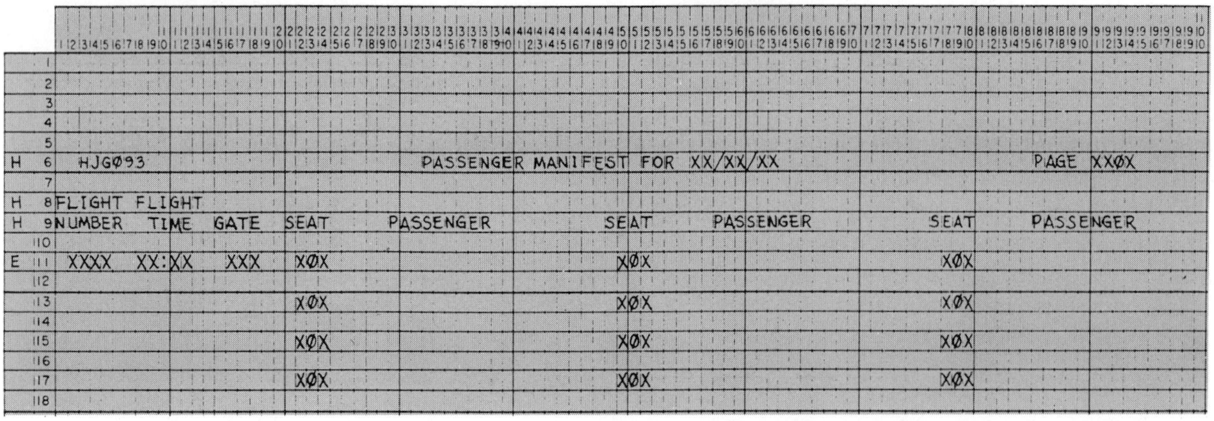

Figure 9-60 Passenger Manifest

Processing Instructions

The Passenger Manifest for each flight will group indicate the flight number, flight time, and departure gate for each flight. In addition, the manifest will contain a listing of all seat numbers available on the flight. The seats are numbered consecutively, beginning with 1. Seat numbers are to be printed in three columns:

1	5	9
2	6	10
3	7	11
4	8	12

Note the arrangement of seat numbers in the columns. The lowest numbered seats are in the first column, and the highest numbered seats in the last column.

PROGRAMMING ASSIGNMENT 4 SALES REPORT

INSTRUCTIONS

Plan, code, enter, and test an RPG program to produce the Sales Report.

INPUT

The format of the Customer Invoice Record is shown in Figure 9-61. Use test data set 23 for this problem.

Note that the invoice data area consists of up to five separate invoice numbers and invoice amounts. Each 13-position invoice area contains a six-position invoice number and a seven-position invoice amount. These areas should be described as alternating-format execution-time arrays.

OUTPUT

Output is the Sales Report, the format of which is shown in Figure 9-62

CUSTOMER INVOICE RECORD						
Field No.	Field Name	Field Description	Field Position	Field Length	Dec. Pos.	Data Class
1	CUSTNO	Customer Number	1–5	5		A
2		Invoice Data	6–70	65		A

Note: The Invoice Data area, positions 6–70 contains information on up to five invoices. The data for each invoice occupies 13 positions. The first six positions contain the invoice number (alphameric) and the remaining seven positions contain the invoice amount, which is a numeric field with two decimal places.

Figure 9-61   Customer Invoice Record

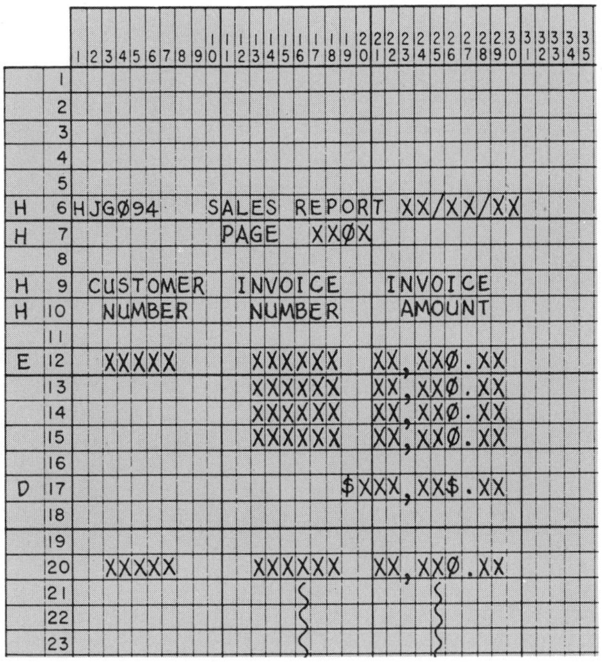

Figure 9-62   Sales Report

Processing Requirements

Using looping techniques and exception output, produce the Sales Report. After all invoices contained in an input record have been processed, print the total amount of all invoices, as shown on line 17 of the printer spacing chart.

Some records do not contain data in all the invoice areas. If a blank invoice number is detected, the processing loop for the input record should be terminated.

Input Data Editing, Internal Subroutines, & Keyed (Indexed) Record Addition

Chapter 3 showed you how to edit numeric output data to make it easier to understand and work with. In this chapter, you learn another form of data editing: editing input data in order to verify that the data being processed by the program is accurate and conforms to the processing requirements of the program. This chapter also demonstrates the techniques that must be used to add new records to a keyed sequence access path (indexed) data file and the use of internal subroutines.

INPUT DATA EDITING

Early in their career, programmers learn the acronym GIGO, which stands for "Garbage In, Garbage Out." This phrase means that if the data being read from an input file is wrong, the output developed by the program will be wrong regardless of how much processing is performed on the input data. **Input data editing** is used to verify that the data records being added, or **loaded**, to a disk file conform to the rules established for the data contents of the file to which the data records are being added. Input data editing techniques are not limited to data record loading but also can be used in any application that requires verification of the accuracy of input data.

Input data editing cannot always assure that the data being added to a file is completely correct. These techniques cannot, for example, test to be sure that a new customer's name is spelled correctly before the data is added to a customer master file. The program has no way of knowing the proper spelling of the name of a person or company, but input data editing can test to be sure that there is a name in the customer name field and can reject the data if no name has been entered. After the name has been added to the customer master file, input data editing can be used to verify that the customer's name is spelled exactly the same way every time the name is entered into the computer.

Input data editing can be used to test for such conditions as blank data fields, zero values in numeric fields that should contain values, and whether the contents of a data field conform to predefined rules. You are already familiar with some of these techniques:

How to use the COMP operation to determine the relative values of two data fields and how, based on indicators set by the COMP operation, to cause messages to print on an output report to indicate the relative value of the fields

How to perform table and array lookup and cause an error message to print if the search argument data cannot be found in the function table or array (Chapter 7)

How to use the CHAIN operation to determine if a record is present in a keyed sequence access path file and, if the required record is not present, how to eliminate some further processing of the input data record containing the invalid key field value (Chapter 8)

The sample program in this chapter will expend your knowledge of input data editing techniques.

═══ SAMPLE PROBLEM DESCRIPTION: PROGRAM HJG10X ═══

The data file flow for program HJG10X, the first sample program, is shown in Figure 10-1. This program adds records to a master listings file used by the Tri-Mount Realty Company. The listings file maintains the records of all properties that Tri-Mount has available for sale.

As you can see, the data flow is quite different from that of the programs you have worked with so far because there are three separate output data files: one disk file and two printed reports. Program HJG10X reads each LISTDATA (listings input) record and subjects the data in the record to a series of input data editing tests. If the data in the record meets all the tested conditions, the record is considered valid and data from the record is added to LISTFILE and printed on AREPORT, the Listings Addition Report.

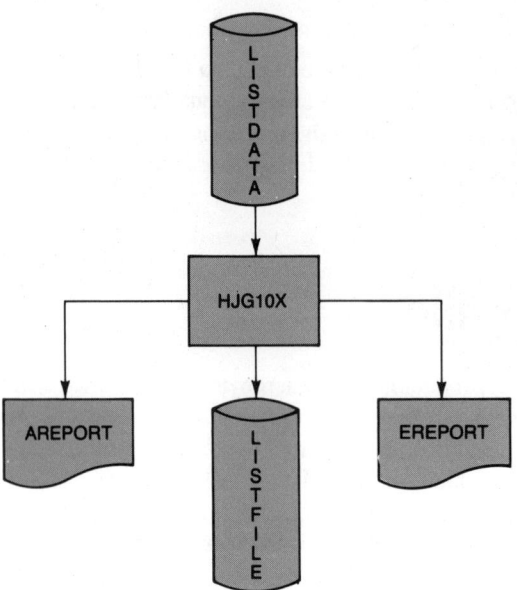

Figure 10-1   Data file flow for program HJG10X

If the data in the record fails to meet one or more of the test conditions, the program neither adds a record to LISTFILE nor prints a line on AREPORT. Instead, it prints a line on EREPORT, the Listings Addition Errors report, for each error condition detected by input data editing.

Note that every input data record appears on one of the two output reports but cannot appear on both. If a record is completely valid, output is printed on AREPORT; If a record is not completely valid, output is printed on EREPORT.

═══ Input

The layout for the LISTDATA records is shown in Figure 10-2. LISTDATA is an arrival sequence data file. The records in LISTDATA have not been edited in any way and can contain data that is not complete or correct based on the standards to be shown in the Processing Requirements portion of the problem description.

LISTINGS INPUT RECORD						
Record Length 120						
Field No.	Field Name	Field Description	Field Position	Field Length	Dec. Pos.	Data Class
1	LISTNO	Listing Identification No.	1–6	6		A
2	LOCATN	Property Location	7–31	25		A
3	TOWN	Town Code	32–33	2		A
4	ZIP	ZIP Code	34–38	5	0	N
5	CONTCT	Contact Person	39–53	15		A
6	PHONE	Telephone Number	54–63	10	0	N
7	EXT	Extension	64–67	4	0	N
8	TYPE	Property Type	68–68	1		A
9	CATEG	Property Category	69–69	1		A
10	BLDSQF	Building Square Footage	70–75	6	0	N
11	LNDSQF	Land Square Footage	76–83	6	0	N
12	LNDACR	Land Acreage	84–87	4	1	N
13	PRICE	Current Asking Price	88–95	8	0	N
14	ACCREP	Account Representative	96–110	15		A

Figure 10-2   LISTDATA record format

The LISTNO field is the unique identifier that has been assigned to each new property listing that is to be added to the listings file. Three fields identify the location of the property being listed: LOCATN contains the street address or other location of the property, and TOWN and ZIP identify the city or town in which the property is located. The Contact Person field contains the name of the owner or other person to be contacted when a potential buyer is interested in the property. The PHONE and EXT fields contain the telephone number and, possibly, the telephone extension of the Contact Person. The TYPE and CATEG fields contain codes that identify the type of property being listed. The BLDSQF, LNDSQF, and LNDACR fields contain information about the size of the property. PRICE is the current sale price being asked for the property. ACCREP may contain the name of the Tri-Mount Realty sales person who is in charge of the sale of the property.

▤ Output

Program HJG10X generates three output files: a disk file and two printed reports.

▸ **LISTFILE Disk Output File**   Figure 10-3 on the next page shows the format of the LISTFILE records. LISTFILE is a keyed sequence access path file containing the record key in positions 2–7, the Listing Identification Number field. Each LISTFILE record contains all the data fields found in the LISTDATA records – and two additional fields: (a) Position 1 contains the status code of A, which indicates that the record is currently active and contains valid data. (b) Positions 112–117 contain the date that the record was added to LISTFILE; the contents of this field will be the current system date (UDATE) when the record was added to LISTFILE.

LISTFILE FILE RECORD						
	Record Length 140		Key Location 2–7			
Field No.	Field Name	Field Description	Field Position	Field Length	Dec. Pos.	Data Class
1		Status Code A	1–1			
2		Listing Identification No.	2–7			
3		Property Location	8–32			
4		Town Code	33–34			
5		ZIP Code	35–39			
6		Contact Person	40–54			
7		Telephone Number	55–64			
8		Extension	65–68			
9		Property Type	69–69			
10		Property Category	70–70			
11		Building Square Footage	71–76			
12		Land Square Footage	77–84			
13		Land Acreage	85–88			
14		Current Asking Price	89–96			
15		Account Representative	97–111			
16		Listing Date	112–117			

Figure 10-3 LISTFILE record format

▶ **AREPORT Output Report** Figure 10-4 shows the report layout for AREPORT, the Listings Addition Report. Note that the report prints only one heading line, shown on line 6 of the printer spacing chart. Each valid input record generates three detail lines, shown on lines 8, 9, and 10 of the chart. Although the first of these three lines provides headings for the Listing Number and Location data fields, it is a detail line controlled by the reading of an input record, not by normal heading processing.

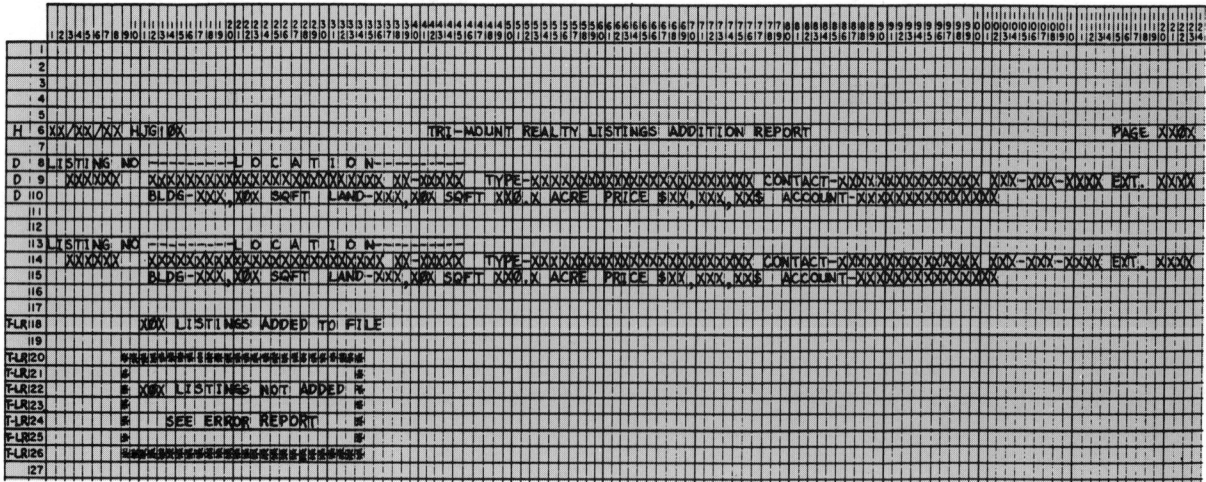

Figure 10-4 Layout of Listings Addition Report

Note also that the second and third detail lines contain constants, such as TYPE- and ACCOUNT-, that are used to identify detail field information. If the data field identified by such a constant is blank or zero, the identifying constant is suppressed and does not print.

Line 18 is a final total count of the number of records added to LISTFILE during execution of the program. Lines 20–26 show an error block, which contains a count of the erroneous input records and prints only if one or more input records contained errors and were not loaded to LISTFILE. If all the input records were valid, lines 20–26 are not printed at the end of the program.

The purpose of the error block is to alert the user of the report that not all the input records were valid. Reports must be designed with the user in mind, and the more information that you give the user of a report the more useful the report will be. When the program code is explained, you will see that only two calculation operations are needed to control printing of the error block.

▸ **EREPORT Output Report**   Figure 10-5 shows the report layout for EREPORT, the Listings Addition Errors report, which consists of three heading lines, shown on lines 6, 7, and 9 of the printer spacing chart, and a series of exception output lines. Each time an error is detected in an input record, the program prints an exception line specifying the type of error. If more than one error is found in a record, only the first error line contains the listing identification number. In other words, the report is group indicated.

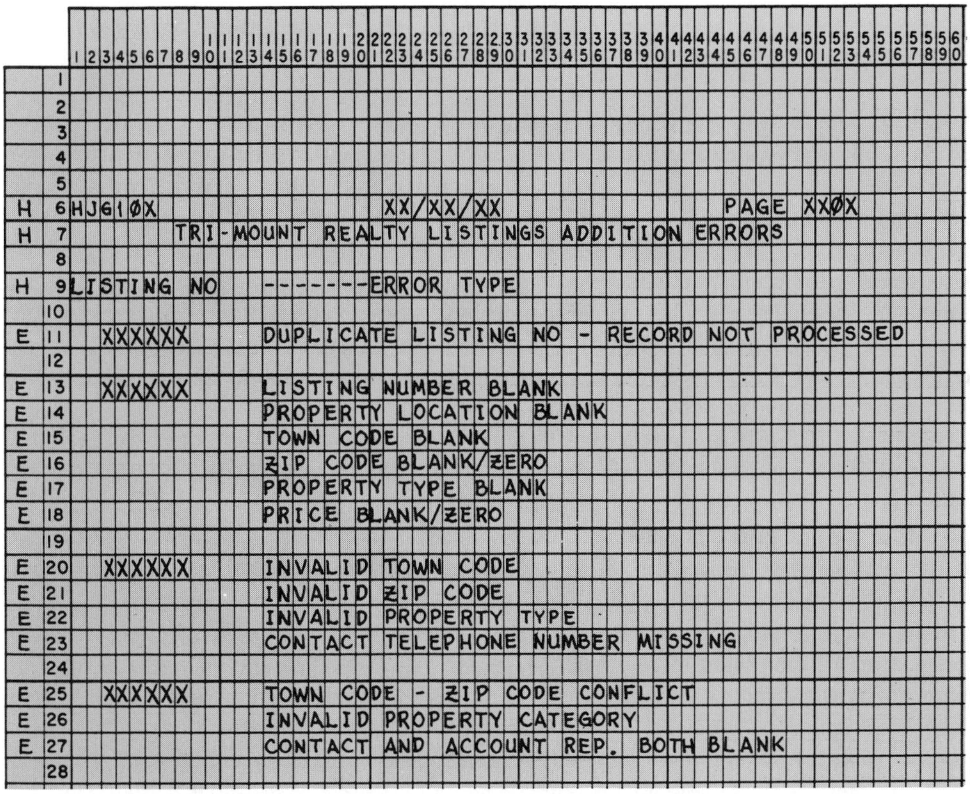

Figure 10-5   Layout of Listings Addition Errors report

It is not possible for a single input record to generate every error message because some errors make it impossible to test for other errors. For example, if the Town Code field is blank (line 15), it is impossible to test the town code and find it to be invalid (line 20).

▶ **Audit Trails** The use of two reports, one listing all valid records and the other listing all records that contain one or more errors, allows the program to generate an audit trail of the input data records. An **audit trail** is a technique by which every input record or transaction appears in printed form on a report. By collecting all the reports pertaining to a specific data file, the user of the file is able to keep track of everything done to the file that affects the data in the file.

A more common form of audit trail is found in cash registers and **point-of-sale terminals** used in stores. When a customer's purchase is rung up, a printed report (the receipt) is generated that shows the amount, date, and time of the sale. This receipt is the customer's audit trail of the transaction with the store. However, this is not the only printed record of the transaction. Most cash registers and point-of-sale terminals also generate another copy of the sales information on a paper tape stored within the machine. This internal tape provides the seller with a complete record, or audit trail, of every transaction that takes place and is rung up. In other words, every transaction that has an effect on the amount of money in the register or terminal is recorded in the form of a printed report, generating a complete audit trail of the day's business.

Point-of-sale terminals also contain small microprocessors and either keep their audit trail on magnetic disk or transfer the transaction information to a centralized computer that maintains an audit trail for all point-of-sale terminals.

An audit trail should be maintained whenever the contents of a data file are altered. Any program that adds new records, deletes unneeded records, or changes data within existing records should generate a complete audit trail. The audit trail should show whether data was added, deleted, or changed, the date the file was altered, and, if the contents of an existing record were changed, both the old and the new data within the record. Audit trails are a critical part of the process of maintaining data files.

▶ **Spooling, The Printing of Multiple Reports** By now, you may have several questions about the way that program HJG10X handles the two printed reports. How can one printer print two reports at the same time? If the program is printing two reports, how does it keep from mixing up the output lines and printing information for both valid and invalid records on the same page? The answer is quite simple: The program does not print both reports at the same time even though it appears to.

Although early business computers were limited and able to print only a single report from a program, almost all computers used today eliminate this problem by a process called spooling. The acronym **SPOOL** stands for **simultaneous peripheral operations on line**. By this process, the computer is able to perform simultaneous output operations (two printed reports, in this example) on the same peripheral device (the printer) by storing the output report data on an on-line device (a disk drive).

When program HJG10X, or any program producing printed reports, is executed, as the figure shows, the output data for AREPORT and EREPORT does not go directly to the printer. Instead, the output records (the print lines) are stored on disk (Figure 10-6) until the program finishes executing. When the program has ended, the report data is sent to the printer (Figure 10-7). The use of spooling operations is totally transparent to both the programmer and the person using the program. Spooling is under complete control of the computer's operating system software, and no special instructions or RPG code are needed to use the spool function.

In addition to permitting the generation of several reports by a single program, spooling enables all people using the computer to use the printer more efficiently. In particular, spooling eliminates the device lock-up that occurred before spooling techniques were developed. Older computers assigned an output device, such as the printer, to the first program that needed it. Once the printer was assigned, the device was locked up, or totally controlled, by that program. Even if a program only generated final totals at the end of a job, if the job took two hours to run, the printer was unavailable to any other program for the entire two-hour period. The printer remained idle even though no printing took place until the program ended, and no other program could access the printer.

When spooling techniques are used, this does not happen. All programs generating printed reports send the output data to the disk area used by spool. As the programs finish, their respective reports are sent to the printer. The report generated by the first program to finish is, generally, printed first, the report from the second program prints second, and so on. When spooling is used, the computer is able to operate the printer in the most efficient manner and to minimize the time that a computer user must wait for printed output.

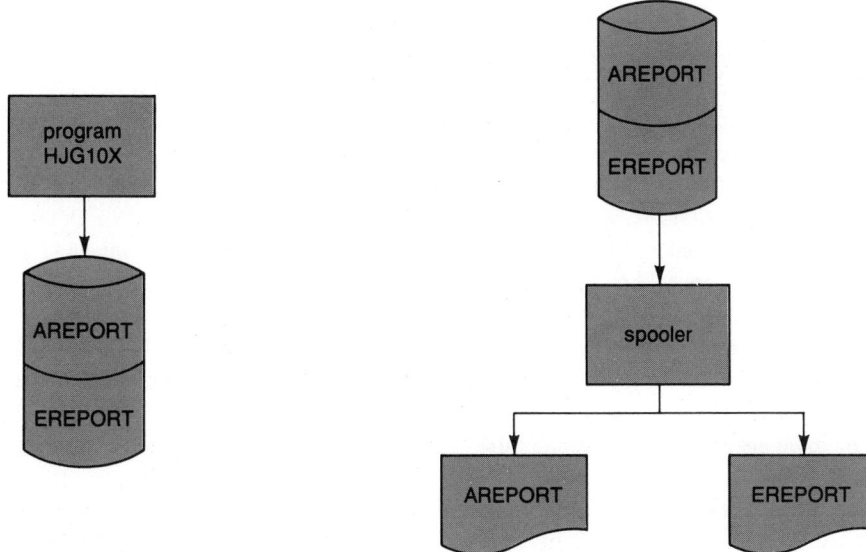

Figure 10-6   Spooling: report to disk file   Figure 10-7   Spooling: disk to printer

▤ Processing Requirements

Program HJG10X tests each LISTDATA input data record for all the following conditions. If all are met, the program writes an output record to the LISTFILE disk file and prints a three line audit trail record on AREPORT. If any of the conditions is not met, the program produces an error line on EREPORT that indicate the type of data error detected. The first error line printed for an input record contains the listing identification number as shown on the EREPORT report layout. The conditions tested are the following:

1. The listing identification number must not be duplicated within LISTFILE. If an input record contains a listing identification number that already appears in a LISTFILE record, no further testing is performed on the input record.
2. The following input data fields must not be blank.

LISTNO	Positions 1–6
LOCATN	Positions 7–31
TOWN	Positions 32–33
ZIP	Positions 34–38
TYPE	Position 68
PRICE	Positions 88–95

   In addition, ZIP and PRICE, which are numeric fields, must not contain a value of zero.
3. Town code (TOWN) and ZIP code (ZIP) must agree based on the following table:

AS	01430		TM	01468
BA	01436		WE	01473
ET	01438		WI	01475
FI	01420		WS	01477
GA	01440			

4. Any town or ZIP code not listed in the preceding table is invalid. If either the town or the ZIP code is invalid, do not attempt to perform test 3 to determine if the two codes agree.
5. The property type code must be R, C, or L.
6. If the property type is R, the category (position 69) must be S or M.
7. If the property type is C, the category must be M, O, or G.
8. If the property type is L, the category must be blank.
9. If the contact person (position 39–53) is not blank, the telephone number (positions 54–63) cannot be blank.
10. Either the Contact Person field, the Account Representative (positions 96–110) field, or both must contain an entry. An input record cannot be blank in both these fields.

The output constants used to identify the CONTCT, EXT, BLDSQF, LNDSQF, LNDACR, and ACCREP fields are printed only if the fields they identify contain data. If one or more of the these fields is blank or zero, neither the field nor its identifying constant is printed.

The hyphens used to separate the three portions of the Contact Telephone Number field are printed only if the preceding portion of the telephone number is printed.

The output constant printed in positions 53–76 of the second detail line for each valid record is based on the contents of the TYPE and CATEG fields. The valid combinations of property type and property category, along with the output constant to be printed for each valid combination, are shown in Figure 10-8.

Property Type	Property Category	Output Constant
R	S	RESIDENTIAL-SINGLE
R	M	RESIDENTIAL-MULTI
C	M	COMMERCIAL-MANUFACTURING
C	O	COMMERCIAL-OFFICE
C	G	COMMERCIAL-GENERAL
L	Blank	LAND

Figure 10-8   Valid TYPE and CATEG code combinations

≡ PROGRAM SPECIFICATIONS FOR PROGRAM HJG10X ≡

Programs using input data editing techniques often appear far more complex than they actually are. In most programs of this type, the program code becomes somewhat repetitious because the program must perform similar tests on several different data fields. For example, once you understand the technique used to determine if one required input field is blank and to print the necessary error message, you will understand the technique used to test the other five required input fields.

Input editing programs do, however, use many different general-purpose indicators to represent error conditions. Because it can be confusing to keep track of the meanings of these indicators, it is useful to use indicator summary sheets. Figure 10-9 shows the indicator summary for the sample program; use it for reference as you study the program code that follows.

Figure 10-9   Indicator Summary for program HJG10X

RPG   INDICATOR SUMMARY

IBM International Business Machines Corporation

Figure 10-9 (1)

Line	Form Type	Record Identifying	Input Field	Calculation Result and Command Key	Halt and User	Control Level and Overflow	FUNCTION OF INDICATORS
01	F*	ID	F	C	H	L	FUNCTION OF INDICATORS
02	F*	Ø1 -	-	-	-	-	LISTDATA RECORD IDENTIFICATION
03	F*	Ø2 -	-	-	-	-	LISTFILE RECORD IDENTIFICATION
04	F*		20	-	-	-	CONTCT BLANK/ZERO
05	F*		21	-	-	-	PHONE BLANK/ZERO
06	F*		22	-	-	-	PH1 BLANK/ZERO
07	F*		23	-	-	-	EXT BLANK/ZERO
08	F*		24	-	-	-	CATEG BLANK/ZERO
09	F*		25	-	-	-	BLDSQF BLANK/ZERO
10	F*		26	-	-	-	LNDSQF BLANK/ZERO
11	F*		27	-	-	-	LNDACR BLANK/ZERO
12	F*		28	-	-	-	ACCREP BLANK/ZERO
13	F*			40	-	-	VALID RECORD INDICATOR
14	F*			51	-	-	EXCPT CONTROL-DUPLICATE LISTING NO.
15	F*			52	-	-	EXCPT CONTROL-BLANK LISTING NO.
16	F*			53	-	-	EXCPT CONTROL-BLANK PROPERTY LOCATION
17	F*			54	-	-	EXCPT CONTROL-BLANK TOWN CODE
18	F*			55	-	-	EXCPT CONTROL-BLANK/ZERO ZIP CODE

Figure 10-9 (1)

RPG   INDICATOR SUMMARY

IBM International Business Machines Corporation

Line	Form Type	Record Identifying	Input Field	Calculation Result and Command Key	Halt and User	Control Level and Overflow	FUNCTION OF INDICATORS
01	F*	ID	F	C	H	L	FUNCTION OF INDICATORS
02	F*			56	-	-	EXCPT CONTROL-BLANK PROPERTY TYPE
03	F*			57	-	-	EXCPT CONTROL-BLANK/ZERO PRICE
04	F*			58	-	-	EXCPT CONTROL-INVALID TOWN CODE
05	F*			59	-	-	EXCPT CONTROL-INVALID ZIP CODE
06	F*			60	-	-	EXCPT CONTROL-INVALID PROPERTY TYPE
07	F*			61	-	-	EXCPT CONTROL-CONTACT PHONE NO. MISSING
08	F*			62	-	-	EXCPT CONTROL-TOWN/ZIP CONFLICT
09	F*			63	-	-	EXCPT CONTROL-INVALID PROPERTY CATEGORY
10	F*			64	-	-	EXCPT CONTROL-CONTACT/REP. BOTH BLANK
11	F*			65	-	-	TOWN CODE LOKUP VALID
12	F*			66	-	-	ZIP CODE LOKUP VALID
13	F*			67	-	-	TOWN/ZIP CODE LOKUP VALID
14	F*			68	-	-	TOWN/ZIP CONFLICT
15	F*			69	-	-	PROPERTY TYPE 'R'
16	F*			70	-	-	PROPERTY TYPE 'C'
17	F*			71	-	-	PROPERTY TYPE 'L'
18	F*			72	-	-	INVALID PROPERTY TYPE

Figure 10-9 (2)

continued

RPG INDICATOR SUMMARY

```
F#  Indicators                    Circle Indicators Used:

Line                              FUNCTION OF INDICATORS
    F.  ID  F   C   H   L      FUNCTION OF INDICATORS
    F.          73  -   -   -  PROPERTY CATEGORY 'S'
    F.          74  -   -   -  PROPERTY CATEGORY 'M'
    F.          75  -   -   -  PROPERTY CATEGORY 'O'
    F.          76  -   -   -  PROPERTY CATEGORY 'G'
    F.          77  -   -   -  OVERFLOW CONTROL
    F.      80  -   -   -      LISTNO BLANK
    F.      81  -   -   -      LOCATN BLANK
    F.      82  -   -   -      TOWN   BLANK
    F.      83  -   -   -      ZIP BLANK/ZERO
    F.      84  -   -   -      TYPE BLANK
    F.      85  -   -   -      PRICE BLANK/ZERO
    F.      N86 -   -   -      DUPLICATE LISTNO
    F.      99  -   -   -      ERROR IN INPUT FILE
    F.                  L1 -   CONTROL BREAK - LISTNO
    F.                  LR -   END OF JOB
    F.                  1P -   FIRST PAGE HEADING CONTROL
    F.                  OF -   OVERFLOW CONTROL - EREPORT
```
*Number of sheets per pad may vary slightly.

Figure 10-9 (3)

RPG INDICATOR SUMMARY

```
F#  Indicators                    Circle Indicators Used:

Line
    F.  ID  F   C   H   L      FUNCTION OF INDICATORS
    F.                  OV -   OVERFLOW CONTROL - AREPORT
```

Figure 10-9 (4)

▤ Control and File Description Specifications

Figure 10-10 shows the Control and File Description Specifications form for the sample program. As you can see, LISTDATA has been described as an arrival sequence file containing records that are 120 characters long, blocked in groups of four records.

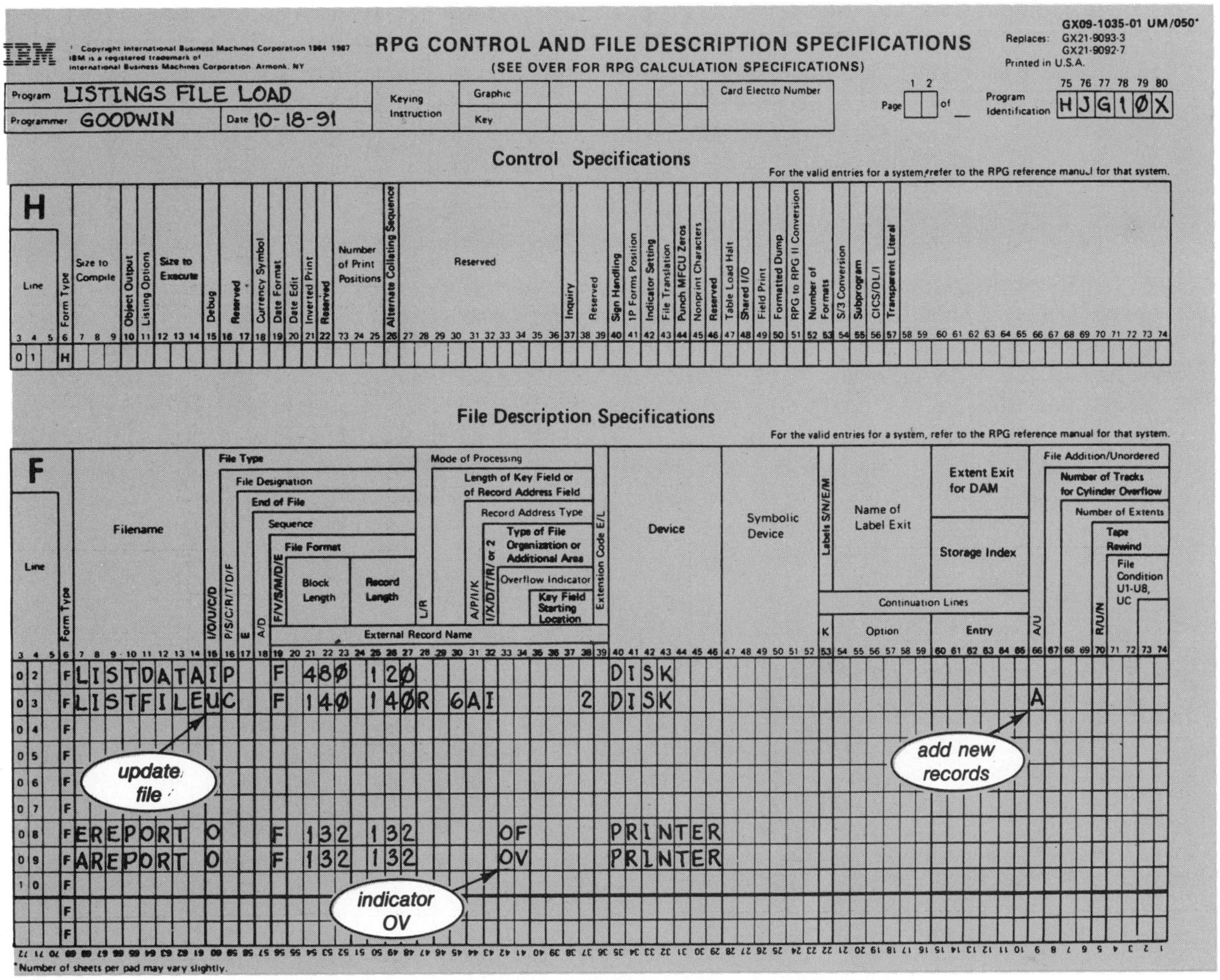

Figure 10-10 Control and File Description Specifications

▶ **Update Files (Type U)** The file description for LISTFILE contains two new entries. The File Type entry U in position 15 specifies that LISTFILE is an update file. An **update file** is a disk file that is both read from and written to in the same program. Although the program specifications show LISTFILE as an output file, the processing requirements specify that "the listing Identification Number may not be duplicated within LIST-FILE". To determine if a specific listing identification number already exists within LISTFILE, it is necessary to perform a random read of the file using a CHAIN operation (note the entry C in position 16). As the file is both read from and written to, it cannot be specified as an output file. RPG does not permit output files to be read. To permit both reading from and writing to the file, the file must be specified as an update file by entering a U in position 15. Update files must be described on both the Input and the Output Specifications forms.

▶ **Record Addition Entry** The sample program adds new records to LISTFILE. To permit records to be added to an existing data file, the File Addition area (position 66) must contain the entry A. The A entry specifies that new records may be written out to a disk file. If this entry is omitted, the program halts when the first attempt is made to add a new record to the file. As you will see, the File Addition area works in conjunction with a record addition entry used on the Output Specifications form.

▸ **Multiple Overflow Indicators** In Chapter 2 you found that RPG supports eight different overflow indicators (OA, OB, OC, OD, OE, OF, OG, and OV). Only one of these (OF) has been used in all the examples so far because indicator OF is considered the standard overflow indicator. Program HJG10X generates two separate output reports and, therefore, requires two separate overflow indicators. Note that indicator OF has been assigned as the overflow indicator for EREPORT, whereas indicator OV has been specified for AREPORT.

Extension Specifications

The Extension Specifications form for the sample program (Figure 10-11) shows that the program uses two tables, described in the separate table format, to verify the Town Code and ZIP Code fields. TABTN contains the nine valid town codes, and TABZIP contains the nine valid ZIP codes. The first TABTN entry corresponds to the first TABZIP entry, the second TABTN entry to the second TABZIP entry, and so on. These tables are compile-time tables, as specified by the entry in positions 33–35 and the lack of an entry in positions 11–26.

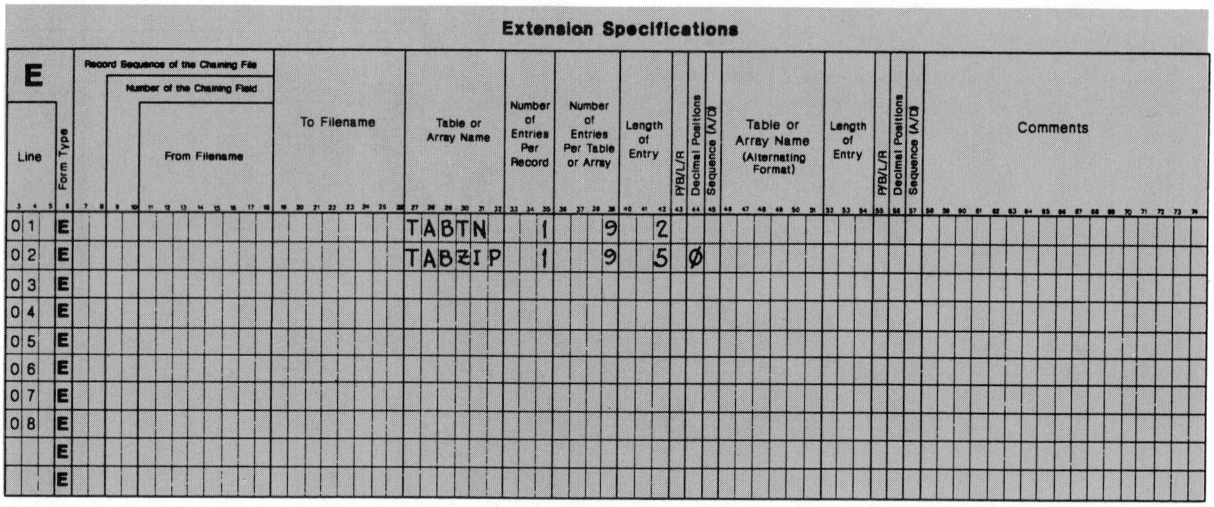

Figure 10-11   Extension Specifications

Input Specifications

Figure 10-12 shows the Input Specifications form for the sample program. As you can see, both LISTDATA and LISTFILE have been described.

▸ **LISTDATA Input Description** The description of LISTDATA does not require any new entries. Note that the PHONE field (positions 54–63) has been redefined into its three separate components, PH1, PH2, and PH3. Fifteen of the fields have indicators specified in the ZERO or BLANK area, positions 69–70. Indicators 80–85 represent error conditions, that is, blank or zero values in the six data fields that must contain nonblank or nonzero entries.

Indicators 20–28 are used to test for blank or zero values in fields that can contain these entries but require special processing if a blank or zero entry is found. For example, if the LNDACR field is blank, and indicator 27 is turned on, the indicator is used to suppress printing of the identifying output constant on AREPORT.

Note that indicator L1 has been specified as a control level indicator to be turned on when the LISTNO field changes, even though the program specifications do not require control breaks or group totals. The L1 indicator is used to perform group indication on the first error line printed for each input record and, in addition, is used to control spacing between groups of error message lines.

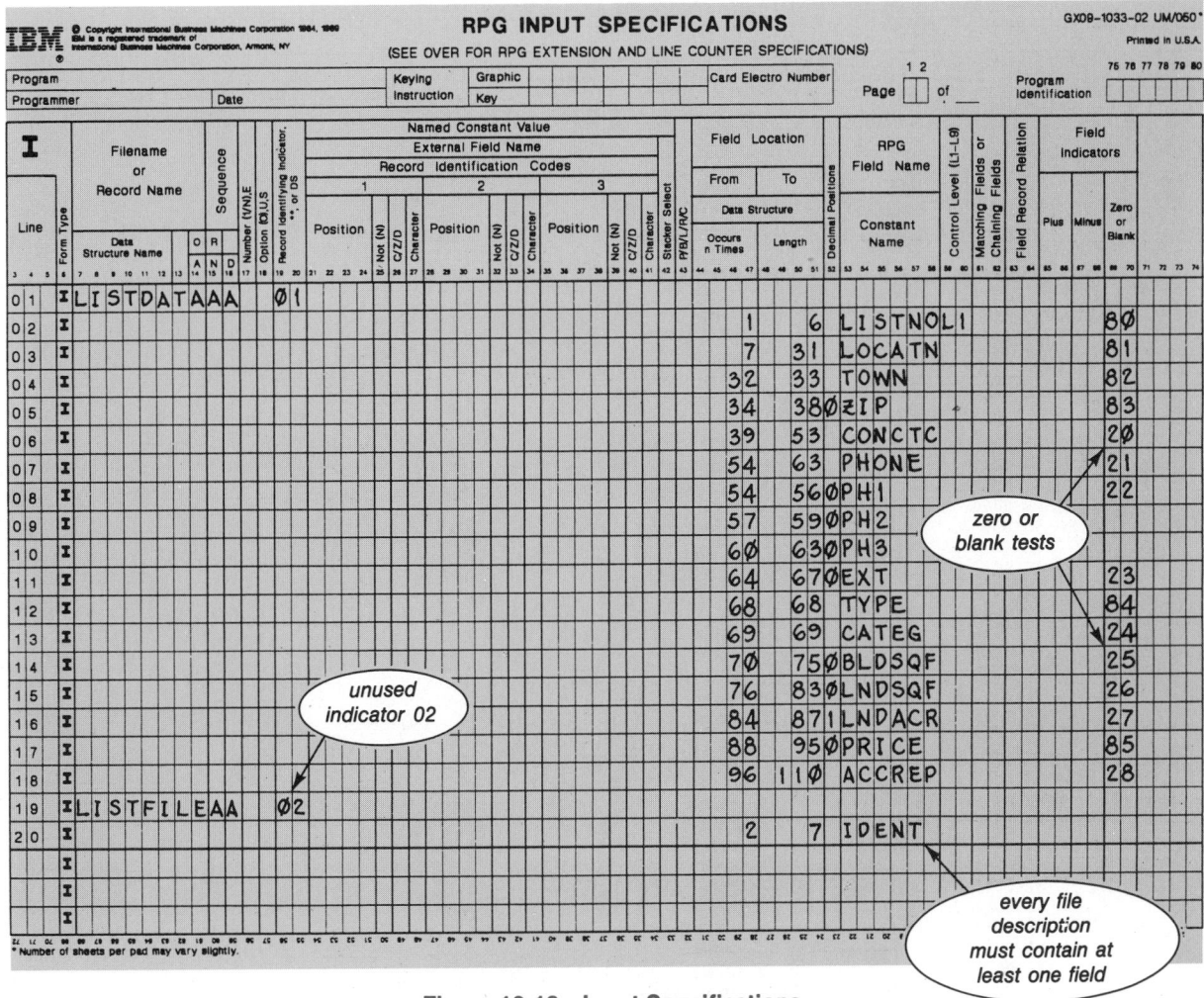

Figure 10-12   Input Specifications

▶ **LISTFILE Input Description**   As was stated earlier, LISTFILE must be described on the Input Specifications form because it is read to determine if a new record contains a listing identification number that already exists within LISTFILE. Although no LISTFILE data fields are used, RPG requires that at least one field be described for every input or update file. The description of the IDENT field in positions 2–7 of the record satisfies this requirement. Note also that indicator 02 has been specified as the record-identifying indicator for LISTFILE.

Neither the IDENT field nor indicator 02 is used in the calculation or output portions of the program. Most versions of RPG generates warning messages to advise you that indicator 02 and the IDENT field are defined but not used. These messages cannot be avoided and, after you verify that you meant to define but not use these elements, can be ignored. Remember, that a warning message does not always point out an error. Warning messages often indicate unusual, but not necessarily incorrect, programming techniques.

═══ CALCULATION SPECIFICATIONS FOR PROGRAM HJG10X ═══

The calculation specifications portion of the compilation listing for this sample program (Figure 10-13 on the next page) can be used as reference as each part of the calculations is discussed in the pages that follow. Note that the calculations begin on line 28 of the program and continue through line 116. For each of the separate error tests, the line numbers on the coding sheets in the examples correspond to the line numbers on the compilation listing.

Figure 10-13 Calculation specifications listing for Program HJG10X

```
HJG10X                              IBM PC      RPG II          Version 3.5

        ....+....1....+....2....+....3....+....4....+....5....+....6....+....7....

  28 0028 C    01            SETON              40
  29 0029 C    80            SETON              52
  30 0030 C    52            EXCPT
  31 0031 C    52            EXSR OFLOW
  32 0032 C    52            SETOF              52
  33 0033 C    N80    LISTNO  CHAINLISTFILE        86
  34 0034 C    N80N86        SETON              51
  35 0035 C    51            EXCPT
  36 0036 C    51            EXSR OFLOW
  37 0037 C    51            SETOF              51
  38 0038 C    N80N86        GOTO END
  39 0039 C    81            SETON              53
  40 0040 C    53            EXCPT
  41 0041 C    53            EXSR OFLOW
  42 0042 C    53            SETOF              53
  43 0043 C    82            SETON              54
  44 0044 C    54            EXCPT
  45 0045 C    54            EXSR OFLOW
  46 0046 C    54            SETOF              54
  47 0047 C    83            SETON              55
  48 0048 C    55            EXCPT
  49 0049 C    55            EXSR OFLOW
  50 0050 C    55            SETOF              55
  51 0051 C    84            SETON              56
  52 0052 C    56            EXCPT
  53 0053 C    56            EXSR OFLOW
  54 0054 C    56            SETOF              56
  55 0055 C    85            SETON              57
  56 0056 C    57            EXCPT
  57 0057 C    57            EXSR OFLOW
  58 0058 C   -57            SETOF              57
  59 0059 C    N82    TOWN    LOKUPTABTN            65
  60 0060 C    N82N65        SETON              58
  61 0061 C    58            EXCPT
  62 0062 C    58            EXSR OFLOW
  63 0063 C    58            SETOF              58
  64 0064 C    N83    ZIP     LOKUPTABZIP          66
  65 0065 C    N83N66        SETON              59
  66 0066 C    59            EXCPT
  67 0067 C    59            EXSR OFLOW
  68 0068 C    59            SETOF              59
  69 0069 C    65 66  TOWN    LOKUPTABTN    TABZIP   67
  70 0070 C    67    TABZIP  COMP ZIP           6868
  71 0071 C    68            SETON              62
  72 0072 C    62            EXCPT
  73 0073 C    62            EXSR OFLOW
  74 0074 C    62            SETOF              626768
  75 0075 C                  SETOF              697071
  76 0076 C    N84    TYPE    COMP 'R'           727269
  77 0077 C    N84 72 TYPE    COMP 'C'           727270
  78 0078 C    N84 72 TYPE    COMP 'L'           727271
  79 0079 C    72            SETON              60
  80 0080 C    60            EXCPT
  81 0081 C    60            EXSR OFLOW
  82 0082 C    60            SETOF              6072
  83 0083 C                  SETOF              737475
  84 0084 C                  SETOF              76
  85 0085 C    N24    CATEG   COMP 'S'              73
  86 0086 C    N24    CATEG   COMP 'M'              74
  87 0087 C    N24    CATEG   COMP 'O'              75
  88 0088 C    N24    CATEG   COMP 'G'              76
  89 0089 C                  SETON.             63
  90 0090 C    69 73
  91 0091 COR 69 74
  92 0092 COR 70 74
  93 0093 COR 70 75
  94 0094 COR 70 76
```

Figure 10-13 (1)

```
HJG10X                        IBM PC      RPG II        Version 3.5

        ....+....1....+....2....+....3....+....4....+....5....+....6....+....7....

    95 0095 COR 71 24             SETOF                         63
    96 0096 C    63               EXCPT
    97 0097 C    63               EXSR OFLOW
    98 0098 C    63               SETOF                         63
    99 0099 C    N20 21           SETON                         61
   100 0100 C    61               EXCPT
   101 0101 C    61               EXSR OFLOW
   102 0102 C    61               SETOF                         61
   103 0103 C    20 28            SETON                         64
   104 0104 C    64               EXCPT
   105 0105 C    64               EXSR OFLOW
   106 0106 C    64               SETOF                         64
   107 0107 C         END         TAG
   108 0108 C    40   ADDS        ADD  1       ADDS    30
   109 0109 C    N40  ERRORS      ADD  1       ERRORS  30
   110 0110 CSR       OFLOW       BEGSR
   111 0111 CSR                   SETOF                      40
   112 0112 CSR 77                SETOF                      77OF
   113 0113 CSR OF                SETON                      77
   114 0114 CSR                   SETOF                      L1
   115 0115 CSR                   SETON                      99
   116 0116 CSR                   ENDSR
```

Figure 10-13 (2)

Exception-Controlled Output Records

As the exception output portion of the compilation listing shows (Figure 10-14), the program contains 14 different output lines that can be printed based on errors detected in the input data. Note that each exception line is controlled by a different indicator. The first exception line is controlled by indicator 51, the second by indicator 52, and so on.

Figure 10-14   Exception Output Specifications for EREPORT

```
HJG10X                        IBM PC      RPG II        Version 3.5

        ....+....1....+....2....+....3....+....4....+....5....+....6....+....7....

   217 0217 O        EF11    51 L1
   218 0218 O        ORF 1   51NL1
   219 0219 O                L1      LISTNO      8
   220 0220 O                OF      LISTNO      8
   221 0221 O                             35 'DUPLICATE LISTING NO -'
   222 0222 O                             56 'RECORD NOT PROCESSED'
   223 0223 O        EF11    52 L1
   224 0224 O        ORF 1   52NL1
   225 0225 O                L1      LISTNO      8
   226 0226 O                OF      LISTNO      8
   227 0227 O                             33 'LISTING NUMBER BLANK'
   228 0228 O        EF11    53 L1
   229 0229 O        ORF 1   53NL1
   230 0230 O                L1      LISTNO      8
   231 0231 O                OF      LISTNO      8
   232 0232 O                             36 'PROPERTY LOCATION BLANK'
   233 0233 O        EF11    54 L1
   234 0234 O        ORF 1   54NL1
   235 0235 O                L1      LISTNO      8
   236 0236 O                OF      LISTNO      8
   237 0237 O                             28 'TOWN CODE BLANK'
   238 0238 O        EF11    55 L1
   239 0239 O        ORF 1   55NL1
   240 0240 O                L1      LISTNO      8
   241 0241 O                OF      LISTNO      8
```

Figure 10-14 (1)

continued

```
HJG10X                            IBM PC        RPG II         Version 3.5

          ....+....1....+....2....+....3....+....4....+....5....+....6....+....7....

        242 0242 O                                       32 'ZIP CODE BLANK/ZERO'
        243 0243 O        EF11      56 L1
        244 0244 O        ORF 1     56NL1
        245 0245 O                  L1    LISTNO      8
        246 0246 O                  OF    LISTNO      8
        247 0247 O                                       32 'PROPERTY TYPE BLANK'
        248 0248 O        EF11      57 L1
        249 0249 O        ORF 1     57NL1
        250 0250 O                  L1    LISTNO      8
        251 0251 O                  OF    LISTNO      8
        252 0252 O                                       29 'PRICE BLANK/ZERO'
        253 0253 O        EF11      58 L1
        254 0254 O        ORF 1     58NL1
        255 0255 O                  L1    LISTNO      8
        256 0256 O                  OF    LISTNO      8
        257 0257 O                                       30 'INVALID TOWN CODE'
        258 0258 O        EF11      59 L1
        259 0259 O        ORF 1     59NL1
        260 0260 O                  L1    LISTNO      8
        261 0261 O                  OF    LISTNO      8
        262 0262 O                                       29 'INVALID ZIP CODE'
        263 0263 O        EF11      60 L1
        264 0264 O        ORF 1     60NL1
        265 0265 O                  L1    LISTNO      8
        266 0266 O                  OF    LISTNO      8
        267 0267 O                                       34 'INVALID PROPERTY TYPE'
        268 0268 O        EF11      61 L1
        269 0269 O        ORF 1     61NL1
        270 0270 O                  L1    LISTNO      8
        271 0271 O                  OF    LISTNO      8
        272 0272 O                                       37 'CONTACT TELEPHONE NUMBER'
        273 0273 O.                                      45 'MISSING'
        274 0274 O        EF11      62 L1
        275 0275 O        ORF 1     62NL1
        276 0276 O                  L1    LISTNO      8
        277 0277 O                  OF    LISTNO      8
        278 0278 O                                       33 'TOWN CODE - ZIP CODE'
        279 0279 O                                       42 'CONFLICT'
        280 0280 O        EF11      63 L1
        281 0281 O        ORF 1     63NL1
        282 0282 O                  L1    LISTNO      8
        283 0283 O                  OF    LISTNO      8
        284 0284 O                                       29 'INVALID PROPERTY'
        285 0285 O                                       38 'CATEGORY'
        286 0286 O        EF11      64 L1
        287 0287 O        ORF 1     64NL1
        288 0288 O                  L1    LISTNO      8
        289 0289 O                  OF    LISTNO      8
        290 0290 O                                       37 'CONTACT AND ACCOUNT REP.'
        291 0291 O                                       48 'BOTH BLANK'
```

Figure 10-14 (2)

In Chapter 9, the exception output lines were controlled only by the EXCPT operation in the program calculations. However, that technique cannot be used in program HJG10X because each of the 14 exception lines must be controlled and printed under different circumstances. If the exception lines were not indicator controlled, all 14 lines would print every time an EXCPT operation was performed. To control exception line printing, each line is conditioned by a different indicator.

Whenever an error is detected in the calculations, the indicator controlling a specific exception output line is turned on by a SETON operation, an EXCPT operation is performed to print the line, and the controlling indicator is then turned off. You will see this pattern of SETON, EXCPT, and SETOF repeated several times in the calculations.

Valid-Record Indicator

Line 28 in Figure 10-15 turns on indicator 40 at the beginning of the processing of each input record. Indicator 40 functions as a valid-record indicator. Any error condition detected by the program causes indicator 40 to be turned off. At the end of the detail calculations, if indicator 40 is still on, the record is treated as a valid record, and indicator 40 controls printing to AREPORT and the addition of a record to LISTFILE. If indicator 40 is not on, no data is added to LISTFILE, and no output is printed on AREPORT. The SETON in line 28 assures that indicator 40 is on at the beginning of each detail calculation cycle.

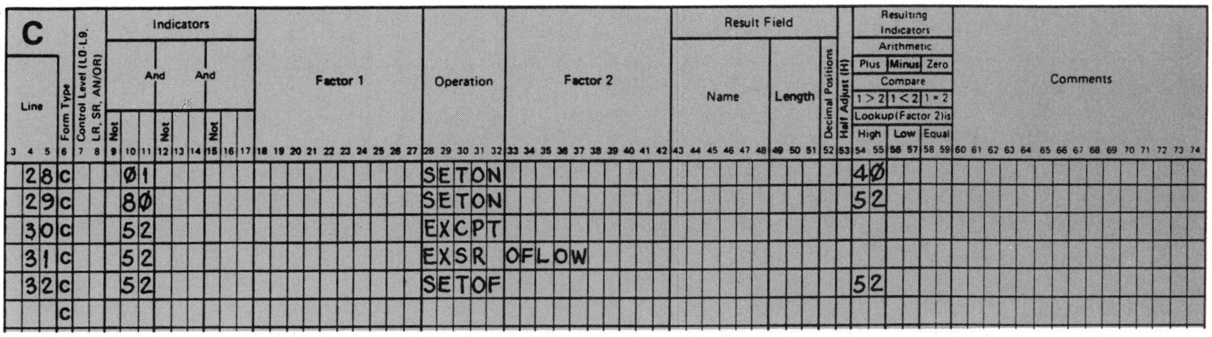

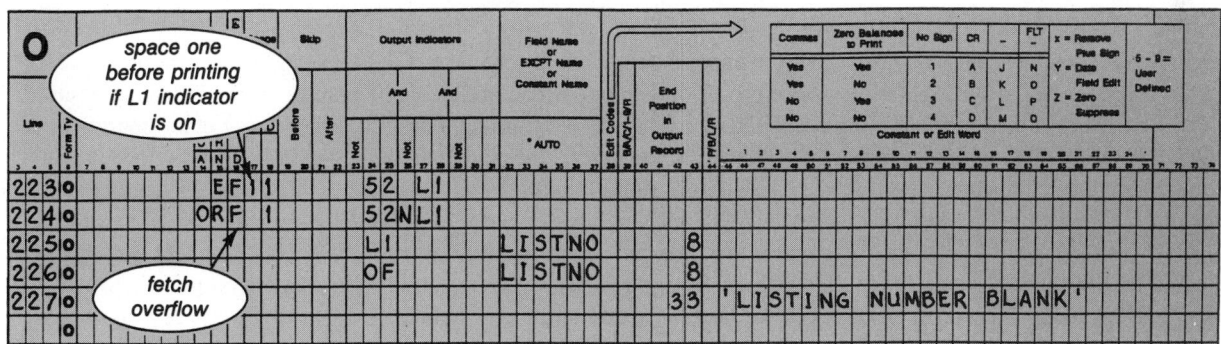

Figure 10-15 Valid-record indicator and LISTNO validity test

Blank LISTNO Field Test

Lines 29–32, also shown in Figure 10-15, control the printing of the LISTING NUMBER BLANK error message if the LISTNO field is blank. The output specifications for the message are shown in Figure 10-16. Note that the error message is controlled by indicator 52 but also uses indicator L1. When this message prints, if indicator L1 is on, the printer spaces once before the line prints and once after printing. If indicator L1 is not on, the printer does not space before printing the line; it spaces only after printing is performed. Note also that the L1 and OF indicators are used to perform group indication of the LISTNO field.

Figure 10-16 Listing number error exception lines

Although the error line is controlled by indicator 52, indicator 80 is the input field indicator used to specify a blank LISTNO field. Line 29 of the calculations (see Figure 10-15) causes indicator 52 to turn on if indicator 80 is on, that is, if LISTNO is blank. Note that the next three calculation operations are controlled by indicator 52. Line 30 performs an EXCPT operation under control of indicator 52. If line 30 is executed, only the exception output line controlled by indicator 52 is printed. As a brief look at Figure 10-14 shows, none of the other exception output lines can print because each of them is controlled by a different, and separate, indicator.

▸ **Subroutine Execution** Line 31 of the calculations uses an EXSR (EXecute SubRoutine) operation to perform an internal subroutine. An **internal subroutine** is a series of operations that are executed only if they are requested or **called** by an instruction within the main, top-down series of calculation operations. Generally, internal subroutines are used whenever the same series of operations must be executed at different points in the calculations. Rather than repeat the same calculations several times, these operations are coded in the form of an internal subroutine and called when needed. Figure 10-17 illustrates the logic of internal subroutine usage.

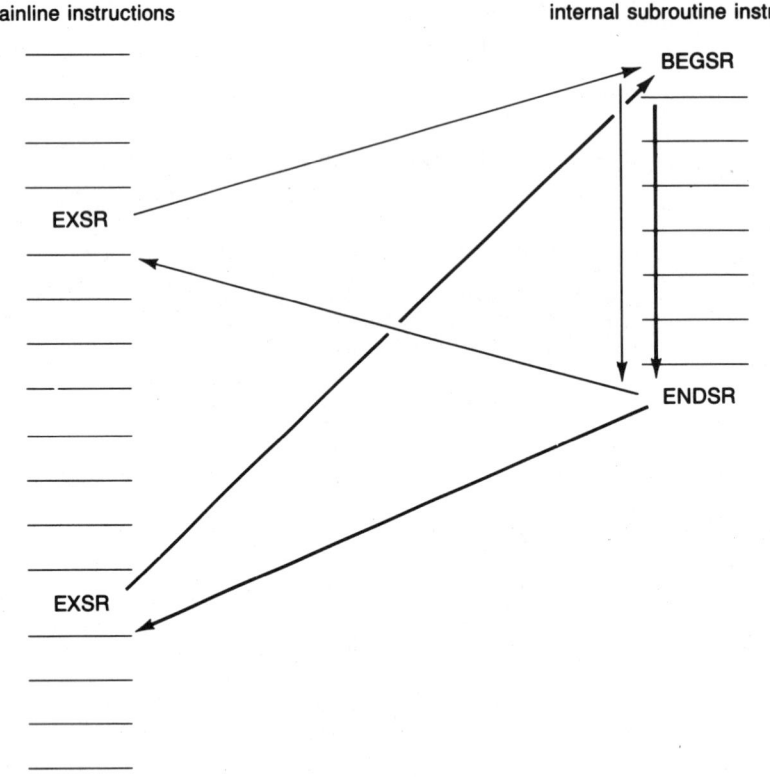

Figure 10-17 Example of internal subroutine

As you can see, when the main sequence of operations reaches the EXSR operation, the program immediately proceeds to the BEGSR (BEGin SubRoutine) operation, which marks the beginning of an internal subroutine. The BEGSR is similar to the TAG operation in that it is a go-to point and does not perform any other operation. Once the program flow has reached the beginning of the subroutine, the operations within the subroutine are executed in a top-down manner until the ENDSR (END SubRoutine) operation is reached. The ENDSR causes the program to return to the operation following the EXSR that caused the subroutine to be executed.

As Figure 10-17 shows, the same subroutine can be accessed by several EXSR operations. Regardless of which EXSR called the subroutine, the program always returns to the operation following the correct EXSR. RPG and RPG II require that all subroutines be located at the end of the calculations and that every line of a subroutine be identified by an entry SR in positions 7–8. Enhanced RPG II, RPG III, and RPG/400 do not require the SR entry in every subroutine line. Your instructor or data center manager can give you the needs of the compiler you are using. Figure 10-18 summarizes the EXSR, BEGSR, and ENDSR operations. RPG also supports another type of subroutine, the **external subroutine**. An external subroutine is a separate program, often in machine language, that is called and executed by an RPG program but does not become part of the program.

EXSR Operation Summary

The EXSR operation causes the program to execute an internal subroutine. Any number of EXSR statements can reference the same subroutine. After all operations in the subroutine are executed, the program will return to the calculation that follows the EXSR operation. The EXSR can be conditioned by indicators in positions 7–19. If no indicators are used, the subroutine will always be executed.

Control Level Indicators	Indicators	Factor 1	Operation Name	Factor 2	Result Field	Resulting Indicators		
7–8	9–17	18–27	28–32	33–42	43–53	54–55	56–57	58–59
optional	optional	blank	EXSR	required	blank	blank	blank	blank

---

BEGSR Operation Summary

The BEGSR operation marks the beginning of an internal subroutine. The name used in Factor 1 must be unique. Each subroutine must be identified by a separate name. The name used in a BEGSR operation cannot be the same as the name used with a TAG operation.

Control Level Indicators	Indicators	Factor 1	Operation Name	Factor 2	Result Field	Resulting Indicators		
7–8	9–17	18–27	28–32	33–42	43–53	54–55	56–57	58–59
SR	blank	required	BEGSR	blank	blank	blank	blank	blank

optional
3X FORMAT

Figure 10-18   EXSR, BEGSR, and ENDSR summary

continued

ENDSR Operation Summary

The ENDSR operation marks the end of an internal subroutine. The ENDSR operation causes the program to return to the calculation operation following the EXSR statement that caused the subroutine to be executed. Factor 1 can contain a name that is branched to by a GOTO operation within the subroutine.

Control Level Indicators	Indicators	Factor 1	Operation Name	Factor 2	Result Field	Resulting Indicators		
7–8	9–17	18–27	28–32	33–42	43–53	54–55	56–57	58–59
SR	blank	optional	ENDSR	blank	blank	blank	blank	blank

optional
3X FORMAT

optional
RPG/400

Figure 10-18   (continued)

▸ **OFLOW Subroutine**   The OFLOW subroutine that is executed by line 31 of the calculations is shown in Figure 10-19. Note that all seven lines of the subroutine are identified by SR in positions 7–8. The first line of the subroutine is the BEGSR operation that identifies the subroutine; the subroutine name, OFLOW, is entered in the Factor 1 area. Line 111 turns off indicator 40, the valid-record indicator. This subroutine is executed after every exception output operation used to print an error message. By including the SETOF of indicator 40 in this subroutine, we guarantee that the valid-record indicator is turned off by any error condition.

Lines 112, 113, and 114 control the overflow indicator (OF) used to group indicate the LISTNO field after page overflow. These three instructions use the same technique you learned in Chapter 9.

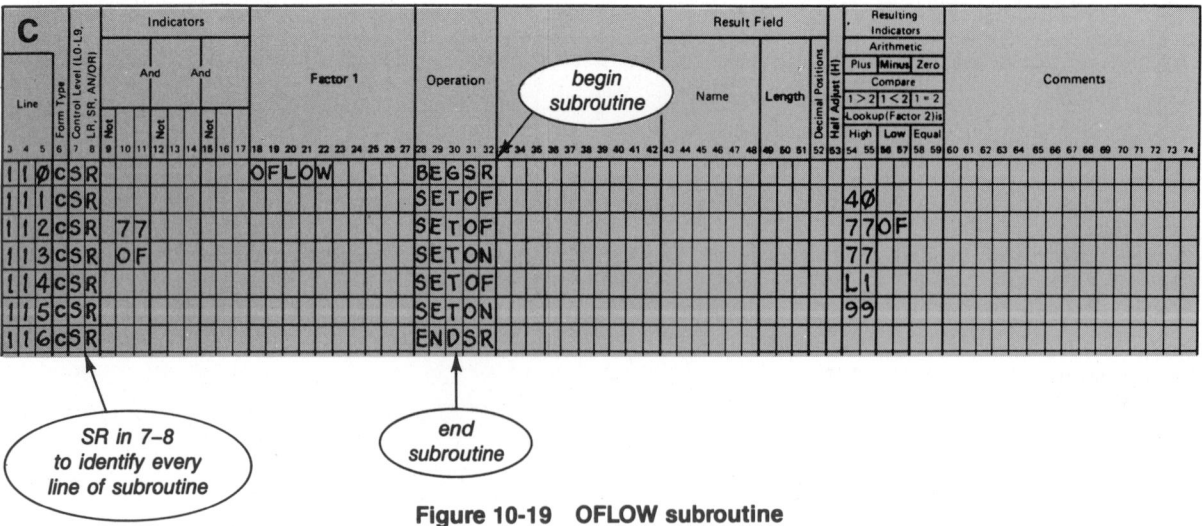

Figure 10-19   OFLOW subroutine

Line 115 sets indicator 99 on any time the subroutine is executed. As you saw, AREPORT contains an error block that must print out at the end of the report if an error occurs in any input data record. If the subroutine is executed at any point in the program, indicator 99, the error indicator, turns on. Because the program does not contain an operation to turn off indicator 99, it stays on for the duration of the program once it is set on. Line 116, the ENDSR operation, marks the end of the subroutine and causes the program to return to line 32 (see Figure 10-15), the line following the EXSR operation.

▸ **Resetting the Error Message Indicator** Because all the operations needed to properly indicate that the LISTNO field is blank have been performed, line 32 uses a SETOF operation to reset the error message indicator. As we proceed through the calculations, you will see the logic we have just discussed repeated several times. Every time an error is identified, the program turns on an indicator, prints an exception line, executes the OFLOW subroutine, and turns off the error indicator to prevent improper printing of the error message.

Duplicate LISTNO Test

Lines 33–38 of the calculations test for a duplicate listing identification number. Figure 10-20 shows the calculation and output specifications used by the test for a duplicate LISTNO field. This test is required because most keyed files cannot contain two or more records identified by the same key field value. If an attempt is made to add a record containing a key field value that already exists in the file, the program halts.

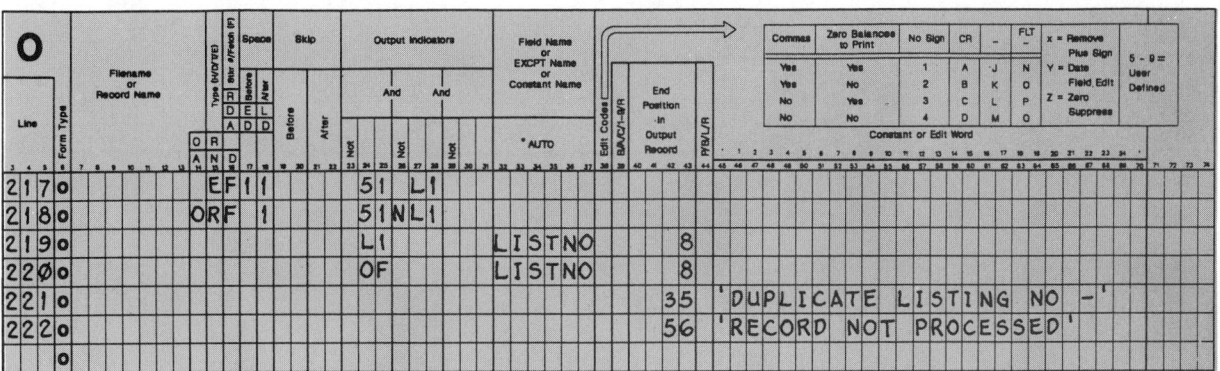

Figure 10-20 Duplicate LISTNO test

The first operation performs a random read of LISTFILE, attempting to read a record identified by the contents of the LISTNO field. Note that this operation is performed only if indicator 80 is not on, meaning that LISTNO is not blank. If the read is unsuccessful, and the record does not already exist in the file, indicator 86 is turned on. Remember that the indicator in positions 54–55 of a CHAIN operation turns on if the requested record is not found. After the CHAIN, if the record is found, the resulting indicator status will be N86.

Line 34, conditioned by indicators N80 (LISTNO not blank) and N86 (record key already in LISTFILE), will SETON indicator 51. Lines 35, 36, and 37 then EXCPT the error message, EXSR the OFLOW subroutine, and SETOF indicator 51. Note that this logic is the same as the error message and indicator reset logic used if LISTNO is blank.

Line 38, also conditioned by N80 and N86, uses a GOTO operation to branch to the end of the calculation tests (line 107), bypassing the remaining tests as specified in the Processing Requirements portion of the problem description.

▤ Remaining Blank Field Tests

Figure 10-21 shows the processing performed if any of the remaining required fields (TOWN, ZIP, TYPE, or PRICE) is blank. Note that in each case the SETON, EXCPT, EXSR, SETOF sequence of operations is performed using the same logic that was used for the previously tested error conditions.

Figure 10-21 Blank field tests

Line	Form Type	Control Level	Indicators (And Not / And Not / And Not)	Factor 1	Operation	Factor 2	Result Field Name	Length	Dec Pos	Half Adjust	Resulting Indicators (Plus/Minus/Zero, High/Low/Equal)	Comments
39	C		81		SETON						53	LOCATION
40	C		53		EXCPT							
41	C		53		EXSR	OFLOW						
42	C		53		SETOF						53	
43	C		82		SETON						54	TOWN CODE
44	C		54		EXCPT							
45	C		54		EXSR	OFLOW						
46	C		54		SETOF						54	
47	C		83		SETON						55	ZIP CODE
48	C		55		EXCPT							
49	C		55		EXSR	OFLOW						
50	C		55		SETOF						55	
51	C		84		SETON						56	PROPERTY TYPE
52	C		56		EXCPT							
53	C		56		EXSR	OFLOW						
54	C		56		SETOF						56	
55	C		85		SETON						57	PRICE
56	C		57		EXCPT							
57	C		57		EXSR	OFLOW						
58	C		57		SETOF						57	

Figure 10-21 (1)

Line	Form Type	Filename or Record Name	Type H/O/T/E/D	Bfr A/Fresh (P)	Space Before	Space After	Skip	Output indicators And And	Field Name or EXCPT Name or Constant Name *AUTO	Edit Codes	End Position in Output Record	Constant or Edit Word
228	O		EF 1 1					53 L1				
229	O	ORF 1						53NL1				
230	O							L1	LISTNO		8	
231	O							OF	LISTNO		8	
232	O										36	'PROPERTY LOCATION BLANK'
233	O		EF 1 1					54 L1				
234	O	ORF 1						54NL1				
235	O							L1	LISTNO		8	
236	O							OF	LISTNO		8	
237	O										28	'TOWN CODE BLANK'
238	O		EF 1 1					55 L1				
239	O	ORF 1						55NL1				
240	O							L1	LISTNO		8	
241	O							OF	LISTNO		8	
242	O										32	'ZIP CODE BLANK/ZERO'
243	O		EF 1 1					56 L1				
244	O	ORF 1						56NL1				
245	O							L1	LISTNO		8	
246	O							OF	LISTNO		8	
247	O										32	'PROPERTY TYPE BLANK'

Figure 10-21 (2)

Line	Form Type	Filename or Record Name	Type H/O/T/E/D	Bfr A/Fresh (P)	Space Before	Space After	Skip	Output indicators And And	Field Name or EXCPT Name or Constant Name *AUTO	Edit Codes	End Position in Output Record	Constant or Edit Word
248	O		EF 1 1					57 L1				
249	O	ORF 1						57NL1				
250	O							L1	LISTNO		8	
251	O							OF	LISTNO		8	
252	O										29	'PRICE BLANK/ZERO'

Figure 10-21 (3)

▤ Valid Town Code Test

Figure 10-22 on the next page shows the processing to test for a valid town code. As you can see, the logic is similar to that used to test for a duplicate LISTNO field. If TOWN is not blank (indicator N82), a LOKUP operation is used to determine if the town code exists in the TABTN table. If the town code cannot be found (N65), the familiar SETON, EXCPT, EXSR, SETOF sequence is performed. Again, the purpose of the OFLOW subroutine is to turn off the valid-record indicator, reset the overflow indicator if needed, and turn on indicator 99, which controls printing of the error block at the end of the program.

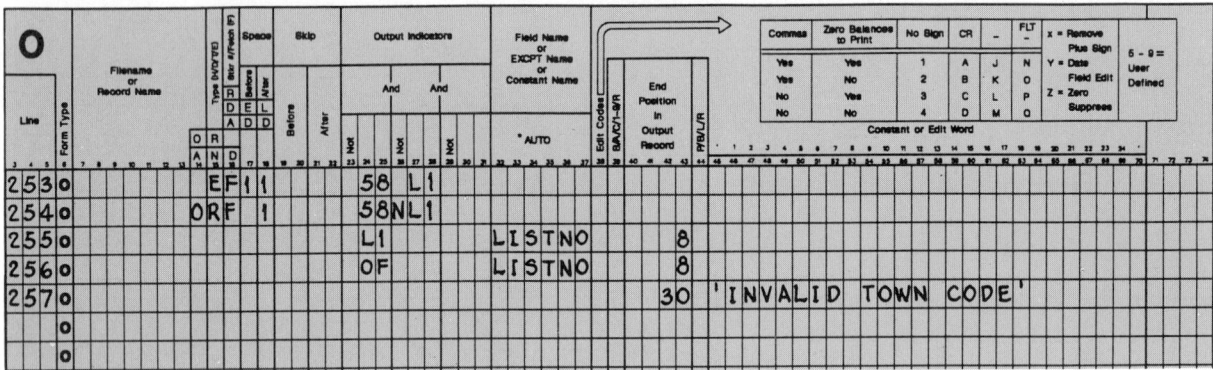

Figure 10-22 Valid town code test

Valid ZIP Code Test

The test for a valid ZIP code, shown in Figure 10-23, is the same type of test used with the town code. Note that neither the town code nor ZIP code test retrieves a function during the LOKUP operation. The purpose of these tests is only to determine if the TOWN and ZIP field contents exist in their respective tables.

▶ **Valid Town and ZIP Code Combination Test** Figure 10-24 shows the coding used to determine if the town code and ZIP code fields contain a valid combination. Line 69 performs a LOKUP operation only if indicators 65 and 66 are both on, indicating that both the town code and ZIP codes are valid.

The LOKUP operation retrieves the ZIP entry that corresponds to the TOWN entry used as the search argument. Line 70 then compares TABZIP, the retrieved ZIP code, with ZIP, the input ZIP Code field. If the two fields are unequal, indicator 68 is turned on. Indicator 68 then sets indicator 62, beginning the repetition of the SETON, EXCPT, EXSR, SETOF sequence.

Note that line 74 sets off indicators 62, 67, and 68. The SETOF of indicators 67 and 68 eliminates the possibility of either indicator being on incorrectly when the next record is processed. This is a variation of the "indicator controlled by another indicator" situation that you learned about as a special problem in comparing.

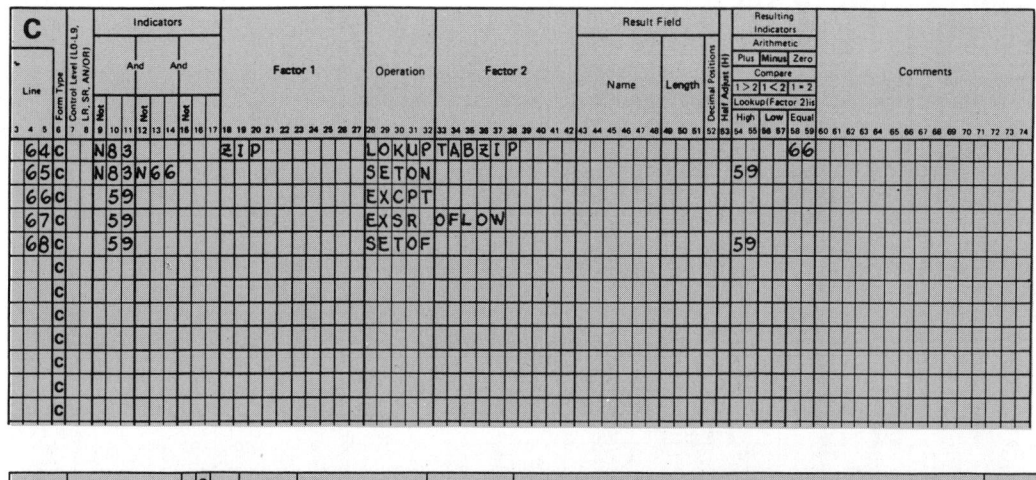

Figure 10-23   Valid ZIP code test

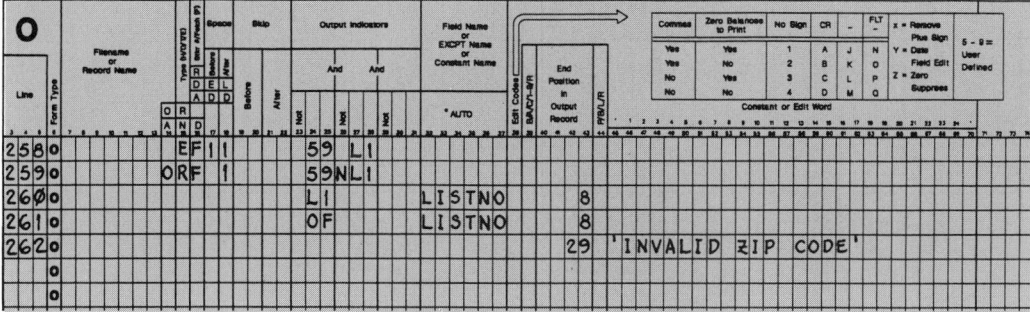

Figure 10-24   Matching town and ZIP code combination test

Valid Property Type Code Test

The code used to determine if the TYPE field contains one of the three valid type code entries is shown in Figure 10-25. In this code, indicator 69 represents type code R, indicator 70 represents type code C, and indicator 71 represents type code L. The first line of code, line 75, sets these three indicators off so as to clear them prior to the three COMP operations that follow.

```
C  Line  Indicators      Factor 1    Operation  Factor 2     Resulting Ind.  Comments
   75C                                SETOF                   697Ø71          CLEAR TYPE IND
   76C   N84              TYPE        COMP       'R'          727269          TEST FOR
   77C   N84 72           TYPE        COMP       'C'          72727Ø            VALID
   78C   N84 72           TYPE        COMP       'L'          727271                TYPE
   79C   72                           SETON                   6Ø              TYPE INVALID
   8ØC   6Ø                           EXCPT
   81C   6Ø                           EXSR       OFLOW
   82C   6Ø                           SETOF                   6Ø72
     C
     C
     C
     C
```

```
O  Line  Filename  Type Space Skip  Output Indicators  Field Name   End Position  Constant
  263O              EF   11           6Ø L1
  264O             ORF    1           6ØNL1
  265O                                L1                LISTNO       8
  266O                                OF                LISTNO       8
  267O                                                               34  'INVALID PROPERTY TYPE'
     O
     O
```

Figure 10-25 Valid property type code test

The three COMP operations, lines 76, 77, and 78, compare the TYPE field with the three valid Type Code entries. In each of the comparisons, if the TYPE field is equal to the Factor 2 literal, the appropriate indicator is turned on. If the TYPE entry is not equal to the literal, indicator 72 is turned on. Note that the three comparisons are performed only if the TYPE field is not blank (indicator N84) and that the second and third comparisons are performed only if the preceding comparison result was not-equal (indicator 72). If, after the three comparisons, indicator 72 is on, showing that the Type Code field entry is not one of the three valid type codes, line 79 sets indicator 60 on. Indicator 60 is then used to control the EXCPT, EXSR, SETOF sequence of operations. Note that the SETOF operation on line 82 also turns off indicator 72. This is another example of clearing an indicator that was set as the result of a prior test.

Valid Property Category Test

Figure 10-26 shows the code used to verify that the property category code entry is one of the four valid codes and matches the property type code. As was stated in the Processing Requirements portion of the problem description, only certain property category codes are valid with each property type code. Recall that a blank Property Category entry is not necessarily an error. The processing requirements state that if the property type is L, the Property Category entry must be blank. Lines 83 and 84 turn off the four indicators (73, 74, 75, and 76) that are used to specify the entry found in the Category Code field.

Lines 85–88 compare CATEG with each of the valid Property Category entries, turning on indicator 73 for code S, indicator 74 for code M, indicator 75 for code O, and indicator 76 for code G. Line 89 then unconditionally turns on indicator 63, the invalid-category indicator.

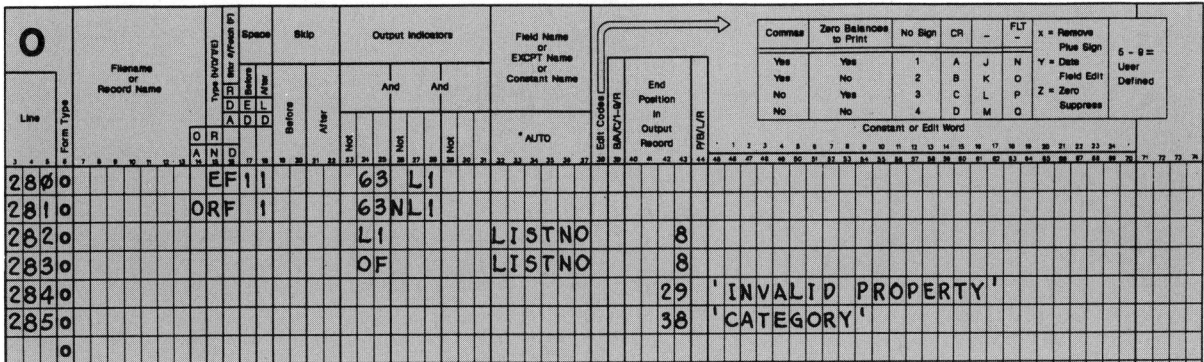

Figure 10-26 Valid property category test

The logic used in this test differs somewhat from the logic used in the previous tests. Because there are six valid combinations of property type and category, the logic used for this error test turns the error indicator on and then, if the combination of property and category codes is valid, turns indicator 63 off. Lines 90–95 link the six possible valid combinations in a series of OR relationships so that if any one of the valid combinations is found in the record, indicator 63 is turned off by the SETOF operation on line 95. If the combination of property and category codes is not valid, and one of the six indicator combinations does not occur, indicator 63 remains on, and the program executes the EXCPT, EXSR, SETOF sequence of operations on lines 96–98.

Contact Telephone Number Test

The processing requirements state that if a contact person is listed, the Contact Telephone Number field may not be blank. Figure 10-27 shows the code used to test for this condition. Line 99 uses two indicators, N20 (Contact Name field not blank) and 21 (Contact Telephone Number field blank) to turn on indicator 61, which then controls lines 100, 101, and 102.

```
 99C   N20 21                SETON                     61
100C      61                 EXCPT
101C      61                 EXSR OFLOW
102C      61                 SETOF                     61
```

```
268O                EF 1     61 L1
269O               ORF 1     61NL1
270O                         L1       LISTNO      8
271O                         OF       LISTNO      8
272O                                             37 'CONTACT TELEPHONE NUMBER'
273O                                             45 'MISSING'
```

Figure 10-27 Contact telephone number test

Contact Name and Account Representative Test

Figure 10-28 shows the code used to verify that the Contact Person field and the Account Representative field are not both blank. Line 103 sets on indicator 64 if indicator 20 (blank Contact Person field) and indicator 28 (blank Account Representative field) are both on. Indicator 64 then controls the last of the EXCPT, EXSR, SETOF sequences used in the calculations.

```
103C   20 28             SETON                     64
104C   64                EXCPT
105C   64                EXSR OFLOW
106C   64                SETOF                     64
```

```
286O        EF11     64 L1
287O       ORF 1     64NL1
288O                 L1      LISTNO     8
289O                 OF      LISTNO     8
290O                                   37 'CONTACT AND ACCOUNT REP.'
291O                                   48 'BOTH BLANK'
```

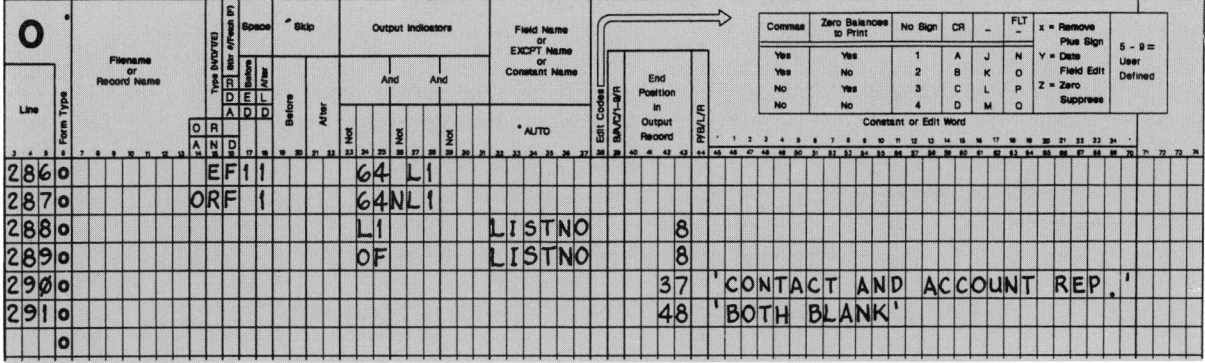

Figure 10-28 Contact name and account representative test

Count of Records Added and Record Errors

After all the tests have been performed, lines 108 and 109 (Figure 10-29) count the number of valid and invalid input records. Remember that indicator 40 was turned on at the beginning of the calculations on line 28 to act as a valid-record indicator. If indicator 40 is still on at the end of the calculations, line 108 adds 1 to the ADDS field, which counts the number of records added to LISTFILE. If indicator 40 was turned off by the OFLOW subroutine, line 109 adds 1 to ERRORS, which counts the number of input records that contain errors. Note that ERRORS is not a count of all the separate errors detected. Line 109 adds 1 to ERRORS only once for each erroneous record, regardless of the number of errors detected.

```
108C   40      ADDS      ADD  1         ADDS    30
109C  N40      ERRORS    ADD  1         ERRORS  30
```

Figure 10-29 Record counts

☰ OUTPUT SPECIFICATIONS FOR PROGRAM HJG10X ☰
☰ AREPORT Output File Specifications

Figure 10-30 shows the Output Specifications forms for AREPORT. Note the use of overflow indicator OV to control overflow headings and indicator 40 to control the printing of the three detail output lines. The only new entry, edit code X, is first shown on line 133 of the first page of output specifications for the file (Figure 10-30).

▸ **Edit Code X** Used with the ZIP, PH1, PH2, PH3, and EXT fields (edit code X), removes the sign of a number and allows the digits to print with no zero suppression. Most computers store the sign of a numeric field as part of the rightmost digit of the field. The rightmost position, because it contains both a digit and a sign, often prints as a letter if no editing is performed. This has not been a problem so far because all the edit codes you have used automatically remove the sign when they perform zero suppression of the field.

In this program, however, several of the numeric fields, such as ZIP code and PH3 cannot be zero suppressed because they must be printed with leading zeros. If these fields are not edited, the possibility exists that the rightmost position will print as a letter. To eliminate this possibility, edit code X is used to remove the sign of the number and allow only the digits to print. Note that edit code X provides no other editing function. It does not insert commas or decimal points or provide zero suppression; it only removes the sign of a number from the rightmost position of the field prior to printing.

▸ **Output Field Control** Note the use of the property type and category code indicators on lines 135–140 to control which of the six possible property type and category constants prints in the second detail line. There is no need to control the TYPE- constant because the output record does not print if the property type and category codes are not a valid combination.

Figure 10-30 AREPORT Output Specifications

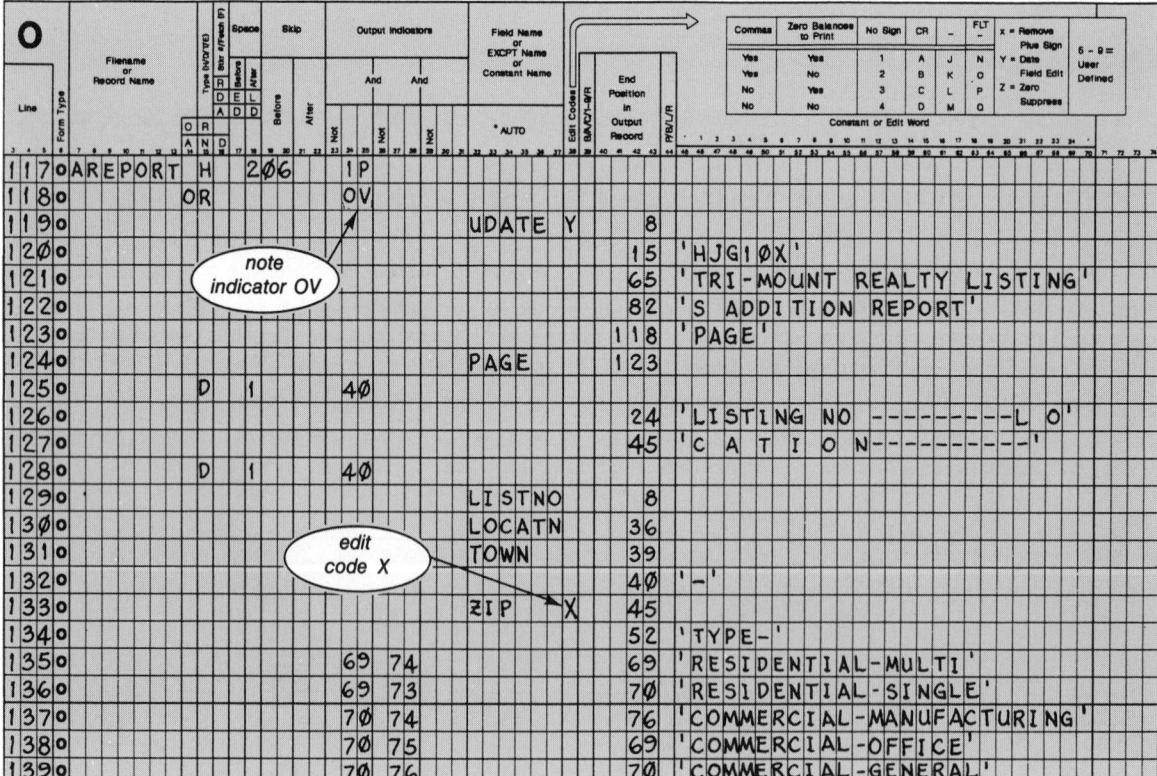

Figure 10-30 (1)

Figure 10-30 (2):

Line	Form Type	Type	Space	Skip	Output Indicators	Field Name / Constant	Edit Codes	End Position	Constant or Edit Word
140	O				71			56	'LAND'
141	O				N20			85	'CONTACT-'
142	O				N20	CONTCT		100	
143	O				N21 N22	PH1	X	104	
144	O				N21 N22			105	'-'
145	O				N21	PH2	X	108	
146	O				N21			109	'-'
147	O				N21	PH3	X	113	
148	O				N21 N23			118	'EXT.'
149	O				N21 N23	EXT	X	123	
150	O	D	3		40				
151	O				N25			25	'BLDG- SQFT'
152	O				N25	BLDSQF2		20	
153	O				N26			47	'LAND SQFT'
154	O				N26	LNDSQF2		42	
155	O				N27	LNDACR2		53	
156	O				N27			58	'ACRE'
157	O							65	'PRICE'
158	O					PRICE	2	77	'$'
159	O				N28			87	'ACCOUNT-'
160	O				N28	ACCREP		102	
161	O	T	2		LR				
162	O					ADDS	Z	11	

Figure 10-30 (2)

Figure 10-30 (3):

Line	Form Type	Type	Space	Skip	Output Indicators	Field Name / Constant	Edit Codes	End Position	Constant or Edit Word
163	O							34	'LISTINGS ADDED TO FILE'
164	O	T	1		LR 99				
165	O							32	'*********************'
166	O							34	'**'
167	O	T	1		LR 99				
168	O							9	'*'
169	O							34	'*'
170	O	T	1		LR 99				
171	O							9	'*'
172	O					ERRORS	Z	13	
173	O							34	'LISTINGS NOT ADDED *'
174	O	T	1		LR 99				
175	O							9	'*'
176	O							34	'*'
177	O	T	1		LR 99				
178	O							9	'*'
179	O							34	'SEE ERROR REPORT *'
180	O	T	1		LR 99				
181	O							9	'*'
182	O							34	'*'
183	O	T		06	LR 99				
184	O							32	'*************************'
185	O							34	'**'

Figure 10-30 (3)

Note also the use of blank field indicators to control the printing of identifying constants. For example, indicator N20 is used on lines 141 and 142 to control printing of both the CONTCT field and the CONTACT- constant that is used to identify the field output.

▶ **Error Block Printing** The seven final total lines controlled by indicators LR and 99 print the error block if any errors were detected by the program. As you saw earlier, indicator 99 is turned on if any error occurs and stays on for the remainder of the program. If indicator 99 is on at the end of the program, meaning that one or more records contained erroneous data, these seven lines are printed. If no errors were detected, the error block is not printed, because indicator 99 is not on.

LISTFILE Output Disk File Specifications

Figure 10-31 shows the output specifications for LISTFILE, the disk output file. Note that the LISTFILE records are written to disk if indicator 40 is on, specifying that the input record contained no errors. Line 186, the record description line, is somewhat different from the output record description lines you have seen so far. The first difference is that there are no spacing or skipping specifications. Space and Skip entries are used only with printed output files and are meaningless with a file going to any device other than PRINTER. Most versions of RPG generate an error message if Space or Skip entries are made for any non-PRINTER file.

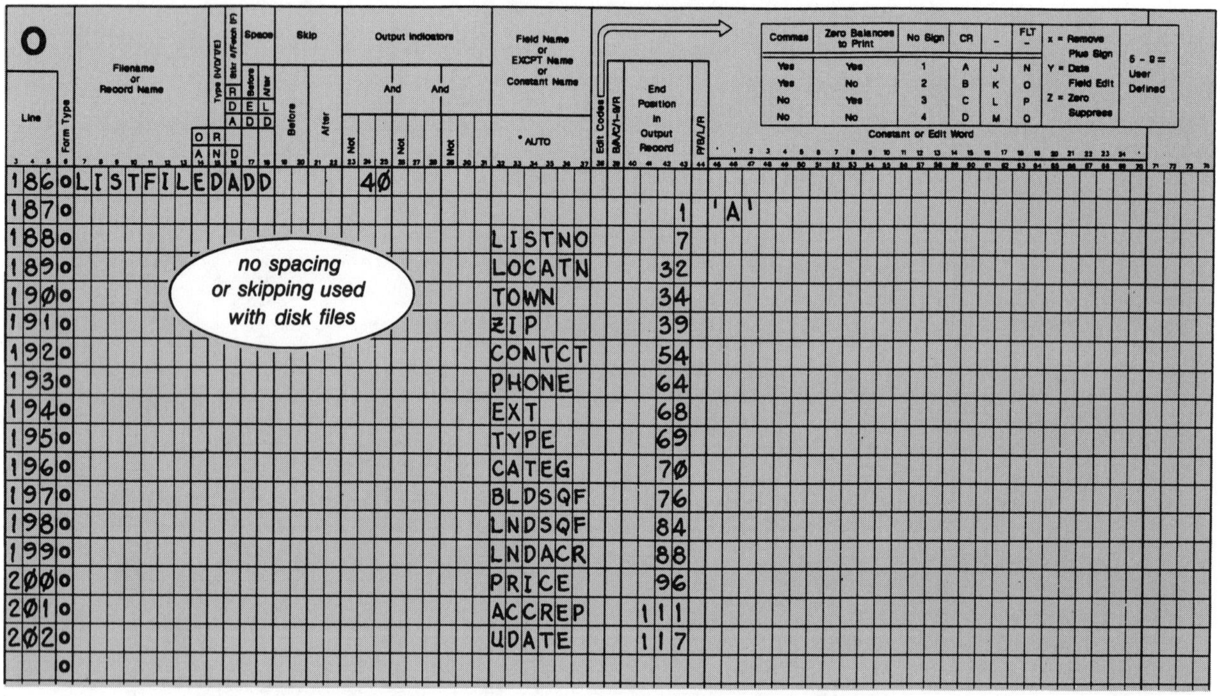

Figure 10-31   LISTFILE Output Specifications

▶ **The Record Addition ADD Entry** The second difference is the entry in positions 16–18, ADD. The ADD entry should not be confused with the ADD operation used in RPG calculations. The output ADD entry specifies that a new output record is being added to a disk output file. This entry works in conjunction with the Record Addition entry A (position 66) that was part of the file description for LISTFILE, as illustrated in Figure 10-32. Both entries must be present for the program to add new records to a disk file.

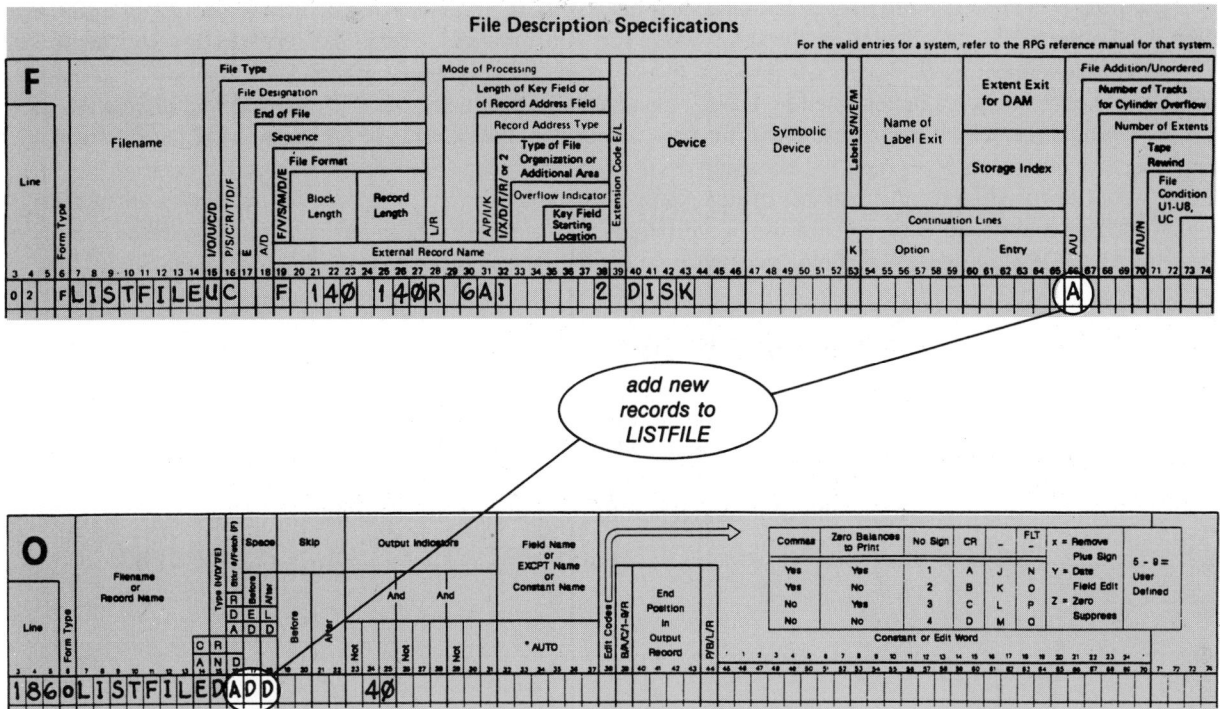

Figure 10-32   Disk record addition

▸ **Output Field Specifications**   As you can see, no edit codes are used with the output fields. Output editing is a method used to make printed output more readable and is, therefore, not normally used with disk file output. Line 187 uses a constant to place the letter A in the Status Code area, as specified by the LISTFILE record layout. Note the use of the UDATE field (line 202) to enter the listing date into positions 112–117 of each output record. This entry identifies the date each record was added to LISTFILE.

▰ EREPORT Output File Specifications

You have already seen the main portion of the EREPORT specifications, the exception output lines. Figure 10-33 shows the heading lines specified for EREPORT. Note that the first heading line does not contain the PAGE field for page numbering. Instead, the PAGE1 field is used.

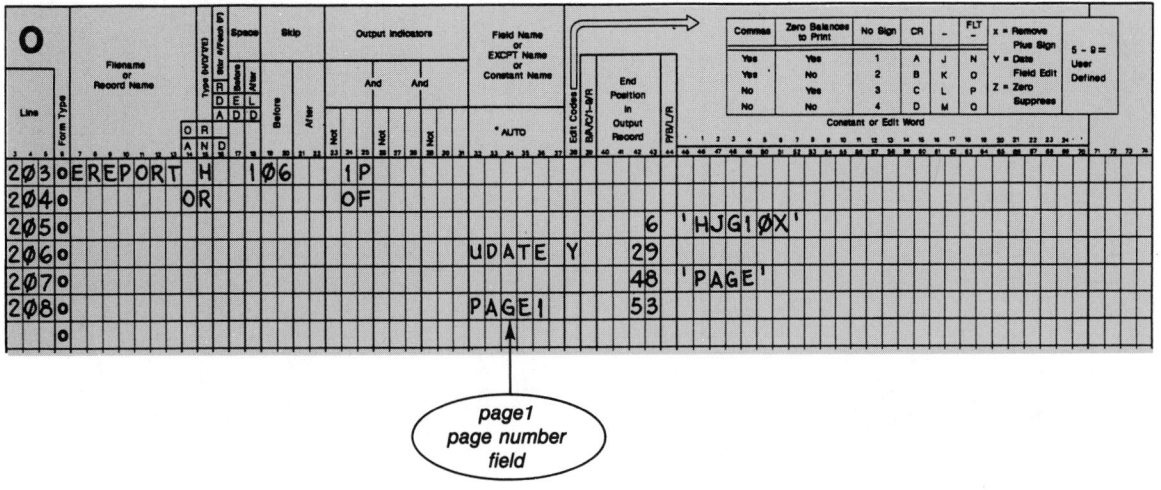

Figure 10-33   Use of PAGE1

RPG provides eight different page-numbering fields: PAGE, PAGE1, PAGE2, ..., PAGE7. Eight different page-numbering fields are provided for the same reason that RPG provides several different overflow indicators. The same page-numbering field cannot be used on two or more different reports. When PAGE is used in a report, the contents of the field are incremented by 1 every time page overflow takes place. If two different reports are created by a program and both reports use PAGE for page numbering, the contents of PAGE are incremented every time overflow occurs on either report. This would result in incorrect page numbering because the contents of PAGE would be based on the total number of pages printed on both reports. To provide for separate page numbering of different reports, RPG permits the use of a different page-numbering field on each report produced. Because AREPORT uses the PAGE field, reserved field PAGE1 is used in the first heading line of EREPORT.

▤ Summary of Program HJG10X

Figure 10-34 shows the complete compilation listing of program HJG10X, the two output reports produced by the program, and a listing of the data records added to LISTFILE by the program.

Figure 10-34   Compilation listing for program HJG10X

```
HJG10X    09-12-91  19:01:50      IBM PC       RPG II        Version 3.5  Page  1

          ....+....1....+....2....+....3....+....4....+....5....+....6....+....7....

          1 0001 H                                                      HJG10X


          2 0002 FLISTDATAIP  F 480 120         DISK
          3 0003 FLISTFILEUC  F 140 140R 6AI   2 DISK                   A
          4 0004 FEREPORT O   F 132 132    OF   PRINTER
          5 0005 FAREPORT O   F 132 132    OV   PRINTER


          6 0006 E                  TABTN  1   9 2
          7 0007 E                  TABZIP 1   9 5 0


          8 0008 ILISTDATAAAA  01
          9 0009 I                            1   6 LISTNOL1    80
         10 0010 I                            7  31 LOCATN      81
         11 0011 I                           32  33 TOWN        82
         12 0012 I                           34  380ZIP        83
         13 0013 I                           39  53 CONTCT      20
         14 0014 I                           54  63 PHONE       21
         15 0015 I                           54  560PH1         22
         16 0016 I                           57  590PH2
         17 0017 I                           60  630PH3
         18 0018 I                           64  670EXT         23
         19 0019 I                           68  68 TYPE        84
         20 0020 I                           69  69 CATEG       24
         21 0021 I                           70  750BLDSQF      25
         22 0022 I                           76  830LNDSQF      26
         23 0023 I                           84  871LNDACR      27
         24 0024 I                           88  950PRICE       85
         25 0025 I                           96 110 ACCREP      28
         26 0026 ILISTFILEAA  02
         27 0027 I                            2   7 IDENT


         28 0028 C    01        SETON              40
         29 0029 C    80        SETON              52
         30 0030 C    52        EXCPT
         31 0031 C    52        EXSR OFLOW
         32 0032 C    52        SETOF              52
         33 0033 C    N80   LISTNO   CHAINLISTFILE   86
         34 0034 C    N80N86    SETON              51
         35 0035 C    51        EXCPT
```

Figure 10-34 (1)

```
HJG10X    09-12-91  19:01:50        IBM PC      RPG II           Version 3.5  Page  2

       ....+....1....+....2....+....3....+....4....+....5....+....6....+....7....

 36 0036 C   51              EXSR OFLOW
 37 0037 C   51              SETOF                         51
 38 0038 C   N80N86          GOTO END
 39 0039 C   81              SETON                         53
 40 0040 C   53              EXCPT
 41 0041 C   53              EXSR OFLOW
 42 0042 C   53              SETOF                         53
 43 0043 C   82              SETON                         54
 44 0044 C   54              EXCPT
 45 0045 C   54              EXSR OFLOW
 46 0046 C   54              SETOF                         54
 47 0047 C   83              SETON                         55
 48 0048 C   55              EXCPT
 49 0049 C   55              EXSR OFLOW
 50 0050 C   55              SETOF                         55
 51 0051 C   84              SETON                         56
 52 0052 C   56              EXCPT
 53 0053 C   56              EXSR OFLOW
 54 0054 C   56              SETOF                         56
 55 0055 C   85              SETON                         57
 56 0056 C   57              EXCPT
 57 0057 C   57              EXSR OFLOW
 58 0058 C   57              SETOF                         57
 59 0059 C   N82      TOWN   LOKUPTABTN                        65
 60 0060 C   N82N65          SETON                         58
 61 0061 C   58              EXCPT
 62 0062 C   58              EXSR OFLOW
 63 0063 C   58              SETOF                         58
 64 0064 C   N83      ZIP    LOKUPTABZIP                       66
 65 0065 C   N83N66          SETON                         59
 66 0066 C   59              EXCPT
 67 0067 C   59              EXSR OFLOW
 68 0068 C   59              SETOF                         59
 69 0069 C   65 66    TOWN   LOKUPTABTN    TABZIP             67
 70 0070 C   67       TABZIP COMP ZIP                      6868
 71 0071 C   68              SETON                         62
 72 0072 C   62              EXCPT
 73 0073 C   62              EXSR OFLOW
 74 0074 C   62              SETOF                         626768
 75 0075 C                   SETOF                         697071
 76 0076 C   N84      TYPE   COMP 'R'                      727269
 77 0077 C   N84 72   TYPE   COMP 'C'                      727270
 78 0078 C   N84 72   TYPE   COMP 'L'                      727271
 79 0079 C   72              SETON                         60
 80 0080 C   60              EXCPT
 81 0081 C   60              EXSR OFLOW
 82 0082 C   60              SETOF                         6072
 83 0083 C                   SETOF                         737475
 84 0084 C                   SETOF                         76
 85 0085 C   N24      CATEG  COMP 'S'                          73
 86 0086 C   N24      CATEG  COMP 'M'                          74
 87 0087 C   N24      CATEG  COMP 'O'                          75
 88 0088 C   N24      CATEG  COMP 'G'                          76
 89 0089 C                   SETON                         63
 90 0090 C   69 73
 91 0091 COR 69 74
 92 0092 COR 70 74
 93 0093 COR 70 75
 94 0094 COR 70 76
 95 0095 COR 71 24          SETOF                         63
 96 0096 C   63              EXCPT
 97 0097 C   63              EXSR OFLOW
 98 0098 C   63              SETOF                         63
 99 0099 C   N20 21          SETON                         61
100 0100 C   61              EXCPT
101 0101 C   61              EXSR OFLOW
102 0102 C   61              SETOF                         61
103 0103 C   20 28           SETON                         64
104 0104 C   64              EXCPT
105 0105 C   64              EXSR OFLOW
106 0106 C   64              SETOF                         64
107 0107 C            END    TAG
108 0108 C   40       ADDS   ADD  1         ADDS    30
109 0109 C   N40      ERRORS ADD  1         ERRORS  30
```

Figure 10-34 (2)

continued

```
HJG10X     09-12-91  19:01:50        IBM PC       RPG II        Version 3.5  Page  3

           ....+....1....+....2....+....3....+....4....+....5....+....6....+....7....
110 0110 CSR          OFLOW     BEGSR
111 0111 CSR          OFLOW     SETOF                    40
112 0112 CSR 77                 SETOF                    770F
113 0113 CSR OF                 SETON                    77
114 0114 CSR                    SETOF                    L1
115 0115 CSR                    SETON                    99
116 0116 CSR                    ENDSR


117 0117 OAREPORT H  206    1P
118 0118 O        OR         OV
119 0119 O                            UDATE Y    8
120 0120 O                                      15 'HJG10X'
121 0121 O                                      65 'TRI-MOUNT REALTY LISTING'
122 0122 O                                      82 'S ADDITION REPORT'
123 0123 O                                     118 'PAGE'
124 0124 O                            PAGE      123
125 0125 O        D  1      40
126 0126 O                                      24 'LISTING NO ---------L O '
127 0127 O                                      45 'C A T I O N----------'
128 0128 O        D  1      40
129 0129 O                            LISTNO     8
130 0130 O                            LOCATN    36
131 0131 O                            TOWN      39
132 0132 O                                      40 '-'
133 0133 O                            ZIP   X   45
134 0134 O                                      52 'TYPE-'
135 0135 O                      69 74           69 'RESIDENTIAL-MULTI'
136 0136 O                      69 73           70 'RESIDENTIAL-SINGLE'
137 0137 O                      70 74           76 'COMMERCIAL-MANUFACTURING'
138 0138 O                      70 75           69 'COMMERCIAL-OFFICE'
139 0139 O                      70 76           70 'COMMERCIAL-GENERAL'
140 0140 O                      71              56 'LAND'
141 0141 O                      N20             85 'CONTACT-'
142 0142 O                      N20   CONTCT   100
143 0143 O                      N21N22 PH1  X  104
144 0144 O                      N21N22         105 '-'
145 0145 O                      N21   PH2   X  108
146 0146 O                      N21            109 '-'
147 0147 O                      N21   PH3   X  113
148 0148 O                      N21N23         118 'EXT.'
149 0149 O                      N21N23 EXT  X  123
150 0150 O        D  3      40
151 0151 O                      N25             25 'BLDG-       SQFT'
152 0152 O                      N25   BLDSQF2   20
153 0153 O                      N26             47 'LAND-       SQFT'
154 0154 O                      N26   LNDSQF2   42
155 0155 O                      N27   LNDACR2   53
156 0156 O                      N27             58 'ACRE'
157 0157 O                                      65 'PRICE'
158 0158 O                            PRICE 2   77 '$'
159 0159 O                      N28             87 'ACCOUNT-'
160 0160 O                      N28   ACCREP   102
161 0161 O        T  2      LR
162 0162 O                            ADDS  Z   11
163 0163 O                                      34 'LISTINGS ADDED TO FILE'
164 0164 O        T  1      LR 99
165 0165 O                                      32 '*************************'
166 0166 O                                      34 '**'
167 0167 O        T  1      LR 99
168 0168 O                                       9 '*'
169 0169 O                                      34 '*'
170 0170 O        T  1      LR 99
171 0171 O                                       9 '*'
172 0172 O                            ERRORSZ   13
173 0173 O                                      34 'LISTINGS NOT ADDED *'
174 0174 O        T  1      LR 99
175 0175 O                                       9 '*'
176 0176 O                                      34 '*'
177 0177 O        T  1      LR 99
178 0178 O                                       9 '*'
179 0179 O                                      34 'SEE ERROR REPORT    *'
180 0180 O        T  1      LR 99
```

Figure 10-34 (3)

```
HJG10X      09-12-91  19:01:50      IBM PC      RPG II        Version 3.5  Page 4

        ....+....1....+....2....+....3....+....4....+....5....+....6....+....7....
        181 0181 O                                        9 '*'
        182 0182 O                                       34 '*'
        183 0183 O          T      06 LR 99
        184 0184 O                                       32 '*************************'
        185 0185 O                                       34 '**'
        186 0186 OLISTFILEDADD        40
        187 0187 O                                        1 'A'
        188 0188 O                           LISTNO        7
        189 0189 O                           LOCATN       32
        190 0190 O                           TOWN         34
        191 0191 O                           ZIP          39
        192 0192 O                           CONTCT       54
        193 0193 O                           PHONE        64
        194 0194 O                           EXT          68
        195 0195 O                           TYPE         69
        196 0196 O                           CATEG        70
        197 0197 O                           BLDSQF       76
        198 0198 O                           LNDSQF       84
        199 0199 O                           LNDACR       88
        200 0200 O                           PRICE        96
        201 0201 O                           ACCREP      111
        202 0202 O                           UDATE       117
        203 0203 OEREPORT H  106    1P
        204 0204 O          OR      OF
        205 0205 O                                        6 'HJG10X'
        206 0206 O                           UDATE Y      29
        207 0207 O                                       48 'PAGE'
        208 0208 O                           PAGE1        53
        209 0209 O          H  2    1P
        210 0210 O          OR      OF
        211 0211 O                                       31 'TRI-MOUNT REALTY LISTING'
        212 0212 O                                       48 'S ADDITION ERRORS'
        213 0213 O          H  2    1P
        214 0214 O          OR      OF
        215 0215 O                                       10 'LISTING NO'
        216 0216 O                                       30 '-------ERROR TYPE'
        217 0217 O          EF11    51 L1
        218 0218 O          ORF 1   51NL1
        219 0219 O                  L1       LISTNO        8
        220 0220 O                  OF       LISTNO        8
        221 0221 O                                       35 'DUPLICATE LISTING NO -'
        222 0222 O                                       56 'RECORD NOT PROCESSED'
        223 0223 O          EF11    52 L1
        224 0224 O          ORF 1   52NL1
        225 0225 O                  L1       LISTNO        8
        226 0226 O                  OF       LISTNO        8
        227 0227 O                                       33 'LISTING NUMBER BLANK'
        228 0228 O          EF11    53 L1
        229 0229 O          ORF 1   53NL1
        230 0230 O                  L1       LISTNO        8
        231 0231 O                  OF       LISTNO        8
        232 0232 O                                       36 'PROPERTY LOCATION BLANK'
        233 0233 O          EF11    54 L1
        234 0234 O          ORF 1   54NL1
        235 0235 O                  L1       LISTNO        8
        236 0236 O                  OF       LISTNO        8
        237 0237 O                                       28 'TOWN CODE BLANK'
        238 0238 O          EF11    55 L1
        239 0239 O          ORF 1   55NL1
        240 0240 O                  L1       LISTNO        8
        241 0241 O                  OF       LISTNO        8
        242 0242 O                                       32 'ZIP CODE BLANK/ZERO'
        243 0243 O          EF11    56 L1
        244 0244 O          ORF 1   56NL1
        245 0245 O                  L1       LISTNO        8
        246 0246 O                  OF       LISTNO        8
        247 0247 O                                       32 'PROPERTY TYPE BLANK'
        248 0248 O          EF11    57 L1
        249 0249 O          ORF 1   57NL1
        250 0250 O                  L1       LISTNO        8
        251 0251 O                  OF       LISTNO        8
        252 0252 O                                       29 'PRICE BLANK/ZERO'
        253 0253 O          EF11    58 L1
        254 0254 O          ORF 1   58NL1
        255 0255 O                  L1       LISTNO        8
```

Figure 10-34 (4)   *continued*

```
  HJG10X     09-12-91  19:01:50      IBM PC      RPG II      Version 3.5  Page  5

            ....+....1....+....2....+....3....+....4....+....5....+....6....+....7....
    256 0256 O                   OF      LISTNO   8
    257 0257 O                                   30 'INVALID TOWN CODE'
    258 0258 O         EF11      59 L1
    259 0259 O         ORF 1     59NL1
    260 0260 O                   L1      LISTNO   8
    261 0261 O                   OF      LISTNO   8
    262 0262 O                                   29 'INVALID ZIP CODE'
    263 0263 O         EF11      60 L1
    264 0264 O         ORF 1     60NL1
    265 0265 O                   L1      LISTNO   8
    266 0266 O                   OF      LISTNO   8
    267 0267 O                                   34 'INVALID PROPERTY TYPE'
    268 0268 O         EF11      61 L1
    269 0269 O         ORF 1     61NL1
    270 0270 O                   L1      LISTNO   8
    271 0271 O                   OF      LISTNO   8
    272 0272 O                                   37 'CONTACT TELEPHONE NUMBER'
    273 0273 O                                   45 'MISSING'
    274 0274 O         EF11      62 L1
    275 0275 O         ORF 1     62NL1
    276 0276 O                   L1      LISTNO   8
    277 0277 O                   OF      LISTNO   8
    278 0278 O                                   33 'TOWN CODE - ZIP CODE'
    279 0279 O                                   42 'CONFLICT'
    280 0280 O         EF11      63 L1
    281 0281 O         ORF 1     63NL1
    282 0282 O                   L1      LISTNO   8
    283 0283 O                   OF      LISTNO   8
    284 0284 O                                   29 'INVALID PROPERTY'
    285 0285 O                                   38 'CATEGORY'
    286 0286 O         EF11      64 L1
    287 0287 O         ORF 1     64NL1
    288 0288 O                   L1      LISTNO   8
    289 0289 O                   OF      LISTNO   8
    290 0290 O                                   37 'CONTACT AND ACCOUNT REP.
    291 0291 O                                   48 'BOTH BLANK'
    292 **
    293 AS
    294 BA
    295 ET
    296 FI
    297 GA
    298 TM
    299 WE
    300 WI
    301 WS
    302 **
    303 01430
    304 01436
    305 01438
    306 01420
    307 01440
    308 01468
    309 01473
    310 01475
    311 01477
    312 /*
    313 /*



        THE FOLLOWING INDICATORS WERE SPECIFIED BUT WERE NEVER
        USED TO CONDITION OPERATIONS

        02


        THE FOLLOWING INDICATORS APPEARED IN THIS PROGRAM

        01  02  20  21  22  23  24  25  26  27  28  40  51  52  53  54
        55  56  57  58  59  60  61  62  63  64  65  66  67  68  69  70
        71  72  73  74  75  76  77  80  81  82  83  84  85  86  99  LR
        L1  1P  OF  OV
No Warning Errors
No Fatal Errors
```

Figure 10-34 (5)

```
HJG10X              09/12/91            PAGE   1
            TRI-MOUNT REALTY LISTINGS ADDITION ERRORS


   LISTING NO ———————ERROR TYPE



      37B00F    TOWN CODE BLANK
                ZIP CODE BLANK/ZERO
                PROPERTY TYPE BLANK
                PRICE BLANK/ZERO
                INVALID PROPERTY CATEGORY
                CONTACT TELEPHONE NUMBER MISSING

      49F83A    PROPERTY LOCATION BLANK
                PROPERTY TYPE BLANK
                TOWN CODE - ZIP CODE CONFLICT
                INVALID PROPERTY CATEGORY


      87F29D    PROPERTY TYPE BLANK
                INVALID TOWN CODE
                INVALID PROPERTY CATEGORY


      93F21H    TOWN CODE - ZIP CODE CONFLICT
                CONTACT AND ACCOUNT REP. BOTH BLANK


      97F38I    INVALID PROPERTY CATEGORY
                CONTACT TELEPHONE NUMBER MISSING


      12A37A    DUPLICATE LISTING NO - RECORD NOT PROCESSED
```

Figure 10-34 (6)

```
09/12/91 HJG10X                   TRI-MOUNT REALTY LISTINGS ADDITION REPORT                    PAGE    1

LISTING NO ———————L O C A T I O N———————
   01X25A  BURNSHIRT INDUSTRIAL PARK TM-01468  TYPE-COMMERCIAL-MANUFACTURING CONTACT-ROY WHEATON        555-9136
           BLDG-125,000 SQFT                        9.0 ACRE  PRICE  $1,500,000


LISTING NO ———————L O C A T I O N———————
   03D41A   21 BULLDOG TERRACE        FI-01420  TYPE-RESIDENTIAL-SINGLE
            BLDG- 1,800 SQFT                        .6 ACRE  PRICE   $102,500  ACCOUNT-TONY GULINO


LISTING NO ———————L O C A T I O N———————
   12A37A   ROUTE 2A                  GA-01440  TYPE-RESIDENTIAL-MULTI        CONTACT-K. BASHAW    508-555-9311
            BLDG- 3,700 SQFT   LAND   27,000 SQFT             PRICE    $99,850  ACCOUNT-TONY GULINO


LISTING NO ———————L O C A T I O N———————
   13A37A   ROUTE 2A AND 101          BA-01436  TYPE-RESIDENTIAL-MULTI        CONTACT-NORM BELIN   508-555-2188
            BLDG- 4,600 SQFT   LAND  103,500 SQFT             PRICE   $187,000  ACCOUNT-TONY GULINO


LISTING NO ———————L O C A T I O N———————
   23D46D   41-55 WALTON WAY          WI-01475  TYPE-LAND                     CONTACT-SCOTT DRAKE   508-555-3000 EXT. 4215
                                        27.0 ACRE  PRICE   $675,000  ACCOUNT-MICHELLE DETLOR


LISTING NO ———————L O C A T I O N———————
   88G34A   THALER HILL ROAD          TM-01468  TYPE-COMMERCIAL-OFFICE        CONTACT-MARTEE RICHARDS 508-555-9876 EXT. 0024
            BLDG- 2,800 SQFT   LAND   40,000 SQFT             PRICE    $103,499


      6 LISTINGS ADDED TO FILE


      ***************************
      *                         *
      *  6 LISTINGS NOT ADDED   *
      *                         *
      *   SEE ERROR REPORT      *
      *                         *
      ***************************
```

Figure 10-34 (7)

continued

```
Filename  RecLen      KeyPo KeyLn                                          Date      Time      Page
LISTFILE  140           2     6                                          09/12/91   8.51

Rec No. Line No. 1... ...10.... ...20.... ...30.... ...40.... ...50.... ...60.... ...70.... ...80.... ...90.... ..100

         1    1   A01X25ABURNSHIRT INDUSTRIAL PARKTM01468ROY WHEATON         55591360000CM1250000000000009001500000
              2             102788

         2    1   A03D41A21 BULLDOG TERRACE        FI01420                   0000RS001800000000000000600102500TONY
              2   GULINO    102788

         3    1   A12A37AROUTE 2A                  GA01440K. BASHAW    5085559311000RM003700002700000000009850TONY
              2   GULINO    102788

         4    1   A13A37AROUTE 2A AND 101          BA01436NORM BELIN   5085552188000RM0046000010350000000187000TONY
              2   GULINO    102788

         5    1   A23D46D41-55 WALTON WAY          WI01475SCOTT DRAKE  50855530004215L 0000000000000027000675000MICH
              2   ELLE DETLOR102788

         6    1   A88G34ATHALER HILL ROAD          TM01468MARTEE RICHARDS50855598760024C00028000004000000000103499
              2             102788
```

Figure 10-34 (8)

≡ PROGRAM HJG10Y: THE ENHANCED EXCPT OPERATION ≡

Figure 10-35 shows the compilation listing for program HJG10Y. This program functions identically to program HJG10X but uses two enhanced RPG functions that are available in RPG III and RPG/400 as well as newer versions of RPG II.

Figure 10-35   Compilation listing for program HJG10Y

```
HJG10Y    09-12-91  19:04:17      IBM PC        RPG II         Version 3.5  Page  1
          ....+....1....+....2....+....3....+....4....+....5....+....6....+....7....

    1 0001 H                                                            HJG10Y


    2 0002 FLISTDATAIP  F 480 120           DISK
    3 0003 FLISTFILEUC  F 140 140R 6AI    2 DISK                A
    4 0004 FEREPORT O   F 132 132     OF    PRINTER
    5 0005 FAREPORT O   F 132 132     OV    PRINTER


    6 0006 E                       TABTN  1  9 2
    7 0007 E                       TABZIP 1  9 5 0


    8 0008 ILISTDATAAA  01
    9 0009 I                                 1   6 LISTNOL1        80
   10 0010 I                                 7  31 LOCATN         81
   11 0011 I                                32  33 TOWN           82
   12 0012 I                                34  38OZIP            83
   13 0013 I                                39  53 CONTCT         20
   14 0014 I                                54  63 PHONE          21
   15 0015 I                                54  56OPH1            22
   16 0016 I                                57  59OPH2
   17 0017 I                                60  63OPH3
   18 0018 I                                64  67OEXT            23
   19 0019 I                                68  68 TYPE           84
   20 0020 I                                69  69 CATEG          24
   21 0021 I                                70  75OBLDSQF         25
```

Figure 10-35 (1)

```
HJG10Y    09-12-91  19:04:17      IBM PC        RPG II          Version 3.5  Page  2

          ....+....1....+....2....+....3....+....4....+....5....+....6....+....7....

   22 0022 I                                          76  830LNDSQF          26
   23 0023 I                                          84  871LNDACR          27
   24 0024 I                                          88  950PRICE           85
   25 0025 I                                          96 110 ACCREP          28
   26 0026 ILISTFILEAA  02
   27 0027 I                                           2    7 IDENT


   28 0028 C    01              SETOF                       656667
   29 0029 C    01              SETOF                       687273
   30 0030 C    01              SETOF                       747576
   31 0031 C    01              SETOF                       86
   32 0032 C    01              SETON                       40
   33 0033 C    80              EXCPTERR2
   34 0034 C    80              EXSR OFLOW
   35 0035 C    N80     LISTNO  CHAINLISTFILE              86
   36 0036 C    N80N86          EXCPTERR1
   37 0037 C    N80N86          EXSR OFLOW
   38 0038 C    N80N86          GOTO END
   39 0039 C    81              EXCPTERR3
   40 0040 C    81              EXSR OFLOW
   41 0041 C    82              EXCPTERR4
   42 0042 C    82              EXSR OFLOW
   43 0043 C    83              EXCPTERR5
   44 0044 C    83              EXSR OFLOW
   45 0045 C    84              EXCPTERR6
   46 0046 C    84              EXSR OFLOW
   47 0047 C    85              EXCPTERR7
   48 0048 C    85              EXSR OFLOW
   49 0049 C    N82     TOWN    LOKUPTABTN                  65
   50 0050 C    N82N65          EXCPTERR8
   51 0051 C    N82N65          EXSR OFLOW
   52 0052 C    N83     ZIP     LOKUPTABZIP                 66
   53 0053 C    N83N66          EXCPTERR9
   54 0054 C    N83N66          EXSR OFLOW
   55 0055 C    65 66   TOWN    LOKUPTABTN      TABZIP      67
   56 0056 C    67      TABZIP  COMP ZIP             6868
   57 0057 C    68              EXCPTERR12
   58 0058 C    68              EXSR OFLOW
   59 0059 C                    SETOF                       697071
   60 0060 C    N84     TYPE    COMP 'R'             727269
   61 0061 C    N84 72  TYPE    COMP 'C'             727270
   62 0062 C    N84 72  TYPE    COMP 'L'             727271
   63 0063 C    72              EXCPTERR10
   64 0064 C    72              EXSR OFLOW
   65 0065 C    24              GOTO BYPASS
   66 0066 C            CATEG   COMP 'S'                    73
   67 0067 C            CATEG   COMP 'M'                    74
   68 0068 C            CATEG   COMP 'O'                    75
   69 0069 C            CATEG   COMP 'G'                    76
   70 0070 C                    SETON                       63
   71 0071 C    69 73
   72 0072 COR 69 74
   73 0073 COR 70 74
   74 0074 COR 70 75
   75 0075 COR 70 76
   76 0076 COR 71 24           SETOF                        63
   77 0077 C    63              EXCPTERR13
   78 0078 C    63              EXSR OFLOW
   79 0079 C    63              SETOF                        63
   80 0080 C            BYPASS  TAG
   81 0081 C    N20 21          EXCPTERR11
   82 0082 C    N20 21          EXSR OFLOW
   83 0083 C    20 28           EXCPTERR14
   84 0084 C    20 28           EXSR OFLOW
   85 0085 C            END     TAG
   86 0086 C    40              ADD  1          ADDS    30
   87 0087 C    N40             ADD  1          ERRORS  30
   88 0088 C            OFLOW   BEGSR
   89 0089 C                    SETOF                        40
   90 0090 C    77              SETOF                        77OF
```

Figure 10-35 (2)

continued

```
HJG10Y     09-12-91  19:04:17        IBM PC        RPG II         Version 3.5  Page  3
          ....+....1....+....2....+....3....+....4....+....5....+....6....+....7....
     91 0091 C    OF              SETON                    77
     92 0092 C                    SETOF                    L1
     93 0093 C                    SETON                    99
     94 0094 C                    ENDSR


     95 0095 OAREPORT H  206   1P
     96 0096 O       OR         OV
     97 0097 O                           UDATE Y    8
     98 0098 O                                     15 'HJG10X'
     99 0099 O                                     65 'TRI-MOUNT REALTY LISTING'
    100 0100 O                                     82 'S ADDITION REPORT'
    101 0101 O                                    118 'PAGE'
    102 0102 O                           PAGE     123
    103 0103 O        D  1    40
    104 0104 O                                     24 'LISTING NO ---------L O '
    105 0105 O                                     45 'C A T I O N----------'
    106 0106 O        D  1    40
    107 0107 O                           LISTNO     8
    108 0108 O                           LOCATN    36
    109 0109 O                           TOWN      39
    110 0110 O                                     40 '-'
    111 0111 O                           ZIP    X  45
    112 0112 O                                     52 'TYPE-'
    113 0113 O             69 74                   69 'RESIDENTIAL-MULTI'
    114 0114 O             69 73                   70 'RESIDENTIAL-SINGLE'
    115 0115 O             70 74                   76 'COMMERCIAL-MANUFACTURING'
    116 0116 O             70 75                   69 'COMMERCIAL-OFFICE'
    117 0117 O             70 76                   70 'COMMERCIAL-GENERAL'
    118 0118 O             71                      56 'LAND'
    119 0119 O        N20                          85 'CONTACT-'
    120 0120 O        N20                 CONTCT   100
    121 0121 O        N21N22              PH1    X 104
    122 0122 O        N21N22                      105 '-'
    123 0123 O        N21                 PH2    X 108
    124 0124 O        N21                         109 '-'
    125 0125 O        N21                 PH3    X 113
    126 0126 O        N21N23                      118 'EXT.'
    127 0127 O        N21N23              EXT    X 123
    128 0128 O        D  3    40
    129 0129 O        N25                          25 'BLDG-        SQFT'
    130 0130 O        N25                 BLDSQF2   20
    131 0131 O        N26                          47 'LAND-        SQFT'
    132 0132 O        N26                 LNDSQF2   42
    133 0133 O        N27                 LNDACR2   53
    134 0134 O        N27                          58 'ACRE'
    135 0135 O                                     65 'PRICE'
    136 0136 O                           PRICE 2   77 '$'
    137 0137 O        N28                          87 'ACCOUNT-'
    138 0138 O        N28                 ACCREP   102
    139 0139 O        T  2    LR
    140 0140 O                           ADDS  Z   11
    141 0141 O                                     34 'LISTINGS ADDED TO FILE'
    142 0142 O        T  1    LR 99
    143 0143 O                                     32 '************************'
    144 0144 O                                     34 '**'
    145 0145 O        T  1    LR 99
    146 0146 O                                      9 '*'
    147 0147 O                                     34 '*'
    148 0148 O        T  1    LR 99
    149 0149 O                                      9 '*'
    150 0150 O                           ERRORSZ   13
    151 0151 O                                     34 'LISTINGS NOT ADDED *'
    152 0152 O        T  1    LR 99
    153 0153 O                                      9 '*'
    154 0154 O                                     34 '*'
    155 0155 O        T  1    LR 99
    156 0156 O                                      9 '*'
    157 0157 O                                     34 'SEE ERROR REPORT     *'
    158 0158 O        T  1    LR 99
    159 0159 O                                      9 '*'
    160 0160 O                                     34 '*'
    161 0161 O        T     06 LR 99
    162 0162 O                                     32 '************************'
    163 0163 O                                     34 '**'
```

Figure 10-35 (3)

```
HJG10Y    09-12-91  19:04:17      IBM PC      RPG II         Version 3.5  Page  4

          ....+....1....+....2....+....3....+....4....+....5....+....6....+....7....

164 0164 OLISTFILEDADD     40
165 0165 O                                1 'A'
166 0166 O                         LISTNO    7
167 0167 O                         LOCATN   32
168 0168 O                         TOWN     34
169 0169 O                         ZIP      39
170 0170 O                         CONTCT   54
171 0171 O                         PHONE    64
172 0172 O                         EXT      68
173 0173 O                         TYPE     69
174 0174 O                         CATEG    70
175 0175 O                         BLDSQF   76
176 0176 O                         LNDSQF   84
177 0177 O                         LNDACR   88
178 0178 O                         PRICE    96
179 0179 O                         ACCREP  111
180 0180 O                         UDATE   117
181 0181 OEREPORT H 106    1P
182 0182 O        OR         OF
183 0183 O                                6 'HJG10X'
184 0184 O                         UDATE Y 29
185 0185 O                               48 'PAGE'
186 0186 O                         PAGE1   53
187 0187 O        H 2        1P
188 0188 O        OR         OF
189 0189 O                               31 'TRI-MOUNT REALTY LISTING'
190 0190 O                               48 'S ADDITION ERRORS'
191 0191 O        H 2        1P
192 0192 O        OR         OF
193 0193 O                               10 'LISTING NO'
194 0194 O                               30 '-------ERROR TYPE'
195 0195 O        EF11   L1   ERR1
196 0196 O        ORF 1  NL1
197 0197 O               L1   LISTNO    8
198 0198 O               OF   LISTNO    8
199 0199 O                               35 'DUPLICATE LISTING NO -'
200 0200 O                               56 'RECORD NOT PROCESSED'
201 0201 O        EF11   L1   ERR2
202 0202 O        ORF 1  NL1
203 0203 O               L1   LISTNO    8
204 0204 O               OF   LISTNO    8
205 0205 O                               33 'LISTING NUMBER BLANK'
206 0206 O        EF11   L1   ERR3
207 0207 O        ORF 1  NL1
208 0208 O               L1   LISTNO    8
209 0209 O               OF   LISTNO    8
210 0210 O                               36 'PROPERTY LOCATION BLANK'
211 0211 O        EF11   L1   ERR4
212 0212 O        ORF 1  NL1
213 0213 O               L1   LISTNO    8
214 0214 O               OF   LISTNO    8
215 0215 O                               28 'TOWN CODE BLANK'
216 0216 O        EF11   L1   ERR5
217 0217 O        ORF 1  NL1
218 0218 O               L1   LISTNO    8
219 0219 O               OF   LISTNO    8
220 0220 O                               32 'ZIP CODE BLANK/ZERO'
221 0221 O        EF11   L1   ERR6
222 0222 O        ORF 1  NL1
223 0223 O               L1   LISTNO    8
224 0224 O               OF   LISTNO    8
225 0225 O                               32 'PROPERTY TYPE BLANK'
226 0226 O        EF11   L1   ERR7
227 0227 O        ORF 1  NL1
228 0228 O               L1   LISTNO    8
229 0229 O               OF   LISTNO    8
230 0230 O                               29 'PRICE BLANK/ZERO'
231 0231 O        EF11   L1   ERR8
232 0232 O        ORF 1  NL1
233 0233 O               L1   LISTNO    8
234 0234 O               OF   LISTNO    8
235 0235 O                               30 'INVALID TOWN CODE'
236 0236 O        EF11   L1   ERR9
237 0237 O        ORF 1  NL1
```

Figure 10-35 (4)

continued

```
HJG10Y     09-12-91  19:04:17        IBM PC        RPG II          Version 3.5  Page  5
           ....+....1....+....2....+....3....+....4....+....5....+....6....+....7....

238 0238 O                    L1      LISTNO       8
239 0239 O                    OF      LISTNO       8
240 0240 O                                        29 'INVALID ZIP CODE'
241 0241 O         EF11       L1      ERR10
242 0242 O         ORF 1      NL1
243 0243 O                    L1      LISTNO       8
244 0244 O                    OF      LISTNO       8
245 0245 O                                        34 'INVALID PROPERTY TYPE'
246 0246 O         EF11       L1      ERR11
247 0247 O         ORF 1      NL1
248 0248 O                    L1      LISTNO       8
249 0249 O                    OF      LISTNO       8
250 0250 O                                        37 'CONTACT TELEPHONE NUMBER'
251 0251 O                                        45 'MISSING'
252 0252 O         EF11       L1      ERR12
253 0253 O         ORF 1      NL1
254 0254 O                    L1      LISTNO       8
255 0255 O                    OF      LISTNO       8
256 0256 O                                        33 'TOWN CODE - ZIP CODE'
257 0257 O                                        42 'CONFLICT'
258 0258 O         EF11       L1      ERR13
259 0259 O         ORF 1      NL1
260 0260 O                    L1      LISTNO       8
261 0261 O                    OF      LISTNO       8
262 0262 O                                        29 'INVALID PROPERTY'
263 0263 O                                        38 'CATEGORY'
264 0264 O         EF11       L1      ERR14
265 0265 O         ORF 1      NL1
266 0266 O                    L1      LISTNO       8
267 0267 O                    OF      LISTNO       8
268 0268 O                                        37 'CONTACT AND ACCOUNT REP.'
269 0269 O                                        48 'BOTH BLANK'
270 **
271 AS
272 BA
273 ET
274 FI
275 GA
276 TM
277 WE
278 WI
279 WS
280 **
281 01430
282 01436
283 01438
284 01420
285 01440
286 01468
287 01473
288 01475
289 01477
290 /*
291 /*




        THE FOLLOWING INDICATORS WERE SPECIFIED BUT WERE NEVER
        USED TO CONDITION OPERATIONS

        02



        THE FOLLOWING INDICATORS APPEARED IN THIS PROGRAM
        01  02  20  21  22  23  24  25  26  27  28  40  63  65  66  67
        68  69  70  71  72  73  74  75  76  77  80  81  82  83  84  85
        86  99  LR  L1  1P  OF  OV
No Warning Errors
No Fatal Errors
```

Figure 10-35 (5)

EXCPT Operation, Enhanced Version

The primary difference between the two programs is that program HJG10Y uses the enhanced EXCPT operation, which permits the use of named exception lines. In the previous sample program, many lines of code were devoted to the SETON and SETOF of the indicators used to control the printing of the proper exception output line.

The enhanced EXCPT operation permits each exception output line to be assigned a name that can be referenced by the EXCPT operation used to print that line. Figure 10-36 shows the portion of the calculation and output specification used to print error messages if the TOWN, ZIP, TYPE, or PRICE field is blank. As you can see, there are several differences between this code and the code shown in Figure 10-21. The SETON and SETOF operations have been eliminated, and the EXCPT and EXSR operations are controlled directly by the zero or blank input field indicator.

```
 41C   82          EXCPTERR4
 42C   82          EXSR OFLOW
 43C   83          EXCPTERR5
 44C   83          EXSR OFLOW
 45C   84          EXCPTERR6
 46C   84          EXSR OFLOW
 47C   85          EXCPTERR7
 48C   85          EXSR OFLOW
   C
```

```
211O        EF11      L1       ERR4
212O       ORF 1    NL1
213O                  L1       LISTNO     8
214O                  OF       LISTNO     8
215O                                     28 'TOWN CODE BLANK'
216O        EF11      L1       ERR5
217O       ORF 1    NL1
218O                  L1       LISTNO     8
219O                  OF       LISTNO     8
220O                                     32 'ZIP CODE BLANK/ZERO'
221O        EF11      L1       ERR6
222O       ORF 1    NL1
223O                  L1       LISTNO     8
224O                  OF       LISTNO     8
225O                                     32 'PROPERTY TYPE BLANK'
226O        EF11      L1       ERR7
227O       ORF      NL1
228O                  L1       LISTNO     8
229O                  OF       LISTNO     8
230O                                     29 'PRICE BLANK/ZERO'
```

Figure 10-36 Named EXCPT operations

The enhanced EXCPT operation specifies a name in the Factor 2 area. This name must be the same as a name used in positions 32–37 of the exception output record description line. When names are used in these areas, the exception operation is referred to as a named EXCPT operation. **Named EXCPT operations** use the Factor 2 and Field Name entries to associate the EXCPT operation with the output record to be written. Named EXCPT operations lessen the amount of code needed in a program by eliminating the SETON and SETOF operations and minimize confusion during programming and program maintenance by providing a name relationship between the EXCPT operation and the output record. The same name can be used on several exception output records, permitting a single EXCPT operation to produce multiple exception output lines. Figure 10-37 summarizes the enhanced version of the EXCPT operation.

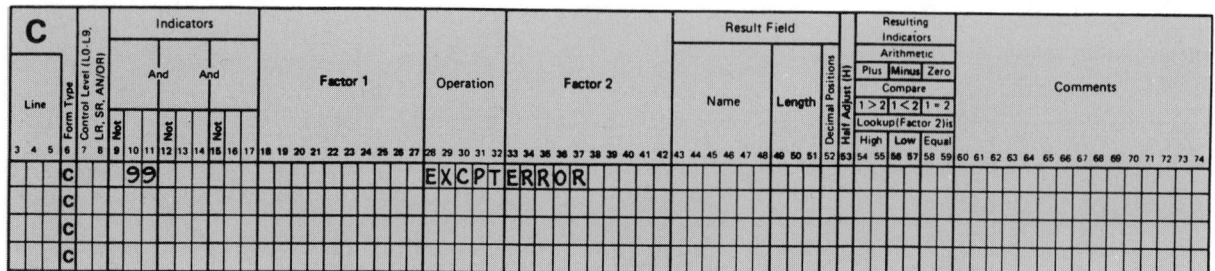

EXCPT Operation Summary, 3X Format

The EXCPT operation causes output records to be written during either detail or total calculation time under control of the object program rather than the RPG fixed logic cycle. The EXCPT operation can be conditioned by indicators in positions 7–17. The output records written must be identified by an entry E in the Type area, position 15. Factor 2 can contain an EXCPT name. This name identifies one or more exception output lines, all of which contain the same name in positions 32–37 of the exception record identification line. An EXCPT name cannot be the same as a file or field name used in the program.

Control Level Indicators	Indicators	Factor 1	Operation Name	Factor 2	Result Field	Resulting Indicators		
7–8	9–17	18–27	28–32	33–42	43–53	54–55	56–57	58–59
optional	optional	blank	EXCPT	required	blank	blank	blank	blank

Figure 10-37   EXCPT operation summary, 3X format

▤ Enhanced Subroutine Coding

Figure 10-38 shows the enhanced version of the subroutine coding used in the sample program. This enhancement is relatively minor and, as you can see, eliminates the need to code the letters SR in positions 7–8 of a subroutine.

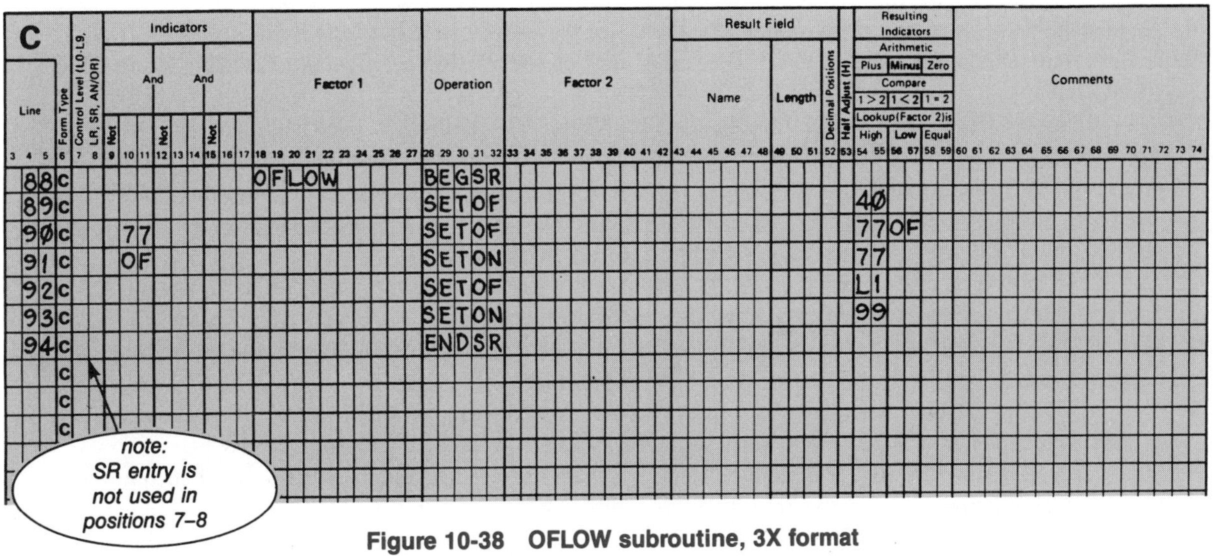

Line	Form Type	Control Level (L0-L9, LR, SR, AN/OR)	And Not	And Not	Factor 1	Operation	Factor 2	Result Field Name	Length	Decimal Positions	Half Adjust (H)	Plus	Minus	Zero	Comments
88	C				OFLOW	BEGSR									
89	C					SETOF						40			
90	C	77				SETOF						77	OF		
91	C	OF				SETON						77			
92	C					SETOF						L1			
93	C					SETON						99			
94	C					ENDSR									
	C														
	C														
	C														

note: SR entry is not used in positions 7-8

Figure 10-38   OFLOW subroutine, 3X format

IN CONCLUSION

This chapter has shown you how to add new records to a keyed file. The data in these files is generally dynamic in nature and changes frequently. In the examples, you added records to a real estate listing file. The records in this file are subject to several different types of change: When property is sold, the listing for the property must be removed from the listing file; new listings must be added to the file; and data fields within records in the file can change.

In Chapter 11 you will learn to perform file maintenance operations, which add, delete, and change records within an existing data file. While studying the RPG program code needed to maintain a data file, you will see how RPG can differentiate between different types of input data records with different data formats and how you can control the processing performed on an input record based on the type of record read. This chapter also will introduce you to the concept of structured RPG programming and several operations that have been added to RPG II, RPG III, and RPG/400 to permit the use of structured programming techniques.

CHAPTER SUMMARY

1. **Input data editing** is a technique used to verify that the data being added to a data file or otherwise processed by a program conforms to the rules established for the data file.
2. Input data editing techniques are not limited to programs that add records to data files. These techniques can be used whenever data verification is needed.
3. Input data editing techniques can test for such conditions as blank data fields, zero values in data fields that require nonzero entries, and whether the contents of a data field conform to predefined rules.
4. An audit trail is a technique that causes every transaction to appear in printed form on a report. An audit trail should be established in any program that changes the contents of a data file and should show exactly what changes were made.
5. **Spooling** permits more efficient use of devices such as printers. Spooling causes output report data to be written to a temporary disk file until the program completes execution and then, when the program is finished, directs the output data to the printer. The use of Spooling eliminates device lock-up, which causes inefficient use of the printer.
6. Programs using input editing techniques often appear to be more complex than they actually are because these programs often perform the same type of processing many times.

7. An **update file** is a disk file that is both read from and written to in the same program.
8. An update file must be described on both the Input and the Output Specifications forms.
9. If a program adds new records to a disk file, an A must be specified in position 66 of the file description specification.
10. If a program produces two or more reports, each report must use a different overflow indicator.
11. An **internal subroutine** is used whenever the same series of instructions must be used at several points in a program. Internal subroutines must appear at the end of the program calculations and must be identified by the letters SR in positions 7–8. RPG and RPG II require this entry in every line of the subroutine. Enhanced versions of RPG II, RPG III, and RPG/400 may not require this entry.
12. The **EXSR** operation causes the program to proceed directly to the beginning of an internal subroutine.
13. The **BEGSR** operation marks the beginning of an internal subroutine.
14. The **ENDSR** operation marks the end of an internal subroutine and causes the program to return to the operation following the EXSR operation that **called** the subroutine.
15. A keyed file usually cannot contain two or more records with the same key field value. If an attempt is made to add a record containing a key field value that already exists in the file, the program may halt.
16. Most computers store the sign of a numeric field as part of the rightmost digit of the field. If such a field is printed without being edited, the rightmost position often prints as a letter.
17. The edit code X removes the sign of a number before printing but performs no other editing functions.
18. Output spacing and skipping specifications are used only with printed output files. If spacing and/or skipping is specified for a disk file, most versions of RPG generate an error message when the program is compiled.
19. The ADD entry in positions 16–18 of the output record description causes the output record to be added to a disk file.
20. If a program produces two or more reports, each report must use a different page numbering field. The eight valid page numbering fields are PAGE, PAGE1, PAGE2, …, .PAGE7.
21. The enhanced EXCPT operation permits each exception output record to be assigned a name that can be referenced by the EXCPT operation used to print that line.
22. When **named EXCPT operations** are used, the same name must appear in Factor 2 of the EXCPT operation and in the name field of the exception output record description.
23. The same name can appear in several exception output records to permit a single EXCPT operation to control multiple output records.

REVIEW QUESTIONS

1. Why is input data editing important in any program that adds records to a file?
2. What is an audit trail? Why is it important that proper audit trails be maintained?
3. How does spooling make computer use more efficient?
4. Why must an update file be described on both the Input and Output Specifications forms even though no data fields are being read from the file?
5. How can internal subroutines be used to make program coding easier and more efficient?
6. How does the use of an internal subroutine differ from the use of GOTO and TAG?
7. What is an external subroutine?
8. Which calculation is executed after the ENDSR operation is reached in an internal subroutine?
9. What editing is performed by the X edit code?
10. What does the ADD entry in positions 16–18 of an output record description do? What other RPG entry must be used if the ADD entry appears in a program?
11. If a program is producing two or more output reports, why must a different page number field (PAGE, PAGE1, etc.) be used on each?
12. How does the enhanced EXCPT operation differ from the standard EXCPT operation?

STUDENT EXERCISES: RPG PROGRAM CODE

1. Code the RPG specifications in Figure 10-39 to determine if the value in the AMOUNT field is between 100.00 and 350.00, inclusive. If the value is within the range, print the named exception line VALID. If the value is outside the range, execute the internal subroutine ERROR.

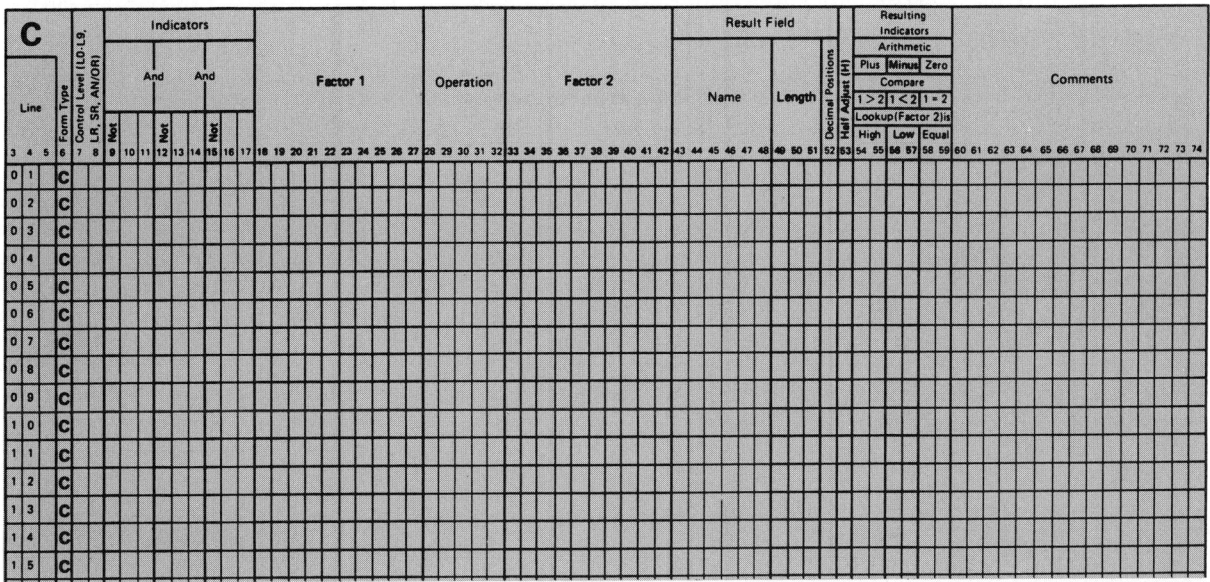

Figure 10-39   Calculation Specifications form

2. Code the RPG specifications in Figure 10-40 to determine if the STATUS field contains the letter A or the letter D. The contents of STATUS have been edited and can contain no other entry. If STATUS contains A, determine if the value in the ACCTNO field is already used as the key field in the ACCOUNTS file. If the key field value is already used in ACCOUNTS execute the DUPREC subroutine.

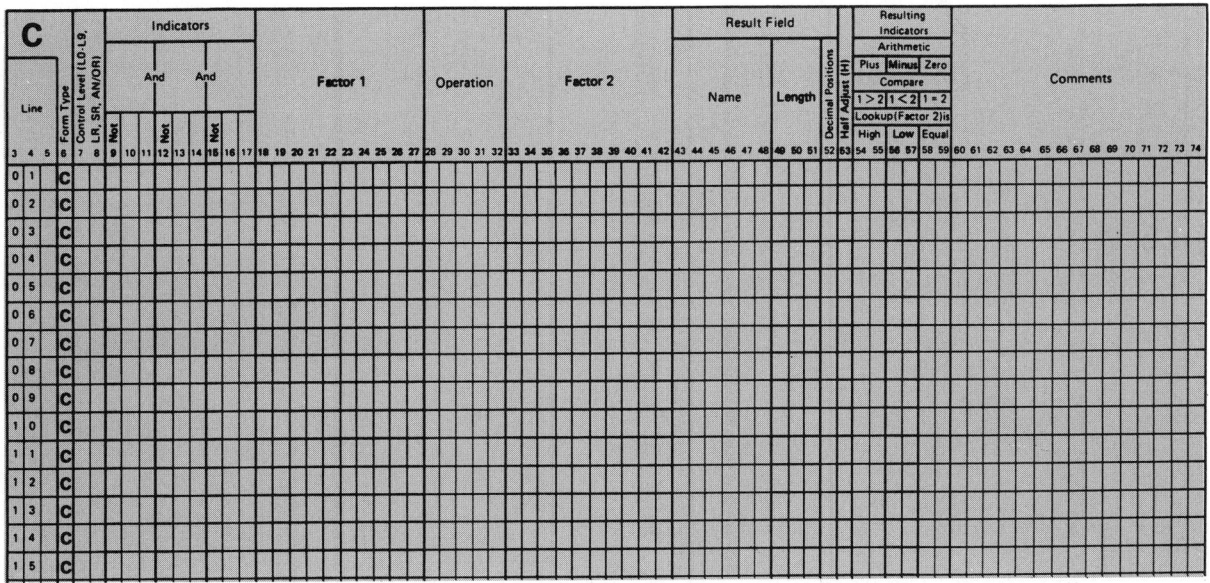

Figure 10-40   Calculation Specifications form

STUDENT EXERCISES: RPG PROGRAM MAINTENANCE

▤ Problem 1

In program HJG10X, if the key field of the record to be added to LISTFILE already exists in LISTFILE, an error message is printed and no further processing is performed on the input record. Modify program HJG10X in Figure 10-41 so that all error testing is performed when this duplicate key condition exists. Explain your modifications and their effect on the program.

Figure 10-41   Compilation listing for program HJG10X

```
HJG10X    09-12-91  19:01:50        IBM PC        RPG II         Version 3.5  Page  1

          ....+....1....+....2....+....3....+....4....+....5....+....6....+....7....

     1 0001 H                                                                  HJG10X


     2 0002 FLISTDATAIP  F 480 120           DISK
     3 0003 FLISTFILEUC  F 140 140R 6AI    2 DISK                    A
     4 0004 FEREPORT  O  F 132 132      OF   PRINTER
     5 0005 FAREPORT  O  F 132 132      OV   PRINTER


     6 0006 E                       TABTN   1   9  2
     7 0007 E                       TABZIP  1   9  5 0


     8 0008 ILISTDATAAA   01
     9 0009 I                                   1    6 LISTNOL1      80
    10 0010 I                                   7   31 LOCATN        81
    11 0011 I                                  32   33 TOWN          82
    12 0012 I                                  34   380ZIP          83
    13 0013 I                                  39   53 CONTCT        20
    14 0014 I                                  54   63 PHONE         21
    15 0015 I                                  54   560PH1          22
    16 0016 I                                  57   590PH2
    17 0017 I                                  60   630PH3
    18 0018 I                                  64   670EXT          23
    19 0019 I                                  68   68 TYPE          84
    20 0020 I                                  69   69 CATEG         24
    21 0021 I                                  70   750BLDSQF        25
    22 0022 I                                  76   830LNDSQF        26
    23 0023 I                                  84   871LNDACR        27
    24 0024 I                                  88   950PRICE         85
    25 0025 I                                  96  110 ACCREP        28
    26 0026 ILISTFILEAA   02
    27 0027 I                                   2    7 IDENT


    28 0028 C     01           SETON                     40
    29 0029 C     80           SETON                     52
    30 0030 C     52           EXCPT
    31 0031 C     52           EXSR OFLOW
    32 0032 C     52           SETOF                     52
    33 0033 C     N80   LISTNO CHAINLISTFILE             86
    34 0034 C     N80N86       SETON                     51
    35 0035 C     51           EXCPT
    36 0036 C     51           EXSR OFLOW
    37 0037 C     51           SETOF                     51
    38 0038 C     N80N86       GOTO END
    39 0039 C     81           SETON                     53
    40 0040 C     53           EXCPT
    41 0041 C     53           EXSR OFLOW
    42 0042 C     53           SETOF                     53
    43 0043 C     82           SETON                     54
    44 0044 C     54           EXCPT
    45 0045 C     54           EXSR OFLOW
    46 0046 C     54           SETOF                     54
```

Figure 10-41 (1)

```
HJG10X      09-12-91  19:01:50      IBM PC       RPG II        Version 3.5  Page  2

            ....+....1....+....2....+....3....+....4....+....5....+....6....+....7....

   47 0047 C    83                  SETON                          55
   48 0048 C    55                  EXCPT
   49 0049 C    55                  EXSR OFLOW
   50 0050 C    55                  SETOF                          55
   51 0051 C    84                  SETON                          56
   52 0052 C    56                  EXCPT
   53 0053 C    56                  EXSR OFLOW
   54 0054 C    56                  SETOF                          56
   55 0055 C    85                  SETON                          57
   56 0056 C    57                  EXCPT
   57 0057 C    57                  EXSR OFLOW
   58 0058 C    57                  SETOF                          57
   59 0059 C    N82       TOWN      LOKUPTABTN                        65
   60 0060 C    N82N65              SETON                          58
   61 0061 C    58                  EXCPT
   62 0062 C    58                  EXSR OFLOW
   63 0063 C    58                  SETOF                          58
   64 0064 C    N83       ZIP       LOKUPTABZIP                      66
   65 0065 C    N83N66              SETON                          59
   66 0066 C    59                  EXCPT
   67 0067 C    59                  EXSR OFLOW
   68 0068 C    59                  SETOF                          59
   69 0069 C    65 66     TOWN      LOKUPTABTN      TABZIP           67
   70 0070 C    67        TABZIP    COMP ZIP                     6868
   71 0071 C    68                  SETON                          62
   72 0072 C    62                  EXCPT
   73 0073 C    62                  EXSR OFLOW
   74 0074 C    62                  SETOF                        626768
   75 0075 C                        SETOF                        697071
   76 0076 C    N84       TYPE      COMP 'R'                     727269
   77 0077 C    N84 72    TYPE      COMP 'C'                     727270
   78 0078 C    N84 72    TYPE      COMP 'L'                     727271
   79 0079 C    72                  SETON                          60
   80 0080 C    60                  EXCPT
   81 0081 C    60                  EXSR OFLOW
   82 0082 C    60                  SETOF                        6072
   83 0083 C                        SETOF                        737475
   84 0084 C                        SETOF                          76
   85 0085 C    N24       CATEG     COMP 'S'                         73
   86 0086 C    N24       CATEG     COMP 'M'                         74
   87 0087 C    N24       CATEG     COMP 'O'                         75
   88 0088 C    N24       CATEG     COMP 'G'                         76
   89 0089 C                        SETON                          63
   90 0090 C    69 73
   91 0091 COR 69 74
   92 0092 COR 70 74
   93 0093 COR 70 75
   94 0094 COR 70 76
   95 0095 COR 71 24              SETOF                          63
   96 0096 C    63                  EXCPT
   97 0097 C    63                  EXSR OFLOW
   98 0098 C    63                  SETOF                          63
   99 0099 C    N20 21              SETON                          61
  100 0100 C    61                  EXCPT
  101 0101 C    61                  EXSR OFLOW
  102 0102 C    61                  SETOF                          61
  103 0103 C    20 28               SETON                          64
  104 0104 C    64                  EXCPT
  105 0105 C    64                  EXSR OFLOW
  106 0106 C    64                  SETOF                          64
  107 0107 C              END       TAG
  108 0108 C    40        ADDS      ADD  1          ADDS     30
  109 0109 C    N40       ERRORS    ADD  1          ERRORS   30
  110 0110 CSR           OFLOW      BEGSR
  111 0111 CSR                      SETOF                          40
  112 0112 CSR 77                   SETOF                          770F
  113 0113 CSR OF                   SETON                          77
  114 0114 CSR                      SETOF                          L1
  115 0115 CSR                      SETON                          99
  116 0116 CSR                      ENDSR


  117 0117 OAREPORT H  206   1P
```

Figure 10-41 (2)

continued

```
HJG10X    09-12-91  19:01:50        IBM PC      RPG II        Version 3.5  Page  3

          ....+....1....+....2....+....3....+....4....+....5....+....6....+....7....

     118 0118 O      OR      OV
     119 0119 O                        UDATE Y     8
     120 0120 O                                   15 'HJG10X'
     121 0121 O                                   65 'TRI-MOUNT REALTY LISTING'
     122 0122 O                                   82 'S ADDITION REPORT'
     123 0123 O                                  118 'PAGE'
     124 0124 O                        PAGE       123
     125 0125 O      D  1    40
     126 0126 O                                   24 'LISTING NO --------L O '
     127 0127 O                                   45 'C A T I O N----------'
     128 0128 O      D  1    40
     129 0129 O                        LISTNO      8
     130 0130 O                        LOCATN     36
     131 0131 O                        TOWN       39
     132 0132 O                                   40 '-'
     133 0133 O                        ZIP   X    45
     134 0134 O                                   52 'TYPE-'
     135 0135 O              69 74                 69 'RESIDENTIAL-MULTI'
     136 0136 O              69 73                 70 'RESIDENTIAL-SINGLE'
     137 0137 O              70 74                 76 'COMMERCIAL-MANUFACTURING'
     138 0138 O              70 75                 69 'COMMERCIAL-OFFICE'
     139 0139 O              70 76                 70 'COMMERCIAL-GENERAL'
     140 0140 O              71                    56 'LAND'
     141 0141 O              N20                   85 'CONTACT-'
     142 0142 O              N20      CONTCT      100
     143 0143 O              N21N22   PH1   X     104
     144 0144 O              N21N22               105 '-'
     145 0145 O              N21      PH2   X     108
     146 0146 O              N21                  109 '-'
     147 0147 O              N21      PH3   X     113
     148 0148 O              N21N23               118 'EXT.'
     149 0149 O              N21N23   EXT   X     123
     150 0150 O      D  3    40
     151 0151 O              N25                   25 'BLDG-      SQFT'
     152 0152 O              N25      BLDSQF2      20
     153 0153 O              N26                   47 'LAND-       SQFT'
     154 0154 O              N26      LNDSQF2      42
     155 0155 O              N27      LNDACR2      53
     156 0156 O              N27                   58 'ACRE'
     157 0157 O                                   65 'PRICE'
     158 0158 O                        PRICE 2    77 '$'
     159 0159 O              N28                   87 'ACCOUNT-'
     160 0160 O              N28      ACCREP      102
     161 0161 O      T  2    LR
     162 0162 O                        ADDS  Z    11
     163 0163 O                                   34 'LISTINGS ADDED TO FILE'
     164 0164 O      T  1    LR 99
     165 0165 O                                   32 '*************************'
     166 0166 O                                   34 '**'
     167 0167 O      T  1    LR 99
     168 0168 O                                    9 '*'
     169 0169 O                                   34 '*'
     170 0170 O      T  1    LR 99
     171 0171 O                                    9 '*'
     172 0172 O                        ERRORSZ    13
     173 0173 O                                   34 'LISTINGS NOT ADDED *'
     174 0174 O      T  1    LR 99
     175 0175 O                                    9 '*'
     176 0176 O                                   34 '*'
     177 0177 O      T  1    LR 99
     178 0178 O                                    9 '*'
     179 0179 O                                   34 'SEE ERROR REPORT     *'
     180 0180 O      T  1    LR 99
     181 0181 O                                    9 '*'
     182 0182 O                                   34 '*'
     183 0183 O      T  06 LR 99
     184 0184 O                                   32 '*************************'
     185 0185 O                                   34 '**'
     186 0186 OLISTFILEDADD      40
     187 0187 O                                    1 'A'
     188 0188 O                        LISTNO      7
     189 0189 O                        LOCATN     32
     190 0190 O                        TOWN       34
     191 0191 O                        ZIP        39
     192 0192 O                        CONTCT     54
```

Figure 10-41 (3)

```
HJG10X    09-12-91  19:01:50      IBM PC      RPG II        Version 3.5  Page  4

          ....+....1....+....2....+....3....+....4....+....5....+....6....+....7....

    193 0193 O                           PHONE    64
    194 0194 O                           EXT      68
    195 0195 O                           TYPE     69
    196 0196 O                           CATEG    70
    197 0197 O                           BLDSQF   76
    198 0198 O                           LNDSQF   84
    199 0199 O                           LNDACR   88
    200 0200 O                           PRICE    96
    201 0201 O                           ACCREP  111
    202 0202 O                           UDATE   117
    203 0203 OEREPORT H  106    1P
    204 0204 O      OR          OF
    205 0205 O                                    6 'HJG10X'
    206 0206 O                           UDATE Y  29
    207 0207 O                                   48 'PAGE'
    208 0208 O                           PAGE1    53
    209 0209 O       H   2     1P
    210 0210 O      OR          OF
    211 0211 O                                   31 'TRI-MOUNT REALTY LISTING'
    212 0212 O                                   48 'S ADDITION ERRORS'
    213 0213 O       H   2     1P
    214 0214 O      OR          OF
    215 0215 O                                   10 'LISTING NO'
    216 0216 O                                   30 '-------ERROR TYPE'
    217 0217 O      EF11       51 L1
    218 0218 O      ORF 1      51NL1
    219 0219 O                  L1       LISTNO    8
    220 0220 O                  OF       LISTNO    8
    221 0221 O                                   35 'DUPLICATE LISTING NO -'
    222 0222 O                                   56 'RECORD NOT PROCESSED'
    223 0223 O      EF11       52 L1
    224 0224 O      ORF 1      52NL1
    225 0225 O                  L1       LISTNO    8
    226 0226 O                  OF       LISTNO    8
    227 0227 O                                   33 'LISTING NUMBER BLANK'
    228 0228 O      EF11       53 L1
    229 0229 O      ORF 1      53NL1
    230 0230 O                  L1       LISTNO    8
    231 0231 O                  OF       LISTNO    8
    232 0232 O                                   36 'PROPERTY LOCATION BLANK'
    233 0233 O      EF11       54 L1
    234 0234 O      ORF 1      54NL1
    235 0235 O                  L1       LISTNO    8
    236 0236 O                  OF       LISTNO    8
    237 0237 O                                   28 'TOWN CODE BLANK'
    238 0238 O      EF11       55 L1
    239 0239 O      ORF 1      55NL1
    240 0240 O                  L1       LISTNO    8
    241 0241 O                  OF       LISTNO    8
    242 0242 O                                   32 'ZIP CODE BLANK/ZERO'
    243 0243 O      EF11       56 L1
    244 0244 O      ORF 1      56NL1
    245 0245 O                  L1       LISTNO    8
    246 0246 O                  OF       LISTNO    8
    247 0247 O                                   32 'PROPERTY TYPE BLANK'
    248 0248 O      EF11       57 L1
    249 0249 O      ORF 1      57NL1
    250 0250 O                  L1       LISTNO    8
    251 0251 O                  OF       LISTNO    8
    252 0252 O                                   29 'PRICE BLANK/ZERO'
    253 0253 O      EF11       58 L1
    254 0254 O      ORF 1      58NL1
    255 0255 O                  L1       LISTNO    8
    256 0256 O                  OF       LISTNO    8
    257 0257 O                                   30 'INVALID TOWN CODE'
    258 0258 O      EF11       59 L1
    259 0259 O      ORF 1      59NL1
    260 0260 O                  L1       LISTNO    8
    261 0261 O                  OF       LISTNO    8
    262 0262 O                                   29 'INVALID ZIP CODE'
    263 0263 O      EF11       60 L1
    264 0264 O      ORF 1      60NL1
    265 0265 O                  L1       LISTNO    8
    266 0266 O                  OF       LISTNO    8
```

Figure 10-41 (4)

continued

```
HJG10X    09-12-91  19:01:50        IBM PC      RPG II          Version 3.5  Page  5

          ....+....1....+....2....+....3....+....4....+....5....+....6....+....7....

    267 0267 O                                       34 'INVALID PROPERTY TYPE'
    268 0268 O        EF11      61 L1
    269 0269 O        ORF 1     61NL1
    270 0270 O                  L1      LISTNO    8
    271 0271 O                  OF      LISTNO    8
    272 0272 O                                       37 'CONTACT TELEPHONE NUMBER'
    273 0273 O                                       45 'MISSING'
    274 0274 O        EF11      62 L1
    275 0275 O        ORF 1     62NL1
    276 0276 O                  L1      LISTNO    8
    277 0277 O                  OF      LISTNO    8
    278 0278 O                                       33 'TOWN CODE - ZIP CODE'
    279 0279 O                                       42 'CONFLICT'
    280 0280 O        EF11      63 L1
    281 0281 O        ORF 1     63NL1
    282 0282 O                  L1      LISTNO    8
    283 0283 O                  OF      LISTNO    8
    284 0284 O                                       29 'INVALID PROPERTY'
    285 0285 O                                       38 'CATEGORY'
    286 0286 O        EF11      64 L1
    287 0287 O        ORF 1     64NL1
    288 0288 O                  L1      LISTNO    8
    289 0289 O                  OF      LISTNO    8
    290 0290 O                                       37 'CONTACT AND ACCOUNT REP
    291 0291 O                                       48 'BOTH BLANK'
    292 **
    293 AS
    294 BA
    295 ET
    296 FI
    297 GA
    298 TM
    299 WE
    300 WI
    301 WS
    302 **
    303 01430
    304 01436
    305 01438
    306 01420
    307 01440
    308 01468
    309 01473
    310 01475
    311 01477
    312 /*
    313 /*



         THE FOLLOWING INDICATORS WERE SPECIFIED BUT WERE NEVER
         USED TO CONDITION OPERATIONS

         02



         THE FOLLOWING INDICATORS APPEARED IN THIS PROGRAM

         01  02  20  21  22  23  24  25  26  27  28  40  51  52  53  54
         55  56  57  58  59  60  61  62  63  64  65  66  67  68  69  70
         71  72  73  74  75  76  77  80  81  82  83  84  85  86  99  LR
         L1  1P  OF  OV
No Warning Errors
No Fatal Errors
```

Figure 10-41 (5)

```
HJG10X              09/12/91              PAGE    1
               TRI-MOUNT REALTY LISTINGS ADDITION ERRORS

   LISTING NO  ------ERROR TYPE


      37B00F      TOWN CODE BLANK
                  ZIP CODE BLANK/ZERO
                  PROPERTY TYPE BLANK
                  PRICE BLANK/ZERO
                  INVALID PROPERTY CATEGORY
                  CONTACT TELEPHONE NUMBER MISSING

      49F83A      PROPERTY LOCATION BLANK
                  PROPERTY TYPE BLANK
                  TOWN CODE - ZIP CODE CONFLICT
                  INVALID PROPERTY CATEGORY

      87F29D      PROPERTY TYPE BLANK
                  INVALID TOWN CODE
                  INVALID PROPERTY CATEGORY

      93F21H      TOWN CODE - ZIP CODE CONFLICT
                  CONTACT AND ACCOUNT REP. BOTH BLANK

      97F38I      INVALID PROPERTY CATEGORY
                  CONTACT TELEPHONE NUMBER MISSING

      12A37A      DUPLICATE LISTING NO - RECORD NOT PROCESSED
```

Figure 10-41 (6)

```
09/12/91 HJG10X                     TRI-MOUNT REALTY LISTINGS ADDITION REPORT                        PAGE    1
LISTING NO ------L O C A T I O N------
  01X25A  BURNSHIRT INDUSTRIAL PARK TM-01468  TYPE-COMMERCIAL-MANUFACTURING CONTACT-ROY WHEATON         555-9136
          BLDG-125,000 SQFT                            9.0 ACRE  PRICE  $1,500,000


LISTING NO ------L O C A T I O N------
  03D41A  21 BULLDOG TERRACE         FI-01420  TYPE-RESIDENTIAL-SINGLE
          BLDG- 1,800 SQFT                           .6 ACRE  PRICE     $102,500  ACCOUNT-TONY GULINO


LISTING NO ------L O C A T I O N------
  12A37A  ROUTE 2A                   GA-01440  TYPE-RESIDENTIAL-MULTI        CONTACT-K. BASHAW     508-555-9311
          BLDG- 3,700 SQFT  LAND   27,000 SQFT            PRICE     $99,850  ACCOUNT-TONY GULINO


LISTING NO ------L O C A T I O N------
  13A37A  ROUTE 2A AND 101           BA-01436  TYPE-RESIDENTIAL-MULTI        CONTACT-NORM BELIN    508-555-2188
          BLDG- 4,600 SQFT  LAND  103,500 SQFT            PRICE    $187,000  ACCOUNT-TONY GULINO


LISTING NO ------L O C A T I O N------
  23D46D  41-55 WALTON WAY           WI-01475  TYPE-LAND                     CONTACT-SCOTT DRAKE   508-555-3000 EXT. 4215
                                                 27.0 ACRE  PRICE    $675,000  ACCOUNT-MICHELLE DETLOR


LISTING NO ------L O C A T I O N------
  88G34A  THALER HILL ROAD           TM-01468  TYPE-COMMERCIAL-OFFICE        CONTACT-MARTEE RICHARDS 508-555-9876 EXT. 0024
          BLDG- 2,800 SQFT  LAND   40,000 SQFT            PRICE    $103,499


      6 LISTINGS ADDED TO FILE

      ****************************
      *                          *
      *  6 LISTINGS NOT ADDED    *
      *                          *
      *   SEE ERROR REPORT       *
      *                          *
      ****************************
```

Figure 10-41 (7)   *continued*

```
Filename  RecLen        KeyPo  KeyLn                                      Date      Time      Page
LISTFILE  140             2      6                                      09/12/91   8.51

Rec No. Line No. 1... ...10.... ...20.... ...30.... ...40.... ...50.... ...60.... ...70.... ...80.... ...90.... ..100

      1   1    A01X25ABURNSHIRT INDUSTRIAL PARKTH01468ROY WHEATON      55591360000CM1250000000000009001500000
          2             102788

      2   1    A03D41A21 BULLDOG TERRACE          FI01420                       0000RS0018000000000000600102500TONY
          2    GULINO   102788

      3   1    A12A37AROUTE 2A                    GA01440K. BASHAW    50855593110000RM003700002700000000099850TONY
          2    GULINO   102788

      4   1    A13A37AROUTE 2A AND 101            BA01436NORM BELIN   50855521880000RM00460001035000000187000TONY
          2    GULINO   102788

      5   1    A23D46D41-55 WALTON WAY            WI01475SCOTT DRAKE  50855530004215L 0000000000000027000675000MICH
          2    ELLE DETLOR102788

      6   1    A88G34ATHALER HILL ROAD            TH01468MARTEE RICHARDS50855598760024C0002800004000000000103499
          2             102788
```

Figure 10-41 (8)

▤ Problem 2

Modify program HJG10X in Figure 10-42 so that it functions only as a data checking program. As such, the program performs all the described tests on the input file, but does not add records to LISTFILE or produce a report showing valid records. The only function of the modified program is to verify the accuracy of the input records based on the problem description for program HJG10X. Explain your modifications and their effect on the program.

Figure 10-42   Compilation listing for program HJG10X

```
HJG10X    09-12-91  19:01:50        IBM PC      RPG II        Version 3.5  Page  1

          ....+....1....+....2....+....3....+....4....+....5....+....6....+....7....

  1 0001 H                                                                HJG10X


  2 0002 FLISTDATAIP  F 480 120           DISK
  3 0003 FLISTFILEUC  F 140 140R 6AI    2 DISK                       A
  4 0004 FEREPORT  O  F 132 132     OF   PRINTER
  5 0005 FAREPORT  O  F 132 132     OV   PRINTER


  6 0006 E                       TABTN  1   9  2
  7 0007 E                       TABZIP 1   9  5 0


  8 0008 ILISTDATAAA  01
  9 0009 I                                       1   6 LISTNOL1        80
 10 0010 I                                       7  31 LOCATN         81
 11 0011 I                                      32  33 TOWN           82
 12 0012 I                                      34  380ZIP           83
 13 0013 I                                      39  53 CONTCT         20
 14 0014 I                                      54  63 PHONE          21
 15 0015 I                                      54  560PH1           22
 16 0016 I                                      57  590PH2
 17 0017 I                                      60  630PH3
 18 0018 I                                      64  670EXT           23
 19 0019 I                                      68  68 TYPE           84
 20 0020 I                                      69  69 CATEG          24
 21 0021 I                                      70  750BLDSQF         25
 22 0022 I                                      76  830LNDSQF         26
 23 0023 I                                      84  871LNDACR         27
```

Figure 10-42 (1)

```
HJG10X    09-12-91  19:01:50       IBM PC      RPG II        Version 3.5  Page  2

          ....+....1....+....2....+....3....+....4....+....5....+....6....+....7....
       24 0024 I                                        88  950PRICE           85
       25 0025 I                                        96 110 ACCREP          28
       26 0026 ILISTFILEAA  02
       27 0027 I                                         2   7 IDENT


       28 0028 C   01             SETON                 40
       29 0029 C   80             SETON                 52
       30 0030 C   52             EXCPT
       31 0031 C   52             EXSR OFLOW
       32 0032 C   52             SETOF                 52
       33 0033 C   N80     LISTNO CHAINLISTFILE         86
       34 0034 C   N80N86         SETON                 51
       35 0035 C   51             EXCPT
       36 0036 C   51             EXSR OFLOW
       37 0037 C   51             SETOF                 51
       38 0038 C   N80N86         GOTO END
       39 0039 C   81             SETON                 53
       40 0040 C   53             EXCPT
       41 0041 C   53             EXSR OFLOW
       42 0042 C   53             SETOF                 53
       43 0043 C   82             SETON                 54
       44 0044 C   54             EXCPT
       45 0045 C   54             EXSR OFLOW
       46 0046 C   54             SETOF                 54
       47 0047 C   83             SETON                 55
       48 0048 C   55             EXCPT
       49 0049 C   55             EXSR OFLOW
       50 0050 C   55             SETOF                 55
       51 0051 C   84             SETON                 56
       52 0052 C   56             EXCPT
       53 0053 C   56             EXSR OFLOW
       54 0054 C   56             SETOF                 56
       55 0055 C   85             SETON                 57
       56 0056 C   57             EXCPT
       57 0057 C   57             EXSR OFLOW
       58 0058 C   57             SETOF                 57
       59 0059 C   N82     TOWN   LOKUPTABTN               65
       60 0060 C   N82N65         SETON                 58
       61 0061 C   58             EXCPT
       62 0062 C   58             EXSR OFLOW
       63 0063 C   58             SETOF                 58
       64 0064 C   N83     ZIP    LOKUPTABZIP              66
       65 0065 C   N83N66         SETON                 59
       66 0066 C   59             EXCPT
       67 0067 C   59             EXSR OFLOW
       68 0068 C   59             SETOF                 59
       69 0069 C   65 66   TOWN   LOKUPTABTN    TABZIP     67
       70 0070 C   67      TABZIP COMP ZIP              6868
       71 0071 C   68             SETON                 62
       72 0072 C   62             EXCPT
       73 0073 C   62             EXSR OFLOW
       74 0074 C   62             SETOF                 626768
       75 0075 C                  SETOF                 697071
       76 0076 C   N84     TYPE   COMP 'R'              727269
       77 0077 C   N84 72  TYPE   COMP 'C'              727270
       78 0078 C   N84 72  TYPE   COMP 'L'              727271
       79 0079 C   72             SETON                 60
       80 0080 C   60             EXCPT
       81 0081 C   60             EXSR OFLOW
       82 0082 C   60             SETOF                 6072
       83 0083 C                  SETOF                 737475
       84 0084 C                  SETOF                 76
       85 0085 C   N24     CATEG  COMP 'S'                 73
       86 0086 C   N24     CATEG  COMP 'M'                 74
       87 0087 C   N24     CATEG  COMP 'O'                 75
       88 0088 C   N24     CATEG  COMP 'G'                 76
       89 0089 C                  SETON                 63
       90 0090 C   69 73
       91 0091 COR 69 74
       92 0092 COR 70 74
       93 0093 COR 70 75
       94 0094 COR 70 76
       95 0095 COR 71 24         SETOF                 63
       96 0096 C   63             EXCPT
       97 0097 C   63             EXSR OFLOW
       98 0098 C   63             SETOF                 63
       99 0099 C   N20 21         SETON                 61
      100 0100 C   61             EXCPT
```

Figure 10-42 (2)

continued

```
HJG10X    09-12-91  19:01:50        IBM PC      RPG II        Version 3.5  Page  3
         ....+....1....+....2....+....3....+....4....+....5....+....6....+....7....
101 0101 C    61                    EXSR OFLOW
102 0102 C    61                    SETOF               61
103 0103 C    20 28                 SETON               64
104 0104 C    64                    EXCPT
105 0105 C    64                    EXSR OFLOW
106 0106 C    64                    SETOF               64
107 0107 C          END             TAG
108 0108 C    40    ADDS      ADD  1      ADDS   30
109 0109 C    N40   ERRORS    ADD  1      ERRORS 30
110 0110 CSR        OFLOW     BEGSR
111 0111 CSR                  SETOF               40
112 0112 CSR 77               SETOF               770F
113 0113 CSR OF              SETON               77
114 0114 CSR                  SETOF               L1
115 0115 CSR                  SETON               99
116 0116 CSR                  ENDSR


117 0117 OAREPORT H 206  1P
118 0118 O       OR       OV
119 0119 O                        UDATE Y    8
120 0120 O                               15 'HJG10X'
121 0121 O                               65 'TRI-MOUNT REALTY LISTING'
122 0122 O                               82 'S ADDITION REPORT'
123 0123 O                              118 'PAGE'
124 0124 O                        PAGE     123
125 0125 O       D 1    40
126 0126 O                               24 'LISTING NO ---------L O '
127 0127 O                               45 'C A T I O N----------'
128 0128 O       D 1    40
129 0129 O                        LISTNO    8
130 0130 O                        LOCATN   36
131 0131 O                        TOWN     39
132 0132 O                               40 '-'
133 0133 O                        ZIP   X  45
134 0134 O                               52 'TYPE-'
135 0135 O              69 74            69 'RESIDENTIAL-MULTI'
136 0136 O              69 73            70 'RESIDENTIAL-SINGLE'
137 0137 O              70 74            76 'COMMERCIAL-MANUFACTURING'
138 0138 O              70 75            69 'COMMERCIAL-OFFICE'
139 0139 O              70 76            70 'COMMERCIAL-GENERAL'
140 0140 O              71               56 'LAND'
141 0141 O              N20              85 'CONTACT-'
142 0142 O              N20   CONTCT   100
143 0143 O              N21N22 PH1   X 104
144 0144 O              N21N22          105 '-'
145 0145 O              N21    PH2   X 108
146 0146 O              N21             109 '-'
147 0147 O              N21    PH3   X 113
148 0148 O              N21N23          118 'EXT.'
149 0149 O              N21N23 EXT   X 123
150 0150 O       D 3    40
151 0151 O              N25              25 'BLDG-      SQFT'
152 0152 O              N25   BLDSQF2   20
153 0153 O              N26              47 'LAND-        SQFT'
154 0154 O              N26   LNDSQF2   42
155 0155 O              N27   LNDACR2   53
156 0156 O              N27              58 'ACRE'
157 0157 O                               65 'PRICE'
158 0158 O                        PRICE 2  77 '$'
159 0159 O              N28              87 'ACCOUNT-'
160 0160 O              N28   ACCREP   102
161 0161 O       T 2    LR
162 0162 O                        ADDS  Z  11
163 0163 O                               34 'LISTINGS ADDED TO FILE'
164 0164 O       T 1    LR 99
165 0165 O                               32 '***********************'
166 0166 O                               34 '**'
167 0167 O       T 1    LR 99
168 0168 O                                9 '*'
169 0169 O                               34 '*'
170 0170 O       T 1    LR 99
171 0171 O                                9 '*'
172 0172 O                        ERRORSZ  13
173 0173 O                               34 'LISTINGS NOT ADDED *'
174 0174 O       T 1    LR 99
175 0175 O                                9 '*'
176 0176 O                               34 '*'
```

Figure 10-42 (3)

```
HJG10X     09-12-91  19:01:50        IBM PC        RPG II          Version 3.5  Page  4

            ....+....1....+....2....+....3....+....4....+....5....+....6....+....7....

177 0177 O         T  1     LR 99
178 0178 O                                          9 '*'
179 0179 O                                         34 'SEE ERROR REPORT    *'
180 0180 O         T  1     LR 99
181 0181 O                                          9 '*'
182 0182 O                                         34 '*'
183 0183 O         T     06 LR 99
184 0184 O                                         32 '************************'
185 0185 O                                         34 '**'
186 0186 OLISTFILEDADD      40
187 0187 O                                          1 'A'
188 0188 O                         LISTNO           7
189 0189 O                         LOCATN          32
190 0190 O                         TOWN            34
191 0191 O                         ZIP             39
192 0192 O                         CONTCT          54
193 0193 O                         PHONE           64
194 0194 O                         EXT             68
195 0195 O                         TYPE            69
196 0196 O                         CATEG           70
197 0197 O                         BLDSQF          76
198 0198 O                         LNDSQF          84
199 0199 O                         LNDACR          88
200 0200 O                         PRICE           96
201 0201 O                         ACCREP         111
202 0202 O                         UDATE          117
203 0203 OEREPORT H  106    1P
204 0204 O     OR           OF
205 0205 O                                          6 'HJG10X'
206 0206 O                         UDATE Y         29
207 0207 O                                         48 'PAGE'
208 0208 O                         PAGE1           53
209 0209 O         H  2     1P
210 0210 O     OR           OF
211 0211 O                                         31 'TRI-MOUNT REALTY LISTING'
212 0212 O                                         48 'S ADDITION ERRORS'
213 0213 O         H  2     1P
214 0214 O     OR           OF
215 0215 O                                         10 'LISTING NO'
216 0216 O                                         30 '-------ERROR TYPE'
217 0217 O         EF11      51 L1
218 0218 O     ORF 1         51NL1
219 0219 O               L1  LISTNO           8
220 0220 O               OF  LISTNO           8
221 0221 O                                         35 'DUPLICATE LISTING NO -'
222 0222 O                                         56 'RECORD NOT PROCESSED'
223 0223 O         EF11      52 L1
224 0224 O     ORF 1         52NL1
225 0225 O               L1  LISTNO           8
226 0226 O               OF  LISTNO           8
227 0227 O                                         33 'LISTING NUMBER BLANK'
228 0228 O         EF11      53 L1
229 0229 O     ORF 1         53NL1
230 0230 O               L1  LISTNO           8
231 0231 O               OF  LISTNO           8
232 0232 O                                         36 'PROPERTY LOCATION BLANK'
233 0233 O         EF11      54 L1
234 0234 O     ORF 1         54NL1
235 0235 O               L1  LISTNO           8
236 0236 O               OF  LISTNO           8
237 0237 O                                         28 'TOWN CODE BLANK'
238 0238 O         EF11      55 L1
239 0239 O     ORF 1         55NL1
240 0240 O               L1  LISTNO           8
241 0241 O               OF  LISTNO           8
242 0242 O                                         32 'ZIP CODE BLANK/ZERO'
243 0243 O         EF11      56 L1
244 0244 O     ORF 1         56NL1
245 0245 O               L1  LISTNO           8
246 0246 O               OF  LISTNO           8
247 0247 O                                         32 'PROPERTY TYPE BLANK'
248 0248 O         EF11      57 L1
249 0249 O     ORF 1         57NL1
250 0250 O               L1  LISTNO           8
251 0251 O               OF  LISTNO           8
252 0252 O                                         29 'PRICE BLANK/ZERO'
253 0253 O         EF11      58 L1
254 0254 O     ORF 1         58NL1
255 0255 O               L1  LISTNO           8
256 0256 O               OF  LISTNO           8
```

Figure 10-42 (4)   *continued*

```
HJG10X    09-12-91  19:01:50        IBM PC      RPG II        Version 3.5  Page  5

          ....+....1....+....2....+....3....+....4....+....5....+....6....+....7....

       257 0257 O                                  30 'INVALID TOWN CODE'
       258 0258 O        EF11      59 L1
       259 0259 O        ORF 1     59NL1
       260 0260 O                  L1   LISTNO      8
       261 0261 O                  OF   LISTNO      8
       262 0262 O                                  29 'INVALID ZIP CODE'
       263 0263 O        EF11      60 L1
       264 0264 O        ORF 1     60NL1
       265 0265 O        ↗         L1   LISTNO      8
       266 0266 O                  OF   LISTNO      8
       267 0267 O                                  34 'INVALID PROPERTY TYPE'
       268 0268 O        EF11      61 L1
       269 0269 O        ORF 1     61NL1
       270 0270 O                  L1   LISTNO      8
       271 0271 O                  OF   LISTNO      8
       272 0272 O                                  37 'CONTACT TELEPHONE NUMBER'
       273 0273 O                                  45 'MISSING'
       274 0274 O        EF11      62 L1
       275 0275 O        ORF 1     62NL1
       276 0276 O                  L1   LISTNO      8
       277 0277 O                  OF   LISTNO      8
       278 0278 O                                  33 'TOWN CODE - ZIP CODE'
       279 0279 O                                  42 'CONFLICT'
       280 0280 O        EF11      63 L1
       281 0281 O        ORF 1     63NL1
       282 0282 O                  L1   LISTNO      8
       283 0283 O                  OF   LISTNO      8
       284 0284 O                                  29 'INVALID PROPERTY'
       285 0285 O                                  38 'CATEGORY'
       286 0286 O        EF11      64 L1
       287 0287 O        ORF 1     64NL1
       288 0288 O                  L1   LISTNO      8
       289 0289 O                  OF   LISTNO      8
       290 0290 O                                  37 'CONTACT AND ACCOUNT REP.
       291 0291 O                                  48 'BOTH BLANK'
       292 **
       293 AS
       294 BA
       295 ET
       296 FI
       297 GA
       298 TM
       299 WE
       300 WI
       301 WS
       302 **
       303 01430
       304 01436
       305 01438
       306 01420
       307 01440
       308 01468
       309 01473
       310 01475
       311 01477
       312 /*
       313 /*




          THE FOLLOWING INDICATORS WERE SPECIFIED BUT WERE NEVER
          USED TO CONDITION OPERATIONS

          02



          THE FOLLOWING INDICATORS APPEARED IN THIS PROGRAM

              01  02  20  21  22  23  24  25  26  27  28  40  51  52  53  54
              55  56  57  58  59  60  61  62  63  64  65  66  67  68  69  70
              71  72  73  74  75  76  77  80  81  82  83  84  85  86  99  LR
              L1  1P  OF  OV
No Warning Errors
No Fatal Errors
```

Figure 10-42 (5)

```
HJG10X              09/12/91           PAGE    1
             TRI-MOUNT REALTY LISTINGS ADDITION ERRORS

    LISTING NO  ———ERROR TYPE


      37B00F     TOWN CODE BLANK
                 ZIP CODE BLANK/ZERO
                 PROPERTY TYPE BLANK
                 PRICE BLANK/ZERO
                 INVALID PROPERTY CATEGORY
                 CONTACT TELEPHONE NUMBER MISSING

      49F83A     PROPERTY LOCATION BLANK
                 PROPERTY TYPE BLANK
                 TOWN CODE - ZIP CODE CONFLICT
                 INVALID PROPERTY CATEGORY

      87F29D     PROPERTY TYPE BLANK
                 INVALID TOWN CODE
                 INVALID PROPERTY CATEGORY

      93F21H     TOWN CODE - ZIP CODE CONFLICT
                 CONTACT AND ACCOUNT REP. BOTH BLANK

      97F38I     INVALID PROPERTY CATEGORY
                 CONTACT TELEPHONE NUMBER MISSING

      12A37A     DUPLICATE LISTING NO - RECORD NOT PROCESSED
```

Figure 10-42 (6)

```
09/12/91 HJG10X                   TRI-MOUNT REALTY LISTINGS ADDITION REPORT                        PAGE    1
LISTING NO ———L O C A T I O N———
 01X25A  BURNSHIRT INDUSTRIAL PARK TM-01468  TYPE-COMMERCIAL-MANUFACTURING CONTACT-ROY WHEATON        555-9136
         BLDG-125,000 SQFT                     9.0 ACRE  PRICE $1,500,000


LISTING NO ———L O C A T I O N———
 03D41A  21 BULLDOG TERRACE       FI-01420  TYPE-RESIDENTIAL-SINGLE
         BLDG- 1,800 SQFT                     .6 ACRE  PRICE   $102,500  ACCOUNT-TONY GULINO


LISTING NO ———L O C A T I O N———
 12A37A  ROUTE 2A                 GA-01440  TYPE-RESIDENTIAL-MULTI        CONTACT-K. BASHAW   508-555-9311
         BLDG- 3,700 SQFT  LAND   27,000 SQFT           PRICE    $99,850  ACCOUNT-TONY GULINO


LISTING NO ———L O C A T I O N———
 13A37A  ROUTE 2A AND 101         BA-01436  TYPE-RESIDENTIAL-MULTI        CONTACT-NORM BELIN  508-555-2188
         BLDG- 4,600 SQFT  LAND   103,500 SQFT          PRICE   $187,000  ACCOUNT-TONY GULINO


LISTING NO ———L O C A T I O N———
 23D46D  41-55 WALTON WAY         WI-01475  TYPE-LAND                     CONTACT-SCOTT DRAKE    508-555-3000 EXT. 4215
                                            27.0 ACRE  PRICE   $675,000  ACCOUNT-MICHELLE DETLOR


LISTING NO ———L O C A T I O N———
 88G34A  THALER HILL ROAD         TM-01468  TYPE-COMMERCIAL-OFFICE        CONTACT-MARTEE RICHARDS 508-555-9876 EXT. 0024
         BLDG- 2,800 SQFT  LAND   40,000 SQFT           PRICE   $103,499


         6 LISTINGS ADDED TO FILE

    ***************************
    *                         *
    *   6 LISTINGS NOT ADDED  *
    *                         *
    *    SEE ERROR REPORT     *
    *                         *
    ***************************
```

Figure 10-42 (7)

continued

```
Filename  RecLen      KeyPo KeyLn                                    Date    Time   Page
LISTFILE  140           2    6                                     09/12/91  8.51

Rec No. Line No. 1... ...10.... ...20.... ...30.... ...40.... ...50.... ...60.... ...70.... ...80.... ...90.... ..100

        1    1    A01X25ABURNSHIRT INDUSTRIAL PARKTM01468ROY WHEATON      55591360000CM125000000000000009001500000
             2              102788

        2    1    A03D41A21 BULLDOG TERRACE      FI01420                  0000RS001800000000000000600102500TONY
             2    GULINO    102788

        3    1    A12A37AROUTE 2A               GA01440K. BASHAW     50855593110000RM0037000002700000000000099850TONY
             2    GULINO    102788

        4    1    A13A37AROUTE 2A AND 101       BA01436NORM BELIN    50855521880000RM00460000103500000000187000TONY
             2    GULINO    102788

        5    1    A23D46D41-55 WALTON WAY       WI01475SCOTT DRAKE   50855530004215L 0000000000000027000675000MICH
             2    ELLE DETLOR102788

        6    1    A88G34ATHALER HILL ROAD       TM01468MARTEE RICHARDS50855598760024C00028000004000000000103499
             2              102788
```

Figure 10-42 (8)

Problem 3

Modify program HJG10Y in Figure 10-43 so that only a single report, headed TRI-MOUNT REALTY –
LISTFILE ADDITION AUDIT is printed. The LISTFILE addition audit contains all the detail, exception, and
total information that currently is printed on both the Listings Addition Report and the Listings Addition Errors
report. Explain your modifications and their effect on the program.

Figure 10-43   Compilation listing for program HJG10Y

```
HJG10Y    09-12-91  19:04:17      IBM PC        RPG II         Version 3.5  Page  1
          ....+....1....+....2....+....3....+....4....+....5....+....6....+....7....

     1 0001 H                                                              HJG10Y

     2 0002 FLISTDATAIP  F 480 120            DISK
     3 0003 FLISTFILEUC  F 140 140R 6AI    2 DISK                A
     4 0004 FEREPORT O   F 132 132      OF    PRINTER
     5 0005 FAREPORT O   F 132 132      OV    PRINTER

     6 0006 E                       TABTN  1  9 2
     7 0007 E                       TABZIP 1  9 5 0

     8 0008 ILISTDATAAA  01
     9 0009 I                              1   6 LISTNOL1        80
    10 0010 I                              7  31 LOCATN          81
    11 0011 I                             32  33 TOWN            82
    12 0012 I                             34  38 0ZIP            83
    13 0013 I                             39  53 CONTCT          20
    14 0014 I                             54  63 PHONE           21
    15 0015 I                             54  56 0PH1            22
    16 0016 I                             57  59 0PH2
    17 0017 I                             60  63 0PH3
    18 0018 I                             64  67 0EXT            23
    19 0019 I                             68  68 TYPE            84
    20 0020 I                             69  69 CATEG           24
    21 0021 I                             70  75 0BLDSQF         25
    22 0022 I                             76  83 0LNDSQF         26
    23 0023 I                             84  87 1LNDACR         27
```

Figure 10-43 (1)

```
        HJG10Y    09-12-91  19:04:17      IBM PC        RPG II        Version 3.5  Page  2

                  ....+....1....+....2....+....3....+....4....+....5....+....6....+....7....

        24 0024 I                                          88 950PRICE          85
        25 0025 I                                          96 110 ACCREP        28
        26 0026 ILISTFILEAA  02
        27 0027 I                                           2   7 IDENT


        28 0028 C   01              SETOF                        656667
        29 0029 C   01              SETOF                        687273
        30 0030 C   01              SETOF                        747576
        31 0031 C   01              SETOF                        86
        32 0032 C   01              SETON                        40
        33 0033 C   80              EXCPTERR2
        34 0034 C   80              EXSR OFLOW
        35 0035 C   N80     LISTNO  CHAINLISTFILE                86
        36 0036 C   N80N86          EXCPTERR1
        37 0037 C   N80N86          EXSR OFLOW
        38 0038 C   N80N86          GOTO END
        39 0039 C   81              EXCPTERR3
        40 0040 C   81              EXSR OFLOW
        41 0041 C   82              EXCPTERR4
        42 0042 C   82              EXSR OFLOW
        43 0043 C   83              EXCPTERR5
        44 0044 C   83              EXSR OFLOW
        45 0045 C   84              EXCPTERR6
        46 0046 C   84              EXSR OFLOW
        47 0047 C   85              EXCPTERR7
        48 0048 C   85              EXSR OFLOW
        49 0049 C   N82     TOWN    LOKUPTABTN                 65
        50 0050 C   N82N65          EXCPTERR8
        51 0051 C   N82N65          EXSR OFLOW
        52 0052 C   N83     ZIP     LOKUPTABZIP                66
        53 0053 C   N83N66          EXCPTERR9
        54 0054 C   N83N66          EXSR OFLOW
        55 0055 C   65 66   TOWN    LOKUPTABTN   TABZIP        67
        56 0056 C   67      TABZIP  COMP ZIP          6868
        57 0057 C   68              EXCPTERR12
        58 0058 C   68              EXSR OFLOW
        59 0059 C                   SETOF                        697071
        60 0060 C   N84     TYPE    COMP 'R'          727269
        61 0061 C   N84 72  TYPE    COMP 'C'          727270
        62 0062 C   N84 72  TYPE    COMP 'L'          727271
        63 0063 C   72              EXCPTERR10
        64 0064 C   72              EXSR OFLOW
        65 0065 C   24              GOTO BYPASS
        66 0066 C           CATEG   COMP 'S'                   73
        67 0067 C           CATEG   COMP 'M'                   74
        68 0068 C           CATEG   COMP 'O'                   75
        69 0069 C           CATEG   COMP 'G'                   76
        70 0070 C                   SETON                      63
        71 0071 C   69 73
        72 0072 COR 69 74
        73 0073 COR 70 74
        74 0074 COR 70 75
        75 0075 COR 70 76
        76 0076 COR 71 24           SETOF                      63
        77 0077 C   63              EXCPTERR13
        78 0078 C   63              EXSR OFLOW
        79 0079 C   63              SETOF                      63
        80 0080 C           BYPASS  TAG
        81 0081 C   N20 21          EXCPTERR11
        82 0082 C   N20 21          EXSR OFLOW
        83 0083 C   20 28           EXCPTERR14
        84 0084 C   20 28           EXSR OFLOW
        85 0085 C           END     TAG
        86 0086 C   40              ADD  1       ADDS    30
        87 0087 C   N40             ADD  1       ERRORS  30
        88 0088 C           OFLOW   BEGSR
        89 0089 C                   SETOF                    40
        90 0090 C   77              SETOF                    770F
        91 0091 C   OF              SETON                    77
        92 0092 C                   SETOF                    L1
        93 0093 C                   SETON                    99
        94 0094 C                   ENDSR
```

Figure 10-43 (2)

continued

```
HJG10Y    09-12-91  19:04:17      IBM PC       RPG II        Version 3.5  Page  3
          ....+....1....+....2....+....3....+....4....+....5....+....6....+....7....

 95 0095 OAREPORT H  206      1P
 96 0096 O        OR          OV
 97 0097 O                        UDATE Y    8
 98 0098 O                                  15 'HJG10X'
 99 0099 O                                  65 'TRI-MOUNT REALTY LISTING'
100 0100 O                                  82 'S ADDITION REPORT'
101 0101 O                                 118 'PAGE'
102 0102 O                        PAGE     123
103 0103 O        D  1      40
104 0104 O                                  24 'LISTING NO ---------L O '
105 0105 O                                  45 'C A T I O N----------'
106 0106 O        D  1      40
107 0107 O                        LISTNO     8
108 0108 O                        LOCATN    36
109 0109 O                        TOWN      39
110 0110 O                                  40 '-'
111 0111 O                        ZIP    X  45
112 0112 O                                  52 'TYPE-'
113 0113 O                  69 74            69 'RESIDENTIAL-MULTI'
114 0114 O                  69 73            70 'RESIDENTIAL-SINGLE'
115 0115 O                  70 74            76 'COMMERCIAL-MANUFACTURING'
116 0116 O                  70 75            69 'COMMERCIAL-OFFICE'
117 0117 O                  70 76            70 'COMMERCIAL-GENERAL'
118 0118 O                  71               56 'LAND'
119 0119 O                  N20              85 'CONTACT-'
120 0120 O                  N20    CONTCT   100
121 0121 O                  N21N22 PH1    X 104
122 0122 O                  N21N22         105 '-'
123 0123 O                  N21    PH2    X 108
124 0124 O                  N21            109 '-'
125 0125 O                  N21    PH3    X 113
126 0126 O                  N21N23         118 'EXT.'
127 0127 O                  N21N23 EXT    X 123
128 0128 O        D  3      40
129 0129 O                  N25              25 'BLDG-       SQFT'
130 0130 O                  N25    BLDSQF2   20
131 0131 O                  N26              47 'LAND-        SQFT'
132 0132 O                  N26    LNDSQF2   42
133 0133 O                  N27    LNDACR2   53
134 0134 O                  N27              58 'ACRE'
135 0135 O                                  65 'PRICE'
136 0136 O                        PRICE 2   77 '$'
137 0137 O                  N28              87 'ACCOUNT-'
138 0138 O                  N28    ACCREP   102
139 0139 O        T  2      LR
140 0140 O                        ADDS  Z   11
141 0141 O                                  34 'LISTINGS ADDED TO FILE'
142 0142 O        T  1      LR 99
143 0143 O                                  32 '************************'
144 0144 O                                  34 '**'
145 0145 O        T  1      LR 99
146 0146 O                                   9 '*'
147 0147 O                                  34 '*'
148 0148 O        T  1      LR 99
149 0149 O                                   9 '*'
150 0150 O                        ERRORSZ   13
151 0151 O                                  34 'LISTINGS NOT ADDED *'
152 0152 O        T  1      LR 99
153 0153 O                                   9 '*'
154 0154 O                                  34 '*'
155 0155 O        T  1      LR 99
156 0156 O                                   9 '*'
157 0157 O                                  34 'SEE ERROR REPORT    *'
158 0158 O        T  1      LR 99
159 0159 O                                   9 '*'
160 0160 O                                  34 '*'
161 0161 O        T    06 LR 99
162 0162 O                                  32 '************************'
163 0163 O                                  34 '**'
164 0164 OLISTFILEDADD      40
165 0165 O                                   1 'A'
166 0166 O                        LISTNO     7
```

Figure 10-43 (3)

```
HJG10Y     09-12-91  19:04:17       IBM PC      RPG II        Version 3.5  Page  4

      ....+....1....+....2....+....3....+....4....+....5....+....6....+....7....
167 0167 O                              LOCATN    32
168 0168 O                              TOWN      34
169 0169 O                              ZIP       39
170 0170 O                              CONTCT    54
171 0171 O                              PHONE     64
172 0172 O                              EXT       68
173 0173 O                              TYPE      69
174 0174 O                              CATEG     70
175 0175 O                              BLDSQF    76
176 0176 O                              LNDSQF    84
177 0177 O                              LNDACR    88
178 0178 O                              PRICE     96
179 0179 O                              ACCREP   111
180 0180 O                              UDATE    117
181 0181 OEREPORT H  106     1P
182 0182 O          OR        OF
183 0183 O                                        6 'HJG10X'
184 0184 O                              UDATE Y  29
185 0185 O                                       48 'PAGE'
186 0186 O                              PAGE1    53
187 0187 O          H   2     1P
188 0188 O          OR        OF
189 0189 O                                       31 'TRI-MOUNT REALTY LISTING'
190 0190 O                                       48 'S ADDITION ERRORS'
191 0191 O          H   2     1P
192 0192 O          OR        OF
193 0193 O                                       10 'LISTING NO'
194 0194 O                                       30 '-------ERROR TYPE'
195 0195 O          EF11      L1        ERR1
196 0196 O          ORF 1     NL1
197 0197 O                    L1        LISTNO    8
198 0198 O                    OF        LISTNO    8
199 0199 O                                       35 'DUPLICATE LISTING NO -'
200 0200 O                                       56 'RECORD NOT PROCESSED'
201 0201 O          EF11      L1        ERR2
202 0202 O          ORF 1     NL1
203 0203 O                    L1        LISTNO    8
204 0204 O                    OF        LISTNO    8
205 0205 O                                       33 'LISTING NUMBER BLANK'
206 0206 O          EF11      L1        ERR3
207 0207 O          ORF 1     NL1
208 0208 O                    L1        LISTNO    8
209 0209 O                    OF        LISTNO    8
210 0210 O                                       36 'PROPERTY LOCATION BLANK'
211 0211 O          EF11      L1        ERR4
212 0212 O          ORF 1     NL1
213 0213 O                    L1        LISTNO    8
214 0214 O                    OF        LISTNO    8
215 0215 O                                       28 'TOWN CODE BLANK'
216 0216 O          EF11      L1        ERR5
217 0217 O          ORF 1     NL1
218 0218 O                    L1        LISTNO    8
219 0219 O                    OF        LISTNO    8
220 0220 O                                       32 'ZIP CODE BLANK/ZERO'
221 0221 O          EF11      L1        ERR6
222 0222 O          ORF 1     NL1
223 0223 O                    L1        LISTNO    8
224 0224 O                    OF        LISTNO    8
225 0225 O                                       32 'PROPERTY TYPE BLANK'
226 0226 O          EF11      L1        ERR7
227 0227 O          ORF 1     NL1
228 0228 O                    L1        LISTNO    8
229 0229 O                    OF        LISTNO    8
230 0230 O                                       29 'PRICE BLANK/ZERO'
231 0231 O          EF11      L1        ERR8
232 0232 O          ORF 1     NL1
233 0233 O                    L1        LISTNO    8
234 0234 O                    OF        LISTNO    8
235 0235 O                                       30 'INVALID TOWN CODE'
236 0236 O          EF11      L1        ERR9
237 0237 O          ORF 1     NL1
238 0238 O                    L1        LISTNO    8
239 0239 O                    OF        LISTNO    8
240 0240 O                                       29 'INVALID ZIP CODE'
241 0241 O          EF11      L1        ERR10
```

Figure 10-43 (4)

continued

```
       HJG10Y    09-12-91  19:04:17        IBM PC      RPG II        Version 3.5  Page  5

                  ....+....1....+....2..:.+....3....+....4....+....5....+....6....+....7....
       242 0242 O      ORF 1   NL1
       243 0243 O              L1      LISTNO    8
       244 0244 O              OF      LISTNO    8
       245 0245 O                                34 'INVALID PROPERTY TYPE'
       246 0246 O      EF11    L1      ERR11
       247 0247 O      ORF 1   NL1
       248 0248 O              L1      LISTNO    8
       249 0249 O              OF      LISTNO    8
       250 0250 O                                37 'CONTACT TELEPHONE NUMBER'
       251 0251 O                                45 'MISSING'
       252 0252 O      EF11    L1      ERR12
       253 0253 O      ORF 1   NL1
       254 0254 O              L1      LISTNO    8
       255 0255 O              OF      LISTNO    8
       256 0256 O                                33 'TOWN CODE - ZIP CODE'
       257 0257 O                                42 'CONFLICT'
       258 0258 O      EF11    L1      ERR13
       259 0259 O      ORF 1   NL1
       260 0260 O              L1      LISTNO    8
       261 0261 O              OF      LISTNO    8
       262 0262 O                                29 'INVALID PROPERTY'
       263 0263 O                                38 'CATEGORY'
       264 0264 O      EF11    L1      ERR14
       265 0265 O      ORF 1   NL1
       266 0266 O              L1      LISTNO    8
       267 0267 O              OF      LISTNO    8
       268 0268 O                                37 'CONTACT AND ACCOUNT REP.'
       269 0269 O                                48 'BOTH BLANK'
       270 **
       271 AS
       272 BA
       273 ET
       274 FI
       275 GA
       276 TM
       277 WE
       278 WI
       279 WS
       280 **
       281 01430
       282 01436
       283 01438
       284 01420
       285 01440
       286 01468
       287 01473
       288 01475
       289 01477
       290 /*
       291 /*



           THE FOLLOWING INDICATORS WERE SPECIFIED BUT WERE NEVER
           USED TO CONDITION OPERATIONS

           02



           THE FOLLOWING INDICATORS APPEARED IN THIS PROGRAM
           01  02  20  21  22  23  24  25  26  27  28  40  63  65  66  67
           68  69  70  71  72  73  74  75  76  77  80  81  82  83  84  85
           86  99  LR  L1  1P  OF  OV
       No Warning Errors
       No Fatal Errors
```

Figure 10-43 (5)

Problem 4

In many situations that involve the addition of records to a data file, the records must be added on an all-or-nothing basis. That is, either the entire group of records is added or none of the records is added. When this type of processing is required, the normal practice is to write the valid input records to a separate, arrival sequence disk file and to add no records to the keyed file. If, at the end of the program no errors were detected, a separate program is used to add the records to the keyed file.

Modify program HJG10Y in Figure 10-44 so that the valid records are written to an arrival sequence file named LISTWORK, rather than being added to LISTFILE. The format of LISTWORK is identical to the format of LISTDATA (Figure 10-2). Note: When records are written to an arrival sequence file, position 66 of the File Description Specification form and the output specification ADD entry are not used because these entries do not apply to arrival sequence files. Explain your modifications and their effect on the program.

Figure 10-44   Compilation listing for program HJG10Y

```
HJG10Y    09-12-91  19:04:17        IBM PC       RPG II          Version 3.5  Page  1

          ....+....1....+....2....+....3....+....4....+....5....+....6....+....7....

        1 0001 H                                                              HJG10Y


        2 0002 FLISTDATAIP  F 480 120              DISK
        3 0003 FLISTFILEUC  F 140 140R 6AI    2 DISK                  A
        4 0004 FEREPORT  O  F 132 132      OF    PRINTER
        5 0005 FAREPORT  O  F 132 132      OV    PRINTER


        6 0006 E                      TABTN   1   9 2
        7 0007 E                      TABZIP  1   9 5 0


        8 0008 ILISTDATAAAA  01
        9 0009 I                                    1    6 LISTNOL1    80
       10 0010 I                                    7   31 LOCATN      81
       11 0011 I                                   32   33 TOWN        82
       12 0012 I                                   34  380ZIP          83
       13 0013 I                                   39   53 CONTCT      20
       14 0014 I                                   54   63 PHONE       21
       15 0015 I                                   54  560PH1          22
       16 0016 I                                   57  590PH2
       17 0017 I                                   60  630PH3
       18 0018 I                                   64  670EXT          23
       19 0019 I                                   68   68 TYPE        84
       20 0020 I                                   69   69 CATEG       24
       21 0021 I                                   70  750BLDSQF       25
       22 0022 I                                   76  830LNDSQF       26
       23 0023 I                                   84  871LNDACR       27
       24 0024 I                                   88  950PRICE        85
       25 0025 I                                   96  110 ACCREP      28
       26 0026 ILISTFILEAA  02
       27 0027 I                                    2    7 IDENT


       28 0028 C    01            SETOF                   656667
       29 0029 C    01            SETOF                   687273
       30 0030 C    01            SETOF                   747576
       31 0031 C    01            SETOF                   86
       32 0032 C    01            SETON                   40
       33 0033 C    80            EXCPTERR2
       34 0034 C    80            EXSR OFLOW
       35 0035 C    N80    LISTNO CHAINLISTFILE           86
       36 0036 C    N80N86        EXCPTERR1
       37 0037 C    N80N86        EXSR OFLOW
       38 0038 C    N80N86        GOTO END
       39 0039 C    81            EXCPTERR3
       40 0040 C    81            EXSR OFLOW
       41 0041 C    82            EXCPTERR4
```

Figure 10-44 (1)

continued

```
HJG10Y      09-12-91  19:04:17      IBM PC       RPG II        Version 3.5  Page  2

            ....+....1....+....2....+....3....+....4....+....5....+....6....+....7....

   42 0042 C    82                  EXSR OFLOW
   43 0043 C    83                  EXCPTERR5
   44 0044 C    83                  EXSR OFLOW
   45 0045 C    84                  EXCPTERR6
   46 0046 C    84                  EXSR OFLOW
   47 0047 C    85                  EXCPTERR7
   48 0048 C    85                  EXSR OFLOW
   49 0049 C    N82     TOWN        LOKUPTABTN                          65
   50 0050 C    N82N65              EXCPTERR8
   51 0051 C    N82N65              EXSR OFLOW
   52 0052 C    N83     ZIP         LOKUPTABZIP                         66
   53 0053 C    N83N66              EXCPTERR9
   54 0054 C    N83N66              EXSR OFLOW
   55 0055 C    65 66   TOWN        LOKUPTABTN      TABZIP              67
   56 0056 C    67      TABZIP      COMP ZIP                        6868
   57 0057 C    68                  EXCPTERR12
   58 0058 C    68                  EXSR OFLOW
   59 0059 C                        SETOF                           697071
   60 0060 C    N84     TYPE        COMP 'R'                        727269
   61 0061 C    N84 72  TYPE        COMP 'C'                        727270
   62 0062 C    N84 72  TYPE        COMP 'L'                        727271
   63 0063 C    72                  EXCPTERR10
   64 0064 C    72                  EXSR OFLOW
   65 0065 C    24                  GOTO BYPASS
   66 0066 C            CATEG       COMP 'S'                            73
   67 0067 C            CATEG       COMP 'N'                            74
   68 0068 C            CATEG       COMP 'O'                            75
   69 0069 C            CATEG       COMP 'G'                            76
   70 0070 C                        SETON                               63
   71 0071 C    69 73
   72 0072 COR  69 74
   73 0073 COR  70 74
   74 0074 COR  70 75
   75 0075 COR  70 76
   76 0076 COR  71 24               SETOF                               63
   77 0077 C    63                  EXCPTERR13
   78 0078 C    63                  EXSR OFLOW
   79 0079 C    63                  SETOF                               63
   80 0080 C            BYPASS      TAG
   81 0081 C    N20 21              EXCPTERR11
   82 0082 C    N20 21              EXSR OFLOW
   83 0083 C    20 28               EXCPTERR14
   84 0084 C    20 28               EXSR OFLOW
   85 0085 C            END         TAG
   86 0086 C    40                  ADD  1          ADDS     30
   87 0087 C    N40                 ADD  1          ERRORS   30
   88 0088 C            OFLOW       BEGSR
   89 0089 C                        SETOF                               40
   90 0090 C    77                  SETOF                               770F
   91 0091 C    OF                  SETON                               77
   92 0092 C                        SETOF                               L1
   93 0093 C                        SETON                               99
   94 0094 C                        ENDSR

   95 0095 OAREPORT H  206      1P
   96 0096 O          OR          OV
   97 0097 O                        UDATE Y     8
   98 0098 O                                   15 'HJG10X'
   99 0099 O                                   65 'TRI-MOUNT REALTY LISTING'
  100 0100 O                                   82 'S ADDITION REPORT'
  101 0101 O                                  118 'PAGE'
  102 0102 O                        PAGE      123
  103 0103 O          D  1      40
  104 0104 O                                   24 'LISTING NO ---------L O '
  105 0105 O                                   45 'C A T I O N----------'
  106 0106 O          D  1      40
  107 0107 O                        LISTNO     8
  108 0108 O                        LOCATN    36
  109 0109 O                        TOWN      39
  110 0110 O                                   40 '-'
  111 0111 O                        ZIP    X  45
  112 0112 O                                   52 'TYPE-'
  113 0113 O                   69 74           69 'RESIDENTIAL-MULTI'
  114 0114 O                   69 73           70 'RESIDENTIAL-SINGLE'
```

Figure 10-44 (2)

```
HJG10Y    09-12-91  19:04:17        IBM PC      RPG II          Version 3.5  Page 3

          ....+....1....+....2....+....3....+....4....+....5....+....6....+....7....

          115 0115 O                70 74              76 'COMMERCIAL-MANUFACTURING'
          116 0116 O                70 75              69 'COMMERCIAL-OFFICE'
          117 0117 O                70 76              70 'COMMERCIAL-GENERAL'
          118 0118 O                71                 56 'LAND'
          119 0119 O                N20                85 'CONTACT-'
          120 0120 O                N20     CONTCT    100
          121 0121 O                N21N22  PH1    X  104
          122 0122 O                N21N22           105 '-'
          123 0123 O                N21     PH2    X  108
          124 0124 O                N21              109 '-'
          125 0125 O                N21     PH3    X  113
          126 0126 O                N21N23           118 'EXT.'
          127 0127 O                N21N23  EXT    X  123
          128 0128 O        D  3    40
          129 0129 O                N25                25 'BLDG-        SQFT'
          130 0130 O                N25     BLDSQF2    20
          131 0131 O                N26                47 'LAND-         SQFT'
          132 0132 O                N26     LNDSQF2    42
          133 0133 O                N27     LNDACR2    53
          134 0134 O                N27                58 'ACRE'
          135 0135 O                                   65 'PRICE'
          136 0136 O                        PRICE 2    77 '$'
          137 0137 O                N28                87 'ACCOUNT-'
          138 0138 O                N28     ACCREP    102
          139 0139 O        T  2    LR
          140 0140 O                        ADDS  Z    11
          141 0141 O                                   34 'LISTINGS ADDED TO FILE'
          142 0142 O        T  1    LR 99
          143 0143 O                                   32 '************************'
          144 0144 O                                   34 '**'
          145 0145 O        T  1    LR 99
          146 0146 O                                    9 '*'
          147 0147 O                                   34 '*'
          148 0148 O        T  1    LR 99
          149 0149 O                                    9 '*'
          150 0150 O                        ERRORSZ    13
          151 0151 O                                   34 'LISTINGS NOT ADDED *'
          152 0152 O        T  1    LR 99
          153 0153 O                                    9 '*'
          154 0154 O                                   34 '*'
          155 0155 O        T  1    LR 99
          156 0156 O                                    9 '*'
          157 0157 O                                   34 'SEE ERROR REPORT     *'
          158 0158 O        T  1    LR 99
          159 0159 O                                    9 '*'
          160 0160 O                                   34 '*'
          161 0161 O        T     06 LR 99
          162 0162 O                                   32 '************************'
          163 0163 O                                   34 '**'
          164 0164 OLISTFILEDADD      40
          165 0165 O                                    1 'A'
          166 0166 O                        LISTNO      7
          167 0167 O                        LOCATN     32
          168 0168 O                        TOWN       34
          169 0169 O                        ZIP        39
          170 0170 O                        CONTCT     54
          171 0171 O                        PHONE      64
          172 0172 O                        EXT        68
          173 0173 O                        TYPE       69
          174 0174 O                        CATEG      70
          175 0175 O                        BLDSQF     76
          176 0176 O                        LNDSQF     84
          177 0177 O                        LNDACR     88
          178 0178 O                        PRICE      96
          179 0179 O                        ACCREP    111
          180 0180 O                        UDATE     117
          181 0181 OEREPORT H  106    1P
          182 0182 O        OR        OF
          183 0183 O                                    6 'HJG10X'
          184 0184 O                        UDATE Y    29
          185 0185 O                                   48 'PAGE'
          186 0186 O                        PAGE1      53
          187 0187 O        H  2      1P
          188 0188 O        OR        OF
          189 0189 O                                   31 'TRI-MOUNT REALTY LISTING'
```

Figure 10-44 (3)

continued

```
HJG10Y    09-12-91  19:04:17       IBM PC      RPG II        Version 3.5  Page  4

          ....+....1....+....2....+....3....+....4....+....5....+....6....+....7....

    190 0190 O                                     48 'S ADDITION ERRORS'
    191 0191 O         H  2      1P
    192 0192 O      OR           OF
    193 0193 O                                     10 'LISTING NO'
    194 0194 O                                     30 '-------ERROR TYPE'
    195 0195 O         EF11      L1      ERR1
    196 0196 O      ORF 1        NL1
    197 0197 O                   L1      LISTNO   8
    198 0198 O                   OF      LISTNO   8
    199 0199 O                                     35 'DUPLICATE LISTING NO -'
    200 0200 O                                     56 'RECORD NOT PROCESSED'
    201 0201 O         EF11      L1      ERR2
    202 0202 O      ORF 1        NL1
    203 0203 O                   L1      LISTNO   8
    204 0204 O                   OF      LISTNO   8
    205 0205 O                                     33 'LISTING NUMBER BLANK'
    206 0206 O         EF11      L1      ERR3
    207 0207 O      ORF 1        NL1
    208 0208 O                   L1      LISTNO   8
    209 0209 O                   OF      LISTNO   8
    210 0210 O                                     36 'PROPERTY LOCATION BLANK'
    211 0211 O         EF11      L1      ERR4
    212 0212 O      ORF 1        NL1
    213 0213 O                   L1      LISTNO   8
    214 0214 O                   OF      LISTNO   8
    215 0215 O                                     28 'TOWN CODE BLANK'
    216 0216 O         EF11      L1      ERR5
    217 0217 O      ORF 1        NL1
    218 0218 O                   L1      LISTNO   8
    219 0219 O                   OF      LISTNO   8
    220 0220 O                                     32 'ZIP CODE BLANK/ZERO'
    221 0221 O         EF11      L1      ERR6
    222 0222 O      ORF 1        NL1
    223 0223 O                   L1      LISTNO   8
    224 0224 O                   OF      LISTNO   8
    225 0225 O                                     32 'PROPERTY TYPE BLANK'
    226 0226 O         EF11      L1      ERR7
    227 0227 O      ORF 1        NL1
    228 0228 O                   L1      LISTNO   8
    229 0229 O                   OF      LISTNO   8
    230 0230 O                                     29 'PRICE BLANK/ZERO'
    231 0231 O         EF11      L1      ERR8
    232 0232 O      ORF 1        NL1
    233 0233 O                   L1      LISTNO   8
    234 0234 O                   OF      LISTNO   8
    235 0235 O                                     30 'INVALID TOWN CODE'
    236 0236 O         EF11      L1      ERR9
    237 0237 O      ORF 1        NL1
    238 0238 O                   L1      LISTNO   8
    239 0239 O                   OF      LISTNO   8
    240 0240 O                                     29 'INVALID ZIP CODE'
    241 0241 O         EF11      L1      ERR10
    242 0242 O      ORF 1        NL1
    243 0243 O                   L1      LISTNO   8
    244 0244 O                   OF      LISTNO   8
    245 0245 O                                     34 'INVALID PROPERTY TYPE'
    246 0246 O         EF11      L1      ERR11
    247 0247 O      ORF 1        NL1
    248 0248 O                   L1      LISTNO   8
    249 0249 O                   OF      LISTNO   8
    250 0250 O                                     37 'CONTACT TELEPHONE NUMBER'
    251 0251 O                                     45 'MISSING'
    252 0252 O         EF11      L1      ERR12
    253 0253 O      ORF 1        NL1
    254 0254 O                   L1      LISTNO   8
    255 0255 O                   OF      LISTNO   8
    256 0256 O                                     33 'TOWN CODE - ZIP CODE'
    257 0257 O                                     42 'CONFLICT'
    258 0258 O         EF11      L1      ERR13
    259 0259 O      ORF 1        NL1
```

Figure 10-44 (4)

```
HJG10Y    09-12-91  19:04:17       IBM PC      RPG II          Version 3.5  Page  5

          ....+....1....+....2....+....3....+....4....+....5....+....6....+....7....
      260 0260 O                 L1    LISTNO      8
      261 0261 O                 OF    LISTNO      8
      262 0262 O                                  29 'INVALID PROPERTY'
      263 0263 O                                  38 'CATEGORY'
      264 0264 O        EF11     L1    ERR14
      265 0265 O        ORF 1    NL1
      266 0266 O                 L1    LISTNO      8
      267 0267 O                 OF    LISTNO      8
      268 0268 O                                  37 'CONTACT AND ACCOUNT REP.'
      269 0269 O                                  48 'BOTH BLANK'
      270 **
      271 AS
      272 BA
      273 ET
      274 FI
      275 GA
      276 TM
      277 WE
      278 WI
      279 WS
      280 **
      281 01430
      282 01436
      283 01438
      284 01420
      285 01440
      286 01468
      287 01473
      288 01475
      289 01477
      290 /*
      291 /*



          THE FOLLOWING INDICATORS WERE SPECIFIED BUT WERE NEVER
          USED TO CONDITION OPERATIONS

          02



          THE FOLLOWING INDICATORS APPEARED IN THIS PROGRAM

          01  02  20  21  22  23  24  25  26  27  28  40  63  65  66  67
          68  69  70  71  72  73  74  75  76  77  80  81  82  83  84  85
          86  99  LR  L1  1P  OF  OV
No Warning Errors
No Fatal Errors
```

Figure 10-44 (5)

STUDENT EXERCISES: PROGRAMMING IN RPG

One of the functions of computer programmers is to design the printed reports generated by the program they are writing. In Chapters 1–9, printer spacing charts that show the format of the output report for each program have been provided as part of the program specifications. Beginning with this chapter, printer spacing charts that show output report formats will not be provided. The design of any needed output reports will be part of the planning stage of each programming assignment.

PROGRAMMING ASSIGNMENT 1
TEST EQUIPMENT MASTER FILE RECORD LOAD

INSTRUCTIONS

Plan, code, enter, and test an RPG program to load new records to the Test Equipment Master File.

INPUT

The format of the Test Equipment Data file is shown in Figure 10-45. Use test data set 1 for this problem.

TEST EQUIPMENT DATA RECORD						
Record Length 65						
Field No.	Field Name	Field Description	Field Position	Field Length	Dec. Pos.	Data Class
1	UNITID	Unit I.D. Number	1–8	8		A
2	DESCR	Unit Description	9–30	22		A
3	LOCAT	Location	36–42	7		A
4	PDATE	Purchase Date	46–51	6	0	N
5	CDATE	Date Last Calibrated	52–57	6	0	N

Figure 10-45   Test equipment data record

OUTPUT

Programming assignment 1 creates three output files. The first is the Test Equipment Master File, a keyed file. The format of the Test Equipment Master File is shown in Figure 10-46. Retain this data file for use in Chapter 11.

TEST EQUIPMENT MASTER FILE RECORD						
Record Length 65		Key Location 1–8				
Field No.	Field Name	Field Description	Field Position	Field Length	Dec. Pos.	Data Class
1		Unit I.D. Number	1–8			
2		Unit Description	9–30			
3		Location	36–42			
4		Purchase Date	46–51			
5		Date Last Calibrated	52–57			
6		Date Loaded	58–63			
7		Status Code A	65–65			

Figure 10-46   Test Equipment Master File record format

The other two output files are printed reports. The first is a record addition report that lists all records added to the Test Equipment Master File. It lists all fields contained in every record added to the file. In addition, the report prints a count of the number of records added to the file and the number of records that contained one or more errors.

The second printed report is a record addition error report. For this assignment, list all errors detected in each input data record based on the tests described in the Processing Requirements section of this problem description. Group indicate the unit identification number of each unit shown on this report. Single space all error messages for a single unit. Double space between units in a manner similar to the spacing used for the two sample programs in this chapter.

Processing Requirements

Test each input data record for the conditions in the following list. If none of the listed conditions is detected, a record is added to the Test Equipment Master File. If one or more of the listed conditions is detected, no addition to the master file is made.

1. The Unit Identification Number must not be duplicated in the Test Equipment Master File.
2. The Unit Identification Number, Description, and Location fields must not be blank.
3. The Purchase Date field must not contain all zeros.
4. If the Date Last Calibrated field contains a date, the date cannot be earlier than the purchase date.
5. Both of the input date fields are in MMDDYY format. The month and day portions of both fields must be valid. Each month entry must be 01–12, and the day entry must be valid for the month. You need not test for leap year because the file does not contain any dates of February 29.

PROGRAMMING ASSIGNMENT 2
EMPLOYEE MASTER FILE LOAD

INSTRUCTIONS

Plan, code, enter, and test an RPG program to load new records to the Employee Master File.

INPUT

The format of the employee payroll file is shown in Figure 10-47. Use test data set 24 for this problem.

EMPLOYEE DATA RECORD						
Record Length 70						
Field No.	Field Name	Field Description	Field Position	Field Length	Dec. Pos.	Data Class
1	EMPLID	Employee Number	1–4	4	0	N
2	LNAME	Last Name	5–19	15		A
3	FNAME	First Name	20–31	12		A
4	SCODE	Sex Code (M/F)	32–32	1		A
5	DTHIRE	Date Hired	33–38	6	0	N
6	DEPTNO	Department Number	39–41	3	0	N
7	PAYCAT	Pay Category (H/S)	42–42	1		A
8	RATCOD	Pay Rate Code	43–44	2	0	N
9	ANNSAL	Annual Salary	45–52	8	2	N
10	HRATE	Hourly Pay Rate	53–57	5	3	N
11	HOURS	Hours Worked Last Pay Period	58–61	4	1	N
12		UNUSED AREA	62–70			

Figure 10-47 Employee Data record format

OUTPUT

Programming Assignment 2 creates three output files. The first is the Employee Master File, a keyed file. The format of the Employee Master File is shown in Figure 10-48. Retain this data file for use in Chapter 11.

EMPLOYEE MASTER FILE RECORD						
Record Length 70			Key Location 1–4			
Field No.	Field Name	Field Description	Field Position	Field Length	Dec. Pos.	Data Class
1		Employee Number	1–4			
2		Last Name	5–19			
3		First Name	20–31			
4		Sex Code (M/F)	32–32			
5		Date Hired	33–38			
6		Department Number	39–41			
7		Pay Category (H/S)	42–42			
8		Pay Rate Code	43–44			
9		Annual Salary	45–52			
10		Hourly Pay Rate	53–57			
11		Current Date	62–67			
12		Status Code A	70–70			

Figure 10-48 Employee Master File Record format

The other two output files are printed reports. The first is a record addition report that lists all records added to the Employee Master File. It lists all fields contained in every record added to the file. In addition, the report prints a count of the number of records added to the file and the number of records that contained one or more errors.

The second printed report is a record addition error report. For this assignment, list all errors detected in each input data record based on the tests described in the Processing Requirements section of this problem description. Group indicate the employee number of each employee record shown on this report. Single space all error messages for a single employee. Double space between employees in a manner similar to the spacing used on the two sample programs in this chapter.

⊨ Processing Requirements

Test each input data record for the conditions in the following list. If none of the listed conditions is detected, a record is added to the Employee Master File. If one or more of the listed conditions is detected, no addition to the master file is made.

1. The employee number must not be duplicated in the Employee Master File.
2. The Employee Number, Last Name, First Name, Date Hired, and Department Number fields must not be blank.
3. Sex code must be either M or F.
4. Pay category must be either H or S.
5. If pay category is H, neither the Pay Rate Code field nor the Hourly Pay Rate field may be blank or zero.
6. If pay category is 'S', the Annual Salary field may not be blank or zero.

PROGRAMMING ASSIGNMENT 3
RENTAL CAR STATUS FILE LOAD

INSTRUCTIONS

Plan, code, enter, and test an RPG program to load new records to the Rental Car Status file.

INPUT

The format of the Rental Car Load file is shown in Figure 10-49. Use test data set 25 for this problem.

RENTAL CAR LOAD RECORD						
Record Length 70						
Field No.	Field Name	Field Description	Field Position	Field Length	Dec. Pos.	Data Class
1	STOCK	Vehicle Stock No.	1–9	9	0	N
2	CHECK	Check Digit	10–10	1	0	N
3	MAKE	Make of Car	11–11	1		A
4	STYLE	Body Style	12–12	1		A
5	EQUIP	Optional Equipment	13–17	5		A
		Air Conditioning	13–13			
		Power Steering	14–14			
		Towing Package	15–15			
		Sun Roof	16–16			
		Automatic Trans.	17–17			
6	STATUS	Vehicle Status	18–18	1		A
7	LICNO	License Number	19–27	9		A
8	NAME	Renter's Name	28–48	21		A
9	PAY	Payment Method	49–50	2		A
10	DOUT	Date Out	51–56	6	0	N
11	NODAYS	Number of Days Rented	57–58	2	0	N
12	DEPST	Deposit Amount	59–62	4	0	N
		UNUSED AREA	63–70			

Figure 10-49   Rental Car Load Record format

OUTPUT

Programming Assignment 3 creates three output files. The first is the Rental Car Status file, a keyed file. The format of the Rental Car Status file is shown in Figure 10-50 on the next page.

The other two output files are printed reports. The first of these is a record addition report that lists all records added to the Rental Car Status file. It lists all fields contained in every record added to the file. Use output constants to specify the Make of Car, Body Style, Optional Equipment, and Vehicle Status fields. In addition, the report prints a count of the number of records added to the file and the number of records that contained one or more errors.

RENTAL CAR STATUS RECORD						
Record Length 70			Key Location 1–10			
Field No.	Field Name	Field Description	Field Position	Field Length	Dec. Pos.	Data Class
		Vehicle Stock No.	1–9			
		Check Digit	10–10			
		Make of Car	11–11			
		Body Style	12–12			
		Optional Equipment	13–17			
		Air Conditioning	13–13			
		Power Steering	14–14			
		Towing Package	15–15			
		Sun Roof	16–16			
		Automatic Trans.	17–17			
		Vehicle Status	18–18			
		License Number	19–27			
		Renter's Name	28–48			
		Payment Method	49–50			
		Date Out	51–56			
		Number of Days Rented	57–58			
		Deposit Amount	59–62			

Figure 10-50 Rental Car Status Record format

The second printed report is a record addition error report. For this assignment, list all errors detected in each input data record based on the tests described in the Processing Requirements section of this problem description.

≡ Processing Requirements

Test each input data record for the conditions in the following list. If none of the listed conditions is detected, a record is added to the Rental Car Status file. Except for condition 11, if one or more of the listed conditions is detected, no addition to the master file is made. If condition 11 is detected, an error message is printed, and the record is added to the Rental Car Status file.

1. The vehicle stock number must not be duplicated in the Rental Car Status file.
2. The STOCK, CHECK, MAKE, STYLE, and STATUS fields must not be blank and must contain valid codes as shown.
3. The Check Digit field must correspond to the Vehicle Stock Number field. To verify the Check Digit field, add together the nine digits of the Vehicle Stock Number field. The rightmost digit of the sum should match the Check Digit field.

4. The valid MAKE entries are

   P   Panther
   T   Tiger
   B   Bearcat
   V   Vulcan

5. The valid STYLE entries are

   C   Convertible
   S   Sedan
   F   Fastback

6. The four makes of car are not all available in every body style. The valid combinations of Make and Body Style are

Panther	Convertible, fastback
Tiger	Sedan, fastback
Bearcat	Convertible, sedan, fastback
Vulcan	Convertible, sedan

   No other combination is valid.

7. The five Optional Equipment fields contain a Y if the vehicle is equipped with the option and an N if the vehicle is not equipped with that option. The invalid optional equipment combinations are

   Fastbacks cannot be equipped with the towing package.
   If a car is equipped with either air conditioning or a towing package, it cannot be equipped with a sun roof.
   If a car is equipped with air conditioning, it must be equipped with power steering and an automatic transmission.

8. The three valid STATUS codes are

   A   Available for rental
   R   Rented, not available
   S   Being serviced, not available

9. If the STATUS code is R, the LICNO, NAME, PAY, and NODAYS fields must not be blank.
10. The valid payment method codes are CA (cash payment) and CR (credit card).
11. If the payment method is CA, the DEPSIT field must be tested to verify a valid deposit amount. Deposit amount is calculated as follows

   If the car is a Panther, Tiger, or Bearcat, the deposit is $50.00 per day. If the car is a Vulcan, the deposit is $35.00 per day.

ELEVEN

Keyed (Indexed) File Updating, Multiple Record Types, & RPG Structured Programming Operations

In Chapter 10 you loaded records to a keyed (indexed) file. Few data files of this type are static. A **static** data file is a file in which the data is subject to a minimal amount of change. Data files that are frequently changed are called **dynamic** files. In this chapter you will study techniques of changing, or **updating**, the contents of keyed files.

TYPES OF FILE UPDATING OPERATIONS

Three types of operations are used to update data files: record addition, record deletion, and record change, all of which can be performed by a single program.

Record Addition

You are already familiar with the record addition function of file updating. The techniques in Chapter 10 for loading records to a keyed file are the same as those used when adding records to an existing file. As you will see in the sample program, the logic of record addition to an existing file is identical to the logic of loading records to a new file.

Record Deletion

Data records are not always permanent. Records are removed from a data file when the data in them is no longer valid or needed. For example, the computer at your school contains one or more records about you in the school's Student Master File. After you graduate, the data in these records will no longer be valid. An update program will be used to remove your record from the Student Master File. The same program may add your information to an Alumni File. The file update technique of record deletion will remove your data from the Student Master File, and record addition techniques will add it to the Alumni File.

Record deletion techniques do not actually remove the data record from the data file. Instead, they insert a delete code into the record. The delete code for a file and the position of the delete code in each file record are defined when the data file is created. Because the techniques of file definition and delete code specification are specific to each type of computer, they are not discussed in this chapter. If you did not receive this information when developing the Chapter 10 programming assignments, you will need it when developing the programming assignments at the end of this chapter.

The **delete code** specifies that a record is no longer active and should be treated as though it had been deleted from the file. This is called **logical deletion** because the delete-marked record continues to exist physically in the data file until the file is reorganized. **File reorganization** is the process that, among other things, removes or **physically deletes** all delete-marked records from a data file. The exact functions performed by file reorganization are machine dependent. Your instructor or data center manager can tell you the functions that are performed by file reorganization on the computer you are using. Some computers have commands that can be used specifically to reorganize a data file and others perform file reorganization automatically every time the operating system software is started, during a process called **initial program load (IPL)** or **booting**.

Because a record is not physically deleted by the file update program, techniques must be used to avoid attempting to delete or change a record that has been marked for deletion. A delete-marked record should be considered to have been already deleted from the file even though it still physically exists as part of the data file.

Record Change

Record change operations modify or alter the contents of one or more fields in an existing record in a data file. RPG can change the contents of any field in a record except the key field. The key field cannot be changed because, as you know, the key identifies the record. The only way in which a key field can be altered is to perform two update operations: a record-deletion operation to remove the old record and then a record-addition operation to create a new record with a different key field value.

Change operations are usually performed by replacing the contents of one or more data fields with new data. Only the field or fields being altered are affected by a change operation. The change operation usually has no effect on the remainder of the data record.

SAMPLE PROBLEM DESCRIPTION

The sample programs in this chapter perform updating operations on PERSFILE, the Personnel Master File. Figure 11-1 shows the data file flow for program HJG11X, the first sample program. As you can see, this program uses three data files:

PERSFILE is the keyed file that is being updated by the program. The bidirectional arrow between PERS-
    FILE and the program indicates that the file is being both read from and written to during program
    execution.
PERSUPDT is an arrival sequence data file that is the primary input file to the program. PERSUPDT
    contains the **update request records**, each of which specifies an update operation to be performed on
    PERSFILE.
PERSREPT is the printed report that provides a complete audit trail of all processing performed by the
    program.

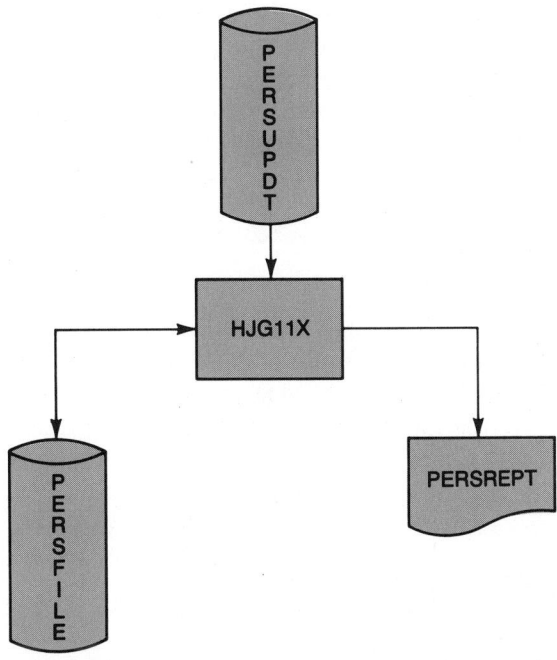

Figure 11-1   Data file flow for program HJG11X

Input

▸ **Personnel Master File**   Figure 11-2 shows the format of PERSFILE, the Personnel Master File. Position 1 contains the status code of the record. Status code A indicates that the record is currently active and has not been marked for deletion. Status Code D specifies that the record has been marked for deletion and is not an active record. There are no other valid status codes.

PERSONNEL MASTER FILE RECORD						
Record Length 40			Key Location 2–10			
Field No.	Field Name	Field Description	Field Position	Field Length	Dec. Pos.	Data Class
1		Status Code	1–1	1		A
2	MAIDNO	I.D. Number	2–10	9		A
3	MANAME	Name	11–30	20		A
4	MABRAN	Military Branch	31–31	1		A
5	MASTAT	Current Status	32–32	1		A
6	MARANK	Rank / Grade	33–33	1		A
7	MAYRS	Length of Service	34–35	2	0	N
8		UNUSED AREA	36–40	5		

Figure 11-2   Personnel Master File format

The Identification Number field (MAIDNO) is the key field of a record and contains a unique identifier. The MANAME field contains the name of the person identified by the record. MABRAN contains a code specifying the military branch in which the person served or is serving. MASTAT contains a code indicating whether the person is in active service or has retired. The MARANK field contains a code specifying the person's rank in the service: enlisted, warrant officer, or officer. The MAYRS field specifies the number of years the person has served in the military.

Because all the data has been fully input edited, you can assume that the data currently contained in PERSFILE is correct in accordance with the rules described in the Processing Requirements section of this problem description.

▶ **Update Request File** The format of the Update Request File, PERSUPDT, is shown in Figure 11-3. Note that the format of this file is identical to the format of PERSFILE. This duplication of format is not necessary when designing a file update program but is commonly done when possible. By using the same format for both files, you can eliminate possible confusion about field locations.

UPDATE REQUEST FILE RECORD						
Record Length 40						
Field No.	Field Name	Field Description	Field Position	Field Length	Dec. Pos.	Data Class
1	TYPE	Update Type Code	1–1	1		A
2	UPIDNO	I.D. Number	2–10	9		A
3	UPNAME	Name	11–30	20		A
4	UPBRAN	Military Branch	31–31	1		A
5	UPSTAT	Current Status	32–32	1		A
6	UPRANK	Rank / Grade	33–33	1		A
7	UPYRS	Length of Service	34–35	2	0	N
8		UNUSED AREA	36–40	5		

Figure 11-3 Personnel Update Request File format

Position 1 of PERSUPDT does not contain a status code but contains an **update request code**. These codes, which can be A, C, and D, represent requests for record addition, record change, and record deletion. No other update request code is valid.

▤ Output

▶ **Updated Personnel Master File** Besides being an input file, the Personnel Master File is also an output file. After the program is executed, PERSFILE may contain new records, delete-marked records, and records in which one or more data fields have been changed.

▶ **Personnel File Update Report** The printer spacing chart and sample output report generated by program HJG11X are shown in Figure 11-4. Note that, with one exception, the program is to print a single exception output line for each input record read from PERSUPDT. The exception is shown on lines 17 and 18 of the printer spacing chart. When a record is changed, the program prints the entire old and new records on two separate lines.

Figure 11-4 Personnel File Update Report format

```
HJG11X                          PERSONNEL FILE UPDATE                    PAGE XXØX

          I.D.                              MILITARY   CURRENT   CURRENT  LENGTH OF
ACTION   NUMBER       PERSONNEL NAME         BRANCH    STATUS    GRADE    SERVICE

XXXXXX  XXX-XX-XXXX  XXXXXXXXXXXXXXXXXX  XXXXXXXXXX  XXXXXXXX  XXXXXXXX   ØX

ADD     213-44-5862  WHEELER, THOMAS     AIR FORCE   ACTIVE    ENLISTED   12

DELETE  337-21-4911  THALER, RICHARD     ARMY        RETIRED   WARRANT    20

CHANGE  481-59-3131  MOES, THOMAS        COAST GUARD ACTIVE    ENLISTED    8    OLD RECORD
                     MOES, THOMAS        COAST GUARD RETIRED   OFFICER    20    NEW RECORD

ADD     526-97-1962  HAYES, CAROLYN      NAVY        ACTIVE    OFFICER     6    DUPLICATE I.D.-RECORD NOT ADDED

ADD     614-38-9412  ---BLANK---         ---BLANK--- --BLANK-- --BLANK--  ZERO  ERROR-NO UPDATE PERFORMED

ADD     639-42-1318  BETTY, LORI         --INVALID-- -INVALID- -INVALID-  10    ERROR-NO UPDATE PERFORMED

CHANGE  658-21-3996                                                            INVALID UPDATE-I.D. NOT ON FILE

DELETE  721-38-4290                                                            INVALID UPDATE-RECORD PREVIOUSLY DELETED

DELETE  736-43-8179                                                            INVALID UPDATE-NAME FIELD MISMATCH

CHANGE  842-31-5967                                  -INVALID- -INVALID-  INVALID ERROR-NO UPDATE PERFORMED

ERROR   934-26-4153  WHEATON, ROY K.     AIR FORCE   ACTIVE    ENLISTED   30    INVALID UPDATE TYPE CODE
                                 (S E P A R A T E  P A G E)

                          PERSONNEL FILE UPDATE SUMMARY
                                   XX/XX/XX

                               VALID  INVALID  TOTAL

              ADDITION REQUESTS  XØX    XØX     XØX

              DELETION REQUESTS  XØX    XØX     XØX

                CHANGE REQUESTS  XØX    XØX     XØX

               INVALID REQUESTS         XØX
```

Figure 11-4 (1)

```
HJG11X                          PERSONNEL FILE UPDATE                    PAGE    1

          I.D.                              MILITARY   CURRENT   CURRENT  LENGTH OF
ACTION   NUMBER       PERSONNEL NAME         BRANCH    STATUS    GRADE    SERVICE

ADD     213-44-5862  WHEELER, THOMAS     AIR FORCE   ACTIVE    ENLISTED   12

DELETE  337-21-4911  THALER, RICHARD     ARMY        RETIRED   WARRANT    20

CHANGE  481-59-3131  MOES, THOMAS        COAST GUARD ACTIVE    ENLISTED    8    OLD RECORD
                                         COAST GUARD RETIRED   OFFICER    20    NEW RECORD

ADD     526-97-1962  HAYES, CAROLYN      NAVY        ACTIVE    OFFICER     6    DUPLICATE I.D.-RECORD NOT ADDED

ADD     614-38-9412  ---BLANK---         ---BLANK--- --BLANK-- --BLANK--  ZERO  ERROR-NO UPDATE PERFORMED

ADD     639-42-1318  BETTY, LORI         --INVALID-- -INVALID- -INVALID-  10    ERROR-NO UPDATE PERFORMED

CHANGE  658-21-3996                                                            INVALID UPDATE-I.D. NOT ON FILE

DELETE  721-38-4290                                                            INVALID UPDATE-RECORD PREVIOUSLY DELETED

DELETE  736-43-8179                                                            INVALID UPDATE-NAME FIELD MISMATCH

CHANGE  842-31-5967                                                            INVALID UPDATE-I.D. NOT ON FILE

ERROR   934-26-4153  WHEATON, ROY K.     AIR FORCE   ACTIVE    ENLISTED   30    INVALID UPDATE TYPE CODE
```

Figure 11-4 (2)

continued

```
                            PERSONNEL FILE UPDATE SUMMARY
                                      11/21/91

                                      INVALID   INVALID   TOTAL

                     ADDITION REQUESTS    1         3        4

                     DELETION REQUESTS    1         2        3

                     CHANGE REQUESTS      1         2        3

                     INVALID REQUESTS                        1
```

Figure 11-4 (3)

Every input record must be accounted for on the output report in order to provide a complete audit trail of all update requests. Line 11 of the printer spacing chart shows the size and format of each output field. Lines 13, 15, 17, and 18 show the output to be generated for each valid add, delete, and change request.

Lines 20–34 show the printed output to be generated if the update request record contains an error condition that is based on the processing requirements of the program. Note that each type of error is identified by an error message beginning in position 86 of the print line. Line 20 shows the record that is printed if a record addition request is invalid because the key field value already exists in PERSFILE. Note that all the data fields in the addition request record are printed. The output line shown on line 22 prints if any required field in an addition request record does not contain data. Line 24 shows the format to be used if any of the three code fields contains an invalid entry. Although the Name field can be erroneous because it is blank (line 22), it cannot contain an invalid entry.

Line 26 shows the error message to be printed if a change request is made for a nonexistent record. Note that only the action type (CHANGE), the I.D. number, and the error message are printed. Line 32 shows the format to be used if a change request contains an invalid code in the Status or Grade fields as well as the message to be printed if the Length of Service field contains an incorrect value.

Line 28 is printed if an attempt is made to delete a record that has been previously marked as deleted or does not exist in PERSFILE. Again, only the action type, I.D. number, and error message are printed. Line 30 shows the output to be printed if a DELETE request is invalid because of a name mismatch. To minimize the possibility of deleting the wrong record, the processing requirements for this program specify that the first five positions of the Name field must be the same before the record can be deleted. This requirement forces a second test of the data prior to marking a record as deleted. This secondary test minimizes the possibility of deleting a record if an incorrect I.D. number is entered because it is unlikely that both the correct and the incorrect records contain the same entry in the first five positions of the Name field.

Line 34 shows the output to be printed in the event of an incorrect update request code. As is the case with a duplicate record addition attempt (line 20), the entire record is printed along with the error message.

Lines 38–49 of the printer spacing chart show the update summary that is printed at the end of the report. Note that this summary prints on a separate page and contains counts of each type of action that was requested and the number of actions that were valid and invalid.

▤ Processing Requirements

▶ **General Processing Requirements**   The processing requirements for each PERSUPDT file record depend, primarily, on the type of input record as determined by the update request code in position 1 of the record. There are, however, several general processing requirements that apply regardless of update request type.

1. All records currently in PERSFILE have been edited and can be assumed to contain valid data.
2. Every PERSUPDT record must be accounted for on the PERSREPT output report in order to provide a complete, accurate audit trail of all processing requests.

3. The Identification Number field in PERSUPDT is never blank and need not be tested for missing data. The Identification Number entries have not, however, been edited to determine if they are valid.

4. Summary counts are made of all update requests, including the number of valid and invalid record addition, record deletion, and record change requests. Also, the number of invalid update request codes are counted.

▶ **Record Addition (Update Request Code A)** A record is added to PERSFILE only if all the following processing requirements are met:

1. The I.D. Number field (UPIDNO) cannot already exist in the Personnel Master File.
2. The Personnel Name field (UPNAME) cannot be blank.
3. The Military Branch field (UPBRAN) must contain one of the following valid codes:

   A   Army
   C   Coast Guard
   F   Air Force
   M   Marines
   N   Navy

   Any other entry in the UPBRAN field is invalid.
4. The Current Status field (UPSTAT) must contain one of the following valid codes:

   A   Active personnel
   R   Retired personnel

   Any other entry in the UPSTAT field is invalid.
5. The Current Grade field (UPRANK) must contain one of the following valid codes:

   E   Enlisted
   W   Warrant Officer
   O   Officer

   Any other entry in the UPRANK field is invalid. The UPRANK entry W (Warrant Officer) is valid only if the Military Branch code is A (Army). An UPRANK of W is invalid with any UPBRAN code other than A.
6. The Length of Service field (UPYRS) must not contain an entry of zero or an entry greater than 30.

▶ **Record Deletion (Update Request Code D)** A record is marked for deletion from PERSFILE only if all the following processing requirements are met.

1. A PERSFILE record cannot be marked for deletion if the status code for the record is already D. Only active records can be marked for deletion.
2. The Identification Number field (UPIDNO) must be the key field value of a currently active PERSFILE record.
3. The first five positions of the Name field in the update request record must exactly match the first five positions of the Name field in the personnel file record that is to be deleted.

▶ **Record Change (Update Request Code C)** A field to be changed is indicated by an entry in that field of the PERSUPDT update request record. If a field is blank, no action is to be taken on that field. If an entry is made in a field, the entry is a request for a change to the field and is processed according to the requirements that follow. Changes can be made to the Personnel Name field, the Current Status field, the Current Grade field, and the Length of Service field. Any entry in the Military Branch field is ignored and no action taken. A PERSFILE record is changed only if all the following processing requirements are met.

1. No modification can be made to the I.D. Number field.
2. If a change to the Current Status field is requested, the status code (UPSTAT) must be valid. See item 4 of the processing requirements for record addition to determine the requirements for this entry.
3. If a change to the Current Grade field is requested, the grade code (UPGRAD) must be valid. See item 5 of the processing requirements for record addition to determine the requirements for this entry.
4. The Length of Service field (UPYRS) must not contain an entry of zero or an entry greater than 30. In addition, the length of service must not decrease, that is, the value in UPYRS cannot be less than the value in MAYRS. An attempt to decrease the length of service is to be considered an invalid entry.

PROGRAM SPECIFICATIONS FOR PROGRAM HJG11X

Control and File Description Specifications

The Control and File Description Specifications form for the sample program is shown in Figure 11-5. No new or different entries are used on this form. PERSUPDT has been described as the primary input file for the program, and PERSFILE is an update file, which is read on a random basis by means of the CHAIN operation.

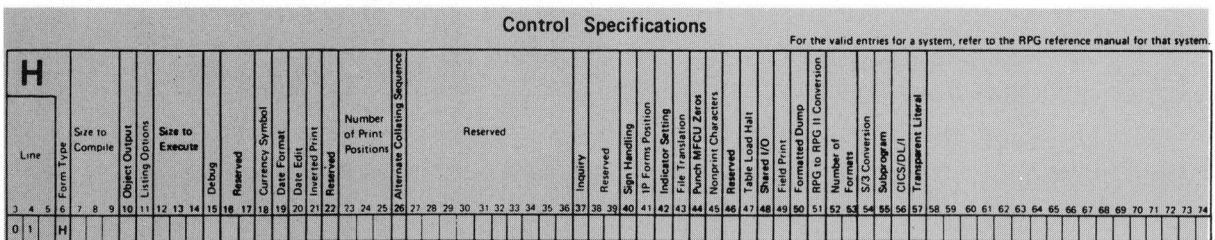

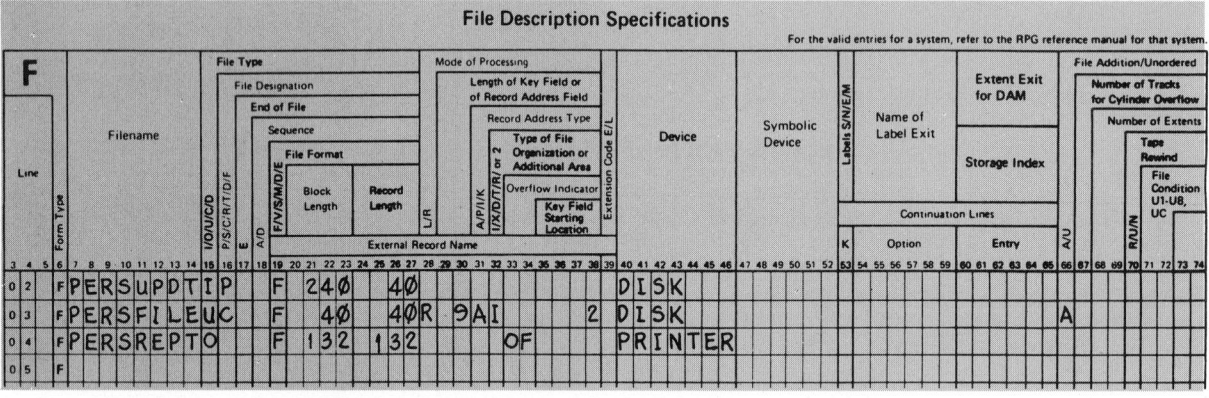

Figure 11-5   Control and File Description Specifications

Indicator Summary Sheets

Update programs, like all programs that edit input, tend to use many indicators. Figure 11-6 shows the indicator summary form for program HJG11X. This illustration can be used for reference as the individual parts of the program are explained.

Figure 11-6   Indicator summary sheets

Figure 11-6 (1)

Line	Form Type	Record Identifying	Input Field	Calculation Result and Command Key	Halt and User	Control Level and Overflow	FUNCTION OF INDICATORS
01	F •	ID	F	C	H	L	FUNCTION OF INDICATORS
02	F •	Ø1	–	–	–	–	– UPDATE REQUEST – RECORD ADDITION
03	F •	Ø2	–	–	–	–	– UPDATE REQUEST – RECORD DELETION
04	F •	Ø3	–	–	–	–	– UPDATE REQUEST – RECORD CHANGE
05	F •	Ø4	–	–	–	–	– ACTIVE PERSFILE RECORD
06	F •	Ø5	–	–	–	–	– DELETED PERSFILE RECORD
07	F •			1Ø	–	–	– EXCPT CONTROL – RECORD ADDITION
08	F •			11	–	–	– EXCPT CONTROL – RECORD DELETION
09	F •			12	–	–	– EXCPT CONTROL – INVALID UPDATE CODE
10	F •			13	–	–	– EXCPT CONTROL – CHANGE ERROR
11	F •			14	–	–	– EXCPT CONTROL – CHANGE ERROR
12	F •			15	–	–	– EXCPT CONTROL – RECORD CHANGE – OLD
13	F •			16	–	–	– EXCPT CONTROL – RECORD CHANGE – NEW
14	F •			41	–	–	– BRANCH = ARMY
15	F •			42	–	–	– BRANCH = NAVY

Figure 11-6 (2)

Line	Form Type	Record Identifying	Input Field	Calculation Result and Command Key	Halt and User	Control Level and Overflow	FUNCTION OF INDICATORS
01	F •	ID	F	C	H	L	FUNCTION OF INDICATORS
02	F •	•		43	–	–	– BRANCH = AIR FORCE
03	F •			44	–	–	– BRANCH = MARINES
04	F •			45	–	–	– BRANCH = COAST GUARD
05	F •			46	–	–	– STATUS = ACTIVE
06	F •			47	–	–	– STATUS = RETIRED
07	F •			48	–	–	– GRADE = ENLISTED
08	F •			49	–	–	– GRADE = OFFICER
09	F •			50	–	–	– GRADE = WARRANT
10	F •			51	–	–	– CHAINED RECORD NOT ON PERSFILE
11	F •			52	–	–	– UPYRS > 3Ø – RECORD ADDITION
12	F •			53	–	–	– UPYRS > 3Ø – RECORD CHANGE
13	F •			86	–	–	– CHANGE REQUEST DATA ERROR
14	F •			88	–	–	– DELETE REQUEST – NAME MISMATCH
15	F •			89	–	–	– INVALID DELETE REQUEST – NOT ON FILE
	F •						
	F •						
	F •						

continued

F* — Circle Indicators Used: (Note: All indicators are not valid with all systems.)

General Indicators	01	02	03	04	05	06	07	08	09
10	11	12	13	14	15	16	17	18	19
20	21	22	23	24	25	26	27	28	29
30	31	32	33	34	35	36	37	38	39
40	41	42	43	44	45	46	47	48	49
50	51	52	53	54	55	56	57	58	59
60	61	62	63	64	65	66	67	68	69
70	71	72	73	74	75	76	77	78	79
80	81	82	83	84	85	86	87	88	89
90	91	92	93	94	95	96	97	98	99

Control Level Indicators: L1 L2 L3 L4 L5 L6 L7 L8 L9
Halt Indicators: H1 H2 H3 H4 H5 H6 H7 H8 H9
External Indicators: U1 U2 U3 U4 U5 U6 U7 U8
Command Key Indicators: KA KB KC KD KE KF KG KH KI KJ KK KL KM KN KP KQ KR KS KT KU KV KW KX KY
Overflow Indicators: OA OB OC OD OE OF OG OV
Special Purpose Indicators: 1P L0 H0 MR *LR RT

Line	Form Type	Record Identifying	Input Field	Calculation Result and Command Key	Halt and User	Control Level and Overflow	
01	F*	ID	F	C	H	L	FUNCTION OF INDICATORS
02	F*			9Ø	-	-	- RECORD ADDITION - BLANK/INVALID DATA FIELD
03	F*			91	-	-	- INVALID GRADE CODE
04	F*			92	-	-	- INVALID STATUS CODE
05	F*			93	-	-	- INVALID BRANCH CODE
06	F*		94	-	-	-	- BLANK UPYRS FIELD
07	F*		95	-	-	-	- BLANK UPRANK FIELD
08	F*		96	-	-	-	- BLANK UPSTAT FIELD
09	F*		97	-	-	-	- BLANK UPBRAN FIELD
10	F*		98	-	-	-	- BLANK UPNAME FIELD
11	F*	99	-	-	-	-	- INVALID UPDATE REQUEST CODE
12	F*					1P	- FIRST PAGE INDICATOR
13	F*					OF	- OVERFLOW INDICATOR
14	F*					LR	- LAST RECORD INDICATOR

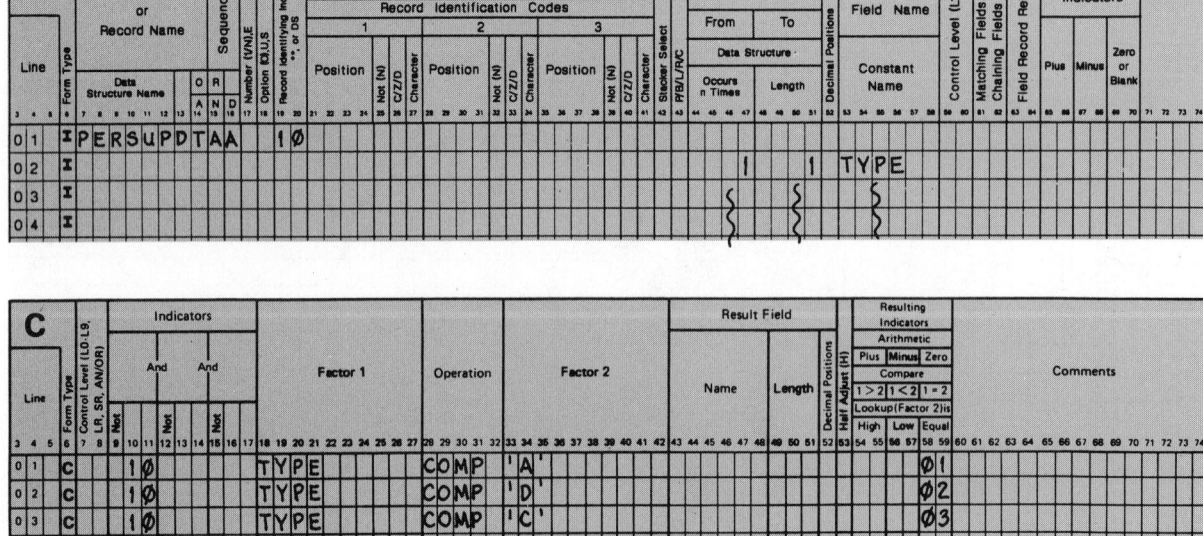

Figure 11-6 (3)

Input Record Type Testing

PERSUPDT, the input file to the sample program contains three types of records, each of which requires different processing in the program. An input record can contain an update request code of A, D, or C, meaning that the record is to cause record addition, record deletion, or record change. To assure that the type of processing will be in accordance with the input record read, the update request code must be tested by the program. One method of testing is shown in Figure 11-7.

I

Line	Form Type	Filename or Record Name	Sequence	Record Identifying Indicator	Field Location From	Field Location To	RPG Field Name
01	I	PERSUPDT	AA	1Ø			
02	I				1	1	TYPE
03	I				⋮	⋮	⋮
04	I				⋮	⋮	⋮

C

Line	Form Type	Indicators	Factor 1	Operation	Factor 2	Result Field	Resulting Indicators High (>)	Resulting Indicators Low (<)	Resulting Indicators Equal (=)
01	C	1Ø	TYPE	COMP	'A'				Ø1
02	C	1Ø	TYPE	COMP	'D'				Ø2
03	C	1Ø	TYPE	COMP	'C'				Ø3
04	C	NØ1 NØ2 NØ3		SETON			99		

Figure 11-7 Simple record type calculations

As you can see, position 1 of the PERSUPDT record has been defined as a field named TYPE. The first four calculation specifications perform a series of comparisons that determine the contents of TYPE. If TYPE = A, indicator 01 is turned on; if TYPE = D, indicator 02 is turned on; if TYPE = C, indicator 03 is turned on; and indicator 99 is turned on if TYPE does not contain any of the three valid update request codes. Although this method can be used for simple testing of the type illustrated in Figure 11-7, comparisons can be difficult to use if the codes being tested are more complex. Consider the following set of record codes:

Record type 1		Record type 2	
X	in position 13	P	in position 13
1	in position 14	3	in position 14
A	in position 15	8	in position 15

Record type 3		Record type 4	
P	in position 13	Any other combination of codes	
5	in position 14		
1	in position 15		

The coding needed to test for these four record types is shown in Figure 11-8. As you can see, these calculations are lengthy and involved. To eliminate the need for these involved comparisons, RPG uses the Record Identification Code area of the Input Specifications form.

Line	Form Type	Control Level	Indicators (And / And)	Factor 1	Operation	Factor 2	Result Field Name	Length	Resulting Indicators	Comments
01	C			POS13	COMP	'X'			25	25-P13=X
02	C		N25	POS13	COMP	'P'			30	30-P13=P
03	C		N25N30		SETON				99	99-INVALID
04	C		N25N30		GOTO	END				
05	C		25	POS14	COMP	'1'			999926	
06	C		25 26	POS15	COMP	'A'			999901	01-TYPE 1
07	C				GOTO	END				
08	C		30	POS14	COMP	'3'			999931	31-P3
09	C		30N31	POS14	COMP	'5'			999932	32-P5
10	C		31	POS15	COMP	'8'			999902	02-TYPE 2
11	C		32	POS15	COMP	'1'			999903	03-TYPE 3
12	C			END	TAG					

Figure 11-8 Complex record type calculations

Record Identification Codes

Figure 11-9 on the next page shows the portion of the Input Specifications form used to determine if the record read from PERSUPDT contains a request for record addition, record deletion, record change, or an invalid update request code.

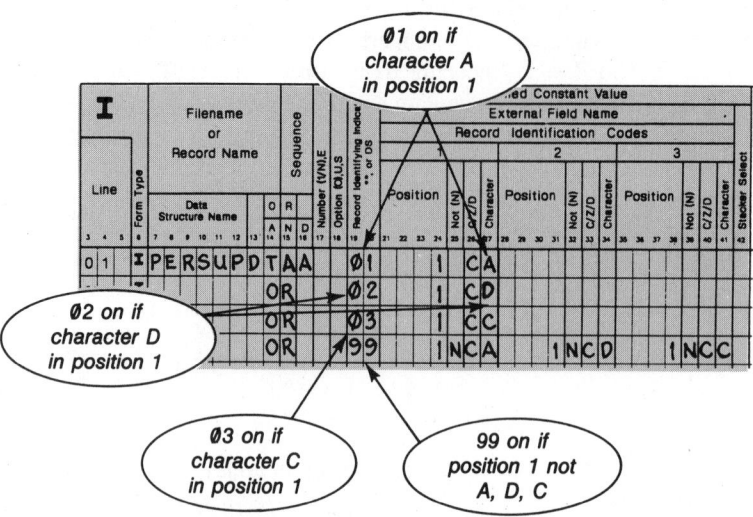

Figure 11-9   Record identification code testing

The Record Identifying Indicator area (positions 19–20) is used in conjunction with the Record Identification Codes area (positions 21–41) to determine the type of record to be processed. The Record Identification Codes area specifies the value or values in a record that identify the **type** of record. There is room in the Record Identification Codes area to specify three different codes in an input record for identification purposes. Positions 21–27 specify the first code to be tested, positions 28–34 the second code, and positions 35–41 the third code. These three areas are used to specify the codes to be tested in a single record. Because the input records in the sample program contain only a single code in each record, the first three lines of record identification code testing use only positions 21–27 (Figure 11-10).

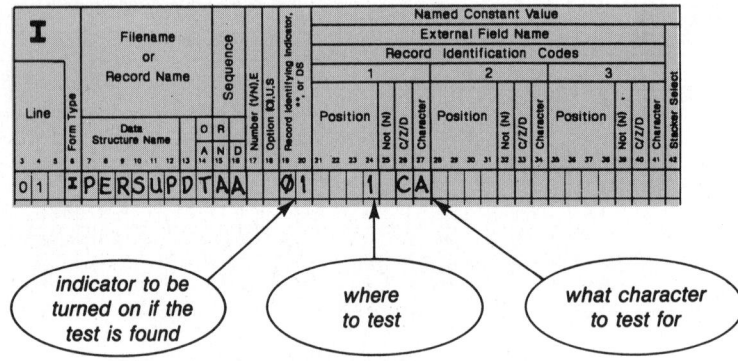

Figure 11-10   Record identification code testing

Positions 21–24 specify the position to be tested in the input record. In Figure 11-10, the value 1 has been entered, right-justified, into this area, specifying that position 1 of the input record is to be tested.

In addition to specifying the position to be tested, the Record Identification Code area also must specify the character being tested for. In Figure 11-10, a C has been entered in position 26 and an A in position 27. The C in position 26 specifies that the position of the input record is to be tested for the character specified in position 27, an A in this example. When the record identification codes specified in positions 21–41 are found, the indicator specified in positions 19–20 of the same line is turned on. Therefore, as a result of the coding specified in this figure, indicator 01 is turned on if the input record contains an A in position 1.

As stated in the problem description, three valid codes can be found in position 1 of an input record: A for record addition, D for record deletion, and C for record change. To specify that several different codes must be tested, multiple record identification code lines must be used (Figure 11-11). The first three lines perform the tests for codes A, D, and C. As you can see, the format of the tests for codes D and C is the same as the format used to test for code A on the first line. Note, however, the use of the word OR in positions 14–15 of the record identification code lines after the first line. The use of the OR entry specifies that any of these entries may be found and that RPG is to perform a series of tests, working from top to bottom, until one of the tests is satisfied. Record identification code testing stops as soon as one of the tested conditions is found.

It is possible that some other character might be found in position 1 of an input record, but any code other than A, D, or C is an error. If the program tests for the three valid characters and an input record contains an invalid entry in position 1, the program halts. *When record identification code testing is used, every possible condition, including invalid codes, must be tested. If an untested condition is found in an input record, the program halts due to an invalid record type.*

Line 4 of the record identification code testing turns on indicator 99 if an invalid update request code is detected. This line specifies that indicator 99 is turned on if the record identification code is NOT A, NOT D, and NOT C. The NOT test is indicated by the letter N in positions 25, 32, and 39. The record identification code tests shown in Figure 11-11 can be summarized as follows:

If there is an A in position 1, turn on indicator 01;
OR if there is a D in position 1, turn on indicator 02;
OR if there is a C in position 1, turn on indicator 03;
OR if neither an A, a D, nor a C is in position 1, turn on indicator 99.

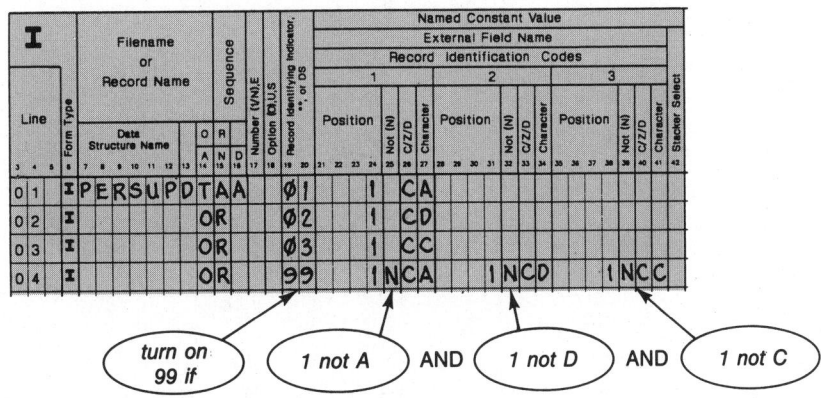

Figure 11-11 Record identification code testing

▶ **Examples of Record Identification Codes** The Record Identification Code entries in positions 21–41 make it possible to test almost any desired configuration. Any character that can be represented by a printed graphic in the Character area (positions 27, 34, and 41) can be tested.

The example in Figure 11-12 is similar to the tests performed on PERSUPDT. If position 80 of the input record contains an A, indicator 01 is turned on. If position 80 does not contain an A, indicator 01 is not turned on.

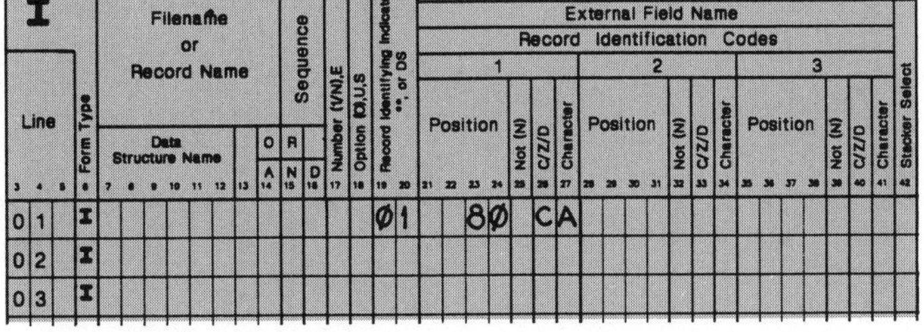

Figure 11-12 Record identification code example

Figure 11-13 illustrates the use of the NOT entry, N, in position 25. This test is the exact reverse of the test in Figure 11-12. In this example, indicator 01 is turned on if position 1 does NOT contain an A. If position 1 contains an A, the indicator is not turned on.

Three tests to be performed on the input record are linked together in an AND relationship in Figure 11-14. Indicator 02 is turned on only if position 1 contains a C AND position 2 contains an A AND position 3 contains a T. If one or more of these characters are missing from the input record, the record-identifying indicator is not turned on. Recall that an AND relationship requires all the conditions to be present for the result to occur.

Figure 11-15 shows the use of more than three tests. Note that the two lines of record identification code tests are linked by the word AND in positions 14, 15, and 16 of the second line. In this example, all five tested characters must be present for indicator 03 to be turned on. Because of the ND entry in positions 15–16 when the AND entry is used, some older versions of RPG do not permit an alphabetic sequence entry of ND to be used in a record identification line.

You have already seen the use of the OR relationship (Figure 11-11). RPG permits the combination of AND and OR relationships in record identification code testing (Figure 11-16). In this example, indicator 14 turns on if positions 1–3 contain the characters CAT or if positions 1–3 contain the characters DOG. Any other combination of characters results in indicator 14 being off.

Refer to Figure 11-8 and the involved series of calculations needed to perform the required tests. Figure 11-17 shows how the same series of tests are performed using record identification code testing. Note that indicator 99 is turned on if the testing does not turn on indicator 01, 02, or 03.

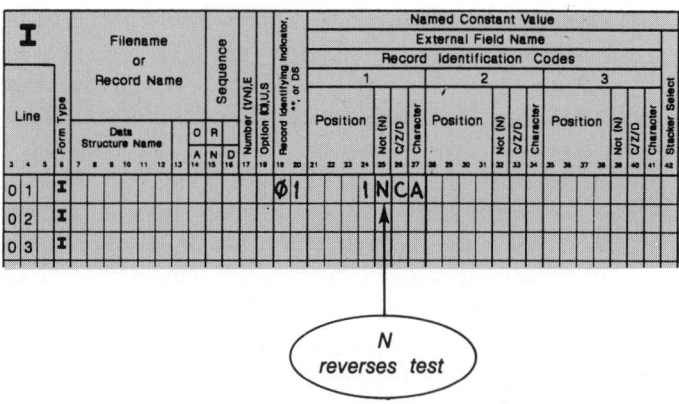

Figure 11-13 Record identification code example

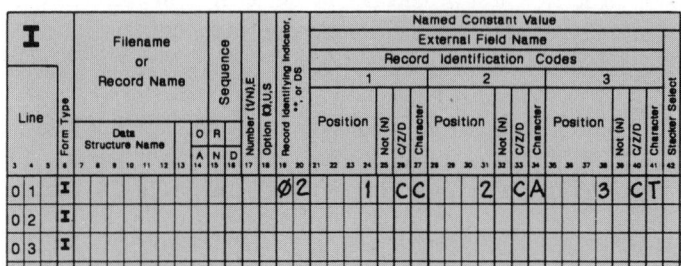

Figure 11-14 Record identification code example

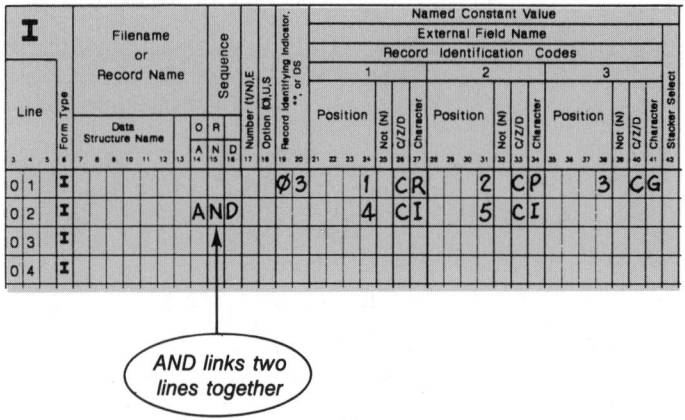

Figure 11-15 Record identification code example

Figure 11-16 Record identification code example

Line	Form Type	Filename or Record Name	Sequence	Record Identifying Indicator	Position (1)	Not (1)	C/Z/D (1)	Character (1)	Position (2)	Not (2)	C/Z/D (2)	Character (2)	Position (3)	Not (3)	C/Z/D (3)	Character (3)
01	I	TESTFILE	AA	Ø1	13		C	X	14		C	1	15		C	A
02	I		OR	Ø2	13		C	P	14		C	3	15		C	8
03	I		OR	Ø3	13		C	P	14		C	5	15		C	1
04	I		OR	99												

Figure 11-17 Record identification code example

Input Specifications for PERSUPDT File

Figure 11-18 shows the input specifications for PERSUPDT. As you can see, record identification code testing has been used to determine if a record contains a record addition code (A in position 1), a record deletion code (D in position 1), or a record change code (C in position 1). In addition, line 04 turns on indicator 99 if the update request code is not one of the valid codes. The use of this line to test for an invalid code and to turn on an indicator if the code is not valid is critical. As was stated earlier, when record identification code testing is performed, every possible combination, including invalid codes, must be tested for. If the program reads an undefined type of record, program execution is halted. RPG assumes that if testing is performed, every type of valid data is specified in the tests. As a result of this, if an undefined record is read, the program assumes the data to be invalid and halts.

Line	Form Type	Filename or Record Name	Sequence	Record Identifying Indicator	Position (1)	Not (1)	C/Z/D (1)	Character (1)	Position (2)	Not (2)	C/Z/D (2)	Character (2)	Position (3)	Not (3)	C/Z/D (3)	Character (3)	From	To	Decimal Positions	RPG Field Name	Field Record Relation	Zero or Blank
01	I	PERSUPDT	AA	Ø1	1		C	A														
02	I		OR	Ø2	1		C	D														
03	I		OR	Ø3	1		C	C														
04	I		OR	99	1	N	C	A	1	N	C	D	1	N	C	C						
05	I																2	1Ø		UPIDNO		
06	I																2	4		UPID1		
07	I																5	6		UPID2		
08	I																7	1Ø		UPID3		
09	I																11	3Ø		UPNAME		98
10	I																31	31		UPBRAN		97
11	I																32	32		UPSTAT		96
12	I																33	33		UPRANK		95
13	I																34	35	Ø	UPYRS		94
14	I																11	15		UPFST5	Ø2	
15	I																					
16	I																					
17	I																					
18	I																					
19	I																					
20	I																					

field record relation

Figure 11-18 Input specifications for PERSUPDT

Note the use of indicators 94–98 to test for blank or zero input fields. The processing requirements of the program specify that fields be tested for missing data. Indicators 94–98 are used for these tests.

▶ **Field Record Relations**   The definition of the PERSUPDT file uses a new entry, located in positions 63 and 64. This area, the Field Record Relation area, associates a field with only one of a series of described record types. This area can only be used if two or more record types are defined. In this program, the first five positions of the Personnel Name field are used to verify the proper I.D. number when a record deletion is requested. The UPFST5 field has been defined, and an entry of 02 has been specified in the Field Record Relation area. This entry specifies that this field exists only when indicator 02 is turned on as a result of record identification testing. If any other indicator (01, 03, or 99) is turned on, no data is moved into the UPFST5 field. RPG assumes that any field not identified by a Field Record Relation entry in positions 63–64 is part of every record type, regardless of record identification code.

Input Specifications for PERSFILE File

The Input Specifications for the Personnel Master File, PERSFILE, show that two record types are described for this file (Figure 11-19). Active records are identified by an A in position 1, and delete-marked records are identified by a D in position 1. Note that there is no test for an invalid record type. Because all the data in PERSFILE has been edited by either the load program that created the file or by this program, which updates PERSFILE, the entries in position 1 can be assumed to be accurate.

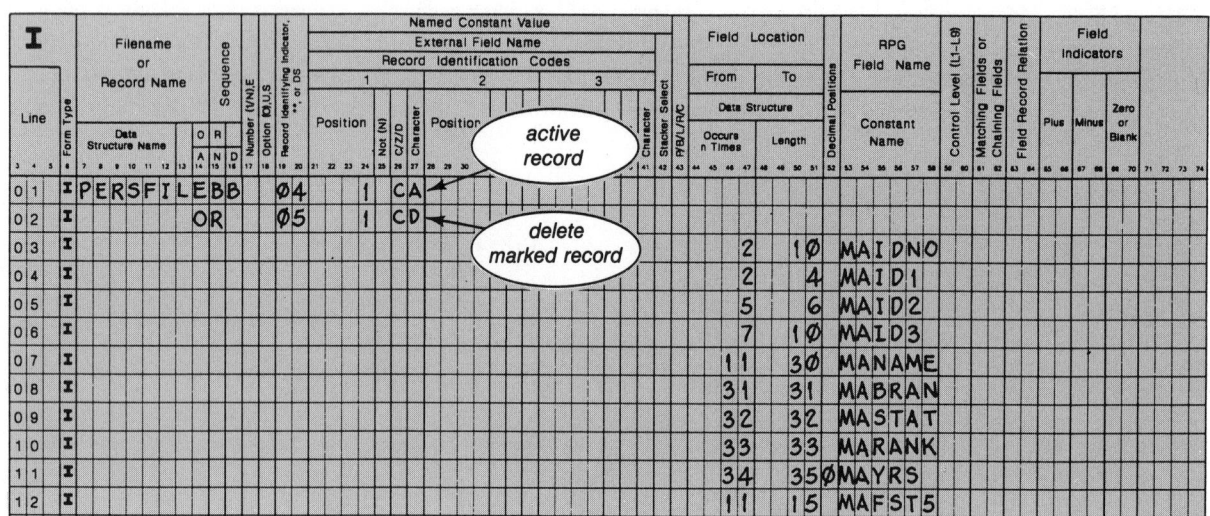

Figure 11-19   Input specifications for PERSFILE

All data fields in PERSFILE are defined in this program, whereas in Chapter 10 it was necessary only to determine if a record key did or did not exist in LISTFILE. When a record is changed in the Personnel File Update, all data from the record currently on file must be printed on the output report. Therefore, it is necessary to define all the PERSFILE fields. As you can see, the field names used in PERSFILE differ from those used in PERSUPDT. Although in some instances it is possible to use the same field name in two different input files, it is poor practice and can lead to program execution errors.

Calculation Specifications

Because the processing of input records read from PERSUPDT varies according to the record identification code in position 1, the calculations for program HJG11X have been structured differently from those in previous programs. Figure 11-20 shows the calculation specifications portion of the compile listing for this program.

Figure 11-20   Calculation specifications listing

```
HJG11X     11-22-91  15:32:05    HJG11X - PERSONNEL FILE UPDATE      Version 3.5

           ....+....1....+....2....+....3....+....4....+....5....+....6....+....7....



 86 0081 C*   MAIN PROCESSING ROUTINE
 87 0082 C*   ----------------------
 88 0083 C   N99       UPIDNO    CHAINPERSFILE             51    READ PERSFILE
 89 0084 C    01                 EXSR ADD                        RECORD ADDITION
 90 0085 C    02                 EXSR DELETE                     RECORD DELETION
 91 0086 C    03                 EXSR CHANGE                     RECORD CHANGE
 92 0087 C          99           EXSR ERROR                      INVALID UPDATE
 93 0088 CLR          ERRADD     ADD  VALADD      TOTADD 30
 94 0089 CLR          ERRDEL     ADD  VALDEL      TOTDEL 30
 95 0090 CLR          ERRCH      ADD  VALCH       TOTCH  30


 98 0092 C*   RECORD ADDITION SUBROUTINE
 99 0093 C*-----------------------------
100 0094 CSR          ADD        BEGSR
101 0095 CSRN97                  MOVE UPBRAN      BRANCH  1       IF NOT BLANK,
102 0096 CSRN97                  EXSR TSTBR                       TEST BRANCH
103 0097 CSRN96                  MOVE UPSTAT      STATUS  1       IF NOT BLANK,
104 0098 CSRN96                  EXSR TSTST                       TEST STATUS
105 0099 CSRN95                  MOVE UPRANK      GRADE   1       IF NOT BLANK,
106 0100 CSRN95                  EXSR TSTGR                       TEST GRADE
107 0101 CSR                     SETOF                  9052      CLEAR INDIC.
108 0102 CSR 94
109 0103 COR 95
110 0104 COR 96
111 0105 COR 97
112 0106 COR 98                  SETON                    90      MISSING DATA
113 0107 CSR 91
114 0108 COR 92
115 0109 COR 93                  SETON                    90      INVALID CODE
116 0110 CSRN94       UPYRS      COMP 30                  52
117 0111 CSR 52                  SETON                    90      YEARS > 30
118 0112 CSRN51                  SETON                    90      DUPLICATE I.D.
119 0113 CSR 90       ERRADD     ADD  1           ERRADD 30       COUNT ERRORS
120 0114 CSRN90       VALADD     ADD  1           VALADD 30       COUNT ADDITIONS
121 0115 CSR                     SETON                    10
122 0116 CSR                     EXCPT                            ADDITION OUTPUT
123 0117 CSR                     SETOF                    10
124 0118 CSR                     ENDSR


127 0120 C*   CHANGE SUBROUTINE
128 0121 C*--------------------
129 0122 CSR          CHANGE     BEGSR
130 0123 CSR                     SETOF                  8653      CLEAR INDIC.
131 0124 CSR 51                  SETON                    13
132 0125 CSR 13                  EXCPT                            PRINT INVALID-
133 0126 CSR                     SETOF                    13        NOT ON FILE
134 0127 CSR 51       ERRCH      ADD  1           ERRCH  30       COUNT ERRORS
135 0128 CSR 51                  GOTO ENDCH                       BYPASS REST OF
136 0129 C*                                                         ROUTINE
137 0130 CSRN96                  MOVE UPSTAT      STATUS          IF NOT BLANK,
138 0131 CSRN96                  EXSR TSTST                       TEST STATUS
139 0132 CSRN95                  MOVE UPRANK      GRADE           IF NOT BLANK,
140 0133 CSRN95                  EXSR TSTGR                       TEST GRADE
141 0134 CSRN94       UPYRS      COMP 30                  53      TEST VALID
142 0135 CSRN94N53    UPYRS      COMP MAYRS               53        YEARS
143 0136 CSR 91
144 0137 COR 92                                                   INVALID CHANGE
145 0138 COR 53                  SETON                    86       REQUEST DATA
146 0139 CSR 86       ERRCH      ADD  1           ERRCH          COUNT ERRORS
147 0140 CSR 86                  SETON                    14
148 0141 CSR 14                  EXCPT                            CHANGE ERROR
149 0142 CSR                     SETOF                    14        OUTPUT
150 0143 CSR 86                  GOTO ENDCH                       BYPASS REST OF
151 0144 C*                                                         ROUTINE
152 0145 C*
153 0146 CSR                     MOVE MABRAN      BRANCH          TEST BRANCH
154 0147 CSR                     EXSR TSTBR
155 0148 CSR                     MOVE MASTAT      STATUS          TEST STATUS
156 0149 CSR                     EXSR TSTST
```

Figure 11-20 (1)

continued

```
HJG11X    11-22-91  15:32:05   HJG11X - PERSONNEL FILE UPDATE      Version 3.5

          ....+....1....+....2....+....3..:.+....4....+....5....+....6....+....7....

  157 0150 CSR                   MOVE MARANK    GRADE           TEST GRADE
  158 0151 CSR                   EXSR TSTGR
  159 0152 CSR                   SETON                    15
  160 0153 CSR                   EXCPT                          PRINT OLD
  161 0154 CSR                   SETOF                    15    RECORD
  162 0155 CSRN96                MOVE UPSTAT    STATUS          IF NOT BLANK,
  163 0156 CSRN96                EXSR TSTST                      TEST STATUS
  164 0157 CSRN95                MOVE UPRANK    GRADE           IF NOT BLANK,
  165 0158 CSRN95                EXSR TSTGR                      TEST GRADE
  166 0159 CSR                   SETON                    16    PRINT NEW
  167 0160 CSR                   EXCPT                           RECORD AND
  168 0161 CSR                   SETOF                    16    CHANGE DISK
  169 0162 CSR       VALCH       ADD  1         VALCH  30       COUNT CHANGES
  170 0163 CSR       ENDCH       TAG
  171 0164 CSR                   ENDSR


  174 0166 C*   RECORD DELETION SUBROUTINE
  175 0167 C*---------------------------
  176 0168 CSR       DELETE      BEGSR
  177 0169 CSR                   SETOF                  8988    CLEAR INDIC.
  178 0170 CSR 51                SETON                    89    NOT ON FILE
  179 0171 CSRN51 05             SETON                    89    PREV. DELETED
  180 0172 CSRN51 04 UPFST5      COMP MAFST5            8888    NAME NOT MATCH
  181 0173 CSR 88                SETON                    89
  182 0174 CSR 89                GOTO NEXT                      BYPASS OF TESTS
  183 0175 CSR                   MOVE MABRAN    BRANCH           TEST BRANCH
  184 0176 CSR                   EXSR TSTBR
  185 0177 CSR                   MOVE MASTAT    STATUS           TEST STATUS
  186 0178 CSR                   EXSR TSTST
  187 0179 CSR                   MOVE MARANK    GRADE            TEST GRADE
  188 0180 CSR                   EXSR TSTGR
  189 0181 CSR       NEXT        TAG
  190 0182 CSR 89    ERRDEL      ADD  1         ERRDEL 30       COUNT ERRORS
  191 0183 CSRN89    VALDEL      ADD  1         VALDEL 30       COUNT DELETES
  192 0184 CSR                   SETON                    11
  193 0185 CSR                   EXCPT
  194 0186 CSR                   SETOF                    11
  195 0187 CSR                   ENDSR


  198 0189 C*   INVALID UPDATE CODE SUBROUTINE
  199 0190 C*--------------------------------
  200 0191 CSR       ERROR       BEGSR
  201 0192 CSRN97                MOVE UPBRAN    BRANCH          IF NOT BLANK,
  202 0193 CSRN97                EXSR TSTBR                      TEST BRANCH
  203 0194 CSRN96                MOVE UPSTAT    STATUS          IF NOT BLANK,
  204 0195 CSRN96                EXSR TSTST                      TEST STATUS
  205 0196 CSRN95                MOVE UPRANK    GRADE           IF NOT BLANK,
  206 0197 CSRN95                EXSR TSTGR                      TEST GRADE
  207 0198 CSRN94.   UPYRS       COMP 30                  52    YEARS > 30
  208 0199 CSR                   SETON                    12
  209 0200 CSR                   EXCPT                          ERROR OUTPUT
  210 0201 CSR                   SETOF                  1252    CLEAR INDIC.
  211 0202 CSR       ERROR       ADD  1         ERROR  30       COUNT INVALID
  212 0203 CSR                   ENDSR


  215 0205 C*   STATUS TEST SUBROUTINE
  216 0206 C*-----------------------
  217 0207 CSR       TSTST       BEGSR
  218 0208 CSR                   SETOF                    92
  219 0209 CSR       STATUS      COMP 'A'                 46 ACTIVE
  220 0210 CSR 46                MOVEL' ACTIVE' STAOUT  9
  221 0211 CSR       STATUS      COMP 'R'                 47 RETIRED
  222 0212 CSR 47                MOVEL' RETIRED'STAOUT
  223 0213 CSRN46N47             SETON                    92 INVALID
  224 0214 CSR 92                MOVEL'-INVALID'STAOUT
  225 0215 CSR 92                MOVE '-'       STAOUT
  226 0216 CSR                   ENDSR


  229 0218 C*   GRADE TEST SUBROUTINE
  230 0219 C*----------------------
  231 0220 CSR       TSTGR       BEGSR
```

Figure 11-20 (2)

```
HJG11X    11-22-91  15:32:05   HJG11X - PERSONNEL FILE UPDATE       Version 3.5

          ....+....1....+....2....+....3....+....4....+....5....+....6....+....7....

     232 0221 CSR               SETOF                    91
     233 0222 CSR        GRADE   COMP 'E'                       48 ENLISTED
     234 0223 CSR 48            MOVEL'ENLISTED'GRAOUT  9
     235 0224 CSR        GRADE   COMP 'O'                       49 OFFICER
     236 0225 CSR 49            MOVEL'OFFICER 'GRAOUT
     237 0226 CSR 41     GRADE   COMP 'W'                       50 WARRANT
     238 0227 CSR 50            MOVEL'WARRANT 'GRAOUT
     239 0228 CSRN48N49N50      SETON                    91     INVALID
     240 0229 CSR 91            MOVEL'-INVALID'GRAOUT
     241 0230 CSR 91            MOVE '-'        GRAOUT
     242 0231 CSR               ENDSR


     245 0233 C* BRANCH TEST SUBROUTINE
     246 0234 C*----------------------
     247 0235 CSR        TSTBR   BEGSR
     248 0236 CSR               SETOF                    93
     249 0237 CSR        BRANCH  COMP 'A'                       41 ARMY
     250 0238 CSR 41            MOVEL'ARMY'     BRAOUT 11
     251 0239 CSR        BRANCH  COMP 'N'                       42 NAVY
     252 0240 CSR 42            MOVEL'NAVY'     BRAOUT
     253 0241 CSR        BRANCH  COMP 'F'                       43 AIR FORCE
     254 0242 CSR 43            MOVEL'AIR'      BRAOUT
     255 0243 CSR 43            MOVE 'FORCE '   BRAOUT
     256 0244 CSR        BRANCH  COMP 'M'                       44 MARINES
     257 0245 CSR 44            MOVEL'MARINES'  BRAOUT
     258 0246 CSR        BRANCH  COMP 'C'                       45 COAST GUARD
     259 0247 CSR 45            MOVEL'COAST'    BRAOUT
     260 0248 CSR 45            MOVE 'GUARD'    BRAOUT
     261 0249 CSRN41N42N43
     262 0250 CANN44N45         SETON                    93     INVALID
     263 0251 CSR 93            MOVEL'--INVALI'BRAOUT
     264 0252 CSR 93            MOVE 'D--'      BRAOUT
     265 0253 CSR               ENDSR
```

Figure 11-20 (3)

The program contains only eight operations in the main processing routine. The remainder of the calculations consists of seven subroutines. Because of the different processing needed for record addition, record deletion, record change, and invalid record types, it would be difficult to code this program in the top-down manner that you have used up to now. Instead, a separate subroutine is executed for each of the four types of input record. In addition, three groups of tests (military branch, current status, and current grade) are performed at several different points in the processing of the input records. Rather than duplicate these tests in the four main subroutines, these tests have been coded as individual subroutines. The seven subroutines used in the program are as follows:

ADD: Record addition subroutine. Determines if the record addition request is valid and, if it is, adds a record to the Personnel Master File and prints an audit trail record. If the request is not valid, an error line is printed on the output report.

DELETE: Record deletion subroutine. Determines if the record deletion request is valid and, if it is, marks a Personnel Master File record for deletion and prints an audit trail record. If the request is not valid, an error line is printed on the output report.

CHANGE: Record change subroutine. Determines if the record change request is valid and, if it is, changes one or more data fields in a Personnel Master File record. If the request is not valid, an error line is printed on the output report.

ERROR: Invalid request subroutine. Processes records that contain an invalid update request code and prints an error line on the output report.

TSTST: Test status subroutine. Determines if a status code is valid and, if it is, moves the literal for the status code into the STAOUT field. If the status code is not valid, the subroutine moves the literal -INVALID- into STAOUT. This subroutine also turns on an indicator to signal that the tested status code is invalid.

TSTGR: Test grade subroutine. Determines if a grade code is valid and, if it is, moves the literal for the grade code into the GRAOUT field. If the grade code is not valid, the subroutine moves the literal -INVALID- into GRAOUT. This subroutine also turns on an indicator to signal that the tested grade code is invalid.

TSTBR: Test military branch subroutine. Determines if a military branch code is valid and, if it is, moves the literal for the branch code into the BRAOUT field. If the military branch code is not valid, the subroutine moves the literal --INVALID-- into BRAOUT. This subroutine also turns on an indicator to signal that the tested military branch code is invalid.

Figure 11-21 diagrams the relationships among these subroutines. Note that the main routine accesses only one of the four subroutines based on the update request code. The three test subroutines, however, can be accessed, or called, from any of the four main subroutines. Recall that RPG subroutine processing always returns the program to the operation following the EXSR operation that caused the subroutine to be executed. Regardless of which of the four main subroutines accesses a testing subroutine, RPG always returns processing to the proper point in the correct calling subroutine.

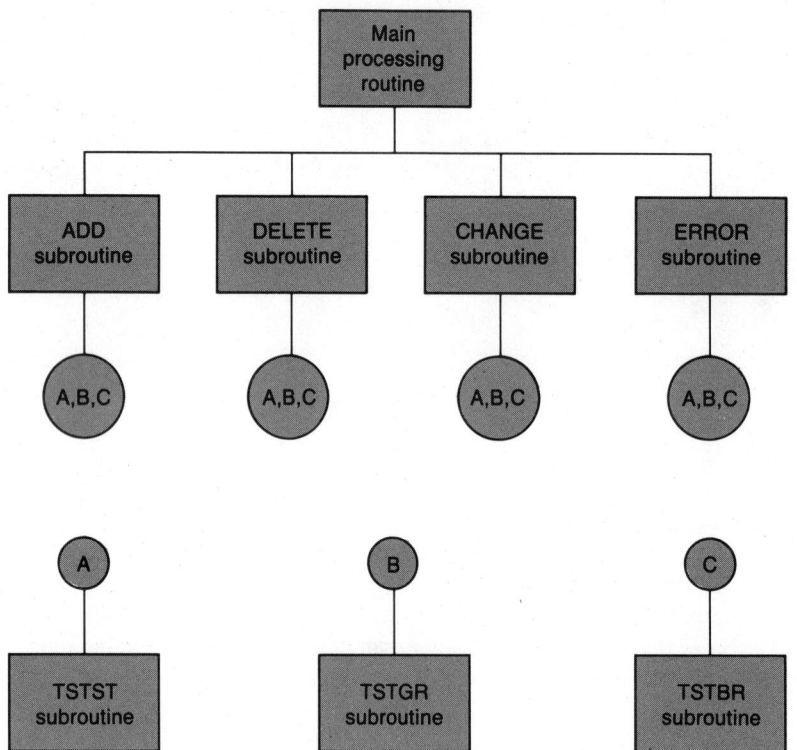

Figure 11-21   HJG11X subroutine relationship

Because of the extensive use of subroutines, the calculations can be thought of as eight separate processing units, or modules. A **program module** is a series of instructions or operations that are treated as a single unit by the program. The word *module* can apply to a subroutine or to any series of consecutive instructions that perform a single function. The calculations in program HJG11X can be thought of as containing seven subroutine modules, all under control of a main processing module. In the explanations that follow you will first be shown the three **low-level subroutines** (subroutines called by other subroutines). This is because the TSTST, TSTGR, and TSTBR subroutines are common to all four main subroutines. After looking at these three simple modules, you will be able to concentrate more easily on the processing performed by the four high-level subroutines.

▸ **TSTST, Test Status Subroutine** The TSTST subroutine used to determine if a status code entry is valid (Figure 11-22) begins by setting indicator 92, the invalid status indicator, off. The STATUS field is then compared with the two valid status codes, A and R. If STATUS contains a valid code, indicators 46 and 47 move a literal (ACTIVE or RETIRED) into the STAOUT field. Note that the Result Field Length entry is made only once, the first time STAOUT is used, on line 04. As you already know, a field is defined only once in an RPG program. After the initial definition is made, there is no need to repeat the length and data class definitions.

Line	Form Type	Control Level (L0-L9, LR, SR, AN/OR)	Not	And	Not	And	Not	Factor 1	Operation	Factor 2	Result Field Name	Length	Decimal Positions	Half Adjust (H)	Resulting Indicators Plus 1>2 High	Minus 1<2 Low	Zero 1=2 Equal	Comments
0 1	C S R							TSTST	BEGSR									
0 2	C S R								SETOF						92			
0 3	C S R							STATUS	COMP	'A'					46			ACTIVE
0 4	C S R	46							MOVEL	'ACTIVE'	STAOUT	9						
0 5	C S R							STATUS	COMP	'R'					47			RETIRED
0 6	C S R	47							MOVEL	'RETIRED'	STAOUT							
0 7	C S R N 46 N 47								SETON						92			INVALID
0 8	C S R	92							MOVEL	'-INVALID'	STAOUT							
0 9	C S R	92							MOVE	'-'	STAOUT							
1 0	C S R								ENDSR									
1 1	C																	

Figure 11-22 TSTST subroutine

If the status code is not valid, line 07 turns on indicator 92, which is used on lines 08 and 09 to move the -INVALID- literal into the STAOUT field. Note the use of both the MOVEL (line 08) and the MOVE (line 09) operations to move a nine-position literal into STAOUT even though the Factor 2 area contains only enough room to move an eight-position literal. By using both a MOVEL and a MOVE operation (Figure 11-23), you can move a literal of more than eight positions. This is similar to the logic used to move the month and year of a date field in program HJG09Y in Chapter 9.

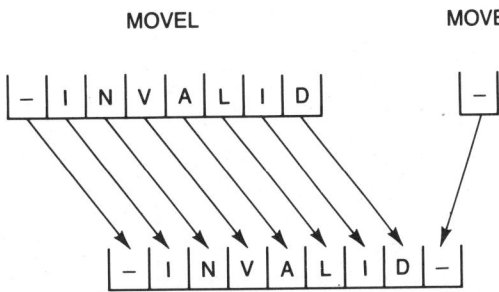

Figure 11-23 Creation of a nine-position literal

You may have noticed that the STATUS field was not defined as part of either of the two input data files. STATUS is a **work field**, a field defined for the temporary storage of data during processing. STATUS can hold the contents of either the UPSTAT or the MASTAT field. If the TSTST subroutine is used to test the contents of UPSTAT, the status code is moved into STATUS prior to executing the subroutine. If the contents of MASTAT are being tested, they are moved into STATUS before the subroutine is executed. By using a work field, you can test either of the two input fields with the same subroutine.

▶ **TSTGR, Test Grade Subroutine** The format of the TSTGR subroutine used to determine if a military grade code is valid (Figure 11-24) is similar to that of the TSTST subroutine. First, the error indicator (91) is turned off, and then a series of comparisons is performed to determine if GRADE (another work field) contains a valid military grade code. If GRADE contains a valid code, one of three literals is moved to the GRAOUT field. If the code contained in GRADE is invalid, the -INVALID- literal is moved.

C		Indicators			Factor 1	Operation	Factor 2	Result Field			Resulting Indicators		Comments
		And	And					Name	Length		Arithmetic / Compare		
Line											Plus Minus Zero 1>2 1<2 1=2 High Low Equal		
01	CSR				TSTGR	BEGSR							
02	CSR					SETOF					91		
03	CSR				GRADE	COMP	'E'					48	ENLISTED
04	CSR	48				MOVE	'ENLISTED'	GRAOUT	9				
05	CSR				GRADE	COMP	'O'					49	OFFICER
06	CSR	49				MOVEL	' OFFICER'	GRAOUT					
07	CSR	41			GRADE	COMP	'W'					50	WARRANT
08	CSR	50				MOVEL	' WARRANT'	GRAOUT					
09	CSR	N48	N49	N50		SETON					91		INVALID
10	CSR	91				MOVEL	'-INVALID'	GRAOUT					
11	CSR	91				MOVE	'-'	GRAOUT					
12	CSR					ENDSR							
13	C												

Figure 11-24 TSTGR subroutine

Note that line 07, which tests for the code W (Warrant Officer) is conditioned by indicator 41. Indicator 41 signals that the military branch code is A for Army. The problem specifications state that a military rank code of W is invalid with any military branch other than Army. By conditioning the test on line 07 with indicator 41, the Warrant Officer indicator (50) can be turned on only if the branch code is A and the grade code is W. If the branch code is other than A, the test is not performed, and indicator 50 is not turned on.

▶ **TSTBR, Test Branch Subroutine** Figure 11-25 shows the TSTBR subroutine that determines if the military branch code is valid. As with the two other testing subroutines, TSTBR begins by turning the invalid branch indicator (93) off and then tests the contents of BRANCH for a valid code. If a valid code is found, the appropriate literal is moved into the BAROUT field. If the code is not valid, the --INVALID-- literal is moved.

▶ **Main Processing Routine** In the main processing routine used in the sample program (Figure 11-26), the first five operations are detail calculations, and the last three are performed at last-record time and are used to calculate final totals of the number of addition, deletion, and change requests processed.

Line 01 performs a random read of the Personnel Master File, PERSFILE, based on the contents of the UPIDNO field. The CHAIN operation turns on indicator 51 if the requested record is not found in PERSFILE. If the requested record is found, indicator 51 is not turned on. Note that this operation is performed only if indicator 99 is not on, meaning that the PERSUPDT record being processed contains a valid update request code. If the update request code is not valid, there is no need to access PERSFILE because the processing of an invalid update request code does not require that PERSFILE be read. The CHAIN operation is performed as part of the main processing routine, rather than as part of the addition, deletion, and change subroutines, because this read must be done as part of the processing of every input record containing a valid update request code. By placing the CHAIN here, you can use indicator 51 in all three update subroutines. In addition, by performing the CHAIN in the main processing routine, the program needs only a single CHAIN operation rather than the three that would be needed if each update subroutine contained a separate random read of PERSFILE.

Line	Form Type	Indicators	Factor 1	Operation	Factor 2	Result Field Name	Length	Resulting Indicators	Comments
01	CSR		TSTBR	BEGSR					
02	CSR			SETOF				93	'
03	CSR		BRANCH	COMP	'A'			41	ARMY
04	CSR	41		MOVEL	'ARMY'	BRAOUT	11		
05	CSR		BRANCH	COMP	'N'			42	NAVY
06	CSR	42		MOVEL	'NAVY'	BRAOUT			
07	CSR		BRANCH	COMP	'F'			43	AIR FORCE
08	CSR	43		MOVEL	'AIR'	BRAOUT			
09	CSR	43		MOVE	'FORCE '	BRAOUT			
10	CSR		BRANCH	COMP	'M'			44	MARINES
11	CSR	44		MOVEL	'MARINES'	BRAOUT			
12	CSR		BRANCH	COMP	'C'			45	COAST GUARD
13	CSR	45		MOVEL	'COAST'	BRAOUT			
14	CSR	45		MOVE	'GUARD'	BRAOUT			
15	CSR	N41N42N43							
16	CAN	N44N45		SETON				93	INVALID
17	CSR	93		MOVEL	'--INVALI'	BRAOUT			
18	CSR	93		MOVE	'D--'	BRAOUT			
19	CSR			ENDSR					
20	C								

Figure 11-25   TSTBR subroutine

Line	Form Type	Indicators	Factor 1	Operation	Factor 2	Result Field Name	Length	Resulting Indicators	Comments
01	C	N99	UPIDNO	CHAIN	PERSFILE			51	READ PERSFILE
02	C	Ø1		EXSR	ADD				RECORD ADDITION
03	C	Ø2		EXSR	DELETE				RECORD DELETION
04	C	Ø3		EXSR	CHANGE				RECORD CHANGE
05	C	99		EXSR	ERROR				INVALID UPDATE
06	CLR		ERRADD	ADD	VALADD	TOTADD	3Ø		
07	CLR		ERRDEL	ADD	VALDEL	TOTDEL	3Ø		
08	CLR		ERRCH	ADD	VALCH	TOTCH	3Ø		
09	C								
10	C								
11	C								
12	C								
13	C								
14	C								
15	C								
16	C								
17	C								
18	C								
19	C								
20	C								

Figure 11-26   Main processing routine

Lines 02–05 execute one of the four main subroutines (ADD, DELETE, CHANGE, or ERROR), based on the record-identifying indicator turned on by the update request code. Because only one of the four record-identifying indicators can be on, only one of these four subroutines can be executed. Remember that record identification checking turns on only one of the possible record-identifying indicators.

Lines 06, 07, and 08 each add two totals to form a third total. As you will see as the individual subroutines are shown, the record addition, record deletion, and record change subroutines count the number of valid and invalid update requests that are processed. Line 06 adds the count of valid record addition requests (VALADD) to the count of invalid record addition requests (ERRADD) to determine the total number of record addition requests (TOTADD). This total is required by the program, as shown on line 43 of the printer spacing chart (see Figure 11-4). In a similar manner, line 07 calculates the total number of record deletion requests, and line 08 calculates the total number of record change requests.

The descriptions of the four main processing subroutines are not in the same order as the EXSR operations that perform them. Because each subroutine in a program is a separate module that performs a distinct function, these subroutines need not be described or explained in any particular sequence. Refer to Figure 11-20. The sequence of the subroutines used when writing the program is one of several, equally valid, subroutine sequences that can be used. The subroutines are, instead, presented in a sequence that is easy to understand, beginning with ERROR, simplest of the four main processing modules, and ending with CHANGE, the most complex of the four.

Invalid Update Code Subroutine The ERROR subroutine (Figure 11-27) is executed when an input record containing an invalid update request code is read. Even though the update request code is invalid, the program must test the contents of the data fields in the record. Lines 02–03 control testing of the military branch field, UPBRAN. Line 02 moves the contents of UPBRAN into BRANCH, the military branch work field. Line 03 then executes the TSTBR subroutine. On completion of the TSTBR subroutine, the BRAOUT field contains either the name of the military branch (ARMY, NAVY, AIR FORCE, etc.) or the literal --INVALID--. Note that these two operations are performed only if indicator 97 is not on, meaning that UPBRAN is not blank. If indicator 97 is on, meaning that UPBRAN is blank, a separate constant, ---BLANK---, is printed under control of indicator 97.

Line	Form Type	Control Level	Indicators	Factor 1	Operation	Factor 2	Result Field Name	Length	Decimal Positions	Resulting Indicators High	Low	Equal	Comments
01	C	SR		ERROR	BEGSR								
02	C	SR	N97		MOVE	UPBRAN	BRANCH						IF NOT BLANK,
03	C	SR	N97		EXSR	TSTBR							TEST BRANCH
04	C	SR	N96		MOVE	UPSTAT	STATUS						IF NOT BLANK,
05	C	SR	N96		EXSR	TSTST							TEST STATUS
06	C	SR	N95		MOVE	UPRANK	GRADE						IF NOT BLANK,
07	C	SR	N95		EXSR	TSTGR							TEST GRADE
08	C	SR	N94	UPYRS	COMP	3Ø				52			YEARS > 3Ø
09	C	SR			SETON					12			
10	C	SR	12		EXCPT								ERROR OUTPUT
11	C	SR			SETOF					12	52		
12	C	SR		ERROR	ADD	1	ERROR	3	Ø				COUNT INVALID
13	C	SR			ENDSR								
14	C												

Figure 11-27 ERROR subroutine

Lines 04–07 use a similar logic to test the contents of the UPSTAT and UPRANK fields. Lines 04 and 06 move the input field contents into a work field, and lines 05 and 07 cause execution of the testing subroutines.

If the UPYRS field is not blank (indicator N94), line 08 compares the contents of UPYRS with 30. If the value in UPYRS is greater than 30, indicator 52 is turned on to denote the error.

Lines 09, 10, and 11 use SETON, EXCPT, and SETOF logic to print an exception output line. Line 11 also turns indicator 52 off to clear it for the next input record and thus eliminates the possibility of incorrect output based on a faulty setting of indicator 52. Line 12 then adds 1 to ERROR, the invalid update request code counter. As you can see, the name of the field (ERROR) is the same as the name of the subroutine. There is no necessary connection between the subroutine name and the counter name. Although two fields cannot have the same name and two subroutines cannot have the same name, RPG does permit a field and subroutine to share a name.

Figure 11-28 shows the output specifications for the print line produced by the ERROR subroutine. Note the use of the three redefinition fields – UPID1, UPID2, and UPID3 – to print the identification number in three sections separated by hyphens.

Line	Form Type	Filename/Record Name	Type	Space/Skip	Output Indicators	Field Name or EXCPT Name or Constant Name	Edit Codes	End Position in Output Record	Constant or Edit Word
01	O		E	2 / 1 2					
02	O							6	'ERROR'
03	O					UPID1		12	
04	O							13	'-'
05	O					UPID2		15	
06	O							16	'-'
07	O					UPID3		20	
08	O				N98	UPNAME		42	
09	O				98			33	'---BLANK---'
10	O				N97	BRAOUT B		55	
11	O				97			55	'---BLANK---'
12	O				N96	STAOUT B		65	
13	O				96			65	'--BLANK--'
14	O				N95	GRAOUT B		75	
15	O				95			75	'--BLANK--'
16	O				N94 N52	UPYRS Z		81	
17	O				94			82	'ZERO'
18	O				52			84	'INVALID'
19	O							109	'INVALID UPDATE TYPE CODE'
20	O								

Figure 11-28 Exception output for ERROR subroutine

Lines 08–18 control printing of the individual fields in the input record. Indicator N98 (UPNAME not blank) controls printing of the UPNAME field. If indicator 98 is on, the literal, ---BLANK--- prints. In a similar manner, the on or off setting of indicators 97, 96, and 95 control printing of the BRAOUT, STAOUT, and GRAOUT fields or of the literal that shows these fields are blank. Line 16 prints UPYRS if indicators 94 and 52 are both off. If indicator 94 is on, the literal ZERO prints instead. If indicator 52 is on, the literal INVALID prints, specifying that the value in UPYRS is greater than 30.

Line 19 causes the printing of the INVALID UPDATE TYPE CODE literal, a required part of this error line.

▸ **Record Deletion Subroutine** Figure 11-29 on the next page shows the DELETE subroutine used to mark a record for deletion. Line 02 turns off indicators 88 and 89, both of which are used as error indicators in this routine. Line 03 turns on indicator 89 if indicator 51 is on. Remember that indicator 51 is turned on by the main processing routine if the requested record is not found by the CHAIN operation. A request to delete a record that is not part of the file is an error.

Line	Form Type	Control Level	Indicators And	And	And	Factor 1	Operation	Factor 2	Result Field Name	Length	Decimal Positions	Resulting Indicators	Comments
01	CSR					DELETE	BEGSR						
02	CSR						SETOF					8988	CLEAR INDIC.
03	CSR		51				SETON					89	NOT ON FILE
04	CSR		N51	05			SETON					89	PREV. DELETED
05	CSR		N51	04		UPFST5	COMP	MAFST5				8888	NAME NOT MATCH
06	CSR		88				SETON					89	
07	CSR		89				GOTO	NEXT					TESTS BYPASS
08	CSR						MOVE	MABRAN	BRANCH				TEST BRANCH
09	CSR						EXSR	TSTBR					
10	CSR						MOVE	MASTAT	STATUS				TEST STATUS
11	CSR						EXSR	TSTST					
12	CSR						MOVE	MARANK	GRADE				TEST GRADE
13	CSR						EXSR	TSTGR					
14	CSR					NEXT	TAG						
15	CSR		89			ERRDEL	ADD	1	ERRDEL	30			COUNT ERRORS
16	CSR		N89			VALDEL	ADD	1	VALDEL	30			COUNT DELETES
17	CSR						SETON					11	
18	CSR		11				EXCPT						
19	CSR						SETOF					11	
20	CSR						ENDSR						

Figure 11-29   DELETE subroutine

If indicator 51 is not on, the requested record is part of PERSFILE. Line 04 uses indicator 51 (requested record exists in PERSFILE) along with indicator 05 to turn on indicator 89, the error indicator. Indicator 05 specifies that a PERSFILE record contains the status code D in position 1, meaning that the record has already been marked for deletion. A request to delete a record that has already been delete-marked is an error.

Line 05 compares UPFST5 with MAFST5 if the record is on file and the status code is A (indicator 04). The processing requirements for record deletion specify that the first five positions of the Name field in the deletion request record match the first five positions of the name field in the Personnel Master File record to verify the match before a record is marked for deletion. Indicator 88 is turned on by line 05 if these two fields do not match. If indicator 88 is turned on, line 06 will then SETON indicator 89, the error indicator.

If, as a result of any of these error tests, indicator 89 is on, line 07 executes a GOTO operation to bypass the remaining operations needed for a valid deletion request. The GOTO operation branches over lines 08–13 and proceeds directly to line 14, the TAG statement.

If the GOTO is not executed, lines 08–13 execute the TSTBR, TSTST, and TSTGR subroutines to set the proper output literals, based on the codes in the Personnel Master File record. Line 15 adds 1 to the deletion error count (ERRDEL) if indicator 89 is on. Line 16 adds 1 to the valid deletion count (VALDEL) if indicator 89 is not on. Lines 17, 18, and 19 then cause the deletion request output operations to be performed.

Figure 11-30 shows the output specifications for the line that is printed as part of the DELETE subroutine. Although the identification number portion of the print line prints under all conditions, the contents of the MANAME, BRAOUT, STAOUT, GRAOUT, and MAYRS fields print only if indicator 89 is not on, indicating a valid record. If the deletion request is not valid, one of the error messages coded on lines 13–18 prints.

Line	Form Type	Filename or Record Name	Type (H/D/T/E)	Stacker/Fetch (F)	Space Before	Space After	Skip Before	Skip After	Output Indicators And/And	Field Name or EXCPT Name or Constant Name	Edit Codes	B/A/CR/-/9/R	End Position in Output Record	P/B/L/R	Constant or Edit Word
01	O		E		2		11								
02	O												7		'DELETE'
03	O									MAID1			12		
04	O												13		'-'
05	O									MAID2			15		
06	O												16		'-'
07	O									MAID3			20		
08	O								N89	MANAME			42		
09	O								N89	BRAOUT		B	55		
10	O								N89	STAOUT		B	65		
11	O								N89	GRAOUT		B	75		
12	O								N89	MAYRS	Z		81		
13	O								51				108		'INVALID UPDATE-I.D. NOT'
14	O								51				116		'ON FILE'
15	O								N51 05				106		'INVALID UPDATE-RECORD'
16	O								N51 05				125		'PREVIOUSLY DELETED'
17	O								88				104		'INVALID UPDATE-NAME'
18	O								88				119		'FIELD MISMATCH'
19	O														
20	O														

Figure 11-30   Exception output for DELETE subroutine

Line	Form Type	Filename or Record Name	Type (H/D/T/E)	Output Indicators And/And	Field Name or EXCPT Name or Constant Name	End Position in Output Record	Constant or Edit Word
01	O		E	11 N89			
02	O					1	'D'
03	O						

Figure 11-31   Disk record deletion

In addition to producing printed output, a valid record deletion request causes a delete code to be written to a PERSFILE record. The output specifications necessary to mark a record on the Personnel Master File for deletion are shown in Figure 11-31. Note that the output specifications simply write D in position 1 of the output record and that the record is written only if indicator 89 (delete request error) is not on. There is no indication of which PERSFILE record is to be deleted, that is, no use of the Identification Number field. How, then, does RPG know which record must be marked for deletion?

The answer is quite simple: *RPG writes the output to the last record that was read from the update file.* As you saw, the main processing routine began by reading a record from PERSFILE. The program then executed the DELETE subroutine and, if there were no errors in the delete request record, wrote a D to the first position of the last record that was read. RPG automatically keeps track of the key field value of the last record read and, when a write operation is performed to the file, writes the output data to the same record. You will see that the same logic is used when a change is made to a PERSFILE record.

▸ **Record Addition Subroutine** Figure 11-32 shows the ADD subroutine, which adds a new record to the Personnel Master File. Lines 02–07 test the contents of the three input code fields. These tests are performed only if the field being tested is not blank. After the tests are completed, line 08 clears the two error indicators used by the subroutine. Lines 09–13 turn on indicator 90 if any of the required input data fields is blank. Lines 14, 15, and 16 turn indicator 90 on if any of the tested code fields contains an invalid code. If the UPYRS field is not blank, line 17 uses a COMP operation to test for an excessive value in the UPYRS field and, if a value greater than 30 is found, turns on indicator 52. If indicator 52 is turned on, line 18 then sets indicator 90 on. Line 19 uses indicator N51 to turn indicator 90 on if the record key requested for addition already exists in PERSFILE. After lines 20 and 21 add 1 to either the ERRADD or the VALADD counts, the program uses SETON, EXCPT, and SETOF logic on lines 22, 23, and 24 to perform all output generated by the record addition request.

Line	Form Type	Control Level	Indicators	Factor 1	Operation	Factor 2	Result Field Name	Length	Resulting Indicators High (Plus)	Low (Minus)	Equal (Zero)	Comments
01	C	SR		ADD	BEGSR							
02	C	SR	N97		MOVE	UPBRAN	BRANCH	1				IF NOT BLANK,
03	C	SR	N97		EXSR	TSTBR						TEST BRANCH
04	C	SR	N96		MOVE	UPSTAT	STATUS	1				IF NOT BLANK,
05	C	SR	N96		EXSR	TSTST						TEST STATUS
06	C	SR	N95		MOVE	UPRANK	GRADE	1				IF NOT BLANK,
07	C	SR	N95		EXSR	TSTGR						TEST GRADE
08	C	SR			SETOF				90	52		CLEAR INDIC.
09	C	SR	94									
10	C	OR	95									
11	C	OR	96									
12	C	OR	97									
13	C	OR	98		SETON				90			MISSING DATA
14	C	SR	91									
15	C	OR	92									
16	C	OR	93		SETON				90			INVALID CODE
17	C	SR	N94	UPYRS	COMP	30			52			
18	C	SR	52		SETON				90			YEARS > 30
19	C	SR	N51		SETON				90			DUPLICATE I.D.
20	C	SR	90	ERRADD	ADD	1	ERRADD	30				COUNT ERRORS
21	C	SR	N90	VALADD	ADD	1	VALADD	30				COUNT ADDS
22	C	SR			SETON				10			
23	C	SR	10		EXCPT							
24	C	SR			SETOF				10			
25	C	SR			ENDSR							

Figure 11-32 ADD subroutine

The format for the PERSREPT output specifications for the line to be printed by a record addition request (Figure 11-33) is similar to that for the lines you have seen in the preceding examples. Note the use of indicators to control the printing of fields within the line. Figure 11-34 shows the output specifications used to add a new record to PERSFILE. This output is controlled by indicators 10 and N90. Indicator 10 signals a record addition request, and indicator N90 signals that no errors were found in the addition request record. As in Chapter 10, the entry ADD in positions 16–18 is necessary to add a record to a keyed file.

Line	Form Type	Filename or Record Name	Type	Space Before/After	Skip	Output Indicators (And/And)	Field Name or EXCPT or Constant Name *AUTO	Edit Codes B/A/C/1-9/R	End Position in Output Record	P/B/L/R	Constant or Edit Word
01	O		E	2		10					
02	O								4		'ADD'
03	O						UPID1		12		
04	O								13		'-'
05	O						UPID2		15		
06	O								16		'-'
07	O						UPID3		20		
08	O					N98	UPNAME		42		
09	O					98			33		'---BLANK---'
10	O					N97	BRAOUT B		55		
11	O					97			55		'---BLANK---'
12	O					N96	STAOUT B		65		
13	O					96			65		'--BLANK--'
14	O					N95	GRAOUT B		75		
15	O					95			75		'--BLANK--'
16	O					N94 N52	UPYRS Z		81		
17	O					94			82		'ZERO'
18	O					52			84		'INVALID'
19	O					N51			106		'DUPLICATE I.D.-RECORD'
20	O					N51			116		'NOT ADDED'
	O					90 51			100		'ERROR-NO UPDATE'
	O					90 51			110		'PERFORMED'
	O										

Figure 11-33   Exception output for ADD Subroutine

Line	Form Type	Filename or Record Name	Type	Space Before/After	Skip	Output Indicators	Field Name or EXCPT or Constant Name *AUTO	End Position in Output Record	P/B/L/R	Constant or Edit Word
01	O	PERSFILE	E	ADD		10 N90				
02	O							1		'A'
03	O						UPIDNO	10		
04	O						UPNAME	30		
05	O						UPBRAN	31		
06	O						UPSTAT	32		
07	O						UPRANK	33		
08	O						UPYRS	35		
09	O									

Figure 11-34   Disk record addition

▸ **Record Change Subroutine**   The CHANGE subroutine (Figure 11-35 on the next page) is the longest, most complicated subroutine in the program. Besides changing one or more of the four PERSFILE fields that can be changed, this subroutine controls the printing of four lines on PERSREPT.

Figure 11-35 CHANGE subroutine

Line	Form Type	Control Level	Indicators (Not)	Factor 1	Operation	Factor 2	Result Field Name	Length	Dec Pos	Resulting Indicators	Comments
01	CSR			CHANGE	BEGSR						
02	CSR				SETOF					86 53	CLEAR INDIC.
03	CSR		51		SETON					13	
04	CSR		13		EXCPT						PRINT INVALID—
05	CSR				SETOF					13	NOT ON FILE
06	CSR		51	ERRCH	ADD	1	ERRCH	30			COUNT ERRORS
07	CSR		51		GOTO	ENDCH					BYPASS REST OF
08	C*										ROUTINE
09	CSR		N96		MOVE	UPSTAT	STATUS				IF NOT BLANK,
10	CSR		N96		EXSR	TSTST					TEST STATUS
11	CSR		N95		MOVE	UPRANK	GRADE				IF NOT BLANK,
12	CSR		N95		EXSR	TSTGR					TEST GRADE
13	CSR		N94	UPYRS	COMP	30				53	TEST VALID
14	CSR		N94N53	UPYRS	COMP	MAYRS				53	YEARS
15	C*										
16	CSR		91								
17	COR		92								INVALID CHANGE
18	COR		53								REQUEST DATA
19	CSR		86	ERRCH	ADD	1	ERRCH			86	COUNT ERRORS
20	CSR		86		SETON					14	
21	CSR		14		EXCPT						CHANGE ERROR
22	CSR				SETOF					14	OUTPUT
23	CSR		86		GOTO	ENDCH					BYPASS REST OF
24	C*										ROUTINE

Figure 11-35 (1)

Line	Form Type	Control Level	Indicators (Not)	Factor 1	Operation	Factor 2	Result Field Name	Length	Dec Pos	Resulting Indicators	Comments
01	CSR				MOVE	MABRAN	BRANCH				TEST BRANCH
02	CSR				EXSR	TSTBR					
03	CSR				MOVE	MASTAT	STATUS				TEST STATUS
04	CSR				EXSR	TSTST					
05	CSR				MOVE	MARANK	GRADE				TEST GRADE
06	CSR				EXSR	TSTGR					
07	CSR				SETON					15	
08	CSR		15		EXCPT						PRINT OLD
09	CSR				SETOF					15	RECORD
10	CSR		N96		MOVE	UPSTAT	STATUS				TEST STATUS
11	CSR		N96		EXSR	TSTST					
12	CSR		N95		MOVE	UPRANK	GRADE				TEST GRADE
13	CSR		N95		EXSR	TSTGR					
14	CSR				SETON					16	PRINT NEW
15	CSR		16		EXCPT						RECORD AND
16	CSR				SETOF					16	CHANGE DISK
17	CSR			VALCH	ADD	1	VALCH	30			COUNT CHANGES
18	CSR			ENDCH	TAG						
19	CSR				ENDSR						

Figure 11-35 (2)

The first part of the subroutine controls the printing of an error line if the identification number of the change request is invalid; the calculations and output exception line specifications are shown in Figure 11-36. This part of the subroutine begins by turning off indicators 86 and 53, the two error indicators. If indicator 51 is on, signaling that the requested record does not exist in PERSFILE, line 03 turns on indicator 13. Indicator 13 then causes the EXCPT operation on line 04 to print the error output line. After line 05 turns off indicator 13, line 06 adds 1 to the error count, and the GOTO on line 07 bypasses the remainder of the CHANGE subroutine.

Line	Form Type	Control Level	Indicators And Not / And Not / Not	Factor 1	Operation	Factor 2	Result Field Name	Length	Decimal Positions	Half Adjust	Resulting Indicators	Comments
01	CSR			CHANGE	BEGSR							
02	CSR				SETOF						8653	CLEAR INDIC.
03	CSR		51		SETON						13	
04	CSR		13		EXCPT							PRINT INVALID-
05	CSR				SETOF						13	NOT ON FILE
06	CSR		51	ERRCH	ADD	1	ERRCH	30				COUNT ERRORS
07	CSR		51		GOTO	ENDCH						BYPASS REST OF
08	C*											ROUTINE
09	C											

Line	Form Type	Filename or Record Name	Type	Space Before/After	Skip Before/After	Output Indicators And Not / And Not / Not	Field Name or EXCPT Name or Constant Name	Edit Codes	End Position in Output Record	P/B/L/R	Constant or Edit Word
01	O		E	2		13					
02	O								7		'CHANGE'
03	O						UPID1		12		
04	O								13		'-'
05	O						UPID2		15		
06	O								16		'-'
07	O						UPID3		20		
08	O								108		'INVALID UPDATE-I.D. NOT'
09	O								116		'ON FILE'

Figure 11-36 Exception output for CHANGE subroutine

The second part of the CHANGE subroutine (Figure 11-37 on the next page) verifies that any requested change contains valid data. Lines 09–12 test the contents of the UPSTST and UPRANK fields. The UPBRAN field is not tested because the problem specifications state that the Military Branch field must not be changed. After line 13 verifies that UPYRS does not contain a value greater than 30, line 14 verifies that the new UPYRS value is not less than the MAYRS value currently stored in the Personnel Master File. After these tests are performed, lines 16–18 turn on indicator 86 if any error was detected. Indicator 86 then adds 1 to the change error count (line 19) and, by controlling lines 20, 21, and 22, prints the error line also shown in Figure 11-37. Line 23 then branches to ENDCH, bypassing the remainder of the CHANGE subroutine.

Line	Form Type	Control Level	And Not	And Not	Not	Factor 1	Operation	Factor 2	Result Field Name	Length	Dec Pos	Resulting Indicators	Comments
09	C	SR	N96				MOVE	UPSTAT	STATUS				IF NOT BLANK,
10	C	SR	N96				EXSR	TSTST					TEST STATUS
11	C	SR	N95				MOVE	UPRANK	GRADE				IF NOT BLANK,
12	C	SR	N95				EXSR	TSTGR					TEST GRADE
13	C	SR	N94				UPYRS	COMP	30				53	TEST VALID
14	C	SR	N94				UPYRS	COMP	MAYRS				53	YEARS
15	C*												
16	C	SR	91										
17	C	OR	92										INVALID CHANGE
18	C	OR	53					SETON					86	REQUEST DATA
19	C	SR	86				ERRCH	ADD	1	ERRCH				COUNT ERRORS
20	C	SR	86					SETON					14	
21	C	SR	14					EXCPT						CHANGE ERROR
22	C	SR						SETOF					14	OUTPUT
23	C	SR	86					GOTO	ENDCH					BYPASS REST OF
24	C*												ROUTINE
	C												

Line	Form Type	Type	Space After	Skip	Output Indicators And And Not	Field Name or EXCPT Name or Constant Name	Edit Codes	End Position in Output Record	Constant or Edit Word
01	O	E	2		14				
02	O							7	'CHANGE'
03	O					UPID1		12	
04	O							13	'_'
05	O					UPID2		15	
06	O							16	'_'
07	O					UPID3		20	
08	O				N96	STAOUT	B	65	
09	O				N95	GRAOUT	B	73	
10	O				53			84	'INVALID'
11	O							109	'ERROR-NO UPDATE PERFORME'
12	O							110	'D'
13	O								

Figure 11-37 Exception output for CHANGE subroutine

The rest of the subroutine controls the printing of the two output lines necessary for a valid change and the actual change of the data in the PERSFILE record. Figure 11-38 shows the calculations needed to print the first of the two change lines and the output specifications for this output line. The three testing subroutines are used to determine the contents in the PERSFILE code fields and to generate the output literals needed for these fields. After the three subroutines are executed, lines 07–09 print the first of the two change lines. This is the line that shows the old record.

Figure 11-39 shows the remainder of the CHANGE subroutine. Calculation lines 10–13 retrieve the literals that represent the codes in the fields being changed. These lines are performed only if there is data in either the UPSTAT or UPRANK fields. Lines 14, 15, and 16 then cause the exception output to be generated.

C	Line	Form Type	Control Level (L0-L9, LR, SR, AN/OR)	Indicators And / And	Factor 1	Operation	Factor 2	Result Field Name	Length	Dec	H	Resulting Indicators	Comments
01		CSR				MOVE	MABRAN	BRANCH					TEST BRANCH
02		CSR				EXSR	TSTBR						
03		CSR				MOVE	MASTAT	STATUS					TEST STATUS
04		CSR				EXSR	TSTST						
05		CSR				MOVE	MARANK	GRADE					TEST GRADE
06		CSR				EXSR	TSTGR						
07		CSR				SETON						15	
08		CSR	15			EXCPT							PRINT OLD
09		CSR				SETOF						15	RECORD

O	Line	Form Type	Filename or Record Name	Type (H/D/T/E)	Space/Skip	Output Indicators And / And	Field Name or EXCPT Name or Constant Name	End Position in Output Record	Constant or Edit Word
01		O		E	1	15			
02		O						7	'CHANGE'
03		O					MAID1	12	
04		O						13	'_'
05		O					MAID2	15	
06		O						16	'_'
07		O					MAID3	20	
08		O					MANAME	42	
09		O					BRAOUT	55	
10		O					STAOUT	65	
11		O					GRAOUT	75	
12		O					MAYRS Z	81	
13		O						95	'OLD RECORD'

Figure 11-38 Exception output for CHANGE subroutine

C	Line	Form Type	Control Level	Indicators And / And	Factor 1	Operation	Factor 2	Result Field Name	Length	Dec	H	Resulting Indicators	Comments
10		CSR	N96			MOVE	UPSTAT	STATUS					TEST STATUS
11		CSR	N96			EXSR	TSTST						
12		CSR	N95			MOVE	UPRANK	GRADE					TEST GRADE
13		CSR	N95			EXSR	TSTGR						
14		CSR				SETON						16	PRINT NEW
15		CSR	16			EXCPT							RECORD AND
16		CSR				SETOF						16	CHANGE DISK
17		CSR			VALCH	ADD	1	VALCH	30				COUNT CHANGES
18		CSR			ENDCH	TAG							
19		CSR				ENDSR							

Figure 11-39 Exception output for CHANGE subroutine   *continued*

After the output operations are performed, line 17 adds 1 to the count of valid change requests. The remaining output specifications are also shown in this figure. When the EXCPT operation on line 15 is executed, the new-record line is printed and the new data is written to the PERSFILE record. Note the use of indicators 94, 95, 96, and 98 to control the output fields that are printed and written to PERSFILE. Remember that the PERSFILE record the program writes to is the record that was read by the CHAIN operation that began the main processing routine.

PERSREPT

Line	Form Type	Filename or Record Name				Type (H/D/T/E)	Stkr A/Fetch (F)	R A N D	D E L	E L A D D	Space Before	Space After	Skip Before	Skip After	Output Indicators							Field Name or EXCPT Name or Constant Name *AUTO	Edit Codes B/A/C/1-9/R	End Position in Output Record	P/B/L/R	Constant or Edit Word
0 1	O					E					2		1 6													
0 2	O																		BRAOUT	B	55		
0 3	O																		STAOUT	B	65		
0 4	O																		GRAOUT	B	75		
0 5	O														N94				UPYRS		81		
0 6	O														94				MAYRS		81		
0 7	O																				95		'NEW RECORD'

PERSFILE

Line	Form Type	Filename or Record Name				Type (H/D/T/E)	Stkr A/Fetch (F)	R A N D	D E L	E L A D D	Space Before	Space After	Skip Before	Skip After	Output Indicators							Field Name or EXCPT Name or Constant Name *AUTO	Edit Codes B/A/C/1-9/R	End Position in Output Record	P/B/L/R	Constant or Edit Word
0 1	O					E							1 6										
0 2	O														N98				UPNAME		30		
0 3	O														N96				UPSTAT		32		
0 4	O														N95				UPRANK		33		
0 5	O														N94				UPYRS		35		
0 6	O																						

Figure 11-39 (continued)

The completed program compile listing and program output (Figure 11-40) includes the printed output report generated by the program and the "before" and "after" listings of PERSFILE. By comparing these data listings with the printed output report, you can see that the requested changes have been made to the contents of PERSFILE.

Figure 11-40   Program HJG11X

```
HJG11X    09-12-91  19:06:15   HJG11X - PERSONNEL FILE UPDATE      Version 3.5  Page  1

          ....+....1....+....2....+....3....+....4....+....5....+....6....+....7....

       3 0002 H                                                                HJG11X


       4 0003 FPERSUPDTIP  F 240  40              DISK
       5 0004 FPERSFILEUC  F  40  40R 9AI      2  DISK                      A
       6 0005 FPERSREPTO   F 132 132      OF     PRINTER
```

```
      52 0050 I*   UPDATE FILE DESCRIPTION
      53 0051 I*-----------------------
      54 0052 IPERSUPDTAA    01   1 CA
      55 0053 I       OR     02   1 CD
      56 0054 I       OR     03   1 CC
      57 0055 I       OR     99  1NCA   1NCD   1NCC
      58 0056 I                                    2  10 UPIDNO
      59 0057 I                                    2   4 UPID1
      60 0058 I                                    5   6 UPID2
      61 0059 I                                    7  10 UPID3
      62 0060 I                                   11  30 UPNAME    98
      63 0061 I                                   31  31 UPBRAN    97
      64 0062 I                                   32  32 UPSTAT    96
```

Figure 11-40 (1)

```
HJG11X   09-12-91  19:06:15   HJG11X - PERSONNEL FILE UPDATE      Version 3.5  Page  2

         ....+....1....+....2....+....3....+....4....+....5....+....6....+....7....

 65 0063 I                                         33  33 UPRANK          95
 66 0064 I                                         34  350UPYRS           94
 67 0065 I                                         11  15 UPFST5     02


 70 0067 I*    PERSONNEL FILE DESCRIPTION
 71 0068 I*---------------------------
 72 0069 IPERSFILEBB   04    1 CA
 73 0070 I        OR   05    1 CD
 74 0071 I                                          2  10 MAIDNO
 75 0072 I                                          2   4 MAID1
 76 0073 I                                          5   6 MAID2
 77 0074 I                                          7  10 MAID3
 78 0075 I                                         11  30 MANAME
 79 0076 I                                         31  31 MABRAN
 80 0077 I                                         32  32 MASTAT
 81 0078 I                                         33  33 MARANK
 82 0079 I                                         34  350MAYRS
 83 0080 I                                         11  15 MAFST5


 84 0081 C*    MAIN PROCESSING ROUTINE
 85 0082 C*    -----------------------
 86 0083 C    N99      UPIDNO    CHAINPERSFILE            51   READ PERSFILE
 87 0084 C    01                 EXSR ADD                      RECORD ADDITION
 88 0085 C    02                 EXSR DELETE                   RECORD DELETION
 89 0086 C    03                 EXSR CHANGE                   RECORD CHANGE
 90 0087 C    99                 EXSR ERROR                    INVALID UPDATE
 91 0088 CLR           ERRADD    ADD  VALADD    TOTADD  30
 92 0089 CLR           ERRDEL    ADD  VALDEL    TOTDEL  30
 93 0090 CLR           ERRCH     ADD  VALCH     TOTCH   30


 96 0092 C*    RECORD ADDITION SUBROUTINE
 97 0093 C*----------------------------
 98 0094 CSR           ADD       BEGSR
 99 0095 CSRN97                  MOVE UPBRAN    BRANCH  1     IF NOT BLANK,
100 0096 CSRN97                  EXSR TSTBR                   TEST BRANCH
101 0097 CSRN96                  MOVE UPSTAT    STATUS  1     IF NOT BLANK,
102 0098 CSRN96                  EXSR TSTST                   TEST STATUS
103 0099 CSRN95                  MOVE UPRANK    GRADE   1     IF NOT BLANK,
104 0100 CSRN95                  EXSR TSTGR                   TEST GRADE
105 0101 CSR                     SETOF                  9052  CLEAR INDIC.
106 0102 CSR 94
107 0103 COR 95
108 0104 COR 96
109 0105 COR 97
110 0106 COR 98                  SETON                  90    MISSING DATA
111 0107 CSR 91
112 0108 COR 92
113 0109 COR 93                  SETON                  90    INVALID CODE
114 0110 CSRN94     UPYRS        COMP 30                52
115 0111 CSR 52                  SETON                  90    YEARS > 30
116 0112 CSRN51                  SETON                  90    DUPLICATE I.D.
117 0113 CSR 90     ERRADD       ADD  1         ERRADD  30    COUNT ERRORS
118 0114 CSRN90     VALADD       ADD  1         VALADD  30    COUNT ADDITIONS
119 0115 CSR                     SETON                  10
120 0116 CSR                     EXCPT                        ADDITION OUTPUT
121 0117 CSR                     SETOF                  10
122 0118 CSR                     ENDSR


125 0120 C*    CHANGE SUBROUTINE
126 0121 C*-------------------
127 0122 CSR           CHANGE    BEGSR
128 0123 CSR                     SETOF                  8653  CLEAR INDIC.
129 0124 CSR 51                  SETON                  13
130 0125 CSR 13                  EXCPT                        PRINT INVALID-
131 0126 CSR                     SETOF                  13    NOT ON FILE
132 0127 CSR 51     ERRCH        ADD  1         ERRCH   30    COUNT ERRORS
133 0128 CSR 51                  GOTO ENDCH                   BYPASS REST OF
134 0129 C*                                                   ROUTINE
135 0130 CSRN96                  MOVE UPSTAT    STATUS        IF NOT BLANK,
136 0131 CSRN96                  EXSR TSTST                   TEST STATUS
```

Figure 11-40 (2)   *continued*

```
HJG11X    09-12-91  19:06:15   HJG11X - PERSONNEL FILE UPDATE        Version 3.5  Page  3

          ....+....1....+....2....+....3....+....4....+....5....+....6....+....7....

137 0132 CSRN95            MOVE UPRANK    GRADE              IF NOT BLANK,
138 0133 CSRN95            EXSR TSTGR                           TEST GRADE
139 0134 CSRN94    UPYRS   COMP 30                      53    TEST VALID
140 0135 CSRN94N53 UPYRS   COMP MAYRS                   53    YEARS
141 0136 CSR 91
142 0137 COR 92                                               INVALID CHANGE
143 0138 COR 53            SETON                        86     REQUEST DATA
144 0139 CSR 86   ERRCH    ADD  1         ERRCH               COUNT ERRORS
145 0140 CSR 86            SETON                        14
146 0141 CSR 14            EXCPT                               CHANGE ERROR
147 0142 CSR              SETOF                         14      OUTPUT
148 0143 CSR 86            GOTO ENDCH                          BYPASS REST OF
149 0144 C*                                                      ROUTINE
150 0145 C*
151 0146 CSR              MOVE MABRAN    BRANCH              TEST BRANCH
152 0147 CSR              EXSR TSTBR
153 0148 CSR              MOVE MASTAT    STATUS              TEST STATUS
154 0149 CSR              EXSR TSTST
155 0150 CSR              MOVE MARANK    GRADE               TEST GRADE
156 0151 CSR              EXSR TSTGR
157 0152 CSR              SETON                         15
158 0153 CSR 15           EXCPT                               PRINT OLD
159 0154 CSR              SETOF                         15      RECORD
160 0155 CSRN96           MOVE UPSTAT    STATUS              IF NOT BLANK,
161 0156 CSRN96           EXSR TSTST                           TEST STATUS
162 0157 CSRN95           MOVE UPRANK    GRADE               IF NOT BLANK,
163 0158 CSRN95           EXSR TSTGR                           TEST GRADE
164 0159 CSR              SETON                         16    PRINT NEW
165 0160 CSR 16           EXCPT                                 RECORD AND
166 0161 CSR              SETOF                         16    CHANGE DISK
167 0162 CSR      VALCH    ADD  1         VALCH 30            COUNT CHANGES
168 0163 CSR      ENDCH    TAG
169 0164 CSR              ENDSR


172 0166 C*    RECORD DELETION SUBROUTINE
173 0167 C*-----------------------------
174 0168 CSR      DELETE   BEGSR
175 0169 CSR              SETOF                       8988    CLEAR INDIC.
176 0170 CSR 51           SETON                         89    NOT ON FILE
177 0171 CSRN51 05        SETON                         89    PREV. DELETED
178 0172 CSRN51 04 UPFST5  COMP MAFST5                 8888    NAME NOT MATCH
179 0173 CSR 88           SETON                         89
180 0174 CSR 89           GOTO NEXT                           BYPASS OF TESTS
181 0175 CSR              MOVE MABRAN    BRANCH               TEST BRANCH
182 0176 CSR              EXSR TSTBR
183 0177 CSR              MOVE MASTAT    STATUS               TEST STATUS
184 0178 CSR              EXSR TSTST
185 0179 CSR              MOVE MARANK    GRADE                TEST GRADE
186 0180 CSR              EXSR TSTGR
187 0181 CSR      NEXT     TAG
188 0182 CSR 89   ERRDEL   ADD  1         ERRDEL 30           COUNT ERRORS
189 0183 CSRN89   VALDEL   ADD  1         VALDEL 30           COUNT DELETES
190 0184 CSR              SETON                         11
191 0185 CSR 11           EXCPT
192 0186 CSR              SETOF                         11
193 0187 CSR              ENDSR


196 0189 C*   INVALID UPDATE CODE SUBROUTINE
197 0190 C*------------------------------------
198 0191 CSR      ERROR    BEGSR
199 0192 CSRN97           MOVE UPBRAN    BRANCH              IF NOT BLANK,
200 0193 CSRN97           EXSR TSTBR                           TEST BRANCH
201 0194 CSRN96           MOVE UPSTAT    STATUS              IF NOT BLANK,
202 0195 CSRN96           EXSR TSTST                           TEST STATUS
203 0196 CSRN95           MOVE UPRANK    GRADE               IF NOT BLANK,
204 0197 CSRN95           EXSR TSTGR                           TEST GRADE
205 0198 CSRN94    UPYRS   COMP 30                      52    YEARS > 30
206 0199 CSR              SETON                         12
207 0200 CSR 12           EXCPT                               ERROR OUTPUT
208 0201 CSR              SETOF                       1252    CLEAR INDIC.
209 0202 CSR      ERROR    ADD  1         ERROR 30            COUNT INVALID
210 0203 CSR              ENDSR
```

Figure 11-40 (3)

```
HJG11X    09-12-91  19:06:15   HJG11X - PERSONNEL FILE UPDATE     Version 3.5  Page  4

         ....+....1....+....2....+....3....+....4....+....5....+....6....+....7....

213 0205 C*   STATUS TEST SUBROUTINE
214 0206 C*-----------------------
215 0207 CSR         TSTST     BEGSR
216 0208 CSR                   SETOF                     92
217 0209 CSR         STATUS    COMP 'A'                       46 ACTIVE
218 0210 CSR 46                MOVEL' ACTIVE' STAOUT 9
219 0211 CSR         STATUS    COMP 'R'                       47 RETIRED
220 0212 CSR 47                MOVEL' RETIRED'STAOUT
221 0213 CSRN46N47             SETON                     92 INVALID
222 0214 CSR 92                MOVEL'-INVALID'STAOUT
223 0215 CSR 92                MOVE '-'      STAOUT
224 0216 CSR                   ENDSR


227 0218 C*   GRADE TEST SUBROUTINE
228 0219 C*-----------------------
229 0220 CSR         TSTGR     BEGSR
230 0221 CSR                   SETOF                     91
231 0222 CSR         GRADE     COMP 'E'                       48 ENLISTED
232 0223 CSR 48                MOVEL'ENLISTED'GRAOUT 9
233 0224 CSR         GRADE     COMP 'O'                       49 OFFICER
234 0225 CSR 49                MOVEL'OFFICER 'GRAOUT
235 0226 CSR 41      GRADE     COMP 'W'                       50 WARRANT
236 0227 CSR 50                MOVEL'WARRANT 'GRAOUT
237 0228 CSRN48N49N50          SETON                     91     INVALID
238 0229 CSR 91                MOVEL'-INVALID'GRAOUT
239 0230 CSR 91                MOVE '-'      GRAOUT
240 0231 CSR                   ENDSR


243 0233 C*   BRANCH TEST SUBROUTINE
244 0234 C*-----------------------
245 0235 CSR         TSTBR     BEGSR
246 0236 CSR                   SETOF                     93
247 0237 CSR         BRANCH    COMP 'A'                       41 ARMY
248 0238 CSR 41                MOVEL'ARMY'   BRAOUT 11
249 0239 CSR         BRANCH    COMP 'N'                       42 NAVY
250 0240 CSR 42                MOVEL'NAVY'   BRAOUT
251 0241 CSR         BRANCH    COMP 'F'                       43 AIR FORCE
252 0242 CSR 43                MOVEL'AIR'    BRAOUT
253 0243 CSR 43                MOVE 'FORCE ' BRAOUT
254 0244 CSR         BRANCH    COMP 'M'                       44 MARINES
255 0245 CSR 44                MOVEL'MARINES'BRAOUT
256 0246 CSR         BRANCH    COMP 'C'                       45 COAST GUARD
257 0247 CSR 45                MOVEL'COAST'. BRAOUT
258 0248 CSR 45                MOVE 'GUARD' BRAOUT
259 0249 CSRN41N42N43
260 0250 CANN44N45             SETON                     93     INVALID
261 0251 CSR 93                MOVEL'--INVALI'BRAOUT
262 0252 CSR 93                MOVE 'D--'    BRAOUT
263 0253 CSR                   ENDSR


264 0254 O*   HEADING LINES
265 0255 O*----------------
266 0256 OPERSREPTH  206  1P
267 0257 O       OR        OF
268 0258 O                           7 'HJG11X'
269 0259 O                          46 'PERSONNEL FILE'
270 0260 O                          55 'UPDATE'
271 0261 O                          80 'PAGE'
272 0262 O                  PAGE     85
273 0263 O       H 1       1P
274 0264 O       OR        OF
275 0265 O                          16 'I.D.'
276 0266 O                          64 'MILITARY    CURRENT'
277 0267 O                          85 'CURRENT  LENGTH OF'
278 0268 O       H 2       1P
279 0269 O       OR        OF
280 0270 O                          17 'ACTION    NUMBER'
281 0271 O                          39 'PERSONNEL NAME'
282 0272 O                          64 'BRANCH    STATUS'
283 0273 O                          84 'GRADE     SERVICE'
```

Figure 11-40 (4)

continued

```
HJG11X    09-12-91  19:06:15   HJG11X - PERSONNEL FILE UPDATE      Version 3.5  Page  5
          ....+....1....+....2....+....3....+....4....+....5....+....6....+....7....


     286 0275 O*    RECORD ADDITION


     287 0276 O*-------------------
     288 0277 O         E  2    10
     289 0278 O                               4 'ADD'
     290 0279 O                    UPID1      12
     291 0280 O                               13 '-'
     292 0281 O                    UPID2      15
     293 0282 O                               16 '-'
     294 0283 O                    UPID3      20
     295 0284 O            N98     UPNAME     42
     296 0285 O             98                33 '---BLANK---'
     297 0286 O            N97     BRAOUT B   55
     298 0287 O             97                55 '---BLANK---'
     299 0288 O            N96     STAOUT B   65
     300 0289 O             96                65 '--BLANK--'
     301 0290 O            N95     GRAOUT B   75
     302 0291 O             95                75 '--BLANK--'
     303 0292 O         N94N52     UPYRS  Z   81
     304 0293 O             94                82 'ZERO'
     305 0294 O             52                84 'INVALID'
     306 0295 O            N51               106 'DUPLICATE I.D.-RECORD'
     307 0296 O            N51               116 'NOT ADDED'
     308 0297 O          90 51               100 'ERROR-NO UPDATE'
     309 0298 O          90 51               110 'PERFORMED'


     312 0300 O*    RECORD DELETION
     313 0301 O*-------------------
     314 0302 O         E  2    11
     315 0303 O                               7 'DELETE'
     316 0304 O                    MAID1      12
     317 0305 O                               13 '-'
     318 0306 O                    MAID2      15
     319 0307 O                               16 '-'
     320 0308 O                    MAID3      20
     321 0309 O            N89     MANAME     42
     322 0310 O            N89     BRAOUT B   55
     323 0311 O            N89     STAOUT B   65
     324 0312 O            N89     GRAOUT B   75
     325 0313 O            N89     MAYRS  Z   81
     326 0314 O             51               108 'INVALID UPDATE-I.D. NOT'
     327 0315 O             51               116 'ON FILE'
     328 0316 O          N51 05              106 'INVALID UPDATE-RECORD'
     329 0317 O          N51 05              125 'PREVIOUSLY DELETED'
     330 0318 O             88               104 'INVALID UPDATE-NAME'
     331 0319 O             88               119 'FIELD MISMATCH'


     334 0321 O*    INVALID UPDATE CODE
     335 0322 O*--------------------
     336 0323 O         E  2    12
     337 0324 O                               6 'ERROR'
     338 0325 O                    UPID1      12
     339 0326 O                               13 '-'
     340 0327 O                    UPID2      15
     341 0328 O                               16 '-'
     342 0329 O                    UPID3      20
     343 0330 O            N98     UPNAME     42
     344 0331 O             98                33 '---BLANK---'
     345 0332 O            N97     BRAOUT B   55
     346 0333 O             97                55 '---BLANK---'
     347 0334 O            N96     STAOUT B   65
     348 0335 O             96                65 '--BLANK--'
     349 0336 O            N95     GRAOUT B   75
     350 0337 O             95                75 '--BLANK--'
     351 0338 O         N94N52     UPYRS  Z   81
     352 0339 O             94                82 'ZERO'
     353 0340 O             52                84 'INVALID'
     354 0341 O                              109 'INVALID UPDATE TYPE CODE'
```

Figure 11-40 (5)

```
HJG11X    09-12-91  19:06:15   HJG11X - PERSONNEL FILE UPDATE      Version 3.5  Page  6

          ....+....1....+....2....+....3....+....4....+....5....+....6....+....7....

357 0343 O*   INVALID CHANGE REQUEST - RECORD NOT ON FILE
358 0344 O*------------------------------------------------
359 0345 O         .  E  2      13
360 0346 O                                             7 'CHANGE'
361 0347 O                          UPID1     12
362 0348 O                                    13 '-'
363 0349 O                          UPID2     15
364 0350 O                                    16 '-'
365 0351 O                          UPID3     20
366 0352 O                                   108 'INVALID UPDATE-I.D. NOT'
367 0353 O                                   116 'ON FILE'


370 0355 O*   INVALID CHANGE REQUEST - ERROR IN NEW DATA
371 0356 O*------------------------------------------------
372 0357 O            E  2      14
373 0358 O                                             7 'CHANGE'
374 0359 O                          UPID1     12
375 0360 O                                    13 '-'
376 0361 O                          UPID2     15
377 0362 O                                    16 '-'
378 0363 O                          UPID3     20
379 0364 O             N96          STAOUT B  65
380 0365 O             N95          GRAOUT B  73
381 0366 O             53                     84 'INVALID'
382 0367 O                                   109 'ERROR-NO UPDATE PERFORME'
383 0368 O                                   110 'D'


386 0370 O*   CHANGE - OLD RECORD
387 0371 O*----------------------
388 0372 O            E  1      15
389 0373 O                                             7 'CHANGE'
390 0374 O                          MAID1     12
391 0375 O                                    13 '-'
392 0376 O                          MAID2     15
393 0377 O                                    16 '-'
394 0378 O                          MAID3     20
395 0379 O                          MANAME    42
396 0380 O                          BRAOUT    55
397 0381 O                          STAOUT    65
398 0382 O                          GRAOUT    75
399 0383 O                          MAYRS  Z  81
400 0384 O                                    95 'OLD RECORD'


403 0386 O*   CHANGE - NEW RECORD
404 0387 O*----------------------
405 0388 O            E  2      16
406 0389 O                          BRAOUT B  55
407 0390 O                          STAOUT B  65
408 0391 O                          GRAOUT B  75
409 0392 O             N94          UPYRS     81
410 0393 O             94           MAYRS     81
411 0394 O                                    95 'NEW RECORD'


414 0396 O*   UPDATE SUMMARY - TOTAL LINES
415 0397 O*------------------------------
416 0398 O         T  106     LR
417 0399 O                                    58 'PERSONNEL FILE UPDATE'
418 0400 O                                    66 'SUMMARY'
419 0401 O         T  2       LR
420 0402 O                          UDATE  Y  55
421 0403 O         T  2       LR
422 0404 O                                    73 'INVALID   INVALID   TOTAL'
423 0405 O         T  2       LR
424 0406 O                                    50 'ADDITION REQUESTS'
425 0407 O                          VALADDZ   56
426 0408 O                          ERRADDZ   64
427 0409 O                          TOTADDZ   72
428 0410 O         T  2       LR
429 0411 O                                    50 'DELETION REQUESTS'
430 0412 O                          VALDELZ   56
431 0413 O                          ERRDELZ   64
432 0414 O                          TOTDELZ   72
```

Figure 11-40 (6)   *continued*

```
HJG11X    09-12-91  19:06:15   HJG11X - PERSONNEL FILE UPDATE    Version 3.5  Page  7

          ....+....1....+....2....+....3....+....4....+....5....+....6....+....7....

433 0415 O        T  2     LR
434 0416 O                                         50 'CHANGE REQUESTS'
435 0417 O                          VALCH Z  56
436 0418 O                          ERRCH Z  64
437 0419 O                          TOTCH Z  72
438 0420 O        T    06  LR
439 0421 O                                         50 'INVALID REQUESTS'
440 0422 O                          ERROR Z  72
443 0424 O*    PERSFILE RECORD ADDITION
444 0425 O*-------------------------
445 0426 OPERSFILEEADD     10N90
446 0427 O                                  1 'A'
447 0428 O                          UPIDNO   10
448 0429 O                          UPNAME   30
449 0430 O                          UPBRAN   31
450 0431 O                          UPSTAT   32
451 0432 O                          UPRANK   33
452 0433 O                          UPYRS    35


455 0435 O*    PERSFILE RECORD DELETION
456 0436 O*-------------------------
457 0437 O        E     11N89
458 0438 O                                  1 'D'


461 0440 O*    PERSFILE RECORD CHANGE
462 0441 O*-------------------------
463 0442 O        E     16
464 0443 O              N98           UPNAME   30
465 0444 O              N96           UPSTAT   32
466 0445 O              N95           UPRANK   33
467 0446 O              N94           UPYRS    35
468 /*
469 /*



          THE FOLLOWING INDICATORS APPEARED IN THIS PROGRAM

          01  02  03  04  05  10  11  12  13  14  15  16  41  42  43  44
          45  46  47  48  49  50  51  52  53  86  88  89  90  91  92  93
          94  95  96  97  98  99  LR  1P  OF
No Warning Errors
No Fatal Errors
```

Figure 11-40 (7)

```
Filename  RecLen      KeyPo  KeyLn                          Date      Time     Page   1
PERSFILE    40          2      9                          09/12/91   15.53

Rec No. Line No. 1... ...10.... ...20.... ...30... ...40.... ...50.... ...60.... ...70.... ...80.... ...90.... ..100

    1    1    A018304839GOODWIN, HAL      FRE06

    2    1    A337214911THALER, RICHARD   ARW20

    3    1    A431587412LEONARD, MARGO     MRE04

    4    1    A481593131MOES, THOMAS       CAE08

    5    1    A526971962HAYES, CAROLYN     NAO06

    6    1    A618792138CARPENTER, JAMES   ARO30

    7    1    D721384290JOHNSON, RAYMOND   FRE06

    8    1    A736438179WILLIAMS, ROBERT   FAE05

    9    1    A751649824RHETT, HERMAN      MRE06
```

PERSFILE
BEFORE PROGRAM EXECUTION

Figure 11-40 (8)

```
Filename  RecLen       KeyPo  KeyLn  KeyP1  KeyL1  KeyP2  KeyL2  KeyP3  KeyL3        Date      Time      Page    1
PERSUPDT   40          NC                                                          09/12/91   15.53

Rec No. Line No. 1... ...10.... ...20.... ...30.... ...40.... ...50.... ...60.... ...70.... ...80.... ...90.... ..100

         1   1   A213445862WHEELER, THOMAS     FAE12

         2   1   D337214911THALER, RICHARD     ARW20

         3   1   C481593131                    RO20

         4   1   A526971962HAYES, CAROLYN      NAO06

         5   1   A614389412                    00

         6   1   A639421318BETTY, LORI         XXX10

         7   1   C658213996                    00

         8   1   D721384290                    00

         9   1   D736438179WHEATON, ROY K.     FAE05

        10   1   C842315967                    DX35

        11   1   X934264153WHEATON, ROY K.     FAE30

                              PERSUPDT
```

Figure 11-40 (9)

```
HJG11X                    PERSONNEL FILE  UPDATE                 PAGE   1

              I.D.                         MILITARY  CURRENT   CURRENT  LENGTH OF
ACTION       NUMBER    PERSONNEL NAME      BRANCH    STATUS    GRADE    SERVICE

ADD       213-44-5862  WHEELER, THOMAS     AIR FORCE  ACTIVE   ENLISTED    12

DELETE    337-21-4911  THALER, RICHARD     ARMY       RETIRED  WARRANT     20

CHANGE    481-59-3131  MOES, THOMAS        COAST GUARD ACTIVE  ENLISTED     8   OLD RECORD
                                           COAST GUARD RETIRED OFFICER     20   NEW RECORD

ADD       526-97-1962  HAYES, CAROLYN      NAVY       ACTIVE   OFFICER      6   DUPLICATE I.D.-RECORD NOT ADDED

ADD       614-38-9412  —BLANK—            —BLANK—  —BLANK—  —BLANK—   ZERO  ERROR-NO UPDATE PERFORMED

ADD       639-42-1318  BETTY, LORI         —INVALID—  -INVALID- -INVALID-   10   ERROR-NO UPDATE PERFORMED

CHANGE    658-21-3996                                                           INVALID UPDATE-I.D. NOT ON FILE

DELETE    721-38-4290                                                           INVALID UPDATE-RECORD PREVIOUSLY DELETED

DELETE    736-43-8179                                                           INVALID UPDATE-NAME FIELD MISMATCH

CHANGE    842-31-5967                                                           INVALID UPDATE-I.D. NOT ON FILE

ERROR     934-26-4153  WHEATON, ROY K.     AIR FORCE  ACTIVE   ENLISTED    30   INVALID UPDATE TYPE CODE
```

Figure 11-40 (10)

```
                    PERSONNEL FILE UPDATE SUMMARY
                           09/12/91

                           INVALID   INVALID   TOTAL

        ADDITION REQUESTS     1         3        4

        DELETION REQUESTS     1         2        3

         CHANGE REQUESTS      1         2        3

        INVALID REQUESTS                         1
```

Figure 11-40 (11)

continued

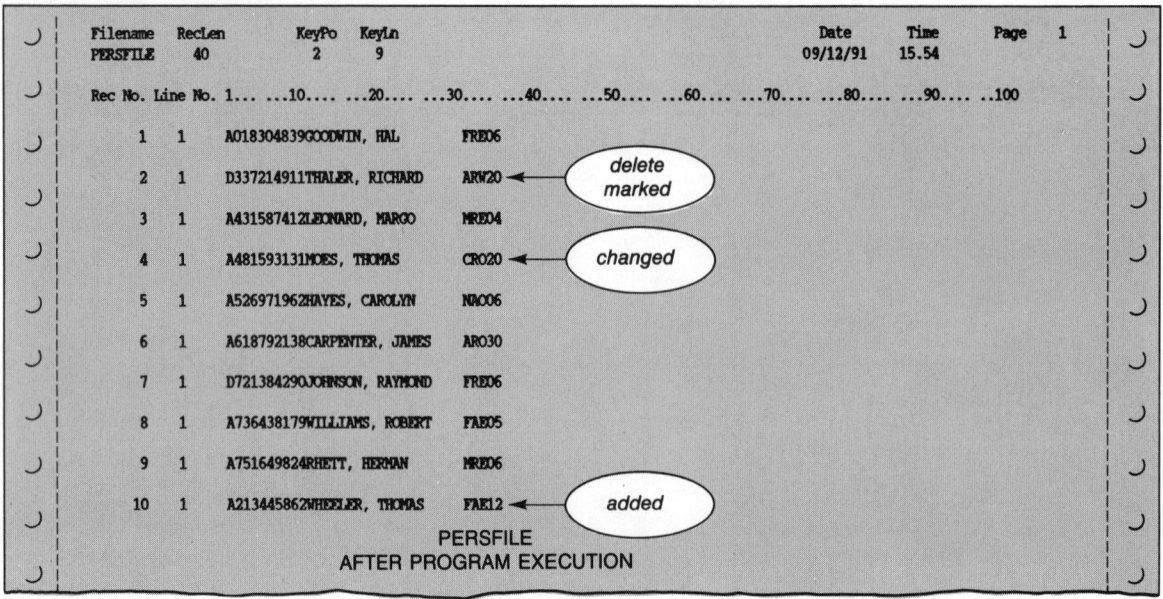

Figure 11-40 (12)

STRUCTURED RPG PROGRAMMING

It has been said that "if carpenters built houses the way that programmers write programs, the first determined termite to come along could destroy civilization." This statement has been made because there have been few standards to guide programmers as they designed and coded programs. Analysts, programmers, and users have viewed every data processing system or program as a unique problem to be solved. Programmers have approached every new project as a never-before-seen problem and have attempted to develop new solutions to each programming problem. All programmers had their special programming techniques that were not to be shared with others.

In recent years, however, attempts have been made to standardize the overall concept of how programs should be developed and the techniques used by programmers in their solutions to problems. The industry has moved away from the individualized approach to what is now called **egoless** programming, an environment in which programmers share techniques and work with standardized methods of problem solution. Structured programming is one such method.

Structured programming is an approach to program design and coding that attempts to make programs easier to understand, code, test, and maintain. A structured program is made up of sequences of operations called structures, and every computer program uses three basic structures: sequential, if-then-else, and do-while or do-until.

The Sequential Structure

The sequential structure (Figure 11-41) performs a series of operations, one after the other, in a top-down sequence. Almost all the programs you have reviewed and written so far have used sequential structure in the calculations.

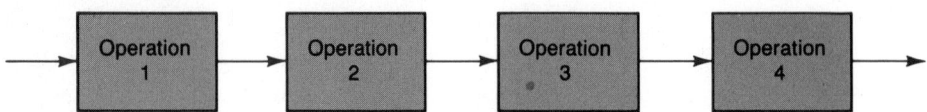

Figure 11-41   Sequential processing structure

The If-Then-Else Structure

The if-then-else structure is comprised of a test and two possible operations that are to be performed on the basis of the result of the test. Consider the following statement and Figure 11-42:

IF the weather forecast is rain,
THEN I will carry my umbrella;
ELSE, I will leave it at home.

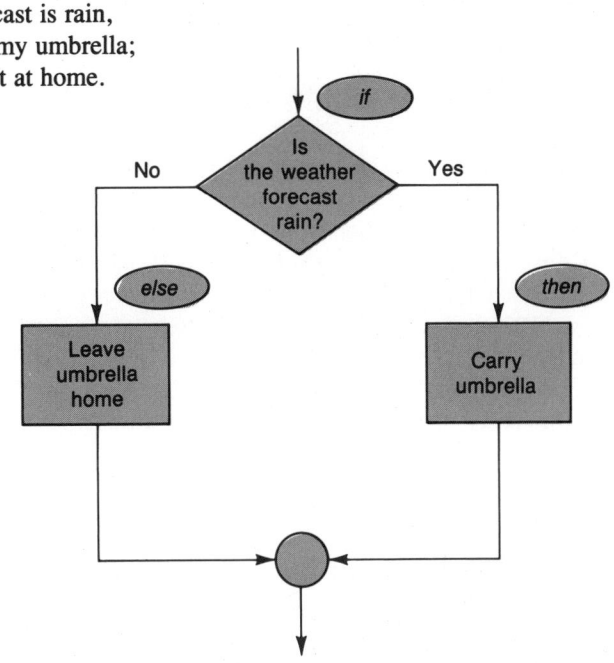

Figure 11-42   IF-then-else processing structure

Note that only one of the possible results of the test can be performed. You can either carry your umbrella or leave it at home. You cannot do both.

Figure 11-43 shows a series of RPG calculations. The COMP operation on line 01 either does or does not turn indicator 22 on. Based on the setting of indicator 22, either lines 02–05, or lines 06–09 are performed.

IF indicator 22 is on,
THEN perform lines 02–05;
ELSE perform lines 06–09.

Line	Form Type	Control Level (L0-L9, LR, SR, AN/OR)	Indicators And			And			Factor 1	Operation	Factor 2	Result Field Name	Length	Decimal Positions	Half Adjust (H)	Resulting Indicators		Comments
0 1	C		Ø1						AMOUNT	COMP	LIMIT					22		IF IND 22 ON:
0 2	C		22							ADD	1	EXCCNT						THEN EXECUTE
0 3	C		22						AMOUNT	SUB	LIMIT	EXCESS						LINES Ø2
0 4	C		22							ADD	EXCESS	TOTEXC						THROUGH Ø5
0 5	C		22							EXSR	OVER							
0 6	C		N22							ADD	1	VALCNT						ELSE EXECUTE
0 7	C		N22							ADD	AMOUNT	TOTAL						LINES Ø6
0 8	C		N22							EXCPT								THROUGH Ø9
0 9	C		N22							EXSR	VALID							
1 0	C																	

Figure 11-43   IF-then-else calculations

The Do-While or Do-Until Structure

When these structures are used, a series of operations is performed repeatedly until some condition causes the repetition to stop. This explanation may sound familiar. It should. In Chapter 9 a definition very similar to this was the definition of a loop. The do-while or do-until structure is the basis for looping techniques and operations.

RPG STRUCTURED PROGRAMMING OPERATIONS

Newer versions of the RPG language contain several operations designed to be used with structured programming techniques. These operations are not standard. Depending on the version of RPG you are using, you may be able to use all, some, or none of these operations. As a general rule, all structured operations are found in RPG III and RPG/400, most of them are available in versions of RPG II that are based on IBM System/36 RPG II Release 5.1 or later, and none of them are available in the original RPG language. If you are using an earlier version of RPG II, consult your instructor or data center manager to determine which of these operations are available on your system. All of the structured operation codes enable you to minimize the number of RPG specifications needed to perform certain functions. In addition, these operations enable you to use fewer indicators in a program and, by eliminating many indicator entries, make the RPG program code easier to read and understand.

The DO Operation

The DO operation performs a series of RPG operations a specified number of times. In its simplest form, the DO operation causes a series of calculations to be executed once without the need for controlling indicators on each calculation that is to be performed.

Figure 11-44 shows two sets of similar calculations. The top set is controlled by indicator 25, which is the resulting indicator of the COMP operation. If indicator 25 is on after the COMP, it conditions each of the calculations that follow and they will execute. If indicator 25 is not on, none of the following operations is performed. The second set of calculations in the figure uses the DO operation to control the calculations. Like the first example, this starts with a COMP operation that may turn on indicator 25. If indicator 25 is on, the DO operation is executed. The DO operation controls the execution of all operations located between the DO and the END operation that marks the end of the range of the DO operation. If indicator 25 is on, every operation between the DO and the END is executed. If indicator 25 is not on, none of these operations is executed.

The DO operation can also be used to control a loop (Figure 11-45). This format of the DO operation generates all the necessary components to control a loop: the control variable, the increment, and the test. Example One in the figure causes the series of operations between the DO and the END to be executed 10 times. The number of times the operations are performed is controlled by the number entered in the Factor 2 area of the DO operation. In this example, RPG generates an internal variable to control the loop and automatically increments the control variable by 1 every time the series of operations is executed.

Example Two in Figure 11-45 shows the same logic. However, a field name has been defined in the Result Field area of the DO operation. This field (X) is used as the control variable and also is available for use in the loop. Example Three also uses a control variable and in addition specifies a starting value and increment value to be used as the DO loop is processed. Factor 1 of the DO operation contains the starting value to be placed in X when the DO begins to execute. The value in Factor 2 of the END statement is the value by which the variable is to be incremented every time the loop executes. In this example, the variable field X starts with a value of 100 and is incremented by 2 every time the loop executes. Execution of the loop ends when X reaches a value of 250.

Two variations of the DO operation can be used to control the execution of a loop a variable number of times based on a specific condition, instead of a fixed number of times. These are the DOWxx (do-while) operation and the DOUxx (do-until) operation.

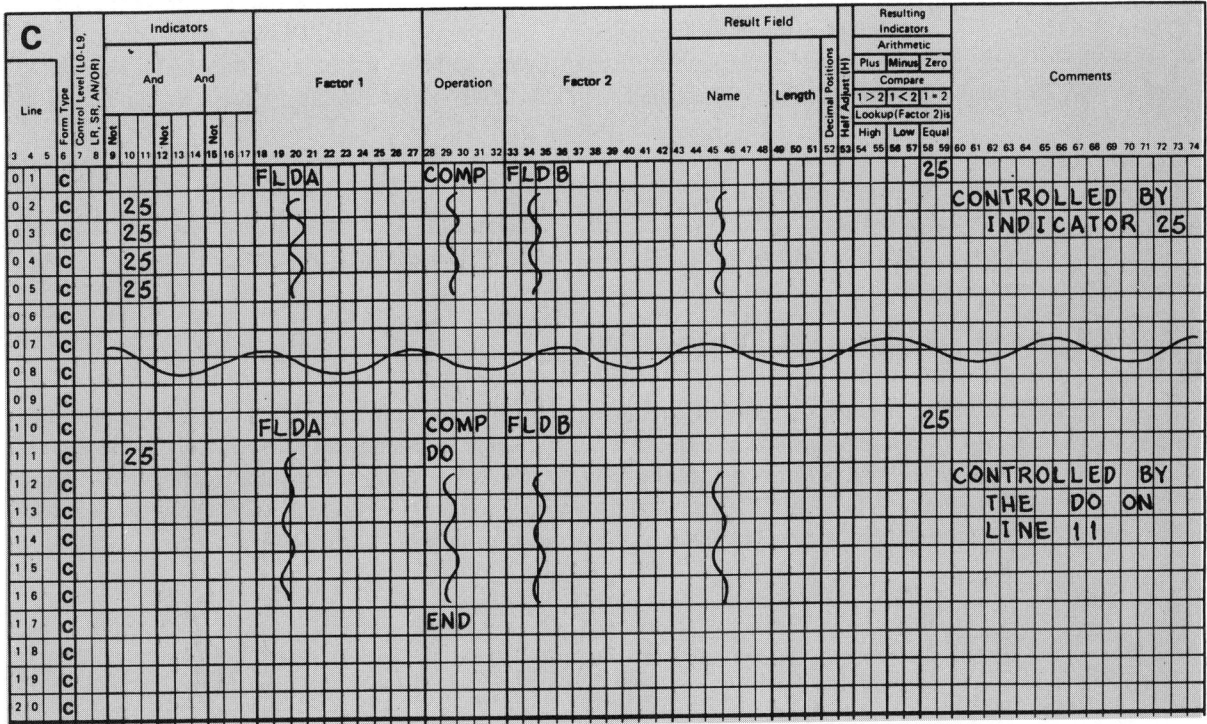

Figure 11-44   The DO operation

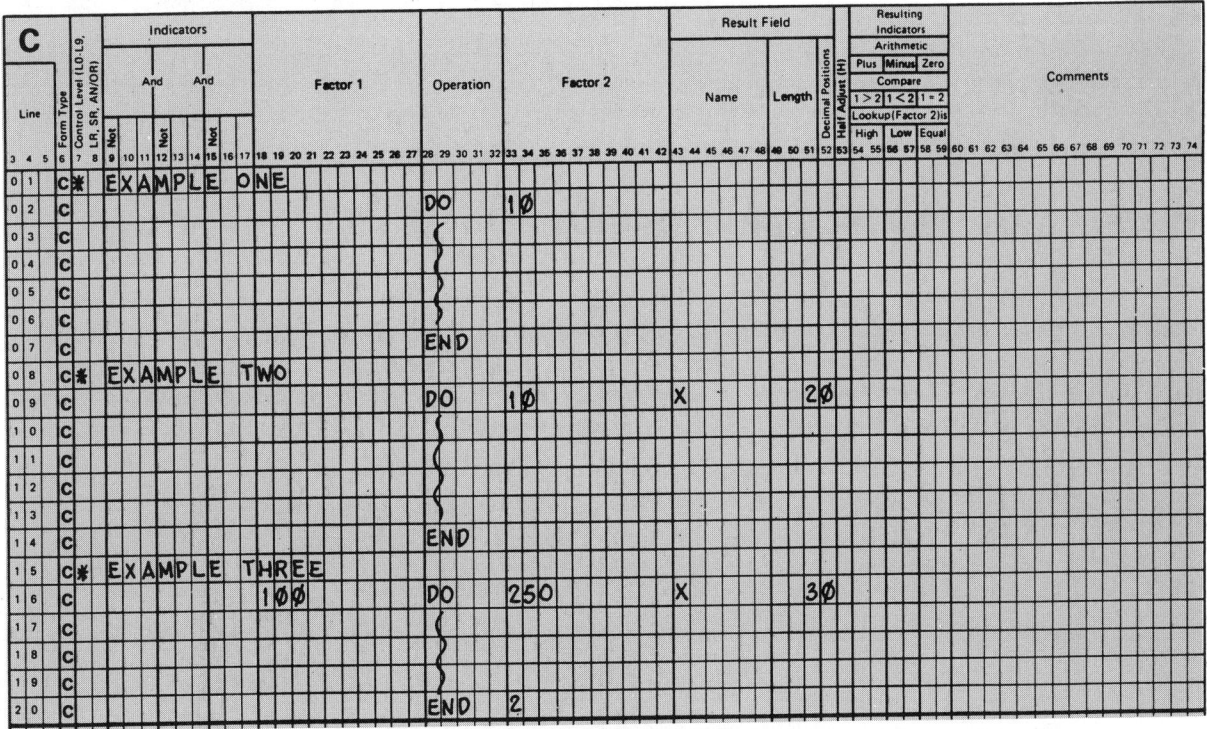

Figure 11-45   DO operation loop control

Note that the operation names end in xx, which represent two characters that are used with DOU and DOW to specify the exact conditions that control the operation. Both the DOUxx and DOWxx operations are controlled by the relationship between the fields specified in the Factor 1 and Factor 2 areas of the operations. The xx specifies the exact relationship being tested. When the DOUxx and DOWxx operations are used, xx can be any of the following:

GT	Factor 1 is greater than Factor 2	NE	Factor 1 is not equal to Factor 2
LT	Factor 1 is less than Factor 2	GE	Factor 1 is greater than or equal to Factor 2
EQ	Factor 1 is equal to Factor 2	LE	Factor 1 is less than or equal to Factor 2

DOUxx, The Do-Until Operation

The DOUxx operation causes a series of operations to be executed until a specified condition is met. The condition can be any of the six relationships just listed. Figure 11-46 is an example of a DOUxx operation that causes the EXCPT operation to be performed until the value in COUNT is equal to the value in NOPACK. If this looks familiar, refer to Figure 9-11. This DOUEQ loop does the same job. Note that the DOU operation automatically performs the incrementation, testing, branching, and termination portions of the loop.

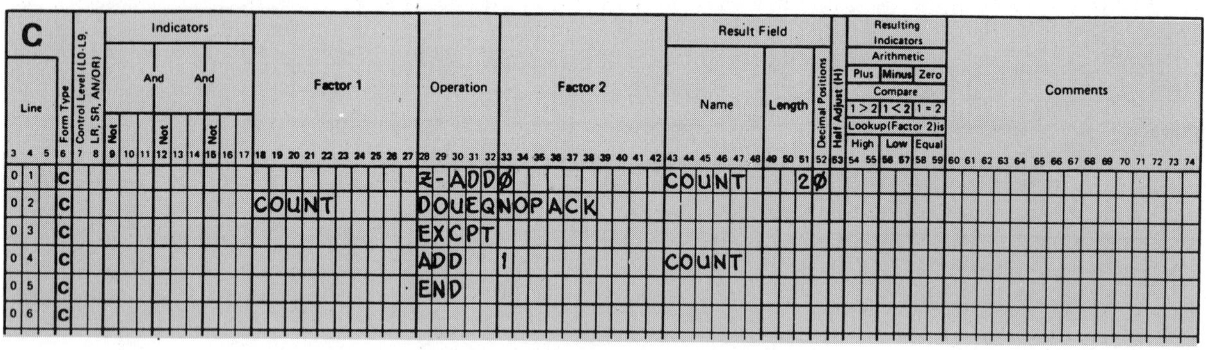

Figure 11-46   DOUxx processing

DOWxx, The Do-While Operation

The DOW operation is similar to the DOU operation. The main difference is that whereas the DOU operation performs a loop until a condition is met, the DOW operation performs a loop while, or as long as, a condition is met (Figure 11-47). Although this example uses the DOWLT operation, any of the six relationships can be used. In this example, the series of operations between the DOWLT and the END operation are executed repeatedly as long as FIELDA is less than FIELDB. The loop stops when FIELDA is no longer less than FIELDB.

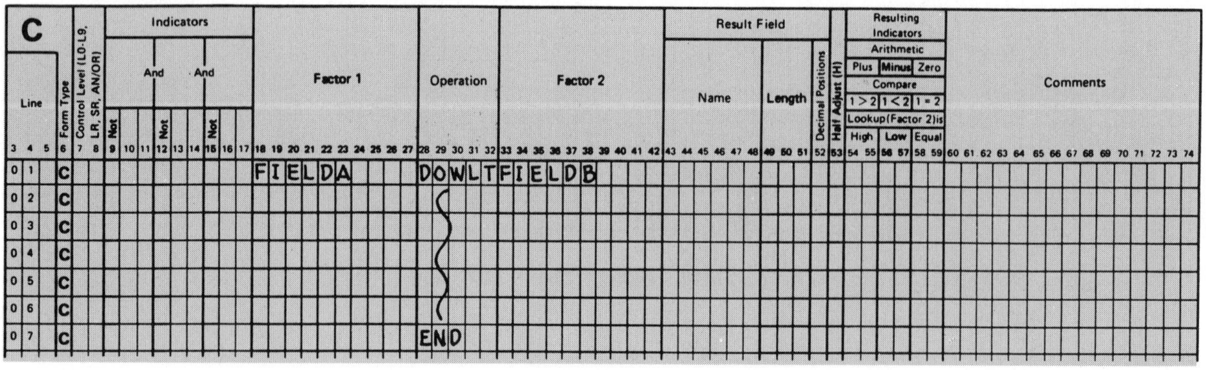

Figure 11-47   DOWxx processing

Figure 11-48 summarizes the three options of the DO operation.

DO Operation Summary

The DO operation causes a series of operations to be performed a fixed number of times. The associated END statement marks the end of the series. Factor 2 specifies the number of times the group is performed. If Factor 2 is blank, the group is executed one time. The Result Field can be used to specify the name of a numeric index field. If no name is used, the DO operation generates an internal index. Factor 1, if used, specifies a starting index value. If Factor 1 is not used, the starting value is 1. Factor 2 of the associated END statement can be used to specify an increment value to be used with the index. If no entry is made, the increment is 1.

Control Level Indicators	Indicators	Factor 1	Operation Name	Factor 2	Result Field	Resulting Indicators		
7–8	9–17	18–27	28–32	33–42	43–53	54–55	56–57	58–59
optional	optional	optional	DO	optional	optional	blank	blank	blank

DOWxx Operation Summary

The DOWxx operation causes a series of operations to be performed one or more times. The associated END statement marks the end of the series. The series of operations will be repeated until the relationship between the Factor 1 and Factor 2 entries specified in the xx positions of the DOWxx operation code is met. After the condition is no longer met, the program will continue with the operation that follows the END statement.

Control Level Indicators	Indicators	Factor 1	Operation Name	Factor 2	Result Field	Resulting Indicators		
7–8	9–17	18–27	28–32	33–42	43–53	54–55	56–57	58–59
optional	optional	required	DOWxx	required	blank	blank	blank	blank

Figure 11-48   DO operation summaries   *continued*

DOUxx Operation Summary

The DOUxx operation causes a series of operations to be performed one or more times. The associated END statement marks the end of the series. The series of operations will be repeated until the relationship between the Factor 1 and Factor 2 entries specified in the xx positions of the DOUxx operation code is met. After the condition is no longer met, the program will continue with the operation that follows the END statement.

Control Level Indicators	Indicators	Factor 1	Operation Name	Factor 2	Result Field	Resulting Indicators		
7–8	9–17	18–27	28–32	33–42	43–53	54–55	56–57	58–59
optional	optional	required	DOUxx	required	blank	blank	blank	blank

END Operation Summary

The END statement marks the end of a CASxx, DO, DOUxx, DOWxx, or IFxx group of operations. The Factor 2 entry can be used only if the END terminates a DO group. In this circumstance, Factor 2 contains the increment value to be applied to the DO group index.

Control Level Indicators	Indicators	Factor 1	Operation Name	Factor 2	Result Field	Resulting Indicators		
7–8	9–17	18–27	28–32	33–42	43–53	54–55	56–57	58–59
optional	optional	blank	END	optional	blank	blank	blank	blank

Figure 11-48   (continued)

IFxx, The IF-Then-Else Operation

The IFxx operation enables you to perform a series of calculations if a specific relationship exists between the Factor 1 and Factor 2 fields specified in the IFxx operation. You can also specify that a second series of calculations is to be performed if the relationship does not exist. Figure 11-49 shows the traditional method of controlling two groups of calculations on the basis of the result of a COMP operation. In this example, if FIELDA is equal to FIELDB, lines 02–06 are executed. If FIELDA is not equal to FIELDB, lines 07–10 are executed.

Line	Form Type	Control Level	Not	Indicators And	Not	And	Not	Factor 1	Operation	Factor 2	Result Field Name	Length	Dec Pos	Half Adj	Resulting Indicators Compare 1>2	1<2	1=2	Comments
0 1	C							FIELDA	COMP	FIELDB							35	
0 2	C		35						EXSR	EQUAL								IF EQUAL
0 3	C		35						EXSR	BIC23								
0 4	C		35						ADD	FIELDA	TOTALA							
0 5	C		35						ADD	FIELDB	TOTALB							
0 6	C		35						EXCPT	LINEEQ								
0 7	C		N35						EXSR	NOTEQL								IF NOT EQUAL
0 8	C		N35						EXSR	C2431								
0 9	C		N35						ADD	FIELDA	TOTALC							
1 0	C		N35						EXCPT	LINUNE								
1 1	C																	

Figure 11-49   RPG calculations

The same series of operations controlled by an IFxx operation is shown in Figure 11-50. If FIELDA is equal to FIELDB the five operations following the IFEQ operation are executed. The ELSE operation on line 07 specifies the beginning of the operations to be performed if the condition tested for by the IFxx operation is not found. Every IFxx statement must be ended by an END statement that marks the end of the range of execution of the IFxx. If you are familiar with COBOL you have noticed that the IFxx statement functions in a manner quite similar to the IF statement in COBOL.

Line	Form Type	Control Level	Not	Indicators And	Not	And	Not	Factor 1	Operation	Factor 2	Result Field Name	Length	Dec Pos	Half Adj	Resulting Indicators	Comments
0 1	C							FIELDA	IFEQ	FIELDB						
0 2	C								EXSR	EQUAL						IF EQUAL
0 3	C								EXSR	BIC23						
0 4	C								ADD	FIELDA	TOTALA					
0 5	C								ADD	FIELDB	TOTALB					
0 6	C								EXCPT	LINEEQ						
0 7	C								ELSE							
0 8	C								EXSR	NOTEQL						IF NOT EQUAL
0 9	C								EXSR	C2431						
1 0	C								ADD	FIELDA	TOTALC					
1 1	C								EXCPT	LINUNE						
1 2	C								END							

Figure 11-50   If-else processing

Figure 11-51 on the next page shows a simple IFxx statement that specifies a series of operations to be performed if the tested condition exists. If FIELDD is less than FIELDE, the operations that follow the IFxx statement are executed. If FIELDD is not less than FIELDE, the program proceeds directly to the operation that follows the END statement. Note that when the IFxx operation is used, any of the six test conditions (GT, LT, EQ, NE, GE, and LE) that were used with the DO operations can be used with the IFxx operation. The IFxx and ELSE operations are summarized in Figure 11-52 (also on the next page).

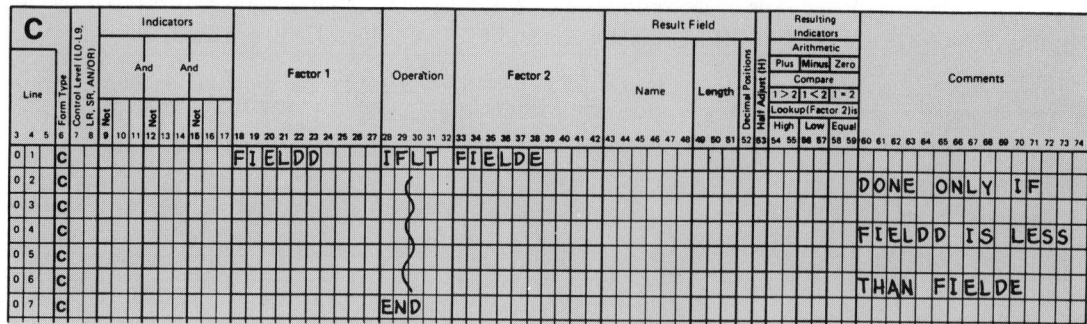

Figure 11-51   IFxx processing

IFxx Operation Summary

The IFxx operation enables a series of operations to be performed if the condition specified in the xx portion of the operation exists between the Factor 1 and Factor 2 entries. If the condition exists, all operations between the IFxx and the following ELSE or END statement will be performed. If the condition does not exist, the program will proceed to the operation following the associated ELSE or END.

Control Level Indicators	Indicators	Factor 1	Operation Name	Factor 2	Result Field	Resulting Indicators		
7–8	9–17	18–27	28–32	33–42	43–53	54–55	56–57	58–59
optional	optional	required	IFxx	required	blank	blank	blank	blank

---

ELSE Operation Summary

The ELSE operation may be used with the IFxx operation. If used, ELSE marks the beginning of the group of operations to be performed if the condition tested by the IFxx operation is not found. Control level indicators may be specified if the ELSE operation is part of a total time IFxx operation. The control level indicators, if used, are for documentation only and do not affect the program.

Control Level Indicators	Indicators	Factor 1	Operation Name	Factor 2	Result Field	Resulting Indicators		
7–8	9–17	18–27	28–32	33–42	43–53	54–55	56–57	58–59
optional	blank	blank	ELSE	blank	blank	blank	blank	blank

Figure 11-52   IFxx operation summary and ELSE operation summary

CABxx, The Compare-and-Branch Operation

The CABxx operation combines a COMP and a GOTO into a single operation that enables you to perform a test and, if the test condition is found, branch to another point in the program. The CABxx operation compares the Factor 1 and Factor 2 fields. If the relationship specified in the xx portion of the operation code is found, the program branches to the TAG named in the Result Field area. The usual rules for both the COMP and the GOTO operations apply to the CABxx operation. This operation is not part of RPG or RPG II and is currently found only in RPG III and RPG/400. Figure 11-53 summarizes the CABxx operation.

CABxx Operation Summary

The CABxx operation compares the value in Factor 1 with the value in Factor 2, testing for the condition specified in the xx position of the operation code. If the tested condition is found, the program branches to the TAG statement specified in the Result Field area. If the condition is not found, the program continues with the next operation. Resulting indicators may be specified. If no Result Field entry is made, the CABxx operation will set resulting indicators and continue with the next operation.

Control Level Indicators	Indicators	Factor 1	Operation Name	Factor 2	Result Field	Resulting Indicators		
7–8	9–17	18–27	28–32	33–42	43–53	54–55	56–57	58–59
optional	optional	required	CABxx	required	optional	optional	optional	optional

Figure 11-53 CABxx operation summary

CASxx, The Compare-and-Execute Subroutine Operation

The CASxx (pronounced "case") operation is similar to the CABxx operation in that it performs a test and then, if the test conditions are met, causes the sequence of operations in the program to be changed. The difference is that the CASxx operation does not cause a GOTO to be executed but causes an EXSR to be executed, performing a subroutine. After the subroutine is executed, the program automatically returns to the point that follows the CASxx operation. Figure 11-54 on the next page shows how program HJG11X could have been coded using the CASxx operation.

As you can see from these portions of the program, the record identification code testing has been eliminated and the TYPE field has been defined in position 1. The calculations, instead of a series of EXSR operations based on different indicators, begin with a series of CASxx operations. Calculation line 01 compares TYPE with A. If TYPE is equal to A, the ADD subroutine specified in the Result Field area is executed. After the ADD subroutine is executed, the program returns to the operation that follows the END statement on line 05. The CASxx does not return control to the statement that follows the CAS operation that executed the subroutine but to the statement after the END of the CAS group of instructions.

```
01   IPERSUPDTAA  01
02   I                                        1   1 TYPE
03   I
04   I
05   I
```

```
01   C           01        TYPE      CASEQ'A'       ADD
02   C           01        TYPE      CASEQ'D'       DELETE
03   C           01        TYPE      CASEQ'C'       CHANGE
04   C           01                  CAS            ERROR
05   C                               END
```

Figure 11-54 Use of the CASxx operation

If the CASEQ on line 01 is not executed, the CASxx on line 02 is performed. If TYPE is equal to D, the DELETE subroutine is executed. If one of the three subroutines tested on lines 01, 02, and 03 is not executed, the program executes the simple CAS operation on line 04 and performs the ERROR subroutine. Figure 11-55 summarizes the CASxx operation.

CASxx Operation Summary

The CASxx operation compares the value in Factor 1 with the value in Factor 2, testing for the condition specified in the xx position of the operation code. If the tested condition is found, the program executes the subroutine named in the Result Field area. A CAS operation with no condition specified as part of the operation is equivalent to an EXSR operation. Resulting indicators may be specified as part of a CASxx operation.

Control Level Indicators	Indicators	Factor 1	Operation Name	Factor 2	Result Field	Resulting Indicators		
7–8	9–17	18–27	28–32	33–42	43–53	54–55	56–57	58–59
optional	optional	optional	CASxx	optional	required	optional	optional	optional

Figure 11-55 CASxx operation summary

≡ IN CONCLUSION ≡

This chapter has shown you how to update a keyed file and has introduced the concept of structured RPG coding and several structured operation codes. Chapter 12 is a two-part chapter about the design and usage of interactive programs. The first part will introduce the concepts of terminal screen panel design that can be applied to any computer system or application. The second part will introduce the IBM System/36 Screen Design Aid utility and will demonstrate the techniques of designing and coding a program that uses terminal input to load records to a data file.

CHAPTER SUMMARY

1. A **static** data file is a file in which the data records are subject to only a minimal amount of change.
2. A **dynamic** data file is one in which the data records require frequent change.
3. **Updating** is the process of changing the contents of a data file. The three common types of file update operations are record addition, record deletion, and record change.
4. The **record addition** update operation adds new records to an existing data file.
5. The **record deletion** update operation does not actually remove a record from a data file. Instead, this operation places a specific code, called a **delete code**, into the record. This operation is called **logical deletion**.
6. The actual removal of a delete-marked record from a file takes place when the data file is reorganized.
7. The **record change** operation alters the contents of one or more data fields in an existing record. The contents of the record key field cannot be changed.
8. The **update request code** specifies the type of update operation to be performed on a file.
9. When **record identification code testing** is used to determine the input record type, every possible record type, including invalid records, must be specified in the record identification testing.
10. When record identification code testing is used in a program, the program halts if an unspecified record type is read.
11. A **program module** is a series of instructions that are treated as a single unit by the program.
12. A **work field** is a field defined for the temporary storage of data within a program.
13. When a change is being made to a disk file, RPG writes the output data to the last record read by the program. Every output operation to a keyed file that does not add a new record to the file must be preceded by a CHAIN operation.
14. **Structured programming** is a method of designing and coding programs so as to make them easier to test and maintain.
15. The three basic structures in a program are the **sequential, if-then-else,** and **do-while or do-until** structures.
16. Newer versions of RPG II, as well as RPG III and RPG/400, support several **structured operations** that are designed to enable RPG programmers to program in a structured manner.
17. Most RPG structured operations incorporate one of six tests into the operation code: the GT, LT, EQ, NE, GE, and LE tests.
18. The **DO, DOUxx,** and **DOWxx** operations are used to control looping in a structured programming environment.
19. The **IFxx** operation allows either of two different sets of operations to be performed, based on the result of the comparison that is part of the IFxx operation.
20. The **CABxx** operation, which is not available in RPG II, combines the functions of the COMP and GOTO operations into a single operation.
21. The **CASxx** operation combines the functions of the COMP and EXSR operations into a single operation.

REVIEW QUESTIONS

1. What is the difference between a static data file and a dynamic data file?
2. What are the three types of file update operations? Explain the function of each.
3. What is the difference between the logical deletion of a record from a data file and the physical deletion of a record from a data file?
4. Why must a test be made for an invalid record type when record identification code testing is performed in a program?
5. What is a program module? Must all program modules be defined as subroutines?
6. What is a work field?
7. Why must an output operation to a disk file, other than a record addition operation, be preceded by a CHAIN operation that reads the file?
8. What is structured programming?
9. What are the six tests, symbolized by the characters xx, that may appear in structured operation codes? Explain each of the tests.
10. What is the difference between a DOUxx and a DOWxx operation?
11. What is the difference between the CASxx and CABxx operations?

STUDENT EXERCISES: RPG PROGRAM CODE

1. On the Input Specification form in Figure 11-56, code the following record identification code tests for an input file named WARBIRDS:

   If an input record contains the letter B in position 7, turn on indicator 01. If an input record contains the letter O in position 7, turn on indicator 02. If an input record contains the letter C in position 7, turn on indicator 03. If an input record contains either the letter P or the letter F in position 7, turn on indicator 04. If position 7 contains any other character, turn on indicator 99.

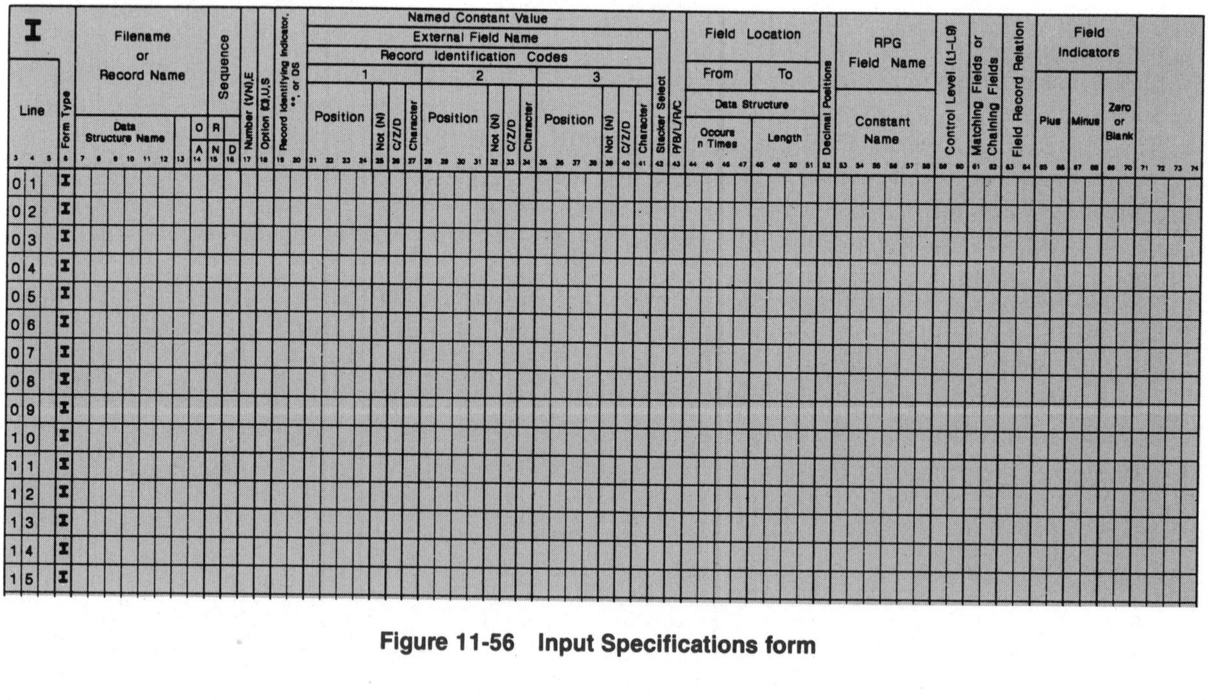

Figure 11-56   Input Specifications form

2. On the Calculation Specifications form in Figure 11-57, using the DO operation, code the necessary instructions to add all the even numbers (2, 4, 6, etc.) between 0 and 100 to a counter named SUMM.

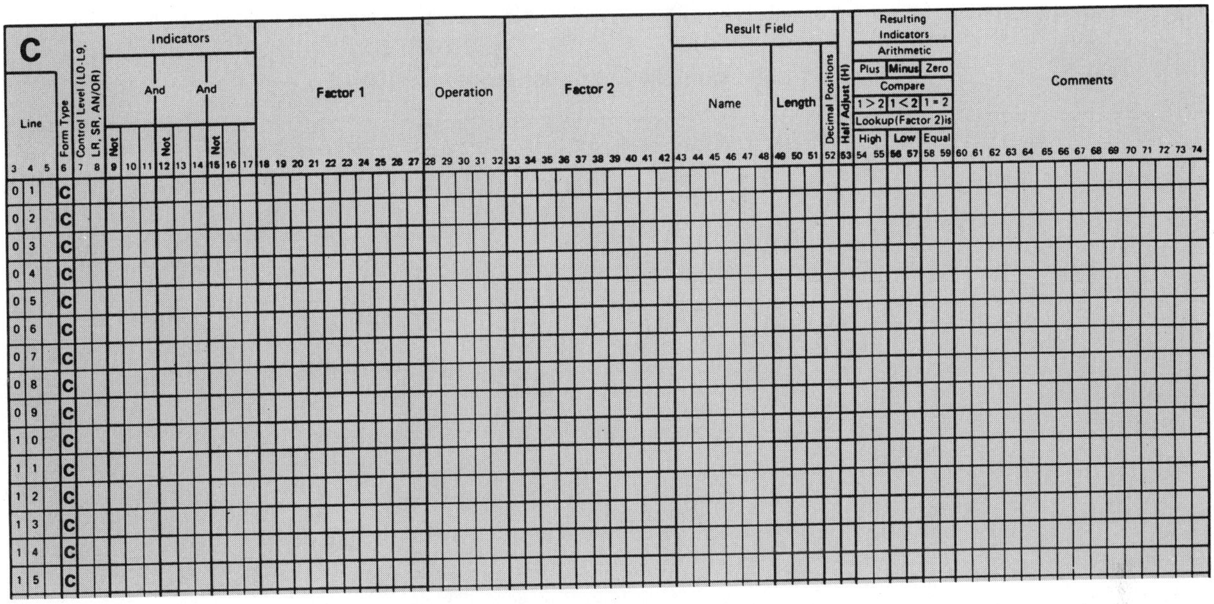

Figure 11-57   Calculation Specifications form

3. On the Calculation Specifications form in Figure 11-58, code a series of instructions, using the IFxx operation, to perform the following:

If the data contained in FIELDX is not greater than the data stored in FIELDZ, add 1 to LCOUNT and add FIELDX to TOTALX. If the data contained in FIELDX is greater than the data stored in FIELDZ, add 1 to HCOUNT and add FIELDZ to TOTALZ.

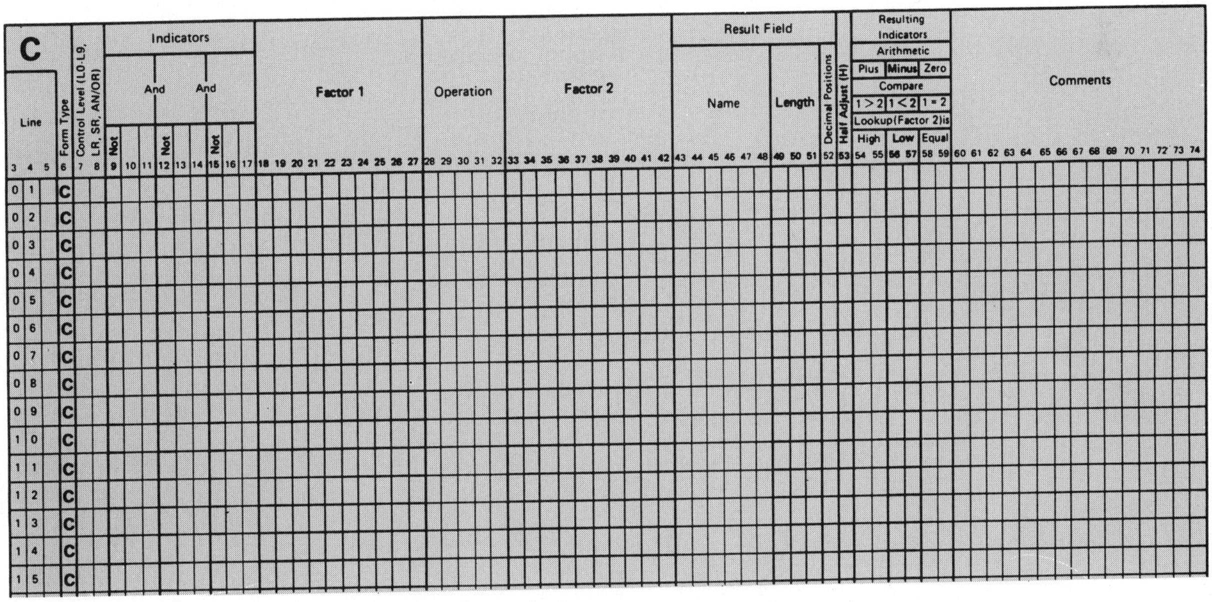

Figure 11-58   Calculation Specifications form

STUDENT EXERCISES: RPG PROGRAM MAINTENANCE

The completed compile listing for program HJG11X, Personnel File Update, appears in Figure 11-59.

Figure 11-59   Compile listing for program HJG11X

```
     HJG11X    09-12-91  19:06:15   HJG11X - PERSONNEL FILE UPDATE        Version 3.5  Page  1

               ....+....1....+....2....+....3....+....4....+....5....+....6....+....7....

       3 0002 H                                                                       HJG11X


       4 0003 FPERSUPDTIP  F 240  40            DISK
       5 0004 FPERSFILEUC  F  40  40R 9AI      2 DISK                         A
       6 0005 FPERSREPTO   F 132 132    OF      PRINTER

       9 0007 F*-----------------------------------------------------------------
      10 0008 F* ID F   C   H   L     FUNCTION OF INDICATORS
      11 0009 F* 01 -   -   -   -  UPDATE REQUEST - RECORD ADDITION
      12 0010 F* 02 -   -   -   -  UPDATE REQUEST - RECORD DELETION
      13 0011 F* 03 -   -   -   -  UPDATE REQUEST - RECORD CHANGE
      14 0012 F* 04 -   -   -   -  ACTIVE PERSFILE RECORD
      15 0013 F* 05 -   -   -   -  DELETED PERSFILE RECORD
      16 0014 F*         10 -   -   -  EXCPT CONTROL - RECORD ADDITION
      17 0015 F*         11 -   -   -  EXCPT CONTROL - RECORD DELETION
      18 0016 F*         12 -   -   -  EXCPT CONTROL - INVALID UPDATE CODE
      19 0017 F*         13 -   -   -  EXCPT CONTROL - CHANGE ERROR
      20 0018 F*         14 -   -   -  EXCPT CONTROL - CHANGE ERROR
      21 0019 F*         15 -   -   -  EXCPT CONTROL - RECORD CHANGE - OLD
      22 0020 F*         16 -   -   -  EXCPT CONTROL - RECORD CHANGE - NEW
      23 0021 F*         41 -   -   -  BRANCH = ARMY
      24 0022 F*         42 -   -   -  BRANCH = NAVY
      25 0023 F*         43 -   -   -  BRANCH = AIR FORCE
      26 0024 F*.        44 -   -   -  BRANCH = MARINES
      27 0025 F*         45 -   -   -  BRANCH = COAST GUARD
      28 0026 F*         46 -   -   -  STATUS = ACTIVE
      29 0027 F*         47 -   -   -  STATUS = RETIRED
      30 0028 F*         48 -   -   -  GRADE = ENLISTED
      31 0029 F*         49 -   -   -  GRADE = OFFICER
      32 0030 F*         50 -   -   -  GRADE = WARRANT
      33 0031 F*         51 -   -   -  CHAINED RECORD NOT ON PERSFILE
      34 0032 F*         52 -   -   -  UPYRS > 30 - RECORD ADDITION
      35 0033 F*         53 -   -   -  UPYRS > 30 - RECORD CHANGE
      36 0034 F*         86 -   -   -  CHANGE REQUEST DATA ERROR
      37 0035 F*         88 -   -   -  DELETE REQUEST - NAME MISMATCH
      38 0036 F*         89 -   -   -  INVALID DELETE REQUEST - NOT ON FILE
      39 0037 F*         90 -   -   -  RECORD ADDITION - BLANK/INVALID DATA FIELD
      40 0038 F*         91 -   -   -  INVALID GRADE CODE
      41 0039 F*         92 -   -   -  INVALID STATUS CODE
      42 0040 F*         93 -   -   -  INVALID BRANCH CODE
      43 0041 F*     94 -   -   -  BLANK UPYRS FIELD
      44 0042 F*     95 -   -   -  BLANK UPRANK FIELD
      45 0043 F*     96 -   -   -  BLANK UPSTAT FIELD
      46 0044 F*     97 -   -   -  BLANK UPBRAN FIELD
      47 0045 F*     98 -   -   -  BLANK UPNAME FIELD
      48 0046 F* 99 -   -   -   -  INVALID UPDATE REQUEST CODE
      49 0047 F*           1P - FIRST PAGE INDICATOR
      50 0048 F*           OF - OVERFLOW INDICATOR
      51 0049 F*           LR - LAST RECORD INDICATOR

      52 0050 I*  UPDATE FILE DESCRIPTION
      53 0051 I*-----------------------
      54 0052 IPERSUPDTAA  01   1 CA
      55 0053 I         OR  02   1 CD
      56 0054 I         OR  03   1 CC
      57 0055 I         OR  99   1NCA     1NCD     1NCC
      58 0056 I                                   2  10 UPIDNO
      59 0057 I                                   2   4 UPID1
      60 0058 I                                   5   6 UPID2
      61 0059 I                                   7  10 UPID3
      62 0060 I                                  11  30 UPNAME    98
      63 0061 I                                  31  31 UPBRAN    97
      64 0062 I                                  32  32 UPSTAT    96
```

Figure 11-59 (1)

```
HJG11X    09-12-91  19:06:15   HJG11X - PERSONNEL FILE UPDATE     Version 3.5  Page  2
          ....+....1....+....2....+....3....+....4....+....5....+....6....+....7....

  65 0063 I                                        33  33 UPRANK          95
  66 0064 I                                        34  350UPYRS          94
  67 0065 I                                        11  15 UPFST5      02


  70 0067 I*   PERSONNEL FILE DESCRIPTION
  71 0068 I*---------------------------
  72 0069 IPERSFILEBB  04   1 CA
  73 0070 I         OR  05   1 CD
  74 0071 I                                         2  10 MAIDNO
  75 0072 I                                         2   4 MAID1
  76 0073 I                                         5   6 MAID2
  77 0074 I                                         7  10 MAID3
  78 0075 I                                        11  30 MANAME
  79 0076 I                                        31  31 MABRAN
  80 0077 I                                        32  32 MASTAT
  81 0078 I                                        33  33 MARANK
  82 0079 I                                        34  350MAYRS
  83 0080 I                                        11  15 MAFST5


  84 0081 C*   MAIN PROCESSING ROUTINE
  85 0082 C*   -----------------------
  86 0083 C    N99    UPIDNO   CHAINPERSFILE           51     READ PERSFILE
  87 0084 C     01             EXSR ADD                       RECORD ADDITION
  88 0085 C     02             EXSR DELETE                    RECORD DELETION
  89 0086 C     03             EXSR CHANGE                    RECORD CHANGE
  90 0087 C     99             EXSR ERROR                     INVALID UPDATE
  91 0088 CLR           ERRADD ADD  VALADD   TOTADD 30
  92 0089 CLR           ERRDEL ADD  VALDEL   TOTDEL 30
  93 0090 CLR           ERRCH  ADD  VALCH    TOTCH  30


  96 0092 C*   RECORD ADDITION SUBROUTINE
  97 0093 C*-----------------------------
  98 0094 CSR     ADD      BEGSR
  99 0095 CSRN97           MOVE UPBRAN   BRANCH 1     IF NOT BLANK.
 100 0096 CSRN97           EXSR TSTBR                 TEST BRANCH
 101 0097 CSRN96           MOVE UPSTAT   STATUS 1     IF NOT BLANK,
 102 0098 CSRN96           EXSR TSTST                 TEST STATUS
 103 0099 CSRN95           MOVE UPRANK   GRADE  1     IF NOT BLANK,
 104 0100 CSRN95           EXSR TSTGR                 TEST GRADE
 105 0101 CSR              SETOF                9052  CLEAR INDIC.
 106 0102 CSR 94
 107 0103 COR 95
 108 0104 COR 96
 109 0105 COR 97
 110 0106 COR 98           SETON                90    MISSING DATA
 111 0107 CSR 91
 112 0108 COR 92
 113 0109 COR 93           SETON                90    INVALID CODE
 114 0110 CSRN94  UPYRS    COMP 30              52     YEARS > 30
 115 0111 CSR 52           SETON                90     YEARS > 30
 116 0112 CSRN51           SETON                90    DUPLICATE I.D.
 117 0113 CSR 90   ERRADD  ADD  1       ERRADD 30    COUNT ERRORS
 118 0114 CSRN90  VALADD   ADD  1       VALADD 30    COUNT ADDITIONS
 119 0115 CSR              SETON                10
 120 0116 CSR              EXCPT                      ADDITION OUTPUT
 121 0117 CSR              SETOF                10
 122 0118 CSR              ENDSR


 125 0120 C*   CHANGE SUBROUTINE
 126 0121 C*-------------------
 127 0122 CSR     CHANGE   BEGSR
 128 0123 CSR              SETOF                8653  CLEAR INDIC.
 129 0124 CSR 51           SETON                13
 130 0125 CSR 13           EXCPT                      PRINT INVALID-
 131 0126 CSR              SETOF                13    NOT ON FILE
 132 0127 CSR 51   ERRCH   ADD  1       ERRCH  30    COUNT ERRORS
 133 0128 CSR 51           GOTO ENDCH                 BYPASS REST OF
 134 0129 C*                                          ROUTINE
 135 0130 CSRN96           MOVE UPSTAT   STATUS       IF NOT BLANK,
```

Figure 11-59 (2)

continued

```
HJG11X    09-12-91  19:06:15   HJG11X - PERSONNEL FILE UPDATE        Version 3.5  Page  3

          ....+....1....+....2....+....3....+....4....+....5....+....6....+....7....

136 0131 CSRN96                     EXSR TSTST                      TEST STATUS
137 0132 CSRN95                     MOVE UPRANK  GRADE              IF NOT BLANK,
138 0133 CSRN95                     EXSR TSTGR                      TEST GRADE
139 0134 CSRN94      UPYRS          COMP 30                  53     TEST VALID
140 0135 CSRN94N53   UPYRS          COMP MAYRS               53       YEARS
141 0136 CSR 91
142 0137 COR 92                                                    INVALID CHANGE
143 0138 COR 53                     SETON                    86      REQUEST DATA
144 0139 CSR 86      ERRCH          ADD  1       ERRCH              COUNT ERRORS
145 0140 CSR 86                     SETON                    14
146 0141 CSR 14                     EXCPT                           CHANGE ERROR
147 0142 CSR                        SETOF                    14      OUTPUT
148 0143 CSR 86                     GOTO ENDCH                      BYPASS REST OF
149 0144 C*                                                         ROUTINE
150 0145 C*
151 0146 CSR                        MOVE MABRAN  BRANCH             TEST BRANCH
152 0147 CSR                        EXSR TSTBR
153 0148 CSR                        MOVE MASTAT  STATUS             TEST STATUS
154 0149 CSR                        EXSR TSTST
155 0150 CSR                        MOVE MARANK  GRADE              TEST GRADE
156 0151 CSR                        EXSR TSTGR
157 0152 CSR                        SETON                    15
158 0153 CSR                        EXCPT                           PRINT OLD
159 0154 CSR                        SETOF                    15      RECORD
160 0155 CSRN96                     MOVE UPSTAT  STATUS             IF NOT BLANK,
161 0156 CSRN96                     EXSR TSTST                       TEST STATUS
162 0157 CSRN95                     MOVE UPRANK  GRADE              IF NOT BLANK,
163 0158 CSRN95                     EXSR TSTGR                       TEST GRADE
164 0159 CSR                        SETON                    16     PRINT NEW
165 0160 CSR                        EXCPT                            RECORD AND
166 0161 CSR                        SETOF                    16     CHANGE DISK
167 0162 CSR         VALCH          ADD  1       VALCH  30          COUNT CHANGES
168 0163 CSR         ENDCH          TAG
169 0164 CSR                        ENDSR


172 0166 C*   RECORD DELETION SUBROUTINE
173 0167 C*--------------------------------
174 0168 CSR         DELETE         BEGSR
175 0169 CSR                        SETOF                    8988  CLEAR INDIC.
176 0170 CSR 51                     SETON                    89    NOT ON FILE
177 0171 CSRN51 05                  SETON                    89    PREV. DELETED
178 0172 CSRN51 04   UPFST5         COMP MAFST5              8888  NAME NOT MATCH
179 0173 CSR 88                     SETON                    89
180 0174 CSR 89                     GOTO NEXT                       BYPASS OF TESTS
181 0175 CSR                        MOVE MABRAN  BRANCH             TEST BRANCH
182 0176 CSR                        EXSR TSTBR
183 0177 CSR                        MOVE MASTAT  STATUS             TEST STATUS
184 0178 CSR                        EXSR TSTST
185 0179 CSR                        MOVE MARANK  GRADE              TEST GRADE
186 0180 CSR                        EXSR TSTGR
187 0181 CSR         NEXT           TAG
188 0182 CSR 89      ERRDEL         ADD  1       ERRDEL 30          COUNT ERRORS
189 0183 CSRN89      VALDEL         ADD  1       VALDEL 30          COUNT DELETES
190 0184 CSR                        SETON                    11
191 0185 CSR                        EXCPT
192 0186 CSR                        SETOF                    11
193 0187 CSR                        ENDSR


196 0189 C*    INVALID UPDATE CODE SUBROUTINE
197 0190 C*--------------------------------------
198 0191 CSR         ERROR          BEGSR
199 0192 CSRN97                     MOVE UPBRAN  BRANCH             IF NOT BLANK,
200 0193 CSRN97                     EXSR TSTBR                       TEST BRANCH
201 0194 CSRN96                     MOVE UPSTAT  STATUS             IF NOT BLANK,
202 0195 CSRN96                     EXSR TSTST                       TEST STATUS
203 0196 CSRN95                     MOVE UPRANK  GRADE              IF NOT BLANK,
204 0197 CSRN95                     EXSR TSTGR                       TEST GRADE
205 0198 CSRN94      UPYRS          COMP 30                  52     YEARS > 30
206 0199 CSR                        SETON                    12
207 0200 CSR                        EXCPT                           ERROR OUTPUT
208 0201 CSR                        SETOF                    1252   CLEAR INDIC.
209 0202 CSR         ERROR          ADD  1       ERROR  30          COUNT INVALID
210 0203 CSR                        ENDSR
```

Figure 11-59 (3)

```
HJG11X    09-12-91  19:06:15   HJG11X - PERSONNEL FILE UPDATE        Version 3.5  Page  4

          ....+....1....+....2....+....3....+....4....+....5....+....6....+....7....


213 0205 C*    STATUS TEST SUBROUTINE
214 0206 C*--------------------------
215 0207 CSR         TSTST    BEGSR
216 0208 CSR                  SETOF                       92
217 0209 CSR         STATUS   COMP 'A'                        46 ACTIVE
218 0210 CSR 46               MOVEL' ACTIVE'STAOUT 9
219 0211 CSR         STATUS   COMP 'R'                        47 RETIRED
220 0212 CSR 47               MOVEL' RETIRED'STAOUT
221 0213 CSRN46N47            SETON                       92 INVALID
222 0214 CSR 92               MOVEL'-INVALID'STAOUT
223 0215 CSR 92               MOVE '-'      STAOUT
224 0216 CSR                  ENDSR


227 0218 C*    GRADE TEST SUBROUTINE
228 0219 C*-----------------------
229 0220 CSR         TSTGR    BEGSR
230 0221 CSR                  SETOF               91
231 0222 CSR         GRADE    COMP 'E'                48 ENLISTED
232 0223 CSR 48               MOVEL'ENLISTED'GRAOUT 9
233 0224 CSR         GRADE    COMP 'O'                49 OFFICER
234 0225 CSR 49               MOVEL'OFFICER 'GRAOUT
235 0226 CSR         GRADE    COMP 'W'                50 WARRANT
236 0227 CSR 50               MOVEL'WARRANT 'GRAOUT
237 0228 CSRN48N49N50         SETON               91     INVALID
238 0229 CSR 91               MOVEL'-INVALID'GRAOUT
239 0230 CSR 91               MOVE '-'       GRAOUT
240 0231 CSR                  ENDSR


243 0233 C*    BRANCH TEST SUBROUTINE
244 0234 C*------------------------
245 0235 CSR         TSTBR    BEGSR
246 0236 CSR                  SETOF               93
247 0237 CSR         BRANCH   COMP 'A'                41 ARMY
248 0238 CSR 41               MOVEL'ARMY'    BRAOUT 11
249 0239 CSR         BRANCH   COMP 'N'                42 NAVY
250 0240 CSR 42               MOVEL'NAVY'    BRAOUT
251 0241 CSR         BRANCH   COMP 'F'                43 AIR FORCE
252 0242 CSR 43               MOVEL'AIR'     BRAOUT
253 0243 CSR 43               MOVE 'FORCE '  BRAOUT
254 0244 CSR         BRANCH   COMP 'M'                44 MARINES
255 0245 CSR 44               MOVEL'MARINES' BRAOUT
256 0246 CSR         BRANCH   COMP 'C'                45 COAST GUARD
257 0247 CSR 45               MOVEL'COAST'   BRAOUT
258 0248 CSR 45               MOVE 'GUARD'   BRAOUT
259 0249 CSRN41N42N43         SETON               93     INVALID
260 0250 CANN44N45            MOVEL'--INVALI'BRAOUT
261 0251 CSR 93               MOVEL'--INVALI'BRAOUT
262 0252 CSR 93               MOVE 'D--'     BRAOUT
263 0253 CSR                  ENDSR


264 0254 O*    HEADING LINES
265 0255 O*---------------
266 0256 OPERSREPTH 206    1P
267 0257 O         OR       OF
268 0258 O                                 7 'HJG11X'
269 0259 O                                46 'PERSONNEL FILE'
270 0260 O                                55 'UPDATE'
271 0261 O                                80 'PAGE'
272 0262 O                       PAGE     85
273 0263 O         H  1     1P
274 0264 O         OR       OF
275 0265 O                                16 'I.D.'
276 0266 O                                64 'MILITARY    CURRENT'
277 0267 O                                85 'CURRENT   LENGTH OF'
278 0268 O         H  2     1P
279 0269 O         OR       OF
280 0270 O                                17 'ACTION    NUMBER'
281 0271 O                                39 'PERSONNEL NAME'
282 0272 O                                64 'BRANCH      STATUS'
283 0273 O                                84 'GRADE     SERVICE'
```

Figure 11-59 (4)

continued

```
HJG11X    09-12-91  19:06:15   HJG11X - PERSONNEL FILE UPDATE      Version 3.5  Page 5
          ....+....1....+....2....+....3....+....4....+....5....+....6....+....7....


    286 0275 O*   RECORD ADDITION


    287 0276 O*-------------------
    288 0277 O        E  2    10
    289 0278 O                                    4 'ADD'
    290 0279 O                      UPID1    12
    291 0280 O                               13 '-'
    292 0281 O                      UPID2    15
    293 0282 O                               16 '-'
    294 0283 O                      UPID3    20
    295 0284 O            N98       UPNAME   42
    296 0285 O             98                33 '---BLANK---'
    297 0286 O            N97       BRAOUT B  55
    298 0287 O             97                55 '---BLANK---'
    299 0288 O            N96       STAOUT B  65
    300 0289 O             96                65 '--BLANK--'
    301 0290 O            N95       GRAOUT B  75
    302 0291 O             95                75 '--BLANK--'
    303 0292 O          N94N52      UPYRS  Z  81
    304 0293 O             94                82 'ZERO'
    305 0294 O             52                84 'INVALID'
    306 0295 O            N51               106 'DUPLICATE I.D.-RECORD'
    307 0296 O            N51               116 'NOT ADDED'
    308 0297 O             90 51            100 'ERROR-NO UPDATE'
    309 0298 O             90 51            110 'PERFORMED'


    312 0300 O*   RECORD DELETION
    313 0301 O*------------------------
    314 0302 O        E  2    11
    315 0303 O                                    7 'DELETE'
    316 0304 O                      MAID1    12
    317 0305 O                               13 '-'
    318 0306 O                      MAID2    15
    319 0307 O                               16 '-'
    320 0308 O                      MAID3    20
    321 0309 O            N89       MANAME   42
    322 0310 O            N89       BRAOUT B  55
    323 0311 O            N89       STAOUT B  65
    324 0312 O            N89       GRAOUT B  75
    325 0313 O            N89       MAYRS  Z  81
    326 0314 O             51               108 'INVALID UPDATE-I.D. NOT'
    327 0315 O             51               116 'ON FILE'
    328 0316 O            N51 05            106 'INVALID UPDATE-RECORD'
    329 0317 O            N51 05            125 'PREVIOUSLY DELETED'
    330 0318 O             88               104 'INVALID UPDATE-NAME'
    331 0319 O             88               119 'FIELD MISMATCH'


    334 0321 O*   INVALID UPDATE CODE
    335 0322 O*------------------------
    336 0323 O        E  2    12
    337 0324 O                                    6 'ERROR'
    338 0325 O                      UPID1    12
    339 0326 O                               13 '-'
    340 0327 O                      UPID2    15
    341 0328 O                               16 '-'
    342 0329 O                      UPID3    20
    343 0330 O            N98       UPNAME   42
    344 0331 O             98                33 '---BLANK---'
    345 0332 O            N97       BRAOUT B  55
    346 0333 O             97                55 '---BLANK---'
    347 0334 O            N96       STAOUT B  65
    348 0335 O             96                65 '--BLANK--'
    349 0336 O            N95       GRAOUT B  75
    350 0337 O             95                75 '--BLANK--'
    351 0338 O          N94N52      UPYRS  Z  81
```

Figure 11-59 (5)

```
HJG11X    09-12-91  19:06:15   HJG11X - PERSONNEL FILE UPDATE    Version 3.5  Page  6
          ....+....1....+....2....+....3....+....4....+....5....+....6....+....7....

352 0339 O                    94                       82 'ZERO'
353 0340 O                    52                       84 'INVALID'
354 0341 O                                            109 'INVALID UPDATE TYPE CODE'


357 0343 O*   INVALID CHANGE REQUEST - RECORD NOT ON FILE
358 0344 O*-------------------------------------------------
359 0345 O       E  2    13
360 0346 O                                              7 'CHANGE'
361 0347 O                           UPID1            12
362 0348 O                                            13 '-'
363 0349 O                           UPID2            15
364 0350 O                                            16 '-'
365 0351 O                           UPID3            20
366 0352 O                                           108 'INVALID UPDATE-I.D. NOT'
367 0353 O                                           116 'ON FILE'


370 0355 O*   INVALID CHANGE REQUEST - ERROR IN NEW DATA
371 0356 O*-------------------------------------------------
372 0357 O       E  2    14
373 0358 O                                              7 'CHANGE'
374 0359 O                           UPID1            12
375 0360 O                                            13 '-'
376 0361 O                           UPID2            15
377 0362 O                                            16 '-'
378 0363 O                           UPID3            20
379 0364 O                    N96    STAOUT B         65
380 0365 O                    N95    GRAOUT B         73
381 0366 O                    53                       84 'INVALID'
382 0367 O                                           109 'ERROR-NO UPDATE PERFORME'
383 0368 O                                           110 'D'


386 0370 O*   CHANGE - OLD RECORD
387 0371 O*---------------------
388 0372 O       E  1    15
389 0373 O                                              7 'CHANGE'
390 0374 O                           MAID1            12
391 0375 O                                            13 '-'
392 0376 O                           MAID2            15
393 0377 O                                            16 '-'
394 0378 O                           MAID3            20
395 0379 O                           MANAME           42
396 0380 O                           BRAOUT           55
397 0381 O                           STAOUT           65
398 0382 O                           GRAOUT           75
399 0383 O                           MAYRS  Z         81
400 0384 O                                            95 'OLD RECORD'


403 0386 O*   CHANGE - NEW RECORD
404 0387 O*---------------------
405 0388 O       E  2    16
406 0389 O                           BRAOUT B         55
407 0390 O                           STAOUT B         65
408 0391 O                           GRAOUT B         75
409 0392 O                    N94    UPYRS            81
410 0393 O                    94     MAYRS            81
411 0394 O                                            95 'NEW RECORD'


414 0396 O*   UPDATE SUMMARY - TOTAL LINES
415 0397 O*------------------------------
416 0398 O       T  106  LR
417 0399 O                                            58 'PERSONNEL FILE UPDATE'
418 0400 O                                            66 'SUMMARY'
419 0401 O       T  2    LR
420 0402 O                           UDATE  Y         55
421 0403 O       T  2    LR
422 0404 O                                            73 'INVALID  INVALID  TOTAL'
423 0405 O*      T  2    LR
```

Figure 11-59 (6)

continued

```
HJG11X     09-12-91  19:06:15   HJG11X - PERSONNEL FILE UPDATE        Version 3.5  Page  7
            ....+....1....+....2....+....3....+....4....+....5....+....6....+....7....
    424 0406 O                                      50 'ADDITION REQUESTS'
    425 0407 O                              VALADDZ 56
    426 0408 O                              ERRADDZ 64
    427 0409 O                              TOTADDZ 72
    428 0410 O        T   2    LR
    429 0411 O                                      50 'DELETION REQUESTS'
    430 0412 O                              VALDELZ 56
    431 0413 O                              ERRDELZ 64
    432 0414 O                              TOTDELZ 72
    433 0415 O        T   2    LR
    434 0416 O                                      50 'CHANGE REQUESTS'
    435 0417 O                              VALCH Z  56
    436 0418 O                              ERRCH Z  64
    437 0419 O                              TOTCH Z  72
    438 0420 O        T      06 LR
    439 0421 O                                      50 'INVALID REQUESTS'
    440 0422 O                              ERROR Z  72
    443 0424 O*    PERSFILE RECORD ADDITION
    444 0425 O*-------------------------
    445 0426 OPERSFILEEADD      10N90
    446 0427 O                                       1 'A'
    447 0428 O                              UPIDNO  10
    448 0429 O                              UPNAME  30
    449 0430 O                              UPBRAN  31
    450 0431 O                              UPSTAT  32
    451 0432 O                              UPRANK  33
    452 0433 O                              UPYRS   35


    455 0435 O*    PERSFILE RECORD DELETION
    456 0436 O*-------------------------
    457 0437 O        E         11N89
    458 0438 O                                       1 'D'


    461 0440 O*    PERSFILE RECORD CHANGE
    462 0441 O*-------------------------
    463 0442 O        E         16
    464 0443 O                  N98      UPNAME  30
    465 0444 O                  N96      UPSTAT  32
    466 0445 O                  N95      UPRANK  33
    467 0446 O                  N94      UPYRS   35
    468 /*
    469 /*



        THE FOLLOWING INDICATORS APPEARED IN THIS PROGRAM

        01   02   03   04   05   10   11   12   13   14   15   16   41   42   43   44
        45   46   47   48   49   50   51   52   53   86   88   89   90   91   92   93
        94   95   96   97   98   99   LR   1P   OF
No Warning Errors
No Fatal Errors
```

Figure 11-59 (7)

▆▆ Problem 1

In addition to the two currently used status codes (A, active; R, retired), two additional codes must be added to program HJG11X: S (reservist) and G (National Guard). In Figure 11-60, show the calculations needed to make these program modifications, and explain the function of the calculations you write.

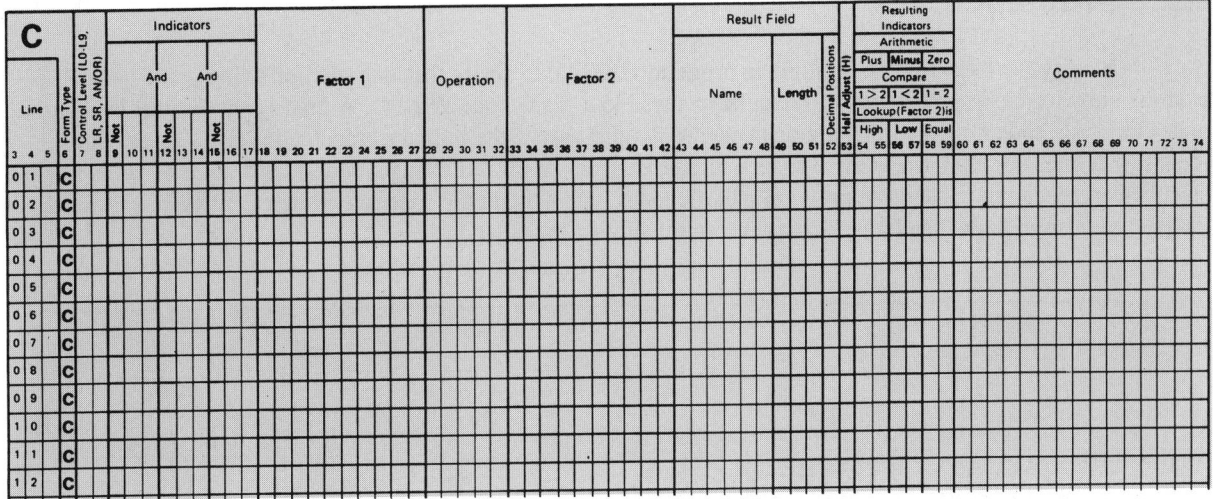

Figure 11-60   Calculation Specifications form

Problem 2

Recently, while performing an update of PERSFILE, the wrong record was changed. To avoid this in the future, the systems analysis staff has decided to expand the testing used to ensure that the correct record is being accessed. To do this, the following modifications must be made to program HJG11X.

1. The name comparison, performed as part of the record deletion subroutine, will be incorporated into the change subroutine as well.
2. In addition to comparing the first five positions of the name field, a comparison will be performed on the branch field in both the deletion and the change subroutines.

In Figure 11-61, show the calculations needed to make these program modifications, and explain the function of the calculations you write. Refer to the listing at the beginning of these exercises in your explanations.

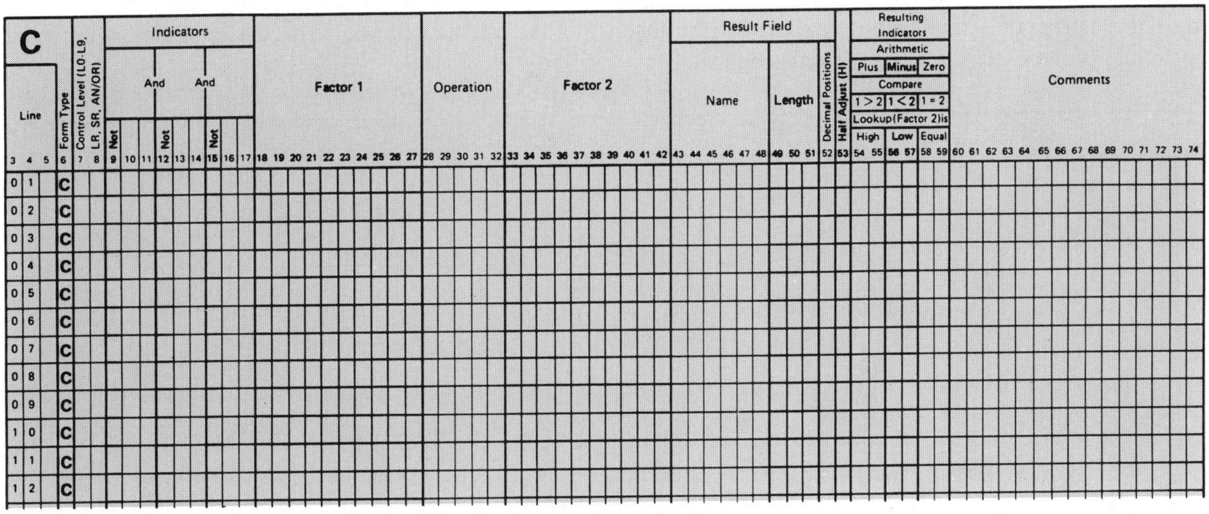

Figure 11-61   Calculation Specifications form

Problem 3

Modify the CHANGE subroutine in program HJG11X to verify that only the following grade code changes are allowed. A grade code of E can be changed to a grade code W or O. A grade code W may be changed only to a grade code O. Recall that a grade code W is valid only if the military branch code is A. Any change request that does not conform to these rules will be treated as an invalid change request. In Figure 11-62, show the calculations needed to make these program modifications, and explain the function of the calculations you write. Refer to the listing at the beginning of these exercises in your explanations.

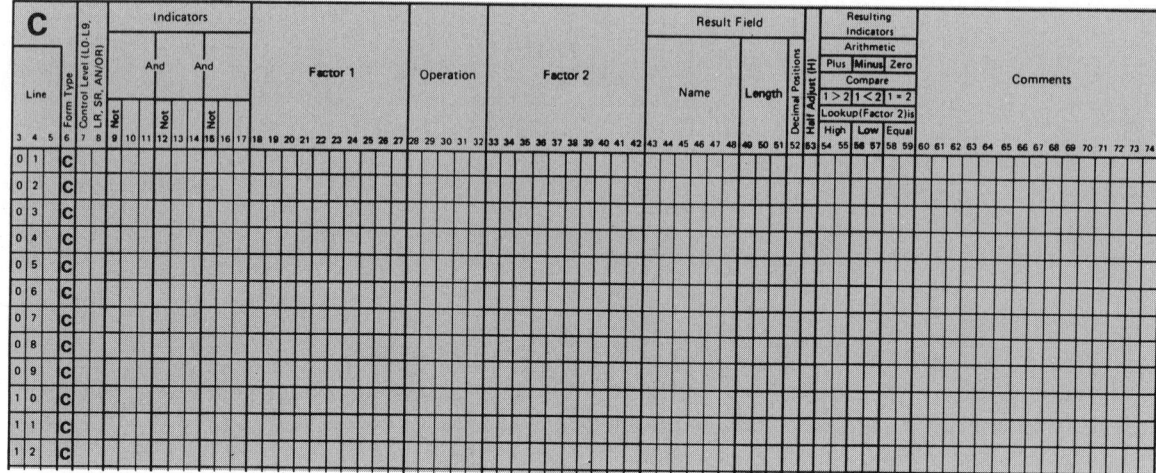

Figure 11-62   Calculation Specifications form

Problem 4

Modify the ADD and CHANGE subroutines in program HJG11X to verify that individuals have sufficient years of service to qualify for their military grade. A minimum of two years of service is needed to qualify as a Warrant Officer (grade code W). A minimum of four years of service is needed to qualify as an Officer (grade code O). If the Years of Service entry is less than the minimum required for the military grade in either a record addition or record change request, the UPYRS field is invalid. In Figure 11-63, show the calculations needed to make these program modifications, and explain the function of the calculations you write. Refer to the listing at the beginning of these exercises in your explanations.

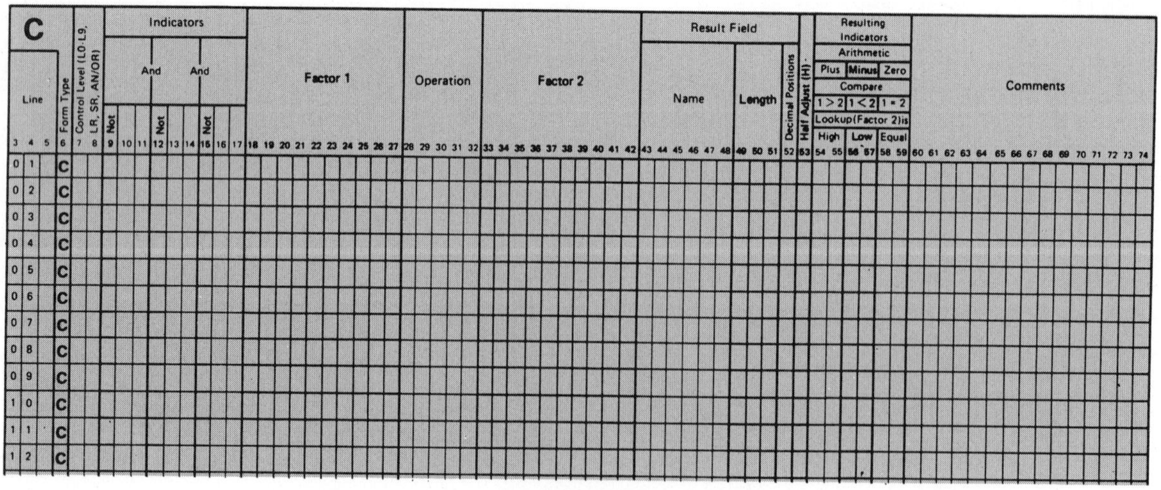

Figure 11-63   Calculation Specifications form

STUDENT EXERCISES: PROGRAMMING IN RPG

The three programming assignments in this chapter are file update programs using the data files developed in Chapter 10. The programming exercises in Chapter 10 directed you to retain the output disk files for use in this chapter. If you did not write the Chapter 10 programming exercises or were not able to save the output files created by those programs, contact your instructor to obtain the necessary data for use in the following programming exercises, which (like those in Chapter 10) require that you plan and design the needed output reports.

PROGRAMMING ASSIGNMENT 1
TEST EQUIPMENT MASTER FILE UPDATE

INSTRUCTIONS

Plan, code, enter, and test an RPG program to update the Test Equipment Master File, the format of which is shown in Figure 11-64.

TEST EQUIPMENT MASTER FILE RECORD						
Record Length 65			Key Location 1–8			
Field No.	Field Name	Field Description	Field Position	Field Length	Dec. Pos.	Data Class
1		Unit I.D. Number	1–8			
2		Unit Description	9–30			
3		Location	36–42			
4		Purchase Date	46–51			
5		Date Last Calibrated	52–57			
6		Date Loaded	58–63			
7		Status Code	65–65			

Figure 11-64   Format of Test Equipment Master File Record

INPUT

The format of the Test Equipment Update File is shown in Figure 11-65. Use test data set 26 for this problem.

OUTPUT

Output from Programming Assignment 1 is to be the updated Test Equipment Master File and a printed report providing a complete audit trail of all update requests. In addition to showing all valid update operations performed on the master file, the report is to list all invalid update requests and the reason that each was determined to be invalid.

TEST EQUIPMENT UPDATE RECORD						
Record Length 65						
Field No.	Field Name	Field Description	Field Position	Field Length	Dec. Pos.	Data Class
1	UNITID	Unit I.D. Number	1–8	8		A
2	DESCR	Unit Description	9–30	22		A
3	LOCAT	Location	36–42	7		A
4	PDATE	Purchase Date	46–51	6	0	N
5	CDATE	Date Last Calibrated	52–57	6	0	N
6		Update Type Code	60–60	1		A

Figure 11-65 Format of Test Equipment Update Record

▤ Processing Requirements

Test each record in the Test Equipment Update File based on the conditions listed for each type of update request. This file has been preedited and contains no invalid update request codes.

▸ **Record Addition (Update Code A)** If none of the following conditions is detected, a record is added to the Test Equipment Master File. If one or more of the listed conditions are detected, no addition to the master file is made. Added records contain the status code A.

1. The Unit Identification Number field must not be duplicated in the Test Equipment Master File.
2. The Unit Identification Number, Description, and location fields must not be blank.
3. The Purchase Date field must not contain all zeros.
4. If the Date Last Calibrated field contains a date, the date cannot be earlier than the Purchase Date field.
5. Both of the input dates are in MMDDYY format. The month and day portions of both dates must be valid. Each month entry must be 01–12, and the day entry must be valid for the month. You need not test for leap year because the file does not contain any dates of February 29.

▸ **Record Deletion (Update Code D)** For a record to be marked as deleted, both the identification number and the description contained in the update request record must match those in the Test Equipment Master File record. If both fields match, the master file record is marked for deletion by changing the Status Code entry to D.

▸ **Record Change (Update Code C)** Only the Location and Date Last Calibrated fields may be changed. If a change is requested to the Date Last Calibrated field, the new date must be later than the date currently in the record. The new date must be tested according to the requirements of test 5 listed under Record Addition.

▤ PROGRAMMING ASSIGNMENT 2
EMPLOYEE MASTER FILE UPDATE

INSTRUCTIONS

Plan, code, enter, and test an RPG program to update the Employee Master File, the format of which is shown in Figure 11-66.

EMPLOYEE MASTER FILE RECORD						
Record Length 70			Key Location 1–4			
Field No.	Field Name	Field Description	Field Position	Field Length	Dec. Pos.	Data Class
1		Employee Number	1–4			
2		Last Name	5–19			
3		First Name	20–31			
4		Sex Code (M/F)	32–32			
5		Date Hired	33–38			
6		Department Number	39–41			
7		Pay Category (H/S)	42–42			
8		Pay Rate Code	43–44			
9		Annual Salary	45–52			
10		Hourly Pay Rate	53–57			
11		Current Date	62–67			
12		Status Code	70–70			

Figure 11-66   Format of Employee Master File Record

INPUT

The format of the Employee Update File is shown in Figure 11-67. Use test data set 27 for this problem.

EMPLOYEE UPDATE RECORD						
Record Length 70						
Field No.	Field Name	Field Description	Field Position	Field Length	Dec. Pos.	Data Class
1	EMPLID	Employee Number	1–4	4	0	N
2	LNAME	Last Name	5–19	15		A
3	FNAME	First Name	20–31	12		A
4	SCODE	Sex Code (M/F)	32–32	1		A
5	DTHIRE	Date Hired	33–38	6	0	N
6	DEPTNO	Department Number	39–41	3	0	N
7	PAYCAT	Pay Category (H/S)	42–42	1		A
8	RATCOD	Pay Rate Code	43–44	2	0	N
9	ANNSAL	Annual Salary	45–52	8	2	N
10	HRATE	Hourly Pay Rate	53–57	5	3	N
11	HOURS	Hours Worked Last Pay Period	58–61	4	1	N
		UNUSED AREA	62–69			
12		Update Type Code	70–70	1		A

Figure 11-67   Format of Employee Update Record

OUTPUT

Output from Programming Assignment 2 is to be the updated Employee Master File and a printed report providing a complete audit trail of all update requests. In addition to showing all valid update operations performed on the master file, the report is to list all invalid update requests and the reason that each was determined to be invalid.

Processing Requirements

▶ **Record Addition (Update Code A)**   Test each input data record for the conditions listed. If none of the listed conditions is detected, a record is added to the Employee Master File. If one or more of the listed conditions are detected, no addition to the master file is made. Added records contain the status code of A. The current date is placed in positions 62–67 of the Employee Master File record.

1. The employee number must not be duplicated in the Employee Master File.
2. The Employee Number, Last Name, First Name, Date Hired, and Department Number fields must not be blank.
3. Sex code must be either M or F.
4. Pay category must be either H or S.
5. If the Pay Category field is H, neither the Pay Rate Code field nor the Hourly Pay Rate field may be blank or zero.
6. If the Pay Category field is S, the Annual Salary field must not be blank or zero.

▶ **Record Deletion (Update Code D)**   For a record to be marked as deleted, both the employee number and the date hired contained in the update request record must match those in the Employee Master File record. If both fields match, the master file record is marked for deletion, by changing the Status Code entry to D. When a record is marked for deletion, the current date is placed in positions 62–67 of the delete-marked record.

▶ **Record Change (Update Code C)**

1. The only fields that can be changed are last name, first name, department number, pay category, pay rate code, annual salary, and hourly pay rate.
2. If a change is made to the Pay Category field, the change must conform to items 4, 5, and 6 listed under Record Addition.
3. If the Pay Category field changes from H to S, the Pay Rate Code and Hourly Pay Rate fields must be changed to zero.
4. If the Pay Category field changes from S to H, the Annual Salary field must be changed to zero.
5. When any change is made to a record, the current date is placed in positions 62–67 of the Employee Master File record.

PROGRAMMING ASSIGNMENT 3
RENTAL CAR STATUS FILE UPDATE

INSTRUCTIONS

Plan, code, enter, and test an RPG program to update the Rental Car Status File, the format of which is shown in Figure 11-68.

INPUT

The format of the Rental Car Update File is shown in Figure 11-69. Use test data set 28 for this problem.

		RENTAL CAR STATUS RECORD				
		Record Length 70	Key Location 1–10			
Field No.	Field Name	Field Description	Field Position	Field Length	Dec. Pos.	Data Class
		Vehicle Stock No.	1–9			
		Check Digit	10–10			
		Make of Car	11–11			
		Body Style	12–12			
		Optional Equipment	13–17			
		Air Conditioning	13–13			
		Power Steering	14–14			
		Towing Package	15–15			
		Sun Roof	16–16			
		Automatic Trans.	17–17			
		Vehicle Status	18–18			
		License Number	19–27			
		Renter's Name	28–48			
		Payment Method	49–50			
		Date Out	51–56			
		Number of Days Rented	57–58			
		Deposit Amount	59–62			

Figure 11-68   Format of Rental Car Status Record

		RENTAL CAR UPDATE RECORD				
		Record Length 70				
Field No.	Field Name	Field Description	Field Position	Field Length	Dec. Pos.	Data Class
1	STOCK	Vehicle Stock No.	1–9	9	0	N
2	CHECK	Check Digit	10–10	1	0	N
3	MAKE	Make of Car	11–11	1		A
4	STYLE	Body Style	12–12	1		A
5	EQUIP	Optional Equipment	13–17	5		A
		Air Conditioning	13–13			
		Power Steering	14–14			
		Towing Package	15–15			
		Sun Roof	16–16			
		Automatic Trans.	17–17			
6	STATUS	Vehicle Status	18–18	1		A
7	LICNO	License Number	19–27	9		A
8	NAME	Renter's Name	28–48	21		A
9	PAY	Payment Method	49–50	2		A
10	DOUT	Date Out	51–56	6	0	N
11	NODAYS	Number of Days Rented	57–58	2	0	N
12	DEPST	Deposit Amount	59–62	4	0	N
13		Update Type Code	63–63	1		A
		UNUSED AREA	64–70			

Figure 11-69   Format of Rental Car Update Record

OUTPUT

Output from Programming Assignment 3 is to be the updated Rental Car Status File and a printed report providing a complete audit trail of all update requests. In addition to showing all valid update operations performed on the master file, the report is to list all invalid update requests and the reason that each was determined to be invalid.

▤ Processing Requirements

▸ **Record Addition (Update Code A)**   Test each input data record for the conditions listed. If none of the listed conditions is detected, a record is added to the Rental Car Status File. Except for condition 11, if one or more of the listed conditions is detected, no addition to the master file is made. If condition 11 is detected, an error message is printed, and the record is added to the Rental Car Status File.

1. The vehicle stock number must not be duplicated in the Rental Car Status File.
2. The STOCK, CHECK, MAKE, STYLE, and STATUS fields must not be blank and must contain valid codes as shown later in this list.
3. The Check Digit field must correspond to the Vehicle Stock Number field. To verify the check digit, add together the nine digits of the vehicle stock number. The rightmost digit of the sum should match the Check Digit field.
4. The valid MAKE entries are

   P   Panther
   T   Tiger
   B   Bearcat
   V   Vulcan

5. The valid STYLE entries are

   C   Convertible
   S   Sedan
   ·F Fastback

6. The four makes of car are not all available in every body style. The valid combinations of make and body style are

   Panther   Convertible, fastback
   Tiger   Sedan, fastback
   Bearcat   Convertible, sedan, fastback
   Vulcan   Convertible, sedan

   No other combination is valid.

7. The five Optional Equipment fields contain a Y if the vehicle is equipped with the option and an N if the vehicle is not equipped with that option. There are several invalid optional equipment combinations:

   Fastbacks cannot be equipped with the towing package.
   If a car is equipped with either air conditioning or a towing package, it cannot be equipped with a sun roof.
   If a car is equipped with air conditioning, it must be equipped with power steering and an automatic transmission.

8. The three valid STATUS codes are

A   Available for rental
R   Rented, not available
S   Being serviced, not available

9. If the STATUS code is R, the LICNO, NAME, PAY, and NODAYS fields must not be blank.
10. The valid payment method codes are CA (cash payment) and CR (credit card).
11. If the payment method is CA, the DEPSIT field must be tested to verify a valid deposit amount. Deposit amount is calculated as follows:
If the car is a Panther, Tiger, or Bearcat, the deposit is $50.00 per day. If the car is a Vulcan, the deposit is $35.00 per day.

▸ **Record Deletion (Update Code D)**   There is no secondary field that must be verified prior to deletion. Record deletion is based upon the vehicle stock number. Deletion request records contain only this nine-digit number. After computing the check digit, use the combination of vehicle identification number and check digit to perform the record deletion.

▸ **Record Change (Update Code C)**   All changes must be based on proper verification of the check digit of the record to be changed. Change request records do not contain a check digit. This digit must be calculated prior to reading the Rental Car Status File and the check digit used as part of the key in the CHAIN operation.

1. No changes can be made to the data fields that describe the vehicle. The only allowable changes are the status changes in the following items (2–4).
2. Vehicle status can be changed from A (available) to S (being serviced). In this case, no further changes are needed to the status file record. In addition, the reverse change (S to A) can also be made with no further processing required on the record.
3. Vehicle status can be changed from A to R (rented) or from S to R. When either of these changes is made, items 9, 10, and 11 listed under Record Addition must be tested and the required entries must be contained in the change request record. If the tested conditions are not met, the change request is not valid.
4. Vehicle status can be changed from R to A or from R to S. If either of these changes is made, positions 19–50 of the record must be changed to blanks, and positions 51–62 of the record must be changed to zeros.

T W E L V E

Interactive Processing, Screen Format Design, Programming, & System/36 Screen Design Aid

All the programming examples up to now have been based on batch processing techniques. In these programs, a group, or batch, of input records is processed with no intervention by the operator after program execution begins. Batch processing has been the most common type of processing in business applications and was the only type of processing available prior to the introduction of the computer terminal or workstation as an input/output device.

The development and introduction of the computer terminal has made it possible to design business programs that are interactive. **Interactive programming** applications develop a dialogue between the computer user and the computer. The word *dialogue* in this case means the same thing as it does in people-oriented terms: a two-way conversation. With interactive programming techniques, the computer user can interact, or "talk," with the computer by using the terminal as an **interface**, a device that allows communication between two machines or between a person and a computer.

Interactive processing techniques do not replace the methods and techniques you have been using; instead, they provide new input and output techniques by which a person and a computer can interact to input the data and obtain the results. This person/machine dialogue enables a user to enter and access information on a **real-time** basis, that is, when needed, rather than having to wait until a group of information requests have been gathered to be processed in a batch.

SCREEN FORMAT DESIGN CONCEPTS

All interactive processing is based on the use of computer terminals or workstations. Although there are some technical differences between a terminal and a workstation, RPG considers them to be the same. Because of this, the term *terminal* is used here to represent either a computer terminal or a computer workstation (Figure 12-1 on the next page). The two parts of a terminal used by the computer user are the keyboard and the screen. The keyboard is the input section of the terminal, and all input is entered through the keyboard. The **screen** is the output unit of a terminal and is the physical surface on which all output data is displayed by an interactive program. The data that is displayed on the screen is called the display.

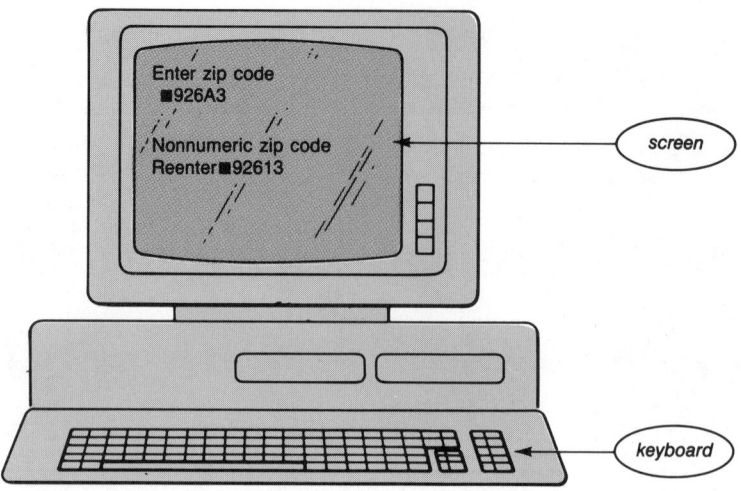

Figure 12-1   Computer terminal

▰▰ Types of Display Formats

A **display**, also called a **panel**, is a predefined group of fields arranged in a predetermined pattern and displayed on a screen. The arrangement of data in a display is called the **display format**, or **format**. Several types of formats are commonly used in business applications, each for a specific interactive application function.

▸ **Menu Format**   The menu format enables the user to choose one of a list of choices (Figure 12-2). In this example, the menu shows 24 numbered choices. The user selects the operation to be performed by entering the appropriate number. The entry 6 would enable the terminal user to send a message, entry 9 to perform an RPG compilation, and entry 24 to sign off, or log off, the terminal. Note that each menu option contains the number

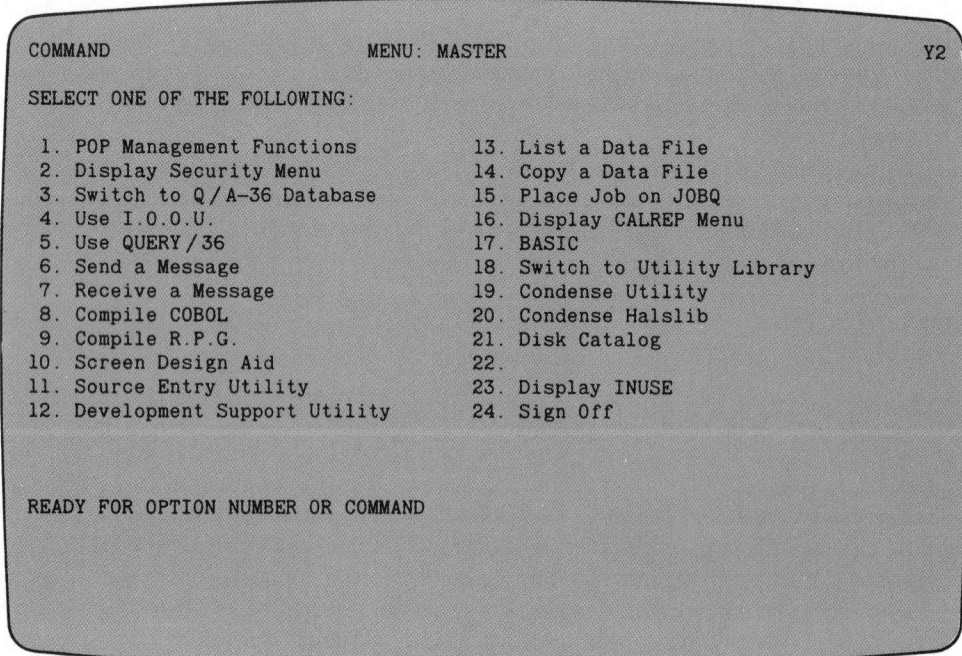

Figure 12-2   Menu format: menu MASTER

that causes the option to be performed and a brief description of what the option does. A number can represent the name of a program or an individual command statement.

Menus make using the computer much easier because the user need not remember, or even know, the command language used by the computer. The user needs only to read the menu and enter the number of the job or command to be run. In addition, because menus reduce the amount of typing necessary to run a job or execute a command, the efficiency of the user increases and the possibility of error is reduced. In the menu in this example, selection of option 21 causes the command CATALOG ALL,F1,,,NAME to be executed. Menus can also be used to cause additional menus to be displayed on the screen. Note that options 2 and 16 cause other menus to be displayed (Figure 12-3). Each of these additional menus contains other options.

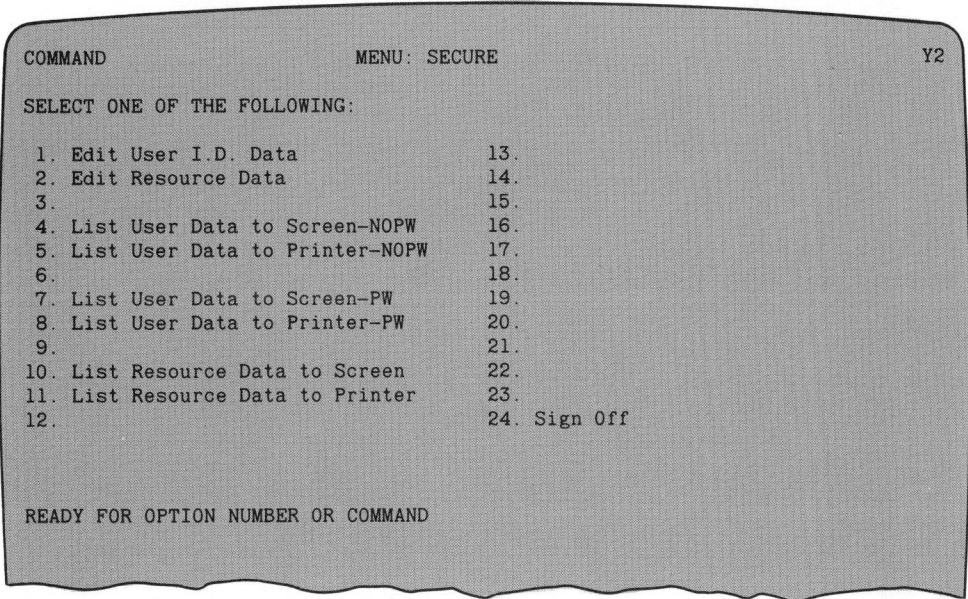

```
COMMAND                    MENU: SECURE                         Y2

SELECT ONE OF THE FOLLOWING:

 1. Edit User I.D. Data              13.
 2. Edit Resource Data               14.
 3.                                  15.
 4. List User Data to Screen-NOPW    16.
 5. List User Data to Printer-NOPW   17.
 6.                                  18.
 7. List User Data to Screen-PW      19.
 8. List User Data to Printer-PW     20.
 9.                                  21.
10. List Resource Data to Screen     22.
11. List Resource Data to Printer    23.
12.                                  24. Sign Off


READY FOR OPTION NUMBER OR COMMAND
```

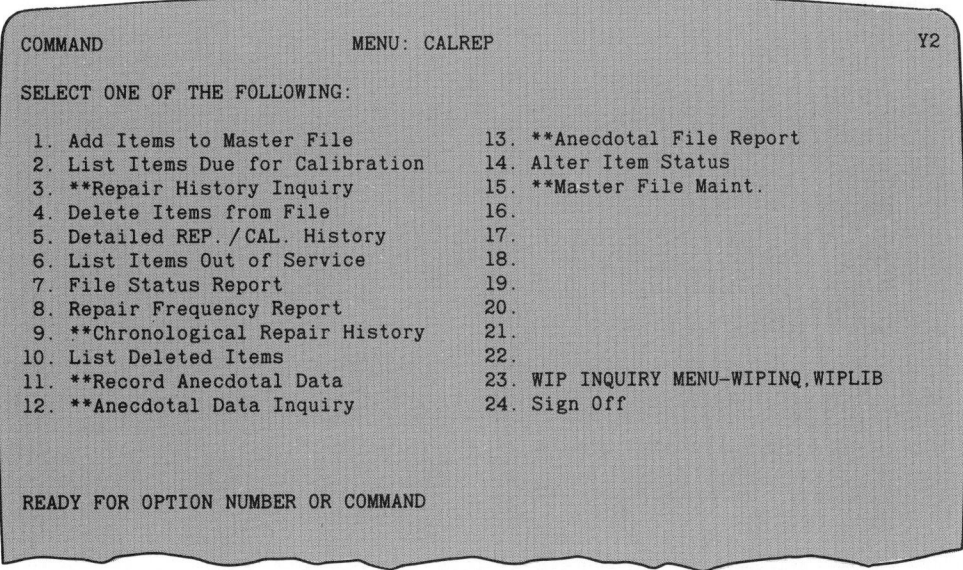

```
COMMAND                    MENU: CALREP                         Y2

SELECT ONE OF THE FOLLOWING:

 1. Add Items to Master File         13. **Anecdotal File Report
 2. List Items Due for Calibration   14. Alter Item Status
 3. **Repair History Inquiry         15. **Master File Maint.
 4. Delete Items from File           16.
 5. Detailed REP./CAL. History       17.
 6. List Items Out of Service        18.
 7. File Status Report               19.
 8. Repair Frequency Report          20.
 9. **Chronological Repair History   21.
10. List Deleted Items               22.
11. **Record Anecdotal Data          23. WIP INQUIRY MENU-WIPINQ,WIPLIB
12. **Anecdotal Data Inquiry         24. Sign Off


READY FOR OPTION NUMBER OR COMMAND
```

Figure 12-3   Menu formats: menus SECURE and CALREP

As you can see, all these menus have one or more option numbers that are not followed by a description. The computer would take no action if any of these undescribed options were entered. These are options that can be activated for use at some later time as the needs of the user change.

▸ **Data Entry Format**   The data entry format enables the user to enter information into the computer. The main portion of a data entry format usually consists of one or more fields into which data can be entered and captions that specify the type of data to be entered. These **captions** serve the same function as headings on a printed report in that they identify the fields.

Some data entry formats (Figure 12-4) enable the user to enter the identifier of a needed record. The entered identifier is then processed by the program and used as a key to retrieve a particular record from a file. This type of data entry format is referred to as an **inquiry format**.

```
        PERSSC12

                    TRANSACTION FILE INQUIRY

                Enter Employee Number . . . . . . . .



                ENTER to perform inquiry
                CMD / 3 to return to previous display
                CMD / 7 to end job
```

Figure 12-4   Data entry inquiry format

Figure 12-5 shows a true data entry format. This format is used to enter information into a data record. Note that in addition to the data fields and captions, a data entry format can also contain information about command keys that can be used with the display. In this example, Command Key 7 is used to end the program. This information is displayed as part of the format at the bottom of the screen.

```
                    TEST EQUIPMENT CALIBRATION
                          ITEM ENTRY

        Calibration Unit ID Number    . . . . . . . . . . . . . . . . . . . .
        Fixed Asset I.D. Number       . . . . . . . . . . . . . . . . . . . .

        Type      . . . . . . . .     Manufacturer  . . . . . . .
        Model     . . . . . . . .     Serial Number . . . . . . . . . . . .

        Location     . . . . .
        Acquisition Date (MMDDYY)     . . . . . . .
        Acquisition Cost              . . . . . . . .

        Date Last Calibrated (MMDDYY)   . . . . . . .
        Calibration Performed By        . . . . . . .
        Calibration Interval (Months)   . . .


        . . . . . . . . . . . . . . . . . . . . . . . . . . .
        Enter Key—Loads This Item Onto File
            CMD / 7—Ends This Load Program
```

Figure 12-5   Data entry format

Information Format   The information format displays **read only** information (Figure 12-6). This type of format does not permit the operator to enter new data; it usually is the result of an entry made in the type of data entry display that is shown in Figure 12-4. After the data entry display is used to accept the identifier, the requested record is displayed using an information format display.

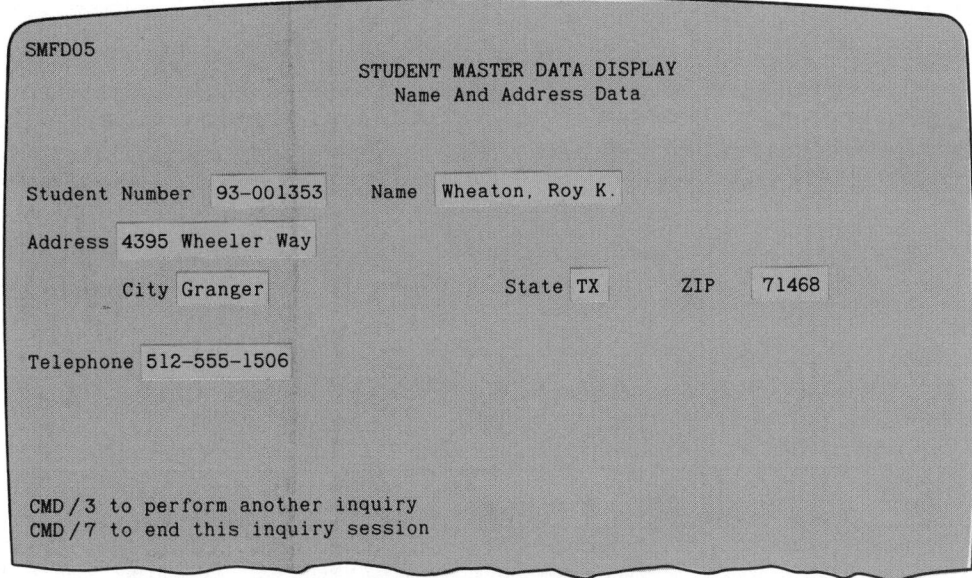

```
SMFD05
                        STUDENT MASTER DATA DISPLAY
                           Name And Address Data


    Student Number  93-001353    Name  Wheaton, Roy K.

    Address 4395 Wheeler Way

         City Granger               State TX      ZIP   71468


    Telephone 512-555-1506




    CMD/3 to perform another inquiry
    CMD/7 to end this inquiry session
```

Figure 12-6   Information format

▸ **Multipurpose Format**   This type of format combines the functions of the data entry and the information formats. A multipurpose format displays requested information (like the information format) but also permits new data to be entered. This format is generally used to update existing data in a file.

▸ **Format Elements**   Every display format is made up of components called **elements**. These elements are the individual units that make up the complete display format. A format does not necessarily contain every type of element. The combination of elements depends on the type of format and the purpose for which it was designed. Figure 12-7 on the next page shows two of the display formats that you have already seen with each of the types of format elements identified.

▸ **Format Identification**   The format identifier is a unique identifier that can be either a heading, centered at the top of the format, or an alphameric identifier, usually at the top left corner of the format. Either or both of these types of identifier can appear in a format, but whichever type is used, every format identification element should be unique. Under no circumstances should two different formats have the same identifier.

▸ **Captions**   Captions in a format are similar to headings in a printed report. Captions are constants used to identify the format, sections of the format, and each element in a format that either displays information or is used for data entry. When captions are used to identify a data entry field or to request information or an action by the user, they are called **prompts**. Captions can appear either over or beside the element or area that the caption identifies.

▸ **Entry Fields**   An entry field is an area of a format into which information can be typed. As data is entered into an entry field, the cursor moves to the next position to be typed. A **cursor** is a special character, usually a high-intensity underline or a vertical rectangle, that indicates the area in the format into which the next character is to be entered. Regardless of its shape, the cursor always shows the next position into which data will be entered.

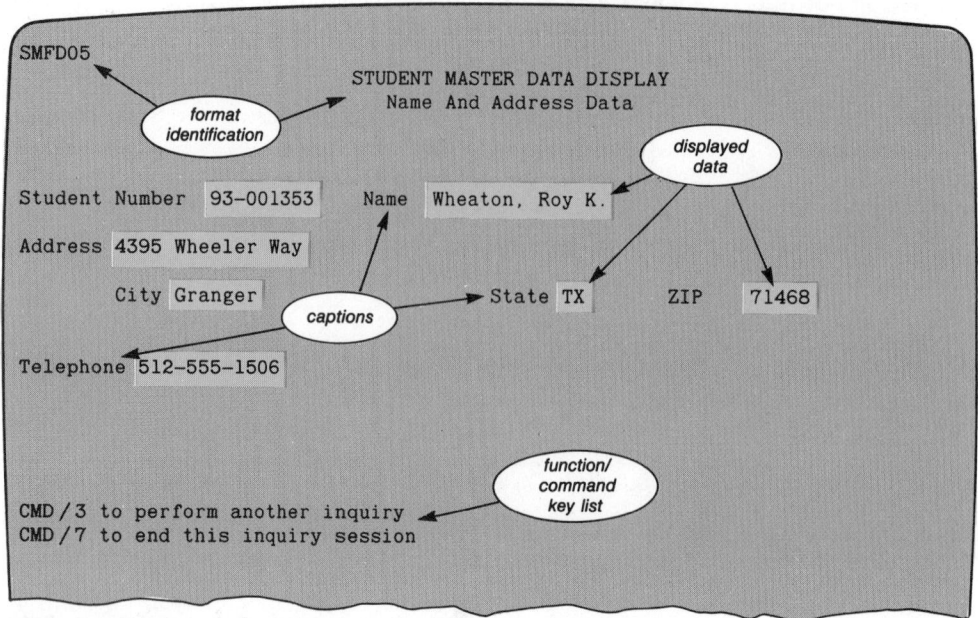

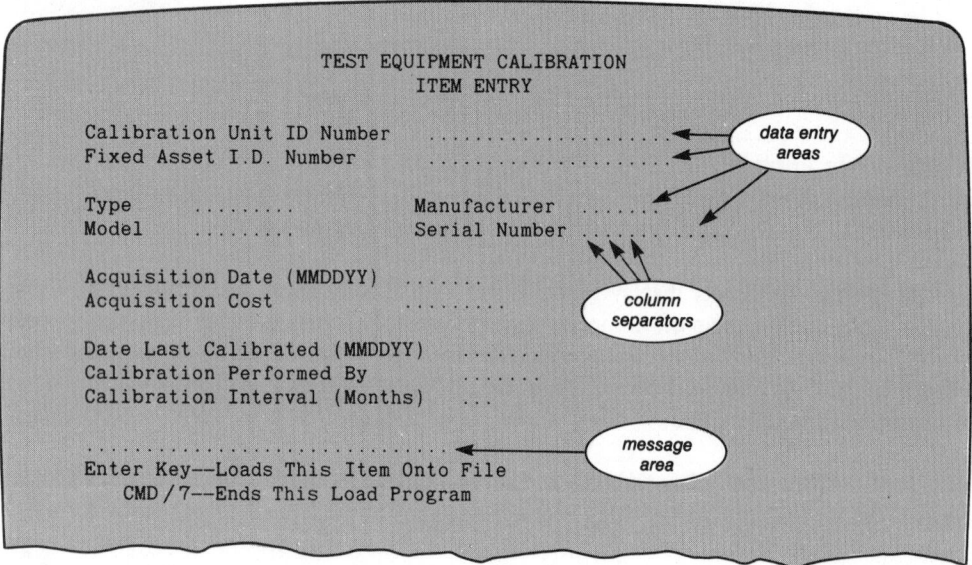

Figure 12-7 Format elements of information and data entry formats

▶ **Message Area** This is an optional area where messages can be displayed to the user, under program control. The message area is most commonly used to indicate errors in data entry and is usually found only in data entry formats. The message area, if used, should be located in the lower portion of the format.

▶ **Command Area** This optional area enables the user to enter standard system commands. Although the location of the command area can, in some cases, be determined by the type of computer you are using, it should, if possible, be placed at the bottom of the display format.

▶ **Function/Command Key List** Most terminals and microcomputers have special keys that are used for program and display format control. These keys are called **Function** or **Command** keys. The Function/Command key list shows which keys are available for use with the format. All Function or Command keys used by the format should be listed in this area with an explanation of their function in the format.

▤ Format Design Considerations

The basic concepts of format design are similar to those you have used when designing a printed report. Just as you used the printer spacing chart to lay out a report, you use the Display Screen Layout Sheet, (Figure 12-8) to plan a display format. This sheet represents the size of a typical display screen. The amount of information that can be placed on a computer display screen is measured in character positions. The Display Screen Layout Sheet is 80 positions across by 24 positions down. Most screens that are used with RPG programming can display up to 24 horizontal lines, each of which can contain up to 80 characters. Although the screens on some newer terminals can display 132 positions on a line, 80 positions is the standard.

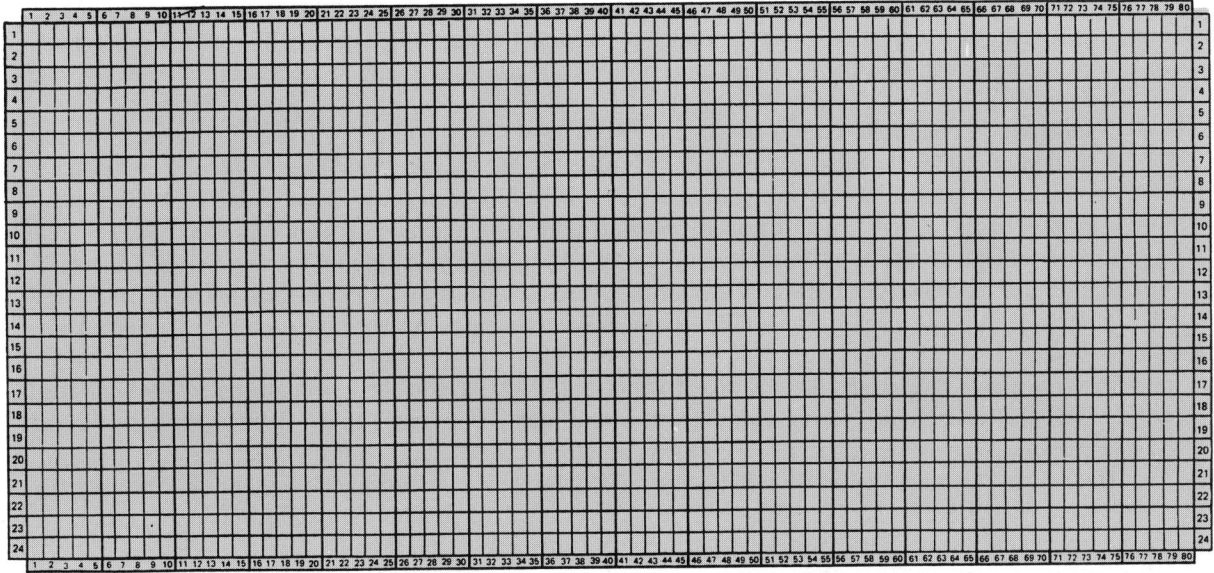

Figure 12-8 Display format layout form

Another system of measuring screens is by the number of individual dots of light or **pixels**, short for **picture elements**, that can be displayed on the screen. When screens are described this way, the numbers that describe screen size are generally quite a bit larger because they define the actual number of dots used to make up the letters and numbers displayed on the screen. For example, the screen being used as this manuscript is prepared is an 80-character by 24-line screen, However, when the screen is used for graphics or pictures, the screen is capable of displaying 800 pixels horizontally and 560 pixels vertically. Generally, the pixel count of a screen is important only when graphic work is performed. As RPG is not capable of generating on-screen graphics, we will discuss screen sizes based on character representation.

Although the design of display formats on a Display Screen Layout Sheer is similar to the design of printed reports, several other factors must be taken into consideration because display screens have capabilities that printers do no have.

▶ **Element Placement** In most versions of RPG that use display formats, each element in the display format is preceded by a **control character**, that marks the beginning of the element. This control character is automatically inserted by the utility program that generates the display format. Control characters are nondisplay characters. **Nondisplay** means that the character does not appear on the screen when the format is displayed. You must leave space for these control characters when you plan your display, and so you must leave at least one space between display elements.

▶ **Case** Display screens can display letters in **uppercase** (CAPITAL) or **lowercase** (small) letters. Normally, format elements should follow English language rules for capitalization of words. If possible, AVOID THE USE OF WORDS DISPLAYED IN ALL CAPITAL LETTERS because they are harder to read. Two exceptions to this are display format headings and acronyms, which should be uppercase, and the description of special-purpose keyboard keys, such as ESC, REPEAT, CTRL, and so on, which should be spelled exactly as they appear on the keyboard.

▸ **Element Attributes** In addition to placement and case, you can assign certain physical characteristics, or **attributes**, to each element in a display format. These attributes control the appearance of an element when it is displayed on the screen. The most common element attributes are the following:

High intensity High-intensity data is brighter than data displayed in the usual way, making it look like **boldface print**. The high-intensity attribute draws attention to important information such as commands, headings, and instructions.

Blink This attribute causes an element on the screen to flash on and off. Blinking fields are very noticeable and can also be used to draw attention to important elements in a display. However, fields using this attribute can be difficult to read and, if overused, can be annoying to the person working with the format.

Nondisplay A nondisplay field is invisible to the operator. The nondisplay attribute can be used for information needed by the program but not by the operator and for information that, when entered, should remain confidential. When you enter your password on your computer, the password probably does not display on the screen. This is the most common example of a nondisplay data entry field. By assigning the nondisplay attribute to the password field, the designer of your sign-on format made it difficult for a person standing behind you to read your password as you enter it. This attribute is called the **protect** attribute by some display format utilities. An element that uses this attribute is called a **protected** element.

Reverse image The usual system of displaying data in a format is to show light characters on a dark background. Reverse image shows dark characters on a light background. This is another method of drawing attention to an element; but, like the blink attribute, it can be annoying if overused.

Underline This attribute can be used to emphasize information or to show the length of a data entry element (like this:_____). Showing the user the length of an input element is important because attempting to enter data beyond the area available often causes an error.

Column separators This attribute is also useful for showing the size of an input element. Column separators are either .s.m.a.l.l. .d.o.t.s. or vertical lines on either side of each character position. The type of column separator available for use in your displays depends on the type of terminal you are using. Column separators do not take up a position in the element but are inserted between the positions.

Color Some computer terminals and most microcomputer monitors use color in display formats. The variety of colors available depends on the kind of terminal or monitor. Color, if used carefully, can draw attention to important elements, identify groups of elements, and identify different types of elements such as captions and data entry fields. If color is misused, it can make a display format very difficult to read and very tiring to work with. Because color is not widely available in RPG programming environments, the remainder of this chapter deals with monochrome, or noncolor capable, display formats.

Not all attributes are compatible with all other attributes. For example, when you design display formats for an IBM System/36, if nondisplay is specified with high intensity, reverse image, or underline, only the nondisplay attribute is used. The other attribute descriptions are ignored. Also, if reverse image, high intensity, and underline are specified for the same element at the same item, an error message occurs. The attribute limitations that apply in your programming environment depend on the type of terminal or microcomputer and the version of RPG that you are using.

Recall that the purpose of the high intensity, blink, reverse image, underline, and color attributes is to call attention to important parts of the format. If these attributes are used too often, they become meaningless to the person using the display format. The old saying that familiarity breeds contempt applies to display format attributes. If too many elements use these attributes, the person using the format begins to ignore the importance of a blinking or reverse image element. Their excess use can also lead to operator fatigue and eyestrain. A well-designed format uses these features sparingly.

▤ Planning a Display Format

When a terminal is used as an interface between a person and a computer, the display format provides the computer's portion of the conversation. The display format must be well planned if the conversation is to be meaningful and productive. A poorly designed format can lead to user fatigue, lack of user attention, and errors.

The rules for display format design are not rigid as those for report design for several reasons. First, a screen has many capabilities not found on most printers. Among these are the blink, reverse image, and nondisplay attributes. Second, a printer is an output-only device with no input capability. A terminal, on the other hand, has both input and output capability. A single display format can be used both to display output data and to enter new data. Because of this dual capability, the rules for format design must be more flexible than those used for an output-only device. The third reason is that although a printed report usually displays a large amount of data, a display format usually displays only a single item or transaction. The concepts used in designing a report showing hundreds or thousands of data records do not necessarily work well when only a single item is displayed. Finally, the physical format of a screen differs from that of a printed report. As was stated earlier, most screens are capable of displaying only 80 characters on a line, instead of the 132 characters on most printed lines. Most screens show a single group of 24 lines instead of the unlimited number of lines available on a printed report. Because of the limited amount of data available to the user at any one time, the use of the space in a display format must be planned very carefully.

The following concepts dealing with the design of display formats should be considered as guidelines, not rules. All these concepts must be balanced against one another to develop a display format that best serves the user of the program.

▶ **Keep It Simple** The more complicated a display format appears, the more difficult it is to work with. When designing a display format, keep in mind the experience level of the person who will be working with the display. You, as a programmer, are comfortable with computers, terminals, and displays. The person using the program you write and the display or displays that the program uses may not have your level of expertise. In fact, the person using your display formats may be uncomfortable with computers in general. Do not overwhelm the user with the quantity of information you can place on a screen at one time. When possible, limit each display format to a single idea or concept. A common mistake of beginning programmers is overuse of some of the fancier attributes such as blink and reverse image.

Most display users fall into two categories: those who use the terminal for extended periods of time and those who use a terminal only occasionally. Users, such as data entry people, who use a terminal for an entire work day can become fatigued and suffer eye strain from the excessive use of attributes and from displays that attempt to pack too much information into a small screen area. As was stated earlier, the excessive use of attributes causes them to be ignored.

Users who use a terminal only occasionally want the display to be clear, complete, and understandable. This group of users may not be highly computer literate and wants to use the terminals simply as a tool. These people want the display they see to provide all the information needed so that they can perform the function that the display was designed for. They do not want to have to use a reference manual or ask questions to get the information they need. Remember that the occasional user is using a display because information is needed or data must be entered quickly. A display format that does not lend itself to quick, total understanding will not only generate information but may also generate unhappy users. Never forget that the primary function of all business data processing is to provide an easy-to-use accurate service to the people using the application program.

▶ **Identify Everything** Every element of a display should be identified. As you learned earlier, every display format should contain a unique identifier either in the form of an alphameric code or a title. Every input or output field should be captioned. Captions can appear either above or to the side of the element being identified. Generally, if the caption is beside the element. the caption should be to the element's left. When you design captions, use full words rather than abbreviations when possible; use *student identification* rather than *stud. I.D.*; use *do not* rather than *don't*.

If a caption is functioning as a prompt to identify information to be entered, make the prompt specific to the type of data to be entered. Rather than a prompt that says *Enter Date*, use a prompt such as *Enter Date (MM/DD/YY)*, which specifies the format in which the date is to be entered. If the data format is specified as part of the prompt, the user is less likely to make data entry errors.

Use column separators to show the number of data positions in an entry field if the length of the field may vary. Name fields and money amount fields are typical of the types of fields that work best when column separators are used. The length of the data in these fields may vary from one record to the next. By providing column separators, you are identifying the number of positions available for the data.

In addition to identifying the fields that appear on the screen, a good display format also shows the command or function keys that can be used with the format and the action taken as the result of each of these keys. The format shown in Figure 12-9 identifies the Command key that can be used with the display and what the key does. Note that the key is identified as it appears on the terminal keyboard. If a display format uses more than one Command key, all of them should be identified. Also note that the action taken by the Enter key is identified. One of the more common mistakes in display format design is the lack of information about the result of pressing the Enter key.

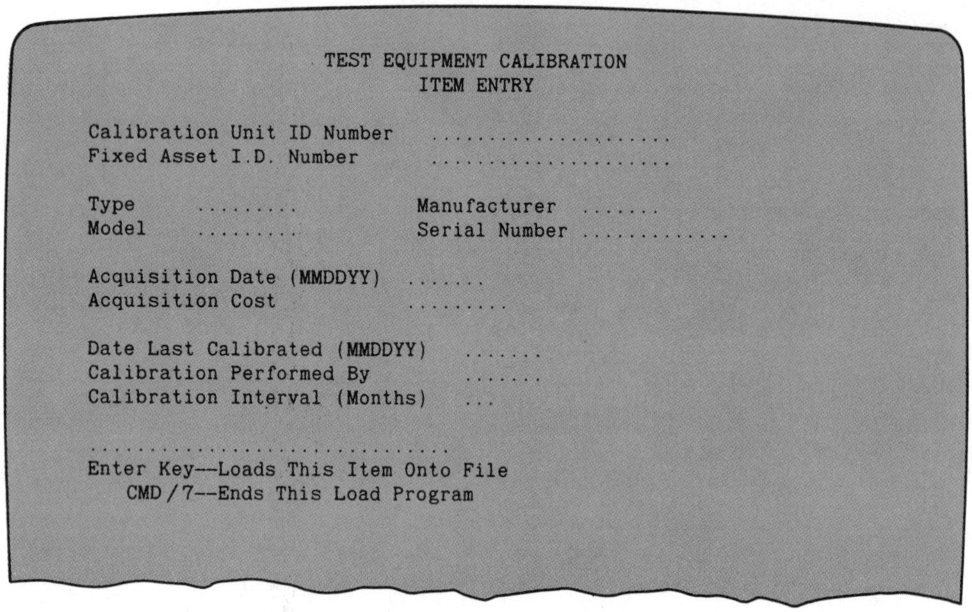

```
                  TEST EQUIPMENT CALIBRATION
                          ITEM ENTRY

Calibration Unit ID Number      ....................
Fixed Asset I.D. Number         ....................


Type         ........      Manufacturer  .......
Model        ........      Serial Number ...........


Acquisition Date (MMDDYY)   .......
Acquisition Cost            ........


Date Last Calibrated (MMDDYY)    .......
Calibration Performed By         .......
Calibration Interval (Months)    ...


..................................
Enter Key---Loads This Item Onto File
    CMD / 7--Ends This Load Program
```

Figure 12-9   Command key identification

▶ **Organize the Format Carefully**   The sequence of entry fields in a data entry format should, when possible, match the sequence of the data fields in the **source document** from which the data is being entered. Figure 12-10 shows a data entry format and the source document from which the data is entered. Note that the field sequence is the same on both. Because of the similarity of sequence, the data entry operator is able to transfer data efficiently from source document to keyboard. Compare this with the format in Figure 12-11 (on page 12.12). In this example, the sequence of fields in the source document does not match the sequence of fields in the display format. As a result, the operator has to search the source document for the needed fields rather than being able simply to follow the document as in Figure 12-10.

Separate areas of the display with blank space. Avoid the use of strings of special characters such as *************** or --------------. The most efficient and least distracting separator is a blank area. The excessive use of strings of characters also can clutter a screen and distract the user from the data.

Note: Boldfaced field names denote required entries; (n/o) denotes numeric only entries.

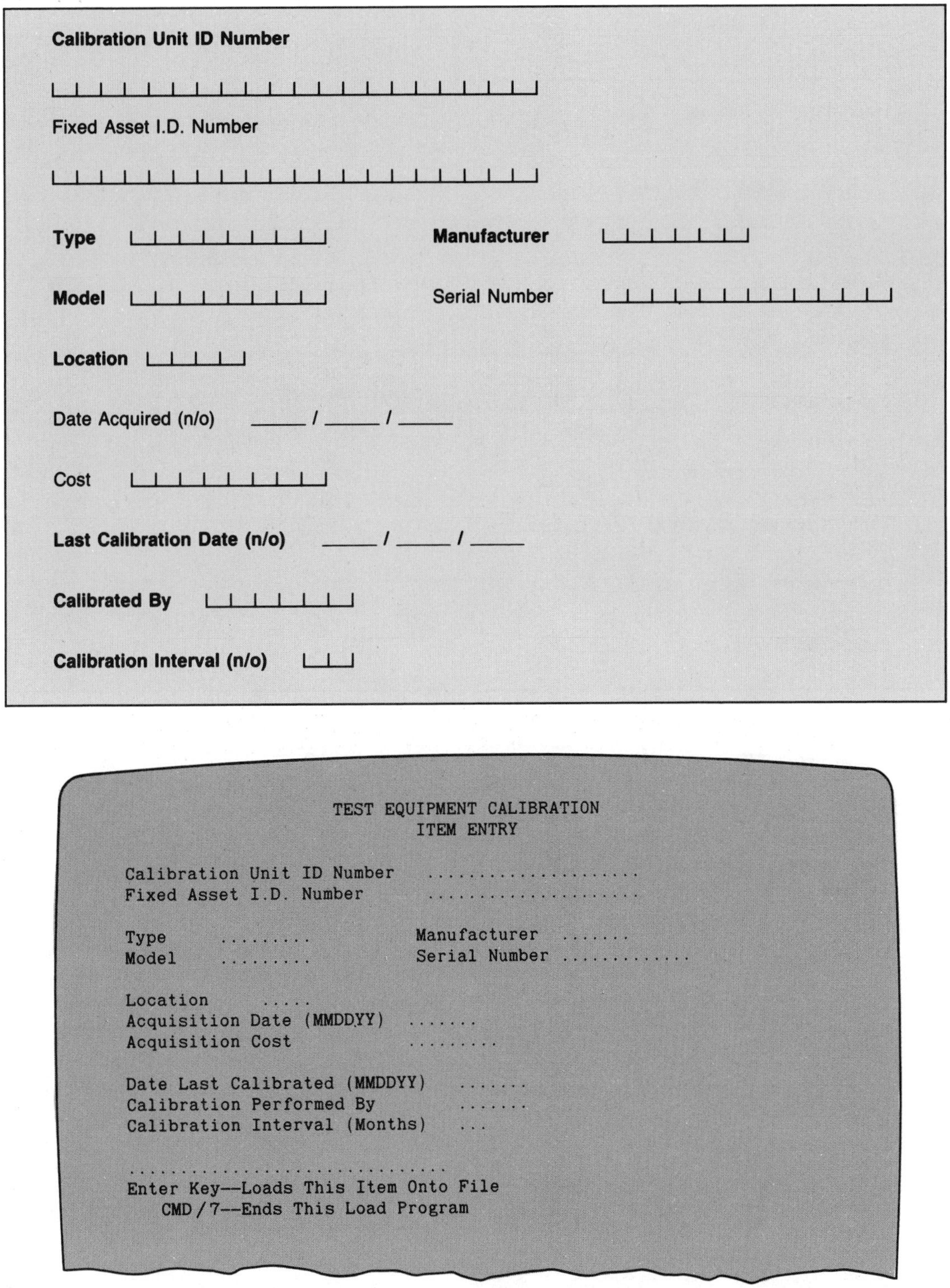

Calibration Unit ID Number

⌊⌊⌊⌊⌊⌊⌊⌊⌊⌊⌊⌊⌊⌊⌊⌊⌊⌊⌊⌊⌊⌊⌊⌊⌊⌊⌋

Fixed Asset I.D. Number

⌊⌊⌊⌊⌊⌊⌊⌊⌊⌊⌊⌊⌊⌊⌊⌊⌊⌊⌊⌊⌊⌊⌊⌋

Type ⌊⌊⌊⌊⌊⌊⌊⌊⌊⌋   **Manufacturer** ⌊⌊⌊⌊⌊⌊⌋

Model ⌊⌊⌊⌊⌊⌊⌊⌊⌊⌋   Serial Number ⌊⌊⌊⌊⌊⌊⌊⌊⌊⌊⌊⌊⌊⌊⌋

Location ⌊⌊⌊⌊⌋

Date Acquired (n/o) _____ / _____ / _____

Cost ⌊⌊⌊⌊⌊⌊⌊⌊⌊⌋

Last Calibration Date (n/o) _____ / _____ / _____

Calibrated By ⌊⌊⌊⌊⌊⌊⌊⌋

Calibration Interval (n/o) ⌊⌊⌋

```
                    TEST EQUIPMENT CALIBRATION
                           ITEM ENTRY

     Calibration Unit ID Number     ....................
     Fixed Asset I.D. Number        ....................

     Type       ........     Manufacturer  .......
     Model      ........     Serial Number ...........

     Location      .....
     Acquisition Date (MMDDYY)  .......
     Acquisition Cost           .........

     Date Last Calibrated (MMDDYY)   .......
     Calibration Performed By        .......
     Calibration Interval (Months)   ...


     ...............................
     Enter Key--Loads This Item Onto File
        CMD / 7--Ends This Load Program
```

Figure 12-10   Source document and display format: same field sequence

Note: Boldfaced field names denote required entries; (n/o) denotes numeric only entries.

Calibration Unit ID Number

|_|_|_|_|_|_|_|_|_|_|_|_|_|_|_|_|_|_|_|_|_|_|_|_|_|_|

Fixed Asset I.D. Number

|_|_|_|_|_|_|_|_|_|_|_|_|_|_|_|_|_|_|_|_|_|_|_|_|_|_|

Type |_|_|_|_|_|_|_|_|_| **Manufacturer** |_|_|_|_|_|_|_|

Model |_|_|_|_|_|_|_|_|_| Serial Number |_|_|_|_|_|_|_|_|_|_|_|_|_|_|_|

Location |_|_|_|_|_|

Date Acquired (n/o) _____ / _____ / _____

Cost |_|_|_|_|_|_|_|_|_|_|

Last Calibration Date (n/o) _____ / _____ / _____

Calibrated By |_|_|_|_|_|_|_|

Calibration Interval (n/o) |_|_|_|

```
                    TEST EQUIPMENT CALIBRATION
                          ITEM ENTRY


        Fixed Asset I.D. Number        .....................

        Calibration Unit ID Number     .....................
        Calibration Interval(Months) ...

        Acquisition Cost               .......
        Date Last Calibrated(MMDDYY) .......
        Calibration Performed By       .......

        Manufacturer  .......   Type      .........  Model    .........
        Serial Number .............

        Acquisition Date (MMDDYY)   .......   Location    .....


        ................................
        Enter Key--Loads This Item Onto File
           CMD / 7--Ends This Load Program
```

Figure 12-11 Source document and display format: different field sequence

Organize the display elements in easy-to-follow columns or lists. Avoid random arrangements of data. Refer to the menus shown in Figures 12-2 and 12-3. Note that the columnar arrangement of the menu choices makes it easier to find the functions and command numbers than would be the case if these items were shown in a scattered format.

Organize groups of common fields in a familiar pattern when possible. Fields arranged in the sequence

Name
Address
City
State
Zip Code

are easier to work with than the same fields arranged in the sequence

State
Zip Code
Name
City
Address

This is because the first sequence of fields is a familiar pattern, and the second is an unfamiliar pattern that must be learned.

▶ **Attributes Usage**   Avoid the overuse of attributes that can complicate a display. However, when these attributes are used, be sure that a specific attribute always means the same thing on any given format. For example, a data entry format may contain some fields that must be entered and others that are optional entries. If reverse image is used to identify the required entry fields, be sure that all required entry fields are in reverse image and that reverse image is not used for any other purpose on that display. Blink should be reserved for those items that must be called to the operators attention, such as error messages.

One last word: Use high intensity sparingly. If it is used excessively, the operator may simply turn the contrast control on the monitor to a lower setting, making the normal-intensity elements of the display more difficult to read. This can lead to errors.

There is one other problem with high-intensity use. If a screen containing high-intensity elements is used for extended periods of time (all day, every day for data entry), the screen may eventually retain a permanent image of the high-intensity areas. This is caused by the image being burned into the chemical coating on the inside of the screen; it is a common problem when video games are played on television sets for extended times. Although this phosphor burn-in does not cause any other problem with the terminal and does not damage the terminal in any other way, the permanent screen image can be distracting to the user.

INTERACTIVE PROGRAMMING WITH SYSTEM/36 SCREEN DESIGN AID

Problem Description

The sample program in this chapter is a data entry program that demonstrates the concepts of interactive programming using screen formats. At first glance, the sample program may appear very complicated; but as you progress through the RPG code needed to develop an interactive program, you will see that very little new RPG code is needed. This program combines many of the techniques that you have mastered and, in some cases, uses them in different ways.

The software used to generate display formats is a separate utility program, not a part of RPG, and thus it varies greatly from one computer to another. For example, the IBM System/36, System/38, and AS/400 computers are members of the same family of minicomputers and use a utility program named Screen Design Aid (SDA) to generate display formats. Even though these three computers are part of the same family, the SDA for the System/36 differs from the SDA used by the System/38 and AS/400.

The remainder of this chapter demonstrates the development of an interactive data entry program on the IBM System/36 because of its wide use and because the most widely used microcomputer versions of RPG use an SDA that is patterned after the System/36 SDA. Even though you may not be using a computer that uses a display format generator similar to the System/36 SDA, the concepts that are used by SDA apply to most display format design utilities. Throughout the remainder of this chapter, any reference to RPG or RPG II pertains to System/36 RPG II unless otherwise indicated.

▸ **Input** Unlike our previous programs, the sample program in this chapter does not use a data file as input. Input to this program is the source document in Figure 12-12, which contains the data to be entered into the computer to add records to the Test Equipment Calibration File.

Note: Boldfaced field names denote required entries; (n/o) denotes numeric only entries.

Figure 12-12   Source document for test equipment calibration file

The Test Equipment Calibration File is used to maintain a record of the equipment used to test the accuracy of the electronics components manufactured by . . . Of Cabbages and Kings, a high-tech firm that manufactures electronic components for use in several aerospace vehicles. As part of the manufacturing process, each component is subjected to several tests by the Quality Control department, which uses specialized testing equipment to assure that each component meets of exceeds the required specifications. To further assure the quality of each component, each piece of test equipment is periodically adjusted or calibrated to assure that the test equipment provides accurate information about the components being tested.

Each source document contains information about one unit of test equipment, which is identified by a calibration unit I.D. number. The fixed asset I.D. number is a secondary identification number and is part of the company's overall equipment inventory system. All applications that work specifically with test equipment use the calibration unit I.D. number as the unit identifier. The Type, Manufacturer, Model, and Serial Number fields contain information that is specific to each piece of test equipment. The Location field specifies where, within the company, the unit is located and used. The Acquisition Date and Acquisition Cost fields contain the date the unit was purchased and its original cost. These values are used, if the unit must be repaired, to determine whether it is more cost effective to repair or to replace the unit. The Date Last Calibrated field specifies when the unit was last tested for accuracy of its readings. The Calibration By field specifies the department or outside company that performs the calibration process on the unit. The calibration interval specifies how often the unit must be calibrated.

Note that several of the fields on the source document have been indicated as **mandatory** entries, which must be made and cannot be left blank, and several have been indicated as numeric only entries, which can contain only numeric data. This source document, as well as several of the problem's processing requirements, will serve as the basis for design of the display format used by the program.

▸ **Output** The first of the two output files created by the sample program is the Test Equipment Calibration File (CAL01), shown in Figure 12-13. As you can see, CALF01 contains all the data fields contained in the source document. One new field, NXTDAT, must be created by the program.

TEST EQUIPMENT MASTER FILE						
Record Length 145			Key Location 5–25 (CALNO)			
Field No.	Field Name	Field Description	Field Position	Field Length	Dec. Pos.	Data Class
1		Status Code A	1–1			
2		Record Code CAL	2–4			
3	CALNO	Calibration ID No.	5–24	20		A
4	TYPE	Unit Type	25–32	8		A
5	MFGR	Manufacturer	33–38	6		A
6	MODEL	Unit Model Number	39–46	8		A
7	SERIAL	Unit Serial Number	47–58	12		A
8	LOCATN	Unit Location	59–62	4		A
9	ACQDAT	Acquisition Date	63–68	6	0	N
10	ACQCST	Acquisition Cost	69–74	6	2	N
11	CALDAT	Date of Last Calibration	75–80	6	0	N
12	NXTDAT	Date of Next Calibration	81–86	6	0	N
13	DONEBY	Calibrated By	90–95	6		A
14	CALINT	Calibration Interval	96–97	2	0	N
15	FAIDNO	Fixed Asset I.D. Number	126–145	20		A

Figure 12-13 Format of test equipment calibration file

The second file created by the program is the Test Equipment Master File Load Report in Figure 12-14. Note that the report layout does not show any error message lines. This is because of one of the advantages of an interactive record addition program over the batch processing type of record addition applications that you have already learned. Because an interactive program develops a dialogue between the user and the computer, the program can identify any input data errors as they occur and immediately generate an on-screen message informing the user of the error. The user can then correct the error and reenter the data. As a result, all incorrect data is detected, or **trapped** by the interactive ability of the program, and so there is no need for error message lines on the report that generates the audit trail of data entered into the file. Interactive data entry applications are able to detect data errors as soon as they are entered and to correct them in real-time, that is, as soon as they are detected.

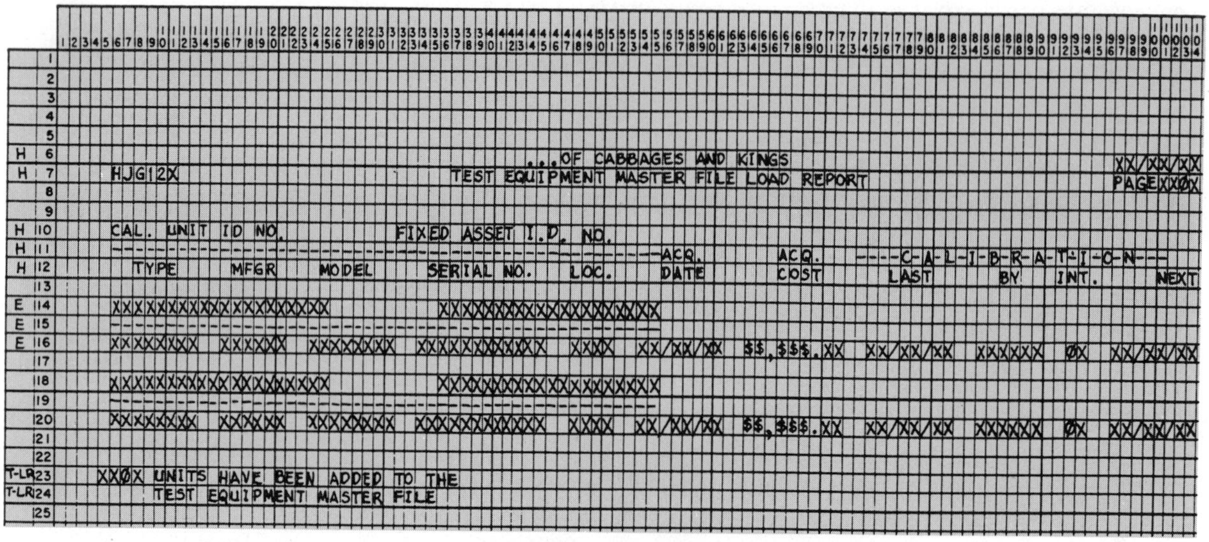

Figure 12-14   **Test Equipment Master File Load Report**

▸ **Processing Requirements**   Program HJG12X generates a data entry display format that contains all entries needed to add records to the Test Equipment Calibration File, based on the following requirements:

1. The program creates one CALF01 record for each source document entered.
2. The key field of each record added is the calibration unit I.D. number. The file must not contain duplicate record keys.
3. The CALN0, TYPE, MFGR, MODEL, LOCATN, CALDAT, DONEBY, and CALINT fields are required. The program does not add a record to CALF01 if one or more of these fields is blank.
4. The ACQDAT, ACQCST, CALDAT, and CALINT fields must contain only numeric data. The program does, however, allow the Acquisition Cost (ACQCST) field to be entered with numeric editing characters. If editing characters are entered, the program removes them from the data field before the record is added to CALF01.
5. If the user attempts to add a record in which required data is missing or a record that contains a duplicate calibration unit I.D. number, the display format generates an error message and enables the user either to correct the error or to enter a different record.
6. In accordance with standard System/36 Command key usage, Command key 7 (CMD/7) terminates execution of the program.

▸ **Format Design**   Before we can begin to discuss the code for the sample program, one new step must be performed: the format design. Recall that the display format in a data entry program should, if possible, match the source document from which the data is entered. Figure 12-15 shows the display format design for the sample program.

Note that the display format is identified by a heading at the top of the layout and that this format does not contain an alphameric identifier in the top-left corner of the display. Remember that a display can be identified by an alphameric code, a heading, or both. By comparing this display layout with the source document, shown in Figure 12-12, you can see that the format has been designed so that the sequence of data is the same on both the source document and the display format. This leads to greater user efficiency when entering data.

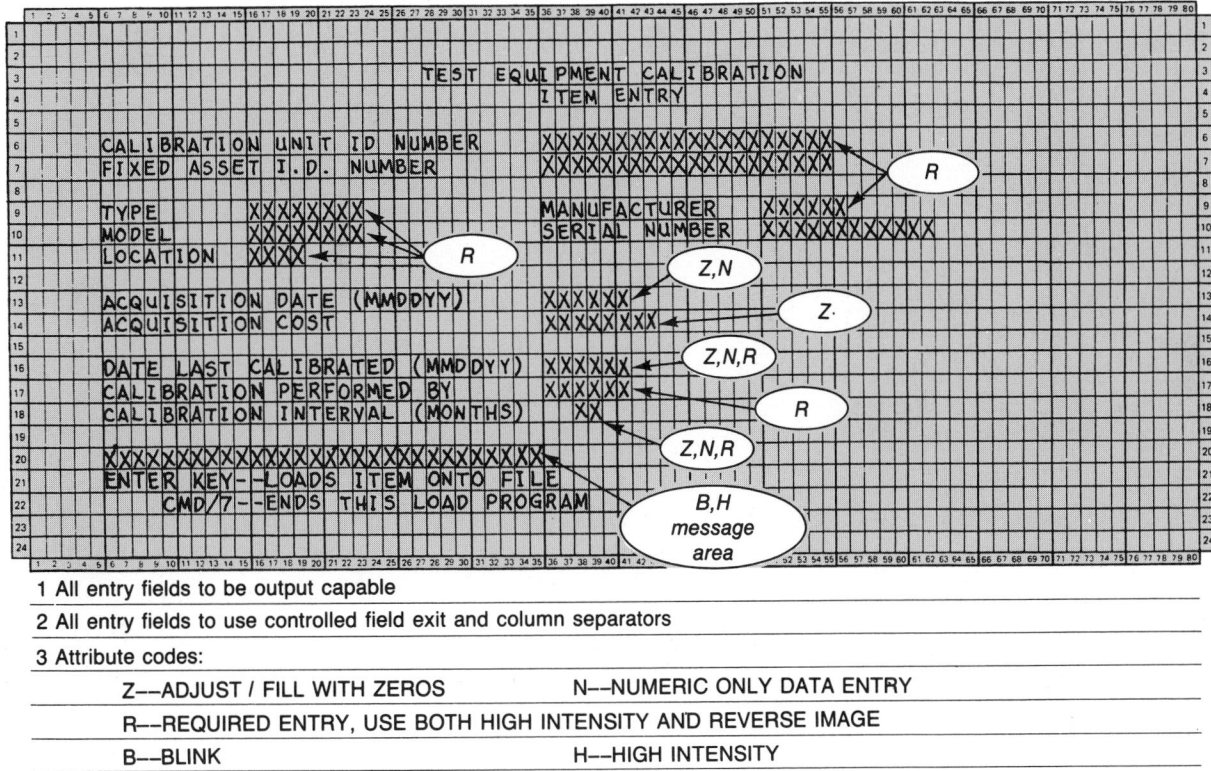

1 All entry fields to be output capable

2 All entry fields to use controlled field exit and column separators

3 Attribute codes:

Z—ADJUST / FILL WITH ZEROS	N—NUMERIC ONLY DATA ENTRY
R—REQUIRED ENTRY, USE BOTH HIGH INTENSITY AND REVERSE IMAGE	
B—BLINK	H—HIGH INTENSITY

Figure 12-15   Display format for CALS01

Note also that several of the elements of the display format are identified by their attributes. Elements that must be in reverse image, blink, and so on are identified. These attribute identifications, which are taken from the problem definition, are used when the Display Format Specifications form is coded to describe the display. Also note that by using the line numbers (located on the left and right sides of the form) and the position numbers (located at the top and bottom of the form), you can identify exactly the positions that each display element will occupy. Also note that at least one space has been left between elements to allow room for the control character that the System/36 inserts at the beginning of each element.

INTERACTIVE PROGRAM LOGIC AND DEVELOPMENT

Interactive Program Logic

Interactive programs, which obtain their input data from a terminal, are very different from the programs that you have seen and written up to now. The most obvious difference is in the logic that these programs use. Figure 12-16 shows steps of the RPG fixed logic cycle that sample program HJG12X uses.

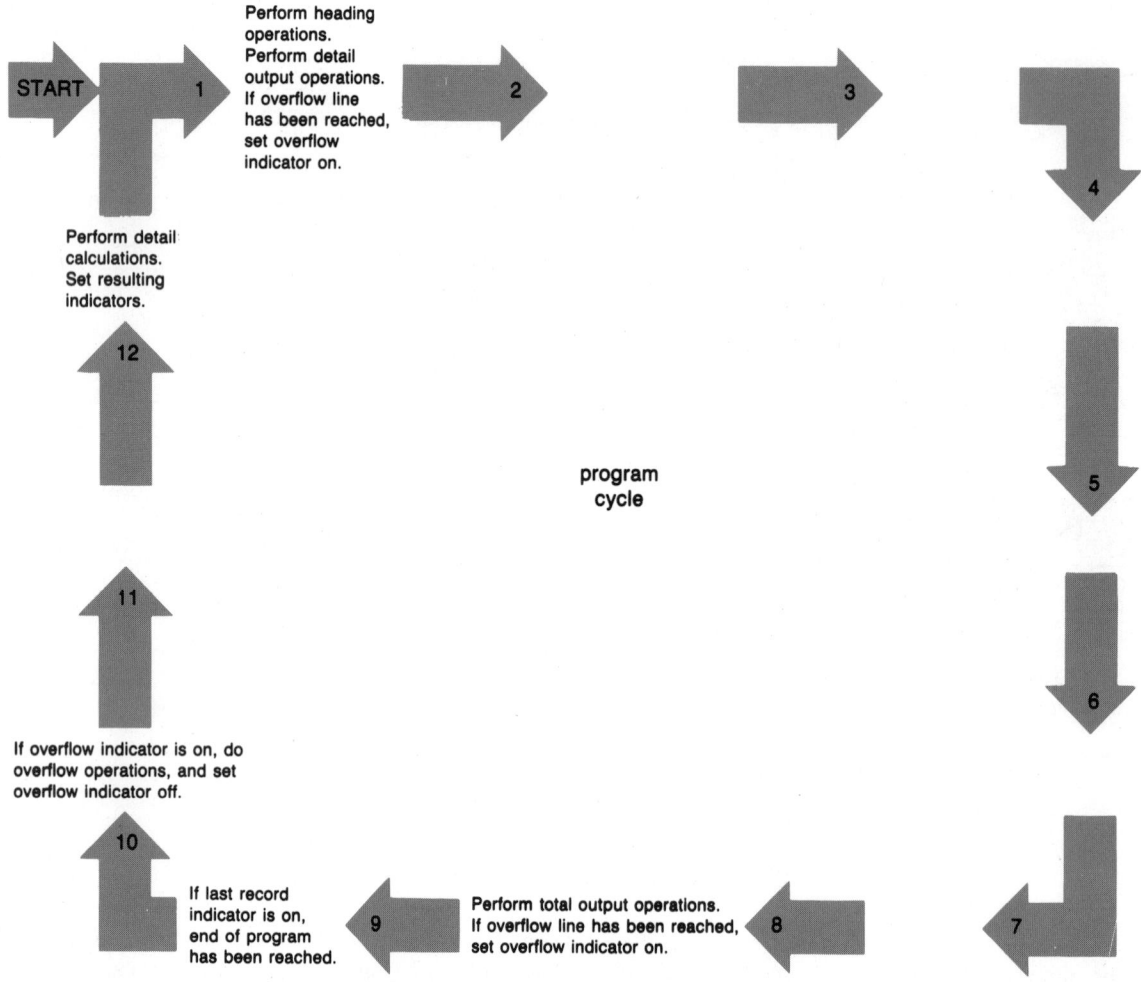

Figure 12-16 **RPG fixed logic cycle for interactive programs**

Several steps of the logic cycle are not shown in this illustration because interactive programs, unlike all previous programs, do not obtain their input data through a fixed input step in the cycle. You have written programs that control output and some input at calculation time. Interactive programs control all input by operations performed at calculation time. The dialogue between the user and the computer is controlled entirely by input and output operations that are performed during the detail calculation portion of the logic cycle.

Interactive Program Development

Most of the new concepts used by interactive programs deal with the entry and compilation of the display format. The specifications needed to describe the display format are coded on the System/36 Display Format Specifications form (Figure 12-17).

The Display Format Specification form contains two specification areas: Display Control and Field Definition. The Display Control, or S, Specification is used to describe information about the entire display format in the same manner that a File Description Specification provides information about an entire data file. Information in the S specification includes the display format name, the area of the screen on which the format is displayed, and the Command and Program Function keys that are used by the display. Every display format used with an RPG program must begin with an S specification.

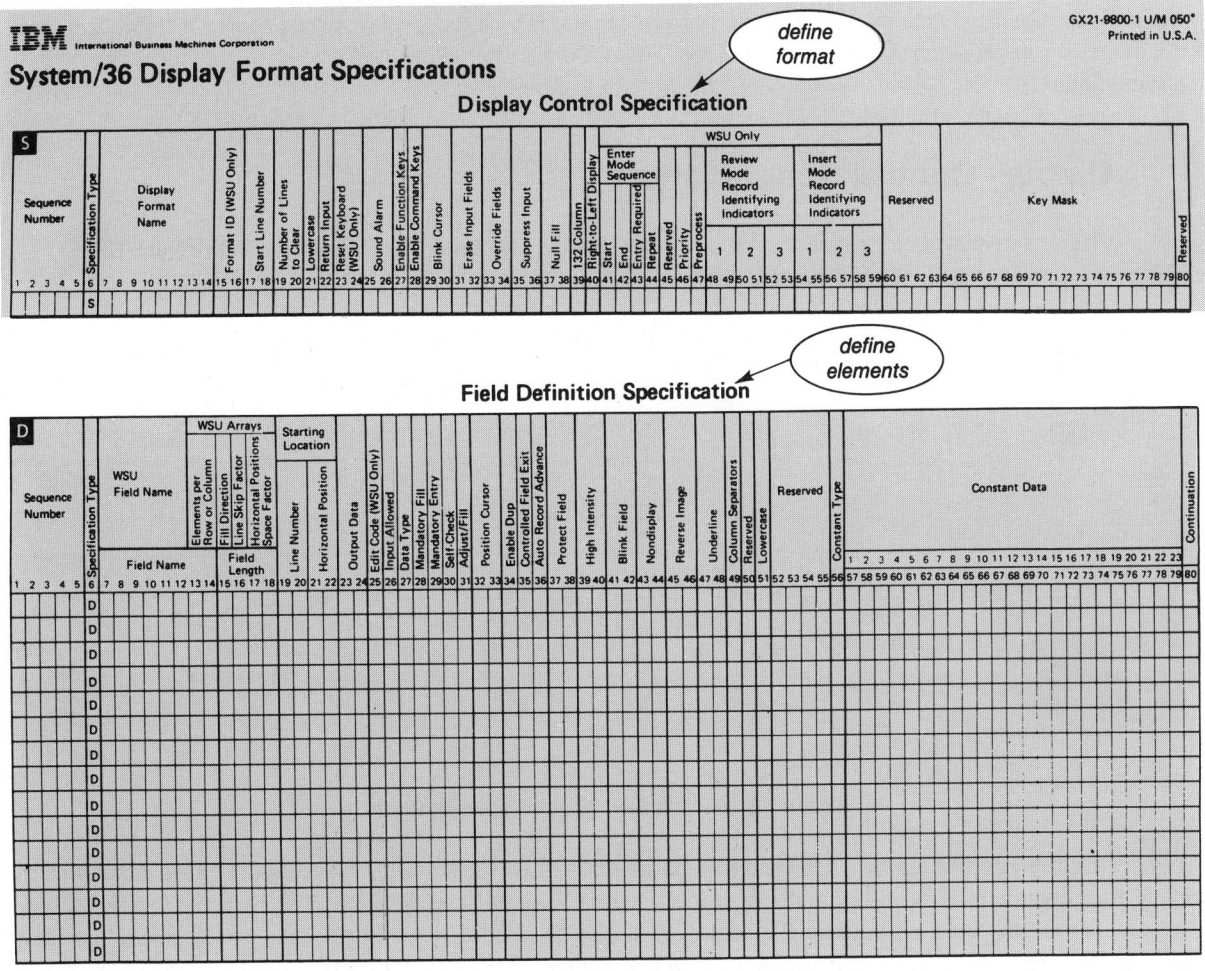

Figure 12-17   System/36 Display Format Specifications

The Field Definition, or D, Specification describes each element that is part of the display format. The D specification contains information such as element location, element attributes, whether the element is an input or output area, and the constants to be used in caption elements. A separate D specification line is used for each element in a display format. The Field Definition Specification form is used in a manner similar to that for the Input and Output Specification forms in RPG.

The Display Format Specification form is not an RPG specification form. These S and D specifications are used with the System/36 **Work Station Utility (WSU)**, the System/36 **Screen Format Generator ($SFGR)**, and the System/36 **Screen Design Aid (SDA)** to develop display format specifications for RPG programs.

In this chapter you will learn to use the Screen Design Aid as a tool for interactive program development. SDA performs several functions that relate to display formats. In the sample program, you will use SDA to compile the S and D specifications into a display load member and to generate the RPG specifications needed to integrate a display format into an RPG program.

DISPLAY FORMAT SPECIFICATIONS FOR PROGRAM HJG12X

The first step in coding an interactive application program is to code the S and D specifications that control the display format or formats used in the program. These specifications are based on the display format layout (Figure 12-15) just as RPG output specifications are based on the printer spacing chart. These specifications are entered into the computer as a source member, using either SEU of DSU, in the same manner as with the RPG programs you have been entering. Do not use the same name for both the display format source member and the RPG program source member. Remember that the System/36 does not allow duplicate source member names in the same library.

Display Control Specification

The first display specification that must be coded is the Display Control Specification (Figure 12-18), which provides information about the entire display format.

Display Control Specification

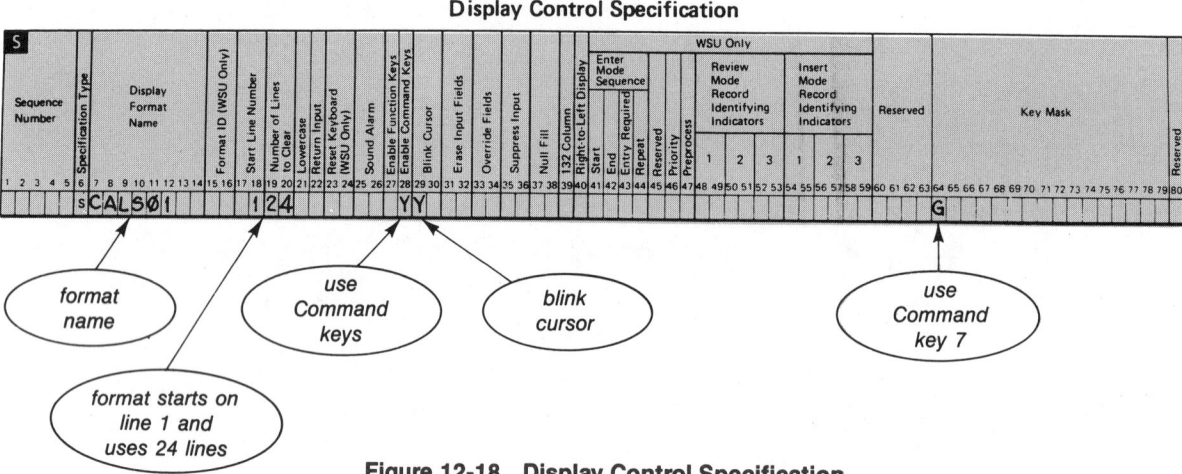

Figure 12-18   Display Control Specification

▸ **Display Format Name**   This entry, in positions 7–14, assigns a name to the display format that you are coding. If a program uses two or more display format names, they must be different. The rules for forming display format names are the same as those for file names. A display format name can be the same as the source member name used for the Display Format Specifications. In this example, the name CALS01 is used for both the source member and the display format.

▸ **Start Line Number**   The entry in positions 17–18 specifies the first screen line used by the display format. You can start a display format at any line on a screen, not just the first. You have seen examples of this if you are using a System/36 and have used the D P command to show the print queue. When any option is taken after a D P is started, the top of the screen remains unchanged, and the bottom half of the screen displays a different format. This is the result of being able to specify a starting line for a format display, In this example, CALS01 uses the entire screen, so the entry 1 has been made in position 18.

▸ **Number of Lines to Clear**   This entry, in positions 19–20, specifies the number of screen lines that are to be cleared before the format is displayed. In this example, all 24 lines are to be cleared. This is similar to a BASIC CLS command in that the entire screen is cleared, and no part of the prior display format is kept. Any number of lines from zero to the maximum number of lines on the screen can be cleared. If this entry is left blank, the entire screen is cleared.

Be sure that the combination of start line number and number of lines to clear does not exceed the size of the screen. If, for example, a display format specifies the clearing of 20 lines starting with line 10, a Terminal error is generated if your terminal cannot display 29 lines.

▸ **Enable Command Keys** The entry Y in position 28 specifies that the program user can use only certain specified Command keys with the display format. This entry has been made because the program specifications state that Command key 7 (CMD/7) is used to indicate the end of the program. As you will see when the RPG code is presented, the program contains code that turns on indicator LR when Command key 7 is used.

If position 28 is left blank, all Command keys are available to the user. When this is done, the program must contain code that specifies what action is to be taken for each of the Command keys, Do not leave this entry blank unless the program you are developing uses all the available Command keys.

▸ **Blink Cursor** The entry Y in position 29 causes the cursor to blink when it is displayed within the format regardless of whether the cursor is shown as a rectangle or as an underline. A blinking cursor is easier to see and work with than a steady cursor.

Note that the Blink Cursor area contains two positions. It is also possible to enter an indicator into this area. If you do this, the cursor blinks only if the entered indicator is on. If the indicator is not on, the cursor is steady. Although this feature draws the user's attention to an area on a display, other features for individual elements, such as the blink, high intensity, and reverse image attributes, can attract a user's attention much more quickly.

▸ **Key Mask** The Key Mask area, positions 64–79, specifies which Command keys are active with the display format being described. The entries made in the Key Mask area are a series of alphabetic characters, each of which represents one Command key. Figure 12-19 shows the alphabetic character that identifies each Command Key to be activated. Note from the examples in the figure that the letters in the Key Mask area are entered with no separation. Also note that these entries need not be in any particular order.

Alphabetic character	Command key	Alphabetic character	Command key
A	1	M	13
B	2	N	14
C	3	P	15
D	4	Q	16
E	5	R	17
F	6	S	18
G	7	T	19
H	8	U	20
I	9	V	21
J	10	W	22
K	11	X	23
L	12	Y	24

Figure 12-19 Command keys and letter codes

As Figure 12-18 shows, a G has been entered in the Key Mask area because Command key 7 is the only active Command key in this display format.

Field Definition Specifications

Recall that each element of a display format must be described by a field definition specification. Each input or output data field and each constant used as a heading or caption must be described by a separate D specification. As is the case with RPG input and output field specifications, the language does not require that these elements be described in any particular order. The accepted practice, however, is to describe display elements in a top-down manner as with all parts of RPG.

Constant Description   The first three elements in the display format are constants. Two of the constants provide the heading for the format, and the third is the caption for the Calibration Unit I.D. Number data entry field. Figure 12-20 shows the D specifications needed to define the first of these three constants.

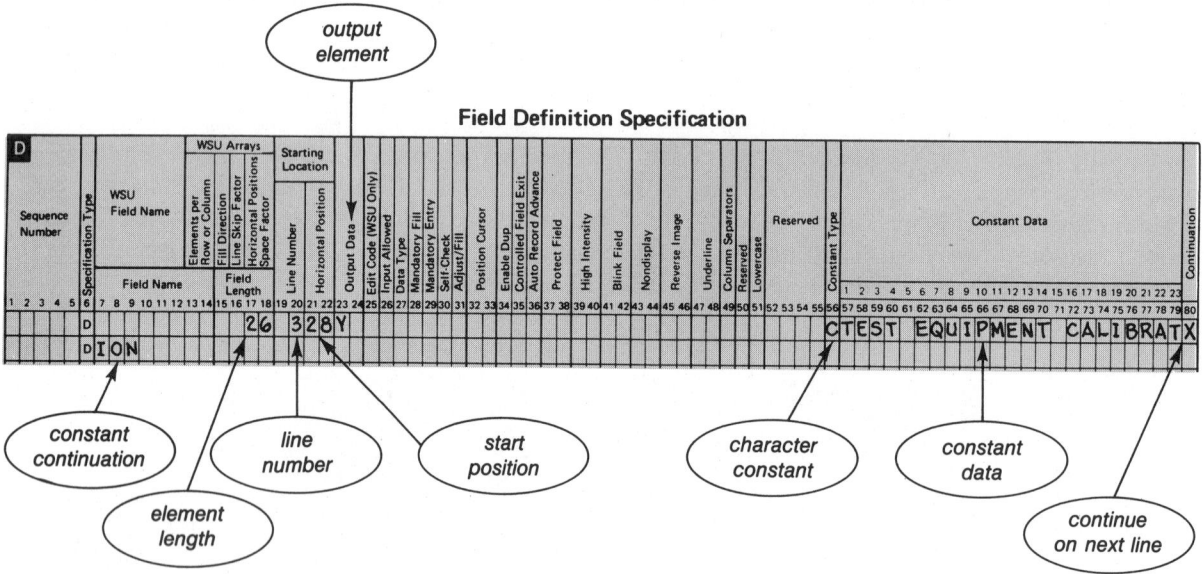

Figure 12-20   Constant definition

The first entry in the constant definition specifies the location of the constant on the screen. These location entries are used for all format elements, both constants and data fields. To properly place an element on the screen, SDA must be provided with three facts about the element: the field length of the element (positions 15–18), the line number on which the element is to be displayed (positions 19–20), and the horizontal position, or start position, of the first position of the element (positions 21–22). Unlike the RPG output specifications, which use a single end-position entry to identify a field location, the D specification uses a start position only. As Figure 12-20 shows, the first heading constant is 26 positions long, is displayed on line 3 of the screen, and begins in position 28 of line 3. Every element of a display must contain these three entries as part of its description.

The Output Data area, positions 23–24 of the D specification, specifies whether the element is an output element and is to be displayed on the screen. If this entry is left blank, the element is not an output element. If a Y is entered in position 23, the element is an output element. If positions 23–24 contain an indicator, the output from the element is performed only if the indicator is on. Because the display must show the heading constant every time the format is displayed, a Y has been entered in position 23.

The entry C in position 56, the Constant Type area, specifies that a constant is to be displayed. The Constant Data area, positions 57–79, specifies the contents of the constant. The constant data to be displayed is entered, left-justified, in the Constant Data area. Note that this area is only 23 positions long. In this example, the constant is 26 characters long, three more than the space available in the Constant Data area. When this problem occurs on an RPG Output Specifications form, the solution is to divide the constant into two separate entries and display them in consecutive print positions. This cannot always be done on the D specification because SDA requires at least one unused position between elements of a display format.

To allow the display of constants greater than 23 positions long, the D specification can continue a constant on a second specification line. **Continuation** is specified by placing an X in position 80 (the Continuation area) of the line to be continued. Figure 12-20 shows that the first 23 characters of the constant (Test Equipment Calibrat) have been entered on the first line, followed by an X in position 80. The remainder of the constant (ion) has been entered on the next line of the specification form. Note that when a constant is continued, the continued portion begins in position 7 of the next line. When constant continuation is used, SDA assumes that the entire second line is an extension of the Constant Data area and ignores the individual areas.

Figure 12-21 shows the completed coding of the first three constants in the display format. Note the use of lowercase letters on the third constant. Constants can be displayed in either uppercase or lowercase letters and are coded exactly as they are to be displayed. This is one of the few instances in which program coding is done in lowercase letters rather than the ordinary practice of using all capital letters.

▸ **Data Field Description** Figure 12-22 shows the entries needed to describe CALNO, the Calibration Unit I.D. Number entry field. Note that the field name (CALNO) has been entered, left-justified, into the Field Name area, positions 7–14. Although this area is eight positions long, only the first six positions can be used for a field name because RPG limits field name length to six positions. This area is eight positions long because these specifications and SDA can be used with other programming languages, some of which allow field names of more than six characters.

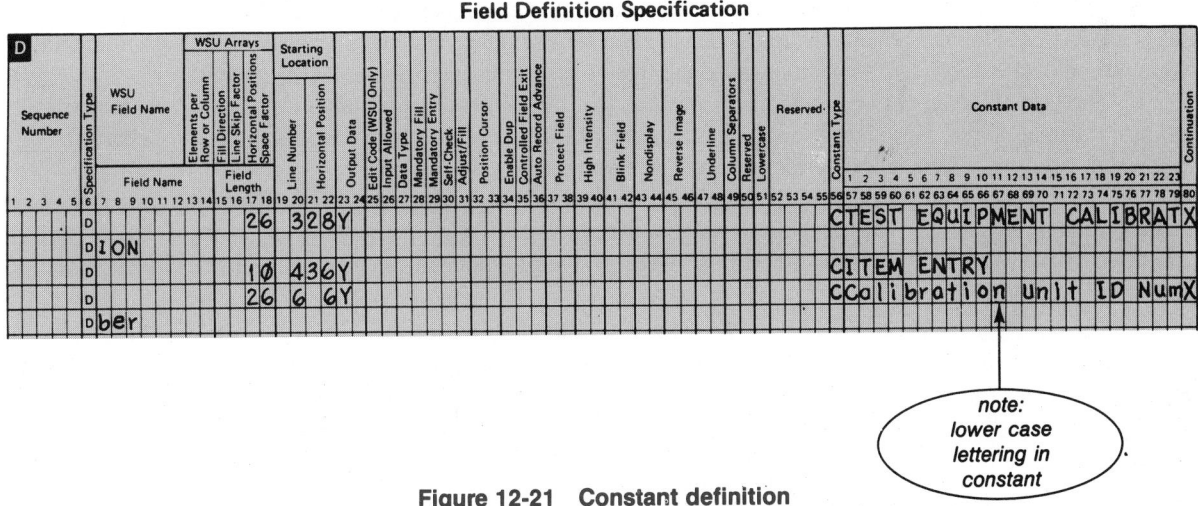

Figure 12-21 Constant definition

Figure 12-22 Field definition

The entries in positions 15–23 specify that CALNO is a 20-position output field that is displayed on line 6, beginning in position 36. The Y in position 26, the Input Allowed area, specifies that CALNO is an input field and that data can be keyed into the area of the screen for use as input to the RPG program. If this entry is not made, data cannot be entered into the field.

The Y entry in position 35, the Controlled Field Exit field, specifies that one of the **field exit keys** must be used to make the cursor leave the field. When controlled field exit is specified, the user cannot simply continue keying from one field to the next. Instead, after the contents of the field have been keyed, one of the field exit keys must be pressed, The most commonly used field exit keys are the Field Advance, Field Exit, Field +, and Field – keys.

Positions 37–48 contain six areas used to specify element attributes. Each of these two-position areas can be used in one of three different ways. If the area is left blank, the attribute is not used with the element being described. If the area contains a Y in the first position (37, 39, 41, 43, 45, or 47), the attribute is used when the element is displayed. If an indicator is entered in the area, the attribute is used only if the indicator is on when the element is displayed. The description of CALNO contains a Y in positions 39 (high intensity) and 45 (reverse image).

Position 49 also describes an element attribute. This is the column separator attribute, which causes separators to be displayed between element positions on the screen. The form of these separators depends on the type of terminal you are using and cannot be changed. As you review the remainder of the D specifications, note that all input elements use the column separator attribute.

Figure 12-23 shows the completed D specifications. The specification entries for the remaining format elements are similar to those you have seen. Note that not all the data input fields use all the attributes that were used with CALNO. Remember that the high intensity and reverse image attributes are used in this example only with required data entry fields. In addition, note the three new entries in positions 27, 31, and 41.

The Data Type entry N in position 27 specifies that the element can contain only numeric characters, commas, decimal points, plus signs, minus signs, and blanks. If the user attempts to enter any other character when using the display format, the system displays an error code on the screen.

This entry is used with the ACQDAT, CALDAT, and CALINT data entry fields. The entry Z in the Adjust/Fill area, position 31, causes data entered into the field to be right-justified and any excess leftmost positions to be filled with zeros. By using the Adjust/Fill entry, the programmer assures that numeric data is placed

Figure 12-23 Field Definition Specifications for CALS01

Field Definition Specification

Specification Type (6)	WSU Field Name / Field Name (7–14)	Field Length (15–18)	Line Number (19–20)	Horizontal Position (21–22)	Output Data (23)	Input Allowed (26)	Controlled Field Exit (35)	High Intensity (39)	Reverse Image (45)	Column Separators (49)	Constant Type (56)	Constant Data (57–79)	Continuation (80)
D		26	3	28	Y						C	TEST EQUIPMENT CALIBRAT	X
D	ION												
D		1Ø	4	36	Y						C	ITEM ENTRY	
D		26	6	6	Y						C	Calibration Unit ID Num	X
D	ber												
D	CALNO	2Ø	6	36	Y	Y	Y	Y	Y	Y			
D		23	7	6	Y						C	Fixed Asset I.D. Number	
D	FAIDNO	2Ø	7	36	Y	Y	Y			Y			
D		4	9	6	Y						C	Type	
D	TYPE	8	9	16	Y	Y	Y	Y	Y	Y			
D		12	9	36	Y						C	Manufacturer	
D	MFGR	6	9	51	Y	Y	Y	Y	Y	Y			
D		5	1Ø	6	Y						C	Model	
D	MODEL	8	1Ø	16	Y	Y	Y	Y	Y	Y			
D		13	1Ø	36	Y						C	Serial Number	

Figure 12-23 (1)

Field Definition Specification

Figure 12-23 (2)

Field Name	Field Length	Line Number	Horizontal Position	Output Data	Input Allowed	Data Type	Mandatory Fill	Mandatory Entry	Self-Check	Adjust/Fill	Position Cursor	Enable Dup	Controlled Field Exit	Auto Record Advance	Protect Field	High Intensity	Blink Field	Nondisplay	Reverse Image	Underline	Column Separators	Reserved	Lowercase	Constant Type	Constant Data
SERIAL		12	10	5	Y	Y																		Y	
		8	11	6																				C	Location
LOCATN		41	11	6	Y	Y				Y					Y				Y					Y	
		25	13	6	Y																			C	Acquisition Date (MMDDYX
Y)																									
ACQDAT		61	33	6	Y	Y	N		Z		Y													Y	
		16	14	6	Y																			C	Acquisition Cost
ACQCST		81	43	6	Y	Y			Z															Y	
		29	16	6	Y																			C	Date Last Calibrated (MX
MDDYY)																									
CALDAT		61	63	6	Y	Y	N		Z		Y					Y				Y				Y	
		24	17	6	Y																			C	Calibration Performed BX
y																									
DONEBY		61	73	6	Y	Y					Y					Y				Y				Y	
		30	18	6	Y																			C	Calibration Interval (MX

Field Definition Specification

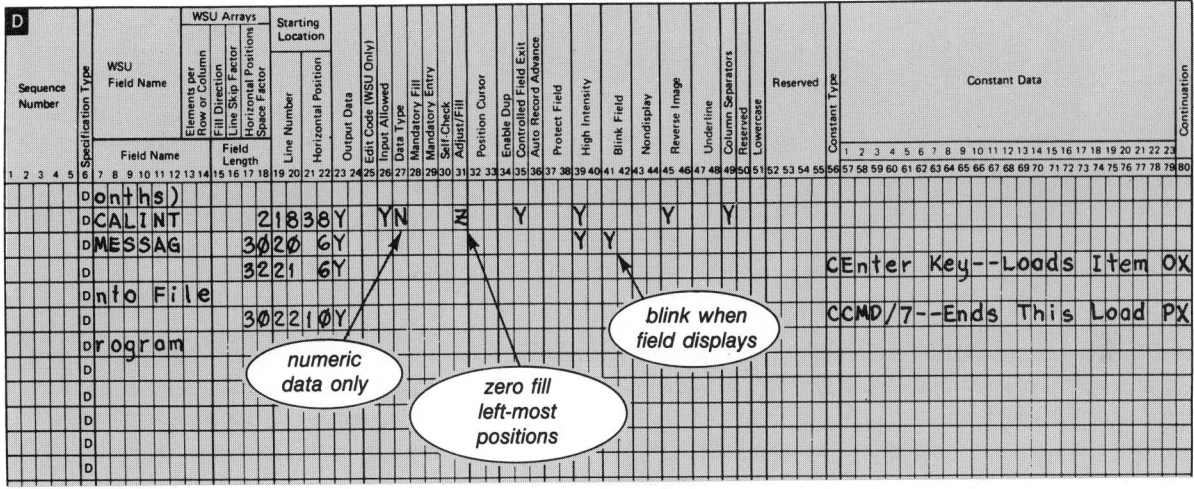

Figure 12-23 (3)

Field Name	Field Length	Line Number	Horizontal Position	Output Data	Input Allowed	Data Type	Mandatory Fill	Mandatory Entry	Self-Check	Adjust/Fill	Position Cursor	High Intensity	Blink Field	Nondisplay	Reverse Image	Underline	Column Separators	Constant Type	Constant Data
onths)																			
CALINT		21	83	8	Y	Y	N		Z		Y	Y				Y		Y	
MESSAG		30	20	6	Y								Y	Y					
		32	21	6	Y													C	Enter Key--Loads Item OX
nto File																			
		30	22	10	Y													C	CMD/7--Ends This Load PX
rogram																			

numeric data only → (position 27)

zero fill left-most positions → (Adjust/Fill position)

blink when field displays → (Blink Field position)

properly within the data field and also relieves the user of the need to place additional zero characters at the beginning of an entered field. Adjust/fill is normally used with numeric data fields.

Note the use of the blink field attribute (Y in position 41) with the MESSAG field. MESSAG contains an error message if a required field is not entered or if an attempt is made to enter a duplicate key. The use of the blink field attribute calls immediate attention to the error message.

SYSTEM/36 SCREEN DESIGN AID

After the display format specifications have been coded, desk checked to ensure their accuracy, and keyed into your library as a source member, the System/36 Screen Design Aid (SDA) converts the source member into a display load member. SDA also generates the RPG file description, input, and output specifications needed to process data using the display format.

▆▆ Display Load Member Generation

SDA can be accessed either from the main help menu or by entering the command SDA. Either method results in the display of the SDA **Main Options** menu (Figure 12-24) on your screen. Select option 2 (Design Display Formats), and the **Format Selection Display**, similar to the one shown in Figure 12-25, will be displayed on your screen. The contents of the top portion of the display, the **Member Name List**, is a list of the source members in your session library.

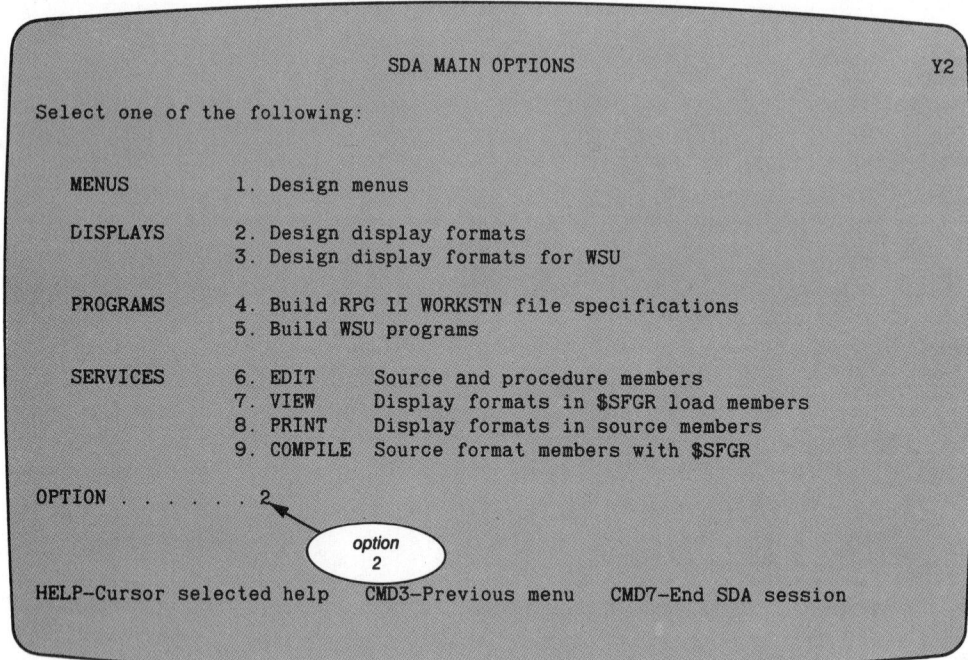

```
                        SDA MAIN OPTIONS                          Y2

     Select one of the following:


        MENUS          1. Design menus

        DISPLAYS       2. Design display formats
                       3. Design display formats for WSU

        PROGRAMS       4. Build RPG II WORKSTN file specifications
                       5. Build WSU programs

        SERVICES       6. EDIT     Source and procedure members
                       7. VIEW     Display formats in $SFGR load members
                       8. PRINT    Display formats in source members
                       9. COMPILE  Source format members with $SFGR

     OPTION . . . . . . 2
                                    option
                                      2

     HELP-Cursor selected help   CMD3-Previous menu   CMD7-End SDA session
```

Figure 12-24   SDA Main Options menu

You must make two entries in the Format Selection display – the Source Format Member Name and the Format Name – as shown in Figure 12-25. The **Source Format Member Name** is the name you assigned to the source member when you used either SEU or DSU to key the S and D specifications into your library. The **Format Name** is the name you assigned to your format when you coded the S specification. In this example, the Source Format Member Name and the Format Name are the same.

After entering the two required names, press the Enter key. SDA then displays the format you have selected (Figure 12-26). This display is generated from the S and D specifications you coded. Note that this format is not exactly the format that will be displayed when your program is run. To make it easier for you to verify the format, SDA performs several functions as an aid to debugging.

First, look at the top heading line. Instead of reading TEST EQUIPMENT CALIBRATION, the line reads TEST;EQUIPMENT;CALIBRATION. SDA inserts semicolons (;) wherever a space has been used within a constant in order to show that the space is part of a constant rather than an unused area of the display. The second function that SDA performs is to show the location of input and output field elements. These elements are shown as a series of letters I or letters O, depending on the way that you have described the field. Note that every position of the screen that is used by the display format contains a character. Any area of the screen that is blank in this display is not used by your format. Carefully compare the generated format with the original display format that you designed. Are all the captions spelled correctly? Are all the captions and input/output elements located correctly? Does the format look as good on the screen as it did on the layout form? After reviewing the format and noting any needed changes, press CMD/9 to continue to the next display. The use of CMD/9 is not shown in Figure 12-26 because the entire display is used to show the format that you have designed and entered. This is one of the rare times that SDA does not list a needed Command key. You must remember that CMD/9 is needed to exit from this format.

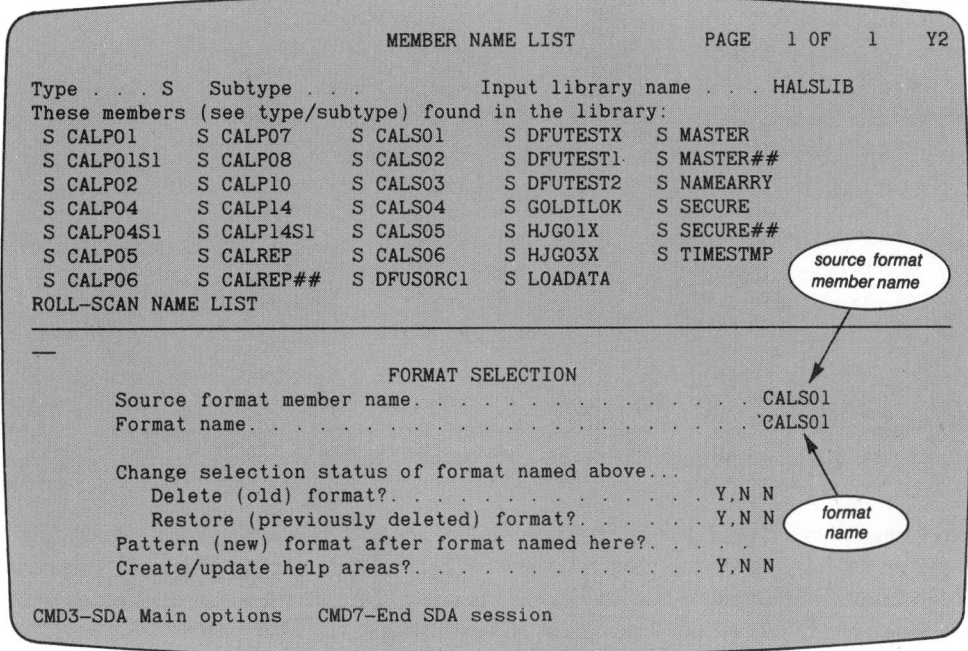

```
                         MEMBER NAME LIST              PAGE   1 OF   1     Y2

Type . . . S   Subtype . . .            Input library name . . . HALSLIB
These members (see type/subtype) found in the library:
 S CALP01      S CALP07      S CALS01      S DFUTESTX    S MASTER
 S CALP01S1    S CALP08      S CALS02      S DFUTEST1    S MASTER##
 S CALP02      S CALP10      S CALS03      S DFUTEST2    S NAMEARRY
 S CALP04      S CALP14      S CALS04      S GOLDILOK    S SECURE
 S CALP04S1    S CALP14S1    S CALS05      S HJG01X      S SECURE##
 S CALP05      S CALREP      S CALS06      S HJG03X      S TIMESTMP
 S CALP06      S CALREP##    S DFUSORC1    S LOADATA
ROLL-SCAN NAME LIST


                         FORMAT SELECTION
      Source format member name. . . . . . . . . . . . . CALS01
      Format name. . . . . . . . . . . . . . . . . . . .`CALS01

      Change selection status of format named above...
         Delete (old) format?. . . . . . . . . . . .  Y,N N
         Restore (previously deleted) format?. . . . .  Y,N N
      Pattern (new) format after format named here?. . . . .
      Create/update help areas?. . . . . . . . . . . .  Y,N N

CMD3-SDA Main options   CMD7-End SDA session
```

source format member name

format name

Figure 12-25 Format Selection display

```
..:...10....:...20....:...30....:...40....:...50....:...60....:...70....:UPDTE

                    TEST;EQUIPMENT;CALIBRATION
                          ITEM;ENTRY

      Calibration;Unit;ID;Number    00000000000000000000
      Fixed;Asset;I.D.;Number       00000000000000000000

      Type       00000000           Manufacturer    000000
      Model      00000000           Serial;Number   000000000000
      Location   0000

      Acquisition;Date;(MMDDYY)      000000
      Acquisition;Cost               00000000

      Date;Last;Calibrated;(MMDDYY)  000000
      Calibration;Performed;By       000000
      Calibration;Interval;(Months);    00

      00000000000000000000000000000000
      Enter;Key--Loads;Item;Onto;File;
         CMD/7--Ends;This;Load;Program;
```

Figure 12-26 CALS01 format display

CMD/9 leads you to the **End of Format Options** display (Figure 12-27). If you note any errors or want to make any changes in the display format, use option 2 to return to the SDA Main Options Menu and exit from SDA. After you have made your changes to the Source Format Member, return to SDA and start this process again.

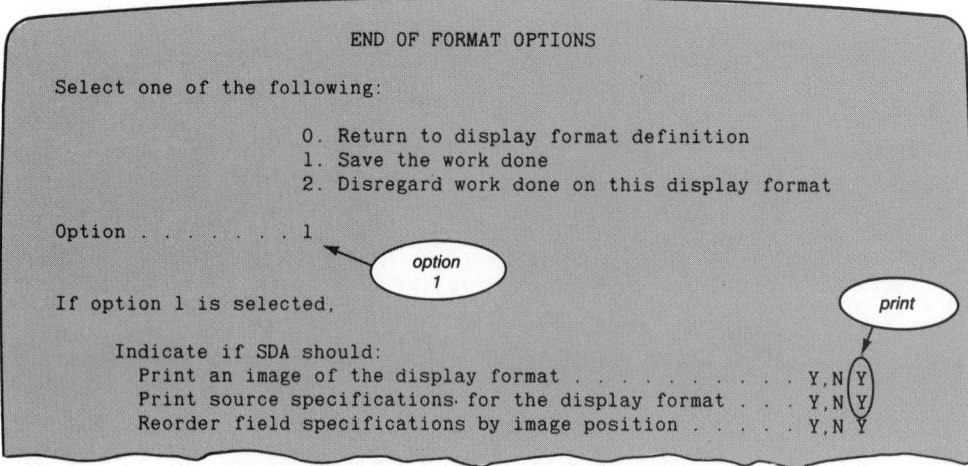

Figure 12-27   End of Format Options display

If the format does not need change or correction, use option 1 to save the format. Before you use the Enter key, however, enter a Y in the two print options at the bottom of the display. This will generate a printout of your display format and a listing of the S and D specifications that generated the format. After making the Y entries and selecting option 1, press the Enter key to go to the Format Name List display (Figure 12-28). If your source member contains only one S specification, use CMD/7 to end the format work and proceed to the **End of Member Options** display (Figure 12-29). Verify that this display shows your correct library name and the correct member name at two different points in the display. Use option 1 to compile the display format specifications and terminate work on the display format. At this point SDA returns you to the SDA Main Options menu. Shortly, SDA sends a message to your terminal informing you that the compilation of the display format specifications either did or did not complete successfully. If the display compilation was not successful, you will receive a listing showing you what errors were detected.

```
                      FORMAT NAME LIST             PAGE   1 OF   1    Y2
Library name . . . . . . . . . . . . . . . . . . . . . . .  HALSLIB
Format member name . . . . . . . . . . . . . . . . . . . .  CALS01
These display formats found in the member:
 U CALS01




ROLL-SCAN NAME LIST
--------------------------------------------------------------------------------
                        FORMAT SELECTION

      Format name. . . . . . . . . . . . . . . . . . . .

      Change selection status of format named above. . . . . .
          Delete (old) format?. . . . . . . . . . . . .  Y,N N
          Restore (previously deleted) format?. . . . .  Y,N N
      Pattern (new) format after format named here?. . . . .
      Create/update help areas?. . . . . . . . . . . .  Y,N N

CMD3-Select new member    CMD7-End format work
```

Figure 12-28   Format Name List display

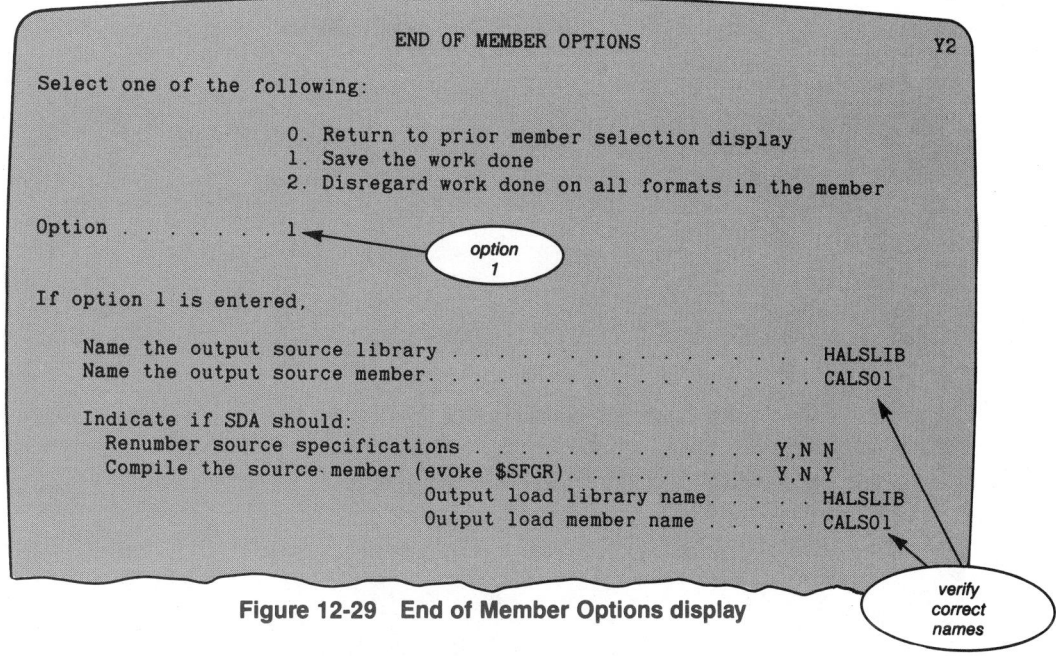

Figure 12-29   End of Member Options display

≡ RPG II Specification Generation

After you have successfully compiled your display format, you can use SDA to generate the RPG specifications needed to describe the display format. A file that is based on an interactive display format is called a **workstation file**. SDA has the ability to read a set of display format specifications containing any number of separate display formats and generate the needed file description, input, and output workstation file specifications.

The process of generating the needed RPG specifications begins at the SDA Main Options menu. Select option 4, **Build RPG II Workstn File Specifications** (Figure 12-30). Option 4 causes the **RPG Program Generation Selection** (Figure 12-31) to be displayed on your screen.

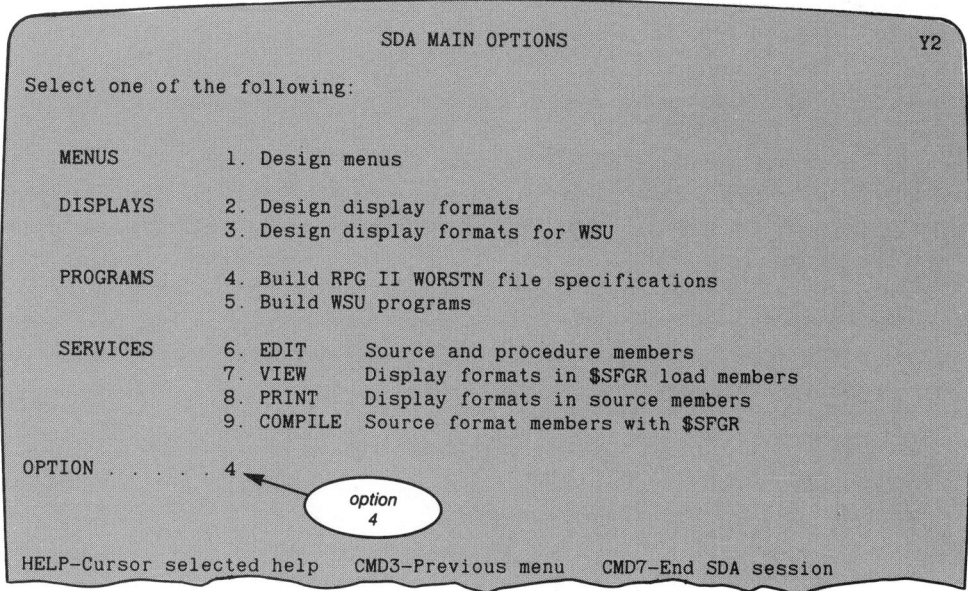

Figure 12-30   SDA Main Options menu

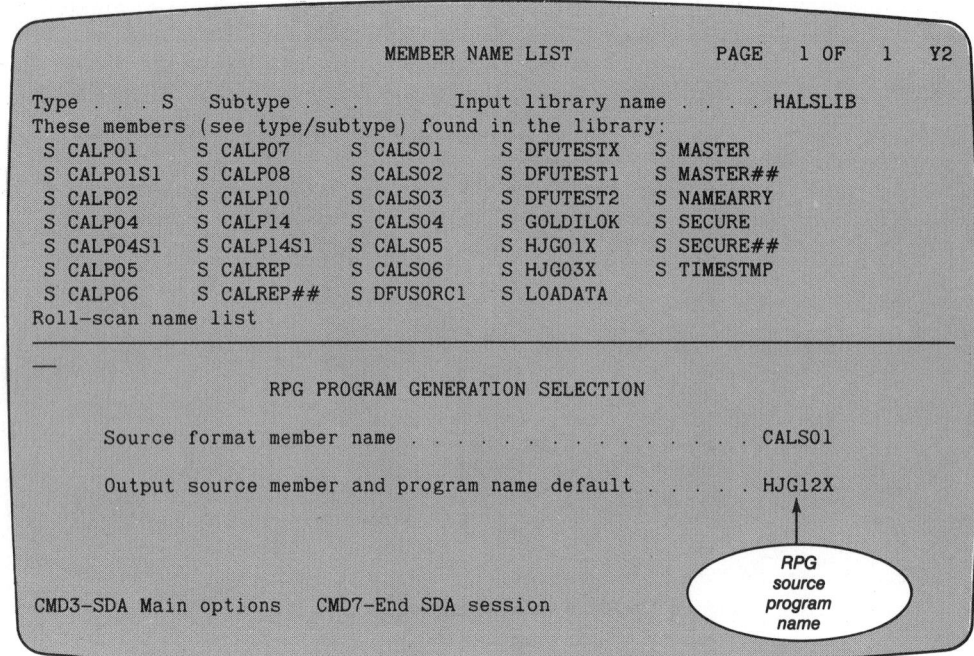

Figure 12-31 RPG Program Generation Selection display

The lower portion of the display requests two names. The first is the Source Format Member Name, which is the name of the source member containing the S and D specifications that describe the display format. The second is the name that you want assigned to the RPG source member that will contain the workstation file specifications. After these two names have been keyed in, press the Enter key to proceed to the **RPG II H and F Specifications Generation** display (Figure 12-32).

This display specifies the program identification that is to appear in positions 75–80 of the H specification of the generated program, as well as the name to be assigned to the workstation file in the generated RPG specifications. This display shows a default name based on the first six positions of the output source member name specified in the previous display (Figure 12-29). You can change this name if you choose.

You must enter a name for the workstation file. In this example, the name CALP01S1 has been entered. Note also that the record length of the workstation file records has been generated by SDA. The last entry of the display is the name of the load format member. This automatically defaults to the name used for the display format source member. After you have made the needed entry to this display, use CMD/9 to continue to the next display. Do not attempt to continue by using the Enter key.

If the display format with which you are working uses numeric input fields, the **RPG II I Specifications Generation** display appears on your screen (Figure 12-33). If the format does not contain numeric input fields, this display does not appear. All the numeric input fields used in the program are shown on this display with a Decimal Positions entry of zero. You must alter the Decimal Positions entry for any field that requires a Decimal Positions entry greater than zero. In this example, the three numeric input fields are all dates, and therefore an entry of zero is valid. After you have made all needed changes, use CMD/9 to continue to the **End of RPG Program Generation Options** display (Figure 12-34 on page 12.32).

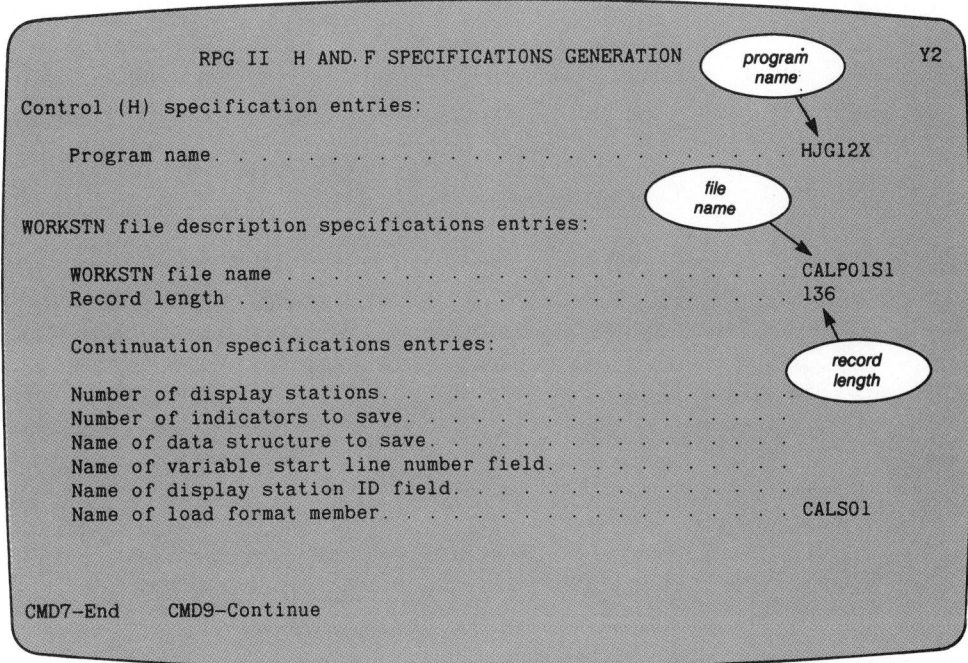

Figure 12-32   RPG II H and F Specifications Generation display

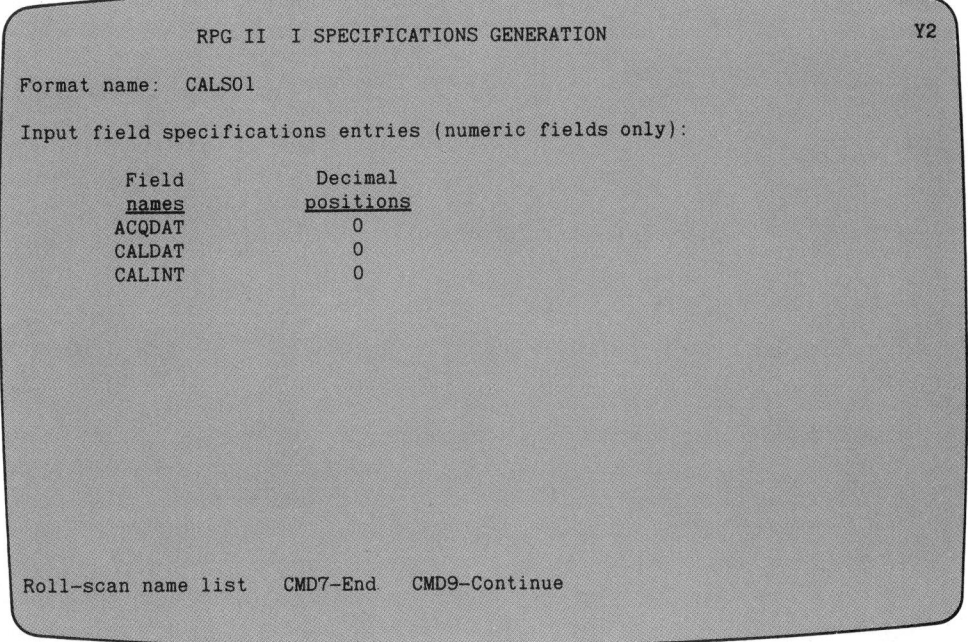

Figure 12-33   RPG II I Specifications Generation display

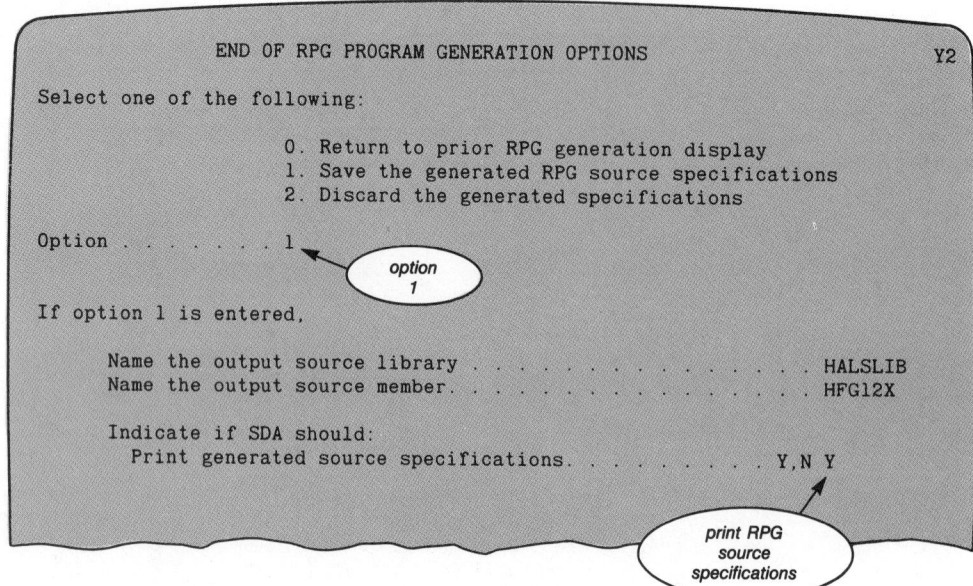

Figure 12-34   End of RPG Program Generation Options display

From this display you have the option of returning to the prior generation display (option 0), discarding the generated specifications (option 2), or saving the generated RPG source specifications (option 1). If you use option 1, verify that the names of the Output Source Library and Output Source Member are correct and enter a Y to cause SDA to print the generated RPG source specifications. Option 1 returns you to the RPG Program Generation Selection display (Figure 12-31). If you need to generate additional RPG specifications you can enter a name and repeat the generation process. If you have completed the needed RPG specification generation, use CMD/7 to end the SDA session and return to your default menu.

What to Do Next

Figure 12-35 shows the generated RPG specifications. Note that they consist of an H specification, a two line F specification, and a series of input and output specifications. These specifications form the basis of the interactive RPG program. They are not a complete program. To these specifications you must add all the remaining code needed for other files, calculations, and so on.

Whether you develop the remainder of the program by adding specifications to these generated workstation file specifications or you integrate these specifications into another source member, you must follow several rules:

1. Do not alter the second input specification (*FORMAT-).
2. Do not alter the second output specification. This specification (K8 ' CALS01   ') is needed by RPG to identify the output format record.
3. Any change to the S or D specifications that changes the location or size of a format element usually affects the RPG specifications for the workstation file. If you make any S or D specifications changes, you must recompile the display format and generate new RPG specifications. *If you perform a regeneration of RPG workstation specifications, do not use the same name for the RPG source member. If you use the same name, your existing RPG source program will be destroyed.* If regeneration is necessary, use a different name (XXXXXX, for example) for the generated RPG source specifications. After generating the source specifications, compare the new specifications against the existing program. If the workstation portions of the programs are not identical, change the full program to match the newly generated specifications. Be careful when regenerating RPG specifications: The use of the same name and the resultant destruction of the existing program is a very easy mistake to make. Remember that any change to the display format probably forces a change in the RPG specifications that control the workstation file.

```
        H                                                                    HJG12X
        FCALP01S1CP F     136        WORKSTN
        F                                      KFMTS   CALS01
        ICALP01S1
        I* FORMAT- CALS01
        I                                 1  20 CALNO
        I                                21  40 FAIDNO
        I                                41  48 TYPE
        I                                49  54 MFGR
        I                                55  62 MODEL
        I                                63  74 SERIAL
        I                                75  78 LOCATN
        I                                79  840ACQDAT
        I                                85  92 ACQCST
        I                                93  980CALDAT
        I                                99 104 DONEBY
        I                               105 1060CALINT
        OCALP01S1D
        O                                     K8 'CALS01
        O                      CALNO     20
        O                      FAIDNO    40
        O                      TYPE      48
        O                      MFGR      54
        O                      MODEL     62
        O                      SERIAL    74
        O                      LOCATN    78
        O                      ACQDAT    84
        O                      ACQCST    92
        O                      CALDAT    98
        O                      DONEBY   104
        O                      CALINT   106
        O                      MESSAG   136
```

Figure 12-35   RPG II specifications generated by SDA

RPG II PROGRAM SPECIFICATIONS FOR PROGRAM HJG12X
File Description Specifications

Figure 12-36 shows the File Description Specifications form for the sample program. Although the file description specifications for the workstation file CALP01S1 were generated by SDA, they are shown here because they contain two new entries, one of which is a change from the generated specifications.

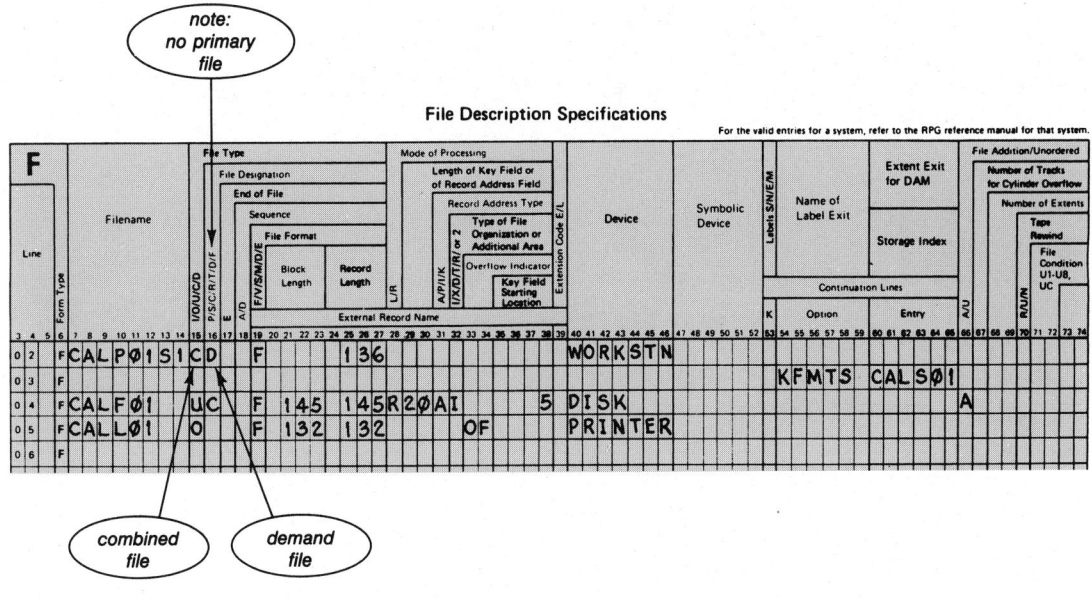

Figure 12-36   File description specifications

▸ **Combined Files** The File Type entry for CALP01S1 is C. A type C file is a **combined file**, which can be used for both input and output. Combined files differ in one important way from update files, also used for both input and output. When you use an update file, you can read a record from the file, modify one or more fields in the record, and then write the updated record back to the file. Combined files do not have this capability. Although a combined file can be both read from and written to, you can not perform a record update on a combined file.

▸ **Demand Files** The second new entry is the File Designation entry of D for CALP01S1. The D entry specifies that the file is a **demand file** and is read by the READ operation rather than RPG fixed logic. The **READ** operation causes RPG to read the next available record in a demand file and, as you will see, causes the input data to be read from the display format. The two remaining file description specifications describe CALF01, the output disk file, and CALL01, the Test Equipment Master Load report. Although these two file descriptions do not contain any new entries, note that CALF01 has been described as an update/chain file (UC, in positions 15–16) because it is read by a CHAIN operation to test for a duplicate key entry.

You may have noticed that a familiar entry that has been used in every RPG program so far is missing. The file descriptions for program HJG12X do not contain a primary file description. This is because all data input is controlled by operations performed during detail calculation time. Because the RPG fixed logic cycle is not used for data input, there is no need for a primary file designation.

Extension Specifications

Figure 12-37 shows the Extension Specifications form for the sample program. The first two arrays, HOLD and OUT, are used by the calculation routine that removes editing characters from the Acquisition Cost (ACQCST) input field. The ERR array is a compile time array that contains the two error messages needed by the display format. Although these messages could be generated by a series of MOVE and MOVEL operations to move literals into the message area, it is easier, because of their length (24 positions), to store the messages in an array and move them to the MESSAG field with a single MOVE operation. In addition, the technique of storing messages in a compile time array makes program maintenance easier.

Extension Specifications

Line	Form Type	Record Sequence of the Chaining File / Number of the Chaining Field	From Filename	To Filename	Table or Array Name	Number of Entries Per Record	Number of Entries Per Table or Array	Length of Entry	P/B/L/R	Decimal Positions	Sequence (A/D)	Table or Array Name (Alternating Format)	Length of Entry	P/B/L/R	Decimal Positions	Sequence (A/D)	Comments
01	E				HOLD		8	1									
02	E				OUT		6	1									
03	E				ERR	1	2	24									
04	E																
05	E																
06	E																
07	E																

Figure 12-37 Extension specifications

Input Specifications

As you can see from the input specifications in Figure 12-38, several modifications have been made to the input specifications that were generated by the SDA. An alphabetic sequence of WS has been added to the first input specification for CALP01S1. In addition, all the fields that are required entries now contain zero/blank indicators in positions 69–70. CALF01 has been described as containing a 145-position record. CALF01 must be described so that the file can be read in order to test for duplicate record keys.

Figure 12-38 Input specifications

Input specification form entries (form type I):

```
01 I* CALP01S1 INPUT SPECIFICATIONS
02 I*--------------------------------
03 I CALP01S1WS
04 I* FORMAT- CALS01          (workstation file)
05 I                              1   20 CALNO            90
06 I                             21   40 FAIDNO
07 I                             41   48 TYPE             91
08 I                             49   54 MFGR             92
09 I                             55   62 MODEL            93
10 I                             63   74 SERIAL
11 I                             75   78 LOCATN           94
12 I                             79   840ACQDAT
13 I                             85   92 ACQCST
14 I                             93   980CALDAT          95
15 I                             99  104 DONEBY          96
16 I                            105  1060CALINT          97
17 I* CALF01 INPUT SPECIFICATIONS
18 I*--------------------------------
19 I CALF01 AA
20 I                              1  145 DATA
```

(added zero/blank indicators)

Note that neither of the files described on the Input Specifications form contains a record-identifying indicator. Neither the calculations nor the output from this program is automatically controlled by the reading of an input record. Because the program does not contain a primary file, RPG proceeds directly to the first detail calculation and begins execution. Because no record is automatically read and, therefore, no record-identifying indicator could be turned on, you cannot control the performance of the calculations by a record-identifying indicator.

Calculation Specifications

The calculations for program HJG12X consist of a main processing loop, which controls the display and reading of the display format. Within the main processing loop, another series of loops performs the removal of editing characters from the ACQCST field. The main processing loop continues to execute until the user presses the CMD/7 key. When CMD/7 is pressed, the calculations turn on indicator LR and terminate loop execution.

▸ **Format Display and Reading** The calculations in Figure 12-39 set the ACQCST field to an initial value of zero, display the format on the screen, read the values that were keyed into the format, and test for end of job.

Calculation specification form entries (form type C):

```
01 C           START      TAG
02 C                      MOVE  *ZEROS    ACQCST
03 C                      EXCPTSCREEN
04 C           NXTONE     TAG
05 C                      READ  CALP01S1
06 C     KG               SETON                       LR
07 C     KG               GOTO  EXIT
08 C
```

Figure 12-39 Calculation specifications: format display and reading

The calculations start with the TAG operation that marks the beginning of the main processing loop. The second operation moves the figurative constant *ZEROS to ACQCST. Although ACQCST contains zeros at the beginning of the program, it must be reset by a calculation operation because it is never used as an output field and cannot, therefore, be reset by an output Blank After entry. If ACQCST is not cleared by moving zeros into it, an incorrect value shows in the ACQCST field in the display.

The third operation is an EXCPT that causes the display format, controlled by the output specifications in Figure 12-40, to be displayed on the screen. Note that the MESSAG field is cleared by the use of a B in position 39. If an error message has been moved into the MESSAG field, the field is cleared after it is displayed, and the message is not redisplayed incorrectly.

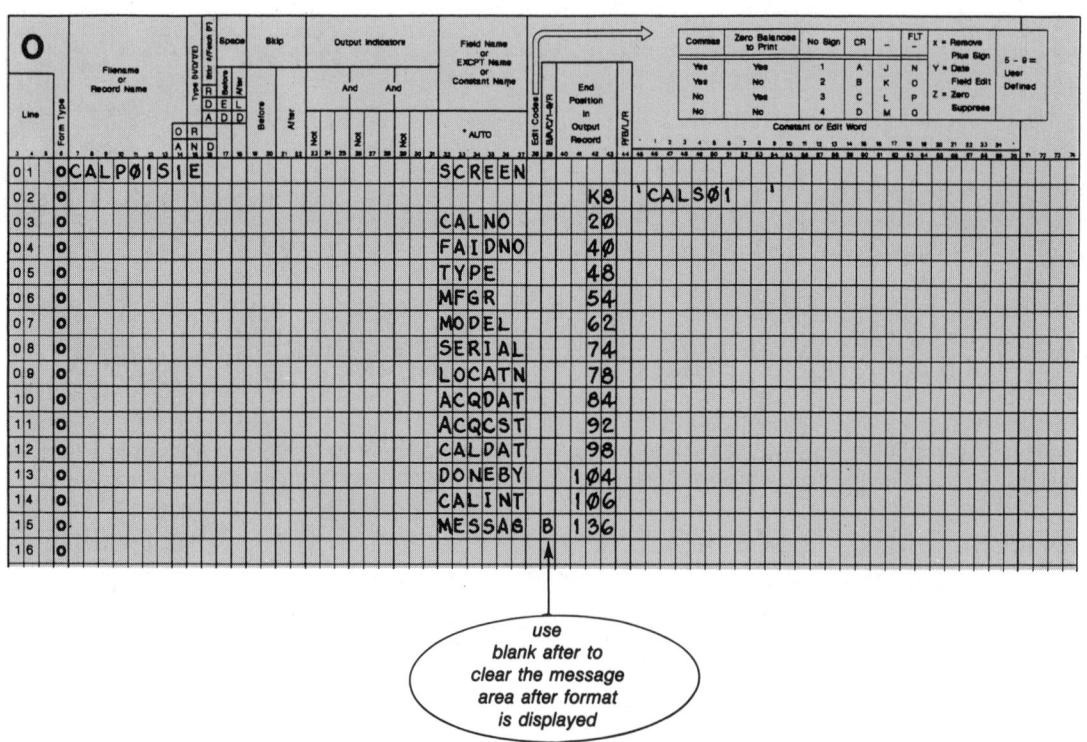

use
blank after to
clear the message
area after format
is displayed

Figure 12-40 Display format output specifications

Refer to Figure 12-39. The operation following the EXCPT is a READ operation that reads CALP01S1. The READ operation causes the data that has been keyed into the data entry input fields (Figure 12-38) to be read and made available for processing. When a READ operation is performed on a workstation file, the program pauses its execution until the user presses either the enter key or a valid Command key. Valid Command keys are those that were defined in the key mask portion of the S specification. The program performs no further processing until one of these keys has been pressed.

The use of the READ operation with a workstation file can cause one of the "you're wrong no matter what you do" situations that can happen with RPG. The READ operation usually requires that at least one resulting indicator be specified. This indicator, however, is not usually needed when READing a workstation file. If you do not specify an indicator, an error message tells you that a required indicator is missing. If you specify the indicator but do not use it, the compiler gives you an un referenced indicator warning. These warnings cannot be avoided but have no effect on the program. Figure 12-41 summarizes the READ operation. As the summary shows, the READ operation can be used for disk files as well as workstation files.

Refer again to Figure 12-39. After one of the valid keys is pressed and the READ operation has been performed, the program proceeds to the next operation. This is a SETON of indicator LR and is controlled by indicator KG. Recall that indicator KG is one of a series of special-purpose indicators used to represent the Command keys. Indicator KG is on if the user pressed the CMD/7 key rather than the Enter key. If KG is on, the program turns on indicator LR and then branches to EXIT, which marks the end of the calculations, thereby ending the main processing loop and terminating the program.

READ Operation Summary

The READ operation causes the next record in a demand file to be accessed during the calculation portion of the RPG fixed logic cycle. If the demand file is a workstation file, the READ operation causes the display format to be read after either the Enter key or a valid Command key is pressed. In addition, the READ operation can be used to perform program-controlled reading of an arrival sequence disk file during the calculation portion of the logic cycle.

Control Level Indicators	Indicators	Factor 1	Operation Name	Factor 2	Result Field	Resulting Indicators		
7–8	9–17	18–27	28–32	33–42	43–53	54–55	56–57	58–59
optional	optional	blank	READ	required	blank	blank	optional	optional

Figure 12-41 Read operation summary

▸ **Data Input Error Testing** The next series of calculations, test for data entry errors (Figure 12-42). The first eight lines causes the contents of ERR,1 (REQUIRED ENTRY MISSING) to be moved into the MESSAG field if any of the required data entry fields is blank, as indicated by indicators 90–97. The next eight lines causes the program to branch back to the beginning of the calculations if a field is blank. These

Line	Form Type	Control Level	Indicators	Factor 1	Operation	Factor 2	Result Field Name	Length	Resulting Indicators (54–55)
01	C		9Ø						
02	C	OR	91						
03	C	OR	92						
04	C	OR	93						
05	C	OR	94						
06	C	OR	95						
07	C	OR	96						
08	C	OR	97		MOVE	ERR,1	MESSAG	24	
09	C		91						
10	C	OR	92						
11	C	OR	93						
12	C	OR	94						
13	C	OR	95						
14	C	OR	96						
15	C	OR	97		GOTO	START			
16	C			CALNO	CHAIN	CALFØ1			2Ø
17	C		N2Ø		MOVE	ERR,2	MESSAG		
18	C		N2Ø		GOTO	START			

Figure 12-42 Calculation specifications: data input error testing

eight lines are one operation controlled by eight indicators. This is not a new technique. You have used this technique before to link two or three lines together. After the branch to START, the program again performs the EXCPT SCREEN operation and redisplays the format. This time, however, the format displays the data that has been keyed in and also the blinking error message. After the blank field has been filled in and the Enter key pressed, the program resumes execution.

After the user enters all required fields and the display has been read, the program uses CALNO to read CALF01 using the CHAIN operation. If indicator 20 is not turned on by the CHAIN, indicating that the CALNO already exists as a record key, the MOVE operation on line 18 moves the contents of ERR,2 (UNIT ID ALREADY ON FILE) to MESSAG, and line 19 causes the program to branch back to START. When the format is displayed, the user can either correct the invalid CALNO entry or enter the data from another source document. After the program has determined that all required data entries have been made and that the key field is not a duplicate, actual processing of the input data can begin.

▸ **Determine Next Calibration Date** The program specifications require that the next calibration date be determined by adding the calibration interval in months to the last calibration date. Figure 12-43 (upper portion) shows the calculations needed to do this.

Line	Form Type	Control Level	And	And	Factor 1	Operation	Factor 2	Result Name	Length	Dec	Resulting Indicators	Comments
01	C					MOVEL	CALDAT	CALMO	20			SEPARATE MONTH
02	C					Z-ADD	CALDAT	NXTDAT	60			MOVE CALDAT TO
03	C*											NXTDAT
04	C					ADD	CALINT	CALMO				ADD INTERVAL
05	C				CALMO	COMP	12				30	MONTH INVALID
06	C		30			SUB	12	CALMO				RESET MONTH
07	C		30			ADD	1	NXTDAT				INCREMENT YEAR
08	C					MOVEL	CALMO	NXTDAT				MOVE MONTH INTO
09	C*											NEXT DATE
10	C											

Line	Form Type	Control Level	And	And	Factor 1	Operation	Factor 2	Result Name	Length	Dec	Resulting Indicators	Comments
01	C					MOVEL	CALDAT	CALMO	20			
02	C					Z-ADD	CALDAT	NXTDAT	60			
03	C*											
04	C					Z-ADD	CALINT	CALMO				
05	C				CALMO	COMP	12				30	
06	C		30			SUB	12	CALMO				
07	C		30			MOVE	NXTDAT	YEAR	20			
08	C		30		YEAR	COMP	99				31	IF YEAR = 99
09	C		30	31		MOVE	'00'	NXTDAT				SET YEAR = 0
10	C		30	N31		ADD	1	NXTDAT				
11	C					MOVEL	CALMO	NXTDAT				

Figure 12-43 Calculation specifications: calculate NXTDAT

On line 01 a MOVEL operation moves the MM portion of CALDAT into a two-position field named CALMO. The Z-ADD operation on line 02 copies the contents of CALDAT into NXTDAT, the Date of Next Calibration field. Line 04 adds CALINT, the calibration interval in months, to CALMO. Line 05 uses a COMP operation to compare CALMO against 12, the greatest possible valid MM value. If CALMO is greater than 12, indicator 30 is turned on signifying an invalid MM value. If indicator 30 is on, line 06 subtracts 12 from CALMO and then adds 1 to NXTDAT, incrementing the year by 1. Line 08, the last line of the routine, then moves the updated MM value in CALMO into NXTDAT with a MOVEL operation.

Computer programs are usually written with an expected useful life of about five years. Because of this, most date routines, such as the one just shown, do not take into consideration the problem that will occur when the year 2000 arrives. Look, for example, at what would happen if the routine were applied to December 3, 1999 (120399). Because the month is 12, the routine resets the month to 01 (010399) and adds one to the year. Because the year is 99, the result of the addition is 010400, January 4, 2000. Note that not only have the month and year been incremented, but the day has been incremented as well. The lower portion of Figure 12-43 shows a modified version of this routine that avoids this problem.

As you can see, if the month is equal to 12, line 07 moves the YY portion of the date to a separate field YEAR, which is compared with 99. If the year is equal to 99, the move operation on line 09 resets the YY portion of NXTDAT to 00. If the year is not equal to 99, the routine proceeds as shown in the upper portion of the figure.

The year 2000 will cause several problems for programs that perform calculations on date fields. Most of these problems will be caused by comparisons because the YY portion of the year 2000 (00) will compare as lower than the YY portion of the year 1999 (99). As you plan and develop programs that may be in use when the millennium arrives, take these potential problems into consideration.

▸ **Elimination of Editing Characters** Figure 12-44 shows the routine to remove editing characters from the ACQCST field. This routine is identical to that presented in Chapter 9.

Line	Form Type	Indicators	Factor 1	Operation	Factor 2	Result Field Name	Length	Decimal Positions	Resulting Indicators (Plus / Minus / Zero)
01	C			MOVEA	ACQCST	HOLD			
02	C			Z-ADD	9	X	1	0	
03	C			Z-ADD	7	Y	1	0	
04	C		LOOP1	TAG					
05	C			SUB	1	Y			50
06	C	50		GOTO	ENDLP				
07	C		LOOP	TAG					
08	C			SUB	1	X			50
09	C	50		GOTO	ENDLP				
10	C		HOLD,X	COMP	'.'				51
11	C	51		GOTO	LOOP				
12	C		HOLD,X	COMP	','				52
13	C	52		GOTO	LOOP				
14	C		HOLD,X	COMP	'$'				53
15	C	53		GOTO	LOOP				
16	C			MOVE	HOLD,X	OUT,Y			
17	C			GOTO	LOOP1				
18	C		ENDLP	TAG					
19	C			MOVEA	OUT	CSTOUT	6	2	
20	C								

Figure 12-44 Calculation specifications: edit character elimination

Data Output to Disk and Printer Figure 12-45 shows the last four calculation specifications. The EXCPT on line 01 causes all four of the ADDDAT exception output records to be created. The first series of output exception specifications adds a record to CALF01. Note the constant 'ACAL', which will be placed in positions 1–4 of the output record as required by the record format. The next series of output exception specifications causes three lines to be printed on the output report. Note that the Blank After area has been used to clear all input fields so that they will be blank when the format is next displayed on the screen.

Figure 12-45 Calculation specifications: record output

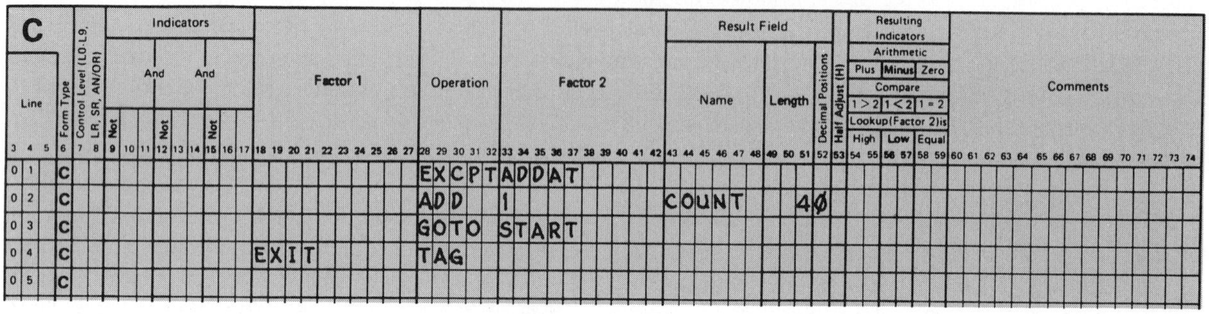

```
01 C                        EXCPTADDDAT
02 C                        ADD  1           COUNT   40
03 C                        GOTO START
04 C              EXIT      TAG
05 C
```

Figure 12-45 (1)

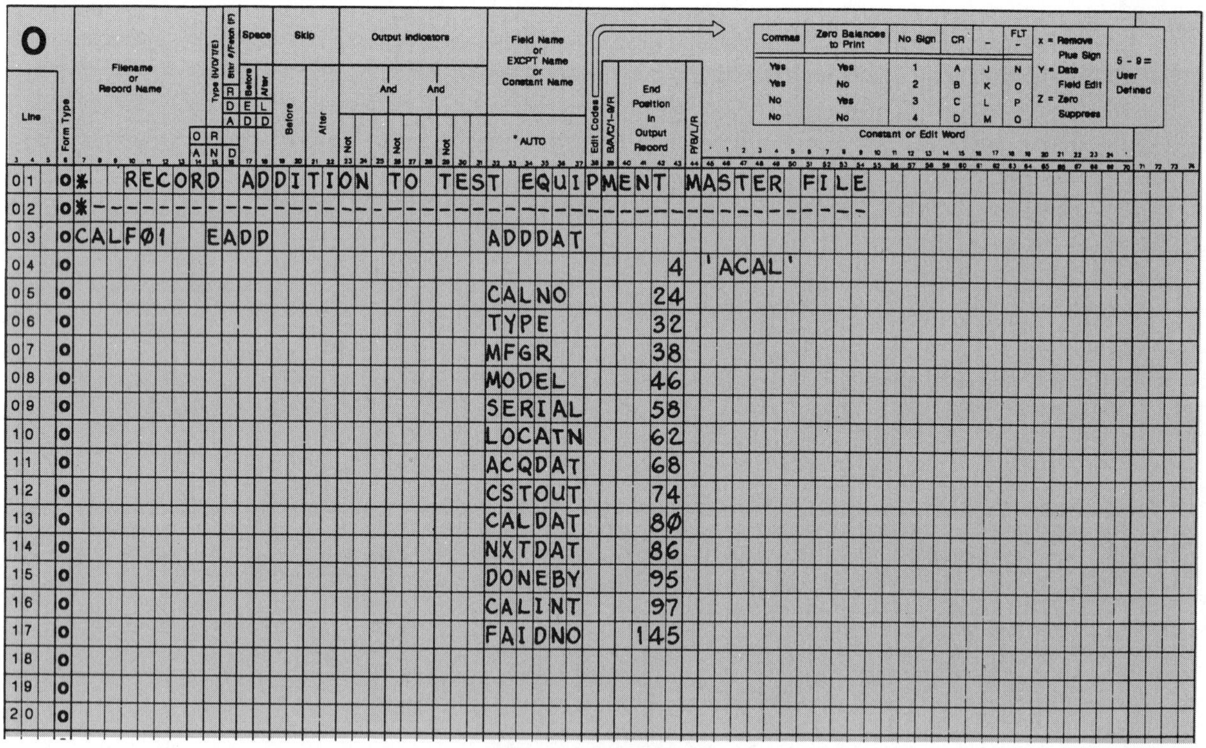

```
01 O*   RECORD ADDITION TO TEST EQUIPMENT MASTER FILE
02 O*-----------------------------------------------------
03 OCALF01  EADD                ADDDAT
04 O                                          4 'ACAL'
05 O                            CALNO        24
06 O                            TYPE         32
07 O                            MFGR         38
08 O                            MODEL        46
09 O                            SERIAL       58
10 O                            LOCATN       62
11 O                            ACQDAT       68
12 O                            CSTOUT       74
13 O                            CALDAT       80
14 O                            NXTDAT       86
15 O                            DONEBY       95
16 O                            CALINT       97
17 O                            FAIDNO      145
18 O
19 O
20 O
```

Figure 12-45 (2)

```
O* RECORD ADDITION DATA LINES
O* --------------------------------
O        E  1              ADDDAT
O                          CALNO   B  25
O                          FAIDNO  B  55
O*
O        E  1              ADDDAT
O                                     29 '------------------'
O                                     53 '------------------'
O                                     55 '--'
O*       E  2              ADDDAT
O                          TYPE    B  13
O                          MFGR    B  21
O                          MODEL   B  31
O                          SERIAL  B  45
O                          LOCATN  B  51
O                          ACQDATY B  61
O                          CSTOUT2 B  72 '$'
O                          CALDATY B  82
O                          DONEBY  B  90
O                          CALINTZ B  94
O                          NXTDATY B 104
```

Figure 12-45 (3)

Line 02 adds 1 to the count of records added to CALF01. Line 03 causes the calculations to branch back to the beginning and restart the loop process. Line 04 is the TAG that is used by the GOTO operation controlled by indicator KG. When this point in the calculations is reached, the loop control of the program is ended, and the RPG fixed logic cycle resumes control. Since indicator LR is on at this time, the program terminates after the final totals have been printed. Figure 12-46 shows the complete compilation listing for program HJG12X.

Figure 12-46 Compilation listing for Program HJG12X

```
   HJG12X    09-12-91  19:08:31      IBM PC      RPG II        Version 3.5  Page 1
        ....+....1....+....2....+....3....+....4....+....5....+....6...+....7....
    1 0001 H                                                              HJG12X

    2 0002 F*------------------------------------------------------------*
    3 0003 F*                                                            *
    4 0004 F* HJG12X - TEST EQUIPMENT MASTER FILE LOAD - DECEMBER 1, 1991 *
    5 0005 F*                                                            *
    6 0006 F* PROGRAM HJG12X ADDS RECORDS TO THE TEST EQUIPMENT MASTER FILE. *
    7 0007 F* INPUT DATA IS KEYED INTO THE PROGRAM USING DISPLAY FORMAT  *
    8 0008 F* CALS01, WHICH IS PART OF CALP01S1. CALP01S1, THE WORKSTATION *
    9 0009 F* FILE, IS A COMBINED DEMAND FILE AND IS READ BY MEANS OF THE *
   10 0010 F* READ OPERATION.  OUTPUT TO THIS FILE IS CONTROLLED BY THE EXCPT *
   11 0011 F* OPERATION.  THE EIGHT INPUT FIELDS WITHIN CALP01S1 THAT USE *
   12 0012 F* ZERO/BLANK INDICATORS ARE REQUIRED ENTRIES.  IF ANY OF THESE *
   13 0013 F* FIELDS DOES NOT CONTAIN DATA THE PROGRAM WILL RE-DISPLAY THE *
   14 0014 F* FORMAT WITH AN ERROR MESSAGE INDICATING THAT REQUIRED DATA IS *
```

Figure 12-46 (1)

continued

```
HJG12X      09-12-91  19:08:31        IBM PC         RPG II          Version 3.5  Page  2

             ....+....1....+....2....+....3....+....4....+....5....+....6....+....7....

15 0015 F*  MISSING.  AN ATTEMPT TO LOAD A RECORD WITH A DUPLICATE KEY       *
16 0016 F*  FIELD WILL ALSO RESULT IN AN ERROR MESSAGE AND RE-DISPLAY OF     *
17 0017 F*  INPUT FORMAT.  THE ACQUISITION COST FIELD MAY BE ENTERED WITH    *
18 0018 F*  DOLLAR SIGN, DECIMAL POINT, AND COMMA AS THE PROGRAM CODE WILL   *
19 0019 F*  DELETE THESE PUNCTUATION MARKS.                                  *
20 0020 F*------------------------------------------------------------------*

23 0022 FCALP01S1CD F     136           WORKSTN
24 0023 F                                         KFMTS  CALS01
25 0024 FCALF01  UC F 145 145R20AI    5 DISK                      A
26 0025 FCALL01   O F 132 132    OF   PRINTER

29 0027 F* ID F  C  H  L   FUNCTION OF INDICATORS
30 0028 F* 01 -  -  -  -  - CALP01S1 RECORD IDENTIFICATION -- UNUSED
31 0029 F* 02 -  -  -  -  - CALF01 RECORD IDENTIFICATION -- UNUSED
32 0030 F*         20 -  - - NON-DUPLICATE CALNO -- VALID TO ADD
33 0031 F*         30 -  - - CALNO > 12 IN ROUTINE TO SET NXTDAT
34 0032 F*         50 -  - - WORK INDICATOR IN ACQCST CONVERSION ROUTINE
35 0033 F*         51 -  - - WORK INDICATOR IN ACQCST CONVERSION ROUTINE
36 0034 F*         52 -  - - WORK INDICATOR IN ACQCST CONVERSION ROUTINE
37 0035 F*         53 -  - - WORK INDICATOR IN ACQCST CONVERSION ROUTINE
38 0036 F*     90 -  -  - - BLANK CALNO FIELD
39 0037 F*     91 -  -  - - BLANK TYPE FIELD
40 0038 F*     92 -  -  - - BLANK MFGR FIELD
41 0039 F*     93 -  -  - - BLANK MODEL FIELD
42 0040 F*     94 -  -  - - BLANK LOCATN FIELD
43 0041 F*     95 -  -  - - BLANK CALDAT FIELD
44 0042 F*     96 -  -  - - BLANK DONEBY FIELD
45 0043 F*     97 -  -  - - BLANK CALINT FIELD
46 0044 F*             1P - FIRST PAGE HEADING CONTROL
47 0045 F*             OF - OVERFLOW HEADING CONTROL
48 0046 F*             LR - LAST RECORD INDICATOR - TURNED ON BY INDICATOR KG
49 0047 F*          KG - - - COMMAND KEY 7 FROM INPUT DISPLAY FORMAT
50 0048 E* THE HOLD AND OUT ARRAYS ARE USED IN THE CONVERSION OF
51 0049 E* INPUT DISPLAY FORMAT ACQUISITION COST DATA TO NUMERIC
52 0050 E* FORMAT.  THE ERR ARRAY CONTAINS ERROR MESSAGES.
53 0051 E*-----------------------------------------------------------
54 0052 E              HOLD     8 1
55 0053 E              OUT      6 1
56 0054 E              ERR    1 2 24

57 0055 I*  CALP01S1 INPUT SPECIFICATIONS
58 0056 I*-------------------------------
59 0057 ICALP01S1WS
60 0058 I* FORMAT- CALS01
61 0059 I                               1  20 CALNO       90
62 0060 I                              21  40 FAIDNO
63 0061 I                              41  48 TYPE        91
64 0062 I                              49  54 MFGR        92
65 0063 I                              55  62 MODEL       93
66 0064 I                              63  74 SERIAL
67 0065 I                              75  78 LOCATN      94
68 0066 I                              79  840ACQDAT
69 0067 I                              85  92 ACQCST
70 0068 I                              93  980CALDAT      95
71 0069 I                              99 104 DONEBY      96
72 0070 I                             105 1060CALINT      97

75 0072 I*  CALF01 INPUT SPECIFICATIONS
76 0073 I*-----------------------------
77 0074 ICALF01  AA
78 0075 I                               1 145 DATA

79 0076 C*  BEGIN PROCESSING AND CLEAR ACQCST FIELD
80 0077 C*-----------------------------------------
81 0078 C         START    TAG
82 0079 C                  MOVE *ZEROS   ACQCST

85 0081 C*  DISPLAY FORMAT
86 0082 C*----------------
87 0083 C                  EXCPTSCREEN
88 0084 C         NXTONE   TAG
```

Figure 12-46 (2)

```
HJG12X      09-12-91  19:08:31      IBM PC      RPG II       Version 3.5  Page  3
            ...+....1....+....2....+....3....+....4....+....5....+....6....+....7....

 91 0086 C*  INPUT FORMAT DATA AND TEST FOR END OF JOB
 92 0087 C*--------------------------------------------------------------
 93 0088 C                        READ CALP01S1
 94 0089 C   KG                   SETON                     LR
 95 0090 C   KG                   GOTO EXIT

 98 0092 C*  IF REQUIRED INPUT DATA IS MISSING MOVE ERROR MESSAGE 1,
 99 0093 C*  RETURN TO START, AND RE-DISPLAY INPUT FORMAT
100 0094 C*--------------------------------------------------------------
101 0095 C     90
102 0096 COR 91
103 0097 COR 92
104 0098 COR 93
105 0099 COR 94
106 0100 COR 95
107 0101 COR 96
108 0102 COR 97            MOVE ERR,1     MESSAG 24
109 0103 C     90
110 0104 COR 91
111 0105 COR 92
112 0106 COR 93
113 0107 COR 94
114 0108 COR 95
115 0109 COR 96
116 0110 COR 97            GOTO START

119 0112 C*  TEST FOR DUPLICATE KEY.  IF DUPLICATE, MOVE ERROR MESSAGE 2
120 0113 C*  AND RETURN TO START TO RE-DISPLAY INPUT FORMAT
121 0114 C*--------------------------------------------------------------
122 0115 C          CALNO    CHAINCALF01            20    VALID TO ADD
123 0116 C   N20             MOVE ERR,2     MESSAG
124 0117 C   N20             GOTO START

127 0119 C*  SET DATE OF NEXT CALIBRATION (NXTDAT)
128 0120 C*--------------------------------------------------------------
129 0121 C                   MOVELCALDAT    CALMO  20    SEPARATE MONTH
130 0122 C                   Z-ADDCALDAT    NXTDAT 60    MOVE CALDAT TO
131 0123 C*                                               NXTDAT
132 0124 C                   ADD  CALINT    CALMO        ADD INTERVAL
133 0125 C          CALMO    COMP 12               30    MONTH INVALID
134 0126 C   30              SUB  12        CALMO        RESET MONTH
135 0127 C   30              ADD  1         NXTDAT       INCREMENT YEAR
136 0128 C                   MOVELCALMO     NXTDAT       MOVE MONTH INTO
137 0129 C*                                               NEXT DATE

140 0131 C*  CONVERT INPUT DISPLAY AMOUNT TO NUMERIC FORMAT
141 0132 C*--------------------------------------------------------------
142 0133 C                   MOVEAACQCST    HOLD
143 0134 C                   Z-ADD9         X      10
144 0135 C                   Z-ADD7         Y      10
145 0136 C          LOOP1    TAG
146 0137 C                   SUB  1         Y            50
147 0138 C   50              GOTO ENDLP
148 0139 C          LOOP     TAG
149 0140 C                   SUB  1         X            50
150 0141 C   50              GOTO ENDLP
151 0142 C          HOLD,X   COMP '.'                    51
152 0143 C   51              GOTO LOOP
153 0144 C          HOLD,X   COMP ','                    52
154 0145 C   52              GOTO LOOP
155 0146 C          HOLD,X   COMP '$'                    53
156 0147 C   53              GOTO LOOP
157 0148 C                   MOVE HOLD,X    OUT,Y
158 0149 C                   GOTO LOOP1
159 0150 C          ENDLP    TAG
160 0151 C                   MOVEAOUT       CSTOUT 62

163 0153 C*  WRITE OUTPUT TO DISK AND PRINTER, ADD TO RECORD COUNT
164 0154 C*--------------------------------------------------------------
165 0155 C                   EXCPTADDDAT
166 0156 C                   ADD  1         COUNT  40
167 0157 C                   GOTO START
168 0158 C          EXIT     TAG
```

Figure 12-46 (3)

continued

```
HJG12X    09-12-91  19:08:31      IBM PC       RPG II        Version 3.5  Page  4

          ....+....1....+....2....+....3....+....4....+....5....+....6....+....7....


169 0159 O*  DISPLAY FORMAT OUTPUT
170 0160 O*----------------------
171 0161 OCALP01S1E              SCREEN
172 0162 O                                  K8 'CALS01
173 0163 O                      CALNO     20
174 0164 O                      FAIDNO    40
175 0165 O                      TYPE      48
176 0166 O                      MFGR      54
177 0167 O                      MODEL     62
178 0168 O                      SERIAL    74
179 0169 O                      LOCATN    78
180 0170 O                      ACQDAT    84
181 0171 O                      ACQCST    92
182 0172 O                      CALDAT    98
183 0173 O                      DONEBY   104
184 0174 O                      CALINT   106
185 0175 O                      MESSAG B 136


188 0177 O*  RECORD ADDITION TO TEST EQUIPMENT MASTER FILE
189 0178 O*---------------------------------------------
190 0179 OCALF01  EADD          ADDDAT
191 0180 O                                   4 'ACAL'
192 0181 O                      CALNO     24
193 0182 O                      TYPE      32
194 0183 O                      MFGR      38
195 0184 O                      MODEL     46
196 0185 O                      SERIAL    58
197 0186 O                      LOCATN    62
198 0187 O                      ACQDAT    68
199 0188 O                      CSTOUT    74
200 0189 O                      CALDAT    80
201 0190 O                      NXTDAT    86
202 0191 O                      DONEBY    95
203 0192 O                      CALINT    97
204 0193 O                      FAIDNO   145


207 0195 O*  HEADING LINES
208 0196 O*--------------
209 0197 OCALL01 H  106   1P
210 0198 O     OR         OF
211 0199 O                              67 '...OF CABBAGES AND KINGS'
212 0200 O                      UDATE Y 104


215 0202 O        H  3    1P
216 0203 O     OR         OF
217 0204 O                              11 'HJG12X'
218 0205 O                              57 'TEST EQUIPMENT MASTER'
219 0206 O                              74 'FILE LOAD REPORT'
220 0207 O                             100 'PAGE'
221 0208 O                      PAGE    104


224 0210 O        H  1    1P
225 0211 O     OR         OF
226 0212 O                              21 'CAL. UNIT ID NO.'
227 0213 O                              55 'FIXED ASSET I.D. NO.'


230 0215 O        H  1    1P
231 0216 O     OR         OF
232 0217 O                              29 '-----------------------'
233 0218 O                              53 '-----------------------'
234 0219 O                              77 '--ACQ.       ACQ.  ----'
235 0220 O                             102 'C-A-L-I-B-R-A-T-I-O-N---'


238 0222 O        H  2    1P
239 0223 O     OR         OF
240 0224 O                              29 'TYPE      MFGR    MODEL'
241 0225 O                              51 'SERIAL NO.   LOC.'
242 0226 O                              70 ' DATE       COST'
243 0227 O                              95 'LAST     BY   INT.'
244 0228 O                             102 'NEXT'
```

Figure 12-46 (4)

```
HJG12X    09-12-91  19:08:31      IBM PC      RPG II        Version 3.5  Page  5

        ....+....1....+....2....+....3....+....4....+....5....+....6....+....7....

247 0230 O*  RECORD ADDITION DATA LINES
248 0231 O*-----------------------------------
249 0232 O         E 1              ADDDAT
250 0233 O                              CALNO  B  25
251 0234 O                              FAIDNO B  55

254 0236 O         E 1              ADDDAT
255 0237 O                                     29 '-------------------'
256 0238 O                                     53 '-------------------'
257 0239 O                                     55 '--'

260 0241 O         E 2              ADDDAT
261 0242 O                              TYPE   B  13
262 0243 O                              MFGR   B  21
263 0244 O                              MODEL  B  31
264 0245 O                              SERIAL B  45
265 0246 O                              LOCATN B  51
266 0247 O                              ACQDATYB  61
267 0248 O                              CSTOUT2B  72 '$'
268 0249 O                              CALDATYB  82
269 0250 O                              DONEBY B  90
270 0251 O                              CALINTZB  94
271 0252 O                              NXTDATYB 104
272 0253 O*  FINAL TOTAL COUNT OF ADDED RECORDS
273 0254 O*-----------------------------------
274 0255 O         T 21     LR
275 0256 O                              COUNT Z   8
276 0257 O                                     30 'UNITS HAVE BEEN ADDED'
277 0258 O                                     37 'TO THE'
278 0259 O         T     01 LR
279 0260 O                                     30 'TEST EQUIPMENT MASTER'
280 0261 O                                     35 'FILE'


283 0263 O*  ERROR MESSAGE ARRAY DATA
284 0264 O*---------------------------
285 **
286 REQUIRED ENTRY MISSING
287 UNIT ID ALREADY ON FILE
288 /*
289 /*


        THE FOLLOWING INDICATORS WERE USED TO CONDITION OPERATIONS
        BUT WERE NEVER SET

        KG


        THE FOLLOWING INDICATORS APPEARED IN THIS PROGRAM

        20  30  50  51  52  53  90  91  92  93  94  95  96  97  LR  1P
        OF  KG
No Warning Errors
No Fatal Errors
```

Figure 12-46 (5)

▤ Program Execution

Program execution in previous examples was transparent to the user, so there has been no need to present information about it. Once program execution began, there was no need for the user or operator to intervene because program execution was fully automatic. However, because program HJG12X is an interactive program, which creates a dialogue between the user and the computer, it is necessary to present the sequence of events that occur when the program executes.

When program execution begins, the user sees the data entry display in Figure 12-47. The user then enters data from the source document into the data entry fields (Figure 12-48). After the data has been keyed, the user presses the Enter key to cause the data to be read into memory by the program. If all entries are valid according to the processing requirements of the program, the user is again presented with an empty data entry screen.

```
                    TEST EQUIPMENT CALIBRATION
                           ITEM ENTRY

     Calibration Unit ID Number
     Fixed Asset I.D. Number

     Type                      Manufacturer
     Model                     Serial Number
     Location

     Acquisition Date (MMDDYY)   000000
     Acquisition Cost            00000000

     Date Last Calibrated (MMDDYY) 000000
     Calibration Performed By
     Calibration Interval (Months)   00


     Enter Key--Loads Item Onto File
        CMD / 7--Ends This Load Program
```

Figure 12-47 CALS01 data entry format

```
                    TEST EQUIPMENT CALIBRATION
                           ITEM ENTRY

     Calibration Unit ID Number     CAL-094
     Fixed Asset I.D. Number

     Type      SCOPE               Manufacturer    AJAX
     Model     37                  Serial Number
     Location  Q-C

     Acquisition Date (MMDDYY)    030690
     Acquisition Cost             00$45.99

     Date Last Calibrated (MMDDYY) 030690
     Calibration Performed By      AJAX
     Calibration Interval (Months)   12


     Enter Key--Loads Item Onto File
        CMD / 7--Ends This Load Program
```

Figure 12-48 CALS01 data entry format after data entry

If one or more required fields was not entered, the format shown in Figure 12-49 is displayed. Note that the user neglected to enter Type and Manufacturer entries and, as a result, the REQUIRED ENTRY MISSING message is displayed in the error message area. After these entries have been keyed in, the Enter key is pressed and the program continues processing.

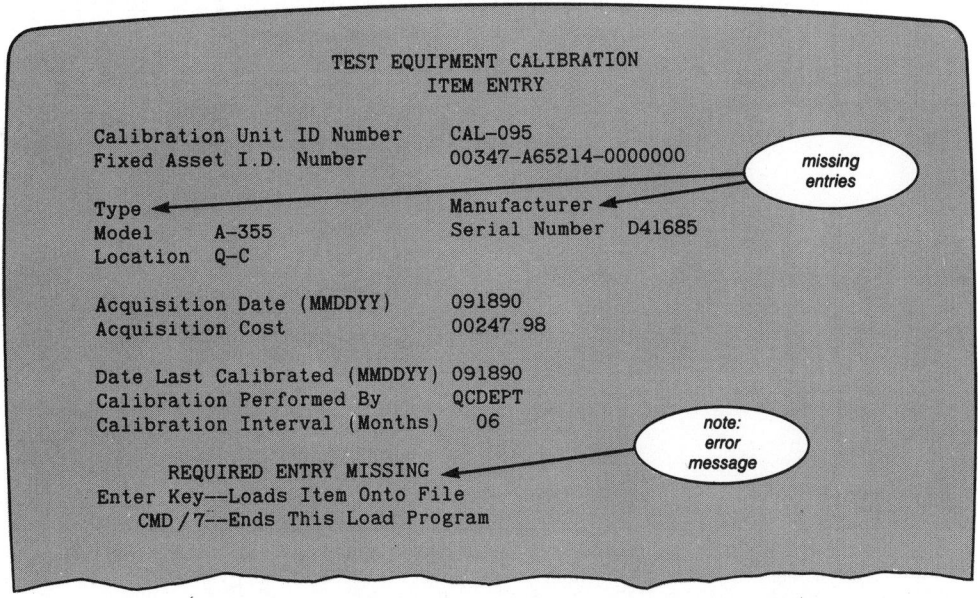

Figure 12-49   CALS01 data entry format: missing data error

Figure 12-50 shows the display as it appears if an attempt is made to enter a record containing a duplicate key. Note that all required entries have been made, but the program has determined that the calibration unit I.D. number is a duplicate of a number that already exists as a key in CALF01. The error message UNIT ID ALREADY ON FILE is displayed to alert the user. After the identification number has been changed, the user presses the enter key to continue processing.

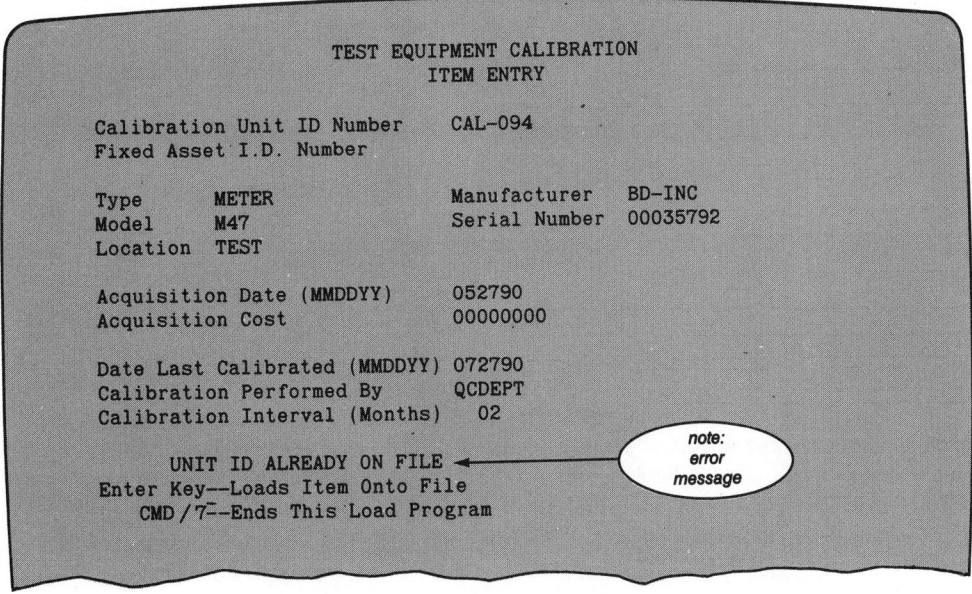

Figure 12-50   CALS01 data entry format: duplicate key error

After all the input data has been entered, the program can be ended by pressing the CMD/7 key when a blank data entry display (Figure 12-47) is on the screen. There is no need to make any data entries when ending the program. In fact, if any entries are made, they will be ignored by the program because the calculations, when indicator KG (CMD/7) is detected, go directly to the end of the processing loop. Figure 12-51 shows the output printed report and a listing of CALF01 after several records have been added.

```
                                        ...OF CABBAGES AND KINGS                      9/03/91
        HJG12X                      TEST EQUIPMENT MASTER FILE LOAD REPORT             PAGE   1


        CAL. UNIT ID NO.              FIXED ASSET I.D. NO.
        ───────────────────────────────────────────────ACQ.    ACQ.    ─── C-A-L-I-B-R-A-T-I-O-N───
           TYPE    MFGR    MODEL    SERIAL NO.  LOC.    DATE     COST    LAST      BY    INT.   NEXT

        CAL-2147
        ─────────────────────────────────────────────────
        METER      ALLIED  A-416    000231587   Q-C   9/18/91            9/18/91  MFGR    6    3/18/92

        CAL-00123457                 000021450096
        ─────────────────────────────────────────────────
        METER      ALLIED  L-315                Q-C   5/27/91   $12.50   7/27/91  QCDEPT  2    9/27/91

        CAL-59217
        ─────────────────────────────────────────────────
        SCOPE      M-VID   216                  F-A   0/00/00            7/23/91  MFGR    6    1/23/92


        3 UNITS HAVE BEEN ADDED TO THE
        TEST EQUIPMENT MASTER FILE
```

```
    Filename   RecLen          KeyPo  KeyLn                                    Date       Time     Page
    CALF01     145               5     20                                    9/03/91     17.09

    Rec No. Line No. 1... ...10.... ...20.... ...30.... ...40.... ...50.... ...60.... ...70.... ...80.... ...90.... ..100

         1    1     ACALCAL-2147          METER   ALLIEDA-416   000231587   Q-C 091890000000091890031891   MFGR  06
              2

         2    1     ACALCAL-00123457      METER   ALLIEDL-315               Q-C 052790001250072790092790   QCDEPT02
              2                           000021450096

         3    1     ACALCAL-59217         SCOPE   M-VID 216                 F-A 000000000000072390012391   MFGR  06
              2
```

Figure 12-51   Output report for program HJG12X and CALF01 file listing

══ IN CONCLUSION ══

The purpose of this chapter has been to introduce you to display format design and to show you an example of the techniques needed to develop interactive RPG programs. This chapter is not a complete treatment of these topics because the scope of display format design is so large that it would require several chapters this size and because the programming of interactive display formats is not standardized and is totally dependent on the hardware and software available to you. If you are not working with a System/36, the first part of the chapter gives you some of the basic tools needed to help you plan and design display formats. If you are working with a System/36, the second part of the chapter introduces the tools needed to develop and use these formats.

Chapter 13 will introduce you to the concepts of updating arrival sequence access path files. The techniques of updating arrival sequence files are not as widely used as the techniques used to update keyed sequence access path files, but they will give you valuable information about the way that RPG works with both primary and secondary files in a program.

CHAPTER SUMMARY

Screen Format Design Concepts

1. **Interactive programming applications** develop a **dialogue** between the user and the computer, using a terminal as the **interface**.
2. The **screen** is the physical surface of a terminal on which information is displayed.
3. A **display**, or **panel**, is a predefined group of fields arranged in a predetermined pattern and displayed on a screen. The specific arrangement of data within a display is called a **display format**.
4. **Captions** are constants used in a format to identify the format and the fields within the format.
5. The separate components of a format are called **elements**.
6. When a caption is used to identify a data entry element or to request a user action, it is called a **prompt**.
7. The **cursor** identifies the area of a format into which the next character will be entered.
8. **Pixels**, or **picture elements**, are the individual dots of light that make up the characters or graphics on a screen.
9. A **nondisplay** element is a part of the display format that does not appear on the screen when the format is displayed.
10. **Attributes** define the physical characteristics and appearance of an element in a format.
11. The excessive use of some attributes can cause them to be ignored by the user, can lead to user fatigue, and can minimize their effectiveness.
12. A well-designed format contains only the information needed to perform the function for which the format was designed.
13. Every data input or output element of a format should be identified by a caption.
14. Data entry formats should be organized in the same sequence as the **source document** from which the data is entered.

Interactive Programming with System/36 SDA

15. **Mandatory entries** are data entry elements that can not be left blank by the user.
16. The **display control (S) specification** provides information about the entire display format being described.
17. The **field definition (D) specifications** provide information about individual elements in a display format.
18. Every set of display format specifications must contain one S specification followed by a series of D specifications.
19. Every element description must contain the Field Length, Line Number, and Horizontal Position entries.
20. A constant element description can be continued on a second D specification by using the Continuation entry X in the first D specification.
21. The System/36 **Screen Design Aid** is used to compile the display format specifications into a load member and to generate the RPG II specifications needed to control the display format.
22. An RPG II file that is based on an interactive display format is called a **workstation file**.
23. The RPG II specifications generated by SDA are not a complete program. Only the F, I, and O specifications needed by the workstation file are generated by SDA.
24. A **combined file** is a file that can be both read from and written to in the same program. When using a combined file, you cannot alter the contents of a specific record (as you can with update files).
25. A **demand file** is a file that is read by the READ operation. The reading of a demand file is not under the control of the RPG fixed logic cycle.
26. When a READ operation is executed, the program pauses until either the Enter key or a valid Command key is pressed by the user.
27. The K indicators specify that a Command key has been pressed by the user.

REVIEW QUESTIONS

Screen Format Design Concepts

1. How does an interactive program differ from a batch processing program in terms of the way that the program is used by the user?
2. What is the difference between a screen and a display?
3. Define *display element.*
4. List and explain the function of each of the following element attributes: (a) high intensity, (b) non-display, (c) reverse image, (d) underline, and (e) column separators.
5. Why should element attributes be used sparingly?
6. What is a source document?

Interactive Programming with System/36 SDA

7. Name the three System/36 utility programs that can use the S and D specifications.
8. What is the purpose of the display control specification?
9. What is the purpose of the field definition specifications?
10. What does the key mask do?
11. Why is constant continuation allowed on the Field Definition Specification form?
12. List and explain the two functions that are performed by System/36 SDA.
13. What is the difference between a combined file and an update file?

STUDENT EXERCISES: DISPLAY FORMAT DESIGN

1. Design a data entry display format based on the source document in Figure 12-52. All fields are mandatory and the Number of Diskettes field is numeric only. Use the form in Figure 12-53 to plan the display format for your design. Indicate any attributes to be used with each element of the display.

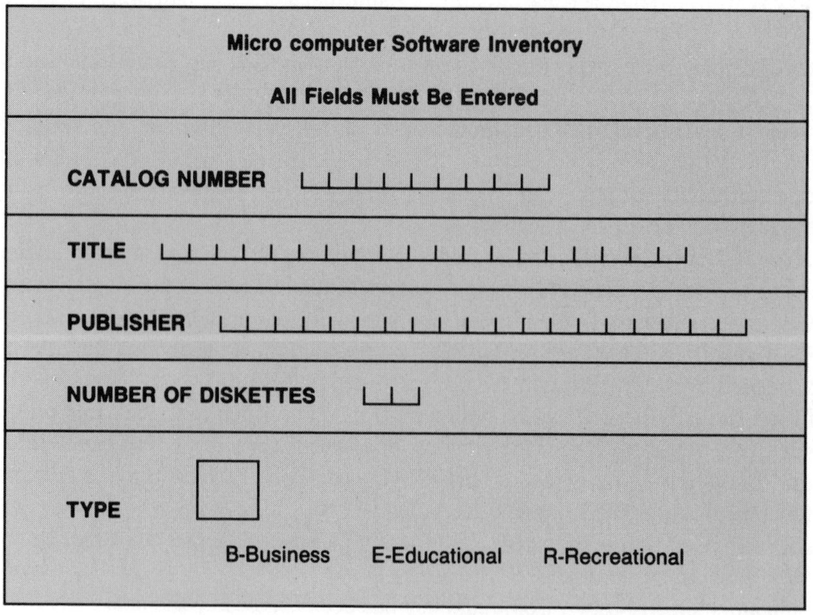
Micro computer Software Inventory

All Fields Must Be Entered

CATALOG NUMBER

TITLE

PUBLISHER

NUMBER OF DISKETTES

TYPE

B-Business E-Educational R-Recreational

Figure 12-52 Microcomputer Software Inventory

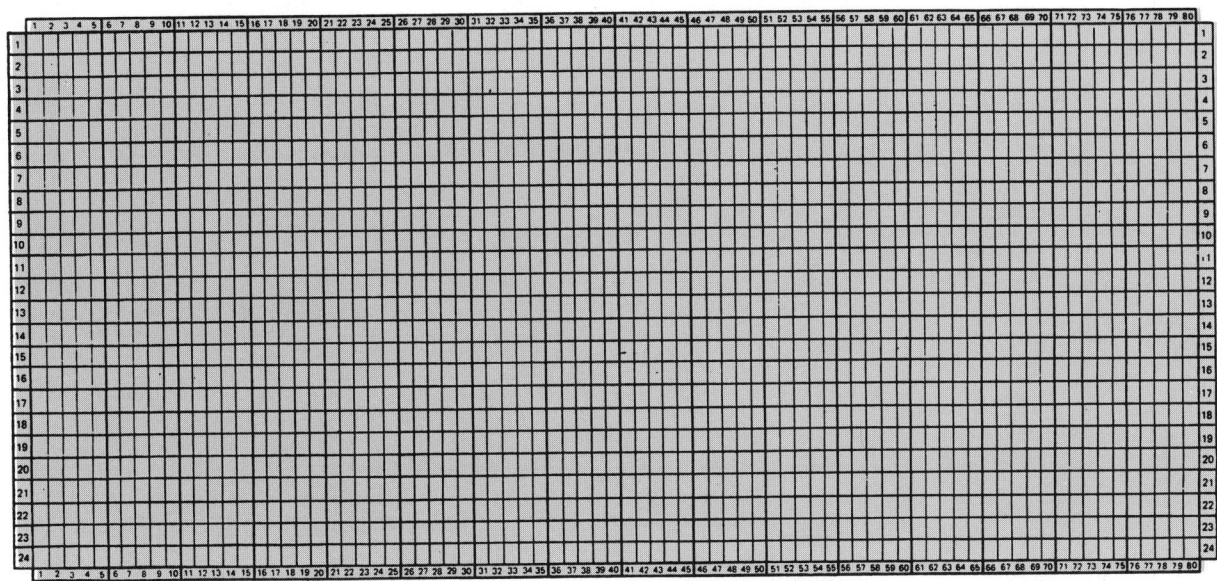

Figure 12-53   Form for display format design

2. Design a data entry display format based on the source document (Mail Order Sales Record) shown in Figure 12-54 on page 12.52. All fields are mandatory entries with the following exceptions:

   The Addr-1 and Addr-2 fields are optional.
   One of the two payment method blocks must contain an entry. Do not specify these areas as mandatory entries.
   If the payment method is check, the Credit Card Payment entries (card type, card number, expiration date, and cardholder's name) are blank.

The Date, Quantity, ZIP, Card Number (if used), and Expiration Date (if used) fields must contain numeric entries. Use the display format layout form in Figure 12-55 on page 12.53 for your design. Indicate any attributes to be used with each element of the display.

Mail Order Sales Record

required

Date _____ / _____ / _____   Order Number [| | | | | | | | | | |]

required

Item Number [| | | | | | |]   Quantity [| | |]

SOLD TO:

Name [| | | | | | | | | | | | | | | | | | | | | | | | | | | |]

Addr-1 [| | | | | | | | | | | | | | | | | | | | | | | | | | |]

Addr-2 [| | | | | | | | | | | | | | | | | | | | | | | | | | |]   (optional)

Addr-3 [| | | | | | | | | | | | | | | | | | | | | | | | | | |]   (optional)

State [| |]   ZIP [| | | | |] [| | | |]

Payment Method: (check one)

Check [ ]   Credit Card [ ]

IF CREDIT CARD PAYMENT: complete all entries below

Card Type [ ]

V-Visa   M-Master Card   A-American Express

Card Number [| | | | | | | | | | | | | | | | |]

Expiration Date [| |] / [| |]

Cardholder's Name [| | | | | | | | | | | | | | | | | | | | | | | | |]

Figure 12-54   Mail order sales document

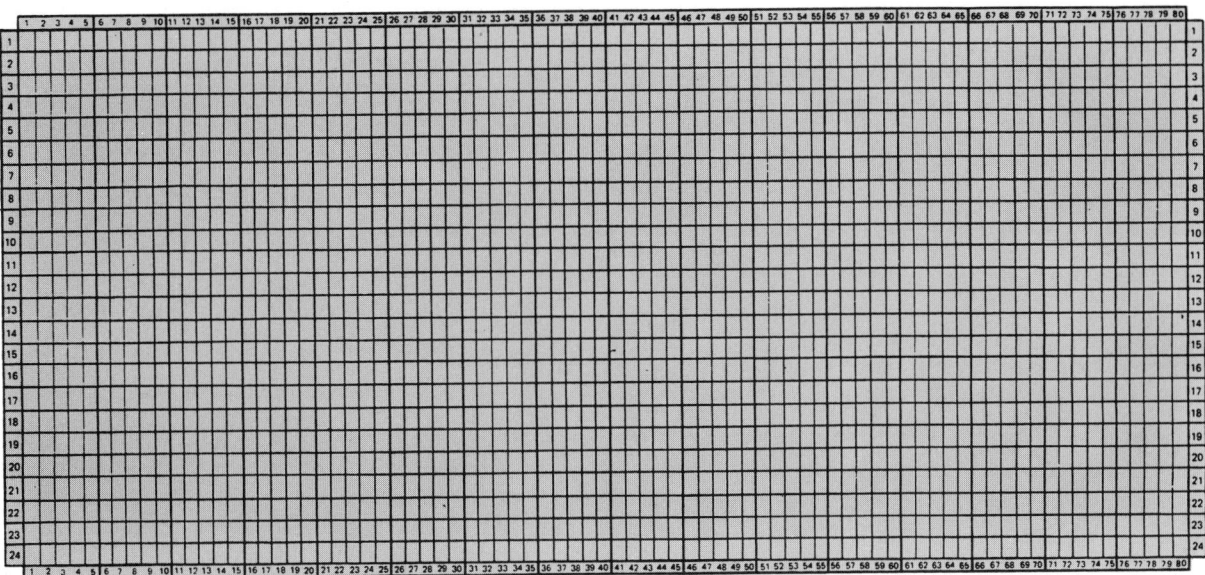

Figure 12-55   Form for display format design

STUDENT EXERCISES: RPG PROGRAM MAINTENANCE

Problem 1

Because program HJG12X has currently been designed and coded, CMD/7 immediately ends the program. If a record has been entered into the display format when CMD/7 is pressed, the program ignores all entered data, turns on indicator LR, and ends the job. Modify the program (in Figure 12-56) so that if a record is entered and CMD/7 is then pressed, the program processes the record and then ends program execution. Explain your modifications and their effect on the program.

Figure 12-56   Compilation listing for program HJG12X

```
0001 H                                                              HJG12X
0002 F*-------------------------------------------------------------*
0003 F*                                                             *
0004 F*  HJG12X - TEST EQUIPMENT MASTER FILE LOAD - DECEMBER 1, 1991  *
0005 F*                                                             *
0006 F*  PROGRAM HJG12X ADDS RECORDS TO THE TEST EQUIPMENT MASTER FILE. *
0007 F*  INPUT DATA IS KEYED INTO THE PROGRAM USING DISPLAY FORMAT  *
0008 F*  CALS01, WHICH IS PART OF CALP01S1.  CALP01S1, THE WORKSTATION *
0009 F*  FILE, IS A COMBINED DEMAND FILE AND IS READ BY MEANS OF THE *
0010 F*  READ OPERATION.  OUTPUT TO THIS FILE IS CONTROLLED BY THE EXCPT *
0011 F*  OPERATION.  THE EIGHT INPUT FIELDS WITHIN CALP01S1 THAT USE *
0012 F*  ZERO/BLANK INDICATORS ARE REQUIRED ENTRIES.  IF ANY OF THESE *
0013 F*  FIELDS DOES NOT CONTAIN DATA THE PROGRAM WILL RE-DISPLAY THE *
0014 F*  FORMAT WITH AN ERROR MESSAGE INDICATING THAT REQUIRED DATA IS *
0015 F*  MISSING.  AN ATTEMPT TO LOAD A RECORD WITH A DUPLICATE KEY *
0016 F*  FIELD WILL ALSO RESULT IN AN ERROR MESSAGE AND RE-DISPLAY OF *
0017 F*  INPUT FORMAT.  THE ACQUISITION COST FIELD MAY BE ENTERED WITH *
0018 F*  DOLLAR SIGN, DECIMAL POINT, AND COMMA AS THE PROGRAM CODE WILL *
0019 F*  DELETE THESE PUNCTUATION MARKS.                            *
0020 F*-------------------------------------------------------------*
0021 F/SPACE
```

Figure 12-56 (1)

continued

```
0023 F                                                        KFMTS  CALS01
0024 FCALF01  UC  F 145 145R20AI      5 DISK                           A
0025 FCALL01  O   F 132 132     OF    PRINTER
0026 F/SPACE
0027 F* ID F   C  H  L    FUNCTION OF INDICATORS
0028 F* 01 -   -  -  -  - CALP01S1 RECORD IDENTIFICATION -- UNISED
0029 F* 02 -   -  -  -  - CALF01 RECORD IDENTIFICATION -- UNUSED
0030 F*        20 -  -  - NON-DUPLICATE CALNO -- VALID TO ADD
0031 F*        30 -  -  - CALNO > 12 IN ROUTINE TO SET NXTDAT
0032 F*        50 -  -  - WORK INDICATOR IN ACQCST CONVERSION ROUTINE
0033 F*        51 -  -  - WORK INDICATOR IN ACQCST CONVERSION ROUTINE
0034 F*        52 -  -  - WORK INDICATOR IN ACQCST CONVERSION ROUTINE
0035 F*        53 -  -  - WORK INDICATOR IN ACQCST CONVERSION ROUTINE
0036 F*     90 -  -  -  - BLANK CALNO FIELD
0037 F*     91 -  -  -  - BLANK TYPE FIELD
0038 F*     92 -  -  -  - BLANK MFGR FIELD
0039 F*     93 -  -  -  - BLANK MODEL FIELD
0040 F*     94 -  -  -  - BLANK LOCATN FIELD
0041 F*     95 -  -  -  - BLANK CALDAT FIELD
0042 F*     96 -  -  -  - BLANK DONEBY FIELD
0043 F*     97 -  -  -  - BLANK CALINT FIELD
0044 F*              1P - FIRST PAGE HEADING CONTROL
0045 F*              OF - OVERFLOW HEADING CONTROL
0046 F*              LR - LAST RECORD INDICATOR - TURNED ON BY INDICATOR KG
0047 F*        KG -  -  - COMMAND KEY 7 FROM INPUT DISPLAY FORMAT
0048 E*  THE HOLD AND OUT ARRAYS ARE USED IN THE CONVERSION OF
0049 E*  INPUT DISPLAY FORMAT ACQUISITION COST DATA TO NUMERIC
0050 E*  FORMAT.  THE ERR ARRAY CONTAINS ERROR MESSAGES.
0051 E*-------------------------------------------------------------
0052 E               HOLD      8 1
0053 E               OUT       6 1
0054 E   ERR      1  2 24
0055 I*  CALP01S1 INPUT SPECIFICATIONS
0056 I*-------------------------------
0057 ICALP01S1WS
0058 I* FORMAT- CALS01
0059 I                             1  20 CALNO      90
0060 I                            21  40 FAIDNO
0061 I                            41  48 TYPE       91
0062 I                            49  54 MFGR       92
0063 I                            55  62 MODEL      93
0064 I                            63  74 SERIAL
0065 I                            75  78 LOCATN     94
0066 I                            79  840ACQDAT
0067 I                            85  92 ACQCST
0068 I                            93  980CALDAT    95
0069 I                            99 104 DONEBY     96
0070 I                           105 1060CALINT    97
0071 I/SPACE
0072 I*  CALF01 INPUT SPECIFICATIONS
0073 I*-----------------------------
0074 ICALF01  AA
0075 I                             1 145 DATA
0076 C*  BEGIN PROCESSING AND CLEAR ACQCST FIELD
0077 C*----------------------------------------------
0078 C          START     TAG
0079 C                    MOVE *ZEROS   ACQCST
0080 C/SPACE
0081 C*  DISPLAY FORMAT
0082 C*----------------
0083 C                    EXCPTSCREEN
0084 C          NXTONE    TAG
0085 C/SPACE
0086 C*  INPUT FORMAT DATA AND TEST FOR END OF JOB
0087 C*-----------------------------------------------------------------
0088 C                    READ CALP01S1
0089 C    KG             SETON              LR
0090 C    KG             GOTO EXIT
0091 C/SPACE
0092 C*  IF REQUIRED INPUT DATA IS MISSING MOVE ERROR MESSAGE 1,
0093 C*  RETURN TO START, AND RE-DISPLAY INPUT FORMAT
0094 C*-------------------------------------------------------------
0095 C    90
0096 COR  91
0097 COR  92
0098 COR  93
0099 COR  94
0100 COR  95
0101 COR  96
```

Figure 12-56 (2)

```
0102 COR 97                     MOVE ERR,1     MESSAG 24
0103 C   90
0104 COR 91
0105 COR 92
0106 COR 93
0107 COR 94
0108 COR 95
0109 COR 96
0110 COR 97                     GOTO START
0111 C/SPACE
0112 C* TEST FOR DUPLICATE KEY.  IF DUPLICATE, MOVE ERROR MESSAGE 2
0113 C*  AND RETURN TO START TO RE-DISPLAY INPUT FORMAT
0114 C*-------------------------------------------------------------
0115 C        CALNO      CHAINCALF01            20     VALID TO ADD
0116 C   N20             MOVE ERR,2     MESSAG
0117 C   N20             GOTO START
0118 C/SPACE
0119 C*  SET DATE OF NEXT CALIBRATION (NXTDAT)
0120 C*----------------------------------------
0121 C                   MOVELCALDAT    CALMO  20     SEPARATE MONTH
0122 C                   Z-ADDCALDAT    NXTDAT 60     MOVE CALDAT TO
0123 C*                                                      NXTDAT
0124 C                   ADD  CALINT    CALMO         ADD INTERVAL
0125 C        CALMO      COMP 12                30    MONTH INVALID
0126 C   30              SUB  12        CALMO         RESET MONTH
0127 C   30              ADD  1         NXTDAT        INCREMENT YEAR
0128 C                   MOVELCALMO     NXTDAT        MOVE MONTH INTO
0129 C*                                                  NEXT DATE
0130 C/SPACE
0131 C*  CONVERT INPUT DISPLAY AMOUNT TO NUMERIC FORMAT
0132 C*-------------------------------------------------
0133 C                   MOVEAACQCST    HOLD
0134 C                   Z-ADD9         X      10
0135 C                   Z-ADD7         Y      10
0136 C        LOOP1      TAG
0137 C                   SUB  1         Y           50
0138 C   50              GOTO ENDLP
0139 C        LOOP       TAG
0140 C                   SUB  1         X           50
0141 C   50              GOTO ENDLP
0142 C        HOLD,X     COMP '.'                   51
0143 C   51              GOTO LOOP
0144 C        HOLD,X     COMP ','                   52
0145 C   52              GOTO LOOP
0146 C        HOLD,X     COMP '$'                   53
0147 C   53              GOTO LOOP
0148 C                   MOVE HOLD,X    OUT,Y
0149 C                   GOTO LOOP1
0150 C        ENDLP      TAG
0151 C                   MOVEAOUT       CSTOUT 62
0152 C/SPACE
0153 C*  WRITE OUTPUT TO DISK AND PRINTER, ADD TO RECORD COUNT
0154 C*-------------------------------------------------------
0155 C                   EXCPTADDDAT
0156 C                   ADD  1         COUNT  40
0157 C                   GOTO START
0158 C        EXIT       TAG
0159 O*  DISPLAY FORMAT OUTPUT
0160 O*-------------------------
0161 OCALP01S1E          SCREEN
0162 O                          K8 'CALS01
0163 O                      CALNO    20
0164 O                      FAIDNO   40
0165 O                      TYPE     48
0166 O                      MFGR     54
0167 O                      MODEL    62
0168 O                      SERIAL   74
0169 O                      LOCATN   78
0170 O                      ACQDAT   84
0171 O                      ACQCST   92
0172 O                      CALDAT   98
0173 O                      DONEBY   104
0174 O                      CALINT   106
0175 O                      MESSAG B 136
0176 O/SPACE
0177 O*  RECORD ADDITION TO TEST EQUIPMENT MASTER FILE
0178 O*-----------------------------------------------
0179 OCALF01 EADD        ADDDAT
0180 O                          4 'ACAL'
```

Figure 12-56 (3)

continued

```
0181 O                         CALNO    24
0182 O                         TYPE     32
0183 O                         MFGR     38
0184 O                         MODEL    46
0185 O                         SERIAL   58
0186 O                         LOCATN   62
0187 O                         ACQDAT   68
0188 O                         CSTOUT   74
0189 O                         CALDAT   80
0190 O                         NXTDAT   86
0191 O                         DONEBY   95
0192 O                         CALINT   97
0193 O                         FAIDNO  145
0194 C/SPACE
0195 O*  HEADING LINES
0196 O*---------------
0197 OCALL01    H  106   1P
0198 O          OR       OF
0199 O                                   67 '...OF CABBAGES AND KINGS'
0200 O                         UDATE Y  104
0201 O/SPACE
0202 O          H   3    1P
0203 O          OR       OF
0204 O                                   11 'HJG12X'
0205 O                                   57 'TEST EQUIPMENT MASTER'
0206 O                                   74 'FILE LOAD REPORT'
0207 O                                  100 'PAGE'
0208 O                         PAGE     104
0209 O/SPACE
0210 O          H   1    1P
0211 O          OR       OF
0212 O                                   21 'CAL. UNIT ID NO.'
0213 O                                   55 'FIXED ASSET I.D. NO.'
0214 O/SPACE
0215 O          H   1    1P
0216 O          OR       OF
0217 O                                   29 '------------------------'
0218 O                                   53 '------------------------'
0219 O                                   77 '--ACQ.      ACQ.    ----'
0220 O                                  102 'C-A-L-I-B-R-A-T-I-O-N---'
0221 O/SPACE
0222 O          H   2    1P
0223 O          OR       OF
0224 O                                   29 'TYPE      MFGR    MODEL'
0225 O                                   51 'SERIAL NO.    LOC.'
0226 O                                   70 ' DATE        COST'
0227 O                                   95 'LAST     BY   INT.'
0228 O                                  102 'NEXT'
0229 O/SPACE
0230 O*  RECORD ADDITION DATA LINES
0231 O*--------------------------
0232 O          E   1          ADDDAT
0233 O                         CALNO  B  25
0234 O                         FAIDNO B  55
0235 O/SPACE
0236 O          E   1          ADDDAT
0237 O                                   29 '------------------------'
0238 O                                   53 '------------------------'
0239 O                                   55 '--'
0240 O/SPACE
0241 O          E   2          ADDDAT
0242 O                         TYPE   B  13
0243 O                         MFGR   B  21
0244 O                         MODEL  B  31
0245 O                         SERIAL B  45
0246 O                         LOCATN B  51
0247 O                         ACQDATB   61
0248 O                         CSTOUT2B  72 '$'
0249 O                         CALDATYB  82
0250 O                         DONEBY B  90
0251 O                         CALINTZB  94
0252 O                         NXTDATYB 104
0253 O* FINAL TOTAL COUNT OF ADDED RECORDS
0254 O*-------------------------------
0255 O          T  21    LR
0256 O                         COUNT Z   8
0257 O                                   30 'UNITS HAVE BEEN ADDED'
0258 O                                   37 'TO THE'
```

Figure 12-56 (4)

```
0259 O        T      01 LR
0260 O                             30 'TEST EQUIPMENT MASTER'
0261 O                             35 'FILE'
0262 O/SPACE 3
0263 O*  ERROR MESSAGE ARRAY DATA
0264 O*------------------------
**
REQUIRED ENTRY MISSING
UNIT ID ALREADY ON FILE
```

Figure 12-56 (5)

Problem 2

The Quality Control department has determined that the current system of assigning two identification numbers, the calibration unit identification number and the fixed asset identification number, to a single unit of test equipment can be confusing when a piece of equipment is used by a department other than the Quality Control department. Modify program HJG12X (Figure 12-57) so that if no calibration unit identification number is entered but a fixed asset identification number is entered, the program uses the fixed asset number as the calibration unit number. If this happens, the program must use FAIDNO to perform the CHAIN to CALF01 and, when the output record is written to CALF01, the contents of the FAIDNO field are placed in both the CALNO and FAIDNO fields. Explain your modifications and their effects on the program.

Figure 12-57   Compilation listing for program HJG12X

```
0001 H                                                            HJG12X
0002 F*------------------------------------------------------------*
0003 F*                                                            *
0004 F*  HJG12X - TEST EQUIPMENT MASTER FILE LOAD - DECEMBER 1, 1991   *
0005 F*                                                            *
0006 F*  PROGRAM HJG12X ADDS RECORDS TO THE TEST EQUIPMENT MASTER FILE. *
0007 F*  INPUT DATA IS KEYED INTO THE PROGRAM USING DISPLAY FORMAT  *
0008 F*  CALS01, WHICH IS PART OF CALP01S1.  CALP01S1, THE WORKSTATION *
0009 F*  FILE, IS A COMBINED DEMAND FILE AND IS READ BY MEANS OF THE  *
0010 F*  READ OPERATION.  OUTPUT TO THIS FILE IS CONTROLLED BY THE EXCPT *
0011 F*  OPERATION.  THE EIGHT INPUT FIELDS WITHIN CALP01S1 THAT USE  *
0012 F*  ZERO/BLANK INDICATORS ARE REQUIRED ENTRIES.  IF ANY OF THESE  *
0013 F*  FIELDS DOES NOT CONTAIN DATA THE PROGRAM WILL RE-DISPLAY THE  *
0014 F*  FORMAT WITH AN ERROR MESSAGE INDICATING THAT REQUIRED DATA IS  *
0015 F*  MISSING.  AN ATTEMPT TO LOAD A RECORD WITH A DUPLICATE KEY  *
0016 F*  FIELD WILL ALSO RESULT IN AN ERROR MESSAGE AND RE-DISPLAY OF  *
0017 F*  INPUT FORMAT.  THE ACQUISITION COST FIELD MAY BE ENTERED WITH  *
0018 F*  DOLLAR SIGN, DECIMAL POINT, AND COMMA AS THE PROGRAM CODE WILL  *
0019 F*  DELETE THESE PUNCTUATION MARKS.                             *
0020 F*------------------------------------------------------------*
0021 F/SPACE
0022 FCALP01S1CD F    136          WORKSTN
0023 F                                        KFMTS  CALS01
0024 FCALF01 UC  F 145 145R20AI    5 DISK               A
0025 FCALL01 O   F 132 132     OF    PRINTER
0026 F/SPACE
0027 F*  ID F  C  H  L    FUNCTION OF INDICATORS
0028 F* 01 -  -  -  -  - CALP01S1 RECORD IDENTIFICATION -- UNISED
0029 F* 02 -  -  -  -  - CALF01 RECORD IDENTIFICATION -- UNUSED
0030 F*        20 -  -  - NON-DUPLICATE CALNO -- VALID TO ADD
0031 F*        30 -  -  - CALNO > 12 IN ROUTINE TO SET NXTDAT
0032 F*        50 -  -  - WORK INDICATOR IN ACQCST CONVERSION ROUTINE
0033 F*        51 -  -  - WORK INDICATOR IN ACQCST CONVERSION ROUTINE
0034 F*        52 -  -  - WORK INDICATOR IN ACQCST CONVERSION ROUTINE
0035 F*        53 -  -  - WORK INDICATOR IN ACQCST CONVERSION ROUTINE
0036 F*  90 -  -  -  - BLANK CALNO FIELD
0037 F*  91 -  -  -  - BLANK TYPE FIELD
0038 F*  92 -  -  -  - BLANK MFGR FIELD
0039 F*  93 -  -  -  - BLANK MODEL FIELD
0040 F*  94 -  -  -  - BLANK LOCATN FIELD
0041 F*  95 -  -  -  - BLANK CALDAT FIELD
0042 F*  96 -  -  -  - BLANK DONEBY FIELD
```

Figure 12-57 (1)

continued

```
0043 F*      97 - - - - BLANK CALINT FIELD
0044 F*              1P - FIRST PAGE HEADING CONTROL
0045 F*              OF - OVERFLOW HEADING CONTROL
0046 F*              LR - LAST RECORD INDICATOR - TURNED ON BY INDICATOR KG
0047 F*      KG - - - COMMAND KEY 7 FROM INPUT DISPLAY FORMAT
0048 E*  THE HOLD AND OUT ARRAYS ARE USED IN THE CONVERSION OF
0049 E*  INPUT DISPLAY FORMAT ACQUISITION COST DATA TO NUMERIC
0050 E*  FORMAT.  THE ERR ARRAY CONTAINS ERROR MESSAGES.
0051 E*----------------------------------------------------------
0052 E               HOLD      8 1
0053 E               OUT       6 1
0054 E               ERR    1  2 24
0055 I* CALP01S1 INPUT SPECIFICATIONS
0056 I*-----------------------------------
0057 ICALP01S1WS
0058 I* FORMAT- CALS01
0059 I                          1  20 CALNO      90
0060 I                         21  40 FAIDNO
0061 I                         41  48 TYPE       91
0062 I                         49  54 MFGR       92
0063 I                         55  62 MODEL      93
0064 I                         63  74 SERIAL
0065 I                         75  78 LOCATN     94
0066 I                         79 840ACQDAT
0067 I                         85  92 ACQCST
0068 I                         93 980CALDAT     95
0069 I                         99 104 DONEBY     96
0070 I                        105 1060CALINT     97
0071 I/SPACE
0072 I* CALF01 INPUT SPECIFICATIONS
0073 I*-----------------------------------
0074 ICALF01  AA
0075 I                          1 145 DATA
0076 C* BEGIN PROCESSING AND CLEAR ACQCST FIELD
0077 C*-----------------------------------
0078 C           START    TAG
0079 C                    MOVE *ZEROS   ACQCST
0080 C/SPACE
0081 C* DISPLAY FORMAT
0082 C*-----------------
0083 C                    EXCPTSCREEN
0084 C           NXTONE   TAG
0085 C/SPACE
0086 C* INPUT FORMAT DATA AND TEST FOR END OF JOB
0087 C*----------------------------------------------------------------------
0088 C                    READ CALP01S1
0089 C     KG             SETON                    LR
0090 C     KG             GOTO EXIT
0091 C/SPACE
0092 C* IF REQUIRED INPUT DATA IS MISSING MOVE ERROR MESSAGE 1,
0093 C* RETURN TO START, AND RE-DISPLAY INPUT FORMAT
0094 C*----------------------------------------------------------
0095 C     90
0096 COR   91
0097 COR   92
0098 COR   93
0099 COR   94
0100 COR   95
0101 COR   96
0102 COR   97             MOVE ERR,1    MESSAG 24
0103 C     90
0104 COR   91
0105 COR   92
0106 COR   93
0107 COR   94
0108 COR   95
0109 COR   96
0110 COR   97             GOTO START
0111 C/SPACE
0112 C* TEST FOR DUPLICATE KEY.  IF DUPLICATE, MOVE ERROR MESSAGE 2
0113 C* AND RETURN TO START TO RE-DISPLAY INPUT FORMAT
0114 C*----------------------------------------------------------
0115 C           CALNO    CHAINCALF01         20   VALID TO ADD
0116 C     N20            MOVE ERR,2    MESSAG
0117 C     N20            GOTO START
0118 C/SPACE
0119 C* SET DATE OF NEXT CALIBRATION (NXTDAT)
0120 C*----------------------------------------------------------
0121 C                    MOVELCALDAT   CALMO  20   SEPARATE MONTH
```

Figure 12-57 (2)

```
0122 C                        Z-ADDCALDAT   NXTDAT  60      MOVE CALDAT TO
0123 C*                                                       NXTDAT
0124 C                        ADD  CALINT   CALMO           ADD INTERVAL
0125 C           CALMO        COMP·12               30      MONTH INVALID
0126 C     30                 SUB  12       CALMO           RESET MONTH
0127 C     30                 ADD  1        NXTDAT          INCREMENT YEAR
0128 C                        MOVELCALMO    NXTDAT          MOVE MONTH INTO
0129 C*                                                       NEXT DATE
0130 C/SPACE
0131 C*  CONVERT INPUT DISPLAY AMOUNT TO NUMERIC FORMAT
0132 C*------------------------------------------------
0133 C                        MOVEAACQCST   HOLD
0134 C                        Z-ADD9        X       10
0135 C                        Z-ADD7        Y       10
0136 C           LOOP1        TAG
0137 C                        SUB  1        Y               50
0138 C     50                 GOTO ENDLP
0139 C           LOOP         TAG
0140 C                        SUB  1        X               50
0141 C     50                 GOTO ENDLP
0142 C           HOLD,X       COMP '.'                      51
0143 C     51                 GOTO LOOP
0144 C           HOLD,X       COMP ','                      52
0145 C     52                 GOTO LOOP
0146 C           HOLD,X       COMP '$'                      53
0147 C     53                 GOTO LOOP
0148 C                        MOVE HOLD,X   OUT,Y
0149 C                        GOTO LOOP1
0150 C           ENDLP        TAG
0151 C                        MOVEAOUT      CSTOUT  62
0152 C/SPACE
0153 C*  WRITE OUTPUT TO DISK AND PRINTER, ADD TO RECORD COUNT
0154 C*--------------------------------------------------------
0155 C                        EXCPTADDDAT
0156 C                        ADD  1        COUNT   40
0157 C                        GOTO START
0158 C           EXIT         TAG
0159 O*  DISPLAY FORMAT OUTPUT
0160 O*---------------------
0161 OCALP01S1E               SCREEN
0162 O                                      K8 'CALS01
0163 O                        CALNO     20
0164 O                        FAIDNO    40
0165 O                        TYPE      48
0166 O                        MFGR      54
0167 O                        MODEL     62
0168 O                        SERIAL    74
0169 O                        LOCATN    78
0170 O                        ACQDAT    84
0171 O                        ACQCST    92
0172 O                        CALDAT    98
0173 O                        DONEBY   104
0174 O                        CALINT   106
0175 O                        MESSAG B 136
0176 O/SPACE
0177 O*  RECORD ADDITION TO TEST EQUIPMENT MASTER FILE
0178 O*---------------------------------------------
0179 OCALF01 EADD             ADDDAT
0180 O                                       4 'ACAL'
0181 O                        CALNO     24
0182 O                        TYPE      32
0183 O                        MFGR      38
0184 O                        MODEL     46
0185 O                        SERIAL    58
0186 O                        LOCATN    62
0187 O                        ACQDAT    68
0188 O                        CSTOUT    74
0189 O                        CALDAT    80
0190 O                        NXTDAT    86
0191 O                        DONEBY    95
0192 O                        CALINT    97
0193 O                        FAIDNO   145
0194 C/SPACE
0195 O*  HEADING LINES
0196 O*---------------
0197 OCALL01  H  106      1P
0198 O         OR         OF
0199 O                                      67 '...OF CABBAGES AND KINGS'
0200 O                        UDATE Y  104
```

Figure 12-57 (3)

continued

```
0201 O/SPACE
0202 O          H  3      1P
0203 O          OR        OF
0204 O                                    11 'HJG12X'
0205 O                                    57 'TEST EQUIPMENT MASTER'
0206 O                                    74 'FILE LOAD REPORT'
0207 O                                   100 'PAGE'
0208 O                          PAGE     104
0209 O/SPACE
0210 O          H  1      1P
0211 O          OR        OF
0212 O                                    21 'CAL. UNIT ID NO.'
0213 O                                    55 'FIXED ASSET I.D. NO.'
0214 O/SPACE
0215 O          H  1      1P
0216 O          OR        OF
0217 O                                    29 '-------------------'
0218 O                                    53 '-------------------'
0219 O                                    77 '--ACQ.      ACQ.  ----'
0220 O                                   102 'C-A-L-I-B-R-A-T-I-O-N---'
0221 O/SPACE
0222 O          H  2      1P
0223 O          OR        OF
0224 O                                    29 'TYPE     MFGR     MODEL'
0225 O                                    51 'SERIAL NO.   LOC.'
0226 O                                    70 ' DATE       COST'
0227 O                                    95 'LAST      BY   INT.'
0228 O                                   102 'NEXT'
0229 O/SPACE
0230 O*  RECORD ADDITION DATA LINES
0231 O*-------------------------
0232 O          E  1           ADDDAT
0233 O                         CALNO  B  25
0234 O                         FAIDNO B  55
0235 O/SPACE
0236 O          E  1           ADDDAT
0237 O                                    29 '------------------------'
0238 O                                    53 '------------------------'
0239 O                                    55 '--'
0240 O/SPACE
0241 O          E  2           ADDDAT
0242 O                         TYPE   B  13
0243 O                         MFGR   B  21
0244 O                         MODEL  B  31
0245 O                         SERIAL B  45
0246 O                         LOCATN B  51
0247 O                         ACQDATYB  61
0248 O                         CSTOUT2B  72 '$'
0249 O                         CALDATYB  82
0250 O                         DONEBY B  90
0251 O                         CALINTZB  94
0252 O                         NXTDATYB 104
0253 O*  FINAL TOTAL COUNT OF ADDED RECORDS
0254 O*-----------------------------------
0255 O          T 21      LR
0256 O                         COUNT Z   8
0257 O                                    30 'UNITS HAVE BEEN ADDED'
0258 O                                    37 'TO THE'
0259 O          T     01  LR
0260 O                                    30 'TEST EQUIPMENT MASTER'
0261 O                                    35 'FILE'
0262 O/SPACE 3
0263 O*  ERROR MESSAGE ARRAY DATA
0264 O*-------------------------
**
REQUIRED ENTRY MISSING
UNIT ID ALREADY ON FILE
```

Figure 12-57 (4)

STUDENT EXERCISES: INTERACTIVE PROGRAMMING IN RPG II

PROGRAMMING ASSIGNMENT 1
BOOK MASTER FILE LOAD

INSTRUCTIONS

Plan, code, enter, and test an interactive RPG program to load new records to the Book Master File.

INPUT

Input is based on the source document (New Book Acquisition) in Figure 12-58. The maximum length of each element can be determined from the Book Master File layout shown in the Output section of this problem description.

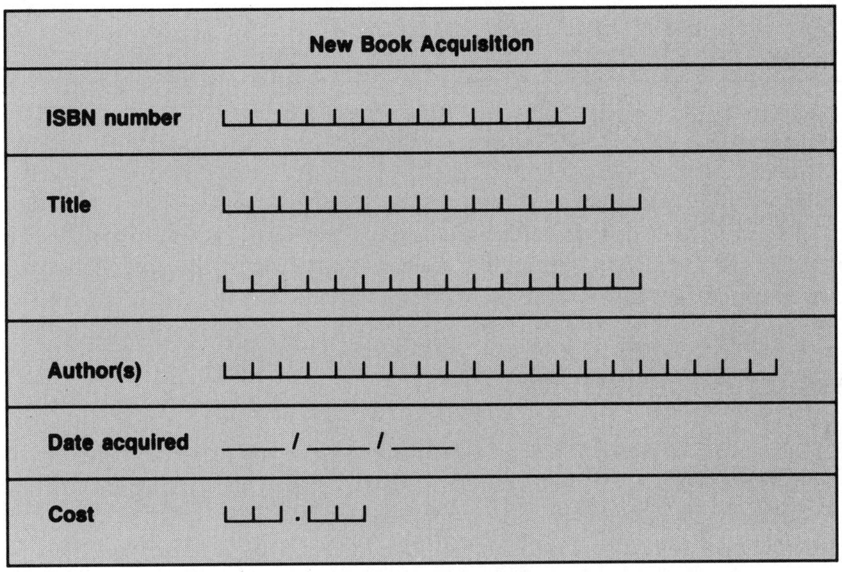
New Book Acquisition

ISBN number

Title

Author(s)

Date acquired ____ / ____ / ____

Cost

Figure 12-58 New Book Acquisition document

No test data set is provided for this program. In addition to designing output reports, programmers are responsible for designing the test data used to verify the accuracy of a program. You must plan and design the test data for this program. Your textbooks and/or school library are convenient sources of test data for this program.

Be sure that as you enter the data, you enter some incorrect data so as to test the input editing functions of the program. Unless otherwise instructed, use the PRINT key to print an image of the data shown on the screen when an error is detected and submit these screen printouts as part of your program. Enter a minimum of ten valid records into the Book Master File.

OUTPUT

Programming Assignment 1 develops two output files. The first is the Book Master File (Figure 12-59). Note that position 80 of each record contains the code A to indicate that the record is active.

BOOK MASTER FILE						
	Record Length 80			Key Location 1–13		
Field No.	Field Name	Field Description	Field Position	Field Length	Dec. Pos.	Data Class
1		ISBN Number	1–13	13		A
2		Book Title	14–43	30		A
3		Author(s)	44–63	20		A
4		Date Acquired	64–69	6	0	N
5		Cost	70–73	4	2	N
6		Status Code A	80–80	1		A

Figure 12-59   Book Master File layout

The second output file is the printed audit report that you will design to show a record of all books added to the Book Master File. This report lists all fields contained in every record added to the file. There is no need to show errors on this audit report because all errors that are detected will cause the program to redisplay the format on the screen with an error message stating the type of error detected.

Processing Requirements

1. The ISBN Number, Title, Author, and Date Acquired fields are mandatory entries. If one or more of these fields is not entered, the program redisplays the format, showing all entered data and an error message indicating that a required entry was not made.
2. ISBN Number must not be duplicated in the Book Master File. Note that the ISBN Number is a 13-character alphameric data field. Include the hyphens as part of the entered field. The ISBN Number is usually found on the cover or the copyright page at the beginning of a book.
3. The Date Acquired and Cost fields must contain numeric data.
4. Use Field Exit keys to leave all data entry fields.
5. End program execution when CMD/7 is pressed while a blank data entry format is displayed. Do not process any input data after CMD/7 is pressed.

PROGRAMMING ASSIGNMENT 2
TEAM ROSTER FILE LOAD

INSTRUCTIONS

Plan, code, enter, and test an interactive RPG program to load new records to the Team Roster File.

INPUT

Input is based on the source document (Team Assignment Data) in Figure 12-60. The maximum length of each element can be determined from the Team Roster File format shown in the Output section of this problem description.

Team Assignment Data

Student Data

Name

Grade

Student Number

Team Data

Season

F - Fall

S - Spring

Sport Code

Position

Number

Sport Codes:

FALL SPORTS

VF-Varsity Football
JF-Junior Varsity Football
CC-Cross Country
VH-Varsity Hockey
JH-Junior Varsity Hockey
MB-Men's Basketball
WB-Women's Basketball

SPRING SPORTS

VB-Varsity Baseball
JB-Junior Varsity Baseball
VS-Varsity Softball
JS-Junior Varsity Softball
MT-Men's Track and Field
WT-Women's Track and Field

Figure 12-60 Team Assignment Data document

As with Programming Assignment 1, you must design the test data for this program. As you enter the data, enter some incorrect data to test the input editing functions of the program. Unless otherwise instructed, use the PRINT key to print an image of the data shown on the screen when an error is detected and submit these screen printouts as part of your program. Enter a minimum of ten valid records into the Team Roster File.

OUTPUT

Programming Assignment 2 develops two output files. The first is the Team Roster File (Figure 12-61).

TEAM ROSTER FILE RECORD						
Record Length 46			Key Location 1–7			
Field No.	Field Name	Field Description	Field Position	Field Length	Dec. Pos.	Data Class
1		Student Number	1–4			
2		Grade	5–6			
3		Season	7			
4		Name	8–32			
5		Jersey Number	33–34			
6		Position	35–36			
7		Sport Code	37–38			

Figure 12-61   Format of Team Roster File Record

The second output file is the printed audit report that you design to list all records added to the Team Roster File. This report shows all fields contained in each added record. Remember that there is no need to show errors on this audit report because all errors that are detected will cause the program to redisplay the format on the screen with an error message stating the type of error detected.

▰ Processing Requirements

1. All fields on the source document are mandatory entries. If one or more of these fields is not entered, the program redisplays the format showing all required data and an error message indicating that a required entry was not made.
2. The record key, consisting of student number, grade, and season, must not be duplicated in the Team Roster File.
3. Grade, student number, and number (jersey number) must contain numeric data.
4. The Sport Code entry must be one of the listed sport codes and must agree with the Season entry (F or S). Hint: Use table lookup to determine if the sport code is valid and agrees with the Season entry.
5. Use field exit keys to leave all data entry fields.
6. End program execution when CMD/7 is pressed while a blank data entry format is displayed. Do not process any input data after CMD/7 is pressed.

PROGRAMMING ASSIGNMENT 3 EMPLOYEE MASTER FILE LOAD

INSTRUCTIONS

Plan, code, enter, and test an interactive RPG program to load new records to the Employee Master File. This programming assignment can be considered either as a new programming assignment or as an advanced exercise in program maintenance. In Chapter 10, a programming assignment loaded records to the Employee Master File using a batch input file. In this programming assignment, you perform the same process, using a display to enter the data. If you did Programming Assignment 2 in Chapter 10, you may find that some portions of the code can be used for this assignment. However, due to the differences in logic between batch processing programs and interactive programs, you will find that the calculation portion of the program will require extensive modification.

INPUT

Input is based on the source document (New Employee Data) in Figure 12-62. The maximum length of each element can be determined from the Employee Master File layout shown in the Output section of this problem description.

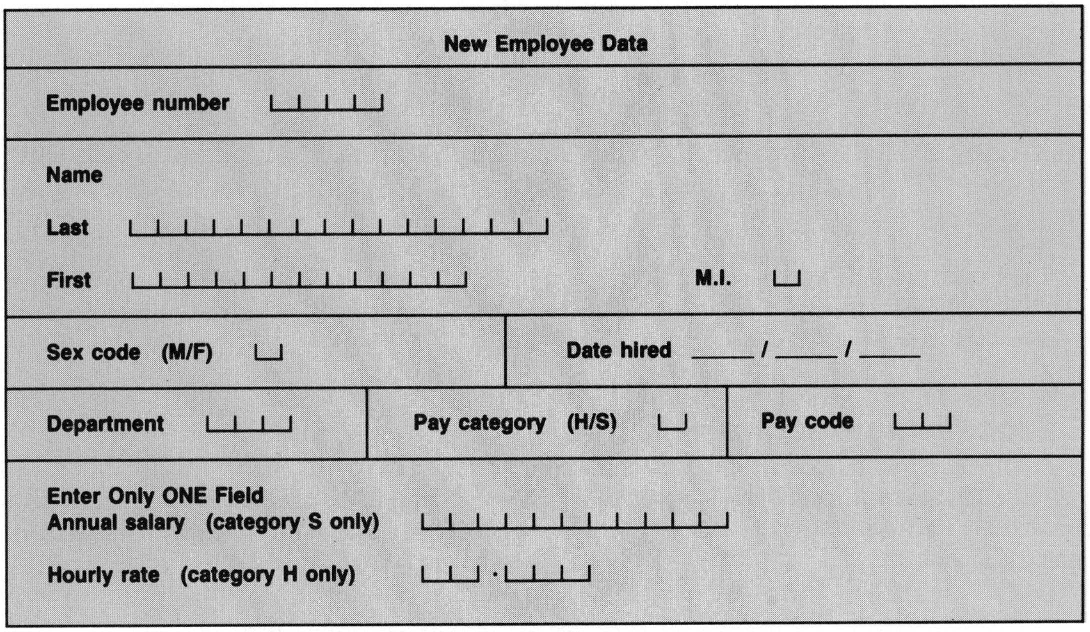
New Employee Data

Employee number

Name

Last

First

M.I.

Sex code (M/F)

Date hired ____ / ____ / ____

Department

Pay category (H/S)

Pay code

Enter Only ONE Field

Annual salary (category S only)

Hourly rate (category H only)

Figure 12-62 New Employee Data document

Use test data set 24 for this program. Unless otherwise instructed, use the PRINT key to print the data on the screen when an error is detected and submit these screen printouts as part of your program.

OUTPUT

Programming Assignment 3 creates two output files. The first is the Employee Master File, the format of which is in Figure 12-63.

EMPLOYEE MASTER FILE RECORD						
Record Length 70			Key Location 1–4			
Field No.	Field Name	Field Description	Field Position	Field Length	Dec. Pos.	Data Class
1		Employee Number	1–4			
2		Last Name	5–19			
3		First Name	20–31			
4		Sex Code (M/F)	32–32			
5		Date Hired	33–38			
6		Department Number	39–41			
7		Pay Category (H/S)	42–42			
8		Pay Rate Code	43–44			
9		Annual Salary	45–52			
10		Hourly Pay Rate	53–57			
11		Current Date	62–67			
12		Status Code A	70–70			

Figure 12-63 Format of Employee Master File Record

The second output file is a record addition report listing all records added to the Employee Master File. This report lists all fields contained in every record added to the file. In addition, the report prints a count of the number of records added to the file.

Processing Requirements

Test each input data record for the following conditions. If none of the listed conditions is detected, a record is added to the Employee Master File. If one or more of the listed conditions are detected, no addition to the master file is made.

1. The employee number must not be duplicated in the Employee Master File.
2. The Employee Number, Last Name, First Name, Date Hired, and Department Number fields must not be blank.
3. Sex code must be either M or F.
4. Pay category must be either H or S.
5. If pay category is H, neither the Pay Rate Code field nor the Hourly Pay Rate field can be blank or zero.
6. If pay category is S, the Annual Salary field cannot be blank or zero.

If any of these error conditions is detected, the program will redisplay the data entry display, showing all entered fields and an error message specifying the error that was detected. In addition to displaying an error message, identify the field or fields in error by using an indicator-controlled blink attribute for the field.

Sequential File Updating Using Matching Records

Recall from Chapter 11 that it is periodically necessary to update a file with current information. The three types of file updating procedures are record addition, record deletion, and record change. An addition takes place when a new record is added to an existing file, a deletion removes a record that is stored in a file, and a change is made to a file whenever a record in the file no longer contains accurate, up-to-date information.

Sequential updating involves reading a sequential master file, which contains the records to be updated, reading a sequential update request file, which contains the update request records, and creating a new, updated master file. As with all update programs, the program also creates an audit report containing a record of every update request and the result of the processing of the request (Figure 13-1).

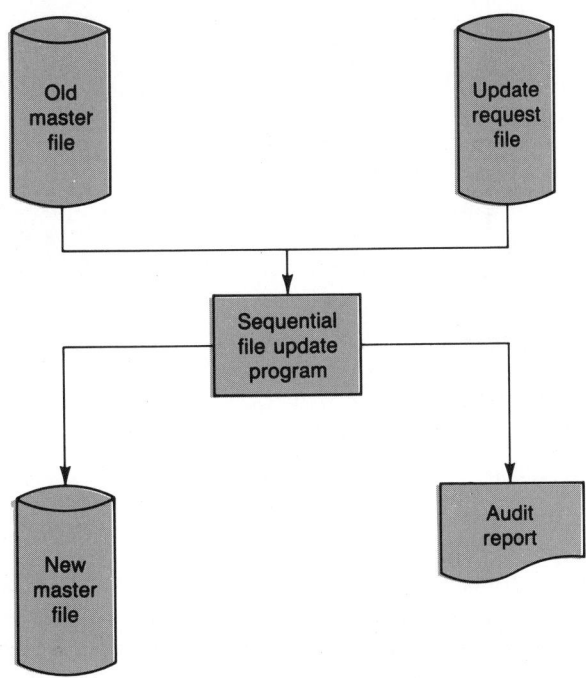

Figure 13-1 File flow for sequential file update

Note in the Figure that the original master file is used only as an input file and that a new version of the file is created by the program as output. This is because records in an arrival sequence path data file cannot be updated "in place." Instead, the entire file must be recreated by the program and will contain unchanged copies of all the original records that were not deleted, the new records that were added, and the new updated contents of records that were changed. To update a sequential file, the program must read and process every record in the file, so sequential file updating is a slower process than the random updating of keyed access path data files. Because of this, sequential updating is generally not used if any other method of file updating is possible.

A sequential data file is an arrival sequence file that is in a particular order based on the contents of a control field. Sequential files are usually placed in sequence by means of a sort utility that is part of your computer's operating system software. A sequential file is not a separate type of file organization or file access path. Sequential file processing treats input data files as arrival sequence access path data files and controls the reading of these files by use of the RPG fixed logic cycle. Sequential file processing is a technique not a file organization method.

SAMPLE PROBLEM DESCRIPTION

The sample program for this chapter illustrates the technique by sequentially updating MSTERIN, the Master Sales File. As the data file flow for program HJG13X shows (Figure 13-2), this sample program reads two input files, MSTERIN, the master file, and UPDATA, the update request file. Both are arrival sequence access path data files. The program produces two output files: MSTEROUT, which is the updated version of the Master Sales File, and REPORT, the update audit report.

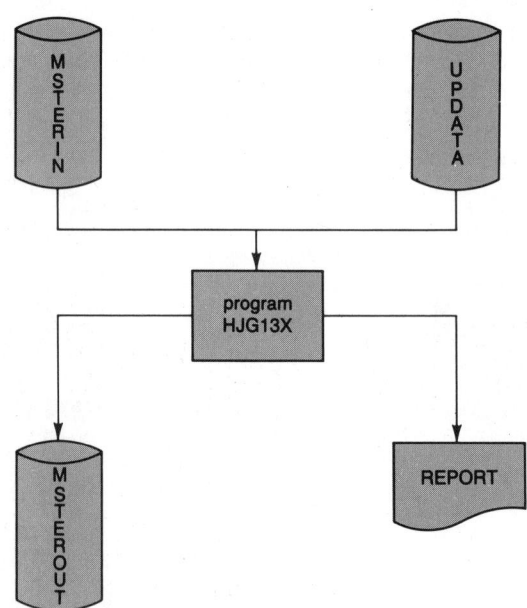

Figure 13-2 File flow for sample program HJG13X

Input

The Master Sales File, the format of which is in Figure 13-3, contains the customer number (MCSTNO), the customer name (MNAME), and the year-to-date sales amount for the customer (MAMT). Note that there is no Status Code field in the record. Sequential file updates do not require setting a deletion code because records are physically deleted during the update process. Remember that this type of file update creates a new data file and, in the process, leaves out the deleted records. As a result, there is no need to use a code to mark a record for physical deletion at some later time.

MASTER SALES FILE RECORD						
Record Length 29						
Field No.	Field Name	Field Description	Field Position	Field Length	Dec. Pos.	Data Class
1	MCSTNO	Customer Number	1–5	5		A
2	MNAME	Customer Name	6–25	20		A
3	MAMT	Sales Amount	26–29	6	2	NP

NP, numeric packed format

Figure 13-3   Format of Master Sales File Record

Figure 13-4 shows the file layout for UPDATA, the update transaction request file. Every addition request record contains the same fields as the master file records. The deletion request records, however, contain only the customer number of the record to be deleted, and the change request records contain only the customer number and sales amount fields. Also, every update request record contains an update code used to specify the type of processing that is to occur. A 1 in the Update Code field indicates that the update request record is an addition to the master file, a 2 indicates a deletion, and a 3 indicates a change to the year-to-date sales amount field in a master record currently on the master file.

UPDATE REQUEST FILE RECORD						
Record Length 33						
Field No.	Field Name	Field Description	Field Position	Field Length	Dec. Pos.	Data Class
1		Update Code	1–1	1		A
2	UCSTNO	Customer Number	2–6	5		A
3	UNAME	Customer Name	7–26	20		A
4	UAMT	Sales Amount	27–33	6	2	N

Figure 13-4   Format of Update Request File Record

Output

Recall that program HJG13X produces two output files. MSTEROUT is the updated version of MSTERIN and uses the same record format as Figure 13-3. The second output file is the Master Sales File Update report (Figure 13-5 on the next page). As was the case when you studied keyed file updating, all update request types, with one exception, produce a single line of output on the audit report. This exception is illustrated on lines 16–17 of the printer spacing chart and shows that when the program makes a change to the Sales Amount field, both the old and the new sales amounts are listed. The audit lines printed for record addition and deletion are illustrated on lines 12 and 14 of the printer spacing chart.

```
H  6  HJG13X        MASTER SALES FILE UPDATE      PAGE XX0X
H  7                     XXXXXXXXX 0X, 19XX
H  9                CUSTOMER
H 10  ACTION        NUMBER       CUSTOMER NAME      AMOUNT
D 12  ADD           XXXXX   XXXXXXXXXXXXXXXXXXXXXX  $XX,XX$.XX
D 14  DELETE        XXXXX   XXXXXXXXXXXXXXXXXXXXXX  $XX,XX$.XX
D 16  CHANGE        XXXXX   XXXXXXXXXXXXXXXXXXXXXX  $XX,XX$.XX  OLD
  17                                               $XX,XX$.XX  NEW
D 19  **ADD         XXXXX   XXXXXXXXXXXXXXXXXXXXXX  $XX,XX$.XX  DUPLICATE CUSTOMER NUMBER
D 21  **DELETE      XXXXX                                      NO MASTER RECORD
D 23  **CHANGE      XXXXX                           $XX,XX$.XX  NO MASTER RECORD
D 25  **********    XXXXX   XXXXXXXXXXXXXXXXXXXXXX  $XX,XX$.XX  INVALID ACTION CODE
```

Figure 13-5   Master Sales File Update Report

Lines 19, 21, 23, and 25 show the output that the program must print if an update request error is detected. Note that these error conditions are the same update error conditions that were tested in the keyed file update program you studied in Chapter 11. Regardless of whether the program is performing a keyed or a sequential update, these four fundamental error conditions must be tested. Every update request record must be tested to determine if it attempts to add a record that already exists in the master file (line 19), attempts to delete or change a record that does not exist in the master file (lines 21 and 23), or contains an invalid update request code (line 25).

Line 7 of each report page shows the report date. This date, as usual, uses the current system date, but instead of showing the date in MM/DD/YY format, the report layout requires the name of the month to be spelled out, the day to appear as a separate field, and the year to be a four-digit field beginning with the digits 19. As a result, the report date does not show 9/18/91 but shows September 18, 1991. Note that this requires that the program be modified on or about January 1, 2000.

Processing Requirements

The processing requirements for each record depend on whether the record is read from MSTERIN or UPDATA and, in the case of UPDATA records, on the update request code in position 1.

▶ **General Processing Requirements**   Several general processing requirements apply regardless of the update request code.

1. Every UPDATA record must be accounted for on the Master Sales File Update report to provide a complete and accurate audit trail of all processing requests.
2. All records currently in MSTERIN have been edited and can be assumed to contain valid data.
3. When a MSTERIN record for which there is no corresponding UPDATA record is read, the complete MSTERIN record is written to the MSTEROUT output file.
4. All UPDATA records have been verified and can, with one exception, be assumed to contain accurate update request data. The exception is the Update Request Code field, which must be tested to ensure that it contains a valid code. If a valid code (1, 2, or 3) is present, the code can be assumed to be correct.

▶ **Record Addition (Update Request Code 1)**   The program adds a new record to the Customer Sales File if the customer number does not already exist in the file.

▸ **Record Deletion (Update Request Code 2)** The program deletes a record from the Customer Sales File if the ÚCSTNO field contains a customer number that is currently contained in the Customer Master File. No further verification is required.

▸ **Record Change (Update Request Code 3)** When a change request is processed, the program updates the contents of the Sales Amount field by adding the contents of the UAMT field in the update request record to the contents of the MAMT field in the Sales Record. The output record written to MSTEROUT contains the original customer number and customer name as well as the newly calculated Sales Amount field.

≡ SEQUENTIAL FILE UPDATING LOGIC ≡

Before examining the RPG entries required to process two input files, you must understand the processing that takes place. The processing consists of four basic steps:

1. The program reads a Master File record.
2. The program reads an Update Request File record.
3. The customer numbers in the master record and the update request record are compared to determine if the master record is equal to, less than, or greater than the update request record.
4. The program processes the data based on the result of the comparison.

The data in the master file and the update request file (Figure 13-6) are now used in a step-by-step analysis of the processing.

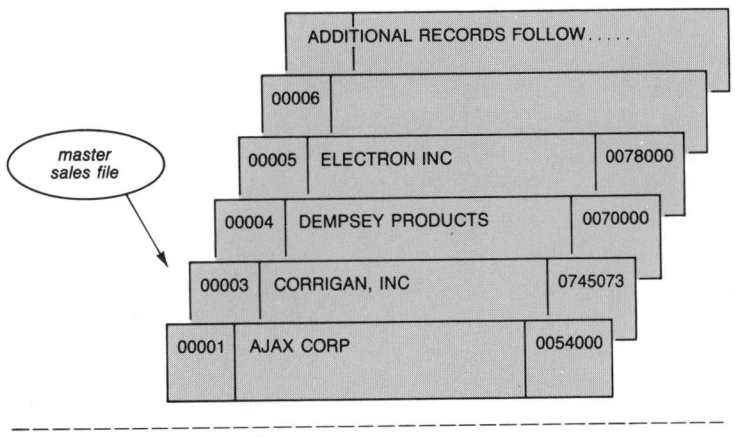

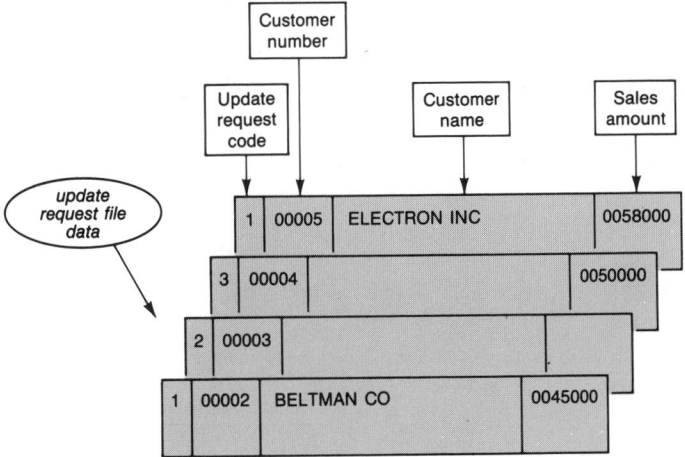

Figure 13-6 Sample update data files

▶ **1. Reading Master and Update Records**   Figure 13-7 shows that the program reads the first record in the update request file and the first record in the master file into main storage. The update request record contains the customer number 00002 and the master record contains the customer number 00001. Remember that these input files are in ascending sequence, that is, each subsequent record in the master file and in the update request file contains a customer number that is higher than the previous customer number. To change or delete a master record, there must be a corresponding update request record, that is, the customer numbers must be the same. This figure also shows that the customer number in the master file (00001) is less than the customer number in the update request file (00002). Therefore, since the update request file is in an ascending sequence, there will never be an update request record with the customer number 00001.

▶ **2. Writing Master Output Record to New Master File**   When the program reads a master record with no corresponding update request, it performs no processing with the master record other than to write the master record data out to the new master file (Figure 13-8).

▶ **3. Reading Another Master Input Record**   Another master input record must now be read to continue the processing. Figure 13-9 shows that the second record of the input master file has been read into the master input area. The customer number in this master record is 00003. This customer number is greater than the customer number in the update request record currently in main storage (00002). Again, because both the update and the master records are sorted in ascending sequence, there can never be a master record with a customer number equal to the customer number in the update request record that was read in Figure 13-7. An unmatched update request record will never be able to delete or change an existing master record. The only valid function of an update request record that does not have a matching customer number in a master record is to add the update request record to the master file as a new customer.

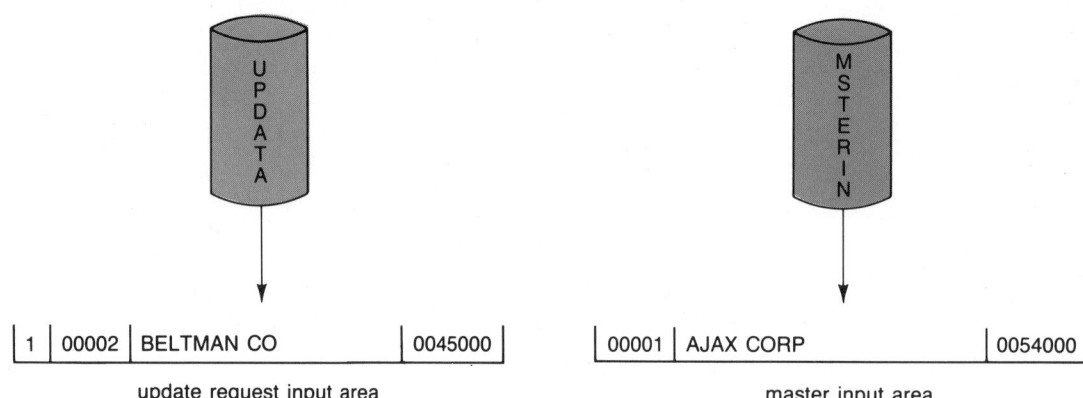

Figure 13-7   Master and update records are read

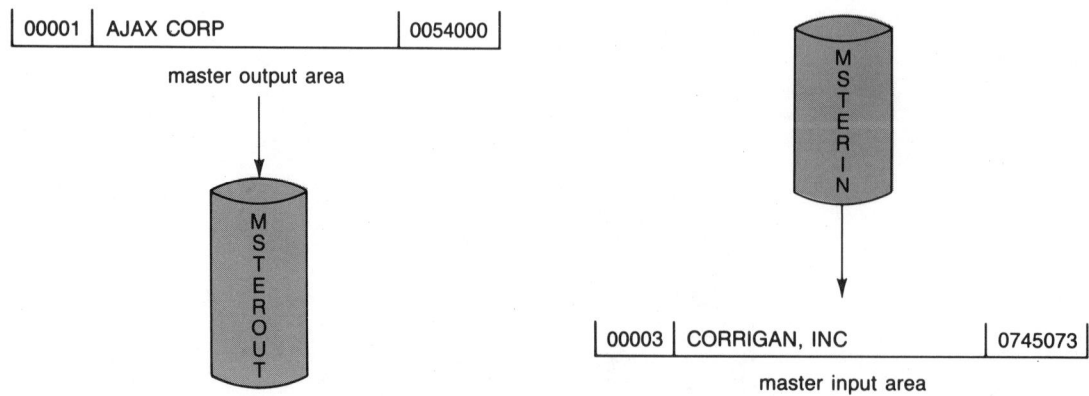

Figure 13-8   Master output record is written

Figure 13-9   Master record is read

Because the customer number in the current update request record (00002) is less than the customer number in the current master record (00003), the update request record can only be added to the master file. For the program to perform a record addition to the master file, the update request code in the update record must be 1. If the code is not 1, the update request record is in error because an add is the only valid operation that can be performed with an unmatched update request record. When an update request record with a low customer number is found, and the update request code is not 1, the program must write an error message on the audit report created by the program. In this example, Figure 13-7 shows that the update request code in the first update request record is equal to 1. Therefore, the program adds the update request record to the new master file.

▶ **4. Adding New Record to Master File** Figure 13-10 shows that the program moves the data in the update request input area to the master output area and then writes the data in the master output area to the new master output file. As is the case with all input data processing, RPG actually moves the data in the update input request area to the input fields for processing and then from the input fields to the output area to be written. For clarity, however, because the moves into and out of the input field areas are automatic and transparent to the programmer, this step is not shown in the illustrations of sequential file update.

▶ **5. Reading Another Update Request Record** After the next update request record is read and placed in the update input area (Figure 13-11), the customer number in the update request record is compared with the customer number in the master record, which is in the master input area, to determine whether it is higher than, lower than, or equal to the master customer number. In this case, customer number 00003, which is contained in the update request record read in Figure 13-11, is equal to the customer number in the master input area (Figure 13-9).

When the customer number in the update request record is equal to the customer number in the master record, one of two types of processing can take place: The update request record may specify that the master record is to be deleted from the new master file or it may specify that the sales amount in the update request record is to be added to the year-to-date sales amount in the old master record. The update code that causes the master record to be deleted is a 2, and the update code that causes the sales amount to be updated is a 3. The update code in Figure 13-11 is 2, indicating that the corresponding master record is to be deleted from the new master file.

Note that a transaction code other than 2 or 3, when the customer numbers are equal, is invalid and causes an error message to be printed on the audit report.

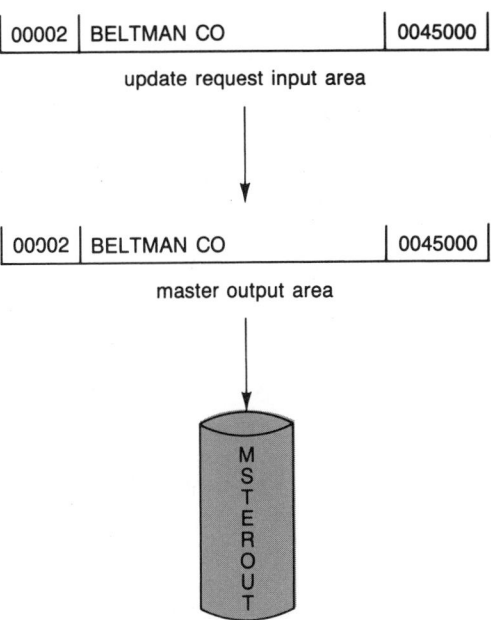

Figure 13-10   New record is added to master file

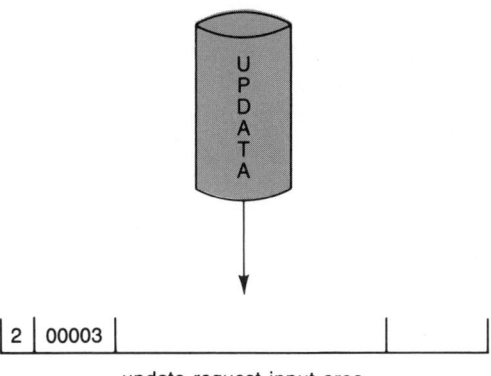

Figure 13-11   Update request record is read

To delete a master record from the new master file, simply do not write it on the new master file. Recall that sequential file updating, unlike keyed file updating, does not require the use of deletion codes within the master file. As the program creates a new master file, records are deleted by omission; a record is deleted by omitting the output operation that would write it to the new master file. This is accomplished by reading a new update request record and reading a master record from the old master file but not writing the old master record, currently in the master input area, to the new master file. Thus, when a master record is to be deleted, the next step is to read another update request record and another master record.

▶ **6. Reading Master and Update Records** As Figure 13-12 shows, the contents of the master input area have been replaced by the contents of master record 00004. Because master record 00003 was not written to the new master file before the data was replaced, the master record is effectively deleted.

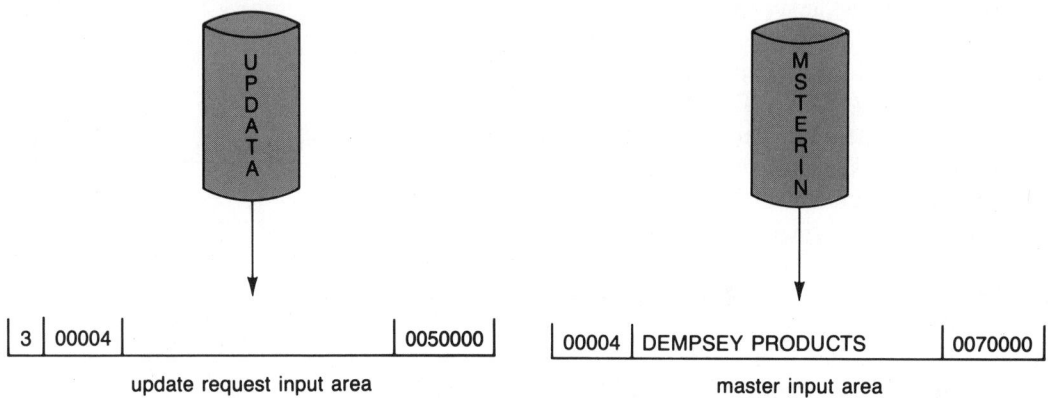

Figure 13-12 Master and update records are read

After the records are read, the program again performs the comparison between the customer numbers in the update request and master records. Figure 13-12 shows that they are equal, that is, the customer number in both the update request record and the master record is equal to 00004. The only valid operations are to delete the master record or to add the sales amount in the update request record to the year-to-date sales amount in the master record. In the example, the update request code is 3, which specifies that the program must add the sales amount in the update request record to the year-to-date sales amount in the master record.

▶ **7. Calculating New Sales Amount** Figure 13-13 shows that the value in the sales amount field in the update request input area is added to the value the year-to-date sales amount field in the master input area. Thus, the year-to-date sales amount in the master record is updated by the sales amount in the update request record.

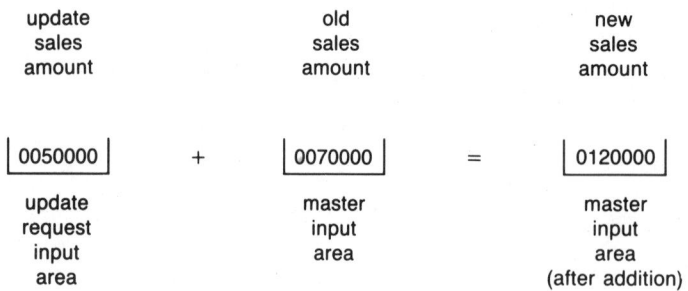

Figure 13-13 New amount is calculated

▸ **8. Writing Updated Master Record to New Output File** As shown in Figure 13-14, the updated master record with the new year-to-date sales amount has been written to the new master file. Because the new master file-record contains a new year-to-date sales amount, the program has completed the processing of the change request.

▸ **9. Reading Update Request Record** The program now reads a new update request record to be processed against a master record (Figure 13-15). After the program has written the updated master record to the new master file, there is no more processing to be performed on the master record currently in the master input area.

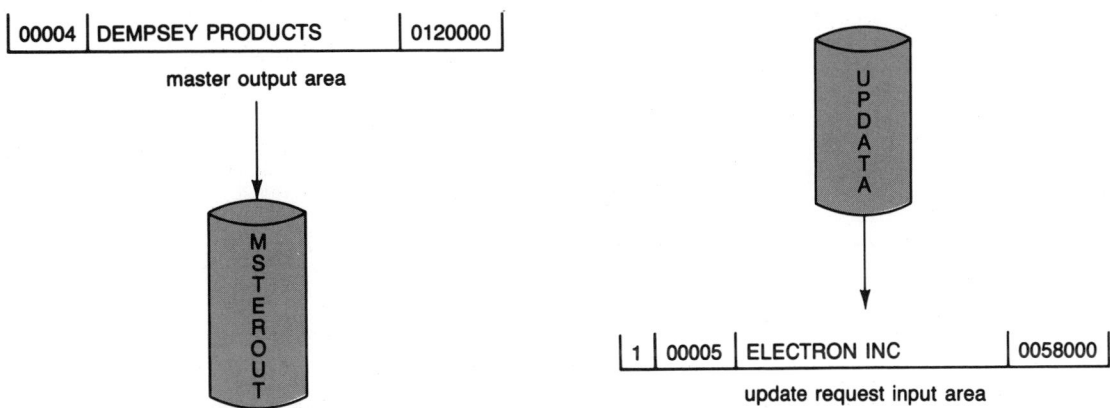

Figure 13-14 **Updated master record is written to new master file**

Figure 13-15 **Update request record is read**

▸ **10. Reading Master Record** Another master record must now be read from the old master file, (Figure 13-16). Note that the next master record contains customer number 00005. After both records have been read, the customer number in the master input record is compared with the customer number in the update request input area (see Figure 13-15). As you can see, the customer numbers are equal.

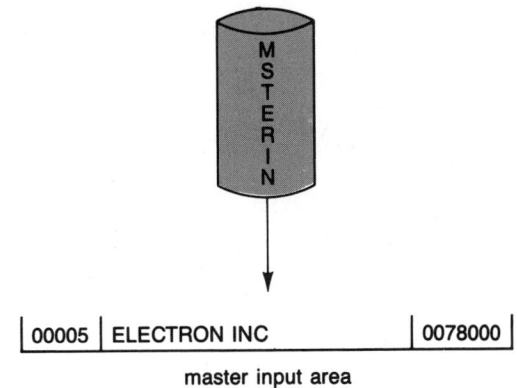

Figure 13-16 **Master record is read**

You already know that when the customer numbers in the master record and the update request record are equal, either of two valid types of processing may take place: the deletion of the master record or the updating of the year-to-date sales amount field. Therefore, the program must determine whether the update request code in the update request record specifies a deletion or an update. In Figure 13-15, the update request code in the record is a 1, which indicates record addition. Adding the update request record to the master file is not valid, however, because there is already a record in the master file that contains the same customer number. Thus, when the update request code indicates an addition and equal customer numbers are found, the update request record is in error.

▶ **11. Printing Error Line on Audit Report** As Figure 13-17 shows, when the customer numbers are equal and the update request code specifies record addition, the error message DUPLICATE CUSTOMER NUMBER is printed on the audit report together with the information contained in the update request record so that the record in error can be identified.

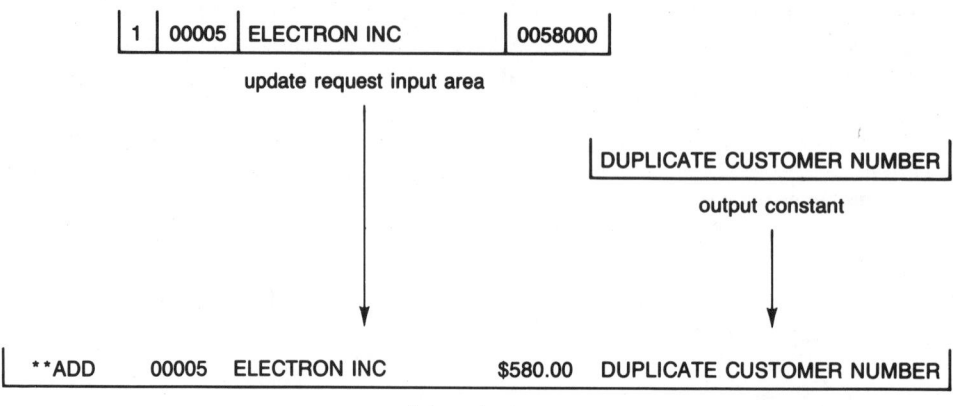

Figure 13-17   Line is printed on audit report

▶ **12. Reading Another Update Request Record** After the program has printed the output line on the audit report, it must read another update request record. As Figure 13-6 shows, the update request record with customer number 00005 is the last update request record. Thus, when the program attempts to read the next update request record, it detects an end-of-file condition. Whenever two input files are being processed, the program does not usually end when only one of the files has reached end-of-file. Thus, the program must process the remainder of the master records. This processing consists of writing the master record in main storage to the new master file and then reading the remainder of the records on the master input file and writing them to the new master output file. The program writes the master record with the customer number 00005, which is stored in main storage, to the new master file and then reads and writes the master record containing customer number 00006 (see Figure 13-6). After the program has read and written all records remaining in the input master file, and end-of-file has been detected for the master file as well as the update request file, the program ends.

PROGRAM SPECIFICATIONS FOR PROGRAM HJG13X

File Description Specifications

The four files that are used for the sequential update program are the update request file, the old master file, the new master file, and the printer file for the audit report. The File Description Specifications form for these files is shown in Figure 13-18.

▶ **Secondary File Definition** When a program must perform sequential file updating, an RPG feature called **matching records** is used. The matching records feature performs the type of comparison of control fields, such as the customer number, that was shown in the previous examples. When matching records are used, one of the input files must be defined as the primary file (P in position 16), and the second and all subsequent input files must be defined as secondary files (S in position 16). Note in Figure 13-18 that the master input file is defined as the primary file, and the update request file is defined as the secondary file. In most situations, master files are the primary files in an RPG program.

▶ **Input File Sequence Checking** Whenever two files such as the master file and the update request file are to be matched, they must both be in the same sequence based on the control field. In this example, both

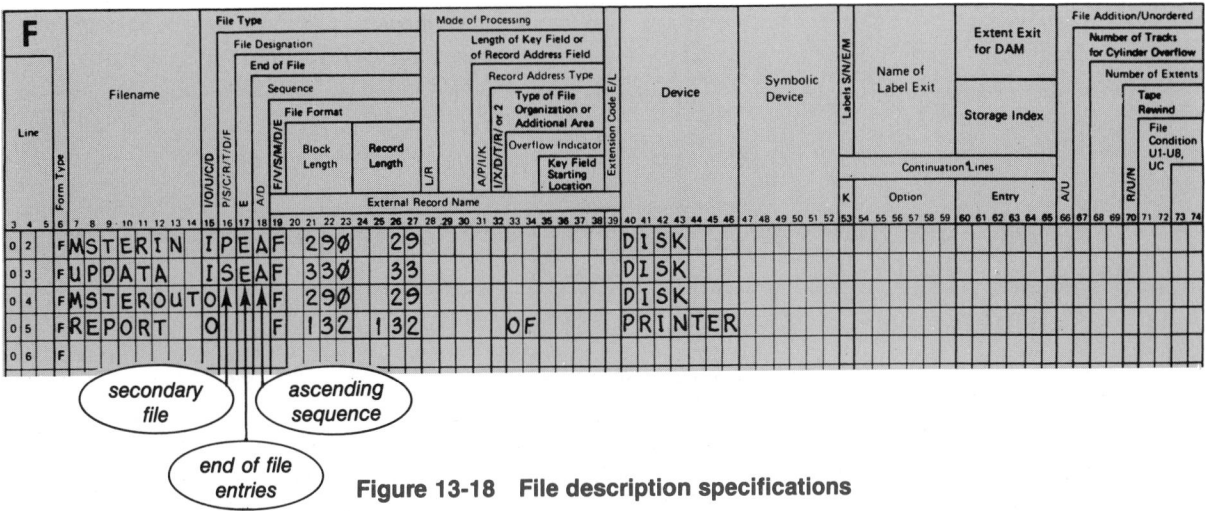

Figure 13-18 File description specifications

files are in ascending sequence by customer number. For a sequential file update to work correctly, the program must verify that the files are in the proper sequence. The process of verifying the sequence of a data file is called **sequence checking**.

Sequence checking is specified by placing the letter A in position 18 (Sequence A/D), signifying that the files are in an ascending sequence and that the program is to check the sequence as each record is read. The letter D in position 18 indicates that the files are in a descending sequence. When sequence checking is specified, the program halts if it reads a record that is not in the specified sequence. Most versions of RPG allow the operator either to terminate the program or to bypass the out-of-sequence record and read the next record from the file. Sequence checking can be performed on any input, update, or combined file that is specified as either a primary or secondary file; it is not limited to update programs that match two input files. The field or fields to be sequence checked within each record are specified in positions 61 and 62 of the Input Specifications form for the file. When sequence checking is specified for a sequential file update program, both files must be in the same sequence, either ascending or descending.

▸ **End-of-File Specifications** Note that the file description specifications for both MSTERIN and UPDATA contain the entry E in position 17. This specifies that the program does not end until all records have been processed from both the primary and secondary input data files. Recall that this must be done to cause the last records of the old master file (MSTERIN) to be written to the new master file (MSTEROUT).

Extension Specifications

Figure 13-19 shows the Extension Specifications form for the sample program. Note that these specifications describe the alternating tables TABMON and TABNAM, which are used to retrieve the name of the current month for use in the second heading line (Figure 13-20 on the next page). The month names are right-justified in the TABNAM array to eliminate extra spaces between the month name and the day when the date is printed.

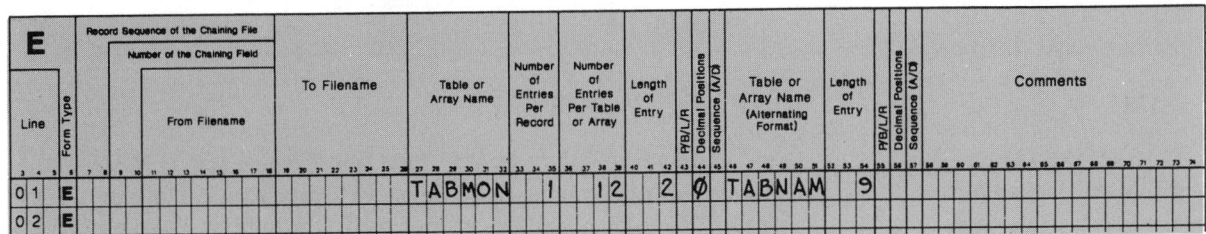

Figure 13-19 Extension specifications

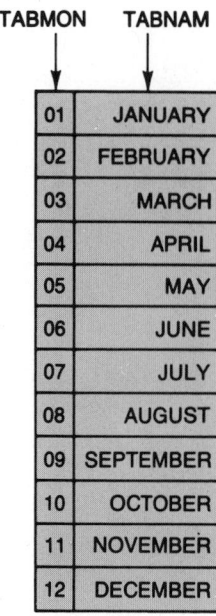

Figure 13-20 Month tables

Input Specifications

Figure 13-21 shows the two input data files MSTERIN and UPDATA, defined in the same manner as has been used in previous programs. Every time the program reads a record from the MSTERIN file, record-identifying indicator 01 is turned on. Every time the program reads a record from the UPDATA file, it turns on either indicator 02, 03, 04, or 99, depending on the update request code in position 1 of the input record.

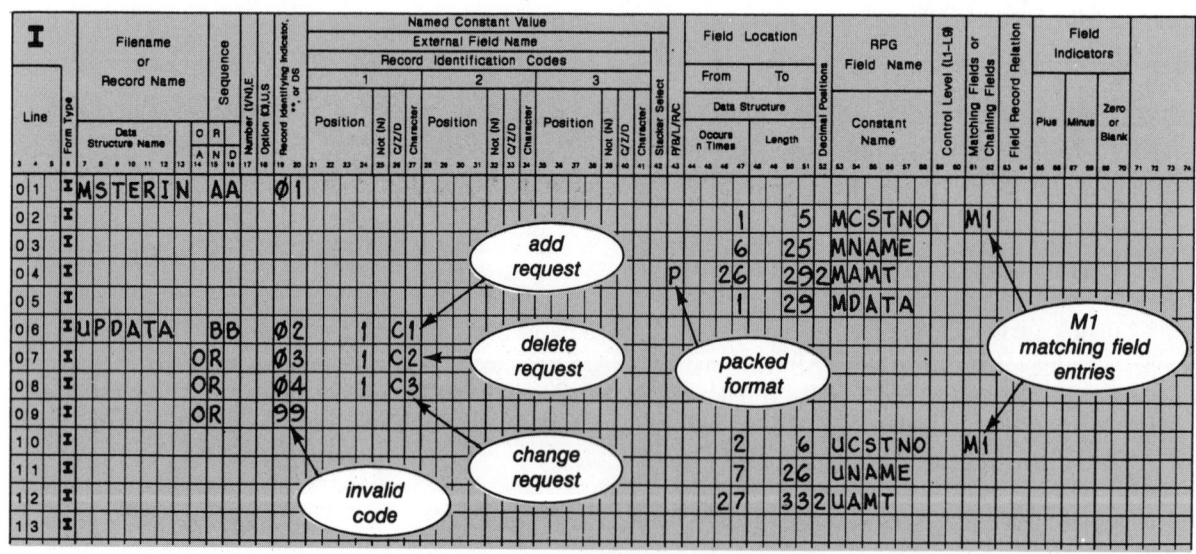

Figure 13-21 Input specifications

▶ **Packed Data Fields** The entry P in position 43 of the MAMT field specifies that data in MAMT is stored in the **packed format**. The packed format is used to minimize the amount of space required to store numeric data fields. Recall that each character of data stored in a computer or on disk requires a separate storage position. This method of data storage is called the **zoned format** because each stored character is represented by two codes, a zone code and a digit code. Figure 13-22 shows a numeric data field with a value of 0012345 stored in the zoned format. Note that each position of memory contains, in the left half, the code F. This code identifies the stored character as one of the digits 0–9. The right half of the memory position contains the numeric digit being stored.

RPG can eliminate up to half of the space needed to store a numeric field by using the packed format instead of the zoned format. This saving is accomplished by eliminating the zone portion of each character and storing two of the digits in each position of memory (Figure 13-23). Note that the data requires only four positions when stored in the packed format. All the zones have been removed, leaving only the digit portion of the characters, as well as the sign of the number in the right half of the rightmost position of the field.

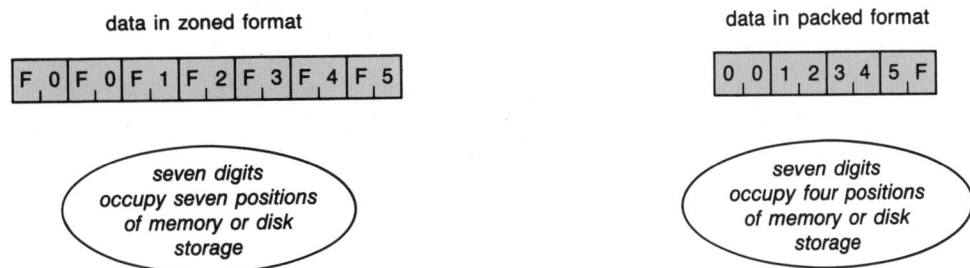

Figure 13-22   Example of zoned data format   Figure 13-23   Example of packed data format

The number of positions needed to store a field in the packed format can be determined by performing one of two simple calculations based on the length of the field in the zoned format. If the number of digits in the zoned format field is an even number (2, 4, 6, 8, etc.), divide the number of digits by two and add one to the result; this gives the minimum length of the field in the packed format. If the number of digits in the zoned format field is an odd number (1, 3, 5, 7, etc.), divide the number of digits by two and round the answer up to the next whole number. The file layout for MSTERIN (Figure 13-3) specified that MAMT is to be stored in the packed format.

For RPG to work properly with the data stored in MAMT, the program must specify that the field is packed. This is done by the entry P in position 43 of the field description (see Figure 13-21). If this entry is not made for a field stored in the packed format, the program cannot properly process the data. Likewise, if this entry is made for a field that is not stored in the packed format, the program cannot process the data properly.

▸ **Matching Field Entries**   The entry M1 in positions 61–62 (Matching Fields or Chaining Fields) of the MCSTNO (line 02) and UCSTNO (line 10) field definitions specifies that these fields are to be used in the matching operation when the two records are read. These entries specify that the data contained in the Customer Number field in positions 1–5 of each MSTERIN record is to be compared against the contents of the Customer Number field in each UPDATA record to determine which record is to be processed next. The M1 entry specifies that the field is the first or only field to be used in the comparison.

It is possible to use as many as nine different fields to form the value to be compared. The entries for these fields are numbered M1–M9. When more than one field is used for matching records, the highest numbered field is considered the major field; for instance, if three fields are numbered M1, M2, and M3, then the M3 field is the high-order field, the M2 field is in the center, and the M1 field is in the low-order position. Figure 13-24 on the next page shows a set of input specifications using three matching fields. Note that RPG combines the three separate input fields into a single field in order to make the comparison. Although the three fields are combined for comparison, they are still treated as three separate fields throughout the remainder of the program. As the illustration shows, the matching fields do not have to occupy the same positions in both input records, nor do the fields have to be in the same sequence. However, fields that have the same matching field identification (M1, M2, M3, etc.) must have the same length and data class.

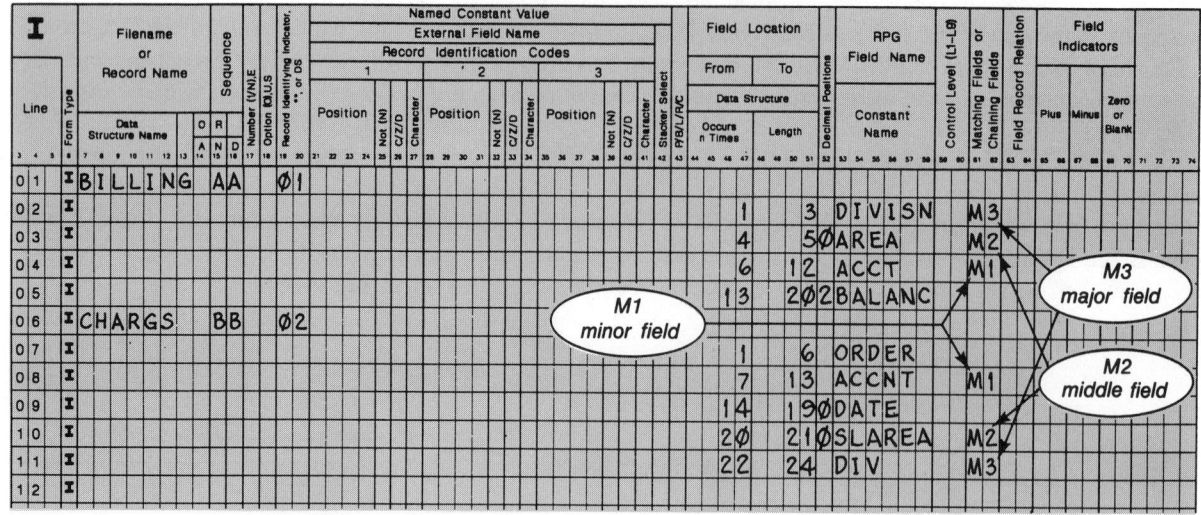

BILLING RECORD INPUT AREAS

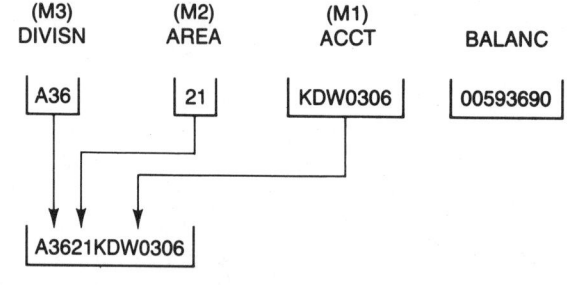

BILLING RECORD MATCHING AREA

—————————————————————————————————

CHARGS RECORD INPUT AREAS

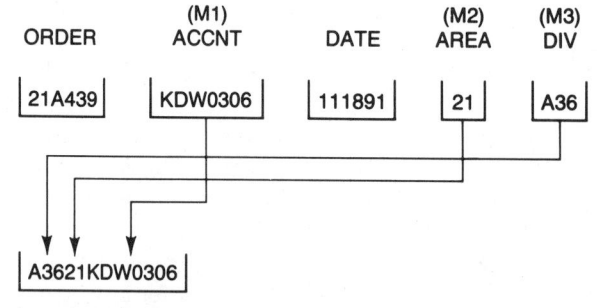

CHARGS RECORD MATCHING AREA

—————————————————————————————————

MATCHING RECORD COMPARISON

| A3621KDW0306 | = | A3621KDW0306 |

BILLING RECORD MATCH FIELDS EQUAL CHARGS
RECORD MATCH FIELDS——
INDICATOR MR IS TURNED ON

Figure 13-24   Multiple matching field specifications

▸ **MR Indicator** Whenever the program detects matching fields, that is, whenever the data in the fields identified on the Input Specifications form as matching fields by the entries M1, M2, and so on are equal, the **MR indicator** is turned on. When the MR indicator is on, it means that a record in the primary file has a value in its matching field equal to the value in the matching field of a record in the secondary file. It is through the use of the MR indicator that the program can detect an equal condition, as illustrated in the sequential file update examples.

To determine if a matching condition has occurred, that is, if the matching field in the primary file is equal to the matching field in the secondary file, the program reads a record from each file and compares the matching fields. If they are equal, the MR indicator is turned on. The record from the primary file is then moved to the input fields for processing, and the record-identifying indicator for the primary record is turned on. After the record from the primary file has been processed, the matching record from the secondary file is moved to the input fields, and its record-identifying indicator is turned on. *When there are matching records, the record from the primary file is always processed before the record from the secondary file.*

When the MR indicator is used in a sequential update, the combination of the MR indicator and the record-identifying indicator dictates the status of the update operation and which record is to be processed next. The indicators used in the sample program and their meanings are given in the following table.

Indicators	Meaning
01,MR	A master record with a matching update request record
02,MR	An add record with a matching master record
03,MR	A delete record with a matching master record
04,MR	A change record with a matching master record
01,NMR	A master record with no matching update request record
02,NMR	An add update request record with no matching master record
03,NMR	A delete update request record with no matching master record
04,NMR	A change update request record with no matching master record
99	Invalid update request code

The preceding combinations of matching record indicator and record-identifying indicator are used to determine the processing of each record. Based on the meanings of these indicators and the processing illustrated in the example of processing the files, the following actions should be taken when these combinations are found.

Indicators	Action Taken
01,MR	No action taken; no processing is to occur until an update request record is moved to the input fields.
02,MR	This is an error; addition of a record already on the master file was attempted. An entry is made on the audit report, and the old master record is written on the new master file.
03,MR	Another master record and update request record is read. No disk output processing takes place because the old master record is not to be written on the new master file. The program does, however, print a line on the audit report to show the record deletion.
04,MR	The sales amount in the update request record is added to the year-to-date sales amount in the master record, the master record is written on the new master file, and a line is printed on the audit report.
01,NMR	The old master record is written on the new master file because there is no update request record to update the master record.
02,NMR	A valid addition; the data in the update request record is moved to the master output area, the data is written as a new master record in the new master file, and a line is printed on the audit report.
03,NMR	This is an error; an attempt was made to delete a master record that is not on the master file. A line is printed on the audit report.
04,NMR	This is an error; an attempt was made to change a master record that is not on the master file. A line is printed on the exception report.
99	This is an error; a line is printed on the audit report, and a new update request record is read.

These are the only combinations that can occur when updating the master file. These combinations of indicators control the output to the new master file and to the printed audit report. Note that if indicator 99 is on, the status of indicator MR is not tested because indicator 99 represents an invalid update request and is not processed against the master file. The only processing based on indicator 99 is the printing of an error message on the audit report.

Calculation Specifications

Figure 13-25 shows the Calculation Specifications form for the sample program. Line 06 contains the only operation that is part of the sequential file update procedure. If indicators 04 and MR are on, line 06 causes the program to add the update sales amount (UAMT) to the master file sales amount (MAMT), giving the new sales amount (TAMT), which is written to the new master file record. Note that the ADD operation does not use any special options or code when performing arithmetic with MAMT, which is stored in the packed format. When packed data is used in calculation or output operations, RPG performs any steps needed to convert the data to the zoned format. Note also that RPG can perform arithmetic operations between a packed data field (MAMT) and a zoned data field (UAMT).

Line	Form Type	Control Level (L0-L9, LR, SR, AN/OR)	Indicators And Not	Indicators And Not	Indicators And Not	Factor 1	Operation	Factor 2	Result Field Name	Length	Decimal Positions	Half Adjust (H)	Resulting Indicators Plus High	Minus Low	Zero Equal	Comments
01	C		N21				SETON						22			
02	C		21	22			SETOF						22			
03	C		22			UMONTH	LOKUP	TABMON	TABNAM						23	
04	C		22				SETON						21			
05	C*															
06	C		04	MR		MAMT	ADD	UAMT	TAMT	7	2					
07	C															

Figure 13-25   Calculation specifications

▸ **First Record Routine (First Cycle)**   Lines 01–04 are a **first record**, or **one time only**, routine that is performed once at the beginning of the program. Because the program specifications require the printing of the current date in the heading with the month name spelled out, rather than in MM/DD/YY format, special coding is needed at the beginning of the calculations to retrieve the month name. This routine uses a table lookup operation to retrieve the name of the month from the compile time table that contains a list of month names, and it is controlled by indicators 21 and 22.

Line 01 turns indicator 22 on if indicator 21 is off. Because all general-purpose indicators are off at the beginning of program execution, this line is executed the first time that the detail calculation portion of the logic cycle is executed. Line 02 turns indicator 22 off if indicators 21 and 22 are on. Because indicator 21 is not on at the beginning of the program, line 02 does not execute during the first detail calculation cycle.

Line 03 performs the table lookup to retrieve the month name from the table. Note that this operation is performed only if indicator 22 is on, as it is during the first cycle. Because the search argument in the lookup operation is the UMONTH field, and UMONTH always contains a valid month number (01–12), there is no logical need for the use of resulting indicator 23 in positions 58 and 59. However, because the syntax of the LOKUP operation requires that at least one resulting indicator be entered in positions 54–59, indicator 23 has been placed in the EQUAL area. This results in an unreferenced indicator warning in most versions of RPG. Under these circumstances, however, this warning can be ignored.

Line 04 turns indicator 21 on if indicator 22 is on. Because 22 is on at this point in the first detail cycle, indicator 21 is turned on.

▸ **First-Record Routine (Second Cycle)** The second time that the calculations are executed, line 01 is not executed, because indicator 21 is on. Because indicators 21 and 22 are both on, line 02 executes, turning indicator 22 off. Because indicator 22 is off, neither line 03 nor line 04 executes.

▸ **First-Record Routine (Remainder of Program)** The remainder of the program cannot execute lines 01–04. Line 01 cannot execute because indicator 21 is on, and lines 02, 03, and 04 cannot execute because indicator 22 is not on. The result is that the lookup operation on line 03 executes only once, during the first detail cycle. Note that as a result of lines 01–04, indicator 22 is on only during the first detail output cycle. Indicator 22 is not on during all the detail output cycles after the first because its only use is to control the printing of headings on the first page of the audit report.

▤ Output Specifications

▸ **First-Page Heading Control at Detail Time** Figure 13-26 shows the output specifications for the heading lines to be printed on the audit report. Note that the heading lines are not controlled by indicators 1P or OF but by indicator 22 or OF. Recall that indicator 1P turns on and then off before the reading of the first input record. If, the first-page headings, controlled by indicator 1P, were printed before the LOKUP operation had retrieved the month name, the name of the month could not appear on the first page of the report. It would, however, appear on all pages after the first. To print the month name on the first page, the headings are controlled by indicator 22 instead of indicator 1P. Remember that indicator 22 is on only during the first detail output cycle. This results in the first-page headings being printed during the same execution of the logic cycle that prints the first detail output line. Because indicator 22 is not on again after the first detail output cycle, it does not cause headings to be printed again. The headings for all successive pages are controlled by indicator OF, as they have been in all previous programs.

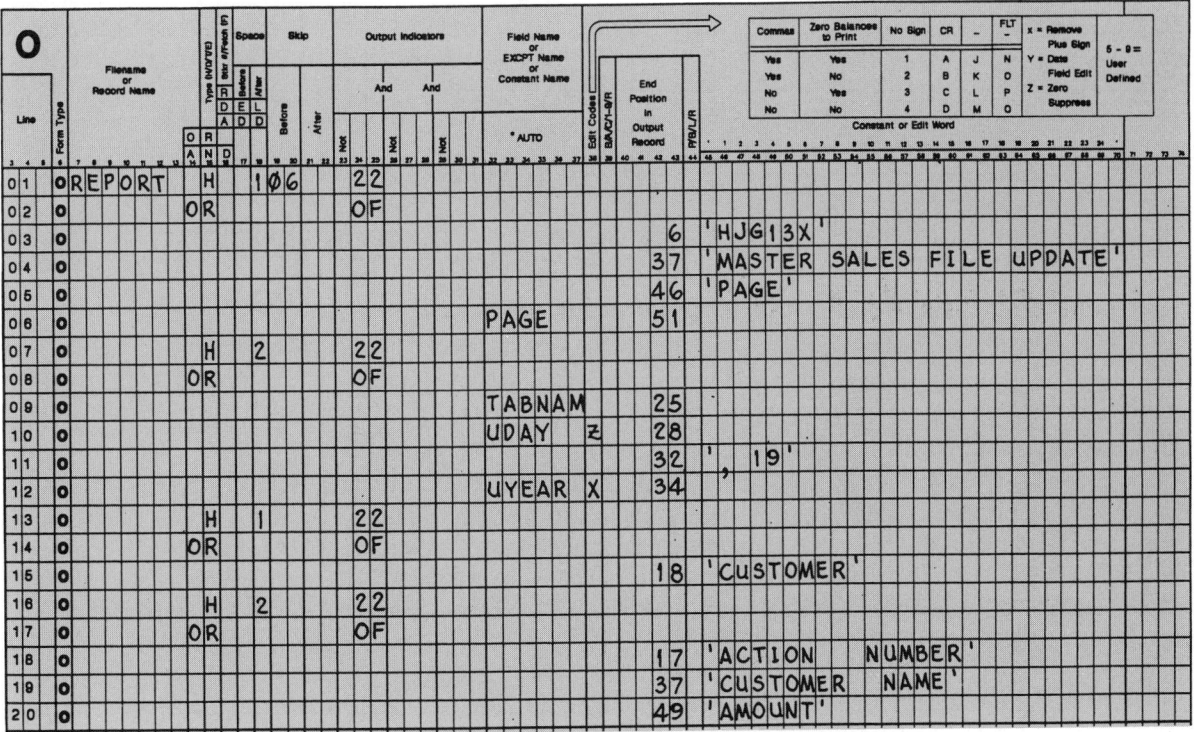

Figure 13-26   Output specifications: headings

Note the use of TABNAM on line 09 to print the month name. This is followed, on line 10, by the field UDAY, which contains the day of the month. The constant ', 19' on line 11 places the comma after the day and also prints the first two digits of the year. As was noted earlier, this program requires maintenance on or about January first of the year 2000. Line 12 uses the UYEAR field to provide the last two digits of the year field in the second heading line.

▶ **Audit Lines for Valid Update Requests**   Figure 13-27 shows the lines that are printed for each of the three valid update requests: record addition, record deletion, and record change. Lines 01–05, controlled by indicators 02 (record addition) and NMR (no matching record in the master file) print the audit line for the addition of a new record to the master file. Note that the three data fields are all taken from the update request record.

Figure 13-27   Output specifications: valid update request lines

Lines 06–10, controlled by indicators 03 (record deletion) and MR (matching record in the master file) print the audit line for a record deletion. Because the record being deleted exists in the old master file, the three field names are taken from the input specification description of the old master file.

Lines 11–19, controlled by indicators 04 (record change) and MR (matching record in the master file) print the two audit lines for record change. The first audit line (specification lines 11–16) contain the information currently in the master file. The second audit line (specification lines 17–19) prints TAMT, the new value in the sales amount field. Note that the two record change lines contain the constants OLD and NEW to identify the values being printed. Also note that the second audit line does not repeat the contents of the customer number and customer name fields.

▶ **Audit Lines for Update Request Errors**   Figure 13-28 shows the lines that are printed when an update request error occurs. Lines 01–07, controlled by indicators 02 (record addition) and MR (matching record in master file), print the audit line for an attempt to add a record containing a customer number that already exists in the master file.

Figure 13-28 Output specifications: invalid update request lines

Line	Form Type	Filename or Record Name	Type	AND/OR	D E L A D D	Space Before/After	Skip Before/After	Output Indicators (And/Not)	Field Name or EXCPT Name or Constant Name *AUTO	Edit Codes	End Position in Output Record	P/B/L/R	Constant or Edit Word
01	O		D			2		02 MR					
02	O										5		'**ADD'
03	O								UCSTNO		17		
04	O								UNAME		40		
05	O								UAMT	1	51		'$'
06	O										71		'DUPLICATE CUSTOMER'
07	O										78		'NUMBER'
08	O		D			2		03NMR					
09	O			OR				04NMR					
10	O							03NMR			8		'**DELETE'
11	O							04NMR			8		'**CHANGE'
12	O								UCSTNO		17		
13	O							04NMR	UAMT	1	51		'$'
14	O										69		'NO MASTER RECORD'
15	O		D			2		99					
16	O										10		'**********'
17	O								UCSTNO		17		
18	O								UNAME		40		
19	O								UAMT	1	51		'$'
20	O										72		'INVALID ACTION CODE'

Lines 08–14, controlled by indicators 03 (record deletion) and NMR (no matching record in master file), or by indicators 04 (record change) and NMR, print the audit line for either an invalid deletion request or an invalid change request. In both cases, indicator NMR specifies that the requested record does not exist in the master file and therefore cannot be deleted or changed. Note the use of the 03NMR and 04NMR indicator specifications to control the printing of individual fields on lines 10, 11, and 13.

Lines 15–20, controlled by indicator 99 (invalid update request code), prints an audit line when the type of update request code cannot be determined based on the code in position 1.

▸ **Output Specifications for New Master File** Figure 13-29 shows the output specifications for the new master file. Because this is a disk output file, there are no entries in the Space and Skip areas, positions 17–22.

Figure 13-29 Output specifications: new master file

Line	Form Type	Filename or Record Name	Type	AND/OR	D E L A D D	Space Before/After	Skip Before/After	Output Indicators (And/Not)	Field Name or EXCPT Name or Constant Name *AUTO	Edit Codes	End Position in Output Record	P/B/L/R	Constant or Edit Word
01	O	MSTEROUT	D					02NMR					
02	O								UCSTNO		5		
03	O								UNAME		25		
04	O								UAMT		29	P	
05	O		D					04 MR					
06	O								MDATA		29		
07	O								TAMT		29	P	
08	O		D					01 NMR					
09	O			OR				02 MR					
10	O			OR				01 MR 99					
11	O								MDATA		29		

Lines 01–04, controlled by indicators 02 (record addition) and NMR (no matching record in master file), cause a record to be added to the new master file. All the field names are from the update request record because all the information for the new record comes from there. No data from the old master file is used. Note the P entry in position 44 of the UAMT field specification, which specifies that UAMT is to be written in the packed format. Although UAMT was read in the zoned format on the Input Specifications form, RPG performs the necessary conversion to the packed format before the data is written out to disk. Although UAMT was defined as a seven-position field, when it is written out in the packed format the data occupies only four positions, 26–29. These are the same four positions used by the MAMT field in the master file.

Lines 05–07, controlled by indicators 04 (record change) and MR (matching record in master file), control the writing of a changed record to the new master file. As you can see, line 06 writes the entire old record to the new master file, and then line 07 overwrites the new sales amount field (TAMT), ending in position 29. As in the addition of a new record, the TAMT field is written out in the packed format as specified by the P entry in position 44.

Lines 08–10 copy data from the old master file directly to the new master file under any of three conditions. The old data is directly copied if indicator 01 (master file record) is on and indicator MR (matching update request record) is off. In addition, an old master file record is written to the new master file if indicator 02 (record addition) and indicator MR (matching master file record) are both on. This condition represents an attempt to add a record containing a customer number that already exists in the master file. When this happens, the update request is ignored, and the old master file record is copied to the new master file.

The third combination of indicators that causes the old master record to be copied to the new master file is 01, MR, and 99. This combination of indicators represents an invalid update request code (indicator 99) that matches (indicator MR) a record on the old master file. When this condition occurs, the program copies the old master record to the new master file.

Figure 13-30 shows the compilation listing for the sample program and the contents of both the old and the new master files.

Figure 13-30   Program HJG13X

```
HJG13X                       SALES FILE UPDATE                    Version 3.5  Page  1

             ....+....1....+....2....+....3....+....4....+....5....+....6....+....7....

      3 0002 H                                                                  HJG13X


      4 0003 F*  OLD MASTER FILE
      5 0004 F*------------------
      6 0005 FMSTERIN IPEAF 290  29          DISK

      9 0007 F*  UPDATE REQUEST FILE
     10 0008 F*--------------------
     11 0009 FUPDATA   ISEAF 330  33          DISK

     14 0011 F*  NEW MASTER FILE
     15 0012 F*------------------
     16 0013 FMSTEROUTO  F 290  29            DISK

     19 0015 F*  AUDIT REPORT
     20 0016 F*--------------
     21 0017 FREPORT   O   F 132 132    OF    PRINTER


     22 0018 E*  MONTH NUMBER (TABMON) AND MONTH NAME (TABNAM) TABLES
     23 0019 E*---------------------------------------------------------
     24 0020 E                        TABMON  1 12  2 0 TABNAM  9


     25 0021 I*  OLD MASTER FILE
     26 0022 I*------------------
     27 0023 IMSTERIN AA  01
     28 0024 I                                   1    5 MCSTNO M1
     29 0025 I                                   6   25 MNAME
     30 0026 I                                 P 26  292MAMT
     31 0027 I                                   1   29 MDATA
```

Figure 13-30 (1)

```
HJG13X                        SALES FILE UPDATE              Version 3.5  Page  2

           ....+....1....+....2....+....3....+....4....+....5....+....6....+....7....

34 0029 I*  UPDATE REQUEST FILE
35 0030 I*----------------------
36 0031 IUPDATA    BB  02    1 C1
37 0032 I         OR  03    1 C2
38 0033 I         OR  04    1 C3
39 0034 I         OR  99
40 0035 I                                         2   6 UCSTNO M1
41 0036 I                                         7  26 UNAME
42 0037 I                                        27 332UAMT


43 0038 C*  FIRST RECORD ROUTINE TO CONTROL FIRST PAGE HEADINGS
44 0039 C*-----------------------------------------------------
45 0040 C   N21               SETON                        22
46 0041 C   21 22             SETOF                        22
47 0042 C*  LOOKUP OF MONTH NAME
48 0043 C*----------------------
49 0044 C   22      UMONTH    LOKUPTABMON    TABNAM         23
50 0045 C   22                SETON                        21

53 0047 C*  CALCULATE NEW TOTAL SALES AMOUNT
54 0048 C*----------------------------------
55 0049 C   04 MR   MAMT      ADD UAMT       TAMT    72


56 0050 O*  HEADING LINES
57 0051 O*---------------
58 0052 OREPORT  H 106      22
59 0053 O         OR        OF
60 0054 O                                    6 'HJG13X'
61 0055 O                                   37 'MASTER SALES FILE UPDATE'
62 0056 O                                   46 'PAGE'
63 0057 O                           PAGE    51
64 0058 O         H   2      22
65 0059 O         OR        OF
66 0060 O                           TABNAM  25
67 0061 O                           UDAY  Z 28
68 0062 O                                   32 ', 19'
69 0063 O                           UYEAR X 34
70 0064 O         H   1      22
71 0065 O         OR        OF
72 0066 O                                   18 'CUSTOMER'
73 0067 O         H   2      22
74 0068 O         OR        OF
75 0069 O                                   17 'ACTION    NUMBER'
76 0070 O                                   37 'CUSTOMER   NAME'
77 0071 O                                   49 'AMOUNT'

80 0073 O*  RECORD ADDITION LINE
81 0074 O*-----------------------
82 0075 O         D   2      02NMR
83 0076 O                                    5 'ADD'
84 0077 O                           UCSTNO  17
85 0078 O                           UNAME   40
86 0079 O                           UAMT  1 51 '$'

89 0081 O*  RECORD DELETION LINE
90 0082 O*-----------------------
91 0083 O         D   2      03 MR
92 0084 O                                    8 'DELETE'
93 0085 O                           MCSTNO  17
94 0086 O                           MNAME   40
95 0087 O                           MAMT  1 40 '$'

98 0089 O*  RECORD CHANGE LINES
99 0090 O*----------------------
100 0091 O        D   1      04 MR
101 0092 O                                    8 'CHANGE'
102 0093 O                           MCSTNO  17
103 0094 O                           MNAME   40
104 0095 O                           MAMT  1 51 '$'
105 0096 O                                   56 'OLD'
106 0097 O        D   2      04 MR
107 0098 O                           TAMT  1 51 '$'
108 0099 O                                   56 'NEW'

111 0101 O*  ADDITION ERROR LINE
112 0102 O*----------------------
113 0103 O        D   2      02 MR
```

Figure 13-30 (2)

continued

```
HJG13X                         SALES FILE UPDATE                 Version 3.5  Page  3

               ....+....1....+....2....+....3....+....4....+....5....+....6....+....7....

 114 0104 O                                        5 '**ADD'
 115 0105 O                              UCSTNO    17
 116 0106 O                              UNAME     40
 117 0107 O                              UAMT  1   51 '$'
 118 0108 O                                        71 'DUPLICATE CUSTOMER'
 119 0109 O                                        78 'NUMBER'

 122 0111 O*   DELETION AND CHANGE ERROR LINES
 123 0112 O*-----------------------------------
 124 0113 O            D  2      03NMR
 125 0114 O            OR         04NMR
 126 0115 O                       03NMR           8 '**DELETE'
 127 0116 O                       04NMR           8 '**CHANGE'
 128 0117 O                              UCSTNO   17
 129 0118 O                       04NMR   UAMT  1 51 '$'
 130 0119 O                                       69 'NO MASTER RECORD'

 133 0121 O*   INVALID UPDATE REQUEST LINE
 134 0122 O*------------------------------
 135 0123 O            D  2      99
 136 0124 O                                       10 '**********'
 137 0125 O                              UCSTNO   17
 138 0126 O                              UNAME    40
 139 0127 O                              UAMT  1  51 '$'
 140 0128 O                                       72 'INVALID ACTION CODE'

 143 0130 O*   DISK RECORD ADDITION
 144 0131 O*-----------------------
 145 0132 OMSTEROUTD         02NMR
 146 0133 O                              UCSTNO    5
 147 0134 O                              UNAME    25
 148 0135 O                              UAMT     29P

 151 0137 O*   DISK RECORD CHANGE
 152 0138 O*---------------------
 153 0139 O            D         04 MR
 154 0140 O                              MDATA    29
 155 0141 O                              TAMT     29P

 158 0143 O*   COPY OLD DISK RECORDS TO NEW FILE
 159 0144 O*-----------------------------------
 160 0145 O            D         01NMR
 161 0146 O            OR        02NMR
 162 0147 O            OR        01 MR 99
 163 0148 O                              MDATA    29


 166 0150 O*   MONTH TABLES
 167 0151 O*---------------
 168 **
 169 01  JANUARY
 170 02  FEBRUARY
 171 03    MARCH
 172 04    APRIL
 173 05      MAY
 174 06     JUNE
 175 07     JULY
 176 08   AUGUST
 177 09SEPTEMBER
 178 10  OCTOBER
 179 11 NOVEMBER
 180 12 DECEMBER
 181 /*
 182 /*



        THE FOLLOWING INDICATORS WERE SPECIFIED BUT WERE NEVER
        USED TO CONDITION OPERATIONS

        23



        THE FOLLOWING INDICATORS APPEARED IN THIS PROGRAM

           01  02  03  04  21  22  23  99  OF  MR
No Warning Errors
No Fatal Errors
```

Figure 13-30 (3)

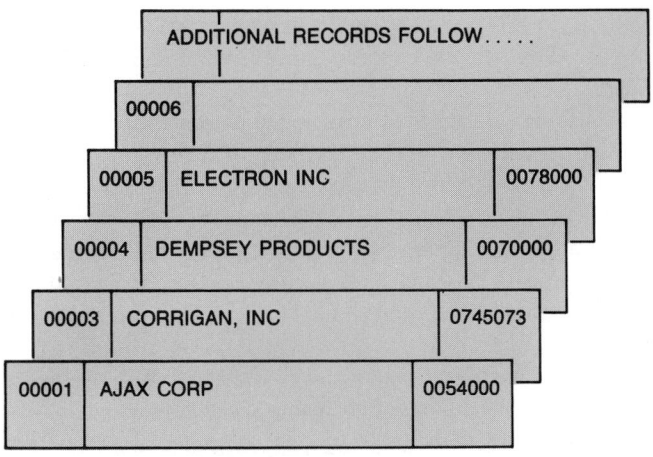

old master sales file

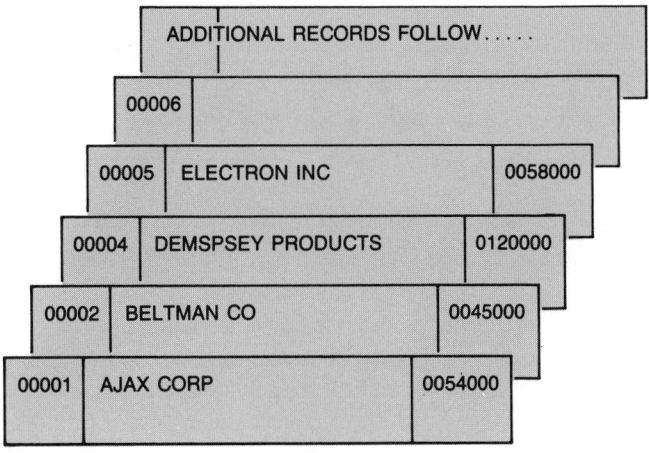

new master sales file

Figure 13-30 (4)

IN CONCLUSION

This is the last chapter to present components of the RPG language based on a sample program. Chapter 14 presents several components of the language as separate topics. These RPG components are found only in RPG III and RPG/400 and therefore may not be available on the machine you are using.

CHAPTER SUMMARY

1. **Sequential file updating**, unlike the random updating of keyed access path data files, creates a complete new version of the updated file.
2. A **sequential data file** is an arrival sequence file that is processed in a specific order that is based on the contents of a control field. A sequential data file is not a type of file organization but is a technique of file processing.
3. The logic of sequential file updating is based on comparison of the control field values in the file being updated and in the update request file.

4. Sequential file updating deletes records by not copying the master record to the new master file.
5. When sequential file updating is performed, the program must copy all master records that are not updated to the new master file.
6. **Matching record** techniques cause the control field value in the master file to be compared against the control field value in each update request record.
7. When the control field value in the master record matches the control field value in the update request record, the program turns on **indicator MR**.
8. Both data files used in a sequential file update must be in the same sequence, based on the same control fields. **Sequence checking** is the process by which RPG verifies that the file records are in the correct sequence. Sequence checking is specified by the entry of either A or D in position 18 of the file description specification for each file.
9. Both files used in a sequential file update must have an end-of-file entry (E in position 17) of their file description specifications to fully process both data files before the program ends.
10. The **packed format** can be used to minimize the amount of space needed in a disk file for numeric data files.
11. RPG automatically performs any needed conversions from the packed format to the zoned format or the zoned format to the packed format before numeric data is processed.
12. If information in a report heading must be based on the result of data input or calculation operations, the first heading cannot be controlled by indicator 1P.
13. A **first-record routine** is executed only once, during the first detail cycle, and is not executed again during the program.

REVIEW QUESTIONS

1. Why is it necessary for a sequential file update program to create a new master file as output?
2. What is a sequential data file? How does it differ from an ordinary arrival sequence access path data file?
3. What valid operations can be performed when the control field in an update request record is equal to the control field in a master record? When the control field in an update request record is not equal to the control field in a master record?
4. How is sequence checking specified in an RPG program? If the program detects that a record is out of sequence, what two options can the operator use?
5. Why must the end-of-file entry be used for both files in a program performing sequential file update?
6. How does the use of the packed format minimize the amount of space needed to store a numeric data file? How is the length of the packed format field determined from the length of the zoned format field?
7. What is the relationship between the Matching Field entries made on the Input Specifications form and the MR indicator?
8. Why cannot indicator 1P be used to control the first-page headings when the headings must contain the result of an input or calculation operation?

STUDENT EXERCISES: RPG PROGRAM CODE

1. Write the input specifications, using the form in Figure 13-31, to define the following master file data record:

Positions	Field Description
1–3	Division
4–10	Part number
11–30	Description
31–36	Date manufactured
37–41	Quantity

The records in this master file are to be matched with fields in update request records based on the following fields: high order, Division; intermediate, Part Number; low order, Date Manufactured. The name of this file is INVMAS.

Line	Form Type	Filename or Record Name / Data Structure Name	O R / A N D	Sequence	Number (1/N)/E	Option (O),U,S	Record Identifying Indicator, **, or DS	Named Constant Value / External Field Name / Record Identification Codes — Position 1	Not (N)	C/Z/D	Character	Position 2	Not (N)	C/Z/D	Character	Position 3	Not (N)	C/Z/D	Character	Stacker Select	P/B/L/R/C	Field Location — From / Occurs n Times	To / Length	Decimal Positions	RPG Field Name / Constant Name	Control Level (L1–L9)	Matching Fields or Chaining Fields	Field Record Relation	Plus	Minus	Zero or Blank
0 1	I																														
0 2	I																														
0 3	I																														
0 4	I																														
0 5	I																														
0 6	I																														
0 7	I																														
0 8	I																														
0 9	I																														
1 0	I																														
1 1	I																														
1 2	I																														

Figure 13-31 Input Specifications form

2. Using the form in Figure 13-32, write the corresponding entries for the following update request records:

Positions	Field Description
1–7	Part number
11–30	Description
40–42	Division
56–60	Quantity
75–80	Date manufactured

The update request code is located in position 81 of the update request records. The valid update request codes are: A, record addition; D, record deletion; C, record change. The name of this file is INVUPD.

Line	Form Type	Filename or Record Name / Data Structure Name	O R / A N D	Sequence	Number (1/N)/E	Option (O),U,S	Record Identifying Indicator, **, or DS	Named Constant Value / External Field Name / Record Identification Codes — Position 1	Not (N)	C/Z/D	Character	Position 2	Not (N)	C/Z/D	Character	Position 3	Not (N)	C/Z/D	Character	Stacker Select	P/B/L/R/C	Field Location — From / Occurs n Times	To / Length	Decimal Positions	RPG Field Name / Constant Name	Control Level (L1–L9)	Matching Fields or Chaining Fields	Field Record Relation	Plus	Minus	Zero or Blank
0 1	I																														
0 2	I																														
0 3	I																														
0 4	I																														
0 5	I																														
0 6	I																														
0 7	I																														
0 8	I																														
0 9	I																														
1 0	I																														
1 1	I																														
1 2	I																														

Figure 13-32 Input Specifications form

3. Based on the following processing requirements, write the output specifications needed to create the new master file. Use the form in Figure 13-33. You can assume that all necessary calculations have been correctly coded.

When a change request is processed the program updates the contents of the Quantity field by adding the contents of the Quantity field in the update request record to the contents of the Quantity field in the master record. The output record written to the new master file contains all the original master file data as well as the newly calculated Quantity field (QUATOT).

All records currently in INVMAS have been edited and can be assumed to contain valid data.

When an INVMAS record for which there is no corresponding INVUPD record is read, the complete INVMAS record is written to the new output file.

All INVUPD records have been verified and can, with one exception, be assumed to contain accurate update request data. The exception is the Update Request Code field, which must be tested to assure that it contains a valid code. If a valid code (A, D, or C) is present, the code can be assumed to be correct.

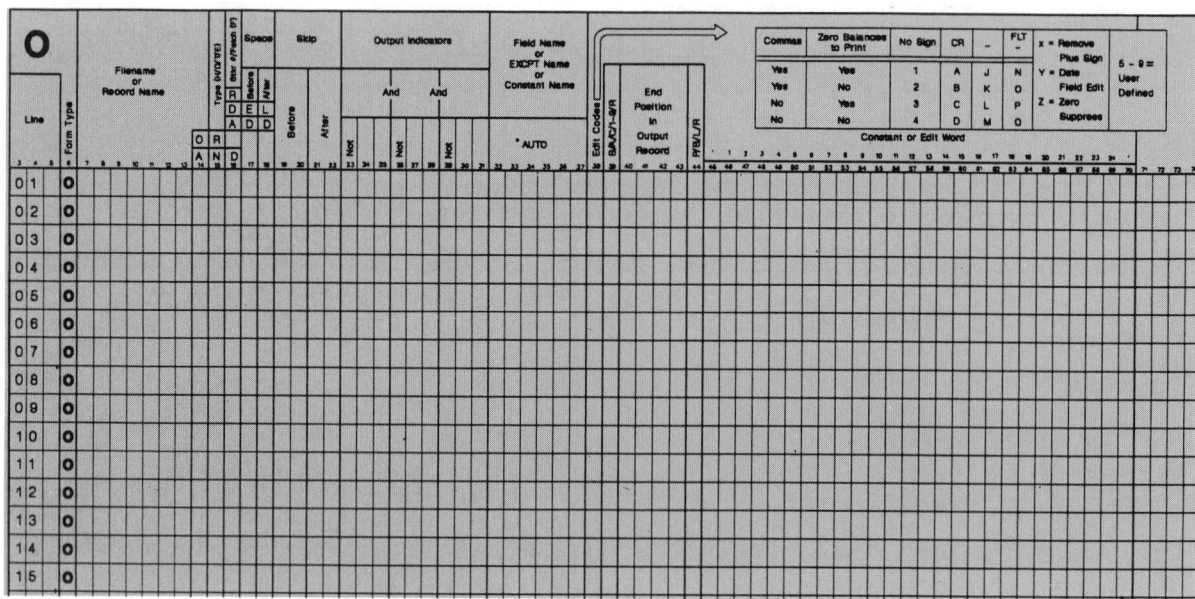

Figure 13-33   Output Specifications form

STUDENT EXERCISES: RPG PROGRAM MAINTENANCE

▤ Problem 1

Because a sequential update program using matching record techniques does not alter the original master file, this type of update program can be written so that the program halts if an error condition occurs. Then, after the data has been corrected, the program can be restarted from the beginning. Program HJG13X prints an error message if an update request record contains an invalid update request code and then continues processing the remainder of the two files. Modify program HJG13X (using Figure 13-34) so that after printing the error line, the program will stop processing if

    1. an invalid update request code is detected, or

    2. an attempt is made to add a duplicate record to the master file.

Specify where in the program you would insert the necessary calculations. Specify the insertion point by listing the two line numbers between which the code should be placed. Refer to Figure 13-30 to determine the line numbers.

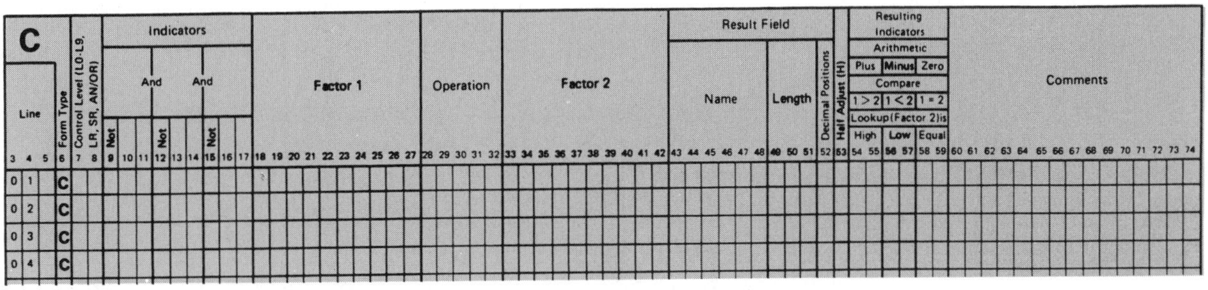

Figure 13-34   Calculation Specifications form

Problem 2

In the Calculation Specifications form in Figure 13-35, write the code needed to count each type of update request processed by the program. Account for every possible update request whether valid or invalid. In addition, count the total number of valid update requests and the total number of invalid update requests. Specify where in the program you would insert the calculations. Specify the insertion point by listing the two line numbers between which the code should be placed. Refer to Figure 13-30 to determine the line numbers.

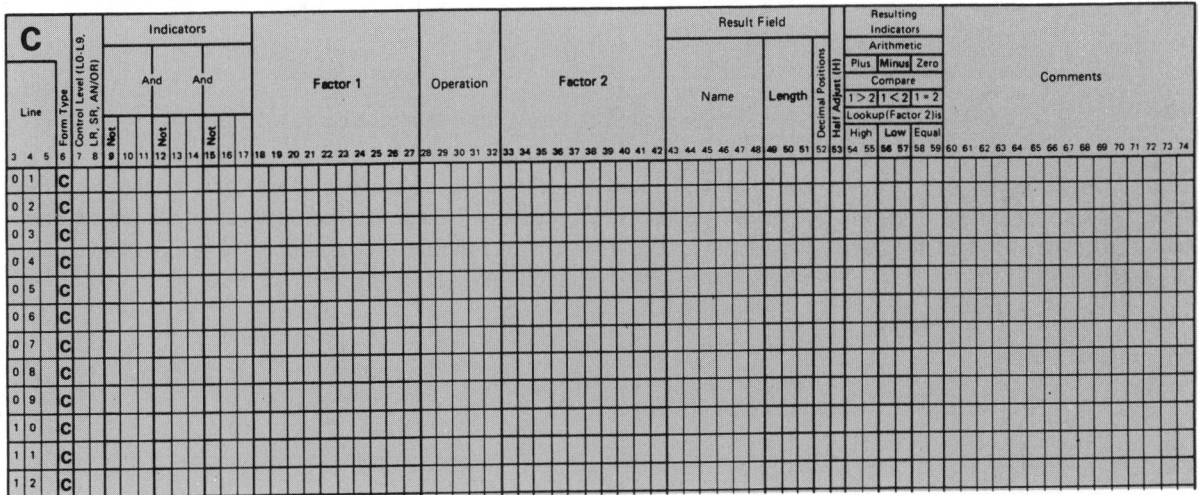

Figure 13-35   Calculation Specifications form

STUDENT EXERCISES: PROGRAMMING IN RPG

The following programming assignments are sequential file update versions of programming assignments in Chapter 11. The master file data is identical to that in the master files used in Chapter 11, the only difference being that the format has been changed from keyed access path to arrival sequence access path. In addition, the update files are identical to those in the update request files in the Chapter 11 assignments.

PROGRAMMING ASSIGNMENT 1
TEST EQUIPMENT MASTER FILE UPDATE

INSTRUCTIONS

Plan, code, enter, and test an RPG program to update the Test Equipment Master File, the format of which is shown in Figure 13-36. To obtain an arrival sequence version of the master file, you can either use your computer's file copy utility or write an RPG program to copy the keyed sequence master file into an arrival sequence file.

TEST EQUIPMENT MASTER FILE RECORD						
Record Length 65						
Field No.	Field Name	Field Description	Field Position	Field Length	Dec. Pos.	Data Class
1		Unit I.D. Number	1–8	8		A
2		Unit Description	9–30	22		A
3		Location	36–42	7		A
4		Purchase Date	46–51	6	0	N
5		Date Last Calibrated	52–57	6	0	N
6		Date Updated	58–63	6	0	N
		UNUSED AREA	65–65			

Figure 13-36 Format of Test Equipment Master File

The Date Updated field is to contain the date that the record was added to the Test Equipment Master File or the date on which the record was last updated by a change operation. If a record is copied from the old master file to the new master file, this is not considered an update operation, and the program does not change the contents of this field.

INPUT

The format of the Test Equipment Update File is shown in Figure 13-37. Use test data set 26 for this file.

TEST EQUIPMENT UPDATE RECORD						
Record Length 65						
Field No.	Field Name	Field Description	Field Position	Field Length	Dec. Pos.	Data Class
1		Unit I.D. Number	1–8	8		A
2		Unit Description	9–30	22		A
3		Location	36–42	7		A
4		Purchase Date	46–51	6	0	N
5		Date Last Calibrated	52–57	6	0	N
6		Update Type Code	60–60	1		A

Figure 13-37 Format of Test Equipment Update File

OUTPUT

Output from Programming Assignment 1 is to be the updated Test Equipment Master File and a printed report providing a complete audit trail of all update requests. In addition to showing all valid update operations performed on the master file, the report is to list all invalid update requests and the reason that each was determined to be invalid.

Processing Requirements

Test each record in the Test Equipment Update File based on the following conditions, which are listed for each type of update request. This file has been preedited and contains no invalid update request codes.

Record Addition (Update Code A)

If none of the conditions listed is detected, a record is added to the Test Equipment Master File. If one or more of the listed conditions are detected, no addition to the master file is made.

1. The unit identification number must not be duplicated in the Test Equipment Master File.
2. The Unit Identification Number, Description, and Location fields must not be blank.
3. The Purchase Date field must not contain all zeros.
4. If the Date Last Calibrated field contains a date, the date cannot be earlier than the Purchase Date.
5. Both of the input date fields are in MMDDYY format. The month and day portions of both fields must be valid. Month entries must be 01–12, and the day entry must be valid for the month. You need not test for leap year because the file does not contain any dates of February 29.

Record Deletion (Update Code D)

For a record to be deleted, both the identification number and the description contained in the update request record must match those in the Test Equipment Master File record. If both fields match, the master file record is deleted.

Record Change (Update Code C)

Only the Location and Date Last Calibrated fields can be changed. If a change is requested to the Date Last Calibrated field, the new date must be later than the date currently in the record. The new date must be tested according to the requirements of test 5 listed earlier under Record Addition.

PROGRAMMING ASSIGNMENT 2
EMPLOYEE MASTER FILE UPDATE

INSTRUCTIONS

Plan, code, enter, and test an RPG program to update the Employee Master File, the format of which is shown in Figure 13-38 on the next page. To obtain an arrival sequence version of the master file you can either use your computer's file copy utility or write an RPG program to copy the keyed sequence master file into an arrival sequence file.

EMPLOYEE MASTER FILE RECORD						
Record Length 70						
Field No.	Field Name	Field Description	Field Position	Field Length	Dec. Pos.	Data Class
1		Employee Number	1–4	4	0	N
2		Last Name	5–19	15		A
3		First Name	20–31	12		A
4		Sex Code (M/F)	32–32	1		A
5		Date Hired	33–38	6	0	N
6		Department Number	39–41	3	0	N
7		Pay Category (H/S)	42–42	1		A
8		Pay Rate Code	43–44	2	0	N
9		Annual Salary	45–52	8	2	N
10		Hourly Pay Rate	53–57	5	3	N
11		Date Updated	62–67	6	0	N
		UNUSED AREA	70–70			

Figure 13-38   Format of Employee Master File

The Date Updated field is to contain the date that the record was added to the Employee Master File or the date on which the record was last updated by a change operation. If a record is copied from the old master file to the new master file, this is not considered an update operation, and the program does not change the contents of this field.

INPUT

The format of the Employee Update file is shown in Figure 13-39. Use test data set 27 for this file.

EMPLOYEE UPDATE RECORD						
Record Length 70						
Field No.	Field Name	Field Description	Field Position	Field Length	Dec. Pos.	Data Class
1		Employee Number	1–4	4	0	N
2		Last Name	5–19	15		A
3		First Name	20–31	12		A
4		Sex Code (M/F)	32–32	1		A
5		Date Hired	33–38	6	0	N
6		Department Number	39–41	3	0	N
7		Pay Category (H/S)	42–42	1		A
8		Pay Rate Code	43–44	2	0	N
9		Annual Salary	45–52	8	2	N
10		Hourly Pay Rate	53–57	5	3	N
11		Hours Worked Last Pay Period	58–61	4	1	N
		UNUSED AREA	62–69			
12		Update Type Code	70–70	1		A

Figure 13-39   Format of Employee Update File

OUTPUT

Output from Programming Assignment 1 is the updated Employee Master File and a printed report providing a complete audit trail of all update requests. In addition to showing all valid update operations performed on the master file, the report is to list all invalid update requests and the reason that each was determined to be invalid.

Processing Requirements

Record Addition (Update Code A)

Test each input data record for the conditions listed. If none of the listed conditions is detected, a record is added to the Employee Master File. If one or more of the listed conditions are detected, no addition to the master file is made. The current date is placed in positions 62–67 of the Employee Master File record.

1. The employee number must not be duplicated in the Employee Master File.
2. The Employee Number, Last Name, First Name, Date Hired, and Department Number fields must not be blank.
3. Sex code must be either M or F.
4. Pay category must be either H or S.
5. If pay category is H, neither the Pay Rate Code field nor the Hourly Pay Rate field may be blank or zero.
6. If pay category is S, the Annual Salary field must not be blank or zero.

Record Deletion (Update Code D)

For a record to be deleted, both the employee number and the date hired contained in the update request record must match those in the Employee Master File record. If both fields match, the master file record is deleted.

Record Change (Update Code C)

1. The only fields that can be changed are the Last Name, First Name, Department Number, Pay Category, Pay Rate Code, Annual Salary, and Hourly Pay Rate fields.
2. If a change is made to the Pay Category field, the change must conform to items 4, 5, and 6 listed earlier under Record Addition.
3. If the pay category changes from H to S, the Pay Rate Code and Hourly Pay Rate fields must be changed to zero.
4. If the pay category changes from S to H, the Annual Salary field must be changed to zero.
5. When any change is made to a record, the current date is placed in positions 62–67 of the Employee Master File record.

PROGRAMMING ASSIGNMENT 3
RENTAL CAR STATUS FILE UPDATE

INSTRUCTIONS

Plan, code, enter, and test an RPG program to update the Rental Car Status File, the format of which is shown in Figure 13-40 on the next page. To obtain an arrival sequence version of the master file, you can either use your computer's file copy utility or write an RPG program to copy the keyed master file into an arrival sequence file.

RENTAL CAR STATUS FILE RECORD						
Record Length 70						
Field No.	Field Name	Field Description	Field Position	Field Length	Dec. Pos.	Data Class
		Vehicle Stock No.	1–9			
		Check Digit	10–10			
		Make of Car	11–11			
		Body Style	12–12			
		Optional Equipment	13–17			
		Air Conditioning	13–13			
		Power Steering	14–14			
		Towing Package	15–15			
		Sun Roof	16–16			
		Automatic Trans.	17–17			
		Vehicle Status	18–18			
		License Number	19–27			
		Renter's Name	28–48			
		Payment Method	49–50			
		Date Out	51–56			
		Number of Days Rented	57–58			
		Deposit Amount	59–62			

Figure 13-40 Format of Rental Car Status File

INPUT

The format of the Rental Car Update File is shown in Figure 13-41. Use test data set 28 for this problem.

OUTPUT

Output from Programming Assignment 3 is the updated Rental Car Status File and a printed report providing a complete audit trail of all update requests. In addition to showing all valid update operations performed on the master file, the report is to list all invalid update requests and the reason that each was determined to be invalid.

RENTAL CAR UPDATE FILE RECORD						
Record Length 70						
Field No.	Field Name	Field Description	Field Position	Field Length	Dec. Pos.	Data Class
1	STOCK	Vehicle Stock No.	1–9	9	0	N
2	CHECK	Check Digit	10–10	1	0	N
3	MAKE	Make of Car	11–11	1		A
4	STYLE	Body Style	12–12	1		A
5	EQUIP	Optional Equipment	13–17	5		A
		Air Conditioning	13–13			
		Power Steering	14–14			
		Towing Package	15–15			
		Sun Roof	16–16			
		Automatic Trans.	17–17			
6	STATUS	Vehicle Status	18–18	1		A
7	LICNO	License Number	19–27	9		A
8	NAME	Renter's Name	28–48	21		A
9	PAY	Payment Method	49–50	2		A
10	DOUT	Date Out	51–56	6	0	N
11	NODAYS	Number of Days Rented	57–58	2	0	N
12	DEPST	Deposit Amount	59–62	4	0	N
13		Update Type Code	63–63	1		A
		UNUSED AREA	64–70			

Figure 13-41   Format of Rental Car Status Update File

Processing Requirements

Record Addition (Update Code A)

Test each input data record for the conditions listed. If none of the listed conditions is detected, a record is added to the Rental Car Status File. Except for condition 11, if one or more of the listed conditions are detected, no addition to the master file is made. If condition 11 is detected, an error message is printed, and the record is added to the Rental Car Status File.

1. The vehicle stock number must not be duplicated in the Rental Car Status File.
2. The STOCK, CHECK, MAKE, STYLE, and STATUS fields must not be blank and must contain valid codes, as shown later in this list.
3. The Check Digit field must correspond to the vehicle stock number. To verify the check digit, add together the nine digits of the Vehicle Stock Number field. The rightmost digit of the sum should match the Check Digit field.

4. The valid MAKE entries are

   P   Panther
   T   Tiger
   B   Bearcat
   V   Vulcan

5. The valid STYLE entries are

   C   Convertible
   S   Sedan
   F   Fastback

6. The four makes of car are not all available in every body style. The valid combinations of make and body style are

   Panther   Convertible, Fastback
   Tiger   Sedan, fastback
   Bearcat   Convertible, sedan, fastback
   Vulcan   Convertible, sedan

   No other combination is valid.

7. The five Optional Equipment fields contain a Y if the vehicle is equipped with the option and an N if the vehicle is not equipped with that option. There are several invalid optional equipment combinations:

   Fastbacks cannot be equipped with the towing package.
   If a car is equipped with either air conditioning or a towing package, it cannot be equipped with a sun roof.
   If a car is equipped with air conditioning, it must be equipped with power steering and an automatic transmission.

8. The three valid STATUS codes are

   A   Available for rental
   R   Rented, not available
   S   Being serviced, not available

9. If the STATUS code is R, the LICNO, NAME, PAY, and NODAYS fields must not be blank.
10. The valid payment method codes are CA (cash payment) and CR (credit card).
11. If the payment method is CA, the DEPSIT field must be tested to verify a valid deposit amount. Deposit amount is calculated as follows:

    If the car is a Panther, Tiger, or Bearcat, the deposit is $50.00 per day. If the car is a Vulcan, the deposit is $35.00 per day.

═══ Record Deletion (Update Code D)

There is no secondary field that must be verified prior to deletion. Record deletion is based on the vehicle stock number. Deletion request records contain only this nine-digit number. After computing the check digit, use the combination of vehicle identification number and check digit to perform the record deletion.

⊨ Record Change (Update Code C)

All changes must be based on proper verification of the check digit of the record to be changed. Change request records do not contain a check digit. This digit must be calculated prior to reading the Rental Car Status File and the check digit used as part of the key in the CHAIN operation.

1. No changes may be made to the data fields that describe the vehicle. The only allowable changes are the status changes in this listed.
2. Vehicle status can be changed from A (available) to S (being serviced). In this case, no further changes are needed to the Rental Car Status File record. In addition, the reverse change (S to A) can also be made with no further processing required on the record.
3. Vehicle status can be changed from A to R (rented) or from S to R. When either of these changes is made, items 9, 10, and 11 of the Record Addition specifications must be tested, and the required entries must be contained in the Change Request record. If the tested conditions are not met, the change request is not valid.
4. Vehicle status can be changed from R to A or from R to S. If either of these changes is made, positions 19–50 of the record must be changed to blanks, and positions 51–62 of the record must be changed to zeros.

RPG III & RPG/400 Enhancements

This chapter introduces components found in RPG III and RPG/400 that are not available in RPG II.

FILE DESCRIPTION SPECIFICATIONS

Externally Described Files

Until recently, all data processed by a computer was stored in separate data files, each of which contained a series of similar records. As you now know, each of the records in a file contains information about a single transaction, and in some business applications, several different data files are needed to provide all the information required by a program. For example, your school probably uses several different files that contain information about you, such as a student master file, a student schedule file, a student attendance file, and a student grade file.

Recent advances in data storage have made it possible to organize all the information about a specific item or person into a single data file called a **database**. This database contains the information that was formerly stored in all the individual data files. The database contains, in addition to the data, a series of descriptions of the fields contained in the database. RPG III and RPG/400 can access database storage systems. Because the information that describes the fields in the database is contained within the database and need not be defined in the program, these files are referred to as **externally described files**. In RPG III and RPG/400, the type of file description you have used so far is called a program described file. **Program described files** perform all file and field descriptions within the application program and do not rely on an external database for descriptions.

Because externally described files already contain the needed field descriptions, data modification in a business application system is considerably easier. Take, for example, the four files that contain information about you. Each of these files probably contains your student number, year of graduation, and name. If any of these items changes, a file maintenance program must update your record in all four files. Contrast this with an externally described file that contains all the information about you. Only a single update operation is required to make the change, thus reducing (in this example) the time needed to update your information by 75%. Furthermore, if a field description changes, you need only make a change to one database description rather than to all the programs that use the changed field. In addition to reducing program and file maintenance time, databases make data security easier. It is far simpler to control access to the data in a single database than it is to control access to a number of separate data files.

Figure 14-1 shows the **Data Description Specifications form** used for externally described files. The R in position 17, Name Type area, identifies STDTL as the name of the record format being described. The PFILE(STUDNT) entry, which begins in position 45, specifies that the data fields for this record type are part of the STUDNT physical file (the disk database). The following entries describe the individual fields that are contained in the STDTL record format. Note that the rules for field definition (name, length, and data class) remain the same as for RPG. The field name is entered in positions 19–24, the length in 30–34, and the data class is identified by the entry or lack of entry in position 37. The TEXT entry, which begins in position 45 of each field definition, provides a narrative description of the field.

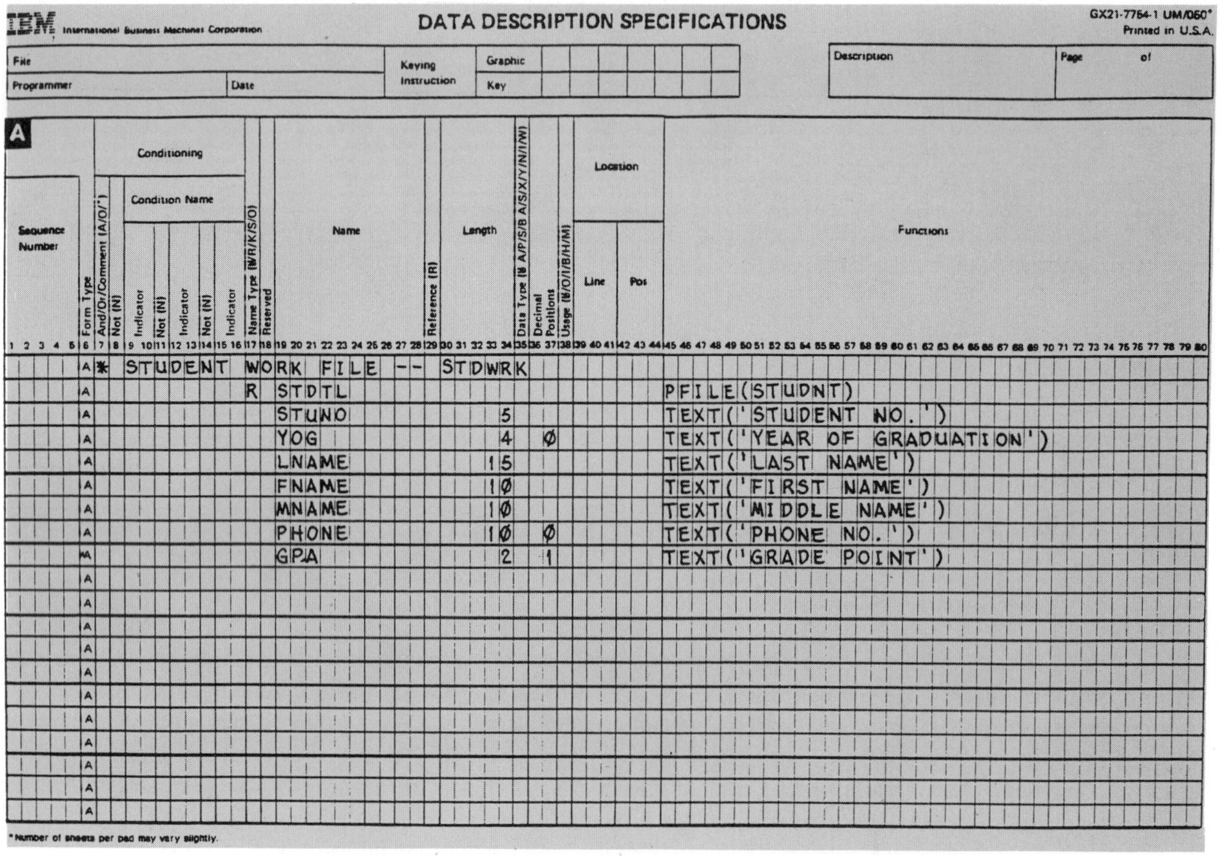
IBM International Business Machines Corporation — DATA DESCRIPTION SPECIFICATIONS — GX21-7764-1 UM/050* Printed in U.S.A.

Form Type	Name Type	Name	Length	Decimal Positions	Functions
A*		STUDENT WORK FILE -- STDWRK			
A	R	STDTL			PFILE(STUDNT)
A		STUNO	5		TEXT('STUDENT NO.')
A		YOG	4	Ø	TEXT('YEAR OF GRADUATION')
A		LNAME	15		TEXT('LAST NAME')
A		FNAME	1Ø		TEXT('FIRST NAME')
A		MNAME	1Ø		TEXT('MIDDLE NAME')
A		PHONE	1Ø	Ø	TEXT('PHONE NO.')
A		GPA	2	1	TEXT('GRADE POINT')

*Number of sheets per pad may vary slightly.

Figure 14-1 Data Description Specifications form

After this data description is complete and is stored by the computer, any reference in an RPG application program to STDWRK causes this data description to be retrieved and included in the program.

Figure 14-2 shows File Description Specification form for STDWRK. As you can see, most of the entries are familiar. STDWRK is an input, primary file that is stored on DISK. Two of the entries are new. The File Format entry E in position 19 specifies that STDWRK is an externally described file. The entry K in position 31 specifies that STDWRK is accessed by its key field. However, several entries that you have seen in every file description so far are missing. There are no entries to describe the record length, block length, and type of file organization. Because this is an externally described file, RPG III or RPG/400 retrieves these descriptions from the database itself. Recall that all the descriptions of an externally described file are stored in the database and are not repeated in the program that is using the database.

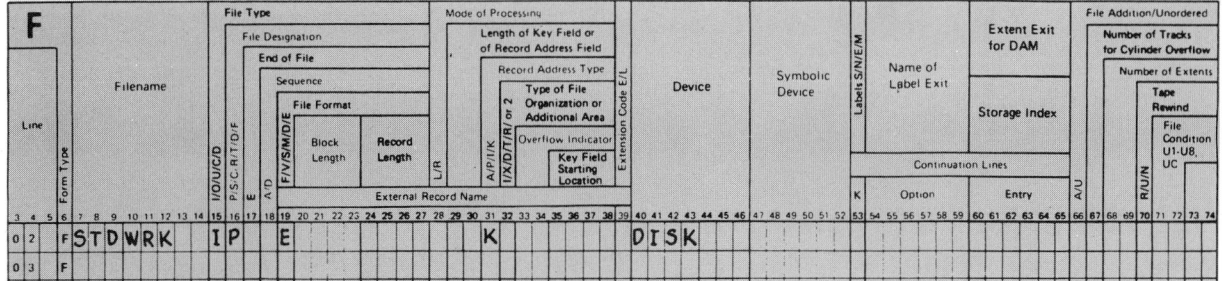

Figure 14-2 Externally described file description specification

Subfiles

RPG III and RPG/400 permit the use of subfiles to minimize the number of input and output operations performed by a terminal. A **subfile** is a group of individual data records that is read from or written to a terminal in a single operation. Figure 14-3 shows a display that contains 14 records. To display this format using the techniques in Chapter 12, you would either perform a minimum of 14 output operations or read 14 input records, move the data from each record to a separate data field, and then display the entire format.

```
Part Identification Search

Search Pattern_____

Part      Description                              Inventory Location

XXXXXX    XXXXXXXXXXXXXXXXXXXXXXXXXXXXXXXX         XXXXXXXXXXXXXXXXXX
XXXXXX    XXXXXXXXXXXXXXXXXXXXXXXXXXXXXXXX         XXXXXXXXXXXXXXXXXX
XXXXXX    XXXXXXXXXXXXXXXXXXXXXXXXXXXXXXXX         XXXXXXXXXXXXXXXXXX
XXXXXX    XXXXXXXXXXXXXXXXXXXXXXXXXXXXXXXX         XXXXXXXXXXXXXXXXXX
XXXXXX    XXXXXXXXXXXXXXXXXXXXXXXXXXXXXXXX         XXXXXXXXXXXXXXXXXX
XXXXXX    XXXXXXXXXXXXXXXXXXXXXXXXXXXXXXXX         XXXXXXXXXXXXXXXXXX
XXXXXX    XXXXXXXXXXXXXXXXXXXXXXXXXXXXXXXX         XXXXXXXXXXXXXXXXXX
XXXXXX    XXXXXXXXXXXXXXXXXXXXXXXXXXXXXXXX         XXXXXXXXXXXXXXXXXX
XXXXXX    XXXXXXXXXXXXXXXXXXXXXXXXXXXXXXXX         XXXXXXXXXXXXXXXXXX
XXXXXX    XXXXXXXXXXXXXXXXXXXXXXXXXXXXXXXX         XXXXXXXXXXXXXXXXXX
XXXXXX    XXXXXXXXXXXXXXXXXXXXXXXXXXXXXXXX         XXXXXXXXXXXXXXXXXX
XXXXXX    XXXXXXXXXXXXXXXXXXXXXXXXXXXXXXXX         XXXXXXXXXXXXXXXXXX
XXXXXX    XXXXXXXXXXXXXXXXXXXXXXXXXXXXXXXX         XXXXXXXXXXXXXXXXXX
XXXXXX    XXXXXXXXXXXXXXXXXXXXXXXXXXXXXXXX         XXXXXXXXXXXXXXXXXX

ENTER—See More Terms                   CMD/7—End Search
```

Figure 14-3 Subfile display format

Subfile techniques enable you to read a predefined number of records from a database file, create a subfile of output records, and then send the entire subfile to the terminal screen in a single output operation. Subfiles are defined on the Data Description Specifications form in a manner similar to the description of externally described files.

CALCULATION SPECIFICATIONS

A number of operations that can be specified on the Calculation Specifications form perform functions that may be useful in a given application. The following sections deal with operations that have not been covered previously in the text.

CALL (Call a Program) Operation

Just as internal subroutines make it possible for you to specify a group of calculations that are executed under the control of the EXSR operation, CALLed programs can be executed under control of another program. The CALL operation, summarized in Figure 14-4, causes RPG to call (execute) another program, usually a machine-language program. When the CALL operation is performed, control is passed to the CALLed program for as long as the CALLed program executes. When the CALLed program is complete, control passes back to the original program, which resumes execution with the statement following the CALL.

CALL Operation Summary (RPG III and RPG/400)

The CALL operation causes the program named by the data field, literal, or array element specified in Factor 2 to be executed. In addition, Factor 2 may contain the name of the library that contains the program. If both a library and a program name are specified, the library name must be specified first, followed by the program name. The two names must be separated by a slash (LIB/PROG). If a literal is specified in Factor 2, the length of the literal cannot exceed eight characters. If a field name is used in Factor 2, the field length cannot exceed 21 characters. An indicator may be used in positions 56–57 to be set on for an error return from the CALLed program. An indicator may be used in positions 58–59 to show that the CALLed program ended with indicator LR on. Factor 2 may contain the name of a parameter list used to communicate information between the current program and the CALLed program.

Control Level Indicators	Indicators	Factor 1	Operation Name	Factor 2	Result Field	Resulting Indicators		
7–8	9–17	18–27	28–32	33–42	43–53	54–55	56–57	58–59
optional	optional	blank	CALL	required	optional	blank	optional	optional

Figure 14-4   CALL operation summary (RPG III and RPG/400)

In Figure 14-4, the CALL operation on line 01 causes program PROGRMX to execute if indicators 21, 22, and 23 are all on. The example on line 03 executes program ERROR if indicator LR is on and indicator 26 is not on.

CLOSE (Close Files) Operation

If a program no longer needs a file for processing, that file can be released from the program by the CLOSE statement, which is summarized in Figure 14-5. File closing might be performed by a program that will continue to execute for some time after it no longer needs a specific file. Rather than tie up an unneeded file and make it unavailable to other users, the programmer can release the file for use by others by using the CLOSE operation. After a file has been closed, the program ignores any further reference to the file unless the file has been made available for processing again by the use of an OPEN operation.

Line		Form Type	Control Level (L0-L9, LR, SR, AN/OR)	And		And		Factor 1	Operation	Factor 2	Name	Length	Decimal Positions	Half Adjust (H)	Resulting Indicators			Comments
0 1		C							CLOSE*ALL									
0 2		C																
0 3		C							CLOSEFILEB						99		CLOSE ERROR
0 4		C	17						GOTO CLOSERR								

CLOSE Operation Summary (RPG III and RPG/400)

The CLOSE operation closes a file by making it unavailable to the program for further processing unless an OPEN operation is executed for the file. A program may contain more than one CLOSE operation for the same file. If a CLOSE is executed for a file that has already been closed, the operation is ignored. Factor 2 must contain the name of the file to be closed. If the key word *ALL is specified in Factor 2, all program files are closed at once. If an indicator is specified in positions 56–57, the indicator will be turned on if the CLOSE operation does not complete successfully.

Control Level Indicators	Indicators	Factor 1	Operation Name	Factor 2	Result Field	Resulting Indicators		
7–8	9–17	18–27	28–32	33–42	43–53	54–55	56–57	58–59
optional	optional	blank	CLOSE	required	blank	blank	optional	blank

Figure 14-5　CLOSE operation summary (RPG III and RPG/400)

DEFN (Field Definition) Operation

The *LIKE DEFN operation, summarized in Figure 14-6, is used to define a new data field based on the description of some other data field. Because the DEFN operation is a form of compiler directive statement and is not a true calculation operation, any entry made in positions 7–8 is for documentation purposes only and is ignored when the program is run. The definition of a new field is, in fact, performed during program compilation. *LIKE DEFN only creates a data field and does not load data into it.

Assuming that FLDA is six positions long with two decimal places, the three examples in Figure 14-6 provide the following results:

Line 01 Six-position field with two decimal places
Line 02 Eight-position field with two decimal places
Line 03 Four-position field with two decimal places

Line	Form Type	Factor 1	Operation	Factor 2	Result Field Name	Length	Decimal Positions
01	C	*LIKE	DEFN	FLDA	FLDB		
02	C	*LIKE	DEFN	FLDA	FLDC	+	2
03	C	*LIKE	DEFN	FLDA	FLDD	–	2
04	C						

DEFN Operation Summary

The DEFN operation, when used with *LIKE in Factor 1 defines a field based on the description (length and data class) of another field. Factor 2 must contain the name of the field on which the definition is based. The Result Field must contain the name of the new field being defined. Positions 49–51 may be used to change the length of the new field. A plus sign (+) in position 49 indicates a field length increase, a minus sign (–) indicates a decrease in length. When this feature is used, positions 50 and 51 must contain the number of positions being added to or deleted from the field. The number of decimal positions cannot be changed.

Control Level Indicators	Indicators	Factor 1	Operation Name	Factor 2	Result Field	Resulting Indicators		
7–8	9–17	18–27	28–32	33–42	43–53	54–55	56–57	58–59
optional	blank	*LIKE	DEFN	required	required	blank	blank	blank

Figure 14-6 DEFN operation summary

▱ DELET (Delete Record) Operation

The DELET operation removes a record from an update data file. The DELET operation, summarized in Figure 14-7, does not mark a record for deletion but, makes the record unavailable for access or processing by the computer. Once a record has been removed by a DELET operation, it cannot be retrieved.

C	Form Type	Control Level (L0–L9, LR, SR, AN/OR)	Indicators And Not / And Not	Factor 1	Operation	Factor 2	Result Field Name	Length	Decimal Positions	Half Adjust (H)	Resulting Indicators	Comments
01	C			002137	DELET	EMPFILE					21	
02	C											
03	C			PARTNO	DELET	PARTMAST					99	
04	C											

DELET Operation Summary (RPG III and RPG/400)

The DELET operation deletes a record from an update data file. Factor 1 must contain the key that identifies the record to be deleted. Factor 2 must contain the name of the update file that contains the record. An indicator specified in positions 54–55 will be turned on if the record to be deleted is not found in the file. An indicator specified in positions 56–57 will be turned on if the DELET operation does not delete the record. This can happen if the user requesting the record deletion does not have proper security access to the data file.

Control Level Indicators	Indicators	Factor 1	Operation Name	Factor 2	Result Field	Resulting Indicators		
7–8	9–17	18–27	28–32	33–42	43–53	54–55	56–57	58–59
optional	optional	required	DELET	required	blank	optional	optional	blank

Figure 14-7   DELET operation summary

Line 01 in Figure 14-7 shows the deletion of a record by the use of a literal in Factor 1. When this operation is executed, the EMPFILE record with a key of 002137 is permanently deleted from EMPFILE. Note the use of indicator 21 to show the attempt to remove a nonexistent record. The example on line 03 shows the use of a field name to control record deletion. In this example, the contents of the PARTNO field determine the record to be deleted from PARTMAST. Indicator 99 is turned on if the DELET attempt fails for any reason other than an attempt to delete a record that does not exist. Although this operation is considered an RPG III and RPG/400 operation, it is available in some versions of RPG II.

▤ EXFMT (Execute Format) Operation

In Chapter 12 you used an output operation (EXCPT) followed by an input operation (READ) to display and then read a display format. The EXFMT operation, summarized in Figure 14-8, combines both of these steps into a single operation. The EXFMT operation shown on line 01 causes the FORMT1 format to be displayed on a screen and then, when either the Enter key or a valid Command key is pressed, performs the read operation.

EXFMT Operation Summary (RPG III and RPG/400)

The EXFMT operation is valid only when used with workstation files and is a combination of a WRITE followed by a READ operation to the same file. The EXFMT operation is valid only when used with externally described, full-procedural, combined workstation files. Factor 2 must contain the name of the format that is to be written and then read. An indicator may be specified in positions 56–57 to indicate that the EXFMT operation did not complete successfully. When this happens, input fields controlled by the format are not changed by the EXFMT operation.

Control Level Indicators	Indicators	Factor 1	Operation Name	Factor 2	Result Field	Resulting Indicators		
7–8	9–17	18–27	28–32	33–42	43–53	54–55	56–57	58–59
optional	optional	blank	EXFMT	required	blank	blank	optional	blank

Figure 14-8   EXFMT operation summary

▤ FORCE (Force a File to Be Read) Operation

The program in Chapter 13 showed how multiple files are processed by the RPG fixed logic cycle. RPG offers one more alternative, that of specifying the next file from which an input record is to be read, regardless of the record that would normally be read by the RPG logic cycle. The example in Figure 14-9 illustrates the FORCE operation, which has several limitations:

1. The first record processed in the program cannot be forced; it will be the record chosen by the fixed logic.
2. The FORCE operation can be issued only during detail calculation time; it cannot be issued during total processing.
3. A FORCE operation is in effect only for the next input cycle. After the next cycle, the control over which input record is processed reverts to the normal RPG logic.
4. If a FORCE operation is specified for a file that has already reached end of file, no record is retrieved from the file. Instead, the normal RPG processing logic determines the next record to be retrieved for processing.

Like the DELET operation, FORCE is available in some versions of RPG II.

FORCE Operation Summary

The FORCE operation overrides the RPG fixed logic cycle and specifies the name of the file from which the next record is to be read. FORCE can only be used with primary or secondary files. A FORCE operation may be specified only during detail time, not at total time. If more than one FORCE operation is executed, all but the last will be ignored. Factor 2 must specify the name of the file from which the next record is to be read.

Control Level Indicators	Indicators	Factor 1	Operation Name	Factor 2	Result Field	Resulting Indicators		
7–8	9–17	18–27	28–32	33–42	43–53	54–55	56–57	58–59
blank	optional	blank	FORCE	required	blank	blank	blank	blank

Figure 14-9   FORCE operation summary

OPEN (Open File for Processing) Operation

The OPEN operation, summarized in Figure 14-10, causes a data file to be opened (made available for processing) under control of the application program rather than the RPG fixed logic cycle. The example on line 01 causes file FILEB to be available for processing by the program. The OPEN operation can be used to reopen a file that was terminated by the CLOSE operation. Note that an attempt to OPEN a file that is already open results in an error condition.

OPEN Operation Summary (RPG III and RPG/400)

The OPEN operation makes the file named in Factor 2 available for processing by the program. The file named in Factor 2 cannot be a primary, secondary, or table file. If an indicator is specified in positions 56–57, the indicator will be turned on if the OPEN operation does not complete successfully. If a file is to be opened for the first time by an OPEN statement, rather than the RPG fixed logic cycle, the file description specification must contain an entry of UC (user control) in positions 71–72. If an OPEN statement is executed for a file that is already open, an error will occur.

Control Level Indicators	Indicators	Factor 1	Operation Name	Factor 2	Result Field	Resulting Indicators		
7–8	9–17	18–27	28–32	33–42	43–53	54–55	56–57	58–59
optional	optional	blank	OPEN	required	blank	blank	optional	blank

Figure 14-10 OPEN operation summary

UPDAT (Modify Existing Record) Operation

The UPDAT operation, summarized in Figure 14-11, is similar to the EXCPT output operation used to change a record read by a CHAIN operation when updating a keyed access path data file. An UPDAT operation must follow a valid input operation such as READ, CHAIN, or the read of a primary or secondary record by the RPG fixed logic cycle.

Do not attempt to use the UPDAT operation to modify a primary or secondary file record at total time. At this point in the RPG logic cycle, the data in the fields area may not correspond to the record in the input area because a new record has been read. At this point, UPDAT would modify the current record, which has been read into the input area, with data from the preceding record stored in the fields areas.

UPDAT Operation Summary (RPG III and RPG/400)

The UPDAT operations modifies the last record read from an update file. No input or output operation may be performed between the read and UPDAT operations. Factor 2 must contain the name of the file or record format (required if an external file description is used) to be updated. The Result Field must contain a data structure name if a file name is specified in Factor 2. The program will write the update record to the file directly from the data structure. The Result Field must be blank if Factor 2 contains a record format name. If an indicator is specified in positions 56–57, the indicator will be turned on if the UPDAT does not execute successfully.

Control Level Indicators	Indicators	Factor 1	Operation Name	Factor 2	Result Field	Resulting Indicators		
7–8	9–17	18–27	28–32	33–42	43–53	54–55	56–57	58–59
optional	optional	blank	UPDAT	required	optional	blank	optional	blank

Figure 14-11 UPDAT operation summary

WRITE (Create New Records) Operation

The WRITE operation, summarized in Figure 14-12, writes a new record to a data file. If WRITE is used with a disk file, position 66 of the file description specification must contain an A to permit records to be added to the file.

WRITE Operation Summary (RPG III and RPG/400)

The WRITE operation adds a new record to a file. Factor 2 must contain the name of a file or record format (required if an external file description is used). The Result Field must contain a data structure name if a file name is specified in Factor 2. The program will write the new record to the file directly from the data structure. The Result Field must be blank if Factor 2 contains a record format name. If an indicator is specified in positions 56–57, the indicator will be turned on if the WRITE does not execute successfully.

Control Level Indicators	Indicators	Factor 1	Operation Name	Factor 2	Result Field	Resulting Indicators		
7–8	9–17	18–27	28–32	33–42	43–53	54–55	56–57	58–59
optional	optional	blank	WRITE	required	optional	optional	required	required

Figure 14-12   WRITE operation summary

⊟ *IN Indicator Key Word

RPG III and RPG/400 enable you to access, refer to, and manipulate most indicators in a manner similar to the way that data fields are accessed. This indicator access is done by means of the *IN array and the *INxx key word.

▸ **The *IN Array**   RPG III and RPG/400 contain a predefined array consisting of 99 one-position elements. Each of these elements represents one of the 99 general-purpose indicators. The 99 elements of the *IN array can only contain the values zero or one. A value of zero in an *IN array element specifies that the associated indicator is off, and a value of one specifies that the indicator is on. If any value other than zero or one is placed in an element of the *IN array, the result of using the indicator referenced by the element is unpredictable. You can use the array elements *IN,01 through *IN,99 as input fields in a data record, as output fields, or in any operation in which array elements can be used.

▸ **The *INxx Data Field** The *INxx data field is a predefined, one-position alphameric data field in which xx represents any RPG III or RPG/400 indicator except indicator 1P. Like the elements in the *IN array, the *IN data field can be used in any place that a one-position field is valid. *INxx cannot, however, be used in a SORTA operation.

Figure 14-13 shows the use of the *IN array. In example 1, the MOVEA operation on line 01 saves the settings of indicators 11–25 by moving the contents of *IN,11 through *IN,25 into a 15-position area named HOLD. After the program executes the SUBRT1 subroutine, the MOVEA operation on line 03 restores the original setting of the 15 saved indicators. You can use this technique in a large program that requires the use of more than 99 general-purpose indicators. By saving a set of indicators prior to execution of a subroutine, the same indicators can be used to represent different conditions within the subroutine.

Example	Line	Form Type	Indicators	Factor 1	Operation	Factor 2	Result Field Name	Length	Decimal Positions	Comments
1	01	C			MOVEA	*IN,11	HOLD	15		SAVE 11-25
	02	C			EXSR	SUBRT1				
	03	C			MOVEA	HOLD	*IN,11			RESTORE 11-25
	04	C*								
2	05	C			MOVEA	'ØØØØØ'	*IN,36			SET OFF 36-4Ø
	06	C		35	ADD	SWITCH	X	2	Ø	X-IND TO SET ON
	07	C			MOVE	'1'	*IN,X			SETON ONE IND.
	08	C	36		EXSR	SUB36				36-4Ø
	09	C	37		EXSR	SUB37				
	10	C	38		EXSR	SUB38				EXECUTE ONE
	11	C	39		EXSR	SUB39				SUBROUTINE
	12	C	4Ø		EXSR	SUB4Ø				
	13	C								

Figure 14-13 Use of the *IN array

In example 2, the MOVEA operation on line 05 turns indicators 36–40 off by moving zeros into *IN,36 through *IN,40. The SWITCH field, used on line 06, contains a value from 1 through 5. This value, when added to 35, determines which of the five indicators must be turned on. The MOVE operation on line 07 turns on the indicator specified by the value in X. Lines 08–12 cause one of the five possible subroutines to be executed, depending on which indicator was turned on by the ADD and MOVE operations.

*ALL Key Word

Recall that RPG contains two key words, *BLANK and *ZERO, which can generate a group of blanks or zeros that can be used for comparing or to clear a data field. In addition, RPG III and RPG/400 contain the *ALL key word. The key word *ALL'x' generates a series of the character or characters that are specified within the apostrophes. If multiple characters appear within the apostrophes, the result field will contain multiple repetitions of the characters. Figure 14-14 on the next page shows the result of two MOVE operations using the *ALL key word.

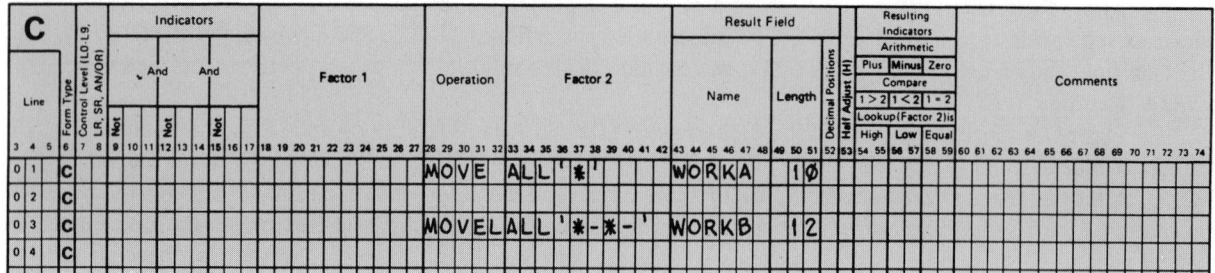

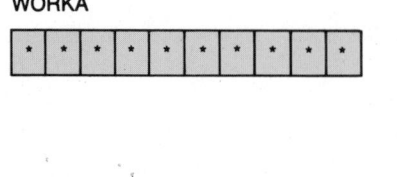

WORKA

WORKB

Figure 14-14   Use of the *ALL key word

*HIVAL and *LOVAL Key Words

*HIVAL and *LOVAL are used to load a field with either the highest or the lowest values possible in the character set used by the computer. These key words are similar to the HIGH-VALUE and LOW-VALUE figurative constants in COBOL. Which characters are generated by these key words depends on the data class of the result field that is to contain the values. Figure 14-15 shows the values that are generated by using *HIVAL and *LOVAL with numeric and alphameric data fields. Note that these examples are based on IBM System/38 and AS/400 architecture. If you are using a different computer, the results will depend on the internal data storage system used by your system.

Key Word	Data Class	Characters Generated
*HIVAL	Alphameric	Highest possible system value: hexadecimal 'FF'
*HIVAL	Numeric	All nines, positive sign
*LOVAL	Alphameric	Lowest possible system value: hexadecimal '00'
*LOVAL	Numeric	All nines, negative sign

Figure 14-15   *HIVAL and *LOVAL values

≡ IN CONCLUSION ≡

RPG is an extremely valuable tool in business application programming. Although RPG was originally designed as a simple tool for the conversion of punched card applications to early computers, it has grown through RPG II, RPG III, and RPG/400 into a sophisticated language for the solution of business data processing problems. RPG has become the primary programming language for IBM's midrange computer family and is now being used with microcomputers in many installations. You can expect that with the development of RPG/400 and the inclusion of RPG in IBM's System Application Architecture that the use of RPG-based programming will continue to expand.

REVIEW QUESTIONS

1. What is a database?
2. List three advantages gained from the use of externally described files.
3. What is a subfile?
4. Describe the processing that occurs when a CALL operation is executed.
5. What is the difference between logical deletion of a record by marking the record with a delete code and the deletion of a record by using the DELET operation?
6. What operations take place when an EXFMT operation is executed?
7. What is represented by each element of the *IN array?
8. What would be in HOLD1, a ten-position alphameric field, after the contents of *ALL' + –' is moved into it?

RPG Coding Checklist
& Programming Standards

RPG CODING CHECKLIST

This list of common problems is meant to help you avoid some of the errors that students are likely to make. If you use this list carefully as an aid to desk checking before you key your program into the system, it will help to eliminate some of these popular mistakes.

Some items in this list refer to RPG functions you may not yet know. Simply bypass them until these areas make sense to you. This list is based on IBM's version of RPG, and some items may not apply to other versions of the language.

General Items

1. Specification sequence must be H, F, E, L, I, C, and O.
2. Enter the form type (position 6) of the specification if the entry utility does not enter it for you when you enter a program.
3. Do not describe unused areas of the input and output records.
4. Any given field should be described only once, whether on the Input, Extension, or Calculation Specifications forms.
5. Comment lines must have an asterisk (*) in position 7.

Control Specifications

1. The Control specification should be the first specification in the program.
2. Be sure to use the correct program identification (positions 75–80) for the program. Depending on the version of RPG and the compiler functions you choose, an incorrect entry can cause the object program to be generated with an unexpected name.

File Description Specifications

1. File names (positions 7–14) must be left-justified.
2. File names (positions 7–14) must begin with an alphabetic character.
3. File type (position 15) must be I, O, C, U, F, or D.
4. File designation (position 16) is not used with output-only files.
5. If block length (positions 20–23) is used, it must be an exact multiple of record length.
6. Record length (positions 24–27) for disk files must match the record length of the file.
7. If multiple printer files are used, each must have a different overflow indicator (positions 33–34).
8. Be sure to use the extension code (position 39) when describing a preexecution time table, preexecution time array, or record address file.
9. If indexed (keyed) files are used, be sure that the Key Field Start Location entry (positions 35–38) and the Length of Key Field entry (positions 29–30) match the format of the file.
10. The Device entry (positions 40–46) and the Symbolic Device entry (positions 47–52, if used) must be valid for the system and the input/output device being used.

File Extension Specifications

1. The time of table or array loading is determined by which entries are used. Use the proper entries for the type of table or array you are describing.
2. The names of tables accessed by the LOKUP operation must begin with the letters TAB.
3. If alternating compile time tables or arrays are described, the data for them must be set up in alternating form at the end of the program.
4. Compile time tables and arrays are placed at the end of the source program and each is preceded by an ** record (positions 1–2).
5. Compile time tables and arrays must appear at the end of the program in the sequence that they are described in the File Extension Specifications.

Input Specifications

1. The first specification must be a record description entry.
2. Record description (positions 7–42) and field description (positions 43–70) must not appear on the same line.
3. File names must not be those of output files.
4. File names and field names must be left-justified.
5. Record description entries should have a Sequence entry (positions 15–16).
6. The alphabetic Sequence entry ND (positions 15–16) should not be used because of possible conflict with an AND entry in positions 14–16. The alphabetic Sequence entry DS is reserved for use with data structures.
7. Field location (positions 44–51) must be within the record length established in the file description specification.
8. The maximum length of a numeric field is 15 for zoned-numeric (30 in RPG/400), 8 for packed-decimal (16 in RPG/400), and 4 for binary.
9. The number of decimal positions in a numeric field cannot exceed the length of the field.
10. The maximum length of an alphanumeric field is 256.
11. Field names (positions 53–58) must begin with an alphabetic character.
12. The field indicators PLUS (positions 65–66) and MINUS (positions 67–68) must not be used with alphanumeric fields.

Calculation Specifications

1. All detail time calculations must precede all total time calculations.
2. All subroutines must appear at the end of the calculations.
3. Operation codes must be left-justified in the Operation area (positions 28–32) and spelled correctly.
4. Field names and literals must be left-justified in the Factor areas (positions 18–27, and 33–42).
5. Alphanumeric literals must be enclosed in apostrophes; numeric literals must not.
6. Rules for field definition are the same as for the Input Specifications form.
7. Move and compare operations work differently with numeric and alphanumeric data. Be sure you understand the rules or check the manual.
8. Most operations prohibit the use of one numeric factor and one alphanumeric factor. Be sure you know which operations permit mixed data classes. The most common errors of this type involve the use of the COMP and LOKUP operations.
9. Arithmetic operations must use numeric data fields or numeric literals as factors. However, some versions of RPG permit alphanumeric result fields.
10. The COMP, SETON, SETOF, and LOKUP operations require the use of a resulting indicator (positions 54–55, 56–57, and 58–59). The CHAIN and READ operations usually use one.
11. Resulting indicators (positions 54–59) must not be used with BEGSR, DEBUG, EXCPT, EXSR, and GOTO.
12. Conditioning indicators (positions 9–17) must not be used with BEGSR, ENDSR, and TAG operations.
13. The factors in a LOKUP operation must have the same length and data class.
14. MVR must immediately follow its related DIV operation, must have conditioning indicators identical to the preceding DIV operation, and must not be used if the result of the DIV operation was half-adjusted.
15. Calculation resulting indicators (positions 54–59) are not reset until the same calculation is performed again. Be especially careful when a COMP operation is conditioned by the result of a previous COMP.
16. No general-purpose indicator should be used to represent more than one condition.
17. Output exception record names must not be duplicates of field names.

Output Specifications

1. The first specification must be a record description entry.
2. Each record description entry must have a Type entry (position 15).
3. Record descriptions (positions 7–37) and field descriptions (positions 23–70) must not appear on the same line.
4. A file name must be that of an output, update, full-procedural, or combined file.
5. All file and field names used must have been previously defined in the program or be reserved RPG key words.
6. File and field name must be left-justified.
7. The end position (positions 40–43) of field must not exceed the record length.
8. Editing may be used only with numeric fields.
9. With the exception of the floating dollar sign and asterisk fill, edit codes (position 38) and edit words (positions 45–70) are not compatible.
10. Constants and edit words must be left-justified and enclosed in apostrophes.
11. The editing of numeric data usually causes a field to consume more space in the output record than the defined field length. Calculate the additional space needed to prevent the overlap of output fields.

12. Normally, editing is done only to printed reports. If you want to edit output data to any other medium, stop and reconsider. You are probably wrong.
13. The Blank After entry (position 39) causes a field to be cleared as soon as the data has been transferred to the output medium. If the same field is used more than once as output, be sure to blank-after only on the last processed entry.
14. If multiple printer files are used and page numbering is required, each must use a different Page Number field (PAGE, PAGE1, PAGE2, etc.).
15. Space and Skip enteries can be used only with printed output files.

RPG PROGRAMMING STANDARDS

These standards will help train you in good programming practices, comparable to industry standards. Although every computer installation has its own set of standards, the standards presented here are typical of those found in data processing departments. You must remember that these standards are not language rules but are uniform methods of handling programming situations. Their purpose is to make programming less an individual art and more a standardized science. Some standards apply in every case; for others there are exceptions that must be judged from experience.

Purpose

To develop RPG programs that conform to accepted programming and documentation practices.

Policy on Standards

1. All programs will follow these RPG Programming Standards unless exceptions are made by the data processing instructor.
2. These standards will remain in force until changed by the data processing instructor.
3. Deviation from these standards must be approved by the data processing instructor.

Program Documentation

1. When a program is submitted for grading, all the following items will be included:
   a. Source program listing
   b. Printer layout form for printed output
   c. Printed report(s) produced by the program
   d. File dumps of disk files produced by the program
   e. Input record layouts
   f. An RPG indicator summary, included in the source program if the program uses more than three general-purpose indicators
   g. A listing of any procedure or job control statements, if they are needed to execute the program
   h. Any special machine setup or operation instructions required to execute the program
2. Standard identifying information will appear at the front of each source program as a series of comments. This identifying information will include programmer name, student number (if available), program name, date submitted, and a brief description of program purpose.
3. The general format of report headings should include
   a. Program I.D. to left of run date
   b. Run date in upper left
   c. Report title in center
   d. Page number in upper right

⊟ Program I.D.

1. This six-character identification is formatted as follows:

   XXXYYZ

   Where XXX represents the three initials of the programmer; YY is the chapter number from which the program was taken and Z is the practice program number in the chapter.

⊟ Indicator Usage

1. Do not assign indicators in a random manner. Group general-purpose indicators according to their use in the program. A typical grouping of indicators is as follows:

Range	Type	Where Defined
01–19	Record-identifying indicator	Input positions 19–20
20–39	Field indicators	Input positions 65–70
40–79	Resulting indicators	Calculations positions 54–59
80–98	Error conditions in program	
99	Invalid input data type	Input positions 19–20

2. Use OF for the overflow indicator if only one overflow indicator is needed.
3. Avoid using H1–H9 whenever possible.
4. Do not use an indicator to represent more than one condition.
5. Eliminate unreferenced indicators from diagnostic listing whenever possible.

⊟ Control Specification

Leave the Core Size to Execute entry blank on the RPG Header record when compilation and execution size are the same, unless this causes an error message to be generated.

⊟ File Description Specifications

1. First statements will contain standard program identification documentation as listed under item 3 of Program Documentation.
2. On the File Description Specifications form, a file name used for a disk file should be the same as the file label whenever possible.

File Extension Specifications

1. Precede each definition with a comment describing the table or array being defined.
2. For tables:
   a. Be as descriptive as possible in assigning table names.
   b. Each set of related table input records should use the alternating format with an argument preceding its corresponding function. Only one argument/function pair should be in each record.
   c. When practical, allow for extra entries at the end of a table.
   d. Define tables as sequential. The look up operation will be faster for entries not found in table.
3. For arrays: One-position names should be avoided. However, when using a one-position array name, be as descriptive as possible; for example, do not use X and Y for rate of pay and for deductions – use R and D.

Line Counter Specifications

Do not use this specification unless ordinary page overflow (66-line page, overflow on line 60) is not used.

Input Specifications

1. Precede each Record Definition entry (positions 7–43) with a comment record stating the name and record identification code (if applicable) of the input record.
2. Do not define a field as numeric (entry in position 52) unless the field is used in calculations or is edited on the output specifications.
3. Eliminate unreferenced field names from diagnostic listing, where possible.
4. Enter field names in ascending sequence by their record location.
5. If multiple record types exist in an input file, code an entry at the end of the input specifications to identify all invalid data records.
6. Use OR lines rather than multiple record I.D. lines when possible. Do not describe unnecessary input records.

Calculation Specifications

1. Describe each group of logically related calculations with comment statements.
2. Bypass calculations for all nonpertinent records by branching to the label END located at the end of detail calculation specifications.
3. Subroutines should be described and separated by comment statements.
4. A routine used more than once should be executed as a closed subroutine using EXSR.
5. Move the reserved field name *ZERO (or *ZEROS) to set a numeric field to a value of zero. Set alphameric fields to spaces by moving the reserved field name *BLANK (or *BLANKS). If these reserved names are not available, an alternate method is to clear numeric fields by using the Z-ADD to add zero to the field or to clear alphameric fields by moving a blank field of equal or larger size into it.
6. Some versions of RPG require that both factors be used in all arithmetic operations even if the arithmetic is being performed between a single factor and the result field. If you are using this type of compiler, use the same field name in factor 1 and in the result field.
7. For comparing a field with more than six constants, use a table lookup operation or an array processing loop rather than separate literals.

Output Specifications

1. Precede each Record Definition entry (positions 7–37) with a comment statement describing the record.
2. The general sequence will be heading, detail, total, and exception. All output pertaining to one file should be grouped.
3. The record definition for the first heading line causes a skip to the first normal print line prior to printing.
4. Use edit codes (position 38) rather than edit words whenever possible.
5. When designing printed reports, include the run date (UDATE), program I.D., and page number as part of the page headings. Usually, program I.D. appears in the top-left corner and page number in the top-right corner.

RPG Debugging Techniques

Because no two RPG application programs are identical, there can be no hard and fast rules governing program debugging. The debugging of each program must be based on the purpose of the program, the types of specifications included in the program, and the particular entries used in the specifications. This appendix presents generalized guidelines that can be used during the debugging process.

Debugging should proceed in two phases. First, all syntax errors that were detected during the compilation should be resolved. Note that the preceding sentence says that these errors should be *resolved*, not eliminated. In some cases, several of which have been mentioned in the text, you cannot eliminate warning messages. When the rules of RPG syntax prevent you from eliminating a warning message, you have no choice but to leave the condition that caused the warning in the program.

After all error messages have been resolved, you can proceed to the testing for and resolution of logic errors in the program. If, during the correction of logic errors, your correction causes additional error messages to be generated during a compilation, you must resolve these syntax errors before continuing with logic testing.

Syntax Error Resolution Guidelines

1. Resolve all terminal errors before attempting to resolve warning errors. Because a terminal error causes the specification containing the error to be ignored by the compiler, a terminal error often causes the erroneous generation of a warning error.
2. Resolve errors starting with the first error specification in the program and proceed sequentially from top to bottom. Usually, an error in the description of a file or field results in the generation of an error message for every specification that references the same file or field. If you attempt to resolve errors from the bottom up, you may encounter error messages on specification lines that appear correct. Often these lines *are* correct. For example, if a terminal error is made in an input field specification, RPG ignores the field definition. Because RPG has not defined the field, any reference to the field in either the calculation or the output specifications is marked as an error, an attempt to use an undefined field.

3. Remember that the rules of RPG sometimes cause warning messages when, in fact, no error exists. For example, RPG arithmetic operations determine the required length of a result field based on the rules of mathematics. If the result field defined in the program is short, according to these rules, a warning message is generated to remind you that the result field may not be long enough. If, based on the program specifications, you have used the correct length for the result field, you can, in most cases, ignore this warning. Do not, however, fall into the familiarity-breeds-contempt trap. Do not automatically ignore these messages. Every RPG compiler message should be checked, regardless of how often the message appears.

═══ LOGIC ERROR RESOLUTION GUIDELINES ═══

The detection and correction of logic errors is based on a careful comparison of the actual program output with the expected program output. This comparison should be based on three questions:

▸ Did the program fail to produce any output that it should have produced? Are any fields, records, or files missing?

▸ Did the program produce any output that it should not have produced? Were any unneeded fields, records, or files produced?

▸ Is all program output correct? If the correct fields, records, and files were produced, do they contain the proper data based on your analysis of the input test data?

To detect and correct all logic errors, you must "play computer." Because neither the computer nor the compiler can detect logic errors, you must do the job yourself. Analyze each input record, perform all calculations that the program should perform, and determine the output that the program should have generated. Compare your output data with the data that the program generated and determine if they are the same. If your forecasted output data exactly matches the program output for the first input record, the last input record, and several other input records in the file, the program is probably functioning correctly.

If the program accumulates final totals, you must add up at least one full column of numbers to determine if the final total is correct. If the program performs control breaks, verify the control break totals for at least two of each type of control break.

When testing a program that produces a disk output file or updates an existing disk file, you must work with printouts of the output disk file. For an update program, you must use "before" and "after" printouts of the file to determine exactly what updating was performed on the file. By comparing the before printout with the update request file printout, you can determine exactly what actions should have been performed on the file. By comparing your forecast of the file update with the actual updated file (the after printout), you can determine if the update was performed correctly. Remember that when testing an update program you must restore the master file to its original condition before every test.

DEBUGGING AIDS

The DEBUG Operation

The DEBUG operation, summarized in Figure B-1, is used to provide information about the status of a program while the program is executing. The DEBUG operation, which can be placed at any point in the calculations, produces one or more output records, generally printed lines, that list all the indicators that are on when the DEBUG is performed and, optionally, show the contents of the data field named in the Result Field area of the DEBUG operation. Figure B-2 shows an output report that contains the result of a DEBUG operation.

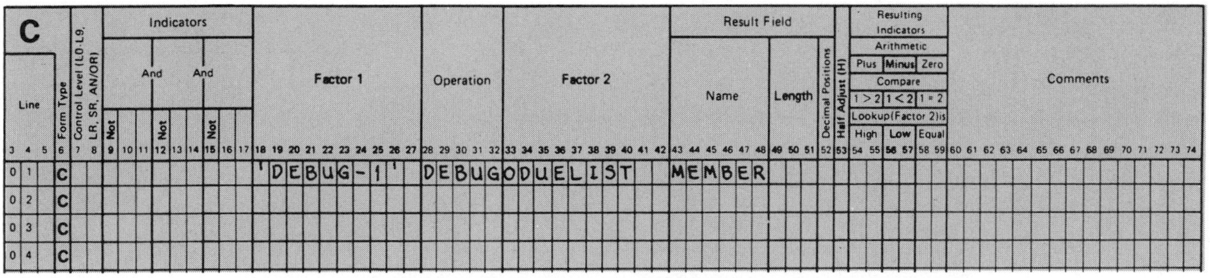

DEBUG Operation Summary

The DEBUG operation will cause one or more records containing information about the current status of the program to be written. As many DEBUG operations as are needed can be specified in the program calculations. Factor 1 may contain a literal or field name used to identify the output DEBUG records. Factor 2 may contain the name of the output file to which the DEBUG statements are to be written. If Factor 2 is not used, the DEBUG statements are written to the system console. The Result Field may contain the name of a data field, array, or table, the contents of which will be written as part of the DEBUG output. All DEBUG statements will produce a list of all indicators that are on when the DEBUG is executed.

Control Level Indicators	Indicators	Factor 1	Operation Name	Factor 2	Result Field	Resulting Indicators		
7–8	9–17	18–27	28–32	33–42	43–53	54–55	56–57	58–59
optional	optional	optional	DEBUG	optional	optional	blank	blank	blank

Figure B-1   DEBUG operation summary

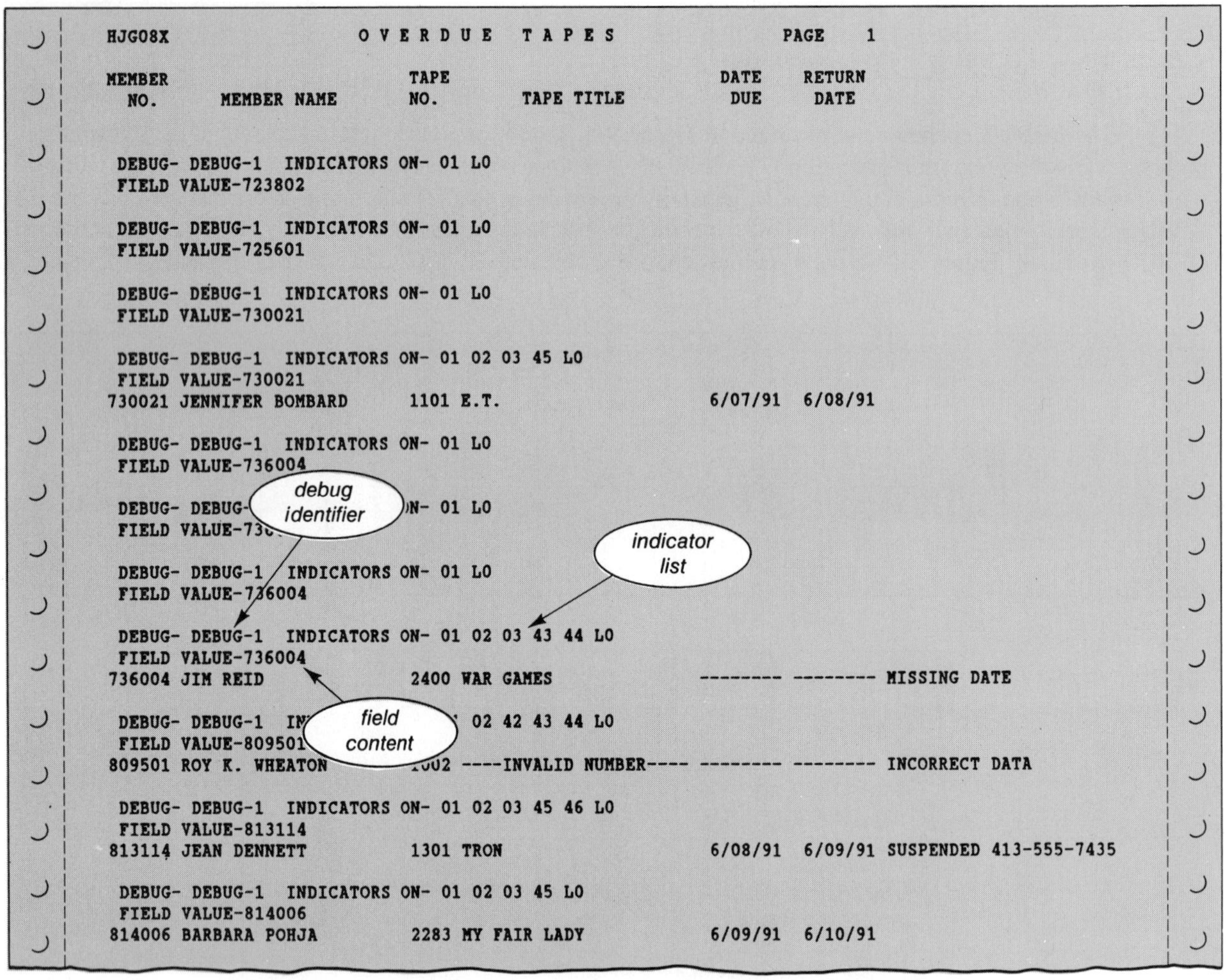

```
HJG08X                    O V E R D U E   T A P E S                 PAGE    1

MEMBER                         TAPE                           DATE    RETURN
  NO.      MEMBER NAME         NO.       TAPE TITLE            DUE      DATE

 DEBUG- DEBUG-1  INDICATORS ON- 01 LO
 FIELD VALUE-723802

 DEBUG- DEBUG-1  INDICATORS ON- 01 LO
 FIELD VALUE-725601

 DEBUG- DEBUG-1  INDICATORS ON- 01 LO
 FIELD VALUE-730021

 DEBUG- DEBUG-1  INDICATORS ON- 01 02 03 45 LO
 FIELD VALUE-730021
730021 JENNIFER BOMBARD       1101 E.T.                       6/07/91  6/08/91

 DEBUG- DEBUG-1  INDICATORS ON- 01 LO
 FIELD VALUE-736004

 DEBUG- DEBUG-                N- 01 LO
 FIELD VALUE-73

 DEBUG- DEBUG-1  INDICATORS ON- 01 LO
 FIELD VALUE-736004

 DEBUG- DEBUG-1  INDICATORS ON- 01 02 03 43 44 LO
 FIELD VALUE-736004
736004 JIM REID               2400 WAR GAMES                  -------- -------- MISSING DATE

 DEBUG- DEBUG-1  IN              02 42 43 44 LO
 FIELD VALUE-809501
809501 ROY K. WHEATON           002 ----INVALID NUMBER---- -------- -------- INCORRECT DATA

 DEBUG- DEBUG-1  INDICATORS ON- 01 02 03 45 46 LO
 FIELD VALUE-813114
813114 JEAN DENNETT           1301 TRON                       6/08/91  6/09/91 SUSPENDED 413-555-7435

 DEBUG- DEBUG-1  INDICATORS ON- 01 02 03 45 LO
 FIELD VALUE-814006
814006 BARBARA POHJA          2283 MY FAIR LADY               6/09/91  6/10/91
```


Figure B-2 DEBUG operation output

Compare this output report with the sample program output shown in the Chapter 8 sample program. The report shown in Figure B-2 is the same report, produced by the same program. The only difference is the addition of the DEBUG operation specified in Figure B-1, which was added as the last program calculation. Note that the DEBUG operation produced two output lines for each input record read by the program.

The first DEBUG line contains the identifier DEBUG-1. If multiple DEBUG operations are used in a program, you can avoid confusion by specifying a different Factor 1 identifier for each. The first DEBUG line also contains a list of all indicators that were on when the DEBUG operation was performed. This list can be used to tell you the exact status of all program indicators at any point in the program. The second DEBUG line contains the name of the field specified in the Result Field area of the DEBUG, in this example the Member Number field.

To use DEBUG operations in a program, you must specify a 1 in position 15 of the program's H specification. If you do not specify a 1 in position 15, all DEBUG operations in the program will be ignored by the compiler.

Debugging Templates

The debugging template is another aid to the debugging process. It makes the compilation listing easier to read by enabling you to see the format of each type of specification line as you look at the listing.

The IBM RPG Debugging Template is a foldable plastic card on which are printed the field headings for each of the RPG specifications forms. The fields are printed in the same size as a standard compilation listing, that is, ten characters per inch. When needed, the debugging template is placed under the line of the listing that you are reviewing. By aligning the specification form character on the debugging template with the corresponding letter on the compilation listing, you can identify every field on the compilation listing line. Figures B-3 and B-4 show the use of the debugging template to review a calculation specification and an output specification.

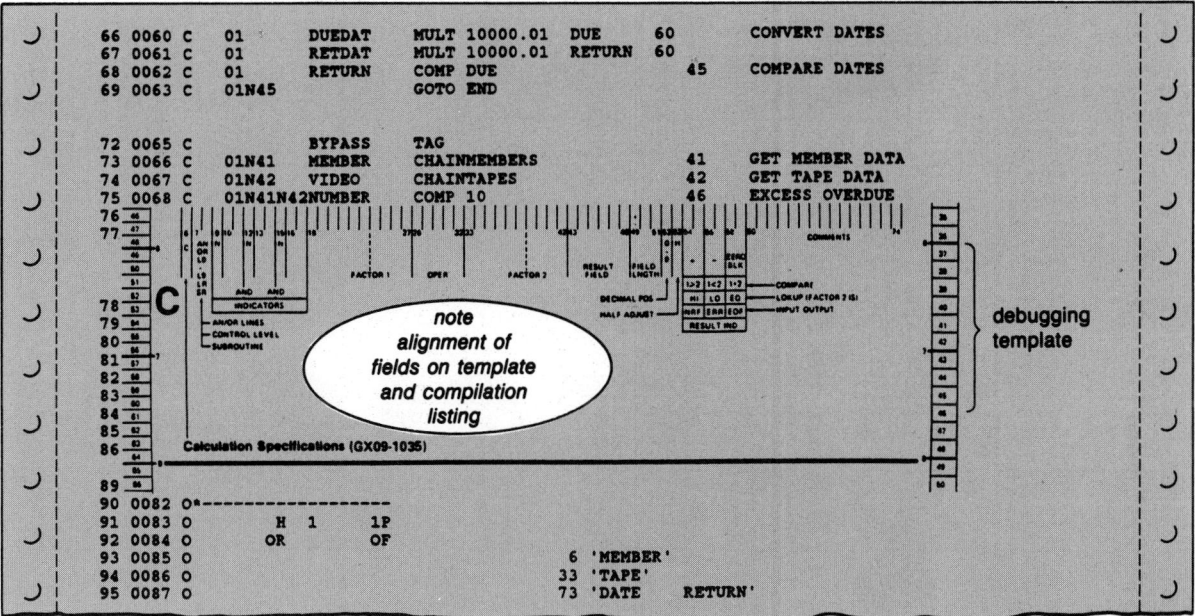

Figure B-3   Debugging template use

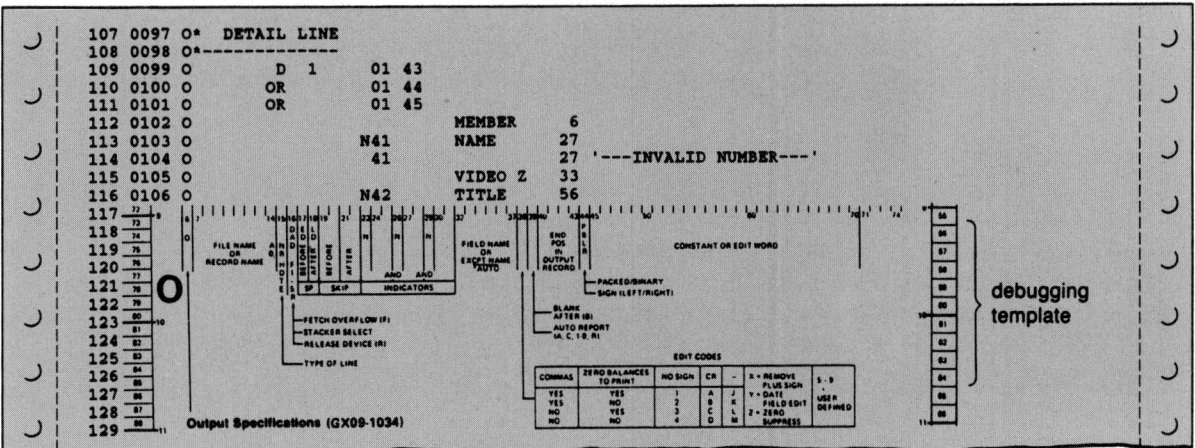

Figure B-4   Debugging template use

Another type of template is the RPG-rule series manufactured by HEXCO, Inc. of Hunt, Texas. An RPG-rule is a stainless steel ruler, approximately 15 1/2 inches long by 2 inches wide, on which are engraved templates of all RPG specifications forms. As Figure B-5 shows, an RPG-rule contains additional information such as internal machine data codes. Although the HEXCO RPG-rule is more expensive than the IBM Debugging Template, it has the advantage of durability; and because it is made of steel, it holds listings flat on a desk or work surface while you work with them.

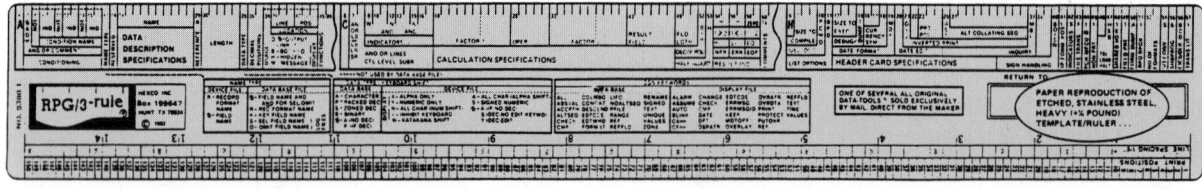

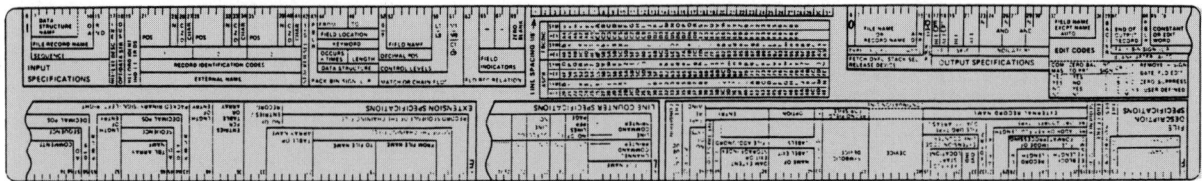

Figure B-5   HEXCO RPG/3-rule

RPG Operation Code Summary

ADD Operation Summary: Non-3X Format

The value of the field or literal specified in Factor 2 is added to the value of the field or literal specified in Factor 1. The sum is placed in the Result Field. Neither Factor 1 nor Factor 2 is changed by the ADD operation.

ADD Operation Summary: 3X Format

The value of the field or literal specified in Factor 2 is added to the value of the field or literal specified in Factor 1. The sum is placed in the Result Field. Neither Factor 1 nor Factor 2 is changed by the ADD operation. If Factor 1 is not specified, Factor 2 is added to the Result Field, and the sum is placed in the Result Field.

BEGSR Operation Summary

The BEGSR operation marks the beginning of an internal subroutine. The name used in Factor 1 must be unique. Each subroutine must be identified by a separate name. The name used in a BEGSR operation cannot be the same as the name used with a TAG operation.

CABxx Operation Summary (RPG III and RPG/400)

The CABxx operation compares the value in Factor 1 with the value in Factor 2, testing for the condition specified in the xx position of the operation code. If the tested condition is found, the program branches to the TAG statement specified in the Result Field area. If the condition is not found, the program continues with the next operation. Resulting indicators may be specified. If no Result Field entry is made, the CABxx operation will set resulting indicators and continue with the next operation.

CALL Operation Summary (RPG III and RPG/400)

The CALL operation causes the program named by the data field, literal, or array element specified in Factor 2 to be executed. In addition, Factor 2 may contain the name of the library that contains the program. If both a library and a program name are specified, the library name must be specified first, followed by the program name. The two names must be separated by a slash (LIB/PROG). If a literal is specified in Factor 2, the length of the literal cannot exceed eight characters. If a field name is used in Factor 2, the field length cannot exceed 21 characters. An indicator may be used in positions 56–57 to be set on for an error return from the CALLed program. An indicator may be used in positions 58–59 to show that the CALLed program ended with indicator LR on. Factor 2 may contain the name of a parameter list used to communicate information between the current program and the CALLed program.

CASxx Operation Summary

The CASxx operation compares the value in Factor 1 with the value in Factor 2, testing for the condition specified in the xx position of the operation code. If the tested condition is found, the program executes the subroutine named in the Result Field area. A CAS operation with no condition specified as part of the operation is equivalent to an EXSR operation. Resulting indicators may be specified as part of a CASxx operation.

CHAIN Operation Summary

The CHAIN operation reads one record from a keyed sequence access path file. Factor 1 may be either a literal or a field name containing the key field value of the record to be read. Factor 2 is the name of the file containing the record. The Result Field is not used. Positions 54 and 55 should contain an indicator that is turned on if the record identified in Factor 1 is not present in the file. If no indicator is specified in positions 54 and 55 and the requested record is not found, the program stops but can be restarted.

CLOSE Operation Summary (RPG III and RPG/400)

The CLOSE operation closes a file by making it unavailable to the program for further processing unless an OPEN operation is executed for the file. A program may contain more than one CLOSE operation for the same file. If a CLOSE is executed for a file that has already been closed, the operation is ignored. Factor 2 must contain the name of the file to be closed. If the key word *ALL is specified in Factor 2, all program files are closed at once. If an indicator is specified in positions 56–57, the indicator will be turned on if the CLOSE operation does not complete successfully.

COMP Operation Summary

The COMP operation compares the value in Factor 1 with the value in Factor 2. Both factors must have the same data class. Fields are automatically aligned prior to the comparison. At least one resulting indicator must be specified. Comparison results are as follows:

High	Factor 1	> Factor 2
Low	Factor 1	< Factor 2
Equal	Factor 1	= Factor 2

DEBUG Operation Summary

The DEBUG operation will cause one or more records containing information about the current status of the program to be written. As many DEBUG operations as are needed can be specified in the program calculations. Factor 1 may contain a literal or field name used to identify the output DEBUG records. Factor 2 may contain the name of the output file to which the DEBUG statements are to be written. If Factor 2 is not used, the DEBUG statements are written to the system console. The Result Field may contain the name of a data field, array, or table, the contents of which will be written as part of the DEBUG output. All DEBUG statements will produce a list of all indicators that are on when the DEBUG is executed.

DEFN Operation Summary

The DEFN operation, when used with *LIKE in Factor 1 defines a field based on the description (length and data class) of another field. Factor 2 must contain the name of the field on which the definition is based. The Result Field must contain the name of the new field being defined. Positions 49–51 may be used to change the length of the new field. A plus sign (+) in position 49 indicates a field length increase, a minus sign (–) indicates a decrease in length. When this feature is used, positions 50 and 51 must contain the number of positions being added to or deleted from the field. The number of decimal positions cannot be changed.

DELET Operation Summary (RPG III and RPG/400)

The DELET operation deletes a record from an update data file. Factor 1 must contain the key that identifies the record to be deleted. Factor 2 must contain the name of the update file that contains the record. An indicator specified in positions 54–55 will be turned on if the record to be deleted is not found in the file. An indicator specified in positions 56–57 will be turned on if the DELET operation does not delete the record. This can happen if the user requesting the record deletion does not have proper security access to the data file.

DIV Operation Summary: Non-3X Format

The value in the field or literal specified in Factor 1 is divided by the value in the field or literal specified in Factor 2. The quotient is placed in the Result Field. Neither Factor 1 nor Factor 2 is changed as a result of the DIV operation. If Factor 1 is zero, the quotient is zero. Factor 2 cannot be zero; if it is, the program stops immediately.

DIV Operation Summary: 3X Format

The value in the field or literal specified in Factor 1 is divided by the value in the field or literal specified in Factor 2. The quotient is placed in the Result Field. Neither Factor 1 nor Factor 2 is changed as a result of the DIV operation. If Factor 1 is zero, the quotient is zero. Factor 2 cannot be zero. If it is, the program stops immediately. If Factor 1 is not specified, the Result Field is divided by Factor 2, and the quotient is placed in the Result Field.

DO Operation Summary

The DO operation causes a series of operations to be performed a fixed number of times. The associated END statement marks the end of the series. Factor 2 specifies the number of times the group is performed. If Factor 2 is blank, the group is executed one time. The Result Field can be used to specify the name of a numeric index field. If no name is used, the DO operation generates an internal index. Factor 1, if used, specifies a starting index value. If Factor 1 is not used, the starting value is 1. Factor 2 of the associated END statement can be used to specify an increment value to be used with the index. If no entry is made the increment is 1.

DOUxx Operation Summary

The DOUxx operation causes a series of operations to be performed one or more times. The associated END statement marks the end of the series. The series of operations will be repeated until the relationship between the Factor 1 and Factor 2 entries specified in the xx positions of the DOUxx operation code is met. After the condition is met, the program will continue with the operation that follows the END statement.

DOWxx Operation Summary

The DOWxx operation causes a series of operations to be performed one or more times. The associated END statement marks the end of the series. The series of operations will be repeated until the relationship between the Factor 1 and Factor 2 entries specified in the xx positions of the DOWxx operation code is met. After the condition is no longer met, the program will continue with the operation that follows the END statement.

ELSE Operation Summary

The ELSE operation may be used with the IFxx operation. If used, ELSE marks the beginning of the group of operations to be performed if the condition tested by the IFxx operation is not found. Control level indicators may be specified if the ELSE operation is part of a total time IFxx operation. The control level indicators, if used, are for documentation only and do not affect the program.

END Operation Summary

The END statement marks the end of a CASxx, DO, DOUxx, DOWxx, or IFxx group of operations. The Factor 2 entry can be used only if the END terminates a DO group. In this circumstance, Factor 2 contains the increment value to be applied to the DO group index.

ENDSR Operation Summary

The ENDSR operation marks the end of an internal subroutine. The ENDSR operation causes the program to return to the calculation operation following the EXSR statement that caused the subroutine to be executed. Factor 1 may contain a name that is branched to by a GOTO operation within the subroutine.

EXCPT Operation Summary: Non-3X Format

The EXCPT operation causes output records to be written during either detail or total calculation time under control of the object program rather than the RPG fixed logic cycle. The EXCPT operation can be conditioned by indicators in positions 7–17. The output records must be identified by the entry E in the Type area, position 15.

≡ EXCPT Operation Summary: 3X Format

The EXCPT operation causes output records to be written during either detail or total calculation time under control of the object program rather than the RPG fixed logic cycle. The EXCPT operation can be conditioned by indicators in positions 7–17. The output records written must be identified by the entry E in the Type area, position 15. Factor 2 can contain an EXCPT name, which identifies one or more exception output lines, all of which contain the same name in positions 32-37 of the exception record identification line. An EXCPT name cannot be the same as a file or field name used in the program.

≡ EXFMT Operation Summary (RPG III and RPG/400)

The EXFMT operation is valid only when used with workstation files and is a combination of a WRITE followed by a READ operation to the same file. The EXFMT operation is valid only when used with externally described, full-procedural, combined workstation files. Factor 2 must contain the name of the format that is to be written and then read. An indicator may be specified in positions 56-57 to indicate that the EXFMT operation did not complete successfully. When this happens, input fields controlled by the format are not changed by the EXFMT operation.

≡ EXSR Operation Summary

The EXSR operation causes the program to execute an internal subroutine. Any number of EXSR statements can reference the same subroutine. After all operations in the subroutine are executed, the program returns to the calculation that follows the EXSR operation. The EXSR can be conditioned by indicators in positions 7–19. If no indicators are used, the subroutine is always executed.

≡ FORCE Operation Summary

The FORCE operation overrides the RPG fixed logic cycle and specifies the name of the file from which the next record is to be read. FORCE can only be used with primary or secondary files. A FORCE operation may be specified only during detail time, not at total time. If more than one FORCE operation is executed, all but the last will be ignored. Factor 2 must specify the name of the file from which the next record is to be read.

≡ GOTO Operation Summary

The GOTO operation causes a branch to another instruction. The instruction being branched to must be immediately preceded by a TAG operation. The GOTO may cause a branch to a previous or succeeding operation. A GOTO may not be used to branch from a detail time operation to a total time operation or from a total time operation to a detail time operation. Factor 2 must contain the name of the operation to which the branch is being made. This same name must be used in Factor 1 of the TAG operation to which the branch is being made. Factor 1 and the Result Field are not used by the GOTO operation.

≡ IFxx Operation Summary

The IFxx operation enables a series of operations to be performed if the condition specified in the xx portion of the operation exists between the Factor 1 and Factor 2 entries. If the condition exists, all operations between the IFxx and the following ELSE or END statement will be performed. If the condition does not exist, the program will proceed to the operation following the associated ELSE or END.

LOKUP Operation Summary

The LOKUP operation performs a search for a specific element in a table or array. The table or array to be searched is named in Factor 2. Factor 1 is the search argument. If table lookup is being performed, the function table can be named in the Result Field area. If array lookup is being performed, the Result Field area cannot be used. At least one resulting indicator must be used with the LOKUP operation.

MOVE Operation Summary

The MOVE operation transfers data from the Factor 2 field to the Result Field, one character at a time, starting with the rightmost position of the fields. The contents of Factor 2 are not changed. If Factor 2 is longer than the Result Field, the leftmost characters of Factor 2 are not transferred. If Factor 2 is shorter than the Result Field, the leftmost characters of the Result Field are not changed.

MOVEA Operation Summary

The MOVEA operation transfers data from Factor 2 to the Result Field, starting with the leftmost position of each. At least one array must be used by the MOVEA operation. Element boundaries within the array or arrays being used are ignored, and data transfer proceeds, one character at a time, from left to right. If Factor 2 and the Result Field area are not the same length, the MOVEA operation stops when the shorter of the two areas has been completely used. The rules of data movement are similar to those of the MOVEL operation.

MOVEL Operation Summary

The MOVEL operation transfers data from the Factor 2 field into the Result Field, one character at a time, starting with the leftmost position of the fields. The contents of Factor 2 are not changed. If Factor 2 is longer than the Result Field, the rightmost characters of Factor 2 are not transferred. If Factor 2 is shorter than the Result Field, the rightmost characters of the Result Field are not changed.

MULT Operation Summary: Non-3X Format

The contents of the field or literal specified in Factor 1 are multiplied by the contents of the field or literal specified in Factor 2. The product is placed in the Result Field. Neither Factor 1 nor Factor 2 is changed by the MULT operation.

MULT Operation Summary: 3X Format

The value in the field or literal specified in Factor 1 is multiplied by the value in the field or literal specified in Factor 2. The product is placed in the Result Field. Neither Factor 1 nor Factor 2 is changed by the MULT operation. If Factor 1 is not specified, the Result Field is multiplied by Factor 2, and the product is placed in the Result Field.

MVR Operation Summary

The MVR operation causes the remainder created by the preceding DIV operation to be moved into the field specified as the Result Field. Factors 1 and 2 must be blank. MVR cannot be used if the quotient of the preceding DIV operation was half-adjusted.

≣ OPEN Operation Summary (RPG III and RPG/400)

The OPEN operation makes the file named in Factor 2 available for processing by the program. The file named in Factor 2 cannot be a primary, secondary, or table file. If an indicator is specified in positions 56–57, the indicator will be turned on if the OPEN operation does not complete successfully. If a file is to be opened for the first time by an OPEN statement, rather than the RPG fixed logic cycle, the file description specification must contain an entry UC (user control) in positions 71–72. If an OPEN statement is executed for a file that is already open, an error will occur.

≣ READ Operation Summary

The READ operation causes the next record in a demand file to be accessed during the calculation portion of the RPG fixed logic cycle. If the demand file is a workstation file, the READ operation causes the display format to be read after either the Enter key or a valid Command key is pressed. In addition, the READ operation can be used to perform program-controlled reading of an arrival sequence disk file during the calculation portion of the logic cycle.

≣ READE Operation Summary

The READE operation retrieves the next sequential record from the full procedural file named in Factor 2 if the key of the record matches the contents of the field or literal specified in Factor 1. If the key field value does not match, the required indicator specified in positions 58–59 is turned on, and no record is retrieved. This same indicator is also turned on when the end of the Factor 2 file is reached. If an indicator is specified in positions 56–57, the indicator will be turned on if the READE operation does not complete.

≣ READP Operation Summary

The READP operation reads the prior record from a full procedural file. Factor 2 must contain the name of the file to be read. An indicator must be specified in positions 58–59. This indicator will be turned on when no prior record exists in the file (beginning of file, or BOF, condition).

≣ SETLL Operation Summary

The SETLL operation enables the programmer to set a lower limit or starting point for the processing of a full-procedural or demand (RPG II only) file. The Factor 1 field name or literal must contain the lower limit value being set. Factor 2 must contain the name of the file for which the lower limit is being set. RPG III and RPG/400 permit the following indicator usage:

Positions 54-55	Factor 1 greater than highest file key value
Positions 56-57	Error in SETLL operation execution
Positions 58-59	Record key in Factor 2 file equals Factor 1 value

≣ SETOF Operation Summary

The SETOF operation turns off all indicators specified in positions 54–55, 56–57, and 58–59. At least one resulting indicator must be specified in a SETOF operation.

SETON Operation Summary

The SETON operation turns on all indicators specified in positions 54–55, 56–57, and 58–59. At least one indicator must be specified as part of a SETON operation.

SORTA Operation Summary

The SORTA operation sorts the elements of the array named in Factor 2 into either ascending or descending sequence based on the entry (A or D) in position 45 of the extension specification for the array. If no sequence entry was made on the Extension Specifications form, the array is sorted in ascending sequence. If an alternate array was specified on the same extension specification, the alternate array is not sorted by the SORTA operation.

SUB Operation Summary: Non-3X Format

The value of the field or literal specified in Factor 2 is subtracted from the value of the field or literal specified in Factor 1. The difference is placed in the Result Field. Neither Factor 1 nor Factor 2 is changed by the SUB operation. Subtracting a field from itself can be used to set a field to a value of zero.

SUB Operation Summary: 3X Format

The value of the field or literal specified in Factor 2 is subtracted from the value of the field or literal specified in Factor 1. The difference is placed in the Result Field. Neither Factor 1 nor Factor 2 is changed by the SUB operation. Subtracting a field from itself can be used to set a field to a value of zero. If Factor 1 is not specified, Factor 2 is subtracted from the Result Field, and the difference placed in the Result Field.

TAG Operation Summary

The TAG operation names an operation being branched to by a GOTO operation. Factor 1 contains the name assigned to the operation, which must be the same as the name used in Factor 2 of the associated GOTO operation. The same name must not be used for two or more TAG operations. Factor 2 and the Result Field are not used by the TAG operation. The indicators area (positions 9–17) must be blank.

TIME Operation Summary

The TIME operation retrieves the system time and can also, if specified, retrieve the system date. The system time of day is based on the 24-hour clock. The Result Field must be a numeric field, either 6 or 12 positions long, with no decimal places. If the Result Field is 6 positions long, the TIME operation will place the system time in the field in HHMMSS format, where HH = hour, MM = minute, and SS = second. If the Result Field is 12 positions long, it will contain the system time in positions 1–6 and the system date, in MMDDYY format, in positions 7–12.

UPDAT Operation Summary (RPG III and RPG/400)

The UPDAT operations modifies the last record read from an update file. No input or output operation may be performed between the read and UPDAT operations. Factor 2 must contain the name of the file or record format (required if an external file description is used) to be updated. The Result Field must contain a data structure name if a file name is specified in Factor 2. The program will write the update record to the file directly from the data structure. The Result Field must be blank if Factor 2 contains a record format name. If an indicator is specified in positions 56–57, the indicator will be turned on if the UPDAT does not execute successfully.

WRITE Operation Summary (RPG III and RPG/400)

The WRITE operation adds a new record to a file. Factor 2 must contain the name of a file or record format (required if an external file description is used). The Result Field must contain a data structure name if a file name is specified in Factor 2. The program will write the new record to the file directly from the data structure. The Result Field must be blank if Factor 2 contains a record format name. If an indicator is specified in positions 56–57, the indicator will be turned on if the WRITE does not execute successfully.

XFOOT Operation Summary

XFOOT adds the contents of all the elements of the numeric array named in Factor 2 and places the sum in the Result Field. Factor 2 must be a numeric array. Factor 1 cannot be used.

Z-ADD Operation Summary

Factor 2 is added to a field of zeros. The sum is then placed into the Result Field. Factor 1 is not used.

Z-SUB Operation Summary

Factor 2 is subtracted from a field of zeros, and the result is placed into the Result Field. This result is the negative of the Factor 2 value. Factor 1 is not used.

System/3X & AS/400 Program Development Aids

Every computer system that supports a version of the RPG language contains some program development software that aids you in the entry and compilation of your programs. Although it is impossible to list every program development aid available on all computer systems, the aids used by the three current members of the System/3X family are typical of the program development aids found on most computer systems.

System/36

The System/36 supports two program entry utilities, the Source Entry Utility (SEU) and the Development Support Utility (DSU). SEU is a line editor that enables you to enter or modify one source program specification at a time. DSU is a full screen editor that displays and allows you to work with several lines at once. SEU, because it is a part of the System/36 operating system software, is available on all System/36 computers. DSU is an extra-cost item and is not, therefore, available on all System/36 machines.

The System/36 RPG II compiler, accessed by the command RPGC, can be used to compile your program and either generate a paper listing of the compilation or return the compile listing to your terminal. The Screen Design Aid (SDA) is used to develop display formats and the RPG II code needed to use these formats in an interactive programming application.

The System/36 supports two general-purpose RPG II program development commands. The first of these, RPGP, displays a general-purpose programming menu on your terminal screen. From this menu you can enter a new source program, modify an existing program, and compile an RPG II source program. The second command, RPGONL, enables you to enter or modify a source program and then immediately compile the source code. For further information on these two program development utilities, see Chapter Three of the System/36 reference manual *Programming in RPG II*.

System/38

The System/38 supports a series of program development aids that are similar to those on the System/36. System/38 SEU, however, is different from SEU on the System/36. Whereas System/36 SEU is a line editor, System/38 SEU is a full screen editor that can display as many as 12 lines of source code at once.

The System/38 compiler command is CRTRPGPGM (CReaTe RPG ProGram). This command causes a compilation menu to be displayed that shows the compiler options available.

AS/400

The Application System/400 uses a single tool, the Programming Development Manager (PDM), to access all program development tools available on the system. The PDM menu, accessed by the STRPDM (STaRt Programming Development Manager) command, provides you with an interface to the SEU, DFU, and SDA utilities as well as the AS/400 RPG compilers. The AS/400, under the direction of PDM, can compile programs written in RPG II, RPG III, or RPG/400.

RPG Fixed Logic
Flowcharts & Indicator Timing

═══ FLOWCHARTS ═══

This appendix contains the complete RPG fixed logic flowchart, which includes the flowcharts for general logic (Figure E-1), matching record logic (Figure E-2), overflow logic (Figure E-3), look-ahead logic (Figure E-4), and RPG exception/error handling logic (Figure E-5). Note that these flowcharts are based on the latest version of RPG, which is RPG/400. Earlier language versions may not contain all the features on these flowcharts.

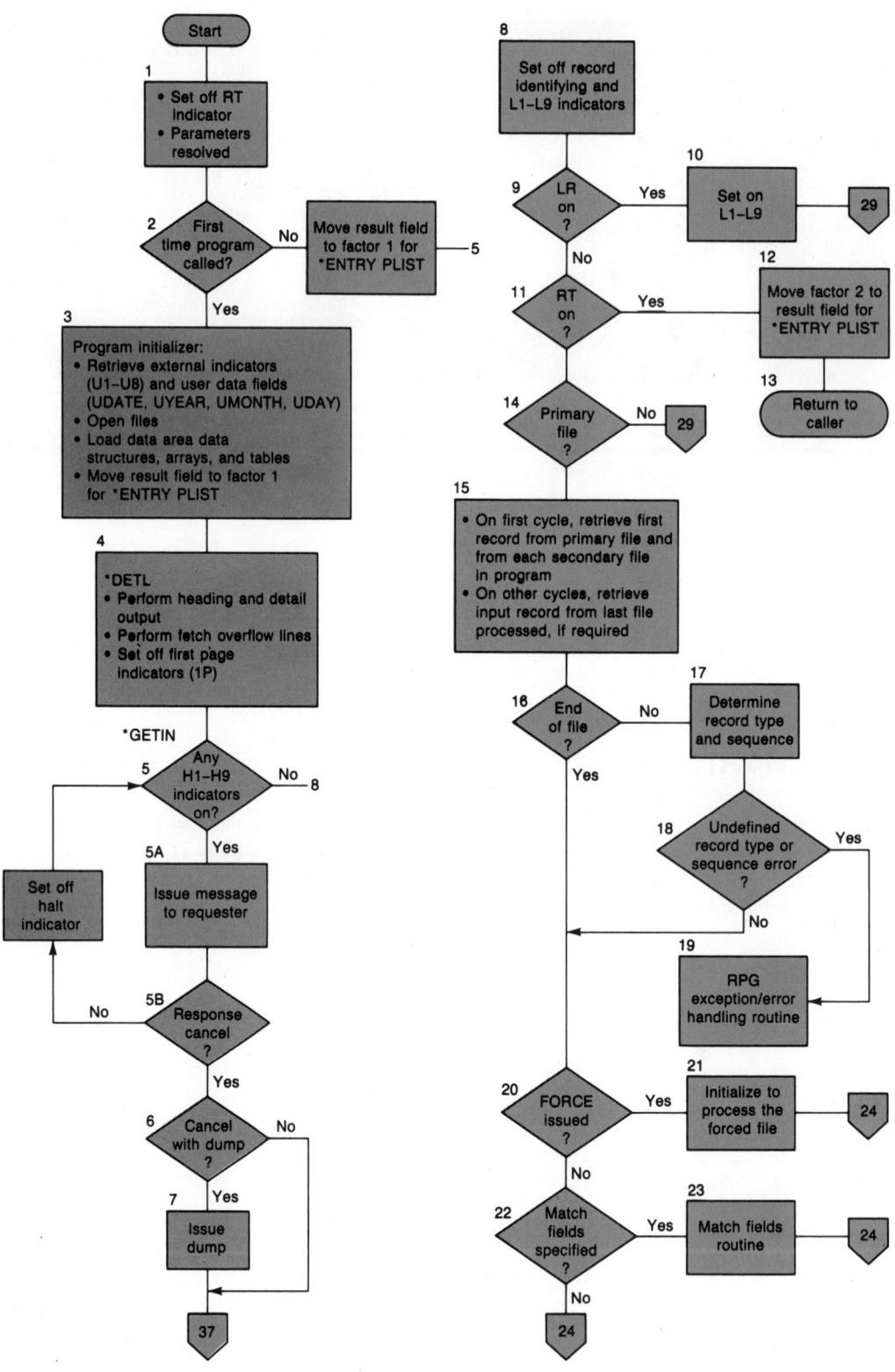

Figure E-1 (A)   RPG general logic flow

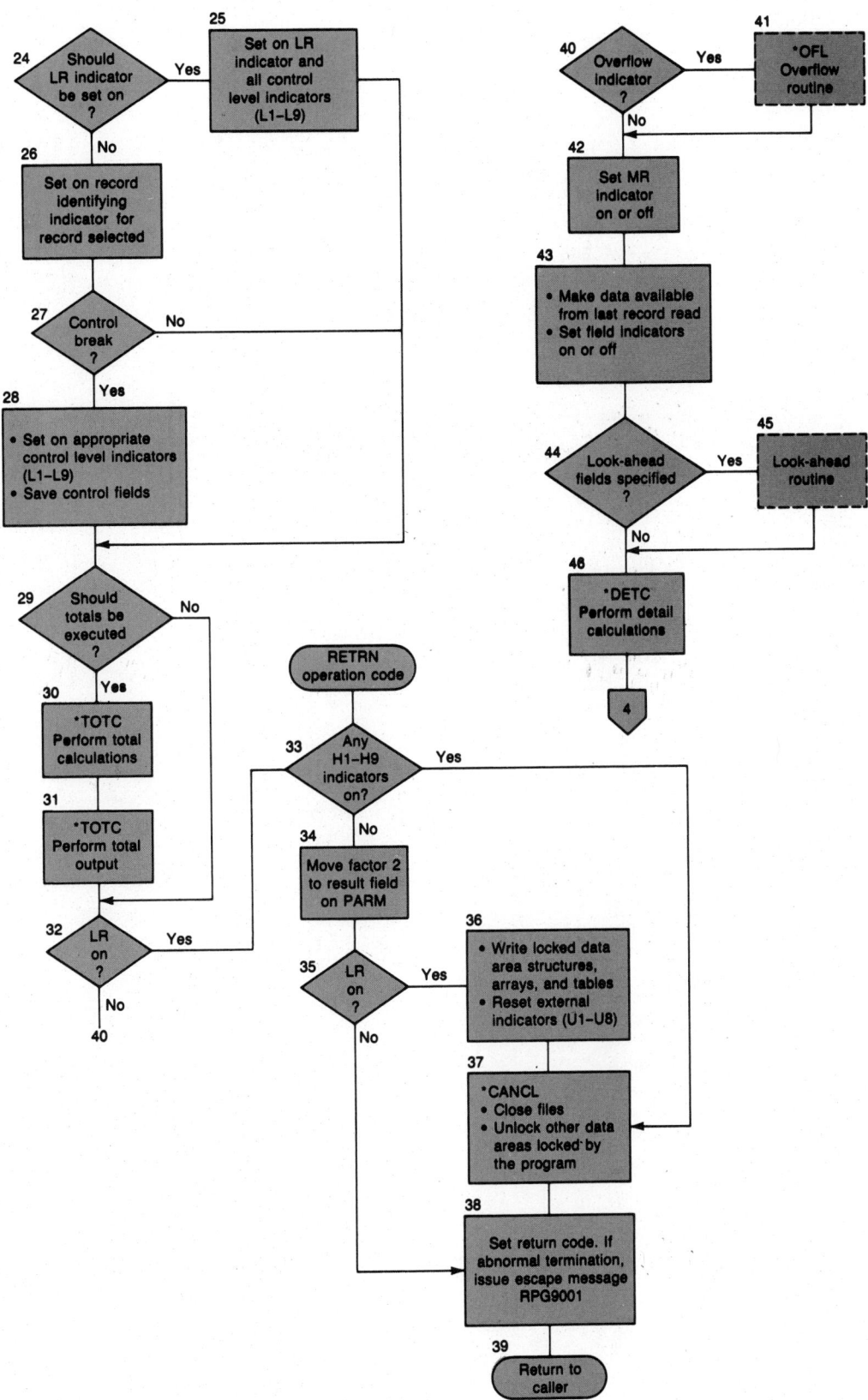

Figure E-1 (B)

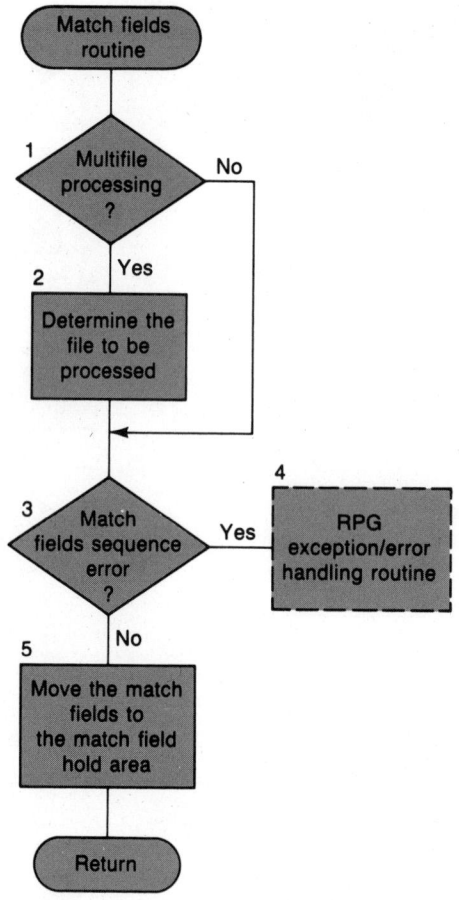

Figure E-2 RPG matching record logic flow

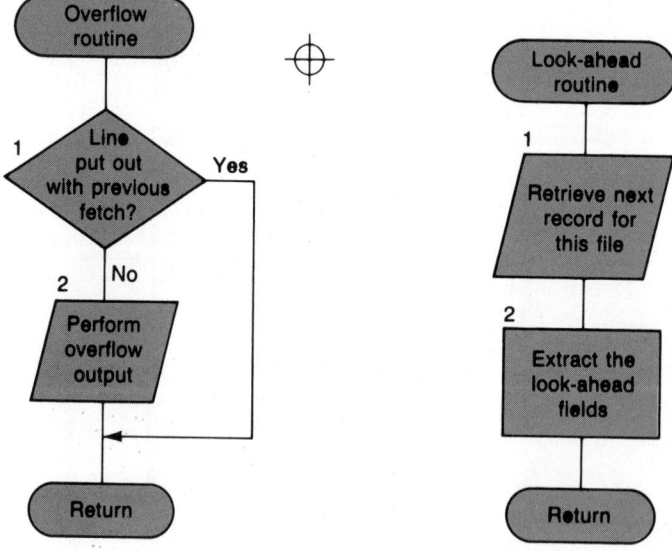

Figure E-3 RPG overflow logic flow   Figure E-4 RPG look ahead logic flow

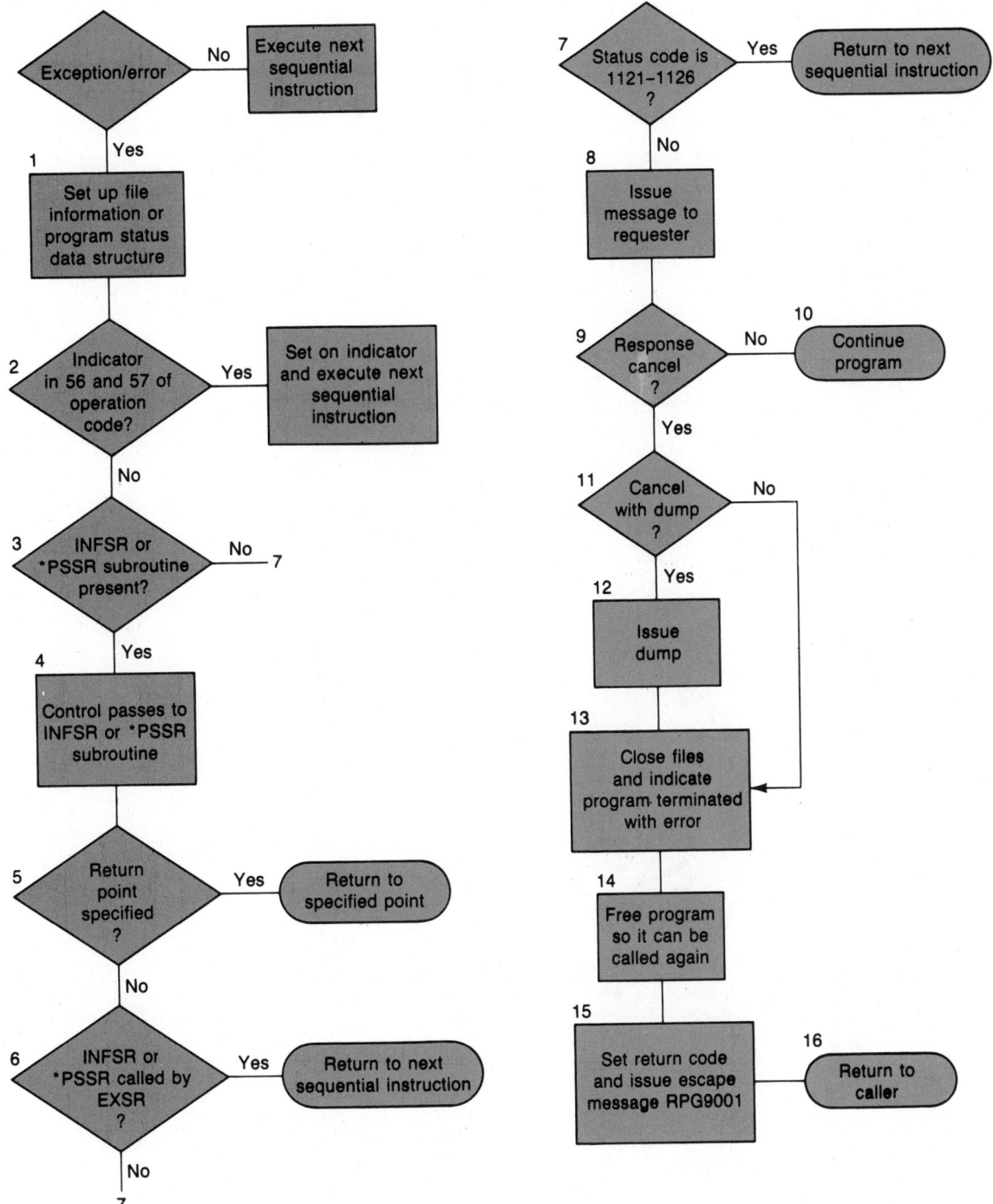

Figure E-5   RPG exception/error handling logic flow

≡ INDICATOR USE AND TIMING ≡

Figure E-6 shows the conditions under which each type of indicator is set on or off within an RPG program.

Indicator Type	Set On	Set Off
Overflow	When overflow line is reached	After heading and detail lines are completed
Record identifying	After primary/secondary or full-procedural record has been read	Before primary/secondary record is read during next processing cycle
Control level	When control field value changes	At end of next detail cycle
Field indicator	When input field meets tested condition	Before next test of same input field
Resulting indicator	When calculation is performed and tested condition exists	When calculation using same resulting indicator is performed
Function key	When corresponding function key is used	By SETOF operation
H1–H9	As specified by programmer	When SETOF by programmer or if continue option is used by operator
1P	At beginning of program before first input record is read	At beginning of program before first input record is read
LR	After all primary and secondary records are processed or by programmer	By programmer
MR	If the contents of all primary and secondary match fields are equal	After all calculations and output operations are completed for all records of the matching group

Figure E-6 When indicators are set on and off

Figure E-7 shows the location within an RPG program at which each type of indicator can be defined and used.

	User Defined	01–99		H1–H9	L1–L9	LR		OA–OG, OV
D	Overflow indicator F specification, positions 33–34							X
E	Record identifying I specification, positions 19–20	X		X	X	X		
F	Control level I specification, positions 59–60				X			
I								
N	Field indicators I specifications, positions 65–70	X		X				
E								
D	Resulting indicators C specifications, positions 54–59	X		X	X			X

	RPG Defined		IP			LR	MR	
	Internal indicators		X			X	X	

		01–99	1P	H1–H9	L1–L9	LR	MR	OA–OG, OV
U	Field record relation I specification, positions 63–64	X		X	X		X	
S	Control Level C specification, positions 7–8				X	X		
E	Conditioning indicators C specification, positions 9–17	X		X	X	X	X	X
D	Output indicators O specification, positions 23–31	X	X	X	X	X	X	X

Figure E-7   Indicator definition and use summary

APPENDIX F

Additional Topics

FILE DESCRIPTION SPECIFICATIONS

Full Procedural Files

A **full procedural** file is a data file that combines the functions of both chained and demand files. A full procedural file does not use the RPG fixed logic cycle but is read and written under complete control of the RPG program calculations. Although you may use full procedural files in RPG II, you must use them in RPG III and RPG/400 in place of chained and demand files. RPG III and RPG/400 do not permit the File Designation entries C or D, for chained and demand files. All the operations you have learned that use chained and demand files can be used with Full procedural files. Figure F-1 shows the definition of a full procedural file. Note the entry F in position 16, the File Type area.

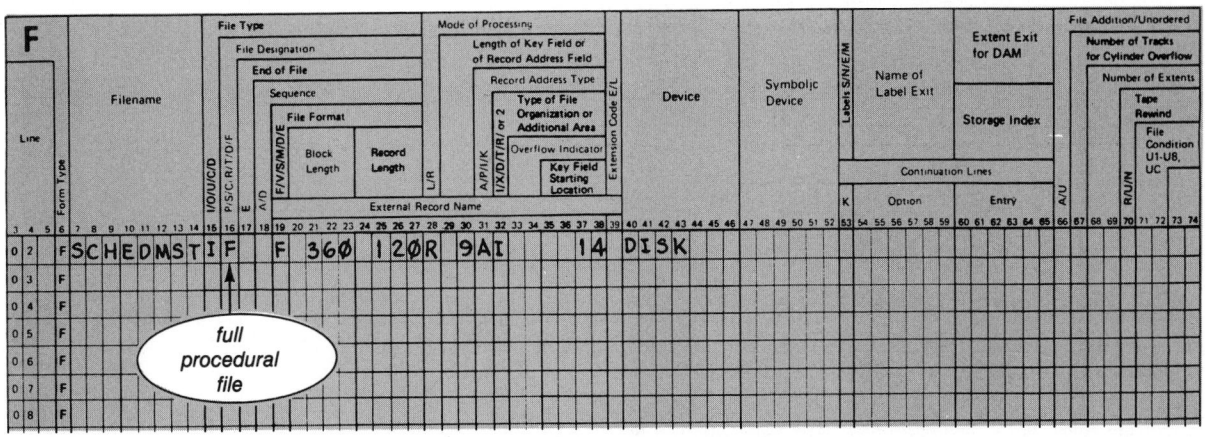

Figure F-1   Full procedural file description

LINE COUNTER SPECIFICATIONS

The **Line Counter Specifications form** was originally designed for use with older printers, which used a paper tape loop to control the movement of forms through the printer. This paper tape loop contained special punched holes that identified specific points on the form, such as the first printing line and the overflow line. IBM printers do not use these tape loops to control form movement because current versions of RPG use a default for the size of the form and the overflow line. IBM RPG assumes that the form is 11 inches (66 lines) long and that the overflow line is line 60 of the form.

The Line Counter Specifications form is used only if the form is not of standard length or if the program requirements demand that the overflow line be changed from line 60 to some other point on the form, as might be the case when special forms such as invoices or checks are printed. Versions of RPG supported by vendors other than IBM may require the use of the Line Counter Specification form. Your instructor or data center manager can provide you with the specific requirements for line counter specification for your computer. Figure F-2 shows the Line Counter Specifications form.

Line Counter Specifications

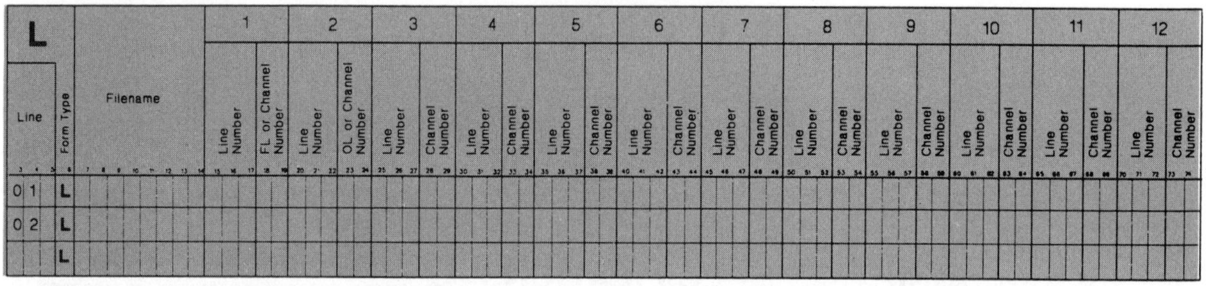

L			1		2		3		4		5		6		7		8		9		10		11		12	
Line	Form Type	Filename	Line Number	FL or Channel Number	Line Number	OL or Channel Number	Line Number	Channel Number	Line Number	Channel Number	Line Number	Channel Number	Line Number	Channel Number	Line Number	Channel Number	Line Number	Channel Number	Line Number	Channel Number	Line Number	Channel Number	Line Number	Channel Number	Line Number	Channel Number
01	L																									
02	L																									
	L																									

Figure F-2 Line Counter Specifications form

Positions 7–14 (Filename) specify the name of the output report for which the default forms assignment must be changed. Positions 15–17 (Line Number area) specify the number of print lines available on the form. The entry in positions 15–17 must be in the range 2–112. A form cannot be one line long, and it cannot be longer than 112 lines. If an entry is made in positions 15–17, you must place FL in positions 18–19 (FL or Channel Number area) to specify that the default form length is being changed.

Positions 20–22 (Line Number area) specify the new overflow line number if the overflow line is being changed. Like the Form Length entry in positions 15–17, this entry must be in the range of 2–112. If an entry is made in positions 20–22, you must place OL in positions 23–24 (OL or Channel Number area) to specify that the default overflow line number is being changed.

A single line-counter specification may change the form length, the overflow line, or both. These changes apply only to the file named in positions 7–14, and do not effect any other output file. The remainder of the Line Counter Specifications form is not used in current versions of RPG II, RPG III, and RPG/400.

INPUT SPECIFICATIONS

Sequenced Multiple Record Types

In some programming applications, the data records in a control group must be in a specific sequence that is based on the record-identification code contained in each input record. Figure F-3 shows a series of input records in which each control group contains a master record (M in position 1), which may be followed by one or more time records (T in position 1). The time records are not required, and some master records are not followed by time records. The master record for employee 10050 is immediately followed by a series of time records for the same employee. As the figure also shows, the first record for the following control group (employee 17329) is a master record, which would be followed by a series of time records. Figure F-4 shows the input specifications needed to test for the proper sequence of records in each control group.

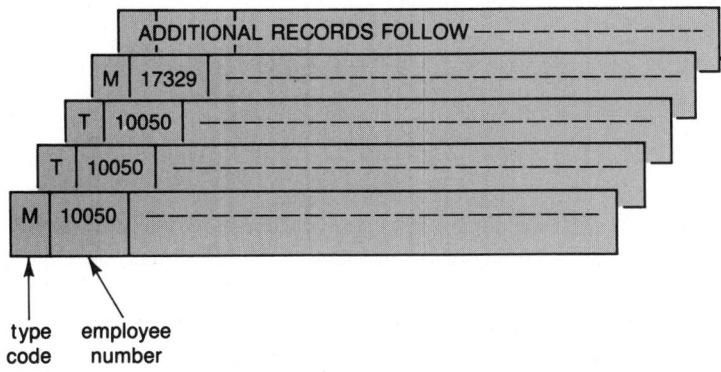

Figure F-3 Sequenced multiple record type file

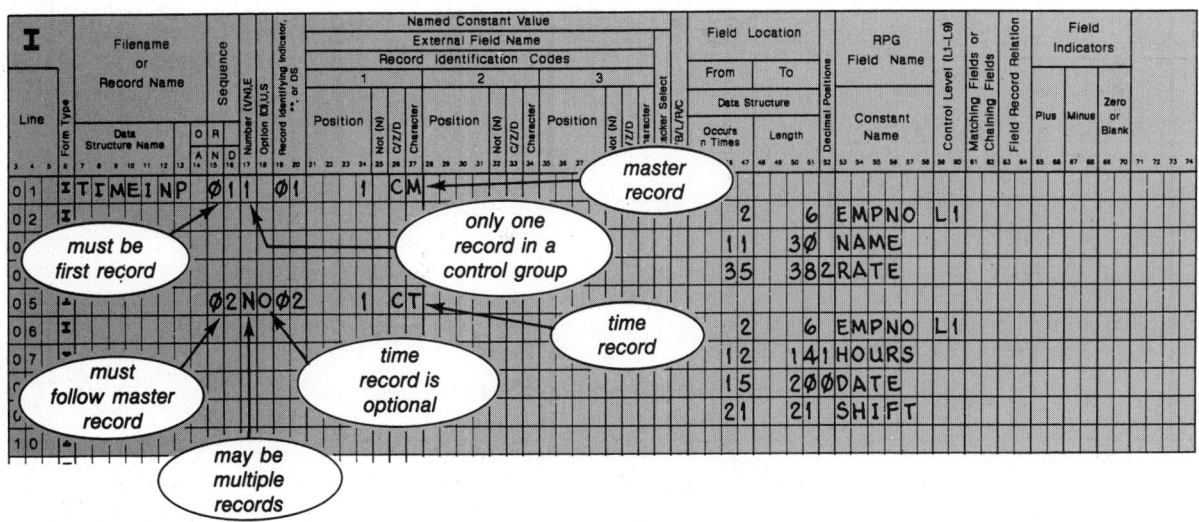

The input specifications show that the name of the file containing the master records and the time records is TIMEINP. In all previous programs, you entered alphabetic values in the Sequence area (positions 15–16) of the Input Specifications form to specify that the input records had no specific sequence. This program, however, contains numeric values in this area because the Sequence area is used to specify the sequence of records in a control group. A control group contains all the consecutive input records that have the same value in the control field. Note in Figure F-4 that the Employee Number field (EMPNO) is the L1 control field. As noted in Figure F-3, in each control group the master record must be first, followed by one or more time records. Enter the value 01 in the Sequence area to indicate that the master record must be the first record of each control group.

Enter the value 02 in the Sequence area of the time record description because the time records are the second record type in the control group. Whenever a numeric value is entered in the Sequence area on the Input Specifications form, the first value must be 01, and each additional value must be incremented in ascending order. If there were four types of records in each control group, they would require Sequence area values of 01, 02, 03, and 04.

When a numeric value is entered in the Sequence area, that is, when the input records must be in a given sequence in a control group, the program also uses the Number area (position 17) and the Option area (position 18).

The Number area is used to specify how many records of the defined type can be in a control group. The Number area must contain one of two possible entries. Enter the number 1 in position 17 if there is only one record of the defined type in each control group. Enter the letter N in position 17 if more than one record of this type may appear in the control group. Since there is only one master record for each control group, the value 1 has been entered in position 17 of the master record description.

Each master record in a control group can be followed by one or more time records. The time record contains the only other valid entry, the letter N in position 17. This entry indicates that if time records exist in the control group, there may be one or more time records following the master record.

As you read earlier, there must be a master record at the beginning of each control group. Whenever a record is required in a control group, you must leave the Option area, position 18, blank on the Input Specifications form. As Figure F-4 shows, position 18 is blank for the master record. The time records, on the other hand, need not always be present. If an employee did not work during the pay period, the file could contain a master record but no time records. When an input record is optional in a control group, enter the letter O in position 18 to specify that the record type is not required.

This example shows that a master record can occur in the file with no following time records but that it is not possible to have time records without a master record, because position 18 is blank for the master record, indicating that one must be present. If RPG detects that a required record type is not present, the program halts.

The record-identifying indicator specified for the master record and the time record are used in the same manner as has been done previously, that is, indicator 01 is turned on when the program reads a master record, and indicator 02 is turned on when the program reads a time record. These indicators can, of course, be tested in both the calculation and output specifications.

▤ Data Structures

A **data structure** is an area of computer memory made up of one or more fields called subfields. Data structures are used to

Define the same area of memory in two or more different ways.

Divide an input field into smaller fields so that the program can reference either the entire field or an individual subfield.

Reorganize input record fields so that they can be referred to more easily.

Data structures must be the last entries coded on the Input Specifications form. The following examples illustrate each of the three types of data structure use.

Define the Same Area in Different Ways   Figure F-5 shows a 55-position data structure that defines one area of memory in two ways. Positions 1–55 are defined as a sales record (SALREC), and positions 1–40 are defined as a return record (RETREC). The advantage gained by using data structures comes from the amount of memory needed to store the input data because a data structure redefines the same area of memory in different ways. This data structure requires only 55 positions of memory regardless of the number of separate records that are defined within it. If the SALREC and RETREC were defined as separate input records, the computer would require 95 positions of memory (40 + 55) to store the input data, almost twice the space needed for the data structure.

Figure F-6 shows the coding needed to describe the data structure. Note that the first line of the data structure entry (line 06) contains the entry DS in positions 19–20. This is a required entry that marks the beginning of data structure definition. The following entries define the subfields within the SALREC and RETREC data structures.

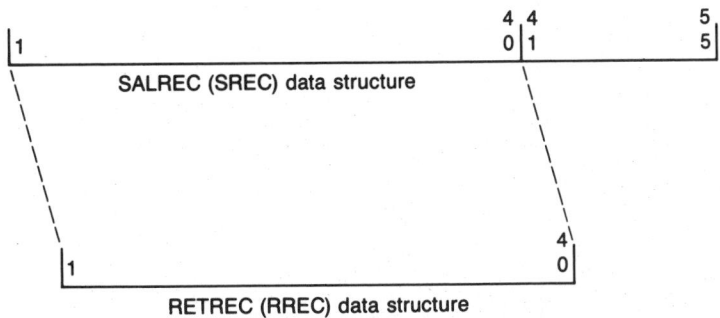

SALREC (SREC) data structure

RETREC (RREC) data structure

Figure F-5   SALREC /RETREC data structure

Line	Form Type	Filename or Record Name / Data Structure Name	Sequence	Number	Record Identifying Indicator or DS	Record Identification Codes	From	To	Dec	RPG Field Name / Constant Name
01	I	SALREC	AA	01		1 N C R				
02	I						1	55		SREC
03	I	RETREC	BB	02		1 C R				
04	I						1	40		RREC
05	I	*								
06	I				DS					
07	I	* SALES FIELDS								
08	I						1	55		SREC
09	I						1	5		SCODES
10	I						6	20		SALENO
11	I						21	35		ACCTNO
12	I						36	41	0	DATE
13	I						42	50	2	SAMT
14	I						51	55		BRNO
15	I	* RETURN FIELDS								
16	I						1	40		RREC
17	I						1	3		RCODES
18	I						4	18		ACCTNO
19	I						19	31		RETNO
20	I						32	40	2	RAMT

Figure F-6   Data structure code for the SALREC/RETREC data structure

▸ **Divide an Input Field into Smaller Fields**   Figure F-7 on the next page shows a data structure used to subdivide an input record field. The NAME field that is part of the PERSFILE record is 25 positions long. The data structure that follows the input record description defines three subfields for the NAME data structure. Note that this data structure contains a name in positions 7–12 of the first data structure line. When a data structure is used to define subfields within a field, the field name (in this example, NAME) is used to identify the data structure. The data structure name must be the same as the name of the field being divided into subfields.

I	Form Type	Filename or Record Name / Data Structure Name	O/R, AND	Number (1/N), E Option (O),U,S	Record Identifying Indicator, * or DS	Record Identification Codes 1 Position	Not (N)	C/Z/D	Character	Position 2	Not (N)	C/Z/D	Character	Position 3	Not (N)	C/Z/D	Character	Stacker Select / P/B/L/R/C	Field Location From / Occurs n Times	Field Location To / Length	Decimal Positions	RPG Field Name / Constant Name	Control Level (L1-L9)	Matching Fields or Chaining Fields	Field Record Relation	Plus	Minus	Zero or Blank
01	I	PERSFILE	AA	Ø1																		IDNO						
02	I																		1	1Ø		IDNO						
03	I																		11	35		NAME						
04	I																		3Ø	7Ø		ADDRES						
05	I	NAME		DS																								
06	I																		1	12		FIRST						
07	I																		13	13		MINIT						
08	I																		14	25		LAST						
09	I																											

Figure F-7   Data structure code for subdividing the NAME data structure

▸ **Reorganize Input Record Fields**   Figure F-8 shows the use of a data structure to reorganize the fields contained in an input record. The fields in the STUDENT record are in the following sequence: STUDNO, YOG, MAJOR, NAME, and GRPNT. The subfield sequence in the KEYST data structure is MAJOR, GRPNT, STUDNO, and YOG. As you can see, the input field NAME is not part of the data structure. The STDNT subfield includes all positions of the entire data structure, enabling you to use the entire data structure as a single field in calculation or output specifications.

I	Form Type	Filename or Record Name / Data Structure Name	O/R, AND	Number (1/N), E Option (O),U,S	Record Identifying Indicator, * or DS	Record Identification Codes 1 Position	Not (N)	C/Z/D	Character	Position 2	Not (N)	C/Z/D	Character	Position 3	Not (N)	C/Z/D	Character	Stacker Select / P/B/L/R/C	Field Location From / Occurs n Times	Field Location To / Length	Decimal Positions	RPG Field Name / Constant Name	Control Level (L1-L9)	Matching Fields or Chaining Fields	Field Record Relation	Plus	Minus	Zero or Blank
01	I	STUDENT	AA	Ø1		1		C	5	2	N	C	X															
02	I																		3	8		STUDNO						
03	I																		9	1ØØ		YOG						
04	I																		11	12		MAJOR						
05	I																		13	37		NAME						
06	I																		38	4Ø	2	GRPNT						
07	I	KEYST		DS																								
08	I																		1	2		MAJOR						
09	I																		3	5	2	GRPNT						
10	I																		6	11		STUDNO						
11	I																		12	13	Ø	YOG						
12	I																		1	13		STDNT						

Figure F-8   Data structure code for reorganizing fields

CALCULATION SPECIFICATIONS

A number of operations that can be specified on the Calculation Specifications form perform functions that can be useful in a given application. The following sections deal with operations that have not yet been covered in the text.

READE (Read Equal Key) Operation

In the coding example shown on line 01 of the READE operation summary (Figure F-9), the program reads the next sequential record in PROFILE and compares the key field value of the record with the value contained in RECKEY. If the two keys are not equal, the indicator specified in positions 58–59 is turned on. The READE operation requires that an indicator be entered in positions 58–59.

READE Operation Summary

The READE operation retrieves the next sequential record from the full procedural file named in Factor 2 if the key of the record matches the contents of the field or literal specified in Factor 1. If the key field value does not match, the required indicator specified in positions 58–59 is turned on, and no record is retrieved. This same indicator is also turned on when the end of the Factor 2 file is reached. If an indicator is specified in positions 56–57, the indicator will be turned on if the READE operation does not complete successfully.

Control Level Indicators	Indicators	Factor 1	Operation Name	Factor 2	Result Field	Resulting Indicators		
7–8	9–17	18–27	28–32	33–42	43–53	54–55	56–57	58–59
optional	optional	required	READE	required	optional	blank	optional	required

Figure F-9   READE Operation summary

READP (Read Prior Record) Operation

Although the READP operation is part of RPG II, RPG III, and RPG/400, the operation format is slightly different in RPG II. Figure F-10 shows the format of the READP operation. Note that although the Result Field area and positions 54–55 are optional in RPG III and RPG/400, these areas cannot be used and must be blank when the READP is used with RPG II. The READP operation reads the prior record from a full procedural data file. The prior record is the record that precedes the last record read by the normal RPG fixed logic cycle, a CHAIN operation, or a READ operation. An indicator specified in positions 58–59 is turned on when no prior record exists in the file being read by a READP operation. The indicator in positions 56–57 is turned on when a READP operation fails to execute successfully.

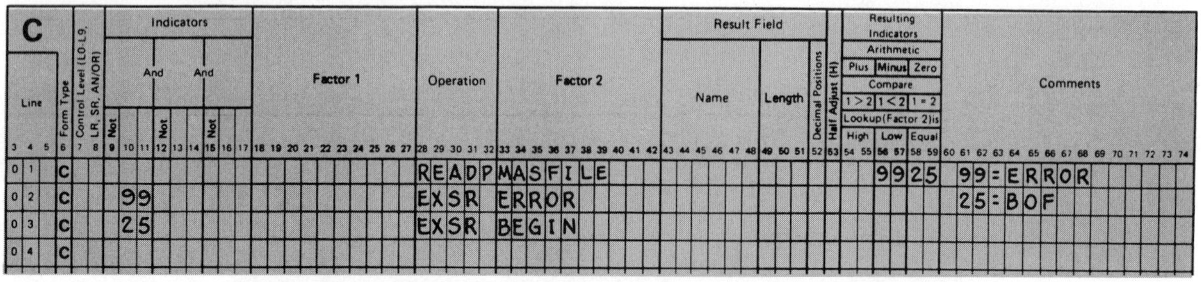

Line	Form Type	Indicators	Factor 1	Operation	Factor 2	Result Field	Resulting Indicators (56–57, 58–59)	Comments
01	C			READP	MASFILE		99 25	99=ERROR
02	C	99		EXSR	ERROR			25=BOF
03	C	25		EXSR	BEGIN			
04	C							

READP Operation Summary

The READP operation reads the prior record from a full procedural file. Factor 2 must contain the name of the file to be read. An indicator must be specified in positions 58–59. This indicator will be turned on when no prior record exists in the file (beginning of file, or BOF, condition).

Control Level Indicators	Indicators	Factor 1	Operation Name	Factor 2	Result Field	Resulting Indicators		
7–8	9–17	18–27	28–32	33–42	43–53	54–55	56–57	58–59
optional	optional	blank	READP	required	optional	blank	optional	required

blank in RPG II

Figure F-10 READP Operation summary

▬ SETLL (Set Lower Limit) Operation

When a full procedural file is read in arrival sequence, processing begins with the first record in the file, based on key field values, and proceeds record-by-record through the file. In some programming applications, you can speed up program execution by specifying the starting point (the first key field value) that is to be processed. The SETLL operation, summarized in Figure F-11, positions the file named in Factor 2 at the next record that has a key field value equal to or greater than the value specified by the field or literal in Factor 1. Arrival sequence processing then proceeds from that record through the file, bypassing all records with a key value lower than the value specified in Factor 1.

SETLL Operation Summary

The SETLL operation allows the programmer to set a lower limit or starting point for the processing of a full procedural or demand (RPG II only) file. The Factor 1 field name or literal must contain the lower limit value being set. Factor 2 must contain the name of the file for which the lower limit is being set. RPG III and RPG/400 permit the following indicator usage:

Positions 54–55   Factor 1 greater than highest file key value
Positions 56–57   Error in SETLL operation execution
Positions 58–59   Record key in Factor 2 file equals Factor 1 value

---

Control Level Indicators	Indicators	Factor 1	Operation Name	Factor 2	Result Field	Resulting Indicators		
7–8	9–17	18–27	28–32	33–42	43–53	54–55	56–57	58–59
optional	optional	required	SETLL	required	blank	optional	optional	optional

Figure F-11   SETLL Operation summary

Figure F-12 is a sample data file keyed on the CUSNO field. Note that there can be multiple records for each customer number. The processing shown in Figure F-13 prints all the records for a specified customer. The program must print all the records for customer 00349A. This value, although shown on line 03 as a literal, could be stored in a data field. The SETLL operation on line 03 positions the file at the first record for customer number 00349A. Because one or more records exist for this customer in CUSFILE, indicator 55 is turned on, and the program does not execute the GOTO operation on line 04. The READE operation on line 06 reads the first record for the customer. Because a record does exist for the customer and is retrieved by the READE operation, indicator 10 is not turned on, and the operations on lines 07 and 08, conditioned by N10, are performed. The EXCPT operation causes a line to be printed, and then the GOTO operation branches back to line 05, causing the READE to be executed again. This loop continues until all records for customer 00349A have been read and processed, at which time indicator 10 is turned on by the READE operation and lines 07 and 08 are not executed, thereby ending the loop.

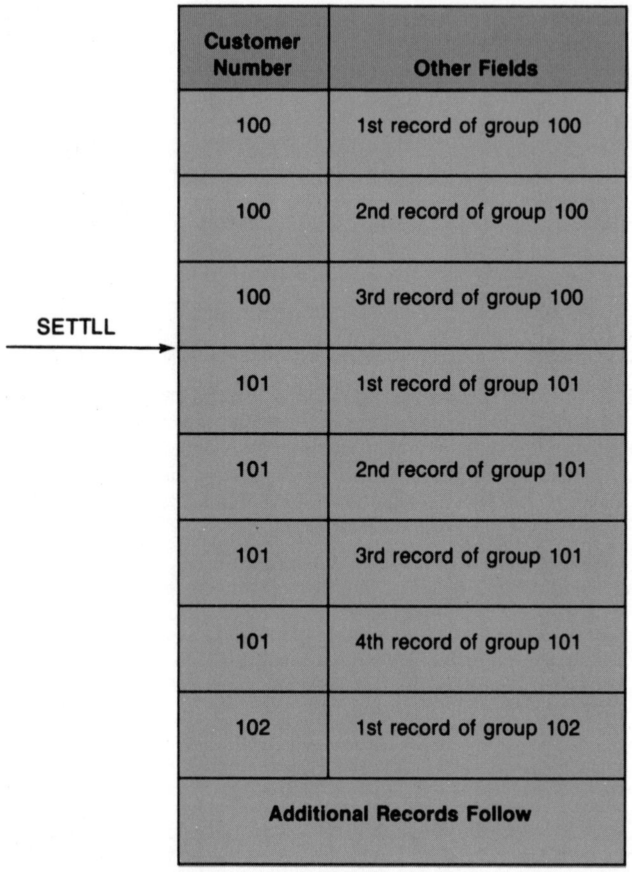

Customer Number	Other Fields
100	1st record of group 100
100	2nd record of group 100
100	3rd record of group 100
101	1st record of group 101
101	2nd record of group 101
101	3rd record of group 101
101	4th record of group 101
102	1st record of group 102
Additional Records Follow	

SETLL → (arrow pointing to the boundary between group 100 and group 101)

Figure F-12   Data file for SETLL operation

SORTA (Sort an Array) Operation

The SORTA operation, summarized in Figure F-14, sorts the elements of an array into ascending or descending sequence based on the sequence entry in position 45 of the extension specification that defined the array. Figure F-15 on page F-12 shows the contents of the ARRX array before and after the execution of a SORTA operation.

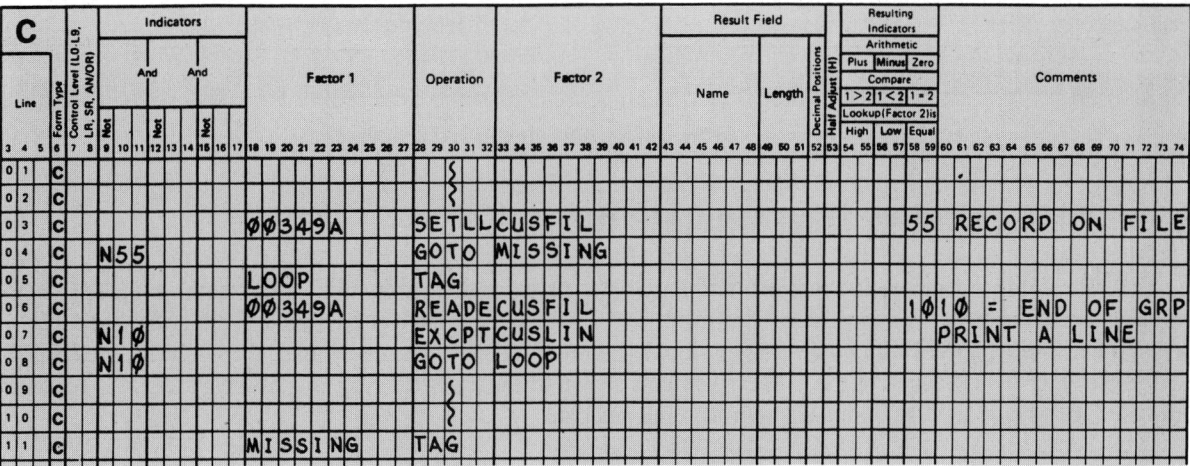

Figure F-13   SETLL coding example

Control Level Indicators	Indicators	Factor 1	Operation Name	Factor 2	Result Field	Resulting Indicators		
7–8	9–17	18–27	28–32	33–42	43–53	54–55	56–57	58–59
optional	optional	blank	SORTA	required	blank	blank	blank	blank

SORTA Operation Summary

The SORTA operation sorts the elements of the array named in Factor 2 into either ascending or descending sequence based on the entry (A or D) in position 45 of the extension specification for the array. If no sequence entry was made on the Extension Specifications form, the array is sorted in ascending sequence. If an alternate array was specified on the same extension specification, the alternate array is not sorted by the SORTA operation.

Figure F-14   SORTA operation summary

ARRX before SORTA operation

| 13 | 45 | 83 | 47 | 95 | 27 | 59 | 82 | 57 | 02 |

ARRX after SORTA operation

| 02 | 13 | 27 | 45 | 47 | 57 | 59 | 82 | 83 | 95 |

Figure F-15   Array before and after SORTA operation

TIME (Time of Day) Operation

The TIME operation, summarized in Figure F-16, accesses the system time-of-day clock and, if requested, also accesses the system data. The result of the TIME operation can be placed in either a 6- or a 12-position numeric data field with no decimal positions. Figure F-17 shows the contents of the CLOCK and TIMDAT fields after the execution of the TIME operations shown in Figure F-16. Note that although CLOCK contains only the time of day, TIMDAT contains both the time and date.

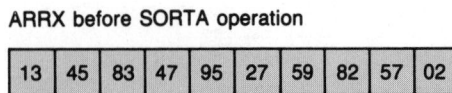

TIME Operation Summary

The TIME operation retrieves the system time and can also, if specified, retrieve the system date. The system time of day is based on the 24-hour clock. The Result Field must be a numeric field, either 6 or 12 positions long, with no decimal places. If the Result Field is 6 positions long, the TIME operation will place the system time in the field in HHMMSS format, where HH = hour, MM = minute, and SS = second. If the Result Field is 12 positions long, it will contain the system time in positions 1–6 and the system date, in MMDDYY format, in positions 7–12.

Control Level Indicators	Indicators	Factor 1	Operation Name	Factor 2	Result Field	Resulting Indicators		
7–8	9–17	18–27	28–32	33–42	43–53	54–55	56–57	58–59
optional	optional	blank	TIME	blank	required	blank	blank	blank

Figure F-16   TIME operation summary

clock

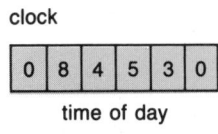

time of day

TIMDAT

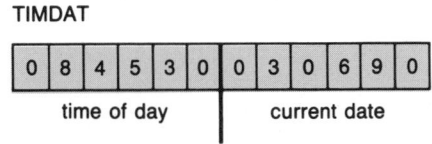

time of day | current date

Figure F-17   Result of TIME operation

Figure F-18 shows a brief routine that can be used to **time stamp** a printed report with the time that the program that created the report ended. The calculation performs the TIME operation at the end of the program under control of indicator LR. This would usually be the last calculation in the program. The Output Specifications form shows the output line that prints the date and time record at the end of the printed report. This output line should be the last output line specified for the report. The combination of the output constants, the system date field (UDATE), and the time field (TIME) prints a line similar to this at the end of the report:

REPORT FINISHED AT 11:04:12 ON 6/06/91

Note that the output specification contains a skip to line 66 (the last line of the page) prior to printing.

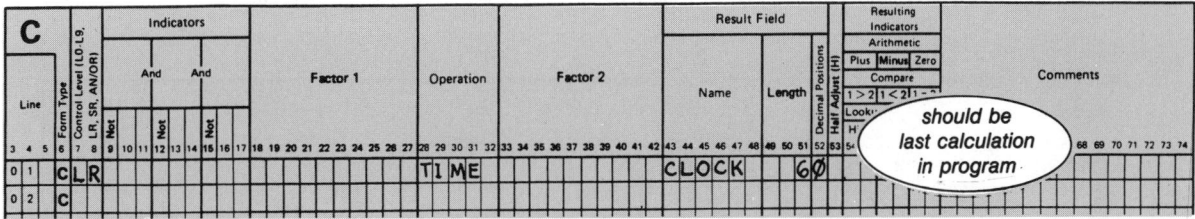

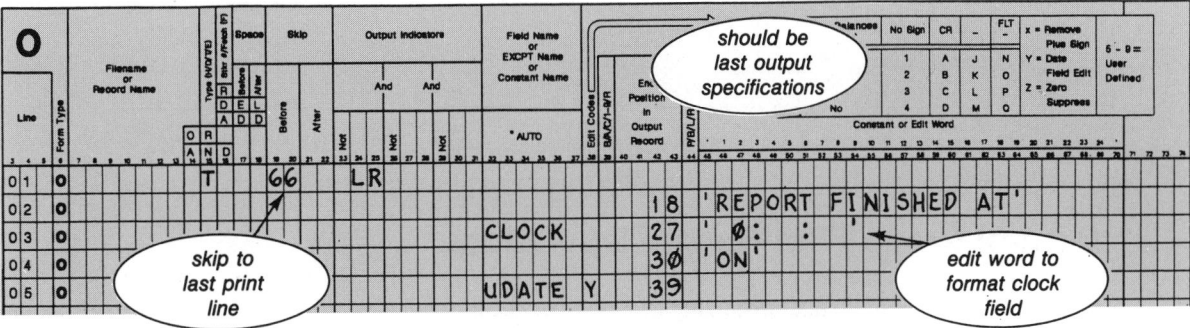

Figure F-18   End-of-job date and time-stamp routine

Z-SUB (Zero and Subtract) Operation

This operation causes the negative of the number contained in the literal or the field in Factor 2 to be placed in the result field specified. This operation is performed after the result field has been set to zeros. Factor 1 is not used in this operation. The Z-SUB operation is used primarily to switch the sign of the field from negative to positive or from positive to negative. Sign switching can also be performed by multiplying the value in Factor 1 by a numeric literal of –1 (minus one). Figure F-19 shows the format of the Z-SUB operation.

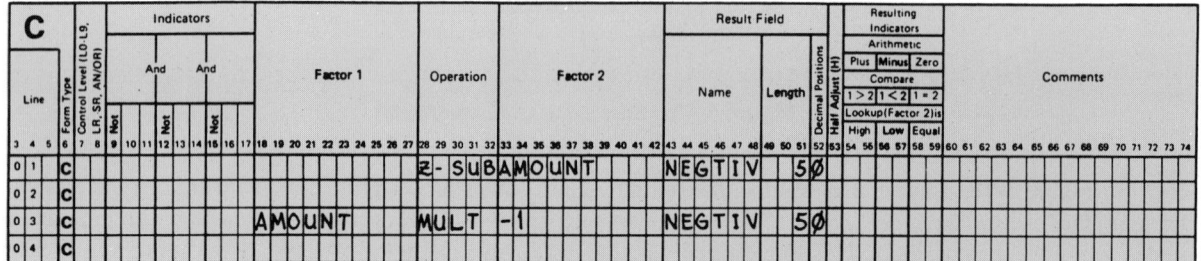

Z-SUB Operation Summary

Factor 2 is subtracted from a field of zeros, and the result is placed into the Result Field. This result is the negative of the Factor 2 value. Factor 1 is not used.

Control Level Indicators	Indicators	Factor 1	Operation Name	Factor 2	Result Field	Resulting Indicators		
7–8	9–17	18–27	28–32	33–42	43–53	54–55	56–57	58–59
optional	optional	blank	Z-SUB	required	required	optional	optional	optional

Figure F-19   Z-SUB operation summary

Control Group First-Record Operations

Some applications require that processing take place at detail calculation time and that processing should occur only on the first input record following a control break. When a control break occurs, the control level indicator that is set on remains on during the detail processing cycle for the next detail input record so that group indication can take place. To specify that a calculation be performed only for the first detail record following a control break, specify the control level indicator in the Indicators area (positions 9–17) of the Calculation Specifications form.

Figure F-20 shows control level indicator L1 specified in the Indicators area, positions 10–11. This results in the SETOF instruction being executed at detail time only if the L1 indicator is on. The L1 indicator is on only for the first detail input record of a new group, that is, the first detail record after a control break has occurred. In this manner, you can specify any processing that must take place only for the first input record of a control group.

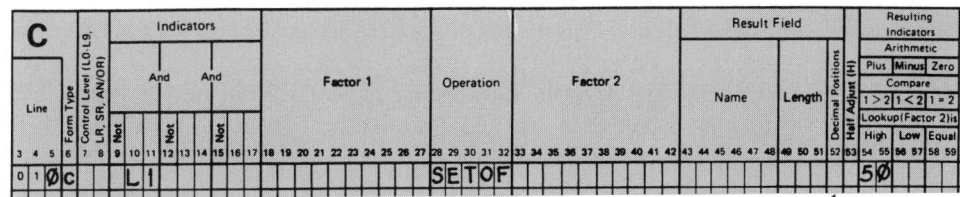

Figure F-20 Control group first-record operations

OUTPUT SPECIFICATIONS

As with the input and calculation specifications, there are several new entries that may be useful on the output specifications.

Edit Words

In previous sample programs in this text, edit codes were used to perform data editing on printed reports. Although this is the preferable method of editing numeric data, RPG offers another method: edit words. An edit word is a set of characters used to indicate the format of an output field. Edit words can perform all the operations performed by edit codes: zero suppression, insertion of commas and decimal points, placement of a negative symbol at the end of a number, and placement of a dollar sign. However, because the edit-word function is more difficult and time-consuming to code, it is usually used only to perform editing operations that cannot be performed by the predefined edit codes.

An edit word is placed in the Constant or Edit Word area, positions 45–70 of the output specification of the field to be edited (Figure F-21). An edit word is a form of constant and, like any output constant, must be enclosed in apostrophes. The following table lists the characters that have special editing functions in an edit word.

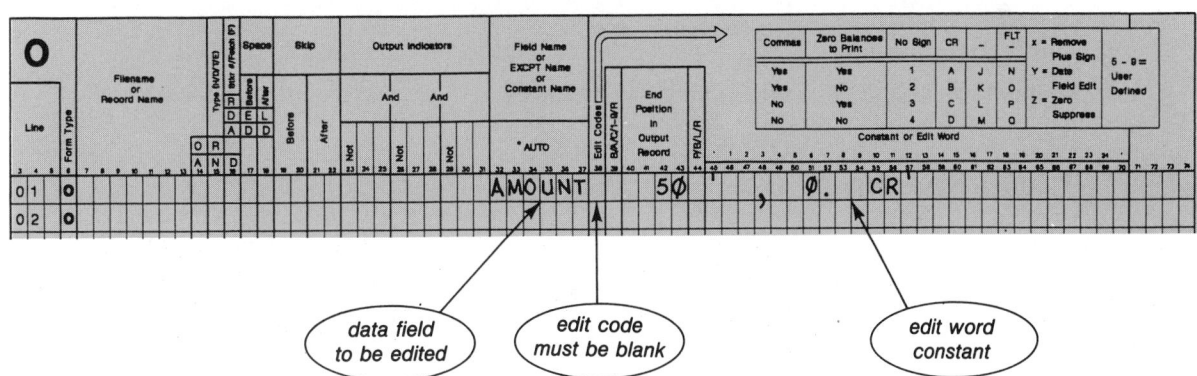

Figure F-21 Edit word placement

Blank A blank is replaced by a character from the field being edited.

Zero The first zero in an edit word marks the rightmost position that is to be zero suppressed. All leading zeros in the data field are replaced by blanks up to the edit word position that contains a zero suppression zero.

Asterisk An asterisk in an edit word performs the same function as a zero, that is, the elimination of leading zeros. However, when an asterisk is used, the leading zeros are not replaced by blanks but are replaced by asterisks. This process is referred to as asterisk fill.

Ampersand An ampersand (&) in an edit word causes a blank space to be inserted in the edited output at the point where the asterisk occurs. This blank does not replace a data character but is inserted between characters.

Comma and **Decimal** Commas and decimal points in an edit word are replaced by blanks if they are placed to the left of the zero suppression zero and if no significant digit has been found. If zero suppression is not active, commas and decimal points are inserted into the edited output field.

Dollar A dollar sign directly before the zero suppression zero causes the output to contain a floating dollar sign. A dollar sign placed in any other location is treated as a constant.

Constants All other characters in an edit word are treated as constants. A constant is inserted into the edited output if zero suppression is not being performed. If zero suppression is being performed, a constant is replaced by a blank.

The number of blanks in an edit word must equal the number of digits in the field to be edited. The only exception to this rule involves the use of zero suppression or asterisk fill. When either a zero or asterisk is used for these functions, the character represents a replacement character, and so the number of blanks in the edit word is reduced by 1. Also note that any constant character that appears to the left of the zero or asterisk in an edit word is replaced by either a blank or an asterisk when either zero suppression or asterisk fill is performed. Figure F-22 shows a series of edit words, the data to be edited, and the result of editing using the specified edit word.

Edit Word	Data	Edited Result
'bbbbb* .bb'	00001234	****12.34
'0AREA&bbb&NO.&bbb-bbbb'	5085551212	bAREAb508bNO.b555-1212
'$bbbbbb**DOLLARS&bb&CTS'	000012345	$****123*DOLLARSb45bCTS
'b0:bb:bb'	144230	14:42:30

Figure F-22   Edit word examples (in these examples, a lowercase b denotes a blank)

▭ *PLACE Key Word

*PLACE is an RPG key word that enables you to write the same output to several different positions in an output record without having to provide names and output positions for each of the entries. When *PLACE is used, all output data between the first output position and the highest previously specified output position is repeated, ending in the end position that is part of the *PLACE output specification. Figure F-23 shows how the *PLACE key word can be used to print a line of 132 hyphens with less code than would be needed by normal coding methods.

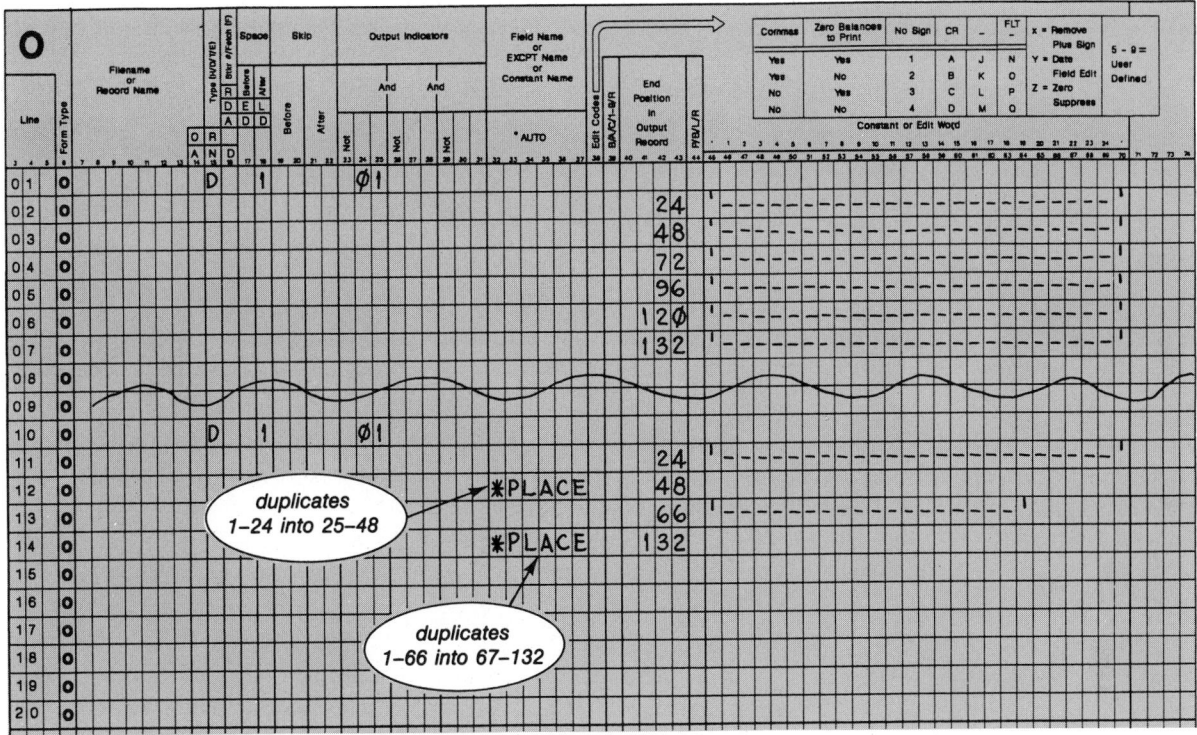

Figure F-23 Use of the *PLACE key word

The upper example uses six output constants to create the 132 hyphens needed to print a complete line. The lower example uses an output constant to place hyphens in positions 1–24 of the line. The constant is followed by a *PLACE output specification that causes all the output in positions 1–24 to be repeated, ending in position 48. The next specification uses an output constant to place hyphens in positions 49–66, and the second *PLACE specification then duplicates positions 1–66 into positions 67–132.

Test Data Sets

▀▀ Test Data Set PE-1

```
          1111111111222222222233333333334444444444555555555566666666667777777778
1234567890123456789012345678901234567890123456789012345678901234567890
```

```
HORACE BELCHER          721 BEMAN RD.          HOLLYWOOD, CA           92736

MYRON ISSON             37 KENNEDY AVE.         WASHINGTON, D.C.        02734

HOMER BRAVO             1776 FLAG DR.           PHILADELPHIA, PA        11771

PAUL NESS               69 STICKLE BLVD.        CHICAGO, IL             44442

NICK L. BAGLEY          10 NEEDLES AVE.         SAN FRANCISCO, CA       99691
```

▀▀ Test Data Set PE-2

```
          11111111112222222222 3
1234567890123456789012345678 90
```

```
10005AMMONIA            0603005000

10982MATCHES            2950020500

22650NUTMEG             2090017000

33569BLEACH             5780922156

44521DETERGENT          0560702178

55903CLEANSER           4217536598

69340SPONGES            0448703905
```

▀▀ Test Data Set PE-3

```
          11111111112222222222
12345678901234567890123456789
```

```
01225STEEL BEAM          0298

22665STEAM GENERATOR     2077

44810ALUMINUM SIDING     0500

52697STEEL SCRAP         1000

66113COUPLING            0499

77221WHEEL, STEEL        1001

81190LIGHTPOST           0750
```

Test Data Set 1

```
             11111111122222222223333333333444444444455555555556666666
    1234567890123456789012345678901234567890123456789012345678901234 5
```

```
1253CDAECAPACITANCE METER          EO LAB1   010186063087
1253CAEAAC/DC VOLTAGE TESTER       EO LAB1   112188063090
1743AMADVOLT OHM AMMETER           EO LAB2   090182073086
1819                               EO LAB1   080581073087
1911FMABDIGITAL PYROMETER          EL LAB3   062170110184
1923CDBBDIGITAL KILOWATT METER               051069030169
1923CSBAPHOTOELECTRIC TACHOMET     EO LAB3   112185113086
2111AMEADIGITAL WATT METER         EL LAB2   020186020188
2143                               EL LAB1   031288093091
2323SPAB2K OHMS/VOLT VOM TEST      EL LAB2   043080102479
2441CSAC10K OHM/VOLT VOM TEST      EO LAB3   100179110190
2642CTAA20K OHMS/VOLT DELUXE                 091086091188
2642GEAEBREADBOARD LAB             EL LAB2   022187022191
2899FMADAC/DC VOLTAGE TESTER       EO LAB2   120188120190
2943CEBADIGITAL PYROMETER          EO LAB1   042086040488
2975CDAEPOWER FACTOR METER         EO LAB3   101089101091
3451                               EO LAB1   101070110186
3563ACBCOSCILLOSCOPE MOD-315P      EO LAB2   110182110187
3711CSBBCAPACITANCE METER          EL LAB3   053085013090
3942                                         061682071683
4001GEBAAC/DC VOLTAGE TESTER       EO LAB2   071988011989
4203CTADBREADBOARD LAB             EO LAB3   080288011689
4705AMACDIGITAL WATT METER         EL LAB2   081579072488
4705SPAAOSCILLOSCOPE MOD-620C      EO LAB3   101386101390
```

Test Data Set 2

```
          1111111111222222222233333333334444444444555555555566666666667
          1234567890123456789012345678901234567890123456789012345678901234567890
```

GEORGE BARROWS	1050 EAST GARDNER ROAD	GARDNER MA	01440
HENRY SINCLAIR	79 CHERRY STREET	PHILADELPHIA PA	19151
MARTHA TURNER	100 NICHOLS AVENUE	HOLYWOOD CA	92343
HELEN ONISCHUCK	40 OLD CENTRE ROAD	DENVER CO	80216
CATHLEEN MAYNARD	666 APPLE LANE	ASPEN CO	80216
MARY JONES	1356 NEEDLES STREET	TUESON AZ	85705
ALLEN SMITH	777 PINEVIEW TERRACE	WASHINGTON D.C.	20009
JOHN SAARI	1890 HOLT ROAD	PHOENIX AZ	85043
JASON LONG	PO BOX 818	ATLANTA GA	30360
MARK FOSTER	200 ALLEN STREET	ROCKPORT ME	04856
HENRIETTA SMITH	16 LOLA LANE	NEW HAVEN CT	06518
MARY-ELLEN PERKINS	1850 PEASE BOULAVARD	TORRINGTON CT	06790
MARY-BETH WERSUK	17 NOWHERE AVENUE	KEENE NH	03431
CHARLOTTE ZAMPONI	66 LOUETTE LANE	PORTSMOUTH NH	03803
SCOTT DENIS	76 TOWNSEND ROAD	TAMPA FL	33619
MARJORY PERKINS	669 TODD STREET	NORTH ADAMS MA	01427
KEITH HARRINGTON	11 AXHOLME ROAD	PORTLAND OR	97227
MATHEW HOLT	1050 PLEASANT STREET	DALLAS TX	75229
ERICKA TAMMY	1011 FIRST STREET	NEW YORK CITY NY	10001
NICOLE MORRIS	EASTSIDE MEADOWS BOX 100ACHARLOTTE NC		28209
TIMOTHY GOODALE	99 FORTY-SECOND STREEET	GARY IN	46405
ROBERT RICKER	44 YORK STREET	OGUNQUIT ME	30907
ANDREW FRANKLIN	111 BAKER AVENUE	VALLEY FORGE PA	19481
ANTHONY DOOLITTLE	6000 BROOK LANE	BALTIMORE MD	21220

▆ Test Data Set 3

```
          1111111111222222222223
  12345678901234567890123456789 0
```

GRAVES, KATHLEEN	88100
KOSKI, MARTHA	88101
TREPANIER, PAUL	88102
EPSTEIN, ANNE	88103
GREENE, ERIKA	88104
CLARK, TIMOTHY	88105
JACKSON, BETSEY	88106
SARRI, HENRY	89200
ADAMS, NICOLE	89201
NADEAU, ANN-MAIRE	89202
CHAPMAN, WILLIAM	89203
TETREAU, CHARLES	89204
D'ENTROMONT, CHRISTOPHER	89205
BALENTINE, STEVE	90300
BISHOP, GLORIA	90301
APGAR, HELEN	90302
FOSTER, ELEN	90303
GARDNER, THOMAS	90304
KARVONEN, TRISHA	90305
STONE, RICHARD	91400
MURPHY, VIOLA	91401
ONISCHUCK, PETER	91402
TANDY, AMY	91403
ROGERS, MARY	91404
BOURQUE, JEFFERY	91405
DAVIS, RANDY	92501
KOZLOSKI, MELISSA	92502
SAVIOR, JENNIFER	92503
ROSS, HENRY	92504
BEAUVIS, BRIAN	92506
FOWLER, NICOLE	93600
RAYMON, JASON	93600
LEGER, MARY	94700
SCOTT, DANNY	94701
CARTER, SARITA	94702
MATNARD, GLORIA	94703
ZAMBLONSKI, CHRIS	94705
CHRISTOFF, DAVID	95800
WARREN, FRED	95801
GIRARD, GREG	95802
HENDERSON, PETER	95804
FRANKHURST, BRETT	95806
DAVIS, KEITH	96900
MCCARTHY, MICHELLE	95807
PARKHURST, EDDIE	95808
LIZOTTE, LENNY	95803
ROULEAU, ELAINE	95805
MATHEWS, CHRISTINE	95809

Test Data Set 4

```
          1111111111222222222233333333334444444444555555555566
 12345678901234567890123456789012345678901234567890123456789012345678901
```

```
010SANDRA ROSE                                    42260 95660

019MICHAEL REGAN JR.                              34555 55080

030MONIQUE THIBODEAU                              48695 23220

032ROSS SANBORN                                   17450 89355

042TAIMI LAMPA                                    28120 03705

068PAUL LA ROSA                                   47000 20445

091ANNE THOMPSON                                  34340 28365

095ERNEST TIGS                                    77225 82805

101CURTIS ALTOBELLI                               62135 76545

104RALPH ALLEN                                    64240 25785

105DOUGLAS ALBERT                                 30055 63680

107CARSON AMERCIAN                                50710 22185

142GARY HAKKARAINEN                               14910 88925

189LLYOD HACKLER                                  35340 89095

184FRANK MANEY                                    46905 88120

249JOHN MANNING                                   02175 41410

273THEODORE MAMMONE                               61350 26750

285BRADLEY HAYES                                  76940 66090

291WALTER POULIN                                  89280 26890

316KEITH STRAW                                    85860 62050

347DELMAR STREETER                                89870 47270

356RAYMOND SWEET                                  54105 66705

430DONALD STILSON                                 20295 35325

464HENRY ZEMICK                                   63290 53040

486IRVING JOYCE                                   24265 43985

497LAWRENCE ZUIDEMA                               54245 59565

509CHESTER YOUNG                                  71295 38515

518BERNARD WILTON                                 39645 88290
```

continued

Test Data Set 4 (continued)

```
524CARL SANDBERG              07895 16485

564HOWARD MILLER              89890 81115

576RENNE WILSON               32355 59240

5985STANLEY WILLIAMS          63870 84145

683JASON WOLFE                55445 24310

698HARRISON RILEY             42260 30660

706BYRON RICHARDS             54285 90860

730ZOEL RICH                  90275 09075

733HARRY PERKINS              08645 08560

773ERIC PERKINS               06840 14425

795MILTON PERA                73040 21725

798HENRY PELTO                46490 49120

803SUSAN PAUL                 84145 34590

816HELEN OSTMAN               65075 52145

821KIM ORSINI                 53655 21285

833EDWARD OBUE                64445 95025

856ELLEN OLDS                 70300 27035

874KENNETH MURPHY             42220 66600

911RICHARD MULLER             13170 43260

978DOUGLAS MUG                21425 64036

984JACK MOORE                 94500 59150
```

Test Data Set 5

```
          1111111111222222222233333333334444444444555555555566
 1234567890123456789012345678901234567890123456789012345678901


          001SYRINGE                     900020008

          005AMMONIA                     100060009

          009STEEL BEAM                  405000052

          034NEEDLES                     300120014

          047MATCHES                     100005024
```

```
130STEAM GENERATOR              205000006

143MASKS                        500050008

176NUTMEG                       700020012

225ALUMINUM SIDING              612000005

255GLOVES                       600150007

273BLEACH                       300030005

294STEEL SCRAP                  506200009

309GOWNS                        500220008

315DETERGENT                    200020003

347COUPLING                     100300010

368SCAPEL                       500100007

370CLEANSER                     600040005

391LIGHTPOST                    503000007

399SPONGES                      400050008

414SCREEN                       900050008

423WINDOW                       300240001

439DOOR                         800750004

443LATCH                        700080010

467PAPER PRESS                  700470007

468PENS                         800005006

477BUILDING BLOCKS              900140023

480AUTOMOBILE MODEL             700250029

488DOOR HANDLE                  600060017

513WRENCH                       200100025

518PIPE WRENCH                  900050033

523SAW                          800120010

551HACK SAW                     200180043

563NAILS                        100040039

568HAMMER                       300100028

576SCREWDRIVER                  500060038

585LEVEL                        300120009

607PLIERS                       100040013

633BROOMS                       600060002
```

continued

Test Data Set 5 (continued)

648DUSTPANS	700040030
650RULER	800010005
694CROSS PENS	600100023
707PAPER	100010004
714CALCULATOR	200200040
766TRAPPER FOLDERS	400010043
837CASSETTE TAPES	300090058
855TAPE RECORDER	500270024
859SWIVEL CHAIRS	700450013
953THREE-HOLE PUNCH	800110020
968CAMERA	501500014

Test Data Set 6

```
1111111111222222222233333333334444444444555555555566666666667
1234567890123456789012345678901234567890123456789012345678901
```

0013ROCHE, MICHAEL	101202101202500000
0015FEN, CARL	202386202386200000
0016RUNN, CLIFFORD	301259001259250780
0017HOLDEN, ARNOLD	401378001378325971
0021HURTZ, RICHARD	200673200000284872
0035MARLBORO, RALPH	301569301569348659
0047WAINO, SCOTT	401250400000782839
0091THONIS, JOHN	101890000890427890
0110TOBIN, GLENN	100456100456324960
0112WHITNEY, SEAN	100127000000786870
0113LALONDE, SPINEY	301345001345428079
0114TWEEDY, LESTER	304873014873003480
0115DAVIS, PAUL	200053200000042800
0116BEAUREGUARD, LYNNE	402345400000000498
0117RIDGEWAY, GEORGE	200579190579000000

```
0118URA, LEE                    401457400057249870

0119DANIELS, FRED               201456000000234280

0120DAWBER, MILDRED             403568403568000000

0200EATON, DAVID                300456300000697280

0231PTAK, ALFRED                300348100920141400

0248BETELGUESE, LENNY           203547202222232050

0250PUCKO, HELEN                104500104500000000

0265PUGH, EUGENE                400346400346042970

02718BRUNDICK, BEN              203984000000897062

0273WERNER, PAULA               300738300738345670

0275EYVES, RONALD               100783099999923456

0281PRIDDLE, LARRY              203759200000000000

0349ELMER, HARRY                203568100000000000

0350STERLING, AUSTIN            210308210308143294

0351COMPTON, LAURA              403459403459870634

0468CONGRAM, PETER              108906100000143942

0500ADAMS, PETE                 403450003453678978

0502AHLSTROM, HAN               212009000009000000

0503GAGNON, HERBERT             406550406550500000

0671GABRENAS, RICK              309833309833428333

0679PARKER, GERALD              412569000000102103

0700FRANTEL, DOUGLAS            204050200000428790

0839ROSEBUSH, LEAH              300348300300101000

0943PARETTE, EDWARD             407890404444999999

1367COUETTE, RALPH              109345109345808072

1373POPP, DIANE                 208394000000005050

1431RENFIELD, RITA              305309300000092800

2117RYAN, WALTER                408398400000100000

2275FENTON, WAYNE               208987208987225022

2702LOLTON, HARRY               304354300000100590

3111LORE, LEO                   208979008979728200

4013MANNY, JEAN                 400783000083928800

4503LOVELACE, LINDSEY           301234000004343280

4686DUGMAN, ARNOLD              400847400847082343
```

Test Data Set 7

```
          11111111112222222222333333333344444444444
          1234567890123456789012345678901234567890123456789012345678
```

```
01846SANDRA ROSE              4310509690004411000201

02337MONIQUE THIBODEAU        5975646594000271000193

03800TONY GULINO              8290633257001853000151

04006SCOTT DRAKE              7722148993001511000201

05273SUE PINTO                4292585138002625000131

06372ALICE LEE                3447429289005309000121

07975WANYE LECUYER            3983266764004870000111

08502LORRAINE LEBLANC         4572415171002704000191

09344NORMAN GOLDMAN           4290816128004446000101

10006SERENE GOLD              8895576150004121000101

11243BENNET BLAKE             8158299436001747000151

12786FRANK BLACK              2278796521005171000161

13303PATRICIA ALTMAN          6562537791006150000171

14259VICTOR CARDINAL          4513148062007987000101

15353LOUIS CARILLO            2833528523004655000191

16593DENNIS GROSS             3796387786006150000121

17161JASON BALD               3249775449002006000181

18720DANIEL THOMASIAN         4554758618004417000151

19420DAVID TIRADO             9720138211004334000031

20058MARTHA CHARTRAND         4269049445003432000091

21563KYE CHI                  3206068537003223000211

22597JOHN HALLMARK            7400338206005937000251

23258PERRY GREEN              3242336274004305000281

24734JONH KADDY               3736817414006939000111

25153JOCELYN KATON            3987778086004990000141

26759PAUL LA FARR             4576278646005993000221

27366DAVID LITTER             3288297800002649000122

28508GLEN LINDER              3204096886005670000271
```

```
29132SALLY LONG          3497407915004150000101

30914ROMEO MAHAR         3730288759004624000291

31200DAN MCCOY           3261377016002228000021

32088KELLY MAYTAG        6593854150002615000131

33743GUY MAYO            8638784459002256000261

34107ISSAC RACZ          3437304639002723000132

35815LAURIE PURO         4461148844002389000160

36548DANA QUIMBY         3270695498003406000221

37732STEPHEN RABY        9701956975002243000181

38330CHRIS PYE           3743658965002726000201

39636KEVIN RHODIN        6539105589003817000271

40848ARTHUR RENDA        9715966294003592000121

41111HOWARD REILY        2549398028006231000242

42570WALTER REID         2572274660003302000211

43999HENRY ROSSA         6596093259002121000280

44534CHRISTINE ROE       4464338837003603000141

45781LEO ROCCA           4529378724003200000261

46100BARBARA SAWYER      7726387379006920000190

47168LINDA SCHMIDT       8635543354001963000230

48323RALPH TOBIN         4010072536001930000171

49176DAVID TOOLIN        4931873373002994000251
```

Test Data Set 8

```
         1111111111222222222233333333334444444444555555555566666666667
123456789012345678901234567890123456789012345678901234567890


0146POWER        CHRIS       M121286532H0100000000056000400

0207FEELEY       LEONARD     M050779532H0500000000036500760

0214KNOWLES      SUSAN       F062284532H0400000000064500230

0442HAIMILA      MICHAEL     M040191420S0801650000000000000

0684SUGAL        RICHARD     M020689109S0702560000000000000
```

continued

▤ Test Data Set 8 (continued)

```
0858STUART        SUE ANNE    F082288328S060345000000000000000
0907HILL          KENNETH     M070782328S030457000000000000000
0916VACHON        ARVID       M010973608H020000000038500390
0919VANN          MARTHA      F022782608H100000000047500525
1051PORELL        GERALD      M043087704S090234000000000000000
1268FIELD         JOHN        M120889570H010000000038500400
1605FIX           JULIE       F032083570H040000000047500390
2106FLAGG         KENNETH     M043090570H020000000047500230
2347FLETCHER      LEO         M090991660S050235000000000000000
2460HENRY         LOUIS       M022967660S030430000000000000000
2526HENEBRY       GLORIA      F022984190S060345000000000000000
2945KATON         BARBARA     F022885190S070219000000000000000
3040CURTIS        OMER        M030185190S100170000000000000000
3113CUSHMAN       PAT         F110877780H080000000023500480
3117FARNWORTH     PAUL        M120579780H070000000025000530
4103GOGUEN        RANDOLPH    M052079520S090685000000000000000
4330LANDRY        RAYMOND     M073086620S090326000000000000000
5140LEWINNER      THERSA      F010189111S040425000000000000000
5833MARINO        DONNA       F102082714H020000000046500170
6076MARR          GERARD      M123091724H030000000047500150
```

▤ Test Data Set 9

```
          1111111111222222222233333333334444444444455555555556
          1234567890123456789012345678901234567890123456789012345678901234567890

          26P7060690DRAKE, SCOTT          1442
          26P7061090RINGWALD, TED         0744
          26P7061490SANDEZ, LOIS          1166
          26P7062390DERONE, JODY          0052
          26P7062490CASTELL, ROBERT       1201
          26P7063090NESMITH, GEORGE       0667
          26P7070390BAILY, TOM            0499
          26P7070390BAILY, TOM            0499
          26P7071190RISBY, SID            0019
```

```
26P7071690LITTLETON, MIKE          0298

26P7071990LACROIX, DARREL          0143

26P7072290JENKINS, PAUL            0016

26P7072390HUXLEY, ALEX             0044

26P7072590HUBBARD, DAWN            0069

26P7072990FISHER, KEVIN            0038

26P7073190BOYD, RENE               0075

30A3061690GULINO, ANTHONY          0684

30A3062090HAIL, BILL               0641

30A3062290ALDEN, PAMELA            0099

30A3062790PORTER, RALPH            0217

30A3063090SINCLAIR, DAVID          0219

30A3072990ROCKWELL, JANET          0041

30A3070990PERKINS, DUNCAN          0719

30A3071190PEPIN, RON               0055

30A3071790MULLINS, DIANE           0622

30A3072590MEMBRENO, PAUL           0116

30A3072890MCPHEE, MARTIN           0076

30A3073190PERRY, SHELDON           0418

46F6061490ROSE, SAM                0907

46F6061990MATTSON, ALPFONZE        0101

46F6062190ROMANO, SHARON           0609

46F6062490KARLTON, RANDY           1228

46F6062890LABATT, GARY             0072

46F6063090FERRIS, PEGGY            0143

46F6070190BRYSON, FRANK            0071

46F6070490TREEWATER, KEN           0169

46F6070990ATKINS, COREY            1294

46F6071190KARR, LESTER             0060

46F6071390LEBARON, CHERYL          1068

46F6071690MOORE, JOHN              0075

46F6072190POWELL, WALTER           0919

46F6072490SMUTHERS, RICH           0440

46F6072690WEAVER, STEPHEN          0606

46F6073090TANNER, PHIL             0421

46F607310GRUTHFIELD, CATHY         0061

52X060490THIBODEAU, MONIQUE        0856

52X1061190SANBORN, ROSS            0747

52X1061990CLEAVES, RODNEY          1112

52X1062690HIT, BRIAN               0406
```

Test Data Set 10

```
            11111111112222
  12345678901234567890123
```

		17B911Q	1720156
		17B012P	1855201
		17B366K	2210215
10A011B	0815085	19A391L	1520105
10A026G	0930100	19A377M	1805121
10A158R	1045250	19A910R	2000100
10A248M	1120105	19A061S	2400087
12A682P	0730126	19A059T	1940108
12A345B	1350137	20B044U	1050091
12A625P	1450211	20B072V	1400190
12A733A	1600285	20B107R	0700121
13B850K	1830220	20B615M	1830170
13B900G	2000267	20B904S	1940200
14A046H	1215185	20B616T	2050277
14A685L	1525200	20B516D	2130185
14A1012	1635090	22A103K	0710111
14A211K	1805111	22A108B	0920121
15A111B	0830112	22A107H	1230211
15A122X	0940129	22A214K	1630180
15A255W	1050276	22A415V	1730175
15A305Y	1205099	22A903S	1930182
15A405I	1415157	22A129G	2035100
15A054C	1900207	22A108A	2145121
15A065N	2200285	26A721M	1040171
17B786J	0940112	26A708G	1250195
17B888O	1100141	26A4240	1430170

Test Data Set 11

```
          11111111112222222222333333333344
          12345678901234567890123456789012345678901

0154673459102589003000400015000005000 1459
0154738206901306001000120002500070000 1083
0154987632100500000000020000500025000 0947
0154194230901500002500100003000065000 0329
0154308512300943000600050001470075000 1099
0154879538701453000700130001690013000 1219
0154577983101890001700060005790065000 0532
0154688102302000004000080006320070000 1456
0154899091201734001300090007670080000 1087
0154995563101623002100070001820050000 0948
0154728935701319000700065004710085000 1243
0154006505601242000900050001930035000 1857
0154741389301080001700084000301002500 0669
1930895321001050000000035904730005000 0327
1930193200501460001000146905030015000 0000
1930329982700390002000181901920025000 0114
1930503478901230002500419004700030000 1930
1930185423900950001800138002500047000 0740
1930706050001070002300157004000059000 0890
1930166236501220001400182301200069000 1250
1930705431701410002800129001140017000 0216
1930212438001090003000100001420035000 0825
1930323590101530002000047003500042000 1213
```

```
1930453093701970001800053001900019000 1382
1930785394202080001700102003000030000 0298
1930439321401840000700120004200010000 1492
4232111111702400003900058701400025000 2189
4232543210001397002500061501200035000 0679
4232987654300540001600091001000025000 1729
4232210957301520000700061605000075000 1449
4232397384100410003400124305000065000 2939
4232451234802020002300198901700080000 3259
4232381469501680001800121401000050000 1989
4232194089201285000750099901500085000 4499
4232893271501090001600100002700070000 1229
4232191919101300002500150001300013000 1919
4232543627101720003500240002000065000 1439
4232389705201830002400380003700007000 1249
4232893257100960002200190006900050000 1669
5940246802401200000700470001400050000 1215
5940353320101150000900175000900055000 1425
5940843961201000001700120000500065000 3235
5940898887602050003900890005000070000 1945
5940312115201900002100830007500025000 4055
5940271223301450000500140001200030000 4360
5940149342200900001300120001000035000 1850
5940789801101250002500590003700040000 1650
5940195451700700000700470003000015000 4340
5940260514800850001700180001500010000 1530
```

Test Data Set 12

```
          11111111112222222222333333333334
          12345678901234567890123456789012345678901234567890
```

```
03211S910256090085090073083100        03221S92090708208907207309109092
03211S910945087092095098084091        03221S92085607901201504304203039
03211S910912056063070064045075        03221S92115806300000000000054025
03211S910667100100099091093099        03221S92091004207908207308409099
03211S910660072074083090088091        03221S92075109808208809009209070
03211S910627086089091072075100        03231R93066806207208207507808063
03211S910605098100100079082097        03231R93065509810009510010000099
03211S910268069078062063052059        03231R93099409509509510010000090
03211S910456072078091088089070        03231R93108307007507908209109071
03211S910402089090069075081075        03231R93060309208408907307209100
03211S911134039043012059040063        03231R93025110007209108410000060
03211S911310730800720750900100        03231R93087805406304302506809071
03211S911172089089089089089089        03231R93114706307208409210000071
03211S911031070063060080078091        03231R93109808408308508208608081
03211S910301083082094100087100        03231R93029310010010009010000100
03211S911400072073074075075077        03231R93001608710009009507309076
03221S921387091100083085100100        03231R93088506305207808008909095
03221S921346083050089072078082        03231R93078307207207207208407075
03221S921207072065060060079078        03241R94034509009508708808508095
03221S921204061082084091073100        03241R94061008709209508508809090
03221S921442059063067073092071        03241R94052507305705506006307071
03221S920684063090090092093080        03241R94048409007206210006507070
03221S921058084072072082092054        03241R94122506907306510007508089
                                       03241R94137707308408907008209091
                                       03241R94065209509909509009909090
                                       03241R94129108208309006907500100
```

Test Data Set 13

```
           1111111111222        MA02016134567826252000
      1234567890123456789012    MA02016136891431910899
                                ME01661061121310720999
 CA04044450062930661099         ME01661061124620801199
 CA04044460051920551999         ME01661061212130110899
 CA05066165116230760799         ME01661063434340222499
 CA05066169121210081099         ME02460101212120361699
 CA05066169311120001699         ME02460101323130381199
 CA05066156567840204945         VA03017148961540852495
 CA06111259898960231099         VA03017149010010990999
 CA06111256867810240899         VA03017149162121101865
 CA06111256891140252999         VA03064150016210091199
 CA06111278891130311199         VT36005446621340104000
 CA07131298861140323099         VT36005446721310060999
 CA07131297762130050898         VT36005447789620071699
 CA07131298888810071299         VT36005446672930901199
 FL10061178911630391099         VT36005489211110800999
 FL10061160000040422999         VT36005486791120601500
 FL10061169999920441899         VT36005487789130411099
 FL10061170001070471689         VT36005486666640303899
 FL10061178888810551099         VT36005479054620321499
 FL20162190909020562099         VT36005478989810600899
 FL20162133333330571199         WI91128391000020111999
 MA00101031142111001000         WI91128391010130141199
 MA00101032262150991800         WI91128310101010181099
 MA02016132666611510999         WI91128360101040362599
```

Test Data Set 14

```
                  1111111111222222222233333
       12345678901234567890234567890123
```

```
060690BOSTON, MA          06281451
060690BOSTON, MA          04041994
060690BOSTON, MA          01102223
060690BOSTON, MA          07471602
060690BOSTON, MA          06441742
060690DENVER, CO          10101491
060690DENVER, CO          07193206
060690DENVER, CO          11141492
060690DENVER, CO          02233005
060990WASHINGTON, DC      04511702
060990WASHINGTON, DC      02512053
060990WASHINGTON, DC      13612454
060990WASHINGTON, DC      21141371
060990WASHINGTON, DC      06172755
060990KNOXVILLE, TN       06691692
060990KNOXVILLE, TN       73113036
060990KNOXVILLE, TN       02142454
060990ORLANDO, FL         10391441
060990ORLANDO, FL         44492895
060990ORLANDO, FL         02812143
060990ORLANDO, FL         02171632
060990ORLANDO, FL         06461772
061290NEW YORK, NY        80192804
```

```
061290NEW YORK, NY          60131502
061290NEW YORK, NY          99181431
061290NEW YORK, NY          42312163
061290GRAND RAPIDS, MI      43822995
061290GRAND RAPIDS, MI      61611712
061290GRAND RAPIDS, MI      59343236
061290GRAND RAPIDS, MI      20601481
061290GRAND RAPIDS, MI      14282976
061290GRAND RAPIDS, MI      82031662
061290GRAND RAPIDS, MI      81912243
061290SAN FRANSISCO, CA     61071361
061290SAN FRANSISCO, CA     91841722
061290SAN FRANSISCO, CA     14422113
061290SAN FRANSISCO, CA     69121732
061590BALTIMORE, MD         83312794
061590BALTIMORE, MD         58612704
061590BALTIMORE, MD         98792745
061590BALTIMORE, MD         40233056
061590AUSTIN, TX            16782213
061590AUSTIN, TX            31641622
061590AUSTIN, TX            24611381
061590AUSTIN, TX            49943166
061590AUSTIN, TX            37832915
061590AUSTIN, TX            86882644
061590HONOLULU, HI          18802033
061590HONOLULU, HI          76911692
```

▱ Test Data Set 15

```
              1111111111222222          1991947844210111009304450
      123456789012345678901234      1991947844212131024300540
                                          1991947844214151007004689
  1300215224177554005000200      1991947844261718006007247
  1300512524111243060001370      1991947844219202005004863
  1300512524120113001901412      1991947844212223004005249
  1300512524112986006401618      1991917944277554000308000
  130051252417088 016001971      1991917944299989000402310
  1300512524107488003001802      1991917944274342003201050
  1300512524110007008901969      1991917972519429004101589
  1300512524102061011208593      1991917972519300001901930
  1300512509620303008404212      1993017972514121003406753
  1300512509605040005106217      1993017972500050009108934
  1300555309642315011201842      1993017972512145004300500
  1300555309623164005501243      1993017972558600001201000
  130055530968375 003500617      1993017972590543001301248
  1300555309668729003000500      1993069972541298003104216
  1300555309690231004501228      1993069972512345004501000
  1301955309609171010002173      1993069972501564008907488
  1301947854932105006501822      1993069966801420009001298
  1301947854939480007502119      1993069966801466003500907
  1301947854906671008002029      1993069966885970000602370
  1301947854966666008204051      1993069966810190001400684
  1301947854953421000501941
  1991947854995683008104214      1993069966867890010700856
  1991947855203859009501243      1993069966800001010901050
```

▤ Test Data Set 16

```
            1111111111      0129903001652002932
    1234567890123456789     0130901001549000696
                            0130901002219001004
    0128901001783102798     0130904002766002788
    0128901001643100742     0130901002076002007
    0128901002702100873     0130902001506000683
    0128902001402105009     0130902002862001245
    0128902002244100752     0130902001654000726
    0128902002486000676     0130903001204010005
    0128903001850100893     0130903001431101004
    0128903001709000431     0130903002131102009
    0128903001658002808     0131901002271100833
    0128903002851101887     0131901002130100924
    0129901002019000461     0131902002103000481
    0129901002157000964     0131902001004100752
    0129901002866001155     0131902001533000756
    0129902002556000682     0131902001367000823
    0129902001499005009     0131903001877001135
    0129902001380101947     0131903002714101807
    0129902002306000903     0131903002066600994
    0129903001152000501     0131903002218003008
    0129903001878000732
```

Test Data Set 17

```
                    1111111
              1234567890123456
```

RICN0001	15	NHNH0267	11
RIMA0002	18	MEVT0268	10
RIME0003	19	MENH0269	09
RINH0004	16	CNCN0334	12
RIRI0005	14	CNMA0334	10
RIVT0006	13	CNNH0334	11
VTCN0008	12	CNNH0344	09
VTMA0067	11	CNRI0411	05
VTME0578	10	CNVT0483	20
VTNH0151	09	MAMA0492	21
VTRI0152	05	MAME0543	19
VTVT0153	04	MANH0567	14
CNCN0154	26	MARI0601	13
CNMA0245	21	MAVT0682	16
CNME0256	16	MEME0799	18
CNNH0257	17	MENH0823	17
CNRI0258	18	MERI0913	03
CNVT0259	19	MEVT1023	30
MACN0261	16	MECN1032	16
MAME0262	15	MEMA1033	15
MARI0263	14	MACN1024	13
VTCN0264	13	NHCN1224	12
NHMA0265	12	NHMA1321	11
		NHME1459	10
		NHNH2221	16
		NHRI2441	16

Test Data Set 18

```
                  1111111111222222          21524804486310310
        12345678901234567890012345          21742354864338400
                                            22463794864496410
        01209270187236010                   22467296344490230
        01267220345077020                   25266255376724235
        01828291213142030                   25262275443706115
        02243502498455040                   26229505976865125
        02863102498508050                   26528386320927405
        03751442498732060                   28377546322453175
        04710682972649070                   28710526322457165
        04751443439316080                   28940856324057203
        05370323451016090                   30933656327170153
        06286553453010100                   35294536328168193
        06355853455383110                   35392277342891143
        07287673455824120                   35769797521972123
        07741023455825130                   41481467724351113
        09395693456377140                   43260077726722093
        09951113458653150                   43720637792895083
        10636393655472009                   44134317891011063
        10921283685473011                   44780408005273053
        11732923688900013                   50409518274632043
        12727713862440160                   61290868382829193
        13658504226400170                   62233658742846183
        13994414252575180                   62290929392185508
        14726974339600190                   62571829863051603
        21259054482510300                   62700579955382097
```

Test Data Set 19

111111	44863104651144
123456789012345	48643386809104
	48644960712242
01872360488219	53431730123257
03450770281085	53444900133089
12131428591234	53767242626323
24984590354350	54437064235344
24985080548297	59768652971346
24987327223327	63209276451204
29726495580120	63224538401234
34393160345099	63224575345276
34510160678343	63240580055087
34530105343169	63271702493324
34553829194287	63281680262234
34558240422109	73428911518328
34558254681321	75219720987316
34563771853233	77243502191134
34586531909187	77267227680198
36554722972256	77928952124350
36854733939243	78910110632256
36889000385111	80052740348213
38624407724226	82746320939236
42264002187256	83828295490126
42525752081234	87428460652168
43396000547215	93922092080086
44825100481233	98630511589088

Test Data Set 20

```
                    1111111111222222222233333333334444444
          1234567890123456789012345678901234567890123456789012345
```

```
88099009001   009080   009089   009093
88101009070   009115   009015   009650
88102010000   119950   009300   009083   009001
88103009065   009091   009075   719550   009950
88104009500   010000   009091   009081   009065
88105009095   009077   009062   009950
88106009580   009120   010010   009001   009083
89200009085   009009   009112   009800   010010
89201009570   009077   009089   009060
89202009095   009081   009001   010010   009500
89203009950   009300   009009   009083   009089
89204009200   009950   009075   009040
89205009067   267890   009580   009950
90300009110   009077   009095   009009
98543009075   009050   009083   009200   009900
90301009120   009072   865723   010000
90302009600   009125   009083   009060
90303009093   009001   009089   009550
90304009097   009800   009072   009001   009015
90305009089   009093   009125
91400009650   010010   009950   009067
91401009062   010000   090200
91402009065   009091   009075   719550   009950
```

91403892074	009200	00950	009075	009040
91404009075	009050	009083	009200	009900
91405009120	009072	867230	01000	
9250109600	009125	009083	009060	
92502009033	009001	009089	009550	
92503009097	009800	009072	009001	009015
92504009095	009081	009001	01001	009500
92506009950	009300	009009	009083	009089
98524009200	009950	009075	009040	
93600009650	010010	009950	009067	
94700009097	009800	009072	009001	009015
94701009070	009115	009015	009650	
94702009001	009080	009089	009093	
94705009110	009077	009095	009009	
95800009200	009950	009075	009940	
95822009950	009300	009009	009083	009089
95804009650	010010	009950	009067	
96900009075	009050	009083	009200	009900
95803009067	009950	010010	009650	
94703009075	009050	009083	009200	009900
95801009095	009077	009062	009950	
95802009093	009001	009089	009550	
95807009600	009125	009083	009060	
95808009040	009075	009950	009200	
95809009085	009009	009112	00980	010010
95806009095	009081	009001	010010	009500

Test Data Set 21

```
          1111111111222222222233333333334444444444555555555566
  12345678901234567890123456789012345678901234567890123456789012345678901
```

```
009001   3GENERAL ENGLISH MECHANICS        ARUNDEL, GEORGE

009009   3C P MECHANICS                    ARVANITAKIS, ROBERT

009015   4C P LITERATURE                   ARYEE, AUGUSTINE

009030   4TECH COMMUNICATIONS              ARZBERGER, DAVID

009040   4TECH LITERATURE                  CAISSIE, LOU

009050   3GENERAL COMMUNICATIONS           HOWARD, TIM

009060   4GENERAL LITERATURE               GRANT, ROB

009062   4C P ENGLISH MECH                 FAVEREAU, LEO

009065   3C P COMMUNICATIONS               DIMEGA, MIKE

009067   4INTRO TO DRAMA                   CLEAVER, COLIN

009070   4COMP MATH                        DAVID, ALEX

009071   4CONSUMER MATH                    ELKINS, GARY

009072   3FUNDAMENTALS OF MATH             HANNEY, RAY

009075   4INTRO TO COMPUTERS               LANDRIE, MARY

009077   4PRE ALGEBRA                      MOECKEL, TIM

009080   4ALGEBRA                          NIGZUS, STEVE

009081   3GEOMETRY                         RAJOTTE, DON

009083   3TRIGONOMETRY                     ST CYR, DAN

009085   4PHOTOGRAPHY I                    TATRO, SHARRON

009088   3PHOTOGRAPHY II                   VIOLETTE, CLIFF

009089   4PERSONAL TYPING                  WINSLOW, HARRY

009090   3WORLD HIST I                     ANTIONIO, GINO

009091   3WORLD HIST II                    BLANCHETTE, CLAIR
```

009093	4MODERN HISTORY	ERRICO, PAUL
009095	3ADOLESCENT TO ADULTHOOD	DELANEY, PAUL
009097	3MARRIAGE AND FAMILY LIFE	CROTEAU, AL
009100	4NATIONAL & WORLD CONCERNS	BARNSWORTH, RAY
009110	4THE U.S. SINCE 1945	GRAHAM, TIM
009112	3LIFE SCIENCE	HAGG, PETE
009115	4ADVANCED LIFE SCIENCE	HENRY, ROB
009120	3EARTH SCIENCE	JAQUES, JOHN
009121	3CURRENT TRENDS IN SCIENCE	KAZMAIER, SAM
009125	3CHEMISTRY	CASTELLA, JACOB
009200	3BIOLOGY	LEBARON, MARK
009300	3PRINC. OF TECHNOLOGY I	LEE, JOHN
009350	4PRINCE. OF TECHNOLOGY II	MACMILLIAN, LISA
009360	4PHYSICS	PISCIOTTA, PAT
009400	4ANATOMY AND PHYSIOLOGY	SMITH, MAY
009500	3CIVICS	WALTERS, ANDI
009550	3U.S. HISTORY I	ROSE, JOHN
009560	4U.S. HISTORY II	THEALL, DAVID
009570	3SOCIOLOGY	WALTON, JACK
009580	4STREET LAW	YOUNG, MIKE
009600	4GEOGRAPHY OF THE U.S.	XARRAS, LEO
009650	4WORLD GEOGRAPHY	FARREL, JIM
009800	3BASIC BUSINESS	GIRARD, MARK
009900	3BUSINESS MANAGEMENT	GROSS, DAN
009950	3SMALL BUSINESS OPERATIONS	HUTTON, THOS
010000	4PHYSICAL EDUCATION	HARRIS, MARK

▤ Test Data Set 22

```
                        1111111111222222222233333333
                  12345678901234567890123456789012345678

                  00019AUTOMOBILE     120989$ 9,750.4006

                  14927COMPUTER SYSTEM061590$34,500.0005

                  12398DRILL PRESS    100791$ 5,000.0008

                  74690CHAINSAW       111789$   685.2709

                  86342TELEPHONE      090193$    84.0004

                  89907TRACTOR        071893$11,600.0010

                  08652HOUSE          101491$97,500.0004

                  38927TELEVISION     012792$   300.0010

                  13182FURNITURE      071589$  1400.0012
```

▤ Test Data Set 23

```
                1111111111222222222233333333334444444444555555555566666666667
      12345678901234567890123456789012345678901234567890123456789012345678901234567890

HF007611000090010061200003552006130000155300
HG666712300150030071240001558007125000325100712600005570071270001901000
MR030201500015040020160001604002017001420400201800001030020190003905000
MS6039422500175500
MT016501000100070050200009507005030000685600504000090050050500001257000
PR129832500001530083260001705008327000310900832800130590083290001905000
RH001011200003580001130001404000114000155500011500016030001160001558000
SR019100000005530010001009007001000201500300100030012060010004013606000
TG007311400022070031150001105003116001320700311700009080000
TH004400000039580040001001259004000200035900400030001060040004001404000
```

Test Data Set 24

```
                  1111111111222222222233333333334444444444555555555566666666667
         1234567890123456789012345678901234567890123456789012345678901234567890

         0146POWER        CHRIS        M121286532H0100000000056000400

         0207FEELEY       LEONARD      M050779532H0500000000036500760

         0214KNOWLES      SUSAN        F062284532H0400000000064500230

         0442HAIMILA      MICHAEL      M040191420S0801650000000000000

         0684SUGAL        RICHARD      M020689109S0702560000000000000

         0858STUART       SUE ANNE     F082288328S0603450000000000000

         0907HILL         KENNETH      M070782328S0304570000000000000

         0916                          M010973608H0200000000038500390

         0919VANN         MARTHA       F022782608H1000000000000000525

         1051PORELL       GERALD       M043087704S0902340000000000000

         1268FIELD        JOHN         M120889570H0100000000038500400

         1605FIX          JULIE        N032083570H0400000000047500390

         2347FLAGG        KENNETH      M043090570H0200000000047500230

         2347FLETCHER     LEO          M090991660S0502350000000000000

         2460HENRY        LOUIS        M022967660F0304300000000000000

         2526HENEBRY      GLORIA       F022984190S0603450000000000000

         2945KATON        BARBARA      F         S0702190000000000000

         3040CURTIS       OMER         M030185190S1001700000000000000

             CUSHMAN      PAT          F110877780H0800000000023500480

         3117FARNWORTH    PAUL         M120579780H0700000000025000530

         4103GOGUEN       RANDOLPH     M052079520S0906850000000000000

         4330LANDRY       RAYMOND      G073086620S0903260000000000000

         5140WHEATON      ROY          M010189111S0404250000000000000

         5142MARINO       DONNA        F102082714F0200000000046500170

         6076MARR         GERARD       M123091724H0300000000047500150
```

Test Data Set 25

```
          1111111111222222222233333333334444444444555555555566666666667
1234567890123456789012345678901234567890123456789012345678901234567890
```

```
0015690012PCYYNYYA
6114567897PCYYYNYR066257412THIBODEAU, MONIQUE    CR102490251250
0432971387TFNYNYNR321495673                      CA113089050250
2976251349TSYYNNYS
3296573216BFYYNNYA
4226323372BOYNYNNP552168329RICE, KIM             CO041991165000
7524129202VFNNNNYR067932441SMITH, KEITH          CR053092170595
0356456920AFYNYNYA
7213961784PFYYNNYA
5371407366TSNYNNNR719343368GULINO, TINA          CA011890050200
0005014146VCYYYNYA
8272884920BMNNNNNR749072741WOODHEAD, JASON       CA090593305000
9418808930VSYYYNYS
6611661241PFYNYNYA
4564317055BCNNYNYR193042101REGAN, SANDRA         CW120989090450
0559021462TFNNYNNA
3428937039BCNNYNYA                               CA091493195000
3122614919TFYYNNYR066131423LAPOINTE, MICHELLE    CR031691241200
4536570897VCYYYNYS
1098436292VFYNNYYA
5447802740VSYYNNYR                               CR072696133500
3837399709TSYYNNYA
```

```
1121131145BCYYNNYR077231699MITOLA, DANIELLE      CR070490030150
2087365438PFNNNYYS
9191535249PCYYYNYA
1050858322PCYYYNYS
6591537208VCNNNYYA
2764580394VSYYNNYR321965432BARRY, MICHAEL        CA022789070245
4293567219TSNNYNYR430528394PECKHAM, ESTER        CR060389120600
4269640809PDYYNNYF836619278AALTO, MIKE           CO      085000
2499001230BFYYYNYA
2230025105PCNYYNYA
6813422958TSYYYNYR019304230LABRIE, MARION        CA091399100500
1355027306VSYYNNYS
3364839815BFYYNNYS
1355342328VAYYNNYR283945678COCHRANE, PETER       CR030793180900
5126440271PFYNYNYA
2281907369VSNYNYNR297836548BILSON, RENEE         CA050391040500
3298463892PCYYYNYR321143116WAGNER, LINDA         CR100889105000
5126435927BCYYNNYS
8674597321TFNNNYYA
0943092074VCNNYYNR456468101SCHULTZ, LEROY        CR101494090315
0943092074BSYYYNYR220322221HARDING, PHILIP       CA091092110550
4569226789BCYYYNYS
```

Test Data Set 26

```
                     1111111111222222222233333333334444444444555555555566666666667
            12345678901234567890123456789012345678901234567890123456789012345678901234567890


            1253CDAECAPACITANCE METER          EO LAB1   010186063087  A
            1743AMADVOLT OHM AMMETER                                   D
            1743FMABDIGITAL PYROMETER                    062170110184  A
            1923CSBAPHOTOELECTRIC TACHOMET                     113086  C
            2111AMEADIGITAL WATT METER         EL LAB2   020186020188  B
            2441CSAC10K OHM/VOLT VOM TEST      EO LAB3                 A
            2642GEADBREADBOARD LAB                                     D
            2642GEAEAC/DC VOLTAGE TESTER                               D
            2943CEBADIGITAL PYROMETER          EO LAB1        040488  M
            2975                                                       D
            3563ACBCOSCILLOSCOPE MOD-317P      EO LAB2   110182110187  A
            3711CSBBCAPACITANCE METER          EL LAB3                 C
            3711GEBAAC/DC VOLTAGE TESTER       EO LAB2   071988011989  A
            4203CTADBREADBOARD LAB                       080288010187  A
            4705AMACDIGITAL WATT METER         EL LAB2        072488  C
            8401NYNXTELEPHONE                                          D
            9641NYNZTELEPHONE                  EL LAB2                 C
```

▤ Test Data Set 27

```
          1111111111222222222233333333334444444444555555555566666666667
 12345678901234567890123456789012345678901234567890123456789012345678901234567890


 0149REESE         WALTER      M121286532H   00000000056000400         A

 0207              LENNY              532S   035000000               C

 0214                          062284                                 D

 0442                          040191                                 D

 0684SUGAL         RICHARD     M020689109S070256000000000000000        A

 0858                          082288                                 D

 0907                                  328S030457000000000000000       C

 1051                                  704S090234000000000000000       C

 1268                          120889                                 D

 2347                          043090                                 D

 2529                          022984190S060345000000000000000        A

 3040CURTIS        OMER                190S100170000000000000000       C

 3117                                  780S070000000025000530         C

 4103                                  520S090685000000000000000       C

 5142BASHAW                            714F020000000046500170         C

 5140WHEATON       ROY                 724H030000000047500150         C

 6984                          123091                                 D
```

Test Data Set 28

```
         1111111111222222222233333333334444444444555555555566666666667
1234567890123456789012345678901234567890123456789012345678901234567890


6114567897PCYYYNYR066257412THIBODEAU, MONIQUE    CR102490255000C
3296573218                                                      D
7524129202VFNNNNYA                                              C
7213961784PFYYNNYF077126412SANBORN, ROSS         CR061590201000C
5371407366                                                      D
9418808930VSYYYNYS499058210LACOUNT, BENOIT       CA121299185000C
3122614919TFYYNNYS                                              C
4536570897                                                      D
3837399710TSYYNNYR303510000MINTY, PAULA          CA081994165000A
2212231145BCYYNNYS                                              A
2087365438                                                      D
2764580394VSYYNNYR321965432BARRY, MICHAEL        CA022789273500A
4293567219                                                      D
6813422951TSYYYNYR019304230LABRIE, MARION        CA091399125000A
1355027306                                                      D
2281907369VSNYNYNR297836548BILSON, RENEE         CA050391043500M
7138263892PCYYYNYR321143116WILLIAMS,JAMES        CR100889100500A
5126435927                                                      B
4569226789BCYYYNYS198911011DUPONT, PAMELA        CA102490355000C
1234567895                                                      D
```

INDEX